John Vivian
Winona State University

The Media of Mass Communication

EIGHTH EDITION

2008 UPDATE

Boston | New York | San Francisco
Mexico City | Montreal | Toronto | London | Madrid | Munich | Paris
Hong Kong | Singapore | Tokyo | Cape Town | Sydney

Editor-in-Chief: Karon Bowers
Series Editorial Assistant: Saunders Robinson
Senior Development Editor: Carol Alper
Associate Editor: Deb Hanlon
Marketing Manager: Suzan Czajkowski
Production Editor: Claudine Bellanton
Editorial Production Service: Stratford Publishing Services
Composition Buyer: Linda Cox
Manufacturing Buyer: JoAnne Sweeney
Electronic Composition: Stratford Publishing Services
Photo Researcher: Julie Tesser
Cover Administrator/Designer: Joel Gendron

For related titles and support materials, visit our online catalog at www.ablongman.com.

Library of Congress Cataloging-in-Publication Data

Vivian, John.
The media of mass communication / John Vivian — 8th ed., 2008 update.
p. cm.
Includes index.
ISBN 0-205-49370-X (alk. paper)
1. Mass media. I. Title.
P90.V53 2008
302.23—dc22
2006100839

Printed in the United States of America

10 9 8 7 6 5 4 3 2 1 RRD-OH 11 10 09 08 07

to Harold Vivian,

my father,

who sparked my curiosity about the mass media at age 5 by asking what was black and white and read all over.

and

to Elaine Vivian,

my mother,

who nurtured this curiosity by keeping the house stocked with books, magazines and reading material of every sort.

Contents

Features List xvi
Preface xviii
About the Author xxvi
Award for Excellence xxvii

PART ONE THE MASS MEDIA

The mass media are the vehicles that carry mass messages. Television is a mass medium. So is the Internet. Magazines too. In all, there are eight major mass media. An entire industry has been built up around each of these major media. This first section of your book includes an introductory chapter and then deals with each of these major mass media.

chapter 1 Mass Media Literacy

Vignette: *Arthur Sulzberger Jr. 1*

Importance of Mass Media 2
Pervasiveness, 2 • Information Source, 3 • Entertainment Source, 3 • Persuasion Forum, 4

Culture and Values 4
Binding Influence, 4 • 500-Channel Universe, 5

Primary Mass Media 6
Print Technology, 6 • Chemical Technology, 8 • Electronic Technology, 8

Technology Melds 9
Print-Visual Integration, 9 • Digital Integration, 10

MSM and New Media 10
Mainstream Media, 10 • New Media, 11

Mass Media Models 11
Hot-Cool Model, 11 • Entertainment-Information Model, 11 • Content-Distribution Model, 12 • Elitist-Populist Model, 13

Economics of Mass Media 14
Economic Foundation, 14 • Economic Imperative, 17 • Mission and Profit, 17 • Perils of Profit and Myopia, 18 • Demassification, 18

Media Conglomeration 19
Media Ownership Consolidation, 19 • Media Ownership Collaboration, 19 • Dubious Effects of Conglomeration, 21 • Positive Effects of Conglomeration, 24 • Conglomeration Cracks, 24

CHAPTER WRAP-UP
QUESTIONS FOR REVIEW
QUESTIONS FOR CRITICAL THINKING
DEEPENING YOUR MEDIA LITERACY
KEEPING UP TO DATE
FOR FURTHER LEARNING

media databank Media Usage 3
media people Christina Saralegui 5
media people Johannes Gutenberg 7
media timeline Media Technology 8
media databank Media Costs 14
media people Rupert Murdoch 20
media databank Biggest U.S. Media Companies 21
media people Vivendi Mastermind 25

chapter  Books

Vignette: *Richard Sarnoff 29*

Influence of Books 30
Books in Human History, 30 • Repository of Culture, 31 • Books in National Development, 31 • Books and Current Issues, 32

Book Industry 33
Scope of Book Industry, 33 • Major Houses, 34 • Book Industry Consolidation, 34 • Small Publishers, 34 • Book Retailing, 35

Book Products 36
Trade Books, 37 • Texts and References, 37 • Graphic Novels, 38

Transformational Formats 39
Paperback Books, 39 • Electronic Books, 40

Book Authors 41
Authoring Process, 41 • Author-Publisher Relations, 43
Book Issues and Trends 44
Blockbusters, 44 • Mass Marketing, 44 • Aliteracy, 46 • Global Online Access, 47 • Google Library Project, 47 • European Response 48
Evaluating Books 48
Populist Measures, 48 • Quality Measures, 49

CHAPTER WRAP-UP
QUESTIONS FOR REVIEW
QUESTIONS FOR CRITICAL THINKING
DEEPENING YOUR MEDIA LITERACY
KEEPING UP TO DATE
FOR FURTHER LEARNING

media timeline Development of Books 31
media people William Holmes McGuffey 32
media people Harriet Beecher Stowe 33
media databank Major Trade Book Publishers 34
media databank Bookstore Chains 36
media people Frank Miller 39
media technology Espresso Machine Brews Books 40
media people Jane Friedman 41
media people J. K. Rowling 42
case study Authors as Franchise: J. D. Robb and Nora Roberts 45

chapter 3 Newspapers

Vignette: *Mary Junck 53*
Importance of Newspapers 54
Newspaper Industry Dimensions, 54 • Content Diversity and Depth, 55
Newspaper Products 56
Broadsheets, 56 • Tabloids, 56
Newspaper Chain Ownership 58
Trend Toward Chains, 58 • Assessing Chain Ownership, 59
National Dailies 60
USA Today, 60 • *Wall Street Journal*, 62 • *Christian Science Monitor*, 64
New York *Times* 65
Newspaper of Record, 65 • New York *Times* Heritage, 65
Hometown Newspapers 67
Metropolitan Dailies, 67 • Hometown Dailies, 68
Future for Dailies 68
Multimedia News, 68 • Newspaper Blogs, 70 • New Efficiencies, 70 • Clustering, 71 • Marketing Databases, 72
Weekly Newspapers 72
Community Weeklies, 72 • Rural Weeklies, 73 • Shoppers, 73
Alternative and Minority Newspapers 73
Counterculture Newspapers, 73 • Black Newspapers, 74 • Foreign-Language Newspapers, 75
Evaluating Newspapers 76
Circulation and Penetration, 76 • Quality Indicators, 77

CHAPTER WRAP-UP
QUESTIONS FOR REVIEW
QUESTIONS FOR CRITICAL THINKING
DEEPENING YOUR MEDIA LITERACY
KEEPING UP TO DATE
FOR FURTHER LEARNING

media databank Largest U.S. Newspapers 55
media technology Newspaper Production 56
media databank Newspaper Chains 58
media databank Newsroom Salaries 60
media timeline Notable Dailies 61
media people George Gilder 69
media databank Best U.S. Newspapers 77

chapter 4 Magazines

Vignette: *Bonnie Fuller 81*
Influence of Magazines 82
Contributing to Nationhood, 82 • National Advertising Medium, 83 • Massive Magazine Audience, 83
Magazines as Media Innovators 84
Investigative Reporting, 84 • Personality Profiles, 84 • Photojournalism, 84
Consumer Magazines 85
Circulation Leaders, 85 • Newsmagazines, 86 • Newspaper Supplements, 87 • Women's Magazines, 88 • Men's Magazines, 88
Non-Newsrack Magazines 89
Sponsored Magazines, 90 • Trade Journals, 91 • Criticism of Trade Magazines, 91 • Newsletters, 92
Magazine Demassification 92
Heyday of Mass Magazines, 92 • Assault from Television, 92 • A Narrower Focus, 93 • Critics of Demassification, 94 • New Competition, 95 • Internet Magazines, 95
Evaluating Magazines 96
Populist Measures, 96 • Quality Measures, 97 • Reader Usage Measure, 98

CHAPTER WRAP-UP
QUESTIONS FOR REVIEW

QUESTIONS FOR CRITICAL THINKING
DEEPENING YOUR MEDIA LITERACY
KEEPING UP TO DATE
FOR FURTHER LEARNING

media timeline Magazines 83
media people Margaret Bourke-White 86
media people DeWitt and Lila Wallace 87
media databank Magazine Advertising Revenue 88
media people Sara Josepha Hale 89
media people Bella Price 90
media people Myles Kovacs 95

chapter 5 Sound Recording

Vignette: Shawn Fanning 101

Influence of Sound Recordings 102
Pervasiveness of Music, 102 • Scope of the Recording Industry, 102

Recording Industry 103
Majors, 103 • Indies, 103

Transforming Innovations 104
Sound Technology, 105 • Performer Influences, 106

Regulatory Pressure 109
Objectionable Music, 109 • Labeling, 109 • Artistic Freedom, 110

Artistic Autonomy 111
A&R Structure, 111 • Music Demassification, 112 • Touring, 112

Streaming Crisis 114
File-Sharing, 114 • iPod, 114 • Pirate Dubbing, 115

Evaluating Recording Companies 117
Populist Measures, 117 • Quality Measures, 118

CHAPTER WRAP-UP
QUESTIONS FOR REVIEW
QUESTIONS FOR CRITICAL THINKING
DEEPENING YOUR MEDIA LITERACY
KEEPING UP TO DATE
FOR FURTHER LEARNING

media databank Recording Companies 103
media people 50 Cent 104
media timeline Recording Formats 105
media timeline Record Industry 107
media technology DualDisc 108
media databank Recorded Music Genres 110
media technology Albums: The Rise and Fall 112
media technology Sound Mixing 113
case study Podcasting: The New Revolution? 116

chapter 6 Movies

Vignette: John Lasseter 121

Importance of Movies 122
Overwhelming Experience, 122 • Cinematic Dream Theory, 123 • Hollywood's Cultural Influence, 123 • Hollywood's New Century, 124

Movie Technology 125
Photography Roots, 125 • D-Cinema, 126

Movie Industry Products 127
Feature Films, 127 • Animated Films, 128 • Documentaries, 130 • Television Production, 132

Movie Industry: Production 132
Major Studios, 132 • Other Studios, 134 • Independent Producers, 134

Movie Industry: Distribution 136
Booking Movies, 136 • Foreign Distribution, 137

Movie Industry: Exhibition 137
What Edison Wrought, 137 • Exhibition Crisis, 139

Movie Censorship 139
Early Licensing, 139 • Government Intimidation, 140 • Movies and First Amendment, 141 • Current Movie Code, 142

Media Literacy and Movies 143
Box Office and Grosses, 143 • Movie Criticism, 143

CHAPTER WRAP-UP
QUESTIONS FOR REVIEW
QUESTIONS FOR CRITICAL THINKING
DEEPENING YOUR MEDIA LITERACY
KEEPING UP TO DATE
FOR FURTHER LEARNING

media databank Movie Revenue 125
media timeline Movie Technology 126
media people Mark Cuban 127
media databank Big-Budget Movies 128
media technology Computer-Generated Imagery 129
media people Lourdes Portillo 130
media people Robert Flaherty 131
media databank Major Movie Studios 132
media people Adolph Zukor 133
media people Steven Spielberg 135

media people Bob and Harvey Weinstein 136
media databank Global Box Office 137
media timeline Movie Exhibition 138
media databank Major Movie-House Chains 139
media timeline Movie Censorship 140
media databank Movie Ratings 142

chapter 7 Radio

Vignette: *Paul Harvey* *147*

Influence of Radio 148
Ubiquity, 148 • Scope of Radio Industry, 149

Radio Technology 149
Electromagnetic Spectrum, 149 • Transmitting Voices, 150 • FM Radio, 150

Radio Industry Infrastructure 151
Trusteeship Rationale, 151 • Localism, 152 • Networks, 153

Infrastructure Transition 154
Historical Characteristics, 154 • Deregulation, 155 • Satellite Radio, 156 • New Technologies, 156

Corporate Radio 157
Chain Ownership, 157 • New Corporate Tune, 158

Radio Content 160
Radio Entertainment, 160 • Radio News, 161 • Talk Radio, 163 • Public Radio, 165

Quality on the Air 167
Marketplace Values, 167 • Measuring Quality, 167

Radio Trends 167
High-Definition Radio, 168 • Bundled Transmission, 168

CHAPTER WRAP-UP
QUESTIONS FOR REVIEW
QUESTIONS FOR CRITICAL THINKING
DEEPENING YOUR MEDIA LITERACY
KEEPING UP TO DATE
FOR FURTHER LEARNING

media timeline Radio 151
media people John Brinkley 153
media timeline Radio Networks 154
media technology Airplay for Sale 157
media databank Radio Chains 157
media people Howard Stern 158
case study More Power for Low Power 159
media people Gordon McLendon 161
media databank Radio Formats 162
media people Edward R. Murrow 163
media databank NPR News Audience 165
media people Terry Gross 165
media people Garrison Keillor 166

chapter 8 Television

Vignette: *Steve Jobs* *171*

Television in Transition 172
Television Industry in Crisis, 172 • Cultural Role of Television, 172 • Enduring Television Effects, 173

Television Technology 173
Electronic Scanning, 173 • Cable Delivery Systems, 175 • Satellite Direct, 178 • Video on Demand, 180

Corporate Structure 181
Dual Infrastructure, 181 • Affiliate-Network Relations, 182 • Fragmentation, 187

Economics of Television 189
Network Advertising, 189 • Cable Revenue Streams, 190 • VOD Business Models, 191 • Noncommercial Television, 191

Television Content Issues 192
Quality Quest, 192 • Network Violence, 194 • Government Role, 194

Untethering Television's Future 195
Time Shifts, 195 • Space Shifts, 195 • Advertising Shifts, 195

CHAPTER WRAP-UP
QUESTIONS FOR REVIEW
QUESTIONS FOR CRITICAL THINKING
DEEPENING YOUR MEDIA LITERACY
KEEPING UP TO DATE
FOR FURTHER LEARNING

media people Philo Farnsworth 174
media timeline Television Technology 175
media people Ed Parsons 176
media databank Cable and Satellite Delivery Companies 179
media technology Digital Television 179
media databank Television Chains 181
media people María Celeste Arrarás 183
media people Debra Lee 184

media technology Video on Demand 188
media databank Cross-Ownership 190
media databank Income-Based Viewership 193
media technology Mobile Television 196

chapter 9 The Internet

Vignette: *Sebastian Babolat 201*

Influence of the Internet 202
New Mass Medium, 202 • Scope of the Internet, 203 • New Terminology, 203

Internet Technology 204
Underlying Technologies, 204 • Creating the Internet, 205 • World Wide Web, 206 • Bandwidth, 208

Reshaping the Internet 210
Wi-Fi, 211 • Ultrawideband, 211 • Mesh Networks, 211

Commerce and the Internet 211
Advertising-Free Origins, 212 • Dot-Com Bubble, 212 • Internet Advertising, 212 • Tracking Internet Traffic, 213

Evaluating the Internet 213
Strengths of Internet Sites, 213 • Accuracy, 214

Media Melding 215
Technological Convergence, 215 • Transition Ahead, 215 • Government Deregulation, 217

Public Policy and the Internet 217
Blogs, 217 • Privacy and the Internet, 219 • Cyberpornography, 219 • Universal Access, 220 • Global Inequities, 220

CHAPTER WRAP-UP
QUESTIONS FOR REVIEW
QUESTIONS FOR CRITICAL THINKING
DEEPENING YOUR MEDIA LITERACY
KEEPING UP TO DATE
FOR FURTHER LEARNING

media timeline Internet 203
media people William Shockley 204
media people Vint Cerf 206
media people Tim Berners-Lee 207
media people Marc Andreessen 209
media technology Carbon Nanotubes 210
media databank Movie Advertising 212
case study Do We Need Net Neutrality? 216
media people Glenn Reynolds 219

PART TWO MASS MESSAGES

The mass media carry all kinds of messages—earth-shaking news, frivolous horoscopes, reality television, hard rock, Brahms, and Nike ads. This section of your book takes up the major forms of media messages. Mass messages are not unique to any medium. News, for example, is as much at home in a newspaper as on the Internet and television. Public relations and advertising people don't limit themselves to any single medium to deliver their persuasive messages. To be sure, there are many other forms of mass media messages, but these are the major ones.

chapter 10 News

Vignette: *Naomi Oreskes 225*

Journalism Traditions 226
Colonial Period, 227 • Partisan Period, 227 • Penny Period, 229 • Yellow Period, 232

Concepts of News 234
U.S. Model, 234 • European Model, 234 • Evolving News Models, 235 • Defining Objectivity, 237

Personal Values in News 237
Role of the Journalist, 237 • Journalists' Personal Values, 238 • Journalistic Bias, 240

Variables Affecting News 242
News Hole, 242 • News Flow and News Staffing, 242 • Perceptions About Audience, 242 • Availability of Material, 243 • Competition, 243

Influences on News 243
Advertiser Influence, 244 • Corporate Policy, 244 • Source Pressure, 245

Confidential Sources 245
News on Condition, 245 • Shield Laws, 246 • Parsing Interview Conditions, 248 • Gatekeeping, 248

Journalism Trends 249
Nonstop Coverage, 249 • Live News, 249 • Unedited Blogs, 250 • Exploratory News, 251 • Soft News, 251

Identifying Good Journalism 251
Audience Dimensions, 251 • Evaluative Criteria, 251

CHAPTER WRAP-UP
QUESTIONS FOR REVIEW
QUESTIONS FOR CRITICAL THINKING
KEEPING UP TO DATE
DEEPENING YOUR MEDIA LITERACY
FOR FURTHER LEARNING

media timeline Journalistic Practices 228
media people Benjamin Day 229
media people James Gordon Bennett 231
media people Seymour Hersh 236
media people Ida Wells-Barnett 238
media databank National Public Radio Audience 241
media people Earl Caldwell 246
case study Are Journalists Who Publish Classified Information Criminals? 247
media people Oriana Fallaci 250

chapter 11 Public Relations

Vignette: Peter Diamantis 255

Importance of Public Relations 256
Defining Public Relations, 256 • Public Relations in a Democracy, 257

Origins of Public Relations 258
Moguls in Trouble, 258 • The Ideas of Ivy Lee, 259 • Public Relations on a New Scale, 261 • Lobbyist-Journalist Balance, 261

Structure of Public Relations 263
Policy Role of Public Relations, 263 • How Public Relations Is Organized, 263 • Public Relations Agencies, 264

Public Relations Services 264
Activities Beyond Publicity, 265 • Public Relations and Advertising, 267 • Integrated Marketing, 267

Media Relations 269
Open Media Relations, 269 • Proactive Media Relations, 270 • Ambivalence in Media Relations, 271 • Adversarial Public Relations, 272

Professionalization 274
A Tarnished Image, 274 • Standards and Certification, 276

CHAPTER WRAP-UP
QUESTIONS FOR REVIEW
QUESTIONS FOR CRITICAL THINKING
DEEPENING YOUR MEDIA LITERACY
KEEPING UP TO DATE
FOR FURTHER LEARNING

media timeline Public Relations 258
media people Paul Garrett 262
media databank Public Relations Agencies 264
media people Jack Abramoff 266
media technology Social Media News Release 271
media people Edward Bernays 274
media people Leslie Unger 275

chapter 12 Advertising

Vignette: Bob Greenberg 279

Importance of Advertising 280
Consumer Economies, 280 • Advertising and Prosperity, 280 • Advertising and Democracy, 281

Origins of Advertising 281
Stepchild of Technology, 281 • Industrial Revolution, 282 • Pioneer Agencies, 283

Advertising Agencies 283
Agency Structure, 283 • Agency Compensation, 284 • Advertiser's Role in Advertising, 284

Placing Advertisements 285
Media Plans, 285 • Media Choices, 285

New Advertising Platforms 287
Gaming, 287 • Advergames, 288 • Google Ads, 288

Pitching Messages 289
Importance of Brands, 289 • Lowest Common Denominator, 290 • Market Segments, 290 • Redundancy Techniques, 291 • Under-the-Radar Advertising, 291 • Post-Brand-Name Era, 293

Research and Psychology 293
Motivational Research, 293 • Subliminal Advertising, 294

Advertising Regulation 295
Media Gatekeeping, 295 • Industry Self-Regulation, 296 • Government Regulation, 298

Problems and Issues 299
Advertising Clutter, 299 • Creative Excesses, 299 • Advertising Effectiveness, 299

CHAPTER WRAP-UP
QUESTIONS FOR REVIEW
QUESTIONS FOR CRITICAL THINKING
DEEPENING YOUR MEDIA LITERACY
KEEPING UP TO DATE
FOR FURTHER LEARNING

media databank Largest Advertisers 281
media timeline Development of Advertising 282
media databank Advertising Agencies 284
media databank Advertising Spending by Medium 286
media databank Gaming Ads 288
media people Dave Balter 300
media technology Measuring Creativity 301

chapter 13 Entertainment

Vignette: Jerry Bruckheimer 305

Entertainment in History 306
Pre-Mass Media Roots, 306 • Technology-Driven Entertainment, 306 • Entertainment Genres, 307

Performance as Media Entertainment 308
Authentic Performance, 308 • Mediated Performance, 308

Storytelling as Media Entertainment 309
Genres of Literature, 309 • Trends and Fads, 309

Music as Media Entertainment 311
American Folk Music, 311 • Early Rock 'n' Roll, 312 • Music as Multimedia Content, 312

Sports as Media Entertainment 313
Mass Audiences for Sports, 313 • Audience and Advertiser Confluence, 314 • Sports and the Web, 314

Gaming as Media Content 315
Growing Entertainment Form, 315 • Impact of Gaming, 315

Sex as Media Entertainment 317
Adult Content, 317 • Decency Requirements, 318 • Sexual Content and Children, 318 • Censorship and Gaming, 319

Evaluating Media Content 318
Media Content as Art, 319 • Production-Line Entertainment, 320 • Copycat Content, 320 • Cross-Media Adaptations, 320 • Unpretentious Media Content, 321

CHAPTER WRAP-UP
QUESTIONS FOR REVIEW
QUESTIONS FOR CRITICAL THINKING
DEEPENING YOUR MEDIA LITERACY
KEEPING UP TO DATE
FOR FURTHER LEARNING

media databank Record Sales by Genre 307
media people Protest Musicians 310
media databank Television Episodes 311
media technology Digital DJs 313
media databank Leading Games 315
media people Shigeru Miyamoto 316
media databank Game Publishers 317
media people Nelly 321

chapter 14 Media Research

Vignette: *Susan Whiting 325*

Public-Opinion Sampling 326
The Surveying Industry, 326 • Probability Sampling, 327 • Quota Sampling, 330 • Evaluating Surveys, 330 • Latter-Day Straw Polls, 332

Measuring Audience Size 332
Newspaper and Magazine Audits, 333 • Broadcast Ratings, 333 • Audience Measurement Techniques, 333 • Internet Audience Measures, 334 • Multimedia Measures, 335 • Criticism of Ratings, 336

Measuring Audience Reaction 339
Focus Groups, 339 • Galvanic Skin Checks, 339 • Prototype Research, 340

Audience Analysis 340
Demographics, 340 • Cohort Analysis, 340 • Geodemographics, 341 • Psychographics, 342

Applied and Theoretical Research 343
Media-Sponsored Research, 343 • Mass Communication Scholarship, 344

CHAPTER WRAP-UP
QUESTIONS FOR REVIEW
QUESTIONS FOR CRITICAL THINKING
DEEPENING YOUR MEDIA LITERACY
KEEPING UP TO DATE
FOR FURTHER LEARNING

media timeline Media Research 327
media people George Gallup 329
media people Andy Kohut 331
case study Ratings Technology: A2/M2 Coming to a Cell Phone Near You 334
media databank Cohort Analysis 341

PART THREE MASS MEDIA ISSUES

This final section builds on what you learned in earlier sections about the mass media and about messages that media carry to their audiences. Every chapter is self-contained, so you can explore them in any order your instructor assigns. Each chapter is a springboard to improve your understanding and appreciation of the mass media and their role in every day of our lives as individuals and as a global society.

chapter 15 Mass Communication

Vignette: *Wilbur Schramm 347*

Types of Communication 348
Intrapersonal Communication, 348 • Interpersonal Communication, 348 • Group Communication, 348 • Mass Communication, 349

Components of Mass Communication 349
Mass Communicators, 350 • Mass Messages, 351 • Mass Media, 351 • Mass Communication, 351 • Mass Audiences, 351

Communication Models 351
Role of Communication Models, 352 • Basic Model, 352 • Narrative Model, 352 • Concentric Circle Model, 352

Fundamentals in the Process 354
Stimulation, 354 • Encoding, 354 • Transmission, 355 • Decoding, 355 • Internalization, 355
Players in the Process 356
Gatekeepers, 356 • Regulators, 356 • Gatekeeper-Regulator Hybrids, 357
Impediments to Communication 357
Noise, 357 • Filters, 358
Results of Mass Communication 359
Amplification, 359 • Feedback, 359 • Effects, 360
CHAPTER WRAP-UP
QUESTIONS FOR REVIEW
QUESTIONS FOR CRITICAL THINKING
DEEPENING YOUR MEDIA LITERACY
KEEPING UP TO DATE
FOR FURTHER LEARNING

media people David Sarnoff 350

chapter 16 Mass Media Effects

***Vignette:** Orson Welles 363*
Effects Studies 364
Powerful Effects Theory, 364 • Minimalist Effects Theory, 365 • Cumulative Effects Theory, 366 • Third-Person Effect, 367 • Future Theories, 367
Uses and Gratifications Studies 368
Challenges to Audience Passivity, 368 • Surveillance Function, 368 • Socialization Function, 369 • Diversion Function, 369 • Consistency Theory, 370
Individual Selectivity 370
Selective Exposure, 370 • Selective Perception, 371 • Selective Retention and Recall, 371
Socialization 372
Media's Initiating Role, 372 • Role Models, 372 • Stereotyping, 373 • Socialization via Eavesdropping, 374
Media-Depicted Violence 375
Learning About Violence, 375 • Media Violence as Positive, 375 • Prodding Socially Positive Action, 376 • Media Violence as Negative, 376 • Catalytic Theory, 377 • Societally Debilitating Effects, 378 • Media Violence and Youth, 378 • Tolerance of Violence, 380 • Violence Studies, 381
Media Agenda-Setting for Individuals 383
Media Selection of Issues, 383 • Intramedia Agenda-Setting, 383
Media-Induced Anxiety and Apathy 384
Information Anxiety, 384 • Media-Induced Passivity, 385
CHAPTER WRAP-UP
QUESTIONS FOR REVIEW
QUESTIONS FOR CRITICAL THINKING
DEEPENING YOUR MEDIA LITERACY
KEEPING UP TO DATE
FOR FURTHER LEARNING

media timeline Understanding Mass Media Effects 366
media people Steve Schild 367
media people Kathleen Rutledge 374
media timeline Mass Communication and Violence 376
media people Peggy Charren 379
media people Sam Peckinpah 380
media people George Gerbner 382

chapter 17 Mass Media and Society

***Vignette:** Marshall McLuhan 389*
Mass Media Role in Culture 390
Elitist versus Populist Values, 390 • The Case Against Pop Art, 392 • Pop Art Revisionism, 392
Social Stability 394
Media-Induced Ritual, 394 • Media and the Status Quo, 395 • Media and Cognitive Dissonance, 396 • Agenda-Setting and Status Conferral, 397 • Media and Morality, 397
Cultural Transmission 400
Historical Transmission, 400 • Contemporary Transmission, 401
Mass Media and Fundamental Change 402
Human Alienation, 402 • Television and the Global Village, 403
CHAPTER WRAP-UP
QUESTIONS FOR REVIEW
QUESTIONS FOR CRITICAL THINKING
DEEPENING YOUR MEDIA LITERACY
KEEPING UP TO DATE
FOR FURTHER LEARNING

media timeline Mass Communication and Culture 391
media people Shonda Rhimes 395
case study Media Advocacy: Will It Make a Difference? 398
media databank Diversity in the News 399

chapter 18 Global Mass Media

***Vignette:** Jean-Jacques Gomez 407*
Mass Media and Nation-States 408
Global Communication, 408 • Friedman Globalization Model, 409

Global Conglomeration 409
Multinational Companies, 409 • The Internet and Globalization, 410

Effects of Globalization 411
Cultural Subversiveness, 411 • Corporate Ideology, 411

Cultural Intrusion 411
Latter-Day Imperialism, 412 • Non-Downward Media Exchange, 413 • Emerging Global Media, 414 • Insidious Western Influence, 415 • Transnational Cultural Enrichment, 415 • Esperanto, 415

Global Media Models 416
Bipolar Model, 416 • Continuum Model, 416 • Compass Model, 417 • Change Model, 418 • Subsystem Model, 419

Global Media Players 419
News Agencies, 419 • Video News Services, 420 • Syndicates, 421

Global Media Companies 421
U.S.-Based Companies, 422 • Non-U.S. Companies, 422 • Global Media Brand Names, 423

Mass Media in China 424
Chinese Policy, 424 • Chinese Firewall, 425 • Internal Chinese Controls, 425 • Chinese Censorship Apparatus, 425 • Chinese Overt Controls, 426 • Chinese Broadcasting, 426

Distinctive Media Systems 427
Britain, 427 • India, 428 • Japan, 429 • Russia, 429 • Colombia, 430

War Zones 431
Combat Reporting, 431 • Early Lessons, 431 • Pool Reporting, 432 • Embedded Reporters, 433

CHAPTER WRAP-UP
QUESTIONS FOR REVIEW
QUESTIONS FOR CRITICAL THINKING
DEEPENING YOUR MEDIA LITERACY
KEEPING UP TO DATE
FOR FURTHER LEARNING

media people Herbert Schiller 412
media databank Movie Power 414
media databank MTV Subscribers 423
media technology China and EVD 425
media people Jineth Bedoya Lima 430
media people Orhan Pamuk 432

chapter 19 Mass Media and Governance

Vignette: Arnold Schwarzenegger 437

Media Role in Governance 438
Fourth Estate, 438 • Government-Media Relations, 439

Media as Information Sources 441
Direct versus Indirect, 441 • Citizen Preferences, 441

Media Effects on Governance 442
Agenda-Setting, 442 • CNN Effect, 442 • Framing, 443 • Priming, 443 • Media Obsessions, 445

Government Manipulation of Media 446
Influencing Coverage, 446 • Trial Balloons and Leaks, 447 • Stonewalling, 448 • Overwhelming Information, 448

Status of the Watchdog 448
Federal Coverage, 448 • State Coverage, 450 • Campaign Coverage, 451 • Attack Ads, 452

Campaign Blogs 452
Blogs and 2008, 452 • Campaign Blog Research, 452 • Sponsored Blogs, 454

Media-Government Issues 454
Political Favors, 455 • Campaign Advertising, 455 • Free Airtime, 456

CHAPTER WRAP-UP
QUESTIONS FOR REVIEW
QUESTIONS FOR CRITICAL THINKING
DEEPENING YOUR MEDIA LITERACY
KEEPING UP TO DATE
FOR FURTHER LEARNING

media people Donna Brazile 439
media people Helen Thomas 444
media people Tony Snow 449

chapter 20 Mass Media Law

Vignette: Jon Lech Johansen 459

The U.S. Constitution 460
First Amendment, 460 • Scope of the First Amendment, 461

Prior Restraint 461
Public Nuisances, 461 • Allowable Abridgments, 463 • Incitement Standard, 465 • Hate Speech, 466 • Flag Burning, 466

Defamation 466
The Libel Concept, 467 • Reckless Disregard, 467 • Comment and Criticism, 469 • Trespass, Fraud and Libel, 470

Privacy Law 470
Intruding on Solitude, 470 • Harassment, 471

Journalism Law 471
Court Coverage, 471 • Sunshine Laws, 472

Obscenity and Pornography 473
Import Restrictions, 473 • Postal Restrictions, 473 • Communications Decency Act, 474 • Pornography versus Obscenity, 474

Censorship Today 474
Local Censorship, 475 • Library and School Boards, 475

Copyright 476
How Copyright Works, 476 • Infringement Issues, 476 • Piracy, 477

CHAPTER WRAP-UP
QUESTIONS FOR REVIEW
QUESTIONS FOR CRITICAL THINKING
DEEPENING YOUR MEDIA LITERACY
KEEPING UP TO DATE
FOR FURTHER LEARNING

media timeline Landmarks in Media Law 461
media people Jay Near 462
media people Clarence Brandenburg 465
media people Joseph Gutnick 468

chapter 21 Ethics and the Mass Media

Vignette: *Jim DeFede* 481

The Difficulty of Ethics 482
Prescriptive Ethics Codes, 482 • Conflict in Duties, 483 • Promoting Self-Interest, 485

Media Ethics 485
Media Commitment, 485 • Audience Expectation, 485 • Ethics as an Intellectual Process, 486

Moral Principles 486
The Golden Mean, 486 • "Do unto Others," 487 • Categorical Imperatives, 487 • Utilitarian Ethics, 487 • Pragmatic Ethics, 488 • Egalitarian Ethics, 488 • Social Responsibility Ethics, 488

Process versus Outcome 489
Deontological Ethics, 489 • Teleological Ethics, 490 • Situational Ethics, 490

Potter's Box 491
Four Quadrants, 491 • Limitations of Potter's Box, 492

Ethics and Other Issues 493
Differentiating Ethics and Law, 493 • Accepted Practices, 493 • Prudence and Ethics, 493

Unsettled, Unsettling Issues 495
Plagiarism, 495 • Misrepresentation, 496 • Gifts, Junkets and Meals, 500

CHAPTER WRAP-UP
QUESTIONS FOR REVIEW
QUESTIONS FOR CRITICAL THINKING
DEEPENING YOUR MEDIA LITERACY
KEEPING UP TO DATE
FOR FURTHER LEARNING

media people Charlie Gay 484
media timeline Media Ethics 488
media people Ted Cohen 494
media people James Frey 497
case study Prepackaged News: Who Funds Advocacy? 499

Online chapters available at:
www.ablongman.com/vivian8e
Passcode:
BWSVME-CLONK-GROSZ-GIPON-LOBBY-NOOSE
Also available on MyMassCommLab at:
www.mymasscommlab.com

ONLINE CHAPTER

chapter 22 Visual Messages

Vignette: *Al Diaz*

Early Media Illustrations
Engravings • Editorial Cartoons • Comics

Photographic Technology
Invention of Photography • Halftones • Digital Captures

Photography in Mass Communication
Visual Messages • Troublesome Word *Medium*

Cameras, Films and Techniques
Stopping Motion • Celluloid • Smaller Cameras • Faster Film • Instant Photography

Documentary Photography
Mathew Brady • Frontier Photography • Depression Photography

Persuasive Photography
Illustrating Advertisements • Illustrating a Cause Poignantly

Reality Photography
Newspapers • Magazines • Moving Visuals

Evaluating Visual Messages
Images as Evocative • Recognition of Excellence

Visual Issues
Imitative or Creative • Image Ownership • Image Misrepresentation • Access for Photographers • Intruding

CHAPTER WRAP-UP
QUESTIONS FOR REVIEW
QUESTIONS FOR CRITICAL THINKING

media timeline Photography Technology
media timeline Visual Media Breakthroughs
media abroad Germany: Leica Cameras
media people Mathew Brady
media people Margaret Bourke-White
media people Alfred Eisenstaedt

ONLINE CHAPTER

chapter 23 Media and Political Systems

Vignette: *John Twyn*

Four Theories Model

Political Systems • Siebert, Peterson and Schramm

Authoritarian Media

Henry VIII • Authoritarian Control • Effectiveness of Controls • Nature of Truth

Communist Media

Marxist Underpinnings • Marxist Notion of Truth • Media Unified with Government

Libertarian Model

Optimism About the Human Mind • Marketplace of Ideas • First Amendment • Libertarians and Religion

Social Responsibility Model

Challenges to Libertarianism • Hutchins Commission

Freedom and Responsibility

Responsibility versus Profitability • Exceptions to Social Responsibility

Media Future: Political and Media Systems

CHAPTER WRAP-UP
QUESTIONS FOR REVIEW
QUESTIONS FOR CRITICAL THINKING

media abroad Distinguishing Media Systems
media timeline Political Media Models
media abroad Greece and Libertarianism
media people Elijah Lovejoy
media abroad Ombuds

Index 503

Features

case STUDIES

Authors as Franchise: J. D. Robb and Nora Roberts 45
Podcasting: The New Revolution? 116
More Power for Low Power 159
Do We Need Net Neutrality? 216
Are Journalists Who Publish Classified Information Criminals? 247
Ratings Technology: A2/M2 Coming to a Cell Phone Near You 334
Media Advocacy: Will It Make a Difference? 398
Prepackaged News: Who Funds Advocacy? 499

media DATABANK

Media Usage 3
Media Costs 14
Biggest U.S. Media Companies 21
Major Trade Book Publishers 34
Bookstore Chains 36
Largest U.S. Newspapers 55
Newspaper Chains 58
Newsroom Salaries 60
Best U.S. Newspapers 77
Magazine Advertising Revenue 88
Recording Companies 103
Recorded Music Genres 110
Movie Revenue 125
Big-Budget Movies 128
Major Movie Studios 132
Global Box Office 137
Major Movie-House Chains 139
Movie Ratings 142
Radio Chains 157
Radio Formats 162
NPR News Audience 165
Cable and Satellite Delivery Companies 179
Television Chains 181
Cross-Ownership 190
Income-Based Viewership 193
Movie Advertising 212
National Public Radio Audiences 241
Public Relations Agencies 264
Largest Advertisers 281
Advertising Agencies 284
Advertising Spending by Medium 286
Gaming Ads 288
Record Sales by Genre 307
Television Episodes 311
Leading Games 315
Game Publishers 317
Cohort Analysis 341
Diversity in the News 399
Movie Power 414
MTV Subscribers 423

media PEOPLE

Christina Saralegui 5
Johannes Gutenberg 7
Rupert Murdoch 20
Vivendi Mastermind 25
William Holmes McGuffey 32
Harriet Beecher Stowe 33
Frank Miller 39
Jane Friedman 41
J. K. Rowling 42
George Gilder 69
Margaret Bourke-White 86
DeWitt and Lila Wallace 87
Sara Josepha Hale 89
Bella Price 90
Myles Kovacs 95
50 Cent 104
Mark Cuban 127
Lourdes Portillo 130
Robert Flaherty 131
Adolph Zukor 133
Steven Spielberg 135
Bob and Harvey Weinstein 136
John Brinkley 153
Howard Stern 158

Gordon McLendon 161
Edward R. Murrow 163
Terry Gross 165
Garrison Keillor 166
Philo Farnsworth 174
Ed Parsons 176
María Celeste Arrarás 183
Debra Lee 184
William Shockley 204
Vint Cerf 206
Tim Berners-Lee 207
Marc Andreessen 209
Glenn Reynolds 219
Benjamin Day 229
James Gordon Bennett 231
Seymour Hersch 236
Ida Wells-Barnett 238
Earl Caldwell 246
Oriana Fallaci 250
Paul Garrett 262
Jack Abramoff 266
Edward Bernays 274
Leslie Unger 275
Dave Balter 300
Protest Musicians 310
Shigeru Miyamoto 316
Nelly 321
George Gallup 329
Andy Kohut 331
David Sarnoff 350
Steve Schild 367
Kathleen Rutledge 374
Peggy Charen 379
Sam Peckinpah 380
George Gerbner 382
Shonda Rhimes 395
Herbert Schiller 412
Jineth Bedoya Lima 430
Orhan Pamuk 432
Donna Brazile 439
Helen Thomas 444
Tony Snow 449
Jay Near 462
Clarence Brandenburg 465
Joseph Gutnick 468
Charlie Gay 484
Ted Cohen 494
James Frey 497

mediaTECHNOLOGY

Espresso Machine Brews Books 40
Newspaper Production 56
DualDisc 108
Albums: The Rise and Fall 112
Sound Mixing 113
Computer-Generated Imagery 129
Airplay for Sale 157
Digital Television 179
Video on Demand 188
Mobile Television 196
Carbon Nanotubes 210
Social Media News Release 271
Measuring Creativity 301
Digital DJs 313
China and EVD 425

mediaTIMELINE

Media Technology 8
Development of Books 31
Notable Dailies 61
Magazines 83
Recording Formats 105
Record Industry 107
Movie Technology 126
Movie Exhibition 138
Movie Censorship 140
Radio 151
Radio Networks 154
Television Technology 175
Internet 203
Journalistic Practices 228
Public Relations 258
Development of Advertising 282
Media Research 327
Understanding Mass Media Effects 366
Mass Communication and Violence 376
Mass Communication and Culture 391
Landmarks in Media Law 461
Media Ethics 488

Preface

Since the first edition of the *Media of Mass Communication* in 1991, more than a million students have found the book their first academic look at the media environment that so much shapes not only their daily routines but their lives and our whole culture. For a teacher this is gratifying. Through *MMC* and a growing network of colleagues who have adopted the book, my reach as a teacher has been extended far, far beyond the confines of my own classrooms. I am indebted deeply to adopters and their students, who pepper me almost daily with their reactions to the book and with news and tidbits to keep the next edition current.

Shawn Fanning
The courts found his 1998 Napster music-downloading software violated the copyrights of the music owners. Nonetheless, Napster paved the way for other systems that facilitated free and inexpensive public access to music that transformed the music industry at the start of the 21st century.

chapter 5 Sound Recording

In this chapter your will learn:

- Recorded music is omnipresent in our lives.
- The recording industry is dominated by four companies.
- Technology and performers have shaped the recording industry.
- Threats of censorship have been met by self-regulation.
- Technology has given performers new control over their recorded work.
- Apple's iPod and iTunes eased losses from download piracy.
- The recording industry can be evaluated by sales, profits, artistic risk and innovation.

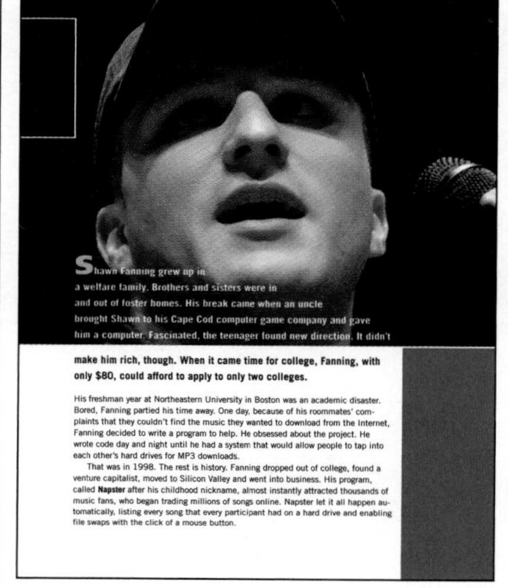

Shawn Fanning grew up in a welfare family. Brothers and sisters were in and out of foster homes. His break came when an uncle brought Shawn to his Cape Cod computer game company and gave him a computer. Fascinated, the teenager found new direction. It didn't make him rich, though. When it came time for college, Fanning, with only $80, could afford to apply to only two colleges.

His freshman year at Northeastern University in Boston was an academic disaster. Bored, Fanning partied his time away. One day, because of his roommates' complaints that they couldn't find the music they wanted to download from the Internet, Fanning decided to write a program to help. He obsessed about the project. He wrote code day and night until he had a system that would allow people to tap into each other's hard drives for MP3 downloads.

That was in 1998. The rest is history. Fanning dropped out of college, found a venture capitalist, moved to Silicon Valley and went into business. His program, called **Napster** after his childhood nickname, almost instantly attracted thousands of music fans, who began trading millions of songs online. Napster let it all happen automatically, listing every song that every participant had on a hard drive and enabling file swaps with the click of a mouse button.

Colorful chapter opening pages bring to life the topic discussed in each chapter. Topical vignettes and learning goals set the stage for the chapter discussion that follows.

The reach of *MMC* is wider than ever. Besides a Canadian edition with co-author Peter Maurin, now going into its fourth edition, translations are in process for students in China, India and Indonesia. In all, *MMC* has been published in 19 variations over the years, each updated to keep students up-to-speed on the ever-changing and fast-changing media of mass communication.

Most gratifying to me is the community that has grown up around *MMC*. These are people, many of whom have become valued friends, whose thoughts have made the book an evolving and interactive project. In countless messages, adopters have shared what works in their classes and how it might work elsewhere. Students write the most, sometimes puzzled over something that deserves more clarity, sometimes with examples to illustrate a point. All of the comments, questions and suggestions go into a mix to add currency and effectiveness with every updated edition.

This edition introduces the role of gaming as a significant new advertising medium. There is the sudden dramatic drop in newspaper circulation, after years of gradual decline. The television industry, once solidly structured around networks and affiliates, is fragmenting into wholly new creation and distribution channels. And are the days of movie-houses numbered? Nobody has figured out the long-term impact of the Internet, but last year's common wisdom, we know this year, is as invalid as a Philo Farnsworth tech manual.

You will find nothing more current than this update to the MMC eighth edition.

How This Book Is Organized

This book has three sections, each intended to examine a different aspect of the mass media.

The Mass Media Chapter 1, "Mass Media Literacy," provides a foundation for understanding the mass media and the dynamics that affect the messages that they transmit. The next eight chapters deal with each of the major mass media—books, newspapers, magazines, sound recordings, movies, radio, television and the Internet.

Mass Messages Then come chapters on the major content forms disseminated by the media to mass audiences. These include news, public relations, advertising and entertainment. Also included is a chapter on media research, with special attention to measuring the audience for mass messages.

Mass Media Issues The rest of the book focuses on specific issues, including the process of mass communication, media effects, the mass media and society, global mass media, media and governance, media law and media ethics.

Using This Book

This edition retains many of the popular features that have helped your predecessors master the subject, as well as introducing some new ones.

- **Introductory Vignettes.** Chapters open with colorful descriptions about people who contributed significantly to the mass media.
- **Learning Goals.** Each chapter begins with learning goals to help you guide your thoughts as you read through the chapter.
- **Study Previews.** To help you prepare for the material ahead, each major section begins with a preview of the concepts to be covered there.
- **Media Online.** The margins contain hundreds of web addresses to guide your learning about the mass media beyond the textbook and the classroom.
- **Running Glossary.** You will also find glossary definitions in the margins, on the same page that the name or concept is introduced in the text.
- **Case Studies.** Many chapters include a new feature, a case study, by my colleague Kay Turnbaugh. These case studies illustrate an issue discussed in the chapter. Each also includes questions to help you sort through the problems presented.
- **Media People.** This feature introduces personalities who have had a major impact on the media or whose story illustrates a major point of media history.
- **Media Technology.** This edition includes boxes that feature media technology breakthroughs and in-progress technology changes.
- **Media Timeline.** This feature helps you see the sequence of important media events and put the events of the chapter in historical context.

Helpful study aids appear throughout: study previews, margin glossary entries, and URLs that point to related content on the Internet.

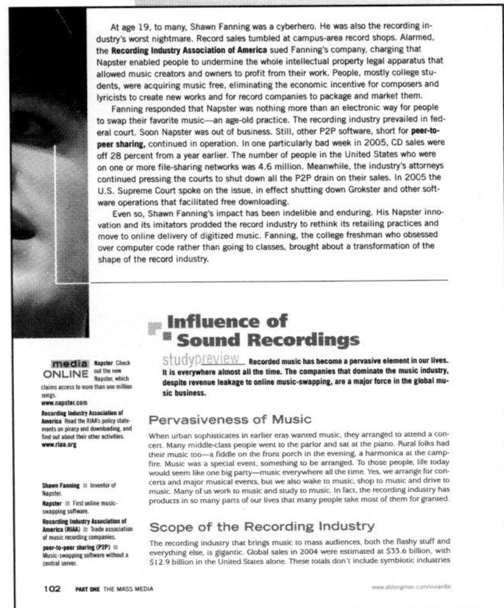

At age 19, to many, Shawn Fanning was a cyberhero. He was also the recording industry's worst nightmare. Record sales tumbled at campus-area record shops. Alarmed, the **Recording Industry Association of America** sued Fanning's company, charging that Napster enabled people to undermine the whole intellectual property legal apparatus that allowed music creators and owners to profit from their work. People, mostly college students, were acquiring music free, eliminating the economic incentive for composers and lyricists to create new works and for record companies to package and market them.

Fanning responded that Napster was nothing more than an electronic way for people to swap their favorite music—an age-old practice. The recording industry prevailed in federal court. Soon Napster was out of business. Still, other P2P software, short for **peer-to-peer sharing,** continued in operation. In one particularly bad week in 2005, CD sales were off 28 percent from a year earlier. The number of people in the United States who were on one or more file-sharing networks was 4.6 million. Meanwhile, the industry's attorneys continued pressing the courts to shut down all the P2P drain on their sales. In 2005 the U.S. Supreme Court spoke on the issue, in effect shutting down Grokster and other software operations that facilitated free downloading.

Even so, Shawn Fanning's impact has been indelible and enduring. His Napster innovation and its imitators prodded the record industry to rethink its retailing practices and move to online delivery of digitized music. Fanning, the college freshman who obsessed over computer code rather than going to classes, brought about a transformation of the shape of the record industry.

Influence of Sound Recordings

studypreview **Recorded music has become a pervasive element in our lives. It is everywhere almost all the time. The companies that dominate the music industry, despite revenue leakage to online music-swapping, are a major force in the global music business.**

media ONLINE **Napster** Check out the new Napster, which claims access to more than one million songs. **www.napster.com**

Recording Industry Association of America Read the RIAA's policy statements on piracy and downloading, and find out about their other activities. **www.riaa.org**

Pervasiveness of Music

When urban sophisticates in earlier eras wanted music, they arranged to attend a concert. Many middle-class people went to the parlor and sat at the piano. Rural folks had their music too—a fiddle on the front porch in the evening, a harmonica at the campfire. Music was a special event, something to be arranged. To those people, life today would seem like one big party—music everywhere all the time. Yes, we arrange for concerts and major musical events, but we also wake to music, shop to music and drive to music. Many of us work to music and study to music. In fact, the recording industry has products in so many parts of our lives that many people take most of them for granted.

Shawn Fanning Inventor of Napster.

Napster First online music-swapping software.

Recording Industry Association of America (RIAA) Trade association of music recording companies.

peer-to-peer sharing (P2P) Music-swapping software without a central server.

Scope of the Recording Industry

The recording industry that brings music to mass audiences, both the flashy stuff and everything else, is gigantic. Global sales in 2004 were estimated at $33.6 billion, with $12.9 billion in the United States alone. These totals don't include symbiotic industries

102 PART ONE THE MASS MEDIA www.ablongman.com/vivianBe

case STUDY

Media Advocacy: Will It Make a Difference?

Book Authors

studypreview **Authors come up with the ideas for many books, but publishers sometimes go looking for an author for a book to fill a hole in the market. The relationship of an author and a publisher is defined in contracts that specify royalties and other conditions and expectations for their partnership.**

media ONLINE **International Digital Publishing Forum** Trade and standards association for the digital publishing industry. Contains e-book best-seller lists. **www.openebook.org**

Authoring Process

No surefire formula exists for writing a successful book. Conventional wisdom at one point noted that books on Abraham Lincoln, on doctors and on dogs usually did well, leading one wag to suggest a book on Lincoln's doctor's dog.

Speculation Many books are written on speculation. The author has an idea, gets it on paper, then hunts for a publisher. That's how Robert Pirsig's *Zen and the Art of Motorcycle Maintenance* came to be. It's a classic case study.

rsig had not had an easy adulthood: mental breakdown, electroshock treatment, ancy. He had grown up expecting more. A high point in his life was working out tionship with his 11-year-old son. From his experiences emerged a gentle philo- y about life. An idea developed in Pirsig's mind for a book that wrapped it all ther.

Finding a publisher was difficult. For more than six years, Pirsig sent out his posal—121 times in all. Publishing houses doubted its commercial potential. It was

media PEOPLE

Jane Friedman

Book Industry Contrarian

Jane Friedman, chief executive at HarperCollins, is unlearning fundamental lessons from her career climb over 30 years. The book industry's future, as Friedman sees it, is not in blockbusters. Big-name authors are risky, she says. Guaranteed advances in the upper six figures, sometimes higher, don't assure that a book won't flop and leave a publisher bleeding red ink.

Friedman sees a new model for publishers that emphasizes long-term profits from what she calls "small books."

Her doubts about blockbusters are understandable. A rule of thumb is 4 percent of new titles earn a good profit, only a few of those make spectacular money. In 2005, for example, only 200 books accounted for 10 percent of U.S. book industry sales. One book, *Harry Potter and the Half-Blood Prince*, with 7 million copies, accounted for 1 percent of the year's total sales.

So what is Friedman's vision? She sees new life for books that now, after their introduction, languish in warehouses until they're shredded to make room for newer titles. With digital storage, these backlist books can remain available indefinitely. With print-on-demand technology, one copy at a time can be printed. Over the long term, Friedman says, many backlist books can generate continuing sales and profits.

Also, she says, small books could sell significantly better if marketed to people with specific interests and who otherwise have no idea the books are available.

Friedman's ideas on targeted marketing are clearly contrarian in an industry where intuitive assessments of manuscripts has been the tradition. She's blunt: "Publishers have never looked at who the consumer is."

The book industry needs to reinvent itself, she says: "Chasing best-sellers is a fool's game."

CHAPTER 2 BOOKS 41

Case Studies explore media issues and provide probing questions.

Media People boxes profile colorful personalities who have had an impact on the media.

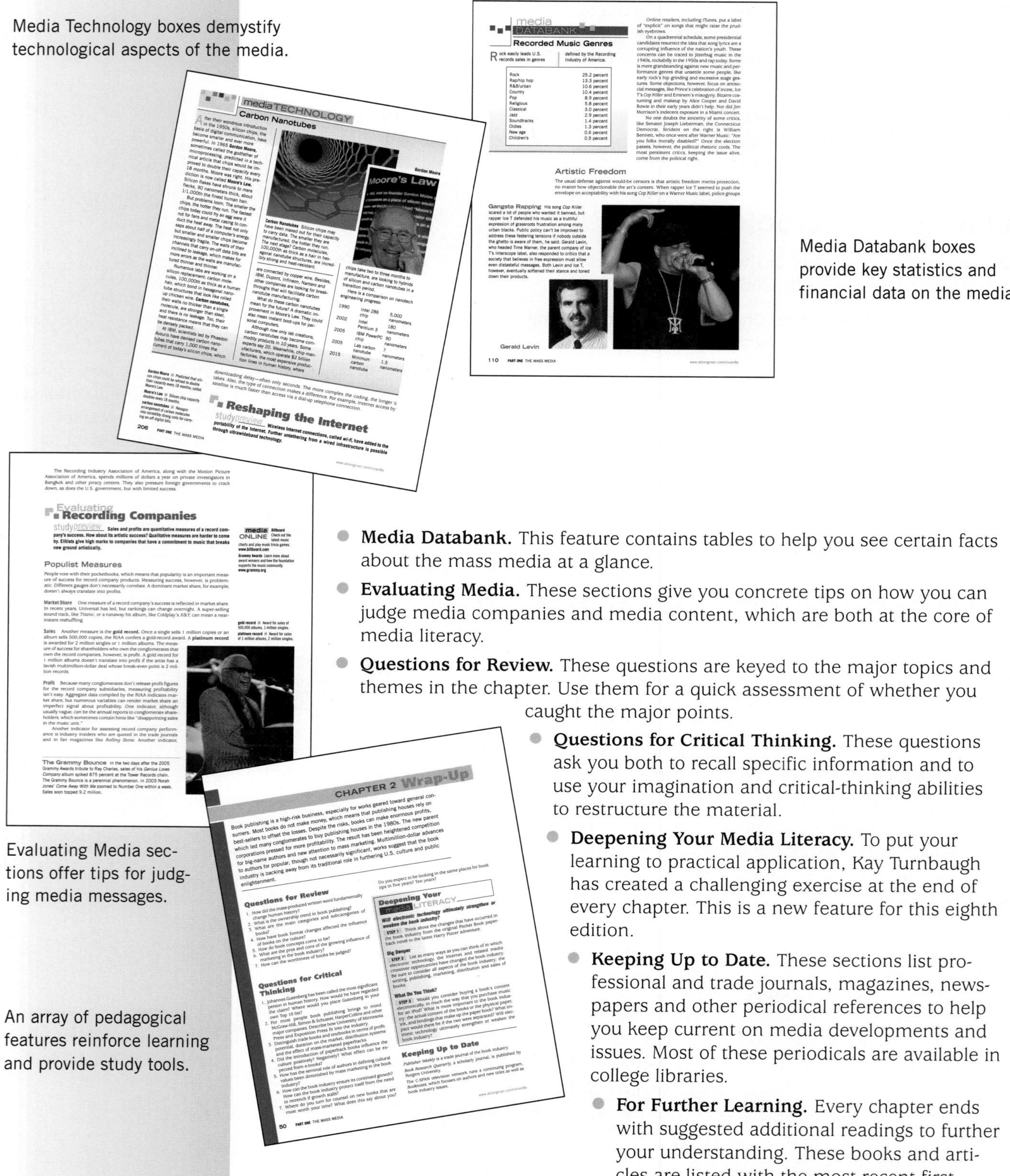

Media Technology boxes demystify technological aspects of the media.

Media Databank boxes provide key statistics and financial data on the media.

Evaluating Media sections offer tips for judging media messages.

An array of pedagogical features reinforce learning and provide study tools.

- **Media Databank.** This feature contains tables to help you see certain facts about the mass media at a glance.
- **Evaluating Media.** These sections give you concrete tips on how you can judge media companies and media content, which are both at the core of media literacy.
- **Questions for Review.** These questions are keyed to the major topics and themes in the chapter. Use them for a quick assessment of whether you caught the major points.
- **Questions for Critical Thinking.** These questions ask you both to recall specific information and to use your imagination and critical-thinking abilities to restructure the material.
- **Deepening Your Media Literacy.** To put your learning to practical application, Kay Turnbaugh has created a challenging exercise at the end of every chapter. This is a new feature for this eighth edition.
- **Keeping Up to Date.** These sections list professional and trade journals, magazines, newspapers and other periodical references to help you keep current on media developments and issues. Most of these periodicals are available in college libraries.
- **For Further Learning.** Every chapter ends with suggested additional readings to further your understanding. These books and articles are listed with the most recent first. Included are seminal, pivotal and leading recent works.

Supplements

Instructor's Resource Manual (IRM). This manual, by Stephen Cebik, is designed to ease time-consuming demands of instructional preparation, to enhance lectures, and to provide helpful suggestions to organize the course. The IRM consists of helpful teaching resources and lecture enrichment including outlines, synopses, glossaries, activities, and at-a-glance guides to the wealth of resources available in the package.

Test Bank. The test bank, by Susan Hunt-Bradford of St. Louis Community College, includes more than 2,500 multiple choice, true/false, matching, fill-in-the-blank, short answer and essay questions.

Computerized Test Bank. The Computerized Test Bank provides test questions electronically through our computerized testing system, TestGen EQ. The fully networkable test-generating software is now available in a multiplatform CD-ROM. The user-friendly interface enables instructors to view, edit and add questions as well as transfer questions to tests and print tests in a variety of fonts. Search and sort features allow instructors to locate questions quickly and arrange them in a preferred order.

MyMassCommLab. MyMassCommLab (www.mymasscommlab.com) is an interactive and instructive online solution for mass communication courses. Designed to be used as a supplement to a traditional lecture course or as an online course, MyMassCommLab combines multimedia, video, activities, research support, tests and quizzes to make teaching and learning fun! Access code required. Please contact your Allyn & Bacon representative for a demo or details.

Careers in Media. This supplement, by Frank Barnas and Mike Savoie, Valdosta State University, profiles employment opportunities in media and points out often overlooked options for students seeking a job in the highly selective and competitive media world. Included is a discussion of portfolio development and valuable appendices with state and job web sites. This supplement is available for your students as a value-pack option with this textbook or sold separately.

VideoWorkshop for Mass Communication. This is a new way for instructors to bring video into the course for maximized learning. This total teaching and learning system includes quality video footage on an easy-to-use CD-ROM plus a Student Learning Guide and an Instructor's Teaching Guide—both with textbook-specific Correlation Grids. The result? A program that brings textbook concepts to life with ease and that helps students understand, analyze and apply the objectives of the course. VideoWorkshop is available for students as a value-pack option with this textbook.

Allyn & Bacon's Mass Communication Interactive Video. Specially selected news segments from ABC news programs include on-screen critical-thinking questions and deal with a variety of media issues and problems to help bring media issues to life in the classroom. The program includes an accompanying video user's guide.

PowerPoint Presentation Package. This package, by Mike Weigold, University of Florida, consists of a collection of lecture outlines and graphic images keyed to every chapter in the text and is available on the Web at the Instructor's Resource Center (www.ablongman.com/irc).

Allyn & Bacon Digital Media Archive for Communication Version 3.0. This collection of communication media images, video and audio clips, lecture resources and web links is available on CD-ROM for Windows and Macintosh and illustrates concepts in all areas of communication.

Allyn & Bacon Mass Communication Video Library. This library of videos, produced by Insight Media and Films for the Humanities and Sciences, includes full-length videos such as *Functions of Mass Communication, Making of a Newspaper, Illusions of News* and *The Truth About Lies*. Some restrictions apply.

Online Bonus Chapters. Two additional chapters: Chapter 22, "Visual Messages," and Chapter 23, "Media and Political Systems" are available on MyMassCommLab and on the secure companion web site, **www.ablongman.com/vivian8e,** which requires a pass-code. (See Table of Contents for your access code to the secure companion web site.)

Allyn & Bacon's Introduction to Mass Communication Study Site. Available at **www.abintromasscomm.com.** This web site features study materials for students taking an introductory mass communication course, including flashcards and a complete set of practice tests for all major topics. Students will also find web links to valuable sites where they can further explore important topics in the field.

Research Navigator™ Guide for Mass Communication, Theatre, and Film. This updated booklet by Ronald Roat, of Southern Indiana University, includes tips, resources, and URLs to aid students conducting research on Pearson Education's research web site, **www.researchnavigator.com.** The guide contains a student access code for the Research Navigator database, offering students unlimited access to a collection of more than 25,000 discipline-specific articles from top-tier academic publications and peer-reviewed journals, as well as the New York *Times* and popular news publications. The guide introduces students to the basics of the Internet and the World Wide Web, and includes tips for searching for articles on the site, and a list of journals useful for research in their discipline. Also included are hundreds of web resources for the discipline, as well as information on how to correctly cite research. The guide is available packaged with new copies of the text.

Study Card for Introduction to Mass Communication. Colorful, affordable, and packed with useful information, Allyn & Bacon/Longman's Study Cards make studying easier, more efficient, and more enjoyable. Course information is distilled down to the basics, helping you quickly master the fundamentals, review a subject for understanding, or prepare for an exam. Because they're laminated for durability, you can keep these Study Cards for years to come and pull them out whenever you need a quick review.

News Resources for Mass Communication—Access Code Card. News Resources for Mass Communication with Research Navigator is one-stop access to keep you abreast of the latest news events and for all of your research needs. Highlighted by an hourly feed of the latest news in the discipline from the New York *Times,* students will stay on the forefront of currency throughout the semester. In addition, Pearson's Research Navigator™ is the easiest way for students to start a research assignment or research paper. Complete with extensive help on the research process and four exclusive databases of credible and reliable source material including the EBSCO Academic Journal and Abstract Database, New York Times Search by Subject Archive, and Financial Times Article Archive and Company Financials, Research Navigator helps students quickly and efficiently make the most of their research time. Access code required.

InterWrite PRS (Personal Response System): Increased Interactivity • Higher Attendance • 100% Participation. Assess your students' progress with the Personal Response System—an easy-to-use wireless polling system that enables you to pose questions, record results, and display those results instantly in your classroom.

Designed by teachers, for teachers, PRS is easy to integrate into your lectures:

- Each student uses a cell-phone-sized transmitter, which students bring to class.
- You ask multiple-choice, numerical-answer, or matching questions during class; students simply click their answer into their transmitter.
- A classroom receiver (portable or mounted) connected to your computer tabulates all answers and displays them graphically in class.
- Results can be recorded for grading, attendance, or simply used as a discussion point.

Acknowledgments

The greatest ongoing contribution to making *The Media of Mass Communication* the most adopted survey textbook in the history of the subject has been made by Carol Alper, senior development editor at Allyn & Bacon. She has not only applied her lively imagination and good sense to the book's contents, but has also coordinated the complexities of moving the manuscript through production. This has all been done with the energetic, hands-on support of Allyn & Bacon's communication editor in chief, Karon Bowers, who has her fingers on the pulse of mass communication instructors nationwide and knows their need for a textbook that offers the latest information and concepts to their students.

Besides my students and colleagues at my academic home, Winona State University, who made contributions in ways beyond what they realize, I am indebted to many students elsewhere who have written thoughtful suggestions that have shaped this edition. They include Niele Anderson, Grambling State University; Krislynn Barnhart, Green River Community College; Mamie Bush, Winthrop University; Lashaunda Carruth, Forest Park Community College; Mike Costache, Pepperdine University; Scott DeWitt, University of Montana; Denise Fredrickson, Mesabi Range Community and Technical College; James Grades, Michigan State University; Dion Hillman, Grambling State University; Rebecca Iserman, Saint Olaf University; Scott Wayne Joyner, Michigan State University; Nicholas Nabokov, University of Montana; Andrew Madsen, University of Central Florida; Scott Phipps, Green River Community College; Colleen Pierce, Green River Community College; June Siple, University of Montana; and Candace Webb, Oxnard College.

I also appreciate the suggestions of other colleagues whose reviews over the years have contributed to *MMC*'s success:

Edward Adams, Brigham Young University
Ralph D. Barney, Brigham Young University
Thomas Beell, Iowa State University
Ralph Beliveau, University of Oklahoma
Robert Bellamy, Duquesne University
ElDean Bennett, Arizona State University
Lori Bergen, Wichita State University
Bob Bode, Western Washington University
Timothy Boudreau, Central Michigan University
Bryan Brown, Missouri State University
Patricia Cambridge, Ohio University
Jane Campbell, Columbia State Community College
Dom Caristi, Ball State University
Michael L. Carlebach, University of Miami
Meta Carstarphen, University of North Texas
Michael Cavanagh, State University of New York at Brockport
Danae Clark, University of Pittsburgh
Jeremy Cohen, Stanford University
Michael Colgan, University of South Carolina
Ross F. Collins, North Dakota State University
James A. Danowski, University of Chicago, Illinois
David Donnelly, University of Houston
Thomas R. Donohue, Virginia Commonwealth University
Michele Rees Edwards, Robert Morris University
Kathleen A. Endres, University of Akron
Glen Feighery, University of Utah
Celestino Fernández, University of Arizona
Donald Fishman, Boston College
Laurie H. Fluker, Southwest Texas State University
Kathy Flynn, Essex County College in Newark, New Jersey
Robert Fordan, Central Washington University
Ralph Frasca, University of Toledo
Mary Lou Galician, Arizona State University
Andy Gallagher, West Virginia State College
Ronald Garay, Louisiana State University
Donald Godfrey, Arizona State University
Neil Gustafson, Eastern Oregon University
Donna Halper, Emerson College
Bill Holden, University of North Dakota

Peggy Holecek, Northern Illinois University
Anita Howard, Austin Community College
Elza Ibroscheva, Southern Illinois University, Edwardsville
Carl Isaacson, Sterling College
Nancy-Jo Johnson, Henderson State University
Carl Kell, Western Kentucky University
Mark A. Kelley, The University of Maine
Wayne F. Kelly, California State University, Long Beach
Donnell King, Pellissippi State Technical Community College
William L. Knowles, University of Montana
John Knowlton, Green River Community College
Sarah Kohnle, Lincoln Land Community College in Illinois
Charles Lewis, Minnesota State University, Mankato
Lila Lieberman, Rutgers University
Amy Lignitz, Johnson County Community College in Kansas
Larry Lorenz, Loyola University
Linda Lumsden, Western Kentucky University
John N. Malala, Cookman College
Reed Markham, Salt Lake Community College
Maclyn McClary, Humbolt State University
Denis Mercier, Rowan College of New Jersey
Timothy P. Meyer, University of Wisconsin, Green Bay
Jonathan Millen, Rider University
Joy Morrison, University of Alaska at Fairbanks
Gene Murray, Grambling State University
Richard Alan Nelson, Kansas State University
Thomas Notton, University of Wisconsin-Superior
Judy Oskam, Texas State University
David J. Paterno, Delaware County Community College
Terri Toles Patkin, Eastern Connecticut State University
Sharri Ann Pentangelo, Purdue University
Deborah Petersen-Perlman, University of Minnesota-Duluth
Tina Pieraccini, State University of New York at Oswego
Leigh Pomeroy, Minnesota State University, Mankato
Mary-Jo Popovici, Monroe Community College
Thom Prentice, Southwest Texas State University
Hoyt Purvis, University of Arkansas
Jack Rang, University of Dayton
Benjamin H. Resnick, Glassboro State College
Ronald Roat, University of Southern Indiana
Patrick Ropple, Nearside Communications
Marshel Rossow, Minnesota State University, Mankato
Julia Ruengert, Pensacola Junior College
Cara L. Schollenberger, Bucks County Community College
Quentin Schultz, Calvin College
Jim Seguin, Robert Morris College
Todd Simon, Michigan State University
Ray Sinclair, University of Alaska at Fairbanks
J. Steven Smethers, Kansas State University
Karen A. Smith, College of Saint Rose
Mark Smith, Stephens College
Howard L. Snider, Ball State University
Brian Southwell, University of Minnesota
Alan G. Stavitsky, University of Oregon
Penelope Summers, Northern Kentucky University
Larry Timbs, Winthrop University
John Tisdale, Baylor University
Edgar D. Trotter, California State University, Fullerton
Helen Varner, Hawaii Pacific University
Rafael Vela, Southwest Texas State University
Stephen Venneman, University of Oregon
Michael Warden, Southern Methodist University
Hazel G. Warlaumont, California State University, Fullerton
Ron Weekes, Ricks College
John Weis, Winona State University
Bill Withers, Wartburg College
Donald K. Wright, University of South Alabama
Alan Zaremba, Northeastern University
Eugenia Zerbinos, University of Maryland

Keeping Current

To you, the student, I want to emphasize that this book is a tool to help you become more intelligent and discerning as a media consumer. If you plan on a media career, the book is intended to orient you to the courses that will follow in your curriculum. This book, though, is only one of many tools for staying on top of the subject for many years to come. A feature at the end of every chapter, Keeping Up to Date, has tips on how to keep current even when your course is over.

Stay in Touch

Please feel free to contact me with questions and also ideas for improving the next edition. My e-mail: jvivian@winona.edu

May your experience with *The Media of Mass Communication* be a good one.

—John Vivian

About the Author

John Vivian is a professor of journalism at Winona State University in Minnesota, where he has taught mass media survey courses for more than 20 years. Previously he taught at Marquette University, the University of North Dakota, New Mexico State University and the University of Wisconsin centers in Waukesha and West Bend. He holds an honorary faculty appointment at the U.S. Defense Information School.

He is a past president of the Text and Academic Authors Association and founder of the Society of Academic Authors. He has been active in the Society of Professional Journalists and College Media Advisers.

His professional media experience began with his hometown newspaper in Kellogg, Idaho, and continued through college at Gonzaga University with United Press International and the Associated Press. After receiving a master's degree from Northwestern University's Medill School of Journalism, he returned to the AP in Seattle, Denver and Cheyenne. Besides Gonzaga and Northwestern, he has done advanced studies at Marquette University, the University of Minnesota and the University of North Dakota.

His work as an Army command information officer earned numerous Minaret, Fourth Estate and other awards. In college he was editor of the Gonzaga *Bulletin*. He was faculty adviser to the Marquette *Tribune* and later founded the multicollege *Winona Campus Life* lab newspaper. He has edited numerous publications, including *The Academic Author*, and several online news sites, including the sa^2 news site for academic authors (sa2.info) and a college news site (indee.info).

Vivian introduced his widely used college textbook, *The Media of Mass Communication*, in 1991. Vivian and coauthor Alfred Lawrence Lorenz of Loyola University in New Orleans wrote *News: Reporting and Writing*, a journalism textbook, in 1995. Vivian's scholarly, professional and trade articles have appeared in many publications, including *American Journalism, American Speech, Journalism Educator, Journalism History, Journalism Quarterly, Masthead* and *Newspaper Research Journal*. He also has written numerous encyclopedia articles.

Award for Excellence

The *Media of Mass Communication* by John Vivian has been awarded the Text and Academic Authors award for excellence. Affectionately called "the Texty," the award has been characterized as the Oscar for textbooks. The award is given to college textbooks in a broad range of academic disciplines that include communication, education and the performing and visual arts. The judges, all veteran textbook authors, evaluate books on four criteria: Is the book interesting and informative? Is the book well organized and presented? Is the book up to date and appealing? Does the book possess "teachability"? The judges gave *The Media of Mass Communication* perfect scores on all criteria. Said one judge: "By all measures, superior." John Vivian said he was especially pleased with the award because fellow textbook authors were the judges. "There is no more meaningful recognition than that which comes from peers," he said.

The Media of Mass Communication was introduced in 1991 and quickly became the most-adopted textbook for introductory mass media and mass communication courses. The book's popularity has grown among college professors and their students with every new edition. The edition marks the 19th variation of the original book, including Canadian editions with coauthor Peter Maurin and translations for students in China, India and Indonesia.

Arthur Sulzberger The New York *Times* chief executive calls himself "platform agnostic." The future of newspapers, as he sees it, is in content regardless of whether the delivery form is ink on paper.

chapter

1 Mass Media Literacy

In this chapter you will learn:

- The mass media are pervasive in our everyday lives.
- Mass media's culturally binding role is diminishing.
- The primary mass media are built on print, chemical and electronic technologies.
- Integration of mass media technologies has transformed their impact.
- Traditional mass media products are being supplemented and replaced.
- Scholars have devised models to explain the mass media.
- Most mass media organizations must be profitable to stay in business.
- Mass media ownership is consolidating.

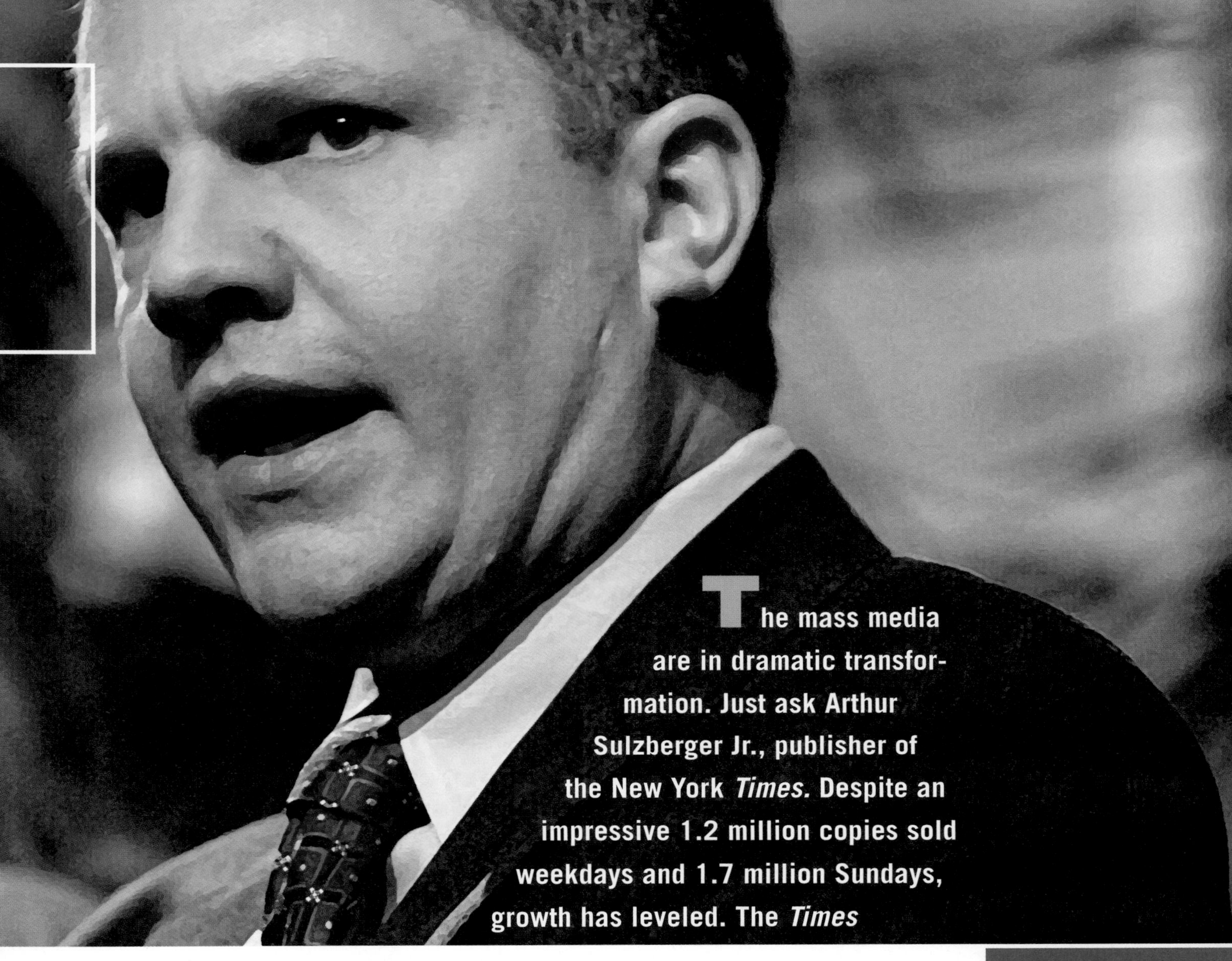

The mass media are in dramatic transformation. Just ask Arthur Sulzberger Jr., publisher of the New York *Times.* Despite an impressive 1.2 million copies sold weekdays and 1.7 million Sundays, growth has leveled. The *Times* might be the world's best newspaper, but as with other traditional media its glamour is fading as the audience and advertisers shift to newer, flashier alternatives. Too, Sulzberger knows that young people, unlike their parents and grandparents, don't read newspapers much.

This might all seem depressing for a newspaper executive whose family has run the *Times* since 1896. Sulzberger himself learned the family business as a *Times* reporter for six years. But he doesn't see himself as a newspaper guy. Sulzberger calls himself a "platform agnostic." It's an insightful term. He sees the *Times* as being not so much in the newspaper business as in the news business. The content generated by the *Times,* which has 1,200 journalists in the New York newsroom alone, is the company's greatest asset. Their coverage, their stories, which can be called *messages,* are the key. Less relevant is the medium, or platform, that conveys the messages.

As a platform agnostic, Sulzberger is jockeying both daringly and gingerly among options for delivering messages. The company has invested heavily in its NYTimes.com

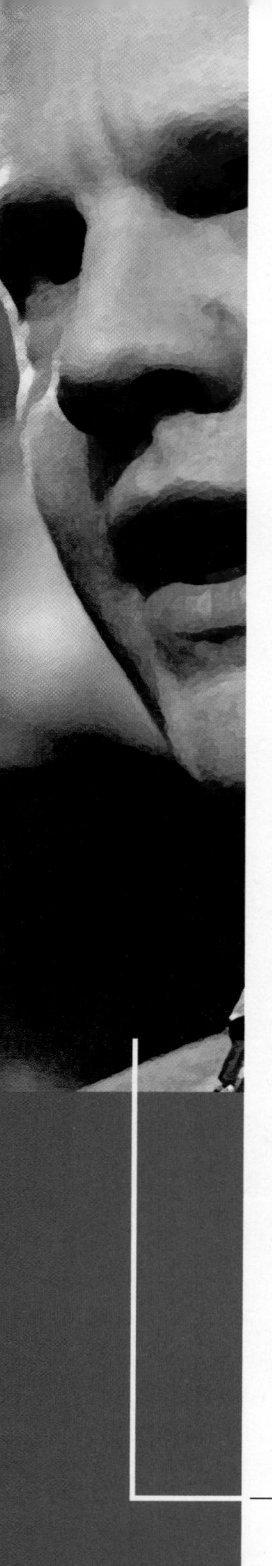

and Boston.com web sites, which score 35 percent profit margins some months—all from advertising. Imagine earning that kind of interest on your checking account.

There is an audience for news. Growth for the *Times'* online ventures is projected to climb to as high as 40 percent a year. NYTimes.com gets 18 million hits a day, better than 10 times the number of copies of the newspaper that are sold.

In a bid for the under-30 set, the company has bought into a giveaway tabloid, *Metro Boston.*

In television the company produces acclaimed pieces for *Frontline, Nova* and other programs. The company has put $100 million into a partnership with Discovery Communications to create the Discovery Times cable channel.

None of this is entirely new. The *Times* has long been involved in other media, including books, magazines, radio and television, adroitly testing the waters of nonnewspaper vehicles, moving in and out as lessons are learned. It was the *Times,* for example, that created the celebrity magazine *Us Weekly.* Now the company is out of the magazine business. In television it owns eight stations.

Sulzberger recognizes, of course, that newspapers aren't about to disappear. Most of the company's revenues are from the flagship newspaper, and although flat, the revenues are a hefty $3 billion a year. Sulzberger also knows that the newspaper industry is healthy. The most profitable chains, such as Gannett and Knight-Ridder, have profit margins of 25 percent.

Sulzberger has created a *Times* national edition, the first U.S. metro daily to do so. The national edition is printed on 20 presses scattered across the country for home delivery to compete for readers and advertisers against *USA Today* and the *Wall Street Journal* as well as magazines and television. Abroad, the company has bought 100 percent control of the Paris-based *International Herald Tribune,* a favorite of travelers and expatriates, with 240,000 subscribers in 180 countries. The company also owns the venerable Boston *Globe* and 15 small dailies, mostly in Massachusetts and Florida.

The common denominator in Sulzberger's strategy is high-quality journalism. No company spends more on news-gathering, an estimated $300 million a year. Nor does any other company have a larger news staff. The *Times* has more Pulitzer Prizes—seven in 2002 alone, six for its coverage of the 9/11 terrorism attack the year before. In the power centers of government and business the *Times* is a must-read.

Since the *Times* was founded in 1851 the paper's tradition has been that investing in journalism will yield its own rewards. The founders 150-some years ago didn't think much beyond their medium, the newspaper, for distributing news. Sulzberger does. The future for distribution, he says, is broadband media like the Internet. In the meantime the *Times* has legs in multiple media—print, video and the Internet.

Importance of Mass Media

studypreview **Mass media are usually thought of as sources of news and entertainment. They also carry messages of persuasion.**

Pervasiveness

Mass media are pervasive in modern life. Every morning, millions of Americans wake up to clock radios. Political candidates spend most of their campaign dollars on television ads to woo voters. The U.S. consumer economy depends on advertising to create mass markets. American children see 30,000 to 40,000 commercial messages a year. With mass media so influential, we need to know as much as we can about how they work. Consider:

- Through the mass media we learn almost everything we know about the world beyond our immediate environs. What would you know about Baghdad or Hurricane Katrina or the Super Bowl if it were not for newspapers, television and other mass media?
- An informed and involved citizenry is possible in modern democracy only when the mass media work well.
- People need the mass media to express their ideas widely. Without mass media your expression would be limited to people within earshot and those to whom you write letters.
- Powerful forces use the mass media to influence us with their ideologies and for their commercial purposes. The mass media are the main tools of propagandists, advertisers and other persuaders.

media DATABANK

Media Usage

The media research firm Veronis Suhler Stevenson reported television easily led other media in the average hours of consumer use per person in 2004. Veronis projected even more television viewing by 2008.

Television	3,584 hours
Radio	1,035 hours
Internet	189 hours
Recorded music	180 hours
Daily newspapers	169 hours
Magazines	118 hours
Books	107 hours
Home video	78 hours

Information Source

The most listened-for item in morning newscasts is the weather forecast. People want to know how to prepare for the day. The quality of their lives is at stake. Not knowing that rain is expected can mean getting wet on the way home or not being prepared for a slower commute on rain-slick roads. There used to be a joke that the most important thing the mass media did was to tell us whether a tornado was coming or whether the Russians were coming.

The heart of the media's informing function lies in messages called **news.** Journalists themselves are hard pressed to agree on a definition of news. One useful definition is that news is reports about things that people want or need to know. In the United States, reporters usually tell the news without taking sides.

Advertising also is part of the mass media's information function. The media, especially newspapers, are bulletin boards for trade and commerce. People look to supermarket advertisements for specials. Classified advertisements provide useful information.

Entertainment Source

The mass media can be wonderful entertainers, bringing together huge audiences not otherwise possible. More people cried at the movie *Titanic* than read all of the dozens of books about the tragedy. More people hear Nine Inch Nails on CDs or the radio than ever attend one of the group's concerts. Count the seats in Jimmy Buffet's bar in Key West, even calculate standing-room-only crowds, and contrast that with the audience for his signature song, *Margaritaville,* in even one television appearance.

Almost all mass media have an entertainment component, although no medium is wholly entertainment. The thrust of the U.S. movie industry is almost all entertainment,

news ■ Nonfiction reports on what people want or need to know.

but there can be a strong informational and persuasive element. Even the most serious newspaper has an occasional humor column. Most mass media are a mix of information and entertainment—and also persuasion.

Persuasion Forum

People form opinions from the information and interpretations to which they are exposed, which means that even news coverage has an element of persuasion. The media's attempts to persuade, however, are usually in editorials and commentaries whose persuasive purpose is obvious. Most news media separate material designed to persuade from news. Newspapers package their opinion articles in an editorial section. Commentary on television is introduced as opinion.

The most obvious of the media messages designed to persuade is advertising. **Advertisements** exhort the audience to action—to go out and buy toothpaste, cornflakes and automobiles. **Public relations** is subtler, seeking to persuade but usually not to induce immediate action. Public relations tries to shape attitudes, usually by persuading mass media audiences to see an institution or activity in a particular light.

Culture and Values

study preview **Historically, mass media treatment of socially divisive issues has helped to create new consensus. This culturally binding media role may be fading. The exponential growth in media channels in recent years has created separate nests where like-minded people find enduring support for their perspectives and prejudices, which solidifies diversity at the expenses of consensus.**

Binding Influence

The mass media bind communities together by giving messages that become a shared experience. In the United States a rural newspaper editor scrambling to get an issue out may not be thinking about how her work creates a common identity among readers, but it does. The town newspaper is something everyone in town has in common. In the same way what subway riders in Philadelphia read on their way to work in the morning gives them something in common. A shared knowledge and a shared experience are created by mass media, and thus they create a base for community.

The same phenomenon occurs on a national level. News coverage of the 9/11 attacks on the World Trade Center and the Pentagon bound Americans in a nationwide grieving process. Coverage of the death of Princess Diana prompted a global dialogue on celebrity coverage.

Stories on misdeeds help us figure out what we as a society regard as acceptable and as inexcusable. News coverage of the impeachment of President Clinton did this. So did coverage of major lapses in the government response to the Hurricane Katrina disaster in Louisiana, Mississippi and Alabama, which forced President Bush to order the firing of the director of the Federal Emergency Management Administration. On a lesser scale so did the hypocrisy that was revealed in 2003 in stories about the gambling habits of conservative moralist William Bennett, a former U.S. secretary of education, and about the drug addiction of talk show host Rush Limbaugh, who for years had stridently advocated harsh crackdowns on sellers and users of drugs. The lists of people convicted of underage alcohol consumption, a staple in many small-city newspapers, keep the question before the public about whether the legal drinking age should be 21 or 18 or whether there should be any restriction at all or, at the other extreme, a return to prohibition. At many levels the mass media are essential for the ongoing process of society identifying its values.

advertisements ■ Messages intended to persuade people to buy.

public relations ■ Messages intended to win support.

Cristina Saralegui

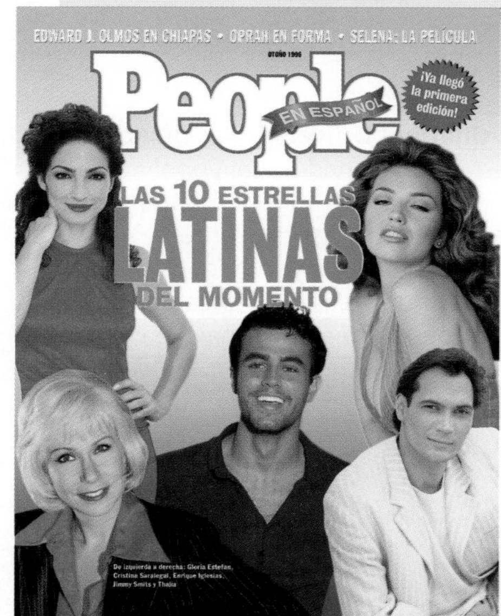

The Cristina Show
When *People* magazine launched its Spanish language edition, Cristina Saralegui made the cover as one of the leading Latinas of the day. Saralegui, lower left, is the reigning host of the dominant U.S.-produced show on Spanish-language television stations in the United States.

Among Hispanic-Americans there is no more trusted television figure than Cristina Saralegui, whose signature media empire is led by her Univision network television show. In a poll on role models, Saralegui outranked Oprah Winfrey and Jose Ramos with Latin-heritage women. Over 15-plus years the show has earned 10 Emmies. Viewership extends beyond the United States to Europe and Latin America.

Saralegui was born into the media in her native Cuba, a granddaughter of Latin American magazine magnate Francisco Saralegui. At age 12, after Castro came to power, Saralegui and her family joined thousands of other Cuban exiles in Miami. After college at the University of Miami she went into an internship with *Vanidades,* the leading Latin America women's magazine, which had been founded by her grandfather.

In 1979 she was named editor of Hearst's *Cosmopolitan en Español,* the Spanish-language version of Helen Gurley Brown's magazine for young, single women. After 10 years she struck out on her own, creating her namesake *Cristina Show* at Univison.

Soon followed *Cristina La Revista,* a monthly women's magazine focusing on the Latino *gente* with lots of celebrity news, personal interviews and success stories. Then came *Cristina Opina,* a daily radio program. Her media enterprises all are marked by an upbeat theme that's both inspirational and motivational. She has causes. Arriba la Vida Foundation works on AIDS awareness and education.

Even in a media world that is increasingly demassified and focusing on audience segments, niche mass audiences can be gigantic. The audience of Cristina Saralegui's television show has been estimated at 100 million worldwide.

The importance of the mass media in binding people into nationhood is clear in every revolution and coup d'état around the world. The leaders try to take over the national media system right away as an essential vehicle to unify the population behind their cause and silence the opposition. When the United States invaded Baghdad in 2003, a priority was to get television back on the air. Until the invasion a priority of Saddam Hussein's regime was to keep the service going despite severe bombing. Rebel radio is always a target in contested areas. Once a crisis is over, except in dictatorial regimes, the media fade as a propagandist tool and become a common reference point for their huge audiences.

Cristina Saralegui Web site of journalist Cristina Saralegui, with links to her talk show and magazine. **www.cristinaonline.com/english**

You might ask whether the media, in covering controversies, are divisive. The answer: No. Seldom do the media create controversy. They merely cover it. Thorough coverage, over time, helps to bring about societal consensus—sometimes for change, sometimes not. For example, most Americans once opposed legalizing abortion, but today, after exhaustive media attention, a majority consensus has emerged that abortions should be available legally. The same is true of many fundamental issues, such as women's rights, racial integration and government budget priorities.

500-Channel Universe

Less than a quarter century ago, for most people the choices for a daily news recap in the United States were the three major television networks, a local newspaper and radio headlines on local stations. The news in those not-so-distant days was edited for general audiences from a detached, neutral perspective. Those media sources still exist, largely in their traditional form. But three revolutionary technologies have changed the media environment dramatically:

- Satellite communication
- Digitized messages
- The Internet

The explosion of media sources, called the **500-Channel Universe,** was first hailed for the way it added to the marketplace of messages and loosened the oligopoly of relatively few media sources. Darker questions have since arisen. Studies are finding that few people scan their new choices to expose themselves to the diverse content. It may be a 500-channel universe, but in the case of television hardly anybody goes beyond the 15 or so channels that coincide with their interests and biases. So instead of being the vehicle for social cohesion that the media used to be, the reality is that new channels, including thousands on the Internet, reinforce what separates us on the cutting-edge issues by which society defines its values.

The media may be becoming a vehicle less for the traditional consensus-building than for building walls around societal niches.

Primary Mass Media

studypreview **Mass production of the written word became possible with an invention by Johannes Gutenberg in the 1440s, which transformed human existence in ways he never imagined. The legacy of Gutenberg's technology includes books, newspapers and magazines. Later came media rooted in chemical and electronic technology.**

Print Technology

The introduction of mass-produced books in the 15th century marked a turning point in human history. Before then, books were handwritten, usually by **scribist** monks who copied existing books onto blank sheets of paper letter by letter, one page at a time. These scribists could turn out only a few hand-lettered books in a lifetime of tedium.

In the mid-1400s **Johannes Gutenberg,** a tinkerer in what is now Germany, devised an innovation that made it possible to print pages using metal letters. Gutenberg's revolutionary contribution was in applying metallurgy to the printing process, which went back to ancient China. The idea for **movable metal type** occurred to Gutenberg in the mid-1430s. Instead of using wood, which often cracked in the pressing process, he experimented with casting individual letters in a lead-based alloy. He built a frame the size of a book's page and then arranged the metal letters into words. Once a page was filled—with letters and words and sentences—he put the frame into a modified wine press, applied ink, laid paper and pressed. The process made it possible to produce dozens, even hundreds or thousands, of copies.

Gutenberg's impact cannot be overstated. The duplicative power of movable type put the written word into wide circulation and fueled quantum increases in literacy. One hundred years after Gutenberg, the state of communication in Europe had undergone a revolution. Elaborate postal systems were in place. Standardized maps produced by printing presses replaced hand-copied maps, with all their inaccuracies and idiosyncrasies. People began writing open letters to be distributed far and wide. Newspapers followed. The exchange of scientific discoveries was hastened through special publications. Johannes Gutenberg stands at a dividing point in the history of humankind. A scribist culture preceded him. The age of mass communication followed.

500-Channel Universe ■ Fanciful term for the growth in media channels available in recent years.

scribist ■ Monks who copied books manually.

Johannes Gutenberg ■ In the mid-1400s, devised revolutionary printing process using metal letters.

movable metal type ■ Small blocks of type arranged into words, lines and pages.

Johannes Gutenberg

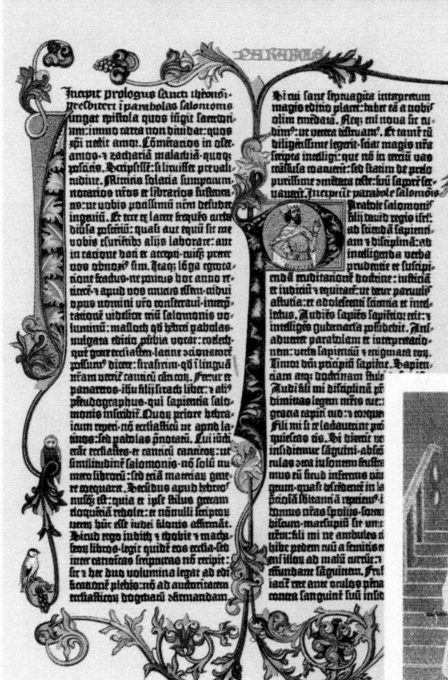

Gutenberg Masterpiece

First Mass-Produced Written Word Johannes Gutenberg and his assistants could produce 50 to 60 imprints an hour with their modified wine press, but Gutenberg's real contribution was movable metal type, which expedited the putting together of pages and opened the age of mass communication.

Johannes Gutenberg was eccentric—a secretive tinkerer with a passion for beauty, detail and craftsmanship. By trade he was a metallurgist, but he never made much money at it. Like most of his fellow 15th-century Rhinelanders (people from an area in present-day Germany), he pressed his own grapes for wine. As a businessman, he was not very successful, and he died penniless. Despite his unpromising combination of traits, quirks and habits—perhaps because of them—Johannes Gutenberg wrought the most significant change in history: the mass-produced written word. He invented movable metal type.

Despite the significance of his invention, there is much we do not know about Gutenberg. Even to friends he seldom mentioned his experiments, and when he did, he referred to them mysteriously as his "secret art." When he ran out of money, Gutenberg quietly sought investors, luring them partly with the mystique he attached to his work. What we know about Gutenberg's "secret art" was recorded only because Gutenberg's main backer didn't realize the quick financial return he expected on his investment and sued. The litigation left a record from which historians have pieced together the origins of modern printing.

The date when Johannes Gutenberg printed his first page with movable type is unknown, but historians usually settle on 1446. Gutenberg's printing process was widely copied—and quickly. By 1500, presses all over Western Europe had published almost 40,000 books.

Today, Gutenberg is remembered for the Bibles he printed with movable type. Two hundred **Gutenberg Bibles,** each a printing masterpiece, were produced over several years. Gutenberg used the best paper. He concocted an especially black ink. The quality amazed everybody, and the Bibles sold quickly. Gutenberg could have printed hundreds more, perhaps thousands. With a couple of husky helpers he and his modified wine press could have produced 50 to 60 page sheets an hour. However, Johannes Gutenberg, who never had much business savvy, concentrated instead on quality. Forty-seven Gutenberg Bibles remain today, all collector's items. One sold in 1978 for $2.4 million.

Today the primary mass media whose technologies descend from Gutenberg are **books, magazines** and **newspapers.** They all come from printing presses, but they can be distinguished according to four categories: binding, regularity, content and timeliness.

	Books	Magazines	Newspapers
Binding	Stitched or glued	Stapled	Unbound
Regularity	Single issue	At least quarterly	At least weekly
Content	Single topic	Diverse topics	Diverse topics
Timeliness	Generally not timely	Timeliness not an issue	Timeliness important

Although these distinctions are helpful, they cannot be applied rigidly. For example, timeliness is critical to *Time* and *Newsweek,* even though they are magazines. Sunday

Gutenberg Bibles ■ Bibles printed by Gutenberg with movable type. Surviving Bibles are all collector's items.

books ■ One-time, bound publications of enduring value on a single topic.

magazines ■ Ongoing bound publications of continuing value with diverse topics.

newspapers ■ Unbound publications, generally weekly or daily, with diverse, timely content.

media TIMELINE

MEDIA TECHNOLOGY

1446 Primal Event Johannes Gutenberg devised movable metal type, permitting mass production of printed materials.

1455 Books Johannes Gutenberg printed the first of his Bibles using movable type.

1690 Newspapers Ben Harris printed *Publick Occurrences,* the first newspaper in the English colonies.

1741 Magazines Andrew Bradford printed *American Magazine* and Benjamin Franklin printed *General Magazine,* the first magazines in the English colonies.

1877 Recording Thomas Edison introduced the phonograph, which could record and play back sound.

1888 Movies William Dickson devised the motion picture camera.

1895 Radio Guglielmo Marconi transmitted the first message by radio wave.

1927 Television Philo Farnsworth invented the tube that picked up moving images for live transmission.

1969 Web The U.S. Defense Department established the computer network that became the Internet.

newspaper supplements such as *Parade* are magazines but are not bound. Over the past 30 years, book publishers have found ways to produce "instant books" on major news events within a couple of weeks so that their topics can be timely. The *National Enquirer* has characteristics of both a newspaper and a magazine.

Chemical Technology

The technology of movies is based on photographic chemistry. Movies are a **chemical medium.** Although a lot of video production, including some prime-time television, is shot on videotape and stored electronically, Hollywood still makes most movies on strips of transparent celluloid that are "pulled through the soup"—a technology that dates back to 1888.

In some respects, chemical technology is not only archaic but also expensive. Studios make as many as 6,000 copies of major releases and ship them from movie house to movie house in cumbersome metal boxes. The freight bills alone are astronomical. How much easier—and cheaper—it would be to transmit movies via satellite to movie houses, a system that would cut film and distribution costs by perhaps 85 percent.

As digital technology improves and costs come down, movies are shifting from chemical to electronic technology. But don't hold your breath.

Electronic Technology

Television, radio and sound recordings flash their messages electronically. Pioneer work on **electronic media** began in the late 1800s, but they are mostly a 20th-century development. Unlike print messages, television and radio messages disappear as soon as they are transmitted. Although it is true that messages can be stored on electronic disks and on tape and by other means, they usually reach listeners and viewers in a nonconcrete form. Television is especially distinctive because it engages several senses at once with sound, sight and movement.

The newest mass medium, the web, combines text, audio and visuals—both still and moving—in a global electronic network.

chemical medium ■ Underlying technology for movies is photographic chemistry.

electronic media ■ Recordings, radio, television or web, whose messages are stored electronically for transmission and retrieval.

Technology Melds

studypreview **For more than 400 years the mass media were largely word-driven. The few visuals were carved woodcuts. An integration of photographic technology transformed the media in the late 1800s, changing dramatically how great numbers of people saw the world. Now digital technology is changing traditional media forms in new ways.**

Joseph Níepce French inventor of a light-sensitive photo process in 1826.

Frederick Ives Invented halftones in 1876.

halftone A conversion of a photograph into tiny dots for reproduction on printing presses.

visual literacy An understanding of images to interpret their meaning and significance.

Print-Visual Integration

The chemical technology used in traditional photography was discovered almost 200 years ago. In 1727 experimenters realized that silver nitrate darkens when exposed to light. A hundred years later, in 1826, French scientist **Joseph Níepce** discovered he could create a fixed image by exposing a light-sensitive, silver-coated copper plate to iodine or mercury vapors. The discovery culminated centuries of experiments to capture and preserve an image. Although Níepce could create a photographic image, he didn't figure out how to make copies. Without copies, the images could not be communicated widely. The only visuals in the mass media of the time—books, magazines and newspapers—continued to be engraved line drawings and not many of them. There was nothing photographic.

The breakthrough that melded the printing press with photographic technology came in 1878. **Frederick Ives** at Cornell University divided a photograph into a microscopic grid, each tiny square with a raised dot to register a separate tonal gray from a photograph; the bigger the dot, the more ink it would transfer to the paper and the darker the gray would be. The grid, cast into metal, was called a **halftone.** At the typical reading distance, 14 inches, the human eye couldn't make out the grid, but the eye could see the image created by the varying grays. Two years later, the New York *Daily Graphic,* a newspaper, adapted Ives' process to high-speed printing and published a halftone image. This was revolutionary. In numbers never before imagined, people could not only read about the world beyond their immediate horizon but also see it.

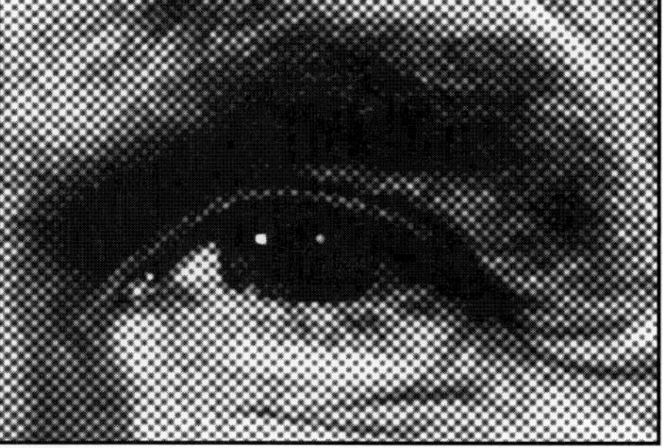

Inked Dots
In the halftone process, invented by Frederick Ives in the 1870s, bigger dots transfer more ink to the printed page for dark parts of a halftone. Smaller dots are lighter. In some respects, the halftone grid is akin to computer-screen pixels with each dot, or pixel, contributing to the larger whole.

During this same period work with motion pictures was coming together, largely at inventor Thomas Edison's laboratories in New Jersey. In 1891 Edison began producing movies. This compounded the impact of visuals as a component of the mass media. There is no better illustration of the impact of visuals that noting the way early movie-goers, in a wholly new experience, would duck in horror when a locomotive came at them on screen, no matter how jerky, scratchy and black-and-white the image was. **Visual literacy,** a sophistication in interpreting photographic images, would come slowly.

Frederick Ives

Digital Integration

Digital technology was devised in the 1950s, first for telephone communication upgrades, but not until 1983, when recorded music was introduced on CDs, did the public perceive the significance. Suddenly, recorded music had unprecedented clarity. When **Marc Andreessen** introduced the **Netscape** Internet browser in 1993, the number of people with home access to digitized media content swelled. Dazzled at new possibilities, entrepreneurs poured $1 trillion into an infrastructure to support the **dot-com** industry, named for the ".com" suffixes used by commercial sites on the Internet.

The inflated dot-com bubble burst in 2000. In the crash most upstart dot-com enterprises went belly-up. Still, the potential of a new age of mass communication was obvious. Caught in the great dot-com implosion were book, magazine, newspaper, radio and television companies that already had begun moving content online. The most dramatic shift was in downloadable music, an area in which the technology of Internet distribution so leapfrogged the existing recording industry infrastructure that some experts predicted that the industry would free-fall out of existence. The dive in CD sales leveled off, however, and by embracing the new technology, the recording industry began to recover.

Meanwhile, digitized technology is eclipsing the technological roots of the mass media. The legacy of Gutenberg, Ives, Edison and the others is no longer their technology but the business models and infrastructure that grew from their technology and shaped the corporate and culture icons of the modern mass media. Even when printing presses are gone, there will still be businesses whose products include the great novels, reference works, textbooks and news. Likewise, the digitization of broadcasting and Hollywood means merely a change in delivery of media messages.

MSM and New Media

studypreview **Mass media can be divided into mainstream and new media categories. The distinction is imperfect for purposes of neat, clean pigeonholing but can help to make some sense of changing ownership, content and audience patterns, and technology.**

CNET Links to technology stories and videos, product reviews and price comparison feature.
www.cnet.com

Sirius Satellite radio with over 120 commercial-free channels. Categories include music, news, entertainment and sports.
www.sirius.com

Mainstream Media

The fragmentation of the mass media into new forms has blurred distinctions. There was a time when identifying a media product was relatively easy. Everybody knew what a newscast looked like. ABC, CBS and NBC offered the master models. Today the mass media comprise an oddball bevy of sources, from which massive percentages of people pick up their knowledge of the day's events. Young people opt more for Jon Stewart, Conan O'Brien and David Letterman. Political right-wingers like Fox News. Techno-nerds go to C-NET.

The term **mainstream media,** sometimes abbreviated as MSM, has been coined to help navigate an evolving landscape. Although the term is rather elastic, it usually distinguishes traditional media forms and sources from new ones.

Ownership In terms of ownership, the major media companies—Time Warner, Viacom, Disney and their ilk—are mainstream. In contrast are startups with novel business plans. Then there are anarchical arrays of products on the web, some of which are creating new molds. Blogs, highly personalized and often quirky, definitely are not MSM. Satellite radio companies XM and Sirius, using technology in new ways, are hardly MSM with their potential to upend the radio industry as we've known it for three-quarters of a century.

Technology The term "MSM" also distinguishes technology-based platforms. Television and magazines are mainstream, clearly defined and traditional. Wi-Fi and other technology-wrought newcomers, definitely not MSM, sometimes are called **new media.**

Marc Andreessen ■ Invented the Netscape browser.

Netscape ■ An Internet browser that broadened web access widely.

dot-com ■ A term for businesses that were started to capitalize on Internet technology.

mainstream media (MSM) ■ Established media companies and products.

new media ■ Upstart media companies and media products resulting from new technology.

New Media

Innovation is not new to the mass media. The Beadle Brothers, who introduced dime novels before the Civil War, were the new media of their day, profoundly changing the U.S. book market. Today, innovations outside the mainstream include broad, sometimes fuzzy categories like alternative media, underground media and high-tech media.

Alternative Media Radio stations geared to neighborhood service with low-power transmitters, now licensed by the Federal Communications Commission, have made possible a level of interactivity with their audiences not possible for traditional stations that seek large audiences to draw advertising and pay the bills. These low-power stations, many staffed with volunteers, are alternative voices in the radio universe.

Underground Media The generation-defined, antiestablishment press of the 1970s was one form of new media, living on in free-distribution weekly form. The emphasis is heavy on local, live entertainment, usually bar-centered; reformist social and political perspectives; outrageous, often ribald humor; and a high quotient of street vulgarities and sexual innuendo. These aren't your grandmother's media products.

High-Tech Media Technology creates new possibilities. Think what iPods are doing to record shops and radio listenership. Cybercafes are giving way to Wi-Fi. For better and worse, Internet bloggers have widened participation in public affairs journalism.

Mass Media Models

studypreview **Scholars have devised numerous ways to dissect and categorize the mass media. These include the hot-cool, entertainment-information, content-distribution and elitist-populist models. Each offers insights, but all of them have shortcomings in explaining the mass media.**

Hot-Cool Model

One model that helps to explain the mass media divides them into hot and cool categories. Books, magazines and newspapers are **hot media** because a high degree of thinking is required to use them. To read a book, for example, you must immerse yourself to derive anything from it. You must concentrate and tune out distractions. The relationship between you and the medium is intense—or hot. The same is true of magazines and newspapers, which require the audience to participate actively in the communication process.

In contrast, some media allow the audience to be less actively involved, even passive. These are **cool media.** Television, for example, requires less intellectual involvement than do the hot media. In fact, television requires hardly any effort. When radio is played mostly as background, it doesn't require any active listener involvement at all. It's a cool medium. Radio is warmer, however, when it engages listeners' imaginations, as with radio drama.

Are movies hot or cold? In some ways, movies are like television, with simultaneous visual and audio components. But there are essential differences. Movies involve viewers completely. Huge screens command the viewers' full attention, and sealed, darkened movie-house auditoriums shut out distractions. On a hot-cool continuum, movies are hot. What about a movie played at home on television? Cool.

Entertainment-Information Model

Many people find it helpful to define media by whether the thrust of their content is entertainment or information. By this definition newspapers almost always are considered

hot media ■ Print media, which require intimate audience involvement.

cool media ■ Can be used passively.

Infotainment
Celebrities and their ordeals and antics have risen on the scale of newsworthiness as the gap between news and entertainment has narrowed. When an angle-seeking paparazzo squirted actor Tom Cruise with water from a handheld "microphone" in a London crowd, Cruise's confrontational response made newscasts everywhere.

an information medium, and audio recording and movies are considered entertainment. As a medium, books both inform and entertain. So do television and radio, although some networks, stations and programs do more of one than the other. The same is true of magazines, some titles being geared more for informing and some more for entertaining.

Although widely used, the entertainment-information dichotomy has limitations. Nothing inherent in newspapers, for example, precludes them from being entertaining. Consider the weirdest supermarket tabloids, which are newspapers but which hardly anybody takes seriously as an information source. The neatness of the entertainment-information dichotomy doesn't work well with mainstream newspapers either. Most daily newspapers have dozens of items intended to entertain. Open a paper and start counting with "Garfield" and the astrology column.

The entertainment-information dichotomy has other weaknesses. It misses the potential of all mass media to do more than entertain and inform. The dichotomy misses the persuasion function, which you read about earlier in this chapter. People might consider most movies to be entertainment, but there is no question that Steven Spielberg has broad social messages even in his most rollicking adventure sagas. In the same sense, just about every television sitcom is a morality tale wrapped up in an entertaining package. The persuasion may be soft-pedaled, but it's everywhere.

Dividing mass media into entertainment and information categories is becoming increasingly difficult as newspapers, usually considered the leading information medium, back off from hard-hitting content to woo readers with softer, entertaining stuff. For better or worse this same shift is also taking place at *Time* and *Newsweek*. This melding even has a name that has come into fashion: **infotainment.**

Although the entertainment-information model will continue to be widely used, generally it is better to think in terms of the major media functions—to entertain, to inform and to persuade—and recognize that all media do all of these things to a greater or lesser degree.

Content-Distribution Model

Many dynamics in mass media behavior today can be visualized in a model that divides media functions into message creation and message distribution. It's the **content-distribution model.** Some companies are heavily into creating content, like producing movies, publishing books and putting out magazines. Other companies are heavily into distribution, like operating movie houses, bookstore chains and cable systems. The heaviest players, including Time Warner, News Corporation, General Electric and Disney, are building stakes in both content creation and distribution. Consider these examples:

infotainment ■ Melding of media role as purveyor of information and entertainment.

content-distribution model ■ Divides functions of media companies into a creation category, like producing a television program, to a distribution function, like delivering the program on a cable system.

Media Company	A Content Unit	A Distribution Unit
Time Warner	Cable News Network	Time Warner Cable
News Corporation	20th Century Fox	Sky Global
General Electric	Universal Studios	NBC
Disney	Disney Studios	ABC

Controlling both content creation and distribution, called **vertical integration,** was once considered a violation of U.S. antitrust laws. In 1948 the U.S. Supreme Court forced Hollywood studios to sell off their national movie-house chains. The Court ruled that controlling the movie business all the way from creation to final movie-house showing stifled competition. Later the Federal Communications Commission forbade the Big Three television networks to own the shows they aired. The commission's reasoning was the same, although the ban was relaxed in 1995 after cable channels had cut into the Big Three's one-time dominance.

In general, the government has backed off on the vertical integration issue. Some critics, including media commentator Steven Brill, blame politics: "Today's media landscape is filled with giants who are some of the key players in the modern Washington landscape of lobbying and campaign cash."

The worst downside of vertical integration is that the companies that own the entire process are inclined to favor internally produced products. When Steven Brill created the Court TV channel, for example, he felt forced to sell part of his company to three giant cable system operators, including Time Warner, to get his channel on the cable systems. In short, an outsider is disadvantaged. Newspapers in the Gannett chain, for example, must carry the parent company's supplement magazine *USA Weekend. Time* magazine carries a medical column by Sanjay Gupta of corporate sibling CNN. Upstart cable channels are squeezed off cable systems whose corporate parents own their own channels.

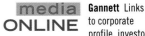

Gannett Links to corporate profile, investor information and services, Gannett newspapers (including *USA Today*), television stations and affiliate companies.
www.gannett.com

Time Magazine Online version of *Time* Magazine; includes headlines from the current magazine, an archive of past issues, and links to CNN headlines.
www.time.com/time

CNN Contains current news stories as well as weather, entertainment, sports, business and more.
www.cnn.com

Elitist-Populist Model

An ongoing tension in the mass media exists between advancing social and cultural interests and giving broad segments of the population what they want. This tension between extremes on a continuum takes many forms:

- Classical music versus pop music.
- Nudes in art books versus nudes in *Playboy* magazine.
- A Penelope Fitzgerald novel versus a pulp romance.
- A PBS documentary on crime versus Fox Television's *Cops.*

At one end of the continuum is serious media content that appeals to people who can be called **elitists** because they believe that the mass media have a responsibility to contribute to a better society and a refinement of the culture, regardless of whether the media attract large audiences. At the other end of the continuum are **populists,** who are entirely oriented to the marketplace. Populists believe that the mass media are at their best when they give people what people want.

The mass media have been significant historically in shaping social and cultural values. Media that are committed to promoting these values generally forsake the largest possible audiences. For years in New York City the serious-minded *Times,* which has no comics, lagged in street sales behind the *Daily News,* a screaming tabloid that emphasizes crime and disaster coverage, loves scandals and sex, and carries popular comics. The *Times* can be accused of elitism, gearing its coverage to a high level for an audience that appreciates thorough news coverage and serious commentary. The *Daily News,* on the other hand, can be charged with catering to a low level of audience and providing hardly any social or cultural leadership. The *Daily News* is in the populist tradition.

A lot of media criticism can be understood in the context of this elitist-populist continuum. People who see a responsibility for the mass media to provide cultural and intellectual leadership fall at one extreme. At the other extreme are people who trust the

New York Times Online version of the New York *Times* with the latest headlines and searchable archives.
www.nytimes.com

New York Daily News Online version of the New York *Daily News,* complete with current headlines, sports and entertainment.
www.nydailynews.com

vertical integration ■ A single corporation or individual's total control over production that can stifle competition. Example: An auto manufacturer that owns iron ore mines, steel plants, manufacturing plants and dealerships.

elitists ■ Focus on media responsibility to society.

populists ■ Applaud media that attract a large following.

general population to determine media content through marketplace dynamics. Certainly, there are economic incentives for the media to cater to mass tastes.

Most mass media in the United States are somewhere in the middle of the elitist-populist continuum. Fox Television offers some serious fare, not only hyped crime recreations, and the New York *Times* has a sense of humor that shows itself in the wit of its columnists and in other ways.

Economics of Mass Media

study preview **With few exceptions the U.S. mass media are privately owned and must turn profits to stay in business. Except for books, sound recordings and movies, most media income is from advertising, with lesser amounts directly from media consumers. These economic realities are potent shapers of media content.**

Economic Foundation

The mass media are expensive to set up and operate. The equipment and facilities require major investment. Meeting the payroll requires a bankroll. Print media must buy paper by the ton. Broadcasters have gigantic electricity bills to pump their messages through the ether.

To meet their expenses, the mass media sell their product in two ways. Either they derive their income from selling a product directly to mass audiences, as do the movie, record and book industries, or they derive their income from advertisers that place advertisements for mass audiences that the media provide, as do newspapers, magazines, radio and television. Newspapers and magazines are hybrids with both audience and advertising revenue streams. In short, the mass media operate in a capitalistic environment. With few exceptions they are in business to make money.

Media Costs

Advertisers pay for space and time in the mass media to reach the audience that the media attract. The larger the audience, the more the media charge. An exception is a premium charge for narrow audiences, which can be far more expensive to reach per capita. Here is a sample of rates for major U.S. media for one-time placements:

Fox, *2005 Super Bowl XXXIII*	30-second spot	$2,400,000
CBS, *Survivor: Vanuatu*	30-second spot	412,000
NBC, *The Apprentice*	30-second spot	410,000
ABC, *Monday Night Football*	30-second spot	307,000
Time	Full page	380,500
Rolling Stone	Full page	154,500
Wall Street Journal	Full page	172,500
New York *Times*	Sunday full page	94,300

Advertising Revenue Advertisers pay the mass media for access to potential customers. From print media, advertisers buy space. From broadcasters they buy time.

Generally, the more potential customers a media company can deliver to advertisers, the more advertisers are charged for time or space. Fox claimed 86.1 million households tuned in for the 2005 Super Bowl, and 30-second spots for the 2005 game went for $2.4 million. A spot on a daytime program, with a fraction of the Super Bowl audience, typically goes for $85,000. *Time* magazine, claiming a 4.6 million circulation, charges $380,600 for a full-page advertisement. If *Time*'s circulation were to plummet, so would its advertising rates. Although there are exceptions, newspapers, magazines, television and radio support themselves with advertising revenues.

Book publishers once relied solely on readers for revenue, but that has changed somewhat. Today, book publishers charge for film rights whenever Hollywood turns a book into a movie or a television program. Publishing houses now profit indirectly from the advertising revenue that television networks pull in from broadcasting movies.

Movies too have come to benefit from advertising. Until the 1950s movies relied entirely on box-office receipts for profits, but movie-makers now calculate what profits they can realize not only from movie-house traffic but also from selling to television and the home video market. High-tech DVDs are replacing VHS tapes, increasing what was already the lion's share of movie producers' income. Today, movie-makers even pick up advertising directly by charging commercial companies to include their products in the scenes they shoot, although the revenue is relatively minor.

Circulation Revenue Although some advertising-supported mass media, such as network television, do not charge their audiences, others do. When income is derived from the audience, it's called **circulation** revenue. *Wall Street Journal* readers pay 75 cents a copy at the newsrack. *Rolling Stone* costs $4.95. Little if any of the newsrack charge or even subscription revenue ends up with the *Wall Street Journal* or *Rolling Stone*. Distribution is costly, and distributors all along the way take their cut. For some publications, however, subscription income makes the difference between profit and loss.

Direct audience payments have emerged in recent years in broadcasting. Cable and satellite subscribers pay a monthly fee. Audience support is the basis of subscription television such as commercial-free HBO. Noncommercial broadcasting, including the Public Broadcasting Service and National Public Radio, relies heavily on viewer and listener

circulation ■ Number of copies of a publication that circulate.

Award-Winning Advertisements

To reach potential customers, advertisers buy space or time in mass media that can deliver audiences. It's the ads themselves, however, that drive home the sales pitch—but first they must get attention. Print ads that did this best in 2003 were "Rebirth" by the ad agency TBWA, Paris, for Sony PlayStation, honored with the Grand Prix Award at the Cannes international advertising festival, and another by the agency Hopper Galton, for the Discovery Channel documentary "Age of Terror," winner of the Cannes Golden Lion award.
Courtesy Discovery Networks Europe. Photo by Ernst Fischer.

TERRORISM HAS CHANGED THE WAY WE VIEW THE WORLD
'AGE OF TERROR' Global terrorism in context.
The first of four documentaries starts tonight at 9.30.
Discovery
CHANNEL

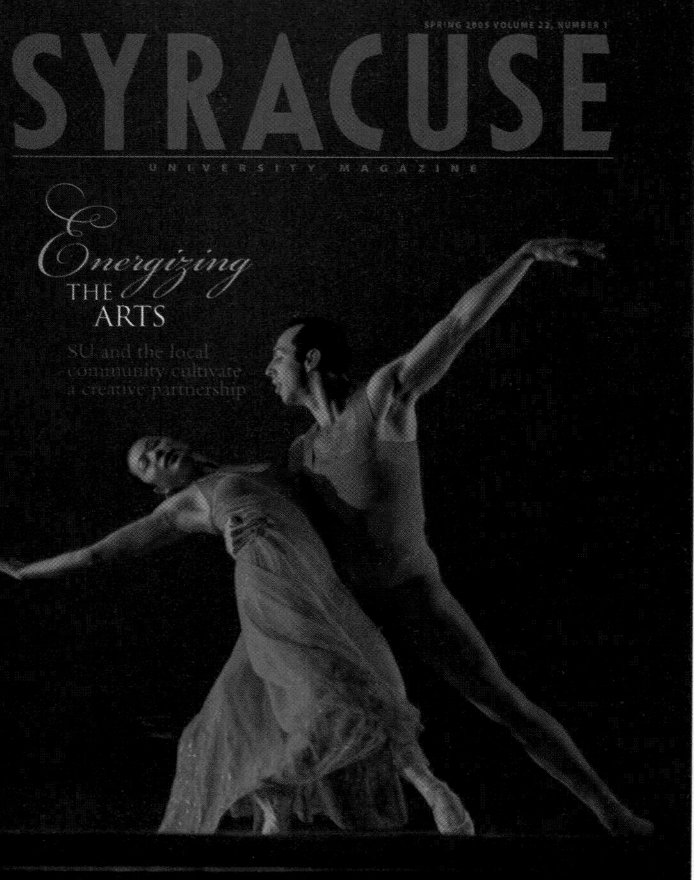

SPRING 2005 VOLUME 22, NUMBER 1
SYRACUSE
UNIVERSITY MAGAZINE
Energizing THE ARTS
SU and the local community cultivate a creative partnership

Image Publication
Some media products are advertising-free, financed by an organization with a message. Most universities issue glossy magazines for alumni and benefactors to tell the good story of the institution. Many corporations and other institutions do the same for shareholders, major customers, employees and other constituencies.

contributions. Record-makers, movie-makers and book publishers depend on direct sales to the consumer.

Besides advertising and circulation revenue, some media units derive income from other sources. PBS, for example, has a thriving catalog mail-order business.

Audience Donations Audience donations are important to some media operations. Public radio and television stations, which carry no advertising, solicit their audiences for contributions. On-air fund drives, usually running as many as four weeks a year, raise as much as 30 percent of many stations' budgets. Why do listeners and viewers cough up $50 or more for public-station programming when so much free media content is available? During their fund drives, the stations stress their heavy emphasis on public affairs and highbrow cultural content, which is hard to find in advertising-supported media. The stations then state, quite frankly, that the continuance of the programming depends on volunteer contributions.

Private Support The *Christian Science Monitor,* which maintains an expensive staff of foreign correspondents, has lost money for 30 years. Neither advertising nor subscription income is sufficient to meet expenses. In recent years the newspaper has been $12 million to $16 million in the red a year. The losses were made up, as always, by the Christian Science church, which sees part of its mission as providing high-quality news coverage of world affairs. Similarly, the Unification Church of the Reverend Sun Myung Moon underwrites the money-losing Washington *Times.*

Private support, largely from philanthropic organizations and large corporations, helps to keep the Public Broadcasting Service and National Public Radio on the air. The Federal Communications Commission does not allow PBS, NPR or their affiliate stations to accept advertising, although sponsor acknowledgments are OK.

Government Subsidies The idea of government support for the mass media might seem contrary to the democratic ideal of a press that is fiercely independent of government, if not adversarial. The fact, however, is that Congress has provided as much as $286 million a year in tax-generated dollars for a quasi-government agency, the Corporation for Public Broadcasting, to funnel to the nation's noncommercial television and radio system. Buffers are built into the structure to prevent governmental interference in programming. The buffers seem generally to have worked. Some states, including Minnesota, New Mexico and Wisconsin, provide state tax dollars for noncommercial broadcasting.

Some states require regulated industries, such as insurance companies, to buy space in the state's newspapers to publicize their financial reports. Although these reports, called *legal advertisements* or **legals,** are in tiny agate type, the same size as classified ads, the fees from them are important income for many publications. Some publications also have an indirect subsidy from school boards and other government units that are required by law to publish their minutes and sometimes budgets and other documents. These too are called legals.

Public Broadcasting Service (PBS) Links to feature stories, news, programs and television schedules.
www.pbs.org

National Public Radio (NPR) Links to radio programs, schedules, stations and news stories.
www.npr.org

Government Advertising The U.S. government pours tremendous amounts of money into the mass media through advertising. In 2005 the government was the 25th largest advertiser, spending $1.3 billion. Government advertising includes ads for the postal service and military recruiting.

Government funding of the media also occurs at lower levels. Some states, for example, have large budgets for advertising to bring in tourists. Business magazines, such as *Forbes,* regularly contain multipage advertising sections from states that want companies to relocate.

legals ■ Government-required paid notices.

Government Sponsorship

Government agencies are getting more bang for the buck with athletic sponsorships. The Army says recruiting at race events, begun in 2003 with a $16 million commitment to NASCAR driver Jerry Nadeau, generated 20,000 inquiries and at least 300 enlistments in six months. Contacts averaged $31, compared to $50 for some television advertisements. The Postal Service has put $40 million over several years into sponsoring the Lance Armstrong bicycle racing team.

Economic Imperative

Economics figures into which messages make it to print or the airwaves. To realize their profit potential, the media that seek large audiences choose to deal with subjects of wide appeal and to present them in ways that attract great numbers of people. A subject that interests only small numbers of people does not make it into *Time* magazine. ABC, to take another example, drops programs that do not do well in the television ratings. This is a function of economics for those media that depend on advertising revenue to stay in business. The larger the audience, the more advertisers are willing to pay for time and space to pitch their goods and services.

Even media that seek narrow segments of the population need to reach as many people within their segments as possible to attract advertisers. A jazz radio station that attracts 90 percent of the jazz fans in a city will be more successful with advertisers than will a competing jazz station that attracts only 10 percent.

The economic imperative also drives cost containment. In some cases, cost-cutting goes so far as to mislead the audience. The bottom-line-obsessed Sinclair television chain, for example, not only shares segments among its stations but also has identical news sets at the stations. An anchor in Flint, Michigan, will toss to another anchor for national news or weather as if that other anchor were in the same studio. What viewers are usually not told is that those other anchors are at Sinclair's headquarters near Baltimore.

Media that do not depend on advertising also are geared to finding large audiences. For example, a novel that flops does not go into a second printing. Only successful movies generate sequels.

Mission and Profit

Like other businesses that are successful in the long term, media companies adapt to changing environments. One of the most adroit movers in the ever-changing media landscape is E. W. Scripps, which grew out of its namesake's Cleveland, Ohio, newspaper in the late 1800s. Scripps made his mark by introducing evening papers at a time when most dailies came out in the morning. The company rode the wave of newspapers as the dominant media of the era, but Scripps' successors founded television stations in the 1940s. In the 1950s the company expanded into syndicated comics, which created major revenue streams for Snoopy and other pop-culture likenesses. While maintaining its newspaper base in 18 markets, Scripps in the 1980s bought local cable television systems. In the 1990s, for a relatively modest $17 million, Scripps bought a television production company and build HGTV into an immensely profitable cable and satellite channel. In 2005 profits from HGTV and sibling lifestyle channels brought in more revenue than the company's newspapers. Among media companies in 2005, the company's annualized return for five years averaged an unusually strong 10.9 percent.

Unlike Scripps, whose history is building on its assets, some financially successful media companies move in and out of media segments. Lee Enterprises, fourth largest among newspaper chains, has sold of all its television properties. The New York Times Company has been in and out of magazines and books. News Corporation has gone beyond newspapers, its base, into television with Fox and into books with HarperCollins but shed Harpers' long-time interest in textbooks. There is no one-size-fits-all model.

Perils of Profit and Myopia

The drive to attract advertising can affect media messages in sinister ways. For example, the television station that overplays the ribbon-cutting ceremony at a new store is usually motivated more by a desire to please an advertiser than by a commitment to reporting news. The economic dependence of the mass media on advertising income gives considerable clout to advertisers, which may threaten to yank advertising out of a publication if a certain negative story appears. Such threats occur, though not frequently.

At a subtler level, lack of advertiser support can work against certain messages. During the 1950s, as racial injustice was emerging as an issue that would rip the nation apart a decade later, U.S. television avoided documentaries on the subject. No advertisers were interested.

Demassification

demassification ■ Media focus on narrower audience segments.

The idea that the mass audience is the largest number of people who can be assembled to hear mass messages is changing. Most media content today is aimed at narrow, albeit often still large, segments. This phenomenon is called **demassification.**

Alternative Media The Carl's Jr. and Hardee's fast-food chains have dropped traditional media advertising and gone after hard-to-reach young men with the Carlsjr.com web site. It's an entertainment-loaded site. Visitors find games and videos in a bachelor-pad setting. Features on the wide-screen TV include the notorious Paris Hilton car-wash sequence.

This demassification process, the result of technological breakthroughs and economic pressures, is changing the mass media dramatically. Radio demassified early, in the 1950s, replacing formats designed to reach the largest possible audiences with formats aimed at sectors of audience. Magazines followed in the 1960s and the 1970s, and today most of the 12,000 consumer magazines in the United States cater only to the special interests of carefully targeted groups of readers. Today, with dozens of television program services via cable or satellite in most U.S. households, television also is going through demassification.

The effects of demassification are only beginning to emerge. At first, advertisers welcomed demassification because they could target their pitches to groups of their likeliest customers. The latest trend in demassification has advertisers producing their own media to carry their messages by mail to potential customers who, through computer sorting and other mechanisms, are more precisely targeted than magazines, newspapers, television and radio could ever do. The new **alternative media,** as they are called, include:

- Sponsored web sites with games and other lures to attract return visits.
- Direct mail catalogs and flyers to selected addresses.
- Television commercials at the point of purchase, such as screens in grocery store shopping carts.
- Place-based media, such as magazines designed for distribution only in physicians' waiting rooms.
- Telemarketing, in which salespeople make their pitches by telephone to households determined by statistical profiles to be good potential customers.
- E-mail marketing.

If advertisers continue their shift to these and other alternative media, the revenue base of magazines, newspapers, radio and television will decline. Wholly new ways to structure the finances of these media will be necessary, probably with readers, listeners and viewers picking up the bill directly rather than indirectly by buying advertised products, which is the case today.

Media Conglomeration

studypreview **Giant corporations with diverse interests have consolidated the U.S. mass media into relatively few hands. One result is that new talent and messengers have a harder time winning media attention.**

Media Ownership Consolidation

The trend toward **conglomeration** involves a process of mergers, acquisitions and buyouts that consolidates the ownership of the media into fewer and fewer companies. The deep pockets of a wealthy corporate parent can see a financially troubled media unit, such as a radio station, through a rough period, but there is a price. In time the corporate parent wants a financial return on its investment, and pressure builds on the station to generate more and more profit. This would not be so bad if the people running the radio station loved radio and had a sense of public service, but the process of conglomeration often doesn't work out that way. Parent corporations tend to replace media people with career-climbing, bottom-line managers whose motivation is looking good to their supervisors in faraway cities who are under serious pressure to increase profits. In radio, for example, management experts, not radio people, end up running the station, and the quality of media content suffers.

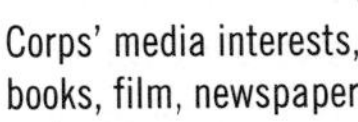

News Corporation Links to News Corps' media interests, including books, film, newspapers, cable, film and more. **www.newscorp.com**

Media Ownership Collaboration

Besides consolidation of media ownership, the remaining media companies have joint deals. Walt Disney invested $30 million in the celebrity magazine *Us Weekly,* owned by magazine

alternative media ■ Emerging, narrowly focused advertising vehicles.

conglomeration ■ Combining of companies into larger companies.

mediaPEOPLE

Rupert Murdoch

Media Mogul
Murdoch has built an empire combining media content creation companies and global distribution.

People love to hate media mogul Rupert Murdoch. Although his News Corp. is only one of many media companies gobbling up other media outlets, Murdoch's name has become synonymous with media power. Former CBS executive Howard Stringer has called him "the leader of a new Napoleonic era of communications." Critics claim that his emphasis on corporate profits is changing the foundation of media, and his competitors work hard to keep up with him.

Murdoch's family controls 30 percent of News Corp.'s shares, worth $12 billion in 2003. The dynasty began with the Australian newspaper chain established by Murdoch's father, who passed his business on to his son in 1952. Now approaching 80, Rupert Murdoch is training his children to take over for him.

Murdoch began by acquiring several British newspapers and then some in the United States. He bought the venerable U.S. book publisher Harper & Row, which he rechristened HarperCollins to fit with his British publishing interests. To qualify to own U.S. television stations, he became a U.S. citizen. That, in the 1980s, allowed him to create Fox as the fourth U.S. television network, which some said couldn't be done, and dovetail it with his recently acquired 20th Century Fox movie and television production studio. He bought the parent company of *TV Guide.* He created the Sky and Star satellite systems in Britain and Asia. Two-thirds of the world's population—3 billion people—watch StarTV, which shows programming that Murdoch's company creates or buys. In 2003 he acquired control of DirecTV, the major U.S. satellite television delivery service.

The expansion gave Murdoch the components to establish the first global system for content creation and delivery under a single corporate umbrella. This is the Murdochian significance—a grip on distribution that competitors don't have. With his unmatched array of media interests Murdoch can cross-market his products in newspapers, magazines, films, books and television. Critic James Fallows cited how the Murdoch media empire synchronizes production, publicity and support: "They supply the content—Fox movies (*Titanic, The Full Monty, There's Something About Mary*), Fox TV shows (*The Simpsons, Ally McBeal, When Animals Attack*), Fox-controlled sports broadcasts, plus newspapers and books. They sell the content to the public and to advertisers—in newspapers, on the broadcast network, on cable channels. And they operate the physical distribution system through which the content reaches the customers." Murdoch's satellite systems distribute News Corporation content in Europe and Asia.

Critics fret that Murdoch media controls too much of the world's media content and note that News Corp. entities have a politically conservative slant. Murdoch calls that balderdash. Using early 2004 data, he once pointed to U.S. talk radio, in which he has no part, and noted how lopsided it is, with 300-plus hours of nationally syndicated conservative talk a week versus five hours of liberal talk. The media, himself included, Murdoch says, merely offer what people want: "Apparently conservative talk is more popular."

There is plenty of evidence that the ideology that drives Murdoch is mostly profits and financial growth. Stories abound about Murdoch killing or facilitating content to benefit his bottom line. When he said in a speech that advanced communications technology would threaten totalitarian regimes, he was surprised to find that he had angered the Chinese government, which was hardly his intention. The Chinese threatened to pull the plug on Murdoch's StarTV transmissions into China. Desperate to remove his StarTV profits from jeopardy, Murdoch immediately arranged for his book-publishing subsidiary to publish a book by Deng Xiaoping's daughter. He also cancelled another book that would probably have provoked the Chinese. Knowing that the Chinese were displeased with the independent news reporting on the BBC World Service, Murdoch dropped the BBC from StarTV's program lineup for China. It worked: Murdoch's Chinese franchise was saved.

magnate Jann Wenner, whose publications also include *Rolling Stone*. In exchange for Disney's investment, *Us* trumpets Disney projects. Any time Disney doesn't like *Us* coverage, it can back out of the relationship. Critics don't like these kinds of deals: "He who pays the piper calls the tune." Can *Us* readers expect anything but platitudes and puff about Disney? What about the *Us*-branded material that, as part of the deal, is run on Disney-owned ABC television and radio? ABC News One distributes a 90-second weekly segment, "The Us Report," highlighting stories in the latest issue of the magazine, to 200-some local television station affiliates. Also as part of the deal, the ABC television show *Good Morning America* carries *Us* material. *Us* has a link on an ABC News web site.

Biggest U.S. Media Companies

	Media Revenue
Time Warner	$37.0 billion
Viacom	21.5 billion
Comcast	20.1 billion
Disney	17.4 billion
NBC Universal	12.5 billion
News Corporation	11.4 billion
DirecTV	9.8 billion
Cox	8.6 billion
EchoStar	6.7 billion
Clear Channel	6.5 billion

Webs of media collaboration are everywhere. There are units of Time Warner, owner of CNN, that have joint deals with rival Fox—despite the highly visible personal animosity between CNN founder Ted Turner and Fox owner Rupert Murdoch. Flying under most people's radar is the fact that Fox also has deals with ABC; with NBC, which is owned by General Electric; and with CBS, which is owned by Viacom, whose properties include a movie studio that competes with 20th Century Fox.

Do these sound like monopolies? The U.S. Justice Department thinks not. To use its trust-busting authority, the Justice Department needs to find collusion to fix prices. Media critic Ken Auletta, who studied the growing web of collaboration, concluded that fast-changing technology works against the restraints on competition that would make price-fixing likely. As the Justice Department sees it, people have more ways than ever before to receive media messages.

More serious than sinister economic impact, says Auletta, is the potential for self-serving control of content, particularly journalism: "Is NBC likely to pursue a major investigative series on its partner Microsoft? Is Fox News going to go after its partner TCI? Is a junior ABC news producer going to think twice before chewing on the leg of a Disney partner?" Writing in the *New Yorker*, Auletta noted that Steven Brill complained that Time Warner had tried three times to wield its clout as part-owner of his law publications to influence coverage.

Dubious Effects of Conglomeration

Critics such as **Ben Bagdikian** say that conglomeration affects the diversity of messages offered by the mass media. Speaking at the Madison Institute, Bagdikian portrayed conglomeration in bleak terms: "They are trying to buy control or market domination not just in one medium but in all the media. The aim is to control the entire process from an original manuscript or new series to its use in as many forms as possible. A magazine article owned by *the company* becomes a book owned by *the company*. That becomes a television program owned by *the company*, which then becomes a movie owned by *the company*. It is shown in theaters owned by *the company*, and the movie sound track is issued on a record label owned by *the company*, featuring the vocalist on the cover of one of *the company* magazines. It does not take an angel from heaven to tell us that *the company* will be less enthusiastic about outside ideas and production that it does not own, and more and more we will be dealing with closed circuits to control access to most of the public."

Ben Bagdikian ■ Critic of media consolidation.

THE NEW MEDIA MONOPOLY

A COMPLETELY REVISED AND UPDATED EDITION WITH SEVEN NEW CHAPTERS

BEN H. BAGDIKIAN

"NO BOOK ON THE MEDIA HAS PROVED AS INFLUENTIAL TO OUR UNDERSTANDING OF THE DANGERS OF CORPORATE CONSOLIDATION TO DEMOCRACY AND THE MARKETPLACE OF IDEAS AS THE MEDIA MONOPOLY; THIS NEW EDITION BUILDS ON THAT WORK AND SURPASSES IT." —ERIC ALTERMAN, AUTHOR OF WHAT LIBERAL MEDIA?

Media Critic
Ben Bagdikian, called "one of the most considerate voices in journalism today," says that huge media companies are ever more profit-obsessed. Their corporate strategies, he says, often sacrifice high-quality content and public service on the altar of increasing profits. Bagdikian has amassed distressing data on conglomeration in his book *The New Media Monopoly.*

Ben Bagdikian

Bagdikian can point to the growing vertical integration among media corporations. In vertical integration a single company owns every step from production to distribution and then after-markets—and profits at every step of the way. An example is the *X Files,* a television series produced by 20th Century Fox Television, a unit of Rupert Murdoch's News Corp. The original episodes, which cost $2.5 million each, played well on Murdoch's Fox television network affiliates and attracted top advertising dollars. There also were profits from local advertising inserted by Fox-owned stations. The episodes created additional advertising revenue when showed later on Murdoch's FX cable network. Then there were the merchandise tie-ins when the series was in its prime-time peak. Still in reruns and being licensed abroad, the episodes are expected to generate $62.5 million each over a projected eight-year period. That's a 25-fold return on the initial investment, plus a spin-off movie.

Nobody begrudges a company making a profit. The difficulty comes when the recycling displaces creative new entries in the mass media marketplace. NBC executive Don Ohlmeyer concedes that a vertically integrated network is disinclined "in even considering projects in which they don't own a financial interest." Independent Hollywood producers, who once competed to produce network shows, are finding themselves out of the loop. The result, says Gary Goldberg, creator of *Spin City* on ABC: "You see this blandness and similarity to the shows. Consumers are the ones who get hurt."

One of the negative effects of conglomeration occurs when a parent company looks to its subsidiaries only to enrich conglomerate coffers as quickly as possible and by any means possible, regardless of the quality of products that are produced. This is especially a problem when a conglomerate's subsidiaries include, for example, widget factories, cherry orchards, funeral homes and, by the way, also some book companies. The top management of such diverse conglomerates is inclined to take a cookie-cutter approach that deemphasizes or even ignores important traditions in book publishing, including a sense of social responsibility. Many of these conglomerates focus on profits alone. One result, according to many literary critics, has been a decline in quality.

Quality Headquarters push subsidiaries to cut costs to increase profits, a trend that has devastated the quality of writing and editing. Fewer people do more work. At newspapers, for example, a reporter's story once went through several hands—editor, copy editor, headline writer, typesetter, proofreader. At every stage, the story could be improved. In today's streamlined newsrooms, proofreaders have been replaced by spell-check software, which not only introduces its own problems but also lacks the intelligence and judgment of a

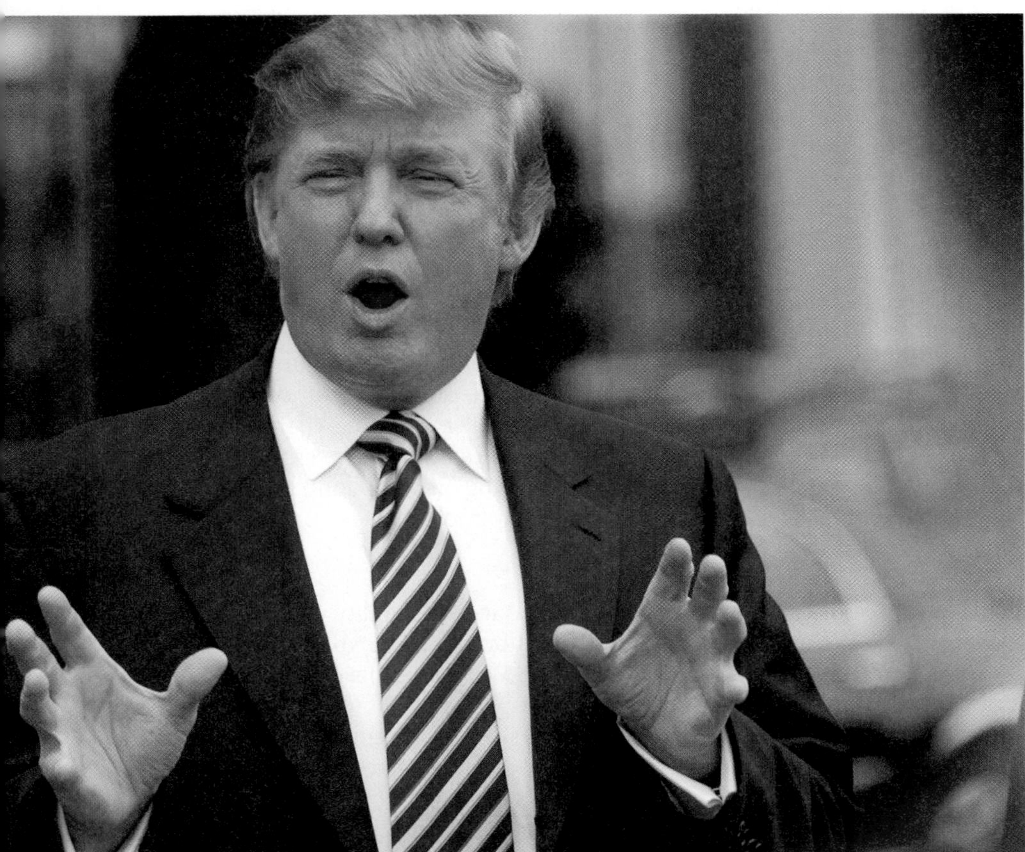

Cross-Promotion
Mega-media companies like NBC Universal are finding more ways to cross-promote their products. NBC tied teaser trailers to its Universal movies before launching its television reality series *The Apprentice* with Donald Trump.

good proofer. The jobs of the reporter and the typesetter have been consolidated. In many newsrooms, so have the jobs of copy editors and headline writers.

Los Angeles *Times* reporter Tom Rosentiel, writing in the *Columbia Journalism Review,* tells how reporters, pressured to increase productivity, take shortcuts to generate more copy: "Newspapers and newsmagazine interviews today are increasingly conducted over the phone, with reporters assembling stories as much as reporting them, combining elements from electronic transcripts, data bases and television. A growing number of major events, reporters acknowledge, are covered without going to the scene. The stories . . . lack the advantage of serendipity or the authenticity of having been there."

In the book industry, media critic Jacob Weisberg has documented how several major publishers, including Simon & Schuster and Random House, have routinely eliminated important stages in the editing process to rush new titles to print and turn quicker profits. In a revealing article in the *New Republic,* Weisberg lists these results of the accelerated schedules:

- Factual errors, both major and minor, that in earlier times, he says, would have been caught by careful editing.
- Loose, flabby writing from deadline-pressured writers who once could rely on editors to tighten their work. Some books, Weisberg says, are running 100 pages longer than they should.

Sameness You can fly from the East to the West Coast on the same day and read the same Associated Press stories word for word. Newspaper publishers learned long ago that sharing stories via the AP could reduce costs. The resulting economics came at the cost of less diversity in content.

Cultural sociologists fret about the sameness. In recorded music, for example, major record companies often encourage artists to imitate what is already popular. The result is that derivative music squeezes original artists and material out of the marketplace or at least makes it more difficult for these artists to find an audience. Sociologists think that the movement of culture in new directions is slowed by this process.

Barry Diller, who created popular television programs at ABC and later at Fox, says that the problem is the profit-driven trend to recycle existing material for a quick buck. In a speech to magazine executives, Diller pointed out the short-sightedness of recycling: "Taking a movie like *Jurassic Park* and turning it into a video game, that's repackaging. Taking a bestseller and putting it on tape, that's repackaging. Taking magazine articles and slapping them on-line, word for word, that's repackaging." He then likened repackaging to strip mining: "After you've extracted the riches from the surface, there's nothing left."

Among local media, at once fiercely competitive, managers have found economies in sharing resources. Television stations, for example, are offering weather forecasts to radio stations in exchange for on-air promotions of their programs. There are similar television-newspaper swaps for weather. Some television stations have created new revenue streams by recycling their newscast content for airing on competing stations, which thereby avoid the expense of operating their own newsrooms. These practices reduce the diversity of media content, adding to a sameness.

Corporate Instability Conglomeration also has introduced instability. Profit-driven corporate parents are quick to sell subsidiaries that fall short of profit expectations even for a short term or just to raise cash. In 2003 AOL Time Warner realized that it had taken on more than it could handle and put Warner Books up for sale. However, bids were too low, and Time Warner reversed its decision. Typically in unstable situations, uncertainty diverts energy and focus from ongoing projects. Some projects are put on hold. There is uncertainty about new projects. Employees, with sudden career jitters, look for jobs elsewhere. None of this serves the media consumer well.

Positive Effects of Conglomeration

At the end of World War II, the mainline book-publishing business was dominated by family-run publishing houses, all relatively small by today's standards. Although there are still hundreds of small publishers in the United States, consolidation has reduced the industry to six giants. Depending on whom you ask, the conglomeration has been a godsend or a disaster. Looking at the effects positively, the U.S. book industry is financially stronger:

- Parent corporations have infused cash into their new subsidiaries, financing expensive initiatives that were not financially possible before, including multimillion-dollar deals with authors.
- Because parent corporations often own newspapers, magazines and broadcast companies, book publishers have ready partners for repackaging books in additional media forms.
- Many of the new parent corporations own book companies abroad, which helps to open up global markets.

In today's business climate the lure of market dominance and profit, often on a global scale, keeps driving the concentration of media companies into fewer and fewer conglomerates.

Conglomeration Cracks

Pell-mell conglomeration among media companies might have peaked. Shareholders in Vivendi, the erstwhile French media conglomerate, discovered in 2002 that big isn't always better when, after rapid expansion, the empire verged on collapse. Vivendi sold off Universal to General Electric, which melded the movie studio into its NBC. Vivendi's

mediaPEOPLE

Vivendi Mastermind

They called Jean-Marie Messier an acquisition binger. The French business executive couldn't buy enough companies to put under his Vivendi corporate umbrella. He amassed French companies in the television, book-publishing, newspaper and telephony industries as well as a motley bunch of companies elsewhere. Messier then turned to the United States. In a three-year period beginning in the late 1990s, he expanded the Vivendi fold to include the Universal movie studio, the MCA record empire, the book publisher Houghton Mifflin, the Sci-Fi Channel and USA Network, and a diverse group of other U.S. enterprises, including the Universal theme parks.

Messier didn't call himself a binger. In countless interviews he spoke of his vision of a media company that would dominate the globe. He bought telephone companies in many countries, eyeing their networks as a means for sending Vivendi-produced content to customers. He also saw endless possibilities for recycling content. A Vivendi book, for example, could become a Vivendi movie with Vivendi music, spinning off Vivendi albums, as well as a television series, then action toys.

Where was Messier getting the money for these acquisitions? Vivendi actually was a newly concocted name for an old French company that built and operated municipal water systems. The company expanded overseas as a utility operator and became a huge cash generator. The cash flow enabled Messier to get loan after loan to finance ever-more acquisitions.

Jean-Marie Messier

Suddenly, in 2001 it fell apart. Terribly overextended, Vivendi was on the verge of missing debt payments. Even so, with bankruptcy imminent, Messier continued negotiating for even more acquisitions. But it was over. The company's board of directors fired him and brought in new executives, who mapped out a plan to sell off parts of the company to pay off loans. Among the first to go was U.S. book publisher Houghton Mifflin, which Messier had bought for $2.2 billion in 2001. One year later in a fire sale, Houghton was sold for $1.7 billion. Major parts of Universal went to General Electric, which folded them into its NBC. Also on the block was an assortment of other Messier-acquired properties, including utility systems in the Middle East and Asia, a garbage disposal in Colombia, and MathBlaster computer software.

Messier was the poster child for the 1990s notion that the future of the mass media resided in companies that controlled the most production, distribution and retail outlets for programming and other content. He might have been right, his fate an aberration en route to a new age of global media giants. At the same time the idea that the future belonged to mega-media companies was being reconsidered. Some other giant consolidations of the 1990s had problems. AOL Time Warner jettisoned Warner Music and took the "AOL" out of its name. Bertelsmann of Germany backed out of its expansion.

Houghton Mifflin book-publishing unit was bought by an investor group. Other units went on the auction block too.

Although Vivendi's situation was extreme, it was not alone among troubled media giants that had grown through mergers and acquisitions in the 1980s and 1990s. The union of Time Warner and America Online was heralded at the time for the anticipated synergies from which both partners would supposedly derive advantages. But Time ended up trying to sell AOL when it not only underperformed on expectations but also yielded few offsetting benefits. Viacom executives have toyed with spinning off their fast-growth MTV Networks unit, which includes Nickelodeon and the BET network, rather than letting their future be hobbled by CBS and other Viacom entities whose growth has slowed.

Whether the era of giant conglomerates dominating the mass media is fading is not clear. It could be that recent sell-offs are fine-tuning adjustments of their holdings by parent companies, with subsidiaries merely moving from one megacorporate home to another. What is clear is that major media corporations are more cautious about finding acquisitions that are good fits than were Vivendi and Time Warner.

Vivendi Universal Links to Vivendi Universal's media holdings including TV, film, publishing, games and music.
www.vivendiuniversal.com

CHAPTER 1 Wrap-Up

The mass media are the vehicles that carry messages to large audiences. These media—books, magazines, newspapers, records, movies, radio, television and the Internet—are so pervasive in modern life that many people do not even notice their influence. Because of that influence, however, we should take time to understand the mass media so that we can better assess whether they are affecting us for better or worse.

Questions for Review

1. How are the mass media pervasive in our everyday lives?
2. How do the mass media contribute to social consensus and also to divisiveness?
3. What are the three technologies on which the primary mass media are built?
4. What was the effect of the integration of printed mass media and photography? How about digitization?
5. What is the difference between mainstream media and new media?
6. What are the models that scholars have devised to explain the mass media?
7. How do mass media organizations make money to stay in business?
8. Is conglomeration good for mass media consumers?

Questions for Critical Thinking

1. Which mass media perform the informing purpose best? The entertaining purpose? The persuading purpose? Which of these purposes does the advertising industry serve? Public relations?
2. Why do revolutionaries try to take over the mass media right away?
3. The effectiveness of messages communicated through the mass media is shaped by the technical limitations of each medium. A limitation of radio is that it cannot accommodate pictures. Is it a technical limitation that the New York *Times* does not carry comics or that most radio news formats limit stories to 40 seconds? Can you provide examples of content limitations of certain media? What are the audience limitations that are inherent in all mass media?
4. For many years CBS television programs drew a generally older and more rural audience than did the other networks. Did that make CBS a niche-seeking mass media unit? Did it make the CBS audience any less heterogeneous?
5. Some people are confused by the terms *cool media* and *hot media* because, in their experience, radios and television sets heat up and newspapers are always at room temperature. What is the other way of looking at hot and cool media?
6. Which is more important to the U.S. mass media: profits or doing social good? What about the goals of supermarket tabloids like the *National Enquirer?*
7. Which mass media rely directly on consumer purchases for their economic survival? Advertising provides almost all the revenue for commercial radio and television stations, but indirectly consumer purchases are an important factor. In what way?
8. Are any types of mass media not dependent on advertising or consumer purchases?
9. Is media baron Rupert Murdoch a villain or a visionary? Consider the evidence that supports these observations by media critic James Fallows: Murdoch has a powerful instinct for mass taste. Murdoch has an appreciation of technology. Murdoch has a strong concept of strategic business structure. Murdoch has a knack for exploiting political power.

Deepening Your media LITERACY

How do you become more media literate?

STEP 1 Think of your favorite commercial on television.

Dig Deeper

STEP 2 People who are media literate consume media with a critical eye. They evaluate sources, intended purposes, techniques and deeper meanings. Answer these questions about your favorite commercial:

1. Why is this ad effective? Write a list of the persuasion techniques it uses.
2. Who is the intended audience? Who will benefit from this commercial?
3. Does it sell more than a product? Is the product or image a step in a vertical integration?
4. Does it help you to identify any social values? Which ones? Does it glamorize a way a life? Does it bind a community?
5. How does it attempt to shape our perception of reality?
6. What is the elitist view of this TV ad? What is the populist view?

What Do You Think?

STEP 3 Media are most powerful when they operate at an emotional level. Do you think most viewers would be able to separate fact from fantasy in this ad? Does your favorite commercial tell you anything truly useful about the product? Do you think it's fair for a commercial to attempt to shape our behavior or attitudes?

Keeping Up to Date

Many mass media developments abroad are tracked in the monthly London-based *Censorship Index.*

Newsmagazines including *Time* and *Newsweek* cover major mass media issues more or less regularly, as do the New York *Times,* the *Wall Street Journal* and other major newspapers.

Periodicals that track the mass media as business include *Business Week, Forbes* and *Fortune.*

The Journal of Media Economics focuses on economic policy issues.

For Further Learning

Thomas Friedman. *The World Is Flat: A Brief History of the 21st Century.* Farrar, Straus & Giroux, 2005.

Friedman, a Pulitzer-winning news reporter, sees humankind as being in a third phase of globalization in which mass media technology is a prime driver.

Sumner Redstone with Peter Knobler. *A Passion to Win.* Simon & Schuster, 2001.

This is the autobiography of Viacom's architect, published by his Simon & Schuster subsidiary and marketed heavily through his Blockbuster video rental chain.

Richard E. Foglesong. *Married to the House: Walt Disney World and Orlando.* Yale University Press, 2001.

Foglesong, a scholar, offers a well-documented assessment of a media company's corporate heavy-handedness.

Benjamin M. Compaine and Douglas Gomery. *Who Owns the Media? Competition and Concentration in the Mass Media Industry,* Third edition. Erlbaum, 2000.

The authors update the 1979 and 1992 editions with details on further concentration, more attention to the cable and home video business, and a discussion of the effect of technological convergence.

Mark Crispin Miller. "Can Viacom's Reporters Cover Viacom's Interests?" *Columbia Journalism Review* (November–December 1999), pages 48–50.

Miller, a leading critic of media conglomeration, looks at the 1999 merger of Viacom and CBS.

Samuel P. Winch. *Mapping the Cultural Space of Journalism: How Journalists Distinguish News from Entertainment.* Praeger, 1998.

Winch, a mass communication scholar, tackles infotainment as a media trend.

Erik Barnouw and others. *Conglomerates and the Media.* The New Press, 1998.

The reflections of broadcast historian Erik Barnouw and other media thinkers in a New York University lecture series are collected here. The theme is negative toward conglomerates, with abundant examples of corporate owners who have used their power to influence media content for their financial benefit.

Ben Bagdikian. *The Media Monopoly,* Fifth edition. Beacon, 1997.

Bagdikian, perhaps the best-known critic of media conglomeration, includes data on the digital revolution in this update of his classic work.

Mark Crispin Miller. "Free the Media." *Nation* (June 3, 1996), pages 9–28.

Professor Miller worries about what's happening to news as it becomes a tinier component than ever in the new mass media conglomerates, whose interests are primarily in the defense and entertainment industries. Miller focuses on Disney (ABC), General Electric (NBC), Westinghouse (CBS) and Time Warner (CNN).

Richard Sarnoff

Random House is among book-publisher leaders in exploring digital delivery—no paper, no ink.

chapter

2 Books

In this chapter you will learn:

- We learn the lessons of past generations mostly from books.
- A few large, growing companies dominate the book industry worldwide.
- Books fall into broad categories: trade books and textbooks.
- Transformational book formats include paperbacks and e-books.
- Most book concepts come from authors.
- Book marketing has grown as a driver of the book industry.
- Books can be judged by populist and elitist measures.

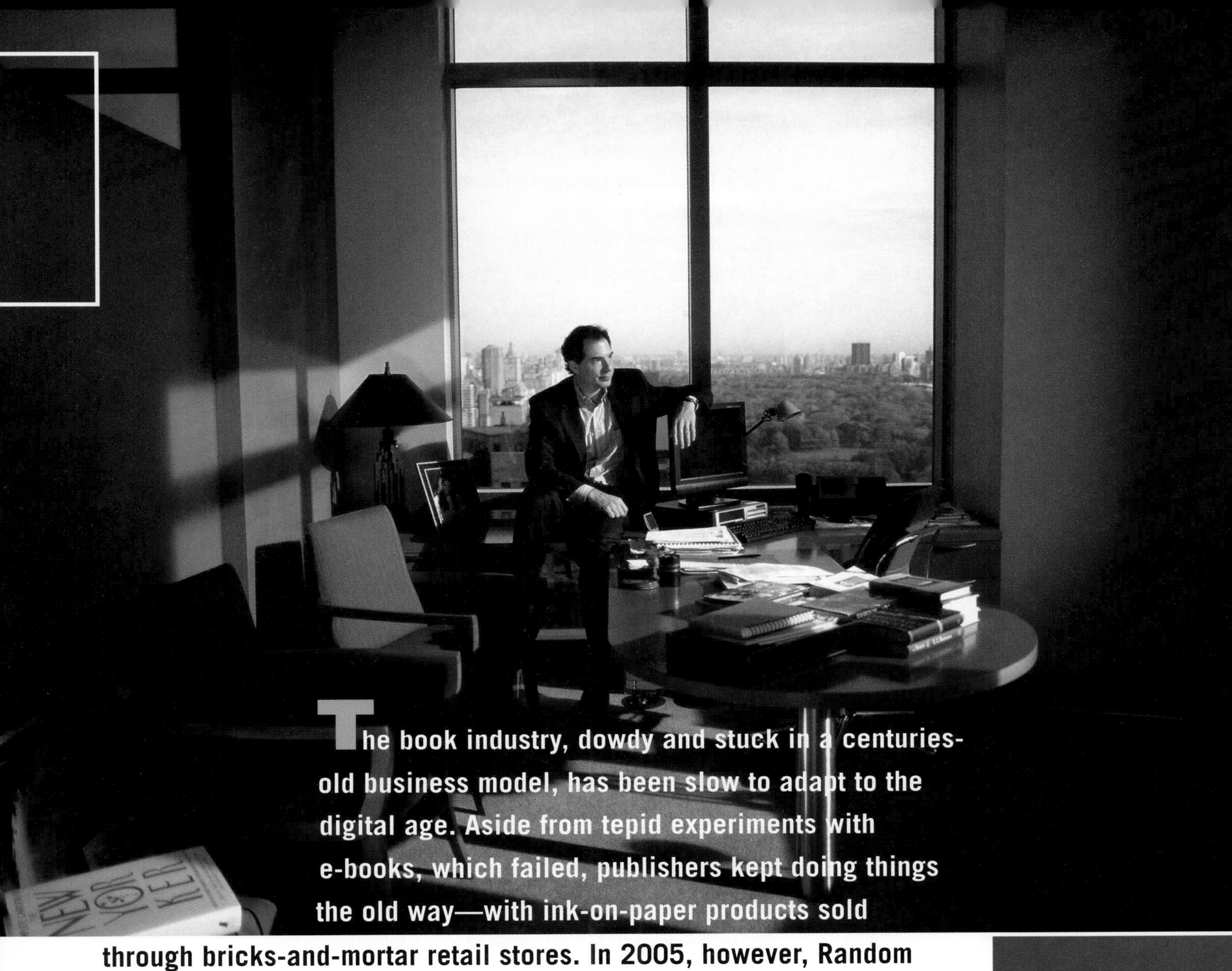

The book industry, dowdy and stuck in a centuries-old business model, has been slow to adapt to the digital age. Aside from tepid experiments with e-books, which failed, publishers kept doing things the old way—with ink-on-paper products sold through bricks-and-mortar retail stores. In 2005, however, Random House, the largest U.S. book publisher, announced initiatives to catch up. Richard Sarnoff, president of corporate development, pointed to what had happened in the record music, where digital technology almost instantly upended the industry in the early 2000s: "Technology was adopted before there was a business model."

To Sarnoff, Random House needed to embrace new technology, rethinking all the old ways of doing business. Ever heard of the dodo bird?

Sarnoff put together new ways to deliver books to consumers—directly via the Internet. For starters, Random House began selling book access online at four cents a page, mostly pay-per-view peeks to encourage sales of print versions. It was a step toward retailing access to whole books online straight from the publisher to the consumer with no intermediary bookstore.

Low-resolution screen technology, which doomed the first e-book products, doesn't worry Sarnoff. By 2008 he expects a break-through that will make reading devices as eyeball-friendly as books. And readers are waiting, he says. Young people, computer-turned as they are, do not have the visceral connection with books that earlier generations have.

Sarnoff is striking out in serveral directions. Random House has bought into a company that delivers education content to cell phones. It has investments also in a download and CD service company. How these initiatives will shake out, and whether they will be the heart of a new business model, remains to be sorted out.

Does Richard Sarnoff have the answers? See whether the first online book you read has a Random House imprint.

Influence of Books

studypreview **Mass-produced books, first introduced in the mid-1400s, changed human history by accelerating the exchange of ideas and information among more people. Books have endured as a repository of culture. They are the primary vehicle by which new generations are educated to their society's values and by which they learn the lessons of the past.**

Books in Human History

After devising movable metal type in the 1440s, Johannes Gutenberg applied himself to printing Bibles. It was no small task. With six hand-operated presses, Gutenberg and his helpers printed one page at a time, first one side, then, after the ink had dried, the other side. Inks were made on site. The paper was a thin-pounded animal skin. In all, Gutenberg produced only 200 copies of the Bible. The Gutenberg Bibles were incredible masterpieces with woodcut initial letters in magnificent colors. The bindings were so good that some still survive, albeit as museum pieces.

Despite the daunting difficulties of the new technology, printing presses sprouted across Europe. By 1490 at least one printing press was operating in every major city. The impact cannot be overstated.

Scientific Progress The impact of the printing press on scientific inquiry was explosive. Scientists had been stymied by delays in learning what their colleagues were thinking and learning. With mass-produced reports on their work, scientists could build on each other's discoveries. This ushered in the Scientific Revolution, which took off in the 1600s and has been transforming our existence ever since.

Social Reform The cost of producing books dropped dramatically with mass production, making the printed word available beyond the socially elite. Exposed to new ideas, people honed their focus on the human condition and social structures and governance in new ways. Revolutionary ideas took root. Martin Luther advanced his Protestantism with printed materials. Tracts and treatises promoting free inquiry came into circulation. It can be asked whether the Renaissance, a period of intellectual, artistic and cultural awakening in the 1500s and 1600s, could have come to fruition without the printing press.

media ONLINE **e-Books from Random House**

Browse for your favorite titles.
www.contentlinkinc.com

Literacy Although the first works using Gutenberg technology were in Latin, soon books and other materials were printed in native languages. Geoffrey Chaucer's classic

media TIMELINE

DEVELOPMENT OF BOOKS

1440s Johannes Gutenberg printed Bibles using movable type.

1638 Puritans established Cambridge Press.

1836 William Holmes McGuffey began writing influential reading textbooks.

1850s A distinct American literature emerged in novels.

1895 Congress established the Government Printing Office.

1971 Michael Hart began Project Gutenberg online archives.

1995 Amazon.com launched.

1998 E-book introduced.

2000 Stephen King issued a novella as a downloadable book.

2005 Google began scanning all books ever published in English for online access.

2005 Print-on-demand machines introduced in bookstores.

Canterbury Tales, although written in 1387, was read by relatively few people until the Gutenberg printing press arrived in England. Chaucer's book, in fact, was the first printed in the English language.

Repository of Culture

The longevity of the printed word in bound volumes exceeds that of all the traditional media. University libraries are measured, for example, by the volumes on the shelves. Books last, which has made them the primary vehicle through which past generations still speak to us and pass on their experiences, observations and lessons. Books are the primary repository of human culture.

Books in National Development

Books were valued in the colonial period. In Massachusetts in 1638 the Puritans set up **Cambridge Press,** the first book producer in what is now the United States. Just as today, personal libraries were a symbol of the intelligentsia. Thomas Jefferson's personal library became the basis for the Library of Congress. **John Harvard** of Cambridge, Massachusetts, was widely known for his personal collection of 300 books, a large library for the time. When Harvard died in 1638, he bequeathed his books to Newtowne College, which was so grateful that the college was renamed for him. Today it is Harvard University.

William Holmes McGuffey's reading textbook series brought the United States out of frontier illiteracy. More than 122 million of McGuffey's readers were sold beginning in 1836, coinciding with the boom in public-supported education as part of the American credo.

In the mid-1800s U.S. publishers brought out books that identified a distinctive new literary genre: the American novel. Still widely read are Nathaniel Hawthorne's *The Scarlet Letter* (1850), Herman Melville's *Moby-Dick* (1851), Harriet Beecher Stowe's *Uncle Tom's Cabin* (1852) and Mark Twain's *Huckleberry Finn* (1884).

Today, most of the books that shape our culture are adapted to other media, which expands their influence. Magazine serialization put Ronald Reagan's memoirs in more hands than did the publisher of the book. More people saw Carl Sagan on television than have read his books. Stephen King's thrillers sell spectacularly, especially in paperback, but more people see the movie renditions. Books have a trickle-down effect through other media, their impact being felt even by people who cannot or do not read them. Although people are more in touch with other mass media day to day, books are the heart of creating U.S. culture and passing it on to new generations.

Harriet Beecher Stowe Center
Contains extensive documentation on the life of Harriet Beecher Stowe. Includes a teacher and student resource section.
www.harrietbeecherstowe.org

Cambridge Press ■ First publisher in the British American colonies.

John Harvard ■ Owned a major personal library.

William Holmes McGuffey ■ Wrote influential reading textbooks in the 1830s and 1840s.

mediaPEOPLE

William Holmes McGuffey

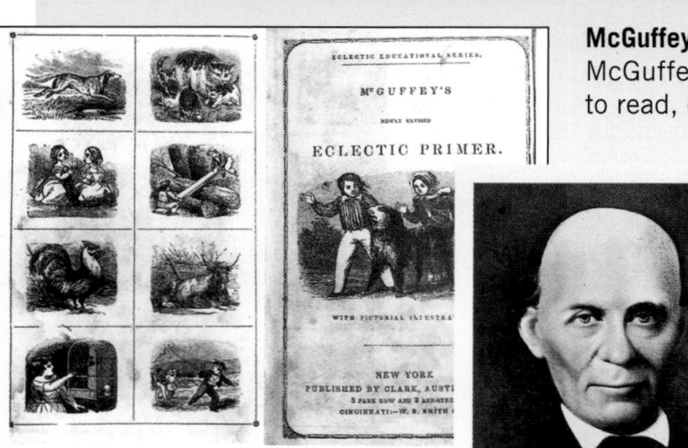

McGuffey Readers For a century McGuffey's readers taught children to read, contributing to quantum increases in literacy. The first book in the McGuffey series appeared in 1836.

Just out of college, William Holmes McGuffey arrived at Miami University in Ohio on horseback in 1826. In his saddle bags were a few books on moral philosophy and languages. At the university he tested his theories about education on neighborhood kids who gathered on his porch next to the campus. McGuffey confirmed that children learn better when sentences are accompanied by a picture. He also noted that reading out loud helps and that spelling is not very important in learning to read. McGuffey took notes on his observations and tested his ideas on other age groups. He also collected a mass of stories from a great variety of places.

In 1833 the Truman & Smith publishing company was scouting for someone to write a series of readers and found McGuffey. He culled his favorite stories for the new reader. Many were from the Bible, and most made a moral point. In 1836 the first of McGuffey's *Eclectic Readers* appeared. McGuffey still had lots of material that he had used with the children on his porch, and a second, a third and a fourth reader followed. Truman & Smith marketed the books vigorously, and they soon had a national following.

As the years went on, many editors had a hand in revisions, and McGuffey had less and less direction regarding their content. McGuffey's brother Alexander completed the fifth and sixth readers in the series between 1843 and 1845 while McGuffey was busy with his teaching.

McGuffey's *Eclectic Readers* sold more than 122 million copies. A version was still being produced for school use in 1920. Today some are still in print for home schooling.

Books and Current Issues

New York Times Best Sellers List Link to the current New York *Times* Best Sellers lists. Includes categories such as fiction, nonfiction, children and advice. **www.nytimes.com/pages/books/bestseller**

Books frame much of our dialogue on current issues. In the 2004 elections even the pundits lost track of the number of campaign books. President Bush himself joked that he had worked wonders for the economy: "Look what I've done for the book industry." At one point 15 titles on the New York *Times* best-seller list were about the Bush administration. Our emerging understanding of the shape of a new world order has been influenced by Thomas Friedman's 2004 work *The World Is Flat: A Brief History of the 21st Century.* Although published in 2001, sociologist Barbara Ehrenreich's *Nickel and Dimed,* which chronicled her struggle living incognito on minimum-wage jobs across the United States, still informs the debate on public policy regarding the poor and social justice. Ehrenreich's work harks back to *Black Like Me,* in which a white man, John Howard Griffin, wrote of how he had masqueraded as a black man in the American South in the 1950s. *Black Like Me* helped to fuel the nascent Civil Rights movement. No one disputes the continuing impact of Rachel Carson's *Silent Spring,* published in 1962, on environmentalism; Ralph Nader's *Unsafe at Any Speed,* in 1963, on consumerism; or Charles Darwin's *On the Origin of Species,* in 1859, on biology.

Historians favor the book for constructions of the past, which are essential for our understanding of the present. Less than adoring views of U.S. history, for example, have yielded more accurate and telling understandings of the formation of the Republic. Recent revisionist works include Ian Williams' *Rum: A Social and Sociable History of the Real Spirit of 1776,* Gary Nash's *The Unknown American Revolution: The Unruly Birth of Democracy and the Struggle to Create America* and Tom Tucker's *Bolt of Fate: Benjamin Franklin and His Electric Kite Hoax.*

Great literature, by definition, gives us new insights into ourselves and the people and world around us.

mediaPEOPLE

Harriet Beecher Stowe

In 1862 with the Civil War in progress, **Harriet Beecher Stowe,** who described herself "as thin and dry as a pinch of snuff," found herself invited to a White House reception. "Why, Mrs. Stowe, right glad to meet you," said President Abraham Lincoln, as he rose from his chair. "So you're the little woman who wrote the book that made this great war. Sit down, please."

Ten years earlier, Stowe's *Uncle Tom's Cabin,* an account of slave life, had become the first blockbuster in U.S. book publishing—an evocative novel that rang so true that it crystallized public opinion on the simmering issue of abolition of slavery.

Harriet Beecher Stowe

Uncle Tom's Cabin In one scene from *Uncle Tom's Cabin,* a child is being ripped from his mother after being sold at a slave auction. The 1851 magazine story by Harriet Beecher Stowe, soon issued as a book, heightened feelings against slavery.

Abolitionists welcomed the sympathy that the book stirred for their cause. In slave states, however, the reception was different. University of Virginia students burned the book. Peddlers who were discovered to have the book in their stock were driven out of town. Southern critics claimed that the book was inaccurate or at least misrepresented slavery. Regarding broken-up slave families, a theme of the book, they said it was cruelly overdrawn.

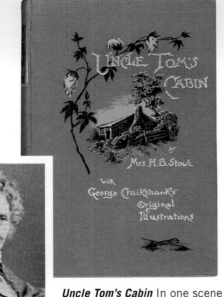

Even so, there was no stopping *Uncle Tom's Cabin.* Translations appeared in almost 40 languages in Europe, five in French alone.

Some latter-day critics have problems with Stowe's story. They say that Stowe portrayed black people as subservient by nature, even obsequious. Also, critics object to a sympathetic, albeit passing, treatment of black colonization. The criticism, however, fails to dilute the book's fundamental impact: Stowe propelled the abolitionist cause to center stage.

Uncle Tom's Cabin transformed the book industry. Sales established a benchmark to measure future publishing endeavors. The book began in 1851 as a serial in an abolitionist publication, the *National Era.* When the book appeared, 10 months later, it was an immediate success, with 20,000 copies sold within three weeks. By January 1853 the number sold had reached 200,000. One royalty check for three months was $10,500—more than any author in the United States or Europe had ever received for such a short period.

With 165,000 books a year being published in the United States, not all contribute equally to our society and our culture. Even so, the best that the book industry issues is a mighty force.

Book Industry

study preview **Mergers and acquisitions have reduced the book industry to fewer and fewer companies, all with global interests. Even so, small publishing houses continue, many profitably, in niches.**

Scope of Book Industry

The number of new books is skyrocketing. New titles totaled 195,000 in the United States in 2004, a 14 percent increase. Sales at 710 million copies were up 9.3 percent. Despite studies that document a decline in reading, consumer spending on books, increasing about 3.5 percent a year, is expected to reach $46.5 billion in the United States in 2009. The growth has eased off from the 4.8 percent of 2005.

The output of adult fiction zoomed 43.1 percent in 2004 to more than 25,000 titles. The Book Industry Study Group, which puts together these numbers, said that novels averaged 359 pages in 2005, a 24-page increase over 10 years. Prices have been largely stable, hardcover novels averaging $25.08 in 2004.

Harriet Beecher Stowe ■ Author of *Uncle Tom's Cabin,* the first blockbuster in U.S. book publishing.

Major Trade Book Publishers

Following are sales in the $8.4 billion U.S. trade book market, by publisher, in 2003:

	U.S. Sales	Corporate Parent
Random House	$ 1.4 billion	Bertelsmann (Germany)
HarperCollins	920 million	News Corp. (Australia)
Penguin	902 million	Pearson (Britain)
Simon & Schuster	693 million	Viacom (United States)
Warner	390 million	Lagardere (France)

Major Houses

Publishing houses think of themselves as widely recognized brand names: Simon & Schuster, Doubleday, HarperCollins, Penguin. To most people, though, a book is a book is a book, no matter the publisher—although there are exceptions, such as Harlequin, which is almost a household word for pulp romances. Scholars are exceptions. Their vocabularies are peppered with publishers' names, perhaps because of all the footnotes and bibliographies they have to wade through.

Major houses once had distinctive personalities that flowed from the literary bent of the people in charge. Scribner's, for example, was the nurturing home of Tom Wolfe, Ernest Hemingway and F. Scott Fitzgerald from the 1920s into the 1950s and very much bore the stamp of Charles Scribner and his famous editor Maxwell Perkins. Typical of the era, it was a male-dominated business, everybody wearing tweed coats and smoking pipes. Today the distinctive cultures have blurred as corporate pride has shifted more to the bottom line.

media ONLINE

Random House Contains an author of the week column, as well as descriptions of newly published fiction, nonfiction and children's books. Also contains headlines from the book publishing industry.
www.randomhouse.com

HarperCollins Includes history of the venerable publishing house, from the days when it published Mark Twain, the Brontë sisters, Thackery and Dickens through John Kennedy and Martin Luther King Jr.
www.harpercollins.com

Penguin USA Web site of publisher Penguin. Allows you to browse and shop by author or special interest. Also contains links to e-books.
www.penguinputnam.com

Simon Says Web site of the brand name publisher Simon & Schuster. Allows you to search by author, title or category; also contains newsletters and a children's section.
www.simonsays.com

Oxford University Press Link to the world's largest university press.
www.oup.co.uk

Harvard University Press University publisher of books in the humanities and social and natural sciences.
www.hup.harvard.edu

Book Industry Consolidation

As with other mass media industries, book publishing has undergone consolidation, with companies merging with each other, acquiring one another, and buying lists from one another. Some imprints that you still see are no longer stand-alone companies but part of international media conglomerates. Random House, a proud name in U.S. book publishing, is now part of the German company Bertelsmann. The company also owns the Bantam, Dell and Doubleday imprints, among other media subsidiaries, including numerous magazines.

Harcourt was sold to Reed Elsevier of Europe and Thomson of Canada in 2001. Half of Simon & Schuster, once the world's largest book publisher, was sold to Pearson, a British conglomerate, in 1999. St. Martin's Press is now part of Holtzbrinck of Germany. HarperCollins is in the hands of Rupert Murdoch, whose flagship News Corp. has its headquarters in Australia. Warner Books became part of French publishing giant Lagardere in 2006. In short, fewer and fewer companies are dominating more and more of the world's book output.

Small Publishers

While conglomerates and major houses dominate the book industry, thousands of other publishers exist, mostly small. These houses have niches that the major houses, by and large, don't bother with. Some put out only a handful of books.

Small Presses By some counts, there are 12,000 book-publishing companies in the United States. The catalogs of most contain only a few titles. Among these small presses are some important regional publishers that publish only low-volume books with a long life. Other small presses specialize in poetry and special subjects for limited audiences that wouldn't otherwise be served.

University Presses As part of their mission to advance and disseminate knowledge, universities have been in the publishing industry since as far back as 1478. That's when

Oxford University Press, the oldest English-language book publisher, was founded. Ninety-nine university presses exist in the United States today, most of them founded to publish works that wouldn't be feasible for a commercial publisher. Their contribution has been notable. Harvard University Press, for example, brought out *The Double Helix* by James Watson, as well as poetry of Ezra Pound.

As university budgets have tightened, some university presses have disappeared. Others are under pressure to move into trade books to offset their losses and even turn a profit. Some have found profitable niches in regional histories, travelogues and cookbooks.

Vanity Presses It's easy for an author to get a book published—if the author is willing to pay all expenses up front. Family histories and club cookbooks are a staple in this part of the book industry. So are many who's-who books and directories, which list names and then are sold to those whose names are in the books.

Some book publishers, called **vanity presses,** go further by soliciting manuscripts and letting the author infer that the company can make it a best-seller. These companies direct their advertising at unpublished authors and promise a free manuscript review. A custom-addressed form letter then goes back to the author, saying, quite accurately, no matter how good or how bad the manuscript, that the proposed book "is indicative of your talent." The letter also says the company would be pleased to publish the manuscript. Most vanity companies do little beyond printing, however. Their ability to promote and distribute a book is very limited, although an occasional best-seller emerges.

It can be argued that vanity publishers unscrupulously take advantage of unpublished authors who don't know how the book industry works. It can be argued too that a legitimate service is being provided. Ed Uhlan of Exposition Press, one of the largest vanity publishers, wrote an autobiographical book, *The Rogue of Publishers Row,* which details how slight the chance is that vanity press clients can make money. When he began including a free copy with the materials he sent inquiring authors, incredible as it seems, his business actually increased.

Book Retailing

The largest U.S. book retailer, Barnes & Noble, accounts for one of every eight books sold. The company's outlets are its namesake superstores and also its smaller B. Dalton mall stores. Barnes & Noble dwarfs its competitors by almost every measure. Its distribution center stocks 600,000 titles. Also Barnes & Noble is the largest retailer in the nation of magazines, newspapers and calendars.

Book retailing has undergone rapid change. Traditionally, shops were owned by local merchants. In Boston, the first seat of intellectualism in the North American British colonies, booksellers were important people in the community who knew their customers individually. Shops carried distinctive inventories. That customer-driven model of book retailing, through **independent bookstores,** worked for almost 250 years. Sales reps from publishers made individual calls on shop owners to chat about their wares, and the owners ordered what they knew their customers would want. Although independents still exist, they comprise fewer than one of five bookstores.

Book Clubs Some inroads against independents came with book clubs. The **Book-of-the-Month Club,** the oldest has shipped more than 500 million books since 1926. Originally, the club saw its market as small-town and rural people who lacked handy bookstores. The club offered packages of free books to entice people to join—on condition that they buy future books. The club used a **negative option** system: Members were sent descriptions of new titles 12 to 15 times a year. Unless they rejected a proposed offering, it was sent automatically. Typically, the club moves 200,000 copies of its featured selection.

Dozens of other book clubs followed, some specializing in narrow fields. Later, record clubs used a similar model.

Direct Mail Several media companies, including Reader's Digest, Time, Meredith and American Heritage, sell books by mail. Promotional literature is sent to people on carefully selected mailing lists, and customers order what they want. Professional and

vanity presses ■ Publishers that charge authors to publish their manuscripts.

independent bookstores ■ Bookstores that are not part of a chain.

Book-of-the-Month Club ■ The oldest book club.

negative option ■ Automatic book club shipments unless the subscriber declines in advance.

Bookstore Chains

The number of stores of major U.S. bookstore chains:

Borders	1,260
Barnes & Noble	842
Family Christian	315
Books-A-Million	202
Hastings	148

academic publishing houses, whose products wouldn't find space on bookstore shelves, market primarily through the mail. These publishers buy mailing lists from professional organizations, which, loaded with good prospects for particular titles, usually ensure a profitable number of orders by return mail.

Mall Stores With the growth of mass merchandising and shopping malls in the 1970s, several bookstore chains emerged. Typified by B. Dalton and Waldenbooks, which together had 2,300 stores at their peak, these chains ordered books in huge lots from the publishers and stocked their stores coast to coast with identical inventories. Often, the chains bought books even before they were printed, basing their decisions on publishers' promises for promotional blitzes and big discounts for bulk purchases. When huge stocks arrived, the mall stores had to move them—sometimes going to extraordinary steps with displays and discounts to fulfill their own projections and sometimes without consideration for a book's literary qualities. Suddenly, bookselling became marketing-driven with flashy displays and other incentives prodding customers to buy—hardly the customer-driven way of doing business that litterateurs would prefer. Whatever their deficiencies, mall stores were in tune with the times. They sold a lot of books, although they too had a comeuppance with the advent of superstores.

Borders Includes inventory search, book recommendations, store locator and events.
www.bordersstores.com

Barnes & Noble In addition to best-seller lists and book recommendations, also contains a new and used textbook section.
www.barnesandnoble.com

Family Christian Web site for this retailer of books, music, software and apparel.
www.familychristian.com

Books-A-Million Discount seller of books, magazines and calendars.
www.booksamillion.com

Hastings Web site for superstore Hastings, which sells books, videos, music, software and DVDs.
www.gohastings.com

Superstores Marketing-driven book retailing entered a new dimension, literally, with stand-alone superbookstores in the 1990s. Barnes & Noble, Crown, Borders and Books-A-Million built 900 humongous stores, some bigger than grocery supermarkets and stocking 180,000 titles. The superstores do more than sell books. Part of their appeal has been to become community centers of sorts, with cafes, lectures, children's programs and poetry readings. The best news, though, was that their gigantic inventories meant that people could find just what they needed—an improvement over the mall stores, albeit a big blow to the remaining independents.

Web Shopping A start-up Seattle company, Amazon.com, created an online bookstore in 1995 with 1 million titles—far more than even the largest superstore. In 1997 Barnes & Noble entered the online business, and soon both stores were claiming more than 2.5 million titles. Those sites and other online bookstores are far more than ordering mechanisms. They carry personalized recommendations, book reviews, author biographies, chatrooms and other attractions. When competition was strongest, the online services offered steep discounts, sometimes 40 percent off retail, and made inroads into the book sales of traditional bookstores and superstores. In 2003 Amazon was earning $1 billion per quarter, its first full-year profit. Aggressive pricing, an expanded product line and free shipping pushed profits up in 2004.

Book Products

studypreview **When most people think about books, fiction and nonfiction aimed at general readers come to mind. These are called trade books, which are a major segment of the book industry. Also important are textbooks, which include not only schoolbooks but also reference books and even cookbooks. There are countless ways to further dissect book products, but textbooks and trade books are the major categories.**

Trade Books

The most visible part of the $28.8 billion a year that the U.S. book publishing industry produces is **trade books.** These are general-interest titles, including fiction and nonfiction, that people usually think of when they think about books. Trade books can be incredible best-sellers. Since it was introduced in 1937, J. R. R. Tolkien's *The Hobbit* has sold almost 40 million copies. Margaret Mitchell's 1936 *Gone With the Wind* has passed 29 million. Most trade books, however, have shorter lives. To stay atop best-seller lists, Stephen King, J. K. Rowling, Danielle Steel and other authors have to keep writing. Steel, known for her discipline at the keyboard, produces a new novel about every six months.

Although publishing trade books can be extremely profitable when a book takes off, trade books have always been a high-risk proposition. One estimate is that 60 percent of them lose money, 36 percent break even and 4 percent turn a good profit. Only a few become best-sellers and make spectacular money.

Texts and References

Although the typical successful trade book best-seller can be a spectacular moneymaker for a few months, a successful **textbook** has a longer life with steady income. For example, Curtis MacDougall wrote a breakthrough textbook on journalism in 1932 that went through eight editions before he died in 1985. Then the publisher brought out a ninth edition, with Robert Reid bringing it up to date. This gave MacDougall's *Interpretative Reporting* a life span of more than 60 years. Although textbook publishers don't routinely announce profits by title, *Interpretative Reporting* undoubtedly has generated more income than many trade book best-sellers.

Textbooks, the biggest segment of the book market, include reference and professional books, college textbooks, and elementary and high school textbooks and learning materials.

Professional and Reference Books Dictionaries, atlases and other reference works represent about 10 percent of textbook sales. Over the years the Christian Bible and Noah Webster's dictionary have led reference book sales. Others also have had exceptional, long-term success that rivals trade books. Even after Benjamin Spock died in 1998, his *Baby and Child Care,* introduced in 1946, kept on selling. Total sales are past 50 million. Next on the list: *The Better Homes and Gardens Cookbook.*

College Textbooks College textbooks sell in great numbers, mostly through the coercion of the syllabus. Although textbooks are written for students, publishers pitch them to the professors who then order them for their students. Students, although the ultimate consumer, don't choose them, which may partly explain the hard feelings students have toward textbooks.

The resentment is usually directed at the college store, which many students are sure gouges them. The fact is that suspicions about bookstore gouging are misplaced. Markups typically are 20 to 30 percent—not out of line in retailing in general. From that markup, the store must meet payroll, rent and other expenses. Nor do publishers get rich. The industry's return on investment is not wickedly high, as investors will attest.

Contributing to the perception that textbooks are overpriced is that most students, until college, have had their schoolbooks provided free. Picking up the tab for the first time, except for $5 paperbacks, is a shock.

El-Hi Books Learning materials for elementary and high schools, known as the **el-hi** market, have unique marketing mechanisms. In most states, school districts are allowed to use state funds to buy books only from a state-approved list. This means that publishers gear books toward acceptance in populous states with powerful adoption boards. If the California adoption board is firm on multiculturalism, textbook publishers will take a multicultural approach to win California acceptance. Multiculturalism then becomes a theme in books for less influential states in the adoption process. If Texas, another key adoption state, insists that creationism be recognized, then so it will be in biology books for the whole nation.

trade books ■ General-interest titles, including fiction and nonfiction.

textbooks ■ Educational, professional, reference titles.

el-hi ■ Elementary and high school book market.

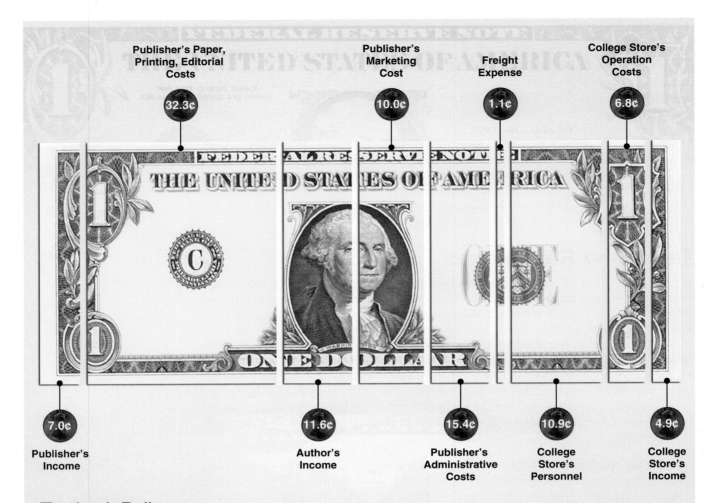

Publisher's Paper, Printing, Editorial Costs 32.3¢

Publisher's Marketing Cost 10.0¢

Freight Expense 1.1¢

College Store's Operation Costs 6.8¢

Publisher's Income 7.0¢

Author's Income 11.6¢

Publisher's Administrative Costs 15.4¢

College Store's Personnel 10.9¢

College Store's Income 4.9¢

Textbook Dollar

Students grumble about textbook costs, which fuel suspicions about profiteering. By most business and retail standards, however, profits are slim. The National Association of College Stores says pre-tax profits on new textbooks average 7.1 percent for publishers and 4.5 percent for retailers. Author royalties average 11.6 percent. For used books, however, the breakdown is drastically different. College stores often have twice the markup. On used books, there are no expenses for manufacturing, publishing house overhead, author royalties or marketing.

DC Comics Publisher of Superman, Batman and many more comics for adults and children.
www.dccomics.com

Marvel This creator of Spider-Man and Captain America comics owns over 5,000 proprietary characters.
www.marvel.com

Graphic Novels

Since the 1930s comic books have been an enduring genre. The greatest contribution was the superhero, beginning in 1938, when Jerry Siegel and Joe Shuster created Superman for DC Comics, followed by Bob Kane's Batman in 1941. A competitor, Marvel, introduced Captain America to fight Nazis during World War II. Marvel found later success with Spider-Man and X-Men.

The term *comic book* came from the first issues in the 1930s, which were bound editions of the "funnies" that had appeared in newspapers since the late 1880s. Although a hybrid of print and image communication that lends itself to all kinds of content, the comic book traditionally has been a male-read medium with superheroes. DC and Marvel dominate, with about $350 million annual sales in the $500 million market. Their greatest influence in recent years has been in licensing their characters for Hollywood movies.

graphic novels ■ Comic book format, usually longer with more sophisticated themes.

Comic books have long included condensations of classical literature, historical fiction and other subgenres. The 1980s brought a distinct variation called **graphic novels.** These had pretensions beyond a juvenile market. Frank Miller began his Sin City series

mediaPEOPLE

Frank Miller

With his Sin City series, Frank Miller helped define the difference between comic books and graphic novels. His lead character was an angst-ridden noir antihero, his scenes set in urban alleys or the dark of night, his story lines and dialogue cinematic and violent—all in contrast to the one-dimensional, Technicolor comic books like Superman and Batman. Miller wrote and sketched the Sin City series over 10 years beginning in 1991.

Book to Movie Author Frank Miller makes a point with movie director Robert Rodriguez in the production of the graphic novel *Sin City* for the screen.

Hollywood saw movie possibilities. Miller's lowlife Sin City characters, the tough cops and sultry babes, and his portrayal of the urban underground were ready-made for the big screen. Miller turned a deaf ear. He was bitter about Hollywood's creative control of his *Robocop 2* screenplay in 1990. Although a box-office success, the movie wasn't his. Miller refused to be sucked in again, whatever the offer.

He was intrigued, however, when maverick director Robert Rodriguez made a no-lose offer. Rodriguez, notoriously independent of the Hollywood establishment, proposed a one-day sample shot at his Austin, Texas, lot. If Miller liked what he saw, they would strike a deal. Miller loved the result, a stark three-minute sequence from *The Customer Is Always Right,* an early Sin City episode. He and Rodriguez signed a deal as codirectors. The three-minute sequence, starring Josh Hartnett and Marley Shelton, became the opener for the 2005 release of the first Sin City movie.

of dark urban tales in 1991. His peek into the criminal underground fascinated readers and led to a 10-year run. Art Spiegelman's *Maus: A Survivor's Tale,* which detailed his complex relationship with his father, a Holocaust survivor, won a 1992 Pulitzer Prize.

Transformational Formats

studypreview **Paperback books as low-cost alternatives to hardcover books democratized reading. Although off to a bumpy start, e-books promise to be the next transformation format for books.**

Paperback Books

The book industry is wrongly perceived as hidebound, even dowdy. Through history, books have been innovative in meeting the changing needs of the times. During the U.S. Civil War thousands of troops in the field had idle time for reading, and several innovative publishers introduced low-cost books that soldiers could afford. They were coverless and lightweight, easy to pack in a knapsack when marching orders arrived.

The modern paperback was introduced in the United States by **Robert de Graff** in 1939. The nation was well into the Depression, and traditional books were beyond the means of many people. His **Pocket Books,** unabridged softcover titles that easily fit into a purse or pocket, cost only 25 cents. Within two months, sales reached 325,000 copies. Almost everybody could afford a quarter for a book. "The paperback democratized reading in America," wrote Kenneth Davis in his book *Two-Bit Culture: The Paperbacking of America.*

Robert de Graff ■ Originated Pocket paperbacks in the United States in 1939.

Pocket Books ■ First modern U.S. paperbacks.

Electronic Books

Book publishers dallied in the early 2000s with **e-books,** portable devices the size of notebooks whose hard drives could hold multiple books—entire personal libraries, in fact. The devices never caught on, perhaps, some said, because reading on-screen is harder on the eyes than reading on paper. Also, there is something comfortable about holding a book, as opposed to a device that whirs, albeit quietly, and occasionally blinks and needs a power supply. Still, the quest to plant books in a cyberworld continues.

The Google search-engine company, rapidly expanding into new enterprises, toyed with renting copies of books online for a week at a time. Readers would pay 10 percent of a book's retail price for one week of online access. By design the books would not be downloadable to avoid cutting into sales. Also, publishers and authors would share in the online revenue.

Also, new e-book devices are coming along. In 2006 Sony introduced the Sony Reader at less than $400, a nine-ounce, pocketbook-size device that stores as many as 80 books. For 2007 Philips of the Netherlands offered Readius, itself smaller than a cellphone but with a screen that unfurls to the size of a printed page. Another Dutch company, iRex, introduced the magazine-size *iLiad,* which has a stylus for making notes in the margins.

Next Generation
The Readius e-reader has a five-inch diagonal screen that's larger than its palm-size container. The screen unfurls.

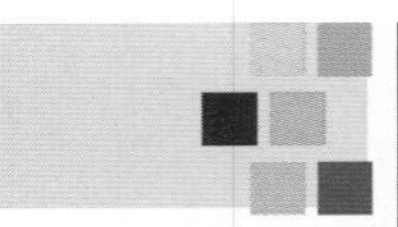

mediaTECHNOLOGY

Espresso Machine Brews Books

Espresso Book Machine Onsite book production in retail stores has been introduced with the Espresso Machine. The print-on-demand machine can produce 15 to 20 copies in an hour but as few as one as the customer waits.

It looks like a copy machine. You choose the title, insert your credit card, press the print-on-demand button, and in less than 10 minutes out pops a bound book, ready to read. Built by the World Bank's InfoShop, it's called the Espresso Machine. And just like making cups of coffee, it can produce 15 to 20 library-quality paperback books in an hour, in any language, in quantities as few as one.

Launched in 2006, the Espresso Machine was the first to fully automate the entire book publishing process, including binding. Print jobs can be initiated from the machine or from any locally connected computer using a web browser.

The World Bank, which isn't really a bank, decided the book-brewing machine fit its mission to reduce global poverty and improve living standards worldwide. Through its two development institutions owned by 184 member countries, the "bank" provides low-interest loans, interest-free credit and grants to developing countries for education, health, infrastructure and communications.

Hafed Al-Ghwell, the InfoShop's manager, said he's hoping that publishers from around the globe will bring literature to World Bank's Espresso Machine. "For the first time, we now have an inexpensive means for a two-way communication by bringing the voices from the developing world to those of us in developed countries."

Espresso Machine advantages include eliminating the costs of shipping, warehousing, returning and pulping unsold books. Globally, the Espresso Machine will allow simultaneous availability of new books and provide an inexpensive source of information for all countries. For the small publisher or self-publisher it will mean a requested book would never be out of stock or out of print.

"By the time all books are digitized over the next few years, we will have replaced the 500-year-old Gutenberg system," said Jason Epstein, former Editorial Director of Random House and a main supporter of the Espresso. "Everyone will have access to the machine and will be able to download any book ever printed."

Book Authors

studypreview **Authors come up with the ideas for many books, but publishers sometimes go looking for an author for a book to fill a hole in the market. The relationship of an author and a publisher is defined in contracts that specify royalties and other conditions and expectations for their partnership.**

media ONLINE **International Digital Publishing Forum** Trade and standards association for the digital publishing industry. Contains e-book best-seller lists. **www.openebook.org**

Authoring Process

No surefire formula exists for writing a successful book. Conventional wisdom at one point noted that books on Abraham Lincoln, on doctors and on dogs usually did well, leading one wag to suggest a book on Lincoln's doctor's dog.

Speculation Many books are written on speculation. The author has an idea, gets it on paper, then hunts for a publisher. That's how Robert Pirsig's *Zen and the Art of Motorcycle Maintenance* came to be. It's a classic case study.

Pirsig had not had an easy adulthood: mental breakdown, electroshock treatment, itinerancy. He had grown up expecting more. A high point in his life was working out a relationship with his 11-year-old son. From his experiences emerged a gentle philosophy about life. An idea developed in Pirsig's mind for a book that wrapped it all together.

Finding a publisher was difficult. For more than six years, Pirsig sent out his proposal—121 times in all. Publishing houses doubted its commercial potential. It was

e-books Portable electronic devices for on-screen reading of books downloaded from the Web.

mediaPEOPLE

Jane Friedman

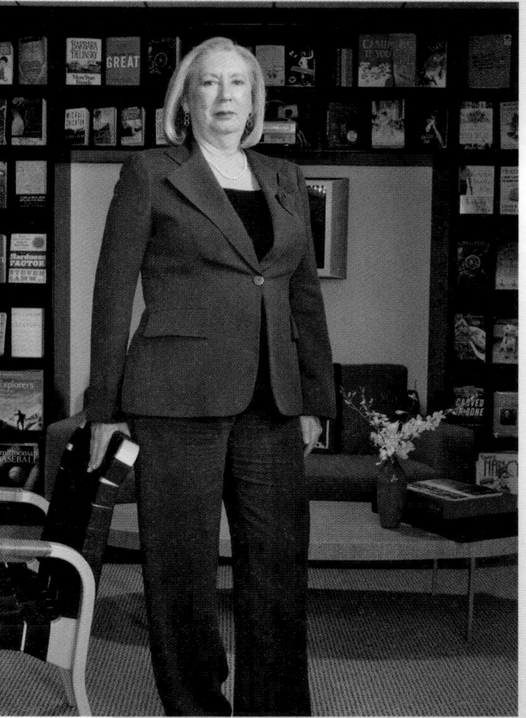

Book Industry Contrarian

Jane Friedman, chief executive at HarperCollins, is unlearning fundamental lessons from her career climb over 30 years. The book industry's future, as Friedman sees it, is not in blockbusters. Big-name authors are risky, she says. Guaranteed advances in the upper six figures, sometimes higher, don't assure that a book won't flop and leave a publisher bleeding red ink.

Friedman sees a new model for publishers that emphasizes long-term profits from what she calls "small books."

Her doubts about blockbusters are understandable. A rule of thumb is 4 percent of new titles earn a good profit, only a few of those make spectacular money. In 2005, for example, only 200 books accounted for 10 percent of U.S. book industry sales. One book, *Harry Potter and the Half-Blood Prince,* with 7 million copies, accounted for 1 percent of the year's total sales.

So what is Friedman's vision?

She sees new life for books that now, after their introduction, languish in warehouses until they're shredded to make room for newer titles. With digital storage, these backlist books can remain available indefinitely. With print-on-demand technology, one copy at a time can be printed. Over the long term, Friedman says, many backlist books can generate continuing sales and profits.

Also, she says, small books could sell significantly better if marketed to people with specific interests and who otherwise have no idea the books are available.

Friedman's ideas on targeted marketing are clearly contrarian in an industry where intuitive assessments of manuscripts has been the tradition. She's blunt: "Publishers have never looked at who the consumer is."

The book industry needs to reinvent itself, she says: "Chasing best-sellers is a fool's game."

a meandering, sometimes confusing manuscript that operated on many levels. At one level it was written around a motorcycle trip that Pirsig and his son had taken from Minnesota westward. At another level it was a highly cerebral exploration of values. Finally, the 122nd time that Pirsig mailed out the manuscript, it attracted the attention of James Landis, an editor at the William Morrow publishing house. The offbeat title was enticing, and Landis saw literary merit in the book. He decided to take a flier. Morrow published the book in 1974. Landis cautioned Pirsig against getting his hopes up. But *Zen and the Art of Motorcycle Maintenance* turned out to be the right book at the right time. Written in a soul-searching, soul-baring style, it touched readers emerging from

mediaPEOPLE

J. K. Rowling

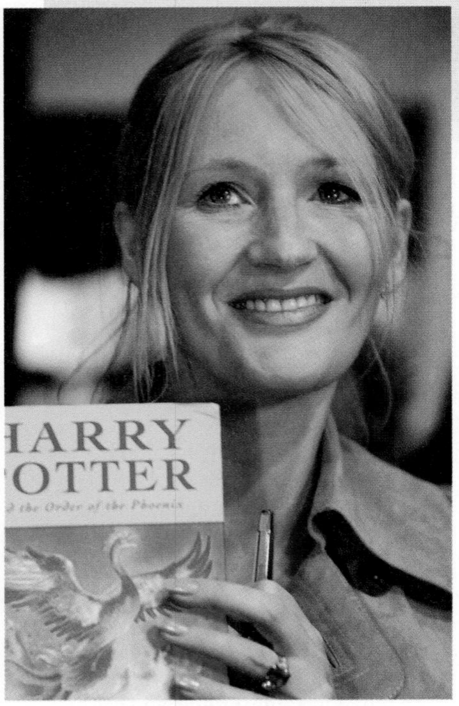

J. K. Rowling She has Harry Potter moving to a conclusion.

Joanne Rowling always liked telling stories. At age 5, maybe 6, she wrote her first book. The plot centered on a rabbit called Rabbit, who came down with the measles and was consoled by a giant bee. Her name: Miss Bee. All through school Rowling regaled her school chums with stories.

After college she took a job in London, but her mind was elsewhere. On the boring train ride into the city every day, a story took form in her mind. At work she scribbled notes. At lunch she pulled her thoughts together on other pads.

Knowing that her obsession with the story was getting in the way of her work, Rowling quit. She left for a teaching job in Portugal. Returning to Britain a year later, she had half a suitcase of manuscript pages. A year later, in 1997, when Rowling was 28, the book, *Harry Potter and the Sorcerer's Stone,* was done.

Rowling hoped the book would find a loyal, albeit probably small, following. At 309 pages the adventure story, about a boy wizard named Harry Potter, seemed a bit heavy for the Nintendo generation. She was wrong.

Word spread fast among kids. *Harry Potter* was a great story. Best of all, it was something their parents and teachers weren't telling them to read. It was their discovery, which gave it an allure somewhat like that of Nancy Drew and the Hardy Boys for earlier generations. Then adults too began reading *Harry Potter.*

J. K. Rowling kept sequels coming. For her sixth book, *Harry Potter and the Half-Blood Prince,* the U.S. publisher, Scholastic, printed a record 10.8 million copies for the first run. Before the book was issued, bookseller Barnes & Noble had received orders from 750,000 customers wanting more than one copy. Presales at Amazon.com totaled 560,000, and opening-day sales broke all records.

At least one of the Harry Potter books was on the New York *Times* best-seller fiction list for 81 weeks straight. It was squeezing other works off the list. The *Times* responded by creating a separate best-seller list for children's books.

The books have had detractors. Conservative religious leaders fretted that Harry was involved in magic, even witchery. Some schools banned the books. This gave the books a forbidden fruit attraction.

Although they are popular, are the Harry Potter books good literature? Will they have the enduring recognition of, say, books by Robert Louis Stevenson? Or will they wear thin on a second reading, like Nancy Drew mysteries?

Rowling's fast-paced plots certainly are hard to put down. She has good guys and bad guys and also complex characters. The stories are scary, riveting even. Rowling's love of funny names adds charm—such as the evil Lord Voldemort (rhymes with "moldy wart").

How did Rowling come up with these names? "I was born in Chipping Sodbury General Hospital, which I think is appropriate for someone who collects funny names," she says. Harry Potter, it seems, was incubating in J. K. Rowling's mind from her earliest moments.

the Haight-Ashbury flower child era. It became a best-seller. Not just a flash sensation, it had sales exceeding 100,000 a year for 20 years and remains in print.

Every year, by one estimate, 30,000 manuscripts written on speculation arrive at the nation's trade publishing houses. Many do not receive even a cursory review. Nine out of 10 are rejected. Of the survivors, only a fraction make it to print.

Publisher Initiative While many authors seek publishers, as Pirsig did, it can also work the other way. When Warner Books saw profit potential in a sequel to Margaret Mitchell's enduring *Gone With the Wind,* it auditioned several leading authors. Alexandra Ripley was the choice. *Scarlett* resulted. Barbara Tuchman's *Guns of August,* about the start of World War I, had a similar origin. A publisher, Macmillan, recognized a dearth of titles on the war and went looking for an author. Tuchman, an accomplished journalist, was an obvious choice. She liked the proposal.

Author-Publisher Relations

Under copyright law, authors are like other creators of intellectual property and almost always own what they write. A publisher's responsibility is to edit and polish the manuscript and then to manufacture, distribute and market the book.

Royalties Authors usually give publishers the ownership of the book in exchange for these services. In a contractual arrangement, authors receive a percentage of their book's income, a **royalty.** The publisher takes the rest to cover expenses and, if a book does well, to make a profit.

In trade publishing, a typical royalty rate is 15 percent of the cover price, although publishers, seeking to trim expenses, have whittled at the standard in recent years. In textbooks the percentage is also 15 percent, but because the royalty is calculated from a wholesale, not retail, price it is actually more typically 11½ percent. Some authors have the negotiating clout for much greater royalties. Stephen King's is reportedly at 50 percent. Two textbook coauthors negotiated 21¾ percent for a promising cutting-edge work in the sciences.

Authors usually receive an **advance** of money from a publisher when they sign a contract. The idea of an advance is to tide an author over until royalties begin coming in. The advance then is deducted from the author's first royalty income. The Hollywood star system that has taken root in trade publishing, however, has changed the concept of advances. To sign big-name authors, publishers regularly offer authors more advance money than is likely to be earned in royalties and never ask for the advance back. Some observers doubted, for example, that former President Bill Clinton's 2004 memoirs, *My Life,* for which publisher Knopf gave a $12 million advance, would ever **earn out.** Knopf executives could not have been more pleased that *My Life* sold 1.2 million copies in the first two weeks.

Risk is involved in book publishing. For most books a publisher invests the same upfront money in editing, production and marketing whether the book sells well or bombs. Authors take a risk too because their advances are repayable, although advances are often forgiven if a book doesn't earn out. Why forgiven? Because publishers recognize their vulnerability to author lawsuits claiming that they marketed a book badly if it doesn't earn out.

Agents Most authors, except for textbooks, hire an **agent** to find an appropriate publisher and negotiate the contract. Typically, agents earn their keep with a 10 percent commission taken from the author's royalties. This arrangement encourages agents to negotiate the best terms possible for the author, at the same time knowing from experience when pushing too hard for certain terms can break a deal.

royalty ■ Author's share of a book's income.

advance ■ Upfront money for an author to sign a contract with a publisher.

earn out ■ When royalty income to an author exceeds the advance.

agent ■ Person who represents an author in finding a publisher and in negotiating a contract.

Book Issues and Trends

study preview **Book publishers' quest for blockbuster profits and concomitant new focus on marketing have diminished literary and other quality measures. Retailers, including giant Wal-Mart, have become gatekeepers on distribution. Also troubling for the book industry is a growing disinterest in reading.**

Blockbusters

Nobody denies the importance of Harriet Beecher Stowe's *Uncle Tom's Cabin.* More Americans read it than any other book between 1852 and the Civil War. It stirred antislavery passions that, some say, led to the war. The book sold an unprecedented 100,000 copies a month in the first three months it was out—the first blockbuster novel.

Publishers ever since have put the quest for blockbusters above all else, say book industry critics. The quest has snowballed, becoming so frenzied and also calculated that, according to the critics, the industry focuses myopically on creating blockbusters, which means slighting and even ignoring works of merit that might not be as profitable.

Although some critics overstate their case, there is no question that conglomeration has accelerated the blockbuster mania. Parent companies, under shareholder pressure to increase profits, incessantly seek a greater return from their book company subsidiaries. They put people in charge who will focus on that task. The bottom-line orientation fuels the concern among elitists that mediocre and even bad stuff ends up displacing good stuff in the marketplace.

In an important book, *The Death of Literature,* Alvin Kernan makes the case that the increasingly consumer-oriented book industry is stunting good literature. Worse, says Kernan, the lower level to which books are written, edited and marketed is undermining cultural standards by placing less of a premium on high literacy.

Indeed, major houses put growing emphasis on clever acquisitions, big-name authors and heavy promotion. Purists complain that blockbuster authors get multimillion-dollar deals before even writing a word because of the Hollywood-like star system that publishers have created to sell books through the author's name, not necessarily the quality of the book.

Publishing executives respond that producing books with limited popular appeal would put them out of business. Their argument: Without attention to profits, the industry would constrict—and where would cultural enhancement be then?

Mass Marketing

Evidence abounds that major houses have forsaken a balance on the elitist-populist continuum. The current classic example is the $600,000 that Warner Books spent to promote *Scarlett,* Alexandra Ripley's 1991 sequel to *Gone With the Wind.* Litterateurs called the book mediocre at best, but Warner's orchestrated promotional campaign created a mass market. The book, although now forgotten, was the year's top seller despite dubious literary merit. Critics say that by channeling so many resources into the Ripley book, Warner either underpromoted or bypassed other works, including some of undoubtedly greater merit. We'll never know.

For sure, success has moved beyond the province of the literary-minded. More and more, the criteria that preoccupy publishing houses in choosing titles are these related questions: Will it sell? How can we make it sell? Too, big retailers choose whether to stock a book on the basis of bulk discounts, publisher promotion budgets and big-name authors—not literary quality.

media ONLINE **Nora Roberts** Official web site for author Nora Roberts, who also writes as J. D. Robb. **www.noraroberts.com**

Selection Criteria In deciding which books to sign, some publishing house editorial committees consider how photogenic the author will be in television interviews. An

case STUDY

Authors as Franchise: J. D. Robb and Nora Roberts

Book publishers have found ways to make money with mediocre products. Nobody would argue, for example, that Harlequin-type romances are great literature, yet the cliché genre generates 2,100 new titles, almost all paperbacks, and $1.4 billion a year in the United States. By 1992 Appalachian housewife Eleanor Jean Robertson, writing as Nora Roberts, had become a leading romance writer. She pumps out six or more romances a year, all formulaic stories with cheesy Fabio covers. Names and settings change, but in every book a rather ordinary but sensitive, bright and finely featured young woman meets a hunky guy with intense eyes that can melt her heart. After explosive sexual encounters they marry and live happily ever after.

At the Putnam publishing house, executives Phyllis Grann and Leslie Gelbman hatched a plan to compound the success of the Nora Roberts franchise. They asked Roberts to produce three longer manuscripts a year with slightly more intricate plots and complex characters. The scheme included upscale covers that wouldn't embarrass a reader at the checkout counter. The classier books sold for $22—triple the $7 Fabio paperbacks. For Roberts' 100th book, *Montana Sky,* Putnam invested in television advertisements, rare for the book industry at the time. The publisher pressed book chains for flashy, front-of-the-store displays. In days sales of *Montana Sky* passed the 100,000 mark, the industry threshold for hardback best-sellers. Sales went on to pass 2 million.

Not content with merely repackaging their Nora Roberts franchise, Grann and Gelbman talked Roberts into an additional series of grisly murder mysteries. To avoid diluting Roberts' huge romance following, they asked the author to come up with a second pen name. Thus was launched the J. D. Robb books: "J" for Roberts' son Jason and "D" for her son Dan. Robb? Well, it was close to her existing nom de plume, Roberts, and to her real name, Robertson. The new In Death series was loosely linked with Eve Dallas, a cop, and Roarke, a billionaire with a fortune of murky origin. Amid steamy escapades they solved murders—all in a slightly edgy setting in New York City in the year 2059. The books—19 of them by 2005—carried thematic titles like *Divided in Death* and *Portrait in Death.* Cumulative sales topped 17 million. The In Death series' success, again, was marketing magic. At the end of every new Dallas-Roarke installment was an excerpt from the next book, like a movie preview.

Then came another marketing ploy. In a dramatic departure from the tradition of secrecy surrounding pen names, the decision was made to uncover J. D. Robb. Posters went up in stores: "Guess who J. D. Robb really is?" In 2001 J. D. Robb was outed. The goal was to lure romance addicts to the J. D. Robb murder series and murder mystery addicts to the Nora Roberts romance series.

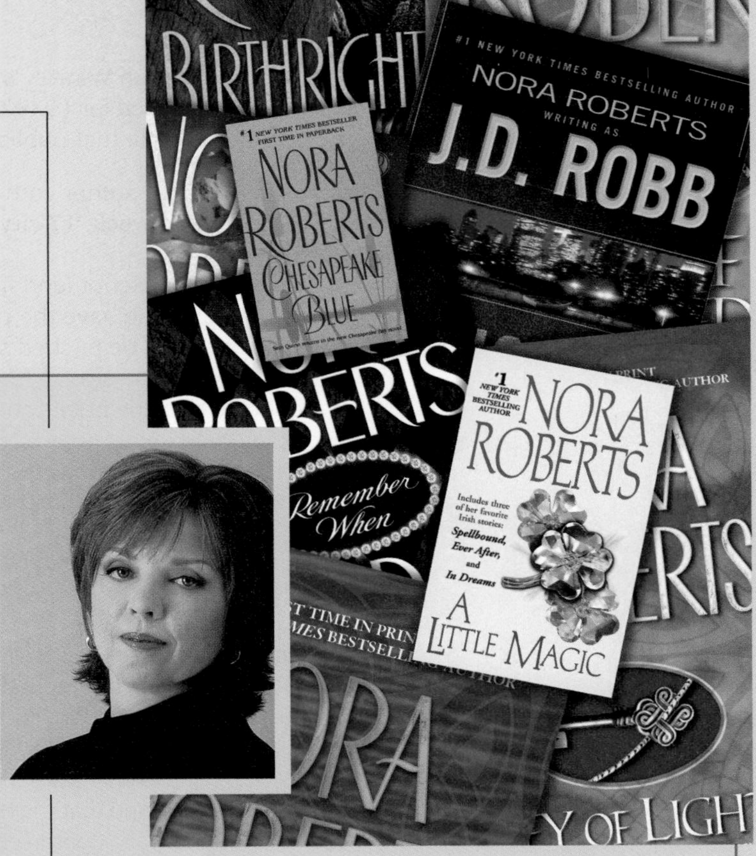

Two Styles, Two Names When products become commodities, like toothpaste, when one is much like the other, marketing, advertising and promotion seek to create the perception of a difference. When romance novels with their look-alike covers had become mere commodities under brand-name imprints like Harlequin and Silhouette, publisher Leslie Gelbman and editor Phyllis Grann conceived a plan to elevate best-selling author Nora Roberts from the pack by tweaking and repackaging the product. It worked. Then came crossing genres by adding murder mysteries to the Robertson genre under the nom de plume J. D. Robb.

The promotion of Nora Roberts as a brand name includes T-shirts, blankets and book bags. The Nora Roberts web site attracts 110,000 visitors a month. A monthly newsletter goes out free to 50,000 fans, promoting the latest title. For $16 there is the 450-page *Official Nora Roberts Companion,* updated annually, on her characters, plots and trivia. Her early titles are reissued on a cycle with new covers. Mel Gibson holds movie rights for the In Death stories. The shareholders of the publishing house, now Putnam subunit Bantam, could not be more pleased. Roberts-Robb book sales reached 50 million copies a year by 2005. The commercial success of the Roberts-Robb franchise, however, was hardly a mark of literary excellence. It was due to clever marketing, not to genius or innovation in content.

WHAT DO YOU THINK?

1. Why do you think books with the same plots and mediocre writing are often more popular than good literature?
2. Is it fair to readers to market mediocre books so heavily?

appearance on Oprah Winfrey's show can make all the difference. Toni Morrison's *Song of Solomon* languished for 19 years on the market before she appeared on *Oprah* in 1996. Among other criteria that publishers use in choosing authors:

- How would the author come across on radio?
- Would a three-week, 17-city sweep on local talk shows at the launch of a book add to sales?
- Does the manuscript lend itself to a screenplay?
- Would the movie have the potential for profitable soundtrack possibilities?
- Could the book be pitched so that a book club would choose it as a monthly selection?
- Could the book be priced so that Wal-Mart would use a prominent point-of-purchase display?
- How enticing can the cover be?
- How much would magazine serialization boost sales?

If any of these criteria speaks to literary quality, it's only tangentially. Charles Scribner and Maxwell Perkins would cringe.

Promotion Humorist Art Buchwald captured how book marketing can run amok. Noting how lascivious covers and hyped subtitles contribute to paperback sales, Buchwald once suggested that *Snow White and the Seven Dwarfs* be subtitled "The Story of a Ravishing Blonde Virgin Held Captive by Seven Deformed Men, All with Different Lusts."

Creating controversy sells. In a classic case, Stein & Day, the publisher of Elia Kazan's *The Arrangement*, found that the book was being criticized as too explicit. In fact, the Mount Pleasant, Iowa, Library Board sent back its copy as too racy for its shelves. Stein & Day's president mailed a letter to the Mount Pleasant *News*, offering a free copy to everyone in the community, urging them to read the book and decide for themselves. Eight hundred people ordered their free copy, which generated a bundle of publicity. Sales soared nationally.

After Mel Gibson's movie *The Passion of the Christ*, sales of *The Dolorous Passion of Our Lord Jesus Christ*, which had been slogging along at 3,000 in 2002, jumped to 14,000. Ironically, another book with no connection to the film, *The Passion of Jesus Christ*, sold 1.6 million in 2004.

Aliteracy

The United States claims a **literacy** rate of 97 percent, among the highest in the world. Yet there is growing evidence that Americans, particularly young people, are reading less. A 2004 study by the National Endowment for the Arts, *Reading at Risk*, found that fewer than half of American adults read literature, loosely defined as fiction or poetry. That was a 10 percent decline over 20 years. For young adults, the drop was 28 percentage points. It's not that people can't read, which would be illiteracy. Instead, people are increasingly **aliterate**, which means they can read but don't.

The findings of the National Endowment for the Arts study, although alarming, can be overstated. The fact is that adult fiction titles grew 43.1 percent in 2004 to more than 25,000 titles, which means perhaps that fewer people are reading more. Too, as book industry spokesperson Patricia Schroeder has noted, people in serious times spend less time with fiction and more with biography, history, current events and other nonfiction. Clearly more time is spent on alternatives to books, like on-screen news and blogs.

Improved e-books, with ambient light that eliminates flickering, may bring people back to literature.

literacy ■ Ability to read

aliterate ■ Choosing not to read although able to do so.

Unsuitable at Wal-Mart

The extent of Wal-Mart's control over books, and also magazines and music, is hard to quantify. The company doesn't announce its bans, but cases surface through other sources. In 2004 this included two satirical works, by comedians George Carlin and Jon Stewart. The bans suggest some humorless executives at Wal-Mart's Bentonville, Arkansas, headquarters have taken on the task of deciding what people in the company's vast customer base can choose. Critics call the Wal-Mart decision-making paternalistic.

Global Online Access

study preview **The search-engine company Google and publishers are in a kerfuffle over a project to digitize all the books in the English language. Not to be left behind, countries with other languages have launched their own scanning projects for works in their languages.**

Google Library Project

Nobody doubts the sky's the limit for imaginativeness at the search-engine company Google. A Google project that boggles the mind is the Library Project. With piles of cash from multiple income streams, Google is scanning and digitizing all the works in four great U.S. academic libraries and one in Britain for online access for people all over the globe. That's 15 million titles, a quantity impossible for a mere mortal to conceptualize. So immense is the project that, although begun in 2005, its projected completion is years away.

The project faces obstacles. Many publishers fear losing control of their inventories if Google is storing every word ever published on Google servers. The Association of American

Publishers has sued to halt the project, claiming that the material publishers produce is their property under copyright laws for works going back 75 years. Google says it has no intention of publishing protected works but means only to provide an indexing service for finding passages. If nothing else, publishers hope to delay the Google project to buy time to play catch-up in the digitizing of books.

European Response

The Goggle project began with digitizing all the books in the English language. "What about French literary works?" asked an alarmed French President Jacques Chirac, who regards himself as the guardian of French culture. The British Library and the National Lottery launched the Collect Britain project. The European Commission plans to digitize and preserve records of Europe's heritage, including books, film fragments, photographs, manuscripts, speeches and music to be available online to all European citizens.

Evaluating Books

study preview **A book's value can be measured by best-seller lists, though neither precisely nor qualitatively. Other measures include external recognition through awards and independent reviews.**

Best-seller ■ 75,000 copies hardcover, 100,000 paperback.

Populist Measures

Jacques Chirac
The French president is worried that the Google Print Library, focusing on digitizing every book in English, will subsume French cultural presence in the world.

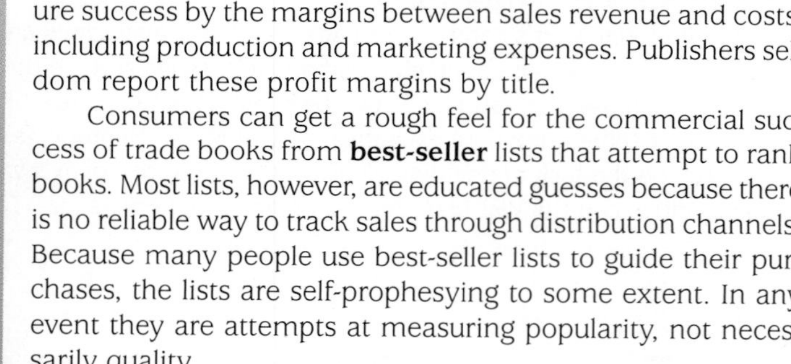

Book publishers, obsessive about their bottom lines, measure success by the margins between sales revenue and costs, including production and marketing expenses. Publishers seldom report these profit margins by title.

Consumers can get a rough feel for the commercial success of trade books from **best-seller** lists that attempt to rank books. Most lists, however, are educated guesses because there is no reliable way to track sales through distribution channels. Because many people use best-seller lists to guide their purchases, the lists are self-prophesying to some extent. In any event they are attempts at measuring popularity, not necessarily quality.

Quality Measures

Qualitative measures are available for people who have a disdain for populist best-seller lists. Among respected prizes:

- **National Book Award:** For fiction, poetry and young people
- **Nobel Prize:** For literature
- **PEN/Faulkner Award:** For U.S. fiction
- **Pulitzer Prize:** For fiction, nonfiction and poetry
- **William Holmes McGuffey Award:** For textbooks

A prestigious prize, such as a Pulitzer, can propel a book into best-seller status on the basis of merit. Yes, elitists are forced to admit, solid works can be best-sellers.

October 8, 2006

THE NEW YORK TIMES BOOK REVIEW

Best Sellers

This Week	FICTION	Last Week	Weeks On List
1	**THE THIRTEENTH TALE,** by Diane Setterfield. (Atria, $26.) A biographer struggles to discover the truth about an aging writer who has mythologized her past.	1	2
2	**THE BOOK OF FATE,** by Brad Meltzer. (Warner, $25.99.) The apparent murder of a presidential aide reveals Masonic secrets in Washington and a 200-year-old code invented by Thomas Jefferson.	2	3
3	**THE MISSION SONG,** by John le Carré. (Little, Brown, $26.99.) An English translator, born in Congo, is sent by British intelligence to work for a corporate syndicate that wants to subvert Congolese elections.		1
4	**RISE AND SHINE,** by Anna Quindlen. (Random House, $24.95.) The lives of two New York sisters, one the host of a television show and the other a social worker.	4	4
5	**JUDGE & JURY,** by James Patterson and Andrew Gross. (Little, Brown, $27.99.) An aspiring actress and an F.B.I. agent join forces against a powerful mobster.	5	8
6	**THE GUY NOT TAKEN,** by Jennifer Weiner. (Atria, $24.95.) Stories about women and relationships from the author of "In Her Shoes."	8	3
7	**IMPERIUM,** by Robert Harris. (Simon & Schuster, $26.) A fictional life of Marcus Cicero, the Roman statesman and orator, as told by a household slave.		1
8	**THE MEPHISTO CLUB,** by Tess Gerritsen. (Ballantine, $25.95.) A Boston medical examiner and a detective must solve a series of murders involving apocalyptic messages and a sinister cabal.	3	2
9	**DARK CELEBRATION,** by Christine Feehan. (Berkley, $23.95.) Carpathians from around the world join together to oppose their enemies' plot to kill all Carpathian women.	6	3
10	**WORLD WAR Z,** by Max Brooks. (Crown, $24.95.) An "oral history" of an imagined Zombie War that nearly destroys civilization.	11	2
11	**THE RIGHT ATTITUDE TO RAIN,** by Alexander McCall Smith. (Pantheon, $21.95.) The third novel featuring the philosopher Isabel Dalhousie is a mystery about the meaning of happiness.		1
12	**THE EMPEROR'S CHILDREN,** by Claire Messud. (Knopf, $25.) A group of privileged 30-somethings try to make their way in literary New York just before 9/11.	9	4
13	**THE AFGHAN,** by Frederick Forsyth. (Putnam, $26.95.) To foil a Qaeda plot, a British operative masquerades as a Taliban commander just released from Guantánamo.	10	5
14	**RICOCHET,** by Sandra Brown. (Simon & Schuster, $25.95.) A detective is attracted to a judge's wife who he suspects is not telling the truth about a fatal shooting.	7	6
15	**A SPOT OF BOTHER,** by Mark Haddon. (Doubleday, $24.95.) The world of a mild-mannered British family man falls apart; from the author of "The Curious Incident of the Dog in the Night-Time."	12	2

This Week	NONFICTION	Last Week	Weeks On List
1	**I FEEL BAD ABOUT MY NECK,** by Nora Ephron. (Knopf, $19.95.) A witty look at aging from a novelist and screenwriter ("When Harry Met Sally").	2	8
2	**THE GREATEST STORY EVER SOLD,** by Frank Rich. (Penguin, $25.95.) A Times columnist attacks the Bush administration's approach to message management.		1
3	**THE CONFESSION,** by James E. McGreevey. (Regan, $26.95.) The former New Jersey governor comes out.		1
4	**MARLEY & ME,** by John Grogan. (Morrow, $21.95.) A newspaper columnist and his wife learn some life lessons from their neurotic dog.	1	49
5	**THE WORLD IS FLAT,** by Thomas L. Friedman. (Farrar, Straus & Giroux, $30.) A columnist for The Times analyzes 21st-century economics and foreign policy.	4	77
6	**STATE OF EMERGENCY,** by Patrick J. Buchanan. (Thomas Dunne/St. Martin's, $24.95.) The conservativ[e] commentator argues against unchecked immigration.	5	5
7	**LETTER TO A CHRISTIAN NATION,** by Sam Harris. (Knopf, $16.95.) The author of "The End of Faith" responds to Christians' arguments in defense of their beliefs.		
8	**I SHOULDN'T EVEN BE DOING THIS!** by Bob Newhart (Hyperion, $23.95.) A memoir by the comedian.		
9	**FREAKONOMICS,** by Steven D. Levitt and Stephen J. Dubner. (Morrow, $25.95.) A maverick scholar and a journalist apply economic theory to almost everything		
10	**THE LOOMING TOWER,** by Lawrence Wright. (Knopf, $27.95.) The road to 9/11 as seen through the lives of terrorist planners and the F.B.I. counterterrorism chief who died in the attacks.		
11	**THE GOD DELUSION,** by Richard Dawkins. (Houghton Mifflin, $27.) An Oxford scientist asserts that belief in God is irrational and that religion has done great harm in the world.		
12	**HUBRIS,** by Michael Isikoff and David Corn. (Crown, $25.95.) The planning and marketing of the invasion of Iraq, featuring the president, administration officials, neoconservatives, Iraqi exiles and credulous journalists.		
13	**FIASCO,** by Thomas E. Ricks. (Penguin Press, $27.95.) How the Bush administration's and the military's failure to understand the developing Iraqi insurgency contributed to its further growth.		
14	**AIR AMERICA: THE PLAYBOOK,** by David Bender, Chuck D, Thom Hartmann et al. (Rodale, $26.95.) Essays, transcripts and interviews from "a bunch of left-wing media types."		
15	**THE WAY WE WERE,** by Paul Burrell. (Morrow, $25.95.) Diana's former butler reminisces.		
16*	**THE LOST,** by Daniel Mendelsohn. (HarperCollins, $27.95.) A critic tracks down the story of a great-uncle and his family, who were killed in the Holocaust.		

Rankings reflect sales, for the week ended Sept. 23, at almost 4,000 bookstores plus wholesalers serving 50,000 other retailers, statistically weighted such outlets nationwide. An asterisk (*) indicates that a book's sales are barely distinguishable from those of the book above. A dagger (†) indicates bookstores report receiving bulk orders. Expanded rankings are available at The New York Times on the Web: nytimes.com/books.

Best-Sellers

People in the book business track the list in the trade journal *Publishers Weekly.* The most quoted list, in the New York *Times,* ranks books by general categories. Critics say that the *Times* gives too much weight to highbrow independent bookstores and that its list undervalues a lot of paperback fiction. The *Wall Street Journal* list uses an index feature to show the relative sales of books on its lists. *USA Today* also has a weekly list, but it is a hodgepodge of formats and genres that, say critics, makes it a list of oranges and apples.

Campus Best-Seller List

The *Chronicle of Higher Education,* a weekly newspaper read mostly by college administrators and faculty, checks campus bookstores at selected universities for best-sellers among students. It bears some semblance to the New York *Times* weekly best-seller list, but there are differences that reflect issues and subjects with special attraction for people who frequent campus shops.

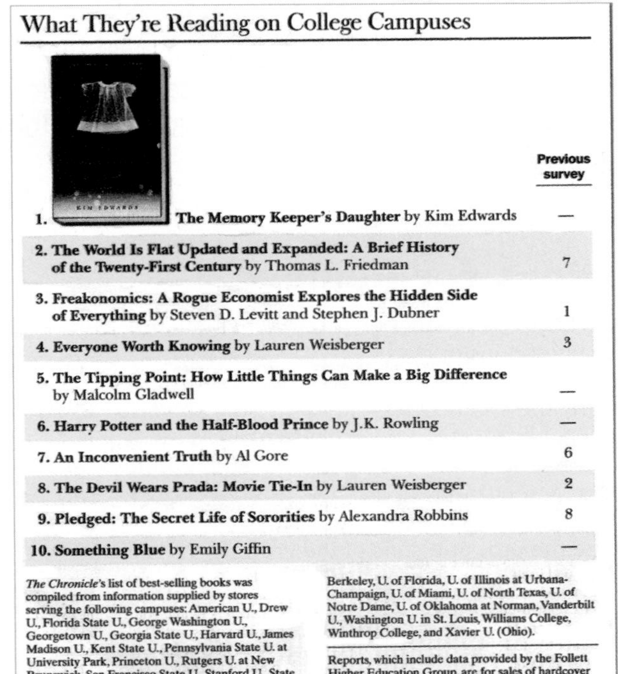

What They're Reading on College Campuses

		Previous survey
1.	**The Memory Keeper's Daughter** by Kim Edwards	—
2.	**The World Is Flat Updated and Expanded: A Brief History of the Twenty-First Century** by Thomas L. Friedman	7
3.	**Freakonomics: A Rogue Economist Explores the Hidden Side of Everything** by Steven D. Levitt and Stephen J. Dubner	1
4.	**Everyone Worth Knowing** by Lauren Weisberger	3
5.	**The Tipping Point: How Little Things Can Make a Big Difference** by Malcolm Gladwell	—
6.	**Harry Potter and the Half-Blood Prince** by J.K. Rowling	—
7.	**An Inconvenient Truth** by Al Gore	6
8.	**The Devil Wears Prada: Movie Tie-In** by Lauren Weisberger	2
9.	**Pledged: The Secret Life of Sororities** by Alexandra Robbins	8
10.	**Something Blue** by Emily Giffin	—

The Chronicle's list of best-selling books was compiled from information supplied by stores serving the following campuses: American U., Drew U., Florida State U., George Washington U., Georgetown U., Georgia State U., Harvard U., James Madison U., Kent State U., Pennsylvania State U. at University Park, Princeton U., Rutgers U. at New Brunswick, San Francisco State U., Stanford U., State U. of New York at Buffalo, U. of California at Berkeley, U. of Florida, U. of Illinois at Urbana-Champaign, U. of Miami, U. of North Texas, U. of Notre Dame, U. of Oklahoma at Norman, Vanderbilt U., Washington U. in St. Louis, Williams College, Winthrop College, and Xavier U. (Ohio).

Reports, which include data provided by the Follett Higher Education Group, are for sales of hardcover and paperback trade books in August.

Another guide to quality for enduring titles is their appearance in numerous series of great works. Also, for contemporary works in a given field many people follow book reviews in trade journals and specialized publications. Among general publications with great elitist followings for their book reviews are the New York *Times,* which puts out a weekly magazine on books, and the *Wall Street Journal.*

Some book clubs are a guide to quality. For many years Book-of-the-Month Club relied on a board of independent authorities to choose titles. A BOMC endorsement was important. Even so, being a matter of judgment, even of collective judgment, the BOMC imprimatur was not infallible. The club missed John Steinbeck's *Grapes of Wrath.*

CHAPTER 2 Wrap-Up

Book publishing is a high-risk business, especially for works geared toward general consumers. Most books do not make money, which means that publishing houses rely on best-sellers to offset the losses. Despite the risks, books can make enormous profits, which led many conglomerates to buy publishing houses in the 1980s. The new parent corporations pressed for more profitability. The result has been heightened competition for big-name authors and new attention to mass marketing. Multimillion-dollar advances to authors for popular, though not necessarily significant, works suggest that the book industry is backing away from its traditional role in furthering U.S. culture and public enlightenment.

Questions for Review

1. How did the mass-produced written word fundamentally change human history?
2. What is the ownership trend in book publishing?
3. What are the main categories and subcategories of books?
4. How have book format changes affected the influence of books on the culture?
5. How do book concepts come to be?
6. What are the pros and cons of the growing influence of marketing in the book industry?
7. How can the worthiness of books be judged?

Questions for Critical Thinking

1. Johannes Gutenberg has been called the most significant person in human history. How would he have regarded the claim? Where would you place Gutenberg in your own Top 10 list?
2. For most people book publishing brings to mind McGraw-Hill, Simon & Schuster, HarperCollins and other major companies. Describe how University of Minnesota Press and Exposition Press fit into the industry.
3. Distinguish trade books and textbooks in terms of profit potential, duration on the market, distribution systems and the effect of mass-marketed paperbacks.
4. Did the introduction of paperback books influence the culture positively? Negatively? What effect can be expected from e-books?
5. How has the seminal role of authors in defining cultural values been diminished by mass marketing in the book industry?
6. How can the book industry ensure its continued growth? How can the book industry protect itself from the need to retrench if growth stalls?
7. Where do you turn for counsel on new books that are most worth your time? What does this say about you? Do you expect to be looking in the same places for book tips in five years? Ten years?

Deepening Your media LITERACY

Will electronic technology ultimately strengthen or weaken the book industry?

STEP 1 Think about the changes that have occurred in the book industry from the original Pocket Book paperback novel to the latest Harry Potter adventure.

Dig Deeper

STEP 2 List as many ways as you can think of in which electronic technology, the Internet and related media crossover opportunities have changed the book industry. Be sure to consider all aspects of the book industry: the writing, publishing, marketing, distribution and sales of books.

What Do You Think?

STEP 3 Would you consider buying a book's content electronically, in much the way that you purchase music for an iPod? What is more important to the book industry: the actual content of the books or the physical paper, ink, and bindings that make up the paper book? What impact would there be if the two were separated? Will electronic technology ultimately strengthen or weaken the book industry?

Keeping Up to Date

Publisher Weekly is a trade journal of the book industry.

Book Research Quarterly, a scholarly journal, is published by Rutgers University.

The C-SPAN television network runs a continuing program, *Booknotes,* which focuses on authors and new titles as well as book industry issues.

Fortune magazine ranks industrial companies in April and service companies in May.

Subtext is a biweekly newsletter on the book industry.

Many general-interest magazines, including *Time* and *Newsweek,* cover book industry issues when they are topical, as do the New York *Times,* the *Wall Street Journal* and other major newspapers.

In recent years the *New Republic* has been especially enterprising in covering book industry practices as they change.

For Further Learning

Diane Cole. "Publish or Panic," *U.S. News & World Report* (March 13, 2006), pages 46–53.

Cole, a reporter, offers a current overview of book industry issues with special focus on prospects for small publishers.

National Endowment for the Arts. *Reading at Risk: Literary Reading in America.* Washington, 2005.

Charles Brownstein. *Eisner/Miller: A One-on-One Interview.* Dark Horse, 2005.

Graphic novelists Will Eisner and Frank Miller, both with roots in comic books, discuss their craft, with rich detail on issues and personalities.

Arthur Klebanoff. *The Agent: Personalities, Publishing and Politics.* Texere, 2002.

Klebanoff, owner of the Scott Meredith Agency, offers insights into the literary agent business in an anecdote-laden account of working with celebrity authors.

Michael Korda. *Making the List: A Cultural History of the American Bestseller 1900–1999.* Barnes and Noble, 2001.

Korda, longtime editor at Simon & Schuster, argues that bestseller lists are telling indicators of social values as they change. Korda is informed, witty and provocative.

Diana Athill. *Stet: An Editor's Life.* Grove, 2001.

Athill, one of her era's great book editors, looks back from retirement at her work with Jack Kerouac, Norman Mailer, V. S. Naipaul, John Updike and others. She offers insight into an editor's role in successful, acclaimed works.

Jerome Rothenberg and Steven Clay, editors. *A Book of the Book: Some Works and Projections About the Book and Writing.* Granary, 2001.

Rothenberg and Clay have assembled observations, many esoteric, on attempting to define the book on many levels, including its role as a medium of mass communication.

Bradford W. Wright. *Comic Book Nation: Transforming American Culture.* Johns Hopkins, 2001.

Wright, a scholar, writes insightful, entertaining political and cultural history.

Robert Spector. *Amazon.Com: Get Big Fast.* HarperBusiness, 2000.

Spector, a reporter, chronicles the dot-com success of Jeff Bezos at Amazon.com.

André Schiffrin. *The Business of Books: How International Conglomerates Took over Publishing and Changed the Way We Read.* Verso, 2000.

Schiffrin, a veteran publishing house executive, indicts the handful of global companies that have taken over U.S. publishers for putting profits above cultural responsibility. Among loads of evidence, Schiffrin tells of his own unpleasant departure as managing director of Pantheon when he and his bosses at Random House, the parent company, saw profit goals differently.

Betsy Lerner. *The Forest for the Trees.* Riverhead, 2000.

Lerner, a former editor at Houghton Mifflin and three other major publishers, explains how authors get published.

Elizabeth L. Eisenstein. *The Printing Press as an Agent of Change: Communications and Cultural Transformation in Early-Modern Europe,* two volumes. Cambridge University Press, 1980.

Eisenstein offers a thorough examination of the advent of printing and how it changed even how we see ourselves.

Mary Junck

She returned to her Iowa roots but not for life on a farm. Junck heads the growing Lee Enterprises newspaper chain.

chapter 3 Newspapers

In this chapter you will learn:

- Newspapers are the major source of news for most Americans.
- Most U.S. newspapers are owned by chains, for better or worse.
- The United States is largely a nation of local and regional newspapers, with only three national dailies.
- The most highly regarded U.S. newspaper is the New York *Times.*
- Most of the leading U.S. newspapers are metropolitan dailies, which have dwindled in number with population and lifestyle shifts.
- Television and retailing changes have cut into newspaper display advertising, and newspapers may lose their dominance as an advertising medium.
- Community newspapers, especially suburban weeklies, are booming as people continue moving out of core cities.
- Thriving newspapers include counterculture, black and Spanish-language papers aimed at narrow segments of readers.

Don't tell Mary Junck that newspapers are past their prime as a mass medium. Since 1999, when she took over the Lee Enterprises newspaper chain, she has kept pre-tax earnings pushing 30 percent. Circulation declines have been turned around at some Lee newspapers, stemmed at others. At most of the company's 58 dailies, circulation is growing. Through acquisitions, the daily newspaper circulation at Lee papers leaped 75 percent in one recent year. The most recent acquisition was Pulitzer, Inc. with 14 dailies and 100 weeklies. Pulitzer became a key part of Lee's future in June 2005 when a $1.5 billion merger was completed.

Lee, headquartered in Davenport, Iowa, is committed to newspapers. In 1999 it sold all its television stations to concentrate on newspapers. It bought up weeklies and specialty periodicals by the score, bringing the total to 175. Then, after shopping carefully for more dailies, Lee bought the 16-daily Howard chain, including the 92,000-circulation Escondido, California, *North County Times,* which became Lee's largest newspaper. Not far behind are the Lee dailies in Munster, Indiana, and Lincoln, Nebraska. In 2004 came the Pulitzer acquisition, which included the St. Louis *Post-Dispatch.*

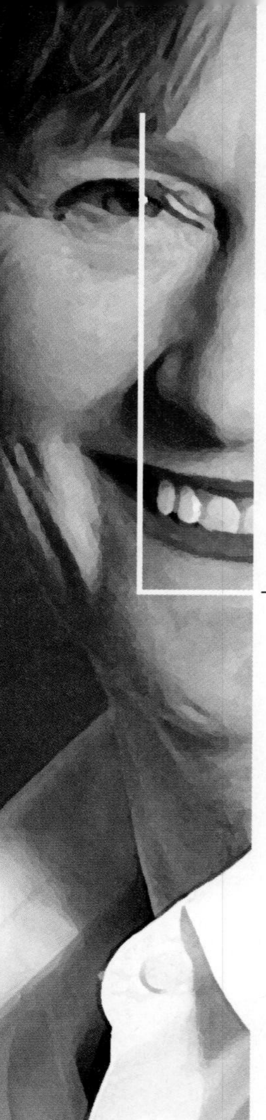

Junck, reared an Iowa farm girl, says the secret to success for 21st-century newspapers includes a strong emphasis on local news. Her academic background is journalism. She edited the yearbook at Valparaiso University in Indiana and then earned a master's in journalism at the University of North Carolina. Then she rose into newspaper management in advertising. At Lee she created the position of vice president for news to help local editors strengthen their coverage. This was at a time when many U.S. newspapers, facing declining advertising revenue in a sour economy, were cutting back on newsroom budgets.

If anyone asks Junck about Lee's priorities, she whips out a business card with a five-point mission statement. There, prominently, is, "Emphasize strong local news." Other Junck priorities: "Grow revenue creatively and rapidly. Improve readership and circulation. Build our online future. Exercise careful cost controls."

Importance of Newspapers

study preview **Newspapers are the primary mass medium from which people receive news. In most cities no other news source comes close to the local newspaper's range and depth of coverage. This contributes to the popularity and influence of newspapers.**

Newspaper Industry Dimensions

The newspaper industry dwarfs other news media by almost every measure. More than one out of three people in the United States reads a newspaper every day, far more than tune in the network news on television in the evening. The data are staggering:

- About 1,570 daily newspapers put out 52.4 million copies a day, more on Sundays. Because each copy is passed along to an average of 2.2 people, daily newspapers reach 116 million people a day.
- Weekly newspapers put out 50 million copies. With their estimated pass-along circulation of four people a copy, these newspapers reach somewhere around 200 million people a week.

Perhaps because television has stolen the glitz and romance that newspapers once had, the significance of newspapers is easy to miss. But the newspaper industry is large by every measure. In an article marveling at an issue of a newspaper as "the daily creation," the Washington *Post*'s Richard Harwood, writing about his own newspaper, said: "Roughly 11,000 people are involved in the production and distribution each day, enough bodies to fill all the billets of an Army light infantry division." Although Harwood stretched to include even the delivery boys and girls in his startling number, his point is valid: In Washington and everywhere else, newspapers far outdistance other news media in the number of people who gather, edit and disseminate news.

Newspapers are the medium of choice for more advertising than competing media. For advertising, daily newspapers attracted $44.9 billion in 2004. Over-air television stations were second at $42.5 billion.

Except for brief downturns in the overall economy and an occasional exceptional situation, daily newspapers have been consistently profitable enterprises through the 20th century. Less than double-digit returns on investment are uncommon. As a mass medium, the newspaper is not to be underrated.

Largest U.S. Newspapers

The Audit Bureau of Circulations, which tracks newspaper circulation, has documented a steady erosion in newspaper circulation, although a brief spike was reported after the September 11, 2001, terrorist attack. In the six months that ended March 31, 2003, there was another net loss of 0.1 percent in both daily and Sunday categories. Here are the nation's largest newspapers by circulation:

	Daily	**Sunday**
USA Today	2,200,000	2,600,000*
Wall Street Journal	2,100,000	1,800,000**
New York *Times*	1,100,000	1,700,000
Los Angeles *Times*	843,000	1,200,000
New York *Daily News*	715,000	787,000
Washington *Post*	678,000	966,000
New York *Post*	686,000	453,000
Chicago *Tribune*	573,000	951,000
Houston *Chronicle*	547,000	738,000
Long Island *Newsday*	481,000	574,000

*Weekend edition issued as Friday edition.
**Weekend edition issued Saturdays.

Content Diversity and Depth

In most communities, newspapers cover more news at greater depth than competing media. A metropolitan daily such as the Washington *Post* typically may carry 300 items and much more on Sundays—more than any Washington television or radio station and at greater length. City magazines in Washington, for example, offer more depth on selected stories, but the magazines are published relatively infrequently and run relatively few articles. Nationally, no broadcast organization comes close to the number of stories or the depth of the two major national newspapers: the *Wall Street Journal* and *USA Today*.

Newspapers have a rich mix of content—news, advice, comics, opinion, puzzles and data. It's all there to tap into at will. Some people go right for the stock market tables, others to sports or a favorite columnist. Unlike radio and television, you don't have to wait for what you want.

People like newspapers. Some talk affectionately of curling up in bed on a leisurely Sunday morning with their paper. The news and features give people something in common to talk about. Newspapers are important in people's lives, and as a medium they adapt to changing lifestyles. The number of Sunday newspapers, for example, grew from 600 in the 1970s to almost 900 today, reflecting an increase, at least for a few years, in people's weekend leisure time for reading and shopping. Ads in weekend papers are their guide for shopping excursions.

All this does not mean that the newspaper industry is not facing problems from competing media, new technology and ongoing lifestyle shifts. But to date, newspapers have reacted to change with surprising effectiveness. To offset television's inroads, newspapers have put new emphasis on being a visual medium and have shed their drab graphics for color and aesthetics. To accommodate the work schedule transition of Americans over recent decades from factory jobs starting at 7 a.m. to service jobs starting at 9 a.m., newspapers have emphasized morning editions, now that more people have a little extra time in the morning, and phased out afternoon editions, because more people are at work later in the day. Knowing that the days of ink-on-paper technology are limited, the newspaper industry is well along into a transition to web delivery.

Some problems are truly daunting, such as the aversion of many young people to newspapers. Also, chain ownership has raised fundamental questions about how well newspapers can do their work and still meet the profit expectations of distant shareholders.

Newspaper Products

studypreview **Over years, the size and formats of newspapers grew as printing technologies improved and paper and printing supplies became plentiful. In recent years the size has progressively shrunk as paper costs have risen and tastes have changed.**

Broadsheets

The first modern newspapers in the Penny Press period were pint size. Ben Day's pioneering New York *Sun* of 1833 was the size of a handbill. As large, steam-powered presses were introduced and as paper supplies became plentiful, page sizes grew into what came to be called **broadsheets.** Some were so wide that pages had nine two-inch columns per page, although 50-inch paper, folded into 25-inch wide pages, became standard until the 1980s.

To save costs the newspaper industry settled on a trimmer new size, called **SAU,** short for **standard advertising unit,** in the 1980s. The SAU format made it easier for big advertisers to place ads in multiple papers, all with standardized dimensions. The introduction of SAU precipitated an almost universal change to a six-column format, in contrast with the formerly dominant eight-column format. The saving in newsprint cost was significant. A downside was that there was less room for news and other content.

Tabloids

The word **tabloid** has a tawdry, second-rate connotation from papers featuring eye-catching but sensationalizing headlines, but newspaper people use the word in a clinical sense for a half-size newspaper that is convenient to hold. Ironically, considering the association of the words *tabloid* and *sensationalism,* none of the papers in the sensationalistic Yellow Press Period were tabloids—with the exception of a one-day experiment by New York publisher Joseph Pulitzer on the first day of the 20th century to illustrate the newspaper of the future.

Inspired by sensationalistic sheets that were the rage in London, two scions of the Chicago *Tribune* fortune, Joseph McCormick and Joseph Patterson, created the **New York *Daily News*** in 1919 as a photo-strong tabloid. Its wacky news selection and emphasis on

media ONLINE **New York Daily News** Check out the daily headlines (in English and Spanish) as well as entertainment, New York borough news and sports. **www.nydailynews.com**

broadsheet ■ A newspaper format with full-size pages; typically six columns wide and 22 or 24 inches long.

standard advertising unit (SAU) ■ A trimmer newspaper broadsheet format with standardized dimensions; introduced in the 1980s.

tabloid ■ A newspaper format with pages half the size of a broadsheet; typically five columns wide and 14 to 18 inches long; *tab* for short; not necessarily sensationalistic despite a connotation the term has acquired.

New York *Daily News* ■ Defined *tabloid* in public thinking as word for sensationalism; founded 1919.

mediaTECHNOLOGY

Newspaper Production

The Industrial Revolution, which began mechanizing manufacturing in the 1600s, reached the newspaper industry in the mid-1800s. Steam-powered presses became the rage. And paper, suddenly manufactured in rolls, not sheets, made press runs of thousands of copies an hour possible. Although the process has been refined, newspaper presses today, more than 150 years later, use the same technology—huge presses at central locations running hour after hour to get each day's issue into distribution. It's all labor intensive. Distribution itself is complex and also labor intensive—getting papers dropped at thousands of individual delivery points by, say, 6:30 a.m.

Digital printing may change all this.

Instead of trucks fanning out at predawn from a single giant printing plant with hundreds of thousands of copies of the day's paper, imagine something like photocopiers scattered throughout the paper's circulation area. Each machine spits out only a few hundred copies.

Richard Rinehart, operations executive at the Raleigh, North Carolina, *News & Observer,* sees lots of untapped potential in digital printing beyond the economics. With smaller, lighter, faster and more flexible presses, digital technology opens capabilities far beyond a typical copy machine. Digital printers at scattered sites, he says, can be programmed to augment their local news with subscriber-chosen add-ons—regional grocery ads included for 617 Maple Street, sports news and comics for 618 Maple, financial news and classified ads for 619, and so on.

By when? The year 2020 is realistic, says Rinehart.

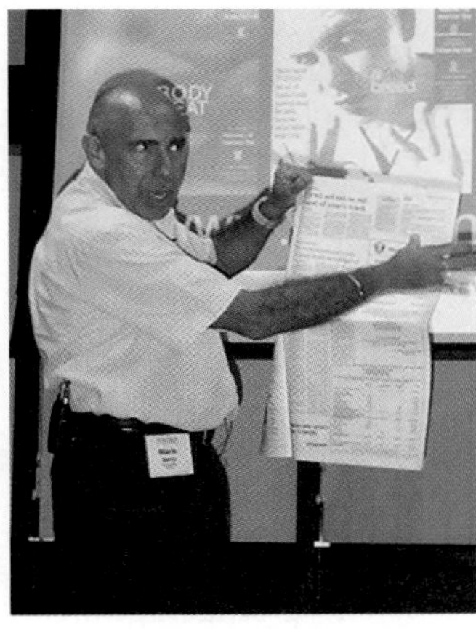

Mario Garcia On the cutting edge of newspaper design.

Downsizing Broadsheet newspapers, usually with six columns to a page, are dabbling with handier tabloid editions like the Chicago *Tribune*'s *RedEye*. A single standard for tabloid page sizes is expected to be adopted by newspaper publishers to make it easier for advertisers. Right now there are four sizes, the most popular being the roughly 8½ by 11 inches and the 17-inch deep Berliner.

crime, sex and disaster made it a quick success. Although shunned by the newspaper establishment, the *Daily News* quickly found a following. Soon it had the largest circulation in the country and redefined the term *tabloid* in popular lexicon. There were a few imitators, mostly in cities with commuters, who preferred the handy size to read in their cramped bus and train seats on the way to work.

Some dailies that switched to the tabloid size, including the *Christian Science Monitor,* were clearly serious about their journalism. But for most of the 20th century, tabs were the exception. By 2001, there were only three dozen.

In recent years, with continuing readership declines, especially among young adults, newspaper executives have discovered through surveys that people prefer compact newspapers. The world's leading newspaper designer, **Mario Garcia,** is traversing the country and the globe for comprehensive redesigns. Garcia's team is making two to three broadsheet-to-tabloid conversions a month. There have been predictions that the only broadsheet left in the United States in 20 years will be the *Wall Street Journal*.

Laura Gordon, in charge of a Dallas *Morning News* tabloid variation called *Quick,* makes the point that tabloids are portable in ways that broadsheets aren't: "We call it the Taco Test, the idea that you can have a newspaper open and have a taco at Taco Bell without going into other peoples' space."

Some dailies, including the San Francisco *Examiner,* have taken a sudden plunge. Others are testing the water. The broadsheet Chicago *Tribune* has a RedEye tabloid edition geared to commuters. Not to be outdone, the Chicago *Sun-Times,* historically a tabloid, rolled out a Red Streak edition that's snappier and more tightly edited. In London the *Times* has twin versions: one broadsheet, one tabloid. The *Independent* switched completely. Other papers have converted inside sections to tabloid to get a feel for what a fuller transition will be like.

media ONLINE

Mario Garcia Site of Garcia Media, the design firm started by Mario Garcia to help clients develop effective visual tools and communication strategies.
www.mariogarcia.com

Quick Visit the site that bills itself as a pop culture, news and social networking site for young adults in the Dallas/Forth Worth area.
www.quickdfw.com

RedEye The daily news that seeks to inform, entertain and provoke young Chicago city dwellers.
www.redeyechicago.com

Red Streak With personals and a restaurant guide on the home page, this daily delivers news and more to Chicago's young adults.
www.chicagoredstreak.com

Mario Garcia ■ Newspaper design expert who champions tabloid formats.

Still, the word *tabloid* carries a stigma. Garcia said in an interview with the trade journal *Editor & Publisher* that one of his newspaper publisher clients wanted a tabloid prototype designed but couldn't handle the word *tabloid:* "He told me, 'You can do a tabloid—but don't call it a tabloid.'" Alternatives include *compact newspaper* and *laptop newspaper.*

Newspaper Chain Ownership

study preview **Through the 20th century, newspapers have been incredibly profitable, which, for better or worse, encouraged chain ownership. Today, chains own most U.S. newspapers.**

Trend Toward Chains

William Randolph Hearst ■ Chain owner who dictated contents of all his newspapers.

newspaper chain ■ Company that owns several newspapers.

Gannett ■ A leading U.S. newspaper chain with 90 dailies.

Reasoning that he could multiply profits by owning multiple newspapers, **William Randolph Hearst** put together a chain of big-city newspapers in the late 1880s. Although Hearst's chain was not the first, his empire became the model in the public's mind for much that was both good and bad about **newspaper chains.** Like other chains, Hearst expanded into magazines, radio and television. The trend toward chain ownership continues, and today 160 chains own four of every five dailies in the United States. Chain ownership is also coming to dominate weeklies, which had long been a bastion of independent ownership.

Newspaper profitability skyrocketed in the 1970s and 1980s, which prompted chains to buy up locally owned newspapers, sometimes in bidding frenzies. Single-newspaper cities were especially attractive because no competing media could match a local newspaper's large audience. It was possible for new owners to push ad rates up rapidly. Local retailers, with no place else to put ads, had to go along. The profit potential was enhanced because production costs were falling dramatically with less labor-intensive back-shop procedures, computerized typesetting and other automation. Profits were dramatic. Eight newspaper companies tracked by *Forbes* magazine from 1983 to 1988 earned the equivalent of 23.9 percent interest on a bank account. Only soft drink companies did better.

The **Gannett** media conglomerate's growth typifies how newspapers became chains and then grew into cross-media conglomerates. In 1906 the chain consisted of six upstate

Newspaper Chains

Here are the largest U.S. newspaper chains, ranked by number of dailies, with a sample of their major properties:

	Daily Circulation	Number of Dailies
McClatchy Miami *Herald,* Sacramento *Bee,* Minneapolis *Star Tribune,* Charlotte *Observer*	9.5 million	44
Gannett *USA Today,* Des Moines *Register,* Detroit *News,* Louisville *Courier-Journal*	7.6 million	90
Lee Enterprises St. Louis *Post-Dispatch,* Tucson *Daily Star,* Lincoln *Journal Star*	1.7 million	58
Tribune Company Los Angeles *Times,* Chicago *Tribune,* Baltimore *Sun,* Long Island *Newsday*	2.8 million	11
New York Times New York *Times,* Boston *Globe,* Florida dailies	1.7 million	26
Newhouse Cleveland *Plain Dealer,* New Orleans *Times-Picayune,* Newark *Star Ledger*	2.9 million	26
Dow Jones *Wall Street Journal,* Ottaway Newspapers	2.5 million	16

New York newspapers. By 1982 Gannett had grown to more than 80 dailies, all profitable medium-size newspapers. Swimming in money, Gannett launched *USA Today.* Gannett not only absorbed *USA Today*'s tremendous start-up costs for several years but also had enough spare cash to outbid other companies for expensive metropolitan newspapers. In 1985 and 1986 Gannett paid $1.4 billion for the Detroit *News,* Des Moines *Register* and Louisville *Courier-Journal.* Along the way, Gannett acquired Combined Communications, which owned 20 broadcasting stations. Today Gannett owns 99 daily newspapers, 39 weeklies, 16 radio stations, 21 television stations, 130 web sites, the largest billboard company in the nation and the Louis Harris polling organization. It bought a Sunday newspaper magazine supplement, *This Week,* beefed it up and renamed it *USA Weekend.* No longer just a newspaper chain, Gannett has become a mass media conglomerate.

Assessing Chain Ownership

Is chain ownership good? The question raised in Hearst's time was whether diverse points of view were as likely to get into print if ownership were concentrated in fewer and fewer hands. Although all the Hearst newspapers were once required to run editorials written in the home office, such is an exception to most chain practices. Newspaper chains are more oriented to profits than manipulating public dialogue on a large scale. Executives at the headquarters of most chains focus on management and leave news coverage and editorials to local editors. While **local autonomy** is consistent with U.S. journalistic values, a corporate focus on profits raises a dark new question: Are chains so myopic about profits that they forget good journalism? The answer is that the emphasis varies among chains.

Journalistic Emphasis Some chains, such as the New York Times Company, whose properties include the flagship *Times* and the Boston *Globe,* are known for their journalism. The *Times* won a record seven Pulitzers, most for its coverage of the September 11, 2001, attack on the World Trade Center.

Balanced Emphasis Most chains are known for undistinguished though profitable newspapers. This is an apt description for Gannett, the largest U.S. chain, measured by circulation.

Profit Emphasis Several chains, including Donrey and American Publishing, have a pattern at new acquisitions of cutting costs aggressively, reducing staffs and trimming news coverage. It is not uncommon for a new chain owner to fire veteran reporters and editors, in some cases almost halving the staff. To save newsprint, some chains cut back the number of pages. They hire inexperienced reporters right out of college, pay them poorly and encourage them to move on after a few months so they can be replaced by other eager but inexperienced, and cheap, new reporters. The result is a reporting staff that lacks the kind of local expertise that is necessary for good journalism. Only the shareholders benefit.

In general, the following realities of chain ownership work against strong local journalistic enterprise:

Absentee Ownership Chain executives are under pressure to run profitable enterprises, which works against good, aggressive journalism that can strain a newsroom budget. Under **absentee ownership** the top chain executives do not live in the communities that are short-changed by decisions to emphasize low-cost news.

Transient Management The local managers of newspapers owned by chains tend to be career climbers who have no long-term stake in the community their newspaper serves. News executives generally are not promoted from within a newspaper but are appointed by corporate headquarters. Generally they have short-term goals to look good to their corporate bosses so that they can be promoted to better-paying jobs with more responsibility at bigger newspapers in the chain.

local autonomy ■ Independence from chain headquarters.

absentee ownership ■ Company headquarters in a faraway city.

Newsroom Salaries

Reporters, photographers and copy editors at 116 U.S. and Canadian newspapers are represented in contract negotiations by the **Newspaper Guild.** Reporters at the New York *Times* had the most lucrative Guild contract in 2004, more than $1,450 a week, $75,000 a year, with two years' experience. Many earn more for merit, in bonuses and for working odd hours.

The lowest Guild salary for experienced reporters was $387 a week at the Utica, New York, *Observer-Dispach.*

The Guild average was $857, almost $45,000 a year. The average for all newspapers, including more than 1,400 nonunion papers, is impossible to calculate because there's no reliable data-gathering mechanism.

	Salary per week
New York *Times*	$1,450 after two years
Boston *Globe*	1,260 after five years
Philadelphia *Inquirer* and *Daily News*	1,225 after five years
Chicago *Sun Times*	1,190 after five years
Minneapolis *Star Tribune*	1,180 after five years
Cleveland *Plain Dealer*	1,130 after four years
Honolulu *Advertiser* and *Star-Bulletin*	1,120 after five years
St. Paul, Minn., *Pioneer Press*	1,110 after five years
Pittsburgh *Post-Gazette*	1,110 after six years
San Francisco *Chronicle*	1,090 after six years

Weak Entry-Level Salaries The focus of newspaper chains on keeping costs down to enhance profits has worked against strong salaries for journalists. By 2004 entry-level salaries typically were $17,000 to $19,000 at small chain-owned dailies. The result has been a brain drain. Many talented reporters and editors leave newspapers for more lucrative jobs in public relations and other fields.

High Newsroom Turnover Cost-conscious policies at many chain newspapers encourage newsroom employees to move on after a few pay raises so that they can be replaced by rookies at entry-level salaries. This turnover can denude a newsroom of people who are knowledgeable about the community the newspaper serves, thus eroding coverage.

National Dailies

study preview **Although a nation of mostly local newspapers, the United States has two firmly established dailies. The flashy *USA Today,* founded in 1982, overcame doubters to become the largest circulation daily in the United States. Close behind is the *Wall Street Journal.***

media ONLINE **USA Today** From news to sports to day in pictures, this site offers as much depth as the print version of this national newspaper. **www.usatoday.com**

USA Today

A strict format, snappy visuals and crisp writing give ***USA Today*** an air of confidence and the trappings of success, and the newspaper has its strengths. In less than a decade, circulation reached 1.6 million. By 2005 *USA Today* was at 2.3 million, passing the *Wall Street Journal.* Gannett executives exude sureness about long-term prospects. The optimism is underscored by the confident if not brash page one motto: "The Nation's Newspaper."

Unlike most U.S. dailies, *USA Today* has built its circulation mostly on single-copy sales and bulk sales, not individual subscriptions. *USA Today* sells mostly to business travelers who are on the road and want a quick fix on the news. Many of *USA Today*'s sales

Newspaper Guild ■ Collective bargaining agent at 134 U.S., Canadian newspapers.

USA Today ■ Garnett national daily founded in 1981.

Allen Neuharth ■ Creator of *USA Today.*

are at airport newsracks, where many buyers are corporate executives and middle-management travelers away from home. Gannett offers deep discounts to upscale hotels to buy the papers in bulk and slip them under guests' doors as a free morning courtesy. Stories strain to be lively and upbeat to make the experience of reading the paper a positive one. Most *USA Today* stories are short, which diverts little of a reader's time from pressing business. The brevity and crispness of *USA Today,* combined with the enticing graphics and the razzle-dazzle compendium of blurbs that earned the newspaper the derisive nickname "McPaper" after being introduced in September 1982.

While being true to founder **Allen Neuharth's** original concept, *USA Today* also has evolved. In the mid-1990s editor David Mazzarella introduced longer, weightier stories and depth and enterprise coverage, albeit without sacrificing the blurblike short stories that gave readers a quick fix on the news. In 1999 a new editor, Karen Jurgensen, began fine-tuning the newspaper in a third phase. Without sacrificing the original snappy graphic personality, Jurgenson has pushed reporters to scoop competitors on major stories and to emphasize thoroughness and depth in their enterprise coverage. Although Jurgenson doesn't have the resources to match the

NOTABLE DAILIES

1851 Henry Raymond founded the New York *Times.*

1889 Newsletter editors Charles Dow and Edward Jones founded the *Wall Street Journal.*

1908 Religious leader Mary Baker Eddy founded the *Christian Science Monitor.*

1919 Joseph Patterson and Robert McCormick founded the New York *Daily News.*

1955 Bohemian New York literati founded the *Village Voice.*

1982 Gannett's Allen Neuharth founded *USA Today.*

www.usatoday.com THE NATION'S NEWSPAPER 75 CENTS

SPORTS SCORES

Wednesday, October 26, 2005

USA TODAY

NO. 1 IN THE USA

Mara's imprint on NFL

Legendary New York Giants owner dies Tuesday at 89, 1, 11C

Bond begins

Casino Royale, the first film with Daniel Craig playing James Bond, will explore the spy's origins, 6D

'I was like a tornado that got out of hand'

Pacers' Ron Artest says he's wiser after turmoil of last season. Interview, 1C

Style gurus assess NBA fashions, 7C

Special report

Death toll reaches 2,000

Homes of the fallen. Map, 9A

Bush: Sacrifices will continue, 9A

Newsline

Consumer confidence tugs on stocks

Rosa Parks: The power of one

Public symbol, private person, 2A

Editorial: A right to fairness, 11A

Parks' legacy in classrooms, 8D

Mood is sour on Bush, Congress

Poll finds discontent with both parties

Letters home FROM IRAQ

Heartfelt words from some of the war dead show the world the hopes and fears of those who were lost

Cover story

Wilma's impact lingers

As the fading storm fuels another in New England, millions in Florida face power outages and destruction, 3A

Retiring well takes work

living longer living better

Iraqi constitution passes, tally shows

Money: New wave of gas sippers coming

Sports: Michelle Wie gets kind message

Life: Benefits of eating fish weighed

Thursday: The new Nicolas Cage

You want nutrition info with th

Food at McDonald's soon will wear calorie, fat figures on its packaging

Burger's nutritional bite

USA TODAY Snapshots®

Dating or the dog?

>THIS IS THE WAY TO ENSURE 99.999% RELIABILITY. >THIS IS NORTEL nortel.com

Allen Neuharth

Graphics Innovator Since its founding in 1982, *USA Today* has had a profound impact on many other newspapers. The most obvious influence has been to establish newspapers as a strong visual medium with color and graphics integrated with words. The newspaper's weather coverage and high story counts also have been widely imitated. *USA Today* is designed for travelers and as a "second buy" for people who have already read their hometown daily. Subscriptions are only a small part of *USA Today's* circulation. Most sales are in distinctive TV-shaped newsracks and in airports, hotels and places where travelers pick it up for a quick fix on the news. Guaranteed in every issue are at least a few sentences about what's happening in news and sports from every state in the Union.

Sunday, 1,357,556
Daily, 1,193,297

DAILY NEWS EXTRA EDITION

NEW YORK'S PICTURE NEWSPAPER

Vol. 9. No. 173 Pages — New York, Friday, January 13, 1928 — 2 Cents

DEAD!

(Copyright: 1928: by Pacific and Atlantic photos)

RUTH SNYDER'S DEATH PICTURED!—This is perhaps the most remarkable exclusive picture in the history of criminology. It shows the actual scene in the Sing Sing death house as the lethal current surged through Ruth Snyder's body at 11:06 last night. Her helmeted head is stiffened in death, her face masked and an electrode strapped to her bare right leg. The autopsy table on which her body was removed is beside her. Judd Gray, mumbling a prayer, followed her down the narrow corridor at 11:14. "Father, forgive them, for they don't know what they are doing?" were Ruth's last words. The picture is the first Sing Sing execution picture and the first of a woman's electrocution.

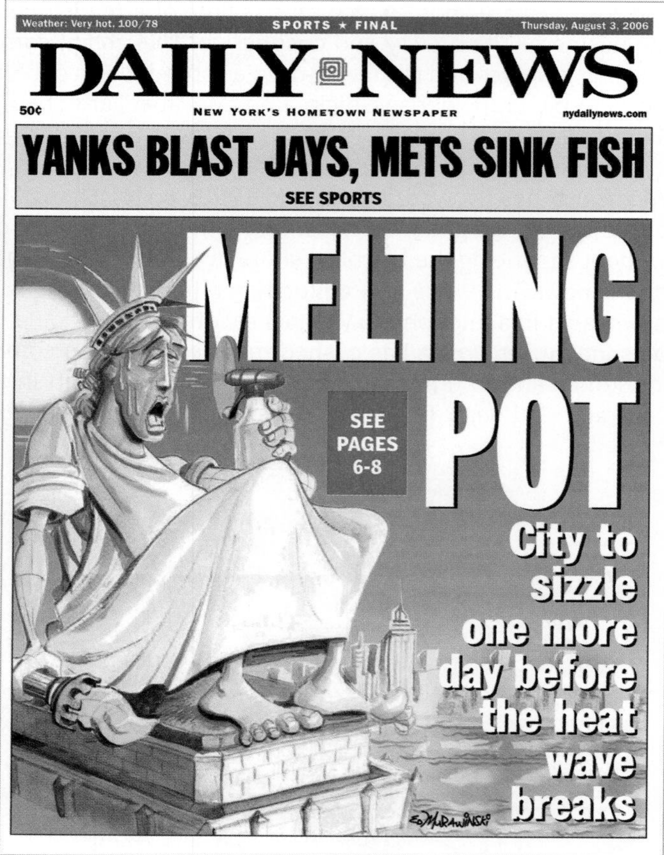

Weather: Very hot. 100/78 — SPORTS ★ FINAL — Thursday, August 3, 2006

DAILY NEWS

50¢ — NEW YORK'S HOMETOWN NEWSPAPER — nydailynews.com

YANKS BLAST JAYS, METS SINK FISH

SEE SPORTS

MELTING POT

SEE PAGES 6-8

City to sizzle one more day before the heat wave breaks

Smudgy Heritage The word "tabloid" is correct for any newspaper with half-size pages, but it picked up an unseemly connotation. The New York *Daily News,* launched in 1919, dwelled on sensational stories and flashy headlines that shouted for street sales—as with its exclusive, unauthorized photo of Ruth Snyder, the first woman executed in U.S. history. The word "tabloid" was sullied by papers like the *Daily News* that focused on the bizarre and sensational. Today a growing number of dailies are switching to tabloid formats because readers find them convenient, although there is a wariness about what to call them. Variations include "compact newspapers" and "laptop newspapers." Examples include the San Francisco *Examiner.* The Chicago *Tribune* has started a *RedEye* tabloid edition geared to commuters. Not to be outdone, the Chicago *Sun-Times,* historically a tabloid, rolled out a *Red Streak* edition that's snappier and more tightly edited.

largest news organizations, she has enough to break important stories on a regular basis: 400 reporters, 20 U.S. bureaus and four foreign bureaus.

The introduction of *USA Today* came at a time when most newspapers were trying to distinguish themselves from television news with longer, exploratory and interpretive stories. While some major newspapers such as the New York *Times* and the Los Angeles *Times* were unswayed by *USA Today*'s snappy, quick-to-read format, many other newspapers moved to shorter, easily digested stories, infographics and more data lists. Color became standard. *USA Today* has influenced today's newspaper style and format.

Wall Street Journal

Wall Street Journal ■ Second largest U.S. daily newspaper.

Charles Dow ■ Cofounder of *Wall Street Journal* in 1882.

Edward Jones ■ Cofounder of *Wall Street Journal* in 1882.

The ***Wall Street Journal,*** until recently the nation's largest newspaper, began humbly. **Charles Dow** and **Edward Jones** went into business in 1882. They roamed the New York financial district for news and scribbled notes by hand, which they sent by courier to their clients. As more information-hungry investors signed up, the service was expanded into a newsletter. In 1889 the *Wall Street Journal* was founded. Advertisers eager to reach *Journal* readers bought space in the newspaper, which provided revenue to hire correspondents in Boston, Philadelphia and Washington. By 1900 circulation had reached 10,000, and it grew to 30,000 by 1940.

The *Wall Street Journal* might have remained a relatively small albeit successful business paper had it not been for the legendary **Barney Kilgore,** who joined the newspaper's San Francisco bureau in 1929. Within two years Kilgore was the *Journal*'s news editor and in a position to shift the newspaper's journalistic direction. Kilgore's formula was threefold:

- Simplify the *Journal*'s business coverage into plain English without sacrificing thoroughness.
- Provide detailed coverage of government but without the jargon that plagued Washington reporting most of the time.
- Expand the definition of the *Journal*'s field of coverage from "business" to "everything that somehow relates to earning a living."

The last part of the formula, expanded coverage, was a risk. Critics told Kilgore that the newspaper's existing readers might switch to other financial papers if they thought the *Journal* was slighting business. Kilgore's vision, however, was not to reduce business coverage but to seek business angles in other fields and cover them too. It worked. Today, with circulation at 1.8 million, the *Journal* is the second largest U.S. daily.

The *Journal* puts significant resources into reporting. It is not unusual for a reporter to be given six weeks for research on a major story. This digging gives the *Journal* big

media ONLINE **Wall Street Journal** Headlines are free, but you'll have to subscribe to see the full articles on this national newspaper's site. **http://online.wsj.com**

Barney Kilgore ■ Created the modern *Wall Street Journal.*

Is That Your Baby Speaking Chinese?
The imperfect English of a child may be good grammar elsewhere
SCIENCE JOURNAL | A7

Checking Out Of Innkeeping
B&Bs turn into private homes as rising costs pinch operators
WEEKEND | W1

Working Out Your Anxiety
Some therapists combine talk with sports and exercise
WEEKEND | W1

THE WALL STREET JOURNAL.

© 2006 Dow Jones & Company. All Rights Reserved

WSJ.com FRIDAY, AUGUST 11, 2006 · VOL. CCXLVIII NO. 35 · ★★★★ $1.00

Interested Parties
In Internal Probes Of Stock Options, Conflicts Abound

Directors' Ties Can Complicate Job of Assuring the Public Investigation Is Thorough

Sorting It Out at UnitedHealth

What's News—

Business and Finance *World-Wide*

Blurred Fingerprints
U.K. Terror Plot Points to New

Alleged Scheme to Blow Up Flights May Be Hybrid Of Locals and al Qaeda

Explosives Disguised as Drinks

Home Ground

Possums Are Playing Upside-Down Role In Florida Elections

Panhandle Marsupial Event Is Vital Campaign Stop; Jeb Bush Was a Regular

Notice to Readers

INDEX

–Markets–

–Online Today–

Airline Terror Plot

INSIDE

Barney Kilgore

Drab but Read The *Wall Street Journal,* the nation's largest daily, relies on its reputation for accurate and thorough reporting and good writing to attract readers. Every day the front page looks the same, with lengthy general-interest stories beginning in Columns 1, 4 and 6. Barney Kilgore shaped the *Journal*'s distinctive look and approach to coverage after taking over as editor in the 1930s. Circulation today exceeds 1.8 million.

breaks on significant stories. Although a serious newspaper, the *Journal* is neither stodgy nor prudish. Lengthy page one pieces range from heavy-duty coverage of national politics to such diverse and unexpected stories as a black widow spider outbreak in Phoenix, archaeological research into human turds to understand lifestyles of lost civilizations, and how the admiral of landlocked Bolivia's navy keeps busy.

The *Wall Street Journal* has 500 editors and reporters, but not all are at the newspaper's Manhattan headquarters. The *Journal* has 37 foreign and 14 domestic bureaus, and its European and Asian editions have their own staffs.

The challenge for the *Journal* has been finding a balance between its original forte—covering business—and its expanding coverage of broader issues. It is a precarious balance. Numerous business publications, including *Business Week* and the Los Angeles-based *Investor's Daily,* vie for the same readers and advertisers with more compact packages, and numerous other national publications, including the newsmagazines, offer general coverage. So far, the *Journal* has succeeded with a gradual broadening of general coverage without losing its business readers. In 2004, to broaden its appeal further, the *Journal* added a Saturday edition.

Christian Science Monitor

Mary Baker Eddy ■ Founded the *Christian Science Monitor* in 1908.

Mary Baker Eddy, the influential founder of the Christian Science faith, was aghast at turn-of-the-century Boston newspapers. The Boston dailies, like papers in other major U.S. cities, were sensationalistic, overplaying crime and gore in hyperbolic battles to steal readers from each other. Entering the fray, Eddy introduced a newspaper with a different

Constructive Journalism

Since its 1908 founding, the *Christian Science Monitor* has emphasized solution-oriented journalism. The *Monitor,* based in Boston, began as an antidote to sensationalistic newspapers, emphasizing accurate and truthful coverage to help people address serious problems facing humankind.

'To injure no man, but to bless all mankind'

BOSTON · MONDAY SEPTEMBER 25, 2006

ETHICAL CONSUMING
Travel globally, spend locally
CURRENTS, 13

ONE DOLLAR

This winter, cost of heating homes is forecast to drop

A HOMEOWNER could save as much as $250 on heating bills over last year.

By RON SCHERER
STAFF WRITER

NEW YORK – With the first chill of autumn in the air, some homeowners are cranking up their heat for the first time since this spring. Many will get a pleasant surprise when they look at their bills: They may be slightly lower.

Since last year at this time, the ...as at the wellhead ... percent, and the home heating oil is ... If prices were to ...ese levels – and if ...ot overly cold – ...d save as much as ...ith last year, some ...timate.

...uivalent of a major ... the same as right ...e government sent ...ody," says Dennis ...conomist for the ...ion in Washington. ...hat it particularly ...and lower-income

See **HEAT** *page 10*

Vote nears on 700-mile border fence

THE SENATE THIS WEEK takes up a bill that would erect a security fence along one-third of the US-Mexico border.

By GAIL RUSSELL CHADDOCK
STAFF WRITER

WASHINGTON – Azul-Cristian Caravaggio made it to Washington from her home in Chattanooga, Tenn., about sundown on Friday – too late to see any senators. But by Monday, when the Senate returns, she says that she and other protesters will be on a hunger strike and chained to a half-ton, 28-foot wall they set up in a Senate park.

This will be the last week of votes on Capitol Hill before November elections, and one will be whether to build a 700-mile fence along the 1,920-mile US border with Mexico. She wants senators to vote no.

"Whatever is done, people will find a way to knock it down, go under or around it. There will be thousands more deaths on the border," she says.

It's a prelude to the final moves on immigration in the 109th Congress. Since last spring, the House and Senate have gridlocked over competing

See **FENCE** *page 10*

ANDY NELSON – STAFF

HOUSE SPEAKER: Dennis Hastert spoke last week of a 'border security crisis in America.'

ELECTION 2006

MELANIE STETSON FREEMAN – STAFF

THE CANDIDATE: Keith Ellison (c.) visits a Somali mall in Minneapolis. He was recently elected the Democratic nominee in the Fifth District.

Contender may become first Muslim in US Congress

By AMANDA PAULSON
STAFF WRITER

MINNEAPOLIS – When Keith Ellison arrives at the Karmel Square, one of Minneapolis's Somali malls, a rock star might as well be walking by the bustling stalls of bright fabrics, jewelry, phone cards, and videos.

People laugh and cheer as they hug Mr. Ellison and pat him on the back. Some speak quickly in Somali as an interpreter translates, and others offer congratulations in fluent English.

"Asalamu aleikum, brothers," Ellison says with a smile. "Thanks for voting."

He is not Somali, or even an immigrant, but for these voters, Ellison is one of their own. After his victory in this month's Democratic primary in the Fifth District, he's likely to become the first Muslim elected to Congress. He would also be the first black congressman to come from Minnesota.

The distinctions are ones Ellison tries

See **ELLISON** *page 4*

DESPITE GAINS, NORTH KOREANS DISILLUSIONED

FOOD, FUEL, and know-how are flowing into the totalitarian state, but citizens are dispirited.

By ROBERT MARQUAND
STAFF WRITER

SEOUL, SOUTH KOREA – Mrs. Park is North Korean salt of the earth. Until the 70-year-old was stripped, beaten, and charged with dissent, Park and her family were patriotic, loyal, ordinary. They were true believers in the ruling Kim family's "juche" ideology, which holds that Korea must be separate from all nations and that total obedience is owed to the Kim family. Park's eight kids worshiped Kim Il Sung, the "father of their minds." When Kim died and millions perished in an epic famine, the Parks didn't panic. They wrote a letter to Kim Jong Il, volunteering to farm – something only a pure and loyal family would dare in North Korea.

Yet today Mrs. Park (not her real name) is in South Korea, an escapee. Her family is broken. So are her ideals. She's been captured in China – sent home to the North, made to endure camps, and witness horrific acts. She had gone to China in 2000 only to feed her family. But her world got turned upside down.

The significance of Park's story may be how typical it is. In the past decade many North Korean families have had their state-enforced high ideals shattered, according to refugees and nongovernmental and

See **NORTH KOREA** *page 11*

...snooping ...ies, like Hewlett- ...n their employees. ...ethical? **2**

...xt leader Shinzo ...ucceed Junichiro ...pan's next prime ...rrow. **6**

...s next move south Lebanon, the ...ry commanders ...ategies. **7**

& extended coverage
csmonitor.com

40114>

8 79021 00000 5

Mary Baker Eddy

mission. Her ***Christian Science Monitor,*** founded in 1908, sought to deal with issues and problems on a higher plane and to help the world come up with solutions.

Nobody, least of all Mary Baker Eddy, expected such an intellectually oriented newspaper to make money, at least not right away, so the church underwrote expenses when subscriptions, newsstand sales and advertising revenue fell short. The *Monitor* sought subscriptions nationwide and abroad, and it developed a following. Though edited in Boston, the *Monitor* was conceived as an international, not a local, newspaper, and it became the first national daily newspaper in the United States.

The *Christian Science Monitor* tries to emphasize positive news, but it also deals with crime, disaster, war and other downbeat news, and it has won Pulitzer Prizes for covering them. The thrust, though, is interpretive, unlike the sensationalistic newspapers to which Mary Baker Eddy wanted an alternative. The *Monitor* does not cover events and issues to titillate its readers. Rather, as veteran *Monitor* editor Erwin Canham explained, the newspaper's mission is "to help give humankind the tools with which to work out its salvation." The *Monitor* is not preachy. In fact, only one plainly labeled religious article appears in each issue. The *Monitor* seeks to lead and influence by example.

The *Monitor*'s circulation peaked at 239,000 in 1971, when public interest in news was high, especially interest in the domestic turmoil over the war in Vietnam. Since then, circulation has slipped. The *Monitor* has never developed a firm advertising base, relying instead on church subsidies. But Christian Science membership has slipped too. With the church's overall income estimated at only $8.5 million a year, it's not clear how much longer the church can afford to carry out Mary Baker Eddy's goal of a strong Christian Science presence in the news media.

media ONLINE **Christian Science Monitor** This international daily newspaper professes that its ownership by a church, rather than a corporate conglomerate, gives it an independent voice in journalism.
www.csmonitor.com

New York *Times*

study preview **The reputation of the New York *Times* rests largely on its attempt to be a newspaper of record. Outstanding reporting through its history also has contributed to its standing. Today, the newspaper seeks to be both a major regional newspaper and, through a national edition, a national newspaper.**

Newspaper of Record

Not a librarian anywhere would want to be without a subscription to the **New York *Times,*** which is one reason that the *Times* boasts at least one subscriber in every county in the country. Since its founding in 1851, the *Times* has had a reputation for fair and thorough coverage of foreign news. A large, widely respected staff covers Washington. It is a newspaper of record, printing the president's annual state of the union address and other important documents in their entirety. The *Times* is an important research source, in part because the *Times* puts out a monthly and annual index that lists every story. More than 100 years of the *Times* pages are available online in many libraries. The editorials are among the most quoted.

In an attempt to attract younger readers, the *Times* has followed the lead of other newspapers by adding some lighter fare to the serious coverage. In 2005 a Thursday style section was launched that includes more lifestyle-oriented advertising. The *Times* even added a 10-page "Funny Pages" section at the front of the glitzy Sunday *Magazine* that includes work by graphic artists, serialized genre fiction and a venue for humor writers called "True-Life Tales." The serious book review section and one of the world's most popular crossword puzzles remain.

media ONLINE **New York Times** Check out the site that has won awards for its design and strong news content. Link to the Sunday magazine or book review, or get today's headlines.
www.nytimes.com

New York *Times* Heritage

From its founding in 1851 the New York *Times* was a serious newspaper, but its journalistic reputation was cemented in the 1870s when courageous reporting brought down the city government.

Christian Science Monitor ■ Boston-based national U.S. newspaper.

New York *Times* ■ Most respected U.S. hometown daily.

Old Gray Lady

True to the graphic spirit of the 19th century, when it rose in eminence, the New York *Times* is sometimes called the Old Gray Lady of American journalism. Even after color photos were added in 1997, the *Times* had a staid, somber visual personality. The coverage, writing and commentary, however, are anything but dull, and it is those things that have made the *Times'* reputation as the world's best newspaper. The paper is distinguished by international and Washington coverage, which is drawn mostly from its own staff reporters rather than the news services that most other newspapers rely on. Among Sunday features is the colorful, splashy New York *Times Magazine,* which runs lengthy examinations on serious issues. Sunday's edition also has a serious book review magazine. The New York *Times* crossword puzzle is one of the most popular in the world. The *Times* carries no comics or horoscopes, which contributes to the tone and mystique that set the newspaper apart.

The New York Times Book Review

Left Behind

By William Kennedy

THE ROAD

Ron Rosenbaum's passion for Shakespeare

The New York Times Magazine

Are We Driving Elephants Crazy?

By Charles Siebert

"All the News That's Fit to Print"

The New York Times

VOL. CLV . . No. 53,702 NEW YORK, THURSDAY, SEPTEMBER 14, 2006 ONE DOLLAR

Interior Official Assails Agency For Ethics Slide

At Oil Lease Hearing, a Broad Attack

PANEL IN SENATE BACKS BUSH PLAN FOR MONITORING

DOMESTIC EAVESDROPPING

But Resistance of G.O.P. Senators Is Stiffening on Terror Tribunals

Cuomo Smiles, Pirro Gleams, And War Is On

As Parents Go Unpaid, Gaza Children Go Hungry

Cut Off From Funds, Region Is Enduring Economic Collapse

INSIDE

First Through Gates of Ellis I., She Was Lost. Now She's Found.

Philanthropy Google's Way: Not the Usual

Tweed Scandal City Council member **William Marcy Tweed** had built a fortune with fraudulent streetcar franchises, sales of nonexistent buildings to the city, and double billing. In 1868 it all got worse: Tweed and like-minded crooks and scoundrels were swept into city offices in a landslide election, and the fraud grew like a spider-web. The *Times* launched an exposé in 1870, which prompted Tweed to call on the *Times'* largest advertisers to withdraw their advertising. Tweed also spread whispers that the city could reclaim the *Times* building because the ownership of the land was in doubt. Neither the management of the *Times* nor the main reporter on the story, **George Jones,** was deterred. With documents leaked from a disgruntled city employee the *Times* reported that the Tweed Gang had robbed the city of as much as $200 million. Desperate, Tweed sent an underling to offer Jones $5 million in hush money—a bribe to back off. Jones refused and sent the underling packing: "I don't think the devil will ever make a higher bid for me than that."

Eventually, Tweed fled to Spain. When caught and returned for trial, he was quoted as saying: "If I were 20 or 30 years younger, I would kill George Jones with my own bare hands." Tweed died in jail two years later, in 1878.

William Marcy Tweed ■ Corrupt New York leader in the 1860s and 1870s who was exposed by the New York *Times.*

George Jones ■ New York *Times* reporter on the Tweed Ring scandal.

L. B. Sullivan ■ Alabama police commissioner who sued the New York *Times* for libel over a 1960 antiracial segregation advertisement.

Sullivan Libel Case In 1960, in the heat of the U.S. racial desegregation tensions, **L. B. Sullivan,** the Montgomery, Alabama, police commissioner, was incensed at criticism in an advertisement in the New York *Times* that promoted racial integration. He sued for libel and won in Alabama courts. The *Times* could have acquiesced, paid the court-ordered settlement and put the issue behind it, but the *Times* chose an expensive appeal to the U.S. Supreme Court to prove a First Amendment principle about free expression. The decision in ***Times* v. *Sullivan*** came in 1964, establishing new rules on libel and untethering the U.S. news media from self-imposed restraints that had discouraged important albeit controversial reporting.

Pentagon Papers After being leaked a copy of a secret government study on U.S. policy in the Vietnam war, the *Times* conducted an exhaustive examination of the documents and decided to run a series of articles based on them. The government ordered the *Times* to halt the series, creating a showdown between a free press and the secretive Nixon administration. Not to be intimidated, the *Times* took the so-called **Pentagon Papers** case to the U.S. Supreme Court, arguing that the people in a democracy need information to make intelligent decisions on essential issues like war and peace. The Supreme Court sided with the *Times*, adding new legal obstacles to government censorship temptations and further establishing the importance of the *Times* in U.S. history.

Jayson Blair The courage of the *Times* throughout its history has enabled it to survive occasional blemishes, like the 2003 scandal in which plagiarism and serial fabrications by reporter **Jayson Blair** were found. But even in the Blair scandal the *Times* was the first to reveal the irregularities. The paper assigned eight reporters to an internal investigation, whose exhaustive report ran four full pages and led eventually to the resignation of top editors who had missed Blair's transgressions.

Hometown Newspapers

study preview **The United States has 1,570 daily newspapers, most oriented to covering hometown news and carrying local advertising. Big-city dailies are the most visible hometown newspapers, but medium-sized and small dailies have made significant strides in quality in recent decades and have eroded the metro newspapers' outlying circulation.**

Metropolitan Dailies

In every region of the United States there is a newspaper whose name is a household word. These are metropolitan dailies with extensive regional circulation. In New England, for example, the Boston *Globe* covers Boston but also prides itself on extensive coverage of Massachusetts state government, as well as coverage of neighboring states. The *Globe* has a Washington bureau, and it sends reporters abroad on special assignments.

When experts are asked to list the nation's best newspapers, the lists inevitably are led by the New York *Times*. Other newspapers with a continuing presence include the Baltimore *Sun*, Chicago *Tribune*, Dallas *Morning News*, Houston *Chronicle*, Los Angeles *Times*, Miami *Herald*, Minneapolis *Star Tribune*, Philadelphia *Inquirer*, St. Louis *Post Dispatch* and Washington *Post*.

Here are snapshots of leading metro dailies:

Washington *Post* The **Washington *Post*** cemented its reputation for investigative reporting by breaking revelation after revelation in the 1972 Watergate scandal, until finally Richard Nixon resigned the presidency in disgrace. The *Wall Street Journal*, New York *Times* and Los Angeles *Times*, all with large Washington staffs, compete aggressively with the *Post* for major federal stories, but the *Post* remains the most quoted newspaper for government coverage.

With the demise of the afternoon Washington *Daily News* and the *Star*, the *Post* was left the only local newspaper in the nation's capital, which upset critics who perceived a liberal bias in the *Post*. This prompted the Unification Church of the Reverend Sun Myung Moon to found the **Washington *Times*** as a rightist daily. The *Times* has only a fraction

Times* v. *Sullivan ■ 1964 case that relaxed libel restriction on the news media in covering public policy.

Pentagon Papers ■ Secret government study that, when reported in the New York *Times*, led to a Supreme Court decision that discouraged censorship.

Jayson Blair ■ Reporter who committed serial fabrications in the New York *Times*.

Washington *Post* ■ Established reputation covering Watergate.

Washington *Times* ■ Conservative newspaper.

of the *Post*'s 733,000 circulation, but its scrappy coverage inserts local excitement into Washington journalism, as does its incessant sniping at the *Post* and *Post*-owned *Newsweek* magazine.

Los Angeles *Times* The **Los Angeles *Times*** edged out the declining New York *Daily News* in 1990 as the nation's largest metropolitan daily when circulation reached 1.3 million. By many measures, the *Times* is huge. A typical Sunday edition makes quite a thump on the doorstep at four pounds and 444 pages.

The *Times* has 1,300 editors and reporters, some in 22 foreign bureaus and 13 U.S. bureaus. Fifty-seven reporters cover the federal government in Washington alone. To cover the 1991 war against Iraq, the *Times* dispatched 20 reporters and photographers to the Gulf region, compared with 12 for the New York *Times* and 10 for the Washington *Post,* the traditional leading U.S. metro dailies for foreign coverage.

The *Times'* reputation was built under Otis Chandler, who rode the wave of boom times beginning in the 1960s. Chandler put journalism first, building an extraordinary staff and expanding coverage. That heritage was undermined after he retired. In 1995 others in the Chandler family, seeking greater profits, hired a chief executive from outside the newspaper business. The *Times* began slipping on many fronts, capped by an ethics scandal in which the newspaper promoted the Staples sports arena in a secret deal in which it profited from Staples advertising. In 2000, the Tribune Company, owner of the Chicago *Tribune* and several other major papers, acquired the Los Angeles *Times,* replaced the top management and began restoring staff morale and the newspaper's old vigor.

Hometown Dailies

With their aggressive reporting on national and regional issues, the metro dailies receive more attention than smaller dailies, but most Americans read **hometown dailies.** By and large, these locally oriented newspapers, most of them chain-owned, have been incredibly profitable while making significant journalistic progress since World War II.

Fifty years ago, people in small towns generally bought both a metropolitan daily and a local newspaper. Hometown dailies were thin, and coverage was hardly comprehensive. Editorial pages tended to offer only a single perspective. Readers had few alternative sources of information. Since then, these smaller dailies have hired better-prepared journalists, acquired new technology and strengthened their local advertising base.

Hometown dailies have grown larger and more comprehensive. The years between 1970 and 1980 were especially important for quantum increases in news coverage. A study of 10 hometown dailies, with circulations ranging from 60,000 to 542,000, found that the space available for news, called the *news hole,* more than doubled between 1964 and 1999. Many hometown dailies also gave much of their large news holes to bigger and more diverse opinion sections. Most editorial sections today are smorgasbords of perspectives.

Future for Dailies

study preview **Newspapers are putting more resources into Internet editions, more and more of them staffed for 24-hour-a-day updating. Newsrooms are experimenting with blogs to attract readers. Even so, declines in newspaper circulation and advertising are necessitating significant cost-cutting.**

Multimedia News

Los Angeles *Times* ■ Largest-circulation U.S. hometown daily.

hometown daily ■ Edited primarily for readers in a defined region.

Newspaper people used to think of packaging the news in editions but now less so. Following readers to the Internet, many newsrooms have added 24/7 coverage with not only the written word but also video and audio. When Kevin Fagan of the San Francisco *Chronicle* served as a media witness at an execution, he immediately recorded his

mediaPEOPLE

George Gilder

Do newspapers and other word-based print media have a future? Media seer George Gilder puts his money on word-based media over television, which relies on visuals to tell stories.

As Gilder sees it, people who see the communication of the future as primarily video have missed the fact that video works better than words for only an extremely narrow range of messages: "Video is most effective in conveying shocks and sensations and appealing to prurient interests of large miscellaneous audiences. Images easily excel in blasting through to the glandular substances of the human community; there's nothing like a body naked or bloody or both to arrest the eye."

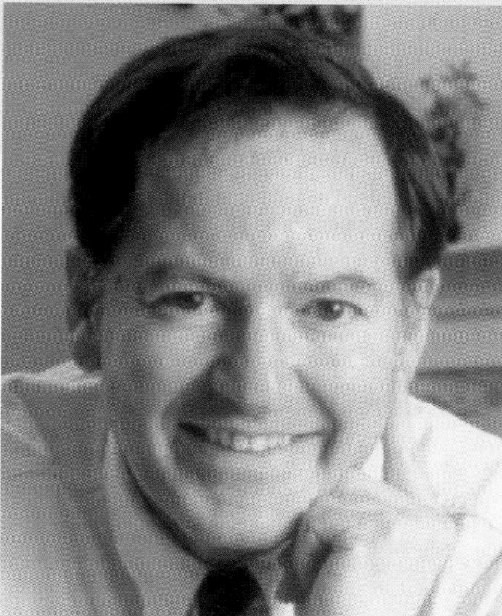

Wordless Society Ahead? No, says futurist George Gilder, not even the generation raised on MTV can communicate effectively without words. Visuals can enhance but not replace them, he says.

However, human communication goes far beyond shock scenes and sensual appeals, he says, noting that people communicate mostly through words.

The printed product you receive on your doorstep every morning may seem like a technological dinosaur from Johannes Gutenberg's time. The fact, however, is that newspapers are well into the digital age. Reporters dip into digitized data for source material and write stories on computers. Editors edit stories and lay out pages electronically. It is in final production that old technology reigns, with multimillion-dollar presses that consume tons and tons of newsprint and barrels and barrels of ink. In delivery too, with minimum-wage carriers entrusted to get the product to readers, newspapers lag.

That is changing. In the vanguard of changing to electronic production, rather than printing, and to electronic delivery, rather than "paperboys and the local newsstand," are newspapers ranging from modest circulation weeklies in the Dakotas to the lofty New York *Times.* Some online editions offer only word-for-word versions of what is in the print editions or just selected stories, but some newspapers are repackaging stories to take advantage of opportunities that electronic delivery offers. Still, true to their tradition, the online newspapers remain word-based. Visuals are a useful accoutrement but seldom the heart of the message.

Even as newspaper circulation withers, as it has in recent years, newspaper companies will survive. They are well positioned to dominate the future of news because, in almost every community, they have the largest, most sophisticated staffs for gathering and telling local news. That resource is unmatched by even the largest television or other news operations.

---

observations for a voice report on the web site. Only later did he write a story for the next edition of the newspaper.

Everywhere, it seems, newspaper reporters are augmenting their pen and pad with audio and video equipment. In newsrooms, the first online staffs in the 1980s merely repackaged news from the latest edition, but now online editors are being integrated into newsroom planning for continuous online coverage somewhat in the spirit of 24/7 cable news networks and all-news radio stations. The Chicago *Tribune* has created a new position with the title *editor of continuous news.*

The new newspaper sites not only are geared to breaking news but, without the limitations of space in the print product, can offer more detail. For a major 2006 series on high-school dropout rates, the Los Angeles *Times* included charts of data on every school, which would have been impossible to fit in the newspaper. There was room for more photos online, the text of a controversial algebra graduation test that many students were fumbling, and a reader discussion board.

The early newspaper web sites were **shovelware,** the print content simply posted online—or shoveled without regard for the potential of the web as a distinctive medium. Today, newspapers in the multimedia vanguard are sensitizing reporters to think 24/7. The Roanoke, Virginia, *Times* puts web editors before a video camera for five-minute web

shovelware ■ Computer-delivered products without modification from the linear original.

updates in the afternoon. Other papers aim webcams at reporters at their desks for updates. It's sometimes clunky compared to slick television sets but has an authenticity. It also may signal the end of newspaper reporters and editors as unseen gatherers and purveyors of news. A lot of the new web content has a broadcast-like personality thrust.

Newspaper Blogs

Newspapers are joining the blog revolution with reporters and columnists putting in their two bits and interacting online with readers. *USA Today* hosts reader chatrooms on a wide range of subjects. Says editor Ken Paulson: "It's about responding to news."

Newspaper-sponsored blogs are not without difficulties, among them the traditional U.S. journalistic premise that news needs to be presented in a detached, neutral tone. Joe Strupp, writing in the trade journal *Editor & Publisher,* put it this way: "Reporting can stray into the quicksand of opinion—leaving many writers wishing they had kept their mouths shut." At this point in the evolution of news blogging, the idea is for reporters to go beyond carefully crafting stories and engaging in a spontaneous dialogue to add dimension, background and interpretation—more than is in their print coverage.

New Efficiencies

Even with a transition well underway to news delivery on the Web, the newspaper industry derives most of its revenue from its signature product—ink on paper. But the traditional 20 to 30 percent return on investment, typical of the most profitable newspaper chains, is in trouble. Circulation nationwide dropped 2.6 percent in one recent six-month period. Of the 20 largest newspapers, 18 reported losses, many significant. Advertising is off, most notably automotive. Attempting to maintain profit levels, the industry has stepped up cost-cutting.

Some cuts seem comical. To save $23,000, the Phildelphia *Inquirer* and *Daily News* dropped a contract with a company that maintained office greenery. Watering, henceforth, was added to the duties of employees whose desks were nearest the plants.

One major newspaper eliminated staples in its weekend television magazine, which might seem as trivial as putting office greenery at risk but which saved a not-unsubstantial $1 million. More seriously, the industry eliminated 2,000 jobs in 2005 and, like much of U.S. industry, trimmed insurance and other employee benefits.

A Manga Touch Some U.S. newspapers, trying to lure young people into a newspaper habit, are running manga strips that draw from the style of trendy Japanese comic books. Will the pet ferret in *Peach Fuzz* do what Snoopy didn't? *Boondocks* also has a cutting-edge touch of its own.

Other cuts tracked by the trade journal *Editor & Publisher:*

- **Fewer editions.** Newspapers have reduced the number of editions edited for segments of their readership. Editions for outlying areas and suburb clusters are fewer. The so-called bulldog editions, which morning newspapers once put out the preceding afternoon for street sales, have become a historical footnote.
- **Smaller pages.** To reduce expenses for newsprint, a major raw material, newspapers have narrowed their pages substantially. Among the last holdouts with larger pages, the New York *Times* is trimming pages 1½ inches in 2008. Another holdout, the *Wall Street Journal,* trimmed page width from 15 inches to 12 in 2007.
- **Fewer pages.** Newspapers are producing fewer pages by reorganizing sections, which almost always is heralded, a tad disingenuously, as a redesign for a more reader-friendly presentation. The Charlotte, North Carolina, *Observer* cut 20 pages a week, down to 480 total, and saved $1 million in newsprint. Nationwide, newsprint consumption dropped 2.6 million tons from 2000 to 2005, partly a function of circulation declines and partly of fewer pages.
- **Lighter newsprint.** Many newspapers have switched to lighter paper, from the old standard 48.8 grams per square meter to 45. Publishers hope that readers won't much notice the wimpy feel and muddy tone.
- **Outsourced printing.** Just as the book and magazine industries did long ago, newspapers are looking to avoid the huge capital expenditures needed to replace aging presses. Commercial printers as an option are being considered by at least one major newspaper, the San Francisco *Chronicle*. Replacing old presses can mean $50 million easily for a newspaper, much more for a metro like the *Chronicle*. Outsourcing has been a long-time practice among weeklies. There also are newspapers, especially dailies in the same chain, that reduced their investment in production equipment by running off the same presses.
- **Content cuts.** Many newspapers have stopped daily stock-market lists, going weekly instead. The Madison *State Journal* in Wisconsin saved 15 pages a week. Television lists are being abbreviated. The Wilmington, Delaware, *News Journal* reduced its tabloid television magazine from 32 pages to 24. The syndicates that provide opinion columns and other features have seen a decline because newspapers have less space to fill.
- **Fewer bureaus.** The Louisville *Courier-Journal* closed three outstate bureaus. The Bridgeport, Connecticut, *Post* replaced many salaried staff reporters with part-time "stringers" who are paid by the inch. Industrywide, foreign bureaus are smaller and fewer. The Tribune Company, whose properties include the Los Angles *Times,* Chicago *Tribune* and *Newsday,* consolidated all its newspapers' Washington bureaus into one.
- **Shared content.** Chain newspapers routinely scan content from sibling papers to get double-duty out of coverage.

Even with budget cutbacks, remains uncertain whether the newspaper industry can return to its 20th-century profit levels. The reality is that newspapers, if assessed as ink-on-paper products, are artifacts of a mature industry. The industry in general recognizes its core product is news and other content—not the medium, ink on paper. The challenge is shifting delivery to other means, a process already underway with the web.

Clustering

Once newspaper chains bought available papers anywhere they could find them. No more. Today, chains try to acquire newspapers with adjoining circulations to cut costs. By the year 2000, more than 400 dailies—about a quarter of the total—were in what is called a **cluster.** Among its 26 papers the Newhouse chain, for example, has eight dailies across southern Michigan. The papers come off the same press, reducing the expense of having several multimillion-dollar presses at the individual newspapers. In some clusters editors are not in the hometown but 30 or even 70 miles away. Clustering eliminates competition for advertisers that seek customers in several communities because cluster papers offer merchants a one-stop place to run all their ads.

clustering ■ Buying newspapers with adjoining circulations to cut operating costs.

Clusters have downsides. Critics say that out-of-town supervising editors lose touch with the communities that the papers serve. Also, editors face pressure to look for stories that can go in multiple papers, reducing news-gathering expenses—and also reducing the traditional local orientation, a historic hallmark of U.S. newspapers. Overall, fewer voices are present in the marketplace.

Proponents argue that clustering creates economies that can save newspapers that otherwise would go under.

Marketing Databases

As a condition for access to their web news sites, a growing number of newspapers are requiring visitors to register. Access is free in exchange for personal information that enables the paper to create a single customer database for print subscribers and e-mail subscribers as well as Internet visitors for news and classifieds with breakdowns to identify personal interests.

Tacoda Systems, a database and marketing management company, took an early lead in creating software for newspapers to compile databases that give advertisers a source of readers. This capability is especially attractive for advertisers with products that lend themselves to direct marketing. Also, these Tacoda databases give newspapers a chance to enter direct marketing themselves.

Aside from selling almanacs and occasional other news-related products, newspapers have kept to their primary business: news. This may need to change if advertising revenue for newspapers declines, as expected, with the already occurring emergence of more competing outlets for advertisers to reach potential customers. As media visionary **Barry Diller** sees it, all of the major mass media will go to direct marketing of their own inventories of consumer products to create revenue streams to replace the loss of traditional advertising. Diller's own operations, including the Home Shopping Network on television, as well as his USA television network, already are a prototype for other media, including newspapers, to enter the business of retailing products alongside their traditional news and entertainment content.

Weekly Newspapers

study preview **Many community weekly newspapers, especially in fast-growing suburbs, are thriving.**

Community Weeklies

Weekly newspapers are making strong circulation gains, especially in suburban communities, and some have moved into publishing twice a week. In all, almost 8,000 weekly newspapers are published in the United States, with circulation approaching 50 million. Weeklies are received in almost 60 percent of the nation's households, up almost one-third from 1970.

To the discomfort of metro dailies, many advertisers are following their customers to the suburban weeklies. Advertisers have found that they can buy space in weeklies for less and reach their likeliest customers. Ralph Ingersoll, whose weeklies give fits to the daily Long Island *Newsday* in New York, explained it this way in an interview with *Forbes:* "If you're an automobile dealer on Long Island, you can pay, say, $14,000 for a tabloid page in *Newsday,* most of which is wasted because the people that get it will never buy a car in your neck of the woods, or you can go into one of the weekender publications and pay a few hundred dollars and reach just the people likely to drive over to your shop."

Some weeklies, particularly those in upscale suburbs, offer sophisticated coverage of community issues. Others feature a homey mix of reports on social events such as who visited whom for Sunday dinner. The success of these weeklies sometimes is called **telephone book journalism** because of the emphasis on names, the somewhat over-

Tacoda Systems ■ A marketing company that has software for newspapers to integrate circulation and internet customer databases.

Barry Diller ■ Television entrepreneur who sees the mass media's financial future shifting to direct sales of products.

telephone book journalism ■ Listing readers' names.

drawn theory being that people buy papers to see their names in print. Weeklies have in common that they cover their communities with a detail that metro dailies have neither staff nor space to match. There is no alternative to keeping up with local news.

Rural Weeklies

Rural weeklies generally have fallen on rough times. Part of their problem is the diminishing significance of agriculture in the national economy and the continuing depopulation of rural America. In communities that remain retail centers, rural weeklies can maintain a strong advertising base. However, the Main Street of many small towns has declined as improved roads and the construction of major retail stores like Wal-Mart draw customers from 40 to 50 miles away. In earlier days those customers patronized hometown retailers, who placed significant advertising in hometown weeklies. Today many of these Main Street retailers, unable to compete with giant discount stores, are out of business.

Shoppers

Free-distribution papers that carry only advertisements have become increasingly important as vehicles for classified advertising. In recent years **shoppers** have attracted display advertising that earlier would have gone to regular newspapers. Almost all shoppers undercut daily newspapers on advertising rates. The number of shoppers has grown to about 1,500 nationwide, and they no longer are merely an ignorable competitor for daily newspapers for advertising.

By definition, shoppers are strictly advertising sheets, but beginning in the 1970s some shoppers added editorial content, usually material that came free over the transom, such as publicity items and occasional self-serving columns from legislators. Some shoppers have added staff members to compile calendars and provide a modicum of news coverage. Most of these papers, however, remain ad sheets with little that is journalistic. Their news-gathering efforts and expenses are minuscule compared with those of a daily newspaper.

Alternative and Minority Newspapers

study preview **Most newspapers attempt broad coverage for a broad audience, but more specialized newspapers are important in the lives of many people. These include counterculture, black and Spanish-language newspapers, many of which are expanding and prospering today.**

Counterculture Newspapers

A group of friends in the Greenwich Village neighborhood of New York, including novelist **Norman Mailer** and **Don Wolf,** decided to start a newspaper. Thus in 1955 was born the ***Village Voice,*** a free-wheeling weekly that became a prototype for a 1960s phenomenon called the **alternative press** and that has continued to thrive.

In its early days the *Village Voice* was a haven for bohemian writers of diverse competence who volunteered occasional pieces, some lengthy, many rambling. Many articles purported to be investigative examinations of hypocritical people and institutions, but, as *Voice* veteran Nat Hentoff has noted, nobody ever bothered to check "noisome facts," let alone the "self-righteous author." The *Voice* seemed to scorn traditional, detached, neutral reporting. Despite its flaws, the amateurism gave the *Voice* a charm, and it picked up readership.

The *Voice* today is more polished and journalistically serious. The characteristics that made it distinctive in its early history, and that were picked up by other **counterculture newspapers,** include:

media ONLINE **The Village Voice** This alternative newsweekly has won numerous awards, including three Pulitzer Prizes. It maintains its no-holds-barred philosophy on which it was founded 50 years ago. **www.villagevoice.com**

shopper ■ An advertising paper without news.

Norman Mailer ■ Among the founders of *Village Voice.*

Don Wolf ■ Among the founders of *Village Voice.*

Village Voice ■ Model for contemporary alternative press.

alternative press ■ Generally anti-establishment publication for a young alienated audience.

counterculture newspapers ■ Challenge, defy mainstream values.

media ONLINE **National Association of Black Journalists** The NABJ is the largest media organization for people of color in the world. **www.nabj.org**

- Antiestablishment political coverage with a strong antimilitary slant.
- Cultural coverage that emphasizes contrarian music and art and exalts sex and drugs.
- Interpretive coverage focusing more on issues of special concern to alienated young people.
- Extensive entertainment coverage and listings of events.
- A conversational, sometimes crude style that includes four-letter words and gratuitous expletives for their shock value.
- Extensive personal ads for dating and sex liaisons.

By delivering a loyal readership that was hard to reach through mainstream media, many counterculture newspapers became fat with advertising. Today, about 100 alternative newspapers are published in the United States. Many are prospering. With a circulation of 172,000, the *Village Voice* is widely available in big-city newsracks and by mail throughout the country.

Black Newspapers

The ongoing integration of black and white people in U.S. society has eroded the role of black newspapers since World War II, but 172 black newspapers remain in publication. In all, the black newspapers have a circulation of 3.6 million, a ratio of about 1:10 to the nation's black population. At their peak after World War II, black newspapers included three nationally distributed dailies, from Baltimore, Chicago and Pittsburgh, whose combined circulation approached 600,000. The black dailies today, the Atlanta *Daily World,* **Chicago *Daily Defender*** and New York *Daily Challenge,* together have a circulation of 106,000, almost all local.

Black newspapers have been important in the U.S. civil rights movement. Frederick Douglass's ***North Star,*** founded in 1847, was a strident abolitionist sheet before the Civil War. W. E. B. DuBois' ***Crisis,*** founded in 1910, was a militant voice for black advancement. Today, most black newspapers crusade for causes in the tradition of their early predecessors, but the focus is more on neighborhood social, church and sports events. The tone is moderate.

Chicago *Daily Defender* ■ Daily black newspaper that continues with probing journalism.

North Star ■ Antislavery black newspaper founded 1847 by Frederick Douglass.

Crisis ■ Black newspaper founded 1910 by W. E. B. DuBois.

Prospects for black newspapers generally do not appear strong. Only 15 percent of the advertising placed in

THE NORTH STAR.

VOL. 1. NO. 23. ROCHESTER, N. Y., FRIDAY, JUNE 2, 1848.

Freedom Fighter

Antislavery orator Frederick Douglass, himself a former slave, created the *North Star* in 1847 to promote the abolitionist movement. The *North Star* was one of the most influential black newspapers, especially in dismantling the notion, prominent at the time, of natural racial inferiority. The newspaper was well written and edited, and within four years it became self-sustaining.

black media, including television, radio and magazines, goes to newspapers. Media scholar James Tinney found that middle-income blacks look to establishment newspapers rather than black newspapers for information, even while relying on other black institutions, such as the church and universities, for spiritual and intellectual stimulation.

media ONLINE **National Association of Hispanic Journalists** The NAHJ is dedicated to the recognition and professional advancement of Hispanics in the news industry. **www.nahj.org**

Asian American Journalists Association The AAJA provides support for Asian American and Pacific Islander journalists. The Association also strives for accurate news coverage of Asian American and Pacific Islander issues. **www.aaja.org**

Native American Journalists Association The NAJA supports Native journalists and seeks to promote Native culture. **www.naja.com**

Foreign-Language Newspapers

Through every wave of immigration, newspapers in foreign languages have sprouted to serve newcomers to the United States in their native tongue. In 1914 there were 140 foreign-language dailies published in the United States. About one-third were German, led by New York *Vorwarts* with a circulation of 175,000. The U.S. German-language press withered during World War I when its loyalty was challenged, but, like other foreign-language newspapers, it undoubtedly would have eventually disappeared anyway as the immigrants assimilated into the mainstream culture.

Today, the fast-growing Hispanic minority represents about one of every 15 Americans, and although most Hispanics are bilingual, six daily newspapers and about 150 weeklies are published in Spanish. In general, these newspapers are thriving. The Knight-Ridder newspaper chain publishes ***El Nuevo Herald*** as a Spanish-language daily in Miami and sells 67,000 copies. In New York, the Gannett chain operates the 63,000-circulation daily *El Diario-La Prensa*. Most Spanish-language newspapers are owned by Hispanics, but the presence of the gigantic, profitable Knight-Ridder and Gannett chains bespeaks the commercial viability of these papers.

El Nuevo Herald ■ Leading Spanish-language daily, Miami.

GRATIS

PRIMERA PLANA

CLASIFICADOS, PÁGINA 38 • TELE-GUÍA, PÁGINA 38 • ¡VAMOS A GOZAR!, PÁGINA 27 • HORÓSCOPO, PÁGINA 26

NUEVO MUNDO

NOTICIAS • ENTRETENIMIENTO • FAMILIA

Tradición y cambio definen a la Misión

El histórico barrio de San Francisco enfrenta nuevas transfor...

Familia acoge a hijos de hermana asesinada

EL MUNDO

Critican a gobierno mexicano por fuga de narcotraficante

¡A GOZAR!

Comienza Festival Tet

KNIGHT RIDDER

日米タイムズ

Nichi Bei Times

JAPANESE AMERICAN DAILY NEWS

フジモリ氏、チリで拘束

Nikkei Who Visited Nikkei Cubans to Report Back on Nov. 13

Japanese Rubik's Cube Contestant Breaks Own World Record

Fujimori Arrested in Chile After Ending 5-Year Exile in Japan

Community Briefs

Arts & Entertainment

Okinawa, Kanagawa Governors Tell Gov't They Reject Realignment Plans

Keeping Posted

Japan Today

Pacific Ties

News in Different Languages The landscape of foreign-language newspapers has evolved through U.S. history with immigration patterns. The first was Benjamin Franklin's *Zeitung* in 1732 for a growing German population. Today the most common foreign-language newspapers are in Spanish in parts of the country with large Hispanic populations. The large Japanese-American population in San Francisco has the *Nichi Bei Times*.

SANADOR. Joe Ortega cura a padres e hijos. **LATINO PROUD**

GLORIA ROMERO TRABAJA DÍA A DÍA PARA BRINDARTE MEJORES NIVELES DE VIDA. **LATIN POWER**

VIVE PARA CONTAR SU HAZAÑA
GALIA MOSS DESAFÍO A LA NATURALEZA Y NOS CUENTA CUÁLES FUERON SUS SECRETOS. **MEXICO NOW**

BUENOS DÍAS ★ NÚMERO 86

VERIFIED AUDIT CIRCULATION www.verifiedaudit.com

FRONTERAS
DE LA NOTICIA

MUNDIAL ALEMANIA 2006

FELIZ DERROCHE
AFUERA DE LAS CANCHAS, LA DANZA DE LOS MILLONES SE BAILA SIN FRENO. LA TV GANA Y LOS FANÁTICOS DESPILFARRAN.
SPORTS

GOL CON MAGIA
NO TE PIERDAS UN NUEVO CAPÍTULO DE LA TIRA CÓMICA DEL ASTRO DE BRASIL, RONALDINHO.
COMICS

LA 'CACERÍA' DE LOS FANÁTICOS
ESTUVIMOS CON LOS MINUTEMEN EN LA FRONTERA Y COMPROBAMOS SU MISIÓN.
COVER STORY

APÚNTATE
Directivos afinan detalles para el juego del Real Madrid contra el Real Salt Lake. Infórmate sobre los boletos. **LOCAL NEWS**

ADEMÁS: EL HORÓSCOPO DE MADAME MYSTIC ¥ SERVICIOS, EMPLEOS, CLIMA

Fronteras

Newspapers in heavily Spanish-speaking U.S. areas have taken on *Fronteras de la Noticia,* a tabloid magazine produced by Danilo Black in Mexico, mostly for free distribution in stores and schools. The newspapers sell advertising local space and have two pages available to insert local news and other content. *Fronteras* is a new revenue stream for newspaper companies outside their main product.

The profitability of Spanish-language newspapers is fueled partly by the desire of many national advertisers to tap into the large Hispanic market. The newspapers' penetration, however, is not especially high. In heavily Hispanic Los Angeles, *La Opinion* has a circulation of only 55,000 a day. In Miami the competing *El Herald* and *Diario las Americas* together sell only 130,000 copies a day. In New York *El Diario-La Prensa* and *Noticias del Mundo* together have a circulation of less than 130,000 in a metropolitan area with 2.5 million Hispanic people.

Whether Spanish-language newspapers will disappear, as did earlier foreign-language newspapers, is uncertain. Although assimilation is occurring, many Hispanics are intent on maintaining their distinctive cultural identity and resist adopting English. Also, there is more sympathy for multiculturalism in the society than there was in the past. For the foreseeable future, Spanish-language newspapers will have a strong following among the continuing influx of people from Latin America and the Caribbean. With this immigration and a high fertility rate, the U.S. Hispanic population is growing about 4 percent a year.

Evaluating Newspapers

study preview **Quantitative measures of a newspaper's success include circulation and penetration. How to judge quality? Rankings and awards are indicators, although they are imperfect. You yourself can evaluate whether the newspaper gives adequate resources to coverage.**

media ONLINE

National Lesbian and Gay Journalists Association The NLGJA seeks to keep its members informed of key issues, provide mentoring and career opportunities, and promote accurate coverage of lesbian, gay, bisexual and transgender news.
www.nlgja.org

El Nuevo Herald The Spanish language newspaper of Miami.
www.miami.com/mld/elnuevo

El Diario-La Prensa The Gannett chain publishes this New York Spanish-language daily.
www.eldiariony.com/noticias/index.aspx

Circulation and Penetration

Once upon a time, measuring a newspaper's marketplace success against its competition was simple. The paper with the largest circulation won. Today, though, hardly any cities have competing dailies. Even so, numbers count. Is circulation growing? Declining? Because almost every newspaper reports its circulation to an auditing agency, you can track circulation year to year, even quarter to quarter.

Even more significant comparative data come from comparing **penetration.** Penetration is the percentage of people or households that gets the paper. The ABC circulation auditing agency doesn't collect penetration data, but fairly reliable penetration is easy to calculate: Divide the circulation by the population. Seeking precise penetration data can get tricky. How you measure the circulation area, for example, can make a difference. There are other variables too. Even so, simple math can give you a good indicator of whether a newspaper's acceptance in the marketplace is improving.

penetration ■ Percentage of persons or households that a newspaper reaches in its circulation area.

Overall, penetration has slipped badly. In 1950, 356 copies of daily newspapers were printed for every 1,000 people in the United States. By 1995 the number was down to

Best U.S. Newspapers

About 100 leading newspaper editors dispersed across the 50 states voted the New York *Times* the top newspaper in the nation in 1999. *Columbia Journalism Review* magazine, which sponsored the survey, asked editors to evaluate reporting, writing, editing, graphics, integrity, accuracy, fairness, vision, innovation, influence in the community and influence on the broader journalistic community. Of the three national papers, the *Wall Street Journal* was third, *USA Today* 12th. The *Christian Science Monitor* did not show. Also, the survey was conducted before the Staples Arena scandal marred the reputation of the Los Angeles *Times.*

1. New York *Times*
2. Washington *Post*
3. *Wall Street Journal*
4. Los Angeles *Times*
5. Dallas *Morning News*
6. Chicago *Tribune*
   Boston *Globe* (tie)
8. San Jose *Mercury News*
9. St. Petersburg *Times*
10. Baltimore *Sun*

234—a 34.2 percent drop. The penetration decline has been masked by population growth. Daily circulation nationwide, at 56 million today, is down only about 8 percent since 1950.

Quality Indicators

Being subjective, indicators of quality are problematic. *Time* magazine once did an often-quoted annual ranking. Now carefully considered rankings occasionally show up in *American Journalism Review* and other media critique journals. In these rankings, consider the fine print so you know the criteria that were used. Also, check for the qualities that impressed the evaluator.

Awards are an indicator too, though hardly perfect. The most prestigious award, the Pulitzer, is not the result of what most people assume—a thorough search for the best. The Pulitzer committee, like most awards groups, looks only at nominated work. Some newspapers, including the Los Angeles *Times,* have full-time employees who do nothing but assemble and submit glossy nomination materials.

With most journalistic contests accepting only self-nominated works, does bad work sometimes win? No, the quality of submissions is almost always high. Eager for bragging rights, most newspapers enter worthy pieces. But not all publications enter, so questions can be raised whether it's truly the best that's even considered.

Too, awards committees seldom do much legwork. Occasionally, as a result, there is an embarrassment. Everyone involved is still red-faced over the 1981 Pulitzer awarded to the Washington *Post*'s Janet Cooke. Afterward, it was learned that Cooke had fabricated her news story. The *Post* made her give the prize back. She left the newspaper and faded into journalistic obscurity.

Here are some quality indicators:

News Hole What percentage of the space in the newspaper goes to news? This is called the **news hole.** From a reader's perspective the bigger the news hole, the better. Discount postal rates are available only to newspapers that cap advertising at 70 percent. Many publications push the limit to maximize revenue, sometimes shorting readers on news coverage, commentary and other non-ad content.

news hole ■ Space in a publication after ads are inserted.

Content Because local coverage is more costly than stories from news agencies, a good measure of quality is whether a newspaper has extensive local coverage or loads up with wire stories. Is local coverage thorough? Is it accurate? Does the newspaper have its own state capitol reporter? Its own Washington bureau?

Staff What kind of professionals report and edit the newspaper? Seasoned reporters who know the community well? Or beginners? Does the newspaper offer competitive salaries for the best talent? Salary scales are available on newspapers with collective-bargaining agreements.

Management Does top management have a permanent stake in the community? Or does leadership rotate in and out, with individuals focusing on making a name in order to move up in the corporate structure?

CHAPTER 3 Wrap-Up

Numerous, once-powerful newspapers have disappeared since the middle of the last century, among them the Chicago *Daily News,* Los Angeles *Herald Examiner,* New York *Herald Tribune,* Philadelphia *Bulletin* and Washington *Star.* U.S. dailies, which numbered 1,745 in 1980, are down to 1,570. Other media, particularly television and its evening newscasts, have siphoned readers away from evening newspapers. Can newspapers survive? Even if people were to stop buying newspapers tomorrow, newspaper organizations would survive because they have an asset that competing media lack: the largest, most skilled newsroom staffs in their communities. The presses and the ink-on-newsprint medium for carrying the message may not have a long future, but newspapers' news-gathering capability will endure.

Questions for Review

1. Describe how newspapers are important in the lives of most Americans.
2. Explain the rise of newspaper chains. Have they been good for readers?
3. Why is the United States a nation mostly of provincial newspapers?
4. Why is the New York *Times* regarded as the best U.S. newspaper?
5. Many metropolitan daily newspapers have lost circulation, and some have shut down. Why?
6. What challenges to their dominance as a news and advertising medium do newspapers face?
7. Community newspapers, especially suburban weeklies, are booming. Why?
8. What kinds of newspapers aimed at narrow audience segments are prospering?

Questions for Critical Thinking

1. The United States is called a nation of provincial newspapers. Is the label correct? Do the *Wall Street Journal, USA Today* and *Christian Science Monitor* fit the provincial characterization?
2. How can you explain the declining number of U.S. newspapers and their losses in market penetration in view of the newspaper industry's profitability?
3. How have newspapers met challenges to their advertising revenue from radio, television, direct mail and shoppers?
4. Can you explain why a greater percentage of U.S. newspapers are published for morning reading, not afternoon?
5. Identify advantages and disadvantages in the consolidation of U.S. newspapers, daily and weekly, into chains and cross-media conglomerates.
6. Can you identify how *USA Today* has changed U.S. newspapers by comparing an issue of your hometown paper today with an issue from the 1970s?
7. How have improvements in U.S. newspapers led to fewer households taking more than a single newspaper?
8. Considering the business orientation that makes newspaper chains so profitable, does it seem unusual that someone like Al Neuharth, whose background was in journalism rather than business, led Gannett through its incredible and profitable growth?

Deepening Your media LITERACY

Can a newspaper have a personality?

STEP 1 Get copies of two different newspapers, daily or weekly.

Dig Deeper

STEP 2 Make a list of the following characteristics for each publication:

1. How big is the news hole? An easy way to calculate this is to measure the total number of inches in each column of type, from the top of the page to the bottom, and multiply by the number of columns across the page. Multiply this number by the total number of pages. Then measure the number of inches of non-advertising material and figure the percentage of non-advertising content—that's your news hole.
2. How much of the news is staff written? How much comes from news services?
3. How diverse is the opinion section?
4. Is the publication chain-owned or independent?
5. What word or phrase describes the overall look of the publication?
6. What kind of news does it carry? Local, sports, entertainment, other?

What Do You Think?

STEP 3 Write down a few words or a phrase that describes the personalities of the publications you investigated. Answer these questions: Can you determine the politics of the publisher or editor from reading the newspaper? What text or images led you to this conclusion? Can you determine who the perceived audience of a publication is by reading it? What values it expresses? It is said that a truly successful newspaper belongs to the community. Do you think that's true for the newspapers you studied?

Keeping Up to Date

Editor & Publisher is a weekly trade journal for the newspaper industry.

mediainfo.com. The trade journal *Editor & Publisher* launched this web site in 1997 to cover the emerging online news industry. www.mediainfo.com

Newspaper Research Journal is a quarterly dealing mostly with applied research.

Presstime is published monthly by the American Newspaper Publishers Association.

For Further Learning

Robin Gerber. *Katharine Graham: The Leadership Journey of an American Icon.* Portfolio, 2005.

Gerber portrays the Washington *Post* publisher as a case study for female success in a corporate environment.

Gene Roberts and Thomas Kunkel, editors. *Breach of Faith: A Crisis of Coverage in the Age of Corporate Newspapering.* University of Arkansas, 2003.

This collection of essays notes that newspapers have become more glitzy than ever but formulaic and bland under new pressures from giant corporate owners.

Mark Fitzgerald. "Farewell to the Gay '90s," *Editor & Publisher* (October 2, 2000), pages 32–35.

The demise of a Chicago and a downstate Illinois gay newspaper prompted Fitzgerald, *E&P*'s editor at large, to write this update on the gay newspaper phenomenon. He finds 237 nationwide.

Greg Mitchell. "Readers Support Bush, Say Coverage Was Good," *Editor & Publisher* (November 6, 2000), pages 7–9, and "Bird in the Hand for Bush," pages 24–27.

Mitchell, an *E&P* editor, reports on studies commissioned by the trade journal on how voters perceived news coverage of the 2000 presidential campaigns and on newspaper endorsements of candidates. Among his findings: People don't like editorial endorsements, and most publishers favored Bush, but editors endorsed Gore.

David Nasaw. *The Chief: The Life of William Randolph Hearst.* Houghton Mifflin, 2000.

Nasaw, a historian, wrote the definitive biography of the newspaper magnate. It draws heavily on letters and interviews of surviving family members, employees and acquaintances. Nasaw works hard at being detached and neutral, which gives the work, like the times, a pro-business edge.

Conrad Black. "Manager's Journal: Don't Write Off Newspapers Yet," *Wall Street Journal* (March 6, 2000), page A30.

The chair of Hollinger International, a Canada-based newspaper company, argues that newspapers have an enduring asset: authoritative content. Even so, Black says, newspapers need to be involved with both print and web products.

David Laventhol. "America's Best Newspapers," *Columbia Journalism Review* (November/December 1999), pages 14–16.

Leading editors rank the top 21 newspapers in the United States plus five other papers that are emerging as leaders.

Lawrence N. Strout. *Covering McCarthyism: How the Christian Science Monitor Handled Joseph R. McCarthy, 1950–1954.* Greenwood, 1999.

Drawing on his doctoral dissertation, Strout tracks the *Monitor*'s balanced, solution-oriented coverage with comparisons to coverage by other leading newspapers.

Carl Sessions Stepp. "The State of the American Newspaper: Then and Now," *American Journalism Review* 21 (September 1999): 7, pages 60–75.

Stepp gives an excellent comparison of the quality of content of 10 hometown dailies from 1964 to 1999.

Anne Colamosca. "Pay for Journalists Is Going Up," *Columbia Journalism Review* (July/August 1999), pages 24–29.

Colamosca provides an update on salaries at newspapers, magazines, broadcast operations and new media.

Jack Bass. "The State of the American Newspaper: Newspaper Monopoly," *American Journalism Review* 21 (July–August 1999): 6, pages 64–86.

Bass examines why newspaper created ownership clusters in the 1990s and the results.

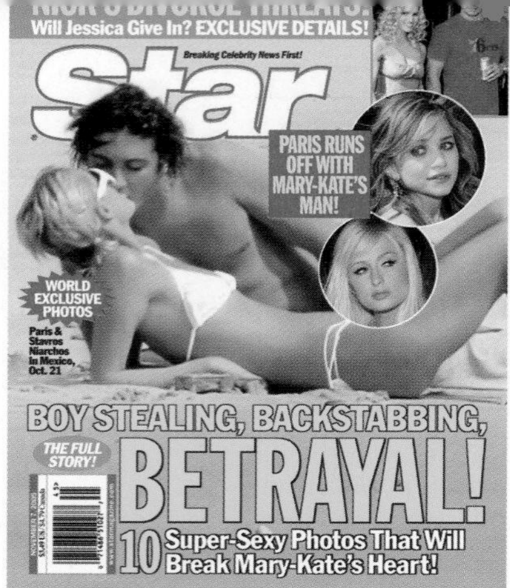

Fuller's New Star In charge at American Media publications, Bonnie Fuller unveiled her remake of the supermarket tabloid *Star* for a 2004 run against celebrity titles *People, Us Weekly* and *InStyle.* For respectability Fuller threw out the classified advertising and most customer-direct advertising, about half of the magazine's ad pages. She promised advertisers a 116-page publication, compared to the previous 80, and set aside 40 pages for ads, compared to the previous 24. Fuller went cutesy with labels for some features, like "Star Bucks," with celebrities photographed in acts of public consumption; "The Stars Are Out," with celebrities at parties and occasions and "Doctor to the Stars," with health and beauty tips.

chapter 4 Magazines

In this chapter you will learn:

- Magazines have contributed importantly to U.S. culture.
- Magazines have been journalistic, visual innovators.
- Most newsrack magazines aim at narrow audience segments.
- Sponsored magazine and trade journals outnumber newsrack magazines.
- Magazines continue to demassify.
- Magazines may be losing their influence in shaping the future.
- Few magazines meet elitist standards for excellence.

Magazine editor Bonnie Fuller has a magic touch. In her six years as editor, she turned *Flare* into the largest fashion magazine in Canada. Then, in New York, she relaunched *YM,* a magazine geared toward young women ages 15 to 24, more than doubling its circulation from 700,000 to more than 1.7 million. In 1994 Fuller joined Hearst Magazines where she launched the French fashion, beauty and lifestyle magazine *Marie Claire* for U.S. readers. Initial circulation of 250,000 rocketed past 500,000. Then Hearst put Fuller in charge of *Cosmopolitan,* which was still riding high on the sex-and-the-single-girl themes of Helen Gurley Brown after more than 30 years—quite an act to follow.

As the new *Cosmo* editor, Fuller utilized reader focus groups to guide her in making changes and additions. She included articles on AIDS and sexual harassment and, no holds barred, any issue of concern and relevance to young women, at the same time maintaining the saucy, sexy Helen Gurley Brown tone. In Fuller's first year, *Cosmo* circulation flourished and drew more advertising. Fuller was named 1997 Editor of the Year by the trade magazine *Advertising Age.* From 1998 to 2001 she served as editor of *Glamour.*

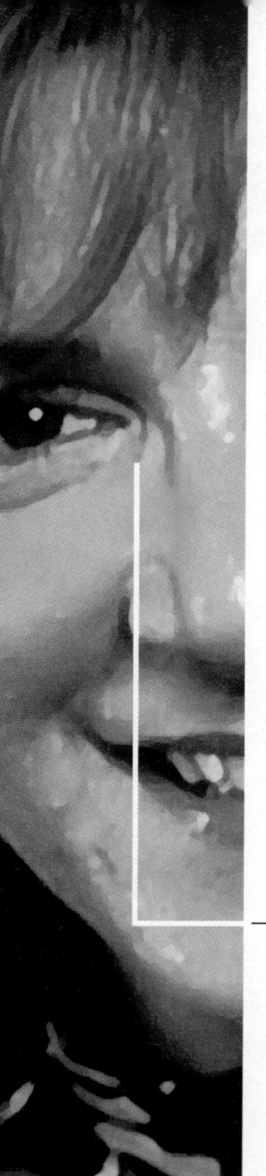

What next? Fuller took on the editorship of the celebrity magazine *Us Weekly,* which had floundered for years against Time Warner's *People.* Almost instantly, *Us* became a pop culture must-read.

At the risk of being labeled a serial job-hopper, in 2003 Fuller switched to tabloid publisher American Media. At American Media she not only was editing one title but was also editor-in-chief for all the company's magazines. It was a new level of responsibility. Said Fuller: "A chance to do this isn't going to necessarily come up in two years, in three years. It came up now." How could the era's most successful magazine editor stoop as low as American Media's *National Enquirer* and *Star?* Her stock answer in myriad interviews was the same: "Don't fool yourself. Every news outlet is doing tabloid stories."

A hands-on editor, Fuller first tackled American Media's supermarket pulp tabloid *Star.* Coverlines suddenly were less gee-whiz and more upbeat. To reposition *Star,* she had it printed on glossy paper. She shunned old *Star*-type scoops that, while tantalizing, often turned out to be untrue. A successful celebrity magazine, she said, needs credibility.

Would Fuller succeed? The circulation of the *Star* she inherited at first slipped below 1.2 million, but by 2005 it was up to 1.6 million in an increasingly competitive field of celebrity magazines. The question was whether, fully Fuller-ized, the magazine could top *People* at 3.5 million. Fuller was confident, saying that her target after *Star* would be to rejuvenate American Media's recently acquired *Men's Fitness* and *Muscle and Fitness* and a motley group of other titles, including Latino magazines, *Natural Health, Globe* and perhaps even American Media's flagship *National Enquirer.*

Influence of Magazines

study preview **Today, as through their whole history, the major magazines constitute a mass medium through which the distinctive U.S. culture is brought to a national audience. At their best, periodicals pack great literature and ideas into formats that, unlike books, almost anybody can afford. Magazines are also a national unifier because they offer manufacturers a nationwide audience for their goods.**

Contributing to Nationhood

The first successful magazines in the United States, in the 1820s, were much less expensive than books. People of ordinary means could afford them. Unlike newspapers, which were oriented to their cities of publication, early magazines created national audiences. This contributed to a sense of nationhood at a time when an American culture, distinctive from its European heritage, had not yet emerged. The American people had their magazines in common. The ***Saturday Evening Post,*** founded in 1821, carried fiction by Edgar Allan Poe, Nathaniel Hawthorne and Harriet Beecher Stowe to readers who could not afford books. Their short stories and serialized novels flowed from the American experience and helped Americans establish a national identity.

Saturday Evening Post ■ Early contributor to identifiable U.S. literature.

Postal Act of 1879 ■ Discounted magazine mail rates.

With the **Postal Act of 1879,** Congress recognized the role of magazines in creating a national culture and promoting literacy—in effect, binding the nation. The law allowed a discount on mailing rates for magazines, a penny a pound. Magazines were being media TIMELINE

MAGAZINES

1741 Andrew Bradford printed *American Magazine,* and Benjamin Franklin printed *General Magazines,* the first magazines in the colonies.

1821 *Saturday Evening Post* was launched, ushering in the era of general interest magazines.

1828 Sara Josepha Hale began editing *Ladies' Magazine,* the first women's magazine.

1860s *Harper's Weekly* introduced visual news with Civil War illustrations.

1879 Congress gave discount postal rates to magazines.

1899 Gilbert Grosvenor introduced photographs in *National Geographic.*

1902 Ida Tarbell wrote a muckraking series on Standard Oil in *McClure's.*

1922 DeWitt and Lila Wallace founded *Reader's Digest.*

1923 Henry Luce and Briton Hadden founded *Time,* the first newsmagazine.

1924 Harold Ross founded the *New Yorker* and introduced the modern personality profile.

1936 Henry Luce founded *Life* and coined the term *photo essay.*

1960s Oversize general magazines, including *Life,* folded as advertisers moved to network television.

1962 Hugh Hefner introduced the modern question-and-answer format in *Playboy.*

1996 Time Warner created the Pathfinder web site for its magazines. Others followed.

subsidized, which reduced distribution costs and sparked dramatic circulation growth. New magazines cropped up as a result.

National Advertising Medium

Advertisers used magazines through the 1800s to build national markets for their products, which was an important factor in transforming the United States from an agricultural and cottage industry economy into a modern economy. This too contributed to a sense of nationhood. The other mass media could not do that as effectively. Few books carried advertisements. Newspapers, with few exceptions, delivered only local readership to advertisers.

Massive Magazine Audience

People have a tremendous appetite for magazines. According to magazine industry studies, almost 90 percent of U.S. adults read an average 10 issues a month. Although magazines are affordable for most people, the household income of the typical reader is 5 percent more than the national average. In general, the more education and higher income a person has, the greater the person's magazine consumption.

In short, magazines are a pervasive mass medium. Magazines are not only for the upper crust, however. Many magazines are edited for downscale audiences, which means that the medium's role in society is spread across almost the whole range of people. Even illiterate people can derive some pleasure and value from magazines, which by and large are visual and colorful.

The massiveness of the audience makes the magazine an exceptionally competitive medium. About 12,000 magazines vie for readers in the United States, ranging from general interest publications such as *Reader's Digest* to such specialized publications as *Chili Pepper,* for people interested in hot foods, and *Spur,* for racehorse aficionados. In recent years 500 to 600 new magazines have been launched annually, although only one in five survives into its third year.

Magazines as Media Innovators

studypreview **Magazines have led other media with significant innovations in journalism, advertising and circulation. These include investigative reporting, in-depth personality profiles, and photojournalism.**

Investigative Reporting

Muckraking, usually called "investigative reporting" today, was honed by magazines as a journalistic approach in the first years of the 20th century. Magazines ran lengthy explorations of abusive institutions in the society. It was **Theodore Roosevelt,** the reform president, who coined the term *muckraking.* Roosevelt generally enjoyed investigative journalism, but one day in 1906, when the digging got too close to home, he likened it to the work of a character in a 17th-century novel who focused so much on raking muck that he missed the good news. The president meant the term derisively, but it came to be a badge of honor among journalists.

Muckraking established magazines as a powerful medium in shaping public policy. In 1902 **Ida Tarbell** wrote a 19-part series on the Standard Oil monopoly for ***McClure's.*** **Lincoln Steffens** detailed municipal corruption, and reforms followed. Other magazines picked up investigative thrusts. *Collier's* took on patent medicine frauds. *Cosmopolitan,* a leading muckraking journal of the period, tackled dishonesty in the U.S. Senate. Muckraking expanded to books with **Upton Sinclair**'s *The Jungle.* Sinclair shocked the nation by detailing filth in meat-packing plants. Federal inspection laws resulted. Later, newspapers joined muckraking, but it was magazines that had led the way.

Personality Profiles

The in-depth **personality profile** was a magazine invention. In the 1920s **Harold Ross** of the *New Yorker* began pushing writers to a thoroughness that was new in journalism. They used multiple interviews with a range of sources—talking not only with the subject of the profile but also with just about everyone and anyone who could comment on the subject, including the subject's friends and enemies. Such depth required weeks, sometimes months, of journalistic digging. It's not uncommon now in newspapers, broadcasting or magazines, but before Harold Ross, it didn't exist.

Under **Hugh Hefner,** *Playboy* took the interview in new directions in 1962 with in-depth profiles developed from a highly structured question-and-answer format. This format became widely imitated. *Rolling Stone* uses Q-and-A's regularly, often creating news. In 2003 presidential hopeful Wesley Clark, a retired general, told *Rolling Stone* that a three-star general in the Pentagon had told him that the Iraq invasion was planned only as the beginning of further U.S. invasions in the Middle East and elsewhere, and Clark named the additional target countries. It was a bombshell assertion that made news. Other magazines meanwhile are boiling down the Q-and-A into quick takes. *Time* introduced the "10 Questions" feature in 2002, tightly editing pointed questions and answers to fit on a single page.

Photojournalism

Magazines brought visuals to the mass media in a way books never had. ***Harper's Weekly*** sent artists to draw Civil War battles, leading the way to journalism that went beyond words.

The young editor of the ***National Geographic,*** Gilbert Grosvenor, drew a map proposing a route to the South Pole for an 1899 issue, putting the *Geographic* on the road to being a visually oriented magazine. For subsequent issues, Grosvenor borrowed government plates to reproduce photos, and he encouraged travelers to submit their

muckraking ■ Turn-of-century term for investigative reporting.

Theodore Roosevelt ■ Coined the term *muckraking.*

Ida Tarbell ■ Exposed Standard Oil.

McClure's ■ Turn-of-century muckraking magazine.

Lincoln Steffens ■ Exposed municipal corruption.

Upton Sinclair ■ Exposed the meat-packing industry.

personality profile ■ In-depth, balanced biographical article.

Harold Ross ■ Pioneered the personality profile.

Hugh Hefner ■ Adapted the personality profile to Q-and-A.

Harper's Weekly ■ Pioneered magazine visuals.

National Geographic ■ Introduced photography in magazines.

photographs to the magazine. This was at a time when most magazines scorned photographs. However, Grosvenor was undeterred as an advocate for documentary photography, and membership in the National Geographic Society, a prerequisite for receiving the magazine, swelled. Eventually, the magazine assembled its own staff of photographers and gradually became a model for other publications that discovered they needed to play catch-up.

Aided by technological advances involving smaller, more portable cameras and faster film capable of recording images under extreme conditions, photographers working for the *Geographic* opened a whole new world of documentary coverage to their readers. Among *Geographic* accomplishments were:

- A photo of a bare-breasted Filipino woman field worker shocked some *Geographic* readers in 1903, but Grosvenor persisted against Victorian sensitivities to show the peoples of the world as they lived.
- The first photographs from Tibet, by Russian explorers, appeared in 1905 in an 11-page spread—extraordinary visual coverage for the time that confirmed photography's role in journalism.
- A 17-page, eight-foot foldout panorama of the Canadian Rockies in 1911 showed that photojournalism need not be limited by format.
- The magazine's 100th anniversary cover in 1988 was the first hologram—a three-dimensional photograph—ever published in a mass-audience magazine. It was a significant production accomplishment.

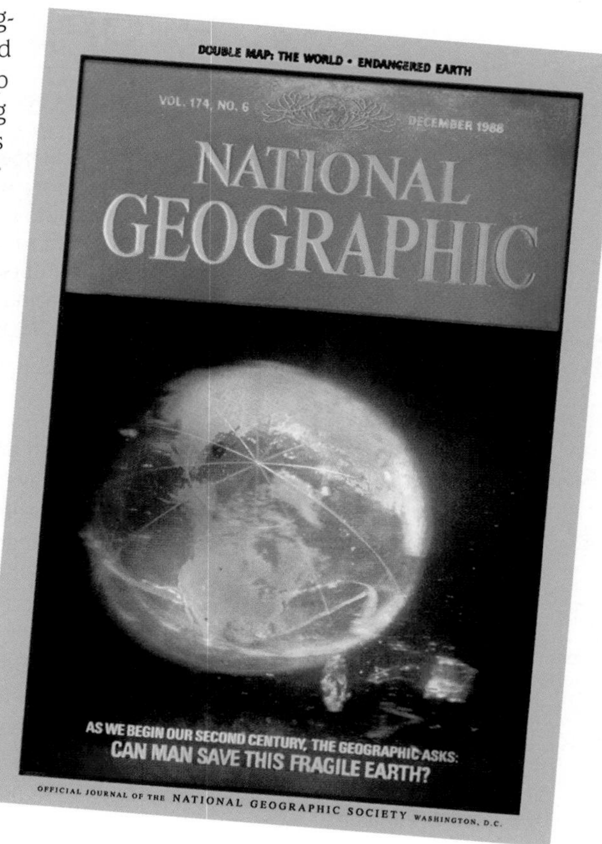

National Geographic
The *Geographic* has remained in the vanguard of magazines photographically. In 1985 the magazine used a hologram, a three-dimentional photograph, of a prehistoric child's skill on its cover—the first ever in a mass-audience magazine. Three years later, for its 100th anniversary, the *Geographic* produced a three-dimensional view of Earth on the first fully holographic magazine cover. The *Geographic* is not only among the oldest U.S. magazines but also, with 6.7 million circulation, among the most read.

Life magazine brought U.S. photojournalism to new importance in the 1930s. The oversize pages of the magazine gave new intensity to photographs, and the magazine, a weekly, demonstrated that newsworthy events could be covered consistently by camera. *Life* captured the spirit of the times photographically and demonstrated that the whole range of human experience could be recorded visually. Both real life and *Life* could be shocking. A 1938 *Life* spread on human birth was so shocking for the time that censors succeeded in banning the issue in 33 cities.

Consumer Magazines

studypreview **The most visible category of magazines is general-interest magazines, which are available on newsracks and by subscription. Called consumer magazines, these include publications like *Reader's Digest* that try to offer something for everybody, but mostly they are magazines edited for narrower audiences.**

Circulation Leaders

Reader's Digest is usually considered to have the largest circulation of any U.S. **consumer magazine,** selling 11.1 million copies a month, not counting foreign editions. However, *Reader's Digest*'s lead in circulation is not technically correct because the circulation of the Sunday newspaper supplement *Parade* is triple that. Also, in recent years, with the graying of America, the magazine ***AARP The Magazine,*** which is sent to members of the American Association of Retired Persons every two months, has reached a circulation of 20 million, considerably ahead of *Reader's Digest*.

The common notion that *Reader's Digest* is the largest magazine stems from its attempt to serve a true mass audience. Unlike *AARP The Magazine,* the *Digest*'s easy-to-read articles cut across divisions of age, gender, occupation and geography. *Reader's Digest* is

consumer magazines ■ Sold on newsracks.

Reader's Digest ■ Largest circulation newsrack magazine.

AARP The Magazine ■ Has the largest circulation but is limited to AARP members.

mediaPEOPLE

Margaret Bourke-White

Fearless Photojournalist Margaret Bourke-White not only would take her camera anywhere but also had a sense of stories that were worth telling photographically. She is remembered mostly for her work in *Life* magazine over 20 years beginning in the mid-1930s.

The oversized *Life* magazine created by Henry Luce was the perfect forum for the work of Margaret Bourke-White. The giant pages, 13½ inches high and opening to 21-inch spreads, gave such impact to photos that they seemed to jump off the page at readers. Bourke-White was there at the beginning, shooting the immense Fort Peck Dam in Montana for *Life*'s first cover in 1936. Over her career, Bourke-White shot 284 assignments for *Life,* many of them enduring images from World War II. These included Holocaust victims in a Nazi concentration camp, great military movements and the leaders of the time in both triumph and defeat. She was among the first great photojournalists.

Bourke-White's photojournalism went beyond the news and emotions of any given day to penetrate the core of great social problems. In collaboration with writer Erskine Caldwell, whom she later married, Bourke-White created a photo documentary on the tragic lives of sharecroppers in the American South. Later, in South Africa, she went underground to photograph gold miners who were known only by numbers. Her haunting photos from the Midwest drought of the 1930s created indelible images in the minds of a generation. These were socially significant projects that moved people and changed public policy.

Margaret Bourke-White was fearless in her pursuit of photography. She took her camera, a weighty Speed Graphic, onto the ledges of skyscrapers to get the feel she wanted in her images. She shot the ravages of the war in Europe from airplanes. She lived her work, and was quoted once as saying, "When I die I want to die living." She died in 1971 at age 67.

---

media ONLINE

Rolling Stone Music news, reviews, photos—if it's key to the scene, *Rolling Stone* has it covered.
www.rollingstone.com

Reader's Digest Sign up for free newsletters, submit a joke or preview the current issue of this widely distributed magazine.
www.rd.com

Time One of the earliest newsmagazines keeps on ticking.
www.time.com

National Geographic Web site of the National Geographic Society, with articles and the pictures that made the magazine famous.
www.nationalgeographic.com

a mass magazine in the truest sense of the word. It tries in every issue to have something for everybody. The Sunday newspaper supplements also are edited for a truly mass audience.

Led by *Reader's Digest,* about 5,300 magazines were published in the United States for newsrack and subscription sales in 2004. A few, including newsmagazines, deal with subjects of general interest. Most, however, have a narrower focus, such as *Motor Trend,* which is geared toward automobile enthusiasts; *Forbes,* which appeals to business people and investors; and *Family Circle,* which targets homemakers.

One thing that consumer magazines have in common is a heavy reliance on advertising. Exceptions include *Consumer Reports,* which wants to be above any suspicion that advertisers influence its reporting; the nondenominational religious magazine *Guideposts* and the feminist magazine *Ms.*

Newsmagazines

Fresh out of Yale in 1923, classmates **Henry Luce** and Briton Hadden begged and borrowed $86,000 from friends and relatives and launched a new kind of magazine: ***Time.*** The magazine provided summaries of news by categories such as national affairs, sports and business. It took four years for *Time* to turn a profit, and some people doubted that the magazine would ever make money, noting that it merely rehashed what daily newspapers had already reported. Readers, however, came to like the handy compilation and the sprightly, often irreverent writing style that set *Time* apart.

A copycat, *Newsweek,* appeared in 1933. So did a third newsweekly, *U.S. News,* the forerunner to today's *U.S. News & World Report.* Despite the competition, *Time,* with 4.1 million copies weekly, has consistently led newsmagazine circulation.

Henry Luce ■ Founder of *Time* and later *Life.*

Time ■ First newsmagazine.

DeWitt and Lila Wallace

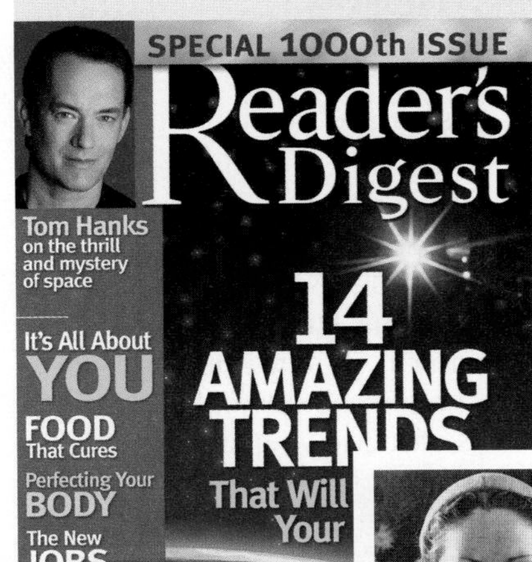

DeWitt and Lila Wallace *Reader's Digest* founders.

DeWitt and Lila Wallace had an idea but hardly any money. The idea was a pocket-sized magazine that condensed informational, inspiring and entertaining nonfiction from other publications—a digest. With borrowed money the Wallaces brought out their first issue of *Reader's Digest* in 1922.

The rest, as they say, is history. In 1947 the *Digest* became the first magazine to exceed a circulation of 9 million. Except for the Sunday newspaper supplement *Parade*, *Reader's Digest* has been the nation's largest-circulation magazine most of the time since then. In 2004 *Reader's Digest*'s circulation was 11.1 million—not counting an additional 12.2 million overseas in 18 languages.

The magazine has remained true to the Wallaces' successful formula. DeWitt and Lila Wallace, children of poor Presbyterian clergy, wanted "constructive articles," each with universal appeal. The thrust was upbeat but not Pollyanna. Digested as they were, the articles could be quickly read. America loved it. More than 90 percent of *Reader's Digest* circulation is by subscription, representing long-term reader commitment.

For its first 33 years, *Reader's Digest* was wholly reader supported. It carried no advertising. Rising postal rates forced a change in 1955. There was scoffing about whether advertisers would go for "postage-stamp-sized ads" in *Reader's Digest* with its diminutive pages, but the scoffers were wrong. The people who decide where to place advertisements never doubted that *Reader's Digest* was well read. Today, advertisers—except for cigarette manufacturers—pay more than $100,000 a page for a color advertisement. Consistent with the Wallaces' standards, cigarette advertisements are not accepted and never have been.

While *Time*, *Newsweek* and *U.S. News & World Report* cover a broad range of subjects, specialized newsmagazines focus on narrower subjects. The largest category is those featuring celebrity news, including the gossipy sort. The supermarket tabloid ***National Enquirer*** focuses on the rich and famous, hyped-up medical research and sensational oddball news and is an incredible commercial success, with 2.1 million in circulation. Time Warner's *People* is at 3.6 million.

Newspaper Supplements

Overlooked sometimes as magazines despite their giant circulations are ***Parade*** and other independently produced newspaper supplements. Newspapers buy the supplements in bulk and stuff them inside their weekend editions. *Parade*, a product of Advance Publications, which also publishes *The New Yorker*, *Women's Wear Daily* and *Modern Bride*, has a circulation of 35.4 million and appears mostly inside Sunday newspapers. The Gannett conglomerate publishes ***USA Weekend***, which its newspapers circulate but which also is sold to non-Gannett papers.

In 2004 Time Warner reinvented its on-again, off-again *Life* magazine, this time as a newspaper supplement for Friday newspapers. Time Warner geared the new *Life*, printed on high-quality paper, for more upscale advertisers than *Parade* and *USA Weekend*, which carried direct-response and consumer-packaged goods advertising.

Rural newspapers also have a supplement, *American Profile*.

Although the newspaper supplements clearly are consumer magazines, they are a separate breed. They don't seek subscribers directly. They need only to convince a newspaper or a newspaper chain to carry them. You don't see them on newsstands, nor do

media ONLINE

Parade Online version of the widely read Sunday supplement.
www.parade.com

USA Weekend Check out the weekly newspaper magazine, with general interest categories such as home and family, personal finance, health and food.
www.usaweekend.com

Life Visit the photo archive for a look at over 22 million classic *Life* photos and magazine covers.
www.life.com

American Profile The regional, weekly supplement with hometown community news.
www.americanprofile.com

National Enquirer ■ Magazine or newspaper?

Parade ■ Largest magazine circulation.

USA Weekend ■ Second largest weekend newspaper supplement.

Magazine Advertising Revenue

These are the leaders among U.S. magazines, not counting foreign editions, based on their 2004 advertising revenue.

Weeklies	
People	$1.3 billion
Sports Illustrated	1.0 billion
Time	1.0 billion
TV Guide	917.6 million
Newsweek	662.4 million
BusinessWeek	430.0 million
Monthlies	
Better Homes & Gardens	588.0 million
Reader's Digest	556.3 million
Good Housekeeping	543.6 million
Cosmopolitan	472.8 million
Woman's Day	449.8 million
Newspaper Supplements	
Parade	616.1 million
USA Weekend	416.3 million
Biweeklies	
Rolling Stone	241.6 million
Bimonthlies	
AARP	200.4 million

you pay for them directly. They are included with the paper.

Women's Magazines

The first U.S. magazine edited to interest only a portion of the mass audience, but otherwise to be of general interest, was *Ladies' Magazine,* which later became *Godey's Lady's Book.* **Sara Josepha Hale** helped start the magazine in 1828 to uplift and glorify womanhood. Its advice on fashions, morals, taste, sewing and cooking developed a following, which peaked with a circulation of 150,000 in 1860.

The *Godey's* tradition is maintained today in the competing magazines *Better Homes & Gardens, Family Circle, Good Housekeeping, Ladies' Home Journal, Redbook, Woman's Day* and the erstwhile *Rosie* (née *McCall's*). While each sister can be distinguished from her siblings, there is a thematic connection: concern for home, family and high-quality living from a traditional woman's perspective.

These traditional women's magazines are sometimes called the **Seven Sisters.** An eighth sister is *Cosmopolitan,* although it may more aptly be called a distant cousin. Under Helen Gurley Brown and later Bonnie Fuller, *Cosmopolitan* has geared itself to a subcategory of women readers: young, unmarried and working. It's the most successful in a large group of women's magazines seeking narrow groups. Among them are *Elle,* focusing on fashion, and *Essence,* for black women. The teen girl market, dominated by *Seventeen* and *YM,* has become crowded with Little Sister spinoffs *Cosmogirl,* the leading newcomer with 1.1 million circulation in 2004, *ElleGirl* and *Teen Vogue.*

Men's Magazines

Founded in 1933, ***Esquire*** was the first classy men's magazine. It was as famous for its pinups as for its literary content, which over the years has included articles from Ernest Hemingway, Hunter S. Thompson and P. J. O'Rourke. Fashion has also been a cornerstone in the *Esquire* content mix.

Hugh Hefner learned about magazines as an *Esquire* staff member, and he applied those lessons when he created ***Playboy*** in 1953. With its lustier tone, *Playboy* quickly overtook *Esquire* in circulation. At its peak *Playboy* sold 7 million copies a month. The magazine emphasized female nudity but also carried journalistic and literary pieces whose merit attracted many readers. Readers who were embarrassed by their carnal curiosity could claim that they bought the magazine for its articles. Critics sniped, however, that *Playboy* published the worst stuff of the best writers. Sociologists credit Hefner with both capitalizing on the post-World War II sexual revolution and fanning it. By 2004, however, *Playboy* seemed tired. Circulation was down to 3.2 million. The publisher of

Sara Josepha Hale ■ Founded first women's magazine.

Seven Sisters ■ Leading women's magazines.

Esquire ■ First classy men's magazine.

Playboy ■ Widely imitated girlie/lifestyle men's magazine.

mediaPEOPLE

Sara Josepha Hale

Sara Hale, widowed with five children, decided to write a novel to put the kids through college. *Northwood,* published in 1826, was one of the first books with America as its setting. The book attracted national attention, and all kinds of literary offers came Hale's way. She decided on the editorship of the new Boston-based *Ladies' Magazine.* Although some magazines of the time had women's sections, no previous magazine had wholly devoted itself to women's interests. Hale's innovations and sensitivities made the magazine and its successor a familiar sight in households throughout the nation for half a century. During her tenure Hale defined women's issues and in indirect ways contributed importantly to women's liberation.

Women's Magazine Pioneer Sara Josepha Hale edited the first magazine designed for women, but just as important was the distinctive content. Whereas many magazines recycled articles from other magazines, mostly from England, Hale prided herself on original content.

As editor of *Ladies' Magazine,* Hale departed from the frothy romance fiction and fashion coverage in the women's sections of other magazines. Her focus was on improving women's role in society. She campaigned vigorously for educational opportunities for women. When Matthew Vassar was setting up a women's college, she persuaded him to include women on the faculty—a novel idea for the time.

No fashion plate, Sara Hale encouraged women to dress comfortably yet attractively—no frills. For herself she preferred black for almost all occasions. When the owners of the magazine thought enthusiastic fashion coverage would boost circulation—and advertising—she went along, but in her own way. She pointed out how impractical and ridiculous the latest fashions were, and some she dismissed as trivial diversions.

Unlike other magazine editors of the time, she disdained reprinting articles from other publications. Hence, *Ladies' Magazine* created opportunities for new writers, particularly women, and enriched the nation's literary output. One issue, in 1843, was produced entirely by women. In her heyday, from the mid-1830s through the 1840s, Hale attracted the best writers to her pages: Ralph Waldo Emerson, Nathaniel Hawthorne, Oliver Wendell Holmes, Washington Irving, Henry Wadsworth Longfellow, Edgar Allan Poe, Harriet Beecher Stowe.

Hale edited *Ladies' Magazine* from 1828 until 1837, when it was merged into the weaker *Godey's Lady's Book.* She moved to Philadelphia to become editor of the new magazine, which retained the *Godey* title. Circulation reached 150,000 in 1860.

copycat *Penthouse* was in bankruptcy. Meanwhile, upstarts like *Maxim* at 2.5 million, *FHM* at 1.1 million and *Stuff* at 676,000 were in an ascendancy despite critics who objected to their raciness. Responding to critics, some retail outlets, notably giant retailer Wal-Mart, ceased stocking some men's titles as well as some women's magazines with provocative covers.

Not all men's magazines dwell on sex. The outdoor life is exalted in *Field & Stream,* whose circulation tops 2 million. Fix-it magazines, led by *Popular Science* and *Popular Mechanics,* have a steady following.

Non-Newsrack Magazines

studypreview **Many organizations publish magazines for their members. Although these sponsored magazines, including *National Geographic, AARP The Magazine* and *Smithsonian,* resemble consumer magazines, they generally are not available at newsracks. In fact, consumer magazines are far outnumbered by sponsored magazines and by trade journals.**

mediaPEOPLE

Bella Price

Herself a mother of four, Bella Price might seem to be a typical Wal-Mart shopper. Well, yes and no. Price is editor of a Time Inc. weekly, *All You,* a women's title, launched in 2004 for sale exclusively at Wal-Mart's 3,100-plus stores. The creation of a one-outlet, nonsubscription magazine was an innovation that was closely watched, then imitated, by competing publishers. American Media, publisher of *Star,* launched its own Wal-Mart title, *Looking Good Now,* in 2005. Hachette Filipacchi created newsstand-only *For Me.*

Bella Price's formula for *All You* was no accidental magic. Time research had identified an unserved audience niche: everyday budget-conscious young mothers who didn't relate easily to the svelte models, designer clothes and $100,000 kitchens of haughty women's magazines. Price fitted models of all shapes with clothes you would find at Wal-Mart and Sears. Her recipes included the cost per serving. How-to items included the mundane. About a piece on how to unblock a toilet, Price told a *Business Week* interviewer: "Even if they have a man around, chances are he's not doing it for them." Price's *All You* had a

Wal-Mart Woman Always scouting for a narrow audience niche to pitch a new magazine, Time Inc. identified an obviously underserved but gigantic audience for which it designed *All You.* The magazine was aimed at women Wal-Mart shoppers. Editor Bella Price focused on issues as pertinent to ordinary people as hanging a derailed closet door and economizing with meal preparation. Available only at Wal-Marts, and at a Wal-Mart price, $1.47 a copy, *All You* quickly was selling 500,000 copies a week.

Bella Price

commonness geared to price-conscious women who dominated the high-traffic Wal-Marts, about 138 million people a week.

In many ways, the *All You* formula made sense. Magazine industry scholar Samir Husni estimated the startup costs at $25 million, about half the average, because Time Inc. needed no costly campaign to lure subscribers. Further, no distributors took a cut. Time ships *All You* directly to Wal-Marts. Some cost savings were passed on to customers with a Wal-Mart-type cover price: $1.47, less than a third of competing women's titles.

Early *All You* issues sold 500,000 copies, not bad for a startup. More important to Time's bottom line, issues soon were bulging with 70 pages of advertising, exceeding projections by 30 percent.

media ONLINE **All You** Online companion to the affordable magazine for value-conscience women. **www.allyou.com**

Sponsored Magazines

The founders of the National Geographic Society decided in 1888 to put out a magazine to promote the society and build membership. The idea was to entice people to join by bundling a subscription with membership and then to use the dues to finance the society's research and expeditions. Within a few years the *National Geographic* had become a phenomenal success both in generating membership and as a profit center for the National Geographic Society. Today, more than 100 years old and with U.S. circulation at 6.7 million, the *Geographic* is the most widely recognized **sponsored magazine** in the nation. Other sponsored magazines include *AARP The Magazine,* published by the American Association of Retired Persons for its members. Its circulation exceeds 20 million. Other major membership magazines include *Smithsonian,* published by the Smithsonian Institute; *VFW,* by the Veterans of Foreign Wars; *American Legion,* and *Elks,* by the Elks lodge.

sponsored magazine ■ Generally non-newsrack magazine, often member supported.

Many sponsored magazines carry advertising and are financially self-sufficient. In fact, the most successful sponsored magazines compete aggressively with consumer magazines for advertising. It is not unusual for an issue of *Smithsonian* to carry 100 pages of advertising.

While advertising has made some sponsored magazines into profit centers for their parent organizations, others come nowhere near breaking even. Typical is *Quill,* which the Society of Professional Journalists publishes as an organizational expense for the good of its membership. The society seeks advertising for *Quill,* but the magazine's relatively small readership has never attracted as much volume or the same types of advertising as the *National Geographic,* the *Smithsonian* or *AARP The Magazine.*

Many sponsored magazines do not seek advertising. These include many university magazines, which are considered something that a university should publish as an institutional expense to disseminate information about research and scholarly activities and, not incidentally, to promote itself. Other sponsored magazines that typically do not carry advertising include publications for union members, in-house publications for employees and company publications for customers. These publications do not have the public recognition of consumer magazines, but many are as slick and professional as consumer magazines. Altogether, they employ far more editors, photographers and writers than consumer magazines do.

Trade Journals

Every profession or trade has at least one magazine, or **trade journal,** for keeping abreast of what is happening in the field. In entertainment *Billboard* provides solid journalistic coverage on a broad range of subjects in music: new recording releases, new acts, new technology and new merger deals. *Billboard* is essential reading for people in the music industry. About 4,000 trade journals cover a mind-boggling range of businesses and trades. Consider the diversity in these titles: *Rock and Dirt, Progressive Grocer, Plastics Technology, Hogs Today* and *Hardware Age.*

Like consumer magazines, the trades rely mostly on advertising for their income and profits. Some charge for subscriptions, but many are sent free to a carefully assembled list of readers whom advertisers want to reach.

Many trade magazines are parts of companies that produce related publications, some with overlapping staffs. McGraw-Hill, the book publisher, produces more than 30 trade journals, including *Chemical Week* and *Modern Hospital.* Another trade magazine company is Crain Communications, whose titles include *Advertising Age, AutoWeek, Electronic Media* and two dozen others.

Criticism of Trade Magazines

Many trade magazine companies, including McGraw-Hill and Crain, are recognized for honest, hard-hitting reporting of the industries they cover, but the trades have a mixed reputation. Some trade magazines are loaded with puffery exalting their advertisers and industries. For years, *Body Fashions,* formerly *Corset and Underwear Review,* unabashedly presented ads as news stories. As many trade journals do, it charged companies to run stories about them and covered only companies that were also advertisers. At some trades, the employees who solicit ads write news stories to echo the ads. These trades tend to be no more than boosters of the industries they pretend to cover. Kent MacDougall, writing in the *Wall Street Journal,* offered this especially egregious example: *America's Textile Reporter,* which promoted the textile industry from a management perspective, once dismissed the hazard of textile workers' contracting brown lung disease by inhaling cotton dust as "a thing brought up by venal doctors" at an international labor meeting in Africa, "where inferior races are bound to be afflicted by new diseases more superior people defeated years ago." At the time, in 1972, 100,000 U.S. textiles workers were afflicted with brown lung. Many trade magazines persist today in pandering to their trades, professions and industries rather than approaching their subjects with journalistic truth-seeking and truth-telling.

Responsible trade journals are embarrassed by some of their brethren, many of which are upstarts put out by people with no journalistic experience or instincts. Because of this, and also because it takes relatively little capital to start a trade magazine, many bad trade magazines thrive. Several professional organizations, including the American

trade journal ■ Keeps members of profession, trade informed.

Business Press and the Society of Business Press Editors, work to improve both their industry and its image. Even so, as former ABP President Charles Mill said, trades continue to be plagued "by fleabag outfits published in somebody's garage."

Newsletters

Even more focused than trade journals are subscription newsletters, a billion-dollar industry. These newsletters are expensive, generally $600 to $1,000 a year, with some as much as $5,000. Why do people pay that much? Where else could Chamber of Commerce executives find the information that's in *Downtown Promotion Reporter?* And no other publication duplicates what's in *Food Chemical News, Beverage Digest* and *Inside Mortgage Finance.* John Farley, vice president of the largest newsletter company, Phillips Publishing, contends that newsletters are the purest form of journalism because they carry little or no advertising: "We're answerable to no one but our subscribers."

Kiplinger Covering personal finance and business forecasts, Kiplinger has been doling out trusted advice for eight decades.
www.kiplinger.com

The first newsletter, launched in 1923, was a weekly update on government news for businesspeople called *Kiplinger Washington Newsletter.* It is still published. Today, more than 5,000 subscription newsletters are published in the United States. A few are daily, such as *Communication Daily,* which covers federal news on electronic media regulation. Not all are print products alone. *Subtext,* which tracks the book industry, puts out a Monday-morning e-mail update to keep subscribers abreast of developments between its biweekly mailed edition. Some newsletters now have subscription web sites.

Magazine Demassification

studypreview **Giant mass-audience magazines, led by *Life,* were major influences in their heyday, but television killed them off by offering larger audiences to advertisers. Today, the magazine industry thrives through demassification, the process of seeking audiences with narrow interests. Critics believe that demassification has changed the role of magazines in society for the worse.**

Heyday of Mass Magazines

Magazines once were epitomized by *Life.* Henry Luce used the fortune he amassed from *Time* to launch *Life* in 1936. The magazine exceeded Luce's expectations. He had planned on an initial circulation of 250,000, but almost right away it was 500,000. *Life* was perfect for its time. At 10 cents a copy, *Life* was within the reach of almost everyone, even during the Great Depression. It had high quality—fiction from the best authors of the day. It had daring—flamboyant photography that seemed to jump off its oversize pages. The term *photo essay* was a *Life* creation.

Imitators followed. *Look,* introduced in 1937, was a knockoff in the same oversize dimension as *Life.* The historic *Saturday Evening Post* and *Collier's* were revamped as oversize magazines.

Assault from Television

The oversize mass-audience magazines do not exist today—at least not as they did in the old days. *Collier's,* bankrupt, published its final issue in 1956. Hemorrhaging money despite a circulation of 4 million, *Saturday Evening Post* ceased publication in 1969. In 1971 *Look* died. *Life* was not able to capitalize on the fact that it suddenly had less competition, and it went out of business the next year. It had lost $30 million over the previous three years. What had happened to the high-flying, oversize, mass-audience magazines? In a single word: television.

Seeing the News Henry Luce's *Life* magazine pioneered photojournalism, beginning with Margaret Bourke-White's haunting shadows of the giant new Fort Peck Dam in Montana for the inaugural issue. When World War II came, *Life* dispatched Bourke-White and other photographers to capture the story, even the horrific details. With people eager for war news, circulation soared.

At its peak, *Life* had a circulation of 8.5 million, but in the 1950s the television networks had begun to deliver even bigger audiences to advertisers. The villain for the giant magazines was not merely television's audience size, but **CPM**—advertising jargon for cost per 1,000 readers, listeners or viewers (the *M* standing for the Roman numeral for 1,000). In 1970 a full-page advertisement in *Life* ran $65,000. For less money an advertiser could have one minute of network television and reach far more potential customers. CPM-conscious advertising agencies could not conscientiously recommend *Life*'s $7.75 CPM when the networks' CPM was $3.60, and advertisers shifted to television.

A Narrower Focus

With the demise of *Life,* doomsayers predicted that magazines were a dying breed of media. However, advertisers withdrew only from magazines with broad readerships. What they discovered was that although it was less expensive to use television to peddle universally used products such as detergents, grooming aids and packaged foods, television, geared at the time for mass audiences, was too expensive for products appealing to narrow groups. Today, relatively few magazines seek a truly mass audience. These include *Reader's Digest* and the Sunday magazine supplements.

Special-interest magazines, whose content focused on limited subjects and whose advertising rates were lower, fit the bill better than either television or the giant mass-audience magazines for reaching customers with special interests. For manufacturers of $7,000 stereo systems, for example, it made sense to advertise in a narrowly focused audiophile magazine such as *Stereo Review.* In the same way, neither mass-audience magazines nor television was a medium of choice for top-of-the-line racing skis, but ski magazines were ideal. For fancy cookware, *Food & Wine* made sense.

Among new magazines that emerged with the demassification in the 1960s were regional and city magazines, offering a geographically defined audience to advertisers. Some of these magazines, which usually bore the name of their city or region, including *New York, Texas Monthly* and *Washingtonian,* offered hard-hitting journalistic coverage of local issues. Many, though, focused on soft lifestyle subjects rather than antagonizing

CPM ■ Cost per thousand.

Magazine Demassification

Advertisers favor magazines that are edited to specific audience interests that coincide with the advertisers' products. Fewer and fewer magazines geared to a general audience remain in business today.

Calvin and Hobbes **by Bill Watterson**

powerful local interests and risking the loss of advertisers. Indeed, hypersensitivity to advertisers is a criticism of today's demassified magazines.

Critics of Demassification

Norman Cousins, once editor of the highbrow *Saturday Review,* criticized demassified magazines for betraying their traditional role of enriching the culture. Cousins said that specialization had diluted the intellectual role of magazines in the society. Advertisers, he said, were shaping magazines' journalistic content for their commercial purposes—in contrast to magazine editors independently deciding content with loftier purposes in mind.

Scholar Dennis Holder put this "unholy alliance" of advertisers and readers this way: "The readers see themselves as members of small, and in some sense, elite groups—joggers, for example, or cat lovers—and they want to be told that they are terribly neat people for being in those groups. Advertisers, of course, want to reinforce the so-called positive self-image too, because joggers who feel good about themselves tend to buy those ridiculous suits and cat lovers who believe lavishing affection on their felines is a sign of warmth and sincerity are the ones who purchase cute little cat sweaters, or are they cat's pajamas." Magazine editors and writers, Holder said, are caught in the symbiotic advertiser-reader alliance and have no choice but to go along.

Norman Cousins and Dennis Holder were right that most consumer magazines today tend to a frothy mix of light, upbeat features, with little that is thoughtful or hard-hitting. However, most readers want to know about other people, particularly celebrities, and about a great many trendy topics. And advertisers want to reach those readers, preferably by steering clear of any controversial magazine coverage that might hurt sales. So profitability for most magazines and their advertisers is locked into providing information their target audiences are interested in rather than serving an indefinable "public interest," which might sometimes be controversial. The emphasis on profits and demassification saddens a number of people who believe that magazines have a higher calling than a cash register. These critics would agree with Cousins, who warned that emphasizing the superficial just because it sells magazines is a betrayal of the social trust that magazine publishers once held. "The purpose of a magazine," he said, "is not to tell you how to fix a leaky faucet, but to tell you what the world is about."

There is no question that demassification works against giving readers any kind of global view. In demassified magazines for auto enthusiasts, as an example, road test articles typically wax as enthusiastically as the advertisements about new cars. These demassified magazines, edited to target selected audiences and thereby attract advertisers, make no pretense of broadening their readers' understanding of substantive issues by exploring diverse perspectives. The narrowing of magazine editorial content appears destined to continue, not only because it is profitable but also because new technologies, such as Time Warner's geodemographic TargetSelect program, make it possible for magazine publishers to identify narrower and narrower segments of the mass audience and then to gear their publications to those narrower and narrower interests.

mediaPEOPLE

Myles Kovacs

In magazine parlance, a hot book is the rising darling of the moment among advertisers. Today it's the automobile-celebrity title *DUB* that has become a lifestyle-defining magazine from the car-crazed southern California urban ghetto. Automaker DaimlerChrysler credits the runaway success of its Chrysler 300 to Myles Kovacs, who created *DUB* at age 25 and who placed the hunky Chrysler sedan in a 50 Cent video and in the magazine.

A car in *DUB* has "street cred," as one Chrysler marketing executive put it. So does Kovacs, who lectures Detroit automakers and other big-league advertisers on reaching the huge urban market. Don't create ghetto imagery around products, he says. Successful products today are about aspiration. Put the products in the Hamptons but, in the case of automobiles, with rims and other urban culture cues.

Next Chrysler entrusted promoting its Dodge Charger to Kovacs. He sports a fiery-red model around East L. A., with 20-inch rims, no less.

Himself multicultural, Myles Kovacs should know whereof he speaks. His lineage is Japanese and Hungarian, but he grew up in a tough Latino 'hood in Los Angeles and is fluent in Spanish. He also knows cars.

In high school Kovacs ran errands at a shop where the rapper Tupac Shakur rimmed his cars. Kovacs eventually designed his own line of rims, which had a with-it cachet.

Kovacs' epiphany for *DUB* came when he was 24 and, while learning the magazine business at an entertainment title, saw a Mercedes owned by country singer Alan Jackson auctioned for an astronomical sum. It all came together. With a couple of buddies he launched *DUB* as a melding of celebrities and automobiles.

Unlike *Motor Trend* and other auto magazines, *DUB* carries no comparison drives or commentary. It's wholly worshipful and uncritical. When Kobe Bryant and Mike Tyson appeared on covers—with cars, of course—the magazine made no mention of their highly publicized legal difficulties.

And the title *DUB?* It's a takeoff of the term for a double-dime bag of pot, which gives the magazine an edginess that ties urban street culture to the ghetto culture of aspiration that Kovacs preaches. He sees no irony in his baggy jeans and $14,0000 diamond-studded watch and a $50,000 Chrysler 300 SRT-8.

The magazine is not only an icon of the currently influential urban street-life culture. Kovacs is building an empire, valued at $50 million in 2005, around the magazine—MTV specials, Midnight Club video games, toys, concerts, car shows, and, yes, rims.

New Competition

An ominous sign for magazines is the cable television industry, which is eating into magazine advertising with an array of demassified channels, such as the ESPN sports channel, the Arts & Entertainment network and the Bloomberg financial news network. The demassified cable channels are picking up advertisers that once used magazines almost exclusively to reach narrow slices of the mass audience with a presumed interest in their products and services.

Another drain on magazine revenue is the growth of direct-mail advertising. Using sophisticated analysis of potential customer groups, advertisers can mail brochures, catalogs, fliers and other material, including video pitches, directly to potential customers at their homes or places of business. Every dollar that goes into direct-mail campaigns is a dollar that in an earlier period went into magazines and other traditional advertising media.

media ONLINE **DUB** What does your car say about you? What are celebrities driving? Check out the "original automotive lifestyles magazine." **www.dubpublishing.com**

Internet Magazines

Consumer and trade magazines adapted quickly to digital delivery in the late 1990s with Internet editions. Time Warner created a massive web site, Pathfinder, for *Time, Sports Illustrated, People* and its other magazines. With substantial original content, Pathfinder wasn't merely an online version of Time Warner magazines but a distinctive product. There were hopes that advertisers would flock to online magazine sites and make them profitable, but ad revenue only trickled in. In 1998 Pathfinder went to subscriptions to

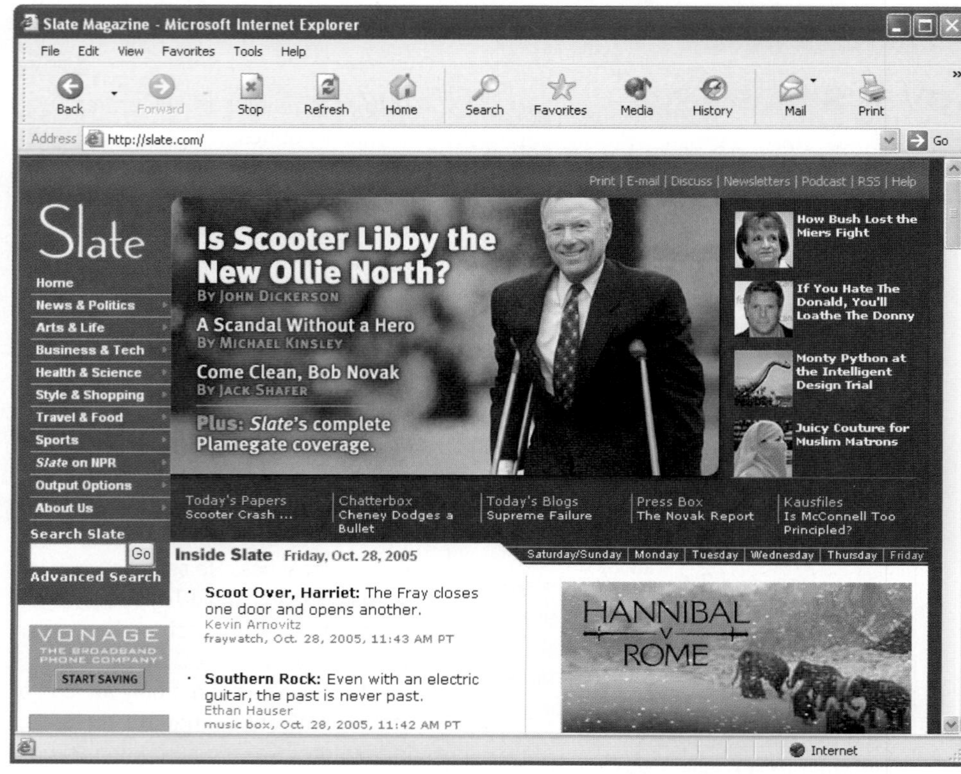

Zine The giant software developer Microsoft moved into developing media content in the 1990s with, among other things, the online magazine *Slate.* To edit the magazine, Microsoft hired Michael Kinsley, known for his commentaries on CNN and his editorship of the political and cultural journal *New Republic.* Kinsley attracted a stable of prestigious, clever writers for the site.

Slate This strictly online magazine covers culture and politics.
www.slate.com

supplement the meager advertising revenues. An access code was issued to *Entertainment Weekly* subscribers for an extra $30 a year. For the *Money* site the fare was $30 to subscribers and $50 to everybody else. All in all, the Pathfinder exercise was not a success.

Microsoft attempted to turn its esoteric, pop *Slate* from a free site to a subscription magazine, but lack of interest on the part of web surfers and competition from free sites forced Microsoft to make *Slate* free again. Time Warner also gave up on Internet subscriptions, made Pathfinder free and set up individual sites for its brand-name magazines. Meanwhile, the number of free web sites offering magazine-type content continues to grow. The proliferation includes thousands of hand-crafted *zines,* as they're called, on the web.

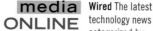

Wired The latest technology news categorized by culture, business and politics.
www.wired.com

New Republic You heard it here first. The New Republic prides itself on reporting political news before it hits the mainstream.
www.tnr.com

Maxim Online version of the popular magazine, complete with entertainment, fashion and loads of photos.
www.maximonline.com

Folio Check out the magazine designed to serve top management in the magazine publishing industry.
www.foliomag.com

study preview **Circulation and advertising revenue are measures of a magazine's populist success. More difficult is finding magazines that regularly fulfill their potential to examine significant issues and make an enduring contribution to a better society.**

Populist Measures

Measures of commercial success in the magazine industry are easy to find. Circulation is one measure. *Parade, USA Weekend, AARP The Magazine* and *Reader's Digest* all score well by that measure. Even more telling as a populist gauge of success is advertising revenue. Advertisers use all kinds of sophisticated research and analysis to determine where their ad dollars are most effectively spent. *People* draws more advertising revenue than any other magazine, $1.3 billion a year—30 percent ahead of *Sports Illustrated,* the distant second.

Total ad pages are another measure. *People* led with 3,705 in 2004, followed by the *New York Times Magazine* at 3,363.

Quality Measures

Critics say that commercial measures recognize magazines that pander to consumerism. Certainly, many magazines today work hard at being magnets for audience niches and for advertisers that seek access to those niches. *Better Homes & Gardens,* for example, offers a lot of predictable content on homemaking that a certain segment of consumers want, and advertisers are lined up to place ads in the magazines to reach those consumers. But is *BH&G* a magazine that makes people think? Or that offers insights into fundamental issues of human existence? Or that contributes to a better world in a broad and enduring sense? Elitists would fault it on all those scores. *Better Homes & Gardens* may be immensely popular and make a lot of money, but, say elitists, it fails at realizing its potential to improve society.

What, then, are measures of excellence that would meet the standards of elitists? Cerebral magazines with long records of commentary and analysis, often in the vanguard of thinking on enduring issues, include *Harper's* and the *Atlantic*. Sometimes called **highbrow slicks,** these magazines steer an editorial course that's not beholden to narrow consumer niches or advertisers. The focus is on social, economic, political and artistic and cultural issues, often analyzed at great length by leading authorities. It should be no surprise that Vannevar Bush's thoughts on possibilities for a worldwide web appeared in the *Atlantic* in 1945—almost 50 years ahead of Tim Berners-Lee's invention of the web. The *New Yorker,* a weekly, prides itself on regularly breaking ground on significant issues in articles that run as long as the editors think is necessary, sometimes the length of a small book.

highbrow slicks ■ Cerebral magazines, edited for the intelligentsia.

Outside of highbrow slicks, significant articles sprout occasionally in commercially oriented magazines. *Time* and *Newsweek* excerpt important new books from time to time. *Wired,* which focuses on future issues, gives cutting-edge thinkers all the space they need to explore their thoughts. Serious journalism appears occasionally in *Esquire, Outside* and other magazines amid all the advertiser-friendly pap but hardly as a staple.

The ideological magazines, like *New Republic, National Review* and *Nation,* frequently are cerebral, but partisanship often clouds their focus.

At another extreme is self-conscious trendiness that doesn't take readers beyond momentary amusement. The gag-oriented *Maxim* and other hip titles that revel in quick cutesiness don't score well with elitists, who look for substance. This is hardly to say that elitists are humorless, but titles that pander to reader self-indulgence without any literary or broader social significance don't score.

Elitists also caution against pseudo-seriousness. Commentator Simon Dumenco, writing in the magazine trade journal *Folio,* cautioned against shallowness masquerading as avant-garde journalism. He cited editors "who dream up 'trend pieces' (more and more women are dating younger guys! more and more women are dating older guys!), commission writers to prove their suppositions." Beware too, Dumenco says, of articles that don't really say much, especially in stage-managed celebrity coverage: "A two-hour lunch, a quick scan of existing clips, a few phone calls to obsequious friends of the celebrity in question, and voilá—you've got a 3,000-word profile."

In short, it's hard to find magazines that consistently meet elitists' standards. The National Magazine Awards, granted by the American Society of Magazine Editors, recognize broad categories of excellence. The trade journal *Folio* sponsors the Ozzie awards for design and the Eddie awards for editorial excellence. Even so, elitists say awards don't address the kinds of measures they prefer. A design award, for example, doesn't mean editorial excellence. An award-winning article in a particular magazine may reflect more on the author than on the magazine as an overall product. In magazines honored for editorial

Eustace Tilley

The *New Yorker* remembers its origins with an annual anniversary cover featuring Eustace Tilley, a character created by Rea Irvin to capture the sophistication of the magazine on its first cover in 1925. The *New Yorker* remains an intelligent, witty and often irreverent weekly whose substantive coverage of political, social, cultural and other issues has maintained its respect among devoted readers.

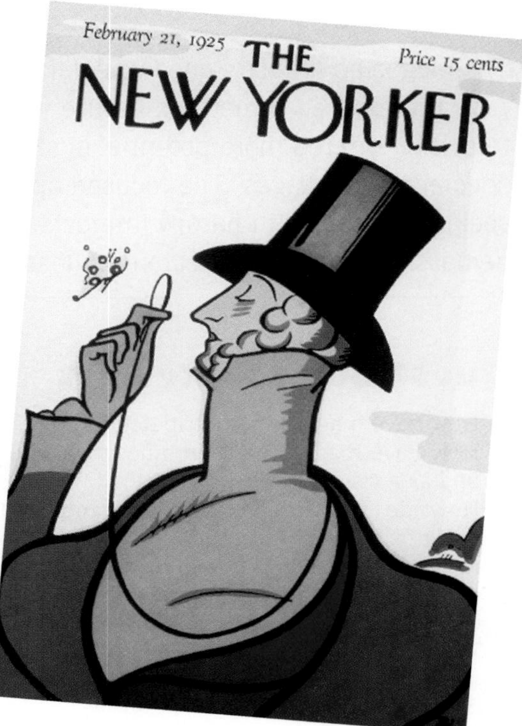

excellence, there may be individual articles that merit a trip to the library or a subscription, but not all measure up. The awards are an imperfect signal of quality.

Reader Usage Measure

A new way of gauging magazine quality, the **Reader Usage Measure,** or **RUM,** was created in 2003 by the magazine industry and Northwestern University media researchers. Thirty-nine statements are put to readers in carefully controlled surveys to ascertain positive and negative reactions. The statements are direct. Answering Yes to these statements contributes to a strong RUM score:

- I get value for my time and money.
- It makes me smarter.
- I often reflect on it.

Conversely, answering Yes to the following statements lowers the RUM score:

- It disappoints me.
- I dislike some of the ads.
- It leaves me feeling bad.

Ellen Oppenheim, a marketing executive with the Magazine Publishers Association, said RUM data provide "a quantitative measure of qualitative information" that transcends circulation, ad pages and ad revenue—all of which are advertising-rooted measures. RUM is a reader-rooted measure that points to a magazine's connectedness to its audience.

The first RUM study included 4,347 readers of 100 leading magazines, which was a large enough sample to provide demographic breakdowns. Black readers, for example, wanted magazines about which they could say, "It touched me" and "It grabbed me visually." Generation Y women, who came of age in the 1990s, gravitate to magazines that help them share experiences. Historically, the great magazines have been edited by people with an intuitive sense for their audiences. With RUM there is concrete information to supplement instinctive knowledge about what attracts an audience.

Reader Usage Measure (RUM) A tool developed by the magazine industry to score reader experience as a guide for designing magazines conceptually and for editing content.

CHAPTER 4 Wrap-Up

The magazine industry once was defined by giant general interest magazines, epitomized by *Life,* that offered something for everybody. Advertisers soured on these oversized giants when television offered more potential customers per advertising dollar. Magazines shifted to more specialized packages. The focused approach worked. Magazines found advertisers who were seeking readers with narrow interests. Now, as other media—particularly television—are demassifying, magazines stand to lose advertisers, which poses new challenges.

Questions for Review

1. How have magazines contributed to U.S. culture?
2. How have magazines been innovative as a journalistic and as a visual medium?
3. How do sponsored magazines and trade journals differ from the consumer magazines available at newsracks?
4. Why are most magazines edited for the special interests of targeted audiences?
5. What is the status of demassification in the magazine industry?
6. Are magazines losing their influence as a shaper of the culture? Explain your answer.
7. Why do elitists criticize magazines that are edited for niches of consumers?

Questions for Critical Thinking

1. What characteristics do these magazine founders have in common: Sara Josepha Hale, Hugh Heffner, Henry Luce, Harold Ross, and DeWitt and Lila Wallace?

2. When U.S. magazines came into their own in the 1820s, they represented a mass medium that was distinct from the existing book and newspaper media. How were magazines different?
3. How was the U.S. identity that emerged in the 19th century fostered by magazines?
4. To some people, the word *muckraking* has a negative tone. Can you make the case that it should be regarded positively? Can you also argue the opposite?
5. Discuss the role of these innovators in contributing to magazines as a visual medium: Gilbert Grosvenor, Margaret Bourke-White and Henry Luce.
6. Can you name at least three consumer magazines in each of these categories: newsmagazines, the Seven Sisters, men's magazines?
7. The late Norman Cousins, a veteran social commentator and magazine editor, worried that trends in the magazine industry were undermining the historic role that magazines have had in enriching the culture. What is your response to Cousins' concerns?
8. Name three magazines of which elitists would approve and explain why.

Deepening Your media LITERACY

Should magazines try for universal appeal, or is it better to have a smaller, specialized audience?

STEP 1 Make a list of characteristics you think make a trade magazine successful. Imagine that you are the publisher of a trade magazine. Write down three things you would tell your editor to do to make the magazine successful. Now think about consumer magazines and make the same lists.

Dig Deeper

STEP 2 Pick a trade magazine and a consumer magazine and make notes on the following characteristics:

1. If you are working with a printed magazine, approximately what percentage of the pages are advertising? If it is an online magazine, count the number of ads.
2. How many stories are in this issue? How long are they? How many are about controversial subjects?
3. How many photos or illustrations are there?
4. What are the demographics of the audience targeted by the style of the writing, the layout and the advertising? Do there seem to be any ties between advertising and the stories?
5. What else do you see that sets this magazine apart?

What Do You Think?

STEP 3 Compare the lists of attributes of a trade magazine and a consumer magazine that you made in Step 2. How do they compare to your ideas in Step 1? Does one of the magazines you looked at do a better job than the others of appealing to its audience? If so, why? Does this correlate with how well a magazine reaches its readers? Do you think it is better to choose to serve a bigger audience or a smaller one?

Keeping Up to Date

Folio is a trade journal on magazine management. Among major newspapers that track magazine issues in a fairly consistent way are the New York *Times*, the *Wall Street Journal* and *USA Today*.

For Further Learning

Myrna Blyth. *Spin Sisters.* St. Martin's, 2005.
Blyth, a former *Ladies Home Journal* editor, criticizes women's service magazines for forsaking their traditional role. Now, she says, they offer a steady diet of shallow content.

Iain Calder. *The Untold Story: My 20 Years Running the National Enquirer.* Miramax, 2004.
Calder, after 23 years at the helm, takes pride in having created a system of inside sources in the entertainment industry that cemented the *Enquirer's* reputation for scoops. Calder celebrates the *Enquirer's* research and enterprise and counters the general notion that the paper plays loose with facts.

Hunter S. Thompson. *Fear and Loathing in America: The Brutal Odyssey of an Outlaw Journalism 1968–1976.* Simon & Schuster, 2000.
The original gonzo journalist offers a collection of letters from his experience interviewing political leaders and pursuing truth in his own distinctive way.

Gregory Curtis. "The End of the Trail," *Brill's Content* (November 2000), pages 76–80.
Curtis recounts his 19 years as editor of *Texas Monthly*, one of the most successful regional magazines of its era.

Jeannette Walls. *Dish: The Inside Story of World Gossip.* Avon/Spike, 2000.
Walls, once a gossip columnist herself, traces the history of gossip and its media of dissemination as far back as *Confidential* magazine in the 1950s.

Sammye Johnson and Patricia Projatel. *Magazine Publishing.* NTC, 2000.
This is an excellent introductory textbook with outstanding examples and illustrations.

Mary Ellen Zuckerman. *History of Popular Women's Magazines in the United States, 1792–1995.* Greenwood, 1999.
Professor Zuckerman reviews how business forces and other forces, including editors, shaped U.S. women's magazines through almost 200 years. They weren't always like this.

Katherine Rosman. "The Secret of Her Success," *Brill's Content* (November 1998), pages 102–111.
Rosman, an associate editor at *Brill's*, is unflattering in assessing the editorial tactics of Bonnie Fuller with her circulation successes at *Flare*, *YM*, *Marie Claire*, *Cosmopolitan* and *Glamour.*

D. M. Osborne. "Paying Respects" *Brill's Content* (October 1998), pages 93–95.
Osborne examines special commemorative issues put out by the entertainment trade magazines *Variety* and *Hollywood Reporter*, like an advertisement-rich issue to mark the 100th *Seinfeld* television show. Her conclusion: He who pays the piper calls the tune.

Shawn Fanning

The courts found his 1998 Napster music-downloading software violated the copyrights of the music owners. Nonetheless, Napster paved the way for other systems that facilitated free and inexpensive public access to music that transformed the music industry at the start of the 21st century.

chapter 5 Sound Recording

In this chapter your will learn:

- **Recorded music is omnipresent in our lives.**
- **The recording industry is dominated by four companies.**
- **Technology and performers have shaped the recording industry.**
- **Threats of censorship have been met by self-regulation.**
- **Technology has given performers new control over their recorded work.**
- **Apple's iPod and iTunes eased losses from download piracy.**
- **The recording industry can be evaluated by sales, profits, artistic risk and innovation.**

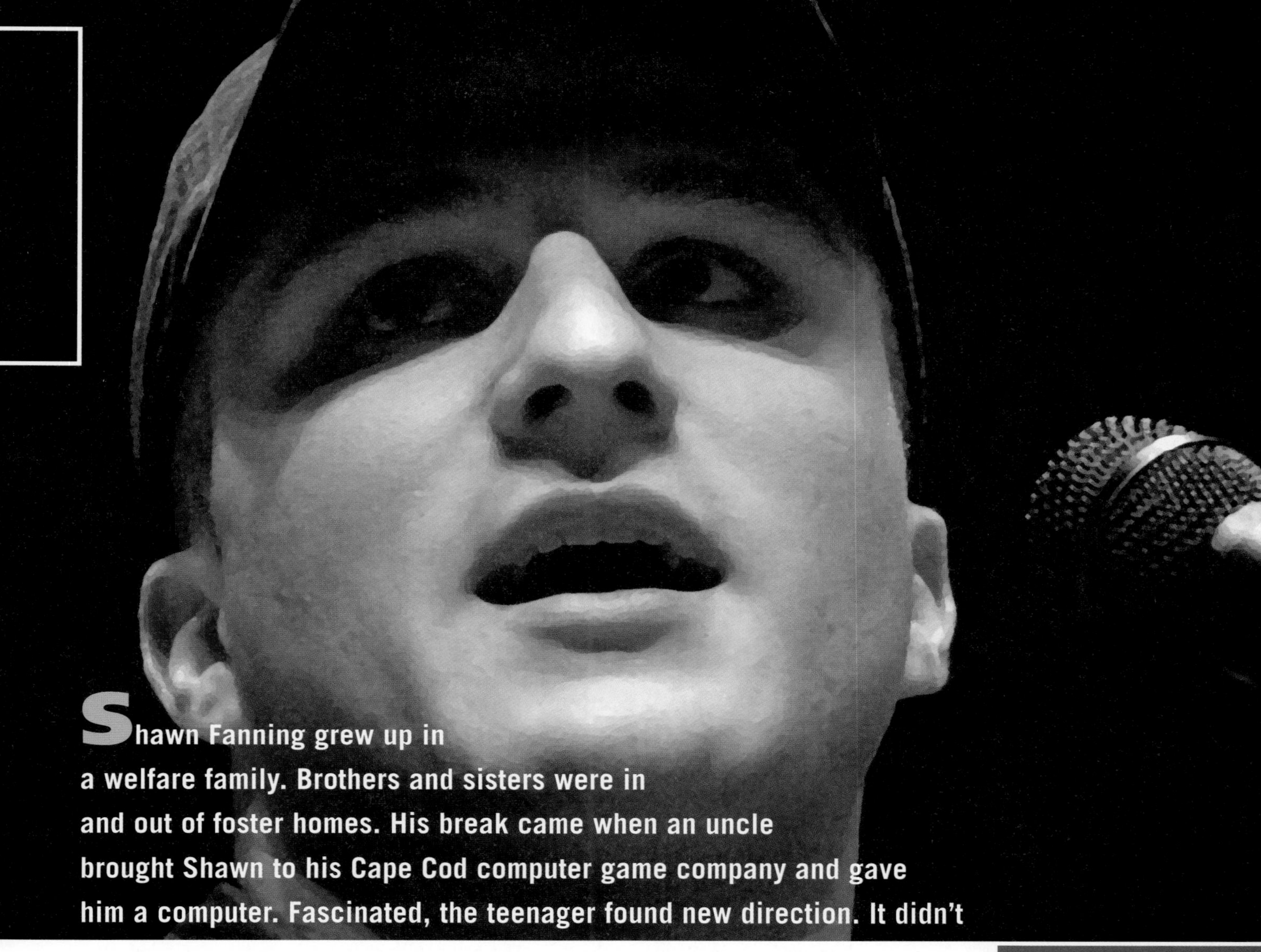

Shawn Fanning grew up in a welfare family. Brothers and sisters were in and out of foster homes. His break came when an uncle brought Shawn to his Cape Cod computer game company and gave him a computer. Fascinated, the teenager found new direction. It didn't make him rich, though. When it came time for college, Fanning, with only $80, could afford to apply to only two colleges.

His freshman year at Northeastern University in Boston was an academic disaster. Bored, Fanning partied his time away. One day, because of his roommates' complaints that they couldn't find the music they wanted to download from the Internet, Fanning decided to write a program to help. He obsessed about the project. He wrote code day and night until he had a system that would allow people to tap into each other's hard drives for MP3 downloads.

That was in 1998. The rest is history. Fanning dropped out of college, found a venture capitalist, moved to Silicon Valley and went into business. His program, called **Napster** after his childhood nickname, almost instantly attracted thousands of music fans, who began trading millions of songs online. Napster let it all happen automatically, listing every song that every participant had on a hard drive and enabling file swaps with the click of a mouse button.

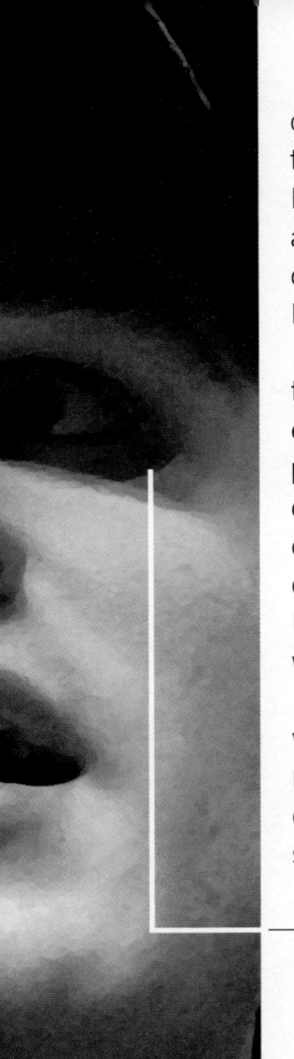

At age 19, to many, Shawn Fanning was a cyberhero. He was also the recording industry's worst nightmare. Record sales tumbled at campus-area record shops. Alarmed, the **Recording Industry Association of America** sued Fanning's company, charging that Napster enabled people to undermine the whole intellectual property legal apparatus that allowed music creators and owners to profit from their work. People, mostly college students, were acquiring music free, eliminating the economic incentive for composers and lyricists to create new works and for record companies to package and market them.

Fanning responded that Napster was nothing more than an electronic way for people to swap their favorite music—an age-old practice. The recording industry prevailed in federal court. Soon Napster was out of business. Still, other P2P software, short for **peer-to-peer sharing,** continued in operation. In one particularly bad week in 2005, CD sales were off 28 percent from a year earlier. The number of people in the United States who were on one or more file-sharing networks was 4.6 million. Meanwhile, the industry's attorneys continued pressing the courts to shut down all the P2P drain on their sales. In 2005 the U.S. Supreme Court spoke on the issue, in effect shutting down Grokster and other software operations that facilitated free downloading.

Even so, Shawn Fanning's impact has been indelible and enduring. His Napster innovation and its imitators prodded the record industry to rethink its retailing practices and move to online delivery of digitized music. Fanning, the college freshman who obsessed over computer code rather than going to classes, brought about a transformation of the shape of the record industry.

Influence of Sound Recordings

studypreview **Recorded music has become a pervasive element in our lives. It is everywhere almost all the time. The companies that dominate the music industry, despite revenue leakage to online music-swapping, are a major force in the global music business.**

media ONLINE **Napster** Check out the new Napster, which claims access to more than one million songs.
www.napster.com

Recording Industry Association of America Read the RIAA's policy statements on piracy and downloading, and find out about their other activities.
www.riaa.org

Pervasiveness of Music

When urban sophisticates in earlier eras wanted music, they arranged to attend a concert. Many middle-class people went to the parlor and sat at the piano. Rural folks had their music too—a fiddle on the front porch in the evening, a harmonica at the campfire. Music was a special event, something to be arranged. To those people, life today would seem like one big party—music everywhere all the time. Yes, we arrange for concerts and major musical events, but we also wake to music, shop to music and drive to music. Many of us work to music and study to music. In fact, the recording industry has products in so many parts of our lives that many people take most of them for granted.

Shawn Fanning ■ Inventor of Napster.

Napster ■ First online music-swapping software.

Recording Industry Association of America (RIAA) ■ Trade association of music recording companies.

peer-to-peer sharing (P2P) ■ Music-swapping software without a central server.

Scope of the Recording Industry

The recording industry that brings music to mass audiences, both the flashy stuff and everything else, is gigantic. Global sales in 2004 were estimated at $33.6 billion, with $12.9 billion in the United States alone. These totals don't include symbiotic industries like fan magazines, music television and radio that, all together, claim revenues approaching $17 billion a year. Then there are concerts, performers' merchandise, sponsorships and a miscellany of related enterprises.

The stakes are big. The first billionaire in Hollywood history, **David Geffen,** became rich by building Geffen Records from scratch, He sold the enterprise for three-quarters of a billion dollars.

Even in leaner times, with major losses to online music swapping, recordings from major acts sell well. Anglo-Dutch recording conglomerate EMI sold 5 million copies of pop singer Robbie Williams' greatest-hits collection. The Beastie Boys' *Hello Nasty* and Janet Jackson's *All for You* both topped 5 million. Two EMI albums by rapper Chingy have approached 4 million copies.

media ONLINE

Universal Music Group The largest presence in sales of recorded music.
http://new.umusic.com

Sony BMG Includes music news and links to the many Sony BMG labels.
www.sonybmg.com

EMI Group Browse EMI's labels and artist sites while listening to music online.
www.emigroup.com

Warner Music Group Links to all of Warner's holdings worldwide.
www.wmg.com

Recording Industry

studypreview **Four major players dominate the global music-recording industry, all with big-name acts. Most of the industry's musical innovations, however, originate with independent recording companies. The indies gave rock 'n' roll its start—rap too.**

Majors

The recording industry is concentrated in four major companies known as the Big Four, which have 84 percent of the U.S. market and 75 percent of the global market. Each of these companies, in turn, is part of a larger media conglomerate.

The Napster-induced crisis in the early 2000s shook up the industry's corporate landscape. Sony and Bertelsmann merged their music units. Bertelsmann, the German company that is the world's fifth largest media company, runs the combined Sony BMG. Alarmed at declining sales in the new file-swapping era, Time Warner sold its Warner Music in 2004 to Edgar Bronfman Jr. and fellow investors. Bronfman, heir to the Seagram liquor fortune from Canada, earlier had run the Universal movie and recording empire but had sold it to the French media conglomerate Vivendi. Although Vivendi, financially overextended, sold off many holdings to solve its own crisis in 2003, it decided to stay the course with Universal Music. There were no buyers anyway. Times were tough in the industry, and prospects for a recovery were cloudy at best.

David Geffen ■ Recording, movie entrepreneur; first self-made billionaire in Hollywood.

indies ■ Independently owned record-making companies; not part of Big Four.

Recording Companies

Four companies dominate the recording industry, although nonmajors, called *indies,* typically claims about 15 percent of U.S. sales—even more globally. This is the global picture, with major acts on the companies' labels:

Universal Music (French) **25.5 percent**
Guns N' Roses (Universal), Jay-Z (Def Jam), Brian McKnight (Motown), George Strait (MCA Nashville), Snoop Dogg (Geffen), Gwen Stefani (Interscope), The Killers (Island)

Sony BMG (German) **21.5 percent**
Bruce Springsteen (Columbia), Jennifer Lopez (Epic), Santa (Legacy), Travis Tritt (Sony Nashville), OperaBabes (Odyssey)

EMI (Anglo-Dutch) **13.1 percent**
Beastie Boys (Capitol), Janet Jackson (Virgin), Tina Turner (Capitol)

Warner Music (U.S.) **11.3 percent**
Doors (Elektra), Boyz N Da Hood (Bad Boy), Twisted Sister (Lava), Lil' Kim (Atlantic)

Indies

For decades a secondary tier of independent recording companies, **indies,** as they were known in industry jargon, struggled against the majors

mediaPEOPLE

50 Cent

An Ambitious Hustler

Curtis Jackson epitomizes all that critics see as right and wrong about the culture of rap that has erupted into a dominant element in pop music, if not pop culture. At 22, after jail time for drug-dealing in the roughest section of Queens, Jackson lucked out through rap friends and landed a contract with Columbia Records. In two weeks he sketched out 36 songs, including his career-launching "How to Rob."

Yes, this is the Curtis Jackson who performs as 50 Cent. But despite the promise of the underground bite of his early Columbia music, his rap career took a hit when he did—9mm bullets in his face, legs and a hand in front of his grandmother's place in Queens. Such is the life of a dealer, a career in itself that allowed the prepubescent kid to buy Air Jordans that his grandma, who reared him, could never afford.

Jackson was months recovering in the hospital. Columbia dropped his contract. But Jackson kept writing, the shooting adding grist to his creative mill. He got back to recording and mixing tapes and caught the ear of Eminem, the reigning king of rap, and Dr. Dre, master-rap producer. Other gangsta labels suddenly were on to 50 Cent too. A bidding war erupted, with 50 Cent going with the new Eminem and Dr. Dre label Aftermath/Shady.

Multiple hits followed, all authentically flowing from Jackson's experience. "I Need Love," a heroin addict yearning desperately for a fix, is pop pap. More explicit is the title "When the Guns Come Out, Somebody's Going to Die Tonight." He made a fortune, with 11 million recordings sold by 2005. Critics say 50 Cent glorifies the drug life. That's not how he sees it: "I was poor for much longer than I been rich, so what do you think I'm going to talk about."

His anthem now is best captured in the title of his super hit "Get Rich or Die Tryin'." His sense of business, honed from age 8 on the streets of Queens, has served Curtis Jackson well. For Reebok he designed G-unit sneakers and earned $20 million. A clothing line brought in $50 million. He has expanded into the Glaceau vitamin water. Hollywood beckoned, teaming *Sopranos* screenwriter Terrace Winter and *In America* director Jim Sheridan for a thinly fictionalized biographical movie, *Hustler's Ambition,* with Curtis Jackson as himself, err, as 50 Cent.

media ONLINE **Indie Centre** An independent label knowledge site, complete with information on starting your own label and getting your music heard. **www.indiecentre.com**

and occasionally produced a hit. When an indy amassed enough successes, it invariably was bought out by a major. The most famous of the indies, Motown, whose name became synonymous with the black Detroit style, maintained its independence for 30 years. In 1988, however, founder Berry Gordy received an offer he could not refuse—for $61 million. Soon Motown was subsumed into the MCA empire, which later became Universal Music.

While struggling indies remain part of the record industry landscape, the latter-day indies are well-funded labels created by major artists who decide to go their own way, with themselves in charge, rather than dealing with cumbersome big studio bureaucracies and machinery. The Beatles did it with Apple. Minnesota-based Prince did it. The Dixie Chicks have done it. Today it's a common route.

Transforming Innovations

studypreview **Technology created the recorded music industry, which goes back to Thomas Edison. Later innovations reshaped recorded products, mostly through playback disks and now digital delivery. Also pivotal in shaping the industry through history have been artistic innovations, some wrought by technology. Some artistic innovations had grassroots origins.**

media TIMELINE

RECORDING FORMATS

Formats for recorded music for consumers have changed dramatically. Some changes represent changed technology. Others represent convenience.

1877 Cylinders
Introduced by Thomas Edison for his Phonograph.

1920s 78-rpm disks
Needle-in-groove technology with 10-inch disks, called platters, became industry standard. Playable on both sides, each with four minutes of music. Disks made of brittle shellac.

1948 33⅓-rpm disks
Columbia introduced disks with microgrooves capable of 30 minutes of music per side. Disks made of vinyl with some flex.

1949 45-rpm disks
RCA introduced small microgroove disks with large spindle hole, used mostly for one song per side. Made of vinyl.

1963 Cassettes
Philips introduced magnetic tape wound on two spindles inside a casing, with the tape pulled through a mechanism to pick up sound. Slightly larger than a pack of cigarettes but thinner.

1966 Eight-tracks cartridges
Somewhat like cassettes. The size of a small paperback book.

1982 Compact disks
Disks, 4.7 inches across, on which sound was recorded digitally for precise reproduction.

1999 MP3s
Technology for downloading music from Internet sources in digital form. Facilitated music-swapping online.

2001 iPod
Apple, using MP3-derived technology, introduced a handheld storage device for a downloaded personal music library.

2005 Dual disks
Music on one side, like a CD, with video performances and other value-added material on the back side, like a DVD.

Sound Technology

For years scientific journals had speculated on ways to reproduce sound, but not until 1877 did anyone build a machine that could do it. That was when U.S. inventor **Thomas Edison** applied for a patent for a talking machine. He used the trade name **Phonograph,** which was taken from Greek words meaning "to write sound."

Thomas Edison Learn more about the inventor who started the march toward today's recording technology. **www.thomasedison.com**

Acoustic Recording The heart of Edison's invention was a cylinder wrapped in tin foil. The cylinder was rotated as a singer shouted into a large metal funnel. The funnel channeled the voice against a diaphragm, which fluttered to the vibrations. A stylus, which most people called a "needle," was connected to the diaphragm and cut a groove in the foil, the depth of the groove reflecting the vibrations. To listen to a recording, you put the cylinder on a player and set a needle in the groove that had been created in the recording process. Then you placed your ear to a megaphonelike horn and rotated the cylinder. The needle tracked the groove, and the vibrations created by the varying depths of the groove were fed through the horn. This process was called **acoustic recording.**

Edison's system contained a major impediment to commercial success: A recording could not be duplicated. In 1887 **Emile Berliner** introduced a breakthrough. Rather than recording on a cylinder covered with flimsy foil, as Edison did, Berliner used a sturdy metal disk. From the metal disk Berliner made a mold and then poured a thermoplastic material into the mold. When the material hardened, Berliner had a near-perfect copy of the original disk—and he could make hundreds of them. Berliner's system, called the Gramophone, led to mass production.

Electrical Recording In the 1920s the Columbia and Victor record companies introduced records based on an electrical system perfected by **Joseph Maxwell** of Bell Laboratories. Metal funnels were replaced by microphones, which had superior sensitivity.

Thomas Edison ■ Built the first audio recorder-playback machine.

Phonograph ■ First recorder-playback machine.

acoustic recording ■ Vibration-sensitive recording technology.

Emile Berliner ■ His machine played disks that could be mass-produced.

Joseph Maxwell ■ Introduced electrical recording in the 1920s.

What Edison Wrought
Prolific inventor Thomas Edison devised a machine that took sound waves and etched them into grooves on a foil drum. Although technologically a breakthrough, the sound was primitive. Only the most obvious tones could be picked up. Whatever few tonal subtleties and soft trills were recorded got lost in playback scratchiness. Firm horns and percussions did well. Marchmeister John Phillip Sousa found an audience.

For listening, it was no longer a matter of putting an ear to a mechanical amplifying horn that had only a narrow frequency response. Instead, loudspeakers amplified the sound electromagnetically.

Digital Recording Record-makers developed a technological revolution in 1978: the **digital recording.** No longer were continuous sound waves inscribed physically on a disk. Instead, sound waves were sampled at millisecond intervals, and each sample was logged in computer language as an isolated on-off binary number. When disks were played back, the digits were translated back to the sound at the same millisecond intervals at which they were recorded. The intervals would be replayed so fast that the sound would seem continuous, just as the individual frames in a motion picture become a moving blur that is perceived by the eye as continuous motion.

By 1983 digital recordings were available to consumers in the form of **compact disks,** silvery 4.7-inch platters. The binary numbers were tiny pits on the disk that were read by a laser light in the latest version of the phonograph: the **CD** player. The player itself converted the numbers to sound.

When the World Wide Web burst into existence in the 1990s, everybody saw the potential to move sound and also animation directly to consumers, the so-called end users, who had been buying music in stores or by mail since the days of Edison and Berliner.

digital recording ■ Recording and playback system using on-off binary code for sound.

compact disk ■ Digital record format; now dominant.

CD ■ Short for "compact disk."

jukebox ■ Coin-operated record player with buttons to select a song.

crooner ■ Singer with a near-humming style for soft, sentimental music.

swooner ■ Singer of music so rapturous that fans would faint.

rockabilly ■ Hybrid of music in the black tradition and hillbilly music; precursor of rock 'n' roll.

Performer Influences

The U.S. recording industry's main product, pop music, has been shaped by changing public tastes.

Dance Music The recording business received a big boost in 1913 when a dance craze hit. Then World War I songs became popular, further fueling demand. Record production totaled 27 million disks in 1914.

Suddenly, the horror of World War I overwhelmed everyone. Casualties in the grueling trench warfare in France totaled 600,000. The United States, which entered the war late, suffered 53,500 battlefield deaths. Then there was the flu pandemic that spread from the Western front, claiming at least 20 million lives, 500,000 of them in the United States. The war was no time for dancing. But when the war ended in 1918, the pent-up craving for good times sent record sales soaring. People danced and danced—no one

media TIMELINE

RECORD INDUSTRY

1877 Thomas Edison introduced a recording-playback device, the Phonograph.

1887 Emile Berliner introduced technology to record disks simultaneously.

1920s Joseph Maxwell introduced electrical microphones and recording system.

1948 Peter Goldmark introduced long-play microgroove vinyl 33⅓-rpm records.

1950s Rock 'n' roll, a new musical genre, shook up the record industry.

1960 Stereo recordings and playback equipment were introduced.

1983 Digital recording on CDs was introduced.

1998 Streaming technology made downloading from the web possible.

2001 Apple introduced handheld iPod MP3-playing device coupled with its online iTunes Music Store, a new model for music retailing.

2005 Recording industry won U.S. Supreme Court case against online music-swapping facilitators, like Grokster, slowing a drain on sales.

more than executives in the recording industry. Sales totaled 107 million discs in 1919.

Jukeboxes The **jukebox** helped the industry through the economically difficult 1930s. The machines, gaudy with colored lights and buttons, some plated with chrome, picked up records from a stack and swiveled them to a mechanism with a pickup needle—all at a nickel a song. Jukeboxes were a marvel to watch and were everywhere—in restaurants, saloons and soda fountains. By 1940 a total of 250,000 jukeboxes were keeping the public interested in recorded music.

The jukebox phenomenon was possible only because of the electrical recording technology introduced by Joseph Maxwell, which improved sound quality markedly. Soft voices and subtle music could be recorded, ushering in an age of **crooners** and **swooners,** as well as recordings by great orchestras that have become legacies. Radio, found in almost every home even during the economic difficulties of the Great Depression, fueled a demand for recordings.

Rockabilly After World War II major record labels groomed singers in the croon-swoon style, typified by Frank Sinatra and Rosemary Clooney. Cavalierly, the majors figured that they could manipulate public tastes to their products. So confident were major labels in their strategy that they were blindsided by the sudden grassroots enthusiasm in the 1950s for Elvis Presley, "the white boy who sang colored," as he was called at the time. In Memphis an independent label, Sun Records, had assembled a lineup consisting of Carl Perkins, Roy Orbison, Johnny Cash and Presley. The music was called **rockabilly,** a linkage of black and hillbilly music.

After months of inroads from rockabilly acts, the major labels scrambled to catch the wave. The major label RCA signed

Elvis Presley

Rock 'n' roll, a new hybrid musical form epitomized by Elvis Presley, took root with independent recording companies. To their peril, major labels tried to ignore the phenomenon, figuring it soon would pass. It didn't. Just when some indies, like Sun, were on the brink of becoming larger players in the recording industry landscape, the majors swept into rock 'n' roll and maintained their dominance in the industry.

mediaTECHNOLOGY

DualDisc

When Bruce Springsteen's 19th album, *Devils & Dust,* was released in 2005, it was on **DualDisc**—a hybrid format with music on one side, like a CD, and video content on the other, like a DVD. Springsteen was the first Top List performer to go with DualDisc, the first major new physical format for recorded music since the compact disk 20 years earlier. Costly, high-end formats like Super Audio CD, SACD for short, and DVD-Audio had been tried in the interim but had not caught on.

Springsteen wasn't first with DualDisc. Pop-punkers Simple Plan had sold almost 1 million copies of their *Still Not Getting Any* on DualDisc a few months earlier. But Springsteen himself was instrumental in bringing new visibility to the format. He insisted that the price of his hybrid album be no more than that of a standard CD. So for the price of a CD, fans got 12 songs, including *The Hitter,* on the CD side and live performances of five songs, including *Reno,* on the DVD flip side.

Sony BMG, which planned 40 DualDisc releases in 2005, saw the format as a way to boost album sales in the face of singles downloads from the Internet. Nobody expected the new format to spur massive new sales, like the CD and earlier formats that prompted people to replace their entire music collections.

DualDisc Bruce Springsteen was among the pioneer performers on DualDisc, a format with music on one side and video performances and other features on the flip side.

media ONLINE

Elvis Presley He ain't nothin' but a hound dog. The official site. **www.elvis.com**

Bruce Springsteen Includes Springsteen music and tour news, as well as an online store of official Springsteen merchandise. **www.backstreets.com**

Presley. Other majors absorbed rockabilly indies. In the nick of time the majors saved themselves from the schmaltzy course they had been following and embraced the new genre, which was coming to be called **rock 'n' roll.**

British Invasion The U.S. record industry was rocked again in the early 1960s, this time by music from Britain. The Beatles caught the ear of a new generation, not only on radio but also with a series of platinum singles and albums. The **British Invasion** was a new wake-up call for U.S. record-makers. The industry's largely insular concept of itself was no longer viable. International licensing agreements to market music became a new way of doing business and introduced a new view of the global potential for U.S. record-makers. All the major U.S. record companies were parts of larger media corporations, like RCA and Columbia Broadcasting, and thus had far more financial muscle than their foreign competitors.

Today exports of U.S. entertainment products, including recorded music, are a major positive factor in the nation's balance of trade with other countries.

Rap As transforming as rock was, so too, 40 years later, was **rap.** Born in the impoverished Bronx section of New York City, this new style of music had an intense bass line for dancing and rhyming riffs, often attitude-strong and rapid-fire, overlaid on the music. Slowly, rap spread to other black urban areas. Indie-produced *Run-D.M.C.* and *King of Rock* were the first black rap albums to break into the U.S. music mainstream. Major record companies soon were signing up rap acts. Controversial groups Public Enemy and N.W.A., using violence and racism as themes, made rap a public issue in the 1990s, which only fanned die-hard enthusiasm.

DualDisc ■ Hybrid CD-DVD format introduced in 2005.

rock 'n' roll ■ Genre marked by incessant beat with guitar as the dominant instrument.

British Invasion ■ Popularity in the United States of the Beatles and other British acts.

rap ■ Rhythm-heavy music genre usually with rapid-fire, attitude-heavy lyrics.

His Own Label The cost and risk of launching a record label once were unthinkable, even for a major artist, but digital recording technology has loosened the control that well-financed record companies had on the industry. Queens-born James Todd Smith, professionally LL Cool J, short for "Ladies Love Cool James," helped to propel rap label Def Jam into the big time among indies in the 1980s. Now, still strong in popularity, LL Cool J has launched his own label, P. O. G. Records.

Regulatory Pressure

studypreview **The record industry has been a scapegoat for social ills. To stay one step ahead of government censorship, the industry has taken a cue from other media groups and introduced self-regulation to head off First Amendment crises.**

media ONLINE **Parental Advisory** News on the latest in music censorship and a brief history of banned music in the United States. **www.ericnuzum.com/banned**

Objectionable Music

Campaigns to ban recorded music are nothing new. In the Roaring Twenties some people saw jazz as morally loose. White racists of the 1950s called Bill Haley's rock "nigger music." War protest songs of the Vietnam period angered many Americans.

Government attempts to censor records have been rare, yet the Federal Communications Commission indirectly keeps some records off the market. The FCC can take a dim view of stations that air objectionable music, which guides broadcasters toward caution. Stations do not want to risk their FCC-awarded licenses.

The FCC has been explicit about obnoxious lyrics. In 1971 the commission said that stations have a responsibility to know "the content of the lyrics." Not to do so, said the commission, would raise "serious questions as to whether continued operation of the station is in the public interest." The issue at the time was music that glorified drugs.

Labeling

In the 1980s complaints about lyrics focused on drugs, sexual promiscuity and violence. **Parents Music Resource Center,** a group led by wives of influential members of Congress, claimed links between explicit rock music and teen suicide, teen pregnancy, parental abuse, broken homes and other social ills. The group objected to lyrics like Prince's *Sister,* which extol incest; Mötley Crüe's *Live Wire,* with its psychopathic enthusiasm for strangulation; Guns N' Roses' white racism; and rap artists' hate music.

The Parents Music Resource Center argued that consumer protection laws should be invoked to require that records with offensive lyrics be labeled as dangerous, like cigarette warning labels or the movie industry's rating system. After the group went to the FCC and the **National Association of Broadcasters,** record companies voluntarily began labeling potentially offensive records: "Explicit Lyrics—Parental Advisory." In some cases the companies printed lyrics on album covers as a warning.

Parents Music Resource Center ■ Crusaded for labels on "objectionable" music.

National Association of Broadcasters ■ Radio, television trade organization.

Recorded Music Genres

Rock easily leads U.S. records sales in genres defined by the Recording Industry of America:

Rock	25.2 percent
Rap/hip hop	13.3 percent
R&B/urban	10.6 percent
Country	10.4 percent
Pop	8.9 percent
Religious	5.8 percent
Classical	3.0 percent
Jazz	2.9 percent
Soundtracks	1.4 percent
Oldies	1.3 percent
New age	0.6 percent
Children's	0.5 percent

Online retailers, including iTunes, put a label of "explicit" on songs that might raise the prudish eyebrows.

On a quadrennial schedule, some presidential candidates resurrect the idea that song lyrics are a corrupting influence of the nation's youth. These concerns can be traced to jitterbug music in the 1940s, rockabilly in the 1950s and rap today. Some is mere grandstanding against new music and performance genres that unsettle some people, like early rock's hip grinding and excessive stage gestures. Some objections, however, focus on antisocial messages, like Prince's celebration of incest, Ice T's *Cop Killer* and Eminem's misogyny. Bizarre costuming and makeup by Alice Cooper and David Bowie in their early years didn't help. Nor did Jim Morrison's indecent exposure in a Miami concert.

No one doubts the sincerity of some critics, like Senator Joseph Lieberman, the Connecticut Democrat. Strident on the right is William Bennett, who once went after Warner Music: "Are you folks morally disabled?" Once the election passes, however, the political rhetoric cools. The most persistent critics, keeping the issue alive, come from the political right.

Artistic Freedom

The usual defense against would-be censors is that artistic freedom merits protection, no matter how objectionable the art's content. When rapper Ice T seemed to push the envelope on acceptability with his song *Cop Killer* on a Warner Music label, police groups

Gangsta Rapping His song *Cop Killer* scared a lot of people who wanted it banned, but rapper Ice T defended his music as a truthful expression of grassroots frustration among many urban blacks. Public policy can't be improved to address these festering tensions if nobody outside the ghetto is aware of them, he said. Gerald Levin, who headed Time Warner, the parent company of Ice T's Interscope label, also responded to critics that a society that believes in free expression must allow even distasteful messages. Both Levin and Ice T, however, eventually softened their stance and toned down their products.

Gerald Levin

and others called for a ban. It was no wonder, with lyrics such as "I got my 12-gauge sawed-off / And I got my headlights turned off / I'm about to dust some cops off." Some defended the album as misunderstood. Gerald Levin, chief executive at Time Warner, catapulted the defense of Ice T to another level with an eloquent defense for artistic liberties as an essential value in a free society. Free expressionists were enthusiastic that Levin had taken a pro-artist stance over a financially safer bottom-line position.

A few months later, however, Levin waffled. He called on Warner artists to begin a dialogue on standards. Fervid support for Levin waned as his position shifted to safer ground for Time Warner: corporate well-being. In the end Levin cut loose Ice T's label from the Warner collection—a more typical, albeit less heroic, action for a media executive. Ever-mindful of potential threats to their industry's autonomy, media executives almost always try to finesse their way out of confrontations that have the potential to precipitate serious calls for government censorship.

A&R (artist and repertoire) ■ Units of recording company responsible for talent.

Artistic Autonomy

study preview **Major labels once dominated the nation's music with expensive talent and recording operations that neither indies nor individual performers could match. Digital recording equipment in the 1980s loosened the majors' artistic control.**

A&R Structure

The heart of the recording industry once was the powerful **A&R** units, short for **artist and repertoire,** at major labels. In an arrogant tyranny over artists A&R executives manufactured countless performers. They groomed artists for stardom, chose their music, ordered the arrangements, controlled recording sessions and even choose their wardrobes for public performances.

In his book *Solid Gold* Serge Denisoff quotes a Capitol executive from the 1950s explaining how the A&R system worked: "The company would pick out 12 songs for Peggy Lee and tell her to be at the studio Wednesday at 8, and she'd show up and sing what you told her. And she'd leave three hours later and Capitol'd take her songs and do any-

Bucking Big Labels
Unlike the era when major labels controlled every aspect of the work of performers like Peggy Lee, low-cost recording equipment today has reduced artist dependence on big recording companies. Among performers who have bucked the Big Label domination of music have been the Dixie Chicks, whose threat to start their own label gave them negotiating leverage.

Peggy Lee

Dixie Chicks

mediaTECHNOLOGY

Albums: The Rise and Fall

The introduction of Apple's handheld digital music player, the iPod, has given new importance to the single song as an art form and as a commercial product. For years the record industry had been thinking of music in terms of albums, typically 12 to 20 songs. Too, many artists regarded their work not as songs but as coherent bodies of music packaged in albums. Even though some people didn't want the whole body of work, they often had no choice but to buy the package. Clunkers were part of the deal.

The iPod is a case study of technology redefining an art form. The iPod was an empowering invention. At Apple's iTunes Music Store, iPod users could buy singles and create their own playlists—not a sequence of music dictated by how a producer had arranged the songs for an album. It seemed that iPods were everywhere. In the three-month run-up to Christmas 2004, 4.6 million iPods were sold.

A technology-driven change that transformed music had happened before—in reverse.

In 1948, when music was recorded and sold on disks, **Peter Goldmark,** the chief engineer at Columbia Records, introduced slow-spinning, **long-play** records, LPs for short. An LP could carry 20 to 30 minutes of music per side, far more than the single song of the dominant format that had been around for two generations.

With LPs record-makers suddenly were able to package multiple songs on a single record, which gave rise to the album. The album itself became a high art form. Producers and performers began thinking of a work not as a song, but as a package of music. They used the term **concept album.** Music critics began reviewing albums, not singles. Goldmark's technological innovation had drastically transformed music conceptually.

thing it wanted with them. That was a time when the artist was supposed to shut up and put up with anything the almighty recording company wanted."

The muscle of the major record companies, aiming for mass market sales, contributed to a homogenizing of U.S. culture. Coast to coast, everybody was humming the same new tunes from Peggy Lee and other pop singers, who served a robotlike role for A&R managers. The A&R structure was a top-down system for creating pop culture. A relatively small number of powerful A&R executives decided what would be recorded and marketed. It was the opposite of grassroots artistry.

Music Demassification

In the 1980s sophisticated low-cost recording and mixing equipment gave individual artists and **garage bands** a means to control their art. The million-dollar sound studio, controlled by major labels and their A&R people, became less important. As little as $15,000 could buy digital recorders and 24-channel mixing boards, plus remodeling the garage, to do what only a major studio could have done a few years earlier. The upshot was liberation for creativity. Artists suddenly had an independence that big recording companies were forced to learn to accommodate. Linda Ronstadt, for example, shifted her recording to a home studio in her basement. Some artists, like LL Cool J, went so far as to create their own labels. The ability of artists to go out on their own gave them clout that was not possible in the A&R heyday. The Dixie Chicks, among others, used this new leverage in negotiating with their labels.

Another result has been greater diversity. A rap fan might never have heard the Dixie Chicks. The music of Barry Manilow is obscure to most Green Day fans. In this sense recorded music has become less of a unifying element in the whole society. The unification, rather, is in subsets of the mass audience.

Peter Goldmark ■ Inventor of long-play records.

long-play (LP) ■ 33⅓-rpm microgroove disks that turned the recorded music industry into conceiving of its products as albums.

concept album ■ Collections of a performer's work with a thematic or stylistic coherency.

garage bands ■ Coined term for upstart performers without a studio contract.

Touring

Big-name performers have found a significant income stream outside of the recording industry by taking their music directly to fans on a new scale. On tour, U2 commands ticket prices from $50 to $170. Prices for the 2005 tours of Paul McCartney and the Rolling Stones were higher. On-tour performances and recorded music sales fuel each

mediaTECHNOLOGY

Sound Mixing

Performance Recording Communicating with sound engineers on stage, Grammy-winning music producer Elliot Scheiner sets up to record the 11-hour Crossroads Guitar Concert from inside a specially outfitted truck trailer outside the Cotton Bowl. The concert went live over the Internet. Scheiner then remixed the performance for a DVD, a television special and a pay-per-view broadcast.

Looking back, it's a wonder we had some of the sophisticated music we did before the late 1980s. Producers back then overlaid sounds from magnetic tapes mounted on numerous spools. So complex and laborious was the process, based on analog recording, that it impeded the genius that goes into great music.

Then producers discovered Apple's drag-and-drop computer technology. With digital instead of analog recording, mixing became easy as moving words on a computer screen. Not only was cutting and pasting quicker, but the creative possibilities far exceeded what had gone before. Complex orchestration that no maestro would have attempted became possible. Was somebody out of tune? Even that was fixable.

The breakthrough was Apple's recording and editing software ProTools. Other programs followed, including Logic Pro and Soundtrack. Dozens of plug-in programs became available with riffs and trills from every instrument imaginable plus sounds that hardly anybody outside the music-mixing industry had ever heard. In 2003 Apple packaged its Garageband software free with its OS X operating system, giving thousands of prerecorded samples to the ordinary computer user. Anybody could mix custom sound tracks.

Although small, the sound market is laden with prestige for software makers. Apple's dominance added to the cachet of its brand name. Among professional musicians Apple has an estimated 90 percent market share. Challengers are emerging, however. Using the competing Windows operating system, Pinnacle's Nuendo and Cakewalk's Sonar have both picked up fans among recording professionals.

other symbiotically, but they are significantly different. A live audience performance consists of audience and performer in the same place and intensely focused on each other, a kind of eyeball-to-eyeball group communication, not mass communication.

Also significant, **touring** is controlled not by recording companies but by concert promotion companies. The largest is a subsidiary of the giant Clear Channel radio chain. To varying degrees the growth of the touring industry has lessened performers' reliance on the recording industry as their main revenue source. This too has contributed to less recording company control and greater artist autonomy.

When music industry analysts assess the revenue streams of performers today, they consider three major factors.

Retail The traditional outlet for recorded music, once mostly free-standing record shops, has shifted to giant retailers like Best Buy. In the post-Napster era traditional retail sales have slipped.

Downloading The new retailing is through download sites like iTunes Music Store, WAM and the resurrected Napster. This is a growing revenue source.

Touring Concerts are big business for performers who can attract sell-out crowds for their shows, especially the techno-spectaculars.

touring ■ Live performances in highly promoted road trips; increasingly important revenue source for big-name performers.

Streaming Crisis

studypreview **Napster and other file-sharing technology that facilitates music-swapping seriously eroded music sales and record industry viability until 2005, when the U.S. Supreme Court intervened. An older problem, pirate dubbing, continues to be a drain on music industry profitability.**

File-Sharing

Shawn Fanning's Napster technology ushered in a frenzy of free music-swapping on the Internet in 2000. Suddenly, record stores found themselves unable to move inventory. Major music retailer Best Buy shut down its Sam Goody's, Musicland and other brand-name stores that had seemed sure money-makers only a few months earlier. The free fall continued. For the first time in its history the record industry was not in control of new technology—unlike the earlier adjustments, when companies exploited developments to goose sales, like switches to high-fidelity and stereo and the introduction of eight-tracks, cassettes and CDs.

The Recording Industry Association of America, which represents recorded music companies, went to court against Napster. A federal judge bought the argument that Napster was participating in copyright infringement by facilitating illicit copying of protected intellectual property. Napster was toast. But other file-swapping mechanisms remained, some harder to tackle. Kazaa, for example, kept moving its operations from one offshore site to another, where legal actions were impossible.

In a surreal initiative in 2003, RIAA began legal action against individuals who downloaded music without paying. The association's goal was a few hundred highly publicized lawsuits, perhaps some showcase trials, to discourage download piracy. In one respect, the strategy backfired, only engendering hard feelings among people who were the industry's greatest consumers.

In another legal maneuver, the industry challenged Grokster and other music-swapping services. The argument was that Grokster was not passively involved in copyright infringements by music-swappers but had actively encouraged the infringements. In 2005 the U.S. Supreme Court agreed in what was quickly hailed as a landmark gain for the recording industry. The decision did not end music-swapping immediately but so hobbled business as usual among swap services that RIAA was confident it had largely stopped the free-swapping drain on its revenues.

media ONLINE

iTunes For a fee, Apple makes music singles available for the iPod and other players.
www.apple.com/itunes

Kazaa This successor to Napster includes a warning label on its site proclaiming its belief in following copyright laws.
www.kazaa.com/us

Morpheus Allows you to download and share music, movies and games.
http://morpheus.com

Grokster Includes information on using peer-to-peer software safely and responsibly.
www.grokster.com

Myspace.com The music section of this community web site includes featured artists, online prerelease songs and music videos.
www.myspace.com

iPod

Another favorable development for the industry was already easing the doomsayers' gloomy scenario: the **iPod.** In 2002 the innovator behind Apple Computer, **Steve Jobs,** introduced a handheld music playback device that he called the iPod, which he quickly followed with the online **iTunes** Music Store. From the iTunes site people could sample a song with a single click and then download with another click for 99 cents. In iTunes' first week, more than 1 million songs were downloaded, juicing a 27 percent spike in Apple stock.

Unlike download-swapping, iTunes wasn't free. But it had advantages. The sound quality was exceptional. Apple used a new format that compressed music efficiently, downloaded faster and consumed less disc space. It was a clean system, without the annoying viruses that affected swap systems like Kazaa, Morpheus and Grokster. Apple benefited too from the guilt trip that RIAA was trying to lay on illegal downloaders.

Jobs began iTunes with huge repertoires from some major labels. Other labels begged to sign on as soon as the iPod-iTunes success was clear. By 2005, 62 percent of all music downloads were from iTunes. To be sure, copycat services spawned quickly. Wal-Mart created WAM. The Napster name was resurrected as a subscription service with unlimited access to downloads, the whole collection playable as long as the subscription was kept current.

iPod ■ Brand name for Apple's handheld digital music device.

Steve Jobs ■ Driving force behind Apple Computer revival, iPod and iTunes.

iTunes ■ Online music store.

iPod The icon of a generation, the Apple iPod not only added new, stylish portability to music but, coupled with iTunes, turned around a decline in recorded music sales. In 2005 Apple introduced a video model with Disney movie snippets and ABC sitcoms for sale from iTunes.

Steve Jobs

Pirate Dubbing

pirate dubbing ■ Illegal duplication of music and movies for black-market sale.

Until the recorded music industry's crisis with downloading, the biggest drain on sales had been criminal music-dubbing. **Pirate dubbing** operations, well financed and organized, have been estimated by the industry to account for 20 to 30 percent of CD sales in the United States. There are no firm figures, but RIAA estimates that the loss globally is $5 billion a year.

The dubbed CDs are from shadowy sources, mostly in Asia but also in other countries, including Saudi Arabia. It is not uncommon for a back-alley Third World pirate operation to have 100 "slave" copying machines going simultaneously 24 hours a day. These pirate operations have no artistic, royalty or promotion expenses. They dub CDs produced by legitimate companies and sell them through black-market channels. Their costs are low, their profits high. Pirate dubs even end up in retail channels, including Wal-Mart at one time.

Apple Math The iPod was not without challenges. A resuscitated Napster, operating within copyright law, argued in ads aimed at Apple that it had a better deal. In Scandinavia, Apple faced legal problems because music from the company's online iTunes store could be downloaded only to Apple iPods, not rival digital music devices. Also, a void in the iTunes repertoire was Beatles music. The Beatles' record label Apple Corps from the 1960s objected in British courts that the Apple Computer logo was confusing to Apple Corps loyalists and refused to release its music for iTunes sales.

case STUDY

Podcasting: The New Revolution?

From VJ to "Podfather" Former MTV VJ Adam Curry has placed himself at the forefront of the podcasting movement as founder of Pod Show Inc. and host of his own podcast.

Bands used to send their singles on a 45-rpm record to radio stations across the country, hoping that a few might play it. Today, musicians who want to reach a global audience send their music on a digital file to podcasters. These are the people who put together their own Internet audio shows, typically an mp3 file, that is delivered to a listener with an iPod, or other audio player, or a computer with an Internet connection and speakers. Listeners can access the podcast at their convenience, and it's free.

As of 2006 there were more than 4,750 podcasters in the music/radio category at Podcast Alley, a directory of podcasts for every type of music from jazz to metal. Chris McIntyre started Podcast Alley to index all the podcasts he could find. Music is only part of what his site indexes. "I truly believe that podcasting is a powerful communication tool and will have a profound effect on the way we communicate in the future," says the Purdue University graduate.

While musicians are hoping for exposure from the new medium, PodShow, Inc. founder Adam Curry is poised to make big bucks from it. "Podfather" Curry and software pioneer Dave Winer developed the computer programs that make podcasting possible. Curry founded PodShow Inc. in January 2005. The same venture capital companies that invested in Yahoo and Google invested $9 million in PodShow Inc.

The mainstream media "are so diluted, so packaged, so predictable. There's so very little that is new or interesting," said Curry in an interview with Martin Miller of the Los Angeles *Times*. "We've lost a lot of social connectedness that used to come from that. And what we're building here is a social media network for human beings." Curry's critics claim the former MTV VJ "promotes himself as a would-be revolutionary for the little guy, but he's actually as profit mad as the corporate giants."

Other companies are jumping on the podcast wagon. Nokia announced in 2006 that some of its new phones would include a podcasting client featuring the PodShow top 10, Podcast Alley Picks and podcasts from Digital Podcast. About the same time Nielsen/NetRatings reported that the number of Americans downloading and consuming podcasts was neck-to-neck with those publishing blogs. About 6.6 percent had recently downloaded an audio podcast, while 4 percent had downloaded a video podcast.

"Thousands of bands are submitting their songs to the Podsafe Music Network. They're connecting with podcasters and listeners, and now they're figuring out that it makes sense to promote shows together and share their audience with each other," said Curry. "This is another way bands are benefiting from the DIY/digital revolution in music."

In place of a mainstream medium, or at least alongside it, will be companies like his and the others that will inevitably follow, Curry believes. As Martin Miller puts it, "They offer what the mainstream media never would or could—a way for regular folk to create and consume their own media content."

WHAT DO YOU THINK?

1. Will podcasting build a "social media network for human beings"?
2. Will podcasting continue to be free to the consumer and to the musician?
3. How do you think podcasting will affect the already beleaguered mainstream recording industry?

The Recording Industry Association of America, along with the Motion Picture Association of America, spends millions of dollars a year on private investigators in Bangkok and other piracy centers. They also pressure foreign governments to crack down, as does the U.S. government, but with limited success.

Evaluating Recording Companies

studypreview **Sales and profits are quantitative measures of a record company's success. How about its artistic success? Qualitative measures are harder to come by. Elitists give high marks to companies that have a commitment to music that breaks new ground artistically.**

media ONLINE **Billboard** Check out the latest music charts and play music trivia games. **www.billboard.com**

Grammy Awards Learn more about award winners and how the foundation supports the music community. **www.grammy.org**

Populist Measures

People vote with their pocketbooks, which means that popularity is an important measure of success for record company products. Measuring success, however, is problematic. Different gauges don't necessarily correlate. A dominant market share, for example, doesn't always translate into profits.

Market Share One measure of a record company's success is reflected in market share. In recent years, Universal has led, but rankings can change overnight. A super-selling sound track, like *Titanic,* or a runaway hit album, like Coldplay's *X&Y,* can mean a near-instant reshuffling.

gold record ■ Award for sales of 500,000 albums, 1 million singles.

platinum record ■ Award for sales of 1 million albums, 2 million singles.

Sales Another measure is the **gold record.** Once a single sells 1 million copies or an album sells 500,000 copies, the RIAA confers a gold-record award. A **platinum record** is awarded for 2 million singles or 1 million albums. The measure of success for shareholders who own the conglomerates that own the record companies, however, is profit. A gold record for 1 million albums doesn't translate into profit if the artist has a lavish multimillion-dollar deal whose break-even point is 2 million records.

Profit Because many conglomerates don't release profit figures for the record company subsidiaries, measuring profitability isn't easy. Aggregate data compiled by the RIAA indicates market share, but numerous variables can render market share an imperfect signal about profitability. One indicator, although usually vague, can be the annual reports to conglomerate shareholders, which sometimes contain hints like "disappointing sales in the music unit."

Another indicator for assessing record company performance is industry insiders who are quoted in the trade journals and in fan magazines like *Rolling Stone.* Another indicator,

The Grammy Bounce In the two days after the 2005 Grammy Awards tribute to Ray Charles, sales of his *Genius Loves Company* album spiked 875 percent at the Tower Records chain. The Grammy Bounce is a perennial phenomenon. In 2003 Norah Jones' *Come Away With Me* zoomed to Number One within a week. Sales soon topped 9.2 million.

also reported in the trade journals, is the promotion and firing of record company executives.

Quality Measures

Media elitists, who argue that the media should lead public taste, not be mere panderers, are not swayed by commercial and popular measures of success. Elitists look to the media, including record companies, to incubate cultural innovation even when it means taking risks.

To be successful, country music lyrics must lament being jilted by a lover and jail time—or so goes one wag's observation that takes note of repetitive themes. And how many times have you ever heard pop rock lyrics without the word "baby"? Although there are exceptions galore, redundant and even tiresome themes seem to work in the marketplace. Many people take comfort in familiar lyrics, instrumentation and even performance styles. But this popularity is hardly satisfying to elitist critics who say the media have a responsibility to push the society's cultural explorations to new levels. To these critics, regurgitation, no matter how pleasant, doesn't count for much. In short, a record company that encourages artistic risk-taking will score well among elitists.

CHAPTER 5 Wrap-Up

The impact of Shawn Fanning's Napster on the music industry, which at one point threatened to force a fundamental restructuring, is a reminder that the mass media are technology-driven. But just as digital Internet technology bedeviled the recording industry, technology has come to its rescue. The Apple iTunes online store that coordinates the mind-meld between personal computers and iPods has reshaped music retailing. The iPod also has allowed the music-recording industry to survive in its traditional form with a few dominant major companies.

Questions for Review

1. How is the music industry integrated into our daily lives?
2. What are major developments in sound recording from Thomas Edison on?
3. What effects are economic pressures having on the corporate structure of the music-recording industry?
4. How have technological innovations in sound recording affected musical styles?
5. How have innovations in music genres and styles threatened the corporate structure of the recording industry?
6. How has the recording industry answered threats of government control on objectionable lyrics?
7. What has happened to the A&R units at major record companies?
8. How was the recording industry threatened by Napster and other software that facilitates online music-swapping?
9. What are examples of populist measures for evaluating record companies? What are some elitist measures?

Questions for Critical Thinking

1. In recent months, how has new recorded music shaped significant human events? Consider music that is inspiring human actions. This might be war music. It might be music that's flowing from a generation or subculture and giving it an identity. It might be a new love song that has become a standard at weddings.
2. What has been the effect of global conglomeration in the record industry on the music you like?
3. Look into your crystal ball to assess how technological changes in the record business will play out in the future.

4. How has the relationship between artists and recording companies changed since World War II? Why has the change occurred?
5. How are measures of commercial and artistic success different in the recorded music business?
6. Why is airplay important to a recording becoming a commercial success? Explain the exceptions.
7. What do you see as a solution to the revenue drain created by MP3 technology on the record industry? If there is no solution, what will happen?
8. Discuss the effect of moralists and others who would like to change the content of some recorded music. How do these people go about trying to accomplish their goals? What common threads have there been to their criticism throughout the 20th century?

Deepening Your media LITERACY

Does popular music reflect our personal identity?

STEP 1 Write down the lyrics of your favorite song. Describe the music of this song.

Dig Deeper

STEP 2 Consider the following:

1. Why do you like these lyrics and this kind of music?
2. What does your preference in music say about you?
3. What do you think this song's fans have in common?
4. Would your parents like this song? Why or why not?
5. Who would find it objectionable?

What Do You Think?

STEP 3 Answer these questions: Does this song or music reflect your life? Does it reflect the lives of its fans? Does it reflect the life of the artist? Do you like this song because you identify with it? Do you think your preference in music reflects your place in society?

Keeping Up to Date

Periodicals and other places for staying abreast:

Billboard. A weekly trade journal

Consumer magazines that track popular music and report on the record industry include *Entertainment Weekly, Rolling Stone* and *Spin*.

For Further Learning

Ethan Brown. *Queens Reigns Supreme.* Anchor, 2005.

Brown traces the roots of many big-name rappers to the 1988 shooting death of rookie cop Edward Byrne, which spurred a police crackdown on Queens drug barons. Many left the drug trade, turning to creating music about what they knew best. Although writing in a detached, neutral journalistic tone, Brown is unsympathetic.

David N. Howard. *Sonic Alchemy: Visionary Music Producers and Their Maverick Recordings.* Hal Leonard, 2004.

Howard, a music historian, sweeps the rock 'n' roll period in treating important music producers, including Arthur Baker, Dr. Dre, Hannett, Glyn Johns, George Martin, Steve Miller, Willie Mitchell, Phil Spector and Brian Wilson.

Jill Jonnes. *Empires of Light: Edison, Tesla, Westinghouse, and the Race to Electrify the World.* Random House, 2003.

Jonnes, a historian, focuses on the rivalry among these three pioneers in electric technology and how their innovations eventually were subsumed in corporate greed.

Stan Cornyn, with Paul Scanlon. *Exploding: The Highs, Hits, Hype, Heroes and Hustler of the Warner Music Group.* Harper, 2002.

Cornyn, an executive with Warner Music for almost 40 years, offers corporate history spiced with cameos by celebrity artitists.

Darryl McDaniels with Bruce Haring. *King of Rock: Respect, Responsibility and My Life with Run-DMC.* St. Martin's, 2001.

Rapper McDaniels offers tales about the early hip-hop period.

James Miller. *Flowers in the Dustbin: The Rise of Rock 'n' Roll, 1947–1977.* Simon & Schuster, 1999.

Miller, an academic who also is a book and music critic, traces rock to earlier origins than most scholars do.

Greil Marcus. *Mystery Train: Images of America in Rock 'n' Roll Music.* Penguin Usapaper Plume, 1997.

Marcus, a rock critic, offers a clever history, albeit with gaps.

Stephen Singular. *The Rise and Rise of David Geffen.* Birch Lane, 1997.

Smoothly written psychobiography that leans on Geffen's distant relationship with his father to explain his career and personal life.

Colin Escort, with Martin Hawkins. *Good Rockin' Tonight: Sun Records and the Birth of Rock 'n' Roll.* St. Martins, 1991.

Discographers Escort and Hawkins update their earlier work on Sam Phillips and his Memphis recording studio.

Dick Hebdige. *Cut 'N' Mix: Culture, Identity and Caribbean Music.* Methuen, 1987.

A history of Caribbean and Jamaican culture and their influence on rap and hip hop.

R. Serge Denisoff, with William Schurk. *Tarnished Gold: The Record Industry Revisited.* Transaction Books, 1986.

Denisoff, a sociologist, examines the recording industry by accepting popular music as a cultural phenomenon within a commercial framework. This is an update of his 1975 book *Solid Gold.*

Steven Hagar. *Hip Hop: The Illustrated History of Break Dancing, Rap Music, and Graffiti.* St. Martin's Press, 1984.

One of the few histories of rap.

Steve Chapple and Reebee Garofalo. *Rock 'n' Roll Is Here to Pay: The History and Politics of the Music Industry.* Nelson-Hall, 1977.

This interpretive look at the music industry is built on the premise that authentic cultural contributions are compromised by profit motives.

Roland Gelatt. *The Fabulous Phonograph: From Tin Foil to High Fidelity.* Lippincott, 1955.

This is a comprehensive history through the Battle of the Speeds and the demise of the 78-rpm record.

John Lasseter

Whatever it takes to get in the spirit, animation genius John Lasseter does.  His successes include the undersea saga *Finding Nemo*.

chapter 6 Movies

In this chapter you will learn:

- Movies have special impact when viewed without interruption in a darkened auditorium.
- Movies are shifting from photographic to digital technology.
- Besides feature films as a Hollywood special, other subspecies of movies include animated films and documentaries.
- The production component of the movie industry is the most visible.
- The distribution component of the movie industry includes marketing and promotion, and booking.
- The exhibition component of the movie industry is in rapid transition from the once dominant movie-house venue.
- Outcries over the violent and sexual content have prompted repeated calls for regulation.

When John Lasseter goes to work, it's almost always in a Hawaiian shirt and on occasion a tiara. And this isn't in Hawaii. Nor Disneyland. But close. Lasseter is the story-telling and artistic genius behind the incredible success of the Pixar animation studio whose run-away box-office movies include *Toy Story, Finding Nemo* and *Cars*. As Pixar's $2.9 million-a-year top executive, Lasseter can wear anything he wants.

In 2006 when Disney shocked Wall Street, paying $7.4 billion to acquire Pixar, Lasseter, at 49, was part of the deal. Now he's running both Disney's animation operation in the Burbank section of Los Angeles and Pixar's in Emeryville 400 miles away in northern California's Silicon Valley.

In ways, the Disney-Pixar merger is a homecoming. Lasseter has Disney roots. As a kid he decided after seeing Disney's *The Sword in the Stone* at a Saturday matinee that he wanted to be an animator. In high school he landed a job as a Jungle Cruise guide at Disneyland. For college he chose Disney-connected California Institute of the Arts. From there it was to Disney as an animator.

In the mid-1980s, when Apple Computer's Steve Jobs bought Pixar from moviemaker George Lucas, Lasseter made the switch to Pixar. He saw Pixar moving to the

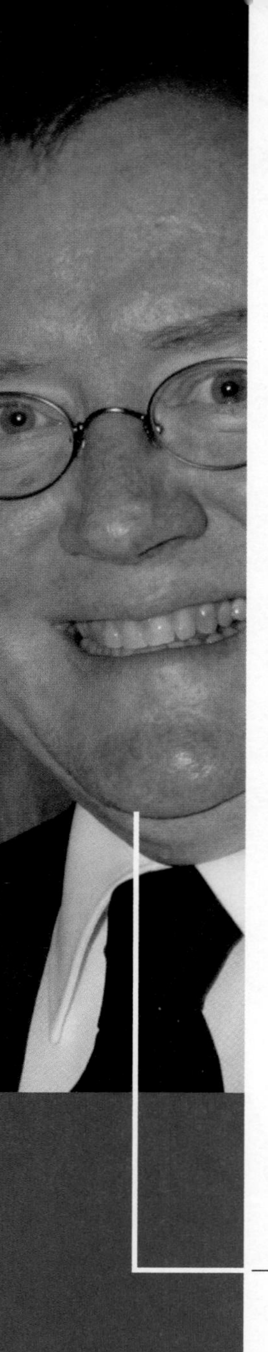

cutting-edge of computer animation for full-length movies—a radical departure from Disney's hand-drawing that was so labor-intensive it took years to produce a movie. It worked. Pixar's *Toy Story* in 1995 was a blockbuster. So was *Finding Nemo,* then *The Incredibles.*

Lasseter hadn't glommed onto computer animation as a way to pump out movies production-line style. Pixar, in fact, averages less than one movie a year. What Lasseter did with computer animation was create the time to polish the stories and characters, which everyone agrees is his genius. One Pixar producer, an old friend, calls Lasseter "a story-teller with a heart."

Unlike at Disney, known for a sluggish bureaucracy and hundreds of animators drawing by hand, Lasseter built small teams with close camaraderie on projects with a high quotient of fun. Animators were encouraged to pick up on Lasseter's wackiness, like converting their cubicles into tiki huts and mini-castles.

Shortcuts were never a production issue. Not uncommonly, production would stop to fix a storyline or a character, even if the change had a domino effect on dozens of scenes already well along. The 2006 movie *Cars* took seven years. Getting details right took time, like mimicking the ride and handling qualities of Sally the Porsche 911 and of Doc Hudson, a 1951 Hornet. The Hudson's color was taken from a paint chip off an original. Rusted and steel parts were salvaged, photographed and studied to be properly duplicated. A production team spent nine days on the road with historian Michael Wallis for an immersion in Route 66 culture, with detailed studies of weathered buildings and billboards, vegetation, and rock formations—and even the clouds.

Thus it was that Pixar productions came slowly, but there was not a box-office clunker among them. Meanwhile, as Pixar rose, Disney made money as distributor of Pixar movies but floundered with a sad series of its own animated features that just didn't catch on. Who remembers the duds *Treasure Island* or *Home on the Range*? Not since the *Lion King* in 1995 had Disney scored with an animated movie.

One of Lasseter's first decisions at Disney after the merger was to cancel *Toy Story 3,* the rights to which Disney had earlier acquired. The story line just wasn't clicking. That shook up the Disney folks. What's next? Everybody, including Disney shareholders, hopes for more great story-telling.

Importance of Movies

study preview **The experience of watching a movie uninterrupted in a darkened auditorium has entranced people since the medium's earliest days, now more than 100 years ago. It's an all-encompassing experience, which has driven perceptions, some accurate, some overstated, about the power of movies to shape cultural values.**

media ONLINE **Pixar Animation Studios** Find out how they do it.
www.pixar.com

Overwhelming Experience

Movies have a hold on people. Sealed in a darkened auditorium, you can't have a more intensive media experience. How powerful can a movie be? It's not unusual for a reviewer to recommend taking a handkerchief. Never will you hear such advice for a music reviewer. And seldom from a book reviewer.

Suspension of Disbelief

People are carrying their experiences and realities with them when they sit down for a movie. As a story-teller, a movie director needs quickly to suck the audience into the plot—to *suspend disbelief,* as novelists call it. Master directors, like James Cameron, best known for *Titanic,* strive to create this new reality in opening scenes to engross viewers in the story as it unfolds.

How do movies have such powerful effects? It's not movies themselves but the theater experience. In the darkened cocoon of a movie house with no distractions, just a giant screen, it's easy to get caught up in the story. It's a phenomenon long recognized by literary critics as **suspension of disbelief.**

Movies, of course, can be shown outdoors at drive-in theaters and on television, but the experience is strongest in a movie house.

Cinematic Dream Theory

Theories abound on the compelling power of movies. The poet Daniel Mark Epstein, commenting on his experience seeing the movie *The Godfather,* noted that Marlin Brando, by rolling his eyes, was able to convey all that the Godfather was thinking. This power was more than the facial expressions of a great actor but something long recognized in movies. The explanation is called **dream theory.**

Colin McGinn, a philosopher, has sought to explain the phenomenon by saying with movies we look *into* rather than *at*. This we also do with water, mirrors, flames and the sky. There is an immaterial quality in movies that McGinn says is lacking in sculpture, theater and the written word. Movies have no texture, no mass, just light playing on a screen. The image is transparent. The image can only be looked *into* or *through*. Referring to the classic *Citizen Kane,* McGinn said the pattern of light on a screen produces an image of Orson Welles as Charles Foster Kane: "We look through the image of Welles toward Kane, and our relationship to Kane is mediated by our imagination." This mediation, so goes the theory, results in an unmatched integration of mind, soul and image.

Why the term *dream theory*? Like dreams, says McGinn, movies mix fantasy and reality. There is a cathartic quality. There is powerful escapism into someone else's mind and soul, a kind of emotional seeing. Terms traditionally associated with Hollywood, even before theorists came up with cinematic dream theory, suggest an underlying truth to the theory. A Hollywood *star,* for example, is akin to a heavenly body visible only by looking *into* rather than *at* the sky. Ever heard Hollywood called the *dream factory?*

suspension of disbelief ■ Occurs when you surrender doubts about the reality of a story and become caught up in the story.

dream theory ■ Seeing a movie involves looking *into* the subject, not *at* the subject, which creates an unmatched union with the mind and soul not only of on-screen characters but also of the director.

Hollywood's Cultural Influence

When Clark Gable took off his shirt in the 1934 movie *It Happened One Night* and revealed that he wasn't wearing anything underneath, American men in great numbers decided that they too would go without undershirts. Nationwide, undershirt sales plummeted.

Whether men prefer wearing underwear is trivial compared with some concerns about how Hollywood portrays U.S. life and its influence, but the Clark Gable experience suggests a powerful cultural influence.

Since the early days, Hollywood has faced incessant criticism that it's a world apart and alien from the rest of U.S. culture. These critics, mostly on the nation's cultural and political right fringe, paint Hollywood as having a leftist agenda for social reform that threatens all that is traditional and good in the society. In the divisive parlance of the red-and-blue politics of contemporary U.S. politics, the critics see Hollywood as blue and Heartland values as red. Although those arguments resonate well with many people, comedian Jon Stewart makes the point that Hollywood is neither blue nor red but green. It's all about making money, as is any business, Stewart says: "Movie people don't sit down and decide to produce movies that Iowa will really hate."

Nonetheless, Hollywood is center stage in the so-called **culture wars** as the nation seeks to identify its values in a changing environment. Scholars keep tracking the sexual and violence content in the mass media, particularly movies, to figure out whether there's a link with changes in acceptable behavior, in tolerance of aberrant behavior, and in social mores. Political leaders, some sincere, some demagogues, frequently rant—most often around election time—that movies corrupt young people. The facts for deciding the legitimacy of the concerns are elusive. The impact of movies? There is much we just don't know.

Even so, nobody can deny that movies are part of our everyday lives in ways we may not even realize. The way we talk, for example, is loaded with movie metaphors. *New Yorker* magazine, introducing an issue on Hollywood, noted: "Our personal scenarios unspool in a sequence of flashbacks, voice-overs and cameos. We zoom in, cut to the chase, fade to black." In South Africa, where indigenous languages have no word for "freeze," bank robbers shout: "Freeze!" Where did they pick that up if not from Hollywood movies?

culture wars ■ Contemporary broad conflict over values, often exploited in political rhetoric, on divisive hot-button social issues, including abortion, race, sexuality.

Hollywood's New Century

Except in super-luxury home theaters, movies played at home, once on VHS machines, now mostly on DVD players, lack the intensity of the move-house experience. Not even a big, big television screen comes close to the enveloping environment of a theater

Poster Child for Culture Wars

Director Ang Lee's sympathetic treatment of homosexual commitment amid social obstacles in *Brokeback Mountain* remained such a divisive issue in 2005 that President Bush felt compelled to deny seeing the film to fend off what would have been the natural followup question: "Did you like the movie?" The argument can be made that filmic treatments help break taboos. The Sidney Portier film *Guess Who's Coming to Dinner* on interracial relationships was so credited in the 1960s.

because of home distractions. The impact is less with mobile video devices, like phones and iPods, that can play movie downloads. Do these technological developments render Hollywood less potent as a shaper of cultural values?

Theater box-office traffic has been dented seriously by home video, a technology introduced in 1977 and growing. Still, theater attendance can be incredible. In its first 10 weeks, the gay theme *Brokeback Mountain,* broaching a sensitive social issue frontally and powerfully, was a box-office leader with $66 million in domestic revenue. Then came the Oscar bump, which prompted more attendance. So volatile was the theme in some quarters that President Bush denied seeing the movie even though the White House had ordered a special print for presidential viewing. Among cultural conservatives there were calls for the faithful not to go lest their values be shaken.

Although home viewing diminishes a movie's impact, it can also be seen as extending the impact. Home and mobile video make movies accessible in more places more of the time. A theater experience even for a heavy-duty fan is but once or twice a week. On an iPod or cell phone it can be every day, with stop-restart options encouraging a fuller integration of Hollywood content with everyday activities not possible before.

There is no denying that home movies are here to stay. Ninety percent of U.S. households have videocassette players, 70 percent DVDs. Television sets are increasingly more attractive with large screens and supersound. Acquiring movies is easy. The largest home-video retailer, Blockbuster, has 5,900 stores in the United States, followed by Movie Gallery/Hollywood Video at 4,500. Wal-Mart has the largest home-video volume. Online rental services like Netflix deliver through the mail.

Movie Revenue

Box-office revenue is only part of the income that a movie can generate. These are conservative and partial income estimates for independent producer Mel Gibson for his *The Passion of the Christ,* which began earning money in 2004.

U.S. box office	$108 million
Overseas box office	100 million
DVD sales	110 million
Pay television	20 million
Soundtrack sales	10 million
Licensing and merchandise	9 million

Movie Technology

study preview **Motion picture technology is based on the same chemical process as photography. The medium developed in the 1880s and 1890s. By the 1930s movie houses everywhere were showing "talkies." Today, chemical-free digital shooting and editing are beginning to transform production, distribution and exhibition.**

media ONLINE

The First Talkie *The Jazz Singer,* with Al Jolson.
www.filmsite.org/jazz.html

Early Cinema An introduction to the first decade of motion pictures.
www.earlycinema.com

Silent Film Society of Chicago A group dedicated to the preservation and presentation of silent films. Provides links to information about silents and places to see them.
www.silentfilmchicago.com

Photography Roots

The technical heritage of motion pictures is photography. The 1727 discovery that light causes silver nitrate to darken was basic to the development of motion picture technology. So was a human phenomenon called **persistence of vision.** The human eye retains an image for a fraction of a second. If a series of photographs capture something in motion and if those photographs are flipped quickly, the human eye will perceive continuous motion.

All that was needed were the right kind of camera and film to capture about 16 images per second. Those appeared in 1888. **William Dickson** of Thomas Edison's laboratory developed a workable motion picture camera. Dickson and Edison used celluloid film perfected by **George Eastman,** who had just introduced his Kodak camera. By 1891 Edison had begun producing movies.

persistence of vision ■ Fast-changing still photos create the illusion of movement.

William Dickson ■ Developed the first movie camera.

George Eastman ■ Devised celluloid film.

media TIMELINE

MOVIE TECHNOLOGY

Three seminal discoveries and inventions made the motion picture possible:

1826 French scientist Joseph Níepce found chemicals to capture and preserve an image on a light-sensitive metal.

1888 William Dickson devised a camera to capture sequential motion.

1891 George Eastman devised flexible celluloid for film that could be run through projectors.

Other innovations:

1922 Fox used sound in newsreels.

1927 *The Black Pirate* with Douglas Fairbanks was the first color movie.

1927 Warner distributed the first talkie, *The Jazz Singer.*

1937 Disney issued the first animated feature, *Snow White.*

1953 20th Century Fox introduced the CinemaScope horizontal screen for *The Robe.*

1999 George Lucas offered a version of *Star Wars: The Phantom Menace* for digital projection.

2006 Ten-year project begins to convert movie theaters to digital projection.

Edison movies were viewed by looking into a box. In France, the **Lumière brothers,** Auguste and Louis, brought projection to motion pictures. By running the film in front of a specially aimed powerful lightbulb, the Lumières projected movie images on a wall. In 1895 they opened an exhibition hall in Paris—the first movie house. Edison recognized the commercial advantage of projection and himself patented the Vitascope projector, which he put on the market in 1896.

D-Cinema

Movie-making has been moving out of photographic technology toward **d-cinema.** George Lucas, director of the Star Wars series, pioneered the shift through his Industrial Light & Magic production house. For his 1999 Star Wars installment *The Phantom Menace,* Lucas shot several scenes with digital equipment, which facilitated integration into digitally created special effects scenes. For exhibition, there were two masters: one on film, which is what most movie-goers saw, and one in digital form, which was shown in a few specially equipped theaters. Thus *The Phantom Menace* became the first major motion picture to be seen in digital form, albeit at only the few theaters then equipped with digital projectors.

Digital advantages were clear. One was that distribution costs could be cut. The trucking of bulky reels, some weighing 85 pounds, from theater to theater was costing $750 million a year. But theater owners, pressed financially by declining box-office traffic, hesitated to invest an average of $100,000 per screen for digital servers, projectors and related equipment. Some owners, notably Mark Cuban, took the plunge. Cuban converted his 270-screen Landmark chain beginning in 2005, saying he would show special events if Hollywood wouldn't supply enough digital movies to fill out his schedules.

DCinema Today Find out the latest in digital advances. **www.dcinematoday.com**

In 2006 the entire movie industry recognized the obvious—that people were becoming more enamored of digital images on computer screens, a trend that was sure to accelerate with the pending television shift to digital transmission. With Hollywood advancing the money, the major movie-house chains began a 10-year project to convert to digital projection equipment at all of the 36,700 screens in the United States and thousands of screens around the world.

Technologically, the industry had come a long way from Níepce, Edison and Eastman.

Lumière brothers ■ Opened the first movie exhibition hall.

d-cinema ■ Digitally filmed, edited, distributed and exhibited movies.

mediaPEOPLE

Mark Cuban

Mark Cuban is a digital believer. Risking big bucks, he created a pioneer company in digital television programming, the HDNet Movies network for satellite delivery. Then he plunged into digital projection for his 270-screen Landmark theater chain. In 2005 he converted the first two of his theaters, in San Francisco and Dallas. By 2007 every Landmark movie house was showing digital movies.

At first executives at the leading exhibition chains showed no daring, regarding Cuban as a mere curiosity. The conventional wisdom was that digital conversion, at $100,000 minimum per screen, was too risky at a time when home-video rentals were sucking box-office traffic away.

Cuban didn't see it that way. He proclaimed that once people saw their first digital movie on a big screen, they would settle for nothing less. His gospel was that digital pulls people into the viewing experience—more vivid colors, no graininess, and an end to inevitable projection-room goofs like reels coming out of sequence. Nor would there be any more distracting focus adjustments or scratchy reels that have been pulled over the sprockets too many times. Cuban said that digital movies would draw people back to movie houses—a salvation for the beleaguered exhibition business.

Cuban's enthusiasm was perhaps too easy to dismiss. His Landmark chain was, to be sure, a blip in the industry—his 270 screens far short of industry leader Regal's 5,600. Too, he had other passions, like his Dallas Mavericks basketball team. But Cuban gauged correctly what the big chains missed—that the huge distribution economies that would come with replacing bulky film canisters with digital signals would lead to Hollywood issuing more digital movies sooner rather than later. One estimate was $568 million a year could be saved in distribution costs. Such savings, Cuban figured, would become—a major incentive for Hollywood to switch.

Cuban was right. In 2006 Hollywood studios and distributors put up the money to begin the conversion of movie screens nationwide. It was a multi-year plan with Hollywood money subsidizing exhibition companies over several years. In effect, those cautious exhibition chain executives who scoffed at Cuban while also eyeing him closely ended up playing catch-up. The Landmark chain was all-digital while the other chains were still converting.

Filmless Movie Houses. He started the major shift to digital exhibition with the conversion of his 270 Landmark theater screens. Here, Cuban and actress Angela Bassett are at a premiere of the film *Akeelah and the Bee.*

Movie Industry Products

studypreview **To most people, the word *movie* conjures up the feature films that are the Hollywood specialty. Subspecies include animated films and documentaries. Also, the historic distinction between Hollywood and television as rivals is melding.**

Feature Films

Movies that tell stories, much in the tradition of stage plays, are **narrative films.** These are what most people think of as movies. They're promoted heavily, their titles and actors on marquees. Most are in the 100-minute range.

A French magician and inventor, Georges Méliès, pioneered narrative films with fairy tales and science-fiction stories to show in his movie house in 1896. Méliès' *Little Red Riding Hood* and *Cinderella* ran less than 10 minutes—short stories, if you will. In 1902 Edwin Porter directed *Life of a Fireman,* the first coherent narrative film in the United

narrative films ■ Movies that tell a story.

Big-Budget Movies

Movie Title	Year	Amount Spent
Titanic	1997	$240 million
Superman Returns	2006	204 million
Chronicles of Narnia	2005	200 million
Terminator 3: Rise of the Machines	2003	175 million
Spider-Man	2002	170 million
Matrix Reloaded	2003	170 million
The Hulk	2003	150 million
Pearl Harbor	2001	140 million
Charlie's Angels: Full Throttle	2003	135 million
Bad Boys II	2003	130 million
Harry Potter and the Sorcerer's Stone	2001	120 million

States. Audiences, accustomed to stage plays and being a distance away from the actors, were distressed, some shocked, at his close-ups, a new technique. They felt cheated at not seeing "the whole stage." Gradually, audiences learned what is called **film literacy,** the ability to appreciate movie-making as an art form with unique-to-the-medium techniques that add impact or facilitate the telling of a story. Porter's next significant film, *The Great Train Robbery,* was shocking, too, for cutting back and forth between robbers and a posse that was chasing them—something, like close-ups, that film can do and the stage cannot. Slowly movies emerged as a distinctive art form.

Talkies At Thomas Edison's lab, the tinkerer William Dickson came up with a sound system for movies in 1889, but it didn't go anywhere. The first successful commercial application of sound was in Movietone newsreels in 1922. But it was four upstart movie-makers, the **Warner brothers,** Albert, Harry, Jack and Sam Warner, who revolutionized **talkies,** movies with sound. In 1927 the Warners released ***The Jazz Singer*** starring Al Jolson. There was sound only for two segments, 354 words total, but audiences in movie houses the Warners equipped with loudspeakers were enthralled. The next year, 1928, the Warners issued ***The Singing Fool,*** also with Jolson, this time with a full-length soundtrack. The Warners earned 25 times their investment. For 10 years no other movie attracted more people to the box office

Color Overtaking *The Singing Fool* in 1939 was a narrative movie with another technological breakthrough, *Gone With the Wind* with color. Although *Gone With the Wind* is often referred to as the first color movie, the technology had been devised in the 1920s, and ***The Black Pirate*** with Douglas Fairbanks was far earlier, in 1925. But *GWTW,* as it's called by buffs, was a far more significant film. *GWTW* marked the start of Hollywood's quest for ever more spectacular stories and effects to attract audiences—the blockbuster.

film literacy ■ Ability to appreciate artistic techniques used for telling a story through film.

Warner brothers ■ Introduced sound.

talkies ■ Movies with sound.

The Jazz Singer ■ First feature sound movie.

The Singing Fool ■ First full-length sound movie.

The Black Pirate ■ First feature movie in color.

Walt Disney ■ Pioneer in animated films.

animated film ■ Narrative films with drawn scenes and characters.

Steamboat Willie ■ Animated cartoon character that became Mickey Mouse.

Snow White and the Seven Dwarfs ■ First full-length animated film.

computer-generated imagery (CGI) ■ The application of three-dimensional computer graphics for special effects, particularly in movies and television.

Animated Films

The 1920s were pivotal in defining genres of narrative films. In his early 20s, **Walt Disney** arrived in Los Angeles from Missouri in 1923 with $40 in his pocket. Walt moved in with his brother Roy, and they rounded up $500 and went into the **animated film** business. In 1928 ***Steamboat Willie*** debuted in a short film to accompany feature films. The character Willie eventually morphed into Mickey Mouse. Disney took animation to full length with ***Snow White and the Seven Dwarfs*** in 1937, cementing animation as a subspecies of narrative films.

Animated films were labor-intensive, requiring an illustrator to create 1,000-plus sequential drawings for a minute of screen time. Computers changed all that in the 1990s, first with digital effects for movies that otherwise had scenes and actors, notably the Star Wars series by George Lucas, then animated features. Disney's *Toy Story* in 1995 was the first movie produced entirely on computers. The new technology, brought to a high level by Lucas' Industrial Light & Magic and Steve Jobs' Pixar, has led to a resurgence in the issuance of animated films after a relatively dormant period.

Recent years have seen huge audiences for *Shrek, Finding Nemo* and *Cars,* among others.

mediaTECHNOLOGY

Computer-Generated Imagery

You can imagine why early moviemaker Alfred Clark used a special effect for his 1895 movie *The Execution of Mary Queen of Scots.* "Illusion" was what special effects were called then. Although audiences were amazed, the effects were nothing like today's *CGI,* the shoptalk abbreviation that movie people use for three-dimensional **computer-generated imagery.**

The first use of three-dimensional CGI in movies was *Futureworld* in 1976. University of Utah grad students Edwin Catmull and Fred Parke created a computer-generated hand and face. There were CGI scenes in *Star Wars* in 1977, but the technology remained mostly an experimental novelty until 1989 when the pseudopod sea creature created by Industrial Light & Magic for *The Abyss* won an Academy Award.

Photorealistic CGI was firmly in place with the villain's liquid metal morphing effects in *Terminator 2,* also by Industrial Light & Magic and also recognized by a 1991 Oscar for special effects.

Computer-generated imagery soon became the dominant form of special effects with technology opening up new possibilities. For stunts, CGI characters began replacing doubles that were nearly indistinguishable from the actors. Crowd scenes were easily created without hiring hundreds of extras. This raised the question of whether movie actors themselves might be replaced by pixels.

Movie commentator Neil Petkus worries that some film-makers may overuse their toy. "CGI effects can be abused and mishandled," Petkus says. "Directors sometimes allow the visual feasts that computers offer to undermine any real content a movie may have had." Petkus faults director George Lucas for going too far in later Star Wars movies: "Any interesting character developments that could have occurred in these movies were overwhelmed by constant CGI action sequences."

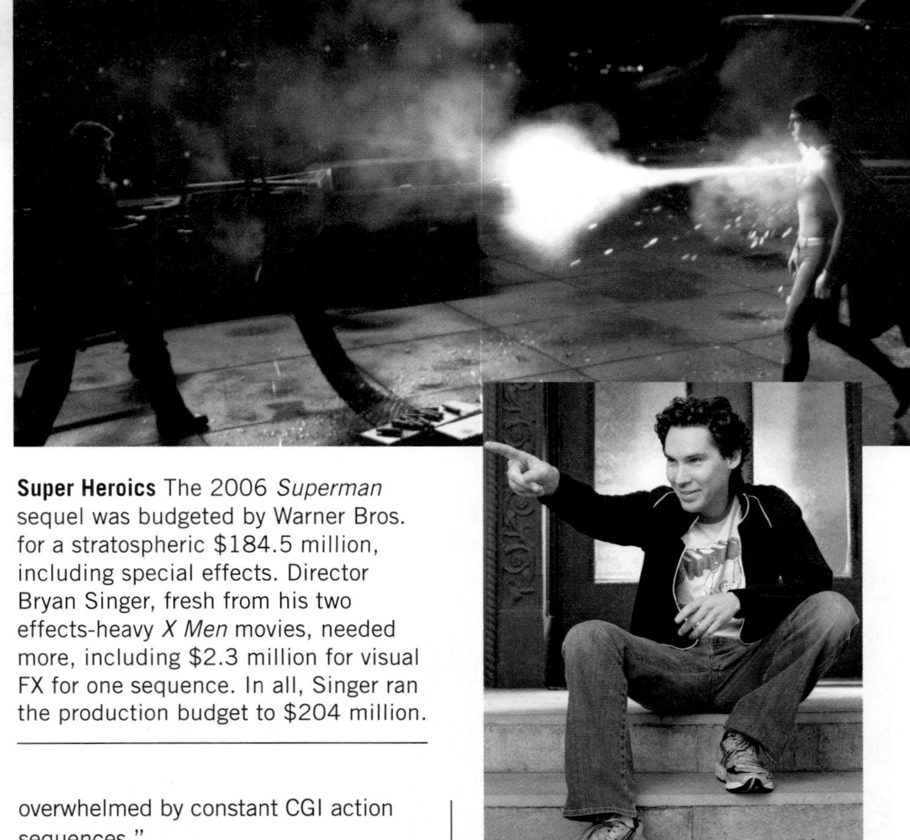

Super Heroics The 2006 *Superman* sequel was budgeted by Warner Bros. for a stratospheric $184.5 million, including special effects. Director Bryan Singer, fresh from his two effects-heavy *X Men* movies, needed more, including $2.3 million for visual FX for one sequence. In all, Singer ran the production budget to $204 million.

Bryan Singer

Movies that overdo CGI can lack the depth of character and nuance that human actors bring to the screen, says Petkus: "How can we relate to a character made up of pixels and mathematical algorithms and not flesh, blood, and emotion? Sure, CGI movies are flashy, but they don't convey the sense of reality that we look for in a good cinematic story."

Another commentator, Matt Leonard, has made the point this way: "There are hundreds of Elvis impersonators in the world, some of which are very good, but none of them are good enough to fool us into thinking Elvis has returned. The closer we get to creating a completely digital character the more our senses seem to alert us to the fact that something is not completely right and therefore we dismiss it as a cheap trick or imitation."

So while CGI characters can make sense for stunt stand-ins or for humanly impossible only-from-Hollywood contortions and feats, they probably don't spell doom for the Screen Actors Guild. About replacing actors, Dennis Muren of Industrial Light & Magic is clear: "Why bother! Why not focus on what doesn't exist as opposed to recreating something that is readily available."

Faster computers and massive data storage capacities have added efficiencies to computer-generated movie imagery, but offsetting the efficiencies has been pressure for greater detail and quality. CGI is labor-intensive. A single frame typically takes two to three hours to render. For a complex frame count on 20 hours or more. The Warner Bros. budget for the 2006 *Superman Returns,* a record $204 million, was eaten up largely with CGI effects.

Morgan Sperlock ■ Maker of point-of-view documentary movies.

documentaries ■ A video examination of a historical or current event or a natural or social phenomenon.

Frank Capra ■ Hollywood movie director who produced powerful propaganda movies for U.S. war effort in World War II.

Why We Fight ■ Frank Capra war mobilization documentary series.

Documentaries

Morgan Sperlock went on a fast-food diet, only Big Macs and other McDonald's fare. It wreaked havoc on Sperlock's body, as anybody can see in his movie *Super Size Me*. The 2003 movie was among a growing number of point-of-view **documentaries.** Documentaries aren't new. Nonfiction film explorations of historical or current events and natural and social phenomena go back to 1922 and Robert Flaherty's look into Eskimo life. Except for propagandist films that found large audiences during World War II, including **Frank Capra**'s seven 50-minute films in the **Why We Fight** series, documentaries have been mostly evenhanded toward their subjects. But not Sperlock's *Super Size*

mediaPEOPLE

Lourdes Portillo

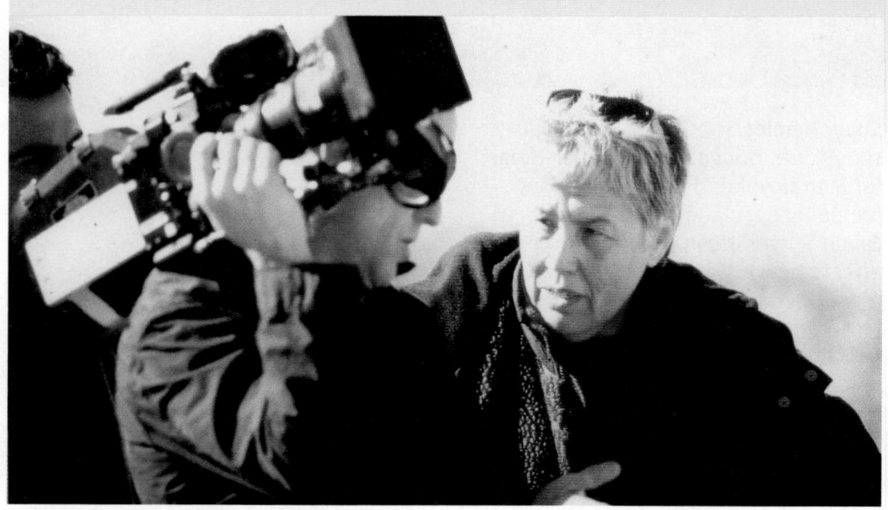

Documentary-Maker As a human rights activist drawn from Hispanic culture, Portillo examines social injustice, especially against women.

Selena Quintanilla's father knew the world was dangerous and wanted so much to protect his daughter. His tragic mistake, as he tells it to film-maker Lourdes Portillo, was sheltering his daughter. He didn't tell Selena about people out there who do horrible things. Selena, the crossover Tejano pop singer, sheltered and naive in her relations with fans and everybody else, was murdered.

In the wrenching documentary *Corpus,* shot home-video style, Portillo interviews the father and people around Selena—even the woman convicted of the murder. The film is part of a body of work that has established Lourdes Portillo as one of the great movie-makers of our era. Yet aside from film aficionados, her name is hardly a household word. That, in a sense, is how Portillo wants it. "I went into film-making not to make money but to say what I wanted to say."

Portillo, Chihuahua-born but living mostly in the United States since her teens, identifies herself as Chicana. She chooses mostly Hispanic subjects, usually women and social injustice.

For what some critics call her most compelling work, *Señorita Extraviada (Missing Woman),* Portillo spent 18 months in the Juarez, where dozens of young women had been murdered. In detective-story style, Portillo details what was happening. During the filming, another 50 women, all brown, young, pretty and unprotected, were killed. That put the total to more than 270 murdered and raped and 450 reported missing.

What was happening in Juarez, a border city across from El Paso, Texas?

In short, Portillo says, Mexican women are disposable: "They are just like raw material—how easy it is to kill and get rid of them and use them." Police, she found, were largely indifferent. Portillo's documentary, however, prompted Mexico President Vicente Fox to order an investigation.

But, again, what was happening? Portillo found the Juarez environment was a layered complexity that included endemic corruption and drug and pornography trafficking, complicated by the social disruptions created by a booming economy. One woman who escaped a brutal encounter, identified only as Maria, told Portillo in a jarring interview that police were participating. Portillo admits she was fearful during her filming not only for her own safety but for the safety of her sources.

Portillo's style, which has been called "filmic poetry," adds to the potency of her stories. The film itself adds to her reputation for treating social injustice, especially against women. That is enough for Portillo. As she puts it, she lights the spark for change and passes the torch: "When you create ripples, that's success."

About her documentaries carrying a point of view, Portillo is unapologetic: "We need a vision that is artistic, that touches people's hearts."

Me nor many other recent opinionated, frequently sarcastic and sometimes darkly comic documentaries.

Relatively in expensive digital film-making equipment has driven the new documentaries. Morgan Sperlock could never have persuaded a major studio for the budget, several million dollars upfront, for a documentary attacking an American icon like McDonald's. Not even Sperlock's record as an MTV producer would have done it. But with a $3,000 digital camera, $5,000 in software and an Apple computer he created his personal statement on fast food. So compelling was *Super Size Me* that 200 theaters showed it and grossed $7.5 million in a month. In all, Sperlock had spent only $65,000 to create the movie.

mediaPEOPLE

Robert Flaherty

Nanook of the North The documentary became a film genre with explorer Robert Flaherty's *Nanook of the North* in 1922. This film was an attempt to record reality—no actors, no props. The film was especially potent not only because it was a new approach and on a fascinating subject but also because, coincidentally, Nanook died of starvation on the ice around the time that the film was released.

Arctic Explorer

Explorer Robert Flaherty took a camera to the Arctic in 1921 to record the life of an Eskimo family. The result was a new kind of movie: the documentary. While other movies of the time were theatrical productions with scripts, sets and actors, Flaherty tried something different: recording reality.

His 57-minute *Nanook of the North* was compelling on its own merits when it started on the movie-house circuit in 1922, but the film received an unexpected macabre boost a few days later when Nanook, the father of the Eskimo family, died of hunger on the ice. News stories of Nanook's death stirred public interest—and also attendance at the movie, which helped to establish the documentary as an important new film genre.

Flaherty's innovative approach took a new twist in the 1930s when propagandists saw reality-based movies as a tool to promote their causes. In Germany the Nazi government produced propaganda films, and other countries followed. Frank Capra directed the vigorous five-film series *Why We Fight* for the U.S. War Office in 1942.

After World War II there was a revival of documentaries in Flaherty's style—a neutral recording of natural history. Walt Disney produced a variety of such documentaries, including the popular *Living Desert* in the 1950s.

Today, documentaries are unusual in U.S. movie houses, with occasional exceptions such as movies built on rock concerts and *March of the Penguins.*

The CBS television network gained a reputation in the 1950s and 1960s for picking up on the documentary tradition with *Harvest of Shame,* about migrant workers, and *Hunger in America.* In the same period the National Geographic Society established a documentary unit, and French explorer Jacques Cousteau went into the television documentary business.

Such full-length documentaries are mostly relegated to the Public Broadcasting Service and cable networks today. The major networks, meanwhile, shifted most documentaries away from full-length treatments. Typical is CBS's *60 Minutes,* a twice-weekly one-hour program of three minidocumentaries. These new network projects combined reality programming and entertainment in slick packages that attracted larger audiences than traditional documentaries.

Television Production

Although once rivals, the movie and television industries have become so intertwined that it is hard to distinguish them. The movie studios all have units devoted to producing television shows. Indeed, some giant media corporations own both movie studios and television networks. The classic movie as narrative film has made concessions to television. Story lines are written to accommodate commercial breaks. The dimension and scale of screens is drastically different, requiring different approaches to directing and editing. But television productions, ranging from high drama to sitcoms, is at its core a variant of the narrative film.

Movie Industry: Production

media ONLINE

Sony Pictures The parent company of the American icon, Columbia Pictures.
www.sonypictures.com

Disney Online Where the magic comes to you.
Disney.com

Paramount Pictures See the trailers of recent releases.
www.paramount.com/

20th Century Fox The Official site for Fox Movies
www.foxmovies.com

Universal Studios Learn about current Universal films, links to projects in projection, and some surprises.
www.universalstudios.com

Warner Brothers More than just "What's up, Doc?"
www.warnerbros.com

studypreview **The movie industry has three major components—production, distribution and exhibition. Most attention goes to production, epitomized in the big-name studios, celebrity directors and actors, and all the attendant glitz.**

Major Studios

The flashy corporate names in the movie business are the big studios that produce movies and also distribute movies from independent producers. Some studios, the brand names, are responsible for about 90 percent of the U.S. movie industry's revenue. They're called the **Big Six**—Columbia, Disney, Paramount, 20th Century Fox, Universal and Warner. These companies are called **studios** because each once maintains acres of stage sets—*studios,* if you will.

In their heyday, the major studios dominated the whole movie industry. Not only did the studios conceive and nurture movies into existence, which is called the **production** component of the industry, they also controlled the distribution of their products and owned many movie houses. The scope of the studios was trimmed in a 1948 U.S. Supreme Court anti-trust opinion called the **Paramount decision,** which forced the major studios of that

Big Six ■ Columbia, Disney, Paramount, 20th Century Fox, Universal and Warner.

studios ■ A company that produces movies, sometimes also involved in distribution.

production ■ Content-creation component of the movie industry.

Paramount decision ■ U.S. Supreme Court 1948 decision for major studios to divest either their production, distribution of exhibition interests, which the Court said constituted too much control of the industry.

Adolph Zukor ■ Creator of celebrity movie star system and the broader studio system.

studio system ■ A mass-production process for movies.

block booking ■ A rental agreement that forces a movie house to accept a batch of movies.

Major Movie Studios

In the high-risk movie business, with drastic revenue swings every weekend of new releases, a ranking of the major studios based on revenue is impossible. A single mega-success can catapult one studio to the top instantly, and a series of flops can push a studio toward insolvency. These, though, are the enduring giants of the industry:

	Corporate Parent	Parent Nationality
Columbia	Sony	Japan
Paramount	Viacom	United States
20th Century Fox	News Corporation	Australia
Universal	General Electric	United States
Walt Disney	Disney	United States
Warner Brothers	Time Warner	United States

mediaPEOPLE

Adolph Zukor

Early movie actors weren't acknowledged with on-screen credits. When fans wrote asking for names, movie-makers didn't answer. They didn't want to contribute to the making of celebrity stars who might demand more than the $15 a day that was the top-dollar rate of the day.

In those fan letters, however, one movie-maker, the Hungarian immigrant **Adolph Zukor,** saw an opportunity. In 1912 he created the Famous Players Company and signed the actors most mentioned in letters to exclusive contracts. Zukor soon had a troupe of stars whose name on the marquee he knew would attract audiences—even to mediocre films. It was costly. Zukor's star Mary Pickford was earning $15,000 a week by 1917, compared to $100 before signing on.

For Zukor the celebrity salaries were an investment. His stars generated many times their salaries at box offices throughout the country. Zukor expanded his enterprise, which eventually became the Paramount studio. There Zukor perfected an assembly-line process for movies that kept not only his popular actors occupied but also staffs of talented directors, editors, writers and technicians. The process was called the **studio system.** Paramount and its competitors soon were pumping out a movie a week. Compromised by production deadlines and budgets, not all the films were gems. In fact, most were formulaic and imitative.

By the mid-1930s the leading movie companies—Columbia, MGM, Paramount, RKO, 20th Century Fox, Universal and Warner—had major investments in acres of studios and sets, hundreds of directors and actors and teams of technicians. Creative latitude was given to some of the best screenwriters and directors, like John Ford and Billy Wilder, but the system, based on a factory model, was designed to churn out quantities of product on predictable schedules. Much of the output was mediocre. But the nation had fallen into a weekly moviegoing habit. At 50 cents or less for a double-feature, even Depression-plagued Americans could afford an evening's escapism. And the money flowed to Hollywood to sustain the system.

Studio System Mastermind

Meanwhile, Zukor's Paramount and the other leading studios acquired movie houses by the hundreds, which gave them control of their product from conception to the final sale. The U.S. Justice Department's antitrust division became concerned when the studios began squeezing independent theatres by renting them the best films only in packages that also included clunkers. The scheme, called **block booking,** was found coercive by the U.S. Supreme Court in the so-called Paramount decision of 1948. The studios were told, in effect, to jettison their owned-and-operated theatres and to end block booking.

The studios barely survived. Their massive investment in facilities and personnel had been based on a guaranteed outlet for their products. Suddenly, they had to compete to get their movies into theatres. Off-site shooting, increasingly feasible with new technology, became common. Underused, the huge sound studios became a liability. High-salaried actors, directors and technicians on ongoing salaries added roughly 30 percent to the cost of every movie.

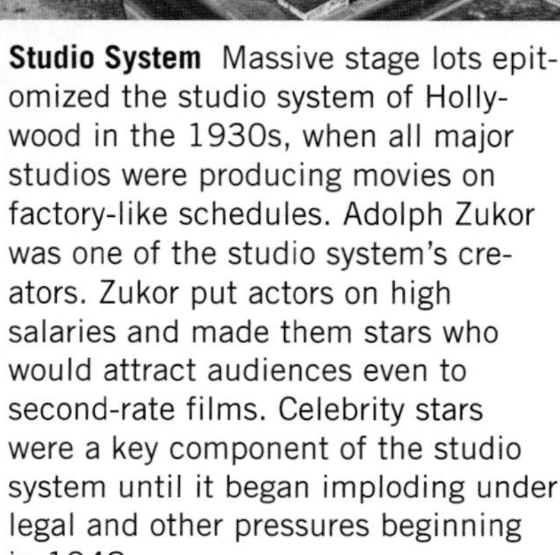

Studio System Massive stage lots epitomized the studio system of Hollywood in the 1930s, when all major studios were producing movies on factory-like schedules. Adolph Zukor was one of the studio system's creators. Zukor put actors on high salaries and made them stars who would attract audiences even to second-rate films. Celebrity stars were a key component of the studio system until it began imploding under legal and other pressures beginning in 1948.

The studios sold their sprawling facilities. In one sign of the times, the RKO facility was sold to the Desilu television production company in 1953 to make television programs exclusively. Meanwhile, studios looked more and more to outside producers and directors to generate movies that studios then picked up and distributed. The system constricted.

The end of the studio system came when large conglomerates bought the studios and imposed new bottom-line expectations. Zukor, one of the original studio moguls, himself was present at the end. He died in 1976 at age 103, still chairman of the board.

time to divest. The studios chose to lop off their theaters, which were sold to other companies. The studios' publicity machines continued to make idols of scriptwriters, directors and actors and simultaneously promoted themselves with glitz. No matter the 1948 setback, the studios maintained a reputation for glamour—and with justification. No other country had such a highly developed movie industry.

Other Studios

A notable player besides the Big Six has been **United Artists.** In 1919 four powerful figures—director D. W. Griffith and box-office darlings Charlie Chaplin, Douglas Fairbanks and Mary Pickford—were concerned that the studios were disproportionately focused on profits and infringing on creativity. They created United Artists. With full creative control, they produced movies that scored well among critics and attracted huge audiences. United Artists has been among only a few insurgent movie companies to make a long-term mark on Hollywood after the giants established themselves early on.

United Artists' financial history, however, has been rocky. It was almost undone by Michael Cimono's out-of-control spending to make *Heaven's Gate* in 1980. A year later the Transamerica insurance company that had acquired United Artists unloaded the studio on MGM. But the amalgamated MGM/UA produced one disaster after another. Whether MGM/UA can break into the Big Six is an open question.

Most upstarts fade quickly or are absorbed by the majors. This happened with Dreamworks, which in the UA spirit was created in 1994 by three Hollywood legends—retired recording executive David Geffen, former Disney executive Jeff Katzenberg and superdirector Steven Spielberg. It was a dream team of well-connected and seasoned Hollywood people who, each with a fortune from successful entertainment industry careers, could bankroll major projects and attract investors. Spielberg's *Saving Private Ryan* in 1998 established an early Dreamworks benchmark for filmic excellence. Then came *Gladiator,* named 2000's best picture at the Academy Awards. In an industry *deja vu,* Geffen, Katzenberg and Spielberg sold their upstart Dreamworks in 2005 to Paramount for $1.6 billion.

Independent Producers

media ONLINE **Newmarket Films** Film distribution company with only one criterion—quality.
www.newmarketfilms.com

United Artists Historical and current information.
www.unitedartists.com/

Before the U.S. Supreme Court's *Paramount* decision in 1948, major studios controlled the entire system. Independent movie-makers did not have much opportunity to get their movies into the distribution and exhibition network. That changed dramatically when the Paramount decision forced a break-up of the majors' control. Today the big studios scout for independent producers to pick up promising movies to distribute. The studios bypass production expenses and cash in on the distribution revenue.

A classic example of a big studio using its distribution muscle with an independent movie was the *Blair Witch Project,* which cost $35,000 to produce. In 1998 the young directors sold the movie for $1.1 million to Artisan Entertainment for distribution. Cleverly promoted by Artisan, within a year the movie was a commercial smash generating revenue of $141 million. At the Sundance Film Festival in Utah and other festivals, many independent producers are in effect auditioning their movies for major studio scouts.

Major studios also bankroll projects from independent producers, whose overhead costs are low. This doesn't mean studio financing is easy to come by, as attested by Spike Lee, the legendary director of black-themed movies, including *Malcolm X*. Even so, Lee has found studio backing for numerous films.

Some actors have succeeded in directing and producing on their own, with varying levels of studio financial backing. These include Clint Eastwood, Tom Hanks and Ron Howard. Then there are independent producers who come from no-where, it seems, and hit a chord that resonates with the public. Michael Moore did it with his bleak documentary on General Motors, *Roger and Me,* and his equally bleak *Bowling for Columbine,* his politically charged *Fahrenheit 9/11,* and most recently *Sicko.*

Independent producers are evidence that major studios have a monopoly on neither originality nor creativity. But as many will tell you, they're outsiders. Ask Daniel Myrick and Eduardo Sánchez, who directed *Blair Witch Project*. Or Spike Lee.

United Artists ■ Upstart artist-directed movie studio, started in 1919.

mediaPEOPLE

Steven Spielberg

Although born in 1946, Steven Spielberg couldn't have made films like *Jaws, E.T.* and *Indiana Jones* if he weren't still a kid himself. At the dinner table when his seven kids were growing up, Spielberg used to start with a few lines from a story that popped into his head, then each of the kids would add a few lines. Where it would go, nobody knew, but everybody kept the story moving.

Spielberg loves stories, especially with ordinary characters meeting extraordinary beings or finding themselves in extraordinary circumstances. Another theme is that of lost innocence and coming-of-age. A persistent theme is parent-child tensions, which has been laid to Spielberg's own distress as a child at his parents divorcing.

Critics, however, see unrealistic optimism and sentimentalism in Spielberg films although they admit exceptions. Certainly *Indiana Jones* is not all that has earned Spielberg his reputation as one of history's great movie-makers. One ranking has him Number One. Twice he has won Academy Awards as best director for *Schindler's List* and *Saving Private Ryan,* both gritty films set in wartime misery. *Schindler* took an Oscar for best picture.

As a kid Spielberg was infected with a love for making movies. At 12 he put two Lionel toy trains on a collision course, turned up the juice to both engines and made a home movie of the crash. By that time he already had shot dozens of short films. For one of them, he coaxed his mother into donning a pith helmet and an Army surplus uniform, and then rolled the film as she bounced the family Jeep through backhill potholes near Phoenix. That was his first war movie.

Later, on a family trip to Los Angeles he lined up an unpaid summer job on the Universal studios lot. He enrolled at California State University in Long Beach in 1965 but interrupted his studies to take a television director job at Universal before finishing his degree. Ironically, Spielberg tried three times for admission to the prestigious film program at the University of Southern California and failed—although in 1994 he was awarded an honorary USC degree.

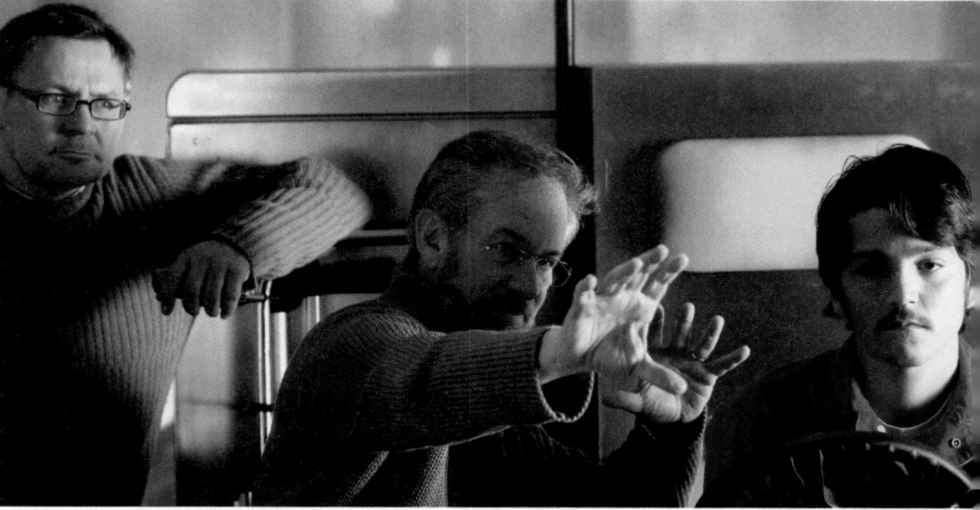

Compelling Storyteller Here, Spielberg makes a point with cinematographer Janusz Kaminski and actor Diego Luna for *The Terminal.* Since *Jaws* in 1975, he has directed movies involving history and science, including many on issues that kids deal with, such as *E.T.* and *Jurassic Park.* Spielberg spends a lot of time in children's hospital wards, working with online links provided by the Starbright Foundation, which he leads.

His films, although wide-ranging in subject, have family-friendly themes with a childlike wonderment. There also are strong emotions, as in the *Schindler* depiction of the horrors of the Holocaust, social and sexual injustice in *The Color Purple,* slavery in *Amistad,* and terrorism in *Munich.* But amid the heavy-duty treatments he mixes in rollicking adventures, like yet another in the Indiana Jones series or *Jurassic Park* sequel.

Spielberg's financial success, $250 million alone for the first *Jurassic Park,* has given him the wherewithal to make whatever movie he wants. Still, he dabbles in other things. For a while he oversaw installments of the NBC television series *E.R.* He has collaborated on a multimedia game called *Steven Spielberg's Director's Chair.* His love of animated cartoons led him to produce *Tiny Toon Adventures* and *Freakazoid.*

In 1994 he teamed with Hollywood legendaries David Geffen and Jeffrey Katzenberg to create Dreamworks, a stand-alone movie studio outside of Hollywood's Big Six. *Amistad* and *Saving Private Ryan* set a benchmark for achievement for the enterprise, which produced acclaimed movies although not in huge numbers. Twelve years later, Geffen, Katzenberg and Spielberg sold Dreamworks to Paramount for $1.6 billion. Before then Spielberg made the *Forbes* magazine ranking of the richest people in the United States with a net worth at $2.7 billion, second among Hollywood figures only to his buddy George Lucas at $3.5 billion.

The sale of Dreamworks, however, didn't mean an end to Spielberg's movie-making. A fourth in the Indiana Jones series was issued in 2007. An Abraham Lincoln bio-pic was coming along. Might we meet the thoroughly ugly but oh-so-lovable E.T., the extra-terrestrial, at least one more time?

media ONLINE

Motion Picture Association of America The voice and advocate of the American motion picture industries.
www.mpaa.org

Video Software Dealers Association A trade association dedicated to advancing the interests of the home entertainment industry.
www.vsda.org

ShowBiz Data Find out about the business side of the movies.
www.showbizdata.com

National Association of Theater Owners This NATO is for theater owners.
www.natoonline.org

Movie Industry: Distribution

study preview **Often overlooked by fans is the distribution component of the movie industry, which includes deciding on release dates, marketing and promotion, and booking films into theaters and coordinating home video and other releases.**

Booking Movies

Opening weekends have become make-it or break-it for movies. If attendance is weak for the theatrical release, powerful word-of-mouth promotion is lost. The task of releasing movies in a competitively open weekend, hitting the mark with the right promotion, and being on the right number of screens in the right places, all these factors are the

media PEOPLE

Bob and Harvey Weinstein

Miramax Founders

Brothers Bob and Harvey Weinstein blew into Hollywood in 1979, introducing themselves as concert promoters from Buffalo, New York. They set up a movie distribution company, Miramax, with a simple premise: Find low-budget independently produced movies and buy them cheap, then promote them lavishly. Finding a niche was tough, but after 10 years of struggling, the Weinsteins hit gold with the biopic *My Left Foot* on Irish writer-painter Christy Brown. An Academy Award nomination as best picture stirred the box office. So did Daniel Day-Lewis's winning the Oscar for best actor.

Also in 1989, Steven Soderbergh's *Sex, Lies and Videotape* earned $20 million at U.S. box offices. Soderbergh had made the film for $1.2 million. Overseas and video sales swelled the profits. Those were the kind of numbers that the Weinsteins had envisioned from the beginning.

There were misses, but Miramax's successes inspired the giant Disney studio to offer to buy Miramax in 1993. The main asset, as Disney saw it, was the Weinsteins' deft cultural touch for edginess—something that stolid Disney sorely lacked. Disney would put up the money to acquire films in which the Weinsteins saw potential, up to $12.5 million each. The Weinsteins were given creative control, subject to veto only if Disney put more than $12.5 million into a project or if something was so edgy as to be rated NC-17. The first success of the arrangement was Quentin Tarantino's *Pulp Fiction* in 1994, an $8 million film that grossed $200 million worldwide. There was an Oscar.

Amid other financial and critical successes, including *Chicago, Good Will Hunting, Kill Bill, Scary Movie 3* and *Shakespeare in Love,* there were Weinstein projects that made Disney uneasy. Disney wasn't keen on *Kids,* a 1995 movie about teenage sex. Then came Michael Moore's Bush-bashing documentary *Fahrenheit 9/11* in 2004. Disney refused to let Miramax distribute the film. Moore went ballistic, charging Disney with cowardliness and censorship. Amid the headlines, the Weinsteins were silent and let Disney roast in the negative publicity that Moore generated. The brothers then bought the rights from Miramax and, acting on their own, arranged for a Canadian distribution company, Lions Gate, to book the movie into theatres.

responsibility of **distribution** units of major studios and stand-alone distribution companies. A great movie can flounder beyond recovery in the marketplace if distribution is fumbled.

media DATABANK

Global Box Office

Movie Title	Year	Amount Earned
Titanic	1997	$1.8 billion
Harry Potter and the Sorcerer's Stone	2001	980 million
Harry Potter and the Chamber of Secrets	2002	880 million
Spider-Man	2002	820 million
Matrix Reloaded	2003	740 million
Pearl Harbor	2001	450 million
Terminator 3: Rise of the Machines	2003	435 million
Bad Boys II	2003	270 million
Charlie's Angels: Full Throttle	2003	260 million
The Hulk	2003	250 million

Foreign Distribution

Hollywood didn't have an edge on European movie-makers until World War I suddenly created a vacuum that the U.S. movie industry filled. That began the pre-eminence of Hollywood in global movie-making. Today, foreign distribution sometimes generates more revenue than domestic box-office sales. Consider these movies early in 2006:

	Domestic	Foreign
King Kong (9 weeks)	$216 million	$325 million
Harry Potter and the Goblet of Fire (13 weeks)	287 million	599 million
Flightplan (21 weeks)	90 million	125 million

Some movies do better domestically, but even then foreign box office is important to the bottom line. In its first 10 weeks, *Brokeback Mountain* grossed $66 million in the United States plus $38 million abroad.

Regional competition for U.S. films has developed. In Mumbai, formerly Bombay, the Indian film industry puts out 900-plus movies a year. These **Bollywood** films, a contrivance of the words *Bombay* and *Hollywood,* are produced mostly for Subcontinent audiences. In Nigeria an emerging film industry called **Nollywood** is emerging. For decades the Canadian government has subsidized Canadian movies, in part in an attempt to counter the intrusion of U.S. cultural influence.

China successfully has muted the cultural influence of Hollywood by allowing only 20 or 21 films a year to be imported for theatrical release. And, yes, the Chinese government has an agency that screens movies for social and political suitability.

Movie Industry: Exhibition

study preview **The movie theater business is under heavy assault from home video sales and rentals. Box-office revenue is off substantially. Financially beleaguered movie-house chains are struggling to adjust to the new realities and also regain customers.**

What Edison Wrought

Thomas Edison demonstrated his **Vitascope** projector in 1896 at a New York concert hall. It was an incredible success. People were awed at *motion* pictures. Although Edison's films were jerky, grainy and soundless and ran only a few minutes, people instinctively wanted to jump back at scenes of ocean waves rolling in lest they be splashed. Soon the first movies houses, if they could be called that, were installed in storefront backrooms.

AMC Theatres Buy tickets online and skip the line in front of the theater. **www.enjoytheshow.com**

distribution The delivery of movies to theaters and other outlets for public consumption.

Bollywood India film industry nickname.

Nollywood Nigerian film industry nickname.

Vitascope An early film projector manufactured by Thomas Edison.

media TIMELINE

MOVIE EXHIBITION

1895 Auguste and Louis Lumière opened a movie house in Paris.

1896 Koster and Bial's Music Hall hosted the first public showing of a motion picture in the United States.

1912 The 3,000-seat Strand Theater, the grandest of movie houses, opened in New York.

1946 U.S. movie box office peaked at 90 million a week.

1970s Multiscreen movie houses, many in the suburbs, became the norm.

1999 Specially equipped movie houses showed *Star Wars: The Phantom Menace* with digital projection.

2000 Several theater chains file for bankruptcy after weak summer season.

2005 Landmark chain begins conversion to digital projection.

2006 U.S. exhibition industry begins conversion to digital.

Some were merely a white sheet stretched on one wall and whatever seating the proprietor could salvage. No traveling carnival was without a movie tent.

The movie exhibition business required little capital—a rented room and second-hand projector. By 1910 about 10,000 of these **nickelodeons** were operating, a nickel for admission. The movies, all silent, were affordable diversion even for newly arrived immigrants. There was no language barrier. What sound there was came when projectionists banged kettles or popped a gram of gunpowder at dramatic moments. Sometimes a piano player provided a bed of music.

Movie Palaces Movie exhibition entered a grand scale in 1914 with the opening of the Strand in Manhattan. With 3,300 seats and with the opulence of the grandest concert halls, the Strand became a model for a wave of gilded downtown theaters with doormen, ushers, lobbies that rivaled the finest hotels, lavish promenades, Roman columns and grand colonnades, and plush velvet wall upholstery. The first air-conditioning was in theaters, using technology invented at Chicago meat-packing plants.

The cost of entry into the exhibition industry suddenly escalated. This gave Hollywood studios, rolling in money from public fascination with increasingly glorious films, the means to finance the construction of new exhibition palaces. By the late 1920s, MGM Paramount, RKO, Twentieth Century Fox and Warner had come to dominate exhibition. Although the other major studios, Columbia, United Artists and Universal, never went into the exhibition business, the oligopoly was clear enough by 1941 that independent owners, being forced by studio-controlled distributors to book inferior films, convinced the U.S. Justice Department to employ anti-trust laws against the studios. In the resulting *Paramount* decision in 1948, the U.S. Supreme Court, in effect, ended coercive studio booking practices.

Neighborhood Movie Houses Meanwhile, neighborhood theaters were sprouting. Although neither as large nor as lavish as the downtown palaces, the neighborhood movie houses were handy and affordable and broadened the base of movie attendance. In 1946, when attendance peaked, 90 million movie tickets a week were sold in the United States. The nation's population was 141 million. Movies were a habit, for many people two or three times a week.

Multiplexes Television in the 1950s hurt movie attendance. Gradually the complex movie exhibition network dwindled. But the surviving exhibition companies, beginning in the 1970s, saw opportunity in moving to the sprawling suburbs, where people had been relocating by the millions. These companies began building a new form of movie house—the **multiplex,** theaters with multiple auditoriums that showed different movies

nickelodeon ■ Small, neighborhood movie theater in early 1900s, generally with 5-cent admission.

multiplex ■ A movie theater with several separate screens.

simultaneously. The new measure of a movie's success was not in how many theaters were booked but on how many screens.

Although hardly on the scale of the Strand, the multiplexes became increasingly upscale. By the late 1990s several chains, expecting continued audience growth, had borrowed heavily to build increasingly ritzy multiplexes. It was overexpansion, which led to bankruptcies.

Exhibition Crisis

The explosive growth of movies on DVD for rental and purchase for home play has struck at movie houses. The impact was thwarted for several years by staggered releases—first to the big screen, then months later to the home market, then to television networks and other venues. The theory was that word-of-mouth from people who saw a new movie on the big screen would goose later DVD sales without damaging the movie-house first-run revenue. The practice placated the skittish exhibition industry, but still the box office slipped. Now movie studios and distributors, eager for revenue from a single promotional splash, have narrowed the interval between **theatrical release** and what used to be aftermarkets to mere weeks.

Major Movie-House Chains

Several movie-house chains overexpanded in the 1990s, borrowing heavily to acquire other chains and to build often-ritzy suburban multiscreen theatres. These are the biggest surviving chains, ranked by the number of their movie houses and the average number of screens per site:

	Movie Houses	Screens per Site
Regal	552	10.6
Carmike	311	11.7
AMC	235	14.1
Loews	226	9.6
Cinemark	191	12.2

The Movie Experience Movie-house owners, led by major chains like Regal and AMC, have responded by improving the theater experience. More posh seats have been installed. Ushers, a fixture from an earlier era, have been hired with special training to quiet unruly movie-goers and even throw them out. On-screen messages implore people to honor traditional theater etiquette. Please check your cell phones at the door. These are attempts to capitalize on the superior experience of watching a film in a theater, in contrast to home.

Cost-Cutting Faced with declining audiences and revenues, exhibitors dragged their feet about converting to digital projection. At $100,000 a screen minimum, conversion wasn't economically doable. In 2006, however, movie studios and distributors agreed to subsidize conversions—and the exhibition industry is in a 21st-century upgrade due to be completed by 2016.

Movie Censorship

studypreview **Nobody doubts the powerful effects of movies, but presumptions about the effects, some wildly, even comically overstated, have led to repeated calls for regulations. Government censorship has been overruled in the courts. Even so, some government leaders have found mechanisms to force restraints on movie content, albeit with uneven success.**

Early Licensing

It was no wonder in Victorian 1896 that a movie called *Dolorita in the Passion Dance* caused an uproar. There were demands that it be banned—the first but hardly last such call against a movie. In 1907 Chicago passed a law restricting objectionable motion pictures. State legislators across the land were insisting that something be done. Worried

theatrical release ■ When a movie opens in movie houses, as opposed to release in DVD, television or other venue.

media TIMELINE

MOVIE CENSORSHIP

1896 *Dolorita in the Passion Dance* raises calls for censorship.

1907 Chicago requires licensing of movies.

1922 Movie industry creates Motion Picture Producers and Distributors of America to regulate content.

1930 Industry creates Motion Picture Production Code.

1934 Catholic bishops create Legion of Decency.

1947 Congressman Parnell Thomas implies that Soviet Communists are in powerful Hollywood positions.

1952 U.S. Supreme Court rules that the movie *The Miracle* has First Amendment protection.

1968 Movie industry creates G through NC-17 (nee X) rating systems.

movie-makers created the **Motion Picture Producers and Distributors of America** in 1922 to clean up movies. **Will Hays,** a prominent Republican who was an elder in his Presbyterian church, was put in charge. Despite his efforts, movies with titillating titles continued to be produced. A lot of people shuddered at titles such as *Sinners in Silk* and *Red Hot Romance*. Hollywood scandals were no help. Actor William Reid died from drugs. Fatty Arbuckle was tried for the drunken slaying of a young actress. When the Depression struck, many people linked the nation's economic failure with "moral bankruptcy." Movies were a target.

Under pressure, the movie industry adopted the **Motion Picture Production Code** in 1930, which codified the kind of thing that Will Hays had been doing. There was to be no naughty language, nothing sexually suggestive and no bad guys going unpunished.

Church people led intensified efforts to clean up movies. The 1930 code was largely the product of Father **Daniel Lord,** a Roman Catholic priest, and **Martin Quigley,** a Catholic layperson. In 1934, after an apostolic delegate from the Vatican berated movies in an address to a New York church convention, U.S. bishops organized the **Legion of Decency,** which worked closely with the movie industry's code administrators.

The legion, which was endorsed by religious leaders of many faiths, moved on several fronts. Chapters sprouted in major cities. Some chapters boycotted theatres for six weeks if they showed condemned films. Members slapped stickers marked "We Demand Clean Movies" on car bumpers. Many theater owners responded, vowing to show only approved movies. Meanwhile, the industry itself added teeth to its own code. Any members of the Motion Picture Producers and Distributors of America who released movies without approval were fined $25,000.

Motion Picture Producers and Distributors of America ■ 1922 Hollywood attempt to establish moral code for movies.

Will Hays ■ Led MPPDA.

Motion Picture Production Code ■ 1930 Hollywood attempt to quiet critical moralists.

Daniel Lord ■ Priest who led a morality crusade against Hollywood.

Martin Quigley ■ Partner of Father Daniel Lord.

Legion of Decency ■ Church listing of acceptable movies.

Hollywood 10 ■ Film industry people who were jailed for refusing to testify at congressional anti-Red hearings.

Government Intimidation

Censorship has not always been through statute. In 1947 Congressman Parnell Thomas, chair of the House Un-American Activities Committee, capitalized on concern over Soviet and communist conspiracies in the country and announced a plan to rout the traitors out of Hollywood. This witch-hunt was as effective as outright censorship. Fearful, Hollywood moguls backed off daring creativity until the heat passed. Some of the industry's most creative people, the so-called Hollywood 10, were barred from working.

In his grandstanding, Thomas summoned 47 screenwriters, directors and actors and demanded answers to accusations about leftist influences in Hollywood and the Screen Writers Guild. Ten witnesses who refused to answer insulting accusations went to jail for contempt of Congress. It was one of the most highly visible manifestations of McCarthyism, a post-World War II overreaction to Soviet communism as a national threat.

The Thomas hearings had longer-lasting deleterious effects. Movie producers, afraid the smear would extend to them, declined to hire the **Hollywood 10.** Other careers were also ruined. One expert identified 11 directors, 36 actors, 106 writers and 61 others who suddenly were unwelcome in their old circles and could not find work.

Among the Hollywood 10 was screenwriter **Dalton Trumbo.** His powerful pacifist novel *Johnny Got His Gun* made Trumbo an obvious target for the jingoist HUAC. After Trumbo refused to answer committee questions, he was jailed. On his release, Trumbo could not find anybody who would accept his screenplays. He resorted to writing under the pseudonym Robert Rich. The best he could earn was $15,000 per script, one-fifth of his former rate. When his screenplay for *The Brave One* won an Academy Award in 1957, "Robert Rich" did not dare show up to accept it.

In a courageous act, **Kirk Douglas** hired Trumbo in 1959 to write *Spartacus.* Then Otto Preminger did the same with *Exodus.* Besides Trumbo, only screenwriter **Ring Lardner Jr.** rose from the 1947 ashes. In 1970, after two decades on the blacklist, Lardner won an Academy Award for *M*A*S*H.*

The personal tragedies resulting from the Thomas excesses were bad enough, but the broader ramification was a paucity of substantial treatments of major social and political issues. Eventually, moviemakers rallied with sophisticated treatments of controversial subjects that, it can be argued, were more intense than they might otherwise have been. It was an anti-McCarthy backlash, which did not occur until the mid-1950s, when Hollywood began to re-establish movies as a serious medium.

Breaking the Hollywood Blacklist
Kirk Douglas challenged the timidity of the Hollywood establishment by hiring blackballed Dalton Trumbo as the screenwriter for *Spartacus.* Then Otto Preminger hired Trumbo for *Exodus.* The success of both films helped to break the ban on hiring the Hollywood 10.

Kirk Douglas

Dalton Trumbo

Movies and First Amendment

In the late 1940s the influence of the policing agencies began to wane. The 1948 Paramount court decision was one factor. It took major studios out of the exhibition business. As a result, many movie houses could rent films from independent producers, many of which never subscribed to the code. A second factor was the movie *The Miracle,* which became a First Amendment issue in 1952. The movie was about a simple woman who was sure Saint Joseph had seduced her. Her baby, she believed, was Christ. Critics wanted the movie banned as sacrilege, but in the ***Miracle* case,** the Supreme Court sided with exhibitors on grounds of free expression. Film-makers became a bit more venturesome.

At the same time, with mores changing in the wake of World War II, the influence of the Legion of Decency was slipping. In 1953 the legion condemned *The Moon Is Blue,* which had failed to receive code approval for being a bit racy. Despite the legion's condemnation, the movie was a box-office smash. The legion contributed to its own undoing with a series of incomprehensible recommendations. It condemned significant movies such as Ingmar Bergman's *The Silence* and Michelangelo Antonioni's *Blowup* in 1966 while endorsing the likes of *Godzilla vs. The Thing.*

Dalton Trumbo ■ Blackballed screenwriter.

Kirk Douglas ■ Had the courage to hire Dalton Trumbo despite anti-Red pressure.

Ring Lardner Jr. ■ Blacklisted screenwriter who reemerged with *M*A*S*H.*

***Miracle* case** ■ U.S. Supreme Court ruled that the First Amendment protected movies from censorship.

Current Movie Code

Movie Ratings A history of how the ratings evolved.
www.mpaa.org/movieratings/about/content.htm

Motion Picture Association of America They rate the movies we all see.
www.mpaa.org

Movie-makers sensed the change in public attitudes in the 1950s but realized that audiences still wanted guidance they could trust on movies. Also, there remained some moralist critics. In 1968 several industry organizations established a new rating system. No movies were banned. Fines were out. Instead, a board representing movie producers, distributors, importers and exhibitors, the **Classification and Rating Administration Board,** placed movies in categories to help parents determine what movies their children should see.

Whether the rating system is widely used by parents is questionable. One survey found that two out of three parents couldn't name a movie their teenagers had seen in recent weeks.

X Rating The CARA code has evolved over the years. Originally the most restrictive rating was X, but the porn industry began using it. Confusion resulted, prompting the Motion Picture Association of America to create NC-17 in 1990 to distinguish non-porn films. X was abandoned to the pornographers.

Even so, NC-17 created a stigma that scuppered the box office. Audiences were wary of them. Exhibitors didn't book them. Paul Verhoeven's flashy and extravagant *Showgirls* in 1995, now a camp classic, flopped in part because its fleshiness garnered an NC-17. To lessen the risk of scaring off movie-goers, studios snipped scenes from films that CARA wanted to slap with the adults-only NC-17.

NC-17 Acceptance The phobia about NC-17 has eased. In 2004 Sony Classics accepted an NC-17 for David MacKenzie's *Young Adam* rather than sanitize the film. Within a few months came Bernardo Bertolucci's *The Dreamers,* with extreme sexuality, and *High Tension,* a French thriller. Both required movie houses to card patrons.

What's happened? The movie industry has rediscovered, as it did in the 1960s, that its economic lifeblood requires it to push boundaries. Edginess keeps audiences interested and sets movies apart as a medium. Also, values change. For better or worse, depending on your perspective, society is increasingly tolerant of media depictions of sex and violence. Important too, exhibitors are less hesitant. Lois Blackburn of Utah-based Westates Theaters said in an interview for the *Christian Science Monitor* that the NC-17 has advantages: "With the R rating, we're always having problems with who's a guardian, who's entitled to bring in someone under 17. This way, if you're not 17, you're not coming in. Period. That's easier and faster for us."

Classification and Rating Administration Board ■ Rates movies on G, PG, PG-13, R, NC-17 scale.

Movie Ratings

The current categories guide parents in directing children to some movies and against others.

- **G:** Suitable for general audiences and all ages.
- **PG:** Parental guidance suggested because some content may be considered unsuitable for preteens.
- **PG-13:** Parental guidance especially suggested for children younger than 13 because of partial nudity, swearing or violence.
- **R:** Restricted for anyone younger than 17 unless accompanied by an adult.
- **NC-17:** No children under age 17 should be admitted.

Media Literacy and Movies

study preview **Populist measures of a movie's success are in box office, aftermarket and merchandise revenue. Critical success is harder to measure. Knowledgeable, sophisticated reviewers are helpful.**

Box Office and Grosses

Weekends are when Hollywood studio executives bite their fingernails. The success or disappointment of their latest offerings are in the weekend box-office tabulations, the week-to-week tallies of how many customers the latest movies attracted. The numbers, gathered at the turnstile, are accurate in and of themselves. Not much can be inferred from them, though. A great new movie could be hurt if it was opening against strong rivals. Inversely, a weak movie may look better in a single weekend's books than it really should. Also, a single weekend's success is only part of the complex formula for a movie to break even financially. Many strong weeks might be needed to offset the costs of an expensive movie. A single good weekend could bring a low-budget movie into black ink right away.

An advance indicator of commercial success, though not entirely reliable, is the number of screens nationwide that a movie shows on. Movie houses choose movies according to what they anticipate will be their popularity. Although exhibitors are savvy about what will play well, they make occasional wrong calls.

The least reliable precursor of a movie's success is the predictable marketing hoopla accompanying a release. Actors and directors who make the talk-show rounds are enthusiastic. How could they be otherwise with their own careers in the balance? Trailers can be misleading. Some previews draw on scenes that don't even make the final cut.

The best check on a movie's popularity is the long-term box-office record. The all-time leader easily is James Cameron's 1997 *Titanic*. Even with long-term, revenue-based data, look at the criteria on which a ranking is based. Some lists are true box office, the revenue from movie-house showings. Others include aftermarket revenue, like video rentals. Some include merchandise income. Some are domestic, some worldwide. Also, with ticket prices approaching $12 in many cities, currency inflation gives newer movies an edge over classics. Has *Titanic* really been more popular than 1939's *Gone With the Wind?*

Movie Criticism

Commercial success doesn't always equate with critical success, which is a subjective rating. Some critics applauded *Titanic*. The technical effects, for example, drew rave comments. The praise, however, wasn't universal. Some critics saw the story line as trite—a bodice-buster cliché that manipulated unsophisticated audiences.

How, then, can a serious media consumer go beyond the box office and the bottom line to assess a movie? Many critics produce immensely helpful reviews and commentary that cut through hype and dazzle to bring a critical, cultivated eye to their reviews. The best reviewers know movies as a medium, including the techniques of the craft. They understand the commercial and artistic dynamics that go into a movie. They know the history of a movie's production, from its seminal moment in a book or whatever the conceptual source.

Where do you find such reviewers? The best sources over the years have included the *New Yorker* magazine and the New York *Times*. Even then, you need to come to know reviewers and their strengths and blind spots. In the end, it is you as a media consumer who makes a critical judgment. This comes from your own increasing sophistication, informed by the dialogue in which the best critics are engaging.

media ONLINE

American Film Institute The quick link feature at this site will get you to AFI's several "100 Years" lists of highlights from the 20th century: 100 movies, 100 heroes and villains, 100 laughs, 100 songs and more.
www.afi.com

The Worst Films of the 20th Century A take-off on AFI's "100 Years" lists, this site has the 100 movies nominated as the worst of the worst.
www.thestinkers.com

Variety Key source of news on the business end of the film industry.
www.variety.com

Internet Movie Database Comprehensive movie database complete with reviews, movie news, showtimes and message boards.
www.imdb.com

MovieWeb Movie information and trailers on the web.
www.movieweb.com

New York Times Movies Movie criticism from the esteemed daily newspaper.
www.nytimes.com/pages/movies

CHAPTER 6 Wrap-Up

Ask anyone what's Hollywood, they'll know. Or they'll think they know. The word *Hollywood,* actually the name of an urban enclave in Los Angeles, is a stand-in for all the magic and glamour of the iconic U.S. movie industry. The word, though, is too vague for a meaningful understanding of an industry whose components largely set their own courses and thrive and shrivel in complex and interconnected relationships. Which is to say that the U.S. movie industry is in simultaneous booms and busts.

The bright side includes the artistic innovation and creativity, as embodied in the annual Oscar awards. Hollywood, at its best, is a beacon of contemporary cultural accomplishment. As an industry, Hollywood contributes mightily to the U.S. balance of trade by exporting its products to eager audiences abroad. No other country does it better.

The impact of technology is still being sorted out. Hollywood distribution companies, including brand-name studios, have embraced home sales and rentals, first with video cassettes and then DVDs. The traditional box office, however, has nose-dived. Can the exhibition business survive? A crash conversion of theaters to digital formats has begun, but whether the costly investment in equipment upgrades will pay off is an unanswered question.

Then there are the cost issues of producing major movies. For studios the risk is high. A series of clunkers can bankrupt a studio, which makes for ongoing drama for industry observers on Wall Street. The big studios, though, have become adept at using their distribution subsidiaries to buy movies, and budget-conscious independent producers and market them at high mark-ups.

Questions for Review

1. Why do movies have such a strong impact on people?
2. What is the role of movie studios in the production and exhibition?
3. What are the major Hollywood studios?
4. What are the advantages of digital technology for the movie industry?
5. How has Hollywood responded to the threat of television?
6. How has Hollywood repeatedly responded to censorship threats?

Questions for Critical Thinking

1. What are the prospects for d-cinema?
2. Epic spectaculars marked one period of movie-making, social causes another and sex and violence another. Have these genres had lasting effect?
3. What were the contributions of William Dickson, George Eastman and the Lumière brothers to early movie-making.
4. What has been the role of these institutions in shaping movie content: Motion Picture Producers and Distributors of America, Legion of Decency and Classification and Rating Administration Board?
5. Describe government censorship of movies in the United States.

Deepening Your media LITERACY

Are the most popular films the best films?

STEP 1 Choose a popular Hollywood movie and an independent or foreign film to compare.

Dig Deeper

STEP 2

1. Read several critical reviews of these movies.
2. Look up the box office receipts of the two movies.
3. Find out how many awards each of these films won.

What Do You Think?

STEP 3 Answer these questions:

1. Do critical acclaim, popularity and film awards go hand in hand?

2. Do you think critical acclaim or winning awards are good ways to measure a film's quality? Why or why not?
3. Are box office receipts the best measure of its success? Why or why not?

Keeping Up to Date

People serious about movies as art will find *American Film* and *Film Comment* valuable sources of information.

Among consumer magazines with significant movie coverage are *Premiere, Entertainment Weekly* and *Rolling Stone.*

Trade journals include *Variety* and *Hollywood Reporter.*

The *Wall Street Journal, Business Week, Forbes* and *Fortune* track the movie industry.

For Further Learning

Colin McGinn. *The Power of Movies.* Pantheon, 2006.

McGinn, a philosopher, builds an easy-to-follow case for the long-analyzed Dream Theory of Cinema to explain the compelling nature of the medium.

Spike Lee, as told to Kaleem Aftab. *Spike Lee: That's My Story and I'm Sticking to It.* Norton, 2005.

An anecdote-full biography of the movie-maker, which has been called "very authorized."

David L. Robb. *Operation Hollywood: How the Pentagon Shapes and Censors Movies.* Prometheus, 2004.

Robb, a veteran Hollywood reporter, chronicles the coerciveness of the government in providing and denying technical support for war movies.

Dade Hayes and Jonathan Bing. *Open Wide: How Hollywood Box Office Became a National Obsession.* Miramax, 2004.

Hayes and Bing, both editors at the movie trade journal *Variety,* examine the role of marketing with *Terminator 3, Legally Blonde 2* and *Sinbad,* each from a different studio, as case studies. They provide a historical context of movie marketing back into the 1950s.

Peter Biskind. *Down and Dirty Pictures: Miramax, Sundance and the Rise of Independent Film.* Simon & Schuster, 2004.

This book chronicles the growth and eventual mainstreaming of independent films and the personalities who made it happen.

Nicholas Jarecki. *Breaking In: How 20 Film Directors Got Their Start.* Broadway, 2002.

Jarecki, who began interviewing directors while himself a film student, spans three generations, including Amy Heckerling (*Clueless*), Peter Farrelly (*Dumb and Dumber*), John Schlesinger (*Midnight Cowboy*) and Edward Zwick (*Glory*).

Bernard F. Dick. *Engulfed: Paramount Pictures and the Birth of Corporate Hollywood.* University Press of Kentucky, 2001.

Dick, a communications professor, places the change in Hollywood culture into another bottom-line industry to the Gulf + Western acquisition of Paramount in 1966. He draws new material, including papers of a former Paramount president.

Paul Buhle and Dave Wagner. *A Very Dangerous Citizen: Abraham Lincoln Polonsky and the Hollywood Left.* University of California Press, 2001.

Buhle and Wagner write a biography of a blacklisted screenwriter who refused to inform on his political associates during the early 1950s Red Scare.

Richard E. Foglesong. *Married to the House: Walt Disney World and Orlando.* Yale University Press, 2001.

Foglesong, a scholar, offers a well-documented assessment of a media company's corporate heavy-handedness.

Emmanuel Levy. *Oscar Fever: The History and Politics of the Academy Awards.* Continuum, 2001.

Levy, a *Variety* reviewer, provides a comprehensive look at the mechanics of the Oscar process, almanac-like detail on nominations, and sociological questions.

Steven DeRosa. *Writing with Hitchcock: The Collaboration of Alfred Hitchcock and John Michael Hayes.* Faber & Faber, 2001.

DeRosa, a film archivist, draws on interviews with Hayes, studio memos and production notes in this indepth examination. DeRosa sees Hayes as the detail researcher for Hitchcock's films and the source of their humor and sophisticated dialogue.

Jon Lewis. *Hollywood v. Hardcore: How the Struggle over Censorship Created the Modern Film Industry.* New York University Press, 2001.

Lewis's detailed history relies on an economic model to explain the U.S. movie industry's repeated attempts at self-restraint and ratings on sexual content.

Peter Lefcourt and Laura J. Shapiro, editors. *The First Time I Got Paid for It: Writers' Tales from the Hollywood Trenches.* Public Affairs, 2000.

This is a collection of 54 articles by screenwriters, including Fay Kanin, William Goldman and Carl Reiner, about breaking into Hollywood.

Paul Harvey
His news and commentary make him, hands down, the most listened-to personality in network radio in the United States.

chapter 7

Radio

In this chapter you will learn:

- Radio is easily accessible, but the audience for traditional stations is slipping.
- Radio technology relies on the electromagnetic spectrum.
- The government regulates traditional radio.
- The 1996 Telecommunications Act profoundly changed radio.
- Large radio-chain corporations have changed the radio industry.
- Music, news and talk are the primary radio content.
- Measures of radio excellence are difficult outside of news.
- Stations are moving rapidly to high-definition delivery.

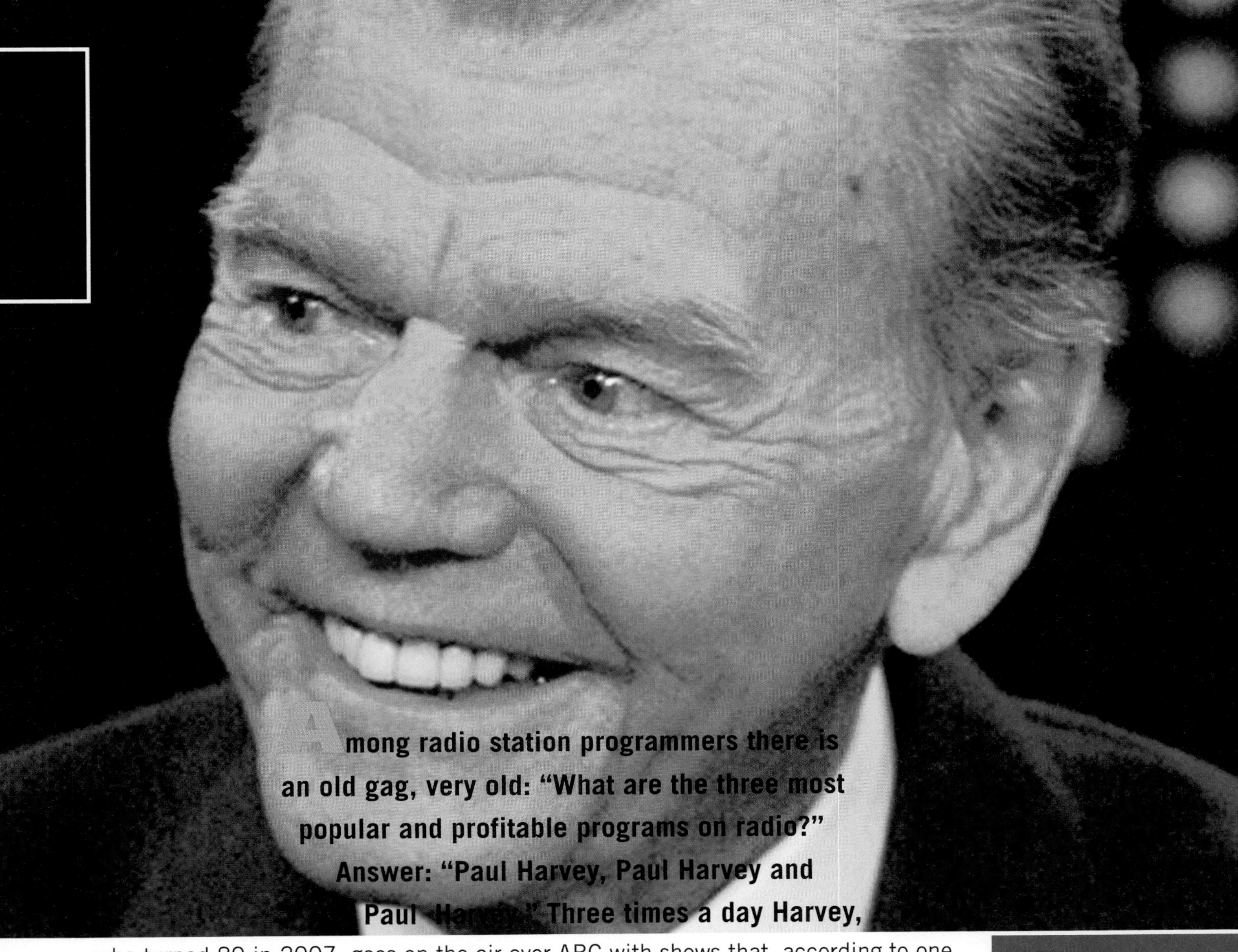

Among radio station programmers there is an old gag, very old: "What are the three most popular and profitable programs on radio?" Answer: "Paul Harvey, Paul Harvey and Paul Harvey." Three times a day Harvey, who turned 89 in 2007, goes on the air over ABC with shows that, according to one estimate, have brought in $1 billion in advertising. He's been with ABC since 1951.

ABC estimates Harvey's audience at 22 million a week, although less exuberant counts are at 15 million. Whatever, he's way ahead of Rush Limbaugh, at 14 million on a good day; Sean Hannity, 12 million; and Michael Savage, Laura Schlesinger and Howard Stern, all clustered at 8 million.

Never heard of Paul Harvey? His audience is skewed to an older set, which he has cultivated with folksy lines, like his ritual Christmas Eve closer: "And remember, it's His birthday—not yours." His signature baritone opener, "Hello! This is Paul Harvey!" followed immediately by, "Stand by for news!" and his dramatic pauses and quirky intonations can be described only as Harveyisms.

His signature style includes seamless segues into commercials that are enthusiastic personal endorsements. General Motors has sold not a few Buicks because of Harvey. And Citrical calcium supplements and Gold Bond medicated creams, also products targeted at older listeners, are among his anointed sponsors. His listeners are loyal to Harvey-endorsed products. One of Harvey's classic lines about his sponsors: "I am fiercely loyal to those willing to put their money where my mouth is."

Harvey's commentaries often hark back through rose-tinted lenses to a better yesteryear. Politically he tilts right.

Harvey broadcasts five-minute morning and 15-minute midday programs, "News and Comment." Since 1976 he also has had a daily series, "The Rest of the Story," obscure but enticing facts behind famous people and events. The programs are carried on 1,200 stations. In addition, Harvey has a thrice-weekly newspaper column and seven books, some drawn from his radio scripts. Paul Harvey's scripts and columns have been reprinted in the Congressional Record more than have those of any other commentator.

Although a studio journalist, Harvey occasionally went into the field after stories in his early years. In 1951, tipped about poor security at the Argonne National Laboratory, Harvey attempted to scale a perimeter fence about 1 a.m., only for his overcoat to get caught on the barbed wire. Security guards found him and turned him over to the FBI.

Harvey's $10 million-a-year ABC contract runs into 2011, when Harvey will be 93. His departure could be a bottom-line shocker to ABC if listeners and advertisers depart with him. When Harvey takes a day off, the network has been substituting Tennessee-folksy former U.S. senator Fred Thompson to see if he catches on. Also, Harvey's son, Paul Aurandt Jr., known on-air as Paul Harvey Jr., writes for his father and sometimes fills in at the microphone. With his father's inflections and pauses, Paul Jr. could make for a smooth transition.

Influence of Radio

studypreview **Radio has become a ubiquitous mass medium, available everywhere, anytime. As an industry, however, there are troubling signs. Radio's primary programming, music, has become available through other devices, many with no advertising. A key radio audience, the segment aged 18 to 24, has fallen off dramatically.**

Ubiquity

Radio is everywhere. The signals are carried on the electromagnetic spectrum to almost every nook and cranny. Hardly a place in the world is beyond the reach of radio.

There are 6.6 radio receivers on average in U.S. households. Almost all automobiles come with radios. People wake up with clock radios, jog with headset radios, party with boomboxes and commute with car radios. People listen to sports events on the radio even if they're in the stadium. Thousands of people build their day around commentators like Paul Harvey. Millions rely on hourly newscasts to keep up to date. People develop personal attachments to their favorite announcers and disk jockeys.

Statistics abound about radio's importance:

- **Arbitron,** a company that surveys radio listenership, says that teenagers and adults average 22 hours a week listening to radio.
- People in the United States own 520 million radio sets. Looked at another way, radios outnumber people 2:1.
- More people, many of them commuting in their cars, receive their morning news from radio than from any other medium.

Although radio is important, cracks are developing in the medium's reach. The audience is slipping from the traditional, federally licensed local stations to iPods, direct-to-listener satellite services, webcasts and cell phones. Yes, 200 million people a week, a sizable number, still tune in at least once a week, but the audience is shifting. The important 18- to 24-year-old listener block fell 22 percent from 1999 to 2004.

Scope of Radio Industry

More than 13,000 radio stations, each licensed by the federal government as a local business, are on the air in the United States. Communities as small as a few hundred people have stations.

Although radio is significant as a $19.1 billion a year industry, its growth seems to have peaked. Revenue, almost entirely from advertising, grew only 1.2 percent in 2003—less than the other major mass media. Big radio chains, like Clear Channel with 1,200-plus stations, remain hugely profitable. The profits, however, are due less to audience and advertising growth, which are stagnant at best, than to the chains' economies of scale and radical cost-cutting.

Too, the big revenue growth of the big chains has been fueled by their acquisitions. When federal caps on chains at 40 stations were dropped in 1996, there was massive consolidation. Chains bought up individually owned stations, and chains bought chains. In effect, the chains now all have bigger shares of a pie that's not growing and may be diminishing. How much is the disparity between big operators and the others? The 20 largest chains, which together own 2,700 stations, brought in $10 billion in advertising in 2003. The remaining 10,000-some stations split the other $9 billion.

Radio Technology

studypreview **Human mastery of the electromagnetic spectrum, through which radio is possible, is only a century old. In 1895 an Italian physicist and inventor, Guglielmo Marconi, was the first to transmit a message through the air. Later came voice transmissions and better sound.**

Electromagnetic Spectrum

Radio waves are part of the physical universe. They have existed forever, moving through the air and the ether. Like light waves, they are silent—a part of a continuing spectrum of energies: the **electromagnetic spectrum.** As early as 1873, physicists speculated that the electromagnetic spectrum existed, but it was an Italian nobleman, **Guglielmo Marconi,** who made practical application of the physicists' theories.

Young Marconi became obsessed with the possibilities of the electromagnetic spectrum and built equipment that could ring a bell by remote control—no strings, no wires, just turning an electromagnetic charge on and off. In 1895, when he was 21, Marconi used his wireless method to transmit codes for more than a mile on his father's Bologna estate. Marconi patented his invention in England, and his mother, a well-connected Irish woman, arranged British financing to set up the Marconi Wireless Telegraph Company.

media ONLINE

Clear Channel Worldwide The giant company that grew from Lowry Mays's single radio station. **www.clearchannel.com**

Electromagnetic Spectrum The spectrum, illustrated and explained. **http://imagine.gsfc.nasa.gov/docs/science/know_l1/emspectrum.html**

Arbitron ■ Radio listener survey company.

electromagnetic spectrum ■ Energy waves on which radio messages are piggybacked.

Guglielmo Marconi ■ Produced the first wireless transmission.

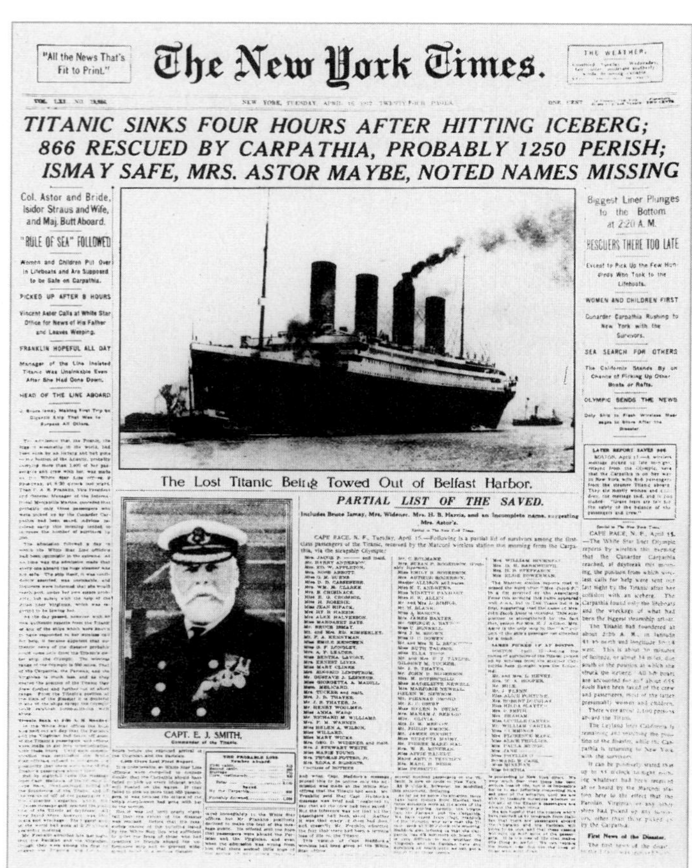
"All the News That's Fit to Print."

The New York Times.

TITANIC SINKS FOUR HOURS AFTER HITTING ICEBERG; 866 RESCUED BY CARPATHIA, PROBABLY 1250 PERISH; ISMAY SAFE, MRS. ASTOR MAYBE, NOTED NAMES MISSING

Col. Astor and Bride, Isidor Straus and Wife, and Maj. Butt Aboard.

"RULE OF SEA" FOLLOWED

Women and Children Put Over in Lifeboats and Are Supposed to be Safe on Carpathia.

PICKED UP AFTER 8 HOURS

Vincent Astor Calls at White Star Office for News of His Father and Leaves Weeping.

FRANKLIN HOPEFUL ALL DAY

Manager of the Line Insisted Titanic Was Unsinkable Even After She Had Gone Down.

HEAD OF THE LINE ABOARD

Biggest Liner Plunges to the Bottom at 2:20 A.M.

RESCUERS THERE TOO LATE

Except to Pick Up the Few Hundreds Who Took to the Lifeboats.

WOMEN AND CHILDREN FIRST

Cunarder Carpathia Rushing to New York with the Survivors.

SEA SEARCH FOR OTHERS

The California Stands By on Chance of Picking Up Other Boats or Rafts.

OLYMPIC SENDS THE NEWS

The Lost Titanic Being Towed Out of Belfast Harbor.

PARTIAL LIST OF THE SAVED.

Includes Bruce Ismay, Mrs. Widener, Mrs. H. B. Harris, and an Incomplete name, suggesting Mrs. Astor's.

CAPT. E. J. SMITH.

Radio Becomes a Household Word

When the *Titanic* sank in 1912, newspapers relied on young radio operator David Sarnoff for information on what was happening in the mid-Atlantic. For 72 hours Sarnoff sat at his primitive receiver, which happened to be on exhibit in a department store, to pick up details from rescue ships. The newspaper coverage of the disaster made *radio* a household word, which paved the way for consumer acceptance over the next few years.

David Sarnoff

Soon oceangoing ships were equipped with Marconi radiotelegraphy equipment to communicate at sea, even when they were beyond the horizon—something never possible before. Marconi made a fortune.

Transmitting Voices

Breakthroughs came quickly. In 1906 a message was sent across the Atlantic. In 1906 **Lee De Forest,** a promoter who fancied himself an inventor, created what he called the **audion tube** to make voice transmission possible. Some say he stole the underlying technology from Canadian inventor **Reginald Fessenden.** Whatever the truth of the matter, it was Fessenden who broadcast the first radio program, also in 1906. From Brant Rock, Massachusetts, where he had a laboratory, Fessenden played some recorded Christmas carols, shocking wireless operators on ships at sea. Instead of the dots and dashes of Morse code, suddenly there was music. De Forest, however, took the limelight with show-off broadcasts from the Eiffel Tower and other stunts. In 1910 De Forest clearly demonstrated radio's potential as an entertainment medium with a magnificent performance by the tenor Enrico Caruso from the New York Metropolitan Opera House.

Lee De Forest ■ Inventor whose projects included the audion tube.

audion tube ■ Made voice transmission possible.

Reginald Fessenden ■ First radio program, 1906.

Edwin Armstrong ■ Invented FM as an alternative transmission method.

frequency modulation ■ FM

amplitude modulation ■ AM

FM Radio

Static-free transmission was developed by **Edwin Armstrong,** a Columbia University researcher. In 1939 Armstrong built an experimental station in New Jersey using a new system called **frequency modulation,** FM for short. FM's system, piggybacking sound on airwaves, was different from the older **amplitude modulation,** or AM method. In time, Armstrong developed FM stereo with two soundtracks, one for each ear, duplicating the sensation of hearing a performance live.

Radio Industry Infrastructure

studypreview The corporate structure of radio in the United States is largely a function of federal regulations. In the 1920s the government began licensing the airwaves, which were declared a public asset. The result was the creation of a local orientation, although the localism became largely a fiction with the growth of networks and sound-alike programming coast-to-coast.

Trusteeship Rationale

Unlike the print media, broadcasting is regulated by the federal government. This is something the government isn't supposed to do under terms of the **First Amendment** to the U.S. Constitution. The First Amendment's wording is unambiguous: "Congress shall make no law . . . abridging the freedom of speech or the press." But an impossible situation, wrought by new radio technology, presented itself in the 1920s. The fledgling radio industry could not solve the problem and begged the government for regulation to sort out the problem.

media ONLINE **Federal Communications Commission** A comprehensive web site with an overview of the agency and links to agency documents. **www.fcc.gov**

Airwave Cacophony Everyone recognized wonderful possibilities for the nascent radio industry in the 1920s. Stations were signing on the air and establishing revenue streams from advertising not only to meet expenses but also to propel the industry's growth. With more stations, however, came a problem. There were not enough frequencies to accommodate all the signals. The airwaves became a deafening cacophony. A station finding itself drowned out would boost its signal to keep listeners, in effect turning up the volume to drown out competing signals in a kind of king-of-the-mountain competition. To be heard, stations were forever jumping to frequencies that were less cluttered at the moment, asking listeners to follow. It was chaos. And without a consistent place on the dial, stations could offer advertisers little assurance about the size of their audience. This impeded the economics for sustaining and growing the industry.

First Amendment ■ Provision in U.S. Constitution against government interference with free citizen expression, including media content.

David Sarnoff ■ His monitoring of the sinking of the *Titanic* familiarized people with radio; later NBC president.

media TIMELINE

RADIO

1895 Guglielmo Marconi transmitted a message by radio.

1906 Lee De Forest created the audion tube that allowed voice transmission.

1912 **David Sarnoff** used radio to learn news of the *Titanic* disaster, putting radio in the public eye.

1920 Westinghouse put KDKA, Pittsburgh, on air as the first licensed commercial station.

1927 Congress created the Federal Radio Communications Commission to regulate radio.

1934 Congress created the Federal Communications Commission to regulate radio, telephone, television. FCC replaced FRC.

1939 Edwin Armstrong put the first FM station on air.

1967 Congress established the Corporation for Public Broadcasting to create a national noncommercial system.

1996 Congress relaxed many government regulations on broadcasting, including ownership caps.

2001 Satellite radio programming direct to listeners launched by XM, followed by Sirius.

Regulation Station owners called on the federal government for a solution. In 1927 Congress established the **Federal Radio Commission.** The commission had authority to specify frequency, power and hours of operation through licenses. But that was not enough to solve the problem. The commission found that 732 stations were on the air, but the technology of the time allowed room for only 568. Through clever sandwiching of signals, daytime-only and nighttime-only operations, the Federal Radio Commission eventually found room for 649 stations.

But therein rested a problem: There still were not enough channels to allow all existing stations to remain in operation. A government agency, through media licensing, had no choice but to take away the megaphone of some stations and deny a megaphone to others who might want to start a station. This was a constitutional issue. The government was de facto interfering in press freedom, in effect putting some stations out of business. Although the First Amendment, written in 1789 used the word "press," everyone assumed that the founders of the republic, had they been able to project themselves 150 years into the future, would have chosen a more inclusive word.

Public Airwaves To sidestep the First Amendment issue, Congress embraced the concept that the airwaves, which carried radio signals, were a public asset and therefore, somewhat like a public park, were subject to government regulation for the public good. The **public airwaves** concept was useful for justifying regulation of the 1927 chaos on the airwaves, but it also was problematic. What criteria would the government use in issuing and denying licenses? Congress came up with another concept: The Federal Radio Commission should award licenses to applicants who best demonstrated that they would broadcast in the **public interest, convenience and necessity.** Today, 80 years later, that standard remains in effect. Government regulates as a trustee for the public good, and station owners, as licensees, are also trustees.

Although the **trusteeship concept** phraseology was high-sounding, some already on-the-air stations that lost licenses cried foul and used the ugly word "censorship." A quack doctor in Kansas, who used his station to sell cure-all potions, went to court on First Amendment grounds. So did a hate-monger preacher who used his church-owned station in Los Angeles as a pulpit. The federal courts ruled glibly that the Federal Radio Commission was acting within its authority, leaving the First Amendment issue for another day.

Localism

The Federal Radio Commission used several mechanisms to guard against broadcasting becoming a one-voice government mouthpiece. There would be no powerful national stations. Stations were licensed to local service areas with local ownership. Further, there were strict limits on how many stations a single person or corporation could own. The goal of **localism** was a diversity of voices.

The law that established the Federal Radio Commission stated explicitly that stations would have First Amendment protection. The fact, however, was that the commission needed to assess station programming in deciding what was in the public interest, convenience and necessity. This inherent contradiction was glossed over during most of U.S. radio history because station license-holders were more than pleased to program whatever it took to satisfy the FRC and its successor, the Federal Communications Commission. That was the tradeoff for stations to retain their licenses and stay in what, by and large, became one of the 20th century's most lucrative businesses. Also, the FCC, which was created in 1934, was gingerly regulating content. Never, for example, did the FCC interfere with format issues, no matter how loud the protests from classical music fans when their favorite station shifted to rock.

Content regulation was mostly measuring the number of minutes per hours of news and public-service announcements, until even that was abandoned in the 1980s. Before Howard Stern, fines for on-air vulgarities were mere wrist-slaps.

Federal Radio Commission ■ Agency to regulate U.S. radio; created in 1927; predecessor of Federal Communications Commission.

public airwaves ■ Concept that broadcast should be subject to government regulation because the electromagnetic spectrum is a public asset.

public interest, convenience and necessity ■ Standard by which the U.S. government grants and renews local radio and television station liscenses.

trusteeship concept ■ Government serves as a trustee for the public's interest in regulating broadcasting; so do the licensed station owners.

localism ■ Issuing broadcast licenses for service to a specified community and its environs.

mediaPEOPLE

John Brinkley

John Brinkley and his bride arrived in Milford, Kansas, population 200, in 1917 and rented the old drug store for $8 a month. Mrs. Brinkley sold patent medicines out front, while Brinkley talked to patients in a back room. One day an elderly gentleman called on "Dr. Brinkley" to do something about his failing manhood. As the story goes, the conversation turned to Brinkley's experience with goats in the medical office of the Swift meat-packing company, a job he had held for barely three weeks. Said Brinkley, "You wouldn't have any trouble if you had a pair of those buck glands in you." The operation was performed in the back room, and word spread. Soon the goat gland surgeon was charging $750 for the service, then $1,000, then $1,500. In 1918 Brinkley, whose only credentials were two mail-order medical degrees, opened the Brinkley Hospital. Five years later he set up a radio station, KFKB, to spread the word about his cures.

Goat Gland Surgeon Eager for publicity, John Brinkley obliges a photographer by placing a healing hand on a supposedly insane patient he is about to cure. Broadcasting such claims from his Kansas radio station, Brinkley developed a wide market for his potions. Because of his quackery, he lost the station in a significant First Amendment case.

Six nights a week, Brinkley extolled the virtues of his hospital over the air. "Don't let your doctor two-dollar you to death," he said. "Come to Dr. Brinkley." If a trip to Milford was not possible, listeners were encouraged to send for Brinkley compounds. Soon the mail-order demand was so great that Brinkley reported he was buying goats from Arkansas by the boxcar. "Dr. Brinkley" became a household word. *Radio Digest* awarded Brinkley's KFKB (for Kansas First, Kansas Best) its Golden Microphone Award as the most popular radio station in the country. The station had received 356,827 votes in the magazine's write-in poll. Brinkley was a 1930 write-in candidate for governor. Harry Woodring won with 217,171 votes to Brinkley's 183,278, but Brinkley would have won had it not been for misspellings that disqualified thousands of write-in ballots.

Also in 1930 the KFKB broadcast license came up for renewal by the Federal Radio Commission, which had been set up to regulate broadcasting. The American Medical Association wanted the license revoked. The medical profession had been outraged by Brinkley but had not found a way to derail his thriving quackery. In fact, Brinkley played to the hearts of thousands of Middle America's listeners when he attacked the AMA as "the meat-cutter's union." At the license hearing, Brinkley argued that the First Amendment guaranteed him freedom to speak his views on medicine, goat glands and anything else he wanted. He noted that Congress had specifically forbidden the FRC to censor. It would be a censorious affront to the First Amendment, he said, to take away KFKB's license for what the station put on the air. Despite Brinkley's arguments, the FRC denied renewal.

Brinkley challenged the denial in federal court, and the case became a landmark on the relationship between the First Amendment and U.S. broadcasting. The appeals court sided with the FRC, declaring that broadcast licenses should be awarded for serving "the public interest, convenience and necessity." It was appropriate, said the court, for the commission to review a station's programming to decide on renewal. Brinkley appealed to the U.S. Supreme Court, which declined to hear the case. The goat gland surgeon was off the air, but not for long. In 1932 Dr. Brinkley, proving himself unsinkable, bought a powerful station in Villa Acuna, Mexico, just across the Rio Grande from Del Rio, Texas, to continue peddling his potions. By telephone linkup from his home in Milford, Brinkley continued to reach much of the United States until 1942, when the Mexican government nationalized foreign-owned property.

Networks

Congress did not foresee the impact of radio networks, which were in their infancy when the Federal Radio Commission was created in 1927. By the 1930s NBC and CBS were piping programs to local stations, called **affiliates,** throughout the land. Although the

John Brinkley ■ Radio quack who challenged government regulation of radio.

affiliates ■ Locally licensed stations that have an affiliation with a network to carry network programming.

media TIMELINE

RADIO NETWORKS

1923 First network was a linkup of a Newark, New Jersey, station and a Schenectady, New York, station to carry the World Series.

1926 RCA formed the NBC network.

1926 NBC bought its main competitor, the AT&T network, and operated it as a second network.

1927 William Paley bought a fledging 16-affiliate network and created CBS.

1934 WGN in Chicago and WOR in New York created Mutual, which, unlike CBS and NBC, offered programs to affiliates on a nonexclusive basis.

1943 NBC sold the old AT&T network, which became ABC.

1950s Importance of networks began fading as stations shifted to recorded music for programming.

2000s The Associated Press network, offering mostly brief newscasts, is the largest network with 1,000 stations.

networks gave local exclusivity to affiliates, one per market, the high quality of the programming amassed unprecedented audiences. Then in 1924 came the Mutual Broadcasting System, which allowed any station to pick up any or all of its programming. Stations became less the forums of local issues and culture that Congress had intended with local licensing. For better or worse, local stations were becoming mere conduits for a powerful emerging national culture.

Localism was further weakened in the 1950s when the networks shifted their emphasis to television and took much of radio's audience with them. Radio stations went almost entirely to recorded music, in effect displacing the original ideal of local talent with music geared for a national audience from the major music-recording centers of New York, Los Angeles and Nashville.

Infrastructure in Transition

study preview **After 70 years of comfortable status quo, the infrastructure of U.S. broadcasting significantly changed with the 1996 Telecommunications Act. The changes were wrought by a general government move away from regulation of the private sector and also by changes in technology.**

Historical Characteristics

Despite wobbly philosophical premises, including the First Amendment dilemma, the broadcast industry was comfortable, making money in bundles, with the infrastructure created by the laws that created the Federal Radio Commission in 1927 and then the FCC in 1934. These were the historical characteristics of the early industry.

Private Sector The industry was privately owned in the U.S. capitalistic tradition. This was in contrast to most other countries, which used the concept of the airwaves being public to create government-sponsored national, not local, broadcast structures.

Advertising Supported The industry was financially self-supporting through advertising, also in the U.S. capitalistic tradition. There were, however, exceptions. In recognition of radio's potential as a cultural force that might not be commercially sustainable, the Federal Radio Commission reserved several frequencies for noncommercial licenses. These licenses went mostly to universities for experimentation with the physics of radiotelegraphy and educational purposes. These stations today go under the name *public radio.*

Engineering Regulation The government held licensees strictly accountable to broadcast precisely within their assigned space on the electromagnetic spectrum to avoid the pre-1927 chaos. This allowed for as many stations as possible to be squeezed into available spectrum.

Ownership Stations were licensed to local owners to encourage diverse content, including news and ideas, on the public airwaves. Some group ownership was permitted, for a maximum of seven stations.

Content The government has never had agents sitting at radio stations to keep things off the air, but the FCC is willing to listen to complaints and does. The possibility of having their licenses yanked, although it rarely happens, is sufficient to keep stations from wandering too far from mainstream social acceptability and business practices.

Although not licensed, networks conform to government expectations for affiliates. The FCC is clear that affiliates are responsible for whatever affiliates retransmit from networks.

Deregulation

Ronald Reagan proclaimed that his presidency would "get government off the backs of business." In 1996, seven years after Reagan left office, it seemed that his **deregulation** dream had come true—at least in broadcasting. With the 1996 Telecommunications Act the age-old limits were relaxed on how many radio stations a single company could own. Right away, radio companies began gobbling one another up in mergers. Today the FCC has no limits on ownership except for a maximum of eight stations in a single market.

The change in the corporate structure of U.S. radio represented a weakening of the trusteeship concept. No longer did the government see that its role as an intermediary for the public was necessary to ensure that the industry performed in the public interest. The trusteeship concept had led to requirements like the Fairness Doctrine, which required stations to air all sides of controversial issues and to air public-service announcements, and even micromanagement details like requiring an identification of a station by call letters and location on the hour and the half-hour. Those requirements were mostly gone by 1996 because one of the premises necessitating the trusteeship role for government, **channel scarcity,** had disappeared. Technology had found ways to squeeze 13,000 stations onto the available electromagnetic spectrum, which was plenty.

In place of the trusteeship concept had emerged a **marketplace concept,** in which the marketplace would have a far greater role in deciding the shape of radio broadcasting. If people were dissatisfied with a station, they had many other stations to go to—in effect voting with a turn of the dial or the press of a preset button. Stations that didn't meet public expectations would, given time, lose listeners and advertisers and cease to be viable businesses. The concept was simple: Let marketplace mechanics serve as a regulator, the people acting directly.

Hardly, however, has government regulation been obviated. There just isn't as much of it. Also, the regulatory mechanisms that were a cocoon that protected the infrastructure of the industry from change is being shed. Even so, the National Association of Broadcasters, which represents radio station owners, as well as television owners, continues to lobby for government maintenance of the status quo to protect its interests. For example, the industry delayed for years the approval for XM and Sirius to use orbiting satellites as platforms for direct-to-listener broadcasting. On that issue, however, the FCC eventually applied the marketplace concept, allowed the satellites to go up and let the people decide.

National Association of Broadcasters Trade association representing the interests of radio and television broadcasters.
www.nab.org

Sirius Satellite radio with over 120 commercial-free channels. Categories include music, news, entertainment and sports.
www.sirius.com

XM Satellite radio with over 150 channels playing commercial-free music, entertainment, sports, weather and traffic.
www.xmradio.com

deregulation ■ A trend in the 1980s and later to reduce government regulation of business.

channel scarcity ■ An insufficiency of radio frequencies that necessitated government regulation in the 1920s.

marketplace concept ■ Allowing people through marketplace mechanism to determine the fate of a business; a successor in broadcasting to the trusteeship concept.

Snoop Dogg Competition between satellite radio service XM and Sirius ratcheted up as the satellite radio market moved toward $6 billion in revenue by 2010. Sirius made a big-budget push for listeners by signing up shock-jock Howard Stern, who debuted in 2006. XM worked at keeping its larger listener base with celebrity endorsements, including Snoop Dogg, for its range of channels.

Satellite Radio

Two **satellite radio** operations, the first national U.S. radio stations, went on the air in 2001. Both Sirius and XM beamed multiple programs from multiple satellites, providing digital-quality sound, much of it commercial free, for a monthly fee ranging between $10 and $13. The companies tried to build an immediate audience by lining up automobile manufacturers to install receivers into new vehicles—about 12 million a year. Both Sirius and XM offered at least a hundred channels—pop, country, news, sports and talk—but also specialized programming like chamber music, Broadway hits, NPR, audio books and gardening tips.

In 2004 Sirius and XM raised the stakes against each other and against traditional over-the-air radio. Sirius signed Howard Stern to a five-year deal worth $500 million, which began in 2006 when his previous contract expired. Stern's **shock jock** act on Sirius is beyond the jurisdiction of the FCC, which licensed only the technical parameters of satellite radio. Signals downlinked from satellites are not considered use of the public's air.

Not to be outdone, XM signed a deal with Major League Baseball to broadcast every big-league game played through 2011, with an option for 2012 to 2014. That deal may be worth as much as $650 million to baseball. Raising their programming bar represents a huge gamble by both satellite firms, which going into 2007 were hemorrhaging money.

While XM and Sirius duke it out, a larger battle is shaping up between satellite radio and what's come to be called **terrestrial radio.** The term was devised to identify the traditional radio industry built around local stations that transmit from towers, in contrast to satellite transmission. Purists with the language object that *terrestrial radio* is a retronym like *print newspapers* and *broadcast television*. But boosted derisively by Howard Stern in hyping his 2006 move to Sirius, the term caught on.

media ONLINE

RadioTime Real-time subscription database of 25,000 radio programs from 140 countries.
www.radiotime.com

The Edge 103.9 Cutting-edge radio station. The Edge's web site plays the latest music releases without commercials.
www.theedge1039.com

New Technologies

In the early 2000s, other technologies were working against the radio industry's infrastructure.

iPod Handheld MP3 players, epitomized by the Apple iPod, siphoned listeners from over-air local radio. With these devices and music downloaded from the Internet or ripped from their own CDs, people are able to create their own playlists—no inane disc-jockey patter, no commercials, no waiting through less-than-favorite tunes for the good stuff.

Podcasting Almost anybody who wanted to create a show could prerecord a batch of favorite music, complete with narration, as an audio file on a personal computer. Then, by adding a hyperlink on a web server, they could let the world download the show for playback on a computer or MP3 player. Whenever the listener links to the server again, a new show from the same source would be downloaded automatically. Podcasting had the potential to make everybody a disk jockey. This too cut into the audience of traditional radio.

On-Demand Radio Like the earlier TiVo device for television, on-demand radio devices have come to market for recording programs for later playback. The leading service, RadioTime, offers a real-time database of 35,000 stations from 140 countries for a $39 annual subscription. Some RadioTime models include an AM-FM tuner to grab local shows that aren't webcast.

satellite radio ■ Delivery method of programming from a single source beamed to an orbiting satellite for transmission directly to individual end-users.

shock jock ■ Announcer whose style includes vulgarities, taboos.

terrestrial radio ■ The industry based on audio transmission from land-based towers, as opposed to transmission via satellite.

mediaTECHNOLOGY

Airplay for Sale

True to its name, the Edge 103-9, an FM station from Phoenix, Arizona, rotates through a playlist of pop music at the edge of what's hot. Its streaming service on the Internet, however, is edgier—commercial-free with music that could be called newer than new. The station sells time to record companies for the latest releases they're pushing. For the station it's a new revenue stream. For listeners the pay-to-play music doesn't sound like commercials, seamlessly fitting into the Edge format. And it's new stuff. Edgy stuff—get it?

The paid-to-play music in the streaming programming replaces some of the commercials that pepper the Edge's over-air programming. Other commercials are covered by the day's most frequent downloads from the iTunes retail music web site. Could there be a more efficient mechanism to keep the station's playlist up-to-date with what's popular?

The other commercials are covered online with music drawn from a playlist of tunes that can't be fit into the over-air programming.

The Edge's mastermind, Scott Fey, has only begun exploring new media technology. Fey says he foresees equipment to allow listeners to press a button whenever they hear a tune they like and download it instantly to their iPod or other MP3 device.

Corporate Radio

study preview **A few corporations dominate the U.S. radio industry, using mostly centralized music and other programming geared to mass tastes. The approach, however, has earned the disapproving moniker "corporate radio" for its bland sameness. The chains have taken steps to win back listeners who have left for alternative sources of music, news and information.**

playlists ■ A list of songs that a radio station plays.

voice tracking ■ A few announcers who prerecord music intros and outros for multiple stations to create a single personality for stations.

Chain Ownership

In a drive to cut costs to maximize profits, the big radio chains consolidated their new properties in the post-1996 era and centralized not only **playlists** but also disk jockeys. Most stations owned by Clear Channel, Viacom and other chains went to formulaic computerized scheduling, with stations each drawing from libraries of only 300 to 400 titles with the same 30 or 40 songs playing most of the time. Through a system called **voice tracking,** a handful of announcers at central sites play the songs over multiple stations in different markets. This robo-programming was efficient.

Also to maximize profits, programming was larded with advertising. Some stations were running 22 minutes of ads an hour, some packages of ads going on for 10 minutes straight. A 2004 study by the investment banking firm J.P. Morgan found an average of 15 minutes an hour of advertising.

media DATABANK

Radio Chains

For years the government restricted a radio company to owning no more than seven AM and seven FM stations, but the restrictions were gradually relaxed. Then the 1996 Telecommunications Act eliminated any cap, except that a single company could own no more than eight stations in a large market. Right away, radio chains began gobbling up stations and also other chains. The 1999 merger of Clear Channel and AMFM created an 838-station group. The FCC then relaxed the limit further. By 2003, Clear Channel owned 1,200-plus stations. These are the biggest radio chains:

Radio Chain	Number of Stations
Clear Channel, San Antonio, Texas	1,231
Cumulus, Atlanta, Georgia	243
Citadel, Las Vegas, Nevada	205
Viacom, New York	183
Entercom, Bala Cynwyd, Pennsylvania	104
Salem, Camarillo, California	83
Cox, Atlanta, Georgia	81
Radio One, Lanham, Maryland	64
Regent, Covington, Kentucky	61
Saga, Grosse Pointe Farms, Michigan	60
ABC, Dallas, Texas	58

mediaPEOPLE

Howard Stern

Howard Stern began his career at Boston University, where he volunteered at the college radio station. His show was canceled after one broadcast. He had spoofed a game show with contestants confessing their worst sins. It was a precursor of Stern's unorthodoxy—a mix of phone chat, much of it inane; music, a lot of it offbeat; and crude, sophomoric shock-talk. His on-air antics earned him the label "shock jock," a new radio programming genre in the 1980s.

No matter how tasteless, Stern amassed a following. He soon had star status and big bucks—and also critics who pushed for federal fines against his on-air vulgarities. At one point, the accumulated unpaid fines totaled $1.7 million. The corporate owner of his flagship New York station had no problem paying the fines from the profits Stern was bringing in.

Still the fines kept coming. A $495,000 fine in 2004 brought his career total to $2.5 million. Analysts say the Viacom-owned Infinity chain, which acquired Stern in its buy-up of stations, cleared $25 million a year in advertising revenue from Stern's show, which played in 40 cities. That was after $70 million in production costs and Stern's $30 million salary. Infinity could afford the fines, but concerned that the government might revoke its stations' licenses, the corporate executives became uneasy. In 2004 they tried putting a lid on Stern.

Shock Jock

Refusing to be bridled, Stern announced he wouldn't renew with Infinity when his contract expired in 2006. Instead he would leave so-called terrestrial radio and go to the unregulated airwaves of the fledgling Sirius satellite radio service. With Sirius, Stern's program would go directly to subscribers, bypassing the traditional delivery mechanism through federally licensed local stations that send their signals from land-based towers.

Typical of his egocentric confidence, Stern declared the death of the traditional infrastructure of U.S. radio with stations licensed to broadcast to local audiences. The future, he said, was in national stations that transmitted directly to individuals—not relayed through local stations. There are two such companies with direct-to-listener services via satellite. XM began broadcasting in 2001, Sirius in 2002.

Howard Stern is not alone in seeing problems for the radio industry as everyone has come to know it since the 1920s. Besides XM and Sirius, handheld iPods and their custom playlists were siphoning away listeners. Chain-owned stations like the 1,200 in Clear Channel ownership, many programmed from afar, were losing listeners. Ten-minute blocks of commercials didn't help. Podcasting was emerging. On-demand radio was coming.

The big operators increased their profits with the formula in the years after the 1996 Telecommunications Act allowed them to amass stations by the dozen, even by the hundreds. Gradually, listeners began to sour on the sameness, which earned a negative label: **corporate radio.** Hit by audience falloff, in part because of iPods and satellite radio, Clear Channel had a sudden wake-up call in 2005.

New Corporate Tune

Shifting a few gears, Clear Channel began striking deals with stations outside its ownership to pick up revenue from advertisers that were following listeners to alternative stations. An example is unorthodox Indie 103, a Los Angeles station whose music mix is personality-driven—pretty much whatever suits a disk jockey at the moment. It's quirky, but it also inspires about 700 listener calls a day. That's an intensity of listener loyalty that robo-radio can't match even with massively larger audiences. Hedging its

corporate radio ■ A disapproving term for programming engineered by radio chains for use in multiple markets.

case STUDY

More Power for Low Power

Ibar "Robert" Mohamed was arrested for operating a tiny unlicensed "pirate" radio station in Queens and Brooklyn. In Fargo, North Dakota, student programming was pulled from the air when radio station KDSU-FM was taken over by the North Dakota Public Radio network.

Today, they're both back on the air. After the Federal Communications Commission froze noncommercial radio licensing in the 1980s, a grassroots movement built over 1,000 pirate stations in protest. Finally, in 2000 the FCC created low-power radio, making licenses available to community groups like libraries, churches and small nonprofits who want to reach a small geographic area. Simple, inexpensive, noncommercial LPFM stations are allowed to operate at 100 watts, which provides an effective radius of approximately 3.5 miles.

Major broadcasters lobbied over the last decade to end most limits on radio ownership and against low-power radio. In 2000 they succeeded in cutting the number of LPFM stations that were planned by 80 percent. The National Association of Broadcasters also insisted on a two-year, $2 million study, which eventually confirmed that the small stations pose no significant interference to the big boys. Following the study the FCC recommended that Congress expand LPFM service, and the Local Community Radio Act of 2005 was introduced in Congress by Senator John McCain.

Mohamed's microstation broadcasts a stream of hit songs from Bollywood musicals and live cricket matches from the Caribbean islands. Mohamed started broadcasting when he was 16, working with his father who was a pioneer at Radio Demerara in Guyana. He describes himself as equal parts engineer, disc jockey and singer.

ThunderRadio started airing music, talk shows and live broadcasts of North Dakota State University athletics in 2004 after the FCC granted a low-power license to a nonprofit group, which passed operations to a student organization. Construction of the radio station cost about $10,000 and was paid by NDSU's student government.

Other success stories include KOCZ in Opelousas, Louisiana, run by the Southern Development Foundation, the first civil rights organization in the United States to own a radio station. The station also hosts the world's largest traditional zydeco music festival. Oroville, California, lost its radio station when Clear Channel purchased it, dismantled it and moved the license to another town. Oroville now has KRBS, which sees itself as a keystone in badly needed downtown revitalization plans.

The public interest in low-power radio stations brings the conflict between public interest and the marketplace into focus. The Radio Act of 1927 gave federal regulators the power to make rules in the "public interest, convenience or necessity." Today, technical advances have made receivers and broadcasting more precise, but back then a cacophony of stations was battling for listeners, and the government decided on a public interest licensing scheme. The broadcaster paid no money for the scarce privilege and received a short-term license and volunteered to serve the public interest.

Low-Power Radio With a low-power federal license and $10,000 from student government, ThunderRadio was on the air at North Dakota State University. Students air music, talk shows and play-by-play sports. Low-power stations have placed over-air broadcasting within the means of neighborhood groups and other organizations that otherwise would never have been able to establish a broadcast presence.

One of the problems with this type of regulation is that Congress never defined exactly "the public interest." Critics say that regulation in the public interest has come to mean whatever is in the interest of regulators at a given time and that industry competition and innovation are often discouraged. Another major criticism of the public trustee system is that it makes a mockery of the First Amendment. These critics say that the FCC was mistaken when it decided there was a scarcity of spectrum, which justified asymmetrical application of the First Amendment by limiting the number of radio stations.

Others bemoan the fact that the cornucopia of choice brought on by the conglomeration of media and enjoyed on the national level is not reflected on the local level. LPFM could change that by bringing local radio back to America.

WHAT DO YOU THINK?

1. Do you agree that the way the FCC interpreted "the public interest" made a mockery of the First Amendment?
2. Do you think market competition benefits the huge media conglomerates more or does it give the little guy the chance he or she deserves?
3. Is the public interest better served by encouraging vigorous market competition? Or is the public better served by the public trustee model of regulation of radio?

course for the future, Clear Channel has bought every minute of Indie 103's available advertising airtime. The deal allowed the station to meet expenses, and Clear Channel made money reselling the time at a premium with the advertising staff that served the chain's existing eight robo-programmed Los Angeles stations.

Clear Channel crafted another deal with the Bush-bashing liberal network Air America that kept the financially failing new operation in business. It's a strange deal indeed for a company whose Texas management strongly supported Bush in the 2004 election. Political ideology, it seemed, was less critical than stopping the leaks of listeners and ad revenue, even small ones, that were breaking out all over the Clear Channel landscape.

Some stations with robo-programming shifted gears in 2005 with **Jack,** a format developed by Rogers Media of Canada that had a decidedly more eclectic mix of music. Jack playlists typically include 1,200 songs. Unlike robo-formulas, few songs get played even once a day in Jack's unlikely patterns, with none of the segues that slide from one tune seamlessly into another. Eight U.S. stations licensed Jack from Rogers in 2005. Others are imitating it. At KSJK in Kansas City, which calls itself 105.1 Jack FM, program director Mike Reilly prides himself on "train wrecks," a collision of unlikely music in sequence: "If you hear MC Hammer go into the Steve Miller Band, I've done my job." It's the kind of programming excitement that people can create on an iPod. In fact, KSJK's print advertising shows an iPod with the line: "I guess you won't be needing this anymore, huh?"

Jack, say critics, is less than it seems. The playlists don't venture beyond what is familiar to listeners. A Jack consultant, Mike Henry, put it this way in a *Wall Street Journal* interview: "You're only challenging them on a stylistic level. You're not challenging them on a familiar/unfamiliar level." Nirvana grunge may butt up against Village People disco, but both are proven pop.

The big chains also have begun trimming commercials, a recognition that they had overdone it and driven listeners away. Radio companies don't like to talk about how much advertising they carry, but a brokerage firm, Harry Nesbitt, said Clear Channel was down to an average 9.4 minutes per hour at its 1,200 stations in 2004. Also, advertisers were encouraged to shorten their spots.

Radio Content

studypreview **Radio programming falls mostly into three categories: entertainment, mostly music; news; and talk. In addition, public radio has created a growing audience for its rich mixture of news and information programming most originating with National Public Radio, Public Radio International and freelance producers.**

Radio Entertainment

The comedies, dramas, variety shows and quiz shows that dominated network-provided radio programming in the 1930s and 1940s moved to television in the 1950s. So did the huge audience that radio had cultivated. The radio networks, losing advertisers to television, scaled back what they offered to affiliates. As the number of listeners dropped, local stations switched to more recorded music, which was far cheaper than producing concerts, dramas and comedies. Thus, radio reinvented itself, survived and prospered.

The industry found itself shaken again in the 1970s when the listeners flocked to new FM stations. Because FM technology offered superior sound fidelity, these became the stations of choice for music. AM listenership seemed destined to tank until, in another reinvention of itself, most AM stations converted to nonmusic formats. From roots in 1961 with programming genius Gordon McLendon, who beamed the first 24/7 news into southern California from XTRA across the border in Tijuana, all-news took off as a format in major cities. So did listener call-in shows with colorful, sometimes bombastic hosts.

Jack ■ An eclectic, somewhat unpredictable musical radio format.

mediaPEOPLE

Gordon McLendon

A crisis hit the U.S. radio history in the 1950s. As comedies, dramas and quiz shows moved to television, so did the huge audience that radio had cultivated. The radio networks, losing advertisers to television, scaled back what they offered to stations. As the number of listeners dropped, local stations switched more to recorded music, which was far cheaper than producing programs.

To the rescue came Gordon McLendon, who perfected a new format, the Top 40, which repeated the day's most popular new music in rotation. McLendon developed the format at KLIF in Dallas, Texas, by mixing the music with fast-paced newscasts, disc jockey chatter, lively commercials and promotional jingles and hype. It was catchy, almost hypnotizing—and widely imitated.

With the portable transistor radios that were coming onto the market and a growing number of automobiles outfitted with radios, Top 40 was right for the times. People could tune in and tune out on the go. Most tunes last only three minutes or so. It was not programming designed for half-hour blocks. It reshaped radio as a medium that began a recovery in a new incarnation even as some observers were writing the medium's epitaph.

McLendon was no one-shot wonder. He also designed so-called beautiful music as a format at KABL, San Francisco, in 1959; all-news at XTRA, Tijuana, Mexico, aimed at southern California, in 1961; and all-classified ads at KADS, Los Angeles, in 1967. In all of his innovations, McLendon was firm about a strict structure. In Top 40, for example, there were no deviations from music in rotation, news every 20 minutes, naming the station by call letters twice between songs, upbeat jingles and no deadpan commercials. McLendon's classified-ad format bombed, but the others have survived.

Gordon McLendon McLendon was a programming genius who devised many niche formats, including all-news, Top 40 and beautiful music.

Radio News

Radio news preceded radio stations. In November 1916, Lee De Forest arranged with a New York newspaper, the *American*, to broadcast election returns. With home-built receivers, hundreds of people tuned to hear an experimental transmission and heard De Forest proclaim: "Charles Evans Hughes will be the next president of the United States." It was an inauspicious beginning. De Forest had it wrong. Actually, Woodrow Wilson was re-elected. In 1920 KDKA signed on as the nation's first licensed commercial station and began by reporting the Harding-Cox presidential race as returns were being counted at the Pittsburgh *Post*. This time, radio had the winner right.

Radio News Forms Radio news today has diverse forms, some drawn from the De Forest notion of drawing listeners to reports on breaking events as they happen, some more focused on depth and understanding. Mostly, though, radio news is known for being on top of events as they happen.

- **Breaking News.** Radio news came into its own in World War II, when the networks sent correspondents abroad. Americans, eager for news from Europe, developed the habit of listening to the likes of Edward Murrow and other giants of mid-20th-century journalism, including Walter Cronkite. As a medium of instantaneous reporting, radio offered news on breakthrough events even before newspapers could issue special extra editions. The term **breaking news** emerged to something to which radio was uniquely suited.

breaking news ■ Reports, often live, on events as they are occurring.

Gordon McLendon The Radio Hall of Fame offers a short biography of the creator of format radio.
www.radiohof.org/pioneer/gordonmclendon.html

Radio News Hear historical news broadcasts at the Radio Days' radio news site.
www.otr.com/news.html

Voice of America This broadcasting service funded by the U.S. government broadcasts news, information, cultural and educational programming.
www.voanews.com

Radio Formats

Country music easily is the leading format of U.S. radio stations although, from 1998 to 2003, 330 stations switched to other formats as defined by the radio industry.

Format	Stations	Trend
Country	2,041 stations	Losing
News/talk/sports	1,579 stations	Gaining
Adult contemporary	1,213 stations	Losing
Religious	1,019 stations	Gaining
Golden oldies	822 stations	Steady
Classic rock	639 stations	Gaining
Spanish	448 stations	Losing
Top 40	444 stations	Gaining
Alternative/modern rock	334 stations	Gaining
Urban contemporary	312 stations	Gaining

- **Headline Service.** In the relatively tranquil period after World War II, with people less intent on news, the radio industry recognized that listeners tuned away from lengthy stories. News formats shifted to shorter stories, making radio a **headline service.** Details and depth were left to newspapers. Gordon McLendon's influential rock 'n' roll format in the 1960s epitomized the headline service, generally with three-minute newscasts dropped every 20 minutes amid three-minute songs, with no story more than 20 seconds, most only two sentences.
- **All News.** As contradictory as it may seem, Gordon McLendon also invented **all-news radio,** also in the 1960s. For the Los Angeles market, McLendon set up a skeletal staff at XTRA across the border in Tijuana to read wire copy nonstop. When XTRA turned profitable, McLendon took over a Chicago station, renamed it WNUS, and converted it to all-news. This was a dramatic departure from the idea of radio as a mass medium with each station trying for the largest possible audience. McLendon's WNUS and later all-news stations sought niche listenerships, finding profitability in a narrow part of the larger mosaic of the whole radio market. Today all-news stations prosper in many large cities, some going far beyond McClenson's low-cost rip-and-read XTRA with large reporting staffs that provide on-scene competitive coverage that goes beyond a headline service.
- **News Packages.** When National Public Radio went on the air in 1970, its flagship *All Things Considered* set itself apart with long-form stories that ignored two premises that had become traditional in radio. These were stories that didn't necessarily have the news peg of breaking news. Also, the stories ran as long as the reporter or producer felt necessary to tell the story, ignoring the premise that radio listeners had extremely short attention spans. The stories, called **news packages,** were slickly produced and reflected a commitment of time and energy in reporting that other news formats lacked. Many personified issues. News packages typically are full of sounds and recorded interviews and are often marked by poignant examples and anecdotes and powerful writing.

headline service ■ Brief news stories.

all-news radio ■ A niche format that delivers only news and related informational content and commentary.

news packages ■ Carefully produced, long-form radio stories that offer depth; hallmark of NPR.

Decline of Radio News Despite the ascendancy of all-news radio and National Public Radio, news is hardly a core element of radio programming anymore. By the 1990s, after the Federal Communications Commissions dropped public service as a condition for license renewal, many stations eliminated their expensive news departments and emphasized low-cost programming based on playing recorded music. Many metropolitan

mediaPEOPLE

Edward R. Murrow

Not long out of college, Edward R. Murrow had a job arranging student exchanges for the Institute of International Education, including a summer seminar for American students and teachers in the Soviet Union. That was in 1932, and it seemed a good job—lots of travel, meeting interesting people, doing something worthwhile. In the early 1950s, though, the demagogic Red Scare-meisters tried to discredit Murrow as somehow being tied to the communist ideology on which the Soviet Union had been founded.

By that time Murrow had established his reputation as a broadcast journalist and was a CBS executive. Though personally offended at being branded a communist sympathizer, Murrow was even more outraged by the anticommunist hysteria that some members of Congress, notably Wisconsin Senator Joseph McCarthy, were stirring up. Many of his network colleagues had been blacklisted. A close friend committed suicide after being falsely accused. In 1954, on his weekly CBS television program *See It Now,* Murrow went after McCarthy, combining his narrative with film clips that exposed the senator's hypocrisy.

Many analysts say that was a pivotal moment in McCarthy's career. His innuendoes and lies, which had caused such great damage, were exposed to the public. Some say that the program, in bringing down one of most recognized members of the Senate, clearly demonstrated television's powerful potential for public affairs.

Murrow had begun with CBS as its representative in Europe, where he covered Adolf Hitler's arrival in Vienna in 1938 when Germany invaded Austria. Realizing that war was imminent in Europe, Murrow persuaded CBS to hire more staff to cover it. He devised the format for the *CBS World News Roundup,* rotating from correspondent to correspondent around Europe for live reports. During World War II he became known for his gripping broadcasts from London. Standing on rooftops with the sounds of sirens, antiaircraft guns and exploding German bombs in the background, he would describe what was happening around him. His reporting had poignancy, color and detail. Here is his description of an Allied air drop over Holland: "There they go. Do you hear them shout? I can see their chutes going down now. Everyone clear. They're dropping just beside a little windmill near a church, hanging there very gracefully. They seem to be completely relaxed like nothing so much as khaki dolls hanging beneath a green lamp shade."

Radio News Icon Edward R. Murrow's World War II coverage from Europe, with bombs in the background during his reports, gave CBS listeners a feel for being there.

One of Murrow's television signatures was an ever-present cigarette. His habit, however, didn't get in his way of his examining the dangers of smoking on *See It Now.* Murrow developed cancer and died in 1965 at age 57.

stations, once major players in news, have cut to just one or two people who anchor brief newscasts during commuting hours. Global and national headlines are piped in from a network, if at all. Some stations don't even commit one person full-time to local news.

media ONLINE **Edward R. Murrow** Part of the PBS American Masters series, this page links to audio of Murrow's most famous broadcasts. **www.pbs.org/wnet/americanmasters/database/murrow_e.html**

Talk Radio

Talk formats that feature live listener telephone calls emerged as a major genre in U.S. radio in the 1980s. Many AM stations, unable to compete with FM's sound quality for music, realized that they were better suited to talk, which doesn't require high fidelity.

Call-in formats were greeted enthusiastically at first because of their potential as forums for discussion of the great public issues. Some stations, including WCCO in Minneapolis and WHO in Des Moines, were models whose long-running talk shows raised expectations. So did *Talk of the Nation* on NPR. However, many talk shows went in other directions, focusing less on issues than on wacky, often vitriolic personalities. Much of the format degenerated into advice programs on hemorrhoids, psoriasis, face-lifts and

Sean Hannity Includes Hannity discussion forums, and book and song clubs.
www.hannity.com

Al Franken Listen live to the Al Franken show on Air America.
www.ofrankenfactor.com

Rush Limbaugh Includes show archives and Limbaugh's recommendations of CDs, books and movies.
www.rushlimbaugh.com

psychoses. Sports trivia went over big. So did pet care. Talk shows gave an illusion of news but in reality were lowbrow entertainment.

Whatever the downside of **talkers,** as they're known in the trade, they have huge followings. **Rush Limbaugh** was syndicated to 660 stations at his peak, reaching an estimated 20 million people a week. Although down to 600 stations by 2003, Limbaugh remained a strong influence among his politically conservative audience until 2003, when it was revealed, incredible as it seemed considering how he reviled drug addiction on the air, that Limbaugh himself had a drug habit. Since returning to the air, Limbaugh's ratings are down in some markets, partially because overwhelmingly conservative talk has some ideological competition. Liberals are also talking, most notably author and former *Saturday Night Live* funny man Al Franken, whose views on the airwaves are drawing listeners tired of talk radio's traditional conservative bent. A survey by a media research organization said that 44 percent of Americans receive most of their political information from talk radio.

Talk Listenership The influence of talkers can be overrated. A 1996 Media Studies Center survey of people who listen to political talk shows found that they are hardly representative of mainstream Americans.

The political talk show audience is largely white, male, Republican and financially well off. It is much more politically engaged than the general population but on the right wing. Also, these people distrust the mainstream media, which they perceive as being biased to the left.

Effect on News Many stations with music-based formats used the advent of news and talk stations to reduce their news programming. In effect, many music stations were saying, "Let those guys do news and talk, and we'll do music." The rationale really was a profit-motivated guise to get out of news and public affairs, which are expensive. Playing records is cheap. The result was fewer stations offering serious news and public affairs programming.

To many people, talk formats leave a perception that there is more news and public affairs on radio than ever. The fact is that fewer stations offer news. Outside of major markets with all-news stations, stations that promote themselves as news-talk are really more talk than news, with much of the talk no more than thinly veiled entertain-

talkers ■ Talk shows.

Rush Limbaugh ■ Most listened-to talk show host in the 1990s.

Joan Kroc ■ Benefactor who fueled NPR expansion with her McDonald's fortune.

National Public Radio ■ Network for noncommercial stations.

Corporation for Public Broadcasting ■ Quasi-government agency that channels funds to noncommercial radio and television.

All Things Considered ■ Pioneer NPR afternoon newsmagazine.

Radio Talkers Sean Hannity has built a major radio audience with a politically right-leaning daily talk show. The Republican enthusiast is carried on 400 ABC radio stations. Most talkers, as these shows are called in the trade, tend to the right, although in 2004, ahead of the presidential election, satirist Al Franken of *Saturday Night Live* fame became the lead host on the new Republican-bashing network Air America.

Al Franken

Sean Hannity

ment that trivializes the format's potential.

Public Radio

Joan Kroc, widow of the founder of the McDonald's fast-food chain, was a faithful radio listener. She especially enjoyed programs from **National Public Radio.** When she died in 2003, Kroc bequeathed $200 million to NPR, sextupling its endowment. The gift is transforming NPR into a powerhouse in radio in ways reminiscent of the networks in their heyday.

National Public Radio had gone on the air in 1970, funded mostly by the **Corporation for Public Broadcasting,** a quasi-government agency to channel federal into noncommercial radio and television as a national resource. Right away NPR created ***All Things Considered,*** a 90-minute newsmagazine for evening drive-time. Many noncommercial stations offered *ATC,* as it's called in the trade, as an alternative to the headline services on commercial stations. The program picked up an enthusiastic albeit small following but grew steadily. In 1979 an early drive-time companion program, ***Morning Edition,*** was launched.

NPR News Audience

The audience of National Public Radio news programs is demographically one that many advertisers would love to reach. But because they air on noncommercial stations that the government prohibits from selling time, there are only sponsorships—no huckstering. NPR's own research, as summed up by *American Journalism Review,* says the NPR news audience is twice as likely than the average American to visit museums, attend theater; go downhill skiing, backpacking and bird-watching; get involved in civic issues; and practice yoga.

Men	54 percent
Women	46 percent
Age 18–34	23 percent
Age 35–54	52 percent
Household income $50,000-plus	75 percent
Never watch television	25 percent

National Public Radio The "bright spot" amid today's decline in radio news. **www.npr.org**

media**PEOPLE**

Terry Gross

"Fresh Air" Terry Gross' interview show has one of the nation's largest radio interview audiences.

In college Terry Gross majored in education, but teaching didn't work out. At a smidgen over five feet, Gross was shorter than most of her Buffalo, New York, eighth-graders. It was tough being an authority figure, she said. She quit after six weeks.

She moved through typing jobs, finally landing at Buffalo radio station WBFO. She loved it. Within three years Gross had moved to WHYY in Philadelphia to produce and host a daily three-hour interview show. Thus, in 1975, began one of radio's longest-running programs: *Fresh Air.*

The show is still based at WHYY but is also carried by 330 National Public Radio network affiliates. Terry Gross typically has 2.9 million people listening to her cerebral interviewing on eclectic subjects as diverse as avant-garde musical forms, breakthrough scholarship and the day's pressing political questions.

As an interviewer, Gross' probing is disarming. Even on tawdry subjects she casts her questions in terms of an intellectual interest that rarely fails to penetrate her subjects. One exception was Monica Lewinsky after the White House sex scandal. Lewinsky walked out of Gross' studio mid-interview. "Too intimate," Lewinsky said.

Over 30 years Gross has conducted more than 5,000 *Fresh Air* interviews.

Garrison Keillor

A Prairie Home Companion Garrison Keillor and his radio company perform *A Prairie Home Companion* on stage live weekly at the old Globe Theater in downtown St. Paul, Minnesota. The show, begun in 1974, romanticizes a small-town agrarian past. It was an overnight cult hit, people packing the 900-seat Globe for every performance and 4 million people tuning in.

With his butterscotch voice, Garrison Keillor purred Hank Snow's *Hello Love* into a radio microphone one Saturday night in 1974. Twenty years after live radio drama, comedy and theater had departed the airwaves, displaced by disk jockeys and records, Keillor was inaugurating a radio show that brought back the good old days for many Americans and intrigued a whole younger generation with gentle stories about Norwegian bachelor farmers, poems and homey music.

The show, *A Prairie Home Companion,* soon went national, attracting 4 million listeners a week, becoming a cult hit among sophisticated noncommercial radio listeners and landing Keillor on the cover *of Time* magazine. Except for a two-year sabbatical, Keillor has been on the air ever since with stories from his fictional Lake Wobegon, somewhere in Minnesota, "where are all the women are strong, all the men are good looking and all the children are above average." Today, the two-hour broadcasts remain a staple at 350 noncommercial radio stations around the country on Saturday evenings—an unlikely time, it would seem, to amass great numbers of people around their radios.

A lot of APHC, as it's known in the trade, is unlikely. There are tongue-in-cheek commercials from Lake Wobegon merchants and the 20-minute monologues about the town's Lutherans and Catholics, old Plymouths and picnics at the lake.

The success of Garrison Keillor's show may rest on its nostalgic feel. As in radio's early days, the show is aired live before an audience. It has spontaneity. It's down-home, not slick—just like local radio used to be in its heyday. It has powerful intimacy and imagery, putting listeners' imaginations to work as they conjure up impressions from the drowsy voices of Keillor and his companions and their old-fashioned sound effects.

Lake Wobegon, "the little town that time forgot and the decades cannot improve," is everybody's hometown. It is rustic, cozy, warm—a refuge in Americana. It is also radio at its traditional old-time best.

media ONLINE

Corporation for Public Broadcasting Provides grants and programs to fund public broadcasting.
www.cpb.org

Public Radio International Not-for-profit creator of public radio programming.
www.pri.org

Today NPR claims more listeners than ratings-leader Rush Limbaugh does on commercial radio. Limbaugh's is the number one stand-alone program at 22 million listeners a week, but NPR does better overall. *Morning Edition* has 13.1 million listeners, and *ATC* has 11.5 million. In news, NPR has a lot to offer. With the Kroc gift and steeper charges to affiliates, the network has built a news staff of 300 in its Washington and Los Angeles bureaus and in 23 U.S. and 14 foreign bureaus. The programs are carried on 773 stations.

Although much of the Kroc endowment has underwritten NPR's growing news operations, the network prides itself on cultural programming too, much of it innovative and experimental, sometimes offbeat. The greatest audience that has evolved, however, has been news-related.

Although NPR is the most visible component of U.S. noncommercial radio, its programs constitute only about one-quarter of the content on its affiliate stations. These stations originate 49 percent of their own programming. Stations also buy about 19 percent of their programming from a competing program service, **Public Radio International.** PRI, a creation of the Minnesota Public Radio network, has the folksy **Garrison Keillor** live-audience variety show *A Prairie Home Companion,* which dates to 1974.

Morning Edition ■ NPR morning newsmagazine.

Public Radio International ■ Program provider for noncommercial stations.

Garrison Keillor ■ Long-running host of *A Prairie Home Companion.*

Quality on the Air

studypreview **With deregulation, radio programming has become more populist, formulaic and bland. Many stations are devoid of local identity. Even so, some stations set themselves apart with local and distinctive content.**

Marketplace Values

Measures of the radio industry include counting the stations in common ownership. It's all in public records maintained by the Federal Communications Commission. Clear Channel is biggest with 1,231 stations, Viacom next at 243. With the post-1996 consolidation of the industry into these giant companies, we have new information on the finances of those whose stock is traded on regulated exchanges. For closely held chains that aren't required to issue financial statements, industry analysts periodically issue reasonably accurate guesstimates on the financial performance.

Audience measures come mostly from the ratings service Arbitron. Because the surveys are paid for by stations that want numbers to persuade advertisers to buy time, Arbitron does not release its findings to the public. The results usually surface, however, when station sales reps pass them out to potential advertisers, although the information is often recast to make particular selling points. Arbitron data are broken down by day parts, like morning drive time, and by audience demographics, like gender and age groupings.

Measuring Quality

Ranking music stations by quality is as subjective as measuring music preferences. On-air performance expectations have become so standardized that even modest-budget stations can offer slick presentation. The distinctive personality has become a rarity, albeit there are notable exceptions like Don Imus, Howard Stern and local equivalents who have built unshakable followings. Mostly, it's all the same all the time—bland, predictable and mindless.

News is another matter. Broadcast societies and other organizations honor outstanding work, an external measure of excellence. These include the **Columbia-DuPont awards** and competitions sponsored by professional groups like the Radio-Television News Directors Association.

Talkers have their fans, but qualitative measures get bogged down in the ideological bent. Right-winger Rush Limbaugh, for example, has glommed on to the word "excellence," and 22 million steady listeners must concur. But outside the faithful, Limbaugh is seen as a ranter whose facts, premises and conclusions wobble regularly. On the left, Al Franken, Randi Rhodes and their friends at Air America are no less lionized and also dismissed as shouters who are prone to cheap shots.

In all the U.S. radio spectrum, the most enthusiasm for continuing excellence rests with what National Public Radio offers steadily: an intelligent curiosity about political, cultural and social issues. There are critics, however, who aren't amused at the mix at public radio stations that includes lowbrow programming. Critics from the political right also perceive a liberal bias in public radio.

Radio Trends

studypreview **The radio industry ignored high-definition, digital transmission until it realized the clarity could help to slow listenership losses. The technology also poses possibilities for bundled transmission to automate the delivery of custom information and services.**

media ONLINE

Canadian Radio-television and Telecommunications Commission Canada's regulatory agency for radio broadcasting.
www.crtc.gc.ca

Arbitron Market research firm that collects radio listenership information.
www.arbitron.com

Columbia-DuPont Awards Administered since 1968, these awards recognize excellence in broadcast journalism.
www.jrn.columbia.edu/events/dupont

Radio-Television News Directors Association Professional organization representing news broadcasters.
www.rtnda.org

Air America Radio Listen to live broadcasts or show highlights. Includes program overviews and schedule.
www.airamericaradio.com

Columbia-DuPont awards ■ Recognitions of excellence in broadcast news.

NTL Guide to Digital Radio for Dummies

A simple-to-understand guide to this complex subject.

www.ntl.com/locales/gb/en/guides/dummies/default.asp

High-Definition Radio

Happy with the heady profits in the 1990s, the radio industry missed an opportunity to upgrade with digital transmission technology. The technology, which would have improved clarity, was deemed too costly at $100,000 a station. What a mistake! Joel Hollander, who came in as chief executive at the Infinity chain in 2005, is frank: "If we had invested three to five years ago, people would be thinking differently about satellite." By 2005, only 300 stations had gone digital.

The largest chains now have all committed to digital conversion. About 2,000 stations will be sending digital signals by 2008. The system requires two transmitters, one for the traditional analog signal and one for the new digital signal, but a new industry-adopted standard, called **IBOC,** short for "in-band, on-channel," allows old-style analog and new-style digital receivers to pick up either signal at the same spot on the dial.

Bundled Transmission

Unlike analog radio, digital signals are encoded as binary 1s and 0s, which means that multiple programs can be **multiplexed** on the same channel. Segments of multiple programs are sent in packets, each coded to be picked out at the receiving end as a single unit and the others ignored. The company that holds the patents on high-definition radio, iBiquity Digital, has a system with which stations can spray six simultaneous messages to listeners, which opens opportunities for stations to regain listeners. Imagine a commuter setting a receiver to a music station with instructions to interrupt for traffic updates embedded in the same signal.

IBOC (in-band, on-channel) ■ A radio industry standard for digital transmission; allows multiple programming on same channel.

multiplexing ■ Sending multiple messages in bundles on the same channel.

Receivers can be designed to store programs, TiVo-like. NPR's *All Things Considered* can be waiting on a commuter's car radio no matter what time the workday ends and the commute home begins.

CHAPTER 7 Wrap-Up

Federal law and regulation shaped the U.S. radio industry in 1927. For 80 years the infrastructure was stable, even with the self-reinvention necessitated in the 1950s when television stole radio's programming, audience and advertisers. The industry also remained in control of new technology like the spectacular success of FM as an alternative in the 1970s. Suddenly, at the dawn of the 21st century, new technologies shook the structure of the industry as listeners opted for cutting-edge alternatives including satellite direct-to-listener radio, iPods, podcasts and on-demand radio. To stem listener losses, mainstream companies have eased their drive for centralized programming and cost-cutting, some trying the new format Jack and copycats. Also, a major investment is being made in high-definition, digital transmission.

Questions for Review

1. What is happening to the number of people who listen to traditional radio?
2. How has radio technology evolved since the pioneering work of Guglielmo Marconi?
3. How has the trusteeship model for broadcast regulation given way to a marketplace model?
4. How has the 1966 Telecommunications Act and new technology reshaped the U.S. radio industry?
5. What is the dominant programming of corporate radio? Has it run its course?
6. How has the mix of entertainment and information changed through the course of radio's history in the United States?
7. What is the promise of high-definition radio?
8. What are measures of excellence in radio?

Questions for Critical Thinking

1. If you were a shareholder in Disney-ABC, how would you view the $10 million-a-year contract that the network has with newscaster and commentator Paul Harvey?

2. How did Howard Armstrong's invention of FM radio transform the landscape of the U.S. radio industry?
3. How did the regulations that were part of the original trusteeship concept for U.S. broadcasting shape the radio industry and its programming?
4. Has the 1966 Telecommunications Act been good for radio?
5. Roughly 18.7 percent of U.S. radio stations play country, easily the leading format. In recorded music sales, however, country is fourth at 10.4 percent of the market, considerably behind rock, rap, hip hop, R&B and urban. How do you explain the discrepancy.
6. Compare the impact of innovations like the Top 40, all-news and Jack formats.
7. What has been the effect of NPR since its inception in 1970?
8. Is it a wise investment for the U.S. radio industry to put probably $13 billion into digital transmission equipment?
9. Has measuring excellence in radio become a pointless task?

Deepening Your media LITERACY

Which concept of ownership of the airwaves is more in the public interest?

STEP 1 The radio industry in the United States is privately owned. In some countries the airwaves are controlled by the government.

1. Think of the U.S. system, which is more and more controlled by chains and corporations.
2. Consider government-controlled radio such as the BBC, the British broadcasting system that is accountable to Parliament and to household license payers and that is often cited as one of the world's most independent news sources and a station in a country that is notorious for censoring media content.
3. Also consider low-power pirate radio and LPFM stations.

Dig Deeper

STEP 2 Each of these models of airwave ownership has pluses and minuses. Make a list of the pros and cons of privately owned airwaves. Make a second list of the pros and cons of government-owned airwaves. Make a third list of the pros and cons of low-power radio.

What Do You Think?

STEP 3 Which model do you think best serves the public interest? Is there some other model, a new one, or a combination of the ones you just analyzed that would do a better job.

Keeping Up to Date

Broadcasting & Cable is a weekly trade journal.

Cinema Journal is a scholarly journal that includes work on radio.

Historical Journal of Film, Radio, and Television is a scholarly journal.

Journal of Broadcasting and Electronic Media is a scholarly quarterly from the Broadcast Education Association.

Journal of Communication is a scholarly quarterly from the International Communication Association.

Journalism and Mass Communication Quarterly is an academic journal from the Association for Education in Journalism and Mass Communication.

Federal Communications Law Journal is a scholarly journal.

R&R is a weekly trade journal, published by Radio & Records, that carries charts and playlists that not only reflect what's getting airtime but also shape what will be getting airtime.

Talkers will keep you posted on talk shows.

For Further Learning

Gerald Eskenazi. *I Hid It Under the Sheets: Growing up with Radio.* University of Missouri, 2006.

Eskenazi, a New York *Times* sports reporter, reminisces about the so-called Golden Era of Radio. His focus is the comedies, quiz shows, soap operas, dramas, mysteries, Westerns and thrillers of the 1930s and 1940s, as well as early radio sports.

Lori Robertson. "Quicker and Deeper," *American Journalism Review* (June/July 2004), pages 30–37.

This is an update on National Public Radio.

Thomas Doherty. "Return With Us Now to Those Thrilling Days of Yesteryear: Radio Studies Rise Again," *Chronicle of Higher Education* (May 21, 2004), pages B12–B13.

Doherty, a broadcast scholar, sees new interest in radio as a social phenomenon in this report on the state of recent scholarship.

Donna Harper. *Invisible Stars: A Social History of Women in American Broadcasting.* Sharpe, 2001.

Harper, a historian, bases this work on interviews with pioneer women broadcasters and their survivors. She also draws on letters and newspaper and magazine articles.

Marc Fisher. "Resurgent Radio," *American Journalism Review* (December 2000), pages 32–37.

Fisher, a Washington *Post* writer on the media, surveys new radio technologies, including satellite and Internet delivery and digital transmission.

Philip M. Seib. *Going Live: Getting the News Right in a Real-Time, Online World.* Rowman & Littlefield, 2000.

Written by a journalism professor, this book looks at how convergence has changed the news-gathering business.

Kevin G. Wilson. *Deregulating Telecommunications: U.S. and Canadian Telecommunications, 1840–1997.* Rowman & Littlefield, 2000.

Wilson, a Canadian communication scholar, reviews evolving regulatory policies historically into the era of converging technologies.

James C. Foust. *Big Voices of the Air: The Battle over Clear Channel Radio.* Iowa State University Press, 2000.

Foust, a journalism professor, offers a history and analysis of federal licensing for 40 superstations to reach rural audiences.

Charles H. Tillinghast. *American Broadcast Regulation and the First Amendment: Another Look.* Iowa State University Press, 2000.

Tillinghast, an entertainment industry lawyer, reviews the history of government regulation and the difficulty it poses for First Amendment advocates.

Jeff Land. *Active Radio: Pacfica's Brash Experiment.* University of Minnesota Press, 1999.

Land details the story of the radio network Pacifica, which chronicled the countercultural movement and broadcast classical music, intellectual roundtables and poetry alongside controversial politics.

Steve Jobs
With show biz flamboyance Steve Jobs keynotes his annual Macworld conference. Can Jobs do for Disney what he did for Apple and Pixar?

chapter 8 Television

In this chapter you will learn:

- **The television industry is under siege from newer media technology.**
- **Technology has driven past infrastructure changes in television.**
- **The business structure of the U.S. television industry is a child of technology.**
- **The U.S. television industry derives revenue from advertising, subscriptions and fees.**
- **Networks are rethinking their old mantra of seeking the largest possible audiences.**
- **Television's future hinges on the impact of mobile, on-demand service.**

Out of a garage Steve Jobs and a buddy built an over-the-top desktop computer, which became the foundation for Apple Computer.

No wonder, when a lot of people think of Jobs, they think computer. Think again. Jobs, now a multibillionaire and in his 50s, has positioned Apple at the convergence point of computers and television and a whole lot of other media channels.

The latest Jobs breakthrough, in 2002, was the iPod portable music device, which triggered a transformation of music retailing and reshaped the music industry. The device morphed into the video iPod in 2005, the first version of which could take 150 hours in video downloads from the Internet.

Meanwhile, Jobs, who ran both Apple and Pixar Animation Studios, known for the blockbuster movies *Toy Story* and *Finding Nemo,* sold Pixar to Disney ABC for an incredible $7.4 billion. The deal made Jobs the largest Disney shareholder. With that came a position on the Disney board of directors, which runs not only Disney but also ABC television.

During preliminaries, with Disney and Pixar still in a dance about merging, Jobs pushed for ABC content to be made available for the video iPod. Negotiations took only three days, unbelievably fast by usual business standards. Mickey Mouse and Goofy features from Disney archives immediately were available on video iPods

at $1.99. So were episodes from ABC's *Desperate Housewives* and *Lost*. Executives at competing television networks saw no choice but to sign on, despite worries about eroding their historic monopoly on distributing programs through their local affiliates.

The Apple innovations under Jobs may not end with handheld devices. Insiders are talking of the living room of 2010 with a single box, an Apple TV, replacing a CD rack, a DVD player, a set-top box and a stereo. An Apple TV, with digital signals from the Internet or wireless relays, could do even more. The one-hour shows now available from Apple's iTunes may soon carry movie-length features. Disney is driving also to move dramatically more content to the Internet. To the consternation of the movie-house industry, this includes releasing movies on the Internet the same day as their theater release.

In this chapter you will learn about the television industry that faces transformation being forced by incredible new technologies. The familiar territory of industry infrastructures in place since the mid-1900s has adjusted to other innovations in the past, including the rise of cable in the 1980s and home-satellite delivery in the 1990s. What's ahead with video on demand? A shakeup like nothing before.

Television in Transition

studypreview **Once television was so influential that its cultural influence was described as "a molder of the soul's geography." The question now is whether television as a medium can retain its social role amid a changing technological environment.**

Television Industry in Crisis

Pixar Watch the trailers and see how they do it.

www.pixar.com

Television transformed the mass media. In the 1950s television, the new kid on the block, forced its media elders, notably movies, radio and magazines, to reinvent themselves or perish. Year by year television entrenched itself in the latter 20th century, first as a hot new medium, then as the dominant medium. Now the industries that developed around television technology are themselves in crisis. They have been overtaken by innovations in delivering video through other channels. Can the television industry reinvent itself? Can the industry get on top of the new technology? Or will television as an industry find itself subsumed, perhaps even replaced, by new competition? High drama is being played out even as you read this chapter.

Cultural Role of Television

Despite questions about how the U.S. television industry will adapt to an era of iPods, blogs and online gaming, the medium itself is hardly on its deathbed. Almost every U.S. household has at least one television set. On average, television is playing about seven hours a day in those households. Many people, sometimes millions, still shape their leisure time around when CBS runs *CSI*. Somewhere around 134 million people assemble ritual-like for the Super Bowl.

As a medium, television can create cultural icons, as Budweiser has demonstrated time and again. A generation remembers the Bud frog, then "Whazzup?" became an icon greeting. Even though many advertisers are shifting their spending to alternative media, Procter & Gamble spends $1.7 billion touting its wares on television, General Motors $1.3 billion.

For important messages to U.S. citizens, President Bush, even though visibly uncomfortable with television, has no more effective pulpit. It is rare for a candidate for public office not use television to solicit support. For information, millions of people look to network news—and also Jon Stewart, Oprah Winfrey, David Letterman and Conan O'Brien.

Fictional television characters can capture the imagination of the public. Perry Mason did wonders for the reputation of the legal profession in the 1960s. Then Mary Tyler Moore's role as a television news producer showed that women could succeed in a male-dominated business. Roles played by Alan Alda were the counter-macho model for the bright, gentle man of the 1970s. The sassy belligerence of Bart Simpson still makes parents shudder.

Enduring Television Effects

Although television can be effective in creating short-term impressions, there also are long-term effects. Social critic Michael Novak, commenting on television at its heyday, called television "a molder of the soul's geography." Said Novak: "It builds up incrementally a psychic structure of expectations. It does so in much the same way that school lessons slowly, over the years, tutor the unformed mind and teach it how to think." Media scholar George Comstock made the point this way: "Television has become an unavoidable and unremitting factor in shaping what we are and what we will become."

Whether the influence ascribed to television by Novak and Comstock will survive the fast-changing media landscape of the 21st century remains to be seen. Nobody, however, is predicting the imminent disappearance of television. The question is whether the television industry may lose its legacy as a mass medium to technological innovations from new media of mass communication.

Television Technology

studypreview **Technology has driven the changing infrastructure of the television industry. The original technology, introduced by Philo Farnsworth, begat the early networks and local affiliates. New major players came in successive waves—cable, satellite-direct and video on demand.**

Electronic Scanning

In the 1920s an Idaho farm boy, **Philo Farnsworth,** came up with the idea of using a vacuum tube to pick up moving images and then display them electronically on a screen. Farnsworth found financial backers, and in 1927 he transmitted the first live moving image from one room in his apartment to another. At age 21 Farnsworth had invented television. Farnsworth's invention was an incredible feat, considering that great corporate research labs, including RCA, were trying to accomplish the same thing.

Zapping Electronics In retrospect the technology seems simple. Farnsworth's camera picked up light reflected off a moving subject and converted the light to electrons. Farnsworth zapped one electron at a time across stacked horizontal lines on a screen. The electrons followed each other back and forth so fast that they seemed to show the movement picked up by the camera.

Philo Farnsworth ■ Invented the electronic technology for television.

mediaPEOPLE

Philo Farnsworth

Television Inventor Thirteen-year-old Philo Farnsworth came up with the concept of live transmission of moving images by zipping electrons back and forth on a screen—just as he was doing, back and forth, in harvesting a potato field. Barely in his 20s, Farnsworth moved from theory to practice with what he called an image dissector.

Philo Farnsworth was 11 when his family loaded three covered wagons to move to a farm near Rigby in eastern Idaho. Cresting a ridge, young Farnsworth, at the reins of one wagon, surveyed the homestead below and saw wires linking the buildings. "This place has electricity!" he exclaimed. Philo obsessed about the electricity, and soon he was an expert at fixing anything electrical that went wrong.

That day when the Farnsworths settled near Rigby, in 1919, was a pivotal moment in young Farnsworth's life that led to technology on which television is based.

The next pivotal moment came two years later when Philo Farnsworth was 13. He found an article saying that scientists were working on ways to add pictures to radio but they couldn't figure out how. He then went out to hitch the horses to a harvesting machine to bring in the potatoes. As he guided the horses back and forth across the field, up one row, down the next, he visualized how moving pictures could be captured live and transmitted to a faraway place. If the light that enables people to see could be converted to electrons and then transmitted one at a time but very fast as a beam, back and forth on a surface, then, perhaps, television could work.

The ideas simmered a few months and then, when he was 14, Farnsworth chalked a complicated diagram for "electronic television" on his chemistry teacher's blackboard. The teacher, Justin Tolman, was impressed. In fact, 15 years later Tolman would reconstruct those blackboard schematics so convincingly that Farnsworth would win a patent war with RCA and cloud RCA's claim that its Vladimir Zworykin invented television.

Farnsworth's native intelligence, earnestness and charm helped to win over the people around him. When he was 19, working in Salt Lake City, Farnsworth found a man with connections to San Francisco investors. With their backing, the third pivotal moment in Farnsworth's work, he set up a lab in Los Angeles, and later in San Francisco, and put his drawings and theories to work. In 1927, with hand-blown tubes and hand-soldered connections, Farnsworth had a gizmo he called the image dissector. It picked up the image of a glass slide and transmitted it. The Idaho farm boy had invented television.

media ONLINE

Philo T. Farnsworth The Farnsworth archives.
http://philotfarnsworth.com

Vladimir Zworykin Exposition about the work of Zworykin.
http://levend.nl/tvmuseum/tvmuseumzworykin/zworykin.htm

Persistence of Vision Experiments that help in understanding of persistence of vision.
www.exploratorium.edu/snacks/persistence_of_vision.html

persistence of vision ■ The eye's ability to retain an image briefly, allowing the brain to fill in gaps between successive images.

As with motion pictures, the system froze movements at fraction-of-second intervals and then replayed them to create an illusion of movement—the **persistence of vision** phenomenon. There was a difference, however. Movies at the time came from a chemical-based photographic process. Television used electronics, not chemicals. Also unlike movies, television images were recorded and transmitted instantly. Movie images were stored on film for later play.

Dual Infrastructure The significance of the Farnsworth technology was quickly recognized. To put it in operation, Congress looked to its experience with radio and instructed the Federal Communications Commission to issue licenses to entrepreneurs to build local stations. These local stations, transmitting signals over the air, became the backbone of the U.S. television industry.

media TIMELINE

TELEVISION TECHNOLOGY

1927 Philo Farnsworth devised a tube that picked up moving images for transmission.

1939 RCA demonstrated television at the New York World's Fair.

1941 Federal Communications Commission adopted a technology standard for U.S. television.

1949 Ed Parsons introduced cable television in Astoria, Oregon.

1952 FCC adopted a compatible color and black-and-white technology standard.

1975 HBO introduced satellite-delivered programming to local cable systems.

1984 DirecTV offered satellite-direct programming to home dishes.

1996 FCC adopted digital standards with a gradual phase-in.

1998 Networks began occasional digital transmissions.

2005 Apple introduced video iPod.

2006 Verizon began V Cast for wireless handheld devices.

2006 AOL created online genre-defined video channels.

2009 FCC required television stations to complete conversion to digital transmission.

Meanwhile, the giant radio networks, first NBC and CBS, later ABC, drew on their radio success to provide programming to the local stations. Thus, the Farnsworth technology spawned a **two-tier system** for the television industry, just like the U.S. structure of radio:

- Local stations that sent signals to viewers.
- National networks that reached viewers only through the local stations.

Into the 1980s this dual infrastructure was a symbiotic money-making bliss for networks and stations. Then came alternate distribution technology—cable.

Cable Delivery Systems

Early television stations were built only in larger cities with a sufficient advertising base for profitability. Because over-air television signals didn't carry great distances, many outlying towns had fuzzy signals. Some were totally out of range. In the late 1940s, a few small-town business operators, some with a smattering of knowledge in electronics from running radio repair shops, saw an opportunity. They hoisted towers on nearby hilltops to catch signals from city stations. They strung a cable down to town and tacked wires on telephone poles up and down alleys to deliver signals to individual subscribers.

CATV The urban television stations were pleased with the upstart **CATV** enterprises, short for *community antenna television*. With no investment, the big-city stations picked up additional listeners, which permitted the stations to charge more to advertisers. Small-town people were enthusiastic to be able to watch Jack Benny.

Although not a technological leap, the locally owned small-town cable systems were a new wrinkle in television delivery. The systems were a minor, relatively passive component in the U.S. television industry. Even into the 1970s nobody sensed what a sleeping giant they were.

Satellite Delivery When the old Time Inc. hired the young **Gerald Levin** as a "resident genius," nobody knew quite what to do with him. Eventually Levin was put in the corporate backwaters to run a subsidiary whose modest claim to fame was beaming

HBO HBO Online. **www.hbo.com**

WTBS The first superstation. **www.tbs.com/tbs17**

Turner Broadcasting Ted Turner's entertainment empire. **www.turner.com**

ESPN The original sports network. **http://espn.go.com**

two-tier system ■ Original infrastructure for U.S. television of local stations with national networks.

CATV ■ Early local cable television systems. Short for *community antenna television.*

Gerald Levin ■ Used orbiting satellite to relay exclusive programs to local cable systems, 1975.

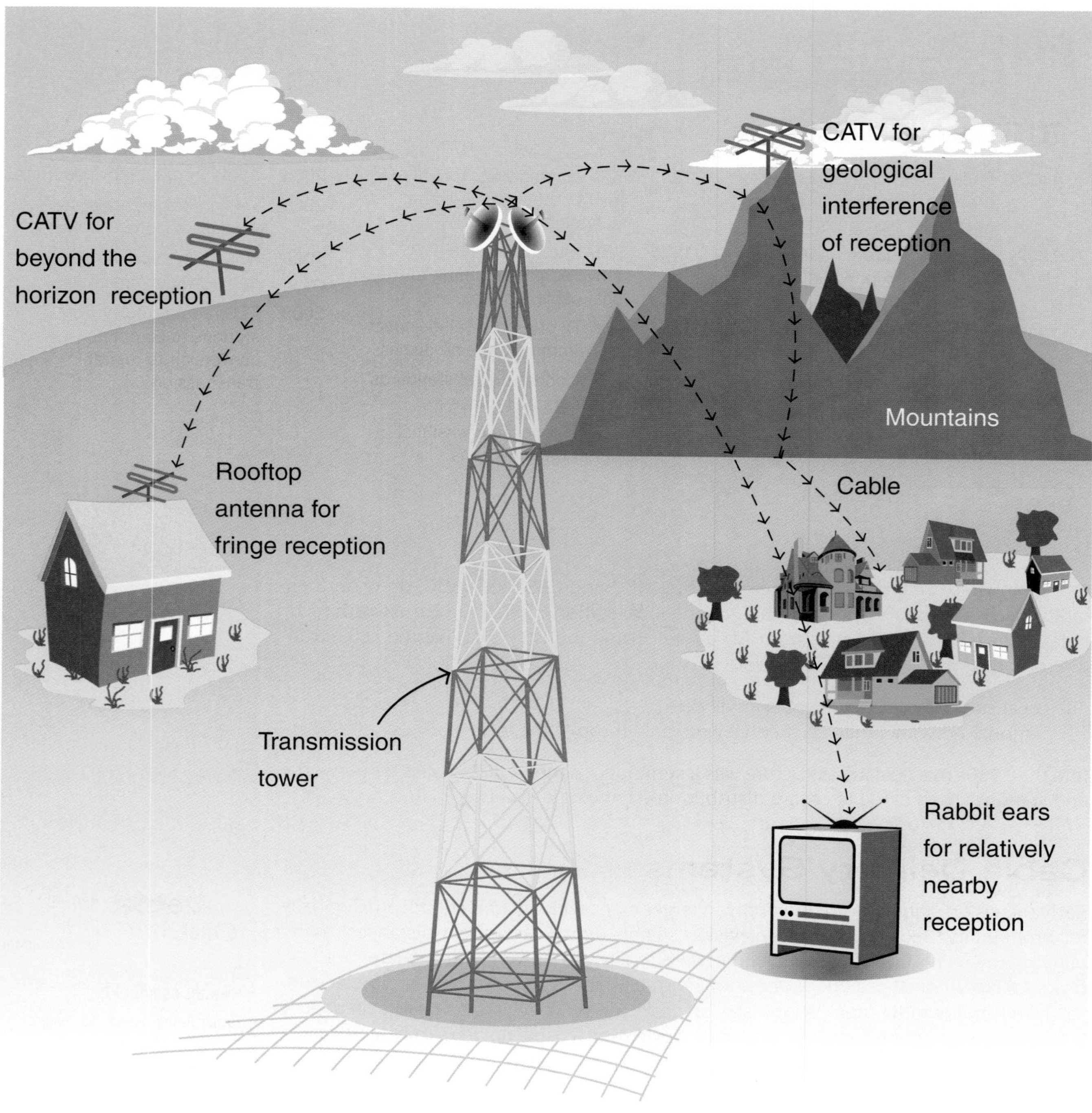

Television Signals Signals transmitted by AM radio stations ricochet off the upper atmosphere and thus follow the curvature of the earth. FM radio and television signals, however, go in straight lines, which gives relatively short range. So while rabbit ears will pick up television within a few miles of a television station, farther away it takes rooftop antennas. Even farther distances require a tall tower, which gave rise to community-antenna systems in far-away places beginning in 1949. Eventually CATV grew into the national cable television industry.

Ed Parsons

In Astoria, Oregon, downriver from Portland at the mouth of the Columbia, **Ed Parsons** had tinkered with radio since he was a kid. Nobody was surprised when he put a local radio station on the air. In 1946 Ed and his wife Grace saw a demonstration of television in Chicago—and Grace was hooked. Two years later, when they heard that a station was going on the air in Seattle, Grace told Ed that if anybody could figure out how to get the television signal from Seattle, 125 miles north,it was him.

Community-Antenna Pioneer

There were problems. One was that television signals travel straight rather than follow the earth's curvature. Reception is chancy beyond 50 miles. Another problem was the 4,000-foot coastal range, which further impeded reception from Seattle.

Parsons, a pilot, took a modified FM receiver and flew around the county to find the Seattle station's audio signal. He also roamed back roads to find a place to raise an antenna, but none was practicable. Then he discovered a suitable signal came in at the roof of the eight-story John Jacob Astor Hotel downtown—a bit more than a stone's throw from his and Grace's apartment.

Parsons jury-rigged an antenna, mounted it on the hotel roof, and strung a line to his living room. On Thanksgiving Day 1948, Grace turned on the set in their living room while Ed, listening to her reports on a walkie-talkie, adjusted the antenna on the Astor Hotel roof until, eventually, the Seattle station came in.

Ed and Grace were little prepared for what happened next. "We literally lost our house. People would drive for hundreds of miles to see television," he said. "You couldn't tell them no." The situation got so bad on Christmas Eve that Parsons chased everybody out and locked the door.

To regain household peace Parsons arranged with the manager of the Astor Hotel to drop a cable down the elevator shaft of the hotel and make a television set available in the lobby. The manager thought it would be good for business. Little did he realize that the television would draw so many people to the hotel lobby that guests wouldn't be able to squeeze their way to the registration desk.

Next Parsons persuaded a music store down the street to put a set in a display window. It, too, seemed like a good idea—until traffic jams prompted the police chief to urge Parsons to try something else. At that point, however, in March 1949, Parsons made history, using cable to connect a television reception antenna with a customer: Cliff Poole's music store.

To alleviate congestion at the store windows, Parsons extended the cable to more stores and taverns and to homes. Within a year Parsons had 25 places hooked up. Six months later there were 75. He charged $125 for installation, then $3 a month.

---

pay-per-view boxing matches to movie houses. Soon Levin was back to his bosses with a scheme to rent a transponder on the Satcom I orbiting satellite. From Satcom, as Levin laid out his vision, signals from his subsidiary, **HBO,** could be amplified and retransmitted down to local cable systems.

The Levin plan was audacious. He was going into space to bypass existing terrestrial technology by which signals were bounced across the country from microwave tower to microwave tower spaced 10 or so miles apart. Satcom would be cheaper, he said.

Unknown was whether cable systems were ready. Cable systems at the time were small-town operations that plucked signals from over-air television stations and sent them by cable to people who couldn't get clear over-air reception with rooftop antennas. There had been little thought since cable's beginnings a quarter century earlier to do anything more, certainly nothing about exclusive programming. Levin argued that cable systems could charge a premium to subscribers for HBO and augment their revenues and give a cut to Time Inc. Back then the nation's cities were not wired. City

Ed Parsons ■ Built first CATV system, Astoria, Oregon, 1949.

HBO ■ First exclusive programming available to cable systems.

Satellite Delivery A technician makes an adjustment on the history-making Satcom communication satellite that relayed HBO signals to local cable systems for delivery to subscribers. HBO thus became the first channel to give cable a distinctive edge in programming. The concept originated with Gerald Levin for Time Inc., which owned HBO and whose successor company still does. The concept jumpstarted the wiring of major U.S. cities for cable.

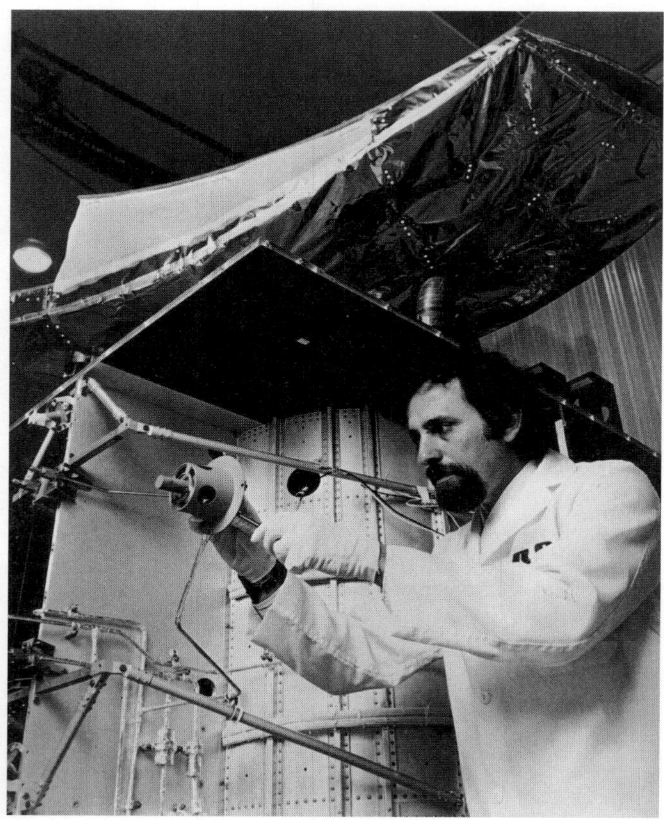

Gerald Levin

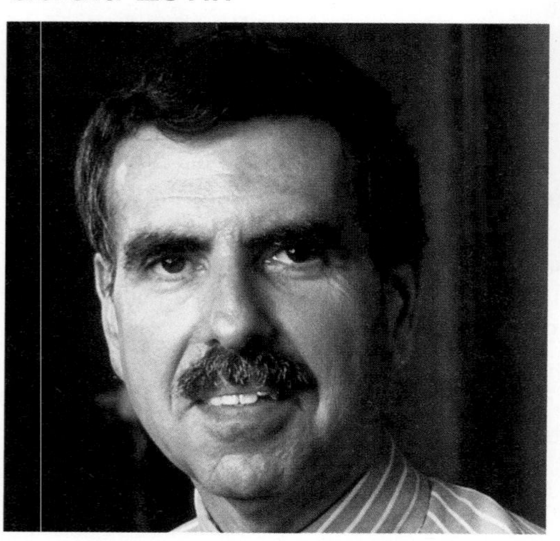

media ONLINE

DIRECTV The first alternative to cable, providing programming access to everyone from the city to suburbs to rural areas.
www.directv.com

The Cable Center Includes a history of cable television and the Cable TV Hall of Fame.
www.cablecenter.org

Dish or Direct A guide to help consumers figure out if satellite makes sense for their homes and, if so, which system would be best.
www.dishordirect.com/sat

Interactive TV Today This company offers a free e-mail newsletter with information on the latest developments in this fast-changing field.
www.itvt.com

Web TV Interactive TV.
www.webtv.com/pc

people didn't need cable. They got clear reception with rabbit-ears that sat on top of their TV sets.

The Levin plan worked. Local cable systems bought into the Levin vision for HBO. Within a year of HBO's 1975 launch, Atlanta television station owner Ted Turner also put his WTBS on satellite. Then Turner broke his own new ground with CNN, a 24/7 news channel. Soon cable systems were hot—or cool, as Turner put it: "I was cable before cable was cool."

With HBO, CNN and other exclusive programming, cable systems found new subscribers in fringe areas who for years had been receiving sometimes-fuzzy content with rooftop antennas. More importantly, investors poured billions of dollars into wiring the nation's cities, where people were clamoring for HBO, CNN and other new cable-exclusive programming.

The near-monopoly that ABC, CBS and NBC and their affiliates had on the medium of television was broken. Again, technology shook up a traditional media infrastructure. Suddenly there were four major players:

- National networks that serviced the local stations.
- Local stations that sent signals to viewers.
- Cable networks that serviced local cable systems.
- Local cable systems.

Satellite Direct

The possibilities for satellite delivery were not lost on **Stanley Hubbard,** who owned television station KSTP in Minnesota. Like almost all network-affiliated stations, KSTP was incredibly profitable, but Hubbard believed it might become a dinosaur in the age of satellite communication. Why should people tune into local stations, which picked up network signals from satellite for retransmission to viewers, when the technology was available for viewers to pick up the signals directly from satellite? Skeptics scoffed, but in 1984 Hubbard joined General Motors, which was in a diversification mode, to offer a **direct broadcast satellite** service. People could pick up signals from almost anyplace with home dishes the size of a large pizza.

Cable and Satellite Delivery Companies

Comcast	Cable	21 million
DirecTV	Satellite	15.4 million
Time Warner	Cable	12.3 million
EchoStar (Dish)	Satellite	11 million
Cox	Cable	6 million
Charter	Cable	6 million
Adelphia	Cable	5 million

Today DBS, as the technology is called, is the fifth component in the fragmenting U.S. television industry—besides the networks serving over-air affiliates, those local affiliates themselves, the cable networks and the cable systems. Together the two U.S. DBS companies, DirecTV and EchoStar, deliver programming to more than 26 million customers. Comcast, the largest multisystem cable chain, has 21 million.

Stanley Hubbard ■ Pioneer of direct-to-viewer satellite television.

direct broadcast satellite (DBS) ■ Transmission of television signals directly from orbiting satellite to viewers without local station or cable system as intermediary.

mediaTECHNOLOGY

Digital Television

Despite the crisp television images available through digital technology, viewers have seemed sufficiently pleased with the old analog quality they grew up with. Even as more digital programming became available starting in 2001, most people kept watching on analog sets. When they bought new sets, most stayed with analog. As recently as 2004, only one digital receiver was sold for every five analog sets.

Why no pell-mell rush to the new technology with super-sharp images, especially considering the usual American fascination with the latest gadgets?

Few over-air local stations promoted digital reception, not even those that offered it. Although the FCC had ordered the digital conversion by the end of 2006, stations were banking that they could delay the costly conversion through a loophole in the Commission's dictum. The FCC, pressed by industry lobbyists, had agreed to exempt stations if 85 percent of the homes in their service area didn't have digital receivers. Also, most cable systems, which deliver signals to more than two of three of U.S. homes, don't have the capacity to deliver digital signals.

The cost of digital receivers also was a deterrent. Although digital sets had dropped dramatically in price, many remained in the neighborhood of $3,000—six times more than a typical analog set.

In a bid to attract cable customers, who receive only analog, satellite-direct provider DirecTV offers some all-digital channels. These include HBO and a special digital channel. Digital subscriptions came slowly although steadily.

When the day arrives that the U.S. television system has converted to digital-only, rendering analog receivers out of date, people with analog receivers can buy set-top converters so they can still watch television. The converters cost about $400. Considering that the average life of a television receiver is 10 years, some working even longer, the actual transition to an all-digital television nation may well not be here until the 2020s.

Video on Demand

Devices for people to watch what they what when they want, **video on demand,** date back to Betamax video tape players introduced by Sony in 1976. Later devices, like **TiVo** digital recorders, provided other options. Today VOD, short for video on demand, has taken multiple forms, further splintering the television industry. Among new VOD services:

Cable VOD Some cable-system operators foresaw the potential of video on demand and have been upgrading their delivery pipelines. The investment is paying off. Comcast, which has been particularly aggressive, scored $100 million in VOD ad revenue in 2005—quintuple the year before. The number of U.S. homes capable of VOD cable service was up to 23.9 million in 2005 and expected to double by 2010.

Satellite VOD Satellite uploads of VOD would be prohibitively expensive. DirecTV and Dish satellite services are forging agreements with telephone companies to compete with satellite VOD services.

Wireless Downloading Cell-phone service provider Verizon rolled out a subscription service in 2006 that offered snippets for subscribers. The number of multimedia cell phones in the United States passed 40 million in 2005, about one in seven. The number is expected to reach 70 million by 2010.

video on demand ■ Mechanisms that allow viewers to play television and video any time they choose.

TiVo ■ A digital recording and playback device for television.

video iPod ■ A handheld Apple device for playing not only music but video at the viewer's choice of time and place.

Computer Downloads The Apple **video iPod,** introduced in 2005, could store as much as 150 hours of video and display the images on a 2.2-inch color screen. The video, downloaded to a computer then transferred to the iPod, gave people the option of taking shows on the road or wherever—and whenever. It was true video on demand, people downloading programs from the Internet to catch any time they wanted. The initial success for iPod video downloads exceeded expectations. Apple sold 8 million downloads of 40 different television series, including *Lost, Laguna Beach* and *CSI,* in the first six months.

Internet Video In 2006 AOL created online channels in a service called In2TV, offering thousands of programs from the archives of the Warner studio, a corporate sibling. Viacom, meanwhile, created MTV Overdrive. In 2005, 5 million viewers saw Live 8 tsunami-relief concerts on AOL. Although AOL viewership was fewer than the 22.4 million on MTV and VH-1 television channels and the 16 million on ABC, the VOD number, roughly 15 percent of the total, was significant. In another telling comparison, MTV's audience for its top-rated *Video Music Awards* was off 22 percent in 2005, but on the new MTV Overdrive service, 13 million people downloaded the show.

Showing on an iPod Near You

The prime-time show *Lost* was among the first network shows to make the early transition to subscription downloading. In the 2005 Disney-Apple alliance, Disney tapped programs from its ABC subsidiary for iPod availability.

Corporate Structure

studypreview **The regulatory mechanism created by Congress for television in the 1930s resulted in a two-tier U.S. television system. Corporate entities that entered television comported with the regulatory infrastructure. Today the infrastructure is under challenge from new corporate players that function largely outside government regulation.**

Dual Infrastructure

With television on the horizon in the 1930s, Congress looked at how its regulation of radio had worked. Congress was pleased with the **Federal Radio Act** of 1927. Licensing had forced tight engineering standards on the nascent industry. Licensing also had encouraged public service in programming. Caps on the number of stations that a single entity could own had precluded chain ownership, which was a bugaboo of the era. By issuing licenses for stations to serve only local communities, the 1927 law had established radio as a local medium, mostly advertising-financed, while at the same time allowing a national programming overlay through the NBC and CBS networks.

If the regulatory system worked for radio, why not television? The **Federal Communications Act** of 1934 tidied up the 1927 law and expanded the scope to television.

Meanwhile, the mastermind behind radio as a mass medium, **David Sarnoff** of the **Radio Corporation of America,** who created the NBC radio network, poured huge resources into research to invent television. For the super-proud Sarnoff, nothing would stop RCA from being first with "radio with pictures," as the concept was called. Learning of Philo Farnsworth's work on the West Coast, Sarnoff sent his chief RCA engineer, **Vladimir Zworykin,** to Los Angeles to call on Farnsworth and reconnoiter. Soon thereafter the RCA labs in New Jersey claimed to have invented television. Farnsworth had to go to patent court to protect his rights. The Idaho farm boy won his patent case, but the RCA publicity machine kept giving the credit to Zworykin. In 1939 RCA demonstrated television at the New York World's Fair with nary a credit to Farnsworth.

The federal government licensed the first television station in 1941. By 1948 heavy-duty **coaxial cables** that were necessary to carry television signals had been laid to the Midwest, and NBC began feeding programs to local stations. The coaxial linkup, with some stretches covered by microwave relays, connected the East and West coasts in 1951.

Local Stations The backbone of the national television system was local stations, squeezed onto the electromagnetic spectrum in a range of **VHF** channels, short for *very high frequency*. The stations were on Channels 2 through 13. To avoid overlapping signals, stations generally were

Federal Radio Act ■ Original law in 1927 for government regulation of U.S. broadcasting.

Federal Communications Act ■ Revision of Federal Radio Act in 1935 to include television.

David Sarnoff ■ Broadcast visionary who built RCA, NBC.

Radio Corporation of America (RCA) ■ Corporate parent of NBC. RCA was heavy in research and development.

Vladimir Zworykin ■ RCA engineer often but erroneously credited as inventor of television.

coaxial cable ■ A high-capacity wire with dual electric-current conductors.

very high frequency (VHF) ■ Original television transmission band was known to consumers as channels 2 to 13.

Television Chains

These companies' over-air stations have the largest reach of the U.S. television audience.

Paxson (West Palm Beach, Florida)	61.8 percent	61 stations
Viacom (CBS) (New York)	42.8 percent	39 stations*
Fox (Los Angeles)	44.4 percent	37 stations*
Univision (Los Angeles)	41.3 percent	36 stations
Tribune (Chicago)	40.1 percent	27 stations
NBC (New York)	38.3 percent	29 stations*
Trinity (Tustin, California)	31.3 percent	23 stations
Sinclair (Hunt Valley, Maryland)	24.1 percent	63 stations
ABC (New York)	23.7 percent	10 stations*
Entarvision (Santa Monica)	19.1 percent	27 stations
Gannett (McLean, Virginia)	17.7 percent	22 stations
Hearst-Argyle (New York)	17.6 percent	34 stations
Belo (Dallas)	13.8 percent	20 stations
Cox (Atlanta)	10.2 percent	15 stations
E. W. Scripps (Cincinnati)	9.9 percent	10 stations

*Does not include affiliates of the network not owned by the network.

spaced at intervals two channels apart—generally six per city. Although there were earlier experimental stations, not until the late 1940s did the building of stations begin in earnest. The first stations, all in larger cities, took affiliations with the fledgling NBC, CBS, ABC and short-lived Dumont network. Larger cities also had unaffiliated independent stations. Noncommercial stations were licensed for educational programming, mostly operated by school districts.

When the VHF channel spectrum became crowded, the FCC, which regulated broadcasting for Congress beginning in 1934, added ultra-high frequency or **UHF** channels 14 to 83. The UHF channels were handicapped because until 1962, television set manufacturers were not required to include the higher channels.

Today over-air television stations operate in 210 U.S. markets. The largest market, New York City, has 7.4 million television households. Los Angeles is second with 5.4 million. The smallest, Glendive, Montana, has 5,150 television households. Although Congress originally favored local ownership, most stations today are parts of chains.

Affiliate-Network Relations

A network affiliation is an asset to local stations. Programs offered by the networks are of a quality that an individual station cannot afford to produce. With high-quality network programs, stations attract larger audiences than they could on their own. Larger audiences mean that stations can charge higher rates for local advertisements in the six to eight minutes per hour the networks leave open for affiliates to fill. Stations also profit directly from affiliations. The networks traditionally shared their advertising revenue with affiliates, paying each affiliate 30 percent of the local advertising rate for time that network-sold advertisements take. Networks, under pressure to reduce costs, have experimented with other formulas, including charging affiliates. But typically, almost 10 percent of a station's income is from the network.

Affiliate-network relations are not entirely money-making bliss. The networks, whose advertising rates are based on the number of viewers they have, would prefer that all affiliates carry all their programs. Affiliates, however, sometimes have sufficient financial incentives to preempt network programming. Broadcasting a state basketball tournament can generate lots of local advertising. The networks also would prefer that affiliates confine their quest for advertising to their home areas, leaving national ads to the networks. Local stations, however, accept national advertising on their own, which they schedule inside and between programs, just as they do local advertising.

The networks have learned to pay more heed to affiliate relations in recent years. Unhappy affiliates have been known to leave one network for another. Television chains such as Group W or Gannett have a major bargaining chip with networks because with a single stroke of a pen they can change the affiliations of several stations. This happened in 1994 when Fox lured 12 stations away from the Big Three networks because of NFL football, eight of the stations from CBS alone.

Networks once required affiliates to carry most network programs, which guaranteed network advertisers a large audience. Most stations were not bothered by the requirement, which dated to network radio's early days, because they received a slice of the network advertising revenue. Even so, the requirement eventually was declared coercive by the FCC, which put an end to it. However, there remains pressure on affiliates to carry a high percentage of network programs. If a station does not, the network might transfer the affiliation to a competing station. At the same time the FCC decision increased the opportunities for affiliates to seek programming from nonnetwork sources, which increased pressure on networks to provide popular programs.

For most of television's history there were three networks that provided programming to local stations. **NBC** and **CBS** were first, but **ABC** grew into a full-fledged competitor. Evenly matched in many ways, the **Big Three** networks had about 200 outlets each, and their programs reached the whole country.

ultra high frequency (UHF) ■ Expanded television transmission band was known to consumers as channels 14 and higher.

NBC ■ National Broadcast Company. Built from NBC radio network under David Sarnoff. One of the Big Three over-air networks.

CBS ■ Columbia Broadcasting System. Built from CBS radio network under William Paley. One of the Big Three over-air networks.

ABC ■ American Broadcasting Company. Built from ABC radio network. One of the Big Three over-air networks.

Big Three ■ ABC, CBS, NBC.

mediaPEOPLE

María Celeste Arrarás

Puerto Rico-born María Celeste Arrarás was a natural for Univision. The Spanish-language television network had bridged the audience gap between Mexican-Americans in the southwest United States, Cuban-Americans in south Florida, and Puerto Ricans in the east. The result was a single delivery platform for advertisers to reach a national Hispanic market. How did Arrarás fit in? With a 1991 honors degree from the University of Puerto Rico-Mayagüez, Arrarás had spent the better part of a decade as a reporter at a Puerto Rico station. Univision, looking for an anchor for the news show *Primer Impacto,* enticed her to Miami. It was giant career step. Univision had the fifth largest network audience in the United States, a distant fifth to be sure but hardly insignificant.

In 2002 Univision's rival, the Telemundo television network, offered Arrarás greater prominence—host and managing editor of a new show *Al Rojo Vivo con María Celeste,* which in English is *Red Hot with María Celeste.* About this time the NBC network bought Telemundo. The easily bilingual Arrarás suddenly had hugely larger-outlets for her journalism. She did segments for the prime-time NBC magazine *Dateline* and reporting for MSNBC. When anchor Katie Couric left NBC's *Today* in 2006, Arrarás moved into a rotating anchor chair.

Although visible mostly as an anchor, Arrarás prides herself on field reporting. Her investigative work includes *El Secreto De Selena,* for which she probed into the death of Tejano singer Selena Quintanilla. The piece included an interview with the woman convicted of the murder. Arrarás did *Crouching Tiger, Hidden Cruelty,* an investigation into how some entertainment animals are treated. Other serious journalism includes the fall of the Soviet Union, the Seoul Olympics, and the 2002 Haiti coup d'etat.

Al Rojo Vivo Telemundo magazine.

There have been foibles, like mistakenly calling Dennis Kucinich a senator in the early 2004 presidential debates. Kucinich had to correct her that he was a mere congressman. For better or worse in terms of her news reputation, Arrarás has done her share of celebrity interviews, including one with heart-throb singer Ricky Martin. There also have been dubious tangents to a news career, like agreeing to judge the 2003 Miss Universe pageant, and acting roles on the Telemundo soap opera *Passions.*

Even so, Arrarás' career coincides with a great movement in the U.S. media toward fragmentation. Her career has made her familiar with millions of U.S. Hispanics. With NBC now in control of Telemundo and looking for ways to wean Hispanic viewers to its flagship product, NBC is finding places for Arrarás in its prime NBC lineup. This perhaps puts Arrarás in the next stage for Spanish-language media in the United States if these minority media, like their predecessors, meld into the mainstream media. It happened with the German-language newspapers of an earlier era, and the Italian papers, and the Norwegian.

Arrarás understands her role in the bigger picture. Asked about why she was on *Today,* Arrarás said: "There are 32 million Latinos in this country, which is the equivalent of the population of Canada. It was inevitable that eventually we would let ourselves be heard and noticed everywhere, including television. That's why I'm here."

NBC Television The federal government licensed the first television stations in 1941, on the eve of U.S. entry into World War II. But when factories converted to war production, no more television sets were manufactured until after peace arrived in 1945. By 1948 the coaxial cables that were necessary to carry television signals had been laid to the Midwest, and NBC began feeding programs to affiliates. The coaxial linkup, with some stretches linked by **microwave relays,** connected the east and west coasts in 1951.

microwave relays ■ Towers reangle over-air signals to match the earth's curvature.

mediaPEOPLE

Debra Lee

Debra Lee finished her Harvard law degree in 1980. That also was year that cable television association executive Robert Johnson put the Black Entertainment Television network, *BET* for short, on cable. Neither Johnson nor Lee had heard of the other, let alone realized they would become partners in growing BET into a leading media and entertainment company targeted to African Americans. Nor did Johnson or Lee see the day when Viacom, the media giant known mostly for CBS, would pay $3 billion to acquire the company.

In 1980 the cable television industry bankrolled Johnson to establish BET to create programming exclusively for local cable systems. Bankroll? It was only $500,000, which wouldn't go far. Johnson started with a two-hour block only on Friday nights. Opening night was the uplifting if not tepid movie *A Visit to a Chief's Son.* Johnson didn't want to rock the boat to start. Most cable operators, he noted, were in white-dominated rural areas and "scared about what programming for the black community would be all about."

Other early programming was cheap stuff, mostly music videos that earned BET the moniker "the black MTV." Then came black collegiate sports and lots of televangelism.

Debra Lee, meanwhile, was clerking in federal court in Washington. Then she joined a corporate law firm. In 1986 she made the jump to BET as vice president and general counsel. Her responsibilities came to include strategic planning. On Lee's watch BET scored consistent growth in revenue and ratings. Original movies, documentaries, and concert specials were funded. News and public affairs, which had been on-again, off-again, became fixtures. There were acquisitions into books and magazines.

BET Team Debra L. Lee, chief of Black Entertainment Television, with her now-retired BET partner Bob Johnson, share the spotlight at the annual 2005 BET Awards in Hollywood.

It was not easy. Along the way Johnson and Lee, both of whom are black, found themselves with critics galore. One vexing issue was whether the BET concept itself was racist. Put baldly, as it was, the question was whether a network called White Entertainment Television would be acceptable.

The music videos, said critics, were mostly rap with many perpetuating negative stereotypes with misogynistic, materialistic and violent themes. BET occasionally banned some stuff, including Little Brother's "Lovin' It" and Eminem's "Just Lose It." Even so, BET kept playing raunchy stuff, although usually late at night.

As inconsistent with cruder rap as it may seem, BET programming was heavy with Christian evangelism, which also attracted critics. Controversial televangelists Robert Tilton and Peter Popoff, who exhort donations for miracles, were BET mainstays.

Also raising eyebrows was the reality show *College Hill,* which tracked female students living together, over a season of episodes. How uplifting for the race were the intimate daily lives of the participants, at historical Southern University the first season in 2004, then at Langston University, then at Virginia State?

Whatever the criticism, Johnson and Lee continued to build the network. Viacom's purchase of BET in 2000 was confirmation of their success. So was the Viacom decision after the acquisition to let Johnson and Lee continue at the helm.

In 2005 Johnson, at 59, retired to run an airline he had bought and to manage other enterprises, including the Charlotte Bobcats and the Charlotte Sting sports franchises. With Viacom's blessing, he turned the BET reins over to Lee. Her title became president and chief operating officer. That made Lee, at 50, the highest ranking African-American woman at Viacom.

NBC innovations included two brainstorms by **Pat Weaver,** an ad executive recruited to the network as a vice president. In 1951 Weaver created a late-night comedy-variety talk show, precursor to the venerable *Tonight Show.* Weaver also created an early morning entry, the still-viable *Today.* With those shows, NBC owned the early morning and insomniac audiences for years. Weaver also authorized special one-shot programs, *spectaculars* as he called them, which preempted regular programs and drew regular viewers from other networks without losing NBC's regulars.

In 1985 **General Electric** bought NBC. During a three-year period, 1982 to 1985, all of the Big Three networks moved out of the hands of the broadcast executives, such as NBC's **David Sarnoff,** who grew up in the business and nurtured these giant influential entities. As it turned out, the Big Three's heyday was over with new competitive pressures from cable and other quarters. The new owners, with their focus on the bottom line and their cost-cutting instincts, fundamentally changed network television for a new era. General Electric bought the Universal movie studio in 2004 and merged it into a new unit, NBC Universal.

NBC One of the original big three networks.
www.nbc.com

CBS Another of the original big three networks.
www.cbs.com

ABC The third of the original big three networks.
http://abc.go.com

FOX 20th Century Fox Television.
www.fox.com

WB-TV The WB Television Network.
www2.warnerbros.com/web/television/index.jsp

UPN-TV United Paramount Network.
www.upn.com

CBS Television CBS was outmaneuvered by NBC in lining up affiliates after World War II but caught up. By 1953 CBS had edged out NBC in audience size by acquiring affiliates and creating popular programs.

The old CBS radio soap operas, transported to television in 1951, were a factor. So was a science fiction anthology, which paved the way for *The Twilight Zone.* Also by 1953 the *I Love Lucy* sitcom series, which eventually included 140 episodes, was a major draw.

CBS established its legacy in television public affairs programming when **Edward R. Murrow,** famous for his live radio reporting from Europe, started *See It Now.* Three years later, when Senator Joseph McCarthy was using his office to smear people as communists when they weren't, it was Murrow on *See It Now* who exposed the senator's dubious tactics. Many scholars credit Murrow with undoing McCarthy and easing the Red Scare that McCarthy was promoting.

The CBS television network was shepherded in its early years by **William Paley,** who had earlier created the CBS radio network. Paley retired in 1982, and Laurence Tisch, a hotel mogul, came into control of CBS. Today, Viacom owns the network.

ABC Television ABC established its television network in 1948 but ran a poor third. Things began changing in 1953 when ABC merged with **United Paramount Theaters,** whose properties included several television stations. The new company went into fast production schedules of programs that were aimed at Hollywood-like mass audiences. Live programming, the hallmark of early network television, was not part of ABC's recipe. By 1969 more than 90 percent of the network's programs were on film, tightly edited and with no live gaffes. It worked. ABC's 1964 fall lineup made national network television a three-way race for the first time.

ABC's growth was pegged largely to two Disney programs: *Disneyland* in 1954 and *The Mickey Mouse Club* in 1955. Another audience builder was ABC's decision not to carry gavel-to-gavel coverage of the national political conventions. That brought criticism that ABC was abdicating its public responsibility, but by leaving the conventions mostly to CBS and NBC, ABC cleaned up in the ratings with entertainment alternatives. ABC picked up more steam in 1961 with its *Wide World of Sports,* a weekend anthology with appeal that extended beyond sports fans. **Roone Arledge,** the network sports chief, created *Monday Night Football* in 1969. Network television was a three-way race again, and in 1975 ABC was leading by a hair.

CapCities Communications, a profitable Kansas City-based television station chain, bought ABC in 1985. The network's parent company operated as ABC/CapCities until Disney bought the operation in 1996. Today it is variously called ABC Disney or Disney ABC.

Pat Weaver ■ Created NBC's *Tonight Show, Today.*

General Electric ■ Current NBC owner.

Edward R. Murrow ■ Reporter who criticized Joseph McCarthy.

William Paley ■ Longtime CBS boss.

United Paramount Theaters ■ Strengthened ABC in 1953 merger.

Roone Arledge ■ Created ABC's *Monday Night Football.*

CapCities Communications ■ Owner of ABC before it was purchased by Disney.

Fox Conventional wisdom through most of television history was that the dominance of NBC, CBS and ABC precluded a fourth network. The only significant attempt at the fourth network, by television-set manufacturer **Allen Dumont,** fizzled in the mid-1950s. Even though the **Dumont network** transmitted 21 hours of prime-time shows to 160 stations at its peak, the other networks had more affiliates. Also, Dumont stations had smaller local audiences, which made the network less attractive to national advertisers.

Then came **Fox.** In 1986 the Australian media mogul **Rupert Murdoch** made a strategic decision to became a major media player in the United States. He bought seven non-network stations in major cities and also the 20th Century Fox movie studio. The stations gave Murdoch the nucleus for a fourth over-air network, and 20th Century Fox gave him production facilities and a huge movie library. Murdoch recruited **Barry Diller,** whose track record included impressive programming successes at ABC, to head the proposed television network.

When Fox went on the air, the signal went to Murdoch's stations and to other independent stations that weren't affiliated with the Big Three. There were doubts whether Fox would make it, but Diller kept costs low. First there was only a late-night talk show. Then Sunday night shows were added, then Saturday night. There was no costly news operation, just relatively low-cost programming. The programs, however, drew a following. Shows like *Married . . . with Children,* featuring the crude, dysfunctional Bundys, and the cartoon series *The Simpsons* attracted mostly young people in their free-spending years, as did new programs like *Beverly Hills 90210* and *Melrose Place.* The young audience made Fox popular with advertisers. Still, Fox stations were almost always the weakest in their markets, which had been the downfall of Dumont, the last previous attempt at a fourth network.

In 1994 Fox outbid CBS for rights to televise half the Sunday National Football league games. With the football contract and a growing bevy of popular prime-time programs, Fox lured affiliates from the other networks. After one Fox raid to pick up affiliates, CBS was left without outlets in several major cities and had to scramble to bring in stations in the less-watched, high-number part of the dial—the UHF stations from Channel 14 and higher—to maintain its promise to advertisers that it could saturate the country with their commercials.

The Murdoch strategy worked. The raids gave Fox almost 200 affiliates, about the same as the other networks, although many were less-watched UHF channels. The UHF disadvantage was softened, however, by growing cable penetration because cable systems assigned their own channel numbers. Still, Fox kept costs low with programs like *Cops* and *America's Most Wanted,* built around live police footage and recreated crime scenes. A news department came in 1996, an essential addition to keep the former CBS and other Big Three affiliates. Even so, the Fox news budget never matched that of other networks. The news operation, in fact, was a spin-off of a separate Murdoch initiative, the Fox News Channel, but even the Fox News budget never came close to that of its main rival, CNN, in the related but separate cable television industry.

CW Seeing the success of Fox, Time Warner launched the **WB Television Network** in 1995 to create an outlet for its Warner Brothers production unit. A week later Viacom announced it was creating UPN, short for **United Paramount Network,** for basically the same reasons. Time Warner and Viacom ended up wishing they hadn't. Not only were both networks slow in getting a prime-time schedule running, the audiences just weren't there in the fragmenting media market. Nor were advertisers, at least not in the quantity or with the enthusiasm that networks had traditionally commanded.

Going into 2006 WB was offering only 12 hours of prime-time programming a week, compared to 21 by ABC, CBS and NBC. On Saturday nights WB was dark, leaving it to affiliates to fill the time with local programming or to buy syndicated programming. The strongest WB program, *Seventh Heaven,* attracted only 3.5 percent of network viewers. Things were worse at UPN. The network was sending only10 hours of prime-time programming to affiliates, much of it less-than-original fare like WWE'S *Smackdown* wrestling and a Friday movie. Ratings were poor. *Everybody Hates Chris,* the strongest program, attracted 3.3 percent of the audience.

Allen Dumont ■ Operated early fourth network.

Dumont network ■ Fourth network, operated 1950–1958.

Fox ■ Network launched in 1986.

Rupert Murdoch ■ Created Fox network.

Barry Diller ■ Created early successful Fox programming.

WB Television Network ■ Network for over-air affiliates from 1995 to 2006.

United Paramount Network ■ Network for over-air affiliates from 1995 to 2006.

My's Telenovelas

For stations that suddenly lost a network affiliation with the merger of UPN and WB, Fox rushed to create My Network. Programming began with English-language novellas from corporate sibling 20th Century Fox. The telenovelas had been intended for Latin America export but were redirected to anchor prime time for the network five nights a week.

Not seeing black ink in their future, Viacom and Time Warner folded UPN and WB into a new broadcast television network, called the **CW network,** for September 2006. The new network, the *C* for *CBS* and the *W* for *Warner,* drew on programming from its predecessors with the target still being the profitable 18–34 age group. Programs included *America's Next Top Model, Veronica Mars, Beauty and the Geek, Smallville,* and *Smackdown.* The goal was to attract viewers from the four established networks.

My Because many cities had both WB and UPN affiliates, one or the other suddenly faced being an orphan without a network affiliation. To address the void, Fox scrambled to piece together another network, called **My Network.** Programming began with two hour-length English-language telenovela, *Desire* and *Secret,* five nights a week. Other programs in the works at Fox sibling 20th Century Fox, originally aimed at syndication, instead were regeared for My. So was a Fox news-produced magazine, *On Scene.*

Fragmentation

The network-affiliate corporate infrastructure of U.S. television was unchallenged money-making bliss for almost 30 years. Then came cable, which avoided most government regulation because it owned the cable that carried programming—not the airwaves that Congress had decreed were public property in 1927 to justify government regulation.

Cable Networks With only 265,000 households at its launch, the first cable network, HBO, barely dented the viewership of over-air stations. But HBO grew. In 1976 Atlanta station owner Ted Turner put his WTBS on satellite as mostly a movie channel for local cable systems. Turner called WTBS a "superstation," which quickly became a money machine. Leveraging the revenue, Turner created CNN, then bought a fledgling competitor and started Headline News as a second 24/7 news service, then TNT as a second movie channel. Seeing the potential, other cable channels soon were competing for space on local cable systems—ESPN for sports, a weather network, music video networks, home-shopping networks. By 2006 there were more than 330 national cable networks.

CW network ■ Network created in 2006 by merger of the WB and UPN.

My Network ■ Formed by Fox in 2006 to serve stations abandoned in the CW, UPN merger.

mediaTECHNOLOGY

Video on Demand

These are pivotal times in the history of television. In 2005 ABC made some shows available at $1.99 for the new Apple video iPod. Next CBS and NBC signed distribution deals for cable and satellite providers to offer select programs as video on demand for 99 cents a show. In 2006 the Warner television studio made a deal to put 14,000 episodes of vintage shows, including *Welcome Back, Kotter, Wonder Woman* and *Kung Fu* free on the America Online subscription service owned by its parent company Time Warner. AOL started with a drama channel, a comedy channel and four others.

These were a dramatic turnaround for the traditional television networks. The networks long had guarded their prime-time and syndication content with proprietary vengeance, in part to protect the money-making franchise of their local over-air affiliates. The fact, however, was that the networks saw additional revenue streams with delivery systems made possible by fast Internet connections. By 2006 about half of U.S. households had the fast broadband connections.

To protect their franchise, the networks encrypted downloads to prevent copying.

Video on Demand Traditional television networks have created a new business model by releasing programs for Internet delivery direct to consumers. One venture, AOL's In2TV, offered Warner episodes of *Welcome Back, Kotter* and other archived television programs. Here actor Freddie Prinze Jr. participates in the 2006 launch of In2TV.

Cable Systems Perceptive observers recognized in 1975 that HBO was leading the way toward a restructuring of the U.S. television industry. On Wall Street, cable systems suddenly were hot. CATV systems were gobbled up in hundreds of acquisitions. What emerged were **multisystem operators,** called MSOs in the industry. These companies, many of them subsidiaries of larger media companies, simultaneously were raising money from investors to wire big cities so cable programming could be offered to larger audiences for a monthly subscription. Today, more than 90 percent of the population of the United States has access to cable, although only about two-thirds of households subscribe.

Comcast catapulted into the largest multisystem operator in 2002 by buying AT&T Broadband and claiming, with earlier acquisitions, more than 21 million subscribers. Time Warner is second at 11 million. The consolidation of cable systems into large ownerships has reduced the number of MSOs nationwide to 25—a far cry from the locally owned autonomous systems that began in the late 1940s.

Satellite-Direct Companies The cost of entry for satellite-direct transmission has limited the number of U.S. operators to two. **DirecTV,** the larger with 14 million subscribers, is controlled by Rupert Murdoch. Murdoch knows the DBS business from his similar satellite services on other continents—Star TV in Asia, B-Sky-B in Britain, Sky Italia in Italy and Foxtel in Australia. In the United States, DirecTV's competitor, the **Dish network,** the trade name for EchoStar, has 11 million subscribers. EchoStar has a fleet of nine satellites in orbit, DirecTV eight.

Both DirecTV and EchoStar are growing, taking subscribers away from cable. In 2003 Dallas became the first major city with more satellite than cable customers. The growth accelerated when the Federal Communications Commission cleared the way for the satellite-delivery companies to include local over-air stations and their network programs among their array of cable channels. Both services also carry pay-per-view movies, pornography and sports packages.

multisystem operator (MSO) A company that owns several local cable-television delivery units in different, usually farflung, communities.

DirecTV Larger of two U.S. satellite-direct companies.

Dish network U.S. satellite-direct tradename of EchoStar.

VOD Companies The video-on-demand industry is too young for us to know which companies will come to dominate. The telephone company Verizon began building its **V Cast** system for cell-phone VOD service in 2006. Apple, meanwhile, was positioning itself with the handheld video iPod and its new Disney ABC connection. In 2006 the Warner television studio made a deal to put 14,000 episodes of vintage shows, including *Welcome Back, Kotter, Wonder Woman* and *Kung Fu* free on the America Online subscription service owned by Time Warner, its parent company. The AOL service, called In2TV, started with a drama channel, a comedy channel and four others. By 2006 about half of U.S. households had fast broadband connections to accommodate larger-than-ever-before downloads from the Internet, like lengthy videos.

Other models for VOD delivery are in development. Local cable systems, which are using their lines for telephone service, have created subscriber call-up services to order video. Satellite-direct services are sampling similar services by using telephone lines for ordering.

Business models are being revised with lessons learned, but profit potential seems everywhere—including advertising. AOLWarner was selling four 15-second commercial spots in its In2TV online video episodes. That was far fewer than 32 in a typical prime-time network show, but the spots were encrypted so viewers could not skip over. In the other initial forays into broadband delivery, AOLWarner gave television networks a 99-cent cut of the $1.99 per episode fee to consumers.

Network affiliates were not pleased, especially with the prime-time shows going out broadband. The networks responded that the Rubicon had been crossed with their earlier decision to sell DVDs of recent programs. There had been no demonstrable drop in viewership at on-air stations due to the DVDs. Edgy station owners were assured that local advertisers would still be attracted to slots set aside in network shows for local commercials.

The VOD revolution has only begun. The cost of entry is so low that almost anyone with a few hundred dollars in software can create videos for VOD distribution. Although big players, like Apple's iTunes, are working to build irresistible packages of programming, nothing precludes the devices from tapping independent program sources or anything on the Internet in what's becoming a cross-media world. Some observers say this is the ultimate democratization of television because the means of content production and distribution is so widely available—in contrast to when television began and it took massive investments to start up a network or even a local station.

Economics of Television

studypreview **The backbone of television economics historically has been the 30-second spot. Even with audiences slipping in recent years, 30-second spots have remained popular enough with advertisers that the networks have kept charging more. Some observers, however, see a softening in demand. Also, with the industry in rapid transition, new players have revenue streams in addition to advertising.**

Network Advertising

The big television networks have become an enigma. While cable networks have nibbled steadily at the audience once commanded by ABC, CBS, Fox and NBC, these major networks still have been able to continue raising their advertising rates. Strange as it seems, advertisers are paying the networks more money than ever to reach fewer viewers.

30-Second Spot Even so, there are signs that advertiser demand for 30-second spots may be softening. Big Four networks are not filling slots as far in advance as they once did. Why? Cable channels, many with relatively low-cost programming, have eased the

V Cast ■ Early cellular television content service, offered by Verizon.

Cross-Ownership

For years, over-air networks resented the intrusion of cable networks as a competitor for national advertising, but the tension cooled as media conglomerates added cable networks to their bevy of holdings. Advertising revenue that the over-air networks lose to cable may still end up in the parent company's coffers. For 2005, for example, NBC's upfront was about the same as the year before, but corporate stablemate Bravo doubled.

Senior sales executives cut deals with advertisers to buy time both on the networks serving air-over affiliates and on the network-owned cable services. Consider that the five major network companies have stable siblings:

	Over-air networks	**Among cable networks**
Disney	ABC	ABC Family Channel, Disney Channel, ESPN, SoapNet
NBC Universal	NBC, Telemundo	Bravo, CNBC, MSNBC, Mun2TV, SciFi Channel, Trio, USA Networks
News Corp.	Fox, My	Fox Movie, Fox New, Fox Sports, Fuel, National Geographic Channel
Time Warner	CW (half ownership)	Cartoon Network, CNN, TBS, Turner Classic Movies, TNT
Viacom	CBS, CW (half ownership)	BET, MTV, MTV2, The N, Nickelodeon, Nick at Night, Noggin, Spike, VH-1

demand with cut-rate pricing while also opening up manifold more slots, albeit for smaller audience slices. Also, doubts have arisen among advertisers about whether pricey 30-second spots on the Big Four are as cost-effective as cable, the Internet and other emerging advertising platforms. In short, the 30-second spot as the economic engine of the television industry may be an endangered species.

Upfront Drama is keen every spring when the networks ask big advertisers to commit themselves upfront to spots in the future year's programming. The networks list shows that they plan to continue, as well as a sample of new programs, and announce their asking price per 30-second spot based on audience projections. Then begins jockeying and bidding between the networks and the agencies that represent advertisers. The **upfront,** as the process is called, locks sponsors into specific shows three to five months ahead of the new season—although contracts generally have options that allow an advertiser to bail out.

For the 2005 season, the networks serving over-air stations obtained $9.1 billion in the upfront. Cable networks, which use the same process, lined up $6.3 billion in commitments.

Eighty percent of a year's commercial time typically gets spoken for in the upfront process. If a show misses the network's projected audience numbers, advertisers are given **make-goods,** the industry's term for additional spots to compensate. If a show turns into a smash hit and exceeds audience forecasts, the price per spot gets jacked higher or, in some cases, if there is no escalation clause, the advertisers end up with a real deal.

upfront ■ Advance advertiser commitments to buy network advertising time.

make-goods ■ Additional time that networks offer advertisers when ratings fall short of projections.

Cable Revenue Streams

Cable systems, going back to CATV, have a core revenue stream from subscribers, who are charged a monthly access fee. Cable networks tap into that revenue stream by charging the local systems to carry their programming. Fees for many cable channels are modest. The Travel Channel is lowest at 7 cents per subscriber per month. These are the highest:

ESPN	76 cents
TNT	64 cents
Nickelodeon	55 cents
CNN	43 cents
MTV	42 cents

When cable networks emerged in the late 1970s, some sought national advertising in competition with the over-air networks. Also, local cable systems went head-to-head with local over-air stations for local advertising.

VOD Business Models

A single model for video-on-demand service has yet to emerge. Verizon charges a monthly access fee for its V Cast. So does AOLWarner for its In2TV. Apple charges by download, one program at a time. There are attempts to integrate paid advertising, including product placement, in VOD content.

Budweiser has gone into entirely new territory with plans for an entire network with company-produced content, as well as content acquired elsewhere, for Internet delivery—all as a platform for promoting Anheuser Busch products. The Budweiser model is free access for consumers with a possible revenue stream from outside advertisers, in addition to in-house Bud ads, contests and promotions.

Noncommercial Television

Corporation for Public Broadcasting
Creating programming for public TV.
www.cpb.org

Many universities and school districts set up stations as noncommercial operations in the 1950s and 1960s to broaden their reach. These stations, as a condition of their licenses from the Federal Communications Commission, could not sell time to advertisers. As educational experiments, the **ETV** stations, as they were called, had mixed results. Most programs were dull lectures. The following was small. In some cities, meanwhile, citizen groups obtained licenses for noncommercial stations. By the late 1960s there were 300 of these stations.

In 1967 a blue-ribbon group, the **Carnegie Commission of Educational Television,** examined the situation and saw a grossly underdeveloped national resource. The commission recommended an alternate concept and used the term **public television** to "serve the needs of the American public." Within months, Congress responded by creating the **Corporation for Public Broadcasting** to develop a national noncommercial broadcasting system for both television and radio. The goal was high-quality programming distinct from that of the commercial networks, which, by their nature, pandered to mass audiences. Thus was born the **Public Broadcasting Service** as a network serving the former ETV stations, most of which shifted to the new public television model.

To pay the bills, public television has cobbled together motley sources of revenue. Until recent years, Congressional appropriations buffered from political control through a quasi-government agency, the Corporation for Public Broadcasting, was a mainstay. As federal funding has declined, the public television system has stepped up its drive for donations from public-spirited corporations and viewers themselves. Although prohibited from selling advertising time, stations can acknowledge their benefactors. These acknowledgments, once bare-bone announcements, have become more elaborate over the years and sometimes seem close to advertising.

Public television has never been much liked by the commercial television industry. Public stations take viewers away, even though relatively few. Also, that public television receives what amounts to government subsidies seems unfair to the commercial stations. The upside of the arrangement for commercial television is that the presence of high-quality programming on public television eases public and government pressure for them to absorb the cost of producing more high-culture fare as a public service that would attract only niche audiences and few advertisers.

educational television (ETV) ■ Stations that supplement classroom lessons, also that extend learning beyond school

Carnegie Commission on Educational Television ■ Recommended ETV be converted to the public television concept.

public television ■ Noncommercial television with an emphasis on quality programs to meet public needs.

Corporation for Public Broadcasting (CPB) ■ Quasi-government agency that channels tax-generated funds into the U.S. noncommercial television and radio system.

Public Broadcasting Service (PBS) ■ Television network for noncommercial over-air stations.

Television Content Issues

study preview Historically the television networks were in a manic quest for numbers—the larger the audience, the more the profits. Emerging now is an emphasis on delivering upscale audience segments that advertisers most covet. Negotiating this transition is an issue of content. So are perennial objections to violence in programming.

Quality Quest

Television rocketed to dominance as a mass medium in the 1950s by delivering unprecedented huge audiences for advertisers. The bigger-is-better philosophy generated advertising revenue although not always quality. Critics talked derisively about Joe Six-Pack programs without subtlety or sophistication that would zip over the heads of the culturally deficient, if not the dolts, in the audience. Sometimes it was called **lowest-common denominator** programming because it was designed to leave nobody out.

By 2006, however, many advertisers were saying size didn't matter so much any more. The concept of quality audience had moved to the fore. Quality? That translates into upscale. To attract big-budget advertisers, the networks realized they needed to pitch programs expected to draw well-heeled viewers. Their hope was to charge premium rates to advertisers seeking hard-to-reach high-income audience niches with messages for five-star hotels and luxury automobiles, not home hair-coloring kits and muffler shops.

At NBC, executives scuttled the sitcom *Committed* to make prime-time room for an edgy-style parody on corporate life, *The Office,* even though *Committed* had attracted far larger audiences. *The Office* came out of the 2004 season ranked 54th. But by delivering upscale viewers, networks could charge advertisers 5 to 20 percent extra. The audience measurement service Nielsen introduced new ratings breakdowns for program viewers in income brackets of $75,000-plus, $100,000-plus and $125,000-plus.

What attracts a quality audience? A consensus has emerged that the characters—even the criminals—need to be upscale. NBC improved the posture of its venerable *Law & Order* by introducing upper-class perpetrators with whom upscale viewers could relate. Upscale viewers also value high production values, sophisticated dialogue and less formulaic story lines.

lowest common denominator Media term drawn from mathematics. Content that someone with an average IQ of 100 or less can appreciate will have a larger potential audience than content that requires a 150 IQ to appreciate.

Law & Order
NBC found an upscale audience that many advertisers sought with the upscale characters in the long-running prime-time series *Law & Order.* The perps in murders may be seedy inside those button-down shirts with silk ties. Audiences related.

Besides wanting to extract more advertising revenue per 30-second spot, the Big Four networks were also in a desperate battle going into 2006 to break out of a ratings deadlock. In 2004 the audience spread among them was 1.4 ratings points. It narrowed to 0.3 in 2005. An unanswered question now is whether the energetic bid for high-income viewers may mean losing the vast mass audience on which the networks traditionally relied.

media DATABANK

Income-Based Viewership

The rankings of prime-time shows vary significantly by audience segments. This is the 2005 season rankings by viewers with $75,000-plus income and by viewers overall.

	$75,000 Viewers	Overall
West Wing (NBC)	1st	33rd
The Apprentice (NBC)	2nd	7th
Boston Legal (ABC)	3rd	14th
The Office (NBC)	4th	54th
Desperate Housewives (ABC)	5th	1st

Network Violence

Everyone agrees that grotesque violence, explicit or graphically implied, is growing in U.S. television, but measures are hard to come by. Parents Television Council, which opposes media-depicted violence, especially on networks providing programs to over-air stations, counted incidents in the 8 to 10 p.m. time slots in 1998 and 2002 and found a 41 percent increase. In the 9 p.m. hour the increase was 134 percent. Parents Television Council has gotten lots of ink with its stats, but critics claim PTC vastly overstates its point. An examination of PTC's 2002 figures, for example, shows 16 acts of violence in the 8 p.m. slot—one explicit and one implied on-screen death, six displays of guns, five fights, 1.4 scenes of blood, 0.8 threats of violence, and 0.35 acts of torture. Is one death a week, on average, too much for dramatic fare?

In election years, like 2008, calls for a government crackdown reach their quadrennial peak. The calls to regulate the violence are framed mostly in terms of protecting children—and to include previously exempt cable networks. Using the protect-the-children framework, regulation advocates note that over-air and cable programs arrive in households side by side. Without limiting violence on both delivery systems, they say, children could not be protected.

There remain First Amendment obstacles to government regulation. Over-air broadcasting historically had been regulated as an exemption to the First Amendment prohibition on government regulation. The premise for the exception is that the public owns

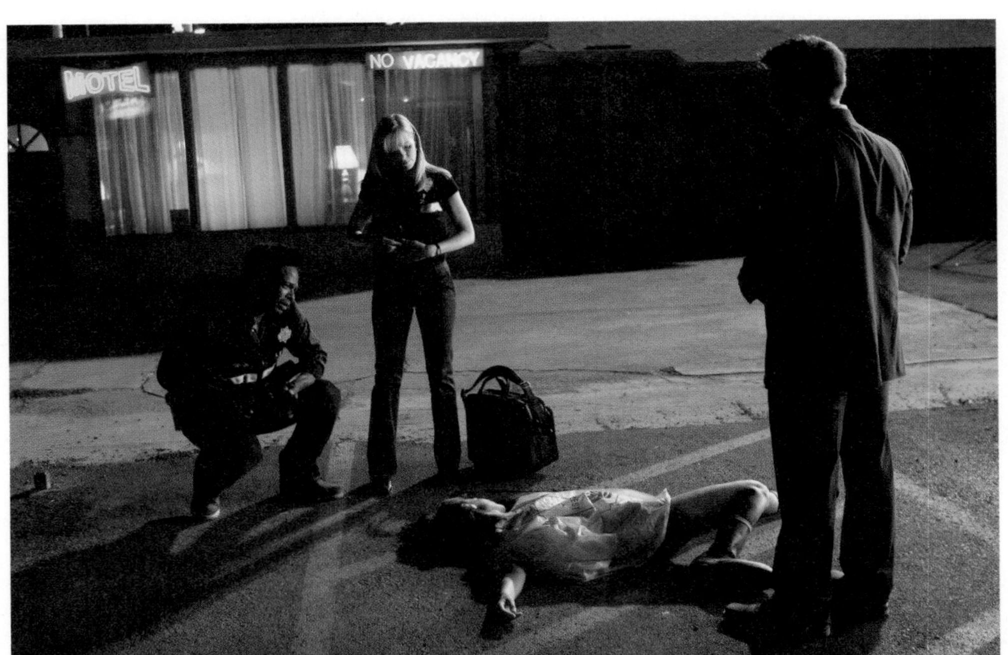

Television Violence

The Jerry Bruckheimer-produced series that attracted huge network television audiences, including *CSI,* have had their share of blood. Should such media-depicted violence, especially considering the great popularity of such shows, be regulated by government? Yes, to protect the children, according to regulation advocates.

the airwaves. But cable systems don't use the public airwaves and presumably have First Amendment protection from government interference with content. Also remaining is the knotty issue of how to shield children from violent fare without violating the constitutional right of adults to watch whatever they want without government interference.

Even so, Congressional and FCC grumbling have put broadcasters on guard. CBS toned down its network premier of the movie *Helter Skelter* to ward off critics. The National Association of Broadcasters talked about reinstating a prime-time "family hour." It all was typical of how mass media respond to threats of government regulation. Eddie Pitts, NAB president, was succinct: "Voluntary industry initiatives are far preferable to government regulations."

Meanwhile, knowing that data were inconclusive on detrimental effects of media-depicted violence, a bill in Congress has proposed giving $90 million to the National Institutes of Health for a five-year study on the effects of media violence on children's cognitive development. If data can demonstrate a link between aggressive child behavior and media violence, then antiviolence restrictions would be easier to put into law and to defend against constitutional challenges in the courts. As Senator Hillary Clinton conceded, the conclusion that violent television begets aggressive children has never been proven empirically: "As parents we know *intuitively* that our young children shouldn't be watching television shows with extreme violence." But, she noted, deleterious effects have never been demonstrated clinically.

Government Role

From time to time, Congress yanks network executives into sweat-box hearings over programming. It happened after performer Janet Jackson somehow lost her bodice during the 2005 Super Bowl halftime show. Occasionally rank language and dramatic themes rankle Congress. The history of these hearing-room confrontations is that the television people promise corrections and future restraints, pleased that their FCC licenses are still intact. And the politicians end up satisfied that their posturing has gone over with their constituents. All becomes copasetic until another day.

The Federal Communications Commission, meanwhile, continues tending to day-to-day issues. Through history the FCC has been astute to steer clear of confrontation over free-press issues that could create a constitutional crisis over whether government belongs in the media regulation business.

The executive branch has been more inclined to meddle in television content. During an early energy crisis, President Nixon had aides float the idea of shutting down most of the nation's television stations during heavy-viewing hours to conserve electricity. Talk about a lead balloon.

Most executive branch meddling has involved public television, which is vulnerable because of tax-dollar support. In 2000 the Republican president, George Bush, put a long-term critic of NPR and PBS in charge of the Corporation for Public Broadcasting. Until he was forced out, Ken Tomlinson worked to force programming with a conservative bent on the Public Broadcasting System. Criticizing documentaries and commentaries by long-time Democrat-connected Bill Moyers, Tomlinson said there needed to be an antidote. Tomlinson finally was forced to resign for intruding too far ideologically into calling the shots for public television content.

In some ways the Tomlinson affair was a replay of a 1972 attempt by President Nixon to curb what he saw as PBS voices on the political left. Nixon vetoed a $154 million funding package for the Corporation for Public Broadcasting. He tried to justify the veto by claiming that CPB had too much network-level influence on the programming of local public stations and that federal money would be better channeled to the stations themselves. Nixon critics pointed out that local stations, even with more direct funding, would be less inclined to develop programs on national issues. The president's goal, said the critics, was to mute robust dialogue on the Nixon agenda. The issue imploded when the Watergate scandal so consumed the Nixon White House that nothing much else got any attention.

The debate over public funding is mostly in Congress, which has begun a phase down of support for the Corporation of Public Broadcasting. The debate is rich. Some argue that the original rationale for public funding in the 1970s was to create quality alternatives to the Big Three networks that then had firm content control on the biggest local stations. Now with cable and satellite-direct services, the so-called 500-Channel Universe provides alternatives aplenty. CPB champions counter that the 500-Channel Universe is almost entirely commercial-driven and would unlikely be hospitable to a lot of what PBS does, including the acclaimed nightly *NewsHour* and the *Front Line* documentaries.

Untethering Television's Future

studypreview **Fundamental changes in the role of television in people's lives are occurring. Time shifting, possible with video on demand, is eroding the social tradition of gathering around the television. A related phenomenon, possible through television's growing portability, is space shifting. People can carry television with them to anywhere—any space—they choose.**

Time Shifts

The centerpiece of television in people's lives in the evening, a social ritual for half a century, is waning, even in prime time. With TiVo-like playback devices, people don't need to tune in at 8 for a favorite sitcom. To be sure, events like sports playoffs, elections and the *American Idol* finale will draw huge, live prime-time audiences. But the end may be in sight for prime-time scheduling for ongoing network series, the historic foundation of network programming.

A fundamental paradigm shift is occurring. Instead of people adapting their daily routines to television's scheduling, people are watching when it suits them. This is audience empowerment. The networks still corral huge audiences for mega-events, like the Super Bowl and *Survivor* finales, and also for major news. But the days are past when icon shows like Milton Berle, *Dallas* and *Seinfeld* had millions glued to the screen at a time dictated by network schedulers.

Space Shifts

The portability of **New Television,** as it might be called, signals a transformation in programming. The old 30-minute blocks assumed an audience being in place, seated for a whole program, and hence the coinage *couch potato.* Thirty-minute blocks were also useful for affiliate breakaways and local patching of programming into network structures. On-the-move audiences, with handheld screens, are neither in place nor freed up in neat 30-minute segments.

Expect **mobisodes,** short episodes for mobile viewers. For Verizon's V Cast service, geared for mobile devices, Fox has created one-minute episodes of its program *24,* something to watch between checking for new e-mail messages or a new online video game.

Verizon V Cast Watch music videos, movie clips, sports highlights—and still make calls with this latest generation of mobile phones.
http://getitnow.vzwshop.com/vcast.home.do

New Television ■ A catchall term that variously includes cable, satellite, handheld and other delivery and reception technology.

mobisodes ■ Mini-episodes, some a mere minute, to fit into short time frames that mobile television viewers have available.

Advertising Shifts

Once the darling of almost every national brand for marketing, 30-second spots on network television are losing luster.

Webisodes One brand-name advertiser that's shifted away from 30-second spots is American Express. In the mid-1900s AmEx put 80 percent of its advertising budget on

mediaTECHNOLOGY

Mobile Television

Cell Phone Television
The comic-strip detective Dick Tracy would have loved cellphone televisions, although they're not yet wrist-watch size. Also, they don't allow instantaneous video exchanges—yet. Downloading can take longer than the snippets play.

The comic-strip detective Dick Tracy wore a two-way wrist TV in the 1950s. The possibilities excited the imagination. In time telephone manufacturers miniaturized hardware sufficiently for palm-held cellular phones to include tiny television screens. But what to watch? In 2005 the phone company Verizon launched V Cast, a $15 a month subscription service offering brief newscasts and clips from the previous night's Jon Stewart show.

The television-equipped cell phones are vastly better than the early battery-powered televisions and their snowy images. They're better too than was the next Tracy-esque innovation: portable video players whose content had to be downloaded from a computer. Still, on-the-go television has a ways to go.

For practical purposes state-of-the-art wireless technology limits shows to a minute or two. Downloading can take longer than the snippets play. It's hardly as easy as turning on a stationary television set at home. There are no TNT movies here—at least not for now. Another limitation is the investment needed to set up mobile television service. At its launch Verizon's V Cast was available only in 30 U.S. metro areas.

Although early in development, the V Cast service carries worth-watching content rounded up from existing sources: NBC and CNN news summaries, ESPN and Fox sports highlights and stock market updates. The closest V Cast has to prime-time entertainment is one-minute episodes of *24: Conspiracy,* a derivative of the Fox television program *24.* Movie studios provide trailers to plug their latest attractions.

For consumers the cost is within the range of many impulse-buy electronic products, some models going for as low as $150 with a two-year subscription. Some have cameras and music and game connections.

---

network spots. By 2005, however, the amount was down to 35 percent. Where have AmEx and other brand-name advertisers diverted their dollars? Some AmEx dollars have stayed with the networks through product mention in scripts, which addresses the TiVo leakage. But much has gone into web initiatives, concert sponsorships, and experiments like stocking blue-labeled bottled water at trendy health clubs to promote its blue card. There have been blue popcorn bags at movie houses and AmEx-sponsored museum exhibits. AmEx has been a leader with **webisodes,** those four-minute mini-movies on the web. In another alternative to television, blue-card logos were everywhere for an AmEx-sponsored concert with Elvis Costello, Stevie Wonder and Counting Crows at the House of Blues in Los Angeles, renamed the House of Blue for the event.

Product Placement Mindful that advertisers are scouting for alternative media, television networks have gone to selling plugs for products and services in scripts. It's not so unlike early radio and 1950s television, when hosts for sponsored programs touted products. For Arthur Godfrey, no tea was as good as Lipton's—and viewers never knew when to expect a plug. This was a leftover from an era when radio advertisers produced their own programs. As the networks took over programs, selling commercial slots to the high-

webisodes ■ Mini-movies, generally four minutes, on the web; usually sponsored and sometimes with the advertiser part of the story line.

Product Placement It was no mistake that contestants on the Game Show Network's *American Dream Derby* swilled Diet Dr. Pepper while discussing strategy. Nor that JellO and other brand names are frequent props built into scripts and stunts for a fee. Product placements, sometimes subtle, sometimes not, have become a vehicle for advertisers to get in your face even if you zap the usual commercials with TiVo or other record-replay devices.

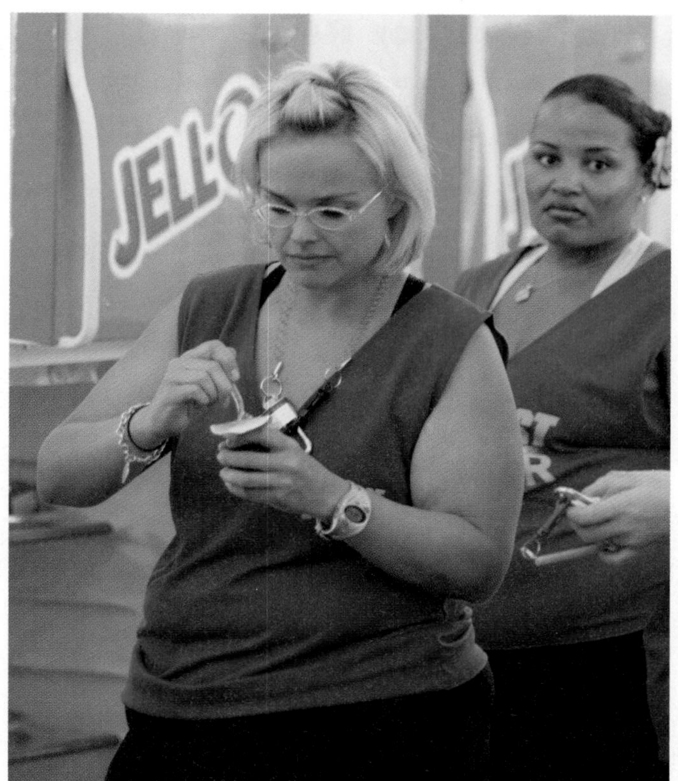

est bidder, a purist distinction between creative control of programming content and advertising became a given. Now the wall has been breached between commercials and pure, pristine, untainted entertainment and drama as creative arts.

In the 1980s Hollywood began selling product mentions in movie scripts. The result was a continuing boiling controversy. The controversy now is back in television, with networks, facing the TiVo drain of viewers who skip the ads, weaving product names into scripts. The presence of Coca-Cola as an *American Idol* prop and Pepsi products in *Survivor* were major-league examples. Despite protests from some producers and calls in Congress for on-air notices, the practice seems destined to stay.

CHAPTER 8 Wrap-Up

People still call television receivers sets. But less so. The idea of television as a stationary appliance or even a piece of furniture is giving way as miniaturization has led to reception on palm-size screens that are so light they can be taken anywhere as easily as, say, a wallet. Television is less a bulky appliance around which people cluster and more a portable device often incorporated with other functions, like telephone, on-demand music, real-time e-mail communication, web access and personal data storage. What does this technological transformation mean for television as we know it? As a medium for moving visuals and sound, now also readable through digital presentation, television is well suited to become the hub of tomorrow's mass communication. The regulatory and corporate structures that have shaped the television industry, however, are vulnerable in a shake-up that is not only under way but accelerating. Cultural habits, like 95 percent of the television households tuning to Milton Berle in the 1950s, or huge audiences amassing ritual-like for the latest *Survivor* finale, seem destined to live on only in fond memories of network executives. We are in a dawning age of television portability and video on demand. For survival the old corporate titans of television must find new ways for doing business.

Questions for Review

1. How extensive has been the influence of television on people in the short term and long term?
2. How is television technology different from movie technology?
3. How has government regulation shaped the television industry?
4. What is the future of the 30-second television commercial?
5. What dynamics influence television content?
6. How will video-on-demand services affect the corporate infrastructure of U.S. television?

Questions for Critical Thinking

1. The business genius behind the NBC television network, RCA's David Sarnoff, valued research to keep ahead on technology. Under new ownership, RCA became merely a manufacturer of electronic goods and eventually was sold to a French company. How could this change from the Sarnoff business model hurt NBC in the emerging video-on-demand era?
2. How did Philo Farnsworth use electronics to pick up moving images and relay them live to faraway screens? How was his invention different from movie technology?
3. Did the two-tier U.S. television system, with locally licensed stations and national networks, make sense when it was put into effect? Does it make sense now? For the future?
4. How do the television networks line up advertising for their coming seasons? What is at stake financially if programs don't meet viewership targets?
5. Elitists fault mass media for pandering to audiences too much and providing too little cultural and artistic leadership. How would elitists evaluate the further fragmentation of the television industry corporate infrastructure and video-delivery systems?
6. Television once was a place-based medium. To watch, people gathered at television sets, usually at home in a living room, and scheduled their daily routines around favorite programs. How has technology changed viewing habits? What effect have these changes had on programming?
7. Jeff Greenfield, publisher of *Branded Entertainment Monthly,* a trade journal, says the screenwriters and actors object to product placement in movies and television only because they don't get a share of the revenue: "This is a shakedown by the writers who want a piece of the pie." How do you square Greenfield's observation with television editor Scott Miller, who argues against product placements, saying he has twisted himself into a pretzel trying to bend plotlines to suit sponsors. Consider too the argument of screenwriters that product placements, when concealed, are de facto dishonest.

Deepening Your media LITERACY

Is television news on the decline?

STEP 1 The big networks have scaled down their global news-gathering systems, creating opportunities for other sources of news. What does this mean for the American news-watching public?

Dig Deeper

STEP 2 Interview three or four of your friends about where they like to get their local news, their global news, their breaking news, their sports news, their entertainment news. How much of it is from the traditional television networks, how much from all-news networks, how much from television newsmagazines and how much from talk shows? How much do they get from sources other than television? If another war were declared tomorrow, where would they turn to get the news about it?

What Do You Think?

STEP 3 Answer these questions:

1. What can you conclude about the state of television news based on your small sample?
2. Do you see any possible trends for the future of television news? Do they match what the experts predict?

Keeping Up to Date

Broadcasting & Cable is a weekly broadcasting trade journal. Coverage of federal regulation, programming and ownership is consistently solid. Every issue includes a comprehensive table on prime-time Nielsens for the six over-air networks.

Electronic Media is a comprehensive broadcast industry trade journal.

Journal of Broadcasting and Electronic Media is a quarterly scholarly journal published by the Broadcast Education Association.

Television/Radio Age is a trade journal.

Videography is a trade journal focusing on production issues in corporate video and production.

Jack Meyer Report, Multichannel News and *Variety* are trade journals.

Consumer magazines that deal extensively with television programming include *Entertainment* and *TV Guide.*

Newsmagazines that report television issues more or less regularly include *Newsweek* and *Time.*

Business Week, Forbes and *Fortune* track television as a business.

Major newspapers with strong television coverage include the Los Angeles *Times,* the New York *Times* and the *Wall Street Journal.*

For Further Learning

J. D. Lasica. *Darknet: Hollywood's War Against the Digital Generation* (Wiley, 2005).

Lasica draws on a wide range of interviews in making a case that the framework for U.S. broadcasting is outdated for the digital age.

Roger P. Smith. *The Other Face of Public Television: Censoring the American Dream.* Algora, 2002.

Smith, a widely recognized television producer, argues that U.S. public television is substantively the same as commercial television, only in a cosmetically different wrapping. Rhetorically he asks whether public television can be truly independent so long as it is dependent on government funding. He concludes with a call for an alternative television production organization endowed with a nongovernment trust fund.

Gary R. Edgerton. *Ken Burns' America: Packaging the Past for Television.* Palgrave, 2002.

Edgerton, a communications professor, is enthusiastic and detailed in examining Burns' documentaries.

Reese Schonfeld. *Me and Ted Against the World: The Unauthorized Story of the Founding of CNN.* HarperCollins, 2001.

Schonfeld, president of CNN for its first three years, claims credit for the original format concept, "fluid news," and argues that the network later lost its way. He is not altogether charitable to Ted Turner, who fired him in an ego clash.

Jennings Bryant and J. Alison Bryant, editors. *Television and the American Family.* Second edition. Earlbaum, 2001.

This collection of articles and essays includes a comprehensive update on research into television portrayals of families, family use of and attitudes toward television, and effects.

Donald Bogle. *Primetime Blues: African Americans on Network Television.* Straus & Giroux, 2001.

Bogle, a media scholar, uses an economic analysis of the television industry for assessing changes in the portrayal of black Americans on U.S. television.

Donna Harper. *Invisible Stars: A Social History of Women in American Broadcasting.* Sharpe, 2001.

Harper, a historian, bases this work on interviews with pioneer women broadcasters and their survivors. She also draws on letters and newspaper and magazine articles.

Peter B. Orlik. *Electronic Media Criticism: Applied Perspectives,* Second edition. Earlbaum, 2000.

Orlik, a scholar, examines tools for assessing television, radio and web content. Orlik includes scripts for analysis.

Clay Calvert. *Voyeur Nation.* Westview, 2000.

Calvert, a communication law scholar, argues that using the First Amendment to defend voyeur television programs debases the value of discourse in a democracy.

Cary O'Dell. *Women Pioneers in Television: Biographies of Fifteen Industry Leaders.* McFarland, 1996.

O'Dell, curator of the Museum of Broadcast Communication at the Chicago Cultural Center, covers Milfred Freed Alberg, Lucille Ball, Gertrude Berg, Peggy Charren, Joan Ganz Cooney, Faye Emerson, Pauline Frederick, Dorothy Fuldheim., Betty Furness, Freida Hennock, Lucy Jarvis, Ida Lupino, Irna Phillips, Judith Walker and Betty White.

Patrick R. Parsons. "Two Tales of a City: John Walson Sr., Mahonoy City, and the 'Founding' of Cable TV." *Journal of Broadcasting & Electronic Media* (Summer 1996). Pages 354–365.

Professor Parsons debunks the often-told story that Walson, of Mahonoy City, Pennsylvania, built the first cable television system. This is historical scholarship of the first order.

Sebastian Babolat
His breezy lessons in French became a podcast hit with 10,000 listeners.

chapter

9 The Internet

In this chapter you will learn:

- **The Internet emerged suddenly in the 1990s as a major mass medium.**
- **Semiconductors and fiber-optic cable are building blocks of Internet technology.**
- **Internet technology is moving rapidly in new directions.**
- **Advertising is driving Internet growth.**
- **Traditional gatekeeping to ensure quality content is less present on the Internet.**
- **Internet technology is blurring distinctions among traditional mass media.**
- **Blogs demonstrate a media democratization, one of many public policy questions posed by the Internet.**

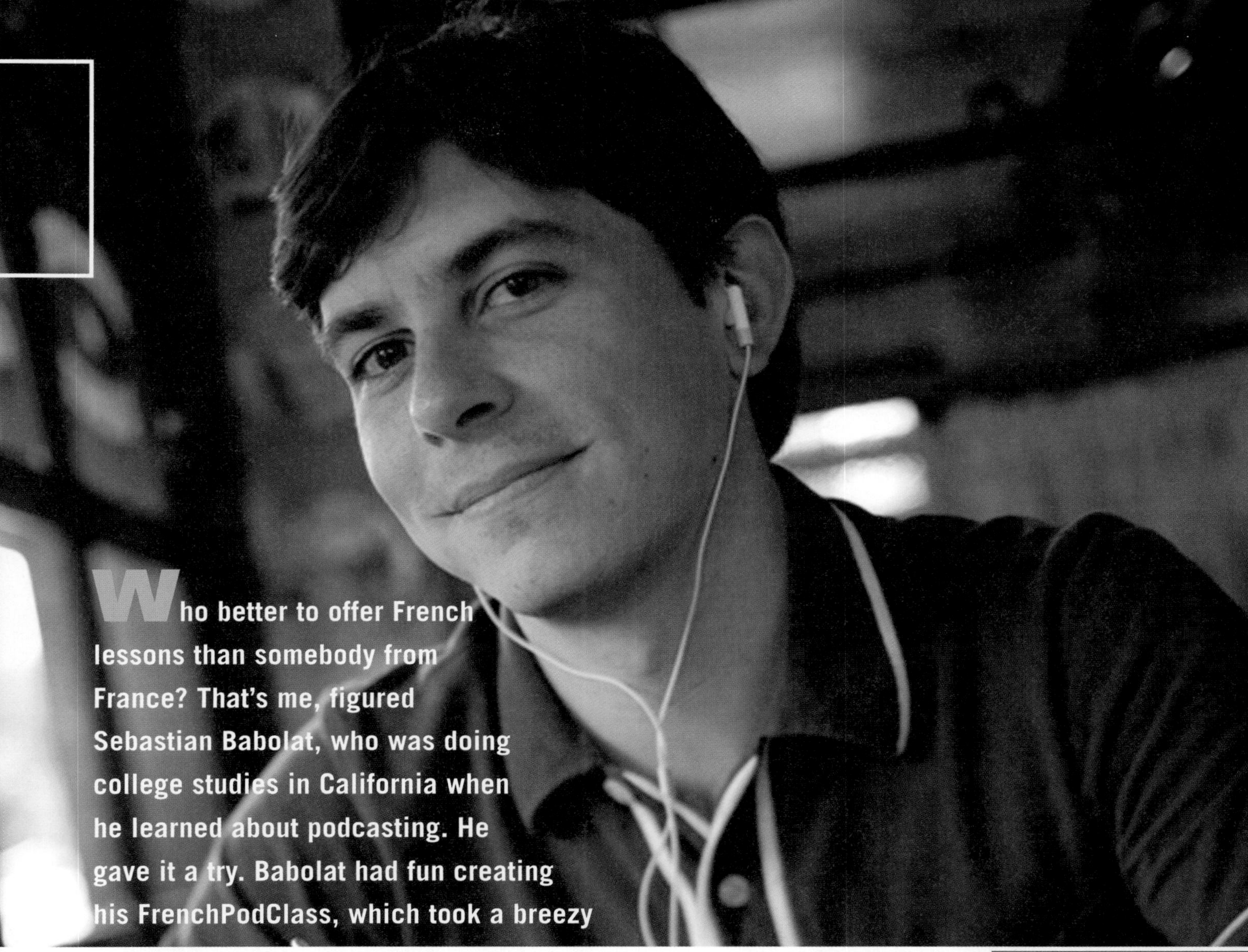

Who better to offer French lessons than somebody from France? That's me, figured Sebastian Babolat, who was doing college studies in California when he learned about podcasting. He gave it a try. Babolat had fun creating his FrenchPodClass, which took a breezy tack with the grammar. Within months the 26-year-old French guy from Monterey had 10,000 listeners. Babolat was among podcast leaders.

Babolat is among an estimated 10,000 people who have capitalized on readily available digital tools—a PC and a few bucks worth of gear—to create digital audio programs on whatever they want and posting them on the web. Subjects cover the spectrum—grunge music and commentary, politics of every stripe, vegan cooking, and, yes, having fun learning French.

Podcasting first was a self-expression tool that grew out of the political blogs that proved to be a low-cost, high-yield communication tool in the 2004 U.S. elections. Inspired by the potential, bloggers devised sites on all kinds of subjects. In 2005 Apple began promoting podcast shows on its iTunes online music store. That's about the time that Bobolat started podcasting for people to brush on their *bonjours*.

Early podcasting has a pristine, noncommercial quality, but the growing audience inevitably took on a commercial cast. Georgia-Pacific, the huge timber company and paper-maker, set up *Mommycast* on parenting with plugs for its Dixie products. Google and others created podcast search engines with sponsored links. Sirius satellite radio hired a former MTV video-jock, Adam Curry, to create a program with his podcast highlights du jour.

Nobody sees a clear course yet for podcasting or whatever next month will bring as the new marvel of the Digital Age. In this chapter you will learn about dynamics that have brought us to where we're at with the Internet, the web and, of course, podcasting. This knowledge will give you tools to keep abreast and perhaps ahead of where it is all is going.

Influence of the Internet

studypreview **The Internet has emerged as the eighth major mass medium with a range of content, especially through web coding, that exceeds that of traditional media in many ways.**

New Mass Medium

From a dizzying array of new technologies, the Internet emerged in the mid-1990s as a powerful new mass medium. What is the Internet? It's a jury-rigged network of telephone and cable lines and satellite links that connect computers. Almost anybody on the planet with a computer can tap into the network. A few clicks of a mouse button will bring in vast quantities of information and entertainment that originate all over the world.

Opsware Check out the products offered by Opsware and read the company bio on founder Marc Andreessen. **www.opsware.com**

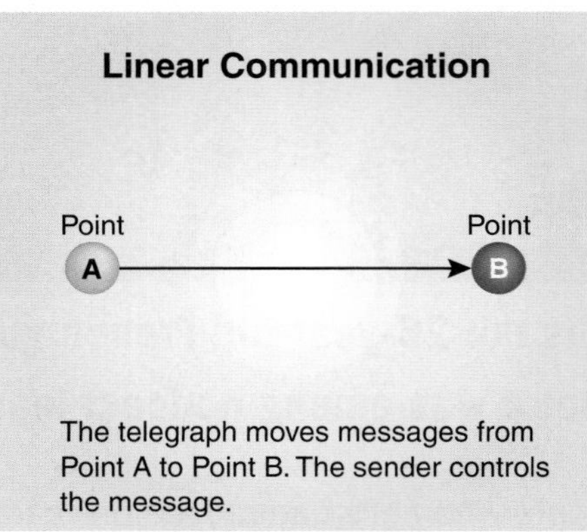

The telegraph moves messages from Point A to Point B. The sender controls the message.

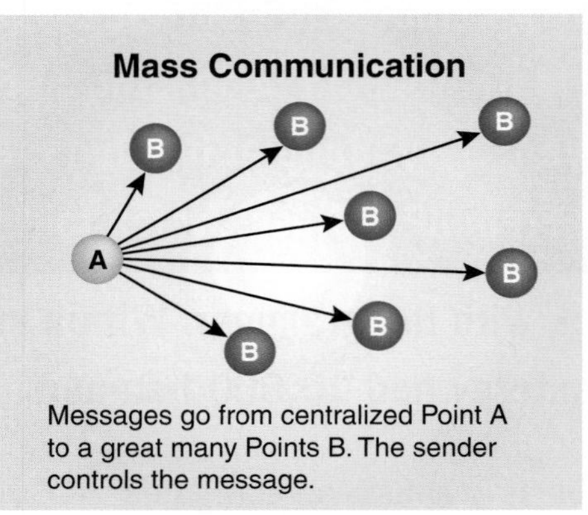

Messages go from centralized Point A to a great many Points B. The sender controls the message.

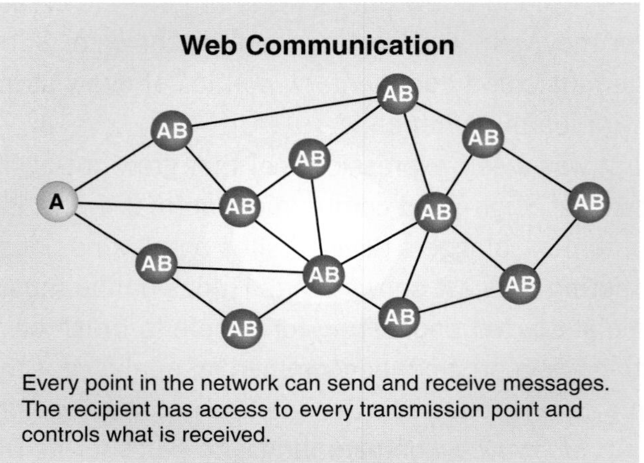

Every point in the network can send and receive messages. The recipient has access to every transmission point and controls what is received.

Whither Mass Communication?

Web communication shifts much of the control of the communication through the mass media to the recipient, turning the traditional process of mass communication on its head. Receivers are no longer hobbled to sequential presentation of messages, as on a network television newscast. Receivers can switch almost instantly to dozens, hundreds even, of alternatives through a weblike network that, at least theoretically, can interconnect every recipient and sender on the planet.

Although in some ways the Internet resembles a traditional mass medium that sends messages from a central transmission point, it is much more. Message recipients are able to click almost instantly from one source to another—from an L.L. Bean catalog to a Disney movie to *USA Today*. In another significant difference from other mass media, the Internet is interactive. It has the capacity for people to communicate outward, not just receive messages, and to do it in real time. Try doing that with a Spielberg movie or the latest Harry Potter sequel.

INTERNET

1969 U.S. military created ARPAnet to link contractors and researchers.

1973 Mead Data Central launched Lexis, the first full-text online legal database.

1978 Mead introduced Nexis, a full-text online news database.

1979 CompuServ began online service to consumers.

1989 Tim Berners-Lee devised coding that made the web possible.

1993 Marc Andreessen created predecessor to Netscape browser.

1996 A race to expand the nation's fiber-optic infrastructure triggered by the U.S. Telecommunications Act.

1997 Rob Malda, a college student, created slashdot.org, "news for news," one of first blogs.

2001 Dot-com bubble burst.

Scope of the Internet

Every major mass media company has put products on the Internet. Thousands of start-up companies are establishing themselves on the ground floor. The technology is so straightforward and access is so inexpensive that millions of individuals have set up their own sites.

How significant is the Internet as a mass medium? Estimates are that the number of users in the United States is well past 200 million—75 percent of the population. In only a few years the Internet has become a major medium for advertising. In 2005 advertisers spent $12.9 billion for space on Internet web sites, up 34 percent from the year before and wholly one-fifth of what was spent on television. A 2004 study found that more than half of new-car buyers based their choice on information they found on the Internet.

The significance of the Internet is measurable in other ways too. There are people who have given up reading the print edition of newspapers and instead browse through the Internet edition. Some of the news sites are updated constantly. Almost every U.S. magazine and newspaper has an **Internet site,** from the venerable but tech-savvy New York *Times* to local papers in the hinterlands.

New Terminology

The terms *Internet* and *web* are often tossed around loosely, leading to lots of confusion. The fundamental network that carries messages is the Internet. It dates to a military communication system created in 1969. The early Internet carried mostly text.

The web is a structure of codes that permits the exchange not only of text but also of graphics, video and audio. Web codes are elegantly simple for users, who don't even need to know them to tap into the web's content. The underlying web codes are accepted universally, which makes it possible for anyone with a computer, a modem and an Internet connection to tap into anything introduced from anywhere on the global web. The term *web* comes from the spidery links among millions of computers that tap into the system—an ever-changing maze that not even a spider could visualize and that becomes more complex all the time.

The prefix ***cyber-*** is affixed almost casually to anything involving communication via computer. *Cyberspace* is the intangible place where the communication occurs. *Cyberporn* is sexual naughtiness delivered on-screen. A *cyberpunk* is a kid obsessed with computer protocols and coding.

The term *cyberspace* was introduced by science-fiction novelist **William Gibson** in his book *Neuromancer*. At that point, in 1984, he saw a kind of integration of computers and human beings. Paraphrasing a bit, here is Gibson's definition of *cyberspace:* "A consensual hallucination experienced daily by billions of people in every nation. A graphic representation of data abstracted from the banks of every computer in the human system. Unthinkable complexity. Lines of light ranged in the nonspace of the mind. Clusters and constellations of data." Gibson got it right.

Internet site ■ Where an institution establishes its web presence.

cyber- ■ Prefix for human connection via computers.

William Gibson ■ Sci-fi writer who coined the term *cyberspace*.

Internet Technology

study preview **The 1947 invention of the semiconductor led to digitization and compression that became building blocks for technology that made the Internet possible. Web coding and the Netscape browser widened access.**

The Time 100: William Shockley
Profile of William Shockley as part of *Time*'s 100 Most Important People of the Twentieth Century.
www.time.com/time/time100/scientist/profile/shockley.html

semiconductor ■ Silicon chips that are used in digitization.

junction transistor ■ Crystal with added impurities that switches on and off at tremendous speed and reliability.

Underlying Technologies

Researchers Walter Brattain, Jack Bardeen and William Shockley at AT&T's Bell Labs knew they were on to something important for telephone communication in 1947. They had devised glasslike silicon chips—pieces of sand, really—that could be used to respond to a negative or positive electrical charge.

Digitization The tiny chips, called **semiconductors,** functioned very rapidly as on-off switches. With the chips the human voice could be reduced to a stream of digits—1 for on, 0 for off—and then transmitted as rapid-fire pulses and reconstructed so fast at the other end that they sounded like the real thing. Digitization dramatically expanded the capacity of telephone systems and revolutionized telephone communication. Brattain, Bardeen and Shockley won a Nobel Prize.

media PEOPLE

William Shockley

Semiconductor Inventors A semiconductor switch can be likened to a tiny triple-decker sandwich. The sandwich, made of silicon, responds to slight variations in electrical current that allow incredibly fast processing of data that have been converted into on-off signals. In addition to speed, the semiconductor ushered in miniaturization of data-processing equipment and storage devices. Since 1947, when Bell Labs engineers devised the semiconductor, it has become possible to store thousands of pages of text on a device as small as a pinhead and to transmit them almost instantly to other devices, like your home computer. The 1956 Nobel Prize went to Bell Labs' Walter Brattain, Jack Bardeen and William Shockley for inventing the semiconductor.

Physicist William Shockley felt cheated. He had developed the theory for the semiconductor, but two Bell Telephone Lab engineers, Jack Bardeen and Walter Brattain, had rigged up the first working transistor. And Shockley wasn't even there to see it happen. Bardeen and Brattain applied electric current to a crystal of germanium, and more power came out than went in.

That momentous event, in 1947, prompted Shockley to throw himself into coming up with further understanding of the phenomenon and figuring out where it might lead. Within a few weeks, Shockley devised the **junction transistor** that, given time, would transform almost every mechanical device that human beings use.

What was the junction transistor? It was a tiny, tiny sandwich of a crystal with impurities added. The crystal could go on and off at tremendous rates with unsurpassed reliability. Almost immediately, telephone engineers saw the potential for the device, which was dubbed the semiconductor, to replace bulky, hot vacuum tubes that were the heart of telephone systems at the time. Those tubes burned out quickly and had to be replaced often, which was expensive. Semiconductors, by contrast, were cool, reliable and long-lived.

In 1956 Shockley founded a research company in Palo Alto, California, and chose silicon instead of germanium for new semiconductors. Silicon, which fundamentally is sand, was cheap. This was the real birth of the semiconductor, and the Shockley Lab was the progenitor of virtually all the semiconductor companies that have come since. In one sense, by locating in Palo Alto, William Shockley created Silicon Valley, the fanciful appellation for the region south of San Francisco that has become the world center of semiconductor and computer research.

Little did they realize, however, that they had laid the groundwork for revolutionizing not just telephonic communication but all human communication.

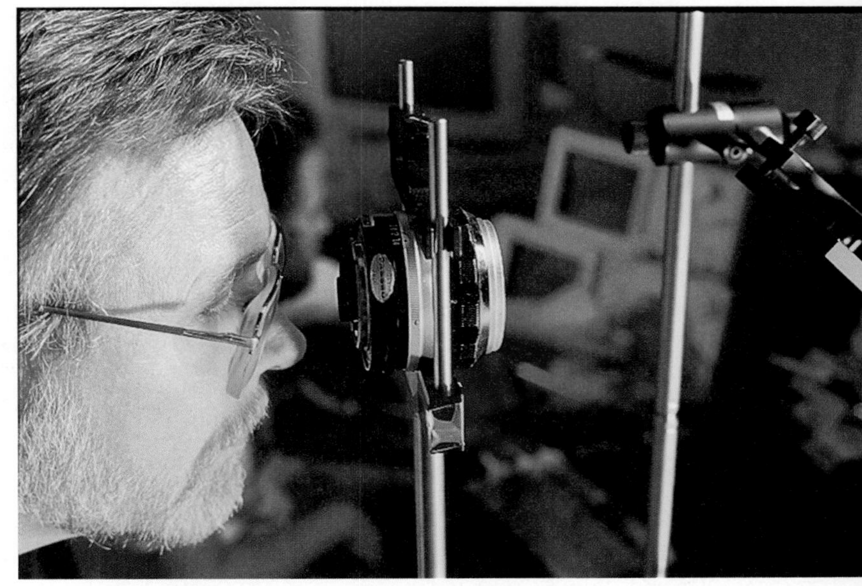

Compression Bell Labs took semiconductors to a new level with **compression** technology in 1965. The on-off digital technology had so compacted messages for transmission that, suddenly, it was possible to break calls into spurts and transmit them simultaneously on a single line, each spurt like a railroad car joining a train on a track and then leaving the train to go to its own destination. People marveled that 51 calls could be carried at the same time on a single wire.

The capacity of the nation's telephone system was dramatically increased without a single new mile of wire being laid.

Miniaturization Semiconductors gradually replaced electrical tubes in broadcast equipment. The idea of a radio as a piece of furniture disappeared with semiconductor-equipped portable radios in the 1950s. But that was only the beginning of miniaturization of all kinds of electrical and mechanical functions. In the emerging field of computers early models used electrical tubes and were housed in entire buildings. Now the movement is toward central units with footprints of less than four square feet. Laptops are a marvel of miniaturization.

There seems no end to miniaturization. The Marquandt Corporation estimates that all the information recorded in the past 10,000 years can be stored in a cube six feet by six feet by six feet. All the 12 million books in the Library of Congress would take fewer than two cubic inches. IBM expects to produce a computer drive that crams an incredible 2 billion digital characters on a thumbtack-size disk. That's equivalent to 2,000 novels.

The Eyeball as a Screen

A Seattle company, Microvision, is hoping to market a device that projects images directly onto the human eyeball. This VRD, short for "virtual retina display," is not much more cumbersome to wear than a pair of glasses, and it gives a sharper image than a 70-millimeter IMAX screen. With VRD, people would not need television or computer screens. Microvision says this device can be made for less than $100.

Creating the Internet

The Internet had its origins in a 1969 U.S. Defense Department computer network called **ARPAnet,** which stood for Advanced Research Projects Agency Network. The Pentagon built the network for military contractors and universities doing military research to exchange information. In 1983 the **National Science Foundation,** whose mandate is to promote science, took over.

This new National Science Foundation network attracted more and more institutional users, many of which had their own internal networks. For example, most universities that joined the NSF network had intracampus computer networks. The NSF network, then, became a connector for thousands of other networks. As a backbone system that interconnects networks, **internet** was a name that fit.

Since then have come upgrades that function side by side with earlier systems:

Abilene **Internet2,** a consortium of universities and corporations, operates this network for researchers. When it opened in 1999, it was four times faster than the original Internet in shuttling data among 200 member universities and several hundred other subscribers. A 2003 upgrade sped things up another two and a half times to 10 gigabits per second.

LambdaRail Another consortium, National LambdaRail, comprising 30 research Universities, opened a 15,000-mile fiber-optic line that runs from New York to Seattle and from Florida to California with several north-south links connecting the two east-west trunks.

It is only time before Lambda's capacity will prove insufficient, which has engineers drooling at the possibility of what they dreamily call **Internet3.** Alas, money is an obstacle. Already Internet2 is too costly for many colleges. Basic connection and membership range from $160,000 to $450,000 a year. The consortiums that built Abilene and Lambda have discussed merging to go to take the next step. An interim possibility is to

compression ■ Technology that makes a message more compact by deleting nonessential underlying code.

ARPAnet ■ Military network that preceded Internet.

National Science Foundation ■ Developed current Internet to give scholars access to supercomputers.

internet ■ A network of computer networks.

Internet2 ■ A network consortium owned by research institutions for fast data transfer.

Internet3 ■ Nickname for ever-faster networks planned for the future.

mediaPEOPLE

Vint Cerf

Father of the Internet

Even as a kid, Vinton Cerf liked technical stuff. When he was 10, back in 1953, he built a volcano out of plaster of paris and potassium permanganate. Then he decorated the mountain with gelatin-coated glycerine capsules and waited for the gelatin to melt. The result: a thermite grenade that impressed and also scared his folks.

Today Cerf is called the Father of the Internet. Although he's uncomfortable with the title, the fact is that he was there. Cerf, "Vint" to his friends, and coresearcher Bob Kahn created the coding that allowed various computers to talk to each other over phone lines. In 1974 Cerf and Kahn, both at the University of California at Los Angeles, published an article explaining their intercomputer language protocols.

Kahn's interests shifted to other things, but Cerf kept working on details for linking the military's Advanced Research Projects Agency network to other networks in a way that would seem seamless to users.

Why does Cerf object to being called the Father of the Internet? "It's not right to think of the Internet as having only one father," he says. "It has at least two, and in reality thousands, because of the number of people who contributed to what it is today." Even so, it was Cerf who took the project to Stanford when he switched universities and shepherded it into maturity through 1982.

Later, in 1992, Cerf created the nonprofit Internet Society that coordinates Internet policy so that the system remains universally useful.

dark fiber ■ Excess telecommunication capacity available for data transfer.

lease **dark fiber,** the unused fiber-optic capacity that commercial telecommunication companies overbuilt in the late 1990s.

World Wide Web

The early Internet created access to lots of data at speeds that were unprecedented. But it was an uninviting place visually. Text and data were in black-and-white and image-free—something only a researcher could love. Even so, there were possibilities to take the new medium in commercial directions.

media ONLINE **LexisNexis** Subscribe to this online database service or use the ala carte option and pay as you go. **www.lexisnexis.com**

Mead The potential of the Internet for tapping into vast databases was recognized by an Ohio company, **Mead Data Central.** In 1973 Mead created **Lexis** with quick access to state and federal statutes, court decisions and other legal documents. A lawyer could tap into Lexis for research and cut back on maintaining and updating the traditional expensive office law library. Because Lexis was delivered via telephone lines whose capacity precluded data-intensive graphics, there was nothing fancy about how Lexis looked—simple text on the computer screen. But it was just what lawyers and legal scholars needed, and they paid handsomely for the service.

Building on its Lexis success, Mead launched **Nexis** in 1978. Nexis was the first online database with national news organizations, including the New York *Times,* the Washington *Post,* the Associated Press and *U.S. News & World Report.* Nexis proved invaluable to researchers, who could search not only recent editions of participating newspapers and magazines but also back issues. Today, Nexis includes thousands of publications from around the world.

Mead Data Central ■ Created Lexis, Nexis.

Lexis ■ First online full-text database; carries legal documents.

Nexis ■ First online database with national news.

Internet service provider ■ Company that charges a fee for online service.

Internet Service Providers A new kind of company, **Internet service providers,** went into business in the 1980s to give ordinary folks a portal to the Internet and help in navigating the Internet's inherent complexity and disorganization. CompuServ was first to provide online service to consumers, but America Online quickly became the leading provider. These companies charged subscription fees for a combination of services—Internet access, e-mail and, most important, a mapping structure to help get to where the user wanted to go among the seemingly infinite number of places to go on the Internet.

The Time 100: Tim Berners-Lee Profile of Tim Berners-Lee as part of *Time*'s 100 Most Important People of the Twentieth Century.
www.time.com/time/time100/scientist/profile/bernerslee.html

Tim Berners-Lee A major breakthrough came from English engineer **Tim Berners-Lee,** who in 1991 devised an addressing system that could connect every computer in the world. The name that Berners-Lee came up with for his system sounded audacious, the **World Wide Web,** but it was accurate—a decentralized global network with the potential, theoretically, for everyone at a computer to communicate with everyone else at a computer anywhere on the planet.

Tim Berners-Lee ■ Devised protocols, codes for the World Wide Web.

World Wide Web ■ System that allows global linking of information modules in user-determined sequences.

Universal resource locator (URL) ■ Address assigned to a page on the Internet.

Berners-Lee's invention was built on three components:

- **Universal resource locators (URL).** Berners-Lee devised an addressing system that gave every computer a unique identifier, much like a postal address that enables mail to be delivered to the right place. The identifiers, URLs, allowed computers connected

mediaPEOPLE

Tim Berners-Lee

Single-handedly, Tim Berners-Lee invented the World Wide Web. Then, unlike many entrepreneurs who have used the Internet to amass quick fortunes, Berners-Lee devoted his life to refining the Web as a medium of communication open to everyone for free.

Berners-Lee, an Oxford engineer, came up with the web concept because he couldn't keep track of all his notes on various computers in various places. It was 1989. Working at CERN, a physics lab in Switzerland, he proposed a system to facilitate scientific research by letting scientists' computers tap into each other. In a way, the software worked like the brain. In fact, Berners-Lee said that the idea was to keep "track of all the random associations one comes across in real life and brains are supposed to be so good at remembering, but sometimes mine wouldn't."

Original Webmaster Tim Berners-Lee and his associates at a Swiss research facility created new Internet coding in 1989, dubbing it the World Wide Web. Today the coding is the heart of global computer communication.

Working with three software engineers, Berners-Lee had a demonstration up and running within three months. As Berners-Lee traveled the globe to introduce the Web at scientific conferences, the potential of what he had devised became clear. The Web was a system that could connect all information with all other information.

The key was a relatively simple computer language known as HTML, short for hypertext markup language, which, although it has evolved over the years, remains the core of the web. Berners-Lee also developed the addressing system that allows computers to find each other. Every web-connected computer has a unique address, a universal resource locator (URL). For it all to work, Berners-Lee also created a protocol that actually links computers: HTTP, short for hypertext transfer protocol.

In 1992 leading research organizations in the Netherlands, Germany and the United States committed to the Web. As enthusiasm grew in the scientific research community, word spread to other quarters. In one eight-month period in 1993, Web use multiplied 414 times. Soon "the Web" was a household word.

As you would expect, Berners-Lee had offers galore from investors and computer companies to build new ways to derive profits from the Web. He said no. Instead, he chose the academic life. At the Massachusetts Institute of Technology he works out of spartan facilities as head of the W3 consortium, which sets the protocol and coding standards that are helping the World Wide Web realize its potential.

It's hard to overrate Berners-Lee's accomplishment. The Internet is the information infrastructure that likely will, given time, eclipse other media. Some liken Berners-Lee to Johannes Gutenberg, who 400 years earlier had launched the age of mass communication with the movable type that made mass production of the written word possible.

in a network to exchange messages. Being "universal," it was a comprehensive and standardized system that became the foundation for the World Wide Web.

- **Hypertext transfer protocol (HTTP).** This is a protocol that allows computers to connect to read Internet files.
- **Hypertext markup language (HTML).** This was a relatively simple computer language that permitted someone creating an Internet message to insert so-called hot spots or links that, if clicked, would instantly switch the on-screen image to something else. For example, a research article could include visible indicators, usually a underline on a term, that with a click of a mouse would move to another article on the subject.

The term **hypertext** was devised by technologist Ted Nugent in his 1962 book *Literary Machines* for a system that would allow people to interrupt themselves while reading through material in the traditional linear way, from beginning to end, and transport themselves nonlinearly to related material. Nugent also called it *nonsequential writing,* but the term *hypertext* stuck.

It was a quarter century later when Berners-Lee devised the HTML coding that made nonsequential reading possible.

Netscape Check out all this browser has to offer, from the latest headline news, to pop culture favorites, to e-mail and Internet service.
www.netscape.com

Netscape The importance of the Berners-Lee innovations for scientists to find sites all around the Internet was a landmark, but for the rest of us the content was geeky stuff. In 1993 the Internet as we know it began to come to life. At the University of Illinois, grad student **Marc Andreessen** developed a software program, **Mosaic,** that improve the interconnections that permitted scientists to browse each other's research.

Enthusiasm for the potential of the **browser,** as it was called, quickly swelled. By tweaking Mosaic, Andreessen and a few colleagues created a new browser, **Netscape,** that could connect any of the three disparate computer operating systems that were becoming commonplace: Microsoft's Windows, Apple's Macintosh OS and Unix. Netscape was a point-and-click system by which anyone with a computer could unlock more content than had ever been conceivable in human history.

Commercialization began. First a few retailers displayed their wares on-screen and took orders online, then shipped their products. The old point-of-purchase concept, catching consumers at the story with displays and posters, took on a whole new meaning. In the new cyberworld the point-of-purchase was not the merchant's shop but the consumer's computer screen.

Hypertext transfer protocol (HTTP) ■ Coding that allows computers to talk with each other to read web pages.

Hypertext markup language (HTML) ■ Language that is used to code for web pages.

hypertext ■ System for nonsequential reading.

Mark Andreessen ■ Devised Netscape browser.

Mosaic ■ Predecessor browser to Netscape.

browser ■ Software that allows access to web sites.

Netscape ■ Browser that made web easily accessible, attractive to personal computer owners.

bandwidth ■ Space available in a medium, such as cable or the electromagnetic spectrum, to carry messages.

Corning Glass ■ Company that developed fiber-optic cable.

fiber-optic cable ■ Glass strands capable of carrying data as light.

Bandwidth

An impediment to the Web realizing its potential was the capacity available on traditional telephone systems for transmitting data. Text was no problem, but as graphics joined the mix, this capacity, called **bandwidth,** became packed and transmissions slowed, sometimes to a crawl. Superdetailed photos required several minutes to traverse from Point A to Point B. The more complex a visual, the more data that are needed to make it blossom at the other end. Theoretically, music could be sent on the Internet, but it was a bandwidth hog. Video was worse.

A combination of technologies are being used to address the bandwidth issues. Some are eliminating choke points in the pipelines. Others are squeezing more data to consume less space.

Fiber-Optic Cable While AT&T was building on its off-on digital technology to improve telephone service in the 1960s, **Corning Glass** developed a cable that was capable of carrying light at incredible speeds—theoretically 186,000 miles per second. It was apparent immediately that this new **fiber-optic cable** could carry far more digitized messages than could the copper wire used for telephones. The messages were encoded as light pulses rather than as the traditional electrical pulses for transmission.

By the 1980s new equipment to convert data to light pulses for transmission was in place, and long-distance telephone companies were replacing their copper lines with fiber optics, as were local cable television systems. With fiber optic cable and other improvements, a single line could carry 60,000 telephone calls simultaneously.

media ONLINE **Timeline of Fiber Optic Cable**
Beginning with Albert Einstein and ending with the Fiber Optic Link Around the Globe, the National Academy of Engineering developed this timeline.
www.greatachievements.org/?id=3706

Multiplexing One innovation that expanded bandwidth was **multiplexing,** a process through which a message was broken into bits for transmission through whichever cables had capacity at the moment. Then the bits are reassembled at the delivery point. So instead of a message getting clogged in a pipeline that's already crammed, tiny bits of the message, called packets, go find alternative paths through whatever pipeline has room. All of this happens in fractions of a second, with the message ending up at its destination faster.

Compression Technology has been devised that screens out nonessential parts of messages so that they need less bandwidth. This is especially important for graphics, video and audio, which are incredibly code-heavy. Coding for a blue sky in a photo, for example, need not be repeated for every dot of color. Even without redundant coding, the sky still appears blue. Unless compressed, audio too is loaded with redundant coding.

Some compression technology further streamlines a message by eliminating details that the human eye or ear will not miss. For example, compression drops sound on a CD that would start dogs howling but that humans cannot hear.

multiplexing ■ Technology to transmit numerous messages simultaneously.

streaming ■ Technology that allows playback of a message to begin before all the components have arrived.

Streaming When a message is massive with coding, such as audio and video, the message can be segmented with the segments stored in a receiving computer's hard drive for replay even before all segments of the message have been received. This is called **streaming.** Most audio and video today is transmitted this way, which means some

mediaPEOPLE

Marc Andreessen

Browser Genius
At 21, Marc Andreessen and a geek buddy created Mosaic, which facilitated web access. Then they trumped themselves by creating Netscape.

At his 240-student high school in New Lisbon, Wisconsin, Marc Andreessen didn't play sports or mingle a lot. He recalls those times as "introverted." Recovering from surgery, he spent his time reading up on computer programming. Back at school, he built a calculator on the library computer to do his math homework.

Later, at the University of Illinois, he honed his interest in computer languages. At his $6.85-an-hour campus job writing computer code, he decided that the web protocols devised by Tim Berners-Lee in Switzerland in 1989 needed a simple interface so that ordinary people could tap in. Marc Andreessen and fellow student Eric Bina spent three months, nights and weekends, writing a program they called Mosaic. It became the gateway for non-nerds to explore the web. After Andreessen graduated, entrepreneur Jim Clark of Silicon Graphics heard about Mosaic and began some exploratory talks with Andreessen. At one point, as Internet folklore has it, Andreessen said: "We could always create a Mosaic killer—build a better product and build a business around it." Andreessen hired geek friends from Illinois, and Netscape was born. It was the pioneer browser for the masses. Andreessen and a bunch of fellow 21-year-olds had democratized the Internet.

Netscape's revenues zoomed to $100 million in 1996. Meanwhile, Microsoft introduced the Explorer browser as a competitor, which hurt. But America Online, the giant content provider, bought Netscape in 1998 and folded it into AOL. Andreessen became a chief resident thinker at AOL, but he didn't cotton well to the New Jersey bureaucracy. By 1999 he was back in Silicon Valley, this time with the idea for a robotic site builder called Loudcloud, which quickly attracted multimillion-dollar bids for its emerging product line. Meanwhile, Loudcloud has been reincarnated as Opsware. Andreessen has moved on to other projects.

mediaTECHNOLOGY

Carbon Nanotubes

After their wondrous introduction in the 1950s, silicon chips, the basis of digital communication, have become smaller and ever more powerful. In 1965 **Gordon Moore,** sometimes called the godfather of microprocessing, predicted in a technical article that chips would be improved to double their capacity every 18 months. Moore was right. His prediction is now called **Moore's Law.** Silicon flakes have shrunk to mere flecks, 90 nanometers thick, about 1/1,000th the finest human hair.

But problems loom. The smaller the chips, the hotter they run. The fastest chips today could fry an egg were it not for fans and metal casing to conduct the heat away. The heat not only saps about half of a computer's energy, but smaller and smaller chips become increasingly fragile. The walls of their channels that carry on-off data bits are inclined to leakage, which makes for more errors as the walls are manufactured thinner and thinner.

Numerous labs are working on a silicon replacement: carbon molecules, 100,000th as thick as a human hair, which bond in hexagonal nanotube structures that look like rolled up chicken wire. **Carbon nanotubes,** their walls no thicker than a single molecule, are stronger than steel, and there is no leakage. Too, their heat resistance means that they can be densely packed.

At IBM, scientists led by Phaedon Avouris have devised carbon nanotubes that carry 1,000 times the current of today's silicon chips, which are connected by copper wire. Besides, IBM, Dupont, Infineon, Nantero and other companies are looking for breakthroughs that will facilitate carbon nanotube manufacturing.

Gordon Moore

Carbon Nanotubes Silicon chips may have been maxed out for their capacity to carry data. The smaller they are manufactured, the hotter they run. The next stage? Carbon molecules, 100,000th as thick as a hair in hexagonal nanotube structures, are incredibly strong and heat-resistant.

What do these carbon nanotubes mean for the future? A dramatic improvement in Moore's Law. They could also mean instant boot-ups for personal computers.

Although now only lab creations, carbon nanotubes may become commodity products in 10 years. Some experts say 20. Meanwhile, chip manufacturers, which operate $2 billion factories, the most expensive production lines in human history, where chips take two to three months to manufacture, are looking to hybrids of silicon and carbon nanotubes in a transition period.

Here is a comparison on nanotech engineering progress:

1990	Intel 286 chip	5,000 nanometers
2002	Intel Pentium 3	180 nanometers
2005	IBM PowerPC chip	90 nanometers
2005	Lab carbon nanotube	7 nanometers
2015	Minimum carbon nanotube	1.5 nanometers

downloading delay—often only seconds. The more complex the coding, the longer it takes. Also, the type of connection makes a difference. For example, Internet access by satellite is much faster than access via a dial-up telephone connection.

Gordon Moore ■ Predicted that silicon chips could be refined to double their capacity every 18 months; called Moore's Law.

Moore's Law ■ Silicon chip capacity doubles every 18 months.

carbon nanotubes ■ Hexagon arrangement of carbon molecules into incredibly strong coils for carrying on-off digital bits.

Reshaping the Internet

studypreview **Wireless Internet connections, called *wi-fi,* have added to the portability of the Internet. Further untethering from a wired infrastructure is possible through ultrawideband technology.**

Wi-Fi

Another wrinkle in interactive media is wireless fidelity technology, better known as **wi-fi.** It untethers laptops and allows Internet access anywhere through radio waves. The coffee chain Starbucks made a splash with wi-fi, encouraging people to linger. Hotels and airports were naturals for wi-fi. In 2004 Iowa installed free wi-fi at interstate highway rest stops. San Francisco installed free wi-fi all over its landmark Union Square.

Municipalities large and small created a wi-fi boom, dubbed **muni wireless,** with wi-fi networks as a utility. In 2005 Mayor Joe Show flicked a switch in Addison, Texas, population 100,000, providing wireless Internet access throughout the Dallas suburb for a subscription fee of $16.95 a month. Three hundred other cities had wireless systems either in place or about to go on-stream as a less expensive alternative for consumers hooked up to the Internet by telephone, cable or satellite.

One justification for municipal wi-fi is to bridge the **digital divide,** the socioeconomic distinction between people in neighborhoods that can afford Internet access and those where they can't. In Philadelphia the plan is to allow low-income people to subscribe for $10 a month, creating new opportunities to tap into mainstream information that can improve quality of life.

Ultrawideband

Short-range wi-fi networks, which become sluggish as more people tap in, will pick up capacity with UWB technology, short for **ultrawideband,** unless opponents prevail. The technology uses existing frequencies, including commercial broadcast channels, but with such lower power that the primary signals seem to be unaffected. In the United States the Federal Communications Commission authorized developers to proceed working on the technology in 2003, despite protests from the aviation industry, which was concerned that frequencies used by on-board collision-avoidance systems could be compromised by crowding. Air safety stands to the jeopardized, according to some tests by the National Aeronautics and Space Administration. Also, wireless carriers including Sprint and Verizon objected to potential interference with existing spectrum occupants.

Mesh Networks

After wi-fi, what? The most anticipated next technology is **dynamic routing,** in which every wireless gadget serves also as a receiver and transmitter to every other wireless device within its range. Messages would just keep moving, hop-skipping invisibly from device to device until each reaches its intended destination. There is no formal network; messages go to whatever device has capacity at the moment—or, rather, the nanosecond. Every wireless device outfitted for dynamic routing would be on call as a stepping stone for however many messages come its way. Engineers say that **mesh networking,** as it is called, using high-speed protocols, will be 15 times faster than currently touted DSL services.

Commerce and the Internet

studypreview **The Internet has emerged as a commercial medium. Some sites are built around products. Others, in a more traditional vein, are designed to attract an audience with content, such as news. The sites sell access to that audience to advertisers.**

wi-fi ■ Wireless fidelity technology.

muni wireless ■ Wi-fi as a public utility.

digital divide ■ The economic distinction between impoverished groups and societal groups with the means to maintain and improve their economic well-being through computer access.

ultrawideband (UWB) ■ Low-power wi-fi system that rides on existing frequencies licensed for other uses.

dynamic routing ■ Technology that makes every wireless device a vehicle for furthering a message along to its destination, rather than moving in a structured network.

mesh networking ■ The ad hoc network created for each single message to reach its destination; also called *dynamic routing.*

Advertising-Free Origins

Before the web, the Internet was a pristine, commerce-free medium. If somebody put out a message that had even a hint of filthy lucre, purists by the dozens, even hundreds, deluged the offender with harsh reminders that commerce was not allowed. By and large, this self-policing worked.

When the web was introduced as an advanced Internet protocol, its potential for commerce was clear almost right away. The World Wide Web Consortium, which sets standards for web protocols, created the dot-com suffix to identify sites that existed to do business. That decision transformed the Internet and our lives.

Dot-Com Bubble

By 1996 Internet traffic was doubling every three months. On an annual basis that was 800 percent growth. In 1996, too, Congress overhauled the nation's telecommunications system, allowing local and long-distance telephone companies to compete with each other and to offer their own local, long-distance, international, data and Internet services. Billions of investment dollars flowed in to finance additional fiber-optic infrastructures. The investment frenzy generated more than $1 trillion to wire the world with extraordinary new capacity.

Meanwhile, seeing no end to the exponential growth in **dot-com** companies, investors poured billions of dollars into ventures for exploiting the Internet's commercial potential. Much of the investment, it turned out, was reckless. The so-called **dot-com bubble** burst in 2001 and 2002 with bankruptcies and a massive scaling down that caught thousands of Internet careers in the downward spiral. Investment portfolios withered with profound implications for pension plans that resulted in many people delaying their retirement. An economic recession followed, lingering for years.

But there was good news. A vast fiber-optic system was in place, with far more capacity than was needed. Nobody was going to dig it up. As Lucent, Global Crossing and other new telecommunications companies went belly up, banks acquired the assets in bankruptcy sales and then sold the fiber-optic networks at 10 cents on the dollar. The new owners operated the networks profitably, having bought them at fire-sale prices. The new owners also installed new transmitter and receiver switches to increase the volume and speed of data moving through the networks.

dot-coms ■ Commercial web sites, so named because their web address ended with the suffix .com.

dot-com bubble ■ Frenzied overinvestment in the telephone and Internet infrastructure and also Internet commerce in late 1990s.

Thomas Friedman, of the New York *Times,* who studied the dot-com phenomenon, described what happened this way: "So as the switches keeping improving, the capacity of all of the already installed fiber cables just keeps growing, making it cheaper and easier to transmit voices and data every year. . . . It's as though we laid down a national highway system where people were first allowed to drive 50 mph, then 60 mph, then 70 mph, then 80 mph, then eventually 150 mph on the same highways without any fear of accidents."

media DATABANK

Movie Advertising

The shift in advertising dollars to online vehicles is illustrated by the ad spending of Hollywood studios to promote new movies. The web has muscled its way to 2.4 percent of the $30.6 billion Hollywood promotion budget, which may seem a small percentage, but for big-city newspapers that once were dominant in the field, it has been a steady erosion—first to television, now to the Internet. Here is the 2004 breakdown by member studios of the Motion Picture Association of America:

Network television	22.9 percent
Spot television	13.3 percent
Newspapers	12.8 percent
Trailers	7.4 percent
Online	2.4 percent
Other media	22.2 percent
Nonmedia promotion	19.0 percent

Internet Advertising

The most visible products during the dot-com bubble were commercial sites that lured investors with the promise that eventually the sites would mature into lucrative advertising-supported enterprises. But building most of these sites into revenue producers took longer than expected. At some sites investors pulled the plug. Others went quietly out of business.

When the bubble burst for so many dot-coms, most remaining sites looked to advertising rather than venture capitalists to sustain them economically. With more than 200 million people with web access in the United States by 2005, and the number growing, the potential for dot-coms to be advertising supported was clear. But many advertisers were hesitant. Advertisers were never quite sure what they were buying. Measuring and categorizing web audiences were not easy tasks.

Tracking Internet Traffic

An impediment to attracting advertisers to the Internet was the difficulty of measuring the audience. Advertisers want solid numbers on which to base decisions on placing their ads. Gradually, the Internet Advertising Bureau and the Advertising Research Foundation developed uniform measurement guidelines. Nielsen, known mostly for surveys on network television audiences, has established monitoring mechanisms.

The most-cited measure of web audiences is the **hit.** Every time someone browsing the web clicks an on-screen icon or on-screen highlighted section, the computer server that offers the web page records a hit. Some companies that operate web sites tout hits as a measure of audience, but savvy advertisers know hits are a misleading indicator of audience size. The online edition of *Wired* magazine, HotWired, for example, records an average of 100 hits from everybody who taps in. HotWired's 600,000 hits on a heavy day come from a mere 6,000 people.

Another measure of web usage is the **visit,** a count of the people who visit a site. But visits too are misleading. At *Playboy* magazine's web site, 200,000 visits are scored on a typical day, but that doesn't mean that *Playboy* cyber-ads are seen by 200,000 different people. Many of the same people visit again and again on a given day.

The **clickthrough** has emerged as a measure. When someone clicks a link to an advertising site, the click is registered and a fee is paid to the site from which the ad visitor came. The gateway site is the Internet equivalent of a newspaper, which charges advertisers for space, or a television station, which charges for airtime.

Some electronic publications charge advertisers by the day, others by the month, others by the hit. But because of the vagaries of audience measurements, there is no standard pricing. Knowing that the web cannot mature as an advertising medium until advertisers can be given better audience data, electronic publications have asked several companies, including Nielsen, to devise tracking mechanisms. But no one expects data as accurate as press runs and broadcast ratings any time soon. In the meantime advertisers are making seat-of-the-pants assessments as to which web sites are hot.

Interactive Advertising Bureau Check out Standards and Guidelines to learn how to determine the success of an online ad campaign.
www.iab.net

Nielsen//Netratings A leader in providing information to help clients determine and execute their Internet business strategies.
www.netratings.com

Evaluating the Internet

study preview **Traditional gatekeeping processes that filter media content for quality are less present in the Internet. Users need to take special care in assessing material they find.**

Strengths of Internet Sites

Several organizations issue awards to excellent Internet sites. The most prestigious are the **Webby** awards, a term contrived from the nickname for the somewhat parallel Emmy awards of television. Many web awards, though, are for design and graphics, not content, although there are many measures of a site's excellence.

hit ■ Tallied every time someone goes to a web page.

visit ■ Tallied for every person who visits a web site.

clickthrough ■ A registered visit to an advertising site from a gateway elsewhere on the Internet.

Webby ■ A major award of excellence for web sites.

Content The heart of all mass media messages is the value of the content. For this, traditional measures of excellence in communication apply, such as accuracy, clarity and coherence.

Navigability Does the site have internal links so that users can move easily from page to page and among various points on the site? Among the mass media, navigability is a quality unique to the Internet.

External Links Does the site connect to related sites on the Internet? The most distinctive feature of the Internet as a mass medium is interconnectivity with other sites on the global network. Good sites exploit this advantage.

Intuitive to Use The best sites have navigational aids for moving around a site seamlessly and efficiently. These include road signs of many sorts, including clearly labeled links.

Loading Times Well-designed sites take advantage of the Internet as a visual medium with images. At the same time, pages should load quickly so users don't have to wait and wait and wait for a page to write itself to their screens. This means the site needs a balance. Overdoing images, which require lots of bandwidth, works against rapid downloads. Absence of images makes for dull pages.

Accuracy

The Internet has been called a democratized mass medium because so many people create Internet content. Almost anybody can put up a site. A downside of so much input from so many people is that the traditional media gatekeepers aren't necessarily present to ensure accuracy. To be sure, there are many reliable sites with traditional gatekeeping, but the Internet is also littered with junk.

Of course, unreliable information isn't exclusive to the Internet. But among older media, economic survival depends on finding and keeping an audience. Unreliable newspapers, for example, eventually lose the confidence of readers. People stop buying them, and they go out of business. The Internet has no such intrinsic economic imperative. A site can be put up and maintained with hardly any capital—in contrast to a newspaper, which requires tons of newsprint and barrels of ink, not to mention expensive presses, to keep coming out. Bad Internet sites can last forever.

To guard against bad information, Internet users should pay special heed to the old admonition: Consider the source. Is the organization or person behind a site reliable? If you have confidence in *USA Today* as a newspaper, you can have the same confidence in its web site. Another news site, no matter how glitzy and slick, may be nothing more than a lunatic working alone in a dank basement somewhere recasting the news with perverse twist and whole-cloth fiction.

In research reports, footnotes or endnotes need to be specific on Internet sources, including URL addresses. This allows people who read a report to go to the source to make their own assessment—just as traditional footnotes allow a reader to go to the library and check a source.

Even with notations, a report that cites Internet sources can be problematic. Unlike a book, which is permanent once it's in print, Internet content can be in continuing flux. What's there today can be changed in a minute—or disappear entirely. To address this problem at least in part, notation systems specify that the date and time of the researcher's Internet visit be included.

In serious research, you can check whether an online journal is refereed. A mission statement will be on the site with a list of editors and their credentials and a statement on the journal's editorial process. Look to see whether articles are screened through a **peer review** process.

peer review ■ A screening mechanism in which scholarly material is reviewed by leaders in a discipline for its merits, generally with neither the author nor the reviewers knowing each other's identity.

Media Melding

study preview **Many mass media as we know them are converging into digitized formats. Complementing and hastening this technological melding are ownership conglomeration and joint ventures. Government deregulation is contributing to a freer business environment that encourages new ventures.**

Technological Convergence

Johannes Gutenberg brought mass production to books. The other primary print media, magazines and newspapers, followed. People never had a problem recognizing differences among books, magazines and newspapers. When sound recording and movies came along, they too were distinctive, and later so were radio and television. Today, the traditional primary media are in various stages of transition to digital form. Old distinctions are blurring.

The cable television systems and the Internet are consolidating with companies in the forefront, such as AT&T. This **technological convergence** is fueled by accelerated miniaturization of equipment and the ability to compress data into tiny digital bits for storage and transmission. And all the media companies, whether their products traditionally relied on print, electronic or photographic technology, are involved in the convergence.

As the magazine *The Economist* noted, once-discrete media industries "are being whirled into an extraordinary whole." Writing in *Quill* magazine, *USA Today*'s Kevin Manay put it this way: "All the devices people use for communicating and all the kinds of communication have started crashing together into one massive megamedia industry. The result is that telephone lines will soon carry TV shows. Cable TV will carry telephone calls. Desktop computers will be used to watch and edit movies. Cellular phone-computers the size of a notepad will dial into interactive magazines that combine text, sound and video to tell stories."

Unanticipated consequences of the new technology are no better illustrated than by Amazon.com. Amazon's site has a growing list of books that people can search internally for the frequency of key terms and phrases. In Scott Ritter's *Solving the Iraq Crises,* Amazon lists 52 pages that contain the term "weapons of mass destruction." A person can call up each of the pages, as well as adjoining pages, to read the paragraphs around the use of the words "weapons of mass destruction," usually several hundred words. Amazon, in the business of selling books, won't let people download whole books, but the service, called **Search Inside,** demonstrates possibilities for the library of the future.

In 2005 Google, the search-engine company, began scanning the entire collections of five major libraries for posting online. Although copyright ownership issues in regard to many works created in the last 75 years remain unresolved, the Google project is underway at Harvard University, the New York Public Library, Oxford University, Stanford University and University of Michigan. When completed, the Google project will allow online access to just about everything ever put between book covers in the history of the English language—15 million titles.

Transition Ahead

Nobody expects the printed newspaper to disappear overnight or for movie houses, video rental shops and over-air broadcasters to go out of business all at once. But all the big media companies have established stakes on the Internet, and in time, digitized messages delivered over the Internet will dominate.

Outside of the Internet itself, major media companies also are trying to establish a future for themselves in reaching audiences in new digital ways. Companies that identify voids in their ability to capitalize on new technology have created joint ventures to ensure they won't be left out. The NBC television network, for example, provides news on Microsoft's MSN online service. All of the regional Bell telephone companies have

technological convergence ■ Melding of print, electronic and photographic media into digitized form.

Search Inside ■ Amazon.com search engine that can find a term or phrase in every book whose copyright owners have agreed to have scanned into a database.

case STUDY

Do We Need Net Neutrality?

Competing Stakes Different components of the U.S. industry, consumer groups and local governments all have stakes in who gets charged for Internet access. Alaska Senator Ted Stevens favors a plan that he says "attempts to strike a balance."

Ten years after President Bill Clinton signed the Telecommunications Act of 1996, Congress took the first serious steps toward rewriting the nation's telecommunications laws, steps that led to a leap off the cliff of controversy.

In the House, a proposal was designed to permit telephone and cable companies to operate Internet and other digital communications services as private networks, free of policy safeguards or governmental oversight. It would permit Internet service providers like AOL to charge fees for almost every online transaction and to prioritize e-mails based on the sender's willingness to pay.

A Senate version raised many of the same public interest concerns as the house bill. It was the most sweeping rewrite in a decade of laws dealing with video, satellite and broadband communications. Alaska Republican Senator Ted Stevens, sponsor of the bill, said that it "attempts to strike a balance between competing industries, consumer groups and local government."

Missing from either proposed legislation was any regulation to ensure what was called *net neutrality,* the shorthand term for free and non-discriminatory Internet access for everyone, everywhere. Companies such as Amazon.com, Google, Yahoo, Intel and Microsoft were lobbying for net neutrality in advance of efforts to rewrite telecommunications laws. Some of the leading minds of the Internet, including founding fathers Tim Berners-Lee and Vint Cerf and network visionary Peter Cochrane, also were urging Congress to consider the consequences of not maintaining net neutrality.

Lobbyists from big telephone companies, such as Verizon and AT&T, and cable companies, such as Comcast, which together provide Internet access to 98 percent of online Americans, claimed that neutrality as a government restriction would stifle competition. The telcos were spending millions of dollars each week on lobbying to write a law that would let them control the Internet, according to Robert McChesney, a University of Illinois professor and founder of Free Press, a bipartisan organization working to increase public participation in crucial media debates. McChesney said the companies were hoping to be able to make websites that don't pay them come through slower, to make them much harder to get, or in some cases, to take them off the Internet altogether. Also, he said, the companies would benefit enormously from new laws that would allow them to charge both the user and the content provider.

Consumer groups and activists raised serious questions about the future of open networks and prospects for real competition on the Internet. They worried about local management of the public right of ways, the red-lining of low income and rural communities and long-term protections for public, education and government access. A law that included red-lining language would allow companies to be discriminatory about which communities they offer their best services to, meaning they could essentially serve just wealthy and middle-class communities.

As these bills and others that would maintain net neutrality and equal access to the Internet were introduced and debated in 2006, most experts agreed that the issues were so complex it could take several years for Congress to agree on how to update the country's telecommunication laws.

"I think what people have to remember is that what excited us all about the Internet was the idea that anyone could start a website at a fairly nominal fee and be competing equally with General Motors, with General Electric, with Rupert Murdoch. We all had a shot at it," said McChesney.

A Seattle *Times* editorial asked: "What happens to services such as iTunes if the telecoms provide a rival music site? Potentially, iTunes could be slowed down while a home-grown proprietary rival gets preferential treatment. How does that serve the consumer? Lawmakers need to insert language that perpetuates the Internet as a breeding ground for divergent voices and services. . . ."

WHAT DO YOU THINK?

1. Is Net neutrality essential to the Internet? Will it stifle competition?
2. Should companies be able to make money by charging both the user and the content provider?
3. How would you rewrite the telecom laws to create more benefits for the U.S. public?

picked up partners to develop video delivery systems. Cable companies have moved into telephonelike two-way interactive communication systems that, for example, permit customers not only to receive messages but also to send them.

Government Deregulation

Until recent years a stumbling block to the melding of digital media was the U.S. government. Major components of today's melded media—the telephone, television and computer industries—grew up separately, and government policy kept many of them from venturing into the others' staked-out territory of services. Telephone companies, for example, were limited to being common carriers. They couldn't create their own media messages, just deliver other people's. Cable companies were barred from building two-way communication into their systems.

In the 1970s government agencies began to ease restrictions on business. In 1984 President **Ronald Reagan** stepped up this **deregulation,** and more barriers came down. The pro-business Reagan administration also took no major actions against the stampede of media company mergers that created fewer and bigger media companies. George Bush, elected in 1988, and Bill Clinton, elected in 1992, continued Reagan's deregulation initiatives and also his soft stance on mergers. The Clinton position, however, was less ideological and more pragmatic. Clinton's thinking was based on the view that regulation and antitrust actions would hamstring U.S. media companies, and other enterprises too, in global competition.

In 1996 Congress approved a new telecommunications law that wiped out many of the barriers that heeded full-bore exploitation of the potential of new media. The law repealed a federal ban against telephone companies providing video programming. Just as significant, cable television systems were given a green light to offer two-way local telephone. The law, the **Telecommunications Act of 1996,** accelerated the competition that had been emerging between telephone and cable television companies to rewire communities for higher-quality, faster delivery of new audio and video services.

Public Policy and the Internet

studypreview **The ability of almost anyone to post content on the Internet poses new public policy questions and issues. This whole new media world is illustrated by the free-wheeling nature of blogs. Media issues of privacy, decency and access are posed in newly critical ways.**

Blogs

In an era when the price of entry to media ownership precludes most mortals, the Internet, although young as a mass medium, is already democratizing mass communication. The rules are new. The most powerful member of the U.S. Senate, Trent Lott, never figured that his career would end under pressure created by a pipsqueak citizen in the hinterlands. It happened.

Joshua Marshall, creator of his own web site, talkingpointsmemo.com, picked up on a speech by Lott that, depending on your view, was either racist or racially insensitive. Lott uttered his comment at the 100th birthday party of Senator Strom Thurmond, once a strong segregationist. Mainstream news media missed how revealing Lott's comments could be read. Not Joshua Marshall. In his **blog** on talkingpointsmemo.com he hammered away at Lott day after day. Other bloggers, also outraged, joined in. Three days later the story hit NBC. Four days later Lott apologized. Two weeks later his Senate colleagues voted him out as majority leader.

The Memory Hole Popular blog that has received as many as four million hits a day.
http://thememoryhole.org

Ronald Reagan ■ President who pushed deregulation.

deregulation ■ Government policy to reduce regulation of business.

Telecommunications Act of 1996 ■ Repealed many limits on services that telephone and cable companies could offer.

blog ■ A web site, generally personal in nature on a narrow subject, such as politics. Short for "web log."

Wonkette.com Ana Marie Cox says she was born to blog. Every day at 7 a.m. she writes 12 items, a self-set quota, on whatever strikes her fancy for her web site wonkette.com. Though from Nebraska, Cox transplanted to Washington and focuses on Capitol gossip. The blog is a must-read in Washington power circles, her satire being funny to some, irritating to others. At Wonkette world headquarters (Cox's spare bedroom) she gets "hate mail," as she calls it, from both liberals and conservatives. As she sees it, she must be doing something right.

Ana Marie Cox

As a blogger who made a difference, Joshua Marshall is hardly alone. Best known is Matt Drudge, whose revelations propelled the Bill Clinton-Monica Lewinsky dalliances in the Oval Office into a national scandal. Another blogger, college student Russ Kirk, at his computer in Arizona, looked for information on government refusals to release photographs of caskets of fallen U.S. soldiers in Iraq and Afghanistan, which he regarded as documents to which the public, himself included, had legal access. Kirk filed a request for the documents under the Freedom of Information Act, then on his web site thememoryhole.org, he posted the photographs of the flag-draped coffins and also of the astronauts who had died in the *Columbia* disaster. The photos became front-page news. At one point Kirk's blog was receiving 4 million hits a day—almost twice the circulation of *USA Today.*

Both the beauty and bane of blogs is their free-for-all nature. On the upside, the web gives ordinary citizens access to mass audiences. It can be a loud and effective megaphone that is outside traditional news media that have resulted from institutionalized practices and traditions. Joshua Marshall's work on Trent Lott is an example of outside-the-box news reporting.

The easy access that bloggers have to mass audiences is also a problem. Most bloggers are amateurs at news, and their lack of experience with journalistic traditions has a downside. It was bloggers, for example, who kept alive a story that presidential candidate John Kerry and an office intern had carried on an affair. So persistent were the bloggers that neither the mainstream news media nor Kerry could ignore it, although Kerry and the intern denied the allegations and there was no evidence that there was anything to it. Kevin Drum, of calpundit.com, calls himself "unedited and unplugged." Although Drum never touched the Kerry intern story and is respected by his followers, his point that bloggers are "unplugged and unedited" is both the good news and bad news about the democratizing impact of the Internet.

Wonkette.com Blog dedicated to news and gossip on the Capitol.
http://wonkette.com

mediaPEOPLE

Glenn Reynolds

Never had Glenn Reynolds thought of himself as a media mogul. Although a young man of strong views, he saw his future as a college prof, not a media star. As a sideline lark in 2001 he set up a web site, Instapundit.com, and tapped out libertarian opinions for anybody who might be interested. At first nobody was.

Blogmeister He never aspired to a major media career, but his blog site Instapundit attracts more hits a day than the average U.S. newspaper's circulation.

Then, a month later, came the September 11 terrorism. People by the thousands turned to the Internet, found Reynolds' impassioned commentaries from Knoxville, Tennessee, and made Instapundit a daily routine. *Wired* magazine has declared his site the world's most popular blog—a shortened word for web log or diary.

At 120,000 visits a day, Reynolds has a larger audience than the average U.S. daily newspaper and more than most cable television pundits. He's prolific, writing 20 to 30 opinion items a day, some fairly long, mostly political. He's also gotten the attention of the traditional media. Fox News has posted his stuff on its site. MSNBC gave him a separate blog on its site.

Reynolds' blog is not alone in its success. Thousands exist, created by individuals who have something to say. Blogs fulfill a promise of the Internet to give people of ordinary means a printing press to reach the world, enriching the dialogue in a free society to an extent once possible only to media moguls and those relatively few whom they chose to print and air.

The Internet is transforming the structure of mass communication.

Privacy and the Internet

The genius of Tim Berners-Lee's original web concept was its openness. Information could be shared easily by anyone and everyone. Therein was a problem. During the web's commercialization in the late 1990s, some companies tracked where people ventured on the Internet. The tracking was going on silently, hidden in the background, as people coursed their way around the Internet. Companies gathering information were selling it to other companies. There was fear that insurance companies, health-care providers, lenders and others had a new secret tool for profiling applicants.

Government agencies began hinting at controls. Late in 1999, Berners-Lee and the web protocol-authoring consortium he runs came up with a new architecture, **P3P,** short for Platform for Privacy Preferences, to address the problem. With P3P people could choose the level of privacy they wanted for their web activities. Microsoft, Netscape and other browser operators agreed to screen sites that were not P3P-compliant. In effect, P3P automatically bypassed web sites that didn't meet a level of privacy expectations specified by individual web users.

Yet to be determined is whether P3P, an attempt at web industry self-regulation, can effectively protect consumers from third parties sharing private information. If P3P fails, Congress and federal agencies might follow through with backup protections.

Cyberpornography

Moralists, many in elected offices, are trying to eradicate indecency from cyberspace, especially if children have access. How serious is the problem? No one is certain how much **cyberpornography** is out there. Although a lot of Internet traffic is to porn sites, Vanderbilt University business professors Donna Hoffman and Thomas Novak estimate

P3P ■ A web protocol that allows users to choose a level of privacy. Short for Platform for Privacy Preferences.

cyberpornography ■ Indecency delivered by computer.

that only one-half of 1 percent of the files available on the Internet could be described as pornographic. How often kids visit those sites is impossible to measure. Some people would argue that even a single child's exposure to pornography is too much and justifies sanctions.

Congress has made three attempts to ban indecency from the Internet, first with the 1996 **Communications Decency Act.** The federal courts found that the law was an unconstitutional restriction on citizen freedom of inquiry. Congress went back to the drawing board and devised the 1998 **Child Online Protection Act.** Again, the courts said no. Although the courts saw protecting children a worthy goal, the restrictions went too far to limit the civil rights of adults.

media ONLINE **Children's Internet Protection Act**
CIPA is a federal law designed to address concerns regarding use of the Internet by children in schools and libraries.

www.fcc.gov/cgb/consumerfacts/cipa.html

The third attempt at legal restrictions, far less aggressive, came in 2000 with the **Children's Internet Protection Act,** which required schools and libraries to install Internet filters to keep children from being able to access sexually explicit content. This time the courts said OK, as long as adults can have the filters disabled for their own use.

Still, policing the Internet, including web sites, presents unique challenges. The nature of the Internet is that it is unstructured and unregulated, and the available material is in ongoing flux. The anarchy of the Internet is its inherent virtue. The immensity of cyberspace is another problem for would-be regulators. The web system that Tim Berners-Lee and his associates devised has infinite capacity.

Among alternatives to protect children are desktop programs that have come on the market to identify objectionable Internet bulletin boards and web sites. **SurfWatch,** for example, blocks access to such sites as soon as they are discovered. Bill Duvall of Los Altos, California, who created SurfWatch, hires college students to monitor cyberspace for sexual explicitness and updates SurfWatch regularly. He identifies five to 10 new smut sites a day.

Commercial online services keep close tabs on what goes on in their bulletin boards and chatrooms, and occasionally excise bawdy material. In addition, the industry is working on a ratings system, somewhat like Hollywood's movie ratings, to help parents to screen things they deem inappropriate for the kids. Since 1993, however, the commercial online services have been able to give their subscribers access to the unregulated Internet. Once out of an online service's gate, subscribers are beyond the protection of the service's in-house standards of acceptability.

Universal Access

Although Internet use is growing dramatically, the fact is that not everybody has access. Those who can afford computers and access fees will benefit tremendously. What about everybody else? This is a profound public policy question, especially in a democracy that prides itself on ensuring equality for every citizen on basic matters like access to information.

One line of reasoning is that the government should not guarantee **universal access.** This rationale draws on the interstate highway system as an analogy. The government builds the roads, but individuals provide the vehicles to drive around on the system.

The counterargument is that access to information will become so essential to everyone's well-being that we could end up with a stratified society of info-rich and info-poor people. Such a knowledge gap hardly is the democratic ideal.

Global Inequities

The exchange of information facilitated by the Internet boosted the United States into unprecedented prosperity going into the 21st century. One measure of efficiency, **diffusion of innovation,** improved dramatically. The time that innovations take to be widely used, which was once 10 years, dropped to one year. Giga Information Group projected that by 2002 businesses would be saving $1.3 trillion because of Internet commerce—an incredible 765 percent gain over five years.

Communication Decency Act ■ 1996 federal law to ban sexual explicitness from the Internet; the courts declared the law unconstitutional on citizen rights.

Child Online Protection Act ■ 1998 federal law to shield children from sexual explicitness on the Internet; the courts declared the law unconstitutional because adult access was impeded.

Children's Internet Protection Act ■ 2000 federal law requires schools and libraries to filter sexually explicit Internet content; the courts endorsed the filters, as long as adults could ask that they be removed.

SurfWatch ■ Software that intercepts indecent material.

universal access ■ Giving everyone the means to use the Internet.

diffusion of innovation ■ Process through which news, ideas, values and information spread.

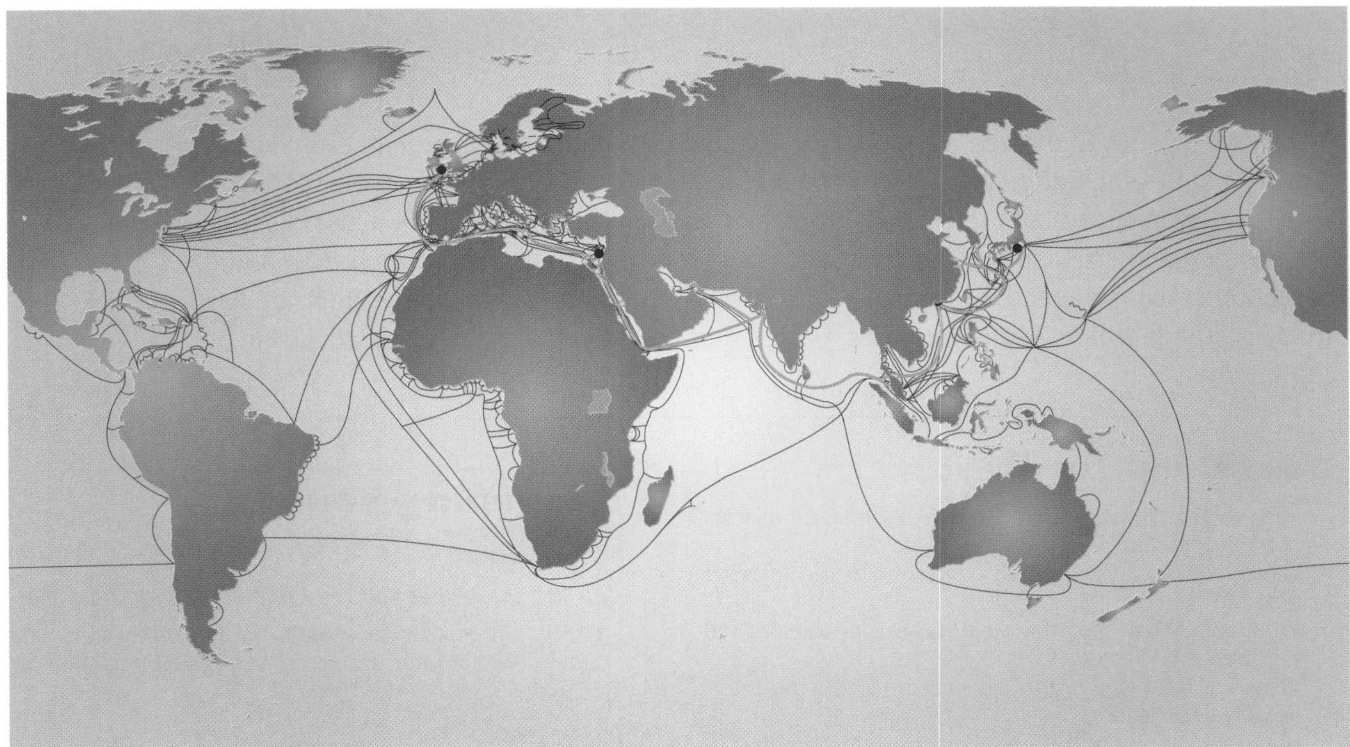

Global Fiber Optics The Fiberoptic Link Around the Globe, "FLAG" for short, is the longest engineering project in human history—a 17,400-mile communication link of England and Japan. The blue lines are other undersea fiber-optic routes that are planned or in place. The world is being wired for faster World Wide Web communication.

A problem, though, is that much of the world isn't well plugged in. All of the Middle East and Africa have only 7.5 million web users in total.

In short, the economic advantages of the Internet may be creating new international inequities. If maximum prosperity depends on free trade in a global economy, as many economists argue, then all of the world must be folded fully into the Internet.

As the technological breakthroughs leapfrog each other, we will see the traditional media shift increasingly to the Internet. Don't expect to wake up one morning, though, and find that the world is paperless and that local television stations have vanished. Just as horses and buggies and the automobile coexisted for 40 years, so will e-books and p-books. Television will still be television as we know it today, with many people satisfied with livingroom sets pretty much as now—although with bigger screens, sharper pictures and movie-house sound quality.

In short, media companies will need to use two redundant modes to maximize the audience. Already we see this with over-air radio stations that stream online, magazines and newspapers on paper and on the Internet, and recordings available at the record store and also downloadable.

Could the Internet lose its diversity? Media mogul Barry Diller, well regarded for his crystal ball on media trends, sees ownership consolidation ahead for the Internet, just like the other media. Citing cable giant Comcast, he said in a *Newsweek* interview: "You can already see at Comcast and others the beginning of efforts to control the home pages that their consumers plug into. It's for one reason: To control a toll bridge or turnstile through which others must pay to go. The inevitable result will be eventual control by media giants of the Internet in terms of independence and strangulation. This is a situation where history is absolutely destined to repeat itself." Most Internet users hope Diller is wrong.

CHAPTER 9 Wrap-Up

The World Wide Web utilizes the global Internet, so computers anywhere can exchange digitized data—including text, visuals and audio. Many media companies are investing heavily in cyberspace, and the expansion of high-capacity fiber-optic cable networks will increase capacity tremendously so that audio and moving visuals are on tap live on any computer screen connected to the Internet. Two-way communication via the Internet already is standard fare. With every passing day, more mass communication is occurring on the Internet.

Questions for Review

1. How can the Internet be defined as a new and distinctive mass medium?
2. What technological breakthroughs made the Internet possible?
3. What are the new directions that technology is taking the Internet?
4. What has been the role of advertising in driving Internet development?
5. How is gatekeeping different on the Internet than in other major mass media?
6. How is the Internet contributing to a melding of the mass media?
7. What public policy questions has the Internet raised?

Questions for Critical Thinking

1. What makes books, magazines, newspapers, sound recordings, movies, radio and television different from one another? What will become of these distinctions in coming years?
2. Trace the development of the technology that has made the web possible.
3. What were the innovations that Tim Berners-Lee introduced that are revolutionizing mass communication?
4. How does hypertext depart from traditional human communication? And does hypertext have a future as a literary form?
5. What obstacles would you have in designing public policy to assure access for every citizen to the Internet?
6. Some people say there is no point in trying to regulate cybersmut. Do you agree? Disagree? Why?
7. Some mass media may be subsumed by the Internet. Pretend you are a futurist and create a timeline for this to happen.

Deepening Your media LITERACY

Can you trust what you read and see on the Internet?

STEP 1 Choose two or three different web sites that you might access for information for a paper, such as Nexis or Wikipedia.

Dig Deeper

STEP 2 Write evaluations of the sites you chose based on the following criteria:

1. How is the site funded? What is the intended purpose of the site? Of the information on the site? Is it user driven or owner/product driven?
2. Does the site appeal to your emotions? If so, how? What other techniques are used to engage the viewer?
3. All media contain ideological and value messages. What are the messages of the site? Are any of them unintended? Are they positive or negative? Are they obvious or intentionally hidden?
4. Does the site use traditional gatekeepers?
5. Does it use a peer review process?

What Do You Think?

STEP 3 Answer these questions: What are the potential drawbacks of using a user-driven site for research? Is the emotional appeal of a site important to a user seeking research information? Are traditional gatekeepers the best way to ensure accuracy on a web site? Why or why not? Is how a site is paid for a fair way to measure its trustworthiness? Why or why not? How could the value messages of a site affect its informational worth?

Keeping Up to Date

Industry Standard is the main trade journal of e-commerce.

The magazine *Wired* offers hip coverage of cyberdevelopments, issues and people.

Trade journals *Editor & Publisher, Advertising Age* and *Broadcasting & Cable* have excellent ongoing coverage of their fields.

InfoWorld covers the gamut of cybernews.

Widely available news media that explore cyberissues include *Time, Newsweek,* the *Wall Street Journal* and the New York *Times.*

Don't overlook surfing the web for sites that track Internet developments.

For Further Learning

Jack Goldsmith and Tim Wu. *Who Controls the Internet? Illusions of a Borderless World.* Oxford University Press, 2006.

Goldsmith and Wu seek cracks in the widespread notion thay governments are powerless at controlling Internet content.

J. Storrs Hall. *Nanofuture.* Prometheus, 2005.

Certain that technology challenges can be overcome, Hall, a futurist with a software background, waxes enthusiastically that the manipulation of individual constructs of atoms can be manufactured to create any and everything.

David Bondanis. *Electrtic Universe.* Crown, 2005.

Bondanis, who teaches mathematical physics at Oxford, offers a parallel to the Internet's quick remaking of the world by chronicling the 19th-century inventions of Michael Faraday, Samuel Morse and Alan Turning.

Urs E. Gattiker. *The Internet as a Diverse Community: Cultural, Organizational and Political Issues,* Earlbaum, 2001.

Gattiker, a Danish scholar, addresses web issues, including national sovereignty.

Alan B. Albarran and David H. Goff, editors. *Understanding the Web: Social, Political and Economic Dimensions of the Internet.* Iowa State University Press, 2000.

Leading scholars contributed analytical articles for this systematic evaluation of the impact of the web on people's lives.

George Gilder. *Telecosm: How Infinite Bandwidth Will Revolutionize Our World.* Free Press, 2000.

In this long-awaited work, high-tech futurist George Gilder begins with fundamentals of physics and then develops his theory that the speed of light is the only limitation on where long-distance human communication can go. We're a long way from there.

Tim Berners-Lee, with Mark Fischetti. *Weaving the Web: The Original Design and the Ultimate Destiny of the World Wide Web by Its Inventor.* HarperSan Francisco, 1999.

Gordon Moore. "*Solid State Physicist:* William Shockley." *Time* (March 29, 1999), pages 193–195.

Moore, who worked for Shockley, explains his thinking, his devices and his quirky paranoia in a *Time* series on leading thinkers of the 20th century.

Tom Standage. *The Victorian Internet.* Walker, 1998.

Standage, a science and technology reporter, traces the evolution of the telegraph in the 1800s, pointing out uncanny parallels with the evolution of the Internet in the late 1900s.

Robert Wright. "The Man Who Invented the Web." *Time* (May 19, 1997), pages 160–164.

Tim Berners-Lee has a hard time with names and recall, which, as this personality profile explains, led to him to create the ultimate archive and recall system—the World Wide Web. The article is based mostly on a penetrating and perceptive interview in which Berners-Lee opens up probably as much as he ever has.

Neal Stephenson. "Mother Earth, Motherboard." *Wired* (December 1996), pages 97–160.

Stephenson, a technology writer, built this lengthy, detailed article on undersea cables around an England-to-Japan journey following the route of the longest cable ever built: FLAG, which is short for Fiber-optic Link Around the Globe. The article is an excellent orientation on cable technology, regulation and ownership for ordinary folks without advanced degrees in engineering, bureaucratic gobbledygook and finance.

Vannevar Bush. "As We May Think." *Atlantic Monthly* (July 1945).

In this seminal article, Bush, president of the Carnegie Institution, proposed a machine for associative retrieval of information—a precursor for the Web.

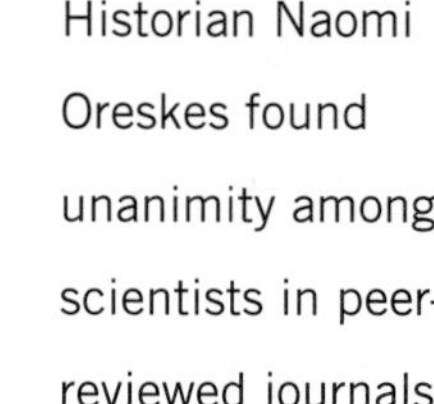

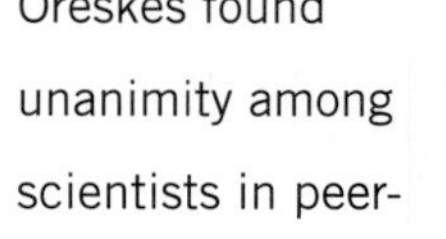

Naomi Oreskes

Historian Naomi Oreskes found unanimity among scientists in peer-reviewed journals that human beings are contributing to global warming. Why, then, are the news media giving so much play to those who see climate change as fiction or who minimize its significance?

chapter 10 News

In this chapter you will learn:

- **Many mass media practices originated during major periods in U.S. history.**
- **The fact-oriented U.S. notion of news is only one model for news.**
- **Journalists bring many personal, social and political values to their work.**
- **Many variables beyond journalists' control affect what ends up being reported.**
- **Factors outside the newsroom influence how news is reported.**
- **Gatekeeping is both essential and hazardous in the news process.**
- **Exploratory reporting and soft news are journalistic trends going in opposite directions.**

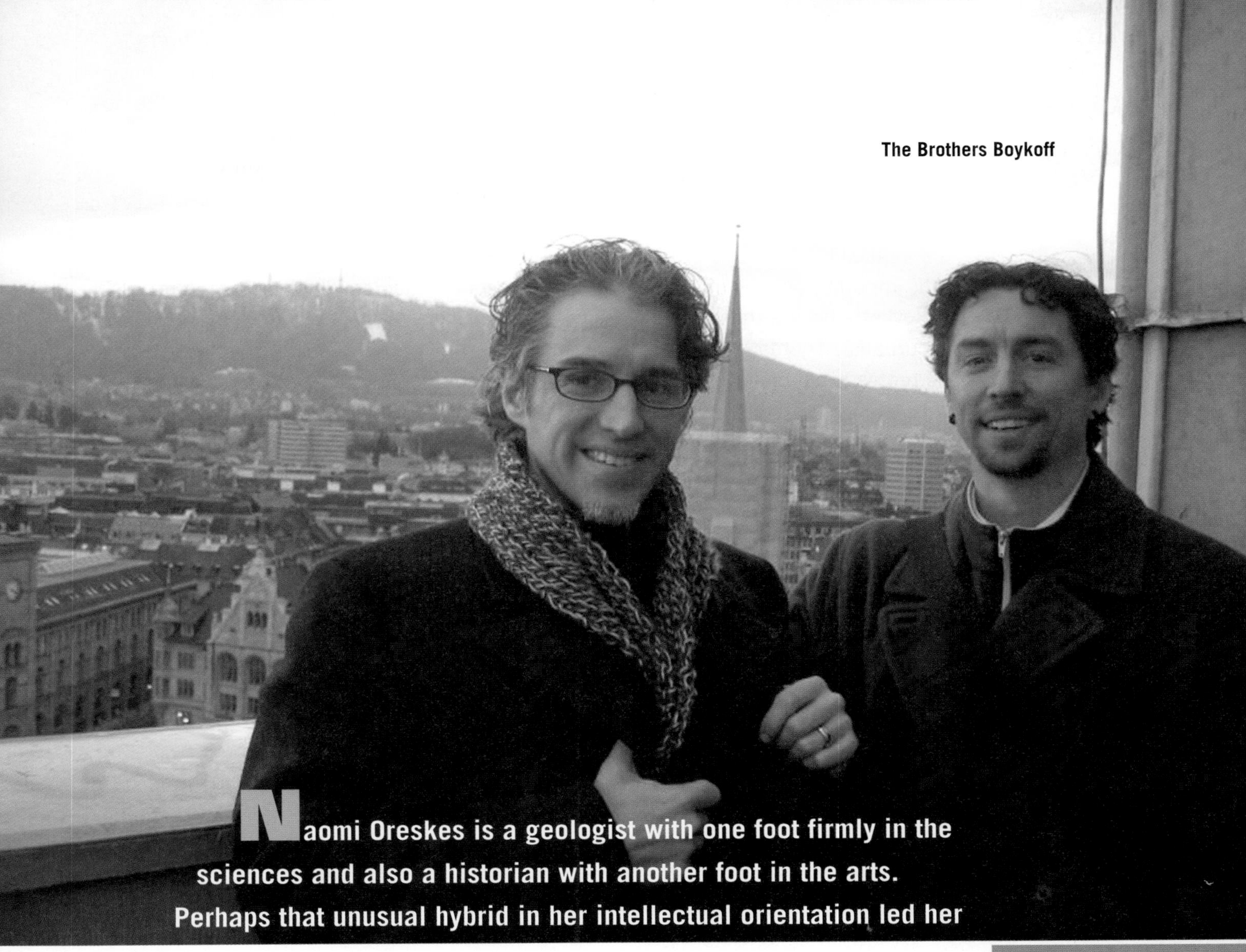

The Brothers Boykoff

Naomi Oreskes is a geologist with one foot firmly in the sciences and also a historian with another foot in the arts. Perhaps that unusual hybrid in her intellectual orientation led her to try to sort through contradictions she was seeing about global warming. For years Oreskes had read scientists expressing alarm in their academic journals about the fate of the planet and that human society was a major culprit. In the news media, however, she found a strong strain of skepticism.

Oreskes went searching for truth, a personal reality check.

She decided to test her impression that scientists were unanimous about global warming. She took the journal *Science* and identified every article on global warming over 10 years. Then she randomly chose 928 articles to analyze. After eliminating articles that weren't relevant to the question, she found none—not one—that disagreed about global warming as a reality with human activity as a cause.

Meanwhile, a separate study of news coverage, also massive, had been launched by brothers Jules Boykoff, a political scientist, and Maxwell Boykoff, a geographer. The Boykoffs reviewed four leading U.S. newspapers, the New York *Times, Wall*

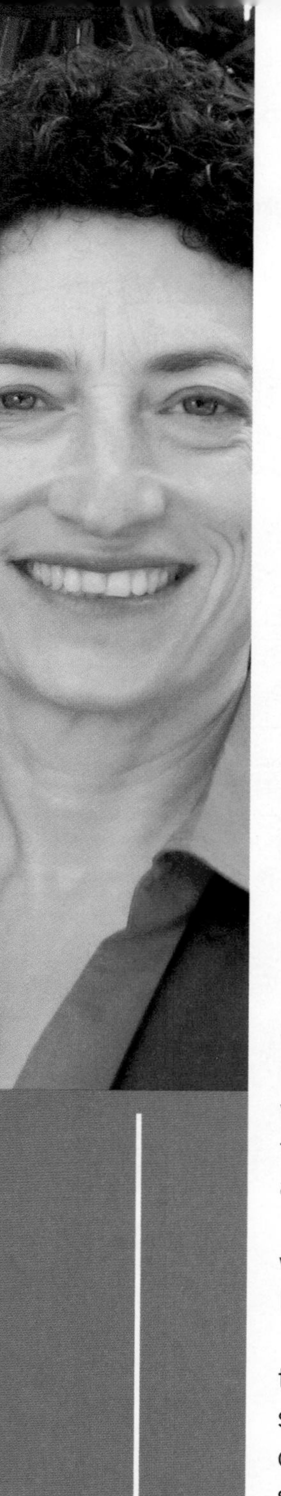

Street Journal, Washington *Post* and Los Angeles *Times* over 14 years and identified 3,542 news items, editorials and other articles on global warming. Randomly they chose 636 articles for analysis. Fifty-three percent, more than half, gave equal weight to the opposing views. The easily inferred impression, they said, was that the scientific community was "embroiled in a rip-roaring debate on whether or not humans were contributing to global warming." The fact is there was no such debate.

How could the news media in their reporting of science be so out of synch with scientists? It's a question at the heart of this chapter on news, which examines definitions of news and, importantly, how media-literate consumers can decide which reporting to trust.

The Boykoffs have a theory about what was wrong: In a sense, as counterintuitive as it seems, journalists try too hard to be fair.

"The professional canon of journalistic fairness requires reporters who write about a controversy to present competing points of view," the Boykoffs explained. "Presenting the most compelling arguments of both sides with equal weight is a fundamental check on biased reporting. But this canon causes problems when it is applied to issues of science. It seems to demand that journalists present competing points of view on a scientific question as if they had equal scientific weight, when actually they do not."

The fairness chink in journalistic armor has given special interests an opportunity to manipulate news by making misleading and even false information easily available to reporters who, dutifully if not mindlessly, apply the principle of fairness. A legion of spokespersons, many funded by special interests, end up with roles in journalists' stories. The Boykoffs cite many examples, one being the New York *Times* quoting a global-warming skeptic that carbon dioxide emissions aren't a threat to the climate but "a wonderful and unexpected gift from the Industrial Revolution."

Who are these special interests? Former Vice President Al Gore, himself a journalist early in his career, has been blunt: "A relatively small cadre of special interests including Exxon Mobil and a few other oil, coal and utilities companies." Why? "These companies want to prevent any new policies that would interfere with their current business plans that rely on the massive, unrestrained dumping of global-warming pollution of the Earth's atmosphere every hour of every day."

The Boykoffs put it this way: "Balanced reporting has allowed a small group of global warming skeptics to have their views amplified." Balanced coverage, according to the Boykoffs, has not translated into accurate coverage.

Are journalists dishonest? Jules Boykoff doesn't blame the journalists. Boykoff notes that giant media companies, intent on improving profits, have cut back on newsroom staffs and labor-intensive investigative reporting. The result: More and more reporters are called upon to be generalists and are being denied time to build expertise on a complex subject such as climate change.

Journalism Traditions

study preview **U.S. journalism has evolved through four distinctive eras: the colonial, partisan, penny and yellow periods. Each of these periods made distinctive contributions to contemporary news media practices.**

Colonial Period

Zenger Trial
Printer John Peter Zenger, in the dock, won his 1735 trial for criticizing New York's royal governor. The victory fed a colonial exuberance that culminated 46 years later in winning the revolution against British rule.

In the American **colonial period, Benjamin Harris** published the first newspaper, ***Publick Occurrences,*** in Boston in 1690. He was in hot water right away. Harris scandalized Puritan sensitivities by alleging that the king of France had dallied with his son's wife. In the colonies, just as in England, a newspaper needed royal consent. The governor had not consented, and Harris was put out of business after one issue.

Even so, Harris' daring was a precursor for emerging press defiance against authority. In 1733 **John Peter Zenger** started a paper in New York in competition with the existing Crown-supported newspaper. Zenger's New York *Journal* was backed by merchants and lawyers who disliked the royal governor. From the beginning, the newspaper antagonized the governor with items challenging his competence. Finally, the governor arrested Zenger. The trial made history. Zenger's attorney, **Andrew Hamilton,** argued that there should be no punishment for printing articles that are true. The argument was a dramatic departure from the legal practice of the day, which allowed royal governors to prosecute for articles that might undermine their authority regardless of whether the articles were true. Hamilton's argument prevailed, and Zenger, who had become a hero for standing up to the Crown, was freed. To the governor's chagrin, there was great public celebration in the streets of New York that night.

Zenger's success against the Crown foreshadowed the explosive colonial reaction after Parliament passed a stamp tax in 1765. The colonies did not have elected representatives in Parliament, so the cry was a defiant "No taxation without representation." The campaign, however, was less ideological than economic. It was led by colonial printers, who stood to lose from the new tax, which was levied on printed materials. Historian **Arthur Schlesinger** has called it the newspaper war on Britain. The newspapers won. The tax was withdrawn. Having seen their potential to force the government's hand, newspapers then led the way in stirring other ill feelings against England and precipitating the American Revolution.

These traditions from the colonial period remain today:

- The news media, both print and broadcast, relish their independence from government censorship and control.
- The news media, especially newspapers and magazines, actively try to mold government policy and mobilize public sentiment. Today this is done primarily on the editorial page.
- Journalists are committed to seeking truth, which was articulated as a social value in Zenger's "truth defense."
- The public comes down in favor of independent news media when government becomes too heavy-handed, as demonstrated by Zenger's popularity.
- In a capitalistic system the news media are economic entities that sometimes react in their own self-interest when their profit-making ability is threatened.

colonial period ■ From the founding of the colonies to the American Revolution.

Benjamin Harris ■ Published *Publick Occurrences.*

Publick Occurrences ■ First colonial newspaper, Boston, 1690.

John Peter Zenger ■ Defied authorities in New York *Journal.*

Andrew Hamilton ■ Urged truth as defense for libel.

Arthur Schlesinger ■ Viewed newspapers as instigating Revolution.

partisan period ■ From the American Revolution at least to the 1830s.

Federalist Papers ■ Essays with diverse views on the form the new nation should take.

Partisan Period

After the Revolution, newspapers divided along partisan lines. What is called the Federalist period in U.S. history is also referred to as the **partisan period** among newspaper historians. Intense partisanship characterized newspapers of the period, which spanned roughly 50 years to the 1830s.

Initially, the issue was over a constitution. Should the nation have a strong central government or remain a loose coalition of states? James Madison, Alexander Hamilton, Thomas Jefferson, John Jay and other leading thinkers exchanged ideas with articles and essays in newspapers. The ***Federalist Papers,*** a series of essays printed and reprinted in newspapers throughout the nation, were part of the debate. Typical of the extreme partisanship of the era were journalists who reveled in nasty barbs and rhetorical

media TIMELINE

JOURNALISTIC PRACTICES

1735 Colonial jury exonerated John Peter Zenger of seditious libel.

1760s Colonial newspapers campaigned against stamp tax.

1833 Ben Day founded New York *Sun,* the first penny newspaper.

1840s James Gordon Bennett pioneered systematic news coverage.

1841 Horace Greeley established the editorial page.

1844 Samuel Morse devised the telegraph, hastening delivery of faraway news.

1880s Joseph Pulitzer and William Randolph Hearst's circulation war led to yellow press excesses.

1916 Presidential returns were broadcast on an experimental New York radio station.

1972 Confidential sources became an issue in reporting the Watergate scandal and other divisive issues.

1980 CNN introduced 24-hour television news.

1992 Albuquerque, New Mexico, *Tribune* launched an online edition.

2005 Confidential sources became an issue again in reporting weapons of mass destruction claims to justify the Iraq war.

excesses. It was not unusual for an ideological opponent to be called a "dog," "traitor," "liar" or "cheat."

After the Constitution was drafted, partisanship intensified, finally culminating lopsidedly when the Federalist party both controlled the Congress and had the party leader, **John Adams,** in the presidency. In firm control and bent on silencing their detractors, the Federalists ramrodded a series of laws through Congress in 1798. One of the things the **Alien and Sedition Acts** prohibited was "false, scandalous, malicious" statements about government. Using these laws, the Federalists made 25 indictments, which culminated in 10 convictions. Among those indicted was **David Bowen,** a Revolutionary War veteran who felt strongly about free expression. He put up a sign in Dedham, Massachusetts: "No stamp tax. No sedition. No alien bills. No land tax. Downfall to tyrants of America. Peace and retirement to the president [the Federalist John Adams]. Long live the vice president [the Anti-Federalist **Thomas Jefferson**] and the minority [the Anti-Federalists]. May moral virtues be the basis of civil government." If only criticisms of recent presidents were so mild! But the Federalists were not of a tolerant mind. Bowen was fined $400 and sentenced to 18 months in prison.

Federalist excesses were at their most extreme when **Matthew Lyon,** a member of Congress, was jailed for a letter to a newspaper editor that accused President Adams of "ridiculous pomp, foolish adulation, selfish avarice." Lyon, an anti-Federalist, was sentenced to four months in jail and fined $1,000. Although he was tried in Rutland, Vermont, he was sent to a filthy jail 40 miles away. When editor Anthony Haswell printed an advertisement to raise money for Lyon's fine, he was jailed for abetting a criminal. The public was outraged at Federalist heavy-handedness. The $1,000 was quickly raised, and Lyon, while still in prison, was re-elected by a two-to-one margin. After his release from prison, Lyon's supporters followed his carriage for 12 miles as he began his way back to Philadelphia, the national capital. Public outrage showed itself in the election of 1800. Jefferson was elected president, and the Federalists were thumped out of office, never to rise again. The people had spoken.

Here are traditions from the partisan period that continue today:

- Government should keep its hands off the press. The First Amendment to the Constitution, which set a tone for this period, declared that "Congress shall make no law . . . abridging freedom . . . of the press."
- The news media are a forum for discussion and debate, as newspapers were in the *Federalist Papers* dialogue on what form the Constitution should take.
- The news media should comment vigorously on public issues.

media ONLINE

Tracing the Story of Journalism A timeline of journalism in the United States. **www.writesite.org/html/tracing.html**

Archiving Early America Explore the world of early America through the media of the day. **www.earlyamerica.com/earlyamerica**

Federalist Papers The original text of the Federalist Papers. View or download the entire plain text version of all the Federalist Papers. **http://memory.loc.gov/ammem/help/constRedir.html**

New York *Sun* See the *Sun* today. **www.nysun.com**

John Adams ■ Federalist president.

Alien and Sedition Acts ■ Discouraged criticism of government.

David Bowen ■ Punished for criticizing the majority party.

Thomas Jefferson ■ Anti-Federalist president.

Matthew Lyon ■ Member of Congress jailed for criticism of President Adams.

- Government transgressions against the news media will ultimately be met by public rejection of those committing the excesses, which has happened periodically throughout U.S. history.

Penny Period

In 1833, when he was 22, the enterprising **Benjamin Day** started a newspaper that changed U.S. journalism: the **New York *Sun*.** At a penny a copy, the *Sun* was within reach of just about everybody. Other papers were expensive, an annual subscription costing as much as a full week's wages. Unlike other papers, which were distributed mostly by mail, the *Sun* was hawked every day on the streets. The *Sun*'s content was different too. It avoided

Benjamin Day ■ Published the New York *Sun*.

New York *Sun* ■ First penny newspaper, 1833.

mediaPEOPLE

Benjamin Day

Years later, reflecting on the instant success of his New York *Sun,* Benjamin Day shook his head in wonderment. He hadn't realized at the time that the *Sun* was such a milestone. Whether he was being falsely modest is something historians can debate. The fact is the *Sun,* which Day founded in 1833, discovered mass audiences on a scale never before envisioned and ushered in the era of modern mass media.

Ben Day, a printer, set up a shop in 1833, but business was slow. With time on his hands, he began a little people-oriented handbill with brief news items and, most important, an advertisement for his printing business. He printed 1,000 copies, which he sold for a penny apiece. The tiny paper, four pages of three columns of type, sold well, so Day decided to keep it going. In six months the *Sun,* the first of a new era of penny papers, had the highest circulation in New York. By 1836 circulation had zoomed to 20,000.

Fifty years later Day told an interviewer that the *Sun*'s success was "more by accident than by design." Even so, the *Sun* was the first newspaper that, at a penny a copy, was within the economic means of almost everyone. He filled the paper with the local police court news, which is the stuff that arouses universal interest. True to its masthead motto, "It Shines for All," the *Sun* was a paper for the masses.

At a penny a copy, Day knew he couldn't pay his bills, so he built the paper's economic foundation on advertising. This remains the financial basis of most mass media today—newspapers, magazines, television and radio. Just as today, advertisers subsidized the product to make it affordable to great multitudes of people.

Today it is technology that makes the media possible. The *Sun* was a pioneer in using the technology of its time: engine-driven presses. The *Sun*'s messages—the articles—were crafted to interest large, diverse audiences, as are mass messages today. Also like today, advertising drove the enterprise financially. The story of Day's *Sun* also demonstrates a reality, as true then as now, that the mass media must be businesses first and purveyors of information and entertainment second.

Mass Media Pioneer When Benjamin Day launched the New York *Sun* in 1833 and sold it for one cent a copy, he ushered in an era of cheap newspapers that common people could afford. Years later his successors pushed circulation past 1 million a week. Today mass media have many of the *Sun*'s pioneering characteristics. These include content of interest to a great many people, a financial base in advertising and easy access.

the political and economic thrust of the traditional papers, concentrating instead on items of interest to common folk. The writing was simple, straightforward and easy to follow. For a motto for the *Sun,* Day came up with "It Shines for All," his pun fully intended.

Day's *Sun* was an immediate success. Naturally, it was quickly imitated, and the **penny period** began. Partisan papers that characterized the partisan period continued, but the mainstream of American newspapers came to be in the mold of the *Sun.*

Merchants saw the unprecedented circulation of the **penny papers** as a way to reach great numbers of potential customers. Advertising revenue meant bigger papers, which attracted more readers, which attracted more advertisers. A snowballing momentum began that continues today with more and more advertising being carried by the mass media. A significant result was a shift in newspaper revenues from subscriptions to advertisers. Day, as a matter of fact, did not meet expenses by selling the *Sun* for a penny a copy. He counted on advertisers to pick up a good part of his production cost. In effect, advertisers subsidized readers, just as they do today.

Several social and economic factors, all resulting from the Industrial Revolution, made the penny press possible:

- **Industrialization.** With new steam-powered presses, hundreds of copies an hour could be printed. Earlier presses had been hand operated.
- **Urbanization.** Workers flocked to the cities to work in new factories, creating a great pool of potential newspaper readers within delivery range. Until the urbanization of the 1820s and 1830s, the U.S. population had been almost wholly agricultural and scattered across the countryside. Even the most populous cities had been relatively small.
- **Immigration.** Waves of immigrants arrived from impoverished parts of Europe. Most were eager to learn English and found that penny papers, with their simple style, were good tutors.
- **Literacy.** As immigrants learned English, they hungered for reading material within their economic means. Also, literacy in general was increasing, which contributed to the rise of mass-circulation newspapers and magazines.

A leading penny press editor was **James Gordon Bennett,** who, in the 1830s, organized the first newsroom and reporting staff. Earlier newspapers had been either sidelines of printers, who put whatever was handy into their papers, or projects of ideologues, whose writing was in an essay vein. Bennett hired reporters and sent them out on rounds to gather information for readers of his New York *Herald.*

Horace Greeley developed editorials as a distinctive journalistic form in his New York *Tribune,* which he founded in 1841. More than his competitors, Greeley used his newspaper to fight social ills that accompanied industrialization. Greeley's *Tribune* was a voice against poverty and slums, an advocate of labor unions and an opponent of slavery. It was a lively forum for discussions of ideas. Karl Marx, the communist philosopher, was a *Tribune* columnist for a while. So was Albert Brisbane, who advocated collective living. Firm in Greeley's concept of a newspaper was that it should be used for social good. He saw the *Tribune* as a voice for those who did not have a voice; a defender for those unable to articulate a defense; and a champion for the underdog, the deprived and the underprivileged.

In 1844, late in the penny press period, **Samuel Morse** invented the telegraph. Within months the nation was being wired. When the Civil War came in 1861, correspondents used the telegraph to get battle news to eager readers. It was called **lightning news,** delivered electrically and quickly. The Civil War also gave rise to a new convention in writing news, the **inverted pyramid.** Editors instructed their war correspondents to tell the most important information first in case telegraph lines failed—or were snipped by the enemy—as a story was being transmitted. That way, when a story was interrupted, editors would have at least a few usable sentences. The inverted pyramid, it turned out, was popular with readers because it allowed them to learn what was most important at a glance. They did not have to wade through a whole story if they were in a hurry. Also, the inverted pyramid helped editors to fit stories into the limited confines of a page—a story could be cut off at any paragraph and the most important parts remained intact. The inverted pyramid remains a standard expository form for telling event-based stories in newspapers, radio and television.

Horace Greeley Info Please encyclopedia information on the famous editor.
www.infoplease.com/ce6/people/A0821713.html

Associated Press An online look at the first 150 years of the Associated Press wire service.
www.ap.org/pages/about/history/history.html

penny period ■ One-cent newspapers geared to mass audience and mass advertising.

penny papers ■ Affordable by almost everyone.

James Gordon Bennett ■ Organized the first methodical news coverage.

Horace Greeley ■ Pioneered editorials.

Samuel Morse ■ Invented the telegraph.

lightning news ■ Delivered by telegraph.

inverted pyramid ■ Most important information first.

mediaPEOPLE

James Gordon Bennett

James Gordon Bennett, a young man seeing the success of Ben Day's penny paper, the New York *Sun,* rounded up $500 and rented a basement. There, in 1835, with a plank across two flour barrels for a desk, a dilapidated press and barely enough type, Bennett produced his own humble penny paper—the New York *Herald,* with pages slightly larger than sheets of a legal pad.

First with News

Bennett quickly recognized that being first with news gave him an advantage over competitors. His obsession with getting news to readers quickly brought an emphasis on timeliness as an important element in the concept of news. It also contributed to the fact-oriented telling of news because reporters rushing to get a dispatch together are too pressed to be analytical.

Bennett made a fetish of timeliness. He used small, fast boats to sail out to Sandy Point, on the coast beyond New York, to pick up parcels of newspapers and letters from arriving oceanic ships and then sail back to the city before the ships themselves could arrive and dock. He beat other papers by hours with fresh news.

In one case Bennett himself went to Halifax, Nova Scotia, where many European vessels landed before continuing down the coast. With a news packet in hand he hired a locomotive to take him to Boston, Worcester and New London, where he took a ferry to Long Island, and then another locomotive to New York. That news was days ahead.

The *Herald* was a quick success, surpassing the circulation of Ben Day's *Sun.*

Bennett never relented in his quest for quick news. After Samuel Morse invented the telegraph in 1844, Bennett instructed reporters to use the infant network that was being built around the country to send back their dispatches without delay.

Several New York newspaper publishers, concerned about the escalating expense of sending reporters to gather faraway news, got together in 1848 to share stories. By together sending one reporter, the newspapers cut costs dramatically. They called their cooperative venture the **Associated Press,** a predecessor of today's giant global news service. The AP introduced a new tone in news reporting. So that AP stories could be used by member newspapers of different political persuasions, reporters were told to write from a nonpartisan point of view. The result was a fact-oriented kind of news writing often called **objective reporting.** It was widely imitated and is still the dominant reporting style for event-based news stories in the U.S. news media.

There are traditions of today's news media, both print and electronic, that can be traced to the penny press period:

- Inverted pyramid story structures.
- Coverage and writing that appeal to a general audience, sometimes by trying to be entertaining or even sensationalistic. It's worth noting that the egalitarian thinking of Andrew Jackson's 1829–1837 presidency, which placed special value on the "common man," coincided with the start of the penny press and its appeal to a large audience of "everyday people."
- A strong orientation to covering events, including the aggressive ferreting out of news.
- A commitment to social improvement, which included a willingness to crusade against corruption.
- Being on top of unfolding events and providing information to readers quickly, something made possible by the telegraph but that also came to be valued in local reporting.
- A detached, neutral perspective in reporting events, a tradition fostered by the Associated Press.

Associated Press ■ Co-op to gather, distribute news.

objective reporting ■ Telling news without bias.

Joseph Pulitzer

William Randolph Hearst

Journalistic Sensationalism

Rival New York newspaper publishers Joseph Pulitzer and William Randolph Hearst tried to outdo each other daily with anti-Spanish atrocity stories from Cuba, many of them trumped up. Some historians say the public hysteria fueled by Pulitzer and Hearst helped to precipitate the Spanish-American War, especially after the U.S. battleship *Maine* exploded in Havana harbor. Both Pulitzer and Hearst claimed that it was a Spanish attack on an American vessel, although a case can be made that the explosion was accidental.

Yellow Period

The quest to sell more copies led to excesses that are illustrated by the Pulitzer-Hearst circulation war in New York in the 1890s, in what came to be known as the **yellow period.**

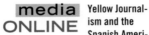

Yellow Journalism and the Spanish American War TNT provided this web site to add background to its television production, *The Roughriders.* **http://alt.tnt.tv/movies/tntoriginals/roughriders/jour.influencewar.html**

National Enquirer You no longer have to stand in line at the supermarket to read this publication. **www.nationalenquirer.com**

Joseph Pulitzer, a poor immigrant, made the St. Louis *Post-Dispatch* into a financial success. In 1883 Pulitzer decided to try a bigger city. He bought the New York *World* and applied his St. Louis formula. He emphasized human interest, crusaded for worthy causes and ran lots of promotional hoopla. Pulitzer's *World* also featured solid journalism. His star reporter, **Nellie Bly,** epitomized the two faces of the Pulitzer formula for journalistic success. For one story Bly feigned mental illness, entered an insane asylum and emerged with scandalous tales about how patients were treated. It was enterprising journalism of great significance. Reforms resulted. Later, showing the less serious, show-biz side of Pulitzer's formula, Nellie Bly was sent out to circle the globe in 80 days, like Jules Verne's fictitious Phileas Fogg. Her journalism stunt took 72 days.

In San Francisco, Pulitzer had a young admirer, **William Randolph Hearst.** With his father's Nevada mining fortune and mimicking Pulitzer's New York formula, Hearst made the San Francisco *Examiner* a great success. In 1895 Hearst decided to go to New York and take on the master. He bought the New York *Journal* and vowed to "out-Pulitzer" Pulitzer. The inevitable resulted. To outdo each other, Pulitzer and Hearst launched crazier and crazier stunts. Not even the comic pages escaped the competitive frenzy. Pulitzer ran the *Yellow Kid,* and then Hearst hired the cartoonist away. Pulitzer hired a new one, and both papers ran the yellow character and plastered the city with yellow promotional posters. The circulation war was nicknamed "yellow journalism," and the term came to be a derisive reference to sensational excesses in news coverage.

yellow period ■ Late 1800s; marked by sensationalism.

Joseph Pulitzer ■ Emphasized human interest in newspapers; later sensationalized.

Nellie Bly ■ Stunt reporter.

William Randolph Hearst ■ Built circulation with sensationalism.

The yellow excesses reached a feverish peak as Hearst and Pulitzer covered the growing tensions between Spain and the United States. Fueled by hyped atrocity stories, the tension eventually exploded in war. One story, perhaps apocryphal, epitomizes the no-holds-barred competition between Pulitzer and Hearst. Although Spain had consented to all demands by the United States, Hearst sent the artist **Frederic Remington** to Cuba to cover the situation. Remington cabled back: "Everything is quiet. There is no trouble here. There will be no war. Wish to return." Hearst replied: "Please remain. You furnish the pictures. I'll furnish the war."

Yellow journalism had its imitators in New York and elsewhere. It is important to note, however, that not all American journalism went the yellow route. **Adolph Ochs** bought the New York *Times* in 1896 and built it into a newspaper that avoided sideshows to report and comment seriously on important issues and events. The *Times,* still true to that approach, outlived the Pulitzer and Hearst newspapers in New York and today is the best newspaper in the world.

The yellow tradition, however, still lives. The New York *Daily News,* founded in 1919 and almost an immediate hit, ushered in a period that some historians characterize as **jazz journalism.** It was just Hearst and Pulitzer updated in tabloid form with an emphasis on photography. Today, newspapers like the commercially successful *National Enquirer* are in the yellow tradition. So are a handful of metropolitan dailies, including Rupert Murdoch's San Antonio, Texas, *Express-News.* It is obvious too in tabloid television interview programs like *Jerry Springer,* which pander to the offbeat, tawdry and sensational.

While not as important in forming distinctive journalistic traditions as the earlier penny papers, yellow newspapers were significant in contributing to the growing feeling of nationhood in the United States, especially among the diverse immigrants who were arriving in massive numbers. Journalism historian Larry Lorenz put it this way: "The publishers reached out to the widest possible audience by trying to find a common denominator, and that turned out to be the human interest story. Similarities among groups were emphasized rather than differences. Readers, in their quest to be real Americans, seized on those common elements to pattern themselves after, and soon their distinctive characteristics and awareness of themselves as special groups began to fade."

Yellow Journalism's Namesake
The Yellow Kid, a popular cartoon character in New York newspapers, was the namesake for the sensationalist "yellow journalism" of the 1880s and 1890s. Many newspapers of the period, especially in New York, hyperbolized and fabricated the news to attract readers. The tradition remains in isolated areas of modern journalism, like the supermarket tabloids and trash documentary programs on television.

Stunt Journalism
When newspaper owner Joseph Pulitzer sent reporter Nellie Bly on an around-the-world trip in 1890 to try to outdo the fictional Phileas Fogg's 80-day trip, stunt journalism was approaching its peak. Her feat took 72 days.

Frederic Remington ■ Illustrator sent by Hearst to find atrocities in Cuba.

Adolph Ochs ■ Developed the New York *Times* as a serious newspaper.

jazz journalism ■ 1920s, similar to yellow journalism.

Concepts of News

studypreview **The contemporary notion that news media content should be objective, prevalent in the United States, is relatively recent. Also, it is a notion not shared in all modern democracies. The word *objectivity* is overused and not very useful. Better is to think of journalism as the process of pursuing truth to tell truth.**

U.S. Model

From colonial times to the mid-1800s, more than 150 years, partisanship largely marked the content of American newspapers. So dominant was opinionated content that U.S. media historians characterize the era before Benjamin Sun introduced his one-cent New York *Sun* in 1833 as the partisan press period.

Two phenomena in the mid-1800s, both rooted in the economics of the newspaper industry, introduced the notion of value-free news—or **objectivity.**

Associated Press Several cost-conscious New York newspaper publishers agreed in 1848 to a joint venture to cover distant news. The Associated Press, as they called the venture, saved a lot of money. It also transformed U.S. journalism in a way that was never anticipated. Inherent in the AP concept was that its stories needed to be nonpartisan to be usable by all of its member newspapers, whose political persuasions spanned the spectrum. The result was an emphasis, some say fetish, on fact-driven journalism devoid of even a hint of partisanship.

Newspaper Economics A second fundamental shift cemented the AP style, often called an objective style: News became profitable—highly so. The fortune that Benjamin Day made with New York *Sun* in the mid-1830s was puny compared with the Pulitzer, Hearst and other news empires that came within 50 years. These super-publishers saw their newspapers as money machines as much as political tools. The bottom line gradually and inevitably gained more weight. The safest route to continue building their mass audiences and enhancing revenue was to avoid antagonizing readers and advertisers. There was money to be made in presenting news in as neutral a tone as possible. Picking up a lesson from the AP, but with a different motivation—to make money rather than save money—profit-driven publishers came to favor information-driven news.

By the early 20th century, when news practices became institutionalized in the first journalism textbooks and in the formation of professional organizations, the notion of a detached, neutral presentation was firmly ensconced. Ethics codes, new at the time, dismissed other approaches as unacceptable and unethical, even though they had been dominant only three generations earlier. The word *objectivity* became a newsroom mantra.

Media Conglomeration By the late 20th century the value-free approach to news was more entrenched in the United States than ever. Most news organizations had become parts of vast media empires that included government-regulated broadcast outlets. A detached, neutral tone in news content was the least apt to upset political leaders and government agencies from whom the media needed favors—like broadcast license renewals, broadcast spectrum access, and consent for more mergers and consolidations that reduced competition and could invite antitrust scrutiny by government.

European Model

objectivity ■ A concept in journalism that news should be gathered and told value-free

The notion that news could be conveyed neutrally, devoid of perspective or values, was peculiarly American. In Europe newspapers traditionally have flaunted their partisanship to attract like-minded readers. The result is flavorful, interesting reporting that flows from a point of view—and, say its defenders, is more truthful than the U.S. model. Leonard Doyle, foreign editor at the *Independent* in London, claims the European model encourages journalists to tell about events as they see them, rather than through the eyes of government officialdom, which can have its own agendas. The U.S. model, by contrast, tends merely to chronicle claims as provided by supposedly credible albeit partisan sources. There is too little attention in the U.S. model, say critics, to sorting through the claims with journalistic analysis.

In a forum sponsored by *Columbia Journalism Review,* Doyle offered striking examples of failures of the U.S. model. One was during the 2002 Afghan war. CNN quoted Pentagon authorities who said that B-52 bombers had dropped dozens of precision-targeted bombs in the Tora Bora area in an attempt to flush out terrorist mastermind Osama bin Laden. That, in itself, was accurate, but CNN missed what the Pentagon had not released: that the bombs had killed 115 people in the village of Kama Ado. The British press, less inclined to merely echo official views, told about the Kama Ado carnage—the whole story.

Doyle says that U.S. journalists' quest for "objectivity" has led to the tying of every fact to a source that can be named. This is a kind of timidity that Doyle says leaves journalists vulnerable to being duped: "The loudest demands for objectivity are made by groups or lobbies who want to ensure that they get equal time." The loudest and most persistent groups make the news. The U.S. approach, as Doyle sees it, is largely clerical and lacking the probing that would serve the audience better by coming closer to truth.

British journalists gloat that their U.S. counterparts uncritically reported the repeated but erroneous claim of President George W. Bush, in pushing for war, that Iraq possessed weapons of mass destruction. The redundancy of the message over many months fueled the early U.S. public support for the war, even though, it turned out, no such weapons existed. To U.S. journalists, Doyle says: "Ask why the God of Objectivity so failed you in your hour of need." The British government had advanced the same claims about weapons of mass destruction, but many British newspapers, openly unfriendly to the government, kept casting doubt on the claim, which tempered British public enthusiasm for the Iraq war. Europeans argue that their model, which places an emphasis on judgment and analysis, yields reporting that comes nearer to truth.

media ONLINE **Columbia Journalism Review** Motto: America's premier media monitor. **www.cjr.org**

Evolving News Models

How did the British and U.S. press, with the same roots historically, end up so different? The newspaper industry in Britain, and the rest of Europe too, never consolidated on the scale of U.S. newspapers. Historically, European papers have found profits by pandering to the political preferences of segments in the mass audience. In contrast, U.S. newspaper ownership consolidated to the point that the United States is a nation of mostly one-paper towns. Now media conglomerates have their feet also in broadcast news. The financial might of U.S. conglomerates, far greater than that of any European news organization, perpetuates itself more easily with blander news coverage. The thrust is to tell news as safely as possible, which means to seek to avoid alienating anybody—readers, advertisers, and, increasingly, government.

The news media in the United States, as European critics see it, lay out information provided by partisans and considers their job done. The result is a cautious and insufficiently critical press. True, the Europeans say, there is breakthrough reporting in the United States, like the Watergate revelations of the 1970s and Seymour Hersh's reports on the atrocities at My Lai in Vietnam and Abu Ghraib prison in Iraq,

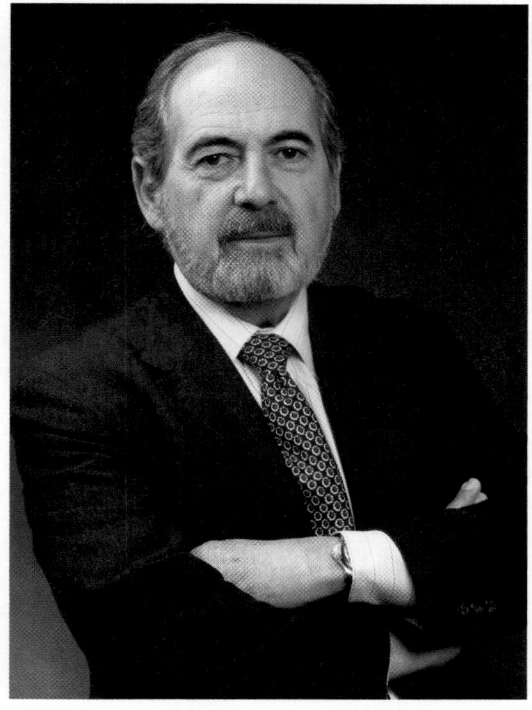

Michael Getler

The fact-orientation of U.S. news, some say obsessions, has a defender in Michael Getler of the Washington *Post.* Getler says the perspective-oriented British model, dominant in much of the world, gets in the way of telling news and leaves readers suspicious about whether they're getting good information. Critics say, however, that the goal of objectivity that underpins the U.S. model is impossible to attain and sometimes obscures truth with an avalanche of facts. Also, according to critics, the U.S. model puts a premium on attributing information to sources, regardless of their truthfulness or accuracy. They point to government sources in time of war as especially suspect.

but they say that these are anomalies and uncharacteristic. It is worth noting, as European critics do, that Hersh's My Lai scoops, unfriendly to the government's Vietnam war policy, were turned away by mainstream papers. Big papers and networks picked them up late, only when they couldn't be ignored. Hersh's Abu Ghraib torture revelations, also unfriendly to government war policy, appeared first in the high-brow *New Yorker* magazine, not the mainstream news press.

Europeans will argue that their newspapers, characterized by reporting that reflects values, is not only livelier but also more effective. Thirty million Brits, out of a population of 58 million, read a morning newspaper—a far higher percentage than in the United States. Too, everyone agrees that British and other European audiences are better informed about public issues and more engaged.

To be sure, some news organizations in Europe don't neatly fit the European model. The British Broadcasting Corporation is famous for straightforward reporting. The *Financial Times* and the *Independent,* among 13 national dailies in Britain, assiduously avoid political leanings. Even so, both BBC and the *Independent* make strong journalistic judgments when supported by the facts more readily than U.S. news media do.

Would journalism in which reporters wear their values on their sleeves work in the United States? A fact is that U.S. audiences are conditioned to expect detached, neutral reporting, even though it is relatively dull and sometimes falls far short of truth. Michael

mediaPEOPLE

Seymour Hersh

Leading Investigative Reporter

Seymour Hersh broke a story about U.S. soldiers wiping out a remote village of civilians during the Vietnam war. Finding official denials everywhere he turned, Hersh tracked veterans to their homes after their tours of duty to piece together an account of the horrible incident. Becoming known as the My Lai Massacre, it led, as it should have, to court martials. But the story so embarrassed the Pentagon that Hersh became a pariah in top Pentagon circles. Even so, he was so respected for his dogged truth-seeking that knowledgeable sources within the Pentagon and the Central Intelligence Agency continued to feed him leads on other stories.

Hersh was no one-shot wonder with his 1969 My Lai stories. En route to becoming one of the pre-eminent investigative reporters of our time, he focused on clandestine operations of U.S. government. These included the CIA's covert role in the overthrow of Salvador Allende in Chile. Hersh exposed secret bombing in Cambodia that had been authorized by presidential aide Henry Kissinger. In 2004 in the *New Yorker* magazine Hersh exposed prisoner abuses at the Abu Ghraib prison in Iraq. Even though the Pentagon's initial response was to label Hersh's Abu Ghraib account "outlandish and conspiratorial," the photos that Hersh showed could not be ignored.

In 1975 when Donald Rumsfeld was President Ford's chief of staff, he and Dick Cheney, a high administration official, exchanged memos on how to contain damaging reporting by Hersh, then with the New York *Times.* In new positions in the second Bush administration—Rumsfeld as secretary of defense, Cheney as vice president—they were no less angry at Hersh. But despite the denials and minimizing reaction statements, the accuracy of Hersh's reporting still was proving unshakable.

No matter how hard the Pentagon tries at the highest levels to make Hersh an outsider, he has become, in fact, an insider. Sources come to him, especially, it seems, midlevel and some senior civilian and military leaders in the defense establishment with grudges against President Bush for ignoring their experience and advice in setting new policy courses, including the Iraq war.

Getler, ombudsman at the Washington *Post,* makes the point that Americans distrust news that's cast in anything but a value-free tone. Readers, he says, "can smell reportorial opinion a mile away" and will then tend to discount the news.

Independent Online version of the British daily.
www.independent.co.uk

Financial Times You can get the headlines and introductions, but need to subscribe for most full-text articles.
http://news.ft.com/home/us

BBC Round-the-clock news from around the world.
http://news.bbc.co.uk/

Seymour Hersh Wikipedia article on the Pulitzer Prize winner in journalism.
http://en.wikipedia.org/wiki/Seymour_Hersh

Defining Objectivity

In U.S. journalism the concept of objectivity is often extolled, but journalists back off the term when pressed. Considering that all human beings, journalists included, have personal values that influence all that they do, objectivity, being value-free, is an impossible ideal. Only someone who is totally amoral can be objective. That means that journalists can do nothing more than work at appearing to be free of any values, which requires playing word games to conceal their values. That, say critics, is a fraud perpetrated on the news audience. It also works against journalists asking tough questions that might hint at personal values. This all suggests that the word "objective" and the concept of objectivity are so problematic that they have limited usefulness. In fact, the Society of Professional Journalists dropped the term *objectivity* from its ethics code in 1996.

A more useful concept, one on which U.S. and Europeans can agree, is that journalists do their best work when they pursue news with the goal of telling truth. What is truth? **Truth** is a broad and accurate understanding, which the Europeans note is far more important than the factual detail on which U.S. journalism obsesses. With truth as the goal, journalists can be honest about the personal values they bring to their work. When the goal is to find truth, values become secondary. In fact, journalists with different values can all have the same goal: truth.

Both the U.S. and European models of news are fact-driven and committed to accuracy. The Europeans argue, however, that facts yield truth only when sorted through and subjected to analysis. *Truth,* a word for broad understanding, does not result automatically from an array of facts or quotes from shouting partisans. In short, the Europeans caution, don't confuse facts and factual accuracy with *truth,* which is broader and more important.

Personal Values in News

studypreview **Journalists make important decisions on which events, phenomena and issues are reported and which are not. The personal values journalists bring to their work and that therefore determine which stories are told, and also how they are told, generally coincide with mainstream American values.**

Role of the Journalist

Even with the values-free pretext under which most U.S. journalism functions, values cannot be wished out of existence. The fact is that journalists make choices. NBC newscaster Chet Huntley, after years of trying to come up with a definition of news, threw up his hands and declared: "News is what I decide is news." Huntley wasn't being arrogant. Rather, he was pointing out that there are no clinical criteria for news that sidestep human judgment on what to put in the paper or on the air. Even if an event has intrinsic qualities as news, such as the prominence of the people involved and the event's consequence and drama, it becomes news only when it's reported. Huntley's point was that the journalist's judgment is indispensable in deciding what is news.

Huntley's conclusion underscores the high degree of autonomy that individual journalists have in shaping what is reported. Even a reporter hired fresh out of college by a small daily newspaper and assigned to city hall has a great deal of independence in deciding what to report and how to report it. Such trust is unheard of in most other fields, which dole out responsibility to newcomers in small bits over a lengthy period. Of course,

truth ■ A broad and accurate understanding.

rookie journalists are monitored by their newsroom supervisors, and editors give them assignments and review their stories, but it is the city hall reporter, no matter how green, who is the news organization's expert on city government.

The First Amendment guarantee of a free press also contributes to the independence and autonomy that characterize news work. Journalists know that they have a high level of constitutional protection in deciding what to report as news. While most reporters will agree on the newsworthiness of some events and issues, such as a catastrophic storm or a tax proposal, their judgments will result in stories that take different slants and angles. On events and issues whose newsworthiness is less obvious, reporters will differ even on whether to do a story.

mediaPEOPLE

Ida Wells-Barnett

Ida Wells bought a first-class ticket for a car at the front of the train, but when the conductor saw she was black, he told her to go to the rear. First-class, he said, was "set apart for white ladies and gentlemen." Wells, a small, sturdy woman, refused. The conductor, who was white, threw her off the train. Wells sued, citing various constitutional guarantees, and won before a Memphis jury. The Tennessee Supreme Court, however, said she was harassing the railroad and overturned the jury verdict.

Social Justice Crusader When she was 21, Ida Wells sued a railroad for throwing her out of a whites-only car. Learning the power of journalism, she went on to a distinguished career as a crusader for racial justice, in particular against the growing 1890s practice of lynching.

The case, in 1885, was among the first involving racial equality in public transportation. The attention her case received made it clear to Wells, a 21-year-old schoolteacher, that the press could be a powerful vehicle to bring about change. She bought into a small weekly newspaper, the *Free Speech,* and began crusading for better schools for black children. The school board, embarrassed, fired her. So she went into journalism full time as editor of her newspaper.

In 1892 a mob lynched three black grocers whose store had been successful against white competitors. Wells pulled out all the stops in her coverage, reporting the details that led to the lynchings and denouncing the community for condoning what had happened. It was thorough, courageous reporting, and it received wide attention. Soon Wells was writing for the New York *Age,* with her articles a fixture in almost all of the nation's 400 black newspapers. She continued her work on lynchings as mob vigilantism, amassing data that they were becoming more common. In 1892 she counted 2,565—triple the number 10 years earlier. She urged black readers to arm themselves for self-protection: "A Winchester rifle should have a place of honor in every home." Her office was attacked.

To continue her crusade, Wells went to England, beyond the mobs' reach, to rail against U.S. racial injustice, including lynchings of black men, on every forum she could find. Her book, *A Red Record,* contained alarming statistics on U.S. lynchings. By now an internationally recognized figure, Wells felt relatively safe to return to the United States on the lecture circuit with the press sure to follow her every word. States began prosecutions for lynchings, and the number declined. Memphis had none for 25 years.

Wells eventually settled in Chicago, where she continued her journalistic crusade for racial justice and other reforms, including women's rights. In fearless pursuit of facts, she went alone to lynchings and riots. Her factual reports, published widely, provided indisputable evidence of injustice and persecution and built general sympathy for both law enforcement and for legislation to correct social wrongs.

Journalists' Personal Values

The journalistic ideal, an unbiased seeking of truth and an unvarnished telling of it, dictates that the work be done without partisanship. Yet as human beings, journalists have personal values that influence all that they do, including their work. Because the news judgment decisions that journalists make are so important to an informed citizenry, we need to know what makes these people tick. Are they left-wingers? Are they ideological zealots? Are they quirky and unpredictable? Are they conscientious?

A sociologist who studied stories in the American news media for 20 years, **Herbert Gans** concluded that journalists have a typical American value system. Gans identified primary values, all in the American mainstream, that journalists use in making their news judgments:

Ethnocentrism American journalists see things through American eyes, which colors news coverage. In the 1960s and 1970s, Gans notes, North Vietnam was consistently characterized as "the enemy." U.S. reporters took the view of the U.S. government and military, which was hardly detached or neutral. This **ethnocentrism** was clear at the end of the war, which U.S. media headlined as "the *fall* of South Vietnam." By other values, Gans said, the communist takeover of Saigon could be considered a *liberation*. In neutral terms, it was a *change in government*.

This ethnocentrism creates problems as the news media become more global. In the 2003 Iraq war, news reporters embedded with U.S. units advancing toward Iraq used the term "the enemy" for Iraqi resistance, which was hardly neutral considering that many Iraqis regarded the invading army as the enemy. It is hard for all people, including journalists, to transcend their own skins.

Commitment to Democracy and Capitalism Gans found that U.S. journalists favor U.S. style democracy. Coverage of other governmental forms dwells on corruption, conflict, protest and bureaucratic malfunction. The unstated idea of most U.S. journalists, said Gans, is that other societies do best when they follow the American ideal of serving the public interest.

Gans also found that U.S. journalists are committed to the capitalist economic system. When they report corruption and misbehavior in U.S. business, journalists treat them as aberrations. The underlying posture of the news coverage of the U.S. economy, Gans said, is "an optimistic faith" that businesspeople refrain from unreasonable profits and gross exploitation of workers or customers while competing to create increased prosperity for all. In covering controlled foreign economies, U.S. journalists emphasize the downside.

It may seem only natural to most Americans that democracy and capitalism should be core values of any reasonable human being. This sense itself is an ethnocentric value, which many people do not even think about but which nonetheless shapes how they conduct their lives. Knowing that U.S. journalists by and large share this value explains a lot about the news coverage they create.

Small-Town Pastoralism Like most of their fellow citizens, U.S. journalists romanticize rural life. Given similar stories from metropolitan Portland and tiny Sweet Home, Oregon, editors usually opt for the small town.

Cities are covered as places with problems; rural life is celebrated. Suburbs are largely ignored. Gans' understanding of small-town pastoralism helped explain the success of the late Charles Kuralt's *On the Road* series on CBS television.

Individualism Tempered by Moderation Gans found that U.S. journalists love stories about rugged individuals who overcome adversity and defeat powerful forces. This is a value that contributes to a negative coverage of technology as something to be feared because it can stifle individuality. Gans again cited the long-running CBS series *On the Road*, in which Charles Kuralt presented pastoral features on rugged individuals. Today the *Everybody Has a Story* series by Steve Hartman serves the same role at CBS.

Herbert Gans ■ Concluded that journalists have mainstream values.

ethnocentrism ■ Seeing things on the basis of personal experience, values.

Everybody Has a Story Giving ordinary Americans the chance to tell their story. **www.cbsnews.com/sections/hartman/main500155.shtml**

Journalists like to turn ordinary individuals into heroes, but there are limits. Rebels and deviates are portrayed as extremists who go beyond another value: moderation. To illustrate this bias toward moderation, Gans noted that "the news treats atheists as extremists and uses the same approach, if more gingerly, with religious fanatics. People who consume conspicuously are criticized, but so are people such as hippies who turn their backs on consumer goods. The news is scornful both of the overly academic scholar and the oversimplifying popularizer; it is kind neither to high-brows nor to low-brows, to users of jargon or users of slang. College students who play when they should study receive disapproval, but so do 'grinds.' Lack of moderation is wrong, whether it involves excesses or abstention."

In politics, Gans says, both ideologues and politicians who lack ideology are treated with suspicion: "Political candidates who talk openly about issues may be described as dull; those who avoid issues entirely evoke doubts about their fitness for office."

Social Order Journalists cover disorder—earthquakes, hurricanes, industrial catastrophes, protest marches, the disintegrating nuclear family and transgressions of laws and mores. This coverage, noted Gans, is concerned not with glamorizing disorder but with finding ways to restore order. Coverage of a hurricane, for example, lasts not much longer than the storm, but coverage of the recovery goes on for days. The media focus is far more on restoring order than on covering death and destruction.

The journalistic commitment to social order also is evident in how heavily reporters rely on people in leadership roles as primary sources of information. These leaders, largely representing the Establishment and the status quo, are the people in the best position to maintain social order and to restore it if there's a disruption. This means government representatives often shape news media reports and thus their audiences' understanding of what is important, "true" or meaningful. No one receives more media attention than the president of the United States, who is seen, said Gans, "as the ultimate protector of order."

Journalistic Bias

Critics of the news media come in many flavors. Conservatives are the most vocal, charging that the media slant news to favor Democrats and liberal causes. Numerous studies, some shoddily partisan, others not, fuel the conservatives' accusations. Althought his work is dated, Ken Walsh of *U.S. News & World Report* is often quoted for a survey that found 50 White House correspondents had voted Democratic and only seven Republican in 1996. To be sure, some news organizations offer partisan spin, for years most notably the Washington *Times.* More recently Fox News took a lesson from the most successful talk-radio shows and intentionally positioned itself to appeal to right-wing viewers.

In general, though, most U.S. newsroom pride themselves on neutral presentation and go to extraordinary lengths to prove it. To avoid confusion between straight news and commentary, newspaper opinion pieces are set apart in clearly labeled editorial sections. Broadcast commentaries are also flagged.

Professional Standards Most news reporters, even those with left or right leanings, profess a zealous regard for detached, neutral reporting. In the United States this is the journalistic creed, embodied in every professional code of ethics. Almost all reporters see their truth-seeking as unfettered by partisanship. In self-flagellating postmortems, they are the first to criticize lapses.

Editors and news directors say they have no political litmus test in hiring reporters. They recruit reporters for their skills and intelligence, not their politics. Joe strupp, who interviewed dozens of editors for the trade journal *Editor & Publisher,* found that editors rely on peer dynamics in the newsroom to keep the focus on complete and thorough reporting, which trumps any ideological bent. At the San Diego *Union-Tribune,* editor

Karin Winter said: "We know how to turn off our affiliation when we walk through the door. It does not come up."

The editing process, an elaborate king of peer review to which virtually all stories are subjected, also works against bias in coverage. Reporters know that the final word on their copy rests with editors, who recognize the main product a newsroom has to offer the audience is accurate, truthful and believable reporting. The media have an economic incentive to tell news straight. Bruce Bartlett of the National Center for Policy Analysis noted that people will cancel their subscriptions if they perceive "liberal claptrap."

National Public Radio Audience

Since its launch in the 1970s, National Public Radio has been accused of leaning to the left politically. True? Not if you judge by the audience, which is usually an indicator because people are attracted to media messages that echo their own views. A study commissioned by NPR asked its listeners to identify themselves politically:

Conservative or very conservative	29 percent
Middle-of-the-road	30 percent
Liberal or very liberal	31 percent

News as Change If the news media indeed are obsessed with avoiding partisan reporting, how do the charges of bias retain currency? A historical reality in the bipolar U.S. political tradition is that the extremes have been conservatives, who by and large prefer things as they are, and liberals, who seek reform and change. Critics who paint the news media as liberal usually are forgetting that news, by its nature, is concerned with change. Everybody, journalists and news media consumers alike, is more interested in a volcano that is blowing its top than in a dormant peak. People are interested congenitally in what is happening, as opposed to what is not happening. Friends don't greet each other: "Hey, what's not new?" News stories on Krakotoa in 1883 hardly meant that journalists favor volcanic eruptions. The fact is that change is more interesting than the status quo, although usually less comforting and sometimes threatening. News is about change—proposed, pending and occurring. And change is not what political conservatism is about.

When journalists write about a presidential candidate's ideas to, for example, eliminate farm subsidies, it's not that journalists favor the proposed change. Rather, it's that the topic is more interesting than stories about government programs that are in place, functioning routinely and unchallenged. In short, to conclude that journalists' concern with change is necessarily born of political bias is to overlook the nature of journalism—and also the natural human interest in what's new.

media ONLINE **National Public Radio** Noncommercial news and entertainment presumed to be from the Left.
www.npr.org

Accuracy in Media View of the news from the Right.
www.aim.org

Watchdog Function Some accusations of journalistic bias originate in confusion between message and messenger. Incumbent office-holders often are quick to blame the media when news is less than hunky-dory. The classic case was in 1968 when the White House was beset unfavorable news. Vice President Spiro Agnew, addicted as he was to fanciful alliteration, called the press "nagging nabobs of negativism." Successive presidential administrations, Democratic and Republican, have been no less gentle in charging the media with bias when news is less than flattering.

The news media frequently are whipping boys for performing their constitutionally implied **watchdog function.** Since the founding of the Republic, journalists have been expected to keep government honest and responsive to the electorate by reporting on its activities, especially shortcomings. Unless the people have full reports, they cannot intelligently discuss public issues, let alone vote knowledgeably on whether to keep or replace their representatives.

This is not to suggest that journalists are perfect or always accurate, especially in confusing situations against deadline. Nor is it to suggest that there are no partisans peppered among reporters in the press corps. But critics, usually themselves partisans, too often

watchdog function ■ The news media role to monitor the performance of government and other institutions of society.

are reflexive with a cheap charge of bias when reporters are, as one wag put it, doing their job to keep the rascals in power honest. In the process of doing their work, journalists sometimes indeed become facilitators of change—but as reporters, not advocates.

Variables Affecting News

studypreview **The variables that determine what is reported include things beyond a journalist's control, such as how much space or time is available to tell stories. Also, a story that might receive top billing on a slow news day might not even appear on a day when an overwhelming number of major stories are breaking.**

News Hole

A variable affecting what ends up being reported as news is called the **news hole.** In newspapers the news hole is the space left after the advertising department has placed all the ads it has sold in the paper. The volume of advertising determines the number of total pages, and generally, the bigger the issue, the more room for news. Newspaper editors can squeeze fewer stories into a thin Monday issue than a fat Wednesday issue.

In broadcasting, the news hole tends to be more consistent. A 30-minute television newscast may have room for only 23 minutes of news, but the format doesn't vary. When the advertising department doesn't sell all the seven minutes available for advertising, it usually is public-service announcements, promotional messages and program notes—not news—that pick up the slack. Even so, the news hole can vary in broadcasting. A 10-minute newscast can accommodate more stories than a 5-minute newscast, and, as with newspapers, it is the judgment of journalists that determines which events make it.

News Flow and News Staffing

Besides the news hole, the **flow** varies from day to day. A story that might be played prominently on a slow news day can be passed over entirely in the competition for space on a heavy news day.

On one of the heaviest news days of all time—June 4, 1989—death claimed Iran's Ayatollah Khomeini, a central figure in U.S. foreign policy; Chinese young people and the government were locked in a showdown in Tiananmen Square; the Polish people were voting to reject their one-party communist political system; and a revolt was under way in the Soviet republic of Uzbekistan. That was a heavy news day, and the flow of major nation-rattling events preempted many stories that otherwise would have been considered news. Heavy news days cannot be predicted. One would have occurred if there had been a confluence on a single day of these 2005 events: Hurricane Katrina, the Samuel Alito nomination to the U.S. Supreme Court, the 2,000th U.S. combat death in Iraq, the Michael Jackson acquittal and the Afghanistan-Pakistan earthquake.

Staffing affects news coverage, for example, whether reporters are in the right place at the right time. A newsworthy event in Nigeria will receive short shrift on U.S. television if the network correspondents for Africa are occupied with a natural disaster in next-door Cameroon. A radio station's city government coverage will slip when the city hall reporter is on vacation or if the station can't afford a regular reporter at city hall.

CNN Money Everything financial and more.
http://money.cnn.com

Wall Street Journal Full of business news and features. Requires a subscription to get more than news briefs.
http://online.wsj.com

MTV Listen to music, watch videos, read up on music news or shop until you drop on this dynamic site.
www.mtv.com

news hole ■ Space for news in a newspaper after ads are inserted; time in a newscast for news after ads.

flow ■ Significance of events worth covering varies from day to day.

staffing ■ Available staff resources to cover news.

Perceptions About Audience

How a news organization perceives its audience affects news coverage. The *National Enquirer* lavishes attention on unproven cancer cures that the New York *Times* treats briefly if at all. The *Wall Street Journal* sees its purpose as news for readers who have special interests in finance, the economy and business. The Bloomberg cable network was established to serve an audience more interested in quick market updates, brief analysis and trendy consumer news than the kind of depth offered by the *Journal*.

The perception that a news organization has of its audience is evident in a comparison of stories on different networks' newscasts. CNN may lead newscasts with a coup d'état in another country, while Bloomberg leads with a new government economic forecast and MTV with the announcement of a rock group's tour.

Availability of Material

The availability of photographs and video also is a factor in what ends up being news. Television is often faulted for overplaying visually titillating stories, such as fires, and underplaying or ignoring more significant stories that are not photogenic. Newspapers and magazines also are partial to stories with strong accompanying visuals, as was shown in an especially poignant way in 1976 when a Boston woman and child sought refuge on their apartment's balcony when the building caught fire. Then the balcony collapsed, and the two fell. The woman died on impact; the child somehow survived. The tragedy was all the more dramatic because it occurred just as firefighters were about to rescue the pair. Most journalists would report such an event, but in this case the coverage was far more extensive than would normally be the case because Stanley Forman of the Boston *Herald-American* had photographed the woman and child plunging to the ground. On its own merits, the event probably would not have been reported beyond Boston, but with Forman's series of dramatic photographs, clicked in quick succession, the story was reported in visual media—newspapers, magazines and television—around the world. Forman won a Pulitzer Prize for the photos.

Radio news people revel in stories when sound is available, which influences what is reported and how. A barnyard interview with the leader of a farmers' organization, with cows snorting in the background, is likelier to make the air than the same leader saying virtually the same thing in the sterile confines of a legislative committee chamber.

Competition

One trigger of adrenaline for journalists is landing a scoop and, conversely, being scooped. Journalism is a competitive business, and the drive to outdo other news organizations keeps news publications and newscasts fresh with new material.

Competition has an unglamorous side. Journalists constantly monitor each other to identify events that they missed and need to catch up on to be competitive. This catch-up aspect of the news business contributes to similarities in coverage, which scholar Leon Sigal calls the **consensible nature of news.** It also is called "pack" and "herd" journalism.

In the final analysis news is the result of journalists scanning their environment and making decisions, first on whether to cover certain events and then on how to cover them. The decisions are made against a backdrop of countless variables, many of them changing during the reporting, writing and editing processes.

Influences on News

study preview **The subtlety of most attempts outside the newsroom to control news coverage makes them difficult to count. Even one is too many. External influence undermines journalists as honest brokers of news and information. Troublesome sources of pressure are advertisers and even media executives and news sources themselves.**

consensible nature of news ■ News organization second-guessing competition in deciding coverage.

Advertiser Influence

Special interests sometimes try to squelch stories or insist on self-serving angles. Usually, these attempts are made quietly, even tacitly, among executives—country-club decision-making. Sometimes the pressure is exerted on media advertising people, who quietly exert influence on the newsroom.

When a Wyoming grocery store was concerned over a warning from a state agency that Bon Vivant vichyssoise was possibly tainted with botulism, the advertising manager at the Laramie *Boomerang,* the only newspaper in town, kept the story out of the paper. A Laramie radio station that aired the story lost the grocery store's advertising.

media ONLINE **Condé Nast Traveler** Find out what kind of news the audience of this magazine gets. **www.concierge.com/cntraveler**

To their credit, most news organizations place allegiance to their audiences ahead of pleasing advertisers, as Terry Berger, president of an advertising agency representing the Brazilian airline Varig, found out from *Condé Nast's Traveler,* a travel magazine. After an article on air pollution in Rio de Janeiro, Berger wrote the magazine, "Is your editorial policy then to see how quickly you can alienate present and potential advertisers and at the same time convince your readers to stick closer to home? I really think that if you continue with this kind of editorial information, you are doing both your readers and your advertisers a disservice. For this kind of information, people read the New York *Times.* I therefore find it necessary to remove *Condé Nast's Traveler* from Varig's media schedule." Unintimidated, the magazine's editor, Harold Evans, did not recant. Not only did Evans print the letter, but he followed with this comment: "Mrs. Berger is, of course, entitled to use her judgment about where she advertises Brazil's national airline. I write not about that narrow commercial issue, but about her assertion that it is a disservice to readers and advertisers for us to print true but unattractive facts when they are relevant. This goes to the heart of the editorial policy of this magazine. . . . We rejoice in the enrichments of travel, but our aim is to give readers the fullest information, frankly and fairly, so they can make their own judgments."

Corporate Policy

No matter how committed journalists may be to truth-seeking and truth-telling, the people in charge have the final word on matters big and small. It is owners, publishers, general managers and their immediate lieutenants who are in charge. Their corporate responsibilities dictate that they are business executives before all else, even if once they were journalists. Executives sometimes make self-serving decisions on coverage that gall the journalists who work for them, but such is how chains of command work.

Lowell Bergman, former executive producer at *60 Minutes,* recalls his days at CBS: "You could not do a story about a supplier or major advertiser. You could try to do it, but you were taking a lot of risks getting close to the limit." At both ABC and CBS, Bergman said, he was told that the networks would not initiate a critical story about the business practices and histories of National Football League team owners. The networks, of course, stood to derive handsome revenue from airing NFL games if they were awarded contracts for play-by-play coverage.

Admonitions not to go near certain stories are not in written policy, although they are real. ABC news people got an unusual overt reminder when Michael Eisner, then chair of Disney, which owns ABC, said in an interview on the NPR program *Fresh Air,* "I would prefer ABC not to cover Disney. I think it's inappropriate." Eisner went on to say that ABC News knew of his preference.

At the time ABC was working on a story about lax hiring screening at Disney World that allowed child molesters onto the payroll. The network decided against airing the story, which detailed an assault on a child at the Disney park.

In fairness it must be said that media owners generally are sensitive to their truth-seeking and truth-telling journalistic responsibilities and assiduously avoid calling the shots on news coverage. Those who answer to a call other than journalistic soundness are within their court-recognized First Amendment rights, which allow media people to exercise their freedom responsibly as well as irresponsibly. Journalists who are bothered by wrongheaded news decisions have three choices: persuade wayward owners of the error of their ways, comply with directives, or quit and go work for a more respectable journalistic organization.

Source Pressure

Journalists sometimes feel external pressure directly. At the courthouse valuable sources turn cold after a story appears that they don't like. A tearful husband begs an editor not to use his wife's name in a story that points to her as a bank embezzler. A bottle of Chivas Regal arrives at Christmas from a sports publicist who says she appreciates excellent coverage over the past year. Most journalists will tell you that their commitment to truth overrides external assaults on their autonomy. Even so, external pressures exist.

The relationship between journalists and publicists can be troublesome. In general, the relationship works well. Publicists want news coverage for their clients and provide information and help reporters to line up interviews. Some publicists, however, are more committed to advancing their clients' interests than to advancing truth, and they work to manipulate journalists into providing coverage that unduly glorifies their clients.

Staging events is a publicity tactic to gain news coverage that a cause would not otherwise attract. Some staged events are obvious hucksterism, such flagpole-sitting stunts by celebrity disk jockeys. Covering such events is usually part of the softer side of news and, in the spirit of fun and games and diversion, is relatively harmless.

Of more serious concern are staged events about which publicists create a mirage of significance to suck journalists and the public into giving more attention than they deserve. For example, consider:

- The false impression created when hundreds of federal workers are released from work for an hour to see an incumbent's campaign speech outside a government office building.
- The contrived photo opportunity at which people, props and lighting are carefully, even meticulously, arranged to create an image on television.
- Stunts that bring attention to a new product and give it an undeserved boost in the marketplace.

Staged events distort a balanced journalistic portrayal of the world. Worse, they divert attention from truly significant events.

Confidential Sources

studypreview **Journalists receive story tips all the time, sometimes confidentially. Although usual journalistic practice is to cite sources, some stories based on confidential tips are so vital that reporters decide to tell them and protect their sources' identities. It's a risky practice that raises doubts about a story's credibility, but journalists generally agree that sometimes there is no alternative.**

News on Condition

Reporters like to identify their sources in their stories. That makes the stories more credible. But what is a reporter to do when a source says, "I've got some information for you but only if you won't use my name." The issue becomes critical if a reporter's perception is that the public good would be served by a story.

In the divisive late 1960s in the United States, with many people perplexed by the antiwar and civil rights movements, reporters drew on confidential sources for insightful articles about what was ripping the country apart. In some cases reporters shielded the names of people whom the police were trying to identify for prosecution for acts of violence. Some judges called reporters in and demanded that they divulge their sources or go to jail for contempt of court. Journalists claimed that they were bound by a higher calling, noting that important stories could not be told if their sources couldn't count on being shielded.

Finally, the U.S. Supreme Court weighed in, ruling that journalists "are not exempt from the normal duty of all citizens" to cooperate in criminal investigations. In related cases, however, the Court said that police and the courts should exhaust every other avenue before pressing journalists on their sources. Still, jail can be a reality when journalists try to shield sources if crimes are involved. In a worst-case situation the consensus among journalists is that the right thing to do is go to jail.

Shield Laws

Several states have adopted **shield laws,** which recognized reporter-source confidentiality. A problem with shield laws is that they require government to define who is a journalist. This raises the specter of the government's deciding who is and who is not a journalist, which smacks of authoritarian press licensing and control. As an example, the Ohio shield law protects "bona fide journalists," who are defined as people employed by or connected to newspapers, radio stations, television stations and news services. Not only is it disturbing when government defines who is a journalist in a free society, but such attempts are destined to fail. The Ohio definition, for example, fails to protect freelance journalists and writers who do their work on their own in the hope they will eventually sell it.

shield laws ■ Allow journalists to protect identification of confidential sources.

mediaPEOPLE

Earl Caldwell

In 1969 with the United States roiling in racial unrest and rioting, Earl Caldwell of the New York *Times* spent 14 months cultivating sources within the Black Panthers organization and produced a series of insightful stories on black activism. A federal grand jury in San Francisco, where Caldwell was assigned, was investigating bombings and other violence blamed on the Black Panthers, and Caldwell's stories caught the jury's attention, especially quotations attributed to unnamed Black Panther leaders, such as "We advocate the direct overthrow of the government by ways of force and violence." The grand jury asked to see Caldwell's notebooks, tapes and anything else that could help its investigation. Caldwell defied the subpoena, saying his appearance before the grand jury would interfere with his relationship with his sources. Furthermore, he had promised these sources that he would not identify them. Journalists watching the showdown were mindful of the historical responsibility of the press as an independent watchdog on government. If Caldwell testified, he in effect would become part of the investigative arm of the government. Tension mounted when a federal judge supported the grand jury, noting that all citizens are required to cooperate with criminal investigations and that journalists are no different.

Defying a Subpoena New York *Times* reporter Earl Caldwell faced jail for defying court orders to reveal the sources of his 1970 articles about urban terrorism. Caldwell argued that he had obtained his information on a confidential basis and that he would not break the covenant he had made with his sources.

A federal appeals judge ruled, however, that "the public's First Amendment right to be informed would be jeopardized by requiring a journalist to submit to secret grand jury interrogation." The government, said the judge, could command a journalist to testify only if it demonstrated "a compelling need." Meanwhile, journalists were running the risk of going to jail for contempt of court for refusing to respond to government subpoenas for their testimony, notes and films. In 1972 the U.S. Supreme Court considered the issue and ruled that journalists "are not exempt from the normal duty of all citizens."

case STUDY

Are Journalists Who Publish Classified Information Criminals?

"Leaking is a matter of White House policy to implement an agenda," says Lanny J. Davis, former special counsel to President Clinton. "That has been the case since the founding of the republic."

But the government claimed that leaks in 2006 jeopardized American lives by giving information to terrorists. The controversial leaks were about secret government programs: the National Security Agency's warrantless wiretapping of terrorism suspects' phone calls and the Treasury Department's tracking of their international banking transactions. In April the CIA fired a senior career officer for supposedly disclosing classified information to reporters, information assumed to include material for Pulitzer Prize-winning articles in the Washington *Post* about the agency's secret overseas prisons for terror suspects.

As the CIA conducted internal investigations of the leaks, the Bush administration explored criminal prosecution for both the source and the publisher of classified information. Traditionally, the government has used espionage laws to fight the practice of leaking. In 2000 anti-leak legislation that would have made it a crime for a government official to disclose classified information was vetoed by President Bill Clinton. In 2006 the Bush administration was preparing a crackdown on intelligence leaks to the media and was considering prosecutions in some of the recent cases. Should the administration pursue the matter, "it could gain a tool that would thoroughly alter the balance of power between the government and the press," reported the New York *Times*.

On the other side of the debate, First Amendment supporters said it was no secret to terrorists that the U.S. government keeps tabs on their telephone calls and bank transactions. And, said Chicago *Tribune* columnist Steve Chapman, if leaking the information truly presented a grave danger to the American people, the government could have asked a federal judge to forbid the newspapers to publish. "The government had plenty of advance notice the leaks were coming. Editors at the *Times* and the *Post* both conferred with officials who tried to dissuade them, and the *Times* held off publishing the NSA story for a year."

Bill Keller, executive editor of the New York *Times,* said in an online note to concerned readers that the founding fathers "rejected the idea that it is wise, or patriotic, to always take the president at his word, or to surrender to the government important decisions about what to publish."

Bill Keller The executive editor of the New York *Times* emerges from a hearing at which he defended publishing information on a secret government program. The government, in an antiterrorism project, had been wiretapping citizen phone calls without the usual civil-liberty safeguards of judicial oversight.

When information about the secret prisons was leaked, former CIA director Porter Goss said he hoped that "we will witness a grand jury investigation with reporters present being asked to reveal who is leaking information. I believe the safety of this nation and the people of this country deserve nothing less."

The government classified 15,294,087 documents in 2004. David Wise, who writes about intelligence and secrecy, pointed out that "officials in Washington talk to reporters every day about matters that may, in some government file cabinet, in some agency, somewhere be stamped with a secrecy classification. How would a reporter be expected to know that he or she was a recipient of classified information, and in theory subject to prosecution . . . ?"

WHAT DO YOU THINK?

1. Should the government pursue criminal prosecution of journalists who publish classified information?
2. How would that alter the balance of power between the government and the media?
3. Should the government or the media decide what to publish during wartime?

Parsing Interview Conditions

Confidential information poses many practical problems for journalists, including misunderstandings that can sour sources. To head off confusion, **Alfred Friendly,** managing editor of the Washington *Post* in the 1960s, put labels on interviewing conditions.

On the Record Journalists prefer information **on the record.** Anything said may be attributed to the source by name. Most stories are told this way.

Off the Record Information offered **off the record** may be given so that a reporter will better understand a confusing or dangerous situation. The information is not to be disseminated, even in conversation. Friendly didn't invent the terms "on the record" and "off the record," but he was the first to codify them, as well as other interview ground rules terms.

Background In Washington and state capitals, where politicians and journalists have a special, well-storied relationship, two other conditions besides on and off the record sometimes come into play. When information is on **background,** what is said may be used as long as the source is not identified. In stories background information takes an attributive like this: "A source close to the governor said. . . ."

Deep Background A related category set up by Friendly was **deep background.** The source's information may be used but with no hint as to its source. As a result, the story must stand on the reporter's reputation alone. In Bob Woodward and Carl Bernstein's Watergate reporting on high-level criminality, their deep background source, Deep Throat, was never mentioned. Deep Throat's confirmation of key information gave the reporters confidence to go ahead with information that they had from other sources but that they could not corroborate without Deep Throat.

Gatekeeping

Although individual reporters have lots of independence in determining what to report and how, news work is a team effort. News dispatches and photographs are subject to changes at many points in the communication chain. At these points, called *gates,* **gatekeepers** delete, trim, embellish and otherwise try to improve messages.

Just as a reporter exercises judgment in deciding what to report and how to report it, judgment also is at the heart of the gatekeeping process. Hardly any message, except live reporting, reaches its audience in its original form. Along the path from its originator to the eventual audience, a message is subject to all kinds of deletions, additions and changes of emphasis. With large news organizations this process may involve dozens of editors and other persons.

The gatekeeping process affects all news. A public relations practitioner who doesn't tell the whole story is a gatekeeper. A reporter who emphasizes one aspect of an event and neglects others is a gatekeeper. Even live, on-scene television coverage involves gatekeeping because it's a gatekeeper who decides where to point the camera, and that's a decision that affects the type of information that reaches viewers. The C-SPAN network's live, unedited coverage of Congress, for example, never shows members of Congress sleeping or reading newspapers during debate, even though such happens.

Gatekeeping can be a creative force. Trimming a news story can add potency. A news producer can enhance a reporter's field report with file footage. An editor can call a public relations person for additional detail to illuminate a point in a reporter's story. A newsmagazine's editor can consolidate related stories and add context that makes an important interpretive point.

Most gatekeepers are invisible to the news audience, working behind the scenes and making crucial decisions in near anonymity on how the world will be portrayed in the evening newscast and the next morning's newspaper.

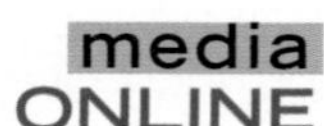

C-SPAN Watch capitol hearings live with streaming video. **www.c-span.org**

You Be the Producer This game from CNN shows you that news producing is not a job for the decision impaired. **www.cnn.com/EVENTS/1996/anniversary/how.things.work/producer.game**

Alfred Friendly ■ Coded conditional interviews as off-record, background, deep background.

on record ■ No restrictions on using information.

off record ■ Absolute embargo on information.

background ■ Information may be used but source may not be identified.

deep background ■ Information cannot be attributed in any way.

gatekeeper ■ Person who decides whether to shorten, drop or change a story en route to the mass audience.

Journalism Trends

study preview **The explosion of 24/7 news on television and the Internet is transforming news-gathering and redefining news practices and audience expectations. Traditional avenues for news, sometimes called mainstream media, were shaken in the 2004 political campaign by individuals, mostly without journalistic training, generally operating alone, who created hundreds of blog sites. Bloggers offer an interconnected web of fascinating reading. Sometimes they score scoops.**

Nonstop Coverage

Reporters for the Associated Press and other news agencies were a breed apart through most of the 20th century. In contrast to most newspaper reporters, who had one deadline a day, agency reporters sent dispatches to hundreds of news organizations, each with its own deadlines. Agency reporters literally had a deadline every minute.

CNN Largest global staff in television reporting. **www.cnn.com**

The advent of all-news radio and then CNN expanded **nonstop coverage** beyond the news agencies. This is no better illustrated than at the White House, where CNN reporters race from an event or interview to a camera for a live stand-up report, often ad-libbing from notes scribbled on the run, and then, adrenaline surging, run back to sources for a new angle or event. This is event-based reporting, which emphasizes timely reports but which has a downside. Going on air a dozen times a day, perhaps more when the news flow is heavy or especially significant, stand-up reporters have scant time to think through implications and context. Theirs is a race to cover events more than to provide understanding. This too was a classic criticism of the news agencies.

The pressures of nonstop coverage have emerged poignantly at National Public Radio, which established its reputation in the 1970s with contemplative and in-depth reporting for its daily flagship, *All Things Considered.* Then NPR added *Morning Edition,* then *Day to Day,* then hourly updates. Reporters were being asked somehow to be contemplative and insightful while also doing endless stand-ups. NPR veteran reporter Nina Totenberg bristled at a planning meeting about her schedule: "If you want me to know anything for me to report, you have to leave me alone a few hours to do it."

In short, nonstop coverage, whatever the advantage of keeping people on top of breaking events, has shortcomings. The pressure for new angles tends to elevate the trivial. Also, context and understanding are sacrificed.

Live News

Over the past 150 years the news media in the United States, elsewhere too, have evolved standard and accepted practices. These practices, taught in journalism schools and institutionalized in codes of ethics, guide reporters and editors in preparing their summaries and wrap-ups. In general the traditional practices worked well when newspapers were the dominant news medium, and they worked well in broadcasting too—until the advent of highly portable, lightweight equipment that enabled broadcasters to carry news events live, bypassing the traditional editing process.

With television cameras focused on the towers of the World Trade Center as they turned into infernos in the 2001 terrorist attack, trapped people began jumping from windows hundreds of feet aboveground. The plunges were desperate and fatal, and audiences viewing the scene live were shocked and horrified. Neither the video nor still photographs were included in most later newscasts or newspapers.

Whatever the virtues of live coverage, a significant downside is that the coverage is raw. Nobody is exercising judgment in deciding what to organize and how to present the material. There is no gatekeeper. Live coverage, of course, obviates the criticism of those who, rightly or wrongly, distrust journalism.

Following live coverage, of course, is time-consuming. Compare, for example, the efficiency of reading or listening to a 60-second report on a congressional hearing or watching the whole four-hour session live.

nonstop coverage ■ News reporting geared to ever-present deadlines, as 24/7 formats.

mediaPEOPLE

Oriana Fallaci

Of necessity, **Oriana Fallaci** grew up fast. A teenager in Mussolini's Italy, she figured out early whose side she was on. She delivered grenades inside cabbage heads for the antifascist resistance. She had a keen sense of who were the good guys and who the bad. Later, as a journalist, she devised interview techniques to smoke them out. She is one of the foremost journalists of our time.

Both intelligent and hardworking, she learns a whole language to conduct interviews in her sources' native tongue. Sometimes she puts six months into preparing for one of her marathon interviews. She flouts danger. In fact, she was shot twice while covering stories in Mexico. She adapts to whatever the situation to get a story.

Although not Muslim, she agreed to wear a Muslim veil, a chador, to interview Iranian leader Ayatollah Khomeini. As an interviewer, she keeps her sights on finding revealing truths about important people through cleverness, disquieting and unexpected questions and persistence.

Those qualities show in Fallaci's famous interview with Ayatollah Khomeini in his Tehran quarters. In deference she wore the chador, which gave her an opportunity for a question that would so unsettle the ayatollah that she learned things no earlier interviewer had about his temper and his temperament. From her own account: "I was wearing the thing, all seven meters of it, pins everywhere, perspiring, and I began to ask him about the chador as a symbol of women's role in Iran." The question penetrated to the core of Khomeini's value system. Off guard, he instantly turned nasty. In a revealing outburst he shouted, "If you don't like the chador, don't wear it, because the chador is for young, proper women!" Insulted, she ripped the veil off: "This is what I do with your stupid medieval rag!" Shocked, the ayatollah shot up and left, with Fallaci calling after him, "Where do you go? Do you go to make pee-pee?" Quick-witted Fallaci's pee-pee after-thought was calculated to elicit further personal revelations, but Khomeini didn't turn around.

Fallaci's detractors see her **caustic interview style** as grand theater. Whatever the criticism, her unconventional approach gives her readers fresh insights into her sources' characters.

Once an interview is under way, Fallaci won't take no for an answer. When Khomeini stomped out, she sat waiting for him to return. Again and again, aides asked her to leave. Finally, Khomeini's son came pleading for her to leave. On his fifth time back, he said Khomeini would see her the next day if she left. By that point, she recalled later, she too needed to pee-pee.

At the appointed hour the next day, Khomeini, faithful to his promise, arrived to continue the interview. And Fallaci, true to her goal, looked him in the eye: "Now Imam, let's start where we left off yesterday. We were talking about my being an indecent woman."

media ONLINE **Investigative Reporters and Editors** Provides educational services to reporters, editors and others interested in investigative journalism. **www.ire.org**

Oriana Fallaci ■ Leading journalistic interviewer.

caustic interview style ■ Adversarial approach to subjects.

blog ■ An amateur web site, generally personal in nature, often focused on a narrow subject, such as politics. Short for "web log."

Unedited Blogs

When *Columbia Journalism Review* created a web site for commentary on reporting of the 2004 presidential campaign, the magazine went out if its way to distance the new site from the thousands of web log sites, called **blogs,** on which amateurs post whatever is on their minds. No, said *CJR,* its campaigndesk.org would be held to the highest journalistic standards. The point was that a lot of irresponsible content gets posted on the web by people without any journalistic training or sense of journalistic standards. The web has made it possible for anyone to create a blog that is as easily accessible as are sites from news organizations that consciously seek to go about journalism right.

No gnashing of teeth, however, will make blogs go away—and their impact is substantial. Blog rumors, gossip and speculation, even when untrue, gain such currency that the mainstream media cannot ignore them. It's become a bronmide, drawn from the tail-wags-dog metaphor, that blogs can wag the media.

Exploratory News

Although in-depth reporting has deep roots, the thrust of U.S. journalism until the 1960s was a chronicling of events: meetings, speeches, crimes, deaths and catastrophes. That changed dramatically in 1972. Two persistent Washington *Post* reporters, **Bob Woodward** and **Carl Bernstein,** not only covered a break-in at the Democratic national headquarters, at a building called the Watergate, but also linked the crime to the White House of Republican President Richard Nixon. The morality questions inherent in the reporting forced Nixon to resign. Twenty-five aides went to jail. The **Watergate** scandal created an enthusiasm for **investigative reporting** and in-depth approaches to news that went far beyond mere chronicling, which is relatively easy to do and, alas, relatively superficial.

Soft News

In contrast to hard investigative reporting came a simultaneous trend toward **soft news.** This included consumer-help stories, lifestyle tips, entertainment news and offbeat gee-whiz items often of a sensational sort. The celebrity-oriented *National Enquirer,* whose circulation skyrocketed in the 1960s, was the progenitor of the trend. Time-Life launched *People* magazine. The staid New York *Times* created *Us.* Newspaper research found that readers liked soft stuff. Soon many dailies added "People" columns. The television show *Entertainment Tonight* focused on glamour and glitz, usually as a lead-in to the evening news on many local stations.

Traditionalists decry the space that soft news takes in many newspapers today, but hard news remains part of the product mix.

media ONLINE

People The latest celebrity news and photos.
http://people.aol.com/people

ET Online Online presence of TV soft news favorite *Entertainment Tonight.*
http://et.tv.yahoo.com

Identifying Good Journalism

study preview **Circulation, ratings, hits and other audience measures are indicators of popularity but not necessarily of quality journalism. News consumers are best guided by criteria such as accuracy, balance and fairness.**

Audience Dimensions

For decades the sensationalizing *National Enquirer* has been the largest-circulation newspaper in the United States. On ABC radio Paul Harvey's entertaining presentation and oddball items drew the medium's largest news audiences. Audience size, of course, is one measure of success, but it's a measure that misses a qualitative question: Is a news product popular because it's good?

For 2.1 million people the *National Enquirer* is good. They keep buying it, every week. Among daily newspapers, the *Wall Street Journal* and *USA Today* are the national circulation leaders—but only with less than half of the *Enquirer*'s circulation. Are they not as good? Is the PBS *Newshour With Jim Lehrer* not as good as the *NBC Nightly News* because its audience is smaller?

The quantitative measures of circulation, reach, penetration, visits and hits, while useful to advertisers, aren't much help for individuals in choosing news sources that meet their needs.

Evaluative Criteria

Rather than following the pack, discerning people develop their own criteria for evaluating news sources. There are no cookie-cutter formulas. One size doesn't fit all. Among criteria to consider:

Accuracy, Balance and Fairness Deadline pressures, at the heart of news reporting, can work against accuracy—and balance and fairness take time. Some errors are

Bob Woodward ■ Bernstein's colleague in the Watergate revelations.

Carl Bernstein ■ Washington *Post* reporter who dug up Watergate.

Watergate ■ Reporting of the Nixon administration scandal.

investigative reporting ■ Enterprise reporting that reveals new information, often startling; most often these are stories that official sources would rather not have told.

soft news ■ Geared to satisfying audience's information wants, not needs.

FAIR Fairness and Accuracy in Reporting.
www.fair.org

Journalism.org Online home of the Project for Excellence in Journalism.
www.journalism.org

forgivable, like those that occur in reporting an airliner hijacking, with all the attendant confusion. Unforgivable are doctored quotes, out-of-context data and slanted editing. The triad of accuracy, balance and fairness comprise a reasonable expectation for news media performance.

Interpretation Are journalists trying to help the audience make sense of what's happening? This interpretive aspect of journalism is tricky because a journalist's individual values are an underlying factor that, by their nature, aren't shared by everyone. The challenge for news consumers is to identify journalists whose judgment they trust to sort through information and present it in a meaningful context.

Original Content News organizations package information from many sources. So much information is available from so many places that some newsrooms, especially in network radio, do nothing more than packaging. They hardly ever send a reporter out on the street, let alone to a war zone. A news organization deserves points for generating its own on-scene reporting. In television news, CNN maintains the largest global staff, which means it draws less than its competitors on news agency reports, pool video and government news releases. CNN has a depth of exclusive material from correspondents and technicians in more places on the globe than any other television news organization.

CHAPTER 10 Wrap-Up

Journalism is an art, not a science. Judgments, rather than formulas, determine which events and issues are reported and how—and no two journalists approach any story exactly the same way. This leaves the whole process of gathering and telling news subject to second-guessing and criticism. Journalists ask themselves all the time whether there are ways to do a better job. All journalists can do is try to find truth and to relate it accurately. Even then, the complexity of modern news-gathering—which involves many people, each with an opportunity to change or even kill a story—includes dozens of points at which inaccuracy and imprecision can creep into a story that started out well.

Questions for Review

1. What contemporary news practices are rooted in the colonial, partisan, penny press and yellow periods of U.S. history?
2. What is the core difference between the U.S. and European concepts of news?
3. What variables beyond journalists' control affect news?
4. What pressures from outside the media affect news reporting?
5. What responsibilities do journalists have as gatekeepers?
6. Is there a contradiction between the two contemporary journalistic trends of exploratory reporting and soft news.
7. What is the downside of a ban on confidential sources in news?

Questions for Critical Thinking

1. The 19-year-old son of the premier of a troubled Central American country in which the CIA has deep involvement died, perhaps of a drug overdose, aboard a Northwest Airlines plane en route from Tokyo to Singapore. On the plane was a young female country-western singer, his frequent companion in recent weeks. The plane was a Boeing 747 manufactured in Washington state. Northwest's corporate headquarters is in Minnesota. The death occurred at 4 a.m. Eastern time. Consider the six elements of news—proximity, prominence, timeliness, consequence, currency and drama—and discuss how this event might be reported on morning television newscasts in Miami, Minneapolis, Nashville, Seattle and the District of Columbia. How about in Managua? Singapore? Tokyo? Rome? Istanbul? Johannesburg? What if the victim were an ordinary college student? What if the death occurred a week ago?
2. Explain news judgment.
3. How do the news hole and news flow affect what is reported in the news media?
4. *Time* and *Newsweek* carry cover stories on the same subject one week. Does this indicate that executives of the magazine have conspired, or is it more likely to be

caused by what Leon Sigal calls *the consensible nature of news*?
5. How does the nature of news provide ammunition to conservatives to criticize the news media as leftist promoters of change?
6. Discuss whether the U.S. news media reflect mainstream American values. Do you see evidence in your news media of an underlying belief that democracy, capitalism, rural small-town life, individualism and moderation are virtues?
7. Do you feel that the mass media revel in disorder? Consider Herbert Gans's view that the media cover disorder from the perspective of identifying ways to restore order.
8. If a college president calls a news conference and makes a major announcement, who are the gatekeepers who determine how the announcement is covered in the campus newspaper?

Keeping Up to Date

Among publications that keep current on journalistic issues are *Columbia Journalism Review, Quill, American Journalism Review,* and *Editor & Publisher.*

Bridging the gap between scholarly and professional work is *Newspaper Research Journal.*

Deepening Your media LITERACY

How important is freedom of the press to you?

STEP 1 Write down your definition of freedom of the press.

Dig Deeper

STEP 2 Imagine that you are a blogger covering the White House and you have uncovered a scandal. Compare how you would cover it with freedom of the press and how that would change without freedom of the press.

What Do You think?

STEP 3 Answer these questions:
1. If you exercise freedom of the press irresponsibly, should your right be revoked?
2. How important is editorial independence to freedom of the press?
3. Do you think freedom of the press and the First Amendment to the U.S. Constitution are important to you and your life as an American? Are they more important to a student, to a parent, to a businessperson, to a journalist, to a politician, to a religious person, to a person who belongs to a minority?
4. How would your life change without freedom of the press?

For Further Learning

Karenna Gore Schiff. *Lighting the Way: Nine Women Who Changed Modern America*. Miramax, 2006.

Schiff, a journalist-lawyer, includes crusaders Ida Wells-Barnett and Mother Jones.

David Walkis, editor. *Killed: Great Journalism Too Hot to Print.* Nation, 2004.

Wallis has compiled great magazine articles that never made it to print, mostly to avoid litigation or not to offend advertisers or the editors' sensitivities. Among the stricken are works by literateurs Betty Friedan, George Orwell and Terry Southern.

"Brits vs. Yanks: Who Does Journalism Right?" *Columbia Journalism Review* (May/June 2004), pages 44–49.

Is it the Yanks who value objectivity, or the Brits, who value their adversarial role.

Kathleen L. Endress. "Help-Wanted Finale: Editor & Publisher Frames Civil Rights Issue," *Journalism and Mass Communication Quarterly* (Spring 2004), pages 7–21.

Endress, a scholar, offers a case study using framing analysis that supports the generalization that the news media, as economic entities, often serve their economic interest above broader interests. The case involves coverage by a newspaper trade journal when gender-denoting sections for help-wanted advertisements were challenged on civil rights grounds.

Nancy Roberts. *The Press and America: An Interpretive History of the Mass Media,* Eighth edition. Allyn & Bacon, 1997.

Nancy Roberts, of the University of Minnesota, updates Edwin and Michael Emery's encyclopedic chronology of American mass media back to its roots in authoritarian England.

Ben Bradlee. *A Good Life: Newspapering and Other Stories.* Simon & Schuster, 1996.

In this memoir veteran Washington *Post* editor Ben Bradlee, the most visible editor of his generation, takes you on an inside expedition through the Kennedy years, the Pentagon Papers, Watergate and the Janet Cooke scandal.

David H. Weaver and G. Cleveland Wilhoit. *The American Journalist: A Portrait of U.S. News People and Their Work,* Second edition. Indiana University Press, 1991.

This comprehensive profile updates the authors' 1986 work and an earlier 1971 study, which also bears reading: John W. C. Johnstone, Edward J. Slawski and William W. Bowman, *The News People: A Sociological Portrait of American Journalists and Their Work.* University of Illinois Press, 1976.

James L. Crouthamel. *Bennett's New York Herald and the Rise of the Popular Press.* Syracuse University Press, 1989.

Jane T. Harrigan. *Read All About It!: A Day in the Life of a Metropolitan Newspaper.* Globe Pequot Press, 1987.

Harrigan, a journalist, tracks hundreds of newspaper people from 6 a.m. through midnight as they produce an issue of the Boston *Globe.* Along the way she explains how journalists decide which events to report.

Herbert J. Gans. *Deciding What's News: A Study of CBS Evening News, NBC Nightly News, Newsweek and Time.* Pantheon, 1979.

A sociologist examines how the values journalists bring to their work affect the news that is reported.

Bob Woodward and Carl Bernstein, *All the President's Men.* Simon & Schuster, 1974.

Indy 500 Airborne
Granger Whitelaw drops into rocket racer at a media event and photo op.
All the traditional tools of promotion are being used to publicize the new Rocket Racing League.

chapter 11 Public Relations

In this chapter you will learn:

- **Public relations is a persuasive communication tool that uses mass media.**
- **Public relations grew out of public disfavor with big business.**
- **Public relations is an important management tool.**
- **Public relations includes promotion, publicity, lobbying, fund-raising and crisis management.**
- **Public relations usually involves a candid, proactive relationship with mass media.**
- **Public relations organizations are working to improve the image of their craft.**

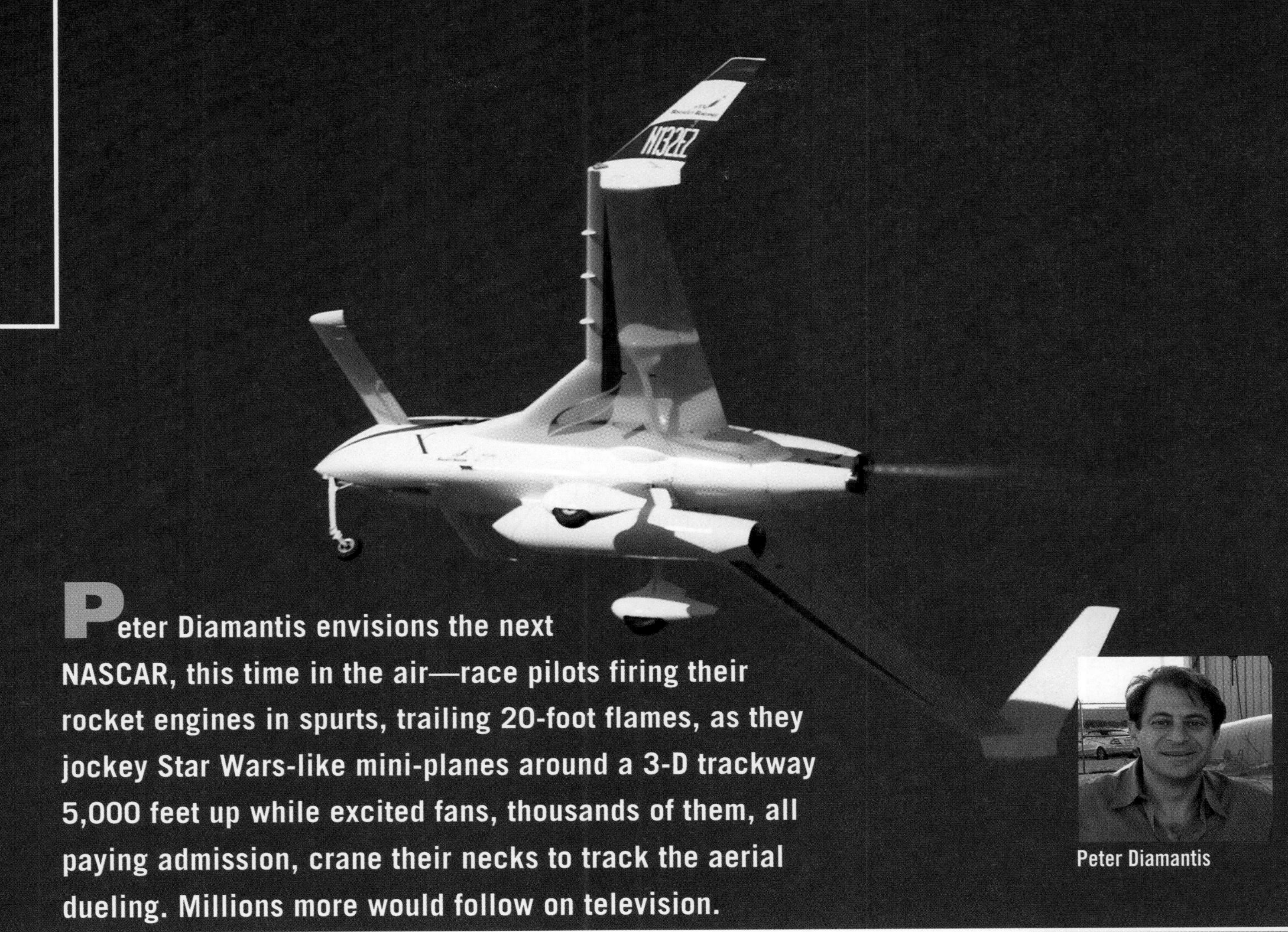

Peter Diamantis envisions the next NASCAR, this time in the air—race pilots firing their rocket engines in spurts, trailing 20-foot flames, as they jockey Star Wars-like mini-planes around a 3-D trackway 5,000 feet up while excited fans, thousands of them, all paying admission, crane their necks to track the aerial dueling. Millions more would follow on television.

Peter Diamantis

Years ago Diamantis, a space-flight enthusiast, founded the $10 million X Prize for suborbital competition. As Diamantis sees it, the next stage for getting the species into space is to spread his excitement at the prospects. What better model than NASCAR, which stirs the adrenalin of millions of people. For his Rocket Racing League, Diamantis faces new financial and technological hurdles. Those he is solving.

He also needs public relations.

The promotion machine is rolling. At a 2005 media event Diamantis unveiled the X-Racer, what he calls the planes, at the league's White Sands spacesport in New Mexico. Space shuttle commander Rick Seafoss was there as chief pilot. In 2006, with four prototype racers, the league took off. The pilots, each with only three minutes of fuel, jockeyed to surpass each other by igniting their engines, then gliding, then restarting over and over again as they roared and soared through virtual tunnels in the sky at 200-plus miles an hour. "It's really the mix of NASCAR excitement and spaceflight," Diamantis said. His enthusiasm and sound bites were perfect. So was partner Granger Whitelaw, an Indianapolis 500 veteran: "It is noth-

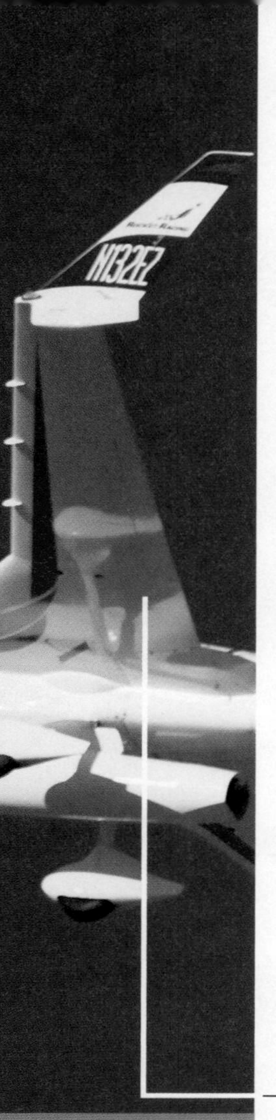

ing like a NASCAR or Indy car—it's 10 times louder." Searfoss was at no loss for sound bites either, calling the crafts "fire-breathing dragons."

In media event after media event, Diamantis and his partners skillfully built enthusiasm for rocket racing. There were demonstrations of the technology. There were attention-getting announcements, like signing Erik Lindbergh, grandson of pioneer aviator Charles Lindbergh, as a Rocket Racing League pilot. Then came the unveiling of handheld global-positioning tracking devices for spectators to add another dimension to their stadium experience. Onboard cameras compound the verisimilitude. No less spectacular were introductions of the satellite-navigation technology to keep planes from colliding, albeit only a few hundred feet apart. Then came the introduction of virtual X-Racing, a video game for fans to race alongside actual flyers during races—all, as Diamantis explained, to engage public interest in human spaceflight.

In many ways Diamantis was his own best promoter, his passion for space travel a consistent theme. The Rocket Racing League, however, was a complex endeavor. Professionals in public relations, who understood how to attract media attention and to craft media messages, were an essential component.

In this chapter you will learn about the practice of public relations, which includes publicity and promotion but also much more, to create support for a wide range of enterprises—and also sometimes to do damage control. With Diamantis the job was easy in some respects because of his genuine enthusiasm for rocket racing as a vehicle to engage public support, especially among young people, for his prime interest—space travel for everyone. The Rocket Racing League, in Diamantis' view, is to speed up aircraft and spacecraft design.

"It's got to be participatory," Diamantis said. "It's about bringing 21st-century racing into people's living rooms."

media ONLINE **X Prize** Tap into our competitive spirits. **www.xprizefoundation.com**

Importance of Public Relations

study preview **Public relations is a persuasive communication tool that people can use to motivate other people and institutions to help them achieve their goals.**

Defining Public Relations

Edward Bernays, the public relations pioneer, lamented how loosely the term **public relations** is used. To illustrate his concern, Bernays told about a young woman who approached him for career advice. He asked her what she did for a living. "I'm in public relations," she said. He pressed her for details, and she explained that she handed out circulars in Harvard Square. Bernays was dismayed at how casually people regard the work of public relations. There are receptionists and secretaries who list public relations on their résumés. To some people, public relations is glad-handing, back-slapping and smiling prettily to make people feel good. Public relations, however, goes far beyond good interpersonal skills. A useful definition is that public relations is a management tool for leaders in business, government and other institutions to establish beneficial *relationships* with other institutions and groups. Four steps are necessary for public relations to accomplish its goals:

public relations ■ A management tool to establish beneficial relationships.

Identify Existing Relationships In modern society institutions have many relationships. A college, for example, has relationships with its students, its faculty, its staff, its alumni, its benefactors, the neighborhood, the community, the legislature, other colleges, accreditors of its programs, perhaps unions. The list could go on and on. Each of these constituencies is called a public—hence the term *public relations*.

Evaluate the Relationships Through research, the public relations practitioner studies these relationships to determine how well they are working. This evaluation is an ongoing process. A college may have excellent relations with the legislature one year and win major appropriations, but after a scandal related to the president's budget the next year, legislators may be downright unfriendly.

Design Policies to Improve the Relationships The job of public relations people is to recommend policies to top management to make these relationships work better, not only for the organization but also for the partners in each relationship. **Paul Garrett,** a pioneer in corporate relations, found that General Motors was seen in unfriendly terms during the Great Depression, which put the giant auto maker at risk with many publics, including its own employees. GM, he advised, needed new policies to seem neighborly—rather than as a far-removed, impersonal, monolithic industrial giant.

Implement the Policies Garrett used the term **enlightened self-interest** for his series of policies intended to downsize GM in the eyes of many of the company's publics. Garrett set up municipal programs in towns with GM plants and grants for schools and scholarships for employees' children. General Motors benefited from a revised image, and in the spirit of enlightened self-interest, so did GM employees, their children and their communities.

Public relations is not a mass medium itself, but PR often uses the media as tools to accomplish its goals. To announce GM's initiatives to change its image in the 1930s, Paul Garrett issued news releases that he hoped newspapers, magazines and radio stations would pick up. The number of people in most of the publics with which public relations practitioners need to communicate is so large that it can be reached only through the mass media. The influence of public relations on the news media is extensive. Half of the news in many newspapers originates with formal statements or news releases from organizations that want something in the paper. It is the same with radio and television.

Public Relations in a Democracy

Misconceptions about public relations include the idea that it is a one-way street for institutions and individuals to communicate to the public. Actually, the good practice of public relations seeks two-way communication between and among all the people and institutions concerned with an issue.

A task force established by the **Public Relations Society of America** to explore the stature and role of the profession concluded that public relations has the potential to improve the functioning of democracy by encouraging the exchange of information and ideas on public issues. The task force made these points:

- Public relations is a means for the public to have its desires and interests felt by the institutions in our society. It interprets and speaks for the public to organizations that otherwise might be unresponsive, and it speaks for those organizations to the public.
- Public relations is a means to achieve mutual adjustments between institutions and groups, establishing smoother relationships that benefit the public.
- Public relations is a safety valve for freedom. By providing means of working out accommodations, it makes arbitrary action or coercion less likely.
- Public relations is an essential element in the communication system that enables individuals to be informed on many aspects of subjects that affect their lives.
- Public relations people can help to activate the social conscience of the organizations for which they work.

Paul Garrett ■ Devised the notion of enlightened self-interest.

enlightened self-interest ■ Mutually beneficial public relations.

Public Relations Society of America ■ Professional public relations association.

media TIMELINE

PUBLIC RELATIONS

1859 Charles Darwin advanced survival-of-the-fittest theory, which led to social Darwinism.

1880s Public became dissatisfied with unconscionable business practices justified with social Darwinism.

1906 Ivy Lee began the first public relations agency.

1917 George Creel headed a federal agency that generated support for World War I.

1927 Arthur Page became the first corporate public relations vice president.

1930s Paul Garrett created the term enlightened self-interest at General Motors.

1942 Elmer Davis headed a federal agency that generated support for World War II.

1951 PRSA adopted an ethics code.

1965 Public Relations Society of America created an accreditation system.

1970s Herb Schmertz pioneered adversarial public relations at Mobil Oil.

Origins of Public Relations

study preview **Many big companies found themselves in disfavor in the late 1800s for ignoring the public good to make profits. Feeling misunderstood, some moguls of industry turned to Ivy Lee, the founder of modern public relations, for counsel on gaining public support.**

Moguls in Trouble

Nobody would be tempted to think of **William Henry Vanderbilt** as good at public relations. In 1882 it was Vanderbilt, president of the New York Central Railroad, who said, "The public be damned," when asked about the effect of changing train schedules. Vanderbilt's utterance so infuriated people that it became a banner in the populist crusade against robber barons and tycoons in the late 1800s. Under populist pressure, state governments set up agencies to regulate railroads. Then the federal government established the Interstate Commerce Commission to control freight and passenger rates. Government began insisting on safety standards. Labor unions formed in the industries with the worst working conditions, safety records and pay. Journalists added pressure with muckraking exposés on excesses in the railroad, coal and oil trusts; on meat-packing industry frauds; and on patent medicines.

The leaders of industry were slow to recognize the effect of populist objections on their practices. They were comfortable with **social Darwinism,** an adaptation of **Charles Darwin**'s survival-of-the-fittest theory. In fact, they thought themselves forward-thinking in applying Darwin's theory to business and social issues. It had been only a few decades earlier, in 1859, that Darwin had laid out his biological theory in *On the Origin of Species by Means of Natural Selection.* To cushion the harshness of social Darwinism, many tycoons espoused paternalism toward those whose "fitness" had not brought them fortune and power. No matter how carefully put, paternalism seemed arrogant to the "less fit."

George Baer, a railroad president, epitomized both social Darwinism and paternalism in commenting on a labor strike: "The rights and interests of the laboring man will be protected and cared for not by labor agitators but by the Christian men to whom God in His infinite wisdom has given the control of the property interests of the country."

William Henry Vanderbilt ■ Embodied the bad corporate images of the 1880s, 1890s with "The public be damned."

social Darwinism ■ Application of Darwin's survival-of-the-fittest theory to society.

Charles Darwin ■ Devised survival-of-the-fittest theory.

Baer was quoted widely, further fueling sentiment against big business. Baer may have been sincere, but his position was read as a cover for excessive business practices by barons who assumed superiority to everyone else.

Meanwhile, social Darwinism came under attack as circuitous reasoning: Economic success accomplished by abusive practices could be used to justify further abusive practices, which would lead to further success. Social Darwinism was a dog-eat-dog outlook that hardly jibed with democratic ideals, especially not as described in the preamble to the U.S. Constitution, which sought to "promote the general welfare, and secure the blessings of liberty" for everyone—not for only the chosen "fittest." Into these tensions at the turn of the century came public relations pioneer Ivy Lee.

The Ideas of Ivy Lee

Coal mine operators, like railroad magnates, were held in the public's contempt at the start of the 1900s. Obsessed with profits, caring little about public sentiment or even the well-being of their employees, mine operators were vulnerable to critics in the growing populist political movement. Mine workers organized, and 150,000 in Pennsylvania went out on strike in 1902, shutting down the anthracite industry and disrupting coal-dependent industries, including the railroads. The mine owners snubbed reporters, which probably contributed to a pro-union slant in many news stories and worsened the owners' public image. Six months into the strike, President Theodore Roosevelt threatened to take over the mines with Army troops. The mine owners settled.

Shaken finally by Roosevelt's threat and recognizing Roosevelt's responsiveness to public opinion, the mine operators began reconsidering how they went about their business. In 1906, with another strike looming, one operator heard about **Ivy Lee,** a young publicist in New York who had new ideas about winning public support. He was hired. In a turnabout in press relations, Lee issued a news release that announced: "The anthracite coal operators, realizing the general public interest in conditions in the mining regions, have arranged to supply the press with all possible information." Then followed a series of releases with information attributed to the mine operators by name—the same people who earlier had preferred anonymity and refused all interview requests. There were no more secret strike strategy meetings. When operators planned a meeting, reporters covering the impending strike were informed. Although reporters were not admitted into the meetings, summaries of the proceedings were given to them immediately afterward. This relative openness eased long-standing hostility toward the operators, and a strike was averted.

Lee's success with the mine operators began a career that rewrote the rules on how corporations deal with their various publics. Among his accomplishments were:

Converting Industry Toward Openness Railroads had notoriously secretive policies not only about their business practices but even about accidents. When the **Pennsylvania Railroad** sought Ivy Lee's counsel, he advised against suppressing news—especially on things that inevitably would leak out anyway. When a train jumped the rails near Gap, Pennsylvania, Lee arranged for a special car to take reporters to the scene and even take pictures. The Pennsylvania line was applauded in the press for the openness, and coverage of the railroad, which had been negative for years, began changing. A "bad press" continued plaguing other railroads that persisted in their secretive tradition.

Turning Negative News into Positive News When the U.S. Senate proposed investigating International Harvester for monopolistic practices, Lee advised the giant farm implement manufacturer against reflexive obstructionism and silence. A statement went out announcing that the company, confident in its business practices, not only welcomed but also would facilitate an investigation. Then began a campaign that pointed out International Harvester's beneficence toward its employees. The campaign also emphasized other upbeat information about the company.

Ivy Lee ■ Laid out fundamentals of public relations.

Pennsylvania Railroad ■ Took Ivy Lee's advice, which favorably changed railroad's approach to public relations.

Ludlow Massacre

Colorado militiamen, called in to augment company guards, opened fire during a 1914 mine labor dispute and killed women and children. Overnight, John D. Rockefeller Jr. became the object of public hatred. It was a Rockefeller company that owned the mine. Even in New York, where Rockefeller lived, there were rallies demanding his head. Public relations pioneer Ivy Lee advised Rockefeller to tour the Ludlow area as soon as tempers cooled to show his sincere concern and to begin work on a labor contract to meet the concerns of miners. Rockefeller ended up a popular character in the Colorado mining camps.

Ivy Lee

Putting Corporate Executives on Display In 1914, when workers at a Colorado mine went on strike, company guards fired machine guns and killed several men. More battling followed, during which two women and 11 children were killed. It was called the **Ludlow Massacre,** and **John D. Rockefeller Jr.,** the chief mine owner, was pilloried for what had happened. Rockefeller was an easy target. Like his father, widely despised for the earlier Standard Oil monopolistic practices, John Jr. tried to keep himself out of the spotlight, but suddenly mobs were protesting at his mansion in New York and calling out, "Shoot him down like a dog." Rockefeller asked Ivy Lee what he should do. Lee began whipping up articles about Rockefeller's human side, his family and his generosity. Then, on Lee's advice, Rockefeller announced that he would visit Colorado to see conditions himself. He spent two weeks talking with miners at work and in their homes and meeting their families. It was a news story that reporters could not resist, and it unveiled Rockefeller as a human being, not a far-removed, callous captain of industry. A myth-shattering episode occurred one evening when Rockefeller, after a brief address to miners and their wives, suggested that the floor be cleared for a dance. Before it was all over, John D. Rockefeller Jr. had danced with almost every miner's wife, and the news stories about the evening did a great deal to mitigate antagonism and distrust toward Rockefeller. Back in New York, with Lee's help, Rockefeller put together a proposal for a grievance procedure, which he asked the Colorado miners to approve. It was ratified overwhelmingly.

Avoiding Puffery and Fluff Ivy Lee came on the scene at a time when many organizations were making extravagant claims about themselves and their products. Circus promoter **P. T. Barnum** made this kind of **puffery** a fine art in the late 1800s, and he had many imitators. It was an age of *puffed-up* advertising claims and fluffy rhetoric. Lee noted, however, that people soon saw through hyperbolic boasts and lost faith in those who made them. In launching his public relations agency in 1906, Lee vowed to be accurate in everything he said and to provide whatever verification anyone requested. This became part of the creed of good practice in public relations, and it remains so today.

Ludlow Massacre ■ Colorado tragedy that Ivy Lee converted into a public relations victory.

John D. Rockefeller Jr. ■ Ivy client who had been the target of public hatred.

P. T. Barnum ■ Known for exaggerated promotion.

puffery ■ Inflated claims.

Public Relations on a New Scale

The potential of public relations to rally support for a cause was demonstrated on a gigantic scale during World War I and again during World War II.

World War I In 1917 President Woodrow Wilson, concerned about widespread antiwar sentiment, asked **George Creel** to head a new government agency whose job was to make the war popular. The Committee on Public Relations, better known as the Creel Committee, cranked out news releases, magazine pieces, posters, even movies. A list of 75,000 local speakers was put together to talk nationwide at school programs, church groups and civic organizations about making the world safe for democracy. More than 15,000 committee articles were printed. Never before had public relations been attempted on such a scale—and it worked. World War I became a popular cause even to the point of inspiring people to buy Liberty Bonds, putting up their own money to finance the war outside the usual taxation apparatus.

World War II When World War II began, an agency akin to the Creel Committee was formed. Veteran journalist **Elmer Davis** was put in charge. The new Office of War Information was public relations on a bigger scale than ever before.

The Creel and Davis committees employed hundreds of people. Davis had 250 employees handling news releases alone. These staff members, mostly young, carried new lessons about public relations into the private sector after the war. These were the people who shaped corporate public relations as we know it today.

George Creel ■ Demonstrated public relations works on a mammoth scale; in World War I.

Elmer Davis ■ Led Office of War Information in World War II.

Lobbyist-Journalist Balance

The rationale for public relations is that everybody, including corporations, should have access to the best counsel available. The best public relations people serve their clients well and honorably, but exceptions abound. In the early 1990s a statehouse reporter for

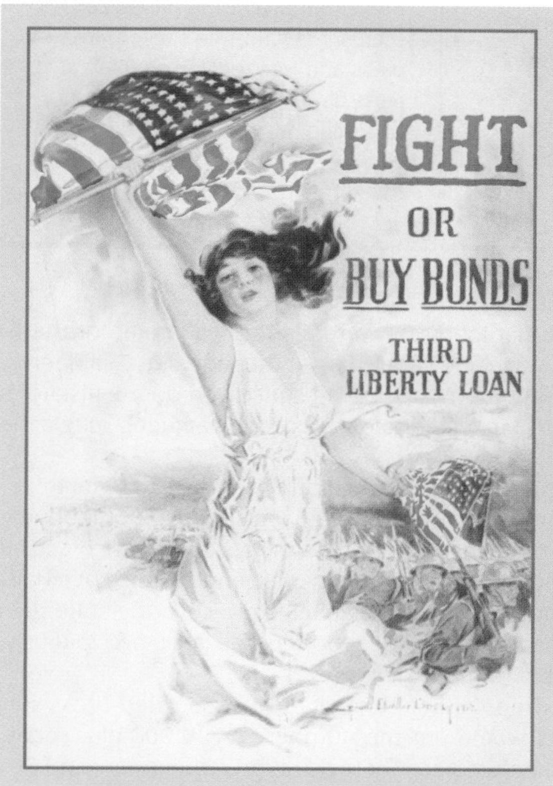

War Popular

World War I did not begin as a popular cause with Americans. There were antidraft riots in many cities. This prompted President Woodrow Wilson to ask journalist George Creel to launch a major campaign to persuade Americans that the war was important to make the world safe for democracy. Within months Americans were financing much of the war voluntarily by buying government bonds. This poster was only one aspect of Creel's work, which demonstrated that public relations principles could be applied on a massive scale.

George Creel

mediaPEOPLE

Paul Garrett

At one of the most precarious times in U.S. history, the Great Depression, Paul Garrett led public relations in new directions to win public support. Amid worries that people—many hungry, all distressed—would see huge corporations as scapegoats and perhaps upend capitalism, Garrett had an unprecedented challenge as General Motors' public relations chief. How precarious was the situation? Sit-down strikes were occurring at GM plants. Discontent was bubbling throughout the country.

Enlightened Self-Interest Paul Garrett, a pioneer in corporate public relations encouraged General Motors to both act in its corporate interest and in the interest of employees and other constituencies. It is possible to serve multiple masters, Garrett said. He called his approach to public relations enlightened self-interest.

Garrett, in the first generation of public relations people who had learned their craft from the government's Creel Committee in World War I, immediately sought to minimize the image of General Motors as some sort of monolithic giant that, being big and distant, was an especially easy target for hate.

To head off problems, Garrett introduced a public strategy: *enlightened self-interest.* It was in GM's self-interest, he argued, to touch the lives of people in personal ways, such as with grants for local schools and scholarships for employees' children. General Motors, of course, nurtured publicity about these corporate good deeds.

Garrett summed it up this way: "The challenge that faces us is to shake off our lethargy and through public relations make the American plan of industry stick. For unless the contributions of the system are explained to consumers in terms of their own interest, the system itself will not stand against the storm of fallacies that rides the air."

Garrett also worked on GM's image at a macro level, aiming for consumers in general to think well of the company. A GM caravan, called the Parade of Progress, traveled from coast to coast in 1936 with a message that new technologies would facilitate progress and social change. In the same spirit, prominent radio announcer Lowell Thomas narrated a feature film, *Previews of Science,* that cast business, big business in particular, in heroic terms. In short, the genius of corporate science and initiative was creating a better tomorrow.

The National Association of Manufacturers caught Garrett's spirit. Garrett worked with the association to tie the public impression of big corporations into warm, albeit fuzzy, notions about Americanism. At a 1939 meeting, the association's public relations division, with Garrett on board, said that its job was to "link free enterprise in the public consciousness with free speech, free press and free religion as integral parts of democracy."

Public relations had become widely embraced as a way to channel the thinking of the country.

---

the Detroit *News,* Jim Mitzelfeld, heard that lobbyists were planning a junket for members of the legislature. Camera in hand, Mitzelfeld showed up at the retreat at Gulf Shores, Alabama, and took pictures of a powerful lobbyist rubbing sunscreen on a legislator's shoulders. "The quintessential lube job," Mitzelfeld told the media watchdog magazine *American Journalism Review.*

Lobbying, as an ethical public relations function, is to offer advice to clients to advance their causes before policymaking bodies such as state legislatures. But lobbying can go too far, as at Gulf Shores. How many inappropriate attempts at influence occur? We'll never know, but indicators are that this is a growing phenomenon in the back halls and fairways of capital cities. Why? Not enough Jim Mitzelfelds are covering state government to catch "lube jobs." The number of statehouse reporters has fallen precipitously, while the number of lobbyists has grown dramatically.

How many lobbyists are there? Extrapolations from a 1990 Associated Press survey of registered state capitol lobbyists would put the number at 120,000-plus today. The figure is probably low because loose enforcement of registration requirements misses lobbyists who never quite get around to registering. At the same time the amount that lobbyists spend is increasing exponentially. Charles Layton and Mary Walton, writing in *American Journalism Review,* said that statehouse lobbying grew from $15 million nationwide in 1986 to $51 million in 1997.

Are journalists like Jim Mitzelfeld looking over the shoulders of lobbyists and legislators to keep things honest? Less and less. Under conglomerate pressure to cut costs, many newspapers have trimmed their statehouse staffs. At Mitzelfeld's Detroit *News,* the full-time staff in Lansing has dropped from six to four. The Detroit *Free Press* and the Lansing *State Journal* have cut full-time staff from three to two. Nationwide, 27 states have fewer reporters covering state government since the early 1990s. The Knight Ridder chain, as an example, cut statehouse coverage 16 percent at its papers.

An important checks-and-balances system is disappearing as the number of lobbyists increases and that of watchdog journalists declines.

Structure of Public Relations

study preview **In developing sound policies, corporations and other institutions depend on public relations experts who are sensitive to the implications of policy on the public consciousness. This makes public relations a vital management function. Besides a role in policymaking, public relations people play key roles in carrying out institutional policy.**

Policy Role of Public Relations

When giant AT&T needed somebody to take over public relations in 1927, the president of the company went to magazine editor **Arthur Page** and offered him a vice presidency. Before accepting, Page laid out several conditions. One was that he have a voice in AT&T policy. Page was hardly on an ego trip. He had seen too many corporations that regarded their public relations arm merely as an executor of policy. Page considered PR itself as a management function. To be effective, Page knew that he must contribute to the making of high-level corporate decisions as well as executing them.

Today, experts on public relations agree with Arthur Page's concept: When institutions are making policy, they need to consider the effects on their many publics. That can be done best when the person in charge of public relations, ideally at the vice presidential level, is intimately involved in decision-making. The public relations executive advises the rest of the institution's leaders on public perceptions and the effects that policy options might have on perceptions. Also, the public relations vice president is in a better position to implement the institution's policy for having been a part of developing it.

How Public Relations Is Organized

No two institutions are organized in precisely the same way. At General Motors 200 people work in public relations. In smaller organizations PR may be one of several hats worn by a single person. Except in the smallest operations, the public relations department usually has three functional areas of responsibility:

External Relations **External public relations** involves communication with groups and people outside the organization, including customers, dealers, suppliers and community leaders. The external relations unit is usually responsible for encouraging employees to participate in civic activities. Other responsibilities include arranging promotional activities like exhibits, trade shows, conferences and tours.

Public relations people also lobby government agencies and legislators on behalf of their organization, keep the organization abreast of government regulations and legis-

media ONLINE

Burson-Marsteller With 24/7 crisis contacts posted on its site, this company works round the clock to protect the reputation of its clients. **www.burson-marsteller.com**

Weber Shandwick Check out the company named 2005 Agency of the Year by *PRWeek*. Weber Shandwick maintains the largest PR network in the world, in terms of number of employees and geographical coverage. **www.webershandwick.com**

Fleishman-Hillard With practice groups ranging from grassroots marketing to homeland security to youth marketing, this international communications firm serves a wide range of clients. **www.fleishman.com**

Edelman Visit the site of the only independent global PR firm. Check out the 6 a.m. blog and get a feel for this free thinking company. **www.edelman.com**

Omnicom Group This strategic holding company for firms specializing in marketing, advertising, communications and media boasts over 5,000 clients worldwide. **www.omnicomgroup.com**

Hill & Knowlton Check out the posted case studies (with real client names) and get a feel for the work this company performs. **www.hillandknowlton.com**

Arthur Page ■ Established the role of public relations as a top management tool.

external public relations ■ Gearing messages to outside organizations, constituencies, individuals.

lation, and coordinate relations with political candidates. This may include fund-raising for candidates and coordinating political action committees.

In hospitals and nonprofit organizations a public relations function may include recruiting and scheduling volunteer workers.

Internal Relations **Internal public relations** involves developing optimal relations with employees, managers, unions, shareholders and other internal groups. In-house newsletters, magazines and brochures are important media for communicating with organizations' internal audiences.

Media Relations Communication with large groups of people outside an organization is practicable only through the mass media. An organization's coordinator of **media relations** responds to news media queries, arranges news conferences and issues news releases. These coordinators coach executives for news interviews and sometimes serve as their organization's spokesperson.

Public Relations Agencies

These are the largest public relations agencies with significant U.S. accounts:

	Global income	Employees worldwide
Edelman	$261 million	1,800
Ruder Finn	92 million	600
Waggener Edstrom	84 million	600
APCO	73 million	400
Text 100	52 million	500
Schwartz	22 million	200
Zeno	20 million	100
Dan Klores	20 million	100
Qorvis	18 million	100
Gibbs & Soell	17 million	100

Public Relations Agencies

Even though many organizations have their own public relations staff, they may go to **public relations agencies** for help on specific projects or problems. In the United States today, hundreds of companies specialize in public relations counsel and related services. It is a big business. Income at global PR agencies like Burson-Marsteller runs about $200 million a year.

The biggest agencies offer a full range of services on a global scale. These agencies will take on projects anywhere in the world, either on their own or by working with local agencies.

Besides full-service agencies, there are specialized public relations companies, which focus on a narrow range of services. For example, clipping services cut out and provide newspaper and magazine articles and radio and television items of interest to clients. Among specialized agencies are those that focus exclusively on political campaigns. Others coach corporate executives for news interviews. Others coordinate trade shows.

Some agencies bill clients only for services rendered. Others charge clients just to be on call. Hill & Knowlton, for example, has a minimum $5,000-a-month retainer fee. Agency expenses for specific projects are billed in addition. Staff time usually is charged at an hourly rate that covers the agency's overhead and allows a profit margin. Other expenses are usually billed with a 15 to 17 percent markup.

Public Relations Services

study preview **Public relations deals with publicity and promotion, but it also involves less visible activities. These include lobbying, fund-raising and crisis management. Public relations is distinct from advertising.**

Activities Beyond Publicity

Full-service public relations agencies provide a wide range of services built on two of the cornerstones of the business: **publicity** and **promotion.** These agencies are ready to conduct media campaigns to rally support for a cause, create an image or turn a problem into an asset. Publicity and promotion, however, are only the most visible services offered by public relations agencies. Others include:

Lobbying Every state capital has hundreds of public relations practitioners whose specialty is representing their clients to legislative bodies and government agencies. In North Dakota, hardly a populous state, more than 300 people are registered as lobbyists in the capital city of Bismarck.

Lobbying has been called a "growth industry." The number of registered lobbyists in Washington, D.C., exceeds 10,000 today. In addition, there are an estimated 20,000 other people in the nation's capital who have slipped through registration requirements but who nonetheless ply the halls of government to plead their clients' interests.

In one sense, lobbyists are expediters. They know local traditions and customs, and they know who is in a position to affect policy. Lobbyists advise their clients, which include trade associations, corporations, public interest groups and regulated utilities and industries, on how to achieve their goals by working with legislators and government regulators. Many lobbyists call themselves "government relations specialists."

The zeal to influence public policy can go too far. In 2005 two prominent Washington lobbyists, Jack Abramoff and Michael Scanlon, both closely tied to the Republican majority in Congress, pleaded guilty to a variety of lobbying excesses. Abramoff had arranged foreign trips and partying for members of Congress and key aides to soften them up for favorable votes on behalf of clients. The money had come from $19 million that six Indian tribes had paid over five years for Abramoff to work his magic on their behalf. Trusting Abramoff was complying with acceptable lobbying practices, the tribes were unaware of what actually was going on. Bribery, of course, is a two-way street, and the news media was full of reports on members of Congress quivering for fear of being implicated publicly and perhaps, like Abramoff and Scanlon, also facing jail time. To the embarrassment of honest practitioners of public relations, Scanlon and Abramoff also had conspired in a self-enriching kickback scheme through inflated billing to the tribes for services that weren't performed.

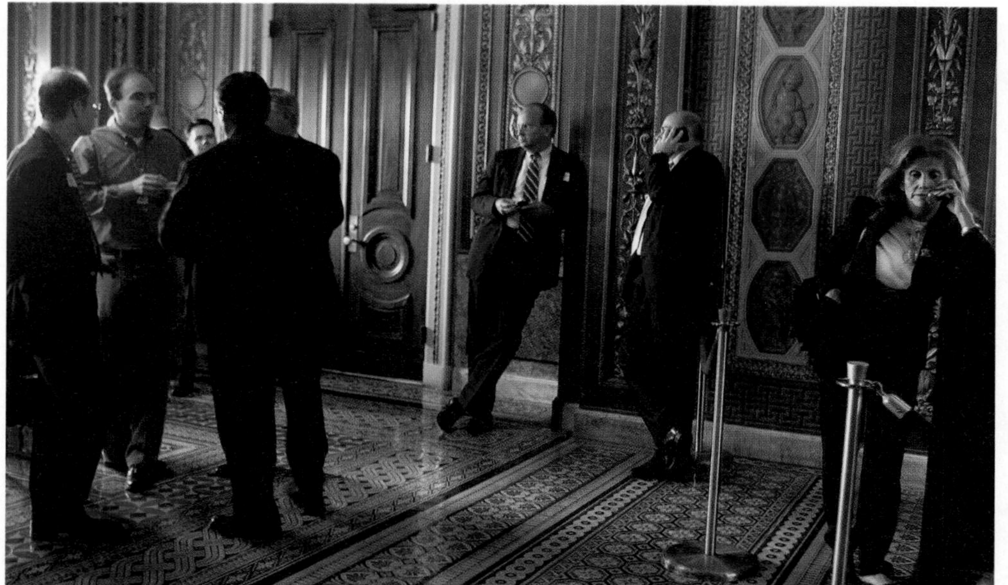

Lobbying Representatives and lobbyists from health-care and insurance concerns join Capitol Hill staffers in the Senate reception room.

media ONLINE

Ketchum Founded in 1923, Ketchum has grown into a full-service public relations firm with offices around the world.
www.ketchum.com

Rowland Check out the colorful, fast-moving site of this international communications firm, whose core competency is corporate reputation.
www.rowland.com

Ogilvy From expert views to case studies to the pressroom, this site gives a thorough look into Ogilvy Public Relations Worldwide.
www.ogilvypr.com

Manning Selvage & Lee What's greater than changing perceptions? Changing minds. Visit this site and read more on the MS&L philosophy of changing minds.
www.mslpr.com

internal public relations ■ Gearing messages to inside groups, constituencies, individuals.

media relations ■ Using mass media to convey messages.

public relations agencies ■ Companies that provide public relations services.

publicity ■ Brings public attention to something.

promotion ■ Promoting a cause, idea.

lobbying ■ Influencing public policy, usually legislation or regulations.

mediaPEOPLE

Jack Abramoff

In college Jack Abramoff was smitten with politics. From his base at Brandeis University, Abramoff rallied Massachusetts college students statewide for Ronald Reagan's presidential bid in 1980. Reagan took the state in an upset. On to Washington, Abramoff rose quickly in the national College Republicans, moving the organization into right-wing activism.

Not all went well. The College Republicans vastly overspent their budget with a poorly conceived direct-mail campaign in 1982. The party elders threw out the free-spending Abramoff. Unsuppressible, Abramoff found a spot running the privately funded Citizens for America, which campaigned for conservative causes. Under the group's banner Abramoff organized some audacious projects. His climactic accomplishment—a convention in a remote part of Angola for a motley bunch of anticommunist guerrillas from disparate Afghanistan, Laos and Nicaragua. The project was costly. The sugar-daddy who financed Citizens for America fired Abramoff for too many liberties with the group's $3 million budget.

In all this, and in a checkered résumé of more Republican-related jobs, mostly in Washington, the young, energetic Abramoff made contacts. His reputation grew rapidly as one of the most influential lobbyists on Capitol Hill and in numerous executive-branch agencies.

By 2000, with Republicans controlling the federal government, Abramoff had amassed the biggest lobbying portfolio in Washington. For the right ambiance to make pitches to members of Congress and top aides and also to acknowledge favors, Abramoff opened two posh restaurants down the street from the Capitol. He bought a fleet of casino boats. He leased four arena and stadium skyboxes. He sponsored golf outings to exclusive St. Andrews in Scotland and to the South Pacific.

The party began imploding in 2003 with revelations by Susan Schmidt of the Washington *Post.* Schmidt tracked $45 million in lobbying fees from Indian tribes that were desperate to protect their casino revenue from possible taxation. There were irregularities galore, including massive overbilling. Abramoff told one aide, for example, to find some way to bill a Choctaw band $150,000 one month: "Be sure we hit the $150k minimum. If you need to add time for me, let me know." The aide responded: "You only had two hours." Abramoff fired back: "Add 60 hours for me."

An avalanche of other revelations followed in what became one of the biggest congressional corruption scandals in history. The scandal was a centerpiece issue in the 2006 elections. Abramoff went to jail. It was not a few members of Congress and their aides who worried about subpoenas for accepting Abramoff's largesse. For lobbyists who conduct themselves honorably, it all was an embarrassing sullying of their craft.

Political Communication Every capital has political consultants whose work is mostly advising candidates for public office in **political communication.** Services include campaign management, survey research, publicity, media relations and image consulting. Political consultants also work on elections, referendums, recalls and other public policy issues.

Image Consulting **Image consulting** has been a growing specialized branch of public relations since the first energy crisis in the 1970s. Oil companies, realizing that their side of the story was not getting across, turned to image consultants to groom corporate spokespersons, often chief executives, to meet reporters one on one and go on talk shows. The groomers did a brisk business, and it paid off in countering the stories and rumors that were blaming the oil companies for skyrocketing fuel prices.

Financial Public Relations Financial public relations dates to the 1920s and 1930s, when the U.S. Securities and Exchange Commission cracked down on abuses in the financial industry. Regulations on promoting sales of securities are complex. It is the job of people in financial PR to know not only the principles of public relations but also the complex regulations governing the promotion of securities in corporate mergers, acquisitions, new issues and stock splits.

political communication ■ Advising candidates, groups on public policy issues, usually in elections.

image consulting ■ Coaching individuals for media contacts.

Fund-Raising Some public relations people specialize in fund-raising and membership drives. Many colleges, for example, have their own staffs to perform these functions. Others look to fund-raising firms to manage capital drives. Such an agency employs a variety of techniques, from mass mailings to telephone soliciting, and charges a percentage of the amount raised.

Contingency Planning Many organizations rely on public relations people to design programs to address problems that can be expected to occur, known as **contingency planning.** Airlines, for example, need detailed plans for handling inevitable plane crashes—situations requiring quick, appropriate responses under tremendous pressure. When a crisis occurs, an organization can turn to public relations people for advice on dealing with it. Some agencies specialize in **crisis management,** which involves picking up the pieces either when a contingency plan fails or when there was no plan to deal with a crisis.

Polling Public-opinion sampling is essential in many public relations projects. Full-service agencies can either conduct surveys themselves or contract with companies that specialize in surveying.

Events Coordination Many public relations people are involved in coordinating a broad range of events, including product announcements, news conferences and convention planning. Some in-house public relations departments and agencies have their own artistic and audio-visual production talent to produce brochures, tapes and other promotional materials. Other agencies contract for these services.

Public Relations and Advertising

Both public relations and advertising involve persuasion through the mass media, but most of the similarities end there.

Management Function Public relations people help to shape an organization's policy. This is a management activity, ideally with the organization's chief public relations person offering counsel to other key policymakers at the vice-presidential level. **Advertising,** in contrast, is not a management function. The work of advertising is much narrower. It focuses on developing persuasive messages, mostly to sell products or services, after all the management decisions have been made.

Measuring Success Public relations "sells" points of view and images. These are intangibles and therefore are hard to measure. In advertising, success is measurable with tangibles, such as sales, that can be calculated from the bottom line.

Control of Messages When an organization decides that it needs a persuasive campaign, there is a choice between public relations and advertising. One advantage of advertising is that the organization controls the message. By buying space or time in the mass media, an organization has the final say on the content of its advertising messages. In public relations, by contrast, an organization tries to influence the media to tell its story a certain way, but the message that actually goes out is up to the media. For example, a news reporter may lean heavily on a public relations person for information about an organization, but the reporter also may gather information from other sources. In the end, it is the reporter who writes the story. The upside of this is that the message, coming from a journalist, has a credibility with the mass audience that advertisements don't. Advertisements are patently self-serving. The downside of leaving it to the media to create the messages that reach the audience is surrendering control over the messages that go to the public.

Integrated Marketing

For many persuasive campaigns, organizations use both public relations and advertising. Increasingly, public relations and advertising people find themselves working to-

contingency planning ■ Developing programs in advance of an unscheduled but anticipated event.

crisis management ■ Helping a client through an emergency.

advertising ■ Unlike public relations, advertising seeks to sell a product or service.

News Release

The workhorse of media relations is the news release, issued to newspapers, broadcast stations and other media to stir reporter interest in covering an event or developing a story or in hope of getting a point of view included in news stories. Studies have found that as many as 90 percent of news stories rely to some extent on information in news releases. Some releases even are reported verbatim, particularly in small-market, low-budget newsrooms.

FOR IMMEDIATE RELEASE

i'm lovin' it

For more information contact:
Walt Riker
630-623-7318
Lisa Howard
630-623-5044

Rashada Jamison
GolinHarris
312-729-4199

McDonald's® Debuts Advertising on the World of Opportunity Under the Golden Arches
New Commercial Shines Spotlight on Power of First Jobs at McDonald's

Chicago, IL – USA (September 21, 2005) – McDonald's today unveiled a new TV commercial that showcases successful individuals whose first jobs were at McDonald's. The *"My First"* spot features people from around the world who started their careers at McDonald's. Among the featured talent at the press conference for the commercial debut were 10-time Olympic track and field medalist Carl Lewis, Canadian fashion photographer Carla LaBrosse, United Kingdom fireman Carl Smeaton, and McDonald's franchisee Leo Lopez from Florida. In addition, A&M recording artist and actress Macy Gray offered her reflections on working her first job at McDonald's in a videotaped message.

The commercial includes crew members from around the world who started at McDonald's, with representation from Australia, Canada, Czech Republic, Germany, Japan, the Netherlands, United Kingdom and the U.S.

The new ad is the latest example of McDonald's ongoing commitment to its people and communicates the many ways McDonald's provides opportunity under the Golden Arches. Opportunity at McDonald's was a key focus of the company's 50th anniversary celebration this past April and is one of McDonald's CEO Jim Skinner's top priorities.

"I worked as a McDonald's crew person and there is so much more to working at McDonald's than people know," said former McDonald's crew member and singer/actress Macy Gray. "The action, the fun, the people, the sense of accomplishment – it truly was My First big break!"

Rich Floersch, McDonald's executive vice president for Human Resources, and Larry Light, McDonald's executive vice president and global chief marketing officer, premiered the commercial during McDonald's Global Human Resources Conference held in Chicago this week and attended by 200 McDonald's HR professionals from 48 countries.

-more-

gether. This is especially true in corporations that have adopted **integrated marketing communication,** which attempts to coordinate advertising as a marketing tool with promotion and publicity of the sort that public relations experts can provide. Several major advertising agencies, aware of their clients' shift to integrated marketing, have acquired or established public relations subsidiaries to provide a wider range of services under their roof.

It is this overlap that has prompted some advertising agencies to move more into public relations. The WWP Group of London, a global advertising agency, has acquired both Hill & Knowlton, the third-largest public relations company in the United States, and the Ogilvy PR Group, the ninth largest. The Young & Rubicam advertising agency has three public relations subsidiaries: Burson-Marsteller, the largest; Cohn & Wolf, the 13th; and Creswell, Munsell, Fultz & Zirbel, the 50th. These are giant enterprises that reflect the conglomeration and globalization of both advertising and public relations.

To describe IMC, media critic James Ledbetter suggests thinking of the old Charlie the Tuna ads, in which a cartoon fish made you chuckle and identify with the product—and established a brand name. That's not good enough for IMC. "By contrast," Ledbetter says, "IMC encourages tuna buyers to think about all aspects of the product. If polls find that consumers are worried about dolphins caught in tuna nets, then you might stick a big 'Dolphin Safe' label on the tins and set up a web site featuring interviews with tuna fishermen." The new wave of IMC, according to one of its primary texts, is "respectful, not patronizing; dialogue-seeking, not monologuic; responsive, not formula-driven. It speaks to the highest point of common interest—not the lowest common denominator."

Public relations and advertising crossovers are hardly new. One area of traditional overlap is **institutional advertising,** which involves producing ads to promote an image rather than a product. The fuzzy, feel-good ads of agricultural conglomerate Archer Daniels Midland, which pepper Sunday morning network television, are typical.

integrated marketing communication ■ Comprehensive program that links public relations, advertising.

institutional advertising ■ Paid space and time to promote institution's image, position.

Media Relations

study preview **Public relations people generally favor candor in working with the news media. Even so, some organizations opt to stonewall journalistic inquiries. An emerging school of thought in public relations is to challenge negative news coverage aggressively and publicly.**

Open Media Relations

The common wisdom among public relations people today is to be open and candid with the mass media. It is a principle that dates to Ivy Lee, and case studies abound to confirm its effectiveness. A classic case study on this point is the Tylenol crisis.

Johnson & Johnson had spent many years and millions of dollars to inspire public confidence in its painkiller Tylenol. By 1982 the product was the leader in a crowded field of headache remedies with 36 percent of the market. Then disaster struck. Seven people in Chicago died after taking Tylenol capsules laced with cyanide. James Burke, president of Johnson & Johnson, and Lawrence Foster, vice president for public relations, moved quickly. Within hours, Johnson & Johnson:

- Halted the manufacture and distribution of Tylenol.
- Removed Tylenol products from retailers' shelves.
- Launched a massive advertising campaign requesting people to exchange Tylenol capsules for a safe replacement.
- Summoned 50 public relations employees from Johnson & Johnson and its subsidiary companies to staff a press center to answer media and consumer questions forthrightly.
- Ordered an internal company investigation of the Tylenol manufacturing and distribution process.
- Promised full cooperation with government investigators.
- Ordered the development of tamper-proof packaging for the reintroduction of Tylenol products after the contamination problem was resolved.

Investigators determined within days that an urban terrorist had poisoned the capsules. Although exonerated of negligence, Johnson & Johnson nonetheless had a tremendous problem: how to restore public confidence in Tylenol. Many former Tylenol users were reluctant to take a chance, and the Tylenol share of the analgesic market dropped to 6 percent.

To address the problem, Johnson & Johnson called in the Burson-Marsteller public relations agency. Burson-Marsteller recommended a media campaign to capitalize on the high marks the news media had given the company for openness during the crisis. Mailgrams went out inviting journalists to a 30-city video teleconference to hear James Burke announce the reintroduction of the product. Six hundred reporters turned out, and Johnson & Johnson officials took their questions live.

To stir even wider attention, 7,500 **media kits** had been sent to newsrooms the day before the teleconference. The kits included a news release and a bevy of supporting materials: photographs, charts and background information.

The resulting news coverage was extensive. On average, newspapers carried 32 column inches of copy on the announcement. Network television and radio as well as local stations also afforded heavy coverage. Meanwhile, Johnson & Johnson executives, who had attended a workshop on how to make favorable television appearances, made themselves available as guests on the network morning shows and talk shows. At the same time Johnson & Johnson distributed 80 million free coupons to encourage people to buy Tylenol again.

The massive media-based public relations campaign worked. Within a year Tylenol had regained 80 percent of its former market share. Today, in an increasingly crowded analgesic field, Tylenol is again the market leader with annual sales of $670 million, compared with $520 million before the cyanide crisis.

media kit ■ A packet provided to news reporters to tell the story in an advantageous way.

James Burke

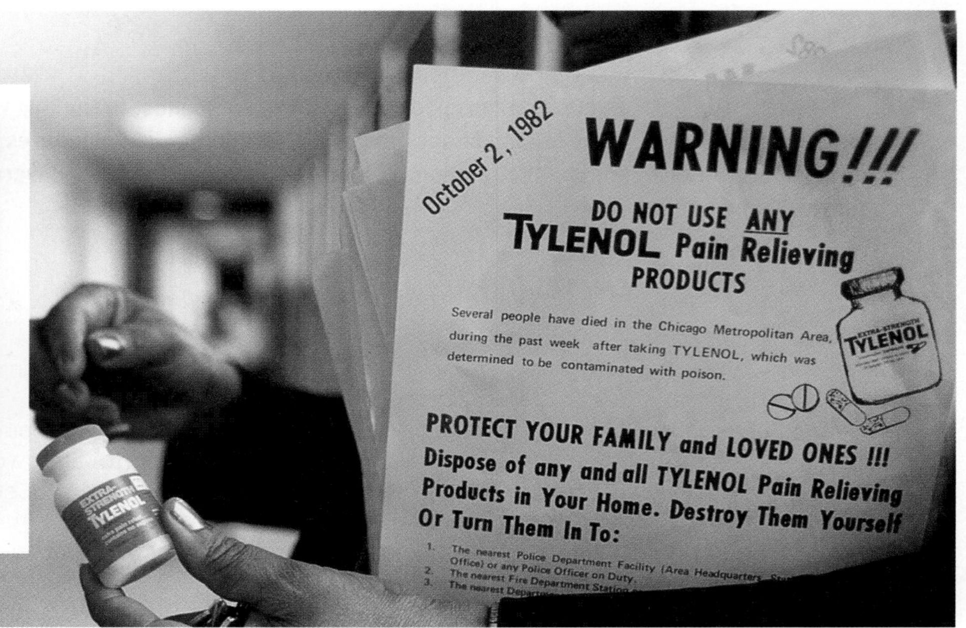

Product-Tampering Crisis When cyanide-laced Tylenol capsules killed seven people in Chicago, the manufacturer, Johnson & Johnson, responded quickly. Company President James Burke immediately pulled the product off retailers' shelves and ordered company publicists to set up a press center to answer news media inquiries as fully as possible. Burke's action and candor helped to restore the public's shaken confidence in Tylenol, and the product resumed its significant market share after the crisis ended. It turned out that it probably was somebody outside Johnson & Johnson's production and distributing system who had contaminated the capsules rather than a manufacturing lapse.

Proactive Media Relations

Although public relations campaigns cannot control what the media say, public relations people can help to shape how news media report issues by taking the initiative. In the Tylenol crisis, for example, Johnson & Johnson reacted quickly and decisively and took control of disseminating information, which, coupled with full disclosure, headed off false rumors that could have caused further damage. This is a good example of **proactive media relations.**

Proactive Crisis Responses A principle in crisis management is to seize leadership on the story. This involves anticipating what journalists will want to know and providing it to them before they even have time to formulate their questions. Ivy Lee did this time and again, and Johnson & Johnson did it in 1982.

For successful crisis management, public relations people need strong ongoing relationships with an organization's top officials. Otherwise, when a crisis strikes, they likely will have difficulty rounding up the kind of breaking information they need to deal effectively with the news media. During the 1991 Persian Gulf war, Pentagon spokesperson **Pete Williams** received high marks as a public relations person for shaping news coverage of the conflict. Williams did this by tapping his close working relationships with Defense Secretary Dick Cheney and the Joint Chiefs of Staff for information favorable to the war effort. At regular news briefings, sometimes several a day, Williams provided so much grist for the journalistic mill that reporters were overwhelmed in putting it together for stories, which reduced the time available for them to go after stories on their own. The war was reported largely as the Pentagon wanted.

White House Read the press briefings from a PR point of view—what is the current administration trying to communicate? **www.whitehouse.gov**

Ongoing Media Relationships Good media relations cannot be forged in the fire of a crisis. Organizations that survive a crisis generally have a history of solid media relations. Their public relations staff people know reporters, editors and news directors on a first-name basis. They avoid hyping news releases on routine matters, and they work hard at earning the trust of journalists.

Many public relations people, in fact, are seasoned journalists themselves, and they understand how journalists go about their work. It is their journalistic background that made them attractive candidates for their PR jobs. Pete Williams, for example, was a television news reporter in Wyoming before making a midcareer shift to join Dick Cheney's staff in Washington when Cheney was first elected to Congress from Wyoming.

proactive media relations ■ Taking initiative to release information.

Pete Williams ■ Tilted news coverage by overwhelming the media with information during the Persian Gulf war.

Sound Operating Principles An underlying strength that helped to see Johnson & Johnson through the Tylenol crisis was the company's credo. The credo was a written vow that Johnson & Johnson's first responsibility was to "those who use our products and services." The credo, which had been promoted in-house for years, said, "Every time a business hires, builds, sells or buys, it is acting *for the people* as well as *for itself,* and it must be prepared to accept full responsibility."

With such a sound operating principle, Johnson & Johnson's crisis response was, in some respects, almost reflexive. Going silent, for example, would have run counter to the principles that Johnson & Johnson people had accepted as part of their corporate culture for years.

Ambivalence in Media Relations

Despite the advantage of open media relations, not all companies embrace the approach. Giant retailer Wal-Mart, as an example, long resisted putting resources into public relations. Founder Sam Walton saw PR as a frill. It didn't fit his keep-costs-minimal concept. By 2005, even with Walton dead, his philosophy remained in place. The company had only a 17-member public relations staff—miniscule in business. How miniscule? Wal-Mart sales exceeded $285 billion, yet the company had but one public relations staffer per $16 billion in earnings. Put another way, the company had one public relations person per 76,000 employees.

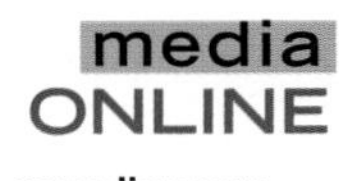

Digg All about user-powered content. Digg it!

www.digg.com

Wal-Mart's spectacular growth, with a new store opening every day in 2005, masked problems. The company was generating legions of critics, whose mantra was epitomized in Anthony Bianco's choice of a title for his Wal-Mart basher book in 2006—*The Bully of Bentonville*. In Irvine, California, voters killed a planned store. Public opposition undid plans in the Queens section of New York City for another store. Reflecting growing employee discontent, there were rumblings to unionize—anathema in the Wal-Mart culture. There was a scandal about illegal aliens doing overnight cleanup work. A class-action suit alleging gender discrimination was filed by some women employees.

Attempts at damage control were clumsy. In 2005 the company invited the news media to an open house at corporate headquarters in Bentonville, Arkansas, for the first time. A clueless senior executive who mounted a stage to open the ceremony became discombobulated when the reporters failed to jump to their feet in cheering enthusiasm, as adoring Wal-Mart employees always had. So ensconced was the executive in the Wal-Mart culture, and with nobody in the company having briefed him on media relations, the guy had no idea that reporters go about their work with a cool, journalistic detachment. Hardly a good show, it could be called public relations disaster.

social media news release Designed for e-mail delivery with image, video and other downloads included, as well as links to blogs and other sites that come later.

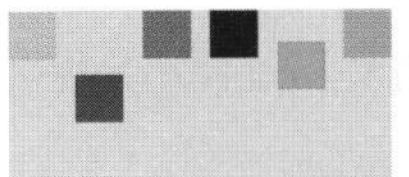

mediaTECHNOLOGY

Social Media News Release

The workhorse of public relations, the news media, made an easy transition to the Internet in the 1990s but pretty much only the medium changed—a mass-delivered e-mail of the standard release that once was snailed. In 2006 a Boston public relations agency, Shift Communications, reinvented the news release for the digital age. Shift's Todd Defren, who devised the new release, called it one-stop shopping for journalists to whom releases are targeted. The release included tech-rich features, including links to blogs that relate to the subject, links to related news releases and sites, videos, downloadable company logos, and videos.

Defren calls it the **social media news release** because it encourages interactive and ongoing communication. With a Shift release posted to the DIGG consumer-generated news site, journalists and bloggers and anyone can click to sites that add to the dialogue. "This gives journalists everything they need in one place," Defren said.

The basis of Defren's invention is the Web 2.0 bevy of Internet services that facilitate the creation of content and exchange of information online. Within months of the Shift creation, which was downloadable free as a template, larger public relations agencies were onto the concept. Giant Eldelman unveiled its variation by the end of the year.

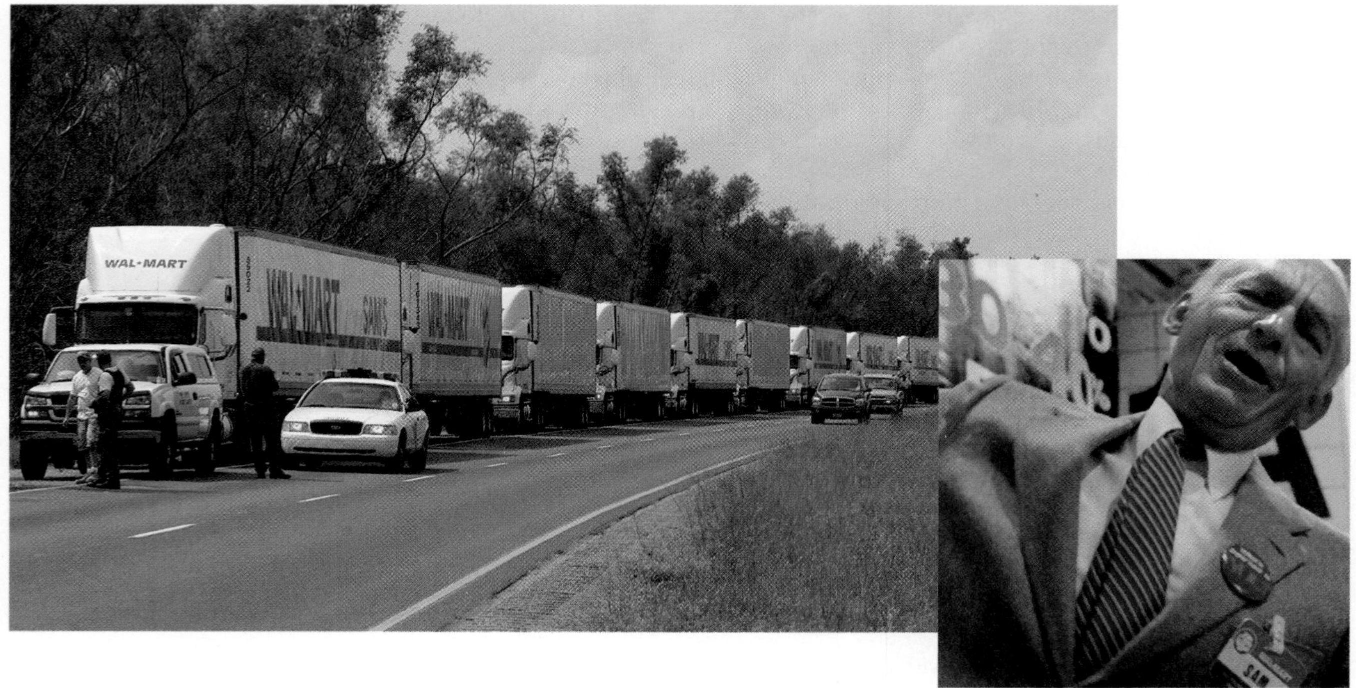

Sam Walton

Still, the Sam Walton notion that actions speak louder than words gave Wal-Mart occasional successes with image. The company upstaged federal agencies in moving relief supplies to the Gulf Coast after Hurricane Katrina. More than 2,400 truckloads of merchandise were dispatched to stricken communities, the first 100 loads of donated merchandise arriving before the fumbling federal mobilization. Wal-Mart drivers also transported water and other essentials.

Occasional image successes, however, weren't doing the job. With a vague sense that something methodical in the public relations spirit was needed, Wal-Mart created an executive position in 2006 with the curious title "senior director stakeholder engagement." The job description had some earmarks of public relations, albeit not quite at the vice-presidential level. Strangely, perhaps in homage to Sam Walton, the words *public relations* appeared nowhere in the job description's 3,000 words. You could, however, read a lot into wording like "an innovative out-of-the-box thinker" and "fundamental changes in how the company does business" and "social responsibility."

Walt-Mart has not been alone in **ambivalent media relations.** Among companies notorious for not even returning calls to journalists are:

- **Amerada Hess,** the huge crude oil and natural gas company.
- **Winn-Dixie,** the Southern supermarket chain.
- **Texas Instruments,** the semiconductor company.

Procter & Gamble is another major U.S. company that generally is tight-lipped about how it conducts its business, with the notable exception of product promotions. Another notable exception was Procter & Gamble's full-scale public relations campaign in the 1980s to squelch persistent rumors that its corporate symbol—the moon and stars—had roots in Satanism.

ambivalent media relations ■ Mix of proactive, reactive and inactive media contacts.

Herb Schmertz ■ Pioneered advertorials.

Adversarial Public Relations

Public relations took on aggressive, even feisty tactics when Mobil Oil decided in the 1970s not to take media criticism lightly any more. **Herb Schmertz,** vice president for Mobil's public affairs, charted a new course by:

- Filing formal complaints with news organizations when coverage was unfair in the company's view.
- Taking Mobil's case directly to the general public with paid advertising, **advertorials,** as they are called, a splicing of the words "advertising" and "editorial," that explained the company's views.
- Sending corporate representatives on media tours to spread Mobil's side to as many constituencies as possible.

Schmertz's energetic counterattacks, an example of **adversarial public relations,** were a departure from conventional wisdom in public relations, which was to let criticism go unanswered or, at most, to complain privately to executives of news organizations that negative coverage is unwarranted. The conventional wisdom was that a public response would only bring more attention to the negative coverage.

In abandoning passivity, Mobil was adapting what sports fans call the Red Auerbach technique. Auerbach, the legendary coach of the Boston Celtics, was known for criticizing referees. He realized he would never get a ref to change a call, but he believed that refs would be less inclined to make questionable calls against the Celtics in the future if they knew that Auerbach would jump all over them. Mobil President Rawleigh Warner Jr. explained the new Mobil policy this way: "People know that if they take a swipe at us, we will fight back."

Schmertz employed the full range of PR tools in 1974 when ABC aired a television documentary that raised critical questions about the U.S. oil industry. Mobil objected first to ABC and then fired off a formal complaint to the National News Council, a volunteer media watchdog group. Mobil claimed 32 inaccuracies and instances of unfairness and requested that the council investigate. Mobil also issued an unusually lengthy news release, quoting from the documentary and offering point-by-point rebuttals.

Six Mobil executives were given a crash course on giving good interviews and sent out to meet the news media. In two years the executives and other Mobil representatives appeared on 365 television and 211 radio shows and talked with 80 newspaper reporters. Schmertz encouraged them to take the offensive. To counter the ABC impression that the oil industry still engaged in the bad practices of its past, Schmertz told executives to stress that such information was outdated. "Put the shoe on the other foot," he said, advising the Mobil executives to say the impression left by the ABC documentary was "comparable to Mobil's producing a documentary about today's television industry and pointing to a 1941 FCC decree requiring RCA to rid itself of one of its networks as evidence of a current conspiracy."

Advertorials were part of Mobil's initiatives. Under Schmertz, as much as $6 million a year went into newspaper and magazine ads explaining the company's position. Mobil also began producing its own television programs on energy issues and providing them free to stations. The programs had a journalistic tone, and many stations ran them as if they were actual documentaries rather than part of Mobil's media campaign.

The jury is still out on whether Schmertz's aggressive sparring is good policy. Most organizations continue to follow the traditional thinking that taking on the media only generates more attention on the original bad news. On the other hand, Schmertz's approach has been tried by some major corporations. Bechtel, Illinois Power and Kaiser Aluminum all have called for independent investigations of stories that reflected badly on them.

Another adversarial approach, though not recommended by most public relations people, is for an offended organization to sever relations with the source of unfavorable news—an **information boycott.** In 1954, in a spectacular pout, General Motors cut off contact with *Wall Street Journal* reporters and withdrew advertising from the newspaper. This approach carries great risks:

- By going silent, an organization loses avenues for conveying its message to mass audiences.
- An organization that yanks advertising to punish detractors is perceived negatively for coercively wielding its economic might.
- An organization that quits advertising in an effective advertising medium will lose sales.

advertorials ■ Paid advertisements that state an editorial position.

adversarial public relations ■ Attacking critics openly.

information boycott ■ Severing ties with news media.

A boycott differs from Schmertz's adversarial approach in an important respect. Schmertz responded to negative news by contributing to the exchange of information and ideas, which is positive in a democratic society. An information boycott, on the other hand, restricts the flow of information. Today, GM's policy has returned to the conventional wisdom of not arguing with anyone who buys paper by the ton and ink by the barrel—with the exception of its suit against NBC for faking the explosion of a GMC truck.

Professionalization

study preview **Public relations has a tarnished image that stems from shortsighted promotion and whitewashing techniques of the late 1800s. Although some dubious practices continue, PR leaders are working to improve standards.**

A Tarnished Image

Unsavory elements in the heritage of public relations remain a heavy burden. P. T. Barnum, whose name became synonymous with hype, attracted crowds to his stunts and shows in the late 1800s with extravagant promises. Sad to say, some promoters still

media PEOPLE

Edward Bernays

After graduation from college in 1912, Edward Bernays tried press agentry. He was good at it, landing free publicity for whoever would hire him. Soon his bosses included famous tenor Enrico Caruso and actor Otis Skinner. Bernays felt, however, that his success was tainted by the disdain in which press agents were held in general. He also saw far greater potential for affecting public opinion than his fellow press agents did. From Bernays' discomfort and vision was born the concept of modern public relations. His 1923 book *Crystallizing Public Opinion* outlined a new craft he called public relations.

Edward Bernays Integrity was important to public relations pioneer Edward Bernays. When he was asked by agents of fascist dictators Francisco Franco and Adolf Hitler to improve their images in the United States, he said no. "I wouldn't do for money what I wouldn't do without money," Bernays said.

Bernays saw good public relations as counsel to clients. He called the public relations practitioner a "special pleader." The concept was modeled partly on the long-established lawyer-client relationship in which the lawyer, or counselor, suggests courses of action. Because of his seminal role in defining what public relations is, Bernays sometimes is called the "Father of PR," although some people say the honor should be shared with Ivy Lee.

No matter, there is no question of Bernays' ongoing contributions. He taught the first course in public relations in 1923 at New York University. Bernays encouraged firm methodology in public relations, a notion that was captured in the title of a book he edited in 1955: *The Engineering of Consent.* He long advocated the professionalization of the field, which laid the groundwork for the accreditation of the sort the Public Relations Society of America has developed.

Throughout his career Bernays stressed that public relations people need a strong sense of responsibility. In one reflective essay, he wrote, "Public relations practiced as a profession is an art applied to a science in which the public interest and not pecuniary motivation is the primary consideration. The engineering of consent in this sense assumes a constructive social role. Regrettably, public relations, like other professions, can be abused and used for anti-social purposes. I have tried to make the profession socially responsible as well as economically viable."

Bernays became the Grand Old Man of public relations, still attending PRSA and other professional meetings past his 100th birthday. He died in 1993 at age 102.

use Barnum's tactics. The claims for snake oils and elixirs from Barnum's era live on in commercials for pain relievers and cold remedies. The early response of tycoons to muckraking attacks, before Ivy Lee came along, was **whitewashing**—covering up the abuses but not correcting them. It is no wonder that the term *PR* is sometimes used derisively. To say something is "all PR" means that it lacks substance. Of people whose apparent positive qualities are a mere façade, it may be said that they have "good PR."

whitewashing ■ Covering up.

flakkers ■ Derisive word for public relations people.

Although journalists rely heavily on public relations people for information, many journalists look at PR practitioners with suspicion. Not uncommon among seasoned journalists are utterances such as "I've never met a PR person I couldn't distrust." Such cynicism flows partly from the journalists' self-image as unfettered truth-seekers whose only obligation is serving their audiences' needs. PR people, on the other hand, are seen as obligated to their employers, whose interests do not always dovetail with the public good. Behind their backs, PR people are called "flaks," a takeoff on the World War II slang for antiaircraft bursts intended to stop enemy bombers. PR **flakkers,** as journalists use the term, interfere with journalistic truth-seeking by putting forth slanted, self-serving information that is not necessarily the whole story.

The journalism-PR tension is exacerbated by a common newsroom view that PR people try to get free news hole space for their messages rather than buying airtime and column inches. This view might seem strange, considering that 50 to 90 percent of all news stories either originate with, or contain information supplied by, PR people. It is also strange considering that many PR people are former news reporters and editors.

mediaPEOPLE

Leslie Unger

Leslie Unger was there at the beginning, when in 1992 the Academy of Motion Picture Arts & Sciences created an in-house communication unit. In her early 20s, after a couple of entry-level public relations jobs, Unger found herself helping run logistics for the Academy Awards. Now, even after so many times through the annual Hollywood extravaganza, Unger at moments can't believe what she's in the middle of. She pinches herself in a reality check: "I'm at the Academy Awards!"

Making Oscar night work right, look good.

Working up to Oscar night occupies Unger full time-plus for five months beginning in November. Her usual seven-person staff is bulked up to 12 to handle news media requests for credentials. In recent years there have been 500 to 600 requests. Only about half are cleared,

For the audience, much of Unger's media-support work is invisible. She decides where individual reporters will be placed so they don't stumble over each other, at least not too much. Interview rooms need to look good on television. Even often-ratty press rooms must be presentable. And are there enough jacks for bloggers and all the laptops?

There are countless meetings with fire and security experts and art directors. The network covering the event has its own marketing and publicity team with which Unger must coordinate. To do it all, Unger has to bring in outside public relations help, most recently from the Dobbin/Bolgla agency in New York.

Unger learned publicity and event management out of college in the public affairs department of the Los Angeles County Public Works Department. Then for a year she was a junior account executive at Ruder Finn, a public relations agency, in Los Angeles. Ruder Finn had handled the Academy Awards account until 1992 when the Academy created an internal communications unit—and Unger made the shift.

The five-month build-up to the climactic Oscar night hardly ends Unger's work. Countless queries come in for days, like, she says, "What was the instrument Sting played?" After a while, though, she moves into less hectic months, an interlude of sorts. She works on Academy programs to promote film appreciation and literacy, the Academy's film archives, and to encourage student movie-making. Those activities include Unger generating a couple of new releases a week—although nothing like the two-a-day rate in the pre-Oscar months.

 and get a feel for the work this company performs.
www.hillandknowlton.com

Ketchum Founded in 1923, Ketchum has grown into a full-service public relations firm with offices around the world.
www.ketchum.com

Rowland Check out the colorful, fast-moving site of this international communications firm, whose core competency is corporate reputation.
www.rowland.com

Ogilvy From expert views to case studies to the pressroom, this site gives a thorough look into Ogilvy Public Relations Worldwide.
www.ogilvypr.com

Manning Selvage & Lee What's greater than changing perceptions? Changing minds. Visit this site and read more on the MS&L philosophy of

public information ■ One alternative word for public relations; others are public affairs, corporate communication.

APR ■ Indicates PRSA accreditation.

No matter how uncomfortable PR people and journalists are as bedfellows, they are bedfellows nonetheless.

Some public relations people have tried to leapfrog the negative baggage attached to the term *PR* by abandoning it. The U.S. military shucked *PR* and tried **public information,** but it found itself still dogged by the same distrust that surrounded "public relations." The military then tried *public affairs,* but that was no solution either. Many organizations have tried *communication* as a way around the problem. Common labels today include the military's current *public affairs* offices and businesses' *corporate communication* departments.

Standards and Certification

The Public Relations Society of America, which has grown to 28,000 members in 114 chapters, has a different approach: improving the quality of public relations work, whatever the label. In 1951 the association adopted a code of professional standards. In a further professionalization step, PRSA has established a certification process. Those who meet the criteria and pass exams are allowed to place **APR,** which stands for "accredited public relations," after their names. About 5,000 PRSA members hold APR status.

Since 1998 the APR program has been operated by the Universal Accreditation Board, which was created for that purpose by PRSA and a consortium of nine other public relations organizations. It is a rigorous process. Nationwide, only 80 to 90 practitioners a year earn the right to use APR with their signatures.

CHAPTER 11 Wrap-Up

When Ivy Lee hung up a shingle in New York for a new publicity agency in 1906, he wanted to distance himself from the huckstering that marked most publicity at the time. To do that, Lee promised to deal only in legitimate news about the agency's clients and no fluff. He invited journalists to pursue more information about the agency's clients. He also vowed to be honest and accurate. Those principles remain the bulwark of good public relations practice today.

Questions for Review

1. What is public relations? How is public relations connected to the mass media?
2. Why did big business become interested in the techniques and principles of public relations beginning in the late 1800s?
3. How is public relations a management tool?
4. What is the range of activities in which public relations people are involved?
5. What kind of relationship do most people strive to have with the mass media?
6. Why does public relations have a bad image? What are public relations professionals doing about it?

Questions for Critical Thinking

1. When Ivy Lee accepted the Pennsylvania Railroad as a client in 1906, he saw the job as "interpreting the Pennsylvania Railroad to the public and interpreting the public to the Pennsylvania Railroad." Compare Lee's point with Arthur Page's view of public relations as a management function.
2. How are public relations practitioners trying to overcome the complaints from journalists that they are flakkers interfering with an unfettered pursuit of truth?
3. What was the contribution of the Committee on Public Information, usually called the Creel Committee, to public relations after World War I?
4. How do public relations agencies turn profits?

5. When does an institution with its own in-house public relations operation need to hire a PR agency?
6. Explain the concept of enlightened self-interest.
7. How did the confluence of the following three phenomena at the turn of the century contribute to the emergence of modern public relations?
   - The related concepts of social Darwinism, a social theory; laissez-faire, a government philosophy; and paternalism, a practice of business.
   - Muckraking, which attacked prevalent abuses of the public interest.
   - Advertising, which had grown since the 1830s as a way to reach great numbers of people.
8. Showman P. T. Barnum epitomized 19th-century press agentry with extravagant claims, such as promoting the midget Tom Thumb as a Civil War general. To attract crowds to a tour by an unknown European soprano, Jenny Lind, Barnum labeled her "the Swedish Nightingale." Would such promotional methods work today? Keep in mind that Barnum, explaining his methods, once said, "There's a sucker born every minute."

Deepening Your media LITERACY

Do press releases serve the public?

STEP 1 Get a copy of a newspaper that you can mark up.

Dig Deeper

STEP 2 Mark all the stories that you think came from press releases, in whole or in part. Choose one of them—it can be on any subject, for example, an upcoming concert or event, an award ceremony or an announcement from a local business.

What Do You Think?

STEP 3 Answer these questions in relation to the press release you chose:

1. How does this story benefit the public? Which public? Who else does it benefit?
2. Is this story, or the part of it that came from a press release, socially responsible?
3. Is the press release proactive?
4. If all the press releases were taken out of the newspaper, how much news would you miss?

Keeping Up to Date

PRWeek is the industry trade journal.

The trade journal *O'Dwyer's PR Services* tracks the industry on a monthly basis.

Other sources of ongoing information are *Public Relations Journal*, *Public Relations Quarterly* and *Public Relations Review*.

For Further Learning

Anthony Bianco. *The Bully of Bentonville.* Currency, 2006.
Bianco, a *BusinessWeek* reporter, gives the corporate culture of Wal-Mart an unfriendly review that suggests serious problems with social responsibility and opportunities for applying techniques of public relations.

Michael L. Kent and Maureen Taylor. "Toward a Dialogic Theory of Public Relations," *Public Relations Review* (February 2002), pages 21–27.
Kent and Taylor, both scholars, draw on a wide range of disciplines to argue for genuine dialogue as a basis for the moral practice of public relations.

Michael S. Sweeney. *Secrets of Victory: The Office of Censorship and the American Press and Radio in World War II.* University of North Carolina Press, 2001.
Sweeney, a scholar, examines the U.S. government's World War II censorship program and attempts to explain its success. Sweeney, once a reporter himself, draws on archival sources.

Robert Jackall and Janice M. Hirota. *Image Makers: Advertising, Public Relations and the Ethos of Advocacy.* University of Chicago Press, 2000.
Jackall and Hirota, a husband-and-wife team, trace the history of advertising and public relations to argue that advocacy has trivialized public and private life.

Rene A. Henry. *Marketing Public Relations.* Iowa State University Press, 2000.
Henry, a regional communications chief with the U.S. Environmental Protection Agency, offers a how-to on creating a demand for public relations services and delivering.

Sally J. Ray. *Strategic Communication in Crisis Management: Lessons from the Airline Industry.* Quorum, 1999.
Ray, a scholar, uses a three-stage model to assess a crisis and develop appropriate messages.

Susan Henry. "Dissonant Notes of a Retiring Feminist: Doris E. Fleishman's Later Years," *Journal of Public Relations Research* (1998), pages l–33.
Henry, a scholar, tracks the last three years of Fleischman's life and career.

Larry Tye. *The Father of Spin: Edward L. Bernays and the Birth of Public Relations.* Crown, 1998.
Tye, a Boston *Globe* reporter, balances appreciation for Bernays' inventiveness with a sober look at its consequences.

Stewart Ewen. *PR! A Social History of Spin.* Basic Books, 1996.
An exhaustive and reflective study of public relations from the evolution of PR through the 20th century.

Scott M. Cutlip. *The Unseen Power: Public Relations—A History.* Erlbaum, 1994.
Cutlip, a pioneer in public relations education, integrates the history of public relations into the larger scheme of U.S. life in this definitive 800-page work.

Lael M. Moynihan. "Horrendous PR Crises: What They Did When the Unthinkable Happened." *Media History Digest* (Spring-Summer 1988), pages 19–25.
Moynihan, a consumer relations specialist, details eight major cases of crisis management through proven public relations principles.

Herbert Schmertz and William Novak. *Goodbye to the Low Profile: The Art of Creative Confrontation.* Little, Brown, 1986.
Combative Herb Schmertz passes on the lessons he learned as Mobil Oil's innovative public relations chief, including how-tos for advertorials and preparation of executives for interviews with journalists.

Ray Eldon Hiebert. *Courtier to the Crowd: The Story of Ivy Lee and the Development of Public Relations.* Iowa State University Press, 1966.
Professor Hiebert's flattering biography focuses on the enduring public relations principles articulated, if not always practiced, by Ivy Lee.

Bob Greenberg
His crystal ball sees advertising not in packaging ads inside entertainment and news but in advertising so compelling that it's why people tune in.

chapter 12 Advertising

In this chapter you will learn:

- Advertising is a keystone in a consumer economy, a democracy and the mass media.
- Most advertising messages are carried through the mass media.
- Advertising agencies create and place ads for advertisers.
- Advertisements are placed with care in media to reach appropriate audiences for advertised products and services.
- New platforms are being used for advertisements.
- Advertising tactics include brand names, lowest common denominators, positioning and redundancy.
- Advertising uses psychology to tap audience interests.
- Advertising messages have shifted from a "buyer beware" to a "seller beware" sensitivity.
- Advertising people need to solve problems created by ad clutter and creative excesses.

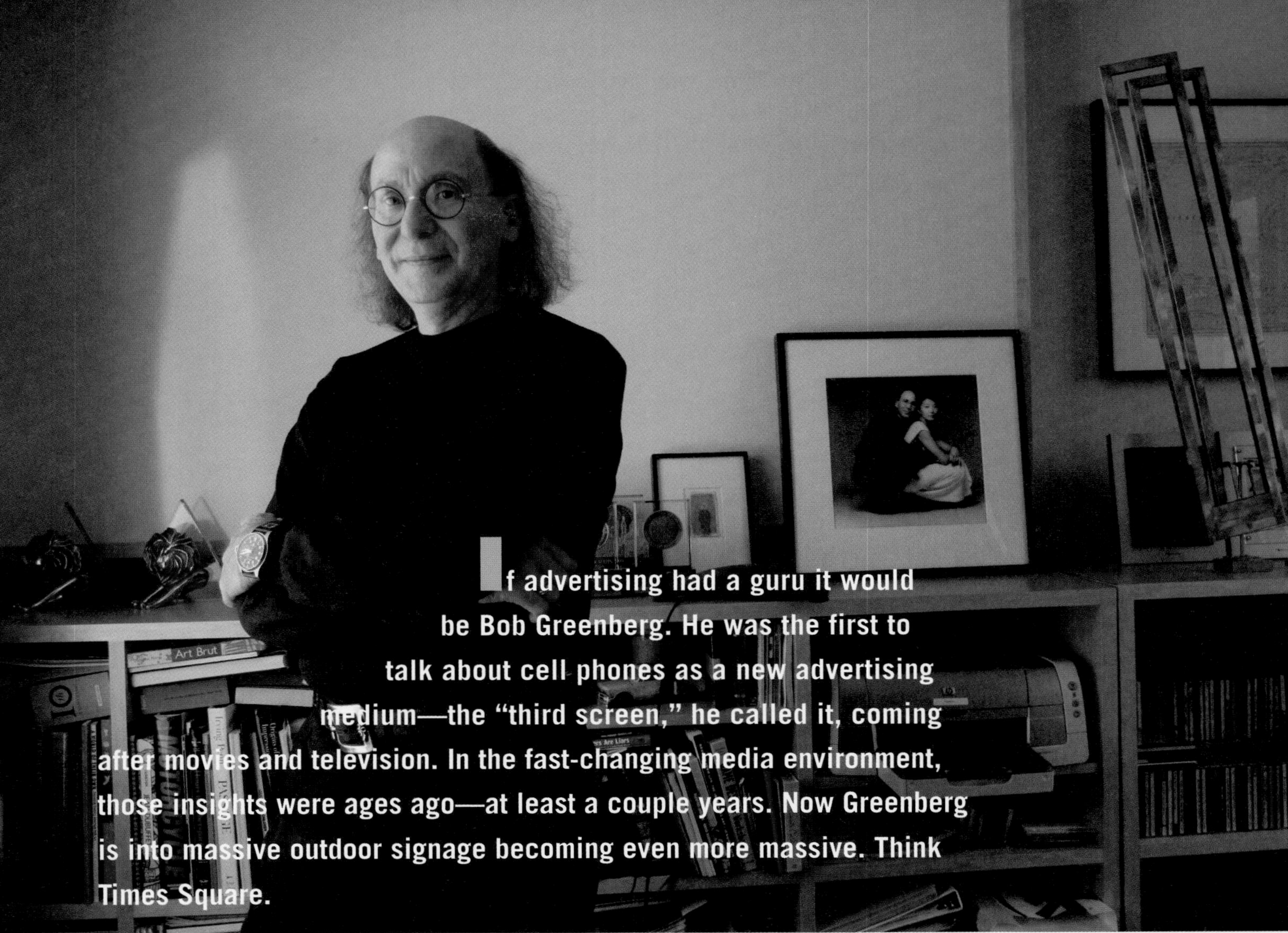

If advertising had a guru it would be Bob Greenberg. He was the first to talk about cell phones as a new advertising medium—the "third screen," he called it, coming after movies and television. In the fast-changing media environment, those insights were ages ago—at least a couple years. Now Greenberg is into massive outdoor signage becoming even more massive. Think Times Square.

Greenberg shares his observations freely, but, no mere armchair commentator, he practices post-mass media advertising at his R/GA agency in New York, part of the global Interpublic agency chain. R/GA designed the Nikeid web site, where footwear freaks can spend hours designing their own. That's customer interactivity that sells products, he said.

The era of entertainment that brought massive audiences to advertising messages is fast-fading, Greenberg says. It's time to think outside the box.

Greenberg pities those ad agency execs who still pitch the 30-second television spot to clients because it's all they know. It's not that television, radio, magazines and newspapers are dead but that their heyday is past and their near-monopoly as carriers of advertising is fading fast. As Greenberg tells it, ad agencies that don't find new models to reach consumers are setting themselves up for extinction.

Greenberg's answer: Rather than ads being sandwiched into entertainment products, the ads themselves must be the entertainment. He's been called a media futurist, but there is evidence the future is now. Samsung and Verizon have tripled their Internet ad budgets. American Express has shifted away from network television.

At R/GA Greenberg has integrated information technologists, data analysts and what he calls "experience designers" into his staff. He must be doing something right. In 2005 he added 85 people to bring the R/GA staff to 400.

Importance of Advertising

study preview **Advertising is vital in a consumer economy. Without it people would have a hard time even knowing what products and services are available. Advertising, in fact, is essential to a prosperous society. Advertising also is the financial basis of important contemporary mass media.**

Consumer Economies

Advertising is a major component of modern economies. In the United States the best estimates are that advertisers spend about 2 percent of the gross domestic product to promote their wares. When the nation's production of goods and services is up, so is advertising spending. When production falters, as it did in the early 2000s, many manufacturers, distributors and retailers pull back their advertising expenditures.

The essential role of advertising in a modern consumer economy is obvious if you think about how people decide what to buy. If a shoe manufacturer were unable to tout the virtues of its footwear by advertising in the mass media, people would have a hard time learning about the product, let alone knowing whether it is what they want.

media ONLINE **Nike** Design your own shoe. **nikeid.com**

Advertising and Prosperity

Advertising's phenomenal continuing growth has been a product of a plentiful society. In a poor society with a shortage of goods, people line up for necessities like food and clothing. Advertising has no role and serves no purpose when survival is the question. With prosperity, however, people have not only discretionary income but also a choice of ways to spend it. Advertising is the vehicle that provides information and rationales to help them decide how to enjoy their prosperity.

Besides being a product of economic prosperity, advertising contributes to prosperity. By dangling desirable commodities and services before mass audiences, advertising can inspire people to greater individual productivity so that they can have more income to buy the things that are advertised.

Advertising also can introduce efficiency into the economy by allowing comparison shopping without in-person inspections of all the alternatives. Efficiencies also can result when advertising alerts consumers to superior and less costly products and services, which displace outdated, outmoded and inefficient offerings.

Said Howard Morgens when he was president of Procter & Gamble: "Advertising is the most effective and efficient way to sell to the consumer. If we should ever find better methods of selling our type of products to the consumer, we'll leave advertising and turn to these other methods." Veteran advertising executive David Ogilvy once made the point this way: "Advertising is still the cheapest form of selling. It would cost you $25,000 to have salesmen call on a thousand homes. A television commercial can do it for $4.69." McGraw-Hill, which publishes trade magazines, has offered research that a salesperson's typical call costs $178, a letter $6.63 and a phone call $6.35. For 17 cents, says McGraw-Hill, an advertiser can reach a prospect through advertising. Although advertising does not close a sale for all products, it introduces products and makes the salesperson's job easier and quicker.

Largest Advertisers

Automotive giant General Motors remained the biggest-spending advertiser in the United States in 2004 at $4 billion, according to data compiled by the trade journal *Advertising Age.* Procter & Gamble was a close second. Other estimates:

Advertiser	Amount spent on advertising
General Motors	$4.0 billion
Procter & Gamble	3.9 billion
Time Warner	3.3 billion
Pfizer	3.0 billion
SBC Communication	2.7 billion
DaimlerChrysler	2.5 billion
Ford Motor	2.5 billion
Walt Disney	2.2 billion
Verizon	2.2 billion
Johnson & Johnson	2.2 billion

Advertising and Democracy

Advertising first took off as a modern phenomenon in the United States, which has given rise to a theory that advertising and democracy are connected. This theory notes that Americans, early in their history as a democracy, were required by their political system to hold individual opinions. They looked for information so that they could evaluate their leaders and vote on public policy. This emphasis on individuality and reason paved the way for advertising: Just as Americans looked to the mass media for information on political matters, they also came to look to the media for information on buying decisions.

In authoritarian countries, by contrast, people tend to look to strong personal leaders, not reason, for ideas to embrace. This, according to the theory, diminishes the demand for information in these nondemocracies, including the kind of information provided by advertising.

Advertising has another important role in democratic societies in generating most of the operating revenue for newspapers, magazines, television and radio. Without advertising, many of the media on which people rely for information, for entertainment and for the exchange of ideas on public issues would not exist as we know them.

Origins of Advertising

studypreview **Advertising is the product of great forces that have shaped modern society, beginning with Gutenberg's movable type, which made mass-produced messages possible. Without the mass media there would be no vehicle to carry advertisements to mass audiences. Advertising also is a product of the democratic experience; of the Industrial Revolution and its spin-offs, including vast transportation networks and mass markets; and of continuing economic growth.**

media ONLINE **John W. Hartman Center for Sales, Advertising and Marketing History** Offers several collections of images of early ads. **http://scriptorium.lib.duke.edu/hartman**

Stepchild of Technology

Advertising is not a mass medium, but it relies on media to carry its messages. **Johannes Gutenberg**'s movable type, which permitted mass production of the printed word, made mass-produced advertising possible. First came flyers. Then advertisements as

Johannes Gutenberg ■ Progenitor of advertising media.

newspapers and magazines were introduced. In the 1800s, when technology created high-speed presses that could produce enough copies for larger audiences, advertisers used these media to expand markets. With the introduction of radio, advertisers learned how to use electronic communication. Then came television.

Flyers were the first form of printed advertising. The British printer **William Caxton** issued the first printed advertisement in 1468 to promote one of his books. In America publisher **John Campbell** of the Boston *News-Letter* ran the first advertisement in 1704, a notice from somebody wanting to sell an estate on Long Island. Colonial newspapers listed cargo arriving from Europe and invited readers to come, look and buy.

Industrial Revolution

The genius of **Benjamin Day**'s New York *Sun,* in 1833 the first penny newspaper, was that it recognized and exploited so many changes spawned by the Industrial Revolution. Steam-powered presses made large press runs possible. Factories drew great numbers of people to jobs in cities that were geographically small areas to which newspapers could be distributed quickly. The jobs also drew immigrants who were eager to learn—from newspapers as well as other sources—about their adopted country. Industrialization, coupled with the labor union movement, created unprecedented wealth, with laborers gaining a share of the new prosperity. A consumer economy was emerging, although it was primitive by today's standards.

A key to the success of Day's *Sun* was that, at a penny a copy, it was affordable for almost everyone. Of course, Day's production expenses exceeded a penny a copy. Just as the commercial media do today, Day looked to advertisers to pick up the slack. As Day wrote in his first issue, "The object of this paper is to lay before the public, at a price within the means of everyone, all the news of the day, and at the same time afford an advantageous medium for advertising." Day and imitator penny press publishers sought larger and larger circulations, knowing that merchants would see the value in buying space to reach so much purchasing power.

National advertising took root in the 1840s as railroads, another creation of the Industrial Revolution, spawned new networks for mass distribution of manufactured goods. National brands developed, and their producers looked to magazines, also delivered by rail, to promote sales. By 1869 the rail network linked the Atlantic and Pacific coasts.

William Caxton ■ Printed the first advertisement.

John Campbell ■ Published the first ad in the British colonies.

Benjamin Day ■ His penny newspaper brought advertising to a new level.

media TIMELINE

DEVELOPMENT OF ADVERTISING

1468 William Caxton promoted a book with the first printed advertisement.

1704 Joseph Campbell included advertisements in the Boston *News-Letter.*

1833 Benjamin Day created the New York *Sun* as combination news and advertising vehicle.

1869 Wayland Ayer opened the first advertising agency, Philadelphia.

1910 Edward Bok of *Ladies' Home Journal* established a magazine advertising code.

1914 Congress created the Federal Trade Commission to combat unfair advertising.

1929 NBC established a code of acceptable advertising.

1942 Media industries created a predecessor to the Ad Council.

1960s Network television surpassed magazines as national advertising medium.

1980s Advertising industry consolidated in mergers, acquisitions.

2003 Store brands emerged as major challenge to brand names.

2004 Thirty-second spot on televised Super Bowl reached $2.5 million.

Pioneer Agencies

By 1869 most merchants recognized the value of advertising, but they grumbled about the time it took away from their other work. In that grumbling, a young Philadelphia man sensed opportunity. **Wayland Ayer,** age 20, speculated that merchants, and even national manufacturers, would welcome a service company to help them create advertisements and place them in publications. Ayer feared, however, that his idea might not be taken seriously by potential clients because of his youth and inexperience. So when Wayland Ayer opened a shop, he borrowed his father's name for the shingle. The father was never part of the business, but the agency's name, N. W. Ayer & Son, gave young Ayer access to potential clients, and the first advertising agency was born. The Ayer agency not only created ads but also offered the array of services that agencies still offer clients today:

- Counsel on selling products and services.
- Design services, that is, actually creating advertisements and campaigns.
- Expertise on placing advertisements in advantageous media.

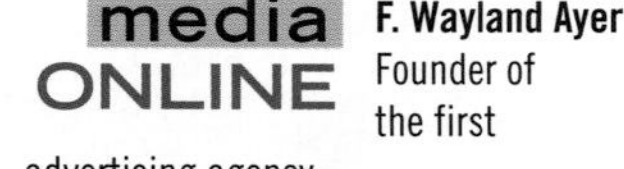

F. Wayland Ayer Founder of the first advertising agency.
www.dvrbs.com/CamdenPeople-FWaylandAyer.htm

Advertising Agencies

study preview **Central in modern advertising are the agencies that create and place ads on behalf of their clients. These agencies are generally funded by the media in which they place ads. In effect, this makes agency services free to advertisers. Other compensation systems are also emerging.**

Agency Structure

Full-service advertising agencies conduct market research for their clients, design and produce advertisements and choose the media in which the advertisement will run. The 500 leading U.S. agencies employ 120,000 people worldwide. In the United States they employ about 73,000. The responsibilities of people who work at advertising agencies fall into these broad categories:

Creativity This category includes copywriters, graphics experts and layout people. These creative people generally report to **creative directors,** art directors and copy supervisors.

Liaison Most of these people are **account executives,** who work with clients. Account executives are responsible for understanding clients' needs, communicating those needs to the creative staff and going back to clients with the creative staff's ideas.

Buying Agency employees called **media buyers** determine the most effective media in which to place ads and then place them.

Research Agency research staffs generate information on target consumer groups, data that can guide the creative and media staffs.

Many agencies also employ technicians and producers who turn ideas into camera-ready proofs, color plates, videotape, audio clips and web-based ads, although a lot of production work is contracted to specialty companies. Besides full-service agencies there are creative boutiques, which specialize in preparing messages; media buying houses, which recommend strategy on placing ads; and other narrowly focused agencies.

Wayland Ayer ■ Founded the first ad agency.

creative directors ■ Key person in ad campaigns.

account executives ■ Agency reps to clients.

media buyers ■ Decide where to place ads.

Advertising Agencies

These are the largest global advertising organizations, all operating numerous subsidiaries, ranked by worldwide revenue:

	Headquarters	Worldwide
Omnicom	New York	$7.5 billion
Interpublic	New York	6.2 billion
WPP	London	5.8 billion
Publicis	Paris	2.7 billion
Dentsu	Tokyo	2.1 billion
Havas	Paris	1.8 billion

These U.S. agencies, all based in New York except Leo Burnett, which is in Chicago, ranked by the revenue from their core advertising clients in the United States. All are part of global conglomerates.

	U.S. Revenue
JWT (WPP)	$469 million
McCann Erickson (Interpublic)	436 million
Leo Burnett (Publicis)	353 million
BBDO (Omnicom)	281 million
Ogilvy & Mather (WPP)	278 million
DDB (Omnicom)	267 million
Grey (WPP)	251 million
FCB (Interpublic)	201 million
Publicis (Publicis)	196 million
Saatchi & Saatchi (Publicis)	196 million

Agency Compensation

Advertising agencies once earned their money in a standard way—15 percent of the client advertiser's total outlay for space or time. On huge accounts, like Procter & Gamble, agencies made killings.

Commissions The 15 percent **commission contract** system broke down in the 1990s when U.S. businesses scrambled to cut costs to become more competitive. Today, according to a guesstimate by the trade journal *Advertising Age*, only 10 to 12 percent of agency contracts use a standard percentage. Agency compensation generally is negotiated. Big advertisers, like P&G, are thought to be paying 13 percent on average, but different agencies handle the company's brands, each in a separate contract. For competitive reasons all parties tend to be secretive about actual terms.

Performance Commission contracts have been replaced largely with **performance contracts.** The advertiser pays an agency's costs plus a negotiated profit. In addition, if a campaign works spectacularly, agencies land bonuses.

Equity In the 1990s dot-com boom a performance contract variation was to pay agencies with shares in the company. **Equity contracts** are chancy for agencies because an advertiser's success hinges on many variables, not just the advertising, but the return for an agency with a soaring client can be stratospheric.

commission contract ■ An advertising agency earns an agreed-upon percentage of what the advertising client spends for time and space, traditionally 15 percent.

performance contract ■ An advertising agency earns expenses and an agreed-upon markup for the advertising client, plus bonuses for exceeding minimal expectations.

equity contract ■ An advertising agency is compensated with shares of stock in an advertising client.

advertising director ■ Coordinates marketing and advertising.

brand manager ■ Coordinates marketing and advertising for a specific brand.

Advertiser's Role in Advertising

Most companies, although they hire agencies for advertising services, have their own advertising expertise among the in-house people who develop marketing strategies. These companies look to ad agencies to develop the advertising campaigns that will help them meet their marketing goals. For some companies the **advertising director** is the liaison between the company's marketing strategists and the ad agency's tacticians. Large companies with many products have in-house **brand managers** for this liaison. Although it is not the usual pattern, some companies have in-house advertising departments and rely hardly at all on agencies.

Placing Advertisements

studypreview **The placement of advertisements is a sophisticated business. Not only do different media have inherent advantages and disadvantages in reaching potential customers, but so do individual publications and broadcast outlets.**

Global Marketing
Knowing the following that Houston Rockets star Yao Ming has in his China homeland, the distributor for the Chinese beer Yanjing paid $6 million for Chinese-language billboards at the Rockets' arena. Thirty 2003 Rockets games were broadcast in China, where millions of viewers saw Houston Yanjing signs. Also, the imported Yanjing beer picked up customers in Houston.

Media Plans

Agencies create **media plans** to ensure that advertisements reach the right target audience. Developing a media plan is no small task. Consider the number of media outlets available: 1,400 daily newspapers in the United States alone, 8,000 weeklies, 1,200 general-interest magazines, 13,000 radio stations and 1,200 television stations. Other possibilities include direct mail, banners on web sites, billboards, blimps, skywriting and even printing the company's name on pencils.

Media buyers use formulas, some very complex, to decide which media are best for reaching potential customers. Most of these formulas begin with a factor called **CPM,** short for cost per thousand. If airtime for a radio advertisement costs 7.2 cents per thousand listeners, it's probably a better deal than a magazine with a 7.3-cent CPM, assuming that both reach the same audience. CPM by itself is just a starting point in choosing media. Other variables that media buyers consider include whether a message will work in a particular medium. For example, radio wouldn't work for a product that lends itself to a visual pitch and sight gags.

Media buyers have numerous sources of data to help them decide where advertisements can be placed for the best results. The **Audit Bureau of Circulations,** created by the newspaper industry in 1914, provides reliable information based on independent audits of the circulation of most newspapers. Survey organizations like Nielsen and Arbitron conduct surveys on television and radio audiences. Standard Rate and Data Service publishes volumes of information on media audiences, circulations and advertising rates.

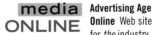

Advertising Age Online Web site for *the* industry magazine with top stories of the day. **www.adage.com**

Audit Bureau of Circulations The world's pre-eminent self-regulatory organization. **www.accessabc.com**

Media Choices

Here are the pluses and minuses of major media as advertising vehicles.

Newspapers The hot relationship that media theorist Marshall McLuhan described between newspapers and their readers attracts advertisers. Newspaper readers are predisposed to consider information in advertisements seriously. Studies show that people, when ready to buy, look more to newspapers than to other media. Because newspapers are tangible, readers can refer back to advertisements just by picking up the paper a second time, which is not possible with ephemeral media like television and radio. Coupons are possible in newspapers. Newspaper readers tend to be older, better educated and higher earning than television and radio audiences. Space for newspaper ads usually can be reserved as late as 48 hours ahead, and 11th-hour changes are possible.

media plans ■ Lays out where ads are placed.

CPM ■ Cost per thousand; a tool to determine the cost effectiveness of different media.

Audit Bureau of Circulations ■ Verifies circulation claims.

Advertising Spending by Medium

This is a projection on how the 2005 advertising pie was divided among major U.S. mass media, including both national and local media:

Television	$65.8 billion
Newspapers	49.6 million
Magazines	13.0 million
Radio	20.0 million
Online	8.8 million

However, newspapers are becoming less valuable for reaching young adults. To the consternation of newspaper publishers there has been an alarming drop in readership among these people in recent years, and it appears that, unlike their parents, young adults are not picking up the newspaper habit as they mature.

Another drawback to newspapers is printing on newsprint, a relatively cheap paper that absorbs ink like a slow blotter. The result is that ads do not look as good as they do in slick magazines. Slick, stand-alone inserts offset the newsprint drawback somewhat, but many readers pull the inserts out and discard them as soon as they open the paper.

Magazines As another print medium, magazines have many of the advantages of newspapers plus longer **shelf life,** an advertising term for the amount of time that an advertisement remains available to readers. Magazines remain in the home for weeks, sometimes months, which offers greater exposure to advertisements. People share magazines, which gives them high **pass-along circulation.** Magazines are more prestigious, with slick paper and splashier graphics. With precise color separations and enameled papers, magazine advertisements can be beautiful in ways that newspaper advertisements cannot. Magazines, specializing as they do, offer more narrowly defined audiences than do newspapers.

On the downside, magazines require reservations for advertising space up to three months in advance. Opportunities for last-minute changes are limited, often impossible.

media ONLINE **Association of Independent Commercial Producers** AICP represent the interests of those who produce commercials in various media. See some of their work.
www.aicp.com

Radio Radio stations with narrow formats offer easily identified target audiences. Time can be bought on short notice, with changes possible almost until airtime. Comparatively inexpensive, radio lends itself to repeated play of advertisements to drive home a message introduced in more expensive media like television. Radio lends itself to jingles that can contribute to a lasting image.

However, radio offers no opportunity for a visual display, although the images that listeners create in their minds from audio suggestions can be more potent than those set out visually on television. Radio is a mobile medium that people carry with them. The extensive availability of radio is offset, however, by the fact that people tune in and out. Another negative is that many listeners are inattentive. Also, there is no shelf life.

Television As a moving and visual medium, television can offer unmatched impact, and the rapid growth of both network and local television advertising, far outpacing other media, indicates its effectiveness in reaching a diverse mass audience.

Drawbacks include the fact that production costs can be high. So are rates. The expense of television time has forced advertisers to go to shorter and shorter advertisements. A result is **ad clutter,** a phenomenon in which advertisements compete against each other and reduce the impact of all of them. Placing advertisements on television is a problem because demand outstrips the supply of slots, especially during prime hours. Slots for some hours are locked up months, even whole seasons, in advance. Because of the audience's diversity and size, targeting potential customers with any precision is difficult with television—with the exception of emerging narrowly focused cable services.

shelf life ■ How long a periodical remains in use.

pass-along circulation ■ All the people who see a periodical.

ad clutter ■ So many competing ads that all lose impact.

Online Services Like many other newspapers in the mid-1990s, the San Jose, California, *Mercury News* established a news web site on the Internet. Editors put news from the newspaper on the web site so that people with computers could pick up news online. Every time an electronic reader connected to the Mercury web site, it was recorded as a **hit.** In 1995, early in web history, the site was receiving 325,000 hits a day, compared with the 270,000 circulation of the newsprint product. The potential of web sites as advertising vehicles has not been lost on newspapers or other organizations, including Microsoft, which also have established news sites online.

One advantage of **online advertising** is that readers can click deeper and deeper levels of information about advertised products. A lot more information can be packed into a layered online message than within the space and time confines of a print or broadcast ad. High-resolution color is standard, and the technology is available for moving pictures and audio.

Advertisers are not abandoning traditional media, but they are experimenting with online possibilities. For mail-order products, orders can be placed over the Internet right from the ad. For some groups of potential customers, online advertising has major advantages. To reach college students, almost all of whom have computer access, online advertising makes sense.

The downside of web site advertising is that the Internet is accessible only to people with computers, modems and Internet accounts. Of course, the percentage of the computer-knowledgeable population is mushrooming and will continue to do so.

All told, alternative media have taken a chunk away from traditional major media.

hit ■ A recorded viewing of a web site.

online advertising ■ Provide messages to computers.

Interactive Advertising Bureau The IAB's mission is to help online and interactive companies increase their revenues.
www.iab.net

New Advertising Platforms

studypreview **Advertisers have discovered video gaming as a platform for reaching potential customers. Some advertisers are building their own games around their products. Search engines like Google are another new advertising platform.**

Gaming

To catch consumers who spend less time with television and more with video games, advertisers have shifted chunks of their budgets to gaming. The potential is incredible. Half of Americans 6 and older play games, and that elusive target for advertisers, men 18 and older, make up 26 percent of the gamers.

For an on-screen plug, advertisers pay typically $20,000 to $100,000 for a message integrated into the game. In gaming's early days, game-makers and product marketers worked directly with each other, but now many ad agencies have gaming divisions that act as brokers.

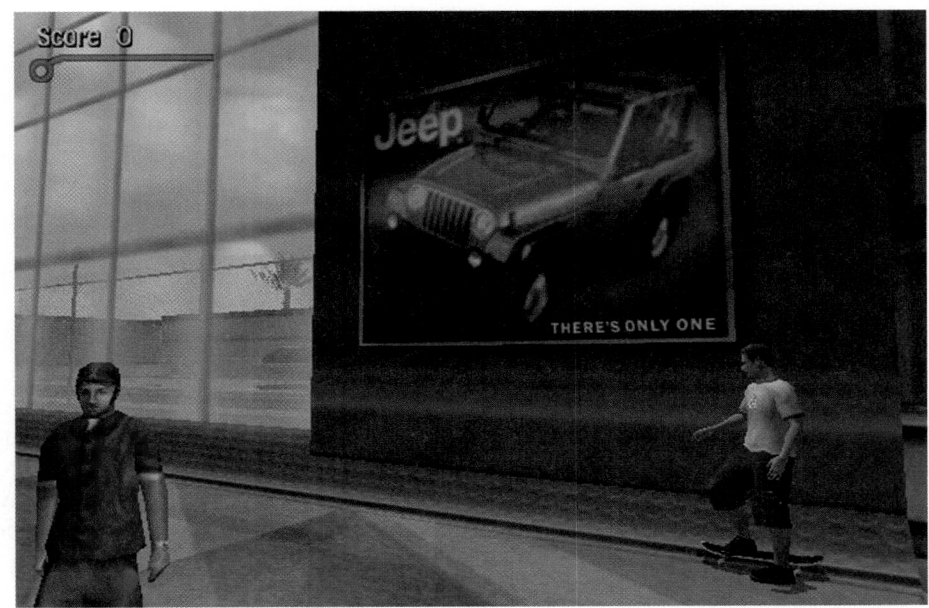

Game Platform Jeep has found video games a new advertising platform. Background billboards on *Tony Hawk's Pro Skater 2* can be updated with new products either as new DVD editions are issued or with downloads for Internet-connected games.

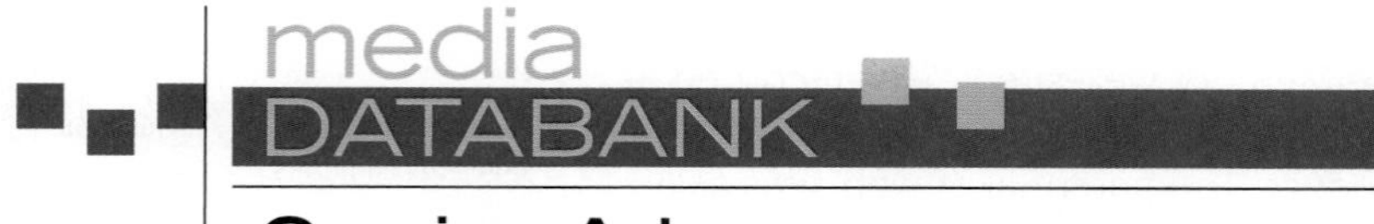

Gaming Ads

Among leading product placements in video games:

Burger King	*Need for Speed Underground 2*
Cingular Wireless	*Need for Speed Underground 2*
Jeep	*Tony Hawk's Pro Skater 2*
Levi Strauss	*NASCAR 2005: Chase the Cup*
Old Spice	*Need for Speed Underground 2*
Proctor & Gamble	*NASCAR 2005: Chase the Cup*

Game ads have advantages, particularly for online games. Messages can be changed instantly—a background billboard for Pepsi can become a movie trailer. One company, Massive, uses unseen interactive coding to identify gamers and adjust plugs that, for example, list stores near specific players and make geographic and other ad content adjustments. Nielsen, known mostly for television ratings, and game publisher Activision have an interactive system for tracking how many players see advertiser impressions—they record how may gamers see an ad and even can measure gamers' recall of an ad.

Although online gaming has advantages for advertisers, there are downsides. Online gaming ads, although generally cost effective, are problematic. Games can take months to develop, requiring far more lead time than advertisers usually have for rolling out a comprehensive multimedia campaign. For simple billboard messages, however, games have the advantage of being instantly changeable.

Advergames

Established brands have created their own games, which appear on their own web sites. In an early **advergame,** as these ads are called, Nike the shoe manufacturer created a soccer game at Nikefootball.com. Kraft Foods had an advergaming race at Candyland.com. A downside: Because advergames are accessible only through a brand's site, they don't make sense for emerging brands.

Google Ads

The Internet search engine Google, capitalizing on its superfast hunt technology, has elbowed into the traditional placement service provided by advertising agencies. Google arranges for advertising space on thousands of web sites, many of them narrowly focused, like blogs, and places ads for its clients on the sites. Every blog visitor who clicks a **sponsored link** placed by Google will go to a fuller advertisement. Google charges the advertiser a **click-through fee.** Google pays the site for every click through. Google matches sites and advertisers, so a search for new Cadillacs doesn't display ads for muffler shops.

Google also places what it calls "advertiser links" on search screens. The New York *Times,* for example, has a license to use Google technology for readers who enter search terms for searches on the *Times* site. The license allows Google to display ads of likely interest whenever a *Times* site reader conducts an internal site search. A search for *Times* coverage of news about Jamaica, for example, will produce links to *Times* stories on Jamaica as well as to advertisements for Caribbean travel elsewhere on the Internet. If a *Times* reader clicks on an ad link, Google pays the *Times* a click-through fee—from the revenue the advertiser paid to Google to place its ads.

Google has quickly become a major player in Internet advertising. Of an estimated $10 billion spent by advertisers for online messages in 2004, Google had $1.9 billion. Nobody was earning more advertising revenue from the Internet.

advergaming ■ A sponsored online game, usually by an established brand at its own site.

sponsored link ■ On-screen hot spot to move to an online advertisement.

click-through fee ■ A charge to advertisers when an online link to their ads is activated; also a fee paid to web sites that host the links.

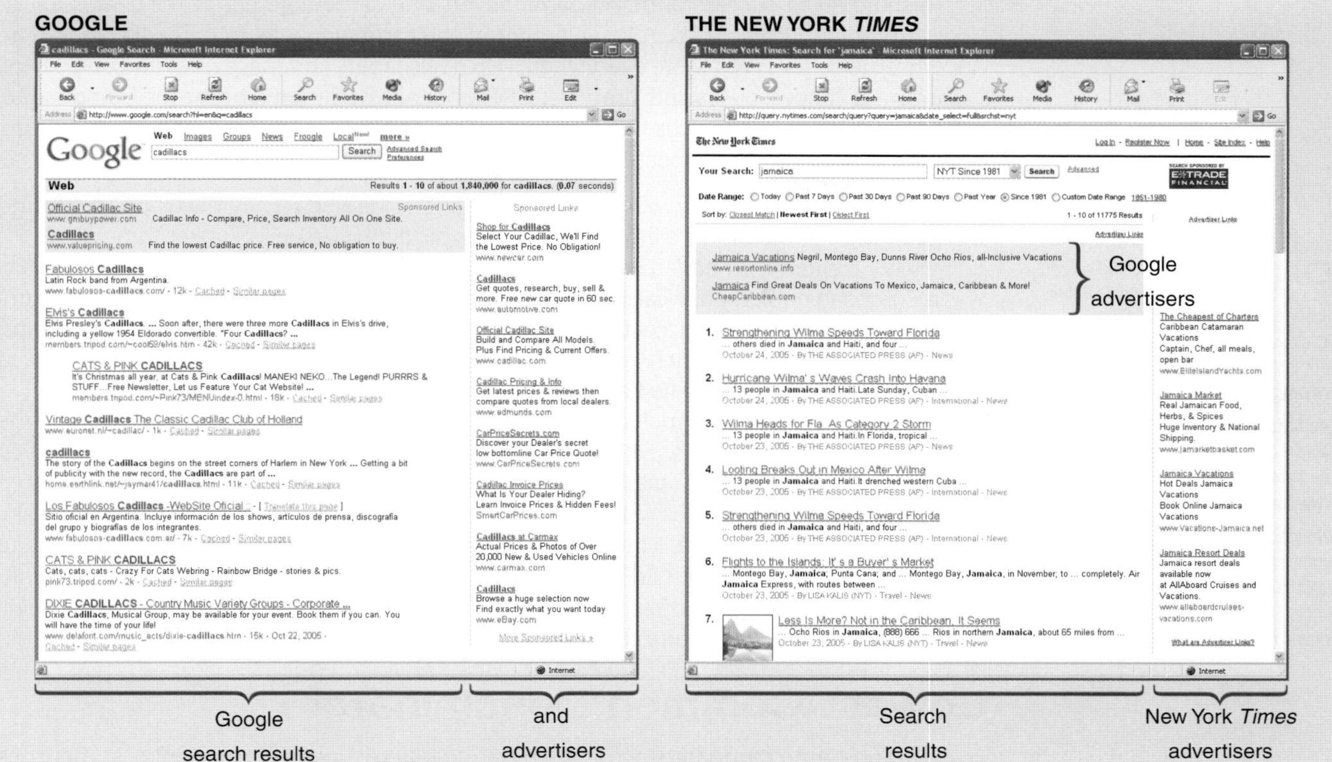

Inside Google's Money Machine Google searches generate links not only to sites that relate to the key word in the search but also links to advertising that relates. A search for information about Cadillacs will generate all kinds of articles about that car, as an example, plus "sponsored links" from places that sell Cadillacs. Google even tries to display ads from dealers that are within an easy drive. The New York *Times* site uses Google technology for on-site searches. Search results are displayed with links to *Times* articles on the subject but also with "advertiser links" to advertiser sites. In its almost instant searches on the *Times* site, Google taps three huge databases to make matches: the *Times* site itself, the advertisers that have paid Google to be sponsors, and the personal computer used to trigger the search.

Pitching Messages

studypreview **When the age of mass production and mass markets arrived, common wisdom in advertising favored aiming at the largest possible audience of potential customers. These are called lowest common denominator approaches, and such advertisements tend to be heavy-handed so that no one can possibly miss the point. Narrower pitches, aimed at segments of the mass audience, permit more deftness, subtlety and imagination.**

Importance of Brands

A challenge for advertising people is the modern-day reality that mass-produced products intended for large markets are essentially alike: Toothpaste is toothpaste is toothpaste. When a product is virtually identical to the competition, how can one toothpaste maker move more tubes?

Brand Names By trial and error, tactics were devised in the late 1800s to set similar products apart. One tactic, promoting a product as a **brand** name, aims to make a product a household word. When it is successful, a brand name becomes almost the generic identifier, like Coke for cola and Kleenex for facial tissue.

brand ■ A nongeneric product name designed to set the product apart from the competition.

Techniques of successful brand-name advertising came together in the 1890s for an English product, Pears' soap. A key element in the campaign was multimedia saturation. Advertisements for Pears' were everywhere—in newspapers and magazines and on posters, vacant walls, fences, buses and lampposts. Redundancy hammered home the brand name. "Good morning. Have you used Pears' today?" became a good-natured greeting among Britons that was still being repeated 50 years later. Each repetition reinforced the brand name.

Brand Image **David Ogilvy,** who headed the Ogilvy & Mather agency, developed the **brand image** in the 1950s. Ogilvy's advice: "Give your product a first-class ticket through life."

Ogilvy created shirt advertisements with the distinguished Baron Wrangell, who really was a European nobleman, wearing a black eye patch—and a Hathaway shirt. The classy image was reinforced with the accoutrements around Wrangell: exquisite models of sailing ships, antique weapons, silver dinnerware. To some seeing Wrangell's setting, the patch suggested all kinds of exotica. Perhaps he had lost an eye in a romantic duel or a sporting accident.

Explaining the importance of image, Ogilvy once said: "Take whisky. Why do some people choose Jack Daniels, while others choose Grand Dad or Taylor? Have they tried all three and compared the taste? Don't make me laugh. The reality is that these three brands have different images which appeal to different kinds of people. It isn't the whisky they choose, it's the image. The brand image is 90 percent of what the distiller has to sell. Give people a taste of Old Crow, and tell them it's Old Crow. Then give them another taste of Old Crow, but tell them it's Jack Daniels. Ask them which they prefer. They'll think the two drinks are quite different. They are tasting images."

media ONLINE

Ogilvy One of the largest marketing communications firms in the world, Ogilvy develops its campaigns on a local level with international flair.
www.ogilvy.com

Leo Burnett Worldwide Check out this colorful site and see what campaigns Leo Burnett is creating.
www.leoburnett.com

What Brand Are You? Enter your name, choose your values and your goals, and they will tell you your brand name.
www.whatbrandareyou.com

Lowest Common Denominator

Early brand-name campaigns were geared to the largest possible audience, sometimes called an LCD, or **lowest common denominator,** approach. The term *LCD* is adapted from mathematics. To reach an audience that includes members with IQs of 100, the pitch cannot exceed their level of understanding, even if some people in the audience have IQs of 150. The opportunity for deft touches and even cleverness is limited by the fact they might be lost on some potential customers.

LCD advertising is best epitomized in contemporary advertising by USP, short for **unique selling proposition,** a term coined by **Rosser Reeves** of the giant Ted Bates agency in the 1960s. Reeves' prescription was simple: Create a benefit of the product, even if from thin air, and then tout the benefit authoritatively and repeatedly as if the competition doesn't have it. One early USP campaign boasted that Schlitz beer bottles were "washed with live steam." The claim sounded good—who would want to drink from dirty bottles? However, the fact was that every brewery used steam to clean reusable bottles before filling them again. Furthermore, what is "live steam"? Although the implication of a competitive edge was hollow, it was done dramatically and pounded home with emphasis, and it sold beer. Just as hollow as a competitive advantage was the USP claim for Colgate toothpaste: "Cleans Your Breath While It Cleans Your Teeth."

Perhaps to compensate for a lack of substance, many USP ads are heavy-handed. Hardly an American has not heard about fast-fast-fast relief from headache remedies or that heartburn relief is spelled R-O-L-A-I-D-S. USP can be unappealing, as is acknowledged even by the chairman of Warner-Lambert, which makes Rolaids, who once laughed that his company owed the American people an apology for insulting their intelligence over and over with Bates' USP slogans. Warner-Lambert was also laughing all the way to the bank over the USP-spurred success of Rolaids, Efferdent, Listermint and Bubblicious.

A unique selling proposition need be neither hollow nor insulting, however. Leo Burnett, founder of the agency bearing his name, refined the USP concept by insisting that the unique point be real. For Maytag, Burnett took the company's slight advantage in reliability and dramatized it with the lonely Maytag repairman.

David Ogilvy ■ Championed brand imaging.

brand image ■ Spin put on a brand name.

lowest common denominator ■ Messages for broadest audience possible.

unique selling proposition ■ Emphasizing a single feature.

Rosser Reeves ■ Devised unique selling proposition.

Jack Trout ■ Devised positioning.

positioning ■ Targeting ads for specific consumer groups.

Market Segments

Rather than pitching to the lowest common denominator, advertising executive **Jack Trout** developed the idea of **positioning.** Trout worked to establish product identities that appealed not to the whole audience but to a specific audience. The cowboy image for Marlboro cigarettes, for example, established a macho attraction beginning in 1958. Later, something similar was done with Virginia Slims, aimed at women.

Positioning helps to distinguish products from all the LCD clamor and noise. Advocates of positioning note that there are more and more advertisements and that they are becoming noisier and noisier. Ad clutter, as it is called, drowns out individual advertisements. With positioning, the appeal is focused and caters to audience segments, and it need not be done in such broad strokes.

Campaigns based on positioning have included:

- Johnson & Johnson's baby oil and baby shampoo, which were positioned as adult products by advertisements featuring athletes.
- Alka-Seltzer, once a hangover and headache remedy, which was positioned as an upscale product for stress relief among health-conscious, success-driven people.

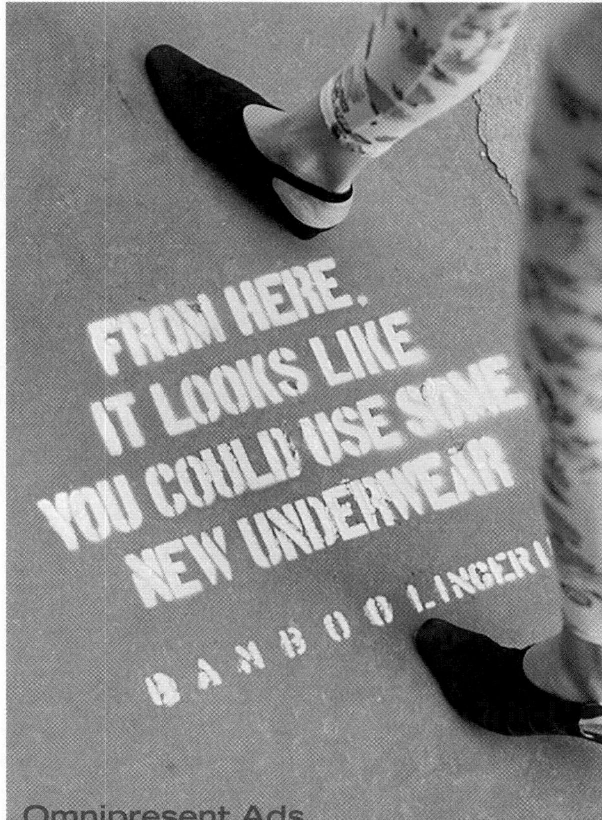

Omnipresent Ads
Bamboo Lingerie's stenciled sidewalk messages may have been unsettling to some folks, but they sold underwear. Like many advertisers worried that their messages are lost in ad-crammed traditional media, Bamboo has struck out for nontraditional territory to be noticed. Regina Kelley, director of strategic planning for the Saatchi & Saatchi agency in New York, said: "Any space you can take in visually, anything you can hear, in the future will be branded."

Redundancy Techniques

Advertising people learned the importance of redundancy early on. To be effective, an advertising message must be repeated, perhaps thousands of times. Redundancy is expensive, however. To increase effectiveness at less cost, advertisers use several techniques:

- **Barrages.** Scheduling advertisements in intensive bursts called **flights** or **waves.**
- **Bunching.** Promoting a product in a limited period, such as running advertisements for school supplies in late August and September.
- **Trailing.** Running condensed versions of advertisements after the original has been introduced, as automakers do when they introduce new models with multipage magazine spreads, following with single-page placements.
- **Multimedia trailing.** Using less expensive media to reinforce expensive advertisements. Relatively cheap drive-time radio in major markets is a favorite follow through to expensive television advertisements created for major events like the Super Bowl.

Marshall McLuhan, the media theorist prominent in the 1960s, is still quoted as saying that advertising is important after the sale to confirm for purchasers that they made a wise choice. McLuhan's observation has not been lost on advertisers that seek repeat customers.

Under-the-Radar Advertising

Inundated with advertisements, 6,000 a week on network television, double since 1983, many people tune out. Some do it literally with their remotes. Ad people are concerned that traditional modes are losing effectiveness. People are overwhelmed. Consider, for example, that a major grocery store carries 30,000 items, each with packaging that screams "buy me." More commercial messages are put there than a human being can handle. The problem is ad clutter. Advertisers are trying to address the clutter in numerous ways, including stealth ads, new-site ads and alternative media. Although not hidden or subliminal, stealth ads are subtle—even covert. You might not know you're being pitched unless you're attentive, really attentive.

barrages ■ Intensive repetition of ads.

flights ■ Intensive repetition of ads.

waves ■ Intensive repetition of ads.

bunching ■ Short-term ad campaign.

trailing ■ Shorter, smaller ads after campaign is introduced.

stealth ads ■ Advertisements, often subtle, in nontraditional, unexpected places.

Stealth Ads So neatly can **stealth ads** fit into the landscape that people may not recognize they're being pitched. Consider the Bamboo lingerie company, which stenciled messages on a Manhattan sidewalk: "From here it looks like you could use some new

Viral Advertising

Automakers have experimented with what's called "viral advertising," producing compelling action stories on the web that viewers will want to pass on, viruslike, to friends. Embedded in story lines, like Ford's "Evil Twin" for its SportKa in Europe, are product messages. BMW estimates that 55.1 million people have seen its "For Hire" series. Honda couldn't be more pleased with its "Cog" mini-story. A Honda executive said: "I have never seen a commercial that bolted around the world like 'Cog' in two weeks."

underwear." Sports stadiums like FedEx Field outside of Washington, D.C., work their way into everyday dialogue, subtly reinforcing product identity.

media ONLINE **Prop Star** An agency that specializes in placing products and brand names in movies and on TV. **www.propstar.com**

Product Placement In the 1980s advertisers began wiggling brand-name products into movie scripts, creating an additional although minor revenue stream for movie-makers. The practice, **product placement,** stirred criticism about artistic integrity, but it gained momentum. Fees zoomed upward. For the 2005 release of *The Green Hornet,* Miramax was seeking an automaker willing to pay at least $35 million for its products to be written into the script, topping the $15 million that Ford paid for its 2003 Thunderbird, Jaguar and Aston Martin lines to be in the James Bond movie *Die Another Day.*

Later, placing products into television scenes gained importance with the advent of **TiVo** and other devices that allow people to record shows and replay them commercial-free at their convenience. By 2004 about 1 million people owned these devices. Their growing popularity worried the television industry, whose business model was dependent on revenue from advertisers to which it guaranteed an audience for ads. With TiVo audiences no longer were trapped into watching commercials. Was the 30-second spot commercial doomed? The television and advertising industries struck product placement deals that went beyond anything seen before. For a fee, products are being built into scripts not only as props but also for both implicit and explicit endorsement.

media ONLINE **Ridiculous Infomercial Review** The web site that gleans laughs from the tacky world of television infomercials. **http://infomercial.tvheaven.com**

Infomercials Less subtle is the **infomercial,** a program-length television commercial dolled up to look like a newscast, a live-audience participation show or a chatty talk show. With the proliferation of 24-hour television service and of cable channels, airtime is so cheap at certain hours that advertisers of even offbeat products can afford it. Hardly anybody is fooled into thinking that infomercials are anything but advertisements, but some full-length media advertisements, like Liz Taylor wandering through CBS sitcoms, are cleverly disguised.

A print media variation is the **'zine**—a magazine published by a manufacturer to plug a single line of products with varying degrees of subtlety. 'Zine publishers, including such stalwarts as IBM and Sony, have even been so brazen as to sell these wall-to-wall advertising vehicles at newsstands. In 1996, if you bought a splashy new magazine called *Colors,* you paid $4.50 for it. Once inside, you probably would realize it was a thinly veiled ad for Benetton casual clothes. *Guess Journal* may look like a magazine, but guess who puts it out as a 'zine: The makers of the Guess fashion brand.

Stealth advertisements try "to morph into the very entertainment it sponsors," wrote Mary Kuntz, Joseph Weber and Heidi Dawley in *Business Week.* The goal, they said, is "to create messages so entertaining, so compelling—and maybe so disguised—that rapt audiences will swallow them whole, oblivious to the sales component."

product placement ■ Writing a brand-name product into a television or movie script.

TiVo ■ A television recording and playback device allows viewers to edit out commercials. A competing device is ReplayTV.

infomercial ■ Program-length broadcast commercial.

'zine ■ Magazine whose entire content, articles and ads, pitches a single product or product line.

Post-Brand-Name Era

Perhaps prematurely, perhaps not, obituaries are being written for brand names—and brand-name advertising. Retailers are pushing **store brands,** on which they typically score 10 percent higher profits. Every time somebody buys Wal-Mart's Ol' Roy dog chow, Purina and other brand-name manufacturers lose a sale. Wal-Mart spends virtually nothing other than packaging costs for in-store displays to advertise Ol' Roy, which has knocked off Purina as top-seller. The store-brand assault has struck at a whole range of venerable brand names: Kellogg's, Kraft, Procter & Gamble and Unilever. Forrester Research, which tracks consumer trends, said in a 2002 report: "Wal-Mart will become the new P&G."

Some brands remain strong, like automobile lines, but many manufacturers of consumer goods, whose advertising has been a financial mainstay of network television and magazines as well as newspapers and radio, have had to cut back on ad spending. P&G spent $13.9 million advertising its Era detergent in 2001, only $5.4 million in 2002. Some manufacturers have dropped out of the brand-name business. Unilever has only 200 brands left, compared to 1,600 in the mid-1990s.

Retail chains, led by Wal-Mart, have the gigantic marketing channels to move great quantities of products without advertising expanses. Some retailers even own the factories. The Kroger chain owns 41 factories that produce 4,300 store-brand products for its grocery shelves.

Before the mega-retailers, brand names gave products an edge—with network television and national magazines carrying the messages. In those days the major networks—ABC, CBS and NBC—delivered messages to millions of consumers with greater effect than could small retailers. Not only are small retailers disappearing, but also the networks can't deliver what they used to. Television systems with 500 channels and the highly diverse web have divided and subdivided the audience into fragments. In a 2003 newsletter to clients the ad agency Doremus noted, despairingly, that "it's almost impossible to get your name in enough channels to build substantial awareness." Willard Bishop Consulting came to a similar conclusion from a study on network television, noting that three commercials could reach 80 percent of one target audience, 18- to 49-year-old women, in 1995. That penetration level required 97 ads in 2000.

In an analysis of the phenomenon *Fortune* magazine writer Michael Boyle said the big superstores are displacing brand-name advertising as the new direct connection to consumers. The new mass channel, he said, is the superstore.

Product Placement
A financial linchpin for the CBS adventure series *Survivor* was integrating identifiable brand-name products into the story lines for a price. Advertisers have gravitated to product placement to counter viewership that's lost to fast-growing options such as TiVo and Replay that viewers can use to bypass commercial messages.

F Research and Psychology

study preview **Freudian ideas about the human subconscious influenced advertising in the 1950s, and research tried to tap hidden motivations that could be exploited to sell products and services. The extreme in appealing to the subconscious, called subliminal advertising, worried many people, but it was an approach whose effectiveness was never demonstrated.**

Motivational Research

Whatever naïveté Americans had about opinion-shaping was dispelled by the mid-20th century. Sinister possibilities were evident in the work of **Joseph Goebbels,** the minister of propaganda and public enlightenment in Nazi Germany. In the Pacific the Japanese beamed the infamous Tokyo Rose radio broadcasts to GIs to lower their morale. Then, during the Korean War, a macabre fascination developed with the so-called brainwashing techniques used on U.S. prisoners of war. In this same period the work of Austrian psychiatrist **Sigmund Freud,** which emphasized hidden motivations and repressed sexual impulses, was being popularized in countless books and articles.

store brands ■ Products sold with a store brand, often manufactured by the retailer. Also called *house brands* and *private labels.*

Joseph Goebbels ■ Nazi propagandist.

Sigmund Freud ■ Examined hidden motivations.

No wonder, considering this intellectual context, advertising people in the 1950s looked to the social sciences to find new ways to woo customers. Among the advertising pioneers of this period was **Ernest Dichter,** who accepted Freud's claim that people act on motivations that they are not even aware of. Depth interviewing, Dichter felt, could reveal these motivations, which could then be exploited in advertising messages.

Dichter used his interviewing, called **motivational research,** for automotive clients. Rightly or wrongly, Dichter determined that the American male was loyal to his wife but fantasized about having a mistress. Men, he noted, usually were the decision makers in purchasing a car. Then, in what seemed a quantum leap, Dichter equated sedans, which were what most people drove, with wives. Sedans were familiar, reliable. Convertibles, impractical for many people and also beyond their reach financially, were equated with mistresses—romantic, daring, glamorous. With these conclusions in hand, Dichter devised advertisements for a new kind of sedan without a center door pillar. The hardtop, as it was called, gave a convertible effect when the windows were down. The advertisements, dripping with sexual innuendo, clearly reflected Dichter's thinking: "You'll find something new to love every time you drive it." Although they were not as solid as sedans and tended to leak air and water, hardtops were popular among automobile buyers for the next 25 years.

Dichter's motivational research led to numerous campaigns that exploited sexual images. For Ronson lighters the flame, in phallic form, was reproduced in extraordinary proportions. A campaign for Ajax cleanser, hardly a glamour product, had a white knight charging through the street, ignoring law and regulation with a great phallic lance. Whether consumers were motivated by sexual imagery is hard to establish. Even so, many campaigns based on motivational research worked.

media ONLINE **The Advertising Archives** Reference source for all those who are interested in art, social history and every product that has been advertised in the last 150 years.
www.advertisingarchives.co.uk

Subliminal Advertising A discussion of subliminal advertising, complete with visual examples.
www.poleshift.org/sublim

Subliminal Advertising

The idea that advertising can be persuasive at subconscious levels was taken a step further by market researcher **Jim Vicary,** who coined the term **subliminal advertising.** Vicary claimed in 1957 that he had studied the effect of inserting messages like "Drink Coca-Cola" and "Eat popcorn" into movies. The messages, though flashed too fast to be recognized by the human eye, still registered in the brain and, said Vicary, prompted movie-goers to rush to the snack bar. In experiments at a New Jersey movie house, he said, Coke sales increased 18 percent and popcorn sales almost 60 percent. Vicary's report stirred great interest, and also alarm, but researchers who tried to replicate his study found no evidence to support his claim.

Despite doubts about Vicary's claims, psychologists have identified a phenomenon they call **subception,** in which certain behavior sometimes seems to be triggered by messages perceived subliminally. Whether the effect works outside laboratory experiments and whether the effect is strong enough to prod a consumer to go out and buy is uncertain. Nevertheless, there remains a widespread belief among the general population that subliminal advertising works, and fortunes are being made by people who peddle various devices and systems with extravagant claims that they can control human behavior. Among these are the "hidden" messages in stores' sound systems that say shoplifting is not nice.

This idea that advertising is loaded with hidden messages has been taken to extremes by **Wilson Bryan Key,** who spins out books alleging that plugs are hidden in all kinds of places for devil worship, homosexuality and a variety of libertine activities. He has accused the Nabisco people of baking the word "sex" into Ritz crackers. At Howard Johnson restaurants, he has charged, placemat pictures of plates heaped with clams portray orgies and bestiality. Though widely read, Key offers no evidence beyond his own observations and interpretations. In advertising circles, Key's views are dismissed as amusing but wacky. The view at Nabisco and Howard Johnson is less charitable.

In 1990 Key's views suffered a serious setback. He was a primary witness in a highly publicized Nevada trial on whether Judas Priest's heavy-metal album "Stained Class" had triggered the suicide of an 18-year-old youth and the attempted suicide of his 20-year-old friend. The families said that the pair had obsessed on a Judas Priest album that dealt with suicide and that one song was subliminally embedded with the words "Do it" over

Ernest Dichter ■ Pioneered motivational research.

motivational research ■ Seeks subconscious appeals that can be used in advertising.

Jim Vicary ■ Made dubious subliminal advertising claims.

subliminal advertising ■ Ads that cannot be consciously perceived.

subception ■ Receiving subconscious messages that trigger behavior.

Wilson Bryan Key ■ Sees subliminal advertising widely used.

Subliminal Messages
Author Wilson Bryan Key is convinced that Madison Avenue hides sex in advertisements to attract attention and sell products. To demonstrate his point, he outlined the human figures that he saw in an orgy in a photograph of clam strips on a Howard Johnson restaurant placemat. Most advertising people dismiss his claims.

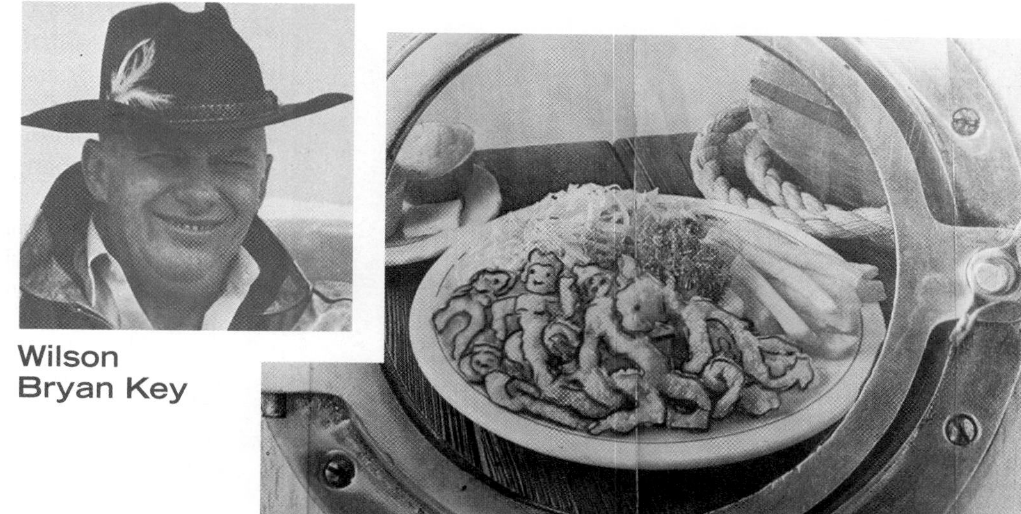

Wilson Bryan Key

Sex in the Clams?

and over. The families' attorneys hired Key as an expert witness to help make their point. From Key's perspective the case did not go well. Millions of television viewers who followed the trial strained to make out the supposed words "Do it," but even when isolated from the rest of the music, they were almost impossible to make out. It turned out the sounds were neither lyrics nor even vocal but rather instrumental effects. Members of Judas Priest testified that they had not equated the sound to any words at all and had inserted it for artistic effect, hardly to encourage suicide. The jury sided with Judas Priest, and Key left town with his wobbly ideas on subliminal messages having taken a serious blow under a jury's scrutiny.

David Ogilvy, founder of the Ogilvy & Mather agency, once made fun of claims like Key's, pointing out the absurdity of "millions of suggestible consumers getting up from their armchairs and rushing like zombies through the traffic on their way to buy the product at the nearest store." The danger of "Vote Bolshevik" being flashed during the *NBC Nightly News* is remote, and whether it would have any effect is dubious.

Advertising Regulation

studypreview **The "buyer beware" underpinning of much of 19th-century advertising has given way to "seller beware." Today, advertising is regulated on many fronts: by the media that carry advertisements, by the advertising industry itself and by government agencies.**

Media Gatekeeping

A dramatic reversal in thinking about advertising has occurred in the 20th century. The earlier ***caveat emptor*** ("let the buyer beware") mindset tolerated extravagant claims. Anybody who believed that the same elixir could cure dandruff, halitosis and cancer deserved to be conned, or so went the thinking. Over the years, owing partly to the growing consumer movement, the thinking changed to ***caveat venditor*** ("let the seller beware"), placing the onus on the advertiser to avoid misleading claims and to demonstrate the truth of claims.

In advertising's early days newspapers and magazines skirted the ethics question posed by false advertisements by saying that their pages were open to all advertisers. Under growing pressure, publications sometimes criticized dubious advertisements

caveat emptor ■ Buyer beware.
caveat venditor ■ Seller beware.

Advertising Globalization

Manufacturers on every continent are seeking markets elsewhere, which is generating accounts and revenues for advertising agencies with international operations. The Gap's new high-fashion outlet in Tokyo's ritzy Ginza district is among thousands of examples. Some of the greatest advertising agency expansion is in China, where by one count 50 foreign agencies are trying to carve a share out of a virtually untapped market of 1.2 billion people. The effect is tremendous. Steven Strasser, writing in *Newsweek,* said: "China cares about its athlete's foot problem. Johnson & Johnson's subsidiary made sure of that. When its recent J&J commercial revealed that a fungus caused the itch, sales of Daktarin fungicidal cream soared from Shanghai to Xian."

editorially, but most did not ban them. **Edward Bok,** who made *Ladies' Home Journal* a runaway success in the 1890s, crusaded against dishonest advertising. In one exposé on Lydia E. Pinkham's remedies for "female maladies," Bok reported that Lydia, to whom women readers were invited in advertisements to write for advice, had been dead for 22 years. Yet the advertisements continued.

In 1929 NBC adopted a code of ethics to preclude false or exaggerated claims. Other networks followed. At the peak of the networks' concern about broadcast standards, it was estimated that half the commercials for products were turned away for violating network codes. Codes for broadcast advertising have come and gone over the years, all voluntary with stations that choose to subscribe.

The print media also have seen a variety of industry-wide codes, all voluntary. Most publications spurn misleading advertisements. Typical is the Minot *Daily News* in North Dakota, which refuses advertisements for "clairvoyance, fortune telling, magnetic healing, doubtful medicines and fake sales." Many college newspapers refuse advertisements from term-paper services. Some metropolitan papers turn away advertisements for pornographic movies.

A case can be made that the media do not go far enough in exercising their prerogative to ban dubious advertisements. Critics argue that on nettling questions, such as the morality of printing ads for carcinogenic tobacco products, with major revenue at stake, many newspapers and magazines sidestep a moral judgment, run the advertisements, and reap the revenue. The critics note, for example, that most commercial broadcasters ran cigarette advertisements until the federal government intervened. The media, so goes the argument, are too devoted to profits to do all the regulating they should.

Industry Self-Regulation

The advertising industry itself has numerous organizations that try, through ethics codes and moral suasion, to eradicate falsity and deception. Besides the explicit purposes of these self-policing mechanisms, advertising people can cite their existence to argue that their industry is able to deal with misdeeds itself with a minimum of government regulation.

Edward Bok ■ Set media standards for ads.

National Advertising Review Council The **National Advertising Review Council** investigates complaints from anybody. When it finds a problem, the council asks the offending advertiser to correct the situation. If that does not work, the council turns its file over to whichever government agency it thinks is appropriate.

Although it is a creation of advertising trade associations, the National Advertising Review Council has earned a reputation as a dispassionate attempt at self-regulation. Its 50 members include 10 people appointed from the public—with no connection to the advertising business. Of the complaints the council investigates, two-thirds typically are found to be deceptive advertising. About half of those advertisements are discontinued or modified under council pressure. The council has no legal authority, but its willingness to go to federal agencies or to state attorneys general, in effect recommending prosecution, is a powerful tool for honesty in advertising.

Codes Typical of codes of advertising trade groups is that of the **American Association of Advertising Agencies,** which says member agencies are expected never to produce ads with:

- False, misleading statements or exaggerations, visual or verbal, including misleading price claims.
- Testimonials from unknowledgeable people.
- Unfair disparagement of competitive products.
- Distorted or insufficiently supported claims.
- Anything offending public decency.

Acceptance of the code is a kind of loose condition of membership—more a statement of the association's values than an enforcement tool.

media ONLINE **National Advertising Review Council** Also known as NARC. **www.narcpartners.org**

American Association of Advertising Agencies The AAAA promotes integrity and ethics in advertising. **www.aaaa.org/eweb/startpage.aspx**

Advertising Educational Foundation Visit the Advertising Educational Foundation to review current issues. **www.aef.com**

Ad Council The Ad Council's web site includes a brief history and list of memorable campaigns: Loose Lips Sink Ships, Friends Don't Let Friends Drive Drunk and Take a Bite Out of Crime. **www.adcouncil.org**

Public Service
On a rotating basis, major U.S. advertising agencies donate their time and creativity on behalf of worthwhile causes. Campaigns against drug misuse have been a recurrent Ad Council theme. So have memorable lines like "Friends Don't Let Friends Drive Drunk," "A Mind Is a Terrible Thing to Waste" and "Only You Can Prevent Forest Fires."

National Advertising Review Council ■ Reviews complaints about ads.

American Association of Advertising Agencies ■ Advertising trade association.

Public Interest Advertising The advertising industry has set up an organization, the **Ad Council,** which creates advertisements free for worthy causes. Since the 1940s the council's existence has helped to offset criticism that the advertising business is an unscrupulous manipulator.

The Ad Council has roots in World War II when the ad industry, major media organizations and advertisers created the War Advertising Council to create ads for the war effort. Advertisers funded the council, agencies created the advertisements gratis and media ran donated time and space for them. The first campaign, to recruit military nurses, stressed: "Nursing is a proud profession." Within weeks 500,000 women applied for the Cadet Nurses Corps—almost eight times more than were needed. After the war the Ad Council was formed to continue *pro bono* work on behalf of socially significant national issues.

Because the ads are well done, the media are pleased to run them as a contribution to the public good. Magazines, newspapers and broadcasters donate about $800 million a year in time and space to the Ad Council's ads.

In a typical year 300 noncommercial organizations ask the Ad Council to take them on. The council chooses a dozen, which are turned over to agencies that rotate their services. The United Way has received continuing support from the council. Other campaigns have included restoring the Statue of Liberty, combating illiteracy and improving U.S. productivity. Campaigns that have left an imprint on the public mind have included:

- Forest fire prevention with the character Smokey Bear.
- Environmental protection with the memorable "Don't be fuelish" slogan.
- Fund-raising for the United Negro College Fund, with the line "A mind is a terrible thing to waste."

Government Regulation

Federal Trade Commission Contains copies of daily press releases, speeches and documents. Also information about the FTCs mission and structure of the agency.
www.ftc.gov

The federal government began regulating advertisements in 1914 when Congress created the **Federal Trade Commission.** The commission was charged with protecting honest companies that were being disadvantaged by competitors that made false claims. Today, nine federal agencies besides the FTC are involved heavily in regulating advertising. These include the Food and Drug Administration, the U.S. Postal Service, the Federal Communications Commission and the Securities and Exchange Commission.

In its early days the Federal Trade Commission went about its work meekly, but fueled by the consumer movement in the 1960s, it became aggressive. Although the agency never had the authority to review advertisements ahead of their publication or airing, the FTC let it be known that it would crack down on violations of truth-in-packaging and truth-in-lending requirements. The FTC also began insisting on clarity so that even someone with low intelligence would not be confused. The FTC took particular aim at the overused word "free." To be advertised as "free," an offer had to be without conditions. The FTC moved further to protect the gullible. It was unacceptable, said the FTC, to leave the impression that actors in white coats speaking authoritatively about over-the-counter drugs and toothpastes were physicians or dentists. When Ocean Spray claimed that its cranberry juice offered "food energy," the FTC insisted that the language be changed to "calories." The FTC clamped down on a claim that Profile bread helped people lose weight, noting that the only difference from regular bread was thinner slices. The FTC pressed the Kroger grocery chain on its claim that it carried 150 everyday items cheaper than the competition, found that the claim was misleading and told Kroger to drop it.

Even with its crackdown, the FTC never ventured into regulating taste. Advertisements in poor taste were allowed, as long as they were not deceptive or unfair. **Puffery** was allowed, as long as there was no misstatement of fact. In borderline cases about what constituted puffery, an advertiser could always appeal to the courts.

The FTC has been less aggressive in regulating advertising since the Reagan administration, which deemphasized government regulation. Consumer activists, however, continue to complain to the FTC and other federal and state agencies and to bring pressure

Ad Council ■ Ad industry group that creates free campaigns for worthy causes.

Federal Trade Commission ■ Regulates advertising.

puffery ■ Legally permissible excesses in advertising.

on the media not to run certain advertisements. Most of the concerns today are to protect impressionable children.

Today, some advertisers—especially the tobacco and liquor industries—face regulation of a different sort. To settle and head off civil lawsuits, tobacco companies have withdrawn advertising aimed at kids. There are fewer pictures of healthy, young people holding a cigarette or taking a puff.

Problems and Issues

studypreview **People are exposed to such a blur of ads that advertisers worry that their messages are being lost in the clutter. Some advertising people see more creativity as the answer so that people will want to see and read ads, but there is evidence that creativity can work against an ad's effectiveness.**

Advertising Clutter

Leo Bogart of the Newspaper Advertising Bureau noted that the number of advertising messages doubled through the 1960s and 1970s, and except for the recession at the start of the 1990s, the trend continues. This proliferation of advertising creates a problem: too many ads. The problem has been exacerbated by the shortening of ads from 60 seconds in the early days of television to today's widely used 15-second format.

At one time the National Association of Broadcasters had a code limiting the quantity of commercials. The Federal Communications Commission let station owners know that it supported the NAB code, but in 1981, as part of the Reagan administration's deregulation, the FCC backed away from any limitation. In 1983 a federal court threw out the NAB limitation as a monopolistic practice.

Ad clutter is less of an issue in the print media. Many people buy magazines and newspapers to look at ads as part of the comparative shopping process. Even so, some advertisers, concerned that their ads are overlooked in massive editions, such as a seven-pound metro Sunday newspaper or a 700-page bridal magazine, are looking to alternative means to reach potential customers in a less cluttered environment.

The clutter that marks much of commercial television and radio today may be alleviated as the media fragment further. Not only will demassification create more specialized outlets, such as narrowly focused cable television services, but there will be new media. The result will be advertising aimed at narrower audiences.

Creative Excesses

Advertisers are reviewing whether creativity is as effective an approach as hard sell. **Harry McMahan** studied **Clio Awards** for creativity in advertising and discovered that 36 agencies that produced 81 winners of the prestigious awards for advertisements had either lost the winning account or gone out of business.

Predicts advertising commentator E. B. Weiss: "Extravagant license for creative people will be curtailed." The future may hold more heavy-handed pitches, perhaps with over-the-counter regimens not only promising fast-fast-fast relief but also spelling it out in all caps and boldface with exclamation marks: **F-A-S-T! F-A-S-T!! F-A-S-T!!!**

A London agency, Naked Communications, set up a New York office in 2005 and became the talk of the industry for eschewing creativity. Rather than catchy slogans and clever jingles, Naked focuses first on strategy, identifying the audience for a product or service, then identifying how to reach that audience. Only then does Naked begin work on the message. As Naked executives put it, the rest of the advertising industry for too long has let the tail wag the dog by going for creative glitz before devising strategy. Naked worked wonders for early clients, including Heineken beer and Honda cars.

media ONLINE

Clio Awards Each year the advertising industry presents the Clio Awards, showcasing the most creative television commercials worldwide.
www.clioawards.com

Adcritic.com Extensive collection of TV commercials in QuickTime format.
www.adcritic.com

Adbusters "A global network of artists, activists, writers, pranksters, students, educators and entrepreneurs who criticize advertising and consumption."
http://adbusters.org

False Advertising A gallery of advertising parody.
http://parody.organique.com

University of Texas-Austin Department of Advertising Home of the Advertising Research Resource Center—the last word in links.
http://advertising.utexas.edu/world

The Cincinnati Consulting Consortium Read all about their new ad agency benchmarking tool.
www.cincconsult.com

Harry McMahan ■ Dubious about ad creativity.

Clio Award ■ Award for advertising creativity.

Advertising Effectiveness

Long-held assumptions about the effectiveness of advertising itself are being questioned. **Gerald Tellis,** a University of Iowa researcher, put together a sophisticated statistical model that found that people are relatively unmoved by television advertisements in making brand choices, especially on mundane everyday products like toilet paper and laundry detergents. Tellis' conclusions began with consumer purchasing studies in Eau Claire, Wisconsin. Not surprisingly, considering its self-interest, the advertising industry has challenged the Tellis studies.

Meanwhile, other researchers have continued work on what makes effective advertising and which media work best. A study by **Yankelovich Partners** found that magazine ads entice only 13 percent of Americans to try new products; newspaper ads, 15 percent; and television ads, 25 percent. The study, with a statistically impressive sample of 1,000 consumers, shook the conventional wisdom that celebrity endorsements work. Only 3 percent of the respondents said that they would try a product on the basis of a celebrity's testimonial. A Yankelovich official, Hal Quinley, explained the dismal report card on advertising's effectiveness on weak credibility. "Advertising has little confidence among consumers," he told the *Wall Street Journal.* "It rates below the federal government." A lot of people trust their friends, however. Six out of 10 would try a new product that was recommended by a friend or relative.

For advertisers the lesson from the Tellis and Yankelovich studies is not that advertising doesn't work but that throwing money into campaigns without careful study can be wasteful. For some products some media are better than others. For new products, according to Yankelovich's findings, free samples are the best way to pique consumer interest. So are cents-off coupons. In short, though, advertising may be overrated. With countless variables affecting consumer decisions, advertisers cannot place total faith in advertising to move their products and services.

Gerald Tellis ■ Dubious about TV ads.

Yankelovich Partners ■ Research group that issued a milestone 1995 study.

mediaPEOPLE

Dave Balter

Out of Skidmore College with a psych degree, Dave Balter set out to be a romance author. Sidetracked, he instead landed jobs on the periphery of advertising in direct-marketing and promotion. In time, seeing the slipping effectiveness of traditional advertising, Balter toyed in his mind with word-of-mouth. Today at his marketing company in Boston he's known around the office as buzz-agent Dave. The company, BzzAgent, is at the vanguard of the explosive word-of-mouth segment of the advertising industry—WOM, for short. BzzAgent handles about 300 campaigns simultaneously. Clients include Levi's Dockers, Anheuser-Busch and Cadbury-Schweppes.

By age 40 Balter, an absolute believer in buzz, had founded the Word-of-Mouth Marketing Association and chaired the association's ethics committee. Dave was in the process of securing a patent on the buzz schemes he had devised at BzzAgent. In 2005 he cemented his place in the evolution of advertising with a book fittingly titled *Grapevine.*

The premise of Balter's system is the universally acknowledged fact that people are more influenced by people around them, no matter how much they're also immersed in traditional advertising messages. BzzAgent signs up volunteers who meet a profile of "influentials," as they're called, and matches them up with a client's products—jeans, perfumes, cheese goodies, you name it—to sample and then chat up among family, friends, associates and anybody else. The buzzing is unscripted, mostly just everyday conversation, although some agents use the Internet to spread the word. The buzz agents file reports on their buzzing and earn buzz points that can be redeemed for rewards. IPods go over well. So do cameras and books.

Balter's agents constitute an army, as many as 117,000 at one point.

Does buzz marketing work? Measures are elusive, but WOM is so cheap compared to buying space and time in traditional media that advertisers figure what's to lose. Anecdotal evidence of the effectiveness abounds. For example, the influential book-retailing trade journal *Publishers Weekly,* after receiving advance proofs of Balter's book *Grapevine,* issued a review that normally would be a death knell: "Balter's gee-whiz, narcissistic writing voice won't help win converts." But Balter also had put 2,000 copies into the hands of buzz agents. The book became a best-selling business title.

mediaTECHNOLOGY

Measuring Creativity

Consumer-products giant Procter & Gamble has adopted a computerized tool to measure the creativity of advertising agencies competing for its accounts. By quantifying creativity, the company hopes to identify agencies that can bring new ideas and imagination to promoting P&G products.

Former P&G executives who formed Cincinnati Consulting Consortium devised the system. Although cloaked in secrecy, it's known that the system assigns points for prizes that agencies win for creativity contests. Awards are weighed according to their prestige. Plugged in, too, are other numbers, including the number of awards for advertising per every dollar that's spent.

Procter & Gamble began applying the tool in 2005 not only to advertising agencies already holding P&G accounts but also to competing agencies. Agencies can expect new pressure to show external confirmation for their creativity.

Nice Smile Actress Nicollette Sheridan, known most recently as a serial divorcee who kept the neighborhood buzzing on television's *Desperate Housewives*, opens an old-fashioned photo booth to promote Crest Whitestrips at a Central Park skating rink in New York. The promotional stunt for the Procter & Gamble Crest product was typical of a new wave of alternatives to traditional media for advertising.

CHAPTER 12 Wrap-Up

The role of advertising in U.S. mass media cannot be overstated. Without advertising, most media would go out of business. In fact, in the 1960s, when advertisers switched to television from the giant general-interest magazines such as *Life* and *Look,* those magazines went under. Today, the rapid expansion of cable networks is possible only because advertisers are buying time on the new networks to reach potential customers. In one sense, advertisers subsidize readers, viewers and listeners who pay only a fraction of the cost of producing publications and broadcasts. The bulk of the cost is paid by advertisers, who are willing to do so to make their pitches to potential customers who, coincidentally, are media consumers.

Besides underwriting the mass media, advertising is vital for a prosperous, growing consumer economy. It triggers demand for goods and services, and it enables people to make wise choices by providing information on competing products. The result is efficiency in the marketplace, which frees more capital for expansion. This all speaks to an intimate interrelationship involving advertising in a democratic and capitalistic society.

Questions for Review

1. Why is advertising essential in a capitalistic society?
2. Trace the development of advertising since the time of Johannes Gutenberg.
3. What is the role of advertising agencies?
4. Why do some advertisements appear in some media and not other media?
5. What are the major tactics used in advertising? Who devised each one?
6. How do advertising people use psychology and research to shape their messages?

7. What are the advantages and the problems of the globalization of the advertising industry?
8. Does advertising still follow the dictum "let the buyer beware"?
9. What are some problems and unanswered issues in advertising?

Questions for Critical Thinking

1. How does the development of modern advertising relate to Johannes Gutenberg's technological innovation? To the Industrial Revolution? To long-distance mass transportation? To mass marketing?
2. Why does advertising flourish more in democratic than in autocratic societies? In a capitalistic more than in a controlled economy? In a prosperous society?
3. What were the contributions to advertising of Wayland Ayer, Rosser Reeves, Jack Trout, Ernest Dichter, Wilson Bryan Key and David Ogilvy?
4. What are the responsibilities of advertising account executives, copywriters, media buyers, researchers, brand managers, ad reps and brokers?
5. What are the advantages of the commission system for advertising agency revenue? Of the fee system? The disadvantages of both?
6. Describe these advertising tactics: brand-name promotion, unique selling proposition, lowest common denominator approach, positioning and redundancy.
7. How is ad clutter a problem? What can be done about it?
8. How has the Ad Council improved the image of companies that advertise, agencies that create advertisements and media that carry advertisements? Give examples.

Deepening Your media LITERACY

How does advertising affect the consumer?

STEP 1 Find a newspaper or magazine with a lot of ads.

Dig Deeper

STEP 2 Make a list of the persuasion techniques used in advertising. Find ads in your publication that best exhibit each technique.

What Do You Think?

STEP 3 Answer these questions:

1. Which ad do you like best? Why?
2. Which ad do you like least? Why?
3. Which ad do you think is most persuasive? Why?
4. Are any of the ads unfair? In what way?

Keeping Up to Date

Advertising & Social Review is a quarterly on the role of advertising in society, culture, history and the economy.

Weekly trade journals are *Advertising Age* and *AdWeek*.

Scholarly publications include *Journal of Marketing Research* and *Journal of Advertising*. The New York *Times* regularly reports on the industry.

The Journal of Consumer Psychology includes analysis, reviews, reports and other scholarship on the role of advertising in consumer psychology.

For Further Learning

Joseph Jaffe. *Life After the 30-Second Spot: Energize Your Brand with a Bold Mix of Alternatives to Traditional Advertising.* Wiley, 2005.

Jaffe, a marketing consultant, criticizes major ad agencies for lack of imagination to adjust to wireless and other new media to meet customers on their terms. He suggests using the Internet, video gaming, word-of-mouth.

Jay Conrad Levinson and Charles Rubin. *Guerrilla Advertising.* Mariner Books, 1998.

These authors show entrepreneurs how they can make a business profitable with only a small marketing budget.

Robbin Lee Zeff and Brad Aronson. *Advertising on the Internet,* Second edition. John Wiley, 1999.

A how-to book about Internet advertising.

Anthony Pratkanis and Elliot Aronson. *Age of Propaganda: The Everyday Use and Abuse of Persuasion.* W. H. Freeman, 1992.

These scholars provide a particularly good, lively status report on "subliminal sorcery."

Mary Billard. "Heavy Metal Goes on Trial," *Rolling Stone* (July 12–26, 1990, double issue), pages 83–88, 132.

Billard examines the events leading to a shotgun suicide of a Nevada youth whose family claimed that subliminal messages in a Judas Priest song led him to do it.

Nancy Millman. *Emperors of Adland: Inside the Advertising Revolution.* Warner, 1988.

This fast-paced book by a Chicago newspaper columnist traces the mergers of advertising agencies in the 1980s and questions whether mega-agencies are good for advertising.

Bob Levenson. *Bill Bernbach's Book: History of the Advertising That Changed the History of Advertising.* Random House, 1987.

Levenson focuses on the creative revolution typified in the Bernbach agency's "Think Small" Volkswagen advertisements in the 1960s and early 1970s.

Michael Schudson. *Advertising: The Uneasy Persuasion: Its Dubious Impact on American Society.* Basic, 1984.

Schudson, a media theorist, challenges the effectiveness of advertising while exploring the ideological impact of advertisements.

Stephen Fox. *The Mirror Makers: A History of American Advertising and Its Creators.* Morrow, 1984.

A look at how the advertising industry grew and changed.

Wilson Bryan Key. *Subliminal Seduction: Ad Media's Manipulation of a Not So Innocent America.* New American Library, 1972.

Sex has a special dimension for Key, who argues that an advertisement for Gilbey's gin has the letters s-e-x carefully carved in ice cubes in an expensive *Time* magazine advertisement. Key offers no corroborating evidence in this and later books, *Media Sexploitation* (New American Library, 1976), *The Clam-Plate Orgy: And Other Subliminal Techniques for Manipulating Your Behavior* (New America, 1980) and *The Age of Manipulation* (Holt, 1989).

David Ogilvy. *Confessions of an Advertising Man.* Atheneum, 1963.

The man who created a leading agency explains his philosophy in this autobiography. In his later *Ogilvy on Advertising* (Vintage, 1985), he offers lively advice about effective advertising.

Jerry Bruckheimer
The signature cinematic feature of his movies and television shows, including *CSI,* is the pace. Shots average 2 to 3 seconds, compared to 8 to 11 only 20 years earlier.

chapter

13 Entertainment

In this chapter you will learn:

- **Mass media technology has magnified the audience for storytelling, music and other entertainment.**
- **Pure performance and mediated performance are different.**
- **The mass media powerfully extend the reach of literature.**
- **Audio technology accelerated the effect of music as a social unifier.**
- **The mass media feed an insatiable demand for more sports and even shape the competition.**
- **The mass media have long trafficked in sexual content and championed the right of adult access.**
- **Creativity in mass media entertainment is compromised by factory-style production techniques.**

One of Hollywood's top-grossing movie producers, Jerry Bruckheimer is on his way to becoming a top-grossing television producer as well.

Bruckheimer has produced fast-paced, swashbuckling, exploding films like *The Rock, Con Air, Pearl Harbor, Pirates of the Caribbean, National Treasure* and *Black Hawk Down* and films about people who made a difference like *Remember the Titans* and *Veronica Guerin.*

Before 1980, the average shot in a mainstream film lasted 8 to 11 seconds, according to film scholar David Bordwell. In Bruckheimer's *Top Gun,* made in 1986, the shots shrank to 3 to 4 seconds. In 1998's *Armageddon* they were 2 to 3 seconds. Jeanine Basinger, historian and chair of film studies at Wesleyan University, says Bruckheimer may have been the first filmmaker to understand how quickly audiences can assimilate images and their meaning. "Bruckheimer movies are the opposite of what his critics say. They're not mindless—they engage a different part of the mind."

Not many people can make the leap from movies to television, but Bruckheimer brought his action-packed brand to shows like *CSI* and its spin-offs, the *Amazing Race* reality shows, and *Without a Trace*. Bruckheimer says he just wants to keep the story moving, and to do that he "takes the air out," just as in his movies, although he likes being able to develop a character through a season of shows.

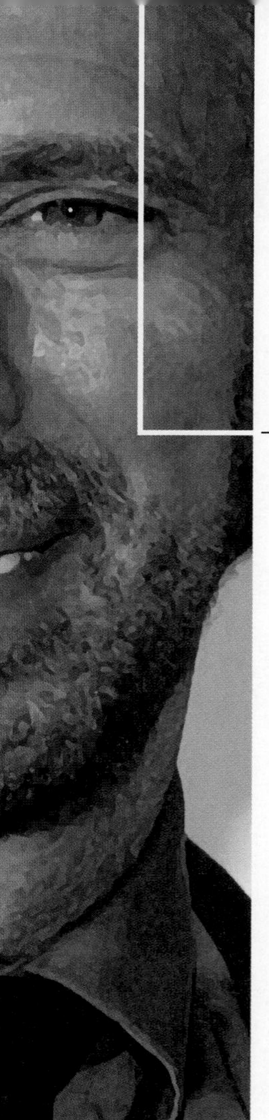

He came to Hollywood in 1972 with a degree in psychology and a successful career as an advertising art director. In 2003 his films earned $12.5 billion in worldwide box-office receipts.

Bruckheimer is "able to make the world's best B movies without condescending to the audience," *Time*'s Joel Stein stays. "His instinct for what excites audiences is eerily perfect."

"We are in the transportation business," says Bruckheimer. "We transport audiences from one place to another." And he does it at high speed.

Entertainment in History

studypreview **The mass media, during their 550-year existence, have magnified the audience for entertainment. Technology has wrought many refinements, but the core categories of media entertainment remain storytelling and music.**

Pre-Mass Media Roots

Entertainment predates the written history of the human species. Around the prehistoric campfire there was music. We know this from Neolithic animal hide drums that archaeologists have unearthed. Certainly, the cave dwellers must have told stories. Who knows when the visual arts began? The record goes back to paintings on cave walls. Through the eons entertainment became higher and higher art. Archaeologists know that the elites of ancient civilizations enjoyed lavish banquets that included performing entertainers—acrobats, musicians and dancers. Sports and athletics became institutionalized entertainment by the time of ancient Greece with the Olympic games and large stadiums. Then came ancient Rome with athletics and competition on an even larger scale. Circus Maximus in Rome could hold 170,000 spectators for chariot races and gladiator games.

Entertainment that has survived the ages includes music, literature, sports and sex. Other breakdowns can be made, like performing arts and visual arts. Some people distinguish entertainment from art, relegating entertainment to a somehow less worthy category. On close examination these distinctions blur, however. Art is in the eye of the beholder, a highly personal and subjective issue.

Technology-Driven Entertainment

What distinguished the Age of Mass Communication, which began with Gutenberg's movable type in the 1440s, was that messages, including entertainment, could be mass produced to reach audiences of unprecedented size. The post-Gutenberg press gave literature wider and wider audiences. But even 200 years after Gutenberg the audience for John Milton's *Paradise Lost,* to take one example, was remarkable for the time but minuscule compared to the audience for every book now on the New York *Times* weekly list of leading titles. Too, literature has taken on diverse forms today, from academic tomes in the Milton tradition to pulp romances and Westerns—and it's not all in printed form.

As media technology leapfrogged into photographic and electronic forms, literature adapted to the new media. Movies extended the reach and the artistic form of books. So did radio and then television. Music, a rare treat in people's lives before audio recording was invented, is everywhere today. Indeed, the impact of the entertainment content of today's

media ONLINE

Main Film Genres A primer on the main genres, subgenres and nongenre categories of film.
www.filmsite.org/genres.html

Music Genres Indiana University offers this list of types of music.
www.music.indiana.edu/music_resources/genres.html

mass media is hard to measure. With television turned on seven hours a day in U.S. homes on average, most of it tuned to entertainment content, it's obvious that people are being entertained more than ever before in history.

Entertainment Genres

To make sense of the gigantic and growing landscape of entertainment in the mass media, people have devised **genres** that are, in effect, subdivisions of the major categories of storytelling and music.

Storytelling Whether novels, short stories, television drama or movies, literature can be divided into genres. Popular genres include suspense, romance, horror, Westerns, fantasy, history and biography. Further slicing and dicing are possible. There are subgenres, such as detective stories. Also, some subgenres cut across two or more genres, such as sci-fi Westerns: Remember the 1999 movie *Wild Wild West?* Some genres are short-lived. In the 1960s a movie genre dubbed *blaxploitation* emerged, for better or worse, with a black racist appeal to black audiences. The genre culminated in the Shaft series, which, although updated in 2003, had been eclipsed by the ongoing racial integration of society.

Music A lot of crossover makes for genre confusion in music. Wanting to define their tastes, aficionados keep reinventing thematic trends. The array of subgenres is dizzying. How is acid rock different from hard rock, from solid rock, from progressive rock, from alternative rock, from power rock, from metal rock? Don't ask. Categorizing is not a neat, clinical task.

Sports Genres are clearest in sports because the rules, although not set in granite, have been agreed on, as have the procedures for revising the rules. Nobody confuses baseball with soccer or the shot put with Formula One auto racing. Attempts at crossover genres, like the wrestling-inspired XFL football experiment, don't do well.

Record Sales by Genre

Rock music has dominated U.S. culture since the 1950s. Following are the current broadly defined genres, but music—like all entertainment—isn't easily pigeonholed. Rock, for example, has subspecies galore that defy any clinical description. Lots of music straddles more than one genre, which has led the radio industry to try to make sense of it all with subcategories like country rock and adult contemporary.

Rock	25.7 percent
Country	14.1 percent
Rhythm and blues	12.8 percent
Rap	10.0 percent
Pop	9.7 percent
Gospel	6.3 percent
Classic	3.3 percent
Jazz	1.9 percent
Movie music	1.7 percent

Perennial Cop Shows The police story, almost always a who-dun-it, is an enduring story genre that spikes periodically in popularity. The latest generation is led by the prime-time CBS series *CSI* and its spinoffs. Here, true to the series' title, characters played by William Petersen and Jorja Fox are at a crime scene investigation.

Performance as Media Entertainment

studypreview **The mass media's entertainment content is performance, but it's not pure performer-to-audience. The media change the performance. Authentic performance is live and eyeball-to-eyeball with the audience. Mediated performance is adapted to meet an unseen and distant audience.**

Authentic Performance

When liberal commentator Al Franken does a routine before a live audience, it's uproariously funny unless his bite hits a raw ideological nerve. That's why conservatives avoid his shows. But in 2004,when Franken took his humor to radio in a talk show on the new Air America network, his humor and bite didn't translate well. On radio he was flat. The fact is that the media change performance. There are many reasons for this.

Audience At a play, whether on Broadway or in a high school auditorium, the audience is assembled for one purpose. It's **authentic performance,** live with the audience on-site. Everyone is attentive to the performance. Nuances are less likely to be missed.

Feedback Performers on stage are in tune with their audience's reactions. There can be reaction and interplay. For the same performance through a mass medium, performers guess—some better than others—at how they are coming across. The fact is, taking television as an example, what resonates in one living room does not resonate in another. Some performers are more gifted at maximizing their impact, but to reach the massive, scattered, heterogeneous mass audience requires pandering to some extent to common denominators. There is less edge.

Technology The equipment that makes mass communication possible is what sets it apart from interpersonal and group communication. Technology imposes its own requirements on performance. The aural beauty of operatic trills in an acoustically optimal concert hall cannot be duplicated in a home stereo, no matter how many woofers it has. Andrew Lloyd Webber's stage musical *Starlight Express,* with roller-skating singers on ramps in front, behind and above the audience, would be a different audience experience in a movie or on television. Media transform a performance. In ways large and small, it becomes a mediated performance.

By definition purists prefer pure, unmediated performance. There will always be a following for Broadway, live concerts and ghost stories around the campfire.

media ONLINE **Playbill** Online version of the well-recognized theatre bill that's been around since 1884.
www.playbill.com

Mediated Performance

In ways we don't always realize, media technology affects and sometimes shapes the messages the media disseminate. The changes to make a **mediated message** work are a function of the technology that makes it possible to reach a mass audience.

Music Edison's mechanical recording technology, which captured acoustic waves in a huge horn, picked up no subtleties. Brass bands and loud voices recorded best. Scratchy background noise drowned out soft sounds. It's no wonder that the late 1800s and early 1900s were marked by popularity of martial music and marching bands. High-pitched voices came through best, which also shaped the popular music of the period.

When Joseph Maxwell's electrical technology was refined in the 1920s, subtle sounds that now could survive the recording and playback processes came into vogue. Rudy Vallee and Bing Crosby were in, John Phillip Sousa was out. Improvements in fidelity beginning in the 1950s meant that music could be played louder and louder without unsettling dissonance—and many rockers took to louder renditions.

genres ■ Broad thematic categories of media content.

authentic performance ■ Live with on-site audience.

mediated message ■ Adjusted to be effective when carried by the mass media.

Movies Media technology profoundly affects art. When audio and film technology were merged to create talkies, movie-makers suddenly had all kinds of new creative options for their storytelling. Directors had more new possibilities when wide screens replaced squarish screens in movie houses. When technology changes the experience for the movie-maker, it also changes the experience for movie-goers.

Sports Technology has dazzled sports fans. Instant replays on television, tried first during an Army-Navy football game in the early 1960s, added a dimension that in-stadium fans could not see. Then came miniature cameras that allowed viewers to see what referees see on the field. Putting microphones on referees, coaches and players let the mass audience eavesdrop on the sounds of the playing field that no one in the stands or sidelines could pick up.

Some digital cable channels allow viewers to select various static camera angles during a game. Viewers, in effect, can participate in creating the media coverage they see. This is a profound development. Watching television, once a largely passive activity, now can involve the viewer at least to some degree.

media ONLINE

Triple Crown Publications The company started in 2001 by self-publishing author Vickie Stringer.
http://writers.aalbc.com/triple_crown_publications.htm

Paradoxa Publishes articles on genre literature. Check out this month's genre.
http://paradoxa.com

History of the Mystery A timeline of mystery stories, detailing the major genres and authors.
www.mysterynet.com/timeline

Storytelling as Media Entertainment

study preview **The media are powerful vehicles for exponentially extending the reach of literature. The most enduring include romances and mysteries, but variations and hybrids come and go in popularity.**

Genres of Literature

Some of literature's storytelling genres have been enduring through the centuries. Shakespeare was neither the first to do romances and mysteries, nor the last. Genres help us make sense of literature, giving us a basis for comparison and contrast. Literature can be categorized in many ways, one as basic as fiction and nonfiction, another being prose and poetry. There are periods: Medieval, Antebellum, Postmodern. There are breakdowns into geographic, ethnic and cultural traditions: Russian, Hispanic and Catholic. Ideologies comprise genres: Marxist, fascist and libertarian. Bookstores use thematic genres to sort their inventory, including mysteries, romances, sports, biographies and hobbies.

Trends and Fads

Genres rise and fall in popularity. Early television was awash with variety shows, which featured a range of comedy, song and dance,

Vickie Stringer

Gangsta Lit Genre Drug dealer Vickie Stringer, during five years in prison, wrote a novel about her outlaw life to publish when she got out. Unable to find a publisher, she printed 1,500 copies and hawked them at hair salons and barber shops and even sold them on street corners. *Let That Be the Reason* found an underground following, which Stringer parlayed into a new genre: Gangsta Lit. Her firm, Triple Crown, now has found itself being raided for authors by St. Martin's Press and other mainstream publishers.

Protest Musicians

Entertainment can be political, potently so. A folk revival was a centerpiece of the anti-Vietnam antiwar movement of the late 1960s into the 1970s. There were counter-singers too, who sold lots of vinyl. "The Ballad of the Green Berets" cast soldiers in a heroic vein. "An Okie from Muskogee" glorified blind patriotism.

This was nothing new. Stephen Foster's "Nothing but a Plain Old Soldier" kept the legend of George Washington going, "The Battle Hymn of the Republic" still moves people. The Civil War generated a spate of patriotic music. The catchy "Over There" did the same in World War I.

It was an off-hand remark, not their music, that made the sassy Dixie Chicks the bad girls among George W. Bush loyalists. In 2003 at the height of enthusiasm for the Iraq war, lead singer Natalie Maines told a London audience that she was "ashamed" that the president was from Texas. Despite the popularity of their music, the Chicks were banned by many radio stations whose managements were cowed by the volume of listener outrage. The Chicks had the last word, however.

Natalie Maines Her off-hand slap at President Bush in a 2003 Dixie Chicks concert was in the vein of a long-running history of protest music. Politics and music can mix potently.

In 2006, with public sentiment shifted against the war, the group rebuffed the angry reaction with "Not Ready to Make Nice" on a CD that opened at Number 28 on *Billboard*'s Hot 100.

Classic rockers Pearl Jam added to the antiwar revival with an album that included "World Wide Suicide," which opened with a newspaper casualty report. Then came the dark lyrics: "Now you know both sides / Claiming killing in God's name / But God is nowhere to be found, conveniently." The new anti-Iraq war repertoire was perhaps most strident with Neil Young's track,"Let's Impeach the President," in which he sings "flip" and "flop" amid Bush quotes. Paul Simon, whose popularity, like Young's, dated to the Vietnam period, entered the antiwar revival in 2006 with the politically tinged album *Surprise.*

Political leaders know the power of incorporating popular music into their campaign personas. Can you imagine a documentary on Franklin Roosevelt without Jack Yellen and Milton Ager's "Happy Days Are Here Again"? The first President Bush paraphrased the Nity Gritty Dirt Band on the campaign trail, then borrowed from Paul Simon's "Boy in the Bubble" to make a point about the economy: "If this age of miracles has taught us anything, it's that if we can change the world, we can change America."

The mobilizing power of recorded music was demonstrated with "We Are the World," the fastest-selling record of the 1980s. Four million copies were sold in six weeks. Profits from the recording, produced by big-name entertainers who volunteered, went to the USA for Africa project. In six months $50 million was raised for medical and financial support for drought-stricken people. "We Are the World," a single song, had directly saved lives.

Willie Nelson has done the same with recordings from his Farm Aid concerts. The worldwide Live Aid concerts were in the same spirit.

In short, music has tremendous effects on human beings, and the technology of sound recording amplifies these effects. The bugle boy was essential to World War II's Company B, but today reveille is digitized to wake the troops. Mothers still sing "Brahms' Lullaby," but more babies are lulled to sleep by Brahms on disc. For romance, lovers today rely more on record music than on their own vocal chords. The technology of sound recording gives composers, lyricists and performers far larger audiences than would ever be possible through live performances.

media ONLINE **TV Variety Shows of the Fifties** Classic television genre. **www.fiftiesweb.com/variety.htm**

The Simpsons Explore the site of the show that has made Springfield a well-known destination. **www.thesimpsons.com**

and other acts. Then came the wave of 1950s quiz shows, then Westerns, then police shows. Going into the 21st century, the television programming fads were talk shows in the style pioneered by Phil Donohue and sustained by Oprah Winfrey, reality shows epitomized by the unending CBS *Survivor* series, and yet another rush of who-done-it police shows.

Some categories are short-lived. A wave of buddy movies was ushered in by *Butch Cassidy and the Sundance Kid* in 1969. Later *Thelma and Louise* spawned girlfriend movies.

Genre trends are audience-driven. People flock to a particular book, song, film or television show and then to the thematic sequels until they tire of it all. Although a lot of genre content is derivative rather than original art, new twists and refinements can reflect artistic fine-tuning by authors, scriptwriters and other creators. People may quibble about whether Francis Ford Coppola's *Godfather* or *Godfather, Part II,* was the better, but almost everyone, including the critics, concur that both were filmic masterpieces. At the same time, nobody serious about creative media content is looking forward to Sylvester Stallone in *Rocky XXXIII.* At some point the possibilities for fresh treatments within a theme are exhausted.

Television Episodes

The Western *Gunsmoke* ran 20 seasons, a record in U.S. television, but the record for the number of prime-time episodes for a series is held by the sitcom *Ozzie and Harriet.* Here are the leaders by episode:

Ozzie and Harriet	435	Sitcom
My Three Sons	380	Sitcom
The Simpsons	352	Sitcom
Dallas	357	Prime-time soap opera

Music as Media Entertainment

study preview **Audio technology accelerated the effect of music as a social unifier. This is no better illustrated than the integration of traditional black music and white hillbilly music into rock 'n' roll, a precursor to the racial integration of U.S. society. The potency of music has been enhanced by its growing role in other media forms, including movies and television.**

American Folk Music

Most music historians trace contemporary popular music to roots in two distinctive types of American folk music, both of which emerged in the South.

Black Music Africans who were brought to the colonies as slaves used music to soothe their difficult lives. Much of the music reflected their oppression and hopeless poverty. Known as **black music,** it was distinctive in that it carried strains of slaves' African roots and at the same time reflected the black American experience. This music also included strong religious themes, expressing the slaves' indefatigable faith in a glorious afterlife. Flowing from the heart and the soul, this was folk music of the most authentic sort.

After the Civil War, black musicians found a white audience on riverboats and in saloons and pleasure palaces of various sorts. That introduced a commercial component into black music and fueled numerous variations, including jazz. Even with the growing white following, the creation of these latter-day forms of black music remained almost entirely with African-American musicians. White musicians who picked up on the growing popularity of black music drew heavily on black songwriters. Much of Benny Goodman's swing music, for example, came from black arranger Fletcher Henderson.

In the 1930s and 1940s a distinctive new form of black music, **rhythm and blues,** emerged. The people who enjoyed this music were all over the country, and these fans included both blacks and whites. Mainstream American music had come to include a firm African-American presence.

Hillbilly Music Another authentic American folk music form, **hillbilly music,** flowed from the lives of Appalachian and Southern whites. Early hillbilly music had a strong colonial heritage in English ballads and ditties, but over time hillbilly music evolved into a genre in its own right. Fiddle playing and twangy lyrics reflected the poverty and hopelessness of rural folk, "hillbillies" as they called themselves. Also like black music, hillbilly music reflected the joys, frustrations and sorrows of love and family. However, hillbilly music failed to develop more than a regional following—that is, until the 1950s,

black music ■ Folk genre from American black slave experience.

rhythm and blues ■ Distinctive style of black music that took form in 1930s.

hillbilly music ■ Folk genre from rural Appalachian, Southern white experience.

when a great confluence of the black and hillbilly traditions occurred. This distinctive new form of American music, called **rockabilly** early on, became rock 'n' roll.

Early Rock 'n' Roll

media ONLINE **Sam Phillips** Tribute page from the Rockabilly Hall of Fame.
www.rockabillyhall.com/SamPhillips.html

Elvis Presley He ain't nothin' but a hound dog. The official site.
www.elvis.com

Allan Freed Disc jockey credited with coining the term "rock 'n' roll."
www.alanfreed.com

Music aficionados quibble about who invented the term *rock 'n' roll.* There is no doubt, though, that Memphis disc jockey **Sam Phillips** was a key figure. From his job at WREC, Phillips found an extra $75 a month to rent a 20-foot-by-35-foot storefront, the paint peeling from the ceiling, to go into business recording, as he put it, "anything, anywhere, anytime." His first jobs, in 1949, were weddings and bar mitzvahs, but in 1951 Phillips put out his first record, *Gotta Let You Go* by blues singer Joe Hill Louis, who played his own guitar, harmonica and drums for accompaniment. In 1951 Phillips recorded B. B. King and then **Jackie Brenston**'s *Rocket 88*, which many musicologists call the first rock 'n' roll record. Phillips sold his early recordings, all by black musicians, mostly in the blues tradition, to other labels.

In 1952 Phillips began his own Sun Records label and a quest to broaden the appeal of the black music he loved to a wide audience. "If I could find a white man who had the Negro sound and the Negro feel, I could make a billion dollars," he said. In a group he recorded in 1954, the Starlight Wranglers, Sam Phillips found Elvis Presley.

Presley's first Sun recording, *That's All Right*, with Scotty Moore and Bill Black, found only moderate success on country radio stations, but Sam Phillips knew that he was onto something. It wasn't quite country or quite blues, but it was a sound that could move both white country fans and black blues fans. Elvis moved on to RCA, a major label. By 1956 he had two of the nation's best-selling records, the flip-side hits *Don't Be Cruel* and *Hound Dog*, plus three others among the year's top 16. Meanwhile, Sam Phillips was recording Carl Perkins, Roy Orbison, Johnny Cash and Jerry Lee Lewis, adding to the distinctively American country-blues hybrid: wild, thrashing, sometimes reckless rock 'n' roll.

The new music found a following on radio stations that picked up on the music mix that Cleveland disk jockey Alan Freed had pioneered as early as 1951—occasional rhythm 'n' blues amid the mainstream Frank Sinatra and Peggy Lee. By 1955 Freed was in New York and clearly on a roll. Freed helped propel Bill Haley and the Comets' *Rock Around the Clock* to number one. Rock's future was cemented when *Rock Around the Clock* was the musical bed under the credits for the 1955 movie *Blackboard Jungle.* Young people flocked to the movie not only for its theme of teen disenchantment and rebellion but also for the music.

media ONLINE **Movie Music** Links to reviews, official and unofficial sites, places to buy soundtracks and more.
www.moviemusic.com/directory

MusicMagic Mixer Show it a song, and it will find others that you're sure to love.
www.predixis.biz

MoodLogic Download the Mix Maker and see what it can do for your MP3s.
www.moodlogic.com

Music as Multimedia Content

Although music often is studied as the content issued by the recording industry, music is hardly a one-dimensional form of media message. Even in pre-mass media eras, going back to prehistoric times, music was integrated with dance and theater. When movies were establishing themselves, music was an important component. Even before movie sound tracks were introduced with the "talkies," many movie houses hired a piano player who kept one eye on the screen and hammered out supportive music. D. W. Griffith's *The Birth of a Nation* of 1915 had an accompanying score for a 70-piece symphony.

Some movies are little more than musical vehicles for popular performers, going back to Bing Crosby and continuing through Elvis Presley and the Beatles. Rare is the modern movie without a significant musical bed. Just count the number of songs in the copyright credits at the end of today's movies.

Early radio recognized the value of music. Jingles and ditties proved key to establishing many brand names. Today many composers and lyricists derive significant

rockabilly ■ Black-hillbilly hybrid that emerged in the 1950s.

Sam Phillips ■ Pioneered rockabilly, rock 'n' roll; discovered Elvis Presley.

Jackie Brenston ■ Recorded *Rocket 88*, first rock 'n' roll record, in 1951.

mediaTECHNOLOGY

Digital DJs

The dwindling universe of radio disk jockeys is taking another blow, this time from software that automatically compiles playlists for iPods and other handheld music players. First to the market was Roxio's Boom Box suite, whose MusicMagic Mixer program can take a single song designated by an iPod owner and scan the whole collection for songs with similar volume, tempo and energy. That's what the best disk jockeys once did in making magical segues and sets.

If you're in an Usher kind of mood, your iPod can sustain it all day by drawing on music like that from your hundreds, even thousands, of digitally stored songs on your device. Or Lucinda Williams or White Stripes.

Another robo-DJ technology, metadata, is used by the company MoodLogic. Thousands of music-lovers' comments on songs have been compiled and sorted to identify collections of songs in iPod files.

Digital DJ software conceivably can create more combinations of music, some even factoring in your past listening patterns, than a single human being could possibly conjure—especially considering the massiveness of iPod files—already up to 15,000 songs on 60-gig models.

Custom Playlists The Roxio Boom Box suite lets music fans scan their recorded music collection for songs with a similar volume, tempo and energy for a custom playlist. Who needs radio? Even a narrowly formatted station can't put together a playlist that's so much you.

income from their work being built into advertisements for television, radio and online. Think about the Intel and NBC tones or the grating: "Hey, Culligan Man."

Sports as Media Entertainment

studypreview **Early on, mass media people sensed the potential of sports to build their audiences, first through newspapers, then through magazines, radio and television. The media feed what seems an insatiable demand for more sports. Why the huge public intrigue with sports? One expert suggests it's the mix of suspense, heroes, villains, pageantry and ritual.**

Mass Audiences for Sports

The brilliant newspaper publisher **James Gordon Bennett** sensed how a public interest in sports could build circulation for his New York *Herald* in the 1830s. Bennett assigned reporters to cover sports regularly. Fifty years later, with growing interest in horse racing, prize fighting, yacht racing and baseball, **Joseph Pulitzer** organized the first separate sports department at his New York *World*. Sportswriters began specializing in different sports.

Audience appetite for sports was insatiable. For the 1897 Corbett-Fitzsimmons heavyweight title fight in remote Nevada, dozens of writers showed up. The New York

James Gordon Bennett ■ New York newspaper publisher in 1830s; first to assign reporters to sports regularly.

Joseph Pulitzer ■ New York newspaper publisher in 1880s; organized the first newspaper sports department.

Times introduced celebrity coverage in 1910 when it hired retired prizefighter John L. Sullivan to cover the Jeffries-Johnson title bout in Reno.

Sports historians call the 1920s the Golden Era of Sports, with newspapers glorifying athletes. Heroes, some with enduring fame, included Jack Dempsey in boxing, Knute Rockne and Jim Thorpe in football, and Babe Ruth in baseball. The 1920s also marked ratio as a medium for sports. In 1921 **KDKA** of Pittsburgh carried the first play-by-play baseball game, the Davis Cup tennis matches and the blow-by-blow Johnny Ray versus John Dundee fight. Sportswriter Grantland Rice, the preeminent sportswriter of the time, covered the entire World Series live from New York for KDKA, also in 1921.

Sports magazines have their roots in *American Turf Register,* which began a 15-year run in Baltimore in 1829. The *American Bicycling Journal* rode a bicycling craze from 1877 to 1879. Nothing matched the breadth and scope of *Sports Illustrated,* founded in 1954 by magazine magnate **Henry Luce.** The magazine, launched with 350,000 charter subscribers, now boasts a circulation of 3.3 million a week.

Although television dabbled in sports from its early days, the introduction of *Wide World of Sports* in 1961 established that television was made for sports and, conversely, that sports was made for television. The show, the brainchild of ABC programming wizard **Roone Arledge,** covered an unpredictable diversity of sports, from Ping-Pong to skiing. In this period, professional athletic leagues agreed to modify their rules to accommodate television for commercial breaks and, eventually, to make the games more exciting for television audiences.

media ONLINE **SI** The online presence of *Sports Illustrated.* **http://sportsillustrated.cnn.com**

Roone Arledge Thorough and well-linked biography of the man who changed TV sports forever. **http://en.wikipedia.org/wiki/Roone_Arledge**

ESPN All sports, all the time, online. **http://espn.go.com**

Television commentator Les Brown explains sports as the perfect program form for television: "At once topical and entertaining, performed live and suspensefully without a script, peopled with heroes and villains, full of action and human interest and laced with pageantry and ritual."

The launching of ESPN as an all-sports network for cable television systems prompted millions of households to subscribe to cable. The success of ESPN spawned sibling networks. Regional sports networks have also emerged, including many created by Fox as major revenue centers.

Audience and Advertiser Confluence

The television networks and national advertisers found a happy confluence of interest in the huge audience for televised sports. This goes back at least to *Friday Night Fights*, sponsored by Gillette, and *Wednesday Night Fights*, sponsored by Pabst beer, in the 1950s. Today, sports and television are almost synonymous. Not only does the Super Bowl pack a stadium, but 90 million U.S. households tune in. The World Cup soccer tournament held every four years draws the largest worldwide television audiences.

In part to keep their names on screen, some firms have bought the rights to put their name on sports stadiums. The value of brand-name exposure at places like the Target Center in Minneapolis, the Bank One Ballpark in Phoenix and Coors Field in Denver is impossible to measure.

Advertiser interest flows and ebbs, as do audiences. The 1950s audience for Wednesday night fights, for example, grew fickle. The phenomenal success of the World Wrestling Federation lost steam after the September 11 terrorist attacks in 2001. Too, there seems to be a saturation point. The WWF's colorful promoter, Vince McMahon, bombed with his new XFL professional football league in 2001. Even with its own rules, designed to add excitement for television audiences, and even with tireless promotion by NBC, it seemed that football fans already had their plates full.

media ONLINE **World Wrestling Entertainment** Formerly known as the World Wrestling Federation. **www.wwe.com**

KDKA ■ Pittsburgh radio station that pioneered sports broadcasting in 1920s.

Henry Luce ■ Magazine publisher known from *Time, Life, Sports Illustrated* and others.

Roone Arledge ■ ABC television executive responsible for *Wide World of Sports* in 1961.

Sports and the Web

Media sports coverage technology keeps evolving. At one time not enough broadcast channels existed in a community to air all the games that interested people. Now audio and video coverage can be web-delivered. Some colleges have arranged for their games to be carried on the web so that faraway alumni can track the touchdowns live.

Gaming as Media Content

studypreview **Computer and video gaming have huge, growing followings that have made them a significant entertainment form. The place of gaming as a media entertainment genre has been confirmed by advertisers, which have shifted budgets to create a presence in gaming.**

Growing Entertainment Form

Nobody could doubt the significance of video games as a media form after 2001. Sales in the United States outpaced movies. In 2004 when Microsoft introduced its Halo2, it was a news event. At 6,800 retailers nationwide, the doors opened at midnight on the release date to thousands of fans waiting in line, some for as long as 14 hours. Within 24 hours sales surpassed $125 million—way ahead of the $70 million opening-weekend box office for the year's leading film *The Incredibles.*

The time enthusiasts spend with video games is catching up with television. Players of Madden NFL 2004 spend an estimated average of 100 hours a year on the game. With 4 million players, that is 400 million hours. The full season of *The Sopranos,* then at its heyday, was claiming 143 million viewing hours. Do the math: *The Sopranos* averaged 11 million viewers for 13 episodes that year.

To catch consumers who spend less time with television and more with video games, advertisers have shifted chunks of their budgets to gaming. The potential is incredible. Half of Americans six and older play games, and that elusive target for advertisers, men 18 and older, make up 26 percent of the gamers.

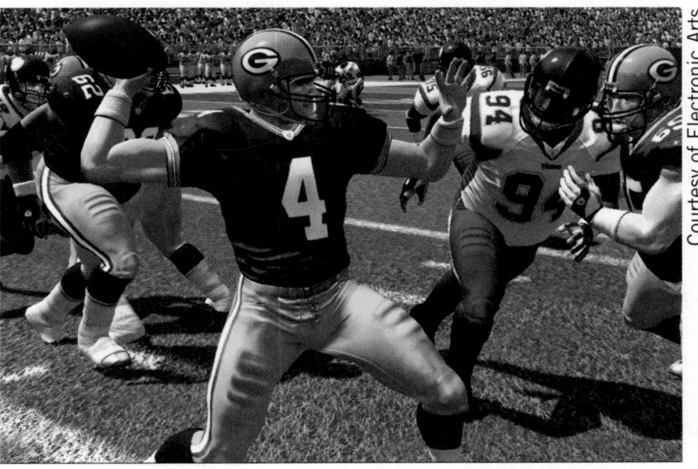
Courtesy of Electronic Arts

Madden NFL
The sudden potency of gaming as a media content form was no better illustrated than with Electronic Arts' Madden NFL 2004, which earned $200 million within four months. The Oscar-winning movie at the time, *Chicago,* took nine months to earn $171 million.

Impact of Gaming

Although gaming is distinctive as a form of media content, market-savvy executives have extended their franchise to other forms. The 2001 movie *Lara Croft Tomb Raider,* adopted from a 1996 game and six sequels, generated $131 million in U.S. box offices. *Resident Evil* grossed $90 million, *Mortal Kombat* $135 million. There is inverse cross-fertilization too. Games have been based on movies, including *James Bond, Matrix, Shrek, Spider-Man* and *Star Wars.* Gaming shows on television and gaming magazines have proliferated.

Leading Games

The leading 2003 video games:

Madden NFL 2004
Pokémon Ruby
Pokémon Sapphire
Need for Speed Underground
The Legend of Zelda: The Wind Waker
Grand Theft Auto: Vice City
Mario Kart: Double Dash
Tony Hawk's Underground
Enter the Matrix
Medal of Honor: Rising Sun

The leading 2003 computer games:

The Sims: Superstar
The Sims Deluxe
Command & Conquer: Generals
Warcraft UUU: The Frozen Throne
The Sims: Makin' Magic
The Sims: Unleashed
SimCity 4
Call of Duty
Age of Mythology
Battlefield 1942

mediaPEOPLE

Shigeru Miyamoto

After the video game classics Donkey Kong, Mario Bros. and The Legend of Zelda, what could Shigeru Miyamoto do for an encore? In 2006 Japanese game-maker Nintendo, where Miyamoto had worked his magic almost 20 years, introduced Wii—a radical hardware departure that literally put gamers into the action. Want to slash a sword through the air? Then extend an arm and slash, and the wireless remote will pick it up on screen. A gentle hula sway? The remote sensor puts your motion on screen. Wii, as Nintendo calls the gizmo, is lots more fun than a joy stick.

The Wii Risk Shigeru Miyamoto, whom some call the superstar of gaming concepts, is seeking to leapfrog competitors with wireless controllers triggered by body motion.

The goal of Wii (pronounced *wee*) was to revolutionize gaming. Nintendo hoped to win back market dominance from Sony's PlayStation and Microsoft's XBox.

Miyamoto began at Nintendo in 1977 as a graphic artist. In 1980 the company, historically a playing-card manufacturer, tried to venture into coin-operated video arcades. The venture flopped. Miyamoto came to rescue with Donkey Kong, which Nintendo quickly plugged into a Nintendo arcade machine in a trial at a U.S. tavern. To everybody's shock the next morning, the coin tray had 1,300 coins. Instantly addicted, the tavern's customers had been pumping quarters nonstop all night. Ninetendo had a winner.

Building on the success, Miyamoto adapted the Donkey Kong character into a game featuring Mario the Italian plumber, who quickly became Nintendo's signature product. Legend of Zelda soon followed, another legendary hit.

Wii moved gaming to new levels of involvement—no more bug-eyed couch-potato joysticking. In the new Zelda installment, aiming a bow and arrow with the wireless remote means aiming a laser beam at the screen. In Tennis, the controller is a racket for wide arcs, low lobs and slices. It's a workout, as in reeling in a virtual fish in another game. There is no button to push. The controller responds to the player's body motions. For the Madden football series, game-maker Electronic Arts the developed a variation for Wii. A gesture hikes the ball to the quarterback. A throwing motion passes the ball. A bullet pass? A hard, fast gesture. Use a slower, less forceful gesture for a loftier, slower lob.

Miyamoto's genius at gaming comes from a fertile mind and sense of adventure. As a kid he roamed the canyons and grassy hills near his home outside Kyoto. One day, as he tells it, he discovered a hole in the ground—the opening to a cave. After building up enough courage to enter, he ventured inside with a lantern, discovering one chamber after another, never knowing what was ahead. Sound like a video game?

In college Miyamoto studied industrial design. He began at Nintendo in 1977 as the company's first graphic artist, albeit an apprentice. There, in 1980, the company president, Hiroshi Yamauchi, asked Miyamoto what he knew about video games. The answer: Not much. Miyamoto had no prior programming experience, but, a quick study, he created Donkey Kong, even composing the music himself on a small electronic keyboard. Suddenly Nintendo not only was on the map in video gaming but was the world leader.

Mario was a character in Donkey Kong who then became his own star in more than 100 games spanning over a dozen gaming platforms. Returning the favor, Donkey Kong made cameo appearances in Mario games.

No one disputes Miyamoto as gaming genius, but it's hardly gone to his head. Despite the multimillion dollar franchises he's created for Nintendo, Miyamoto insists on only an average income. He rides a bicycle to work.

Music ranging from orchestral to hip-hop has replaced the blips and bleeps of early-generation games. For recorded music companies and artists, landing a spot in a game can be stronger exposure than MTV. For Madden NFL 2005, game manufacturer Electronic Arts auditioned 2,500 songs submitted by recording companies. Twenty-one ended up in the game. The Phoenix band Minibosses plays nothing but Nintendo music, note for note.

Not surprisingly, the integration of gaming into larger media conglomerates is under way. The Warner Brothers movie studio now has a movie division. So does Disney's Buena Vista. Sumner Redstone, whose media empire includes CBS and MTV, has bought into

Game Publishers

For the first three months of 2003 these were the leading game publishers, listed by their revenue and with marketshare and leading titles:

Publisher	Revenue	Marketshare
Electronic Arts *Sims, Battlefield, Madden NFL*	$594 million	20.0 percent
Nintendo *Zelda, Metroid, Star Fox, Mario, Donkey Kong*	349 million	11.8 percent
Sony *Rampage, Total Destruction, Treasures of Aht Arhgan*	206 million	6.9 percent
Atari *Matrix, Asteroids, Space Invaders*	183 million	6.2 percent
THQ *Worms, Warriors, Juice, SpongeBob*	177 million	6.0 percent

the Midway gaming company. Hollywood and New York talent agencies have divisions that look for game roles for their client actors.

Sex as Media Entertainment

studypreview **Despite the risk of offending some people's sensitivities, the media have long trafficked in sexual content. Undeniably, there is a market. The media have fought in the U.S. courts for their right to carry sexually explicit content and for the right of adults to have access to it.**

Adult Content

Sexually oriented content has bedeviled the mass media in the United States for longer than anyone can remember. Clearly, there is a demand. Sales of banned books soared as soon as the courts overruled government restrictions, as was no better illustrated than with the Irish classic ***Ulysses*** by James Joyce in 1930. Firm data on the profitability of sexual content are hard to come by, partly because definitions are elusive. *Ulysses*, as an example, is hardly a sex book for most people, yet its sexual content is what once prompted a federal import ban. The definition difficulty gives partisans the opportunity to issue exaggerated estimates of the scope of the sexual media content.

Ulysses for Dummies Designed to help the general reader get over their fear of "difficult" reading. **www.bway.net/~hunger/ulysses.html**

Even so, there is no denying that sex sells. Revenues are difficult to peg precisely, but most estimates are in the range of $8 billion to $10 billion annually for the entire U.S. sex industry, a major part of which is media content. About 8,000 adult movie titles a year are released. Pay-per-view adult movies on satellite and cable television generate almost $600 million in revenue a year.

It was no sleazy outfit that first imported *Ulysses* but the venerable publisher Random House. Today the major purveyors of adult content include Time Warner's HBO and Cinemax, which pipe late-night adult content to multiple-system cable operators including Time Warner. Satellite providers DirecTV and Dish Network offer porn to their subscribers.

Ulysses ■ James Joyce novel banned in the United States until 1930 court decision.

obscenity ■ Sexually explicit media depictions that the government can ban.

pornography ■ Sexually explicit depictions that are protected from government bans.

Miller Standard ■ Current U.S. Supreme Court definition on sexually explicit depictions that are protected by the First Amendment from government bans.

Sam Ginsberg ■ Figure in U.S. Supreme Court decision to bar sales of pornography to children.

Pacifica case ■ U.S. Supreme Court ruling to keep indecency off over-air broadcast stations at times when children are likely to be listening or watching.

Big-name hotel chains pipe adult movies into rooms. In addition, moralists periodically picket Barnes & Noble and other mainstream bookstores to protest the books and magazines they stock.

Decency Requirements

Most media companies have found comfort in the definition of sexually acceptable content that has evolved in free-expression cases in the U.S. courts. Today the courts make a distinction between **obscenity,** which is not allowed, and **pornography,** which the courts find is protected by the First Amendment guarantee not only of free expression but also of adult access to other people's expressions.

How are obscenity and pornography different? Since 1973, when the U.S. Supreme Court decided the case *Miller* v. *California,* the courts have followed the **Miller Standard.** In effect, sexual content is protected from government bans unless the material fails all of these tests:

- Would a typical person applying local standards see the material as appealing mainly for its sexually arousing effect?
- Is the material devoid of serious literary, artistic, political or scientific value?
- Is the sexual activity depicted offensively, in a way that violates state law that explicitly defines offensiveness?

The Miller Standard protects a vast range of sexual content. Only material for which the answer is "yes" to all three Miller questions can be censored by government agencies.

The Miller Standard notwithstanding, the Federal Communications Commission fined CBS $550,000 for the Janet Jackson breast flash during the 2004 Super Bowl halftime. The producer, CBS's Viacom cousin MTV, called the incident a "wardrobe malfunction." About 89 million people were tuned in. Some complained.

Filthy Words

After Pacifica radio station WBAI in New York aired a 12-minute recorded George Carlin monologue, the U.S. Supreme Court authorized government restrictions on indecency at times of the day when children might be listening.

Sexual Content and Children

Although government limits on sexual content gradually eased in the late 20th century, there remained restrictions on media content for children. State laws that forbid the sale of sexually explicit materials to children are exempted from regular First Amendment rules. The U.S. Supreme Court established the childhood exception in 1968 in a case involving a Bellmore, New York, sandwich shop owner, **Sam Ginsberg,** who had sold girlie magazines to a 16-year-old. The local prosecutor went after Ginsberg using a state law that prohibited selling depictions of nudity to anyone under age 17. The U.S. Supreme Court upheld the constitutionality of the state law.

In broadcasting, the U.S. Supreme Court has upheld restrictions aimed at shielding children. After New York radio station WBAI aired a comedy routine by George Carlin with four-letter anatomical words and vulgarities, the Federal Communications Commission, which can yank a station's license to broadcast, took action against the station's owner, the Pacifica Foundation. In the **Pacifica case,** as it came to be known, the U.S. Supreme Court upheld the FCC's limits on indecency during times of the day when children are likely to be listening. Carlin's monologue, *Filthy Words,* had aired at 2 p.m. In response, stations now are careful to keep the raunchiest stuff off the air until late night.

The courts also have upheld laws against sexual depictions of juveniles as exploitative. Many prosecutors come down hard even for the possession of such materials. Child pornography is one of society's last taboos.

Association of Sites Advocating Child Protection Fighting child pornography.
www.asacp.org/index.php

Filthy Words A verbatim transcript of George Carlin's monologue.
www.law.umkc.edu/faculty/projects/ftrials/conlaw/filthywords.html

Censorship and Gaming

Like other entertainment forms, gaming is a lightning rod of concern about the effect of explicit violence and sex on children. The industry devised a voluntary rating system from EC for "early childhood" to AO for "adults only," but critics have called the system a joke among retailers. Three high-visibility U.S. senators, Evan Bayh of Indiana, Hillary Clinton of New York and Joe Lieberman of Connecticut, favored $5,000 fines for every time a retailer violates the code for kids under 17.

Similar attempts to codify ratings through law at the state level have not been viewed kindly in the courts. Since 2001 federal judges have found a lack of compelling evidence from opponents who claim that games like Grand Theft Auto: San Andreas cause harm. If anyone ever demonstrates that a game begets violent behavior, the courts may change their stance. Meanwhile, the First Amendment gives constitutional protection to game-makers as freedom of expression and to game-players as freedom to inquire and explore.

Evaluating Media Content

study preview **By definition, media content is creative, but the quality of the creativity is a matter for debate. Mass-production techniques, pioneered in factories, have been applied in the mass media to supply the incessant commercial demand for content, which is one of many factors working against consistent creative innovation and excellence.**

Media Content as Art

Mass media messages can be art of a high order, as was perhaps no better illustrated than by early film-maker D. W. Griffith. In the 1910s Griffith proved himself a film-making author whose contribution to the culture, for better or worse, was original in scale, content and style. Griffith had something to say, and the new mass medium of film was the vehicle for his message.

In the 1950s, when French New Wave directors were offering distinctive stories and messages, film critic **Andre Bazin** devised the term **auteur** to denote the significant and original cinematic contributions. Bazin's auteurs included Jean Luc Godard, who made *Breathless,* and François Truffaut, who made *The 400 Blows.* Their work was marked by distinctive cinematic techniques—freeze-frames, handheld cameras and novel angles, many of them common in movies now. Perhaps the most famous of these highbrow film-makers who developed a global following was the Swedish director Ingmar Bergman, with *The Seventh Seal* and other dark, moody and autobiographical works.

American film-makers have also contributed to the auteur movement. Among them was Stanley Kubrick, who directed *2001: A Space Odyssey.* Other notable contemporary American film auteurs include Martin Scorsese, whose films include *Taxi Driver* David Lynch, who made *Blue Velvet* and Spike Lee, who focuses on African-American life.

Culturally significant media content is hardly limited to movies. Older media forms, including novels and short stories, have long been home for creative people whose work adds insight to our lives and deepens our understandings and appreciations. The impact of great composers from eras before the mass media has been exponentially

The Godard Experience Timeline, links, in-depth information on his major works.
www.carleton.edu/curricular/MEDA/classes/media110/Friesema/intro.html

Francois Truffaut Learn more about this auteur director.
www4.eou.edu/~wellsm/truffaut.html

Kubrick Multimedia Film Guide Images and sounds from Kubrick's films.
www.indelibleinc.com/kubrick

Spike Lee Brief bio and in-depth film information from Film Bug.
www.filmbug.com/db/980

Andre Bazin ■ French film critic who devised the term *auteur* for significant cutting-edge film-makers.

auteur ■ A film-maker recognized for significant and original treatments.

studio system ■ A production-line movie production system devised by Hollywood in the 1920s.

Harlequin ■ Canadian publisher known for romances with cliché characters, settings and themes; the term is applied generically to pulp romances.

extended through recording, film and television. The printing press greatly expanded the audience for religious scriptures whose messages went back to prehistoric times.

Production-Line Entertainment

To be sure, not all media content is high art. A television soap opera, whatever its entertainment value, lacks the creative genius of Shakespeare's enduring *Romeo and Juliet*. Why can't all media content rank high on an artistic scale? Besides the obvious explanation that not everyone is born a Shakespeare, the modern mass media are commercial enterprises that must produce vast quantities of material. In the 1920s, for example, an insatiable public demand for movies led to the creation of the Hollywood **studio system,** in effect turning movie-making into a factory process. Production quotas drove movie production. The studios, awash in money, hired leading authors of the day, including F. Scott Fitzgerald and William Faulkner, for creative story lines and scripts, but inexorable demands for material drained them. It has been said that Hollywood had some of the most gifted writers of the time doing their weakest work.

Hollywood Renegades Archive A collection of information mostly against block booking and the Hollywood studio system from Society of Independent Motion Picture Producers.
www.cobbles.com/simpp_archive/1film_studio-system.htm

eharlequin Where readers go for passion.
www.eharlequin.com

The factory model, a product of the Industrial Age, extends throughout the media. The Canadian book publisher **Harlequin** grinds out romance novels with their bodice-busting covers. Nobody confuses them with high art. Imagine, also, filling a television network's prime-time obligation, 42 half-hour slots a week. It can't all be great stuff, despite the promotional claims in preseason ramp-ups. Also, many in the mass audience don't want great art anyway.

Copycat Content

Significant amounts of media content are imitative. Copycat sounds abound in material from the recording industry. In network television a sudden success, like ABC's *Who Wants to Be a Millionaire* in 2001, spawned other, albeit less successful, quiz shows. Alas, even *Millionaire* was hardly original. The concept was licensed from an already-running show in Britain.

Cross-Media Adaptations

The demand for content creates a vacuum that sucks up material from other media. Movie studios draw heavily on written literature, from best-selling novels to comic books like *Spider-Man* and *The X-Men*. Conversely, fresh movies sometimes are adapted into book form.

Cross-media adaptations don't always work well. Movie versions of books often disappoint readers. Scenes change. So do characters. Inevitably, a lot is left out. Some of the criticism is unfair because it fails to recognize that movies are a distinct medium. How, for example, could a screenwriter pack everything in a 100,000-word novel into a 100-minute script? These are different media. Passages that work brilliantly in a word-driven medium, like a magazine short story, can fall flat in a medium with visual enhancements. Conversely, the nuances compactly portrayed by a master actor, like Meryl Streep or Jack Nicholson, could take pages and pages in a book and not work as well. Also, movie studio producers, almost always needing to appeal to the widest possible audience, will alter plots, scenes and characters and sometimes even reverse a story line's climactic events.

The Da Vinci Code Official web site for author Dan Brown and his New York *Times* best-seller.
www.danbrown.com/novels/davinci_code/reviews.html

Some cross-media adaptations are commercial disasters. With limited success, movie studios have tried to cash in on the popularity of video games. Despite high expectations, *Super Mario Bros.* flopped in 1993. The explanation? Some critics cite the same difficulties as occur in transferring messages from books to movies. With video games the audience member plays an active role by exercising some control over the story line. Watching a movie, however, is relatively passive.

mediaPEOPLE

Nelly

Crossing over Rapper Nelly and Christina Aguilera in an energetic moment at the MTV Music Video Awards. The performance represented a pinnacle of Nelly's integration of rap into the repertoire of pop. Like many performers before him, he's branched into movies in hopes of more cross-over magic.

Platinum-selling hip-hop performer Nelly, like many recording successes before him, has jumped media into movies. He crossed over for Adam Sandler's 2005 remake of *The Longest Yard*. Nelly, who was christened Cornell Hayes Jr., had come a long way fast. As a teenager he supported himself as a graveyard-shift UPS package sorter in St. Louis and also served up burgers at McDonald's. Music was his passion, and, imbued with rap, he cut a CD on the side, sold copies from the trunk of his car, and finally signed a record deal.

His breakthrough, in 2000 at age 25, was nursery-rhyme hit *Country Grammar*. His first two albums sold 15 million with a populist fantasy theme—fun and partying all the time and lots of lyricizing on pot. He was ambitious. On the same date in 2004 he released two Universal label albums with the curious tandem titles *Sweat* and *Suit*. The music is a favorite of exotic dancers.

Nelly set his sights on other venues, including a clothing line. He bought into a National Basketball Association team. Then movies.

Meanwhile, as with most cross-media performers, he kept one foot in music. Even there, he was a crossover master, melding hard-core rap and sugary pop in an exuberant rolling delivery that bridged a chasm to find sales with fans in both divergent camps.

Unpretentious Media Content

Although critics pan a lot of media content as unworthy, the fact is that lowbrow art and middlebrow art find audiences, sometimes large audiences, and have a firm place in the mix that the mass media offer. There is nothing artistically pretentious in **pulp fiction,** including the Harlequin romances, nor their soap-opera equivalents on television.

pulp fiction ■ Quickly and inexpensively produced easy-to-read short novels.

CHAPTER 13 Wrap-Up

Entertainment content of the mass media draws huge audiences and drives the economics of most media companies. The drama inherent in good storytelling is a major component that dates to prehistoric tribal gatherings around the campfire. The modern-day campfire is books, movies and television. The emotive power of music, which also has prehistoric roots, is another major component of today's mass media entertainment content. So is sports, which has all the fascination of compelling literature to keep people in tune until the outcome reveals itself. Sometimes overlooked as a genre in media content is sex, which probably is best explained by the great mystery of sexuality and insuppressible curiosity.

Mass media are not mere conduits for entertainment. The media themselves shape entertainment. Changes in media technology have thrust musical styles into popularity. Marches lent themselves to early acoustic recording, which couldn't handle subtleties. Crooners had their heyday when electric recording was introduced.

The huge audiences that mass media can attract also shape entertainment content. A regional drama that might go over in an isolated community with a unique culture and local issues might not interest a larger audience. The powerhouse media companies seek content that will attract national and even global audiences, which places a premium on entertainment that travels easily and widely.

Questions for Review

1. What categories of entertainment have endured from prehistoric times and now reach people through mass media?
2. How does the use of genres both both clarify and cloud a serious discussion of the literary content of the mass media?
3. How has recorded music radically changed the social complexion of the United States?
4. How do you explain the obsession that many people have with mass media coverage of sports?
5. How is it that the First Amendment to the U.S. Constitution protects pornography but not obscenity?
6. What changes in mass media technology have reshaped entertainment?
7. Why are creativity and artistry often sacrificed in producing mass media entertainment?

Questions for Critical Thinking

1. Pigeonholing media content into genres involves judgment calls about which informed, clear-thinking people can disagree. Can you make a case for reassigning an example of at least one media product to multiple genres?
2. When do you expect public enthusiasm over *Harry Potter* to fade? *Star Wars? Lord of the Rings?*
3. Do you see any difficulty in defining hip-hop and rap as distinct music genres?
4. Are extreme sports faddish or do you see them as an enduring media genre?
5. Would further miniaturization of electronic media devices serve any purpose for media consumers?
6. What is the downside of media products that are pumped out like widgets from a widget factory?

Deepening Your media LITERACY

Can technology and authenticity co-exist in sports?

STEP 1 Think of your favorite sport. Write a list of the advantages of going to a live event or game. Write a list of the advantages of watching the same event on television. Write a list of the advantages of listening to the same event on the radio.

Dig Deeper

STEP 2 Compare your lists. How does the technology used to bring an event to a television or radio audience change the experience for the spectator? Have aspects of live events of your favorite sport been changed to make it more effective for a television or radio audience? Does that make this sport's events mediated performances?

What Do You Think?

STEP 3 Did television's technology change the live events or games of your favorite sport? Does this add to the experience of the spectator, or does it detract? What about the listening experience on radio? Do you think spectators will continue to go to live events as media technology continues to evolve? Does the mass media's technology make a sporting event any less authentic?

Keeping Up to Date

Rolling Stone carries serious articles on music and movies.

Entertainment Weekly is among an array of fan magazines, many of which are more ga-ga over celebrities than concerned with media issues.

Communication Policy and Law is among scholarly journals that track First Amendment issues, including sexually explicit media content.

Publications that cover artistic aspects of media mass content from time to time include the *Atlantic, Harper's* and the *New Yorker.*

Because the mass media are a major industry, you can find regular coverage of media entertainment issues in the *Wall Street Journal, Forbes, Fortune,* the New York *Times* and other publications.

For Further Learning

Chris Willman. *Rednecks & Bluenecks: The Politics of Country Music.* New Press, 2006.

Willman, a writer for *Entertainment Weekly,* makes a case that as much as country music has a conservative bent, it's driven by the bottom line, not politics. Music Row execs, he argues, are mostly liberals who nurture a brand image of conservativism because it sells.

Neil Swidey. "Family !@%$#%'Ties," Boston *Globe Magazine* (November 27, 2005), pages 48–51, 58–59.

Swidey, a staff writer at the *Globe Magazine,* updates the history of television sitcoms in focusing on comedian Louis C. K.'s 2005 venture *Lucky Louie* on HBO.

Kathleen Krull. *The Book of Rock Stars: 24 Musical Icons That Shine Through History.* Hyperion, 2004.
Krull's informal narrative offers mini-biographies. Her picks include the Beatles, Kurt Cobain, Bob Dylan, Elvis Presley, Janis Joplin, Bob Marley and Jim Morrison.

Glenn C. Altschuler. *All Shook Up: How Rock 'n' Roll Changed America.* Oxford University Press, 2004.
Altschuler, a writer specializing in the media, explores the social effects, including racial integration, of rock from the 1950s on.

Stuart Evey. *ESPN: Creating an Empire.* Triumph, 2004.
Evey, a Getty Oil executive, recounts convincing his Getty colleagues to take a flyer and finance the novel concept of a sports cable network in 1976. He was ESPN's chair until 1985, when he negotiated its sale to ABC television.

Robert L. Hilliard and Michael C. Keith. *Dirty Discourse: Sex and Indecency in American Radio.* Iowa State Press, 2003.
Hilliard and Keith, both communication scholars, trace the course of radio deregulation and changes in FCC decency standards.

Eric Schlosser. "Empire of the Obscene," *New Yorker* (March 10, 2003), pages 60–71.
Schlosser details the career of Reuben Shurman, who built a giant pornography empire and, until late in his life, outfoxed federal agents.

Guthrie P. Ramsey Jr. *Race Music: Black Culture from Bebop to Hip-Hop.* University of California Press, 2003.
Ramsey, a scholar, sees popular music in the United States from the 1940s to 1990s as a window into the diverse American black culture, society and politics.

Steven L. Kent. *The Ultimate History of Video Games: From Pong to Pokemon—The Story Behind the Craze That Touched Our Lives and Changed the World.* Random House, 2001.
Kent, drawing on hundreds of interviews, offers a comprehensive history of video games, from the first pinball machines.

Ronald A. Smith. *Radio, Television, and Big-Time College Sport.* Johns Hopkins University Press, 2001.
An academic treatment of sports and media.

Dolf Zillmann and Peter Voderer. *Media Entertainment: The Psychology of Its Appeal.* Erlbaum, 2000.
A collection of essays about popular culture and media.

Barry Diller. "Don't Repackage, Redefine!" *Wired* (February 1995), pages 82–85.
This is a reprint of a 1994 speech in which media whiz Barry Diller implores magazine executives to focus more on original material and less on repackaging and recycling.

Elliot Gorn and Warren Goldstein. *A Brief History of American Sports.* Hill and Wang, 1993.
An overview of the impact of sports on today's American society.

David Sheff. *Game Over: Press Start to Continue.* Random House, 1993.
Sheff, known perhaps best for exhaustive *Playboy* magazine interviews, tracks the history of video gaming in this and later editions in his Game Over series.

James A. Michener. *Sports in America.* Random House, 1976.
Michener, the epic novelist, turns his attention to the growing mania for sports in U.S. culture.

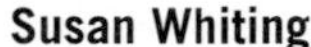

Susan Whiting She defends her Nielsen television viewership tracking, with Charlie Rangel of the New York congressional delegation at her side.

chapter 14 Media Research

In this chapter you will learn:

- **Surveys tell the mass media about their audiences.**
- **The size of mass media audiences is measured by monitoring press runs and sales and by surveying.**
- **Mass media organizations measure the reaction of people to make informed decisions on content.**
- **Audience analysis techniques include demographic, geodemographic and psychographic breakdowns.**
- **Mass media organizations are more interested in applied than theoretical research.**

Susan Whiting had critics waiting when, after 26 years at the Nielsen audience rating service, she was named president. Media mogul Rupert Murdoch was irate. He accused Nielsen of underrating the audience of his Fox television network. Nielsen data, he said, were costing him millions in advertising revenue. Black leader Al Sharpton was storming that urban blacks were underrepresented in Nielsen ratings. Then there were advertisers, which rely on Nielsen. They complained that the data were insufficient to help them make intelligent decisions in negotiating with networks on what to pay for 30-second spots.

Whiting, 47 at the time, had her hands full. The fact is that a lot is at stake in Nielsen television data. It is hardly an overstatement to say that Nielsen is called the most influential company in the television industry. Nielsens are used to determine the price of some $60 billion in television commercials a year. Network shows depend on the Nielsens for renewal. Ad agencies pay for access to Nielsen data. Time Warner itself pays more than $20 million a year, NBC, Viacom and Disney much more.

Whiting, from Quaker roots, joined Nielsen at 21 as a trainee. In 2004, when she was put in charge, Whiting immediately set out to double the number of Nielsen "families," the 5,000 households nationwide that Nielsen taps to measure network viewership.

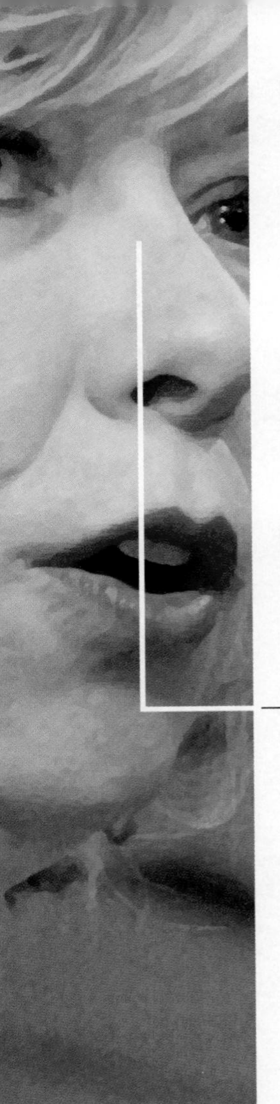

Because the television audience was fragmenting with the growth of cable and satellite television, a larger sample was needed for detailed information on proliferating niche networks.

A perennial complaint against Nielsen is that networks and advertisers have no alternative. There is no competitor. In the 1990s, upset at slipping viewership data from Nielsen, NBC threatened to form a separate service. Nothing came of the grumbling, but later Murdoch, displeased with the Nielsens for his Fox network, decried Nielsen as a monopoly. Murdoch's claim was that Nielsen undercounted urban blacks, which he said were a substantial 25 percent of Fox's audience. An ad in the New York *Times,* headed "Don't Count Us Out," claimed that "flawed" Nielsen numbers could have "a dramatic effect on the diversity of television programming."

Quietly but firmly, Whiting methodically defended Nielsen methodology. Black viewers, she demonstrated, were as accurately represented in new meters being introduced in major cities as they had been by early methods. Simultaneously, she stepped up plans to reduce statistical margins of error and to track where viewers were going in the fragmented universe of television choices.

Public-Opinion Sampling

study preview **The effectiveness of mass media messages is measured through research techniques that are widely recognized in the social sciences and in business. These techniques include public-opinion polling, which relies on statistical extrapolation that can be incredibly accurate. Sad to say, less reliable survey techniques also are used, sullying the reputation of serious sampling.**

The Surveying Industry

Public-opinion surveying is a $5 billion-a-year business whose clients include major corporations, political candidates and the mass media. Today, just as in 1935 when **George Gallup** founded it, the **Institute of American Public Opinion** cranks out regular surveys for clients. Major news organizations hire survey companies to tap public sentiment regularly on specific issues.

About 300 companies are in the survey business in the United States, most performing advertising and product-related opinion research for private clients. During election campaigns, political candidates become major clients. There are dozens of other survey companies that do confidential research for and about the media. Their findings are important because they determine what kind of advertising will run and where, what programs will be developed and broadcast, and which ones will be canceled. Some television stations even use such research to choose anchors for major newscasts.

The major companies:

Nielsen Nielsen Media Research, owned by Dutch publisher VNU, is known mostly for its network television ratings although it does local television ratings in major markets and other sampling too.

Arbitron Arbitron measures mostly radio audiences in local markets.

Gallup The Gallup Organization studies human nature and behavior and specializes in management, economics, psychology and sociology.

Pew The Pew Research Center is an independent opinion research group that studies attitudes toward the press, politics and public policy issues.

media ONLINE

Nielsen Nielsen Media Research, the famous TV ratings company.
www.nielsenmedia.com

Arbitron The radio research people.
www.arbitron.com/home/content.stm

Gallup See results of current and past Gallup polls.
www.gallup.com

Pew National surveys on public opinion.
http://people-press.org

Harris Internet-based public research.
www.harrisinteractive.com

George Gallup ■ Introduced probability sampling.

Institute of American Public Opinion ■ Gallup polling organization.

media TIMELINE

MEDIA RESEARCH

1914 Advertisers, publications created the Audit Bureau of Circulations to verify circulation claims.

1929 Archibald Crossley conducted the first listenership survey.

1932 George Gallup used quota sampling in an Iowa election.

1936 Gallup used quota sampling in a presidential election.

1940s A. C. Nielsen conducted a demographic listenership survey.

1948 Gallup used probability sampling in a presidential election.

1970s SRI introduced VALS psychographics.

1974 Jonathan Robbin introduced PRIZM geodemographics.

2000 Portable People Meters were introduced to track listenership for radio and television, including cable.

2006 Nielsen announced plans to integrate audience measures on numerous devices besides television, including home computers, video game players, iPods and cell phones.

2006 Nielsen announced plans to abandon diaries for local television ratings.

Harris Market research firm Harris Interactive Inc. is perhaps best known for the Harris Poll and for pioneering and engineering Internet-based research methods.

Probability Sampling

Although polling has become a high-profile business, many people do not understand how questions to a few hundred individuals can tell the mood of 250 million Americans. In the **probability sampling** method pioneered by George Gallup in the 1940s, four factors figure into accurate surveying:

Sample Size To learn how Layne College students feel about abortion on demand, you start by asking one student. Because you can hardly generalize from one student to the whole student body of 2,000, you ask a second student. If both agree, you start developing a tentative sense of how Layne students feel, but because you cannot have much confidence in such a tiny sample, you ask a third student and a fourth and a fifth. At some point between interviewing just one and all 2,000 Layne students, you can draw a reasonable conclusion.

How do you choose a **sample size?** Statisticians have found that **384** is a magic number for many surveys. Put simply, no matter how large the **population** being sampled, if every member has an equal opportunity to be polled, you need ask only 384 people to be 95 percent confident that you are within 5 percentage points of a precise reading. For a lot of surveys, that is close enough. Here is a breakdown, from Philip Meyer's *Precision Journalism,* a book for journalists on surveying, on necessary sample sizes for 95 percent confidence and being within 5 percentage points:

Population Size	Sample Size
Infinity	384
500,000	384
100,000	383
50,000	381
10,000	370
5,000	357
3,000	341
2,000	322
1,000	278

At Layne, with a total enrollment of 2,000, the sample size would need to be 322 students.

media ONLINE **Polls** The Gallup poll people explain how they conduct polls. **http://media.gallup.com/PDF/FAQ/HowArePolls.pdf**

American Association for Public Opinion Research Individuals who share an interest in public opinion and survey research. **www.aapor.org**

probability sampling ■ Everyone in population being surveyed has an equal chance to be sampled.

sample size ■ Number of people surveyed.

384 ■ Number of people in a properly selected sample for results to provide 95 percent confidence that results have less than 5 percent margin of error.

population ■ Group of people being studied.

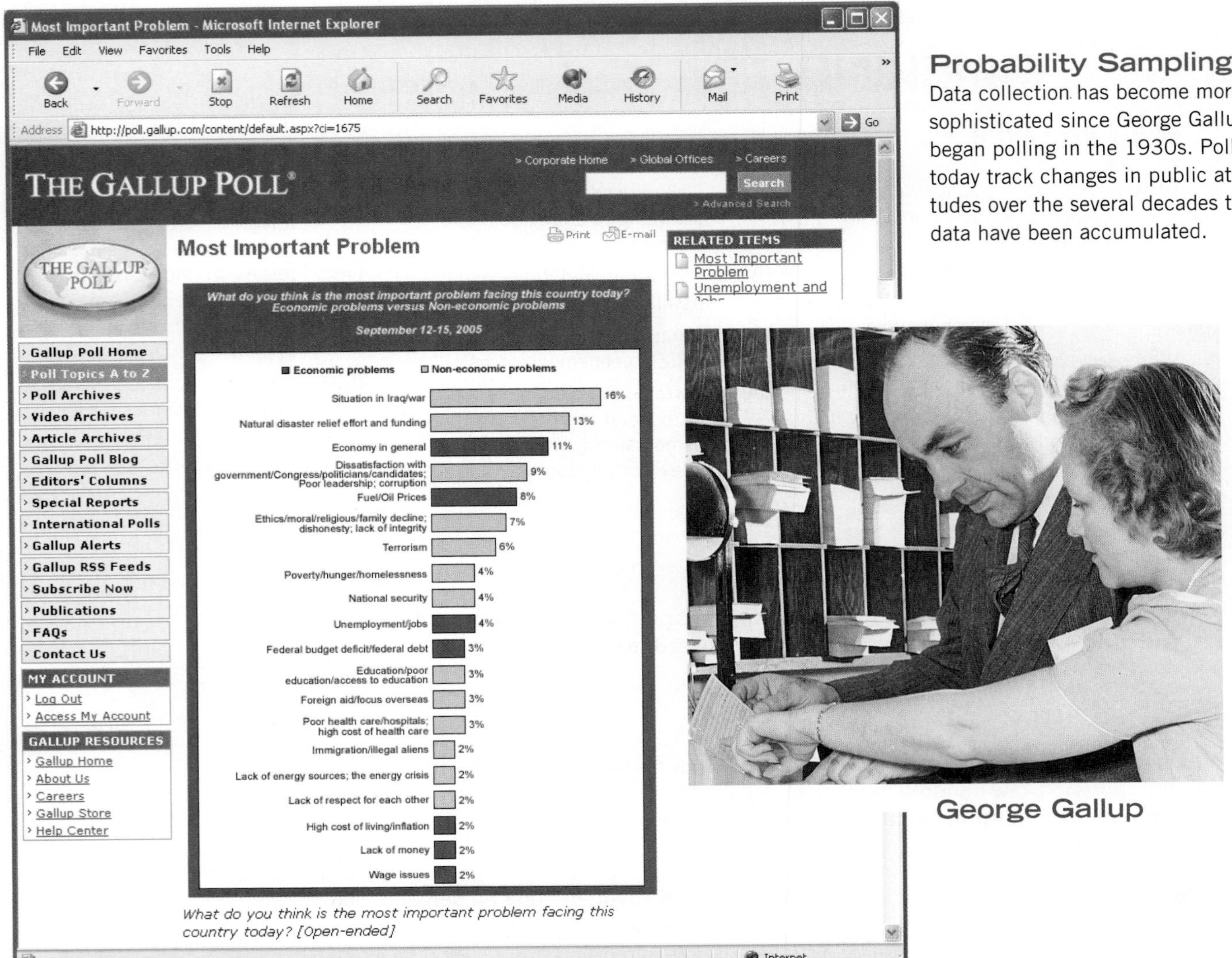

Probability Sampling Data collection has become more sophisticated since George Gallup began polling in the 1930s. Polls today track changes in public attitudes over the several decades that data have been accumulated.

George Gallup

Sample Selection Essential in probability sampling is **sample selection,** the process of choosing whom to interview. A good sample gives every member of the population being sampled an equal chance to be interviewed. For example, if you want to know how Kansans intend to vote, you cannot merely go to a Wichita street corner and survey the first 384 people who pass by. You would need to check a list of the state's 675,000 registered voters and then divide by the magic number, 384:

$$\frac{675{,}000}{384} = 1{,}758$$

You would need to talk with every 1,758th person on the list. At Layne College 2,000 divided by 322 would mean an interval of 6.2. Every sixth person in the student body would need to be polled.

Besides the right sample size and proper interval selection, two other significant variables affect survey accuracy: margin of error and confidence level.

Margin of Error For absolute precision every person in the population must be interviewed, but such precision is hardly ever needed, and the process would be prohibitively expensive and impracticable. Pollsters must therefore decide what is an acceptable **margin of error** for every survey they conduct. This is a complex matter, but in simple terms, you can have a fairly high level of confidence that a properly designed survey with 384 respondents can yield results within 5 percentage points, either way, of being correct.

sample selection ■ Process for drawing individuals to be interviewed.

margin of error ■ Percentage that a survey may be off mark.

George Gallup

George Gallup was excited. His mother-in-law, Ola Babcock Miller, had decided to run for secretary of state. If elected, she would become not only Iowa's first Democrat but also the first woman to hold the statewide office. Gallup's excitement, however, went beyond the novelty of his mother-in-law's candidacy. The campaign gave him an opportunity to pull together his three primary intellectual interests: survey research, public opinion and politics. In that 1932 campaign George Gallup conducted the first serious poll in history for a political candidate. Gallup's surveying provided important barometers of public sentiment that helped Miller to gear her campaign to the issues that were most on voters' minds. She won and was re-elected twice by large margins.

Four years after that first 1932 election campaign, Gallup tried his polling techniques in the presidential race and correctly predicted that Franklin Roosevelt would beat Alf Landon. Having called Roosevelt's victory accurately, his Gallup Poll organization had clients knocking at his door.

Gallup devoted himself to accuracy. Even though he predicted Roosevelt's 1936 victory, Gallup was bothered that his reliability was not better. His method, quota sampling, could not call a two-way race within 4 percentage points. With quota sampling, a representative percentage of women and men was surveyed, as was a representative percentage of Democrats and Republicans, Westerners and Easterners, Christians and Jews and other constituencies.

In 1948 Gallup correctly concluded that Thomas Dewey was not a shoo-in for president. Nonetheless, his pre-election poll was 5.3 percentage points off. So he decided to switch to a tighter method, probability sampling, which theoretically gave everyone in the population being sampled an equal chance to be surveyed. With probability sampling, there was no need for quotas because, as Gallup explained in his folksy Midwestern way, it was like a cook making soup: "When a housewife wants to test the quality of the soup she is making, she tastes only a teaspoonful or two. She knows that if the soup is thoroughly stirred, one teaspoonful is enough to tell her whether she has the right mixture of ingredients." With the new method, Gallup's **statistical extrapolation** narrowed his error rate to less than 2 percentage points.

Even with improvements pioneered by Gallup, public opinion surveying has detractors. Some critics say that polls influence undecided voters toward the front-runner—a bandwagon effect. Other critics say that polls make elected officials too responsive to the momentary whims of the electorate, discouraging courageous leadership. George Gallup, who died in 1984, tirelessly defended polling, arguing that good surveys give voice to the "inarticulate minority" that legislators otherwise might not hear. Gallup was convinced that public-opinion surveys help to make democracy work.

If the survey finds that two candidates for statewide office are running 51 to 49 percent, for example, the race is too close to call with a sample of 384. If the survey says that the candidates are running 56 to 44 percent, however, you can be reasonably confident who is ahead in the race because, even if the survey is 5 points off on the high side for the leader, the candidate at the very least has 51 percent support (56 percent minus a maximum 5 percentage points for possible error). At best, the trailing candidate has 49 percent (44 percent plus a maximum 5 percentage points for possible error).

Increasing the sample size will reduce the margin of error. Meyer gives this breakdown:

Population Size	Sample Size	Margin of Error
Infinity	384	5 percentage points
Infinity	600	4 percentage points
Infinity	1,067	3 percentage points
Infinity	2,401	2 percentage points
Infinity	9,605	1 percentage point

Professional polling organizations that sample U.S. voters typically use sample sizes between 1,500 and 3,000 to increase accuracy. Also, measuring subgroups within the population being sampled requires that each subgroup, such as men and women, Catholics and non-Catholics or Northerners and Southerners, be represented by 384 properly selected people.

Confidence Level With a sample of 384, pollsters can claim a relatively high 95 percent **confidence level,** that is, that they are within 5 percentage points of being on the mark. For

statistical extrapolation ■ Drawing conclusions from a segment of the whole.

confidence level ■ Degree of certainty that a survey is accurate.

many surveys, this is sufficient statistical validity. If the confidence level needs to be higher, or if the margin of error needs to be decreased, the number of people surveyed will need to be increased. In short, the level of confidence and margin of error are inversely related. A larger sample can improve confidence, just as it also can reduce the margin of error.

Quota Sampling

media ONLINE **Roper** Where thinking people go to learn what people are thinking. **www.ropercenter.uconn.edu**

Besides probability sampling, pollsters survey cross-sections of the whole population. This quota sampling technique gave Gallup his historic 1936 conclusions about the Roosevelt-Landon presidential race. With **quota sampling,** a pollster checking an election campaign interviews a sample of people that includes a quota of men and women that corresponds to the number of male and female registered voters. The sample might also include an appropriate quota of Democrats, Republicans and independents; of poor, middle-income and wealthy people; of Catholics, Jews and Protestants; of Southerners, Midwesterners and New Englanders; of the employed and unemployed; and other breakdowns significant to the pollster.

Both quota sampling and probability sampling are valid if done correctly, but Gallup abandoned quota sampling because he could not pinpoint public opinion more closely than 4 percentage points on average. With probability sampling, he regularly came within 2 percentage points.

Evaluating Surveys

Sidewalk interviews cannot be expected to reflect the views of the population. The people who respond to such polls are self-selected by virtue of being at a given place at a given time. Just as unreliable are call-in polls with 800 or 900 telephone numbers. These polls test the views only of people who are aware of the poll and who have sufficiently strong opinions to go to the trouble of calling in.

Journalists run the risk of being duped when special-interest groups suggest that news stories be written based on their privately conducted surveys. Some organizations selectively release self-serving conclusions.

To guard against being duped, the Associated Press insists on knowing methodology details before running poll stories. The AP tells reporters to ask:

- **How many people were interviewed and how were they selected?** Any survey of fewer than 384 people selected randomly from the population group has a greater margin for error than is usually tolerated.
- **When was the poll taken?** Opinions shift over time. During election campaigns, shifts can be quick, even overnight.
- **Who paid for the poll?** With privately commissioned polls, reporters should be skeptical, asking whether the results being released constitute everything learned in the survey. The timing of the release of political polls to be politically advantageous is not uncommon.
- **What was the sampling error?** Margins of error exist in all surveys unless everyone in the population is surveyed.
- **How was the poll conducted?** Whether a survey was conducted over the telephone or face to face in homes is important. Polls conducted on street corners or in shopping malls are not worth much statistically. Mail surveys are flawed unless surveyors follow up on people who do not answer the original questionnaires.
- **How were questions worded and in what order were they asked?** Drafting questions is an art. Sloppily worded questions yield sloppy conclusions. Leading questions and loaded questions can skew results. So can question sequencing.

Polling organizations get serious when someone misuses their findings. In 1998 the Gallup organization publicly told the tobacco industry to stop saying that a 1954 Gallup poll found 90 percent of Americans were aware of a correlation between smoking and cancer. Not so, said Gallup. The question was "Have you heard or read anything recently that cigarette smoking may be a cause of cancer of the lung?" Ninety percent said that

quota sampling ■ Demographics of the sample coincide with those of the whole population.

mediaPEOPLE

Andy Kohut

In college Andy Kohut learned polling from the experts. He first had a part-time job with the Gallup organization in Princeton, New Jersey. Polling fascinated Kohut more than his graduate studies, so he went full-time with Gallup and eventually worked his way up to president. What drew him to Gallup? Kohut, who has a strong sense of civic responsibility, liked Gallup's continuing work on public opinion on the great issues.

Andy Kohut He opted for public-opinion polling that's pristine from commercial underpinnings.

Something bad, from Kohut's perspective, happened in 1988. Gallup was bought by a market research company whose interest was providing data to corporations to push their goods and services more efficiently. Social polling issues were sure to take a back seat.

Eventually, Kohut joined the Los Angeles *Times'* quasi-independent polling organization, the Times Mirror Research Center for People and the Press. Times Mirror had created the center to find how the public perceived the media, what interests people in the news and the relationship among the people, press and politics. In many ways it was like the old Gallup. The Times Mirror studies provided scholars, as well as the media, with new baselines of understanding.

But like the old Gallup, it changed. Times Mirror, with a new bottom-line-focused management, let it be known in 1995 that Kohut's operation was on a cut list. Was there no place left for public policy polling? A philanthropic organization, Pew Charitable Trusts, was concerned about the loss of the Times Mirror polling unit and offered to take it over.

Today, Kohut's work generally is called the *Pew polls.* They are the most widely cited studies on U.S. public opinion. Robert Strauss, in a biographical article, said that the Los Angeles *Times* cites Pew polls every five days on average and the Washington *Post* cites them every six days. Said James Beninger, when he was president of the American Association for Public Opinion: "It is reported in all of the places where people of influence seem to look, the New York *Times* and the like."

What separates Pew polls from others?

- **Impartiality.** Nobody can accuse Pew of being the hireling of special interests.
- **Distribution.** Pew findings are distributed free.
- **Independence.** Unlike news media-sponsored surveys, Kohut isn't driven by deadlines. The polls sometimes make news, but that's residual.
- **Social and political thrust.** Kohut and his staff don't need to weigh whether to do a lucrative marketing survey or an issues poll. Because their focus is on public issues alone, their focus is never diluted.

they were aware of a controversy, but, says Gallup, that doesn't necessarily mean those people believed there was smoking-cancer correlation. Gallup threatened to go to court to refute the flawed conclusion if a tobacco company used it again in any wrongful-death lawsuit. Lydia Saad of Gallup told the *Wall Street Journal* that her organization gives people lots of latitude in interpreting its surveys. But this, Saad added, "really crosses the line."

It is with great risk that a polling company's client misrepresents survey results. Most polling companies, concerned about protecting their reputations, include a clause in their contracts with clients that gives the pollster the right to approve the release of findings. The clause usually reads: "When misinterpretation appears, we shall publicly disclose what is required to correct it, notwithstanding our obligation for client confidentiality in all other respects."

Latter-Day Straw Polls

The ABC and CNN television networks and other news organizations dabble, some say irresponsibly, with phone-in polling on public issues. The vehicle is the **900 telephone number,**

900 telephone number ■ Used for call-in surveys; respondents select themselves to participate and pay for the call.

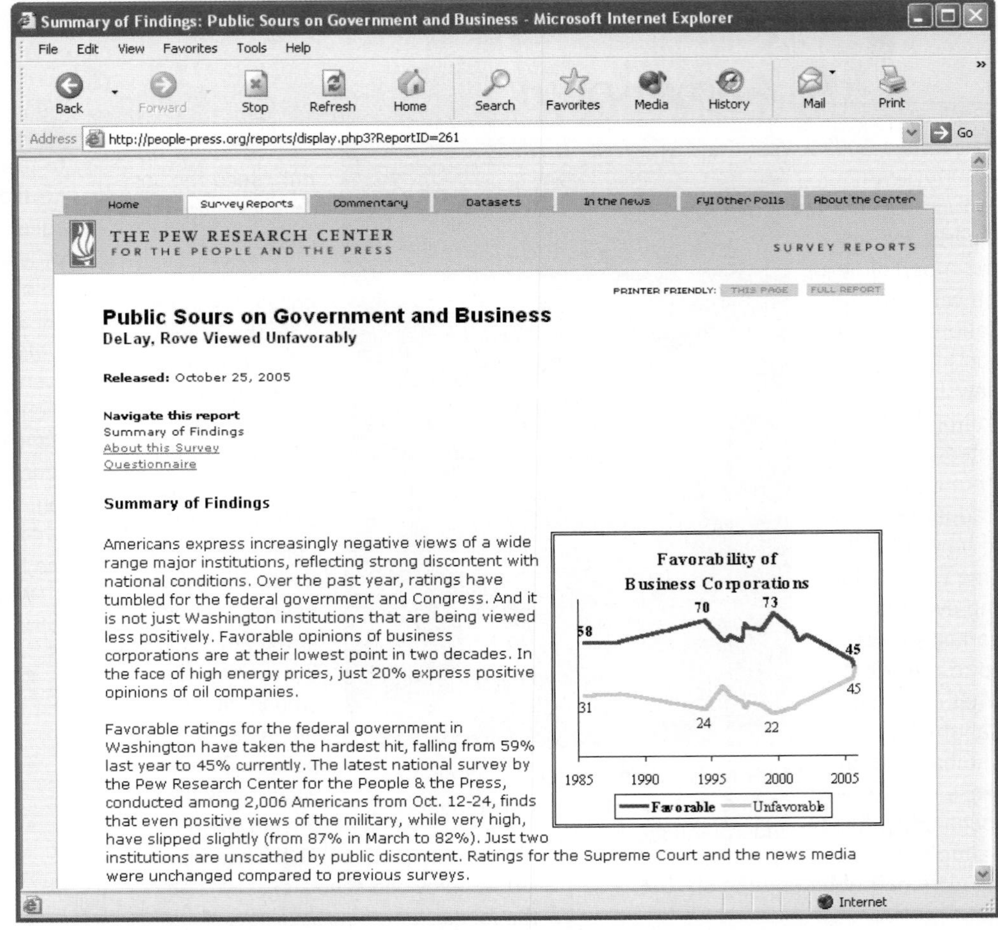

Summary of Findings: Public Sours on Government and Business - Microsoft Internet Explorer

File Edit View Favorites Tools Help

Back Forward Stop Refresh Home Search Favorites Media History Mail Print

Address http://people-press.org/reports/display.php3?ReportID=261 Go

Home | Survey Reports | Commentary | Datasets | In the News | FYI Other Polls | About the Center

THE PEW RESEARCH CENTER FOR THE PEOPLE AND THE PRESS

SURVEY REPORTS

PRINTER FRIENDLY: THIS PAGE FULL REPORT

Public Sours on Government and Business

DeLay, Rove Viewed Unfavorably

Released: October 25, 2005

Navigate this report

Summary of Findings

About this Survey

Questionnaire

Summary of Findings

Americans express increasingly negative views of a wide range major institutions, reflecting strong discontent with national conditions. Over the past year, ratings have tumbled for the federal government and Congress. And it is not just Washington institutions that are being viewed less positively. Favorable opinions of business corporations are at their lowest point in two decades. In the face of high energy prices, just 20% express positive opinions of oil companies.

Favorable ratings for the federal government in Washington have taken the hardest hit, falling from 59% last year to 45% currently. The latest national survey by the Pew Research Center for the People & the Press, conducted among 2,006 Americans from Oct. 12-24, finds that even positive views of the military, while very high, have slipped slightly (from 87% in March to 82%). Just two institutions are unscathed by public discontent. Ratings for the Supreme Court and the news media were unchanged compared to previous surveys.

Pew Poll

The Pew Research Center's polls focus on public policy issues, as reported in this 2005 news release on a tracking poll that found declining public confidence in government and business.

which listeners dial at 50 cents a call to register yea or nay on a question. These **straw polls** are conducted on the Internet too. While they can be fun, statistically they are meaningless.

Just as dubious are the candid camera features, popular in weekly newspapers, in which a question is put to people on the street. The photos of half a dozen individuals and their comments are then published, often on the editorial page. These features are circulation builders for small publications whose financial success depends on how many local names and mug shots can be crammed into an issue, but it is only coincidental when the views expressed are representative of the population as a whole.

These **roving photographer** features are at their worst when people are not given time to formulate an intelligent response. The result too often is contributions to the public babble, not public understanding. The result is irresponsible pseudojournalism.

Measuring Audience Size

study preview **To attract advertisers, the mass media need to know the number and kinds of people they reach. This is done for the print media by audits and for the broadcast media by surveys. Although surveying is widely accepted for obtaining such data, some approaches are more reliable than others.**

Newspaper and Magazine Audits

The number of copies a newspaper or magazine puts out, called **circulation,** is fairly easy to calculate. It is simple arithmetic involving data like press runs, subscription sales and unsold copies returned from news racks. Many publishers follow strict procedures, which

straw polls ■ Respondents select themselves to be polled; unreliable indicator of public opinion.

roving photographer ■ Statistically unsound way to tap public opinion.

circulation ■ Number of readers of a publication.

are checked by independent audit organizations, like the **Audit Bureau of Circulations,** to assure advertisers that the system is honest and circulation claims comparable.

The Audit Bureau of Circulations was formed in 1914 to remove the temptation for publishers to inflate their claims to attract advertisers and hike ad rates. Inflated claims, contagious in some cities, were working to the disadvantage of honest publishers. Today, most newspapers and magazines belong to ABC, which means that they follow the bureau's standards for reporting circulation and are subject to the bureau's audits.

media ONLINE **Audit Bureau of Circulations** Measuring print circulation. **www.accessabc.com**

Broadcast Ratings

Radio and television audiences are harder to measure, but advertisers have no less need for counts to help them decide where to place ads and to know what is a fair price. To keep track of broadcast audiences, a whole **ratings** industry, now with about 200 companies, has developed. **Nielsen Media Research** tracks network television viewership.

Radio ratings began in 1929 when advertisers asked pollster Archibald Crossley to determine how many people were listening to network programs. Crossley checked a small sample of households and then extrapolated the data into national ratings, the same process that radio and television audience tracking companies still use, though there have been refinements.

In the 1940s Nielsen began telling advertisers which radio programs were especially popular among men, women and children. Nielsen also divided listenership into age brackets: 18 to 34, 35 to 49 and 50 plus. These were called **demographic** breakdowns. When Nielsen moved into television monitoring in 1950, it expanded audience data into more breakdowns. Today breakdowns include income, education, religion, occupation, neighborhood and even which products the viewers of certain programs use frequently.

While Archibald Crossley's early ratings were sponsored by advertisers, today networks and individual stations also commission ratings to be done. The television networks pass ratings data on to advertisers immediately. Local stations usually recast the raw data for brochures that display the data in ways that put the station in the most favorable light. These brochures are distributed by station sales representatives to advertisers. While advertisers receive ratings data from the stations and networks, major advertising agencies have contracts with Nielsen, Arbitron and other market research companies to gather audience data to meet their specifications.

Audience Measurement Techniques

The primary techniques, sometimes used in combination, for measuring broadcast audiences are interview, diaries and meters.

Interviews In his pioneer 1929 listenership polling, Archibald Crossley placed telephone calls to randomly selected households. Although many polling companies use telephone **interviews** exclusively, they're not used much in broadcasting anymore. Also rare in broadcasting are face-to-face interviews. Although eyeball-to-eyeball interviewing can elicit fuller information, it is labor-intensive and relatively expensive.

Diaries Nielsen began using **diaries** in the 1950s. Instead of interviews, Nielsen mailed forms to selected families in major markets to list program titles, times, channels and who was watching. This was done in major sweep periods: February, May, July and November. Although diaries were cost-efficient, viewers would forget their duty and then try to remember days later what they had watched. The resulting data were better than no data but were rather muddy.

Meters Meters were introduced in the 1970s as a supplement to diaries to improve accuracy. Some Nielsen families had their sets wired to track what channel was on. Some were issued meters that household members could click so that Nielsen could determine for whom programs have their appeal—men, women, children, oldsters. Some set-top meters even traced who was watching by sensing body mass.

People Meters In 1987 Nielsen introduced **people meters.** These were two-function units, one on the television set to scan the channels being watched every 2.7 seconds

Audit Bureau of Circulations ■ Checks newspaper, magazine circulation claims.

ratings ■ Measurements of broadcast audience size.

Nielsen Media Research ■ Surveys television viewership.

demographic ■ Characteristics of groups within a population being sampled, including age, gender, affiliations.

interviews ■ Face-to-face, mail, telephone survey technique.

diaries ■ Sampling technique in which respondents keep their own records.

people meters ■ Devices that track individual viewers.

case STUDY

Ratings Technology: A2/M2 Coming to a Cell Phone Near You

At first, research companies collected data on television audiences by asking people to fill out a paper diary. Then Nielsen began using its electronic People Meter, which automatically recorded what channel a television set was tuned to.

Now Nielsen is planning to provide ratings for television regardless of the platform on which it is viewed. Its Anytime Anywhere Media Measurement, A2/M2 for short, will assess the new ways that people are watching television, including on the Internet, outside the home and via cell phones, video iPods and other personal mobile devices.

"A2/M2 is the result of extensive consultation with clients, who told us clearly that we should 'follow the video,'" said Nielsen chief executive Susan Whiting.

Nielsen is owned by information provider VNU, and together they own the majority of NetRatings, Inc., a web traffic tracking service. Nielsen and NetRatings want to provide the industry's most comprehensive system for tracking and reporting digital audio and video delivered via the Internet. The companies will use ping-back technology to measure what is delivered online. By 2007 Nielsen plans to install software on computers and laptops owned by people who already are part of the sample audience using People Meters linked to their television sets. Eventually, the company hopes to have a single panel of viewers to measure the relationship among television viewing, web site usage and streaming video consumption. The fused data will provide combined reporting of viewership of broadcast and cable networks and usage of their web sites.

Outside-the-Home Television Measuring television audiences has become a greater challenge with the proliferation of sets in airports, bars and even luxury SUVs. Here, students at Minnesota State University, Mankato, jog on treadmills while watching television and surfing the Net. The Nielsen audience measurement company is working on devices that volunteers wear with them to check even on exposure to billboards. The walking meters, as they're called, pick up an inaudible code embedded in the audio of television, radio and streamed programs—and signals sent out by billboards as they pass by. When people get home, they put the meters in a dock that transmits accumulated data to survey-company computers for aggregation.

and a handheld remote that monitored who was watching. With data flowing in nightly to Nielsen's central computers, the company generates next-day reports, called **overnights,** for the networks and advertisers.

Portable Meters In 2001 Nielsen and Arbitron, which focuses on radio audiences, jointly tested portable meters for people to carry around. The pager-size meters, weighing $2^1/_2$ ounces, were set to pick up inaudible signals transmitted with programs. The goal: to track away-from-home audiences at sports bars, offices and airports and, in the case of radio, cars. Tracking those "lost listeners" could affect ratings. ESPN estimates that 4 million people watch its sports away from home in a typical week. The "walking meters," as they are called, also track commuter radio habits for the first time.

comScore Media Metrix
Leading Internet audience measurement company.

Internet Audience Measures

The leading Internet audience measuring company, **Media Metrix,** uses a two-track system to determine how many people view web sites. Media Metrix gathers data from 40,000 individual computers whose owners have agreed to be monitored. Some of these computers are programmed to track Internet usage and report data back by e-mail. In addition, Media Metrix has lined up other computer users to mail in a tracking disc periodically. In 1998 the Nielsen television ratings company set up a similar methodology. Other companies also are in the Internet ratings business.

overnights ■ Next-morning reports on network viewership.

Media Metrix ■ A service measuring Internet audience size.

Nielsen also is developing and testing new personal meters to measure television viewership away from home, including at work and in bars, restaurants, hotels and airports. Theoretical research includes:

2½-ounce Walking Meter

- **Effects Studies.** Looking at media-triggered behaviors of individuals, groups and institutions.
- **Process Studies.** How the process of mass communication works.
- **Gratifications Studies.** How people use the mass media to meet their needs.
- **Content Analysis.** Finding patterns in media content through measurement and analysis.

The Go Meters are designed to collect audio signatures. One device places metering technology in cell phones, and the other is a customized meter that resembles an MP3 player. Nielsen expects to introduce these meters by the end of 2008. The company also plans to expand the use of electronic metering to smaller television markets and by 2011 to have replaced paper diaries and logs in smaller cities with electronic meters.

The Solo Meter that the company is developing can be used with any portable media system. For wireless, Bluetooth connections, Nielsen is working on a tiny wireless meter that will passively listen to communication between mated devices. For wired systems, Nielsen is building a diminutive in-line meter that will be physically inserted between the device and its earphones. These Solo Meters also will identify viewing by collecting audio signatures.

For advertisers, Nielsen plans to adopt a measure of engagement for television. Engagement assesses how deep an impression an ad or program has made with a viewer. As audiences for programming and advertising grow narrower, the need to make a deeper impression on a smaller group of people becomes more important than the conventional focus on reaching as many people as possible. Recent research points toward the possibility of a link between media engagement and advertising engagement. A survey conducted by Knowledge Networks/Statistical Research found that across all three 24-hour cable news networks, viewers who correctly recalled advertising posted higher media engagement scores than viewers who did not recall any advertising. The object of this new engagement research is to figure out which networks or programs are more likely to deliver an audience receptive to advertising and which ads are more likely to engage a viewer.

As the technology of the mass media continues to progress, audience measurement companies must find ways to keep up. Sometimes that could mean dramatic changes in the way viewership figures are tallied. And that could result in major shifts in the way advertising dollars are spent and received. Stay tuned.

WHAT DO YOU THINK?

1. How do you think the changes in audience tracking technology will change the way advertising dollars are spent?
2. As ways to measure our culture's reaction to the media become more sophisticated, some people fear that Big Brother, the leader of a totalitarian government that censored everyone's behavior, even their thoughts, in George Orwell's classic novel *1984,* is coming. What do you think?
3. Will consumers benefit as much as advertisers from the newest audience tracking technology?

How accurate are Internet ratings? Some major content providers, including CNN, ESPN and Time Warner, claim that the ratings undercount their users. Such claims go beyond self-serving comments because, in fact, different rating companies come up with widely divergent ratings. The question is: Why can't the ratings companies get it right? The answer, in part, is that divergent data flow from divergent methodologies. Data need to be viewed in terms of the methodology that was used. Also, the infant Internet ratings business undoubtedly is hobbled by methodology flaws that have yet to be identified and corrected.

Multimedia Measures

Recognizing that television viewers were increasingly mobile and less set-bound, Nielsen began remaking its ratings system in 2006 to measure the use of personal computers, videogame players, iPods, cell phones and other mobile devices. Nielsen said the program, called **Anytime Anywhere Media Measurement,** or A2/M2 for short, represented a commitment to "follow the vided" with an "all-electronic measurement system that will deliver integrated ratings for television viewing regardless of the platform." Nielsen's chief researcher, Paul Donato, put it this way: "The plan is to try to capture it all."

Anytime Anywhere Media Measurement (A2/M2) ■ Nielsen plan to integrate audience measurements on wide range of video platforms.

An initial step was creating a panel of 400 video iPod users to track the programs they download and watch. Nielson also began fusing data from its television-tracking unit and

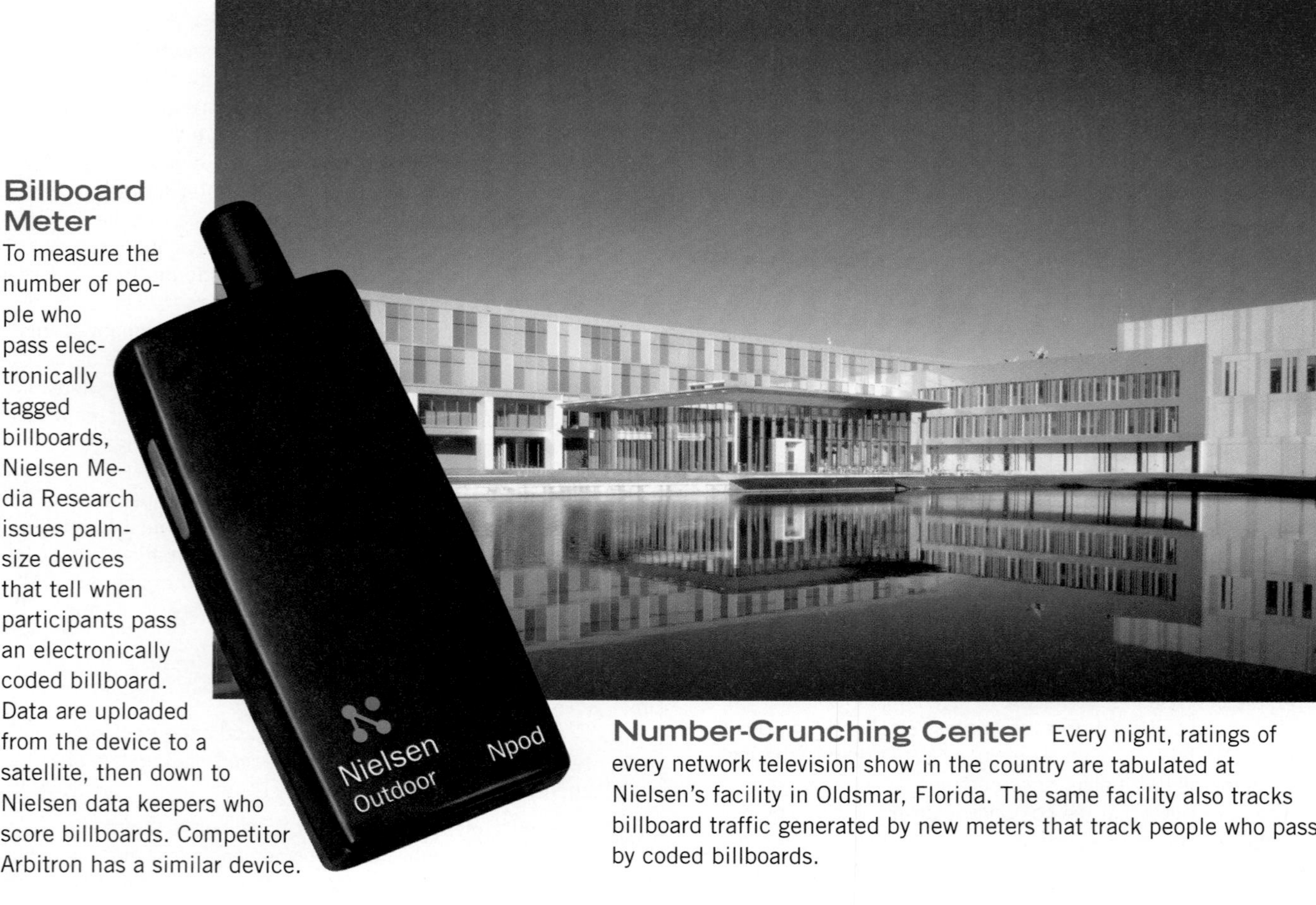

Billboard Meter To measure the number of people who pass electronically tagged billboards, Nielsen Media Research issues palm-size devices that tell when participants pass an electronically coded billboard. Data are uploaded from the device to a satellite, then down to Nielsen data keepers who score billboards. Competitor Arbitron has a similar device.

Number-Crunching Center Every night, ratings of every network television show in the country are tabulated at Nielsen's facility in Oldsmar, Florida. The same facility also tracks billboard traffic generated by new meters that track people who pass by coded billboards.

its Nielsen/Net Ratings unit to measure the relation between conventional television viewing and web-surfing with meters on both television and personal computers.

Nielsen also was developing small devices to capture the audio signatures of video content to figure out what's being watched.

Criticism of Ratings

However sophisticated the ratings services have become, they have critics. Many fans question the accuracy of ratings when their favorite television program is cancelled because the network finds the ratings inadequate. Something is wrong, they say, when the viewing preferences of a few thousand households determine network programming for the entire nation. Though it seems incredible to someone who is not knowledgeable about statistical probability, the sample base of major ratings services like Nielsen generally is considered sufficient to extrapolate reliably on viewership in the 97 million U.S. households.

Ratings and Shares The weekly Nielsens on prime-time network audiences show how each show ranked. The CBS show *CSI* at 9 p.m. Thursday led this week. Second was ABC's *Desperate Housewives* at 9 p.m. Sunday. One measure of audience is the "rating," the percentage of television-equipped households viewing a program. *CSI*'s rating was 17.9. Because 97 million U.S. households have television sets, each percentage point is valued at 970,000 households, which means 17.4 million households were tuned in to *CSI*. A second audience measure, "share," is the percentage of all households with a television on. *CSI* had a 27 share, far outdistancing NBC's *Apprentice* with 11; Fox's *Reunion,* with 4; WB's *Everwood,* 3; UPN's *Eve,* 3; and Pax's *Diagnosis Murder,* 1. The rest of television-equipped U.S. households, 51 percent, were watching something else or nothing at all.

NIELSEN MEDIA RESEARCH

10/31/05–11/06/05

MONDAY

	ABC	CBS	FOX	NBC	PAX	UPN	WB
8:00	68 Wife Swap 4.4 8	**35 King of Queens 6.4 10**			119 DOC-Mon 0.5 1	105 One on One 1.5 2	75 7th Heaven WB 3.5 6
8:30		**46 How I Met Your Mother 5.5 9**				107 All of Us 1.5 2	
9:00	**19 NFL Monday 8.8 14**	22 Two and a Half Men 8.4 13	40 Prison Break 5.9 9		111 Diagnosis Murder-Mon 0.7 1	101 Girlfriends 1.6 2	99 Related WB 1.7 3
9:30	**6 NFL Monday 11.0 19**	30 Out of Practice 6.7 10				106 Half and Half 1.5 2	
10:00		18 CSI: Miami 9.0 15		34 Medium 6.4 11	121 Early Edition 0.4 1		
10:30							

TUESDAY

	ABC	CBS	FOX	NBC	PAX	UPN	WB
8:00	56 According to Jim 5.0 8	**5 NCIS 11.3 17**	55 Bones 5.0 8	38 Biggest Loser 2 6.1 9	120 Diagnosis Murder-Tue 0.4 1	92 America's Next Top Model 2.0 3	82 Gilmore Girls 2.7 4
8:30	61 Rodney 4.8 7						
9:00	**15 Commander in Chief 9.6 14**	29 Amazing Race 8 6.8 10	20 House 8.7 13	24 My Name Is Earl 7.6 11	110 Diagnosis Murder-Tue 0.8 1		95 Supernatural 1.9 3
9:30				51 Office 5.1 8			
10:00	25 Boston Legal 7.4 12	33 Close to Home 6.5 11		**13 Law and Order: SVU 10.2 17**	115 DOC-Tue 0.6 1		
10:30							

WEDNESDAY

	ABC	CBS	FOX	NBC	PAX	UPN	WB
8:00	59 George Lopez 4.9 8	60 Still Standing 4.8 8	58 That 70's Show 4.9 8	**31 E-Ring 6.6 10**	114 Diagnosis Murder-Wed 0.6 1	80 America's Next Top Model 3.1 5	90 One Tree Hill WB 2.1 3
8:30	64 Freddie 4.6 7	50 Yes Dear 5.2 8					
9:00	45 Lost 5.6 9	**10 Criminal Minds 10.4 16**	47 Trading Spouses 5.4 8	54 Apprentice: 5.0 8	109 Diagnosis Murder-Wed 0.8 1	103 Veronica Mars 1.5 2	104 Related-Wed 1.5 2
9:30							
10:00	76 Invasion 3.4 6	**9 CSI: NY 10.6 18**		21 Law and Order 8.6 15	118 DOC-Wed 0.5 1		
10:30							

THURSDAY

	ABC	CBS	FOX	NBC	PAX	UPN	WB
8:00		**7 Survivor: Guatemala 10.9 17**	70 O.C. 4.2 6	49 Joey 5.2 8	113 Diagnosis Murder-Thu 0.6 1	79 Everybody Hates Chris 3.3 5	78 Smallville WB 3.3 5
8:30				44 Will & Grace 5.6 8		94 Love, Inc. 1.9 3	
9:00		**1 CSI 17.9 27**	88 Reunion 2.4 4	27 Apprentice 4 7.3 11	112 Diagnosis Murder-Thu 0.6 1	97 Eve 1.8 3	86 Everwood WB 2.5 4
9:30						98 Cuts 1.7 2	
10:00		**3 Without a Trace 13.3 22**		14 E.R. 9.8 16			
10:30							

FRIDAY

	ABC	CBS	FOX	NBC	PAX	UPN	WB
8:00	72 Supernanny 4.1 7	**23 Ghost 8.2 14**	85 Bernie Mac 2.5 4	39 Dateline Friday 5.9 10	123 America's Most Tal Kids 0.3 1	83 WWE Smackdown 2.6 4	96 What I Like WB 1.8 3
8:30			89 Malcolm in the Middle 2.2 4				100 What I Like WB 1.6 3
9:00	63 Hope & Faith 4.6 8	48 Threshold 5.2 9	81 Killer Instinct 3.0 5	**42 Three Wishes 5.6 10**	122 I Love a Mystery 0.3 0		84 Reba WB 2.5 4
9:30	73 Hot Properties 4.0 7						91 Twins WB 2.0 3
10:00	37 20/20 Friday 6.1 11	**26 Numbers 7.3 13**		43 Law and Order: CI-FRI 5.6 10			
10:30							

SATURDAY

	ABC	CBS	FOX	NBC	PAX	UPN	WB
8:00	62 ABC Saturday Movie of the Week 4.7 8	**53 Crimetime 5.0 9**	77 COPS 3.3 6				
8:30			74 COPS 2 3.6 6				
9:00		**41 Crimetime 5.6 10**	71 AMW: America Fights Back 4.1 7				
9:30							
10:00		**57 48 Hours 4.9 9**			126 World Cup 0.1 0		
10:30							

SUNDAY

	ABC	CBS	FOX	NBC	PAX	UPN	WB
7:00	28 Extreme Makeover Home Ed 6.9 11	**12 60 Minutes 10.3 16**		65 Dateline Sunday 4.5 7	124 Young Blades Sunday 0.2 0		102 Reba Begin WB 1.5 2
7:30			67 King of the Hill 4.4 7				93 Reba Begin Sunday WB 1.9 3
8:00	11 Extreme Makeover Home Ed 10.3 15	**8 Cold Case 10.6 15**	32 Simpsons 6.5 10	36 West Wing 6.1 9	125 Palmetto Pointe 0.2 0		87 Charmed WB 2.4 3
8:30			69 War at Home 4.3 6				
9:00	**2 Desperate Housewives 15.3 22**	17 CBS Sunday Movie 9.1 14	52 Family Guy 5.0 7	16 Law and Order: Crim Intent 9.4 14	117 Diagnosis Murder-Sun 0.5 1		108 Supernatural Sunday WB 1.0 1
9:30			66 American Dad 4.5 6				
10:00	**4 Grey's Anatomy 12.1 19**				116 Sue Thomas, F. B. Eye 0.5 1		
10:30							

It was not always so. Doubts peaked in the 1940s and 1950s when it was learned that some ratings services lied about sample size and were less than scientific in choosing samples. A congressional investigation in 1963 prompted the networks to create the **Broadcast Ratings Council** to accredit ratings companies and audit their reports.

Ratings have problems, some inherent in differing methodologies and some attributable to human error and fudging.

Discrepancies When different ratings services come up with widely divergent findings in the same market, advertisers become suspicious. Minor discrepancies can be explained by different sampling methods, but significant discrepancies point to flawed methodology or execution. It was discrepancies of this sort that led to the creation of the Broadcast Ratings Council.

Slanted Results Sales reps of some local stations, eager to demonstrate to advertisers that their stations have large audiences, extract only the favorable data from survey results. It takes a sophisticated local advertiser to reconcile slanted and fudged claims.

Sample Selection Some ratings services select their samples meticulously, giving every household in a market a statistically equal opportunity to be sampled. Some sample selections are seriously flawed: How reliable, for example, are the listenership claims of a rock 'n' roll station that puts a disk jockey's face on billboards all over town and then sends the disk jockey to a teenage dance palace to ask about listening preferences?

Hyping Ratings-hungry stations have learned how to build audiences during **sweeps** weeks in February, May and November when major local television ratings are done. Consider these examples of **hyping:**

- Radio give-aways often coincide with ratings periods.
- Many news departments promote sensationalistic series for the sweeps and then retreat to routine coverage when the ratings period is over.
- Besides sweeps weeks, there are **black weeks** when no ratings are conducted. In these periods some stations run all kinds of odd and dull serve-the-public programs that they would never consider during a sweeps period.

Respondent Accuracy With handwritten diaries, respondents don't always answer honestly. People have an opportunity to write that they watched *Masterpiece Theater* on PBS instead of less classy fare. For the same reason, shock radio and trash television probably have more audience than the ratings show.

In a project to tighten measurement techniques Nielsen gradually began eliminating diaries in local television markets in 2006. In the 10 largest markets Nielsen redesigned its people meters, which measure both what network shows are being watched and who is in the room watching. The new meters also track local viewing choices. Gradually Nielsen sought to eliminate diaries in smaller markets too.

Zipping, Zapping and Flushing Ratings services measure audiences for programs and for different times of day, but they do not measure whether commercials are watched. Advertisers are interested, of course, in whether the programs in which their ads are sandwiched are popular, but more important to them is whether people are watching the ads.

This vacuum in audience measurements was documented in the 1960s when somebody with a sense of humor correlated a major drop in Chicago water pressure with the Super Bowl halftime, in what became known as the **flush factor.** Football fans were getting off the couch by the thousands at halftime to go to the bathroom. Advertisers were missing many people because although viewers were watching the program many were not watching the ads.

This problem has been exacerbated with the advent of handheld television remote controls and systems like TiVo. Viewers can **zip** from station to station to avoid commercials, and when they record programs for later viewing, they can **zap** out the commercials.

Broadcast Ratings Council ■ Accredits ratings companies.

sweeps ■ When broadcast ratings are conducted.

hyping ■ Intensive promotion to attract an audience during ratings periods.

black weeks ■ Periods when ratings are not conducted.

flush factor ■ Viewers leave during commercials to go to refrigerator, bathroom, etc.

zipping ■ Viewers change television channels to avoid commercials.

zapping ■ Viewers record programs and eliminate commercial breaks.

focus groups ■ Small groups interviewed in loosely structured ways for opinion, reactions.

galvanic skin checks ■ Monitor pulse, skin responses to stimuli.

Measuring Audience Reaction

studypreview **The television ratings business has moved beyond measuring audience size to measuring audience reaction. Researchers measure audience reaction with numerous methods, including focus groups, galvanic skin checks and prototypes.**

Focus Groups

Television consulting companies measure audience reaction with **focus groups.** Typically, an interview crew goes to a shopping center, chooses a dozen individuals by gender and age, and offers them cookies, soft drinks and $25 each to sit down and watch a taped local newscast. A moderator then asks their reactions, sometimes with loaded and leading questions to open them up. It is a tricky research method that depends highly on the skill of the moderator. In one court case an anchor who had lost her job as a result of responses to a focus group complained that the moderator had contaminated the process with prejudicial assertions and questions:

- "This is your chance to get rid of the things you don't like to see on the news."
- "Come on, unload on those sons of bitches who make $100,000 a year."
- "This is your chance to do more than just yell at the TV. You can speak up and say I really hate that guy or I really like that broad."
- "Let's spend 30 seconds destroying this anchor. Is she a mutt? Be honest about this."

Even when conducted skillfully, focus groups have the disadvantage of reflecting the opinion of the loudest respondent.

media ONLINE

The Use and Misuse of Focus Groups By Jakob Nielsen, known in the web world as the "king of usability research."
www.useit.com/papers/focusgroups.html

Guidelines for Conducting a Focus Group The basics, from preparing to after the session.
www.managementhelp.org/evaluatn/focusgrp.htm

Lies, Damn Lies, and Focus Groups Why consumers don't tell the truth about what they want.
www.slate.com/id/2089677

Galvanic Skin Checks

Consulting companies hired by television stations run a great variety of studies to determine audience reaction. Local stations, which originate news programs and not much else, look to these consultants for advice on news sets, story selection and even which anchors and reporters are most popular. Besides surveys, these consultants sometimes use **galvanic skin checks.** Wires are attached to individuals in a sample group of viewers to measure pulse and skin reactions, such as perspiration. Advocates of these tests claim that they reveal how much interest a newscast evokes and whether the interest is positive or negative.

These tests were first used to check audience reaction to advertisements, but today some stations look to them in deciding whether to remodel a studio. A dubious use, from a journalistic perspective, is using galvanic skin checks to determine what kinds of stories to cover and whether to find new anchors and reporters. The skin checks reward short, photogenic stories like fires and accidents rather than significant stories, which tend to be longer and don't lend themselves to flashy video. The checks also favor good-looking, smooth anchors and reporters, regardless of their journalistic competence. One wag was literally correct when he called this "a heartthrob approach to journalism."

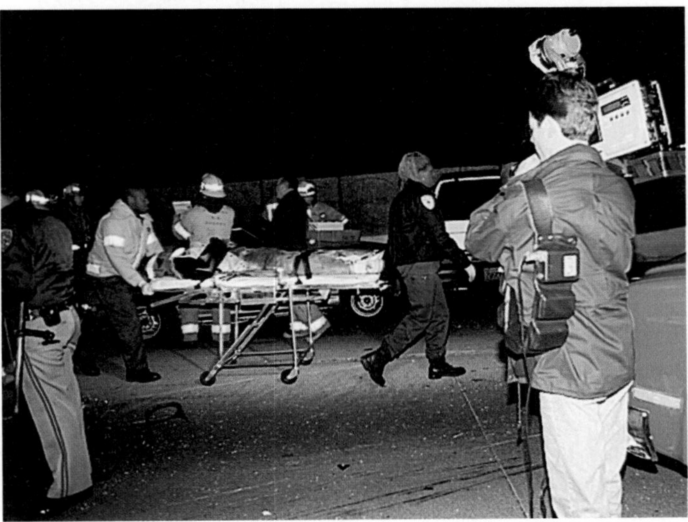

If It Bleeds, It Leads Audience researchers have found newscast ratings go up for stations that consistently deliver graphic video. This has prompted many stations to favor fire stories, for example, even if the fire wasn't consequential, if graphic video is available. The ratings quest also prompts these stations to favor crimes and accidents over more substantive stories, like government budgets, that don't lend themselves to gripping graphics.

Prototype Research

Before making major investments, media executives need as much information as they can obtain to determine how to enhance a project's chances for success or whether it has a chance at all. This is known as **prototype research.** The **American Research Institute** of Los Angeles specializes in showing previews of television programs and even promotional ads to sample audiences. It is a method originated by movie studios, which invite people to advance showings and watch their reaction to decide how to advertise a new film most effectively, how to time the film's release and even whether to re-edit the film.

When Gannett decided to establish a new newspaper, *USA Today,* it created prototypes, each designed differently, to test readers' reactions. Many new magazines are preceded by at least one trial issue to sample marketplace reaction and to show to potential advertisers.

In network television a prototype can even make it on the air in the form of a **pilot.** One or a few episodes are tested, usually in prime time with a lot of promotion, to see whether the audience goes for the program concept. Some made-for-television movies actually are test runs to determine whether a series might be spun off from the movie.

Audience Analysis

study preview **Traditional demographic polling methods divided people by gender, age and other easily identifiable population characteristics. Today, media people use sophisticated lifestyle breakdowns such as geodemographics and psychographics to match the content of their publications, broadcast programs and advertising to the audiences they seek.**

Demographics

Early in the development of public-opinion surveying, pollsters learned that broad breakdowns had limited usefulness. Archibald Crossley's pioneering radio surveys, for example, told the number of people who were listening to network programs, which was valuable to the networks and their advertisers, but Crossley's figures did not tell how many listeners were men or women, urban or rural, old or young. Such breakdowns of overall survey data, called demographics, were developed in the 1930s as Crossley, Gallup and other early pollsters refined their work.

Today, if demographic data indicate a presidential candidate is weak in the Midwest, campaign strategists can gear the candidate's message to Midwestern concerns. Through demographics, advertisers keen on reaching young women can identify magazines that will carry their ads to that audience. If advertisers seek an elderly audience, they can use demographic data to determine where to place their television ads.

While demographics remains valuable today, newer methods can break the population into categories that have even greater usefulness. These newer methods, which include cohort analysis, geodemography and psychographics, provide lifestyle breakdowns.

Cohort Analysis

Marketing people have developed **cohort analysis,** a specialized form of demographics, to identify generations and then design and produce products with generational appeal. Advertising people then gear media messages with the images, music, humor and other generational variables that appeal to the target cohort. The major cohorts are dubbed:

- **Generation X,** who came of age in the 1980s.
- **Baby Boomers,** who came of age in the late 1960s and 1970s.
- **Postwar Generation,** who came of age in the 1950s.
- **World War II Veterans,** who came of age in the 1940s.
- **Depression Survivors,** who came of age during the economic depression of the 1930s.

prototype research ■ Checks response to product still in development.

American Research Institute ■ Movie prototype research.

pilot ■ A prototype television show that is given an on-air trial.

cohort analysis ■ Demographic tool to identify marketing targets by common characteristics.

Generation X ■ Today's 30-something generation.

Baby Boomers ■ Today's 40-something and 50-something generations.

Postwar Generation ■ Today's 60-something generation.

World War II Veterans ■ Today's 70-something and 80-something generations.

Depression Survivors ■ Today's 80-something and 90-something generations.

Cohort analysis has jarred traditional thinking that people, as they get older, simply adopt their parents' values. The new 50-plus generation, for example, grew up on Coke and Pepsi drinks and, to the dismay of coffee growers, may prefer to start the day with cola—not the coffee their parents drank.

The Chrysler automobile company was early to recognize that Baby Boomers aren't interested in buying Cadillac-type luxury cars even when they have amassed the money to afford them. In 1996 Chrysler scrapped plans for a new luxury car to compete with Cadillac and instead introduced the $35,000 open-top 1997 Plymouth Prowler that gave Baby Boomers a nostalgic feel for the hot rods of their youth. Chrysler also determined that graying Baby Boomers preferred upscale Jeeps to the luxo-barge cars that appealed to the Postwar Generation.

Advertising people who use cohort analysis know that Baby Boomers, although now in their 50s, are still turned on by pizzas and the Rolling Stones. In short, the habits of their youth stick with a generation as it gets older. What appealed to the 30-something a decade ago won't necessarily sail with today's 30-something set. David Bostwick, Chrysler's marketing research director, puts it this way: "Nobody wants to become their parents."

Cohort Analysis

Through cohort analysis the Pentagon has characterized population groups from which most recruits come. Using household segments designed by Claritas and widely used in demographic research, the Pentagon identified 18 cohorts to which to target recruiting pitches. About its targets, the Pentagon knew a lot. Ten segments had lower midscale or downscale incomes. Eight were small-town or rural. For eight, a high-school diploma is the highest academic achievement.

Clariitas Cohort	Urbanization	Ethnicity	Income
Upward Bound	Small city	White/Asian	Upscale
Beltway Boomers	Suburban	White/Asian	Upper-middle
Kids and Cul de Sacs	Suburban	White/Asian/Hispanic	Upper-middle
Fast-Track Families	Town/rural	White	Upscale
New Homesteaders	Town/rural	White	Midscale
Big Sky Families	Town/rural	White	Midscale
White Picket Fences	Small city	White/Black/Hispanic	Midscale
Blue Chip Blues	Suburban	White/Black/Hispanic	Midscale
Sunset City Blues	Small city	White	Lower-middle
Young and Rustic	Town/rural	White	Downscale
Kid Country USA	Town/rural	White/Hispanic	Lower-middle
Shotguns and Pickups	Town/rural	White	Lower-middle
Suburban Pioneers	Suburban	White/Black/Hispanic	Lower-middle
Mobility Blues	Small city	Whiter/Black	Downscale
Multicultural Mosaic	Urban	Black/Hispanic	Lower-middle
Old Milltowns	Town/rural	White/Black	Downscale
Family Thrifts	Small city	Black/Hispanic	Downscale
Bedrock America	Town/rural	White/Black/Hispanic	Downscale

Geodemographics

While demographics, including cohort analysis, remain valuable today, new methods can break the population into categories that have even greater usefulness. These newer methods, which include geodemography, provide lifestyle breakdowns.

Computer whiz **Jonathan Robbin** provided the basis for more sophisticated breakdowns in 1974 when he began developing his **PRIZM** system for **geodemography.** From census data Robbin grouped every zip code by ethnicity, family life cycle, housing style, mobility and social rank. Then he identified 34 factors that statistically distinguished neighborhoods from each other. All this information was cranked through a computer programmed by Robbin to plug every zip code into 1 of 40 clusters. Here are the most frequent clusters created through PRIZM, which stands for Potential Rating Index for Zip Markets, with the labels Robbin put on them:

- **Blue-Chip Blues.** These are the wealthiest blue-collar suburbs. These Blue-Chip Blues, as Robbin calls them, make up about 6 percent of U.S. households. About 13 percent of these people are college graduates.
- **Young Suburbia.** Child-rearing outlying suburbs, 5.3 percent of U.S. population; college grads, 24 percent.

Jonathan Robbin ■ Devised PRIZM geodemography system.

PRIZM ■ Identifies population characteristics by zip code.

geodemography ■ Demographic characteristics by geographic area.

- **Golden Ponds.** Rustic mountain, seashore or lakeside cottage communities, 5.2 percent; college grads, 13 percent.
- **Blue-Blood Estates.** Wealthiest neighborhoods; college grads, 51 percent.
- **Money and Brains.** Posh big-city enclaves of townhouses, condos and apartments; college grads, 46 percent.

Geodemographic breakdowns are used not only for magazine advertising but also for editorial content. At Time Warner magazines, geodemographic analysis permits issues to be edited for special audiences. *Time*, for example, has a 600,000 circulation edition for company owners, directors, board chairs, presidents, other titled officers and department heads. Among others are editions for physicians and college students.

Psychographics

media ONLINE **VALS** Take a survey to find out where you fit into the VALS categories.
www.sric-bi.com/VALS/presurvey.shtml

A refined lifestyle breakdown introduced in the late 1970s, **psychographics,** divides the population into lifestyle segments. One leading psychographics approach, the Values and Life-Styles program, known as **VALS** for short, uses an 85-page survey to identify broad categories of people:

- **Belongers.** Comprising about 38 percent of the U.S. population, these people are conformists who are satisfied with mainstream values and are reluctant to change brands once they're satisfied. Belongers are not very venturesome and fit the stereotype of Middle America. They tend to be churchgoers and television watchers.
- **Achievers.** Comprising about 20 percent of the population, these are prosperous people who fit into a broader category of inner-directed consumers. Achievers pride themselves on making their own decisions. They're an upscale audience to which a lot of advertising is directed. As a group, achievers aren't heavy television watchers.
- **Societally Conscious.** Comprising 11 percent of the population, these people are aware of social issues and tend to be politically active. The societally conscious also are upscale and inner directed, and they tend to prefer reading to watching television.
- **Emulators.** Comprising 10 percent of the population, these people aspire to a better life but, not quite understanding how to do it, go for the trappings of prosperity. Emulators are status seekers, prone to suggestions on what makes the good life.
- **Experientials.** Comprising 5 percent of the population, these people are venturesome, willing to try new things in an attempt to experience life fully. They are a promising upscale audience for many advertisers.
- **I-Am-Me's.** Comprising 3 percent of the population, these people work hard to set themselves apart and are susceptible to advertising pitches that offer ways to differentiate themselves, which gives them a kind of subculture conformity. SRI International, which developed the VALS technique, characterized I-Am-Me's as "a guitar-playing punk rocker who goes around in shades and sports an earring." Rebellious youth, angry and maladjusted, fit this category.
- **Survivors.** This is a small downscale category that includes pensioners who worry about making ends meet.
- **Sustainers.** These people live from paycheck to paycheck. Although they indulge in an occasional extravagance, they have slight hope for improving their lot in life. Sustainers are a downscale category and aren't frequent advertising targets.
- **Integrateds.** Comprising only 2 percent of the population, integrateds are both creative and prosperous—willing to try different products and ways of doing things, and they have the wherewithal to do it.

Applying psychographics is not without hazard. The categories are in flux as society and lifestyles change. SRI researchers who chart growth in the percentage of I-Am-Me's, experientials and the societally conscious project that they total one-third of the population. Belongers are declining.

Another complication is that no person fits absolutely the mold of any one category. Even for individuals who fit one category better than another, there is no single mass

psychographics ■ Breaking down a population by lifestyle characteristics.

VALS ■ Psychographic analysis by values, lifestyle, life stage.

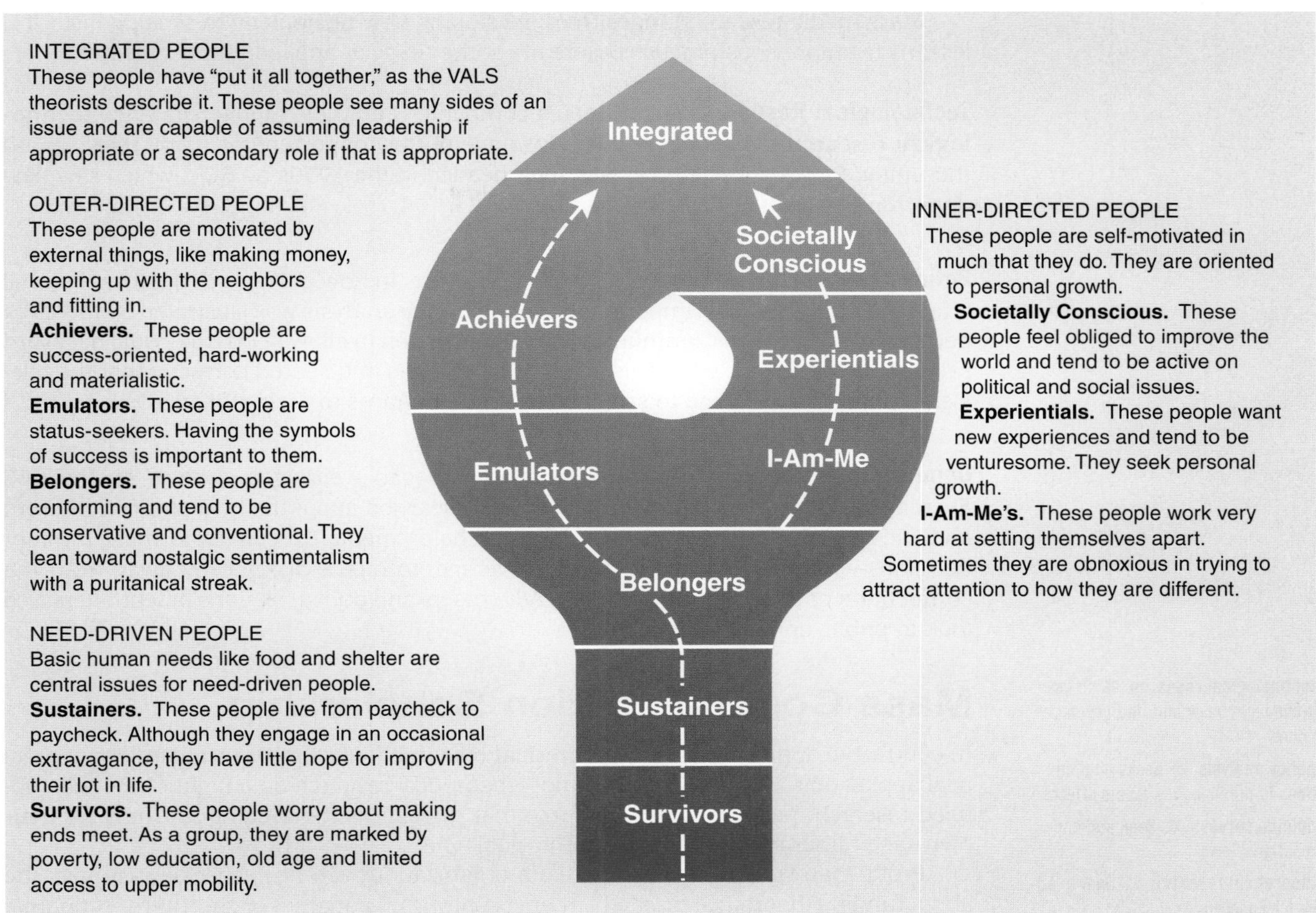

INTEGRATED PEOPLE
These people have "put it all together," as the VALS theorists describe it. These people see many sides of an issue and are capable of assuming leadership if appropriate or a secondary role if that is appropriate.
Integrated
OUTER-DIRECTED PEOPLE
These people are motivated by external things, like making money, keeping up with the neighbors and fitting in.
Achievers. These people are success-oriented, hard-working and materialistic.
Emulators. These people are status-seekers. Having the symbols of success is important to them.
Belongers. These people are conforming and tend to be conservative and conventional. They lean toward nostalgic sentimentalism with a puritanical streak.
Societally Conscious
Achievers
Experientials
Emulators
I-Am-Me
Belongers
Sustainers
Survivors
INNER-DIRECTED PEOPLE
These people are self-motivated in much that they do. They are oriented to personal growth.
Societally Conscious. These people feel obliged to improve the world and tend to be active on political and social issues.
Experientials. These people want new experiences and tend to be venturesome. They seek personal growth.
I-Am-Me's. These people work very hard at setting themselves apart. Sometimes they are obnoxious in trying to attract attention to how they are different.
NEED-DRIVEN PEOPLE
Basic human needs like food and shelter are central issues for need-driven people.
Sustainers. These people live from paycheck to paycheck. Although they engage in an occasional extravagance, they have little hope for improving their lot in life.
Survivors. These people worry about making ends meet. As a group, they are marked by poverty, low education, old age and limited access to upper mobility.

VALS Hierarchy
Developmental psychologists have long told us that people change their values as they mature. Today, many advertisers rely on the Values and Life-Styles model, VALS for short, which was derived from developmental psychology, to identify potential consumers and to design effective messages. Relatively few advertising messages are aimed at survivors and sustainers, who have little discretionary income. However, belongers and people on the divergent outer-directed or inner-directed paths are lucrative advertising targets for many products and services.

medium to reach them. VALS research may show that achievers constitute the biggest market for antihistamines, but belongers also head to the medicine cabinet when they're congested.

Applied and Theoretical Research

study preview **Media-sponsored research looks for ways to build audiences, to enhance profits and to program responsibly. In contrast, mass communication scholarship asks theoretical questions that can yield new understandings, regardless of whether there is a practical application.**

Media-Sponsored Research

Studies sponsored by mass media companies seek information that can be put to use. This is called **applied research.** When broadcasters underwrite research on media violence, they want answers to help make programming decisions. Audience measures and analysis are applied research, which can be put to work to enhance profits.

applied research ■ Usefulness, usually economic, is apparent.

Mass media research ranges from developing new technology to seeking historical lessons from previous practices. Here are some fields of applied media research:

Technological Research Mass media companies and their suppliers finance **technological research** to take economic advantage of new opportunities. Early television in the United States, for example, was spearheaded in the 1930s by RCA, which saw new opportunities for its NBC radio subsidiary.

Policy Analysis The media have intense interests in how changes in public policy will affect their business. The importance of good **policy analysis** was illustrated by the 1979 decision of the Federal Communications Commission to allow people to install backyard satellite dishes to pick up television signals. Analysts anticipated correctly that the television networks would go to satellites to send programs to their affiliates.

Opinion Surveys When anchor Dan Rather began wearing a sweater on the CBS Evening News, ratings improved. The network learned about the "sweater factor" from audience **opinion surveys.** Survey research helps media executives to make content decisions—whether to expand sports coverage, to hire a disk jockey away from the competition or to ax a dubious sitcom. Advertisers and public relations practitioners also look to public-opinion surveys.

Mass Communication Scholarship

In contrast to applied research, **theoretical research** looks for truths regardless of practical application. Scholars consider most theoretical research on a higher level than applied research, partly because the force that drives it is the seeking of truths for their own sake rather than for any economic goal.

Profit motivated as they are, media organizations are not especially enthusiastic about funding theoretical research. There usually is no apparent or short-term economic return from theoretical scholarship. For this reason most theoretical research occurs at major universities, whose institutional commitments include pushing back the frontiers of human knowledge, even if no economic reward is likely. Theoretical research includes:

- **Effect Studies.** Looking at media-triggered behaviors of individuals, groups and institutions.
- **Process Studies.** How the process of mass communication works.
- **Gratifications Studies.** How people use the mass to meet their needs.
- **Content Analysis.** Finding patterns in media content through measurement and analysis.

technological research ■ To improve technology and find new technology.

policy analysis ■ Seeks implications of public policy, future effects.

opinion surveys ■ Seek audience reaction, views.

theoretical research ■ Goal to advance knowledge.

effects studies ■ Impact of media on society, of society on media.

process studies ■ To understand the mass communication process.

gratifications studies ■ To explain why people choose their media outlets.

content analysis ■ Measuring media content to establish a database for analysis.

CHAPTER 14 Wrap-Up

Theoretical research, which mostly is campus-based, and applied research, which the media eagerly fund, use many of the same tools. A unifying tool of these disparate research approaches is public-opinion sampling. It is used to track public opinion, which is essential in public relations work; to learn which television programs are the most watched, which is essential in programming and advertising decisions; and to determine the effects of media and how people use the media, which are scholarly endeavors.

Questions for Review

1. What do surveys tell the mass media about their audiences?
2. How is the size of mass media audiences measured?
3. How is the reaction of people to the mass media measured?
4. What are techniques of audience analysis?
5. Why are mass media organizations more interested in applied than theoretical research?

Questions for Critical Thinking

1. Street-corner polls are based on weak methodology. Explain how quota sampling and probability sampling are improvements.
2. What is the basis for arguments that public-opinion surveys subvert democracy? What is the counter-argument?
3. The Audit Bureau of Circulations and broadcast rating services like A. C. Nielsen and Arbitron are essential media services to advertisers. How are these services similar? How different?
4. How can local television and radio stations manipulate their ratings?
5. Explain how applied research and theoretical research differ.

Deepening Your media LITERACY

Does exit polling have a place in democracy?

STEP 1 Some news organizations have called the results of an election based on exit polling, only to find themselves making red-faced retractions the next morning. Have you ever participated in an exit poll? If so, did you tell the truth about your vote?

Dig Deeper

STEP 2 Critics of polling at election time, including exit polls, say that polling tends to defeat the democratic process. Write a list of reasons why you think they believe this. Write another list of reasons why you think many political leaders believe that polling is beneficial to the democratic process.

What Do You Think?

STEP 3 Evaluate your lists. Do the possible pros for polling outweigh the possible problems? Can you see a way to conduct an exit poll that would not have any influence on the outcome of an election? With the phasing-out of paper ballots in the United States, do you think exit polling could become more or less of a factor in future elections?

Keeping Up to Date

Public Opinion Quarterly is a scholarly publication. *American Demographics* and *Public Opinion* have a lot of general-interest content for media observers.

For Further Learning

Kenneth F. Warren. *In Defense of Public Opinion Polling.* Westview, 2001.

Warren, a pollster, acknowledges that bad polling exists but explains and defends good practices and notes their growing role in democracy.

Dan Fleming, editor. *Formations: 21st Century Media Studies.* Manchester University Press, 2001.

In this collection of essays Fleming lays out the groundwork for students interested in advanced media studies.

James G. Webster, Patricia F. Phalen and Lawrence W. Lichty. *Ratings Analysis: The Theory and Practice of Audience Research,* Second edition. Erlbaum, 2000.

The authors, all scholars, describe the tools used in professional audience research and offer tools for laypeople to assess ratings.

Paula M. Poindexter and Maxwell E. McCombs. *Research in Mass Communication: A Practical Guide.* St. Martin's, 2000.

Poindexter and McCombs offer a textbook on both how to conduct research and how to make use of research findings.

Tom Dickson. *Mass Media Education in Transition: Preparing for the 21st Century.* Erlbaum, 2000.

Dickson offers a history of U.S. mass media education, concluding that fragmentation into warring subspecies, like journalism and advertising, may move the discipline out of the broad mission statements of many universities.

Robert Strauss. "The Man Without a Dog in the Fight." *Trust* Volume 1 (Fall 1998): Issue 2, pages 2–7.

Strauss traces the polling career of Andy Kohut, who has emerged as the most respected pollster on public issues in the United States.

Roger D. Wimmer and Joseph R. Dominick. *Mass Media Research: An Introduction,* Fifth edition. Wadsworth, 1997.

The authors include the history of audience measures and research, including the techniques used in television ratings. Wimmer and Dominick also examine fundamentals of polling techniques.

Shearson A. Lowery and Melvin L. DeFleur. *Milestones in Communication Research: Media Effects,* Third edition. Longman, 1995.

Beginners will find Lowery and DeFleur's chronicle an easy-to-follow primer on developments in mass communication research.

David W. Moore. *The Superpollsters: How They Measure and Manipulate Public Opinion in America.* Four Walls Eight Windows, 1992.

Moore, a pollster and political scientist, sees personal views and values contaminating public-opinion sampling no matter how careful and sophisticated the sampling tools. Offers a history of poll-based news coverage. Also profiles leading pollsters.

Wilbur Schramm
He defined mass communication as an academic discipline.

chapter 15 Mass Communication

In this chapter you will learn:

- The most widely influential form of human communication is through mass media.
- Mass communicators reach mass audiences via mass media through a mysterious process called mass communication.
- Models are imperfect but useful vehicles for seeing how mass communication works.
- Mass communication and other human communication forms have the same fundamentals.
- Media gatekeepers and nonmedia regulators influence media messages.
- Impediments to the success of mass communication include noise and filters.
- The mass media amplify messages to reach large audiences.

Some say Wilbur Schramm created mass communication as a hybrid academic discipline. There is no doubt that Schramm's two influential anthologies shaped two generations of masscom scholars. His *Mass Communications,* compiled in 1949, combined seminal works in the social sciences with works by leading media practitioners and scholars. "It combined diversity of approach with unity of target," Schramm wrote in the introduction. That it did.

Enthusiastic word spread abroad, prompting requests from scholars for copies within a week of the book's release. Demand so outstripped supply that some used copies sold at triple the retail price. Schramm revised the trail-blazing book in 1959, again combining important work from anthropology, economics, political science, psychology and sociology with material from the growing field of mass communication studies.

In the meantime, in 1954, Schramm compiled another anthology, *The Process and Effect of Mass Communication.* Originally, *P&E,* as it was known, was intended as a research methods primer for U.S. information agency employees, but as Schramm pulled material together, it was clear the book had a larger appeal.

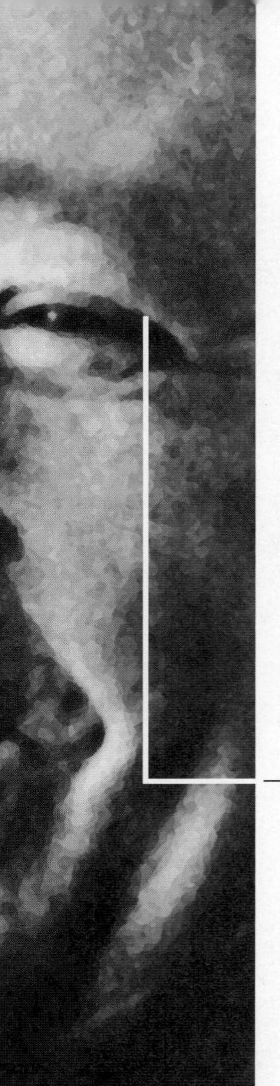

P&E was a worthy successor to the *Mass Communications* anthology, but both remained in demand, and the University of Illinois Press kept reprinting them.

Thirty-one years after *P&E's* introduction, and with the second edition becoming outdated, the University of Illinois Press asked Schramm to do a third edition. His agenda full, Schramm declined but urged that someone do a revision. "The only obligation is to make a book that will be as good for the future as *P&E* was for its time," he said. Schramm was not being immodest. It was a fact, recognized everywhere, that *P&E* had become a mainstay in curricula of emerging mass communication departments throughout the country and abroad.

While Schramm's *Mass Communications* and *P&E* were major contributions, they were in a sense mere warm-ups. When Schramm died in 1987, his legacy included 30 books, 25 of them translated into other languages, and more than 120 research and scholarly papers and treatises. His personal papers, which his family holds, contain 18,722 pages.

The largest collection in his papers is 6,158 pages for his final book, *The Story of Human Communications: Cave Painting to Microchip,* which was in press when he died. The scope of the book, the whole spectrum through history, seemed an appropriate ultimate work for Wilbur Schramm, who was then 80.

Types of Communication

study preview **The communication in which the mass media engage is only one form of communication. One way to begin understanding the process of mass communication is to differentiate it from other forms of communication.**

media ONLINE **Wilbur Schramm** A short biography of Wilbur Schramm. **www.utexas.edu/coc/journalism/SOURCE/j363/schramm.html**

Exploring Nonverbal Communication A scholarly look at communicating without words. **http://nonverbal.ucsc.edu**

Intrapersonal Communication

We engage in **intrapersonal communication** when we talk to ourselves to develop our thoughts and ideas. This intrapersonal communication precedes our speaking or acting.

Interpersonal Communication

When people talk to each other, they are engaging in **interpersonal communication.** In its simplest form, interpersonal communication is between two people physically located in the same place. It can occur, however, if they are physically separated but emotionally connected, like lovers on cell phones.

The difference between the prefixes *intra-* and *inter-* is the key difference between intrapersonal and interpersonal communication. Just as intrasquad athletic games are within a team, intrapersonal communication is within one's self. Just as intercollegiate games are between schools, interpersonal communication is between individuals.

communication ■ Exchange of ideas, information.

intrapersonal communication ■ Talking to oneself.

interpersonal communication ■ Usually two people face to face.

group communication ■ More than two people; in person.

Group Communication

There comes a point when the number of people involved reduces the intimacy of the communication process. That's when the situation becomes **group communication.** A club meeting is an example. So is a speech to an audience in an auditorium.

Group and Mass Communication When Boyz II Men goes on stage, the members are engaging in group communication. A spontaneous relationship with their audience is part of their performance—their communication. In the recording studio Boyz II Men has to adjust their performance intuitively to an audience they cannot see. This lack of immediate feedback is a characteristic of mass communication that separates it from interpersonal and group communication.

Mass Communication

Capable of reaching thousands, even millions, of people is **mass communication,** which is accomplished through a mass medium like television or newspapers. Mass communication can be defined as the process of using a mass medium to send messages to large audiences for the purpose of informing, entertaining or persuading.

In many respects, the process of mass communication and other communication forms is the same: Someone conceives a message, essentially an intrapersonal act. The message then is encoded into a common code, such as language. Then it's transmitted. Another person receives the message, decodes it and internalizes it. Internalizing a message is also an intrapersonal act.

In other respects, mass communication is distinctive. Crafting an effective message for thousands of people of diverse backgrounds and interests requires different skills than chatting with a friend across the table. Encoding the message is more complex because a device is always used—for example, a printing press, a camera or a recorder.

One aspect of mass communication that should not be a mystery is the spelling of the often-misused word *communication*. The word takes no "s" if you are using it to refer to a *process*. If you are referring to a communication as *a thing,* such as a letter, a movie, a telegram or a television program, rather than a process, the word is *communication* in singular form and *communications* in plural. When the term *mass communication* refers to a process, it is spelled without the "s."

Components of Mass Communication

studypreview **Mass communication is the process that mass communicators use to send their mass messages to mass audiences. They do this through the mass media. Think of these as the Five Ms: mass communicators, mass messages, mass media, mass communication and mass audience.**

mass communication ■ Many recipients; not face to face; a process.

mediaPEOPLE

David Sarnoff

Mass Communication Concept David Sarnoff's genius was seeing radio as mass communication.

David Sarnoff had no childhood. In 1901, when he was 10, Sarnoff and his mother and two brothers arrived penniless in New York from Russia. Two days later he had a job as a delivery boy; then he added a newspaper route, then a newsstand. In spare moments he went to the library to read technical books. At 16 he landed a job with American Marconi, which sent him to an island station to exchange messages with ships at sea with the new technology of radio telegraphy. He earned $70 a month, of which $25 went to room and board at a nearby farm. He sent $40 back to his mother.

In 1912 Sarnoff was working at a Marconi demonstration in a New York department store when he picked up the first signals that the steamship *Titanic* had sunk. President Taft ordered every other radio telegraphy station off the air to reduce interference. For the whole world, young David Sarnoff was the only link to the rescue drama unfolding out in the North Atlantic. He stayed at his post for 72 hours straight and then went to another site for better reception until the lists of living and dead were complete.

When he collapsed into bed sometime during the fourth day, Sarnoff, then 21, was a national hero, and "radio" had become a household word. Through Sarnoff the whole world suddenly recognized the importance of radio for point-to-point communication, which was the business American Marconi was into. Sarnoff's most significant work, however, was yet to come.

In 1916 Sarnoff drafted a memo to his boss that demonstrated he grasped a potential for radio that everyone else at Marconi had missed. He proposed building "radio music boxes," to be sold as household appliances so that people at home could listen to music, news, weather and sports. Sarnoff saw profit in manufacturing these home receivers and selling them for $75. His boss scoffed, but Sarnoff kept refining his proposal. By 1920 he had won the ear of the people running the company.

Sarnoff's proposal for radio music boxes demonstrated his genius. He grasped that radio could be more than a vehicle for telegraph-like point-to-point communication. He saw radio as a mass medium, which could send signals from a central source to dozens, hundreds, thousands, indeed millions of people simultaneously. Sarnoff was not alone in conceptualizing radio as a mass medium. Lee De Forest, for example, had been broadcasting music, but as historian Erik Barnouw noted: "Sarnoff translated the idea into a business plan that began with the consumer." That business plan included a financial base for radio in advertising.

Under RCA auspices, Sarnoff went on to build NBC, the first radio network, and then NBC television. He also pioneered the business of mass-producing music for mass audiences with RCA records. From humble origins, through hard work, insight and genius, Sarnoff came to preside for the rest of his life over one of the world's largest and most significant media empires: RCA. He died in 1971.

media ONLINE **The David Sarnoff Library** Everything you wanted to know about this innovative entrepreneur. **www.davidsarnoff.org**

Mass Communicators

The heart of mass communication is the people who produce the messages that are carried in the mass media. These people include journalists, scriptwriters, lyricists, television anchors, radio disk jockeys, public relations practitioners and advertising copywriters. The list could go on and on.

mass communicators ■ Message crafters.

Mass communicators are unlike other communicators because they cannot see their audience. David Letterman knows that hundreds of thousands of people are watching as he unveils his latest Top 10 list, but he can't see them or hear them chuckle and laugh. He receives no immediate feedback from his mass audience. This communicating with an unseen audience distinguishes mass communication from other forms of communication. Storytellers of yore told their stories face to face, and they could adjust their pacing and gestures and even their vocabulary according to how they sensed they were being received. Mass communicators don't have that advantage, although a studio audience, like David Letterman has, is a loose substitute.

Mass Messages

A news item is a **mass message,** as are a movie, a novel, a recorded song and a billboard advertisement. The *message* is the most apparent part of our relationship to the mass media. It is for the messages that we pay attention to the media. We don't listen to the radio, for example, to marvel at the technology. We listen to hear the music.

Mass Media

The **mass media** are the vehicles that carry messages. The primary mass media are books, magazines, newspapers, television, radio, sound recordings, movies and the web. Most theorists view media as neutral carriers of messages. The people who are experts at media include technicians who keep the presses running and who keep the television transmitters on the air. Media experts also are tinkerers and inventors who come up with technical improvements, such as compact discs, DVDs, AM stereo radio and newspaper presses that can produce high-quality color.

Mass Communication

The process through which messages reach the audience via the mass media is called *mass communication.* This is a mysterious process about which we know far less than we should. Researchers and scholars have unraveled some of the mystery, but most of how it works remains a matter of wonderment. For example, why do people pay more attention to some messages than to others? How does one advertisement generate more sales than another? Is behavior, including violent behavior, triggered through the mass communication process? There is reason to believe that mass communication affects voting behavior, but how does this work? Which is most correct—to say that people can be controlled by mass communication? Or manipulated? Or merely influenced? Nobody has the answer.

media ONLINE **Web Journal of Mass Communication Research** Read some of the latest studies in the field. **www.scripps.ohiou.edu/wjmcr**

Mass Audiences

The size and diversity of **mass audiences** add complexity to mass communication. Only indirectly do mass communicators learn whether their messages have been received. Mass communicators are never sure exactly of the size of audiences, let alone of the effect of their messages. Mass audiences are fickle. What attracts great attention one day may not the next. The challenge of trying to communicate to a mass audience is even more complex because people are tuning in and tuning out all the time, and when they are tuned in, it is with varying degrees of attentiveness.

Communication Models

studypreview **Scholars have devised models of the communication process in an attempt to understand how the process works. Like all models, these are simplifications and are imperfect. Even so, these models bring some illumination to the mysterious communication process.**

mass message ■ What is communicated.

mass media ■ Vehicles that carry messages.

mass audiences ■ Recipients of mass messages.

Role of Communication Models

Hobbyists build models of ships, planes, automobiles and all kinds of other things. These models help them see whatever they are modeling in different ways. Industrial engineers and scientists do the same thing, learning lessons from models before they actually build something to full scale. Communication models are similar. By creating a facsimile of the process, we hope to better understand the process.

A reality about models is that they are never perfect. This reality is especially true when the subject being modeled is complex. An architect, for example, may have a model of what the building will look like to passersby, but there also will be models of the building's heating system, traffic patterns, and electrical, plumbing and ventilation systems. None of these models is complete or accurate in every detail, but all nonetheless are useful.

Communication models are like that. Different models illustrate different aspects of the process. The process itself is so complex that no single model can adequately cover it.

Basic Model

Shannon-Weaver Model A thorough look at the basic communication model. **www.cultsock.ndirect.co.uk/MUHome/cshtml/index.html**

Two Bell telephone engineers, **Claude Shannon** and **Warren Weaver,** laid out a **basic communication model** in 1948. They were working on advanced switching systems. The model, fundamentally a simple diagram, gave them a reference point for their work. That model has become a standard baseline for describing the communication process. The Shannon-Weaver model identifies five fundamental steps in the communication process:

- The human stimulation that results in a thought.
- The encoding of the thought into a message.
- The transmission of the message.
- The decoding of the message by the recipient into a thought.
- The internalization of the message by the recipient.

Narrative Model

Yale professor **Harold Lasswell,** an early mass communication theorist, developed a useful yet simple model that was all words—no diagram. Lasswell's **narrative model** poses four questions: Who says what? In which channel? To whom? With what effect?

You can easily apply the model. Pick any bylined story from the front page of a newspaper.

- **Who says what?** The newspaper reporter tells a story, often quoting someone who is especially knowledgeable on the subject.
- **In which channel?** In this case the story is told through the newspaper, a mass medium.
- **To whom?** The story is told to a newspaper reader.
- **With what effect?** The reader decides to vote for Candidate A or B, or perhaps readers just add the information to their reservoir of knowledge.

Claude Shannon ■ Devised a basic communication model, with Warren Weaver.

Warren Weaver ■ Devised a basic communication model, with Claude Shannon.

basic communication model ■ Shows sender, encoding, transmission, decoding, receiver.

Harold Lasswell ■ Devised the narrative model.

narrative model ■ Describes process in words, not schematic.

Thomas Bohn ■ Devised the concentric circle model, with Ray Hiebert, Donald Ungurait.

Concentric Circle Model

The Shannon-Weaver model can be applied to all communication, but it misses some things that are unique to mass communication. In 1974 scholars Ray Hiebert, Donald Ungurait and **Thomas Bohn** presented an important new model—a series of concentric circles with the encoding source at the center. One of the outer rings was the receiving audience. In between were several elements that are important in the mass communication process but less so in other communication processes.

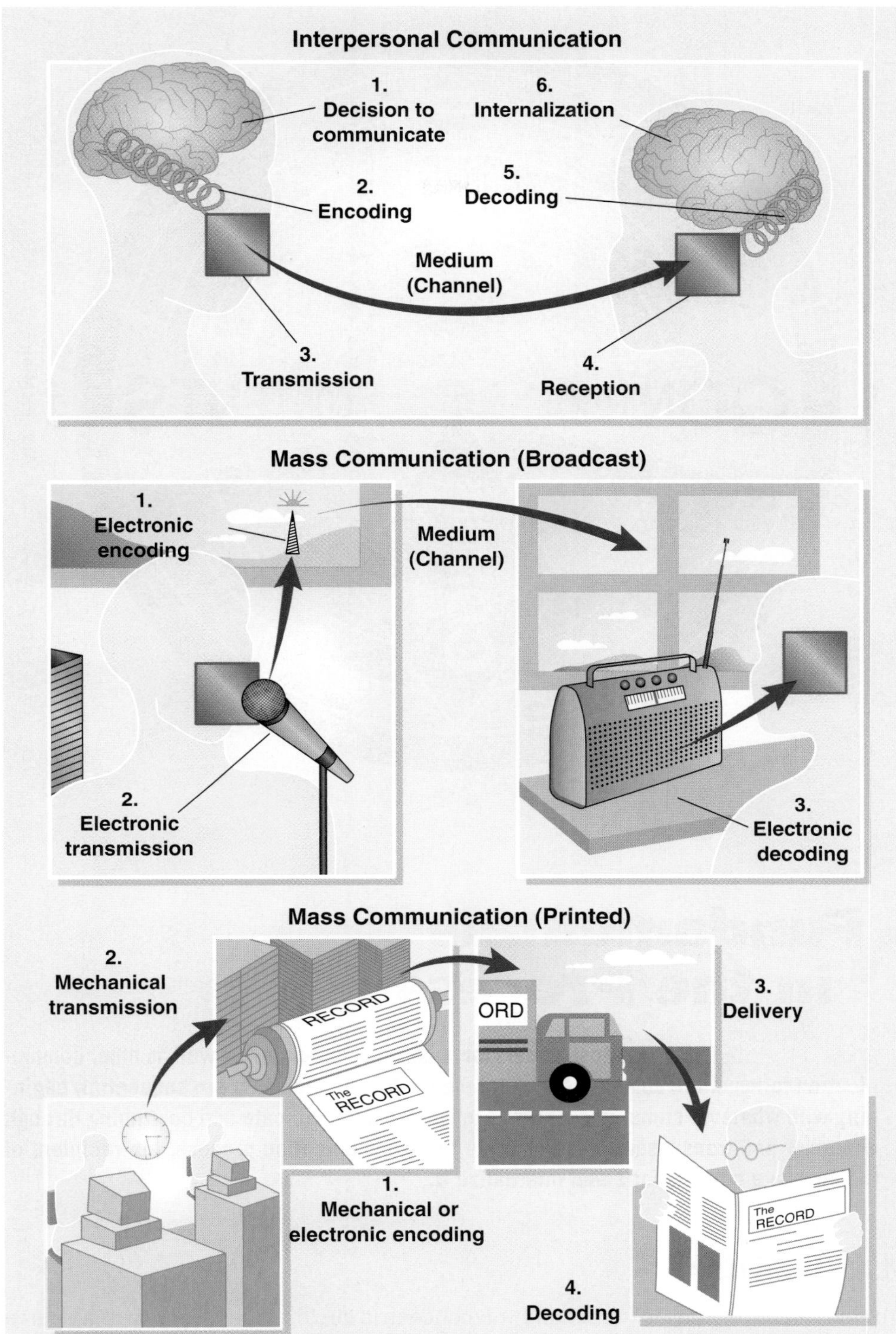

Fundamentals of the Process

Claude Shannon and Warren Weaver reduced communication to fundamental elements in their classic model. Communication, they said, begins in the human mind. Messages are then encoded into language or gesture and transmitted. A recipient sees or hears the message and decodes from the language or other form in which it was transmitted and internalizes it. Those fundamental elements are also present in mass communication except that there is a double encoding and double decoding. In mass communication, not only does the communicator encode the message into language or another form to be communicated but also the message then is encoded technologically for transmission through a mass medium. In radio, for example, the words are encoded into electronic impulses. At the decoding site a piece of machinery—a radio receiver—decodes the impulses into words, which then are decoded again by the human recipient to internalize them. With print media the two steps in decoding are not as obvious because they are so integrated. One is reading the words. The other is converting those representations into concepts.

The **concentric circle model** is one of the most complete models for identifying elements in the mass communication process, but it misses many complexities. It takes only one message from its point of origin, but in reality thousands of messages are being issued simultaneously. Audiences receive many of these messages but not all of them, and the messages are received imperfectly. Feedback resonates back to communicators unevenly, often muted, often ill-based. Gatekeeping too is uneven. In short, there are so many variables that it is impossible to track what happens in any kind of comprehensive way.

concentric circle model ■ Useful radiating model of the mass communication process.

Concentric Circle Model

The scholars who designed the concentric circle model suggest thinking of it as a pebble being dropped in still water. The ripples emanating outward from the communicator go through many barriers before reaching the audience or having any effect. The model takes note of feedback, media amplification, noise and distortion introduced by the media.

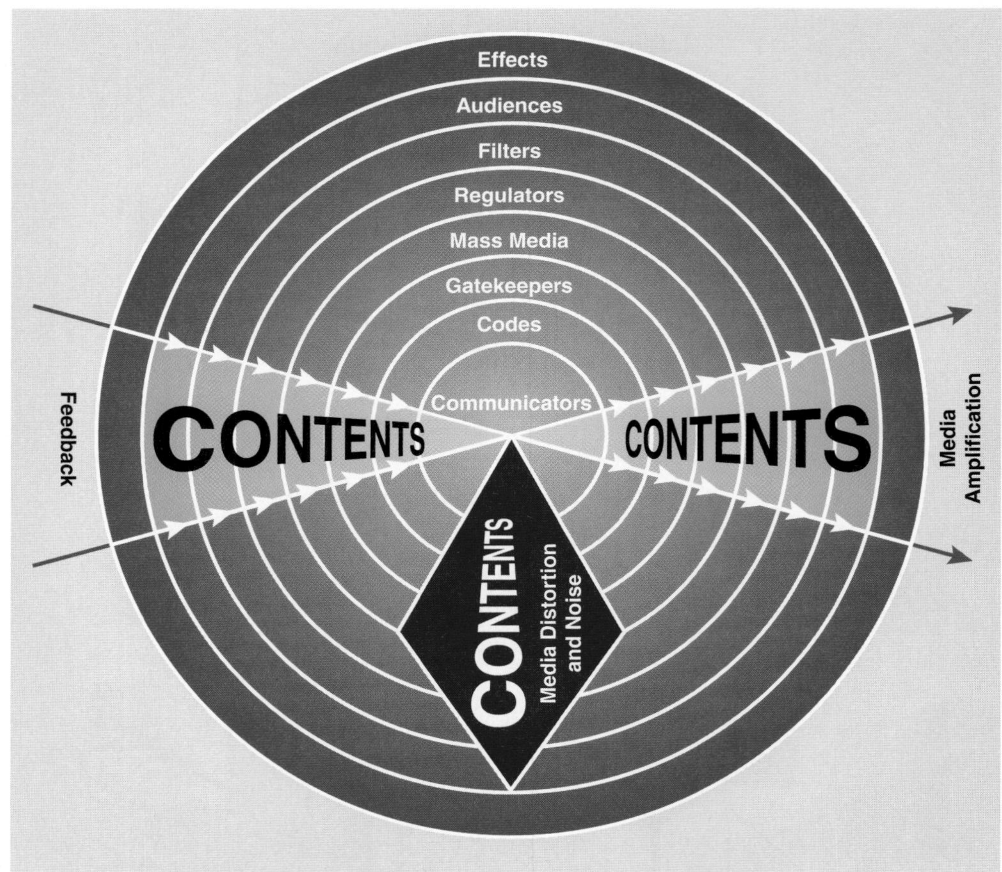

Fundamentals in the Process

studypreview **Most models for mass communication as well as other communication forms share some fundamental elements. The elements are sequential, beginning with whatever stimulates a person to want to communicate and continuing through encoding and transmission. To complete the communication process, the recipient of the message must decode and internalize it.**

Stimulation

Both the Shannon-Weaver model and the concentric circle model begin with a source who is stimulated to want to communicate a message. The **stimulation** can result from many things. Emotions can be stimuli, as can something that is sensed. The stimulation can be as diverse as seeing a beautiful panorama, feeling a draft, hearing a child cry, or smelling dinner.

Encoding

The second step is **encoding.** The source puts thoughts into symbols that can be understood by whoever is destined to receive the message. The symbols take many forms—for example, the written word, smoke signals or pictographs.

stimulation ■ Stirs someone to communicate.

encoding ■ Putting something into symbols.

Transmission

The message is the representation of the thought. In interpersonal communication the message is almost always delivered face to face. In mass communication, however, the message is encoded so that it is suitable for the equipment being used for **transmission.** Shannon and Weaver, being telephone engineers in the 1940s, offered the example of the sound pressure of a voice being changed into proportional electrical current for transmission over telephone lines. In technical terms telephone lines were channels for Shannon and Weaver's messages. On a more conceptual basis the telephone lines were the *media,* in the same way as is the printed page or a broadcast signal.

Decoding

The receiver picks up signals sent by the transmitter. In interpersonal communication the receiver is a person who hears the message, sees it, or both. An angry message encoded as a fist banging a table is heard and perhaps felt. An insulting message encoded as a puff of cigar smoke in the face is smelled. In mass communication the first receiver of the message is not a person but the equipment that picks up and then reconstructs the message from the signal. This mechanical **decoding** is necessary so that the human receiver of the message can understand it. As Shannon and Weaver put it: "The receiver ordinarily performs the inverse operation that was done by the transmitter."

Internalization

In mass communication a second kind of decoding occurs with the person who receives the message from the receiving equipment. This is an intrapersonal act, **internalizing** the message. For this second kind of decoding to work, the receiver must understand the communication form chosen by the source in encoding. Someone who reads only English will not be able to decode a message in Greek. Someone whose

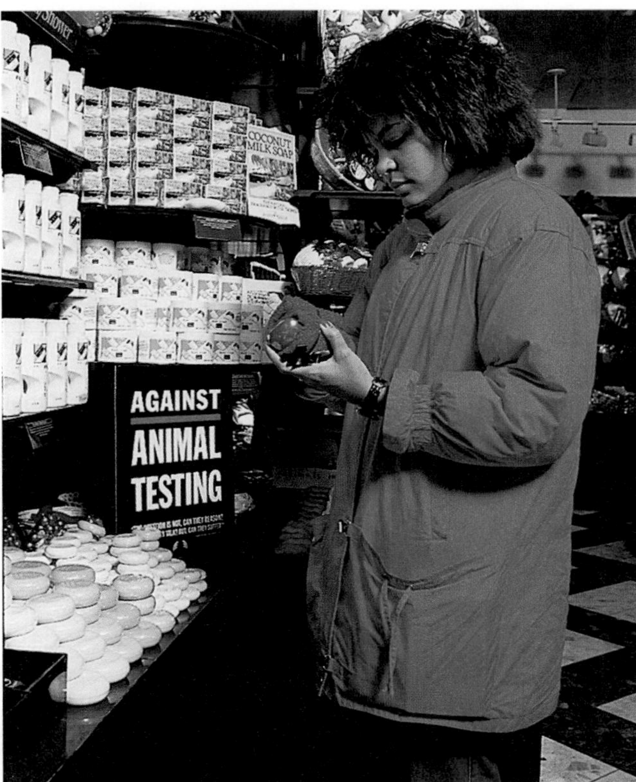

Internalization

A consumer who has seen and heard ads for a product retrieves those messages from memory to weigh whether or not to make a purchase. Those retrieved messages are considered with packaging messages, which are a form of mass communication.

transmission ■ Sending a message.

decoding ■ Translating a symbolic message.

internalizing ■ Making sense of a decoded message.

sensitivities are limited to punk rock will not understand Handel's *Water Music*. In other words, the source and the receiver must have enough in common for communication to occur. This common experience, which can be as simple as speaking the same tongue, is called **homophyly.** In mass communication the encoder must know the audience well enough to shape messages that can be decoded accurately and with the intended effect.

The audience and how it perceives a message are essential in the mass communication process. This is no better illustrated than in a front-page headline in the *National Examiner,* a sensationalizing weekly tabloid: "Cops Think Kato Did It!" Brian "Kato" Kaelin was a pal of O. J. Simpson and had been subjected to police interviewing off and on for months before the Simpson murder trial. Kaelin sued the *Examiner* over the headline. In court, the *Examiner* said the "it" in the headline didn't refer to the murders but to possible perjury. The *Examiner* argued that "it" was explained in a secondary head on Page 1: ". . . He Fears They Want Him for Perjury."

A three-judge federal appeals court sided with Kaelin, saying that *Examiner* readers were likely to infer that the police thought he was a murderer. This was despite the fact that the story made it clear that "it" was perjury, not murder, and also despite the secondary Page 1 head.

The judges noted that the headline came only a week after the widely reported Simpson acquittal and that, in the court's opinion, people who had followed the trial reasonably could have interpreted "it" to be murder. The decision allowed Kaelin to pursue his $15 million legal action against the *Examiner.*

For mass communicators the lesson is that strict, literal meanings are not always enough. Audience inferences are part of the intrapersonal decoding process.

Players in the Process

studypreview **Two great influences on the mass communication process are gatekeepers and regulators. Gatekeepers are media people who influence messages. Regulators are nonmedia people who do the same.**

Gatekeepers

The most visible people in the mass communication process are the communicators. These are the Katie Courics, Danielle Steels and Rush Limbaughs. But mass communication is not a solo endeavor. Dozens, sometimes hundreds, of individuals are involved. A Stephen King thriller passes through several editors before being published. When it's adapted as a screenplay, substantial modifications are made by many other individuals, all expert in the medium of the movie. Later, when it is adapted for television, experts in television as a mass medium make further changes, and so might the network program standards office. Any media person who can stop or alter a message en route to the audience is a **gatekeeper.** Newscast producers are gatekeepers because they decide what is aired and what is not. They make decisions about what to emphasize and what to deemphasize. Magazine and newspaper editors do the same, sorting through hundreds of stories to choose the relatively few that will fit in their publications.

Gatekeepers have tremendous responsibility because they shape the messages that reach us. They even decide which messages don't reach us. When gatekeepers make a mistake, both the communication process and the message suffer.

Regulators

Nonmedia people and institutions that try to influence mass-communicated messages before they reach the audience are **regulators.** The Federal Communications Commission is a government agency that serves as a regulator with its authority to fine radio

homophyly ■ A coding oneness that makes communication possible.

gatekeeper ■ Media people who influence messages en route.

regulators ■ Nonmedia people who influence messages.

and television stations for on-air indecency. The specter of FCC fines keeps most stations in line. Advertisers know the Federal Trade Commission and two dozen other federal regulatory agencies are looking over their shoulders. Local cable commissions throughout the country have a strong voice in what cable systems offer their subscribers.

Regulators in the mass communication process also include **pressure groups.** For several years the Parents Music Resource Center campaigned for controls on recorded music and videos, including album covers, that it found objectionable. The PMRC's plan for a rating system fell apart, but it was influential in persuading record-makers to place warning labels for parents on certain records. The Communications Office of the United Church of Christ prevailed in getting the FCC to yank the license of a racist television station, WLBT, in Jackson, Mississippi. Community groups that threaten media boycotts also are regulators.

media ONLINE **Federal Communications Commission** Government regulators of the media. **www.fcc.gov**

Gatekeeper-Regulator Hybrids

Media trade and professional organizations influence media content. For many years the programming standards of the National Association of Broadcasters influenced what many television stations aired. An NAB maximum on the number of radio commercials per hour became an industry standard. Ethics codes from the Society of Professional Journalists and many other groups of media people have had wide influence.

Are organizations like the NAB and SPJ gatekeepers or regulators? Composed of media people, they would seem to be gatekeepers, but because they do not operate on the front line of making content decisions directly, they have many characteristics of regulators. They are, in fact, **gatekeeper-regulator hybrids** that institutionalize peer pressure among media people to influence media content.

Impediments to Communication

study preview **Some models emphasize things that interfere with a message being communicated. Feedback can influence a communicator to change a message. Noise is transmission interference. Filters are recipient factors that interfere with an easy or correct reception of the message.**

Noise

If speakers slur their words, the effectiveness of their messages is jeopardized. Slurring and other impediments in the communication process before the message reaches the audience are called **noise.** In mass communication, which is based on complex mechanical and electronic equipment, the opportunities for noise interference are countless because so many things can go wrong. Noise occurs in three forms: semantic noise, channel noise and environmental noise.

Semantic Noise Mass communicators themselves can interfere with the success of their own messages by sloppiness. This is called **semantic noise.** Sloppy wording is an example. Slurring is also a semantic impediment to communication.

Channel Noise When you're listening to an AM radio station and static interrupts the transmission, you are experiencing **channel noise.** Other forms of channel noise include smudged ink on a magazine page and a faulty microphone on a television anchor's lapel.

Environmental Noise An intrusion that occurs at the reception site is **environmental noise.** This would include a doorbell interrupting someone's reading of an article or

pressure groups ■ Try to influence media messages, policies; include citizen groups, government agencies.

gatekeeper-regulator hybrids ■ Media trade, professional groups.

noise ■ Impedes communication before message reaches receiver.

semantic noise ■ Sloppy message-crafting.

channel noise ■ Interference during transmission.

environmental noise ■ Interference at reception site.

The Lower case

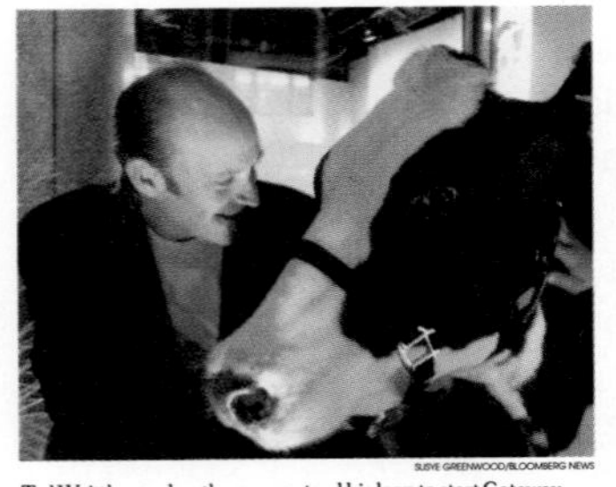

SUSIE GREENWOOD/BLOOMBERG NEWS

Ted Waitt's grandmother guaranteed his loan to start Gateway.

The New York Times 5/20/05

Oozing corpses raising eyebrows

San Francisco Chronicle 5/27/05

Beautification process begins today for pope

Eau Claire (Wis.) *Leader-Telegram* 6/29/05

Legislators spurn domestic partners

Milwaukee Journal Sentinel 5/24/05

Some adults grow into blemishes

The Olympian (Olympia, Wash.) 7/9/05

Weather watchers keep eyes on the sky for meteorologists

Asheville (N.C.) *Citizen-Times* 7/15/05

Documentary filmmaker introduced students to AIDS

Sarasota Herald-Tribune 4/12/05

Former addict has resisted temptation to stay clean

Winona (Minn.) *Daily News* 6/5/05

Vicious animal law considered

The San Francisco Examiner 6/20/05

Police say finger in chili had been given to husband

Milwaukee Journal Sentinel 5/14/05

Endangered ape delivers child

The Indianapolis Star 7/14/05

CJR offers $25 for items published in The Lower case. Please send only original, unmutilated clippings suitable for reproduction, together with name and date of publication, and include your Social Security number for payment.

Semantic Noise In every issue, the *Columbia Journalism Review* delights in reproducing bad headlines and other newspaper gaffes as a reminder to journalists to be more careful. These gaffes are examples of semantic noise, in which ambiguous wording and other poor word choices interfere with clear communication.

shouting kids who distract a viewer from the 6 o'clock news, interfering with the decoding process.

Mass communicators go to special lengths to guard against noise interfering with their messages. For example, in encoding, broadcast scriptwriters avoid "s" sounds as much as possible because they can hiss gratingly if listeners are not tuned precisely to the frequency. Because words can be unintentionally dropped in typesetting, many newspaper reporters write that a verdict was "innocent" rather than "not guilty." It would be a serious matter if noise resulted in the deletion of "not."

To keep noise at a minimum, technicians strive to keep their equipment in top-notch condition. Even so, things can go wrong. Also, mass communicators cannot control noise that affects individual members of their audience—such as the siren of a passing fire truck, a migraine headache or the distraction of a pot boiling over on the stove. Clear expression, whether sharp writing in a magazine or clear pronunciation on the radio, can minimize such interference, but most noise is beyond the communicator's control.

Repetition is the mass communicator's best antidote against noise. If the message does not get through the first time, it is repeated. Rare is an advertisement that plays only once. Radio newscasters repeat the same major news stories every hour, although they rehash the scripts so they will not bore people who heard the stories earlier.

Filters

Unwittingly, people who tune in to mass messages may themselves interfere with the success of the mass communication process. The causes of this interference are known as **filters.**

Informational Filters If someone doesn't understand the language or symbols a communicator uses, the communication process becomes flawed. It is a matter of lacking information to decipher a message, a deficiency called an **informational filter.** This filter can be partly the responsibility of the communicator, whose vocabulary may not be in tune with the audience's. More clearly, though, it is an audience deficiency.

Physical Filters When a receiver's mind is dimmed by fatigue, a **physical filter** is interfering with the mass communication process. A drunk person whose focus fades in and out also suffers from a physical filter. Mass communicators have little control over physical filters.

Psychological Filters If a receiver is a zealous animal rights activist, **psychological filters** likely will affect the reception of news on medical research involving animals. Being on a different wavelength can be a factor. Imagine two women friends going to the movie *Fatal Attraction* together. One woman is married and monogamous; the other is involved with a married man. Having different ideas about and experiences with marital fidelity, which is at the heart of the movie, the women hear the same words and see the same images but see two "different" movies.

filters ■ Receiver factor that impedes communication.

informational filter ■ Receiver's knowledge limits impede deciphering symbols.

physical filter ■ Receiver's alertness impedes deciphering.

psychological filter ■ Receiver's state of mind impedes deciphering.

Results of Mass Communication

study preview **Because mass communication reaches such large audiences, the process amplifies messages like a giant megaphone. Things that are mass communicated stand a better chance of becoming important than things that are not. Mass communication has its greatest influence when it moves people to action.**

Media Amplification

Actress Dana Reeve learned the value of media attention for a cause in the nine years that she helped her husband, actor Christopher Reeve, campaign for legislation and funds for spinal injury research. Remembered mostly for his movie portrayal of Superman, Christopher Reeve made a powerful poster character for his cause. After Christopher's 2004 death, Dana was diagnosed with lung cancer. She applied those lessons to heighten attention for lung cancer awareness and research until her death in 2006.

Amplification

The technology of the mass media gives mass communicators a megaphone. This is something other communicators don't have. A letter writer, for example, generally aims a message at one other person. A magazine writer, in contrast, has the printing press to reach thousands, if not millions, of readers. The printing press is a megaphone. Broadcasters have their transmission equipment. The equipment of the mass media allows mass communicators to **amplify** messages in ways that are not possible with interpersonal or even group communication.

Things that mass communicators choose to communicate have a status conferred on them. This is gatekeeping at work. Stories and views that don't survive the gatekeeping process have little chance of gaining widespread attention. Those that make it through the process have some inherent credibility just because they made it over so many hurdles.

Status conferral can work positively and negatively. For example, it appeared by 2004 that in going to war, the U.S. government had overreacted to suspicions that Iraq possessed weapons of mass destruction. News coverage of U.S. claims about the existence of the weapons, although sometimes sketchy, nonetheless fanned enthusiasm for war. Indeed, *WMD* became a household word that nobody would have recognized even a year earlier. Intensive media coverage of high-budget searches for the weapons after the war kept the issue on the front burner in the 2004 presidential campaigns and into the second term of the Bush administration.

Status conferral is not limited to the news media. Ballads and music, amplified through the mass media, can capture the public's imagination and keep an issue alive and even enlarge it. In World War I catchy songs such as *Over There* helped to rally support for the cause. Fifty years later, *An Okie from Muskogee* lent legitimacy to the hawkish position on the war in Vietnam, while Crosby, Stills, Nash, & Young's *Ohio* expressed some of the sentiments of those opposed to the war. Bob Dylan's 1975 song *Hurricane* reopened the investigation into the murder conviction of Rubin "Hurricane" Carter. Movies also have the power to move people and sustain issues. Sidney Poitier's movies of the 1960s, including *Guess Who's Coming to Dinner,* helped to keep racial integration on the American agenda. The 1988 movie *The Thin Blue Line* led to the exoneration of a death-row inmate.

Feedback

Because mass communication is not the one-way street that the Shannon-Weaver model indicated, later theorists embellished the model by looping the process back on itself.

amplification ■ Spreading a message.

status conferral ■ Credence that a topic or issue receives because of media attention.

Kill Your Television Teacher and former journalist Ron Kaufman of Philadelphia, Pennsylvania, created this web site as a guide to research on the effects of television viewing. **www.turnoffyourtv.com**

The recipient of a message, after decoding, responds. The original recipient then becomes the sender, encoding a response and sending it via a medium back to the original sender, who becomes the new destination and decodes the response. This reverse process is called **feedback.**

In interpersonal communication you know if your listener does not understand. If you hear "Uhh?" or see a puzzled look, you restate your point. In mass communication, feedback is delayed. It might be a week after an article is published before a reader's letter arrives in the newsroom. Because feedback is delayed and because there usually is not very much of it, precise expression in mass communication is especially important. There is little chance to restate the point immediately if the television viewer does not understand. A mass communicator cannot hear the "Uhh?"

An inherent disadvantage of mass communication when compared to interpersonal and group communication is delayed feedback. In interpersonal communication, feedback can be immediate: a quizzical arch of an eyebrow, a hand cupped around an ear to hear better, a fist in the face.

Technology has reduced delays in feedback, but feedback remains an impediment in mass communication that doesn't occur in face-to-face communication. Feedback left on a telephone answering machine, for example, will go unheard until somebody listens to the messages. E-mail can stack up. Faxes can go unread.

Despite feedback as a shortcoming in mass communication, there is an offsetting advantage: efficiency. Other forms of communication, including interpersonal and group, may have the advantage of on-the-spot feedback, but they cannot reach the massive audience of mass communication.

Effects

The whole point of communicating a message is to have an **effect.** A jokester wants to evoke at least a chuckle. A eulogist wants to inspire memories. A cheerleader wants to stir school spirit. The vast size of the mass communicator's audience compounds the potential for powerful effects. Because the potential effect is so great, we need to understand as much as possible about the process that leads to effects.

feedback ■ Recipient's response to the sender.

effect ■ Result of mass communication.

CHAPTER 15 Wrap-Up

Mass communication is a mysterious process. Many scholars have developed theories and models to help us understand some aspects of mass communication, but the process is so complex that we will never master it to the point of being able to predict reliably the outcome of the process. There are just too many variables. This does not mean, however, that the quest for understanding is pointless. The more we know about how mass communication works, the better mass communicators can use the process for good effects and the better media consumers can intelligently assess media messages before using them as a basis for action.

Questions for Review

1. Can you create a sentence that uses the Five Ms: mass communicators, mass messages, mass media, mass communication and mass audiences?
2. What good are mass communication and other models? What do models fail to do?
3. How does mass communication differ from other human communication?
4. How do gatekeepers and regulators influence media messages? How are they different from each other?
5. How do noise and filters impede mass communication?
6. Status conferral is one effect of mass media amplification. How does this work?

Questions for Critical Thinking

1. How is each of these types of communication—intrapersonal, interpersonal, group and mass—difficult to master?
2. All communication involves conceiving, encoding, transmitting, receiving and decoding, but some of these steps are more complicated for mass communication. In what way?
3. Different mass communication models offer different insights into the mass communication process. Describe the different perspectives of these models: Shannon-Weaver, concentric circle and narrative.
4. From your own experience, describe a message that went awry as it moved through the mass communication process. Did the problem involve gatekeepers? Regulators? Noise? Filters?
5. People in the physical sciences can predict with great accuracy how certain phenomena will work. Why will social scientists never be able to do this with the mass communication process?
6. From your own experience, describe how a lack of homophyly has damaged a mass communication attempt.

Deepening Your media LITERACY

What impedes your understanding?

STEP 1 Think about the textbook you have the most trouble understanding. Write down all the factors that can and do interfere with your ability to comprehend the textbook, such as: Is the radio on? Do you come across too many words you don't understand? Is it a subject you like? Is vocabulary a problem?

Dig Deeper

STEP 2 Which of these factors are noise? Which are filters? Why?

What Do You Think?

STEP 3 Answer these questions:

1. Which factor do you think is the biggest impediment to your understanding? Why?
2. Is noise more important to control or are filters? Why?
3. Do you think the textbook author and editors did a good job of finding ways to make their communication of the ideas and facts in the book accessible to their perceived audience? Why or why not?

Keeping Up to Date

Scholarly discussion on the communication process can be found in *Communication Yearbook*, published since 1977, and *Mass Communication Review Yearbook*, published since 1986.

The *Journal of Communication* is a quarterly scholarly publication from Oxford University Press.

For Further Learning

Stephen W. Littlejohn. *Theories of Human Communication*, Fifth edition. Wadsworth, 1996.

Professor Littlejohn traces developments in communication theory and synthesizes the research. One chapter focuses on mass communication.

Denis McQuail and Sven Windahl. *Communication Models for the Study of Mass Communication*, Second edition. Longman, 1993.

McQuail and Windahl show dozens of models from the first 30 years of mass communication research with explanatory comments. Included in the discussion on the narrative, Shannon-Weaver and helix models.

Robert Lichter, Linda S. Richter and Stanley Rothman. *Watching America: What Television Tells Us about Our Lives*. Prentice Hall, 1991.

These authors, affiliated with a nonprofit media watchdog group, relate prime-time television programming to society at large.

Alexis S. Tan. *Mass Communication Theories and Research*. Macmillan, 1986.

Drawing on a growing body of behavioral communication research, Professor Tan explains mass communication functions, processes and effects. Although written for serious advanced students, the book requires no background in communication theory, methodology or statistics.

Marshall McLuhan. *The Gutenberg Galaxy: The Making of Typographical Man*. University of Toronto Press, 1967.

Most of the array of McLuhan's speculations about media effects can be found in this book and in his earlier *Understanding Media: The Extensions of Man* (McGraw-Hill, 1964).

Susan Sontag. "One Cuture and New Sensibility." *Against Interpretation*. Farrar Straus & Giroux, 1966.

Sontag sees pop art as a vehicle for bringing cultural sensitivity to mass audiences.

Orson Welles
Young Orson Welles scared the living daylights out of several million radio listeners with the 1938 radio drama *War of the Worlds.* Most of the fright was short-lived, though. All but the most naïve listeners quickly realized that Martians, marching toward the Hudson River to destroy Manhattan, really had not devastated the New Jersey militia.

chapter 16 Mass Media Effects

In this chapter you will learn:

- **Most media scholars today believe the effects of the mass media generally are cumulative over time.**
- **Individuals choose some mass media over others for the satisfactions they anticipate.**
- **Individuals have substantial control over mass media effects on them.**
- **Mass media have a significant role in helping children learn society's expectations of them.**
- **Scholars differ on whether media-depicted violence triggers aggressive behavior.**
- **The mass media set the agenda for what people are interested in and talk about.**
- **The mass media can work against citizen involvement in political processes.**

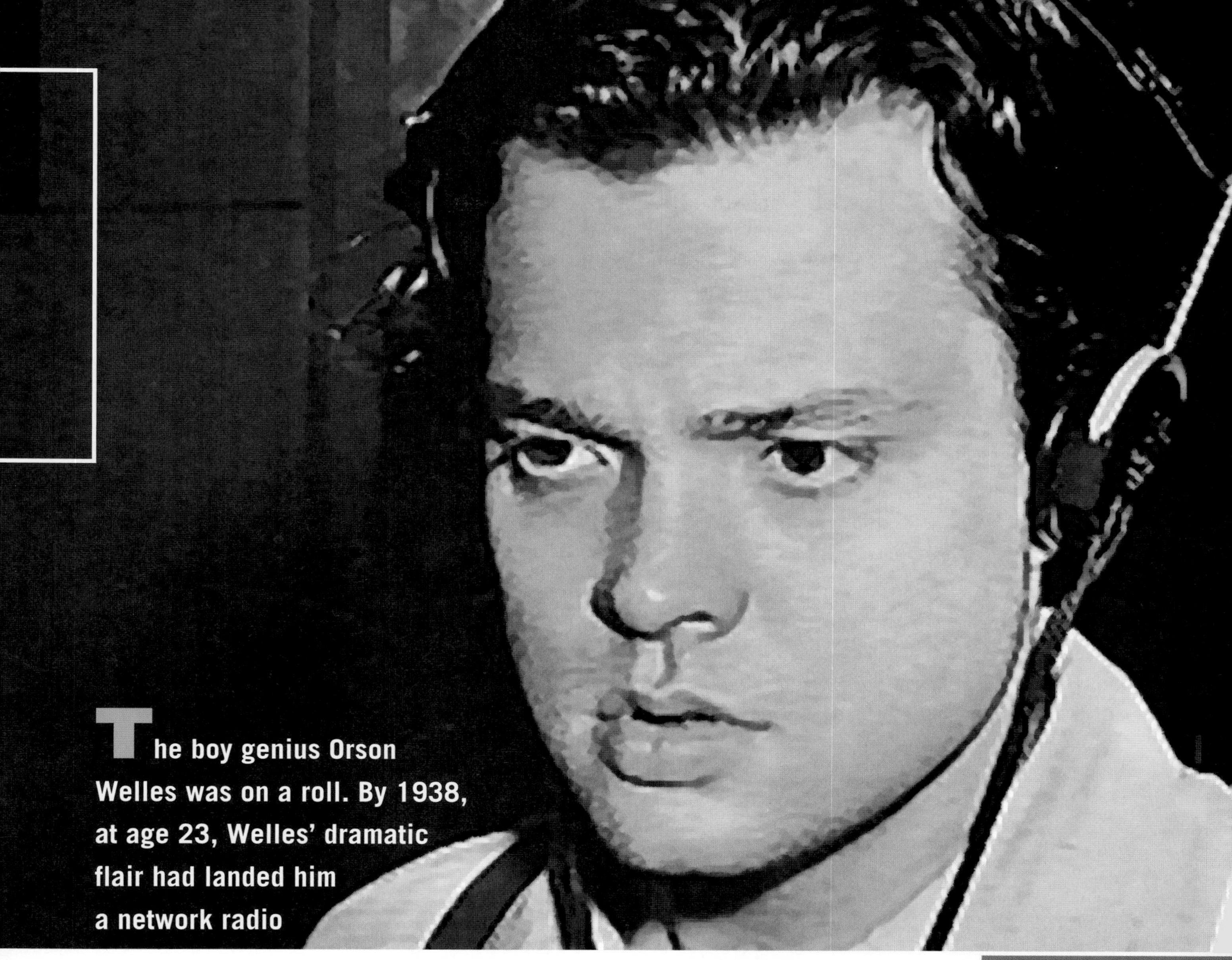

The boy genius Orson Welles was on a roll. By 1938, at age 23, Welles' dramatic flair had landed him a network radio show, *Mercury Theater on the Air,* at prime time on CBS on Sunday nights. The program featured adaptations of well-known literature. For their October 30 program, Welles and his colleagues decided on a scary 1898 British novel, H. G. Wells' *War of the Worlds.*

Orson Welles opened with the voice of a wizened chronicler from some future time, intoning an unsettling monologue. That was followed by an innocuous weather forecast, then hotel dance music. Then the music was interrupted by a news bulletin. An astronomer reported several explosions on Mars, propelling something at enormous velocity toward Earth. The bulletin over, listeners were transported back to the hotel orchestra. After applause the orchestra started up again, only to be interrupted by a special announcement: Seismologists had picked up an earthquake-like shock in New Jersey. Then it was one bulletin after another.

The story line accelerated. Giant Martians moved across the countryside spewing fatal gas. One at a time, reporters at remote sites vanished off the air. The Martians decimated the Army and were wading across the Hudson River. Amid sirens and

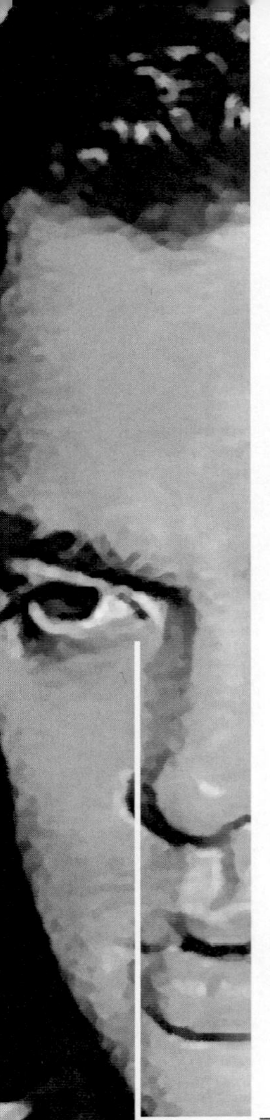

other sounds of emergency, a reporter on a Manhattan rooftop described the monsters advancing through the streets. From his vantage point he described the Martians felling people by the thousands and moving in on him, the gas crossing Sixth Avenue, then Fifth Avenue, then 100 yards away, then 50 feet. Then silence.

To the surprise of Orson Welles and his crew the drama triggered widespread mayhem. Neighbors gathered in streets all over the country, wet towels held to their faces to slow the gas. In Newark, New Jersey, people—many undressed—fled their apartments. Said a New York woman, "I never hugged my radio so closely. . . . I held a crucifix in my hand and prayed while looking out my open window to get a faint whiff of gas so that I would know when to close my window and hermetically seal my room with waterproof cement or anything else I could get a hold of. My plan was to stay in the room and hope that I would not suffocate before the gas blew away."

Researchers estimate that one out of six people who heard the program, more than one million in all, suspended disbelief and braced for the worst.

The effects were especially amazing considering that:

- An announcer identified the program as fiction at four points.
- Almost 10 times as many people were tuned to a popular comedy show on another network.
- The program ran only one hour, an impossibly short time for the sequence that began with the blastoffs on Mars, included a major military battle in New Jersey and ended with New York's destruction.

Unwittingly, Orson Welles and his Mercury Theater crew had created an evening of infamy and raised questions about media effects to new intensity. In this chapter you will learn what scholars have found out about the effects of the mass media on individuals.

media ONLINE **War of the Worlds** Information regarding every version of *The War of the Worlds* ever released, including books, performances, music, movies, television shows, models and games. **www.war-of-the-worlds.org**

Orson Welles ■ His radio drama cast doubt on powerful effects theory.

War of the Worlds ■ Novel that inspired a radio drama that became the test bed of the media's ability to instill panic.

powerful effects theory ■ Theory that media have immediate, direct influence.

Walter Lippmann ■ His *Public Opinion* assumed powerful media effects in 1920s.

Harold Lasswell ■ His mass communication model assumed powerful effects.

Effects Studies

study preview **Early mass communication scholars assumed that the mass media were so powerful that ideas and even ballot-box instructions could be inserted as if by hypodermic needle into the body politic. Doubts arose in the 1940s about whether the media were really that powerful, and scholars began shaping their research questions on assumptions that media effects were more modest. Recent studies are asking about long-term, cumulative media effects.**

Powerful Effects Theory

The first generation of mass communication scholars thought the mass media had a profound, direct effect on people. Their idea, called **powerful effects theory,** drew heavily on social commentator **Walter Lippmann**'s influential 1922 book *Public Opinion.* Lippmann argued that we see the world not as it really is but as "pictures in our heads." The "pictures" of things we have not experienced personally, he said, are shaped by the mass media. The powerful impact that Lippmann ascribed to the media was a precursor of the powerful effects theory that evolved among scholars over the next few years.

Yale psychologist **Harold Lasswell,** who studied World War II propaganda, embodied the effects theory in his famous model of mass communication: *Who, Says what, In* *which channel, To whom, With what effect.* At their extreme, powerful effects theory devotees assumed that the media could inject information, ideas and even propaganda into the public. The theory was explained in terms of a hypodermic needle model or bullet model. Early powerful effects scholars would agree that newspaper coverage and endorsements of political candidates decided elections.

The early scholars did not see that the hypodermic metaphor was hopelessly simplistic. They assumed wrongly that individuals are passive and absorb uncritically and unconditionally whatever the media spew forth. The fact is that individuals read, hear and see the same things differently. Even if they did not, people are exposed to many, many media—hardly a single, monolithic voice. Also, there is a skepticism among media consumers that is manifested at its extreme in the saying "You can't believe a thing you read in the paper." People are not mindless, uncritical blotters.

The most recent comeuppance for the powerful effects theory has Hollywood publicists scratching their heads. Once they saw celebrity magazine covers as powerful promotion vehicles for new films. By 2003, however, this tool wasn't working—at least not reliably. Writing in *Newsweek* magazine, media observer Sean Smith said: "The Jennifer Lopez-Ben Affleck romance made more money for *Us Weekly*, which sold millions of issues with the couple on its covers, than it did for Sony, which lost millions on the couple's movie *Gigli*. This was a shock to both the studio publicity team and the media world. For years the conventional wisdom had been: Get a celebrity on the cover, and people are likely to see her movie." That logic was falling apart with movie after movie. The 2003 *Charlie's Angels: Full Throttle* had a lackluster opening despite the stars being on the cover of *Maxim, Entertainment Weekly, Newsweek* and even—in terms of the Demi Moore-Ashton Kutcher affair—*People* and *Us Weekly*.

Clearly, the powerful effects theory is overrated.

Minimalist Effects Theory

Scholarly enthusiasm for the hypodermic needle model dwindled after two massive studies of voter behavior, one in Erie County, Ohio, in 1940 and the other in Elmira, New York, in 1948. The studies, led by sociologist **Paul Lazarsfeld** of Columbia University, were the first rigorous tests of media effects on an election. Lazarsfeld's researchers went back to 600 people several times to discover how they developed their campaign opinions. Rather than citing particular newspapers, magazines or radio stations, as had been expected, these people generally mentioned friends and acquaintances. The media had hardly any direct effect. Clearly, the hypodermic needle model was off base, and the powerful effects theory needed rethinking. From that rethinking emerged the **minimalist effects theory,** which included:

Two-Step Flow Model Minimalist scholars devised the **two-step flow** model to show that voters are motivated less by the mass media than by people they know personally and respect. These people, called **opinion leaders,** include many clergy, teachers and neighborhood merchants, although it is impossible to list categorically all those who are opinion leaders. Not all clergy, for example, are influential, and opinion leaders are not necessarily in an authority role. The minimalist scholars' point is that personal contact is more important than media contact. The two-step flow model, which replaced the hypodermic needle model, showed that whatever effect the media have on the majority of the population is through opinion leaders. Later, as mass communication research became more sophisticated, the two-step model was expanded into a **multistep flow** model to capture the complex web of social relationships that affects individuals.

Status Conferral Minimalist scholars acknowledge that the media create prominence for issues and people by giving them coverage. Conversely, neglect relegates issues and personalities to obscurity. Related to this **status conferral** phenomenon is **agenda-setting.** Professors **Maxwell McCombs and Don Shaw,** describing the agenda-setting phenomenon in 1972, said the media do not tell people *what to think* but tell them *what*

Paul Lazarsfeld ■ Found voters more influenced by other people than by mass media.

minimalist effects theory ■ Theory that media effects are mostly indirect.

two-step flow ■ Media effects on individuals are through opinion leaders.

opinion leaders ■ Influence friends, acquaintances.

multistep flow ■ Media effects on individuals come through complex interpersonal connections.

status conferral ■ Media attention enhances attention to people, subjects, issues.

agenda-setting ■ Media tell people what to think about, not what to think.

Maxwell McCombs and Don Shaw ■ Articulated agenda-setting theory.

media TIMELINE

UNDERSTANDING MASS MEDIA EFFECTS

1922 Walter Lippmann attributed powerful effects to the mass media.

1938 Hadley Cantril concluded that the "War of the Worlds" panic was drastically overstated.

1940s Mass communication scholars shifted from studying effects to uses and gratification.

1948 Paul Lazarsfeld challenged powerful effects theory in voter studies.

1967 George Gerbner launched his television violence index.

1970s Mass communication scholars shifted to cumulative effects theory.

1972 Maxwell McCombs and Don Shaw concluded that media create public agendas, not opinion.

to think about. This is a profound distinction. In covering a political campaign, explain McCombs and Shaw, the media choose which issues or topics to emphasize, thereby helping set the campaign's agenda. "This ability to affect cognitive change among individuals," say McCombs and Shaw, "is one of the most important aspects of the power of mass communication."

Narcoticizing Dysfunction Some minimalists claim that the media rarely energize people into action, such as getting them to go out to vote for a candidate. Rather, they say, the media lull people into passivity. This effect, called **narcoticizing dysfunction,** is supported by studies that find that many people are so overwhelmed by the volume of news and information available to them that they tend to withdraw from involvement in public issues. Narcoticizing dysfunction occurs also when people pick up a great deal of information from the media on a particular subject—poverty, for example—and believe that they are doing something about a problem when they are really only smugly well informed. Intellectual involvement becomes a substitute for active involvement.

Center for Research on the Effects of Television Based at Ithaca College in New York, the center examines television content and its effect on viewers. **www.ithaca.edu/cretv**

Cumulative Effects Theory

In recent years some mass communication scholars have parted from the minimalists and resurrected the powerful effects theory, although with a twist that avoids the simplistic hypodermic needle model. German scholar **Elisabeth Noelle-Neumann,** a leader of this school, conceded that the media do not have powerful immediate effects but argues that effects over time are profound. Her **cumulative effects theory** notes that nobody can escape either the media, which are ubiquitous, or the media's messages, which are driven home with redundancy. To support her point, Noelle-Neumann cites multimedia advertising campaigns that hammer away with the same message over and over. There's no missing the point. Even in news reports there is a redundancy, with the media all focusing on the same events.

Noelle-Neumann's cumulative effects theory has troubling implications. She says that the media, despite surface appearances, work against diverse, robust public consideration of issues. Noelle-Neumann bases her observation on human psychology, which she says encourages people who feel they hold majority viewpoints to speak out confidently. Those views gain credibility in their claim to be dominant when they are carried by the media, whether they are really dominant or not. Meanwhile, says Noelle-Neumann, people who perceive that they are in a minority are inclined to speak out less, perhaps not at all. The result is that dominant views can snowball through the media and become consensus views without being sufficiently challenged.

To demonstrate her intriguing theory, Noelle-Neumann has devised the ominously labeled **spiral of silence** model, in which minority views are intimidated into silence

narcoticizing dysfunction ■ People deceive themselves into believing they're involved when actually they're only informed.

Elisabeth Noelle-Neumann ■ Leading cumulative effects theorist.

cumulative effects theory ■ Theory that media influence is gradual over time.

spiral of silence ■ Vocal majority intimidates others into silence.

mediaPEOPLE

Steve Schild

A Minnesota e-mail group designed to foster community dialogue, Winona Online Democracy, has instead become home for a few like-minded people who dominate the discussion, according to a 25-month study by St. Mary's University mass communication professor Steve Schild. Although as many as 250 people subscribed to Winona Online Democracy, six writers wrote 31 percent of the messages. In a survey of subscribers, Schild found that fear of being criticized online for their views kept some subscribers from entering the dialogue. "That sounds like the 'spiral of silence' theory developed by social scientist Elisabeth Noelle-Neumann," Schild said. "She predicted that people with unpopular views will go silent rather than continue to oppose prevailing opinion."

Elisabeth Noelle-Neumann

Steve Schild

Schild has noted also that letters to local newspaper opinion pages, where immediate feedback is not possible, were more evenly divided on the issues he studied. On an earlier study that Schild did on a local school referendum, he found that letters to the editor more closely coincided with how the vote went in the election.

Said Schild: "It's easy to keep talking when people in the conversation are on the same side; it's quite another thing when they're divided into opposing camps. What complicates it even more is that the things we are most deeply divided over are the things we most need to talk about."

and obscurity. Noelle-Neumann's model raises doubts about the libertarian concept that the media provide a marketplace in which conflicting ideas fight it out fairly, all receiving a full hearing.

Third-Person Effect

A remnant of now-discredited perceptions that the media have powerful and immediate influence is called **third-person effect.** In short, the theory holds that people overestimate the impact of media messages on other people. Scholar **W. P. Davison,** who came up with the concept in 1983, told a story about a community film board that censored some movies because they might harm people who watch them—even though the board members would deny that they themselves were harmed by watching them. The theory can be reduced to this notion: "It's the other guy who can't handle it, not me."

Davison's pioneering scholarship spawned many studies. Most of the conclusions can be boiled down to these:

- Fears about negative impact are often unwarranted.
- Blocking negative messages is often unwarranted.

third-person effect ■ One person overestimating the effect of media messages on other people.

W. P. Davison ■ Scholar who devised third-person effect theory.

Melvin DeFleur ■ Scholar who concluded that mass communication theory had peaked.

Future Theories

Scholar **Melvin DeFleur,** who has chronicled developments in mass communication theory, is pessimistic about what's happening now in mass communication studies. DeFleur, of Boston University, says recent years have lacked milestones, seminal studies on mass communication, after a rich history of significant studies from the 1930s to the early 1980s. Writing in the scholarly journal *Mass Communication and Society* in 1998, DeFleur said: "When asked by my publisher to revise a book summarizing the existing milestones and adding new ones, I could not identify even one that fit the same criteria as the earlier investigations."

The Golden Age of masscom research, as DeFleur calls it, yielded "important concepts, generalizations and theories that are now part of the accumulated knowledge of how the U.S. media function and the kinds of influence that they have on individuals and society." Among those seminal projects:

- **Payne Fund Studies.** These studies, in the 1930s, established theoretical fundamentals on movies' effects on children.
- **"War of the Worlds" Study.** This 1940 study, by Hadley Cantril, questioned whether the mass media have a bullet effect on audiences. It helped to usher in more sophisticated ways of understanding mass communication.
- **Lazarsfeld Studies.** These studies, in 1940 and 1948, created a new understanding of how mass communication influences people.

Why is mass communication theory dead in the water? DeFleur says that one factor has been a brain drain from universities, where such research took place in earlier times. Corporations now offer much higher salaries than universities—sometimes double and triple—to attract people with doctoral degrees who can do research for their marketing and other corporate pursuits. Scholars are drawn to more practical and lucrative work that may help a detergent manufacturer to choose the right color for packaging the soap but fails to further our understanding of how the mass communication process works.

Uses and Gratifications Studies

study preview **Beginning in the 1940s, many mass communication scholars shifted from studying the media to studying media audiences. These scholars assumed that individuals use the media to gratify needs. Their work, known as uses and gratifications studies, focused on how individuals use mass media—and why.**

Challenges to Audience Passivity

As disillusionment with the powerful effects theory set in after the Lazarsfeld studies of the 1940s, scholars reevaluated many of their assumptions, including the idea that people are merely passive consumers of the mass media. From the reevaluation came research questions about why individuals tap into the mass media. This research, called **uses and gratifications** studies, explored how individuals choose certain media outlets. One vein of research said people seek certain media to gratify certain needs.

These scholars worked with social science theories about people being motivated to do certain things by human needs and wants, such as seeking water, food and shelter as necessities and wanting to be socially accepted and loved. These scholars identified dozens of reasons why people use the media, among them surveillance, socialization and diversion.

Surveillance Function

uses and gratifications ■ Theory that people choose media that meet their needs, interests.

With their acute sense of smell and sound, deer scan their environment constantly for approaching danger. In modern human society, surveillance is provided for individuals by the mass media, which scan local and global environments for information that helps individuals make decisions to live better, even survive.

News coverage is the most evident form through which the mass media serve this **surveillance function.** From a weather report, people decide whether to wear a raincoat; from the Wall Street averages, whether to invest; from the news, whether the president will have their support. Although most people don't obsess about being on top of all that's happening in the world, there is a touch of the news junkie in everybody. All people need reliable information on their immediate environment. Are tornadoes expected? Is the bridge fixed? Are vegetable prices coming down? Most of us are curious about developments in politics, economics, science and other fields. The news media provide a surveillance function for their audiences, surveying the world for information that people want and need to know.

It is not only news that provides surveillance. From drama and literature people learn about great human issues that give them a better feel for the human condition. Popular music and entertainment, conveyed by the mass media, give people a feel for the emotional reactions of other human beings, many very far away, and for things going on in distant places.

media ONLINE **Media Awareness Network** A rich media literacy site from Canada. The section on media research provides many resources for further study. **www.media-awareness.ca**

Socialization Function

Except for recluses, people are always seeking information that helps them fit in with other people. This **socialization function,** a lifelong process, is greatly assisted by the mass media. Without paying attention to the media, for example, it is hard to participate in conversations about how the Yankees did last night, Tom Cruise's latest movie or the current political scandal. Jay Leno's monologues give late-night television watchers a common experience with their friends and associates the next day, as do the latest movie, the evening news and Sunday's football games.

Using the media can be a social activity, bringing people together. Gathering around the radio on Sunday night for the Mercury Theater in the 1930s was a family activity. Television brings people together, huddling around sets in a shared experience like watching 9/11 events unfold or a disabled jet land. Going to the movies with friends is a group activity.

The media also contribute to togetherness by creating commonality. Friends who subscribe to *Newsweek* have a shared experience in reading the weekly cover story, even though they do it separately. The magazine helps individuals maintain social relationships by giving them something in common. In this sense the media are important in creating community, even nationhood and perhaps, with global communication, a fellowship of humankind.

Less positive as a social function of the mass media is **parasocial interaction.** When a television anchor looks directly into the camera, as if talking with individual viewers, it is not a true social relationship that is being created. The communication is one-way without audience feedback. However, because many people enjoy the sense of interaction, no matter how false it is, many local stations encourage on-camera members of the news team to chat among themselves, which furthers the impression of an ongoing conversation with an extended peer group that includes the individual viewer.

This same false sense of reciprocal dialogue exists also among individuals and their favorite political columnists, lovelorn and other advice writers and humorists. Some people have the illusion that the celebrities David Letterman interviews on his program are their friends, and so are Jay Leno's and Larry King's. It is also illusory parasocial interaction when someone has the television set on for companionship.

Diversion Function

Through the mass media, people can escape everyday drudgery, immersing themselves in a soap opera, a murder mystery or pop music. This is the **diversion function.** The result can be stimulation, relaxation or emotional release.

surveillance function ■ Media provide information on what's going on.

socialization function ■ Media help people fit into society.

parasocial interaction ■ A false sense of participating in dialogue.

diversion function ■ Media entertainment.

Stimulation Everybody is bored occasionally. When our senses—sight, hearing, smell, taste and touch—lack sufficient external stimuli, a sensory vacuum results. Following the physicist's law that a vacuum must be filled, we seek new stimuli to correct our sensory deprivation. In modern society the mass media are almost always handy as boredom-offsetting stimulants. It's not only in boring situations that the mass media can be a stimulant. To accelerate the pace of an already lively party, for example, someone can put on quicker music and turn up the volume.

Relaxation When someone's sensory abilities are overloaded, the media can be relaxing. Slower, softer music can sometimes help. Relaxation, in fact, can come through any change of pace. In some situations a high-tension movie or book can be as effective as a lullaby.

Release People can use the mass media to blow off steam. Somehow a Friday night horror movie dissipates the frustration pent up all week. So can a good cry over a tear-jerking book.

Using the mass media as a stimulant, relaxant or release is quick, healthy escapism. Escapism, however, can go further, as when soap opera fans so enmesh themselves in the programs that they perceive themselves as characters in the story line. Carried too far, escapism becomes withdrawal. When people build on media portrayals to the point that their existence revolves on living out the lives of, say, Elvis Presley or Marilyn Monroe, the withdrawal from reality has become a serious psychological disorder.

Consistency Theory

Gratifications scholars learned that people generally are conservative and cautious in choosing media, looking for media that reinforce their personal views. Faced with messages that are consistent with their own views and ones that are radically different, people pay attention to the ones they're comfortable with and have slight recall of contrary views. These phenomena—selective exposure, selective perception, selective retention and selective recall—came to be called **consistency theory.**

Consistency theory does a lot to explain media habits. People read, watch and listen to media with messages that don't jar them. The theory raised serious questions about how well the media can meet the democratic ideal that they be a forum for the robust exchange of divergent ideas. The media can't fulfill their role as a forum if people hear only what they want to hear.

Individual Selectivity

study preview **Individuals choose to expose themselves to media whose perspective and approach reinforce their personal interests and values. These choices, called selective exposure, are consciously made. Similar selectivity phenomena are at work subconsciously in how individuals perceive and retain media content.**

Selective Exposure

People make deliberate decisions in choosing media. For example, outdoors enthusiasts choose *Field & Stream* at the newsrack. Academics subscribe to the *Chronicle of Higher Education.* Young rock fans watch MTV. People expose themselves to media whose content relates to their interests. In this sense, individuals exercise control over the media's effects on them. Nobody forces these selections on anybody.

This process of choosing media, called **selective exposure,** continues once an individual is involved in a publication or a broadcast. A hunter who seldom fishes will

consistency theory ■ People choose media messages consistent with their individual views, values.

selective exposure ■ People choose some media messages over others.

gravitate to the hunting articles in *Field & Stream,* perhaps even skipping the fishing pieces entirely. On a music video channel a hard-rock aficionado will be attentive to wild music but will take a break when the video jock announces that a mellow piece will follow the commercial.

Selective Perception

The selectivity that occurs in actually reading, watching and listening is less conscious than in selective exposure. No matter how clear a message is, people see and hear egocentrically. This phenomenon, known as **selective perception** or **autistic perception,** was demonstrated in the 1950s by researcher Roy Carter, who found that physicians concerned about socialized medicine at the time would hear "social aspects of medicine" as "socialized medicine." Rural folks in North Carolina, anxious for news about farming, thought they heard the words "farm news" on the radio when the announcer said "foreign news."

Selective Perception An introduction to selective perception and how it's used in advertising. **www.ciadvertising.org/student_account/fall_01/adv382j/howardmo/selectiveperception.html**

Scholars Eugene Webb and Jerry Salancik explain it this way: "Exposure to information is hedonistic." People pick up what they want to pick up. Webb and Salancik state that nonsmokers who read an article about smoking focus subconsciously on passages that link smoking with cancer, being secure and content, even joyful, in the information that reinforces the wisdom of their decision not to smoke. In contrast, smokers are more attentive to passages that hedge the smoking-cancer link. In using the mass media for information, people tend to perceive what they want. As social commentator Walter Lippmann put it: "For the most part we do not first see and then define, we define first and then see." Sometimes the human mind distorts facts to square with predispositions and preconceptions.

Selective Retention and Recall

Experts say that the brain records forever everything to which it is exposed. The problem is recall. Although people remember many things that were extremely pleasurable or that coincided with their beliefs, they have a harder time calling up the memory's file on other things.

Selective retention happens to mothers when they tend to deemphasize or even forget the illnesses or disturbances of pregnancy and the pain of birth. This phenomenon works the opposite way when individuals encounter things that reinforce their beliefs.

Nostalgia also can affect recall. For example, many mothers grossly predate when their children abandoned an undesirable behavior like thumb sucking. Mothers tend also to suggest precocity about the age at which Suzy or José first walked or cut the first tooth. In the same way people often use rose-colored lenses, not 20/20 vision, in recalling information and ideas from the media. This is known as **selective recall.**

In summary, individuals have a large degree of control over how the mass media affect them. Not only do individuals make conscious choices in exposing themselves to particular media, but also their beliefs and values subconsciously shape how their minds pick up and store information and ideas. The phenomena of selective exposure, selective perception and selective retention and recall are overlooked by people who portray the mass media as omnipotent and individuals as helpless and manipulated pawns.

The 1938 "War of the Worlds" scare demonstrates this point. The immediate response was to heap blame on the media, particularly Orson Welles and CBS, but panic-stricken listeners bore responsibility too. A Princeton University team led by psychologist **Hadley Cantril,** which studied the panic, noted that radio listeners brought to their radio sets predispositions and preconceptions that contributed to what happened. Among their subconscious baggage:

- A preconception, almost a reverence, about radio, especially CBS, as a reliable medium for major, breaking news.

selective perception ■ People tend to hear what they want or expect to hear.

autistic perception ■ Synonym for *selective perception.*

selective retention ■ Subconsciously, people retain some events and messages, not others.

selective recall ■ People recollect some events and messages for long term but not others.

Hadley Cantril ■ Concluded that there is less media effect than had been thought.

- A predisposition to expect bad news, created by a decade of disastrous global economic developments and another war imminent in Europe.
- Selective perception, which caused them to miss announcements that the program was a dramatization. Although many listeners tuned in late and missed the initial announcement, others listened straight through the announcements without registering them.
- An awe about scientific discoveries, technological progress and new weapons, which contributed to gullibility.
- Memories from World War I about the horror of gas warfare.
- A failure to test the radio story against their own common sense. How, for example, could the Army mobilize for a battle against the Martians within 20 minutes of the invasion?

Socialization

study preview **The mass media have a large role in initiating children into the society. This socialization process is essential to perpetuating cultural values, but some people worry that it can be negative if the media report and portray undesirable behavior and attitudes, such as violence and racism.**

Media's Initiating Role

Nobody is born knowing how to fit into society. This is learned through a process that begins at home. Children imitate their parents and brothers and sisters. From listening and observing, children learn values. Some behavior is applauded, some is scolded. Gradually this culturization and **socialization** process expands to include friends, neighbors, school and at some point the mass media.

In earlier times the role of the mass media came late because books, magazines and newspapers required reading skills that were learned in school. The media were only a modest part of early childhood socialization. Today, however, television is omnipresent from the cradle. A young person turning 18 will have spent more time watching television than in any other activity except sleep. Television, which requires no special skills to use, has displaced much of the socializing influence that once came from parents. "Sesame Street" imparts more information on the value of nutrition than does Mom's admonition to eat spinach.

By definition, socialization is **prosocial.** Children learn that motherhood, baseball and apple pie are valued; that buddies frown on tattling; that honesty is virtuous; and that hard work is rewarded. The stability of a society is ensured through the transmission of such values to the next generation.

media ONLINE **Mediawise** A national resource for research, education and information about the impact of media on children and families.
www.mediafamily.org

The International Clearinghouse on Children, Youth and Media Collects information regarding the effects of media on children.
www.nordicom.gu.se/clearinghouse.php

Role Models

The extent of media influence on individuals may never be sorted out with any precision, in part because every individual is a distinct person and because media exposure varies from person to person. Even so, some media influence is undeniable. Consider the effect of entertainment idols as they come across through the media. Many individuals, especially young people casting about for an identity all their own, groom themselves in conformity with the latest heartthrob. Consider the Mickey Mantle butch haircuts in the 1950s and then Elvis Presley ducktails, Beatle mopheads in the 1960s and punk spikes in the 1980s. Remember all the Spice Girls look-alikes in high school some years ago? This imitation, called **role modeling,** even includes speech mannerisms from whomever is hip at the moment—"Show me the money," "Hasta la vista, baby" and "I'm the king of the world." Let's not forget "yadda-yadda-yadda" from *Seinfeld.*

socialization ■ Learning to fit into society.

prosocial ■ Socialization perpetuates positive values.

role modeling ■ Basis for imitative behavior.

No matter how quirky, fashion fads are not terribly consequential, but serious questions can be raised about whether role modeling extends to behavior. Many people who produce media messages recognize a responsibility for role modeling. Whenever Batman and Robin leaped into their Batmobile in the campy 1960s television series, the camera always managed to show them fastening their seat belts. Many newspapers have a policy to mention in accident stories whether seat belts were in use. In the 1980s, as concern about AIDS mounted, movie-makers went out of their way to show condoms as a precaution in social situations. For example, in the movie *Broadcast News,* the producer character slips a condom into her purse before leaving the house on the night of the awards dinner.

If role modeling can work for good purposes, such as promoting safety consciousness and disease prevention, it would seem that it could also have a negative effect. Some people linked the Columbine High School massacre in Littleton, Colorado, to a scene in the Leonardo DiCaprio movie, *The Basketball Diaries.* In one scene, a student in a black trench coat executes fellow classmates. An outbreak of shootings followed other 1990s films that glorified thug life, including *New Jack City, Juice* and *Boyz N the Hood.*

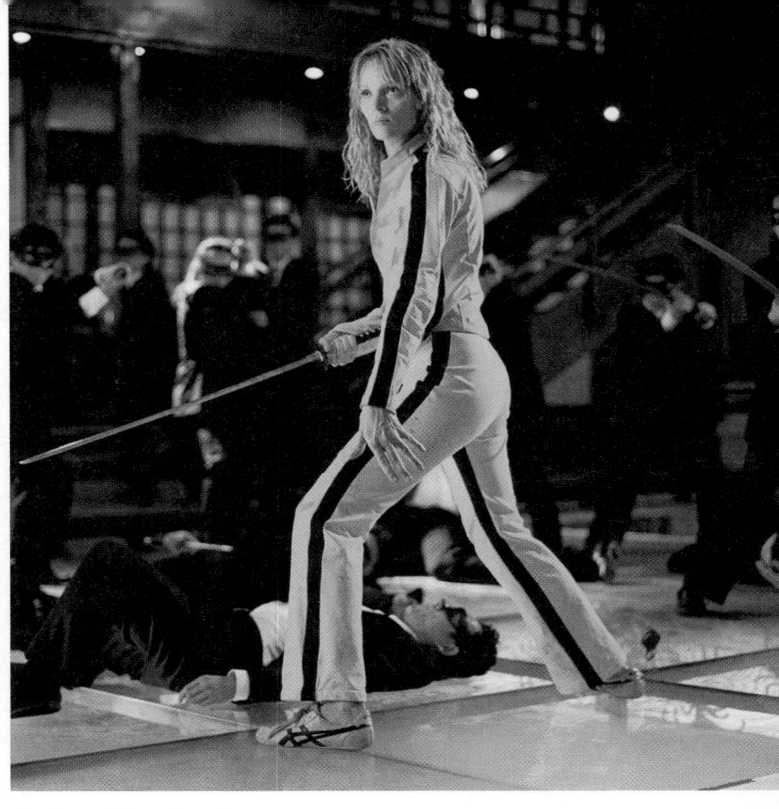

Asics Revival When Uma Thurman slashed her way through Quentin Tarantino's movie *Kill Bill,* the 1949-vintage Asics sneakers she wore, the Onitsuka Tiger model, were suddenly a hit again. In the first quarter after the movie, Asics net profits outperformed $1.8 billion in expectations to $2.6 billion. The question was whether Thurman would wear Asics in the sequel in 2004 and whether interest in the Tiger model could be sustained.

Stereotyping

Close your eyes. Think "professor." What image forms in your mind? Before 1973 most people would have envisioned a harmless, absent-minded eccentric. Today, *The Nutty Professor* movie remake is a more likely image. Both the absent-minded and later nutty professor images are known as stereotypes. Both flow from the mass media. Although neither is an accurate generalization about professors, both have long-term impact.

Stereotyping is a kind of shorthand that can facilitate communication. Putting a cowboy in a black hat allows a movie director to sidestep complex character explanation and move quickly into a story line because movie-goers hold a generalization about cowboys in black hats: They are the bad guys—a stereotype.

Newspaper editors pack lots of information into headlines by drawing on stereotypes held by the readers. Consider the extra meanings implicit in headlines that refer to the "Castro regime," a "Southern belle" or a "college jock." Stereotypes paint broad strokes that help create impact in media messages, but they are also a problem. A generalization, no matter how useful, is inaccurate. Not all Scots are tight-fisted, nor are all Wall Street brokers crooked, nor are all college jocks dumb—not even a majority.

By using stereotypes, the mass media perpetuate them. With benign stereotypes there is no problem, but the media can perpetuate social injustice with stereotypes. In the late 1970s the U.S. Civil Rights Commission found that blacks on network television were portrayed disproportionately in immature, demeaning or comic roles. By using a stereotype, television was not only perpetuating false generalizations but also being racist. Worse, network thoughtlessness was robbing black people of strong role models.

Feminists have leveled objections that women are both underrepresented and misrepresented in the media. One study by sociologist Eve Simson found that most female television parts were decorative, played by pretty California women in their 20s. Worse were the occupations represented by women, said Simson. Most frequent were prostitutes, at 16 percent. Traditional female occupations—secretaries, nurses, flight attendants and receptionists—represented 17 percent. Career women tended to be man-haters or

media ONLINE

Media Stereotypes This educational introduction to media stereotyping details several categories of common stereotypes.
www.media-awareness.ca/english/issues/stereotyping/index.cfm

Young African-Americans against Media Stereotypes Nonprofit organization working for equal and fair exposure of African-Americans in the media.
www.yaaams.org

stereotyping ■ Using broad strokes to facilitate storytelling.

Kathleen Rutledge

To people who criticize the mass media for trafficking in misleading stereotypes, Kathleen Rutledge is a hero. Rutledge, editor of the Lincoln, Nebraska, *Journal Star,* has banned references to sports mascots and nicknames that many American Indians consider insulting. Readers of the *Journal Star,* circulation 74,000, no longer read about the Washington Redskins, just Washington. Instead of the Fighting Sioux, it's just North Dakota. The Cleveland Indians' logo Chief Wahoo, whose weird grin irked Indians, doesn't appear in the newspaper either.

Kathleen Rutledge

Rutledge acknowledges that the policy change rankled some readers when it was announced. In 500-some letters and e-mail messages, readers accused the newspaper of abandoning tradition and succumbing to the leftist politically correct agenda. Leftist? Hardly, responds Rutledge, noting that the *Journal Star* endorsed the self-proclaimed "compassionate conservative" George Bush for president in 2000.

Rather, she says, the newspaper is working hard to recognize diversity. Influxes of people from Latin America, Africa and Asia have changed the Lincoln area. "We've just become more aware of other cultures, other ethnicities," Rutledge said.

Banned in Lincoln Kathleen Rutledge, editor of the Lincoln *Journal Star* in Nebraska, doesn't allow nicknames and mascots that offend many American Indians to appear in the newspaper. Chief Wahoo, mascot of the Cleveland professional baseball team, doesn't appear in the newspaper. Nor does the tribal name Fighting Illini for the University of Illinois athletic teams. In 2005 the National Collegiate Athletic Association stepped up pressure on other college teams to drop Indian nicknames like the Fighting Sioux at North Dakota and the Savages at Southeastern Oklahoma State.

media ONLINE

Media Education Network Started after September 11, 2001, this group fights religious and ethnic stereotypes in the media through education.
www.honestreports.com

Media Action Network for Asian Americans Check out the memo from MANAA to Hollywood, regarding Asian American stereotypes in the media.
www.manaa.org

Media Stereotypes of Young People Even children are stereotyped in the media.
www.childrens-express.org/dynamic/public/d703721.htm

domestic failures. Said Simson: "With nearly every family, regardless of socioeconomic class, having at least one TV set and the average set being turned on seven hours per day, TV has emerged as an important source for promulgating attitudes, values and customs. For some viewers it is the only major contact with outside 'reality,' including how to relate to women. Thus, not only is TV's sexism insulting, but it is also detrimental to the status of women."

Media critics like Simson call for the media to become activists to revise demeaning stereotypes. Although often right-minded, such calls can interfere with accurate portrayals. Italian-Americans, for example, lobbied successfully against Mafia characters being identified as Italians. Exceptions like HBO's Soprano family remain irritants, however. In general, activists against stereotyping have succeeded. Simson would be pleased with the women and black and Latino characters in nonstereotypical roles in popular shows like NBC's *Law & Order* and CBS's *CSI.*

Socialization via Eavesdropping

The mass media, especially television, have eroded the boundaries that people once respected between the generations, genders and other social institutions. Once adults whispered when they wanted to discuss certain subjects, like sex, when children were around. Today, children eavesdrop on all kinds of adult topics by seeing them depicted on television. Though meant as a joke, these lines ring true today to many squirming parents:

> **Father to a friend:** My son and I had that father-and-son talk about the birds and the bees yesterday.
> **Friend:** Did you learn anything?

Joshua Meyrowitz, a communication scholar at the University of New Hampshire, brought the new socialization effects of intergenerational eavesdropping to wide attention with his 1985 book, *No Sense of Place.* In effect, the old socially recognized institution of childhood, which long had been protected from "grown-up issues" like money, divorce and sex, was disappearing. From television sitcoms, kids today learn that adults fight and goof up and sometimes are just plain silly. These are things kids may always have been aware of in a vague sense, but now they have front row seats.

Television also cracked other protected societal institutions, such as the "man's world." Through television many women entered the man's world of the locker room, the fishing trip and the workplace beyond the home. Older mass media, including books, had dealt with a diversity of topics and allowed people in on the "secrets" of other groups, but the ubiquity of television and the ease of access to it accelerated the breakdown of traditional institutional barriers.

Media-Depicted Violence

study preview **Some individuals mimic aggressive behavior they see in the media, but such incidents are exceptions. Some experts argue, in fact, that media-depicted violence actually reduces real-life aggressive behavior.**

Learning About Violence

The mass media help to bring young people into society's mainstream by demonstrating dominant behaviors and norms. This prosocial process, called **observational learning,** turns dark, however, when children learn deviant behaviors from the media. In Manteca, California, two teenagers, one only 13, lay in wait for a friend's father in his own house and attacked him. They beat him with a fireplace poker, kicked him and stabbed him, and choked him to death with a dog chain. Then they poured salt in his wounds. Why the final act of violence—the salt in the wounds? The 13-year-old explained that he had seen it on television. While there is no question that people can learn about violent behavior from the media, a major issue of our time is whether the mass media are the cause of aberrant behavior.

Individuals on trial for criminal acts occasionally plead that "the media made me do it." That was the defense in a 1974 California case in which two young girls playing on a beach were raped with a beer bottle by four teenagers. The rapists told police they had picked up the idea from a television movie they had seen four days earlier. In the movie a young woman was raped with a broom handle, and in court the youths' attorneys blamed the movie. The judge, as is typical in such cases, threw out media-projected violence as an unacceptable scapegoating defense and held the young perpetrators responsible.

Although the courts have never accepted transfer of responsibility as a legal defense, it is clear that violent behavior can be imitated from the media. Some experts, however, say that the negative effect of media-depicted violence is too often overstated and that media violence actually has a positive side.

Media Violence as Positive

People who downplay the effect of media portrayals of blood, guts and violence often refer to a **cathartic effect.** This theory, which dates to ancient Greece and the philosopher

Media Violence Research summary and links to articles on the effects of media violence from an antiviolence parents' organization.
www.lionlamb.org/media_violence.htm

Violence on Television The American Psychological Association provides this page with background on research into the effects of televised violence on children.
www.apa.org/pubinfo/violence.html

Joshua Meyrowitz ■ Noted that media have reduced generational, gender barriers.

observational learning ■ Theory that people learn behavior by seeing it in real life, in depictions.

cathartic effect ■ People release violent inclinations by seeing them portrayed.

media TIMELINE

MASS COMMUNICATION AND VIOLENCE

200 B.C. Aristotle concluded that portrayals of violence have cathartic effect.

1961 Albert Bandura's Bobo doll studies suggested that media violence stirs aggressive behavior.

1963 Wilbur Schramm and associates discredited television as having much effect on most children.

1980s Numerous studies concluded that media violence by itself rarely triggers violence.

1984 Joshua Meyrowitz theorized that television was breaking down gender and generation gaps.

2000 Federal Trade Commission reported that violent fare was being advertised to children despite ratings that it was unsuitable, sparking political calls for restraint but not adding any new research to the core question of whether children are adversely affected.

Aristotle, suggests that watching violence allows individuals vicariously to release pent-up everyday frustration that might otherwise explode dangerously. By seeing violence, so goes the theory, people let off steam. Most advocates of the cathartic effect claim that individuals who see violent activity are stimulated to fantasy violence, which drains off latent tendencies toward real-life violence.

In more recent times, scholar **Seymour Feshbach** has conducted studies that lend support to the cathartic effect theory. In one study, Feshbach lined up 625 junior high school boys at seven California boarding schools and showed half of them a steady diet of violent television programs for six weeks. The other half were shown nonviolent fare. Every day during the study, teachers and supervisors reported on each boy's behavior in and out of class. Feshbach found no difference in aggressive behavior between the two groups. Further, there was a decline in aggression among boys who were determined by personality tests to be more inclined toward aggressive behavior.

Opponents of the cathartic effect theory, who include both respected researchers as well as reflexive media bashers, were quick to point out flaws in Feshbach's research methods. Nonetheless, his conclusions carried a lot of influence because of the study's unprecedented massiveness—625 individuals. Also, the study was conducted in a real-life environment rather than in a laboratory, and there was a consistency in the findings.

Prodding Socially Positive Action

Besides the cathartic effect theory, an argument for portraying violence is that it prompts people to socially positive action. This happened after NBC aired *The Burning Bed*, a television movie about an abused woman who could not take any more and set fire to her sleeping husband. The night the movie was shown, battered-spouse centers nationwide were overwhelmed by calls from women who had been putting off doing anything to extricate themselves from relationships with abusive mates.

On the negative side, one man set his estranged wife afire and explained that he was inspired by *The Burning Bed*. Another man who beat his wife senseless gave the same explanation.

Media Violence as Negative

The preponderance of evidence is that media-depicted violence has the potential to cue real-life violence. However, the **aggressive stimulation** theory is often overstated. The fact is that few people act out media violence in their lives. For example, do you know anybody who saw a murder in a movie and went out afterward and murdered somebody? Yet you know many people who see murders in movies and *don't* kill anyone.

Aristotle ■ Defended portrayals of violence.

Seymour Feshbach ■ Found evidence for media violence as a release.

aggressive stimulation ■ Theory that people are inspired to violence from media depictions.

We need to be careful in talking about aggressive stimulation. Note how scholar Wayne Danielson, who participated in the 1995–1997 National Television Violence Study, carefully qualified one of the study's conclusions: "Viewing violence on TV *tends* to increase violent behavior in viewers, more *in some situations* and less in others. For whatever reason, *when the circumstances are right,* we *tend* to imitate what we see others doing. Our inner resistance to engage in violent behavior *weakens.*"

The study concluded that children may be more susceptible than adults to media violence, but that too was far, far short of a universal causal statement.

Why, then, do many people believe that media violence begets real-life violence? Some early studies pointed to a causal link. These included the 1960 **Bobo doll studies** of **Albert Bandura,** who showed children a violent movie and then encouraged them to play with oversize, inflated dolls. Bandura concluded that kids who saw the film were more inclined to beat up the dolls than were other kids. Critics have challenged Bandura's methodology and said that he mistook childish playfulness for aggression. In short, Bandura and other aggressive stimulation scholars have failed to prove their theory to the full satisfaction of other scholars.

When pressed, people who hold the aggressive stimulation theory point to particular incidents they know about. A favorite is the claim by serial killer Ted Bundy that *Playboy* magazine led him to stalk and kill women. Was Bundy telling the truth? We will never know. He offered the scapegoat explanation on his way to the execution chamber, which suggests that there may have been other motives. The Bundy case is anecdotal, and anecdotes cannot be extrapolated into general validity.

An alternative to aggressive stimulation theory is a theory that people whose feelings and general view of the world tend toward aggressiveness and violence are attracted to violence in movies, television and other media depictions of violence. This alternative theory holds that people who are violent are predisposed to violence, which is far short of saying the media made them do it. This leads us to the **catalytic theory,** which sees media-depicted violence as having a contributing role in violent behavior, not as triggering it.

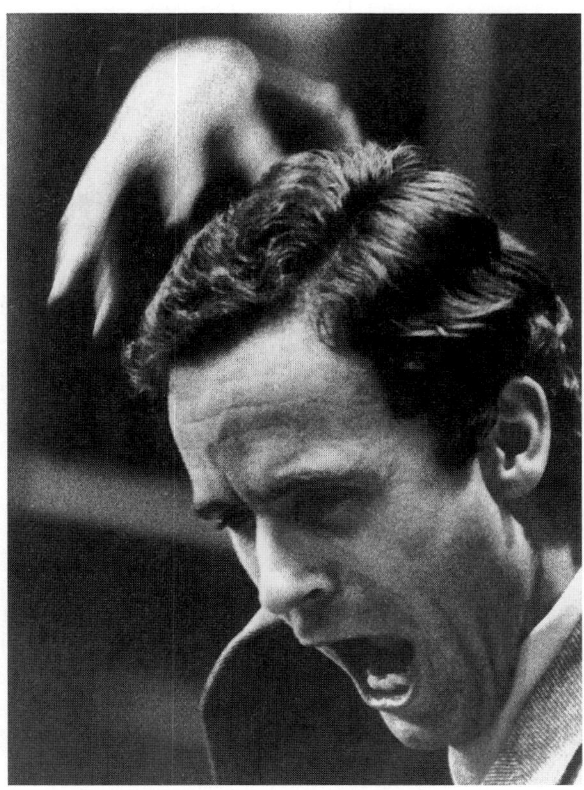

Scapegoating On the eve of his execution, serial killer Ted Bundy claimed that his violence had been sparked by girlie magazines. Whatever the truth of Bundy's claim, scholars are divided about whether media depictions precipitate violent behavior. At one extreme is the view that media violence is a safety valve for people inclined to violence. At the other extreme is the aggressive stimulation theory that media violence causes real-life violence. The most prevalent thinking, to paraphrase a pioneer 1961 study on television and children, is that *certain* depictions under *certain* conditions *may* prompt violence in *certain* people.

Catalytic Theory

Simplistic readings of both cathartic and aggressive stimulation effects research can yield extreme conclusions. A careful reading, however, points more to the media having a role in real-life violence but not necessarily triggering it and doing so only infrequently—and only if several nonmedia factors are also present. For example, evidence suggests that television and movie violence, even in cartoons, is arousing and can excite some children to violence, especially hyperactive and easily excitable children. These children, like unstable adults, become wrapped up psychologically with the portrayals and are stirred to the point of acting out. However, this happens only when a combination of other influences are also present. Among these other influences are:

- **Whether violence portrayed in the media is rewarded.** In 1984 David Phillips of the University of California at San Diego found that the murder rate increases after publicized prizefights, in which the victor is rewarded, and decreases after publicized murder trials and executions, in which, of course, violence is punished.

Bobo doll studies ■ Kids seemed more violent after seeing violence in movies.

Albert Bandura ■ Found media violence stimulated aggression in children.

catalytic theory ■ Media violence is among factors that sometimes contribute to real-life violence.

- **Whether media exposure is heavy.** Researcher Monroe Lefkowitz studied upstate New York third-graders who watched a lot of media-depicted violence. Ten years later, Lefkowitz found that these individuals were rated by their peers as violent. This suggests cumulative, long-term media effects.
- **Whether a violent person fits other profiles.** Studies have found correlations between aggressive behavior and many variables besides violence viewing. These include income, education, intelligence and parental child-rearing practices. This is not to say that any of these third variables cause violent behavior. The suggestion, rather, is that violence is far too complex to be explained by a single factor.

Most researchers note too that screen-triggered violence is increased if the aggression:

- Is realistic and exciting, like a chase or suspense sequence that sends adrenaline levels surging.
- Succeeds in righting a wrong, like helping an abused or ridiculed character get even.
- Includes situations or characters similar to those in the viewer's own experience.

All these things would prompt a scientist to call media violence a catalyst. Just as the presence of a certain element will allow other elements to react explosively but itself not be part of the explosion, the presence of media violence can be a factor in real-life violence but not a cause by itself. This catalytic theory was articulated by scholars **Wilbur Schramm,** Jack Lyle and Edwin Parker, who investigated the effects of television on children and came up with this statement in their 1961 book *Television in the Lives of Our Children,* which has become a classic on the effects of media-depicted violence on individuals: "For *some* children under *some* conditions, *some* television is harmful. For *other* children under the same conditions, or for the same children under *other* conditions, it *may* be beneficial. For *most* children, under *most* conditions, *most* television is *probably* neither particularly harmful nor particularly beneficial."

Societally Debilitating Effects

Media-depicted violence scares far more people than it inspires to violence, and this, according to **George Gerbner,** a leading researcher on screen violence, leads some people to believe the world is more dangerous than it really is. Gerbner calculates that 1 in 10 television characters is involved in violence in any given week. In real life the chances are only about 1 in 100 per *year.* People who watch a lot of television, Gerbner found, see their own chances of being involved in violence nearer the distorted television level than their local crime statistics or even their own experience would suggest. It seems that television violence leads people to think they are in far greater real-life jeopardy than they really are.

The implications of Gerbner's findings go to the heart of a free and democratic society. With exaggerated fears about their safety, Gerbner says, people will demand greater police protection. They are also likelier, he says, to submit to established authority and even to accept police violence as a tradeoff for their own security.

Media Violence and Youth

Nobody would argue that Jerry Springer's television talk show is a model of good taste and restraint. In fact, the conventional wisdom is that such shows do harm. But do they? Two scholars at the University of Pennsylvania, Stacy Davis and Marie-Louise Mares, conducted a careful study with 292 high school students in North Carolina, some from a city and some from a rural area, and concluded from their data: "Although talk shows may offend some people, these data do not suggest that the youth of the U.S. is corrupted by watching them."

One issue was whether talk-show viewing desensitizes teenagers to tawdry behavior. The conventional wisdom, articulated by many politicians calling for television

Wilbur Schramm ■ Concluded that television has minimal effects on children.

George Gerbner ■ Speculated that democracy is endangered by media violence.

mediaPEOPLE

Peggy Charren

Children's Television Peggy Charren, a homemaker and concerned mother, led a campaign in Washington for better kids' television, persuading the Federal Communications Commission, the Federal Trade Commission and Congress that reform was needed. After the Children's Television Act was passed in 1990, Charren disbanded her lobbying group, Action for Children's Television.

After watching television with her two young daughters, Peggy Charren decided that something needed to be done. "Children's television time was filled with cartoon adventures, often violent and rarely creative, in story or animation form," she said. "Youngsters were being told to want unhealthy food and expensive toys." Charren invited neighborhood moms to her living room to discuss the "wall-to-wall monster cartoons." Thus, in 1968, was born Action for Children's Television, which, with Charren in charge, became the most influential non-government entity shaping U.S. television for the next two decades.

The first target was *Romper Room,* a Boston-produced show that was little more than a program-length commercial aimed at kids. The host shamelessly hawked *Romper Room*'s own line of toys from sign-on to sign-off. ACT sponsored a university study of *Romper Room* and was ready to take the findings to the Federal Communications Commission when station WHDH, which produced the show, stopped the host-selling to get Charren off its back—ACT's first victory.

Action for Children's Television then requested meetings with the three big networks, but ABC and NBC said no. Insulted, Charren and her growing organization decided to take their cause to the government. In 1970 ACT became the first public interest group to request a meeting with the FCC. The commission responded by creating a permanent group to oversee children's television issues. With the new government pressure, the National Association of Broadcasters, the major industry trade group, established new standards for children's television. The new guidelines barred host-selling and put a 12-minute per hour cap on commercials during children's television. The lesson for ACT was that government pressure works. "We found that when the regulators make noise, the industry takes action to keep the rules away," Charren said.

There were other battles, but the major victory for Charren and Action for Children's Television was the Children's Television Act of 1990. The law established government expectations for children's programming across a wide range of issues, including advertising, content and quantity. In 1992, to the surprise of many people, Charren announced she was disbanding ACT. After 24 years, she said, ACT has met the objectives that she had set out to accomplish. With the Children's Television Act in effect, the need for ACT had passed. At that point, ACT had 10,000 members.

Through all her crusading for better children's programming, Charren never called for censorship. Her battle cry was choice. "Censorship meant fewer choices. We needed more choice, not less." She did, however, admit to pushing "to eliminate commercial abuses targeted to children."

reform, is that teenagers are numbed by all the antisocial, deviant and treacherous figures on talk shows. Not so, said Davis and Mares: "Heavy talk-show viewers were no less likely than light viewers to believe that the victims of antisocial behavior had been wronged, to perceive that the victim had suffered, or to rate the antisocial behavior as immoral."

Do talk shows undercut society's values? According to Davis and Mares, "In fact, the world of talk shows may be quite conservative. Studio audiences reinforce traditional moral codes by booing guests who flout social norms, and cheering those who speak in favor of the show's theme. So, actually, it looks almost as though talk shows serve as cautionary tales, heightening teens' perceptions of how often certain behaviors occur and how serious social issues are."

mediaPEOPLE

Sam Peckinpah

Nobody is neutral about Sam Peckinpah. For all his Hollywood career he had a reputation of being hard to work with. He was a drunk. Movie critic Pauline Kael, a friend of Peckinpah, recalled his boozing at breakfast, straight up, nothing else. He reviled Hollywood producers. For four years they blacklisted him, but even so, they had to recognize his genius as a director and bring him back.

People split on the most evident part of Peckinpah's legacy: graphic violence. His 1969 Western masterpiece, *The Wild Bunch,* with a gruesome slow-motion fury of death, drew heaps of criticism. He continues to be blamed as the godfather of later Hollywood violence excesses—even today, though he died in 1984.

Friends remember Peckinpah as relishing the part of a bad boy. He worked at riling the producers who backed his movies financially, setting them up like straw men so that he could demonize them. A dismayed producer once wrote him, "I have no idea why you singled me out as an adversary." To which Peckinpah responded, "My problem is, I do not suffer fools graciously and detest petty thievery and incompetence. Other than that, I find you charming, and on occasion, mildly entertaining."

About Peckinpah and producers, Kael said, "He needed their hatred to stir up his own." His rage was his genius.

A theme in Peckinpah's movies is the rebel outlaw, a part he lived. Privately, though, he was thoughtful and considerate even as a cocaine snorter and two-fisted boozer.

Peckinpah's early career was mostly as a writer and director for television Westerns, including *Gunsmoke* and *The Rifleman.* He found in a 1965 television drama, *The Losers*, that slow-motion violence could be a poignant tool.

The themes in Peckinpah's major movies, beginning with *Ride the High Country* in 1962, included noble though flawed men who couldn't survive in a changing world. Mutual male respect, a camaraderie that didn't always come easily, was a staple that was morally more powerful than adversarial forces—a point that he made with tragic and violent punctuations. These themes were at the heart of *The Wild Bunch.* A band of Texas desperadoes allow themselves to be slaughtered by a ruthless Mexican revolutionary rather than betray each other.

After making *The Wild Bunch,* Peckinpah was labeled "Bloody Sam." He hated it. The nickname missed the humanistic sensitivity in his work. It also missed his rage against how dehumanizing changes in the culture assault fundamental morality, an example being his unlikely heroes, the outlaws in *The Wild Bunch.*

Whatever Peckinpah's genius in filmic violence, countless directors—many less skilled, some plainly exploitive—have taken lessons from Peckinpah in racheting up ultraviolence.

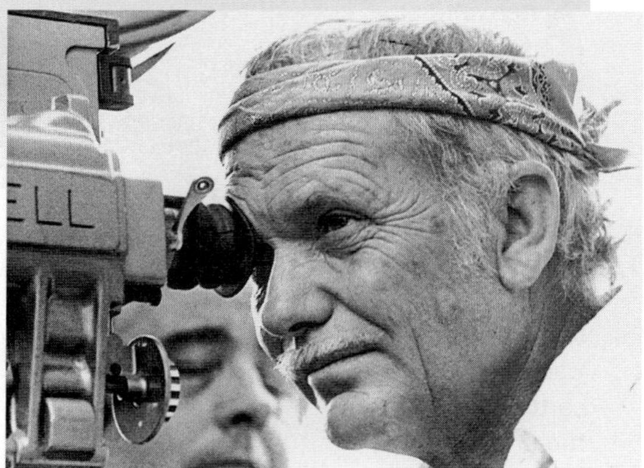

Movie Violence Director Sam Peckinpah is remembered mostly for the graphic violence of his 1969 movie *The Wild Bunch.*

Tolerance of Violence

An especially serious concern about media-depicted violence is that it has a numbing, callousing effect on people. This **desensitizing theory,** which is widely held, says not only that individuals are becoming hardened by media violence but also that society's tolerance for such antisocial behavior is increasing.

Media critics say that the media are responsible for this desensitization, but many media people, particularly movie and television directors, respond that it is the desensitization that has forced them to make the violence in their shows even more graphic. They explain that they have run out of alternatives to get the point across when the story line requires that the audience be repulsed.

Some movie critics, of course, find this explanation a little too convenient for gore-inclined movie-makers and television directors, but even directors who are not inclined to gratuitous violence feel that their options for stirring the audience have become scarcer. The critics respond that this is a chicken-or-egg question and that the media are in no position to use the desensitization theory to excuse increasing violence in their products

desensitizing theory ■ Tolerance of real-life violence grows because of media-depicted violence.

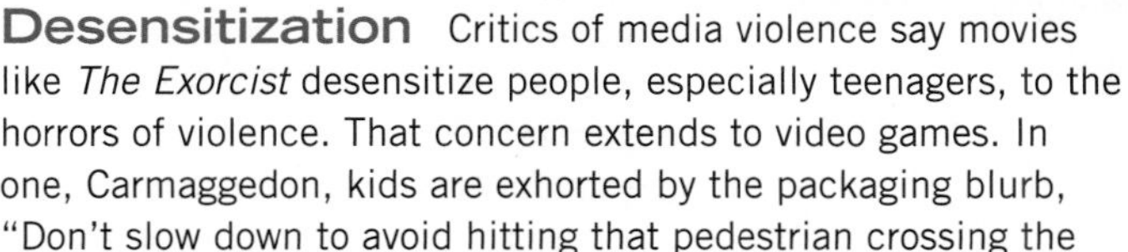

Desensitization Critics of media violence say movies like *The Exorcist* desensitize people, especially teenagers, to the horrors of violence. That concern extends to video games. In one, Carmaggedon, kids are exhorted by the packaging blurb, "Don't slow down to avoid hitting that pedestrian crossing the street—aim, rev up and rack up those points." In one sequence in the Mortal Kombat video game, a crowd shouts encouragement for Kano to rip the heart out of Scorpion, his downed protagonist. Kano waves the dismembered heart at the crowd, which roars approvingly. Although scholars disagree about whether media violence begets real-life violence, most do agree that media violence leaves people more accepting of violence around them in their everyday lives.

if they themselves contributed to the desensitization. And so the argument goes on about who is to blame.

Desensitization is apparent in news also. In 2004 the New York *Times,* traditionally cautious about gore, showed a photo of victims' corpses hanging from a bridge in Fallujah, Iraq. Only a few years earlier there was an almost universal ban on showing the bodies of crime, accident and war victims in newspapers and on television newscasts. Photos of U.S. troops torturing Iraqi prisoners, integral in telling a horrible but important story, pushed back the earlier limits. No mainstream media showed the videotaped beheading of U.S. businessman Nick Berg by terrorists in Iraq, but millions of people found the gruesome sequence online. This desensitizing did not come suddenly with the 2003 Iraq war and its aftermath, but the war clearly established new ground rules.

Undeniable is that violence has had a growing presence in the mass media, which makes even more poignant the fact that we know far less about media violence than we need to. What do we know? Various theories explain some phenomena, but the theories themselves do not dovetail. The desensitizing theory, for example, explains audience acceptance of more violence, but it hardly explains research findings that people who watch a lot of television actually have heightened anxiety about their personal safety. People fretting about their own safety are hardly desensitized.

Violence Studies

The mass media, especially television and movies that deal in fiction, depict a lot of violence. Studies have found as many as six violent acts per hour on prime-time network television. In and of itself, that may seem a lot, but a study at the University of California, Los Angeles, operating on the premise that the issue should not be how much violence

mediaPEOPLE

George Gerbner

George Gerbner worried a lot about media violence. And when he died in 2005, he had been doing this longer than just about anybody else. In 1967 Gerbner and colleagues at the University of Pennsylvania created a television violence index and began counting acts of violence. Today, more than three decades later, the numbers are startling. Gerbner calculated the typical American 18-year-old has seen 32,000 murders and 40,000 attempted murders at home on television.

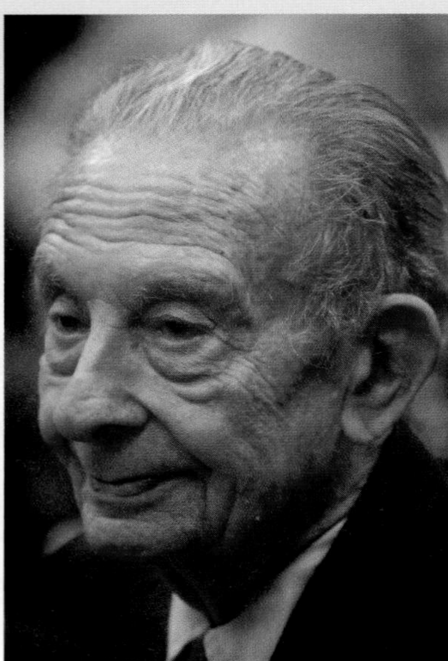

It's a Mean World Scholar George Gerbner, who began tracking television violence in 1967, found that the typical American child sees 32,000 on-screen murders before age 18. The result, he said, is many people see the world as much meaner than it really is.

In a dubious sense, there may be good news for those who fear the effects of media violence. Gerbner's index found no significant change in the volume of violence since the mid-1970s. Maybe it maxed out.

Gerbner theorized that the media violence has negative effects on society. It's what he called "the mean-world syndrome." As he saw it, people exposed to so much violence come to perceive the world as a far more dangerous place than it really is. One of his concerns is that people become overly concerned for their own safety and, in time, may become willing to accept a police state to ensure their personal security. That, he said, has dire consequences for the free and open society that has been a valued hallmark of the American lifestyle.

Are there answers? Gerbner pointed out that the global conglomeration of mass media companies works against any kind of media self-policing. These companies are seeking worldwide outlets for their products, whether movies, television programs or music, and violence doesn't require any kind of costly translations. "Violence travels well," he said. Also, violence has low production costs.

Gerbner noted that violence is an easy fill for weak spots in a television story line. Also, in television, violence is an effective cliff-hanger before a commercial break.

While Gerbner's statistics are unsettling, they have critics who say his numbers make the situation seem worse than it really is. The Gerbner index scores acts of violence without considering their context. That means when Bugs Bunny is bopped on the head, it counts the same as Rambo doing the same thing to a vile villain in a skull-crushing, blood-spurting scene. A poke in the eye on *The Three Stooges* also scores as a violent act.

Despite his critics, Gerbner provided a baseline for measuring changes in the quantity of television violence. Virtually every scholar cites him in the ongoing struggle to figure out whether media violence is something that should worry us all.

is depicted but the context in which it occurs, came to a less startling conclusion: Slapstick comedic violence shouldn't be lumped with a graphic homicide in counting depictions of violence. Nor should a violent storm.

The UCLA research, called the **Violence Assessment Monitoring Project,** concluded in its first year that distressing human violence was much less prevalent than earlier studies counted. Of 121 prime-time episodes, only 10 had frequent violence and only eight had occasional violence. This was after comedic violence and nonhuman violence, such as hurricanes, were screened out. The next year, 1996, found violence in only five prime-time shows—half the number of the year before. Also, most of the shows didn't survive the season. In 1998 the number was down to two series.

The UCLA study added sophistication to counting acts of media-depicted violence but still didn't assess whether the violence affected people. In 1986 scholar **William McQuire** reviewed the literature on mediated violence and found that hardly any of the studies' evidence was statistically reliable. The exception was controlled laboratory studies, for which the statistics were more meaningful but didn't indicate much causality.

Violence Assessment Monitoring Project ■ Conducted contextual nonviolence studies and found less serious media depictions than earlier thought.

William McQuire ■ Found most media violence research flawed.

Media Agenda-Setting for Individuals

studypreview **Media coverage helps to define the things people think about and worry about. This is called agenda-setting. It occurs as the media create awareness of issues through their coverage, which lends importance to those issues. The media don't set agendas unilaterally but look to their audiences in deciding their priorities for coverage.**

Media Selection of Issues

When the New York police wanted more subway patrols, their union public relations person, Morty Martz, asked officers to call him with every subway crime. Martz passed the accounts, all of them, on to newspapers and television and radio stations. Martz could not have been more pleased with his media blitz. News coverage of subway crime, he later boasted, increased several thousand percent, although there had been no appreciable change in the crime rate itself. Suddenly, for no reason other than dramatically stepped-up coverage, people were alarmed. Their personal agendas of what to think about—and worry about—had changed. The sudden new concern, which made it easier for Martz's union to argue for more subway patrols, was an example of media agenda-setting at work. Martz lured news media decision-makers into putting subway crime higher on their lists of issues to be covered. As a result, citizens moved subway crime up on their lists of personal concerns.

The agenda-setting phenomenon has been recognized for a long time. Sociologist **Robert Park,** writing in the 1920s, articulated the theory in rejecting the once-popular notion that the media tell people what to think. As Park saw it, the media create awareness of issues more than they create knowledge or attitudes. Agenda-setting occurs at several levels:

Creating Awareness Only if individuals are aware of an issue can they be concerned about it. Concern about parents who kill their children becomes a major issue with media coverage of spectacular cases. In 1994 Susan Smith, a South Carolina woman, attracted wide attention with her horrific report that her sons, ages 3 and 1, had been kidnapped. The story darkened later when the woman confessed to driving the family car into the lake and drowning the boys herself. Over several days of intense media attention the nation not only learned the morbid details of what happened, but also became better informed about a wide range of parental, family, mental health and legal issues that the coverage brought to the fore.

Establishing Priorities People trust the news media to sort through the events of the day and make order of them. Lead-off stories on a newscast or on Page 1 are expected to be the most significant. Not only does how a story is played affect people's agendas, but so do the time and space afforded it. Lavish graphics can propel an item higher.

Perpetuating Issues Continuing coverage lends importance to an issue. A single story on a bribed senator might soon be forgotten, but day-after-day follow-ups can fuel ethics reforms. Conversely, if gatekeepers are diverted to other stories, a hot issue can cool overnight—out of sight, out of mind.

Intramedia Agenda-Setting

Agenda-setting also is a phenomenon that affects media people, who constantly monitor one another. Reporters and editors many times are concerned more with how their peers are handling a story than with what their audience wants. Sometimes the media

Robert Park ■ Argued that media create awareness.

Agenda Setting A detailed discussion of the theory. **www.agendasetting.com**

harp on one topic, making it seem more important than it really is, until it becomes tedious.

The media's agenda-setting role extends beyond news. Over time, lifestyles and values portrayed in the media can influence not just what people think about but what they do. Hugh Hefner's *Playboy* magazine of the 1950s helped to usher in the sexual revolution. Advertising has created a redefinition of American values by whetting an appetite for possessions and glamorizing immediate gratification.

Even so, individuals exercise a high degree of control in their personal agendas. For decades William Randolph Hearst campaigned with front-page editorials in all his newspapers against using animals in research, but animal rights did not become a pressing public issue. Even with the extensive media coverage of the Vietnam war, polls late in the 1960s found that many Americans still were unmoved. For the most part, these were people who chose to tune out the war coverage. The fact is that journalists and other creators of media messages cannot automatically impose their agendas on individuals. If people are not interested, an issue won't become part of their agendas. The individual values at work in the processes of selective exposure, perception and retention can thwart media leadership in agenda-setting.

Also, media agendas are not decided in a vacuum. Dependent as they are on having mass audiences, the media take cues for their coverage from their audiences. Penny press editors in the 1830s looked over the shoulders of newspaper readers on the street to see what stories attracted them and then shaped their coverage accordingly. Today, news organizations tap the public pulse through scientific sampling to deliver what people want. The mass media both exert leadership in agenda-setting and mirror the agendas of their audiences.

Media-Induced Anxiety and Apathy

studypreview **The pervasiveness of the mass media is not necessarily a good thing, according to some theorists who say a plethora of information and access to ideas and entertainment can induce information anxiety. Another theory is that the news media even encourage passivity by leaving an impression that their reporting is so complete that there's nothing left to know or do.**

Information Anxiety

The New York *Times* had a landmark day on November 13, 1987. It published its largest edition ever: 12 pounds, 1,612 pages and 12 million words. How could anyone, even on a quiet Sunday, manage all that information? One of the problems in contemporary life is the sheer quantity of information technology allows us as a society to gather and disseminate. Even a relatively slender weekday edition of the New York *Times* contains more information than the average person in the 17th century was likely to come across in a lifetime, according to Richard Saul Wurman in his book *Information Anxiety.*

While educated people traditionally have thirsted for information, the quantity has become such that many people feel overwhelmed by what is called **information pollution.** We are awash in it and drowning, and the mass media are a factor in this. Consider college students at a major metropolitan campus:

information pollution ■ Media deluge people with information and no sense of order, priority.

- They pass newspaper vending machines and racks with a dozen different papers—dailies, weeklies, freebies—en route to class.
- On the radio they have access to 40 stations.
- In their mailbox they find a solicitation for discount subscriptions to 240 magazines.

- They turn on their television during a study break and need to choose among 50 channels.
- At lunch they notice advertisements everywhere—on the placemat, on the milk carton, on table standups, on the butter pat, on the walls, on the radio coming over the public-address system, on the pen used to write a check or sign a credit-card receipt.
- At the library and often in their dorm rooms they have almost instant online access through computer systems to more information than any human being could possibly deal with.

Compounding the quantity of information available is the accelerating rate at which it is available. Trend analyst John Naisbitt has made the point with this example: When President Lincoln was shot in 1865, people in London learned about it five days later. When President Reagan was shot in 1981, journalist Henry Fairlie, in his office one block away, heard about the assassination attempt from his London editor who had seen it on television and phoned Fairlie to alert him to go to the scene. On September 11, 2001, the all-day news services were live in real time.

It is no wonder that conscientious people who want good and current data to form their judgments and opinions, even to go about their jobs, feel overwhelmed. Wurman, who has written extensively on this frustration, describes information anxiety as the result of "the ever-widening gap between what we understand and what we think we should understand."

The solution is knowing how to locate relevant information and tune out the rest, but even this is increasingly difficult. Naisbitt reported in *Megatrends* that scientists planning an experiment are spending more time figuring out whether someone somewhere already has done the experiment than conducting the experiment itself.

On some matters, many people do not even try to sort through all the information that they have available. Their solution to information anxiety is to give up. Other people have a false sense of being on top of things, especially public issues, because so much information is available.

Media-Induced Passivity

One effect of the mass media is embodied in the stereotypical couch potato, whose greatest physical and mental exercise is heading to the refrigerator during commercials. Studies indicate that television is on seven hours a day on average in U.S. homes and that the typical American spends four to six hours a day with the mass media, mostly with television. The experience is primarily passive, and such **media-induced passivity** has been blamed, along with greater mobility and access to more leisure activities, for major changes in how people live their lives:

- **Worship services.** In 1955 Gallup found that 49 percent of Americans attended worship services weekly. Today, it is less than 40 percent.
- **Churches and lodges.** The role of church auxiliaries and lodges, such as the Masons, Odd Fellows and Knights of Pythias, once central in community social life with weekly activities, has diminished.
- **Neighborhood taverns.** Taverns at busy neighborhood corners and rural crossroads once were the center of political discussion in many areas, but this is less true today.
- **Participatory sports.** Despite the fitness and wellness craze, more people than ever are overweight and out of shape, which can be partly attributed to physical passivity induced by television and media-based homebound activities.

Although these phenomena may be explained in part by people's increased use of the mass media and the attendant passivity, it would be a mistake not to recognize that social forces besides the media have contributed to them.

media-induced passivity ■ Media entice people away from social involvement.

CHAPTER 16 Wrap-Up

The mass media influence us, but scholars are divided about how much. There is agreement that the media help to initiate children into society by portraying social and cultural values. This is a serious responsibility because portrayals of aberrant behavior like violence have effects, although we are not sure about their extent. This is not to say that individuals are unwitting pawns of the mass media. People choose what they read and what they tune in to, and they generally filter the information and images to conform with their preconceived notions and personal values.

In other respects, too, the mass media are a stabilizing influence. The media try to fit into the lives of their audiences. An example is children's television programs on weekend mornings when kids are home from school but still on an early-rising schedule. The media not only react to audience lifestyles but also contribute to the patterns by which people live their lives, like going to bed after the late news. In short, the media have effects on individuals and on society, but it is a two-way street. Society is a shaper of media content, but individuals make the ultimate decisions about subscribing, listening and watching. The influence issue is a complex one that merits further research and thought.

Questions for Review

1. Why have most media scholars abandoned the powerful effects and minimalist effects theories for the cumulative theory?
2. What is the uses and gratifications approach to mass media studies?
3. Do individuals have any control over mass media effects on them?
4. What role do the mass media have in socializing children?
5. How do scholars differ on whether media-depicted violence triggers aggressive behavior?
6. What is meant when someone says, "The mass media don't tell people what to think as much as tell them what to think about"?
7. Does being informed by mass media necessarily improve citizen involvement in political processes?

Questions for Critical Thinking

1. Although generally discredited by scholars now, the powerful effects theory once had many adherents. How do you explain the lingering popularity of this thinking among many people?
2. Name at least three opinion leaders who influence you on issues that you do not follow closely in the media. On what issues are you yourself an opinion leader?
3. Give specific examples of each of the eight primary mass media contributing to the lifelong socialization process. For starters, consider a current nonfiction best-selling book.
4. Explain how selective exposure, selective perception and selective retention would work in the case of a devout Christian conservative to whom George W. Bush spoke at Bob Jones University, a conservative Baptist college, during the 2000 presidential primaries. Compare how these same people recorded other candidates' campaign speeches in their minds that same day.
5. Discuss the human needs that the mass media help to satisfy in terms of the news and entertainment media.
6. Among the functions that the mass media serve for individuals are diversion and escape. Is this healthy?
7. Explain the prosocial potential of the mass media in culturization and socialization. What about the media as an antisocial force in observational learning?
8. Cite at least three contemporary role models who you can argue are positive. Explain how they might also be viewed as negative. Cite three role models who you can argue are negative.
9. What stereotype comes to your mind with the term *Uncle Remus?* Is your image of Uncle Remus one that would be held universally? Why or why not?
10. How can serious scholars of mass communication hold such diverse ideas as the cathartic, aggressive stimulation and catalytic theories? Which camp is right?

Deepening Your media LITERACY

Reality shows: more than diversion?

STEP 1 From *Survivor* to *The Intern*, *The Bachelor* or *All American Girl*, reality shows have proliferated on American television.

Dig Deeper

STEP 2 Think of your favorite reality show. Think about why you were first attracted to it. Think about why you kept watching it. Think about a reality show that doesn't appeal to you. Why doesn't it? To whom does it appeal?

What Do You Think?

STEP 3 Answer these questions:

1. Has your favorite reality show changed U.S. society, or does it just reflect society?
2. What needs does it gratify?
3. Does it tell you anything about the great human issues?
4. Does it reinforce your personal views? If so, which ones?
5. Do you want to emulate the people on the show? Do you think they are stereotyped?
6. Does the show help its viewers find their place in society?

Keeping Up to Date

The interdisciplinary scholarly journal *Media Psychology,* a quarterly, focuses on theory-based research on media uses, processes and effects.

For Further Learning

Carolyn Byerly and Karen Ross. *Women and Media: A Critical Introduction.* Blackwell, 2005.

Byerly and Ross, communication professors, examine how women have worked inside and outside the mainstream media since the 1970s.

Lewis H. Lapham. *Gag Rule: On the Suppression of Dissent and the Stifling of Democracy.* Penguin, 2004.

Lapham, editor of *Harper's,* blames the news media in part for public acquiescence in the erosion of individual liberties. He is especially critical of the 2001 Patriot Act. Lapham also blames schools and textbooks for letting young people conclude that civic affairs are boring.

Carolyn Kitch. *The Girl on the Magazine Cover.* University of North Carolina Press, 2002.

Kitch, a former women's magazine editor, notes a disconnect between the visual images of women in magazines between 1895 and 1930 and a wave of feminism. The magazines portrayed women as consumers until this wave of feminism dissipated.

Gabriele Griffin. *Representations of HIV and AIDS: Visibility Blues.* Manchester University Press, 2001.

Griffin's subject is a case study in media status conferral.

Elizabeth M. Perse. *Media Effects and Society.* Erlbaum, 2001.

Perse, a communication scholar, offers an advanced overview of studies on media effects, including their effect on public opinion and voting.

Michael Pickering. *Stereotyping: The Politics of Representation.* Palgrave, 2001.

Pickering sees limitations to stereotyping as a social science research concept.

Margaret Gallagher. *Gender Setting: New Media Agenda for Monitoring and Advocacy.* Palgrave, 2001.

Gallagher, writing from a feminist perspective, brings together research on monitoring gender content, images, symbols and values in the mass media.

Donald Bogle. *Primetime Blues: African Americans on Network Television.* Straus & Giroux, 2001.

Bogle, a media scholar, uses an economic analysis of the television industry for assessing changes in the portrayal of black Americans on U.S. television.

Jane D. Brown, Jeanne R. Steele and Kim Walsh-Childers, editors. *Sexual Teens, Sexual Media: Investigating Media's Influence of Adolescent Sexuality.* Erlbaum, 2001.

The authors, all scholars, organize articles from contributors by medium—television, magazines, movies, music and the Internet.

Joshua Meyrowitz. *No Sense of Place: The Impact of Electronic Media on Social Behavior.* Oxford, 1985.

Professor Meyrowitz says television allows everybody, adult and child, to eavesdrop into other generations, which has eroded if not undone intergenerational distinctions that once were essential components of the social structure.

Paul Lazarsfeld, Bernard Berelson and Hazel Gaudet. *The People's Choice: How the Voter Makes Up His Mind in a Presidential Campaign,* Second edition. Bureau of Applied Social Research, 1948.

They questioned the Magic Bullet Theory.

Marshall McLuhan
The controversial Canadian theorist blamed Gutenberg for social alienation, but not all was lost. He also foresaw a transforming global village.

chapter 17 Mass Media and Society

In this chapter you will learn:

- **The mass media seek to reach large audiences rather than to extend cultural sensitivity.**
- **The mass media contribute to stability in the society by providing common rituals.**
- **People communicate with generations into the future and with faraway people through the mass media.**
- **Scholar Marshall McLuhan foresaw television easing the alienation of human beings from their true nature.**
- **Societies that dominate economically and politically export their values elsewhere for better or worse.**

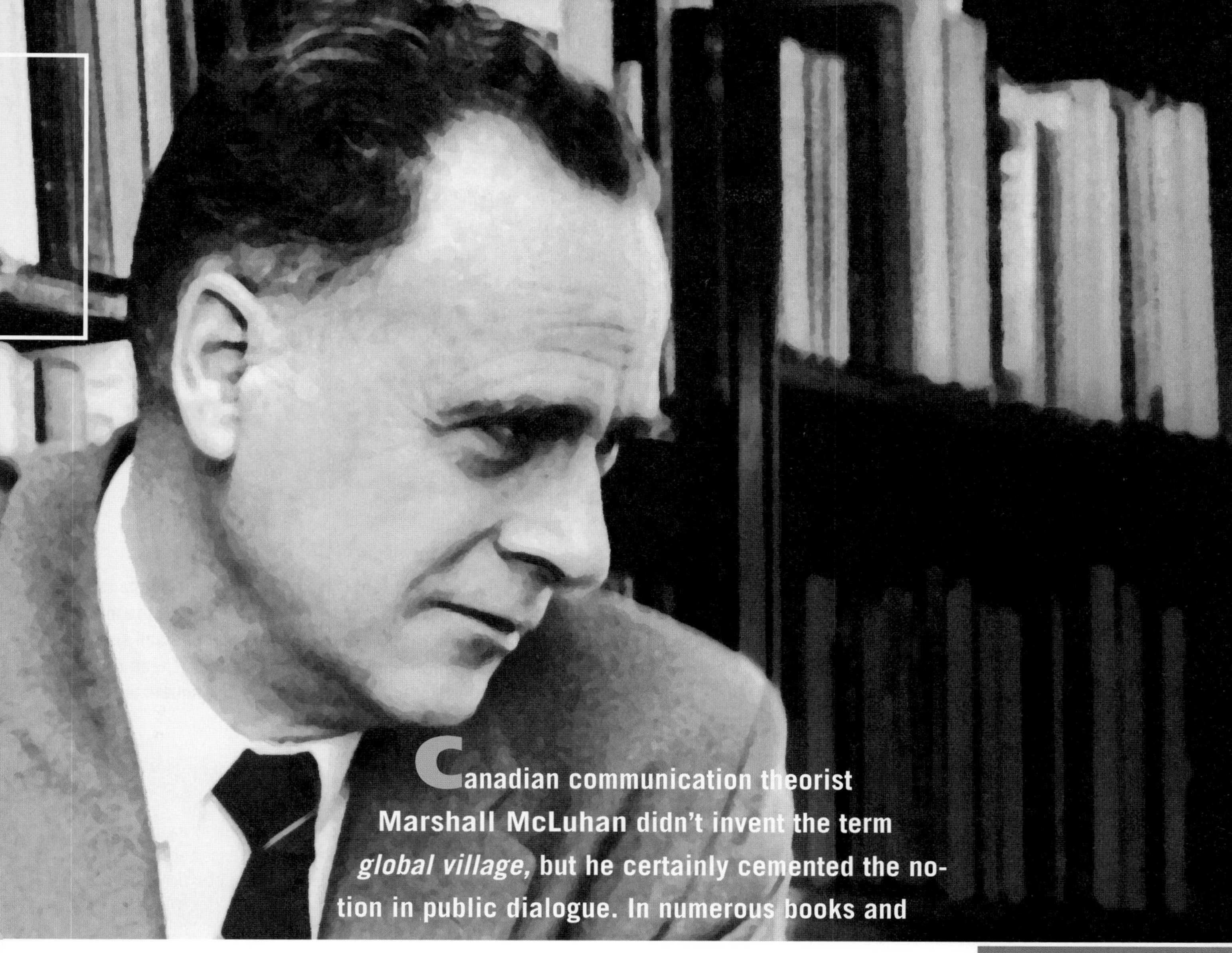

Canadian communication theorist Marshall McLuhan didn't invent the term *global village,* but he certainly cemented the notion in public dialogue. In numerous books and the scholarly journal *Explorations,* which he founded in 1954, McLuhan talked about the world shrinking, at least metaphorically. In an electronically linked world, he said, television could present live information from anywhere to everyone. The result, as he saw it, could change human existence profoundly, reversing a trend that went back to Gutenberg's mass-produced printed word in the 1400s.

As McLuhan saw it, Gutenberg's invention had a dark side. Reading, a skill necessary to partake of print media, is hardly a natural act. It requires so much concentration and focus that it squeezes out other sensory perceptions that a human being would normally sense and respond to. Reading requires you to block out the world around you. For example, if you are really into a book, you might miss a knock on the door.

Television would reverse this perversion of human nature, McLuhan said. With a world connected by live media, people would respond spontaneously—or, as he

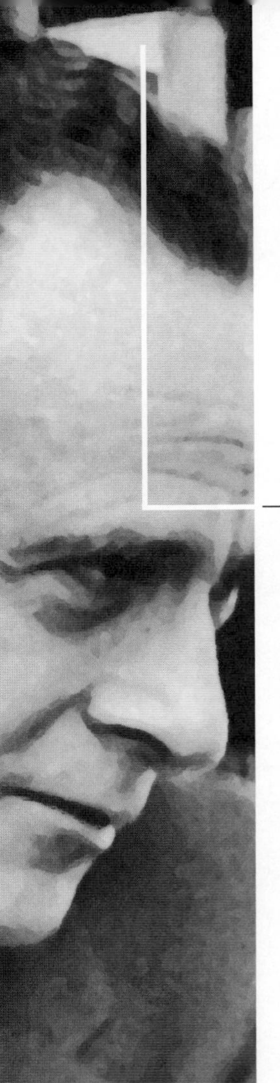

saw it, naturally. Receiving the message would no longer be an isolated, insulated act. This global village, like pre-Gutenberg villages, could help human beings to return to a pristine form of existence, their senses in tune with their surroundings and their responses governed more by instinct than contrivances like reading, which, he said, had alienated human beings from their true nature.

McLuhan, whose works include theoretical best-sellers in the 1960s, was confusing in some of his writing, using concepts and terms in different ways over a long career of thinking about mass communication. Even so, his contributions to our understanding remain bulwarks in many advanced mass communication curriculums even 25 years after his death.

Mass Media Role in Culture

study preview **The mass media are inextricably linked with culture because it is through the media that creative people have their strongest sway. Although the media have the potential to disseminate the best creative work of the human mind and soul, some critics say the media are obsessive about trendy, often silly subjects. These critics find serious fault with the media's concern for pop culture, claiming it squeezes out things of significance.**

Elitist versus Populist Values

The mass media can enrich society by disseminating the best of human creativity, including great literature, music and art. The media also carry a lot of lesser things that reflect the culture and, for better or worse, contribute to it. Over time, a continuum has been devised that covers this vast range of artistic production. At one extreme is artistic material that requires sophisticated and cultivated tastes to appreciate it. This is called **high art.** At the other extreme is **low art,** which requires little sophistication to enjoy.

One strain of traditional media criticism has been that the media underplay great works and concentrate on low art. This **elitist** view argues that the mass media do society a disservice by pandering to low tastes. To describe low art, elitists sometimes use the German word ***kitsch,*** which translates roughly as "garish" or "trashy." The word captures their disdain. In contrast, the **populist** view is that there is nothing unbecoming in the mass media's catering to mass tastes in a democratic, capitalistic society.

In a 1960 essay still widely cited, "Masscult and Midcult," social commentator **Dwight Macdonald** made a virulent case that all popular art is kitsch. The mass media, which depend on finding large audiences for their economic base, can hardly ever come out at the higher reaches of Macdonald's spectrum.

This kind of elitist analysis was given a larger framework in 1976 when sociologist **Herbert Gans** categorized cultural work along socioeconomic and intellectual lines. Gans said that classical music, as an example, appealed by and large to people of academic and professional accomplishments and higher incomes. These were **high-culture audiences,** which enjoyed complexities and subtleties in their art and entertainment. Next came **middle-culture audiences,** which were less abstract in their interests and liked Norman Rockwell and prime-time television. **Low-culture audiences** were factory and service workers whose interests were more basic; whose educational accomplishments, incomes and social status were lower; and whose media tastes leaned toward kung fu movies, comic books and supermarket tabloids.

Marshall McLuhan ■ Blamed human alienation on mass-produced written word.

high art ■ Requires sophisticated taste to be appreciated.

low art ■ Can be appreciated by almost everybody.

elitist ■ Mass media should gear to sophisticated audiences.

kitsch ■ Pejorative word for trendy, trashy, low art.

populist ■ Mass media should seek largest possible audiences.

Dwight Macdonald ■ Said all pop art is kitsch.

Herbert Gans ■ Said social, economic and intellectual levels of audience coincide.

high-, middle- and low-culture audiences ■ Continuum identified by Herbert Gans.

media TIMELINE

MASS COMMUNICATION AND CULTURE

1960s Marshall McLuhan theorized that television could end human alienation caused by print media.

1960s Dwight Macdonald equated pop art and kitsch.

1965 Susan Sontag saw pop art as emotive high art.

1976 Herbert Gans related cultural sensitivity to social and economic status.

Gans was applying his contemporary observations to flesh out the distinctions that had been taking form in art criticism for centuries—the distinctions between high art and low art.

Highbrow The high art favored by elitists generally can be identified by its technical and thematic complexity and originality. High art is often highly individualistic because the creator, whether a novelist or a television producer, has explored issues in fresh ways, often with new and different methods. Even when it's a collaborative effort, a piece of high art is distinctive. High art requires a sophisticated audience to appreciate it fully. Often it has enduring value, surviving time's test as to its significance and worth.

The sophistication that permits an opera aficionado to appreciate the intricacies of a composer's score, the poetry of the lyricist and the excellence of the performance

media ONLINE **The Center for Media and Public Affairs** The web site's Media Monitor includes a political newswatch, economic studies, media factoids, TV studies, late-night comedy counts and more. **www.cmpa.com**

Modernist "Lowbrow" Readers Take a look at the syllabus for a course that explores early-twentieth-century fiction, such as Tarzan, that became popular in other media forms. **www.uweb.ucsb.edu/~seg1/test/lowbrow.html**

Elitist Horror
The National Book Foundation muddied the easy distinctions between elitist and populist literature with a National Book Award to horror novelist Stephen King. In his acceptance speech King acknowledged the flap over his being chosen but called on authors and publishers to "build a bridge between the popular and the literary." Of his 40-plus books King said some are entertainment, some literature. "Just don't ask me to define literature," he added.

sometimes is called **highbrow.** The label has grim origins in the idea that a person must have great intelligence to have refined tastes, and a high brow is necessary to accommodate such a big brain. Generally, the term is used by people who disdain those who have not developed the sophistication to enjoy, for example, the abstractions of a Fellini film, a Matisse sculpture or a Picasso painting. Highbrows generally are people who, as Gans noted, are interested in issues by which society is defining itself and look to literature and drama for stories on conflicts inherent in the human condition and between the individual and society.

Middlebrow **Middlebrow** tastes recognize some artistic merit but without a high level of sophistication. There is more interest in action than abstractions—in Captain Kirk aboard the starship *Enterprise,* for example, than in the childhood struggles of Ingmar Bergman that shaped his films. In socioeconomic terms, middlebrow appeals to people who take comfort in media portrayals that support their status quo orientation and values.

Lowbrow Someone once made this often-repeated distinction: Highbrows talk about ideas, middlebrows talk about things, and **lowbrows** talk about people. Judging from the circulation success of the *National Enquirer* and other celebrity tabloids, there must be a lot of lowbrows in contemporary America. Hardly any sophistication is needed to recognize the machismo of Rambo, the villainy of Darth Vader, the heroism of Superman or the sexiness of Lara Croft.

The Case Against Pop Art

Pop art is of the moment, including things like body piercings and hip-hop garb—and trendy media fare. Even elitists may have fun with pop, but they traditionally have drawn the line at anyone who mistakes it as having serious artistic merit. Pop art is low art that has immense although generally short-lived popularity.

media ONLINE **Pop Art** Index of pop artists. **www.fi.muni.cz/~toms/PopArt/contents.html**

Elitists see pop art as contrived and artificial. In their view, the people who create **popular art** are masters at identifying what will succeed in the marketplace and then providing it. Pop art, according to this view, succeeds by conning people into liking it. When capri pants were the fashion rage in 2006, it was not because they were superior in comfort, utility or aesthetics, but because promoters sensed that profits could be made in touting them through the mass media as new and cashing in on easily manipulated mass tastes. It was the same with pet rocks, Tickle-Me Elmo and countless other faddy products.

The mass media, according to the critics, are obsessed with pop art. This is partly because the media are the carriers of the promotional campaigns that create popular followings but also because competition within the media creates pressure to be first, to be ahead, to be on top of things. The result, say elitists, is that junk takes precedence over quality.

Much is to be said for this criticism of pop art. The promotion by CBS of the screwball 1960s sitcom *Beverly Hillbillies,* as an example, created an eager audience that otherwise might have been reading Steinbeck's critically respected *Grapes of Wrath*. An elitist might chortle, even laugh, at the unbelievable antics and travails of the Beverly Hillbillies, who had their own charm and attractiveness, but an elitist would be concerned all the while that low art was displacing high art in the marketplace and that the society was the poorer for it.

highbrow, middlebrow and lowbrow ■ Levels of media content sophistication that coincide with audience tastes.

popular art ■ Art that tries to succeed in the marketplace.

pop art revisionism ■ Pop art has inherent value.

Susan Sontag ■ Saw cultural, social value in pop art.

Pop Art Revisionism

Pop art has always had a few champions among intellectuals, although the voices of **pop art revisionism** often have been drowned out in the din of elitist pooh-poohing. In 1965, however, essayist **Susan Sontag** wrote an influential piece, "On Culture and the New Sensibility," which prompted many elitists to take a fresh look at pop art.

"All the News That's Fit to Print"

The New York Times

Late Edition

VOL. CLV . . . No. 53,674 — NEW YORK, THURSDAY, AUGUST 17, 2006 — ONE DOLLAR

EYE ON ELECTION, DEMOCRATS RUN AS WAL-MART FOE

A WAGE AND BENEFIT ISSUE

Candidates Mount Attack as Part of Strategy to Stump on Economy

Breaking Through Adoption's Racial Barriers

Lebanon Army Goes Into Area Hezbollah Rules

But No Effort to Disarm Militia Is in the Plans

INSURGENT BOMBS DIRECTED AT G.I.'S INCREASE IN IRAQ

GRIM MILITARY REPORTS

Attacks on U.S. and Iraqi Forces Soar, Wounding More Americans

Schoolteacher Arrested in JonBenet Ramsey Case

Fear — Disgust — Anger — Determination/Anger — Sadness — Sadness

Faces, Too, Are Searched as U.S. Airports Try to Spot Terrorists

NEW YORK POST — 25 CENTS

LATE CITY FINAL

AMAZING FANTASY

FREE INSIDE Spider-Man ORIGINAL comic book FIRST ISSUE

JONBENET SLAY BUST

Teach 'admits' killing her: Thai cops — PAGES 2-3-4-5

Gearing News to Audience
The level of intellectual interest necessary to enjoy elitist news coverage, like that of the New York *Times,* is more sophisticated than that needed to enjoy popular tabloids edited for a broader audience.

Pop Art as Evocative Sontag made the case that pop art could raise serious issues, just as high art could. She wrote: "The feeling given off by a Rauschenberg painting might be like that of a song by the Supremes." Sontag soon was being called the high priestess of pop intellectualism. More significantly, the Supremes were being taken more seriously, as were a great number of Sontag's avant-garde and obscure pop artist friends.

media ONLINE

Susan Sontag Web site for the author and human rights activist who died in 2004.
www.susansontag.com

Batman Tribute Site A tribute to the campy 60s TV series.
www.geocities.com/~1966

Pop Art as a Societal Unifier In effect, Sontag encouraged people not to look at art on the traditional divisive, class-conscious, elitist-populist continuum. Artistic value, she said, could be found almost anywhere. The word "camp" gained circulation among 1960s elitists who were influenced by Sontag. These highbrows began finding a perversely sophisticated appeal in pop art as diverse as Andy Warhol's banal soup cans and ABC's outrageous *Batman.* The mass media, through which most people experienced Warhol and all people experienced *Batman,* became recognized more broadly than ever as a societal unifier.

The Sontag-inspired revisionist look at pop art coincides with the view of many mass media historians that the media have helped bind the society rather than divide it. In the 1840s, these historians note, books and magazines with national distribution provided Americans of diverse backgrounds and regions with common reference points. Radio did the same even more effectively in the 1940s. Later, so did network television.

In short, the mass media are purveyors of cultural production that contributes to social cohesion, whether it be high art or low art.

media ONLINE **Ken Burns on PBS** A master of making "high art" popular on public TV. **www.pbs.org/kenburns**

High Art as Popular While kitsch may be prominent in media programming, it hardly elbows out all substantive content. In 1991, for example, Ken Burns' public television documentary *The Civil War* outdrew low art prime-time programs on ABC, CBS and NBC five nights in a row. It was a glaring example that high art can appeal to people across almost the whole range of socioeconomic levels and is not necessarily driven out by low art. Burns' documentary was hardly a lone example. Another, also from 1991, was Franco Zeffirelli's movie *Hamlet,* starring pop movie star Mel Gibson, which was marketed to a mass audience yet could hardly be dismissed by elitists as kitsch. In radio, public broadcasting stations, marked by highbrow programming, have become major players for ratings in some cities.

Social Stability

study preview **The mass media create rituals around which people structure their lives. This is one of many ways in which the media contribute to social stability. The media foster socialization throughout adulthood, contributing to social cohesion by affirming beliefs and values and helping reconcile inconsistent values and discrepancies between private behavior and public morality.**

Media-Induced Ritual

Northwest Airlines pilots, flying their Stratocruisers over the Dakotas in the 1950s, could tell when the late-night news ended on WCCO, the powerful Minneapolis radio station. They could see lights at ranches and towns all across the Dakotas going off as people, having heard the news, went to bed. The 10 o'clock WCCO news had become a ritual. Today, for people on the East and West coasts, where most television stations run their late news at 11 p.m., the commonest time to go to bed is 11:30, after the news. In the Midwest, where late newscasts are at 10 o'clock, people tend to go to bed an hour earlier and to rise an hour earlier. Like other rituals that mark a society, media-induced rituals contribute order and structure to the lives of individuals.

The effect of media-induced rituals extends even further. Collectively, the lifestyles of individuals have a broad social effect. Consider just these two effects of evening newspapers, an 1878 media innovation:

media ONLINE **Evening News** PBS ponders the fate of evening television news in the face of changing viewer habits. **www.pbs.org/newshour/media/evening_news**

Evening News E. W. Scripps changed people's habits with his evening newspapers, first in Cleveland in 1878, then elsewhere. Soon, evening papers outnumbered morning papers. The new habit, however, was not so much for evening newspapers as for evening news, as newspaper publishers discovered a hundred years later when television siphoned readers away with evening newscasts. The evening ritual persists, even though the medium is changing as evening papers go out of business or retreat to mornings.

Competitive Shopping In the era before refrigeration and packaged food, household shopping was a daily necessity. When evening newspapers appeared, housewives, who were the primary shoppers of the period, adjusted their routines to read the paper the evening before their morning trips to the market. The new ritual allowed time for more methodical bargain hunting, which sharpened retail competition.

Besides shaping routines, ritual contributes to the mass media's influence as a shaper of culture. At 8:15 a.m. every Sunday, half the television sets in Japan are tuned to *Serial Novel,* a tear-jerking series that began in the 1950s. Because so many people watch, it is a common experience that is one element in the identification of contemporary Japanese society. A ritual that marked U.S. society for years was *Dallas,* on Friday at

mediaPEOPLE

Shonda Rhimes

In high school Shonda Rhimes was a hospital candy striper. There she became familiar with hospital goings-on that led her eventually, as a writer after college, to create the television series *Grey's Anatomy*. The show, introduced in 2005, quickly drew close to 20 million viewers and became an anchor for a resurgent ABC lineup. One measure of the show's impact was a new hep word, *McDreamy*, for a heartthrob hunk. It was the nickname that Rhimes dropped into the script for her tousle-haired brain surgeon character Derek Shepherd.

Rhimes' characters have been praised as people next door. The women especially seem plucked from everyday life with intense relationships and romances, often conflicted and silly, sometimes unpredictable. The guys, well, Rhimes calls them fanatasies.

Grey's cast is marked by a rich racial and ethnic mix. Rhimes, herself of black lineage, says that except for her female and male characters, she never wrote diversity into the script. She assumed that casting would be color blind. It wasn't. When agents sent actors for auditions, all were white. "We had to call back and say, excuse me, where are all the actors of color? And they went, 'Oh, so this is a diverse role.' And I said, they're all diverse roles."

Grey's Diversity Anatomy

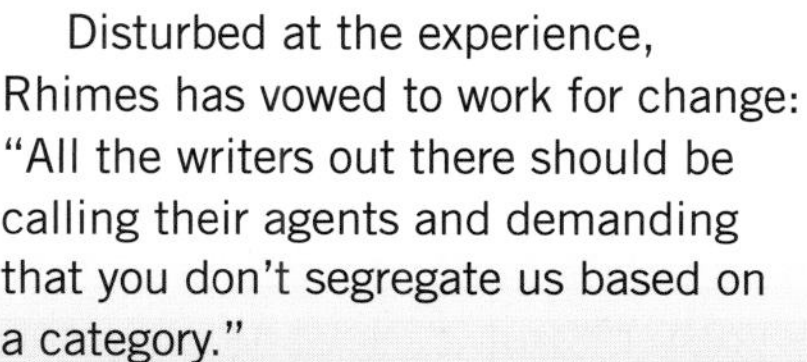

Disturbed at the experience, Rhimes has vowed to work for change: "All the writers out there should be calling their agents and demanding that you don't segregate us based on a category."

For *Grey's*, Rhimes said casting choices were based on chemistry that showed in auditions—not race or ethnicity. For the brain surgeon McDreamy she needed someone witty, caring and also "sexy in a smart way." When Patrick Dempsey, who is white, read the part, Rhimes knew he was right. "It was one of those moments when you're like, 'This is why I'm a writer.' There was just great chemistry." She then molded the script about his ethnicity, as she did too for the other parts.

9 p.m. Eastern time, 8 p.m. Central time. Then came *Survivor* on CBS in 2000. Other rituals are going to Saturday movie matinees, reading a book at bedtime and watching Monday night football.

Media and the Status Quo

Sherry Turkle Dr. Turkle's home page, with a detailed bio and link to MIT's Initiative on Technology and Self. **http://web.mit.edu/sturkle/www**

In their quest for profits through large audiences, the mass media need to tap into their audience's common knowledge and widely felt feelings. Writers for network sitcoms avoid obscure, arcane language. Heroes and villains reflect current morals. Catering this way to a mass audience, the media reinforce existing cultural beliefs and values. People take comfort in learning through the media that they fit into their community and society, which furthers social cohesion. This is socialization continued beyond the formative years. It also is socialization in reverse, with the media taking cues from the society and playing them back.

The media's role in social cohesion has a negative side. Critics say that the media pander to the lowest common denominator by dealing only with things that fit the status quo easily. The result, the critics note, is a thwarting of artistic exploration beyond the mainstream. Critics are especially disparaging of predictable, wooden characters in movies and television and of predictability in many subjects chosen for the news.

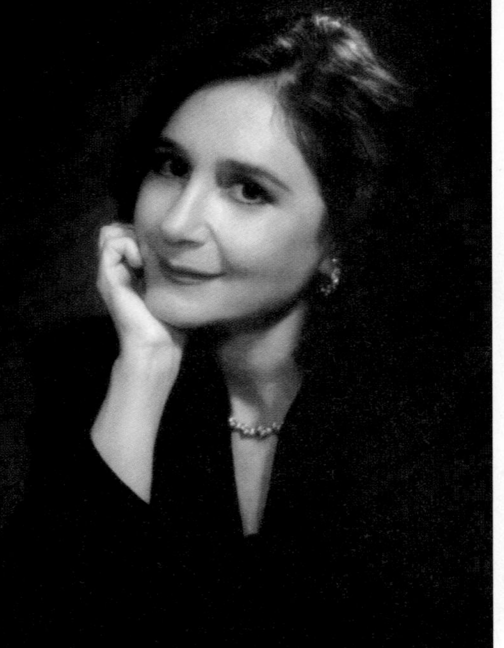

Sherry Turkle

Some people create new personalities for themselves when they're online in Internet chatrooms. This has given rise to computer sociology as a specialized academic field. Sherry Turkle, a professor at the Massachusetts Institute of Technology, is in the vanguard exploring the Internet's influence on behavior. Some people, Turkle has discovered, like the anonymity of the Net to play with personas they wouldn't dare experiment with in face-to-face, real-life situations. Some individuals like their new Net personality so much they integrate it into other aspects of their lives.

A related negative aspect of the media's role as a contributor to social cohesion is that dominant values too often go unchallenged, which means that some wrong values and practices persist. Dudley Clendinen, a newspaper editor who grew up in the South, faults journalists for, in effect, defending racism by not covering it: "The news columns of Southern papers weren't very curious or deep or original in the late 1940s and 1950s. They followed sports and politics actively enough, but the whole rational thrust of Southern culture from the time of John C. Calhoun on had been self-defensive and maintaining. It had to be, to justify the unjustifiable in a society dedicated first to slavery and then to segregation and subservience. Tradition was everything, and the news pages were simply not in the habit of examining the traditions of the South."

Media and Cognitive Dissonance

The media are not always complacent. Beginning in the late 1950s, after the period to which Clendinen was referring, media attention turned to racial segregation. News coverage, literary comment and dramatic and comedy portrayals began to point up flaws in the status quo. Consider the effect, through the mass media, of these individuals on American racism:

- **John Howard Griffin.** In 1959 Griffin, a white journalist, dyed his skin black for a six-week odyssey through the South. His book *Black Like Me* was an inside look at being black in America. It had special credibility for the white majority because Griffin was white.
- **George Wallace.** The mass audience saw the issue of segregation personified in news coverage of Governor George Wallace physically blocking black students from attending the University of Alabama. The indelible impression was that segregation could be defended only by a clenched fist and not by reason.
- **Martin Luther King Jr.** News photographers captured the courage and conviction of Martin Luther King Jr. and other civil rights activists, black and white, taking great risks through civil disobedience to object to racist public policies.
- **Archie Bunker.** Archie Bunker, a television sitcom character, made a laughingstock of bigots.

media ONLINE **Cognitive Dissonance** A briefing on the psychological theory, from Wikipedia. **http://en.wikipedia.org/wiki/Cognitive_dissonance**

To some people, the media coverage and portrayals seemed to exacerbate racial tensions. In the longer run, however, media attention contributed to a new consensus through a phenomenon that psychologists call **cognitive dissonance.** Imagine white racists as they saw George Wallace giving way to federal troops under orders from the White House. The situation pitted against each other two values held by individual racists: segregation as a value and an ordered society as symbolized by the presidency. Suddenly aware that their personal values were in terrible disharmony, or dissonance, many of these racists avoided the issue. Instead of continuing to express racism among family and friends, many tended to be silent. They may have been as racist as ever, but they were quiet or watched their words carefully. Gradually, their untenable view is fading into social unacceptability. This is not to say that racism does not persist. It does and continues to manifest itself in American life though, in many ways, in forms much muted since the media focused on the experiment of John Howard Griffin, the clenched fist of George Wallace and the crusade of Martin Luther King Jr.

When the media go beyond pap and the predictable, they are examining the cutting-edge issues by which the society defines its values. Newsmagazines, newspapers and television, using new printing, photography and video technology in the late 1960s, put war graphically into U.S. living rooms, pointing up all kinds of discrepancies between Pentagon claims and the Vietnam reality. The glamorized, heroic view of war, which had persisted through history, was countered by media depictions of the blood and death. Unable to resolve the discrepancies, some people withdrew into silence. Others reassessed their views and then, with changed positions or more confident in their original positions, they engaged in a dialogue from which a consensus emerged. And the

cognitive dissonance ■ Occurs when people realize their values are inconsistent.

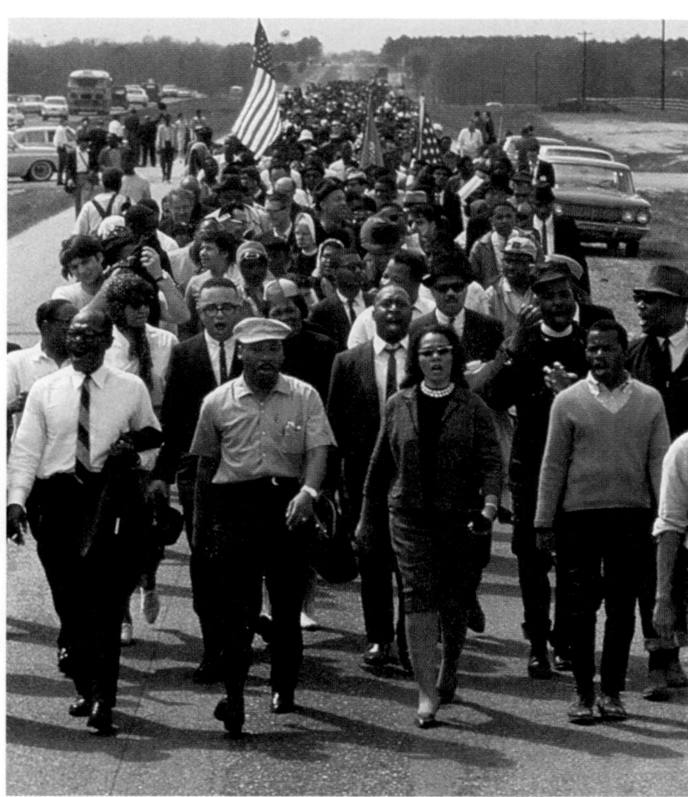

Cognitive Dissonance Many white Americans from racist backgrounds found themselves challenging their own values when the federal government adopted proactive civil rights policies in the 1950s and 1960s. This dissonance escalated as these people followed news coverage of the long-overdue demands of blacks for fair treatment, as in this 1963 march. Some white racists resolved the discrepancy by abandoning racism. Many others simply retreated from discussion on the issue.

United States, the mightiest power in history, began a militarily humiliating withdrawal. It was democracy at work, slowly and painfully, but at work.

During the Iraq war of the 2000s, cognitive dissonance set in between the Bush administration's premise for war, that the Saddam Hussein regime had a trigger finger on weapons of mass destruction, and growing evidence that there were no such weapons. The media attention to the issue forced the Bush administration to back away from its claim.

Agenda-Setting and Status Conferral

Media attention lends a legitimacy to events, individuals and issues that does not extend to things that go uncovered. This conferring of status occurs through the media's role as agenda-setters. It puts everybody on the same wavelength, or at least a similar one, which contributes to social cohesion by focusing our collective attention on issues we can address together. Otherwise, each of us could be going in separate directions, which would make collective action difficult if not impossible.

Examples abound of how media attention spotlights certain issues. An especially poignant case occurred in 1998 when a gay University of Wyoming student, Matthew Shepard, was savagely beaten, tied to a fence outside of town and left to die. It was tragic gay-bashing, and coverage of the event moved gay rights higher on the national agenda. Coverage of the gruesome death was an example of the media agenda-setting and of status conferral.

Women's International News Gathering Service Giving women a voice in the news, WINGS is an independent radio production company producing news and current affairs stories by and about women.
www.wings.org

Project for Excellence in Journalism Initiative started by journalists to raise the standards of American journalism and provide the industry with examples of good journalism.
www.journalism.org

Morality in Media An organization established by a Catholic priest to combat obscenity and uphold decency standards in the media.
www.moralityinmedia.org

Media and Morality

A small-town wag once noted that people read the local newspaper not to find out what is going on, which everybody already knows, but to find out who got caught. The observation was profound. The mass media, by reporting deviant behavior, help to enforce society's moral order. When someone is arrested for burglary and convicted, it reaffirms for everybody that human beings have property rights.

case STUDY

Media Advocacy: Will It Make a Difference?

Immigration Demonstration An estimated 500,000 people took to the streets in Los Angeles to protest a proposal in Congress to criminalize millions of unauthorized workers in the United States from other countries. Critics faulted the news media for picking up the protesters' arguments in the coverage. What all sides agreed on was that news coverage kept the issue on the public agenda.

A few years ago hardly anyone cared, but pick up any newspaper today and you'll find a story about immigration. It's a hot-button issue filled with emotion, conflict and drama. Many claim the immigration debate parallels the debate about black civil rights.

As it did 50 years ago, the news media brought the immigration story to the forefront of American consciousness, and today's media advocacy mirrors the role of the media in the older civil rights movement.

In California in March 2006 a few advocacy groups wanted to organize a protest to a bill introduced by Wisconsin Republican Senator James Sensenbrenner and approved by the House of Representatives. The bill would criminalize millions of unauthorized workers and punish those who helped them, including social and religious groups. It also called for the construction of a wall along the U.S.-Mexico border.

"At the beginning, about 10 groups wanted to organize a protest in Los Angeles," said Noé Hernández, an immigrant rights activist. "Then they invited members of the Spanish press, and everything changed." Radio DJs decided to broadcast a call directly to the community. A Spanish-language newspaper published articles in the days leading up to the protest. TV stations helped mobilize people to go to the protests with announcements of details for participating.

The response to the Latino media campaign stunned the mainstream news media, which stepped up coverage of the movement. An estimated 500,000 people took to the streets of Los Angeles. About 300,000 participated in Chicago. Similar protests were held in other cities across the country. In Atlanta 80,000 Latinos did not show up for work one day as part of a citywide boycott organized by the March 17 Alliance, a coalition of radio broadcasters, religious and community leaders.

The media were criticized, mostly by those who leaned to the right politically. They charged that the news coverage was advocacy. Critics on the left criticized the words used in the media to frame the debate. Saurav Sarkar of Fairness & Accuracy in Reporting said: "The mainstream media helped to set the terms of the debate by endlessly repeating catchphrases and buzzwords like *porous borders* and *comprehensive immigration reform*."

The words most often criticized were *illegal* and *alien*. The National Association of Hispanic Journalists said their use dehumanized people and stereotyped them as having committed a crime. An estimated 40 percent of the group referred to as *illegal immigrants* initially had valid visas but did not return to their native countries when their visas expired. Some former students fell into this category. The National Association of Hispanic Journalists suggested *undocumented immigrant* or *undocumented worker*. The Pew Hispanic Center *suggested unauthorized migrant*.

However it was worded, the media set the country's agenda to debate the immigration question. The question for the media is, will the future show its advocacy played as important a role in changing society as it did a half century ago?

WHAT DO YOU THINK?

1. Should the media be setting the agenda for national debates like the immigration issue?
2. In the black civil rights movement cognitive dissonance helped change society. Do you think the same thing will happen this time?

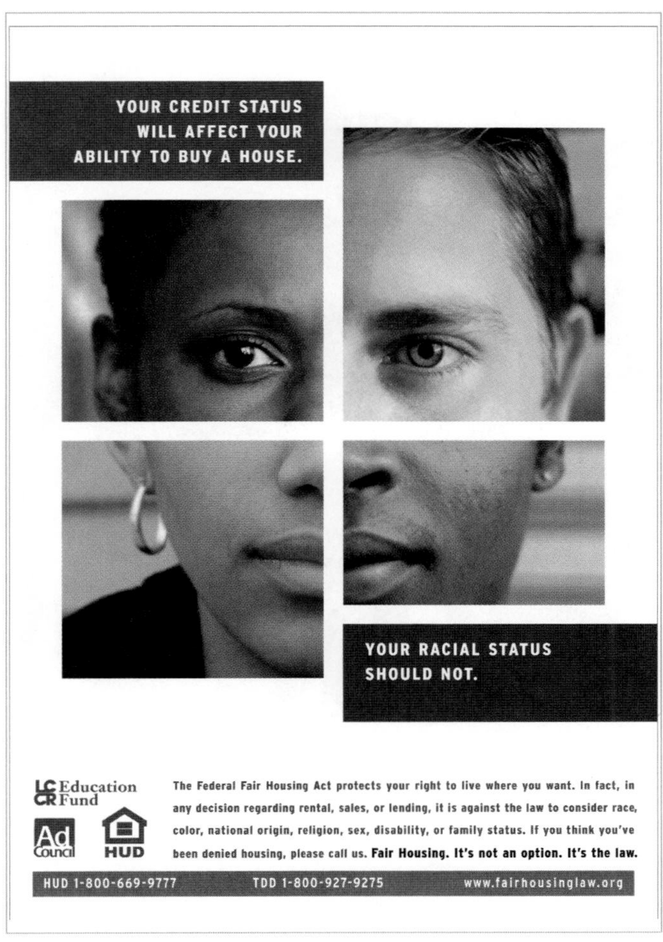

YOUR CREDIT STATUS WILL AFFECT YOUR ABILITY TO BUY A HOUSE.
YOUR RACIAL STATUS SHOULD NOT.
LC CR Education Fund
Ad Council
HUD
The Federal Fair Housing Act protects your right to live where you want. In fact, in any decision regarding rental, sales, or lending, it is against the law to consider race, color, national origin, religion, sex, disability, or family status. If you think you've been denied housing, please call us. Fair Housing. It's not an option. It's the law.
HUD 1-800-669-9777
TDD 1-800-927-9275
www.fairhousinglaw.org

Public Service Major agencies produce public-service advertisements on a rotating basis for the Ad Council. These magazines and newspaper ads, as well as television and radio public-service announcements, are distributed free. The media run them at no charges. The Council chooses about a dozen organizations a year to benefit from the in-house creative genius at the agencies that produce the ads *pro bono.*

Beyond police blotter news, the mass media are agents for reconciling discrepancies between **private actions and public morality.** Individually, people tolerate minor infractions of public morality, such as taking pens home from work. Some people even let life-threatening behavior such as child abuse go unreported. When the deviant behavior is publicly exposed, however, toleration ceases, and social processes come into action that reconcile the deviance with public morality. The reconciling process

private actions and public morality ■ Dichotomy that exposes discrepancies between behavior and values.

Diversity in the News

Experts agree on a number of methods journalists can use to make their stories less discriminatory. You can also use these points to judge the news you see, hear or read.

- Don't generalize. Use quotes or paraphrase what individuals say.
- Get information about the activities of minorities from them.
- Balance coverage of conflicts and negative coverage with coverage of common ground and activities. Don't treat events as typical for a group of people. Find the heroes as well as the victims and villains.
- Provide a forum for all parties in conflict, recognizing that there may be more than two sides involved and the complexity of the conflict may call for including contextual material. Expand expert sources beyond government officials. Don't always rely on the same spokesperson.
- Avoid stereotyping minority groups and individuals. Cover minorities in interaction with other groups. Don't always link certain groups to particular stories.

Cindy Sheehan
Even strident supporters of the Bush war on Iraq could relate at an emotional level to Cindy Sheehan, whose son Casey was killed in combat. This kind of cognitive dissonance can be pivotal in silencing people who otherwise might be vocal on an issue.

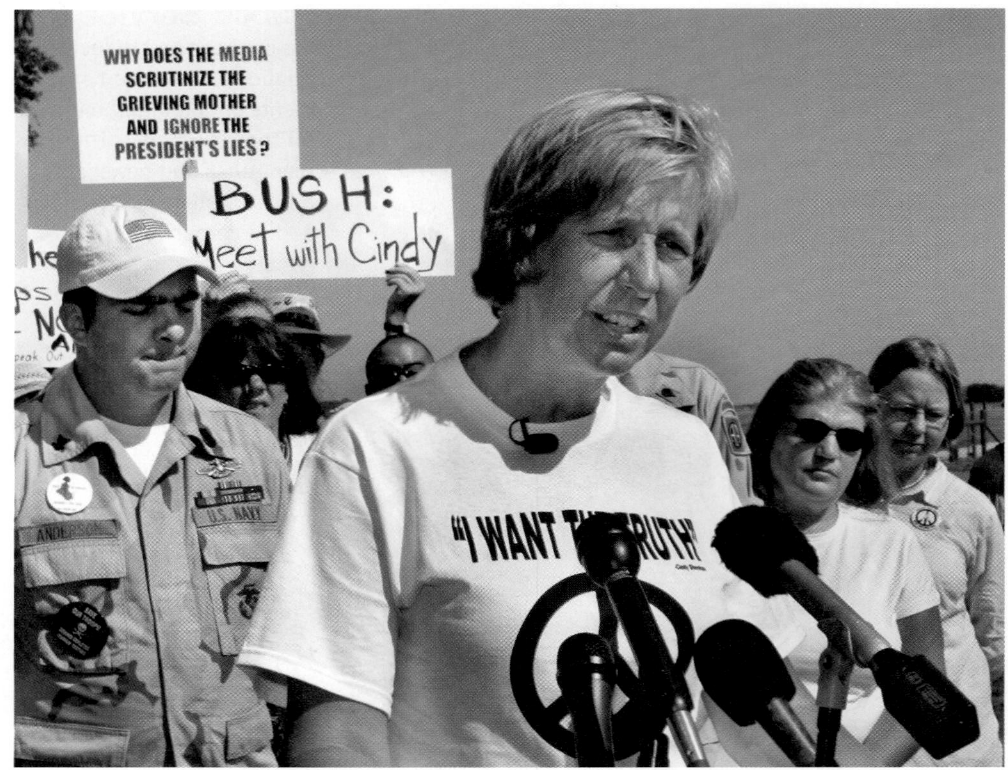

maintains public norms and values. Consider Douglas Ginsburg. In the 1970s Ginsburg, a young law professor, smoked marijuana at a few parties. It was a misdemeanor, but Ginsburg's friends tolerated it, and not a word was said publicly. In 1988, however, when President Reagan nominated Ginsburg to the U.S. Supreme Court, reporter Nina Totenberg of National Public Radio reported Ginsburg's transgressions. Exposed, he withdrew his name. There was no choice. His private action, publicly exposed, could not be tolerated, and his withdrawal maintained public norms and values, without which a society cannot exist.

Cultural Transmission

study preview **The mass media transmit cultural values through history. Past generations talk to us through mass media, mostly books, just as we, often not realizing it, talk to future generations. The media also diffuse values and ideas contemporaneously.**

Historical Transmission

Human beings have a compulsion to leave the wisdom they have accumulated for future generations. There is a compulsion, too, to learn from the past. In olden times, people gathered around fires and in temples to hear storytellers. It was a ritual through which people learned the values that governed their community. This is a form of **historical transmission.**

historical transmission ■ Communication of cultural values to later generations.

Five thousand years ago, the oral tradition was augmented when Middle Eastern traders devised an alphabet to keep track of inventories, transactions and rates of exchange. When paper was invented, clay tablets gave way to scrolls and eventually books, which became the primary vehicle for storytelling. Religious values were passed on in holy books. Military chronicles laid out the lessons of war. Literature provided lessons by exploring the nooks and crannies of the human condition.

Books remain the primary repository of our culture. For several centuries it has been between hard covers, in black ink on paper, that the experiences, lessons and wisdom of our forebears have been recorded for posterity. Other mass media today share in the preservation and transmission of our culture over time. Consider these archives:

- **Museum of Television and Radio** in New York, with 1,200 hours of television documentaries; great performances, productions, debuts and series; and a sample of top-rated shows.
- **Library for Communication and Graphic Arts** at Ohio State University, whose collection includes editorial cartoons.
- **Vanderbilt Television News Archive** in Nashville, Tennessee, with 7,000 hours of network nightly news programs and special coverage such as political conventions and space shots.

Contemporary Transmission

The mass media also transmit values among contemporary communities and societies, sometimes causing changes that otherwise would not occur. This is known as **contemporary transmission.** Anthropologists have documented that mass communication can change society. When Edmund Carpenter introduced movies in an isolated New Guinea village, the men adjusted their clothing toward the Western style and even

contemporary transmission Communication of cultural values to different cultures.

Tommy Lee Mass media attention to cutting-edge performers, especially those with dubious themes, worry traditionalists about disturbing values being transmitted to a new generation. The concern is triggered by the demonstrable effect of other offbeat media subjects, like the relatively trivial imitation of attire and hairstyles, and also the media's less easily documented diffusion of "innovations" that leads eventually to fundamental social change.

Media History Project Promoting the study of media history, from petroglyphs to pixels.
www.mediahistory.umn.edu

The Museum of Broadcast Communications Link to some vast archives of radio and television history.
www.museum.tv

Television News Archive Housed at Vanderbilt University in Nashville, Tennessee, the archives contain more than 30,000 evening news broadcasts.
http://tvnews.vanderbilt.edu

remodeled their houses. This phenomenon, which scholars call **diffusion of innovations,** occurs when ideas move through the mass media. Consider the following:

- **American Revolution.** Colonists up and down the Atlantic seaboard took cues on what to think and how to act from newspaper reports on radical activities, mostly in Boston, in the decade before the Declaration of Independence. These included inflammatory articles against the 1765 Stamp Act and accounts of the Boston Tea Party in 1773.
- **Music, fashion and pop culture.** In modern-day pop culture the cues come through the media, mostly from New York, Hollywood and Nashville.
- **Third World innovation.** The United Nations creates instructional films and radio programs to promote agricultural reform in less developed parts of the world. Overpopulated areas have been targets of birth control campaigns.
- **Democracy in China.** As China opened itself to Western tourists, commerce and mass media in the 1980s, the people glimpsed Western democracy and prosperity, which precipitated pressure on the Communist government to westernize and resulted in the 1989 Tiananmen Square confrontation. A similar phenomenon was a factor in the glasnost relaxations in the Soviet Union in the late 1980s.
- **Demise of Main Street.** Small-town businesses are boarding up throughout the United States as rural people see advertisements from regional shopping malls, which are farther away but offer greater variety and lower prices than Main Street.

Scholars note that the mass media can be given too much credit for the diffusion of innovations. Diffusion almost always needs reinforcement through interpersonal communication. Also, the diffusion is hardly ever a one-shot hypodermic injection but a process that requires redundancy in messages over an extended period. The 1989 outburst for democracy in China did not happen because one Chinese person read Thomas Paine one afternoon, nor do rural people suddenly abandon their local Main Street for a Wal-Mart 40 miles away. The diffusion of innovations typically involves three initial steps in which the mass media can be pivotal:

- **Awareness.** Individuals and groups learn about alternatives, new options and possibilities.
- **Interest.** Once aware, people need to have their interest further whetted.
- **Evaluation.** By considering the experience of other people, as relayed by the mass media, individuals evaluate whether they wish to adopt an innovation.

The adoption process has two additional steps in which the media play a small role: the trial stage, in which an innovation is given a try, and the final stage, in which the innovation is either adopted or rejected.

Mass Media and Fundamental Change

study preview **The detribalization theory says the written word changed tribal communities by deemphasizing interpersonal communication. Written communication engaged the mind, not the senses, and according to the theory, a lonely, cerebral-based culture resulted. Now, as sense-intensive television displaces written communication, retribalization is creating a global village.**

Human Alienation

diffusion of innovations ■ Process through which news, ideas, values, information spread.

An intriguing, contrarian assessment of the media's effects on human society was laid out by Canadian theorist Marshall McLuhan in the 1960s. McLuhan argued that the print media had **alienated** human beings from their natural state. In pre-mass media times, McLuhan said, people acquired their awareness about their world through their own observation and experience and through their fellow human beings, whom they saw face to face and with whom they communicated orally. As McLuhan saw it, this was a pristine communal existence—rich in that it involved all the senses—sight, sound, smell, taste and touch. This communal, tribal state was eroded by the written word, which involved the insular, meditative act of reading. The printing press, he said, compounded this alienation from humankind's tribal roots. The written word, by engaging the mind, not the senses, begat **detribalization,** and the printing press accelerated it.

According to McLuhan, the printed word even changed human thought processes. In their tribal state, he said, human beings responded spontaneously to everything that was happening around them. The written word, in contrast, required people to concentrate on an author's relatively narrow, contrived set of data that led from Point A to Point B to Point C. Following the linear serial order of the written word was a lonely, cerebral activity, unlike participatory tribal communication, which had an undirected, helter-skelter spontaneity.

Television and the Global Village

McLuhan saw television bringing back tribalization. While books, magazines and newspapers engaged the mind, television engaged the senses. In fact, the television screen could be so loaded with data that it could approximate the high level of sensual stimuli that people found in their environments back in the tribal period of human existence. **Retribalization,** he said, was at hand because of the new, intensely sensual communication that television could facilitate. Because television could far exceed the reach of any previous interpersonal communication, McLuhan called the new tribal village a **global village.**

With retribalization, McLuhan said, people will abandon the print media's linear intrusions on human nature. Was McLuhan right? His disciples claim that certain earmarks of written communication—complex story lines, logical progression and causality—are less important to today's young people, who grew up with sense-intensive television. They point to the music videos that excite the senses but make no linear sense. Many teachers say that children are having a harder time finding significance in the totality of a lesson. Instead, children fasten on to details.

As fascinating as McLuhan was, he left himself vulnerable to critics who point out that, in a true nonlinear spirit, he was selective with evidence and never put his ideas to rigorous scholarly examination. McLuhan died in 1980. Today, the jury remains divided, agreeing only that he was a provocative thinker.

alienation ■ Dissatisfaction with individual and cultural deviations from basic nature.

detribalization ■ The removal of humankind from natural, tribal state.

retribalization ■ Restoring humankind to natural, tribal state.

global village ■ Instantaneous connection of every human being.

CHAPTER 17 Wrap-Up

The media contribute both to social stability and to change. A lot of media content gives comfort to audiences by reinforcing existing social values. At the same time, media attention to nonmainstream ideas, in both news and fiction forms, requires people to reassess their values and, over time, contributes to social change.

Questions for Review

1. Why are mass media more interested in reaching large audiences than in contributing to cultural sensitivity?
2. How do the mass media contribute to stability in the society?
3. What are historical and cultural transmission?
4. How did scholar Marshall McLuhan foresee that television would ease the human alienation that he

said was created by the mass-produced written word?

Questions for Critical Thinking

1. Why do the mass media find little room for great works that could elevate the cultural sensitivity of the society?
2. Explain essayist Susan Sontag's point that the mass media bring culturally significant works to mass audiences through the popularization process.
3. Give examples of how people shape their everyday lives around rituals created by the mass media. Also, give examples of how the mass media respond to social rituals in deciding what to present and how and when to present it.
4. Why would a radical social reformer object to most mass media content?
5. How has cognitive dissonance created through the mass media worked against racial separatism in American society since the 1950s?
6. How do the mass media help to determine the issues that society sees as important?
7. How do the media contribute to social order and cohesion by reporting private acts that deviate from public morality? You might want to consider the case of President Bill Clinton and Monica Lewinsky.
8. Give examples of the mass media allowing cultural values to be communicated through history to future societies. Also, give examples of contemporary cultural transmission.
9. Explain scholar Marshall McLuhan's theory that the mass-produced written word has contributed to an alienation of human beings from their true nature. How did McLuhan think television could reverse this alienation?

Deepening Your media LITERACY

Are Christian fundamentalists savvy media users?

STEP 1 The fundamentalist Christian movement in the United States is often in the news, but its members often don't like the way the group is represented. They have taken matters into their own hands and are creating their own media opportunities.

Dig Deeper

STEP 2 James Dobson, perhaps the most powerful figure in the Dominionist movement, is the founder and chairman of Focus on the Family. Dominionists take the beliefs of the Protestant Christian evangelical fundamentalists a bit further. They believe in more than political participation—they believe that it is their destiny to dominate the political process, to govern with a political and judicial system based on the Old Testament. While teaching at the University of Southern California, Dobson wrote *Dare to Discipline,* which encourages parents to spank their children and has sold over 3.5 million copies since its release in 1970. Dobson employs 1,300 people, sends out 4 million pieces of mail each month, and is heard on radio broadcasts in 99 countries. His estimated listening audience is more than 200 million worldwide; in the United States alone he appears on 100 television stations each day. Not all fundamentalists endorse the Dominionist creed, but many on the Christian right believe that Christians are under attack. To counter that "problem," the National Religious Broadcasters Association boasts 1,600-plus members and claims to reach up to 141 million listeners and viewers. NRB President Dr. Frank Wright says that of 13,838 stations in the United States, 15 percent are religiously formatted. He puts it this way: "Does it strike you that we are the first generation in the history of the world that might see every nation, tongue, and tribe reached with the Gospel?"

What Do You Think?

STEP 3 Answer these questions:

1. In this chapter you learned that media attention lends legitimacy to events. How could this apply to the way the Christian right and the Dominionist movement are using the media they control?
2. Do you think the Dominionist movement is counting on cognitive dissonance to convert new followers? If so, how?
3. Christian fundamentalists often make fun of elitists and intellectuals. Why?
4. Have the Dominionists and the fundamental Christian movement benefited from their use of the media? What do you foresee for the movement, the media and society?

Keeping Up to Date

Recommended are *Journal of Popular Culture, Journal of American Culture* and *Journal of International Popular Culture,* all scholarly publications.

For Further Learning

Leo W. Jeffres. *Mass Media Process and Effects,* Second Edition. Waveland. 1994.

Professor Jeffres discusses the variety of perspectives that attempt to understand the mysterious process of mass communication and then focuses on the effects of the media on individuals and society.

Robert M. Liebert, Joyce N. Spatkin and Emily S. Davidson. *The Early Window: Effects on Television on Children and Youth,* Third Edition. Pergamon, 1988.

This compendium covers the broad range of studies on television and children with special emphasis on research into media-depicted violence.

Joshua Meyrowitz. *No Sense of Place: The Impact of Electronic Media on Social Behavior.* Oxford, 1985.

Professor Meyrowitz says television allows everybody, adult and child alike, to eavesdrop into other generations, which has eroded if not undone intergenerational distinctions that once were essential components of the social structure.

Williard D. Rowland Jr. *The Politics of TV Violence: Uses of Communication Policy.* Sage, 1983.

Rowland argues that mass media have used a heavy hand behind the scenes to dilute research fundings that on-screen violence begets real-life violence. Rowland, a scholar, goes back to the Payne studies in the late 1920s.

Wilbur Schramm, Jack Lyle and Edwin Parker. *Television in the Lives of Our Children.* Stanford University Press, 1961.

A seminal work.

Jean-Jacques Gomez
The French judge bridled the Internet by insisting that content remained subject to national laws.

chapter 18 Global Mass Media

In this chapter you will learn:

- **Technology has increased the difficulty of nations to control mass media content.**
- **Mass media are globalizing under a few companies.**
- **Globalization works against indigenous and distinctive media content.**
- **Values from dominant cultures are subsuming other cultures.**
- **Models use diverse variables to sort out national media systems.**
- **News agencies were the first global media operations.**
- **Global media companies are based mostly in the United States and Europe.**
- **Variations exist among national media systems, even in democracies.**
- **China is shielding its population from foreign mass media influences with some success.**
- **Many nations still struggle with the concept of an independent mass media.**
- **Rules for war and combat reporting continue to evolve.**

The heady days of people thinking the Internet was ushering in a new era of human existence came to an abrupt end in 2000. In a Paris courtroom Judge Jean-Jacques Gomez asserted the sovereignty of France over Internet messages crossing into French territory. The judge told the giant Internet portal Yahoo, based in the United States, to conform with a French ban on Nazi memorabilia. Gomez ordered Yahoo immediately to stop giving French surfers access to Nazi auction items. Kicking and screaming, Yahoo complied.

Yahoo's founder, Jerry Yang, had bought into the idea of early Internet gurus who foresaw a new world order. National governments, the traditional major player in human events, would be displaced by the decentralized routing system of the Internet. The Internet had no hubs where governments could assert control—no printing presses, no transmission towers. The result, as these futurists saw it, would be a new empowerment of individuals to govern their own affairs individually through one-on-one global communication and an array of chatroom-like communities so numerous and diverse that government regulation would be impossible. The exuberant vision of these thinkers was a coming world with individuals liberated from the constraints of oppressive societies and from government meddling.

Judge Gomez ruined the party.

It started in February 2000. A fervent opponent of neo-Nazism, French historian Marc Knobel spotted a yahoo.com auction site with hundreds of Nazi items—even replicas of the hydrogen cyanide canisters used in concentration-camp exterminations. How could this be? France had laws that embodied the dominant post-World War II repulsion of the French people against anything Nazi. Yahoo found itself in a French court.

Out of court Yahoo's quick response to Knobel was to get with it. Acting on the notion that a new world order represented by the Internet was at hand, Yahoo believed that laws against individual communication and media content had suddenly become archaic. These laws, as Yahoo saw it, were remnants of the old world order in which nation-states controlled destinies. Yahoo asserted too that it was technically impossible to stop Internet messages at national borders. To regulate against Nazi memorabilia would mean shutting down the Internet and thwarting free expression and the promise of an Internet-facilitated better world.

In Gomez's court, however, Yahoo was less esoteric. Yahoo used a conventional argument that recognized national sovereignty. It was an ironic twist considering Yahoo's government-as-suddenly-irrelevant mindset. Why, Yahoo asked, should France be allowed to impose its laws on a company based in the United States, where the national Constitution allowed for a greater tolerance of obnoxious media content, allowing even the sale of Nazi stuff? Yahoo pointed out that the computers hosting the Nazi auction materials were located not on French soil but in California.

Judge Gomez would have none of it. The presence of Nazi stuff at the Yahoo auction site was an "offense to the collective memory" of France, he said. When Gomez learned that Yahoo in fact was using a Swedish web site to speed up access for French surfers, suddenly the argument that the U.S. Constitution protected Yahoo was entirely irrelevant. Yahoo, it turned out, was in the process of setting up sites all over the globe to mirror the content from its home-base computers. Judge Gomez also learned of new technology that could identify Internet content on the basis of its geographic source. Indeed, messages directed at France could be screened.

In a single court case, Judge Gomez radically reined in the wild optimism prevalent in early Silicon Valley about the Internet as an agent of fundamental social change. True, the Internet was a significant new player in human communication. But not as significant as Yahoo's Jerry Yang once saw it.

Mass Media and Nation-States

study preview **The ability of national governments to control media content is diminishing with the technology that is allowing the globalization of the mass media.**

Global Communication

After the 2005 terrorist subway and bus bombings in London, the British news media flooded the streets and airwaves with stories about the suspects. Understandably, coverage was emotional. When the first arrests were made, the front page of the tabloid *Sun* blared: "Got the Bastards." Then the media went silent. British law forbids news coverage once a criminal charge has been filed. The rationale is not to prejudice potential jurors. It's a silly law by standards in the United States, where jury contamination is avoided through jury selection procedures, jury sequestering and relocation of trials. But the British system has accomplished the same purpose too—until now.

Hungry for news about the terrorism investigation and the people arrested, Britons needed to look no further than the Internet. The Internet's most-used coding structure is called the World Wide Web for a reason. And just down the street, newsstands stocked foreign newspapers and magazines full of ongoing revelations about the suspects. Legally, the imported publications, as well as Internet coverage, could be banned under the 1981 Contempt of Court Act. But how? The logistics would be overwhelming.

Throughout the world, the power that governments once wielded over mass communication has eroded. The challenge for governments, especially in countries with oppressive regimes, is how to impede unwanted messages from outside getting in.

Thomas Friedman
The New York *Times* columnist had an epiphany while in India researching a Discovery documentary: Computer software has so empowered individuals that social, business and other infrastructures are in a fundamental transformation. Friedman calls it Globalization 3.0, the third fundamental change in global power structures in human history.

Friedman Globalization Model

Globalization has been explained in a sweeping historical way by analyst Thomas Friedman of the New York *Times*. Friedman sees three great eras in human society over the past 500 years, beginning with the rise of great nation-states like Spain, England and France.

Nation-States The world shrank, says Friedman, as these powerful governments projected their influence beyond their borders roughly from 1492 to 1800. Nation-states used brawn in the form of horsepower, wind power and eventually steam power to exert their will and facilitate commerce controlled by their citizens.

Multinationals After 1800 multinational companies themselves became the prime drivers of globalized commerce with their own steamships and railroads. The efficiency of long-distance shipping kept improving. In the late 1990s, when communication costs dropped dramatically with new networks of orbiting satellites, multinational companies displaced even more of the power of the nation-states.

Decentralization New communication technology, notably the decentralized Internet, has empowered individuals as never before to chart their own courses. The umbrellas of multinationals and nation-states are becoming less relevant.

media ONLINE **Thomas Friedman** Official web site for this author and New York *Time*'s columnist.
www.thomaslfriedman.com

Global Conglomeration

study preview **Media titan Rupert Murdoch has created the first global content creation and delivery system under a single corporate umbrella, but he's not alone in putting together a global media empire. Many media companies have international operations, though none as comprehensive. Still developing are the ways in which global media companies adapt to the Internet.**

Multinational Companies

The mass media have had international sales for centuries, going back to early book printers. Until the 20th century, however, media companies designed little specifically for export.

media ONLINE **Who Owns What** Prepared by the *Columbia Journalism Review* to show how large media companies control many aspects of mass communication in the United States and around the world.
www.cjr.org/tools/owners

Reader's Digest *Reader's Digest* is now published in more than 20 countries. From the United States web site you can access foreign web versions.
www.rd.com

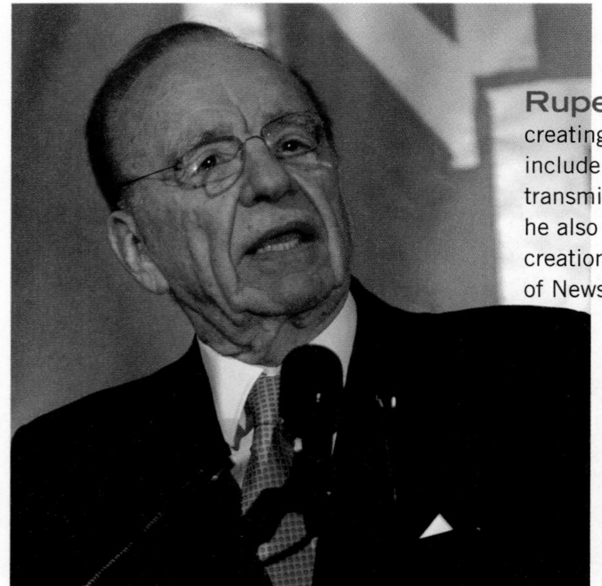

Rupert Murdoch The future of the mass media business is in both creating and distributing content under a single roof—his. Murdoch's companies include the DirectTV, BSkyB and Star TV satellite television with multicontinental transmission. His news and entertainment companies all produce content that he also distributes. The future, as Murdoch sees it, is combining content creation and distribution. Here, Murdoch is addressing the American Society of Newspaper Editors about the future of the news business.

Foreign Branches A new awareness of potential markets abroad came in the 1930s, typified by the *Reader's Digest*'s first foray overseas. The magazine, born in the United States in 1922, had obvious international potential. In 1938 publishers DeWitt and Lila Wallace established a British edition. It was largely the same as the U.S. edition, but British editors replaced some articles. Today, the magazine is published in 18 languages. Some editions are extensively edited for distinct audiences.

In the same spirit U.S. movie producers began eyeing foreign markets in the 1930s and added subtitles or dubbed dialogue.

Acquisitions Another model for international media companies emerged in the 1980s. Media companies began buying up foreign media companies. Bertelsmann of Germany bought its way into many foreign markets. Acquisitions included the RCA and Arista record labels in the United States, then 14 women's magazines bought from the New York *Times,* then the venerable U.S. book company Random House. Other Bertelsmann properties in the United States today include Bantam, Dell and Doubleday books. Bertelsmann has 200 operating units with 44,000 employees in 25 countries.

Mergers Some media companies have found synergies in merging. A merger of Hachette of France and Filapacchi of Italy created cross-fertilization opportunities that generated more profits from existing products. The new company also exported concepts, such as the French fashion magazine *Elle* being adapted for additional markets, including the United States.

Alliances Most media companies rely on other companies for foreign distribution of their content. Viacom, for example, sells its television programs to existing networks and stations in other countries. Several magazine publishers have agreements with native companies to produce and distribute foreign editions.

media ONLINE **News Corporation** Rupert Murdoch's global empire. **www.newscorp.com**

Content-Distribution Model Media mogul **Rupert Murdoch,** known mostly for his 20th Century/Fox movie and Fox television empires, has moved media globalization into new directions by combining media content-creation companies and content-distribution companies under a super-corporate umbrella. Murdoch's orbiting satellites companies, including BSkyB, DirecTV and Star TV, beam signals directly to consumers, bypassing traditional delivery media. With 20th Century and Fox, he also generates content to supply his delivery system—no middlemen.

The content-distribution model is not new. Newspapers, for example, have handled their own distribution historically. Murdoch, however, has implemented the model on an unprecedented global scale.

The Internet and Globalization

New technologies are opening the way for more companies to seek global audiences directly, with no middlemen, at low cost. E-books, for example, don't require expensive presses to produce. Nor do they need massive warehouses or require expensive shipping. Producers of radio and television programs can use streaming instead of having to negotiate complex deals with networks or individual stations for distribution. In short, the Internet can eliminate middlemen.

Rupert Murdoch ■ Australian-born owner of the global company News Corporation.

Easy access to the Internet opens opportunities for upstarts to reach global audiences. Whether new companies can establish Internet followings that compete with the majors, which also have created presences on the Web, isn't clear. With the massiveness of their repertoires the major players certainly have a leg up.

The question for media critics, concerned about conglomeration on a global scale, is whether the Internet will level the playing field to give little guys a chance. The resulting diversity would ease concerns about the media becoming concentrated in only a few hands. If the majors continue to dominate the creation of content, as well as delivery, the critics of conglomeration will have added cause for alarm.

media ONLINE **eBooks.com** View best-selling e-books in all the usual categories, from business to romance to self-help. **www.ebooks.com**

Effects of Globalization

study preview **Foreign ownership worries some media critics. At stake, as these critics see it, is control of the direction of cultural advancement—something they believe should not be farmed out. Other experts say that global media companies are neutral as to content and have no ideological preferences except making money.**

media ONLINE **Media Channel** A nonprofit, public interest supersite dedicated to global media issues. **www.mediachannel.org**

Cultural Subversiveness

Experts disagree about the effect of globalization. Some critics, including respected media commentator Ben Bagdikian, fret that "anonymous superpowers" such as Bertelsmann are a potential threat to U.S. cultural autonomy and the free flow of information and ideas. In his book *The New Media Monopoly* Bagdikian said: "The highest levels of world finance have become intertwined with the highest levels of mass media ownership, with the result of tighter control over the systems on which most of the public depends for its news and information."

Other observers, such as Toni Heinzl and Robert Stevenson at the University of North Carolina, note that many global media companies, including Bertelsmann, have learned to let their local operating companies adapt to local cultures: "Following a global strategy, it is the company's policy to respect the national characteristics and cultural traditions in each of the more than two dozen countries in which it operates. It is impossible to detect even hints of German culture from the product lineup of Bertelsmann's companies abroad. Targeting specific preference of a national public or audience, the company has custom-tailored its products for each country: French culture in France, Spanish culture in Spain, American culture in the United States, and so on." The target is growth.

Corporate Ideology

By and large the agenda of media conglomerates is profits and nothing more. They do not promote ideology. U.S. movie-goers did not see Japanese overtones in Columbia movies or CBS records after the Sony takeover or in MCA products after the Matsushita takeover. At the same time it cannot be ignored that Bertelsmann tried to transplant its successful German geographic magazine *Geo* in the United States in 1979, only to give it up two years and $50 million later when it realized that *National Geographic*'s following was unshakable. In the same vein Murdoch imported British tabloid editors to reshape some of the U.S. newspapers he bought. What can be said with certainty about media globalization is that it is occurring and that observers are divided about its consequences.

Cultural Intrusion

study preview **Some experts claim that the export of U.S. and other Western popular culture is latter-day imperialism motivated by profit and without concern for its**

effect on other societies. The theory is that Third World countries are pawns of Western-based global media companies. Other experts see charges of cultural imperialism as overblown and hysterical.

Latter-Day Imperialism

The great concern about media globalization has been about the flow of values not among developed countries but to developing countries. Critics use the term **cultural imperialism** for this dark side of international communication. Their view is that the media are like the 19th-century European colonial powers, exporting Western values, often uninvited, to other cultures. At stake, these critics say, is the cultural sovereignty of non-Western nations. These critics note that the international communication media have their headquarters in the United States and in the former European colonial powers. The communication flow, they claim, is one way, from the powerful nations to the weak ones. The result, as they see it, is that Western values are imposed in an impossible-to-resist way. A Third World television station, for example, can buy a recycled American television program for far less than it costs to produce an indigenous program.

media ONLINE **Herbert Schiller** Links to information about Herbert Schiller, including magazine interviews where he explains his ideas. **www.scils.rutgers.edu/~favretto/schiller.html**

cultural imperialism ■ One culture's dominance of another.

Herbert Schiller ■ Saw Western cultures subsuming others.

Scholar **Herbert Schiller,** who wrote *Mass Communications and American Empire,* argued that the one-way communication flow is especially insidious because the Western productions, especially movies and television, are so slick that they easily outdraw locally produced programs. As a result, says Schiller, the Western-controlled international mass media preempt native culture, a situation he sees as robbery, just like the earlier colonial tapping of natural resources to enrich the home countries.

India is a fascinating recent example of cultural intrusion, if not cultural imperialism. Until 1991 this nation had only one television network, which ran programs that originated

mediaPEOPLE

Herbert Schiller

Herbert Schiller

Nobody could provoke a debate quite like Herbert Schiller, whether among his college students or in the whole society. As Schiller saw it, corporations in the United States were coming to dominate cultural life abroad. He amassed his evidence in a 1969 book, *Mass Communications and American Empire.* The book sensitized readers to the implications of exporting movies, music and other U.S. media products. It also put leading media companies on notice that Mickey Mouse in Borneo, no matter how endearing, had untoward implications for the indigenous culture. U.S. corporate greed, Schiller said, was undermining native cultures in developing countries. It was an insidious destruction of heritage because U.S. media products were so well produced, so slick, that it was hard for people elsewhere to resist them.

Some scholars argued that Schiller had overstated his case. Media leaders, most of whom hadn't considered the cultural implications of exporting their products, responded with a defensiveness that masked their vulnerability. Theirs was a populist argument that people wanted their products and that the products weren't being forced on anybody. They also missed Schiller's point.

The debate still rages even after Schiller's death in 2000 at age 80. In one sense, he has had the last word. His last book, *Living in the Number One Country: Reflections from a Critic of American Empire,* was published posthumously in May 2000, four months after he died.

in India almost exclusively. Then came Star TV, global media mogul Rupert Murdoch's satellite service from Hong Kong, which carried lots of U.S.-originated programming. Writing in *Media Studies Journal,* India media critic Shailaja Bajpai offered these observations:

- Many Indians were dressing like the Americans they saw on *Baywatch.*
- While Indian boys once wanted to grow up to be great cricket players, they now wanted to shoot baskets like Yao Ming.

Other anecdotal evidence of U.S. culture rubbing off elsewhere is in South Africa. According to Sebiletso Mokone-Matabane, an executive with the Independent Broadcasting Authority there, robbers were shouting "freeze," a word that had no roots in Afrikaans or the indigenous languages, when they stormed into a bank. The robbers had been watching too much U.S. television.

Some media genres translate easily across cultures. Hoping to attract audiences with reality shows, which had been the rage in Europe and the United States in the early 2000s, Middle Eastern television producers tried a variety of adaptations. Some worked, toned down from their progenitors' risque edginess. Sex was verboten. Swearing too. No kissing. In *Fear Factor* the female contestants in the swimming stunts wore full-body wet suits. There were no cameras in the showers. The bedrooms in *Big Brother* were off limits to the opposite sex.

Even so, the relatively tame variations were a lightning rod for defenders of conservative mores. There was even a *fatwa* calling for the banning of *Star Academy,* a show loosely modeled after *American Idol.* One complaint was that contestants were shown shedding tears at winning and losing. Tears of joy, as well as tears of frustration and relief, are not shed publicly in many parts of the Middle East. In Bahrain, besieged with complaints of immorality, Middle East Broadcasting decided that prudence dictated canceling *Big Brother* after two weeks. In general, though, the shows attracted large audiences, especially among young people intrigued with testing the traditional boundaries of acceptable behavior and portrayals.

In Beirut, fans crammed the Lebanese Broadcasting Corporation studios for *Star Academy* to cheer their favorite contestants, who agreed to be confined to a villa with cameras rolling until they were voted out, two at a time, by viewers. Thousands of callers voted every week. That the contestants represented several countries added a homeland excitement.

Mideast Reality Show
Algerian contestant Salma Ghazali sings during a live show of the *Star Academy,* one of the first reality shows to air in the Middle East. Other reality shows, many from Lebanon, are modeled on European and U.S. television and have attracted young viewers.

A dynamic that distinguished the shows from their steamy progenitors in Europe and the United States is that the networks that produced them were seeking pan-Arab audiences. Despite attacks on the programs, there was caution in pressing the limits of acceptability too far. The region includes 22 countries with varying levels of tolerance on acceptability. In an interview with the *Christian Science Monitor, Star Academy*'s producer-director, Roula Saad, found the show's participants could be relied on not to go too far: "They've all grown up in Middle Eastern homes. They know what's acceptable."

Non-Downward Media Exchange

In some ways cultural imperialism is in the eyes of the beholder. Some Latin American countries, for example, scream "cultural imperialism" at the United States but don't object when Mexico exports soap operas to the rest of Latin America, as Brazil and Argentina also do. Although they are exercising a form of cultural imperialism, nobody puts the label on them. Media observer Larry Lorenz, who has studied this phenomenon, explains it this way: "What is occurring is simply internationalism brought on by the ever more sophisticated media of mass communication."

The cultural imperialism theory has other doubters among scholars. The doubters note that the theory is a simplistic application of the now-discredited hypodermic needle model of mass communication. Media messages do not have immediate direct effects.

Also overstated are charges that news from Europe and the United States dominates coverage in other parts of the world. One study found that 60 to 75 percent of the foreign news in the Third World is about other Third World countries, mostly those nearby. While the giant Western news services—AP, Agence France-Presse and Reuters—are the main purveyors of foreign news, the coverage that reaches Third World audiences is extremely parochial.

Movie Power

In ranking the most powerful countries for *Newsweek* magazine in 2003, analyst John Spark used movies as one measure. "Hollywood and Bollywood fantasies of the good life shape the desires of billions," he said in offering these data.

Movie Tickets Sold per Year	
India	2.9 billion
United States	1.4 billion
Indonesia	190 million
France	155 million
Germany	149 million
Japan	145 million
United Kingdom	139 million
Spain	131 million
Mexico	120 million
Canada	113 million
Film Investment	
United States	$14.7 billion
Japan	1.3 billion
United Kingdom	852 million
France	813 million
Germany	687 million
Spain	304 million
Italy	304 million
India	192 million
South Korea	134 million
Canada	133 million
Feature-Film Production	
India	1,200
United States	543
Japan	293
France	200
Spain	137
Italy	130
Germany	116
China	100
Philippines	97
Hong Kong	92

You can derive additional meaning from these numbers by reranking the nations per capita.

Emerging Global Media

Concern about Western cultural imperialism is slowly changing as two related things occur. First, the number of international media players, many in neither Europe nor the United States, is increasing. Second, rather than merely recycling domestic products abroad, U.S.-based media companies are creating new, local-oriented content in the countries where they do business.

For generations prime-time U.S. television shows have been prime-time fare throughout the world, either with subtitles or dubbed awkwardly into local languages. Today, local media people who have mastered Western production techniques are producing local media content. Although production quality in some countries isn't as slick as for U.S. programs, indigenous programs have their own attractions and are siphoning viewers and advertisers from imported fare. Their programs go over big, attracting viewers and advertisers better than imported programs.

Not only is indigenous local programming taking hold in other countries, especially those with a developing middle class, but also many of these emerging media are exporting their material. Throughout Latin America, for example, people watch soap operas produced by TV Globo in Brazil and Televisa in Mexico. The Belgian broadcast company RTL, which once spent most of its programming dollars on imports like *Dallas* and *Dynasty*, now produces most of its own shows. The French TF-1 and Italian Rai Uno television services have cut back substantially on U.S. programs. The turnaround in Europe has been fueled not only by audience preferences for local material but also by a European Union policy that half of each nation's broadcast programming must originate within the EU.

There is also new competition, much of it well financed. In Europe the television service Canal One has teamed up with Bertelsmann of Germany to create a formidable competitor for the whole European audience. TVB in Hong Kong has its eye on dominating media fare to China, Southeast Asia and the Indian Subcontinent. What once were easy pickings for U.S. media companies are now tough markets.

To compete, U.S. media companies are investing in other countries to develop local programming. MTV and ESPN both have built advanced production studios in Singapore. Viacom has relaunched its MTV service to Asia with local hosts. In Europe, U.S. companies are forming local partnerships. NBC, for example, which bought the European Super Channel cable network, has added business news from the *Financial Times,* a London newspaper. NBC has teamed up with TV Azteca in Mexico to tap into local programming and marketing savvy. Time Warner's HBO is in partnership with Omnivision, a Venezuelan cable company, for the HBO Olé pay-television service in Latin America.

While many countries are developing significant local media powerhouses, some countries are decades away from having their own media production facilities, financing and know-how. Their complaint today is not about cultural imperialism solely from the United States but also from media production centers like Bonn, Caracas, Hong Kong, London, Mexico City, Paris and São Paulo.

media ONLINE **RTL Television** Belgium TV.
www.rtl-television.de

HBO-LA In this case, the LA stands for Latin America.
www.hbo-la.tv

Insidious Western Influence

Although more media content is being originated in home countries, some critics say, "Don't be fooled." Shailaja Bajpai, editor of an Indian television magazine, says that Indian TV producers clone U.S. television: "The American talk show has inspired Indian imitations. Never have so many Indians revealed so much about their private lives to such a wide audience. Every day a new show is planned. If nothing else, American television has loosened tongues (to say nothing of our morals). Subjects long taboo are receiving a good airing." Those Indian programs may be produced in India, but the concept is hardly Indian.

Transnational Cultural Enrichment

Some scholars see transnational cultural flow in more benign terms than Herbert Schiller and his fellow cultural imperialism theorists. George Steiner has noted that European and American culture have been enriched, not corrupted, by the continuing presence of Greek mythology over 2,000 years.

Sociologist Michael Tracey makes a similar point in a homey way: "I was born in a working-class neighborhood called Oldham in the north of England. Before the First World War, Oldham produced most of the world's spun cotton. It is a place of mills and chimneys, and I was born and raised in one of the areas of housing—called St. Mary's—built to serve those mills. I recently heard a record by a local group of folk singers called the Oldham Tinkers, and one track was about Charlie Chaplin. This song was apparently very popular with local children in the years immediately after the First World War. Was that evidence of the cultural influences of Hollywood, a primeval moment of the imperialism of one culture, the subjugation of another? It seems almost boorish to think of it that way. Was the little man not a deep well of pleasure through laughter, a pleasure that was simply universal in appeal? Was it not Chaplin's real genius to strike some common chord, uniting the whole of humanity? Is that not, in fact, the real genius of American popular culture, to bind together, better than anything, common humanity?"

Esperanto

Language remains an impediment to seamless media content serving the entire world simultaneously. More than 100 years after Esperanto was devised as an international language with the noble goal of facilitating intercultural communication, only about 2 million people worldwide are conversant—0.48 percent of the number who speak the English language.

The language was the creation of a young Polish physician, Ludovic Zamenhof, who was frustrated at the difficulty people in his own hometown had communicating among themselves. Some spoke Polish, but others spoke German, Russian or Yiddish. Zamenhof's

Esperanto Information about Esperanto in 62 languages. **www.esperanto.net**

solution: Invent a new language that transcended traditional differences. In 1887 Zamenhof introduced his language, Esperanto, a word for "hoping." The world yawned.

His disciples, though, kept the idea alive. Vatican Radio began a weekly shortwave program in Esperanto in 1977. Masses have been said in Esperanto in Roman Catholic churches since 1981. Pope John Paul II addressed the International Catholic Esperanto Union in the language in 1997. The Catholic Church's interest is fueled in part by the loss of Latin as a common language.

What is Esperanto? It uses 700 roots that are common to European languages, such as "floro" for the English "flower" and "familio" for "family." Grammar is straightforward, with no irregular verbs. Pronunciation is phonetic. For most people the language takes one-fifth as long to master as foreign languages.

More important, say Esperanto zealots, is that its multilanguage Indo-European basis, with some touches of Greek, Latin and the Romance languages, helps even the playing field in international communication. In this sense Esperanto is a neutral language, albeit a second language. But it has never caught on enough to be effective. In the United States Esperanto enthusiasts have 26 clubs, all small and local.

Global Media Models

studypreview **Models help us visualize different media systems. Models have different levels of sophistication, such as going from a bipolar model for political systems to a more complex continuum to an even more complex compass. Besides political systems, models can demonstrate media cultural environments, developmental state and other characterizing criteria.**

Bipolar Model

To compare media systems, some scholars use a **bipolar model** with two extremes: authoritarianism at one end and libertarianism at the other. The model demonstrates opposites in an extreme way. Just as east is opposite from west, so is freedom opposite from control. Bipolar models are useful beginning points to separate political systems.

Continuum Model

More sophisticated than a simple bipolar model is a variation called the **continuum model.** The basics of the continuum political system model are bipolar, with the extremes being authoritarianism and libertarianism, but there is an added element of sophistication. The media system of each country is placed not at an extreme but at points along the line. The United States would be near the libertarian end, although not quite at the extreme because, indeed, the U.S. media operate within limitations, like laws of treason, libel and intellectual property and also broadcast regulation. Britain, with more restrictive libel laws than the United States, would still be in libertarian territory on the continuum but not as near the extreme. On the other end would be tinhorn dictatorships and other repressive countries with tight controls on the mass media.

The continuum model recognizes the uniqueness of media systems in different countries. By assessing variables, scholars can plant individual countries on the continuum, which facilitates grouping countries for comparison.

Sometimes the continuum model is represented in maps. One of the most useful for a quick sense of the status of libertarianism is updated regularly by **Freedom House,** a New York organization that tracks media freedom worldwide. Freedom House categorizes media systems as free, partly free and not free and color-codes them on a map of the planet. Other continuum models offer more categories.

bipolar model ■ Portrays extremes as opposites, as libertarian and authoritarian political systems.

continuum model ■ A scale with authoritarianism at one end, libertarianism at the other and media systems at varying points in between.

Freedom House ■ A private agency that tracks media freedom worldwide.

Color-Coding Freedom Freedom House, which tracks the freedom of the new media worldwide, reports relatively few countries where news and information flow freely within and across their borders. Green shows countries that Freedom House regards as free, yellow as partly free, and purple as not free. The number of free countries has grown over 20 years from 31 percent to 40 percent.

media ONLINE **Freedom House** Review Freedom House's annual survey of countries' freedom scores.
www.freedomhouse.org

John Merrill ■ Introduced the compass model, which showed that social responsibility and authoritarianism could be bedmates.

compass model ■ A looped model that juxtaposes traditional authoritarian and social responsibility models.

Compass Model

In his book *The Imperative of Freedom,* scholar **John Merrill** looped the libertarian-authoritarian continuum around so that its ends meet themselves. On the loop Merrill marked the four major philosophical underpinnings as compass points that define the major media systems and their underlying political systems.

Among Merrill's points with the **compass model** is that a social responsibility system might not be just a variation on libertarianism but actually authoritarian. Merrill's compass addresses the troubling question about how to attain a socially responsible media: Who ensures responsibility? If it's government, then we have introduced shades of authoritarianism. If not government, then who?

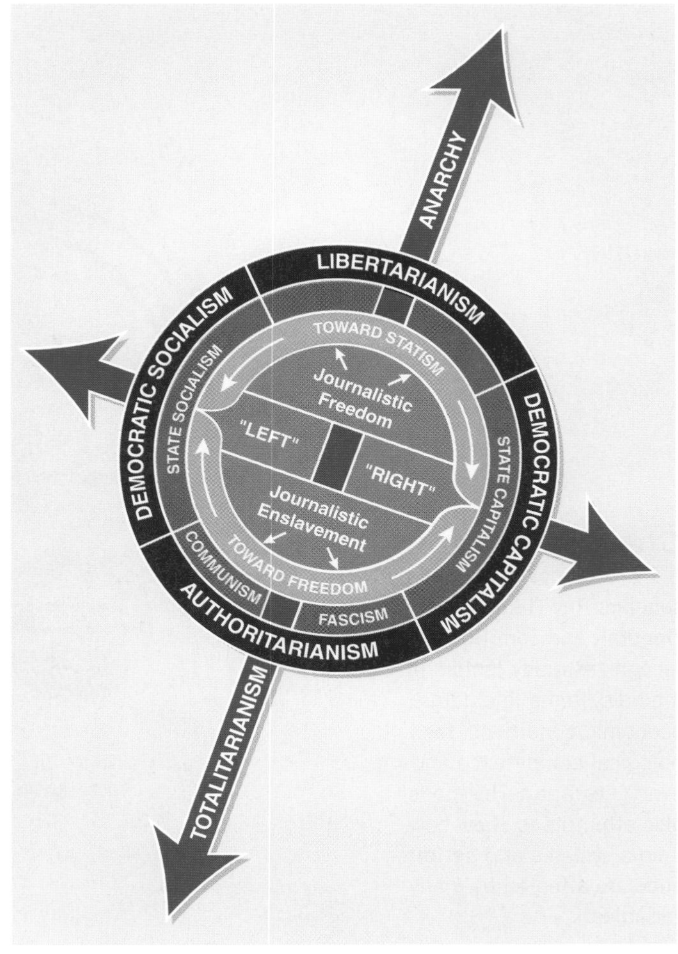

Compass Model
Scholar John Merrill rethought the libertarian-authoritarian continuum to develop this compass model. The result was a graphic representation that a responsible press, if responsibility is by government mandate, is frighteningly close to traditional authoritarianism.

Change Model

The effects of culture and geography on media systems is taken into account in the **change model,** which shows the interaction of many variables on media and systems and performance. One of the best of these models, introduced in 1974 by scholars Ray Hiebert, Don Ungurait and Tom Bohn, takes other variables into account:

- **Economics.** In impoverished parts of the world, such as Chad, few people can afford access to the mass media. There is no advertising. This lack of an economic base means a weak media system that is generally subservient to political leadership. A wealthy elite, of course, may have access to all kinds of media, often from other countries, which helps to maintain its advantage and privilege.
- **Culture.** A country's mass media reflect cultural values. The media of Iran, run by religious fundamentalists, are quite different from the media of India, a democracy that accommodates a diversity of religions. Social norms, mores and values vary from country to country, all with an effect on the mass media. So do language and traditions.
- **Technology.** Outdated equipment can undermine the service that media provide. For print media, poor roads can limit distribution. In much of the Third World, presses are hand-me-downs from more developed countries, not only outdated but also prone to breakdowns.
- **Climate.** In tropical climates, where the kinds of trees used for pulp to make paper can't grow, the print media have extraordinary production expenses for importing paper. Mexico is an example.
- **Geography.** Broadcasters in a mountainous country like Nepal have a hard time getting signals to people living in narrow valleys shielded by steep terrain. This is a factor in the economics of broadcasting and also a station's influence.

change model ■ Shows the effect of mass media on numerous social variables and the effect of those variables on the media.

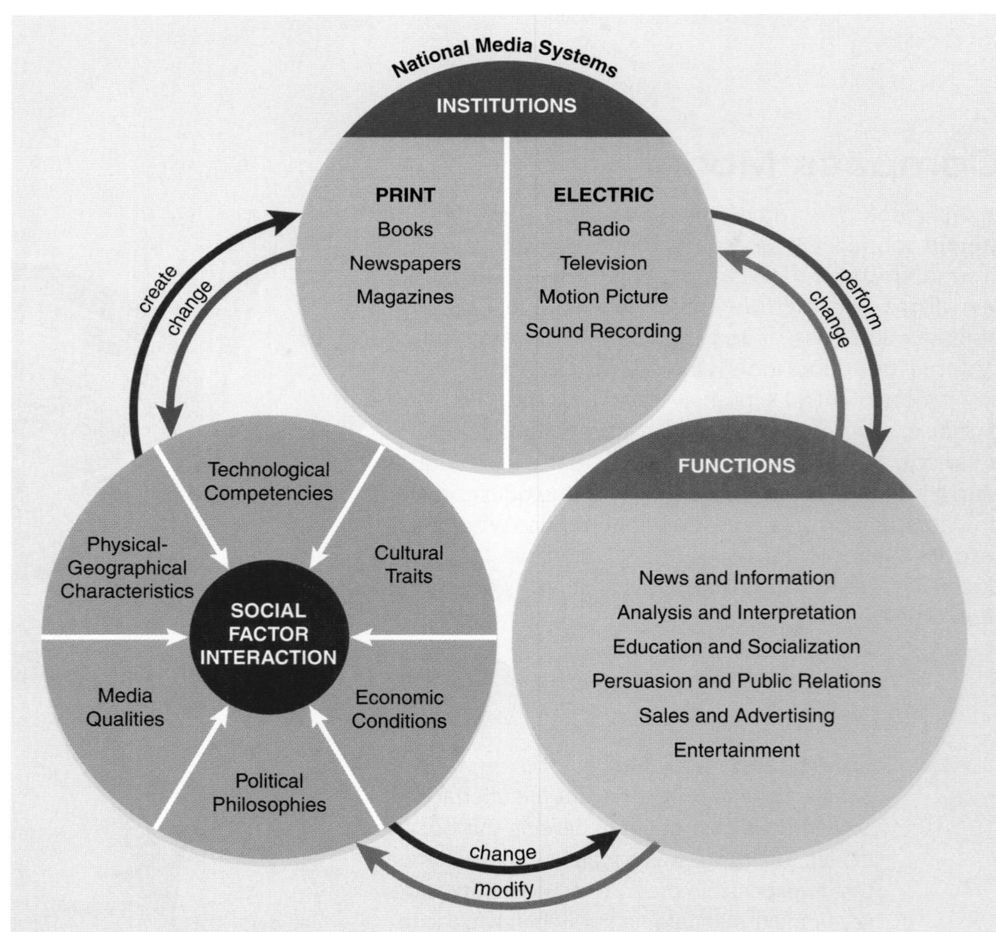

Change Model
A 1974 model developed by scholars Ray Hiebert, Don Ungurait and Tom Bohn recognizes many factors in media systems, including economic conditions, technological competence and even geography. The model also attempts to show how media systems and performance are affected by many variables.

- **Literacy.** If people can't read, the print media are handicapped. In Cameroon, for example, compulsory education goes only to age 12. Even then, one-third of Cameroon's children don't attend school. The literacy rate is only 63 percent.
- **Media.** A country's media infrastructure can be an indicator of other realities. If the primary mass medium is radio, for example, it may be an indicator that low literacy has stunted the growth of the print media. A country wired well for the Internet has a basis for sophisticated delivery of messages of all sorts.

Subsystem Model

The mass media have grown in complexity, especially in economically advanced countries. Some scholars are making a case that it doesn't make sense anymore to evaluate media in the traditional broad terms of major media, like television, magazines and newspapers. Instead, they advocate classifying media by subsystems to understand what's happening. The following are among the elements in a **subsystem model:**

- **Commercial media.** These are the profit-seeking media that have traditionally been the focus of comparative studies.
- **Government media.** Controlled by the government. May coexist with commercial media.
- **Public media.** Financed by citizens and government money to further the public good, like PBS and NPR in the United States.
- **Organizational media.** Aimed at serving nongovernment bodies, such as professional groups, tribes, religions and corporations.
- **Individualized media.** Media customized to an individual's needs and interests, as is possible through the web.
- **Political media.** Used by political parties.

Global Media Players

study preview **The first media companies to extend their operations abroad significantly were news agencies such as the Associated Press, Reuters and United Press. Today, companies that produce all kinds of media messages, not just news, are engaged in finding global markets.**

News Agencies

Hundreds of agencies cover news around the world and sell their accounts to subscribing media organizations. Most of these are national and regional services. The primary global players are Associated Press, Reuters, Agence France-Presse and Interfax.

Associated Press The news anyway you want it—read it, watch it or hear it. **www.ap.org**

Reuters News and financial information. **http://today.reuters.com**

Associated Press The **Associated Press** is the largest news-gathering organization in the world, disseminating 20 million words and 1,000-plus images a day. There are 8,500 subscribers in 112 countries. About 1,500 U.S. daily newspapers, 6,000 television and radio stations and numerous cable systems carry AP news. In addition, about 1,000 radio stations carry newscasts from AP Network News, which is the largest single radio network in the United States. In the United States the AP has 3,700 employees.

The AP is a nonprofit cooperative organization owned by daily newspapers. Each newspaper is obligated to furnish its local stories to the AP for distribution to other AP member newspapers and clients. Each member newspaper owns a share of the company based on its circulation and numerous other factors. Periodically, the expenses are tallied, and member newspapers are billed for their share. Policies are set by member newspapers.

subsystem model ■ Examines media in terms of originator and intended audience.

Associated Press ■ U.S.-based global news service; largest news-gathering organization in the world.

In addition, the AP owns profit-making subsidiaries that offset some costs. Subsidiaries include Press Association, which sells news scripts to television and radio stations; Wide World, which sells pictures from the immense archive that AP built over the years; APTV, which provides global video news coverage to television networks; AP Network, a newscast and actuality service for radio stations; and ARI, which services weeklies, including many college newspapers.

The AP, based in New York, has 142 foreign bureaus in 72 countries. Domestically, the AP operates 123 bureaus in state capitals and major cities. The domestic bureaus provide comprehensive regional and state coverage.

Reuters **Reuters** serves 6,500 media organizations worldwide, including 290 in the United States. Altogether, counting subscribers to its financial and business news services, Reuters has 27,000 subscribers worldwide. The service is offered in 11 languages. There are 120 bureaus in 80 countries. U.S. video clients include CNN and NBC.

media ONLINE **Agence France-Presse** Available in several languages. **www.afp.com/english/home**

Interfax Providing more than just the news, including extensive databases. **www.interfax.com**

Agence France-Presse Paris-based **Agence France-Presse** was founded by Charles Havas in 1835. Using carrier pigeons, Havas supplied Paris newspapers by noon with news that had happened that same morning in London and Brussels.

Today AFP is the third-largest global agency. AFP has 2,000 people in 150 bureaus worldwide, including 850 full-time journalists. Text, photo, audio and video services are transmitted in Arabic, English, French, German, Spanish and Portuguese to 500 newspapers, 350 radio and 200 television clients and to 99 national news agencies that pass AFB stories on to more media outlets. AFP has more than 50 U.S. media clients.

Interfax This Moscow-based news agency was founded as Tass in 1925. Today, reconstituted and renamed **Interfax,** the agency supplies reports in Russian, English, German, Spanish and Arabic. At its peak, the agency claimed 5,500 media and nonmedia subscribers, but the disintegration of communism and the shriveling of Russian influence has meant inevitable declines.

Video News Services

The major U.S. news networks—ABC, CBS, CNN, Fox and NBC—prefer to cover foreign stories with their own crews, but they also subscribe to global video services for stories and pictures that they miss. The largest news video suppliers are, not surprisingly, the world's two largest news services: New York-based Associated Press and London-based Reuters.

media ONLINE **AP Broadcast** Associated Press' broadcast news service. **www.apbroadcast.com**

APTV, a subsidiary of the Associated Press, cemented its leadership by buying Worldwide Television News, WTN for short, in 1998. WTN's owners, including the ABC television network, cashed in for $44 million. The deal left only London-based Reuters as a major AP competitor in the business of providing video feeds for television.

The video news business grew rapidly in the 1990s for several reasons:

Network Cutbacks Beginning in the early 1980s corporate bosses at ABC, CBS and NBC slashed their news divisions' budgets. The cuts forced news executives to make painful decisions. At each network foreign staffing took the hardest hits. At CBS the cuts were wrenching. Since 1938, when it launched its *World News Roundup* radio newscasts with staff reporters in Europe, CBS had prided itself on distinctive foreign coverage.

Critics lamented the decline of the networks' foreign coverage, but others said the foreign staffs were bloated and reductions were overdue. Also, relatively few foreign stories made it on the air. Newscast producers recognized that Americans are not international minded and, all others things being equal, favor domestic over foreign stories.

Reuters ■ British-based global news agency.

Agence France-Presse ■ Paris-based global news agency.

Interfax ■ Russian news agency.

Today, ABC, CBS and NBC operate only a handful of foreign bureaus. From those bureaus reporters fly to hot spots. Always short-staffed, these bureaus miss stories, so producers in New York pick up material from APTV and Reuters. Unlike the other U.S. networks, CNN has expanded its foreign bureaus, but even CNN's foreign staff cannot feed producers enough stories to satisfy the 24-hour news network's voracious appetite. So CNN too leans heavily on the video news services.

Government Deregulation Several European nations have deregulated broadcasting, and entrepreneurs have launched networks and stations. Stephen Claypole, an old Reuters hand who joined the new APTV in 1994, estimates the market for international news will grow 50 percent by early in the 21st century.

Independent Stations Years ago, network-affiliated stations learned that news is a good lead-in to build audiences for other programming. Today, many independent stations have established newscasts that draw on the video news stories for faraway coverage. Affiliates of the Fox network, which didn't offer network news in its first few years of existence, were among subscribers to the video news services to provide at least some distant coverage.

New Technologies The video that APTV and Reuters shoot is digital, which means it can be adapted easily to other media. Reuters, for example, can provide its subscribing newspapers and magazines with stills from its television service. The market will expand as newspapers and magazines continue to shift to digital delivery that includes moving images.

Syndicates

After Union recruiters swept through Baraboo, Wisconsin, and signed up the local boys for the Civil War, **Ansell Kellogg** lacked the staff to get out his four-page Baraboo *Republic,* so he took to borrowing the inside pages of another newspaper. The practice not only saw Kellogg through a staffing crisis, but also sparked an idea to save costs by supplying inside pages at a fee to other short-handed publishers. By 1865 Kellogg was in Chicago providing ready-to-print material for newspapers nationwide. In journalism history Kellogg is remembered as the father of the newspaper **syndicate.**

In the 1880s **S. S. McClure** had a thriving syndicate, putting out 50,000 words a week in timeless features on fashion, homemaking, manners and literature. McClure and other syndicators charged subscribing newspapers a fraction of what each would have to pay to generate such material with its own staff. Features, poetry, opinion and serialized stories by the period's great literary figures, including Jack London, Rudyard Kipling, George Bernard Shaw, Robert Louis Stevenson and Mark Twain, became standard fare in many newspapers through syndication.

Today syndicates seek international audiences, spreading expenses among more subscribers and building new revenue. Some syndicate material doesn't travel easily, like sophisticated humor columns and comic strips that reflect the traditions, experiences and values of a particular culture. It's hard to imagine, for example, that *Family Circle* or *Beetle Bailey* would go over well in south Asia. But other syndicated material is easily adapted to overseas audiences—like Dear Abby and medical advice columns.

Universal Press Syndicate Comics, Dear Abby, and more.
www.amuniversal.com/ups

Global Media Companies

study preview **National origins of companies in the media business are blurring. Sony of Japan owns Columbia Pictures and many leading U.S. record labels under a subsidiary. Sony also owns a share of Time Warner. Bertelsmann of Germany is a big player in U.S. magazines and books. U.S. companies themselves have foreign stakes.**

Ansell Kellogg ■ Founded the first syndicate.

syndicate ■ Provide low-cost, high-quality content to many news outlets.

S. S. McClure ■ Expanded syndicate concept.

U.S.-Based Companies

Five U.S. media rivals have established themselves as major players in other countries.

TimeWarner Get a feel for this award-winning, global media and entertainment company.
www.timewarner.com/corp

Disney Check out upcoming movies, play games or plan a vacation to a Disney theme park.
http://disney.go.com

Viacom Learn more about this diverse, hugely successful entertainment company.
www.viacom.com

NBC Universal Take a sneak peak at NBC TV programs and movies.
www.nbcuni.com

- **Time Warner.** Time Warner, operating in 70-plus countries, is the world's largest media company, with a value ranging as high as $183 billion. Its CNN can reach a billion people in 212 countries. HBO Olé attracts legions of subscribers in Latin America. Warner Brothers' movies and TV shows are distributed worldwide. *Time* publishes editions in Europe, Latin America and the South Pacific.
- **Disney-ABC.** When Walt Disney labored over his primitive animation for *Steamboat Willie* in 1928, he likely didn't dream that his name would forever be attached to a corporate giant. The huge acquisition of ABC in 1995 provided a domestic outlet for Disney Studio productions, which already had gone global. Theme parks in Tokyo, Hong Kong and Paris have added to Disney's world impact.
- **Viacom.** Viacom began as a syndication arm of CBS but a change in Federal Communications required it to be spun off. Ironically, Viacom made so much money recycling television shows that it acquired back CBS in 2001. Viacom's wildly profitable MTV can be tuned in at 400 million homes in 164 countries. Viacom's Paramount Pictures has a vault of 50,000 hours of television shows for international marketing. So successful has been Viacom that its chief, Sumner Redstone, in 2006 broke the company into separate entities, probably with MTV at the heart of one and the other comprising CBS and Paramount.
- **News Corporation.** Beginning with an inherited newspaper in Adelaide, Australia, Rupert Murdoch built a successful chain, then expanded to Europe where he acquired the prestigious *Times* of London. Moving to the United States, Murdoch nabbed 20th Century Fox studios and created the Fox Television Network whose products are distributed by his BSkyB in Europe and Star TV in Asia. With Murdoch's acquisition of control of U.S. satcast company DirecTV in 2003, there's scarcely a television set in the world that a News Corporation satellite can't reach.
- **NBC Universal.** In 2004, General Electric's NBC and Vivendi Universal Entertainment closed a merger that created the fifth-largest media conglomerate, NBC Universal. NBC's television network and cable channels, including Telemundo, joined with Universal's studios and theme parks, and Vivendi's A&M, Geffen, Polygram and Motown labels. Wall Street figures net assets of the new company at $42 billion.

Non-U.S. Companies

Once U.S. media companies held the commanding lead for overseas markets, but home-grown companies are pumping out more content all the time. Some of these companies have become global players themselves.

Bertelsmann Media worldwide.
www.bertelsmann.com

Hachette Filipacchi The U.S. division.
www.hfmmag.com/HachetteUSA

TVB Hong Kong satellite service.
www.tvb.com

TV Globo Brazilian media company.
http://tvglobointernacional.globo.com

Televisa Media giant from Mexico.
www.esmas.com/televisahome

Pearson Educating and entertaining all ages.
www.pearson.com

Reed Elsevier Providing information to professionals around the world.
www.reed-elsevier.com

- **Bertelsmann.** The German company Bertelsmann established itself globally as a book and magazine company. It has 200 subsidiaries in 25 countries, many of them operating under the name they had when Bertelsmann acquired them. In the United States these include Random House, Bantam, Dell and Doubleday books. The company's U.S. interests, jointly owned with Sony since 2003, include RCA Records.
- **Hachette Filipacchi.** The French-Italian company Hachette Filipacchi publishes 74 magazines in 10 countries. This includes the 4.5 million circulation *Woman's Day*, which Hachette acquired when it bought the CBS magazine empire in 1988. Another Hachette magazine in the United States is the fashion magazine *Elle*.
- **Televisa.** Throughout Latin America people watch soap operas, called *telenovelas*. Most of these originate from Televisa, a Mexican media giant.
- **TVB.** Hong Kong-based TVB has started an Asian television-satellite service. This company has plenty to put on the satellite. Its production runs about 6,000 hours a year in both Cantonese and Mandarin.

- **TV Globo.** A Brazilian media company, TV Globo, true to its name, has developed a global audience. Its telenovelas air in all the Spanish-speaking and Portuguese-speaking countries and beyond, including China.
- **Pearson.** Once a British newspaper company, Pearson has sold its papers, except the Financial *Times,* to concentrate on book publishing. One subsidiary, Pearson Education, is the largest educational publisher in the United States. Pearson trade-book imprints include Penguin.
- **Reed Elsevier.** An Anglo-Dutch conglomerate, Reed Elsevier owns the Lexis-Nexis online legal news reference service and publishes more academic journals than any other company. Worldwide, Reed has 36,000 employees. A major revenue source is library subscriptions to its online journals. The California state university library system alone pays $7 million to $8 million a year for Reed journals in an online format.

Global Media Brand Names

The names of global media companies are less well known than their products. The global television service MTV, for example, is much more recognized than Viacom, its U.S.-based owner.

Worldwide, MTV is hard not to find. With a 2005 concert in an abandoned drive-in theater in Johannesburg, headlined by Nigerian Seun Anikulapo and U.S. exports Ludacris and Will Smith, MTV launched its African service. The service, called MTV Base, was the 100th unit for the U.S.-based company outside the United States. Viacom executive Tom Freston, whose province includes MTV, called it the "missing piece." From Johannesburg MTV looks to creating an advertising vehicle reaching into 45 sub-Saharan countries with 675 million people, half 19 or younger.

In all, MTV is in more than 400 million homes in 164 countries. It's in 18 languages. Count it all up, about 1 billion people, about one-sixth of the planet's total, have access to MTV.

MTV So much more than the music videos of the '80s. **www.mtv.com**

Launched in 1981 by Time Warner as a programming service for local cable companies in North America, MTV offered endless music videos and built a following. Viacom bought MTV in 1985 and pushed the franchise globally, adapting formats to regional audiences. In Islamic Indonesia MTV airs calls to prayer. The spin on MTV Latin America hardly has the techno-edginess of MTV Japan and none of the rai on MTV in Morocco or the Afro-Cuban fusion of MTV in Senegal.

For shareholders of Viacom, whose most visible crown jewel in the United States is CBS, MTV is a sweet revenue generator. MTV and fellow corporate subunits, including Nickelodeon, rake in $6.5 billion. Although 80 percent of the revenue is from the United States, MTV Networks International is where the greatest growth is—20 percent a year with Freston shooting for 40 percent.

Global brands see the advantage. Nokia has signed on with MTV Base in Africa, pitching cell phones as a digital download gadget. Microsoft launched its Xbox game player with an MTV splash.

MTV Subscribers

MTV reached 419 million homes worldwide by 2005.

MTV Asia	140.1 million
MTV Europe	125.1 million
MTV United States	87.6 million
MTV Russia	27.1 million
MTV Brazil	18.0 million
MTV Latin America	13.7 million
MTV Canada	8.0 million
MTV Japan	5.4 million
MTV Australia	1.0 million

Mass Media in China

study preview **The struggle between freedom and tyranny plays and replays with the mass media offering case studies on broader issues. Among major nations, China has suppressed challenges to government authority with the most labor-intensive censorship initiative in history.**

Chinese Policy

Chinese authorities were less than amused at the free-wheeling satire of someone on the Internet going by the name Stainless Steel Mouse. The Mouse was tapping out stinging quips about ideological hypocrisy among the country's communist leaders. When government agents tracked the commentaries to Liu Di, a psychology major at a Beijing university, they jailed her for a year without charges. Finally, figuring the publicity about the arrest would chill other free-thinkers into silence, the authorities let Liu Di go—on condition she not return to her old ways.

The government's rationale has been articulated at the highest levels. In a speech President Jiang Zemin put the necessity of absolute government control this way: "We must be vigilant against infiltration, subversive activities, and separatist activities of international and domestic hostile forces. Only by sticking to and perfecting China's socialist political system can we achieve the country's unification, national unity, social stability, and economic development. The Western mode of political systems must never be copied."

firewall ■ A block on unauthorized access to a computer system while permitting outward communication.

Golden Shield ■ Chinese system to control internal Internet communication within the country.

Next Carrying Network (CN2) ■ Fast Chinese Internet protocols built on new technical standards; incompatible with other protocols.

Chinese Firewall

To exclude unwanted Internet communication, the Chinese government has undertaken numerous initiatives. One of them has been likened to a 21st-century version of the Great Wall of China, a 1,500-mile fortress barrier built in ancient times along the Mongolian frontier to keep invaders out.

The Chinese didn't invent their **firewall.** It came from the U.S. network design company Cisco, which devised filters in the early 1990s for corporate clients to filter employee access to the Internet. The goal of these firewalls was productivity, to keep employees equipped with desktop computers from whiling away company minutes, hours even, on sites featuring entertainment and diversions. When Cisco went courting the Chinese as customers, the filters seemed perfect for China to block unwanted material from outside the country. Cisco filters soon were installed at the gateways for Internet messages into China. Here's how it works: The filters subtly "lose" messages from banned sites abroad. If a Chinese user seeks access to a verboten foreign site, an error message or a message saying "site not found" appears on the screen. Whether it's censorship or a technical glitch, the user never knows.

There is dark humor among critics of the Chinese firewall. Noting the role of Cisco, they say: "The modern Great Wall of China was built with American bricks."

Liu Di

Government agents arrested college student Liu Di for her Internet essays, some of which mocked the government. Agents jailed her in a cell with a convicted murderer. After a year she was released subject to "permanent surveillance." She was told never to speak to foreign journalists.

Internal Chinese Controls

To control communication within the country, the Chinese Ministry of Public Security bans Internet service providers from carrying anything that might jeopardize national security, social stability—or even to spread false news, superstition and obscenity. As a condition of doing business in China, the U.S. company Yahoo agreed to the terms in 2002. So have Microsoft and other service providers. The system is called the **Golden Shield.** The shield complements the firewall against unwanted foreign messages by controlling communication inside the country.

Even tighter control is expected through a huge intranet that the Chinese government is building within the country—the **Next Carrying Network.** CN2, as it's called for short, was designed from scratch—unencumbered by the older technical standards that have been cobbled together for the system that serves the rest of the planet. CN2's technical advantages include exceptional capacity and speed. Also, because CN2 uses its own technical standards that are not easily compatible with the global Internet, the system fits neatly with government policy to limit contact with the outside. Communications from abroad can be received on CN2 only after code translations that will stall delivery and, not unimportantly, make them subject to more scrutiny.

Chinese Censorship Apparatus

Because **prior censorship,** reviewing messages before they reach an audience, is hugely labor intensive, seldom in human history has it been practiced on a large scale. Past authoritarian regimes have relied almost wholly on post-publication sanctions with severe penalties against wayward printers and broadcasters to keep others in line. The Chinese, however, are engaging in pre-publication censorship on an unprecedented scale.

Chinese censorship is partly automated. Internet postings are machine-scanned for words and terms like *human rights, Taiwan independence* and *Falun Gong* (a forbidden religious movement) and dropped from further routing. The system catches other terms that signal forbidden subjects, like *oral sex* and *pornography*.

No one outside government has numbers on the extent of human involvement in censorship, but there appears to be significant human monitoring at work. Western organizations, including Reporters Without Borders, occasionally test the Chinese system by posting controversial messages, some with terms that machines can easily spot, some with trickier language. Postings with easy-to-catch terms like *Falun Gong* never make it. Postings with harder-to-spot language but nonetheless objectionable content last a bit longer, although seldom more than an hour, which suggests a review by human eyes.

Who are these censors? How many are there? The consensus among experts outside the country is that China, whose Internet users number 100 million-plus, must be a mas-

prior censorship ■ Government review of content before dissemination.

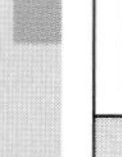

mediaTECHNOLOGY

China and EVD

EVD Shopping Pushed by their government, Chinese firms are shunning technologies developed abroad and developing their own. Here, a poster featuring an EVD player, a Chinese-developed DVD product, beckons mall shoppers in Guangzhou.

Seeking independence from the invented-elsewhere DVD format for movies, the Chinese government is introducing an alternative format, the EVD, short for enhanced versatile discs. The goal is for EVD to become the standard in the giant, growing Chinese market.

The format uses high-definition compression with finer-quality images than DVDs. At $240, players run triple what DVD players cost, but software is cheaper because Chinese film distributors do not need to pay licensing fees to foreign companies that control DVD technology.

Although EVD was conceived as a Chinese format for the Chinese market, the government, as well as manufacturers, would like to develop a global following.

There is nothing standard about formats. DVDs are heading to dominance in the United States, where they are quickly replacing VHS videocassettes. In China a format called VCD, for video compact discs, is dominant for the time being.

Meanwhile, other formats are being developed in Japan, Korea and Europe. These include BluRay and HD DVD-9.

sive censorship bureaucracy. A rare peek into the system appeared in a 2005 interview in *Nanfang Weekend* with a censor in Siquan, Ma Zhichun, whose background is in journalism. Ma discusses his job as an *Internet coordinator* in the municipal External Propaganda Office, where, without identifying himself online as a government agent, he guides discussions in the government's favor. Ma is part of elaborate mechanisms to keep online dialogue on the right track particularly in chatrooms, but like thousands of other propaganda officers throughout the country, Ma is in a position to spot banned postings and report them.

Chinese Overt Controls

Although a lot of Chinese government control of Internet postings is invisible, some is overt. Because users are required to use a government-issued personal identification number to log on, citizens know they're subject to being monitored. Operators of blog sites, which number 4 million, need to register with the government. Cybercafés, which have been woven into the lifestyle of many Chinese, must be licensed. At cybercafés, cameras check over users' shoulders for what's onscreen. Police spend a lot of time in cafés looking over shoulders too.

The government's seriousness about regulating the Internet was unmistakable when thousands of illegal cafés were shut down in a series of sweeps in the early 2000s.

Arrests are publicized, which has a chilling effect. One especially notable case involved Wang Youcai, who, during President Clinton's historic 1998 visit to China, proposed an opposition political party in the U.S. tradition. Wang filed papers to register the China Democratic Party. Within a day, government knocked on his door, interrogated him for three hours, and hauled him away. He was sent to prison for 11 years and ordered into political abstinence for an additional three years for "fomenting opposition against the government."

The later case of Liu Di the Stainless Steel Mouse for satirizing the government was similarly chilling to full and open dialogue.

Chinese Broadcasting

Although political issues are the major focus of Chinese censorship, the government discourages what it sees as a creeping intrusion of Western values and sexuality. In a clampdown on racy radio gab and, lo behold, orange-tinted hair on television, the State Administration for Radio, Film and Television issued an edict: Enough. To television hosts, the order was no vulgarity. That included "overall appearance." Specifically forbidden: "multicolor dyed hair" and "overly revealing clothing." There also were new bans on things sexual. Violence, murder and horrors were out until 11 p.m. So too were "fights, spitting, littering and base language."

The restrictions, which are periodically issued as media stray, were consistent with the communist notion that government and media are inseparably linked in moving the society and culture to a better future. As the Chinese put it, the media are the *houshe,* the throat and tongue, of the ruling Communist Party.

Chinese nationalism takes unexpected turns. Broadcasters, for example, periodically are instructed to use only Mandarin. Foreign words, including Westernisms like *OK* and *yadda-yadda,* are not allowed. Not allowed either were dialects from separatist Taiwan. Also, a strict cap was put on imported soap operas and martial arts programs for television. Imports couldn't constitute more than 25 percent of the total of such programs.

Even in Hong Kong, the British colony that was returned to China in 1997, which was to be governed by different rules that honored its tradition of free expression, Beijing-approved governors were appointed to comport with official policies. Political cartoonists also have been reigned in.

Is government pressure effective? In Fujian province, the hosts of the program *Entertainment Overturning the Skies* gave up their blonde dye jobs after one crackdown. Some television programs imported from Taiwan, the United States and elsewhere suddenly and quietly disappeared. Hong Kong radio is tamer. But clampdowns come and

Mongolian Cow Sour Yogurt Supergirl

An *Idol*-like mania swept China when an upstart television station in remote Hunan province put its show *Supergirl* on satellite. Despite admonitions against lyrics in English and gyrating hips, contestants pushed the envelope of government acceptability to huge audiences. That viewers could vote their preferences by mobile phones raised a specter of nascent democracy in a country where people can't vote for their leadership. Most analysts, however, have concluded that the phenomenon was an anomaly in the tightly controlled society. Even so, winners, who are called Mongolian Cow Sour Yogurt Supergirls, because a dairy sponsored the show, have gone on into singing and modeling careers.

go. Kenny Bloom of the Beijing-based AsiaVision production house told a *Wall Street Journal* interviewer: "Commentators will follow the rules for a couple months, and then their clothes will get tighter and their hair will get wilder."

Even so, legal scholars Jack Goldsmith of Harvard and Tim Wu of Columbia, who have studied government controls on media content globally, say controls do not have to be absolute to be effective. Goldsmith and Wu offer copyright law as an example. Infringements of copyright in, say, illegal music downloads, are inevitable, but the threat of civil or criminal sanctions keep violations at a rate that copyright owners are willing to live with. Such, they note, is the same with the censorious Chinese government. Nobody is so unrealistic to claim that all dissidence can be suppressed. The goal, rather, is to keep dissidence from breaking beyond an easily manageable level.

Distinctive Media Systems

studypreview **Nations organize their media systems differently. Besides advertising, Britain and Japan have distinctive methods for funding some media. Emerging democracies are beset with their own challenges. In Columbia, drug lords have strong sway.**

Britain

Almost everybody has heard of the BBC, Britain's venerable public service radio and television system. Parliament created the British Broadcasting Corporation in 1927 as a government-funded entity that, despite government support, would have as much programming autonomy as possible. The idea was to avoid private ownership and to give the enterprise the prestige of being associated with the crown. The government appoints a 12-member board of governors, which runs BBC. Although the government has the authority to remove members of the board, it never has. BBC has developed largely independently of the politics of the moment, which has given it a credibility and stature that are recognized worldwide.

BBC Listen to the BBC live online.
www.bbc.co.uk

The Beeb, as BBC is affectionately known, is financed through an annual licensing fee, about $230, on television receivers.

BBC is known for its global news coverage. It has 250 full-time correspondents, compared to CNN's 113. The Beeb's reputation for first-rate dramatic and entertainment programs is known among English-speaking people everywhere. The 1960s brought such enduring comedies as David Frost's *That Was The Week That Was* and later *Monty Python's Flying Circus*. Sir Kenneth Clark's *Civilisation* debuted in 1969. Then came dramatic classics like *The Six Wives of Henry VIII*, *War and Peace* and *I, Claudius*.

The great issue today is whether the BBC should leave the government fold. Advocates of privatization argue that BBC could exploit its powerful brand name better if it were privatized. The privatization advocates say that BBC's government ties are keeping it from aggressively pursuing partnerships to make it a global competitor with companies like Time Warner and Rupert Murdoch's News Corporation. But continuing to do business as always, they say, will leave the Beeb in everybody else's dust.

India

The world's largest democracy, India, has a highly developed movie industry that took root by providing affordable entertainment to mass audiences when the country was largely impoverished. The industry, called **Bollywood,** a contrivance of its historic roots in Bombay and the U.S. movie capital Hollywood, is adapting as India moves rapidly out of its Third World past. Today India is becoming a model for new media applications, like wi-fi, as the country brings itself into modern times.

media ONLINE **Bollywood** All the latest music, movie and celebrity news out of Bollywood. **www.bollywoodworld.com**

Bollywood At 85 cents a seat, people jam Indian movie houses in such numbers that some exhibitors schedule five showings a day starting at 9 a.m. Better seats sell out days in advance in some cities. There is no question that movies are the country's strongest mass medium. Even though per capita income is only $1,360 a year, Indians find enough rupees to support an industry that cranks out as many as 1,200 movies a year, twice more than U.S. movie-makers. Most are B-grade formula melodramas and action stories. Screen credits often include a director of fights. Despite their flaws, Indian movies are so popular that it is not unusual for a movie house in a Hindi-speaking area to be packed for a film in another Indian language that nobody in the audience understands. Movies are produced in 16 Indian languages.

The movie mania centers on stars. Incredible as it may seem, M. G. Ramachandran, who played folk warriors, and M. R. Radha, who played villains, got into a real-life gun duel one day. Both survived their wounds, but Ramachandran exploited the incident to bid for public office. He campaigned with posters that showed him bound in head bandages and was elected chief minister of his state. While in office, Ramachandran continued to make B-grade movies, always as the hero.

Billboards, fan clubs and scurrilous magazines fuel the obsession with stars. Scholars Erik Barnouw and Subrahmanyam Krishna, in their book *Indian Film,* characterize the portrayals of stars as "mythological demigods who live on a highly physical and erotic plane, indulging in amours." With some magazines, compromising photos are a specialty.

Bollywood ■ Nickname for India movie industry.

A few Indian movie-makers have been recognized abroad for innovation and excellence, but they generally have an uphill battle against B-movies in attracting Indian audiences. Many internationally recognized Indian films, like those by Satyajit Ray, flop commercially at home.

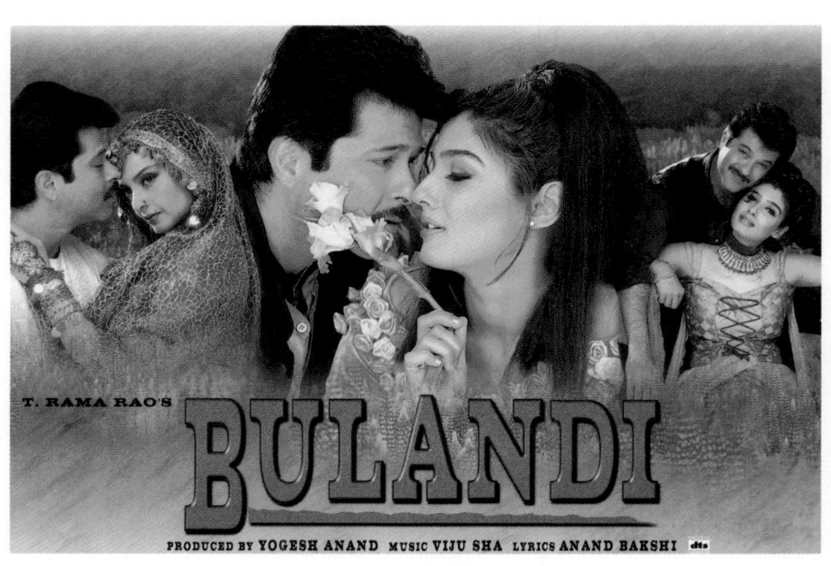

T. RAMA RAO'S
BULANDI
PRODUCED BY YOGESH ANAND MUSIC VIJU SHA LYRICS ANAND BAKSHI

Bollywood
The Indian movie industry, centered in Bombay and sometimes called Bollywood, pumps out an incredible 1,200 movies a year. Although India has some internationally recognized movie-makers, most Bollywood productions are formulaic action movies that critics derisively label "curry westerns."

In the late 1990s Indian movies developed a cult following in the United States. The major Indian movie export market, however, was in Hindi-speaking parts of the world. In Sri Lanka, for example, whose language Sinhalese is closely related to Hindi, the domestic movie industry is overshadowed by imported Indian movies.

Wi-Fi India has taken a lead in linking remote villages with the rest of the world with wireless technology. Villagers and farmers who once had to walk several miles to pay their power bills, now go to a "knowledge center" as it's called—several rooms equipped with desktop computers, connected by wi-fi to the Internet—and pay online. Such "knowledge centers" are being installed in 600,000 villages in a government-entrepreneurial program launched in 2005. Eventually, all 237,000 villages in India large enough to have a governing unit will be equipped.

The Indian experience is a model for extending mass media links into isolated, poverty-ridden areas in Africa and eastern Europe. Farmers can learn market corn prices to decide when it's best to sell. Faraway doctors can diagnose illnesses through digital electrocardiography. In India a company named n-Logue has designed wi-fi kiosks for rural villages at $1,200 a unit, complete with a computer, software, a digital camera, paper and a backup power supply. Kiosks can have ATM banking too.

A remaining obstacle is the diversity in languages in many underdeveloped parts of the world. Google doesn't translate universally.

Japan

Anyone who owns a television set in Japan can expect a knock on the door every couple of months. It is the collector from NHK, the Japan Broadcast Corporation, knocking to pick up a periodic $16 reception fee. This ritual occurs six times a year in 31 million doorways. The reception fee, required by law since 1950, produces $2.6 billion annually to support the NHK network.

NHK is a Japanese tradition. It went on the air in 1926, a single radio station, the first broadcast of which was the enthronement of Emperor Hirohito. Today, NHK operates three radio and two domestic television networks. It also runs Radio Japan, the national overseas shortwave service, which transmits 40 hours of programs a day in 21 languages.

The primary NHK television network, Channel One, offers mostly highbrow programming, which gives NHK its reputation as the good gray network. NHK airs about 600 hours a year of British and U.S. documentaries and dramas from the BBC and PBS. The network prides itself on its news.

Most Japanese viewers, however, spend most of their television time with stations served by four networks, all with headquarters in Tokyo: Fuji, NHK, NTV and Tokyo Broadcasting System. A few independent stations complete Japan's television system.

The commercial stations all offer similar fare: comedies, pop concerts and videos, quiz shows, sports and talk shows. In recent years news has gained importance in attracting viewers and advertisers, encroaching on one of NHK's traditional strengths.

Russia

Optimists expected that the dust of the imploding Soviet empire in 1989 would yield a robust, prosperous free society. In Russia, however, despite occasional signs of new media independence, old ways die hard.

The **NTV** network, part of the country's largest media chain, gained respect as an independent voice for its critical reports on Kremlin policies in the early **perestroika** period. Then in 2000, NTV owner Vladimir Gusinsky was arrested after months of harassment by the Kremlin. Gusinsky was dumped in one of Moscow's filthiest jails. It all smacked of authoritarianism. Embarrassed at the worldwide media attention on the heavy-handedness, the president of Russia, Vladimir Putin, distanced himself from the arrest and called it excessive. Still, it was Putin's administration that had gone after Gusinsky.

Meanwhile, NTV's coverage of a Russian military campaign against Chechen separatists was toned down. From 1994 to 1996 the network had gained respect for fearless

NTV ■ Privately owned Russian television network.

perestroika ■ Russian policy of restructuring institutions in the spirit of candor and openness.

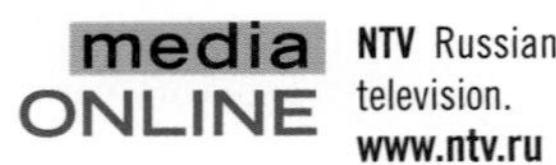

NTV Russian television. **www.ntv.ru**

frontline reporting on stalled Russian tactics in Chechnya. Video showed frightened teenage Russian troops in over their heads against grizzled Chechens. When Russian troops destroyed the town of Grozny, the coverage was not pretty and hardly heroic. As Russian public pressure shifted against the war, the Kremlin opted to act in old ways. NTV was told that its broadcast license was in jeopardy.

The Kremlin underscored its seriousness in 2000 when a Radio Free Europe correspondent from the first Chechen war, Andrei Babitsky, tried again to roam independently for balanced coverage. Suddenly Babitsky's reports stopped. He had been arrested by Russian forces, badly beaten up and jailed for 40 days, which had a chilling effect that showed in all coverage, including NTV's.

It's not just government that has failed in the transition to a free mass media. In 1996 the president of Gusinsky's NTV managed the re-election campaign of President Boris Yeltsin. The infrastructure for independent media wasn't in place. At lower levels, too, many career media people, rewarded for years as loyal Leninists, found themselves suddenly in a strange transitional environment and couldn't deal with it. In many cities local media were beholden to town mayors for office space, equipment and supplies—just as in the old days.

Organized crime and corruption also work against a free media. According to the Committee to Protect Journalists, 34 journalists died doing their work in Russia in the 1990s, mostly in war zones but some murdered elsewhere. Hundreds have reported being attacked.

Colombia

High drama is popular on Colombia radio stations, but it is hardly theatrical. In Colombia thousands of people, both wealthy and ordinary, are kidnap captives. Families go on the air to express love and support in the hope that their kidnapped kin are listening. It makes for powerful radio. Tragically, it's real.

mediaPEOPLE

Jineth Bedoya Lima

In Pursuit of a Story Lima was kidnapped and raped while pursuing a story.

After Jineth Bedoya Lima wrote about executions during a Bogota prison riot, she got word that a paramilitary leader inside the prison wanted to give her his side. "Come alone," she was told. Like all Colombian journalists, Bedoya, 25 at the time, was aware of the dangers of reporting news, especially on subjects sensitive to warring factions. Her editor and a photographer went with her.

As they waited outside the prison, the photographer left to buy sodas, then the editor followed him. When they came back, Bedoya was gone. Guards at the prison gate said they had seen nothing.

Many hours later, a taxi driver found Bedoya at a roadside garbage dump. She said that two men had grabbed her and forced a drugged cloth over her face. She regained consciousness in a nearby house, where her captors taped her mouth, blindfolded her and bound her hands and feet. They then drove her three hours to another city. They said they were going to kill her, as well as several other journalists they named. Then they beat and raped her and threw her out at the dump.

Her story, typical of violence against media people in Colombia, was disseminated widely by the Committee to Protect Journalists. It's a cautionary tale. Bedoya, who believed that she was being trailed months later, was assigned two government bodyguards. Even so, she feels at risk. Why does she still do it? Frank Smyth of CPJ, writing in *Quill* magazine, quoted her: "I love my work, and I want to keep doing it. The worst thing that could happen has already happened."

Drug lords and petty criminals alike have found kidnapping lucrative in a country where anarchy is close to an everyday reality. The mass media are hardly immune. In the 1990s, according to the U.S.-based Committee to Protect Journalists, 31 journalists were killed because of their work. Sixteen others have died in incidents that may or may not be related to their work. In a typical year, six to 10 journalists are kidnapped in a country whose population is less than that of the U.S. Pacific Coast states.

A political satirist, Jamie Garzón, was shot to death in 1999 after a television show. *El Espectador,* a leading newspaper, has armed guards at every entrance and around the perimeter, as do most media operations. Many reporters are assigned bodyguards, usually two, both armed. Two *El Espectador* reporters have fled the country under threat. The editor of another daily, *El Tiempo,* fled in 2000 after supporting a peace movement.

Beset with corruption fueled by the powerful cocaine industry, the government has no handle on assaults against the media. Although hypersensitive to negative coverage, the drug industry is not the only threat to the Colombian media. The Committee to Protect Journalists, Human Rights Watch, Amnesty International and other watchdogs blame renegade paramilitary units and guerrillas, some of whom are ideologically inspired. Also, the Colombian military itself and some government agencies have been implicated.

Radio El Espectador Listen to Colombian radio on the web. **www.espectador.com**

War Zones

studypreview **The need in a democracy for people to be informed doesn't square easily with military necessity in time of war. The United States has tried a wide range of policies for war coverage. The latest, embedded reporters in the 2003 Iraq war, generally worked well from the military, media and public perspectives. All the historic media-government arrangements for war coverage, however, raise the looming question of how global media serving international audiences can be faithful both to truth and to competing national causes.**

Combat Reporting

War is a danger zone for journalists. The Committee to Protect Journalists, which tracks reporters in peril, tallied 54 reporters killed doing their work in 2004—23 in Iraq alone—compared to 13 in 2003. In addition, 22 journalists were kidnapped in Iraq.

Early Lessons

The struggle to find ways for journalists to report from the battlefield without getting in the way or jeopardizing operations is not recent.

Civil War The Civil War was the first with a large contingent of reporters with the armies, about 500. After some fumbling with how to deal with the reporters, the secretary of war, **Edwin Stanton,** ordered that stories go to censors to delete sensitive military matters. In general, the system worked, from Stanton's perspective. Toward the end of the war General William Sherman marched all the way from Chattanooga, Tennessee, through hostile Georgia to the sea at Savannah, a nine-month campaign, without a hint in the press to tip off the Confederacy.

World War II In World War II correspondents wore uniforms with the rank of captain and usually had a driver and a Jeep. The reporters generated lots of field coverage, but the reporting, reflecting the highly patriotic spirit of the times, as evident in reporters even wearing military uniforms, was hardly dispassionate and sometimes propagandist.

Vietnam Reporters had great freedom in reporting the Vietnam war in the 1960s and 1970s. Almost at will, reporters could link up with South Vietnamese or U.S. units and go on patrols. The result, dubbed **rice-roots reporting,** included lots of negative stories on what was, in fact, an unsuccessful military campaign that was unpopular among many

Edwin Stanton ■ Union secretary of state who organized Civil War censorship of sensitive military news.

rice-roots reporting ■ Uncensored field reporting from the Vietnam war.

Orhan Pamuk

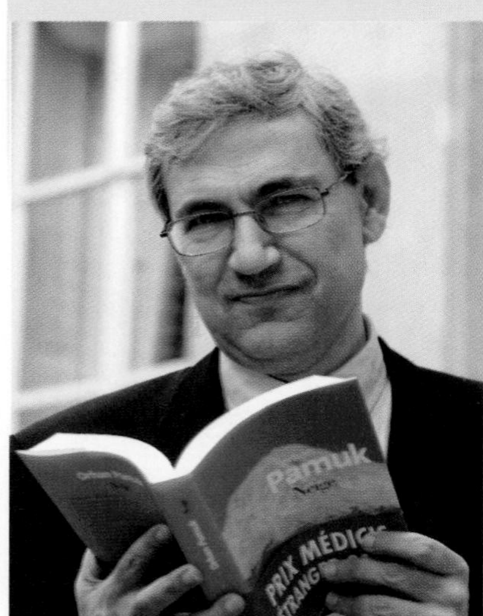

Insulted the State

As a novelist, Orhan Pamuk does what novelists do best—cast pressing problematic issues in such a powerful light that their resolution is hastened. In memoir-style best-sellers Pamuk has explored controversial views of the culture of his native Turkey, particularly tensions between East and West, secularism and Islamism, and past and present. Although Pamuk's works have been lauded for their literary merit, his critics would rather some things be left unsaid. Some Turkish newspapers have editorialized that Pamuk should be "silenced for good." In 2005 he went on trial, charged with the crime of "insulting Turkish identity."

Pamuk personifies the difficulty of many tradition-bound countries in emerging from authoritarianism. Turkey, as an example, is torn between strong nationalism that dates to the Ottoman empire and the need to join the European Union to grow its economy. A condition for European Union membership is embracing fully the Western value of free expression. The European Court of Human Rights has been unequivocal about the right "to criticize public institutions in very strong terms." Although Turkey revised its laws on free expression in 2004, parts of old laws remained intact, including provision in the criminal code against "insulting Turkish identity." At the time of Pamuk's trial, 65 free-expression cases were before the courts in Turkey.

The Pamuk case grew out of an interview in a Swiss newspaper in which he discussed the deaths of 1 million Armenians and 30,000 Kurds in the late Ottoman period, which Western historians call the first genocide of the 20th century but which Turkey officially calls "internecine fighting." Pamuk also said that Turkish security forces shared responsibility for an estimated 30,000 Kurd deaths during separatist fighting in the 1980s and 1990s. Pamuk did not use the hot-button word *genocide,* but he must have realized he was venturing into dangerous territory. About the mass killings, he said: "Nobody but me dares to talk about it."

For fierce Turkish nationalists, this was too much. A provincial governor ordered Pamuk's books burned, including *My Name is Red* and *The White Castle,* all of which had been widely praised elsewhere and contributed to his winning the German Peace Prize for literature in 2005. Despite the attacks and threats, Pamuk was defiant. Awaiting trial he honed in on the Turkish dilemma: "What am I to make of a country that insists that the Turks, unlike their Western neighbors, are a compassionate people, incapable of genocide, while nationalist political groups are pelting me with death threats?"

In 2005 Pamuk's trial was adjourned on technical grounds. But under pressure from ultranationalists the government continued to prosecute other writers, including journalists and scholars.

media ONLINE

War Stories An interactive exhibition from the Newseum.
www.newseum.org/warstories

Tips on War Reporting From the South Asian Journalists Association.
www.saja.org/tipsreportingwar.html

troops and a growing majority at home. For the first time the reporting was filmed for television, with gruesome footage being pumped by the networks into living rooms across the nation on the evening news, deepening opposition to the war.

Commanders didn't like negative reports, which some blamed for losing the public's support for the war. In the end, demoralized, the United States withdrew in defeat—the first war the nation had lost in its history.

Grenada For the next wars, relatively quick incursions, the Pentagon had new rules. In 1983, when the United States took over the Caribbean nation of Grenada, a naval blockade kept reporters out. The war, secretly planned, surprised the news media. Scrambling to get on top of the story but barred from the action, enterprising reporters hired small boats to run the blockade but were intercepted.

Pool Reporting

Major newspapers, the networks and news agencies protested loudly at being excluded from covering the Grenada invasion. Acknowledging that the policy had ridden roughshod over the democratic principles on which the nation was founded, with an informed electorate essential for the system to work, the Pentagon agreed to sit down with news media leaders to devise new ground rules. The result was a **pool system,** in which a corps of reporters would be on call on a rotating basis to be shuttled to combat areas on short notice for the next quick war.

In 1989, when U.S. forces invaded Panama to capture dictator Manuel Noriega on drug charges, the Pentagon activated the pool system and took reporters along. Top military commanders, however, still smarting from their Vietnam experience and blaming the news media, carefully controlled the reporters and their access to information.

Embedded Reporters

The Iraq war, beginning in 2003, was covered by journalists like no other. The U.S. government, after flip-flopping on rules for war correspondents for 50 years, seemed to recognize the futility of trying to manipulate information in the digital age. Months before the invasion the Pentagon chief for media relations, Victoria Clarke, invited news organizations to send reporters to special combat mini-courses to get up to speed—and also into physical shape—to go to war with combat units. These reporters would be embedded in the units to cover combat for the duration of hostilities. The reporters, called **embeds,** would need to supply their own equipment, including vehicles, but would be free to tell the story of the war as they saw it. Commanders were told to let the cameras roll whenever the journalists wanted.

Ground rules were few. Among them was not to disclose unit positions, lest the enemy be tipped to locations. Also, the Pentagon warned that it might need to black out reports for "operational security, success of the mission, and the safety of the people involved."

The Pentagon was pleased with how the new system worked. Yes, the embeds showed the ugliness of war, as well as gaffes. But the invasion went well for the United States and its allies, and the Pentagon concluded that the coverage, perceived by the public as honest and independent, contributed to public enthusiasm for the war during the initial combat phase. The news media were pleased, too, remembering that only 10 years earlier, in the Kuwait war, reporters were kept away from combat and had access only to information fed to them at headquarters briefings.

Critics said the embeds were too limited in their perspective, lacking an overview, and that, losing objectivity, they picked up the gung-ho spirit of the units they were assigned to. The criticism, however, missed the fact that reporters were in regular contact with editors and producers in their home newsrooms, as well as in field newsrooms, who fed them information from other sources. Also, reports from the embeds were integrated into newscasts and stories that presented the broad picture.

pool system ■ Reporters chosen on a rotating basis to cover an event to which access is limited.

embeds ■ A 2003 Iraq war term for reporters accompanying, or embedded with, U.S. military combat units.

Embeds

Victoria Clarke, media relations chief for the U.S. Defense Department, created new rules for war news coverage by allowing news organizations to "embed" reporters with combat units. Embedded reporters were unfettered in filing live battle reports uncensored as long as they followed rules. These included not disclosing unit positions. Here, Clarke and the Defense Department's vice director of operations, Major General Stanley McChrystal, provide a Pentagon briefing on 2003 Iraq war progress.

CHAPTER 18 Wrap-Up

Models to help explain the world's great variety of mass media systems are important in this fast-changing era of globalization. The most useful model focuses on change—how economics, culture, technology and other factors influence media infrastructures and content in an interactive way. Models alone, however, are insufficient to explain media policy in a global context. Economic imperatives are at the heart of understanding why mass media companies behave as they do. The implications are important in explaining media effects on different cultures, both positive and negative.

Questions for Review

1. What does Thomas Friedman's historic globalization model suggest about the future of human society?
2. What ideology do global media companies export?
3. What is the negative connotation of Herbert Schiller's term "cultural imperialism"?
4. How does media globalization work against indigenous and distinctive media content?
5. Is it a problem when values from dominant cultures subsume those of other cultures?
6. How does the continuum model bypass the bipolar model in sophistication?
7. How have global news agencies affected nations they cover for the rest of the world?
8. Where are the major global media companies based?
9. How has the Chinese government shielded its people from foreign cultural values and political dissidence?
10. What are different approaches that have grown up in other countries' media infrastructures?
11. What problems beset media people in countries without independent media?
12. How has the U.S. military accommodated news reporters whose job is to cover war and combat?

Questions for Critical Thinking

1. What does Thomas Friedman's historic globalization model suggest about the future of human society?
2. What can be expected if global consolidation of mass media companies continues?
3. Assess the view that "cultural imperialism" is a loaded term that misses an enriching aspect of transnational communication.
4. Does media globalization necessarily work against indigenous and distinctive media content?
5. Is human civilization moving toward a monolithic culture?
6. Use the subsystem model to explain the mass media in any developing country you choose.
7. Assess the criticism of some Third World leaders that news agencies like AP and Reuters are lackeys of the government in the country where they're based.
8. Why are the biggest global media companies based mostly in the United States and Europe?
9. Were you a closet freedom-fighter in China, what could you do to access foreign Internet sites and communicate within the country with like-minded dissidents?
10. Compare and contrast the U.S., British and Japanese systems of financing their national television networks.
11. What trends can you ascertain about media-government relations worldwide?
12. How can the interests of national security and the battlefield be assured with news reporters covering combat?

Deepening Your media LITERACY

What is the message of the Marlboro Man?

STEP 1 Write down how cultural intrusion differs from cultural imperialism.

Dig Deeper

STEP 2 A basic media literacy skill is to look beneath the surface of a media message. Consider a message such as the Marlboro Man, which has become common in Japan, South Korea and Taiwan, where U.S. tobacco sales increased 24-fold almost overnight after bans on foreign tobacco were lifted in 1987. The New Mexico Literacy Project has compiled a list of questions to deconstruct a media message. Use their questions to look more closely at the Marlboro Man:

1. Who paid for the media? Why?
2. Who is being targeted?
3. What text, images or sounds lead you to this conclusion?
4. What is the literal meaning of the message?
5. What is the unstated or underlying message?
6. What kind of lifestyle is presented? Is it glamorized? If so, how?
7. What values are expressed?
8. What tools or techniques of persuasion are used?
9. What story is not being told?
10. In what ways is this a healthy media message? Or an unhealthy one? Or both?

What Do You Think?

STEP 3 Answer these questions:

1. Is it the responsibility of the company or country that exports a message like the Marlboro Man to make sure that it's a healthy message?
2. How much responsibility should be borne by the viewer?
3. What if the viewer doesn't have access to information about the health risks of smoking?
4. Is exporting the Marlboro Man cultural intrusion or cultural imperialism? Why?

Keeping Up to Date

Index on Censorship. Published in London. Provides monthly country-by-country status reports.

Scholarly journals that carry articles on foreign media systems, international communication and media responsibility include the *International Communication Bulletin, Journal of Broadcasting and Electronic Media, Journal of Communication* and *Journal and Mass Communication Quarterly.*

Professional journals that carry articles on foreign media systems and on media responsibility include *Columbia Journalism Review, Quill* and *American Journalism Review.*

Ongoing discussions on media responsibility also appear in the *Journal of Mass Media Ethics.*

For Further Learning

Micah Garen and Marie-Hélène Carleton. *American Hostage: A Memoir of a Journalist Kidnapped in Iraq and the Remarkable Battle to Win His Release.* Simon & Schuster, 2005.

A first-person account of the kidnapping of Garen and his translator Amir Dosh while doing a documentary.

Thomas L. Friedman. *The World Is Flat: A Brief History of the 21st Century.* Farrar, Straus and Giroux, 2005.

Learn how the digital revolution has made it possible to do business instantaneously with billions of other people across the planet.

Charles Ayres. *War Reporting for Cowards.* Atlantic Monthly Press, 2005.

Ayers, a London *Times* reporter, mixes the frivolous and serious in recounting his experience embedded with an artillery unit in the 2003 U.S. assault into Iraq.

Alan Feuer. *Over There: From the Bronx to Baghdad: A Memoir.* Counterpoint, 2005.

Feuer, of the New York *Times,* covered the Iraq war first from Jordan but finally made it into Iraq. He admits his own foibles as a reporter and also explores the firm hand the military kept on reportage.

Michael S. Sweeney. *Secrets of Victory: The Office of Censorship and the American Press and Radio in World War II.* University of North Carolina Press, 2001.

Sweeney, a scholar, examines the U.S. government's World War II censorship program and attempts to explain its success. Sweeney, once a reporter himself, draws on archival sources.

Daya Kishan Thussu, editor. *Electronic Empires: Global Media and Local Resistance.* Arnold, 1999.

Sixteen essays evaluate media globalization, especially television, from a diverse range of perspectives, including cultural imperialism and audience liberation.

David D. Perlmutter. *Photojournalism and Foreign Policy: Icons of Outrage in International Crises.* Praeger, 1998.

Perlmutter, a mass communication scholar, presents case studies in which photographic images define the public discussion of international issues.

Edward S. Herman and Robert W. McChesney. *The Global Media: The New Missionaries of Global Capitalism.* Cassell, 1997.

A look at the ways market forces are shaping global societies.

Robert W. McChesney. *Corporate Media and the Threat to Democracy.* Seven Stories Press, 1997.

What happens when corporations control the flow of information?

Wolfgang Hoffmann-Riem. *Regulating Media: The Licensing and Supervision of Broadcasting in Six Countries.* Guilford, 1996.

Hoffmann-Riem, a German senator, examines broadcast regulation in six European industrial nations. Well documented.

Jerry W. Knudson. "Licensing Journalists in Latin America: An Appraisal." *Journalism and Mass Communication Quarterly* (Winter 1996), pages 878–889.

Professor Knudson acknowledges the arguments against requiring journalists to be licensed, but argues that the *colegio* system in many Latin American countries has improved professional standards, raised salaries and, in some cases, buffered journalists against dictatorial and military governments.

"Global Views on U.S. Media." *Media Studies Journal* (Fall 1995).

This special issue carries 21 articles on perceptions of U.S. media abroad, including ones by Shailaja Bajpai of India and Sebiletso Mokone-Matabane of South Africa, both of which are cited in this chapter.

John C. Merrill. *An Imperative of Freedom: A Philosophy of Journalistic Autonomy.* Hastings House, 1974.

Merrill, a media scholar, offers a totalitarian-anarchy continuum model of major media systems.

Bernard Cohen. *The Press and Foreign Policy.* Princeton University Press, 1963.

This is the classic treatment of the subject.

Populist Celebration When populist Jesse Ventura was sworn in as governor of Minnesota, Arnold Schwarzenegger was there. Both had built followings through the media in nonpolitical contexts—Ventura in wrestling, Schwarzenegger in bodybuilding, then movies.

chapter

19 Mass Media and Governance

In this chapter you will learn:

- **The U.S. news media are a watchdog on government in the people's behalf.**
- **The news media influence people mostly through opinion leaders.**
- **The mass media are major shapers of the public's agenda of issues.**
- **Government has many tools for manipulating media coverage.**
- **Watchdog performance is uneven, with voids in some government coverage.**
- **Blogs seem important in campaigns, but their effect is not fully understood.**
- **Credibility is at the heart of many unsettled government-media issues.**

Arnold Schwarzenegger had made up his mind. In advance of an appearance on the *Tonight Show* he had told host Jay Leno, his friend, that he wouldn't run for governor of California. On the edge of the set before going on, Schwarzenegger stood chatting with his adviser, George Gorton, who held a news release ready to issue. It began: "I am not running for governor." Then and there, as Gorton tells it, Schwarzenegger changed his mind: "Let's go do it."

The rest, after that August 2003 announcement, became history that raised anew questions about populism and the role of the mass media in the process of representative government. Schwarzenegger was in the tradition of populist candidates, who, as newcomers to politics, rally sectors of the society against existing institutions. "Hasta la vista, baby," Schwarzenegger taunted incumbent Governor Gray Davis, using a famous line from one of his movies. He vowed to clean house at the Sacramento Capitol. To attract support, he drew on public dissatisfaction with record state government deficits, college tuition hikes and higher auto registration fees.

Was Schwarzenegger qualified? His popularity came not from political experience. He had none. When he was a young man, Schwarzenegger was a photogenic,

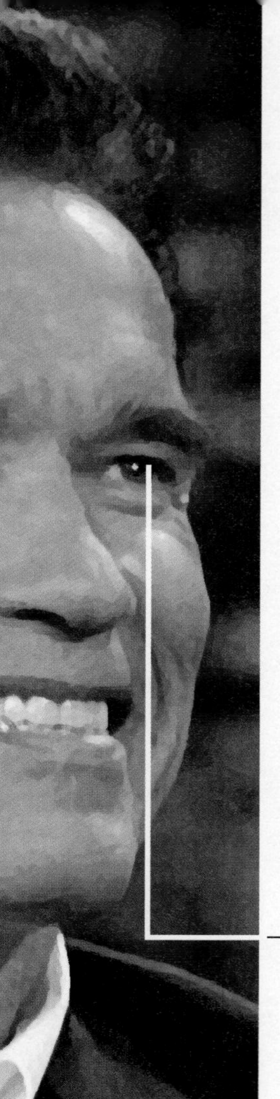

world-class bodybuilder. He later made a fortune in movies, the most successful being high-energy action flicks that were short on dialogue except for pithy deadpan phrases like "Hasta la vista, baby." Critics said that the media made Schwarzenegger—or, perhaps more accurately, Schwarzenegger used the media to create a persona.

Is populism a good thing? Critics note that populist appeals are often simplistic and don't work. When ex-wrestler Jesse Ventura ran for governor of Minnesota, he vowed to return the state's reserve funds to the taxpayers, which drew many people to the polls who had never voted before. Ventura depleted the reserve with tax rebate checks, which were popular until the state ran short of money and entered fiscal chaos. Ventura didn't seek a second term.

Despite downsides, populist candidates can draw new voters to the polls, increasing political participation in the spirit of fuller democracy. Schwarzenegger, for example, proclaimed himself the "people's candidate." The core question, however, is whether people are participating knowledgably and intelligently or responding to simplistic and panacean policy proposals that aren't well thought out. Populism carries a risk of uninformed though popular-at-the-time policy changes that end up doing more harm than good.

The mass media, of course, are key in helping people sort through issues as they participate in the political process. How hard do news reporters push candidates to defend their proposals? How responsible, forthcoming and honest are candidates in their advertising, photo-ops and other media manipulation? These are questions you will be exploring in this chapter on the mass media and governance.

Media Role in Governance

study preview **The news media are sometimes called the fourth estate or the fourth branch of government. These terms identify the independent role of the media in reporting on the government. The media are a kind of watchdog on behalf of the citizens.**

media ONLINE **Welcome to California** The governor's office web site.
www.governor.ca.gov/state/govsite/gov_homepage.jsp

Schwarzenegger.com Visit the Arnold store, and more.
www.schwarzenegger.com/en

Fourth Estate

Medieval English and French societies were highly structured into classes of people called *estates*. The first estate was the clergy. The second was the nobility. The third was the common people. After Gutenberg the mass-produced written word began emerging as a player in the power structure, but it couldn't be pigeonholed as part of one or another of the three estates. In time the press came to be called the **fourth estate.** Where the term came from isn't clear, but **Edmund Burke,** a member of the British Parliament, used it in the mid-1700s. Pointing to the reporters' gallery, Burke said, "There sat a Fourth Estate more important by far than them all." The term remains for all journalistic activity today. The news media report on the other estates, ideally with roots in none and a commitment only to truth.

The fourth-estate concept underwent an adaptation when the United States was created. The Constitution of the new republic, drafted in 1787, set up a balanced form of government with three branches: the legislative, the executive and the judicial. The republic's founders implied a role for the press in the new governance structure when they declared in the Constitution's First Amendment that the government should not interfere with the press. The press, however, was not part of the structure. This led to the

fourth estate ■ The press as a player in medieval power structures, in addition to the clerical, noble and common estates.

Edmund Burke ■ British member of Parliament who is sometimes credited with coining the term *fourth estate.*

mediaPEOPLE

Donna Brazile

A political activist at the age of 9, Donna Brazile went on to become the first African American woman to lead a major presidential campaign. The talented field operative and grass-roots organizer grew up in poverty in a small town near New Orleans and began her political activism campaigning for a city council candidate who promised a playground in her neighborhood. The third of nine children, she was encouraged to follow her dreams by her grandmother.

Political Strategist Although she failed in masterminding Al Gore's presidential campaign in 2000, Donna Brazile has emerged as a respected voice of reason, albeit from a partisan perspective.

On the road to being named Al Gore's campaign manager, Brazile worked on presidential campaigns for Democratic candidates Carter and Mondale in 1976 and 1980, the Reverend Jesse Jackson's first historic bid for the presidency in 1984, Mondale-Ferraro in 1984, Dick Gephardt in 1988, Dukakis-Bentsen in 1988, and Clinton-Gore in 1992 and 1996. It was Gore's 2000 loss to George W. Bush that was the most heartbreaking. Many political observers praised Brazile for her strategic planning and her get-out-the-vote effort, which resulted in Gore winning the popular vote, even though he lost in the electoral college.

Since then Brazile served as a fellow at Harvard's Institute of Politics, where she taught students how a multimillion-dollar presidential campaign is structured, managed and organized. The Gore campaign lost, she says, "because we failed to educate voters, failed to remove structural barriers, failed to have every ballot counted."

In her autobiography, *Cooking with Grease: Stirring the Pots in American Politics,* Brazile named each chapter for a favorite dish, to reflect her lifelong habit of stirring the pot for social change. Now she wants to focus on the themes that have resonated through her life: voter participation, voter education, trying to make the system better and letting people vote without harassment, and she is the founder and managing director of Brazile and Associates, a political consulting and grassroots advocacy firm based in the District of Columbia.

Brazile, in her late 40s, is a contributor and political commentator on CNN's *Inside Politics,* MSNBC's *Hardball* and Fox's *Hannity and Colmes.* She is chair of the Democratic National Committee's Voting Rights Institute, which was established in 2001 to help protect and promote the rights of all Americans to participate in the political process. She told the Detroit *Free Press,* "I talk to the hip-hop generation 24/7, every day of my life. I want to be part of what they see as their vision of this country."

press informally being called the **fourth branch** of government. Its job was to monitor the other branches as an external check on behalf of the people. This is the **watchdog role** of the press. As one wag put it, the founders saw the role of the press as keeping tabs on the rascals in power to keep them honest.

Government-Media Relations

Although the First Amendment says that the government shouldn't place restrictions on the press, the reality is that exceptions have evolved.

Broadcast Regulation In the early days of commercial radio, stations drowned one another out. Unable to work out mutually agreeable transmission rules to help the new medium realize its potential, station owners went to the government for help. Congress obliged by creating the Federal Radio Commission in 1927. The commission's job was to limit the number of stations and their transmitting power to avoid signal overlaps. This the commission did by requiring stations to have a government-issued license

fourth branch ■ The press as an informally structured check on the legislative, executive and judicial branches of government.

watchdog role ■ Concept of the press as a skeptical and critical monitor of government.

that specified technical limitations. Because more stations were broadcasting than could be licensed, the commission issued and denied licenses on the basis of each applicant's potential to operate in the public interest. Over time this criterion led to numerous requirements for broadcasters, in radio and later television, to cover public issues.

Because of the limited number of available channels, Congress tried to ensure an evenhandedness in political content through the **equal time rule.** If a station allows one candidate to advertise, it must allow competing candidates to do so under the same conditions, including time of day and rates. The equal time requirement is in the law that established the Federal Radio Commission and also the 1934 law that established its successor, the Federal Communications Commission. The rule has since been expanded to require stations to carry a response from the opposition party immediately after broadcasts that can be construed as political, like the president's state of the union address.

media ONLINE **Federal Communications Commission** Find out what the FCC is doing today.
www.fcc.gov

The Freedom Forum The Gannett media chain created the Freedom Forum to study and explore media issues, including issues of press freedom, press-government relations and media coverage.
www.freedomforum.org

Internet Law and Regulation A law firm sponsors this site, which it describes as the world's largest Internet case law library.
http://internetlaw.pf.com

From 1949 to 1987 the Federal Communications Commission also required stations to air all sides of public issues. The requirement, called the **fairness doctrine,** was abandoned in the belief that a growing number of stations, made possible by improved technology, meant the public could find plenty of diverse views. Also, the FCC figured the public's disdain for unfairness would undermine the ability of lopsided stations to keep an audience. The commission, in effect, acknowledged the marketplace could be an effective force for fairness—without further need for a government requirement.

Abandonment of the fairness doctrine was part of the general movement to ease government regulation on business. This shift has eased the First Amendment difficulties inherent in the federal regulation of broadcasting. Even so, the FCC remains firm against imbalanced political broadcasting. In 1975, for example, the commission refused to renew the licenses of stations owned by **Don Burden** after learning that he was using them on behalf of political friends. At KISN in Vancouver, Washington, Burden had instructed the news staff to run only favorable stories on one U.S. Senate candidate and negative stories on the other. At WIFE in Indianapolis he ordered "frequent, favorable mention" of one U.S. senator. The FCC declared it would not put up with "attempts to use broadcast facilities to subvert the political process." Although the Burden case is a quarter-century old, the FCC has sent no signals that it has modified its position on blatant slanting.

Print Regulation The U.S. Supreme Court gave legitimacy to government regulation of broadcasting, despite the First Amendment issue, in its 1975 **Tornillo opinion.** Pat Tornillo, a candidate for the Florida Legislature, sued the Miami *Herald* for refusing to print his response to an editorial urging voters to the other candidate. The issue was whether the FCC's fairness doctrine could apply to the print media—and the Supreme Court said no. As the Court sees it, the First Amendment applies more directly to print than broadcast media.

This does not mean, however, that the First Amendment always protects print media from government interference. The Union Army shut down dissident newspapers in Chicago and Ohio during the Civil War. Those incidents were never challenged in the courts, but the U.S. Supreme Court has consistently said it could envision circumstances in which government censorship would be justified. Even so, the court has laid so many prerequisites for government interference that censorship seems an extremely remote possibility.

equal time rule ■ Government requirement for stations to offer competing political candidates the same time and the same rate for advertising.

fairness doctrine ■ Former government requirement that stations air all sides of public issues.

Don Burden ■ Radio station owner who lost licenses for favoring some political candidates over others.

Tornillo opinion ■ The U.S. Supreme Court upheld First Amendment protection for the print media even if they are imbalanced and unfair.

Internet Regulation The Internet and all its permutations, including chatrooms and web sites, are almost entirely unregulated in terms of political content. The massive quantities of material, its constant flux and the fact that the Internet is an international network make government regulation virtually impossible. Even Congress' attempts to ban Internet indecency in 1996 and again in 1999 fell apart under judicial review. The only inhibition on Internet political content is not through government restriction but through civil suits between individuals on issues like libel and invasion of privacy.

Media as Information Sources

studypreview **Most news media influence is through opinion leaders. Newspapers and magazines are especially important to these opinion leaders. For the public, television is the preferred source of national political news. For politically engaged people, talk radio and online media are also significant sources.**

Direct versus Indirect

Many people once saw a direct link between press reports and individual decision-making. Today we know the linkage between the media and individuals generally is less direct. **Paul Lazarsfeld**'s pioneering studies on voter behavior in 1940 and 1948 found most people rely on personal acquaintances for information about politics and governance. Lazarsfeld called this a **two-step flow** process, with **opinion leaders** relying heavily on the news media for information and ideas, and other people relying on the opinion leaders. In reality this is hardly a clinically neat process. The influence of opinion leaders varies significantly from issue to issue and even from day to day, and people who normally don't use the media much may do so at some points and then rely less on opinion leaders. As Lazarsfeld came to recognize the complexity of the process, he renamed it **multistep flow.**

In short, news coverage and media commentary have influence on the public, but usually it is through the intermediaries whom Lazarsfeld called opinion leaders. Lazarsfeld's observation is underscored every time network television reporters talk on-camera with political leaders and refer to the public in the third person as "they," as if *they* aren't even watching. Implicit in the third person is the reporters' and political leaders' understanding that their audience is made up more of opinion leaders than the body politic.

Citizen Preferences

Which media do people use most for political news? Opinion leaders lean heavily on newspapers and magazines, which generally are more comprehensive and thorough than broadcast sources. Not surprisingly, scholar Doris Graber found that better-educated people favor newspapers. Even so, there is no denying that television has supplanted newspapers as the primary source for national news for most people. A TechnoMetrica survey found that people relied more on television than newspapers by a 2:1 margin in the 2000 presidential campaign. For national coverage the television networks present news attractively and concisely.

For local and state political news, however, television isn't as respected. Newspapers, political scientist William Mayer found, are the primary source for most people on local political campaigns. In many communities, local television coverage is superficial and radio coverage almost nonexistent. In state-level gubernatorial and senatorial races, television is favored 5:3 as a primary information source, according to Mayer's 1992 studies—roughly half as much as at the national level.

Media preference studies generally ask people to rank their preference, which can lead to a false conclusion that the second-ranked preference isn't relied on at all. While people may use television most, this hardly means that they don't read newspapers at all. The daily press turns out more than 50 million copies a day nationwide. Also, broadcast assignment editors look to newspapers and magazines, especially those with veteran political reporters and commentaries, for ideas on stories to pursue. Daniel Patrick Moynihan, the former New York senator, once noted that the New York *Times* is the standard by which other media decide what's worth covering.

New York *Times* Setting the standard for what's newsworthy. **www.nytimes.com**

Paul Lazarsfeld ■ Sociologist who concluded that media influence on voters generally is indirect.

two-step flow ■ Media effect on individuals is through opinion leaders.

opinion leaders ■ Media-savvy individuals who influence friends and acquaintances.

multistep flow ■ Political information moves from the media to individuals through complex, ever-changing interpersonal connections.

Media Effects on Governance

study preview **Media coverage shapes what we think about as well as how to think about it. This means the media are a powerful linkage between the government and how people view their government. A negative aspect is the trend of the media to pander to transitory public interest in less substantive subjects, like scandals, gaffes and negative events.**

Agenda-Setting

media ONLINE **Agenda Setting** A detailed discussion of the theory. **www.agendasetting.com**

A lot of people think the news media are powerful, affecting the course of events in godlike ways. It's true that the media are powerful, but scholars, going back to sociologist Paul Lazarsfeld in the 1940s and even Robert Park in the 1920s, have concluded that it's not in a direct tell-them-how-to-vote-and-they-will kind of way. Media scholars Maxwell McCombs and Don Shaw cast media effects succinctly when they said the media don't tell people *what to think* but rather *what to think about*. This has come to be called **agenda-setting.**

Civil Rights The civil rights of American blacks were horribly ignored for the century following the Civil War. Then came news coverage of a growing reform movement in the 1960s. That coverage, of marches and demonstrations by Martin Luther King Jr. and others, including film footage of the way police treated peaceful black demonstrators, got the public thinking about racial injustice. In 1964 Congress passed the Civil Rights Act, which explicitly forbade discrimination in hotels and eateries, government aid and employment practices. Without media coverage the public agenda would not have included civil rights at a high enough level to have precipitated change as early as 1964.

Watergate Had the Washington *Post* not doggedly followed up on a break-in at the Democratic Party's national headquarters in 1972, the public would never have learned that people around the Republican president, Richard Nixon, were behind it. The *Post* set the national agenda.

White House Sex Scandals Nobody would have spent much time pondering whether President Bill Clinton engaged in sexual indiscretions if David Brock, writing in the *American Spectator* in 1993, had not reported allegations by Paula Jones. Nor would the issue have reached a feverish level of public attention without Matt Drudge's 1997 report in his online *Drudge Report* about Monica Lewinsky.

By and large, news coverage does not call for people to take positions, but on the basis of what they learn from coverage, people do take positions. It's a catalytic effect. The coverage doesn't cause change directly but serves rather as a catalyst.

CNN Effect

Television is especially potent as an agenda-setter. For years nobody outside Ethiopia cared much about a devastating famine. Not even after four articles in the New York *Times* was there much response. The Washington *Post* ran three articles, and the Associated Press distributed 228 stories—still hardly any response. The next year, however, disturbing videos aired by BBC captured public attention and triggered a massive relief effort. In recent years many scholars looking at the agenda-setting effect of television vis-à-vis other media have focused on CNN, whose extensive coverage lends itself to study. As a result, the power of television to put faraway issues in the minds of domestic audiences has been labeled the **CNN Effect.**

agenda-setting ■ The process through which issues bubble up into public attention through mass media selection on what to cover.

CNN Effect ■ The ability of television, through emotion-raising video, to elevate distant issues on the domestic public agenda.

A Failure of Government CNN deployed hundreds of staff to the Gulf Coast when Hurricane Katrina struck, documenting not only the disaster but the failure of the federal government to respond adequately. The coverage, including anchor Soledad O'Brien on the scene, kept the failure on the public agenda and forced President Bush to adjust his initially rosy claims about the federal response. The influence of the news media, particularly television, to propel issues powerfully into public consciousness has been dubbed the CNN Effect.

Framing

Related to agenda-setting and the CNN Effect is a process called **framing,** in which media coverage shapes how people see issues. Because the Pentagon allowed news reporters to accompany combat units in the Iraq war of 2003, there was concern that the war coverage might be decontextualized. Critics foresaw coverage focusing on tactical encounters of the combat units, missing larger, strategic stories. In other words, highly dramatic and photogenic stories from combat units might frame the telling of the war story in terms of the minutiae of the conflict. Too, Pentagon war planners were aware that reporters living with combat units would, not unnaturally, see the story from the soldiers' perspective. The Pentagon, in fact, had carefully studied the 1982 war between Britain and Argentina, in which embedded British journalists were entirely reliant on the military not only for access to the battle zone but even for such basics as food. The resulting camaraderie gave a not-unnatural favorable twist to coverage. As it turned out, scholars who analyzed the coverage concluded that the framing from combat zones was largely, though not wholly, as the Pentagon had intended. The tone was favorable to the military and individual combat units. However, the reports from embedded reporters were packaged in larger-perspective accounts that also included material from war protesters, mostly in Europe, and the fractured diplomatic front.

In the 2004 presidential campaign advertising in support of President Bush hammered at inconsistencies in the Senate voting record of Democratic challenger John Kerry. The goal was to frame Kerry in the public mind as wavering and unreliable. The Bush campaign also emphasized consistency on national defense. Kerry, on the other hand, worked at framing Bush as single-minded, if not simple-minded, on military issues and as easily misled, even duped, by ideologues among his advisers.

Partisan framing is the easiest to spot. But news, though usually cast in a dispassionate tone, is also subject to framing. Framing cannot be avoided. Not everything about an event or issue can be compacted into a 30-second television story item or even a 3,000-word magazine article. Reporters must choose what to include and what not to. Whatever a reporter's choices, the result is a framing of how the audience will see the reality.

media ONLINE

CNN See the CNN effect for yourself.
www.cnn.com

BBC An agenda setter for the world.
www.bbc.co.uk

Priming

Media coverage not only creates public awareness but can also trigger dramatic shifts in opinion. An example was the fate of the elder George Bush. In 1991 his approval

framing ■ Selecting aspects of a perceived reality for emphasis in a mass media message, thereby shaping how the audience sees the reality.

mediaPEOPLE

Helen Thomas

Helen Thomas grew up in Detroit, one of nine children of Syrian immigrants. Her father couldn't read or write English. Helen and her brothers and sisters read the newspapers to him. By high school she had decided to be a journalist. After graduating from her hometown Wayne University, she headed to Washington. That was in 1942, and prospects for women in the male-dominated capital press corps were not as bleak as usual because World War II was sucking almost every able-bodied male, including journalists, into the military. Helen Thomas landed a job as a copy girl with the Washington *Daily News* for $17.50 a week. Somehow she survived the pink slips that most women journalists received when men began returning to their old jobs from the war.

In 1961 Helen Thomas switched to the White House. Within a few years she found herself the senior reporter, which meant, by tradition, that she and the Associated Press reporter alternated asking the first question of the president at news conferences. Also, as senior reporter, it fell to her to close news conferences after an agreed-upon 30 minutes by saying, "Thank you, Mr. President."

During her tenure Helen Thomas consistently improved the status of women in journalism and the respect they deserved. She joined the Women's National Press Club, which had been formed in 1908 because the National Press Club refused to admit women even to cover newsworthy speeches. Thomas became president of the women's club in 1960 and kept pressure on its male counterpart to admit women. Finally, in 1971, the National Press Club admitted women.

Things have changed dramatically since then in Washington journalism. Thomas herself was elected president of the National Press Club in 1975, and she broke gender barriers at the Overseas Press Club, the White House Correspondents Association and the Gridiron Club.

Dean of White House correspondents at age 85.

It was the 2006 Gridiron Club dinner that gave Thomas a segue into her most memorable news conference question with President George W. Bush.

Thomas: After that brilliant performance at the Gridiron [dinner], I am . . . *(fellow reporters and Bush break into laughter)*. You're going to be sorry. *(more laughter)*

Bush: Well, then, let me take it back. *(more laughter)*

Thomas: I'd like to ask you, Mr. President, your decision to invade Iraq has caused the deaths of thousands of Americans and Iraqis, wounds of Americans and Iraqis for a lifetime. Every reason given, publicly at least, has turned out not to be true. My question is, why did you really want to go to war? From the moment you stepped into the White House, from your Cabinet—your Cabinet officers, intelligence people, and so forth—what was your real reason? You have said it wasn't oil—quest for oil, it hasn't been Israel, or anything else. What was it?

It was the first time, three years after the U.S.-led invasion of Iraq, that a reporter had capsulized growing frustration at the war in a direct question to President Bush. In a few words, without showing disrespect for the office of the presidency, Thomas had framed a truth-seeking question in a way that was impossible for even the well-rehearsed president to sidestep gracefully. It was a tough question put honestly, directly and poignantly.

It also was the kind of question that Thomas, in her 2006 book, *Watchdogs of Democracy?* argued is too seldom asked anymore. The Washington press corps has gone soft, she argues. She said media owners, beholden to government for broadcast licenses, had incubated a get-along mentality. Tightened news budgets meant short-staffing that precluded lots of labor-intensive journalistic digging. She also blamed government for a growing aggressive tendency to wield its bully-pulpit to discredit news reports and reporters who ventured from the party line.

ratings were at record highs. In 1992 the people thumped him out of office. What had happened? During the Persian Gulf war in 1991, the media put almost everything else on the back burner to cover the war. The president's role in the coverage was as commander-in-chief. Primed by the coverage, the public gave Bush exceptionally favorable ratings. When the war ended, media coverage shifted to the economy, which was ailing, and the president was hardly portrayed heroically. His ratings plummeted, and in 1992 he lost a re-election bid.

In 1991 the media coverage created an environment that primed the public to see the president positively, and in 1992 the environment changed. It was a classic example of **priming,** the process in which the media affect the standard that people use to evaluate political figures and issues. This is hardly to say that the media manipulate the environments in which people see political figures and issues. No one, for example, would argue that the Persian Gulf war should not have been covered. However, the fact is that it was through the media that people were aware of the war and concluded the president was doing a great job.

Media Obsessions

Although critics argue that the media are politically biased, studies don't support this. Reporters perceive themselves as middle-of-the-road politically, and by and large they work to suppress personal biases. Even so, reporters gravitate toward certain kinds of stories to the neglect of others, and this flavors coverage.

Presidential Coverage News reporters and editors have long recognized that people like stories about people, so any time an issue can be personified, so much the better. In Washington coverage this has meant focusing on the president as a vehicle for treating issues. A study of the *CBS Evening News* found that 60 percent of the opening stories featured the president. Even in nonelection years the media have a near-myopic fix on the White House. This displaces coverage of other important government institutions, like Congress, the courts, and state and local government.

Conflict Journalists learn two things about conflict early in their careers. First, their audiences like conflict. Second, conflict often illustrates the great issues by which society is defining and redefining its values. Take, for example, capital punishment, abortion or the draft. People get excited about these issues because of the fundamental values involved.

Part of journalists' predilection for conflict is that conflict involves change—whether to do something differently. All news involves change, and conflict almost always is a signal to the kind of change that's most worth reporting. Conflict is generally a useful indicator of newsworthiness.

Scandals Journalists know too that their audiences like scandal stories—a fact that trivializes political coverage. Talking about coverage of Bill Clinton early in his presidency, political scientists Morris Fiorina and Paul Peterson said: "The public was bombarded with stories about Whitewater, Vince Foster's suicide, $200 haircuts, parties with Sharon Stone, the White House travel office, Hillary Clinton's investments, and numerous other matters that readers will not remember. The reason you do not remember is that, however important these matters were to the individuals involved, they were not important for the overall operation of government. Hence, they have been forgotten."

U.S. Political Scandals Compiled and categorized by Wikipedia. **http://en.wikipedia.org/wiki/Category:U.S._political_scandals**

No matter how transitory their news value, scandal and gaffe stories build audiences, which explains their increase. Robert Lichter and Daniel Amundson, analysts who monitor Washington news coverage, found policy stories outnumbered scandal stories 13:1 in 1972 but only 3:1 in 1992. During that same period news media have become more savvy at catering to audience interests and less interested in covering issues of significance. This also has led to more negative news. Lichter and Amundson found that negative stories from Congress outnumbered positive stories 3:1 in 1972 but 9:1 in 1992.

priming ■ Process in which the media affect the standard that people use to evaluate political figures and issues.

Horse Races In reporting political campaigns, the news media obsess on reporting the polls. Critics say this treating of campaigns as **horse races** results in substantive issues being underplayed. Even when issues are the focus, as when a candidate announces a major policy position, reporters connect the issue to its potential impact in the polls.

Brevity People who design media packages, such as a newspaper or newscast, have devised presentation formats that favor shorter stories. This trend has been driven in part by broadcasting's severe time constraints. Network anchors have complained for years that they have to condense the world's news into 23 minutes on their evening newscasts. The result: short, often superficial treatments. The short-story format shifted to many newspapers and magazines, beginning with the launch of *USA Today* in 1982. *USA Today* obtained extremely high story counts, covering a great many events by running short stories—many only a half-dozen sentences. The effect on political coverage has been profound.

USA Today Leading the trend toward brevity.
www.usatoday.com

The **sound bites** in campaign stories, the actual voice of a candidate in a broadcast news story, dropped from 47 seconds in 1968 to 10 seconds in 1988 and have remained short. Issues that require lengthy explorations, say critics, get passed up. Candidates, eager for airtime, have learned to offer quippy, catchy, clever capsules that are likely to be picked up rather than articulating thoughtful persuasive statements. The same dynamic is available in *USA Today*-style brevity.

Some people defend brevity, saying it's the only way to reach people whose increasingly busy lives don't leave them much time to track politics and government. In one generalization, brevity's defenders note, the short attention span of the MTV generation can't handle much more than 10-second sound bites. Sanford Ungar, the communication dean at American University, applauds the news media for devising writing and reporting styles that boil down complex issues so they can be readily understood by great masses of people. Says Ungar: "If *USA Today* encourages people not to think deeply, or not to go into more detail about what's happening, then it will be a disservice. But if *USA Today* teaches people how to be concise and get the main points across sometimes, they're doing nothing worse than what television is doing, and doing it at least as well."

While many news organizations have moved to briefer and trendier government and political coverage, it's unfair to paint too broad a stroke. The New York *Times*, the Washington *Post* and the Los Angeles *Times* do not scrimp on coverage, and even *USA Today* has come to carry more lengthy articles on government and politics. The television networks, which have been rapped the most for sound-bite coverage, also offer in-depth treatments outside of newscasts—such as the Sunday morning programs.

Candidates have also discovered alternatives to being condensed and packaged. In 2000 both George W. Bush and Al Gore made appearances on Oprah Winfrey's, Jay Leno's and David Letterman's shows and even *Saturday Night Live*.

media ONLINE

Oprah The Oprah Winfrey empire online.
www2.oprah.com

Government Manipulation of Media

study preview **Many political leaders are preoccupied with media coverage because they know the power it can have. Over the years they have developed mechanisms to influence coverage to their advantage.**

horse races ■ An election campaign treated by reporters like a game—who's ahead, who's falling back, who's coming up the rail.

sound bites ■ The actual voice of someone in the news, sandwiched in a correspondent's report.

Influencing Coverage

Many political leaders stay up nights figuring out ways to influence media coverage. James Fallows, in his book *Breaking the News,* quoted a Clinton White House official: "When I

Presidents and the Media Franklin Roosevelt was not popular with most newspaper and magazine publishers. Editorials opposed his election in 1932, and whatever sparse support there was for his ideas to end the Great Depression was fading. Two months after taking office, Roosevelt decided to try radio to communicate directly to the people, bypassing the traditional reporting and editing process that didn't always work in his favor. In his first national radio address, Roosevelt explained the steps he had taken to meet the nation's financial emergency. It worked. The president came across well on radio, and people were fascinated to hear their leader live and direct. Roosevelt's "fireside chats" became a fixture of his administration, which despite editorial negativism, would continue for 13 years—longer than any in U.S. history. John Kennedy used television as Roosevelt had used radio, and every political leader since, for better or worse, has recognized the value of the mass media as a vehicle for governance.

was there, absolutely nothing was more important than figuring out what the news was going to be. . . . There is no such thing as a substantive discussion that is not shaped or dominated by how it is going to play in the press."

The game of trying to outsmart the news media is nothing new. Theodore Roosevelt, at the turn of the 20th century, chose Sundays to issue many announcements. Roosevelt recognized that editors producing Monday newspapers usually had a dearth of news because weekends, with government and business shut down, didn't generate much worth telling. Roosevelt's Sunday announcements, therefore, received more prominent play in Monday editions. With typical bullishness Roosevelt claimed that he had "discovered Mondays." Compared to how sophisticated government leaders have become at manipulating press coverage today, Roosevelt was a piker.

Trial Balloons and Leaks

To check weather conditions, meteorologists send up balloons. To get an advance peek at public reaction, political leaders also float **trial balloons.** When Richard Nixon was considering shutting down radio and television stations at night to conserve electricity during the 1973 energy crisis, the idea was floated to the press by a subordinate. The reaction was so swift and so negative that the idea was shelved. Had there not been a negative reaction or if reaction had been positive, then the president himself would have unveiled the plan as his own.

Trial balloons are not the only way in which the media can be used. Partisans and dissidents use **leaks** to bring attention to their opponents and people they don't much like. In leaking, someone passes information to reporters on condition that he or she not be identified as the source. While reporters are leery of many leakers, some information is so significant and from such reliable sources that it's hard to pass up.

trial balloons ■ A deliberate leak of a potential policy, usually from a diversionary source, to test public response.

leaks ■ A deliberate disclosure of confidential or classified information by someone who wants to advance the public interest, embarrass a bureaucratic rival or supervisor, or disclose incompetence or skullduggery.

It's essential that reporters understand how their sources intend information to be used. It is also important for sources to have some control over what they tell reporters. Even so, reporter-source relationships lend themselves to abuse by manipulative government officials. Worse, the structures of these relationships allow officials to throttle what's told to the people. As political scientists Karen O'Connor and Larry Sabato said: "Every public official knows that journalists are pledged to protect the confidentiality of sources, and therefore the rules can be used to an official's own benefit—but, say, giving reporters derogatory information to print about a source without having to be identified with the source." This manipulation is a regrettable, though unavoidable, part of the news-gathering process.

Stonewalling

When Richard Nixon was under fire for ordering a cover-up of the Watergate break-in, he went months without a news conference. His aides plotted his movements to avoid even informal, shouted questions from reporters. He hunkered down in the White House in a classic example of **stonewalling.** Experts in the branch of public relations called political communications generally advise against stonewalling because people infer guilt or something to hide. Nonetheless, it is one way to deal with difficult media questions.

A variation on stonewalling is the **news blackout.** When U.S. troops invaded Grenada, the Pentagon barred the press. Reporters who hired runabout boats to get to the island were intercepted by a U.S. naval blockade. While heavy-handed, such limitations on media coverage do, for a limited time, give the government the opportunity to report what's happening from its self-serving perspective.

Overwhelming Information

During the Persian Gulf buildup in 1990 and the war itself the Pentagon tried a new approach in media relations. Pete Williams, the Pentagon's chief spokesperson, provided so much information, including video, sound bites and data, that reporters were overwhelmed. The result was that reporters spent so much time sorting through Pentagon-provided material, all of it worthy, that they didn't have time to compose difficult questions or pursue fresh story angles of their own. As a result, war coverage was almost entirely favorable to the Bush administration.

Status of the Watchdog

Covering Politics Better A collection of resources for journalists from the Project for Excellence in Journalism, an initiative of the Pew Charitable Trusts. **www.journalism.org/resources/tools/reporting/politics**

studypreview **News coverage of government has slipped by many measures in recent years, largely because of constricting news organization budgets. Some slack has been picked up by trade journals and specialized newsletters, although they don't address the decline in coverage for general readers.**

Federal Coverage

Coverage of the national government ranges from near-saturation, in covering the president, to dismal at the agencies.

White House White House reporters call it the **body watch.** Befitting the most powerful person on the planet, the media watch and monitor the president more closely than anyone else on earth. When the president goes on a long trip, reporters usually are aboard Air Force One. Generally, a second plane with other reporters is also assigned to the trip.

In the White House is an elaborate press suite, equipped with all the power outlets and ports needed for today's journalistic equipment. The president's staff establishes rules

stonewalling ■ To refuse to answer questions, sometimes refusing even to meet with reporters.

news blackout ■ When a person or institution decides to issue no statements despite public interest and also declines news media questions.

body watch ■ White House term for media tracking of the president 24 hours a day, seven days a week.

of coverage and accredits reporters who are allowed in. An incredible 1,700 reporters have White House credentials. In the Reagan years reporters were free to wander down a hall to the office of the president's **news secretary.** The Clinton administration ended those roaming privileges for a while but later relented. The Bush administration tightened up again when it took over in 2001.

Usually, White House reporters are briefed twice a day. With cameras taping and sometimes the all-news networks broadcasting live, the president's news secretary makes an announcement and fields questions in what is called a **news briefing.** When the president does this, it's called a **news conference.** Practice has varied, but recent presidents have held news conferences as often as twice a week, though President George W. Bush does so less often.

Reporters ask tough questions, and presidents don't relish the grilling. Even so, the news conference has emerged as the only institution for the people to hold the president accountable, short of impeachment and the next election. Reporters see themselves

news secretary ■ Responsible for media relations. In this age of broadcasting, the term *press secretary* is outdated.

news briefing ■ When an assistant makes announcements to reporters and, usually, fields questions.

news conference ■ When a person in charge, like the president, makes announcements to reporters and, usually, fields questions.

mediaPEOPLE

Tony Snow

Tony Snow was a long-haired, flute-playing liberal in college. In 2006 he became George W. Bush's news secretary.

President Bush hoped that Snow's reputation as a journalist would help reverse the president's record-low approval ratings and the White House's battle-prone relationship with the news media.

At Davidson College in North Carolina, Snow wrote for the student newspaper and received an award for creative writing. He was a philosophy major and a member of the debate team, the literary society and the honorary forensics society. He was elected president of the senior class. He participated in late-night debates of philosophical ideas, and he co-authored an underground newspaper that never quite made it to press. On many Friday afternoons he played Jethro Tull's "Aqualung" on his flute. At the time he leaned to the left politically.

After college Snow taught physics and geography in Kenya. He worked as an advocate for the mentally ill and the developmentally disabled in North Carolina, and he was a substitute teacher in subjects ranging from calculus to seventh-grade art.

He began his journalism career in 1979 and worked as an editorial writer, then an editor for several newspapers, including the Detroit *News* and the Washington *Times.* He took a sabbatical from the *Times* to work in the White House for President Bush's father as a speechwriter. He wrote a syndicated column and appeared on radio and television programs including the *McLaughlin Group, Face the Nation, Crossfire* and *Good Morning America.* He was the first host of *Fox News Sunday* and served as the primary guest host of Rush Limbaugh's program.

Opening Up A change of course in White House news relations.

In 2005 surgeons removed Snow's colon after discovering cancer. One doctor joked the high-stress job of White House news secretary might give him heartburn but not cancer.

Snow is not shy about expressing his strong opinions. In fact, although he was firmly identified with conservative politics in much of his journalism career, he had been one of Bush's most unsparing critics. He once remarked, "When it comes to federal spending, George W. Bush is the boy who can't say no."

To those who wondered at Snow being Bush's voice as news secretary, the president had a ready one liner: "I asked him about those comments, and he said, 'You should have heard what I said about the other guy.' "

Snow has been described as "telegenic, supremely self-confident and quick with a zinger," characteristics that brought laughter back to White House news conferences after five years of tight-lipped message control.

Before accepting the job, the former pundit extracted a promise that he would have more access to the Oval Office and more power to shape policy than Bush's past news secretaries. If that truly happens, he should have plenty to say.

White House Briefing Room The next best thing to being part of the White House Press Corps.
www.whitehouse.gov/news

The Nation Political news and opinions.
www.thenation.com

The New Republic A magazine of commentary and essays on political and cultural issues.
www.tnr.com

Thomas You, too, can follow the daily doings of the U.S. Congress, with this service of the Library of Congress.
thomas.loc.gov

Government Resources The National Technology Transfer Institute has compiled a comprehensive list of government departments, independent government agencies and state governments.
www.nttc.edu/resources/government/govresources.asp

American Journalism Review Examines how the media cover specific stories and broader coverage trends.
http://ajr.org/

as surrogates for the citizenry, asking questions that a well-informed citizen would ask. What is said at a news conference is actually a two-way street. As Harry Truman told reporters after leaving the presidency: "For eight years, you and I have been helping each other. I have been trying to keep you informed of the news from the point of view of the presidency. You, more than you realize, have been giving me a great deal of what the people of this country are thinking."

Congress On Capitol Hill the primary reporting focuses on the Senate and House leadership that controls the law-making process through an elaborate committee system. Reporters cover hearings and listen to testimony on major issues, but they also lean on news releases issued by committees, caucuses and members of Congress. Reporters spend a lot of their time interviewing aides and others, sometimes for a scoop, sometimes just to be up-to-speed on emerging issues that will break as major news.

A second tier of reporters covers the Hill for regional stories that the news agencies and television networks pass over but that have hometown importance. A **regional reporter** for the Seattle *Times,* for example, would leave national stories from Congress to the news agencies that serve the *Times* and concentrate instead on stories of local interest—like maritime, timber and aerospace issues in the case of Seattle.

Agencies While the White House remains thoroughly covered, and Congress too, though to a lesser extent, federal agencies are increasingly neglected. The U.S. Department of the Interior is an example. It controls 500 million acres of public land and administers the national parks, the U.S. Bureau of Indian Affairs and the U.S. Fish and Wildlife Service. Its policies and regulations affect key issues such as water rights, mining and logging. Because the Department of the Interior has great effects on western states, it was no surprise, several years back, that several western newspapers, including the Denver *Post,* had reporters posted at the agency, as did the New York *Times* and the Washington *Post*. Today, none does.

When breaking news occurs in a noncovered agency, news bureaus send a reporter over for a story. But the expertise that comes from knowing regular sources day to day is missing. So is the kind of background on agency personalities and policies without which enterprise stories are not possible.

Some of the staffing attrition is due to the introduction of thematic beats, as opposed to building beats. Some editors have opted for health beats that span many agencies, for example, rather than a beat at the Department of Health and Human Services. Even so, fewer reporters are covering the beats that generate regular coverage of your government at work.

Some slack is being picked up by the growing **trade journal** and **newsletter** industry. At the Federal Communications Commission, for example, major agencies and newspapers have only six reporters, but the trade journal *Broadcasting & Cable* keeps its readers up to date. Hundreds of such journals and newsletters come out of Washington for specialized audiences. But because these journals are so focused, typical citizens have less news about federal agencies.

State Coverage

A continuing study headed by Charles Layton for *American Journalism Review* has found distressing drops in reporters covering state government. In 2003 only two newspapers had double-digit staffs in their state capitals: the Newark *Star-Ledger* in New Jersey, with 12, and the Sacramento *Bee* in California, with 10. There was some improvement, though. For example, the Atlanta *Journal and Constitution* went from three to nine. But that was unusual. In California the Los Angeles *Times* dropped from 14 to six. Some chains, meanwhile, continued paring statehouse staffs. Gannett, whose 100 dailies have 7.7 million circulation, fields only 66 statehouse reporters. In the mid-1980s Michigan newspapers had 25 full-time reporters in Lansing, but by 2003 there were merely 12. Furthermore,

regional reporter ■ A reporter assigned by a hometown newsroom to look for regional news in Washington that the news agencies wouldn't cover.

trade journal ■ A magazine edited for people in a specific profession or trade.

newsletter ■ A simple-format informational bulletin covering a narrowly defined field.

many of the reporters are green. At the Indiana Capitol, Lesley Stedman of the Fort Wayne *Journal Gazette* was the senior reporter at age 26 and only two years on the beat.

Not only are newspapers running less news on state government, but with fewer reporters scrambling to cover day-to-day events, there is less investigative and interpretive reporting.

The decline in coverage is serious for several reasons:

- **New Federalism.** Gradually, since the early 1990s, Congress has shifted many programs from federal to state responsibility, in a trend known as the **New Federalism.** More dollars are collected and spent by state government than ever before on education, prisons, welfare and other priorities. The U.S. Bureau of Labor Statistics lists state government as the nation's eighth largest growth industry, spending $854 billion a year, which breaks down to more than $2,000 a person. Yet fewer reporters are tracking what's happening, which means that citizens have less information to form opinions and make judgments on how their government is working.
- **Lobbying.** Private interests have increased **lobbying** dramatically. A 1990 survey by the Associated Press found 42,500 lobbyists registered in the 50 states, an increase of 20 percent in four years. Although no one has repeated the AP study, there is no reason to believe that the number of lobbyists hasn't continued to grow. The growing lobbyist corps outnumbers reporters 150:1 in Georgia's capital, a ratio not untypical of other states. Their job was to create, promote and influence legislation to adjust public policy to their own benefit. Never was there a greater need for media watchdogs.

Campaign Coverage

Critics fault the news media for falling short in covering political campaigns. These are frequent criticisms:

- **Issues.** Reporters need to push for details on positions and ask tough questions on major issues, not accept generalities. They need to bounce one candidate's position off other candidates, creating a forum of intelligent discussion from which voters can make informed choices.
- **Agenda.** Reporters need to assume some role in setting a campaign agenda. When reporters allow candidates to control the agenda of coverage, they become mere conduits for self-serving news releases and images from candidates. **Pseudo-events** with candidates, like visits to photogenic flag factories, lack substance. So do staged **photo ops.** Reporters need to guard against letting such easy-to-cover events squeeze out substantive coverage.
- **Interpretation.** Campaigns are drawn out and complicated, and reporters need to keep trying to pull together what's happened for the audience. Day-to-day spot news isn't enough. There also need to be explanation, interpretation and analysis to help voters see the big picture.
- **Inside coverage.** Reporters need to cover the machinery of the campaigns—who's running things and how. This is especially important with the growing role of campaign consultants. Who are these people? What history do they bring to a campaign? What agenda?
- **Polling.** Poll results are easy to report but tricky and inconsistent because of variations in methodology and even questions. News operations should report on competing polls, not just their own. In tracking polls, asking the same questions over time for consistency is essential.
- **Instant feedback.** Television newsrooms have supplemented their coverage and commentary with e-mail instant feedback from viewers. Select messages are flashed on-screen within minutes. In some programs a reporter is assigned to analyze incoming messages and identify trends. While all this makes for "good television," the comments are statistically dubious as indicators of overall public opinion. Too much can be read into them.

New Federalism ■ The shift in funding and administration of programs from the federal to state government.

lobbying ■ Trying to persuade legislators and regulators to a position.

pseudo-event ■ A staged event to attract media attention, usually lacking substance.

photo op ■ Short for "photo opportunity." A staged event, usually photogenic, to attract media attention.

- **Depth.** With candidates going directly to voters in debates, talk-show appearances and on blogs' reporters need to offer something more than what voters can see and hear for themselves. Analysis and depth add a fresh dimension that is not redundant to what the audience already knows.

Attack Ads

The 2004 presidential campaign spawned **negative ads** in unprecedented quantity. With little regard for facts or truth, Republicans loosely connected to the Bush campaign, under the banner of Swift Boat Veterans for Truth, ripped at the war-hero record of Democratic candidate John Kerry. Then there was the entry in a campaign advertising contest that likened George W. Bush to Hitler, which an anti-Bush group, moveon.org, let sit on its web site for days.

Put an End to Neagative Ads The League of Women Voters of Greater Youngstown compares negative and positive political campaigns. **www.cboss.com/lwv/politicalcampagns.htm**

Negativism was not new in politics. An 1884 ditty that makes reference to Grover Cleveland's illegitimate child is still a favorite among folk singers. Negativism took center stage in 1952 when a Republican slogan "Communism, Corruption, Korea," slammed outgoing President Truman's Korea policy. Two hunkered-down soldiers, portrayed by actors, were lamenting a shortage of weapons. Then one soldier was killed, and the other charged courageously into enemy fire. The **attack ad** demonstrated the potency of political advertising on the new medium of television.

527 Financing The 2004 wave of attack ads were mostly from shadowy groups not directly affiliated with candidates or parties. These groups operated under what was called 527 status in the federal campaign law. Unlike the parties and candidates, the 527s were allowed to collect unlimited money independently. The 527s had raised an incredible $240 million within a month of election day. Although there was widespread disgust at the nastiest 527 ads, experts who tracked polls concluded they had significant influence. When Congress reconvened in 2005, there were cries for reforms to curb the influence of the 527 organizations.

Making Light Amid the 2004 campaign negativity, Senator Russ Feingold of Wisconsin took a different tack—humor. Just as commercial advertising relies largely on evoking chuckles, Feingold did the same and won re-election. Whether easygoing self-deprecation and deft fun-poking are antidotes that will displace attack ads, or at least reduce their role, may be determined by whether 2008 candidates and their advisers have a good sense of humor and also decency and good taste.

Campaign Blogs

studypreview **Some candidate successes in 2004 suggested great potential for campaign blogging, but the jury is out. The early presidential hopefuls for 2008 established blog presences, some energetically, some cautiously. Conventional wisdom on campaign blogging is in a formative stage. Among unanswered questions is whether blogging should be subject to regulations like those for campaign advertising.**

negative ads ■ Political campaign advertising, usually on television, in which a candidate criticizes the opponent rather than extols emphasizes his or her platform.

attack ads ■ A subspecies of negative ads, especially savage in criticizing an opponent, many playing loose with context and facts.

blog ■ Web sites with commentary, links to related pages on other sites, interactive exchanges, and reportage.

blogosphere ■ The universe of blog sites.

Blogs and 2008

Nobody knows the role that **blogs** will take in coming political campaigns. Lessons from the 2004 and 2006 experiences are too fragmentary for firm conclusions. Even so, some 2008 presidential hopefuls, led by John Edwards, charged head-first into the **blogosphere,**

Markos Moulitsas Zúniga

4.8 Million Visitors

Leading blogs include *Daily Kos,* with links to leftist, liberal and Democratic bloggers. U.S. Army vet Markos Moulitsas Zúniga, who later went to law school, is attracting 4.8 million visitors a month according to Nielsen tracking service. That's more than the populations of Iowa and New Hampshire combined, which raises questions whether blogsophere may be more important than primaries for determining which presidential candidates sink and which swim.

that unpredictable Internet free-for-all, as if it were the keystone of their candidacies. Edwards posted his own blog regularly and plugged the site repeatedly at speaking engagements for keeping in touch. He invited other bloggers to get interactive with him. Also, he posted regularly on other blogs.

The retired general Wesley Clark also was intense at blogging. Other earlier bloggers included Hillary Clinton, Bill Frist, Russ Feingold, Newt Gingrich, Barack Obama and Tom Vilsack, although they tended to caution in their postings. Rival candidate staffs are always scouting for goofed-up facts, misstatements and gaffes to exploit later. Wary of minefields they could be laying for themselves later, some candidates hedged their bets in the early 2008 campaign. They created blog presences for themselves but posted only prepared material—speeches, talking points and other stuff that had been vetted through speechwriters, consultants and advisers.

David Perlmutter, a political analyst at Louisiana State University who studies blogs, says prepackaging doesn't work. Bloggers, he says, are a "community of debaters," not passive message recipients: "Woe to the candidate whose supposedly first-person blog is outed as a prepackaged set of talking points created by a committee." Perlmutter noted that Hillary Clinton's safely worded comments "read more like press releases than real posts."

What, then, was the political wisdom of Edwards and the spontaneity of his energetic blogging? Perlmutter notes that Edwards had given up his U.S. Senate seat and returned to North Carolina. He was out of the loop of the national news media. He had little to lose even with high-risk blog exchanges. The same with Wesley Clark.

In some ways, Edwards and Clark were in a position like the relatively unknown Howard Dean in 2004. With no place else to go, Dean went online and portrayed himself as a populist outsider. The former Vermont governor shocked campaign orthodoxy by registering 600,000 supporters online and raising $20 million. Unable to rally big-buck supporters to $1,000-a-plate fundraisers in grand hotel ballrooms, Dean went blogging. His fund-raising "dinners" were nibbling on a turkey sandwich while pecking away at a keyboard in blog correspondence on issues as thousands of supporters—and the curious—linked in. Dean suddenly was a major player for the Democratic nomination, although he fizzled after the Iowa primary as John Kerry and John Edwards picked up steam.

Campaign Blog Research

Political strategists are the first to admit that the rule book is still being written on how candidates can utilize blogs effectively. That makes the 2008 elections a testbed for exploring a wide range of hypotheses. At this point, this much is known:

- **Early momentum.** Bloggers tend to decide early who to support and, conversely, who to oppose. The decisions come even before caucuses and primaries, which suggests that candidates would do well to curry blog favor as soon as possible.

  Although bloggers settle on loyalties early, they are not blind loyalists. You can ask Illinois Senator Dick Durbin about this. He lost substantial blog support after suggesting that Nazi-like techniques were being used on prisoners at Guantanámo.
- **Continued presence.** A long-term commitment is necessary for candidates to earn blog support. Trust and respect comes from an ongoing blog presence and interaction. A single post won't do. Nor even a few.
- **Blog as news sources.** The traditional news media lean on information on frequently visited blogs for tips on trends. Thus blogs have become a factor in campaign news coverage that transcends their individual habitués.
- **Niche audience.** Blog readers are unimpressed with traditional messages geared for mass audiences, like one-size-fits-all television ads. Bloggers may represent a large audience but not a mass audience in the old-fashioned sense. Bloggers are a niche audience. They value individual interaction and authenticity. Says Perlmutter: "The essence of blogging, after all, is personal connections between participants—the ability to talk and talk back, the interplay of argument and critique."
- **Intent readership.** Bloggers are attentive readers who make themselves incredibly well-informed. These aren't mere headline-readers. Their information-heavy stature would suggest that many are opinion leaders among family, friends and associates. Bloggers influence the voting of non-bloggers.
- **Bloggers vote.** A study by the Pew Center for People and the Press found, for example, that most of the early online supporters of Howard Dean indeed voted in November even though he had washed out.

Sponsored Blogs

As a subspecies in the culture, bloggers are purists who would bristle at the idea of being bought. Even so, a Trojan horse among partisan bloggers are sites that are beholden financially to candidates. It was learned after the 2004 election that John Thune, who was seeking a South Dakota seat in the U.S. Senate, had given money to two seemingly independent prominent bloggers who attacked incumbent Tom Daschle. Thune won. The Thune-financed sites gave no hint to their sponsorship.

Unlike paid advertisements in publications and on television and radio, ads and videos on blogs are not covered by campaign law. Identifying the sponsor is not required. Campaign funds that go to blogs are reported by law as campaign expenditures, but the reports, being quarterly, provide data to the public in some cases, as in South Dakota, only after the election is over.

Media-Government Issues

studypreview **Serious questions of trust are at stake as media owners become more business oriented. Other issues: Can news be trusted if reporters pick up outside income from special interests? Does political advertising pander to emotional and superficial instincts? Should television be required to give candidates free airtime? Should we look to the Internet to make government instantly responsive to the public will?**

Political Favors

Public confidence in media coverage suffers whenever doubts arise about whether the media are truly the public's watchdogs on government. Such doubts have grown as media control has been concentrated in fewer hands through conglomeration and with the concomitant growth in media leaders being business people first and media people second. Rupert Murdoch, whose media empire includes the Fox television network, lost tremendous credibility when it was discovered he had offered House Speaker Newt Gingrich $4.5 million for a yet-unwritten manuscript to be published by Murdoch's HarperCollins book subsidiary. At the time Murdoch was facing a federal challenge to his ownership of Fox. Book industry experts said there was no way Gingrich's book could earn $4.5 million—and, in fact, it flopped. When the deal was exposed, Murdoch and Gingrich both backpedaled and proclaimed Murdoch's problems on the Hill and the book deal were unfortunate coincidences.

Whatever the truth of the Murdoch-Gingrich deal, the interplay of media and government raises questions about whether the media are more responsive to their financial interest or to the public interest. Murdoch once yanked BBC off his StarTV satellite service to China after Chinese government leaders objected to BBC coverage. At the time Murdoch had numerous business initiatives needing Chinese government approval. In a similar incident, in 1998, Murdoch canceled publication of a forthcoming book from HarperCollins because of passages that were critical of China's human rights record. Murdoch's action became known only because the author, the respected former British governor of Hong Kong, went public with his objections.

It's impossible to know how many media decisions are driven by business rather than public interests because the participants don't advertise them as such. Such decisions become public only through roundabout ways, and while the participants are embarrassed, it doesn't seem they derive any lessons and change their ways—at least not in the case of Rupert Murdoch.

Media Monitors Network Online forum for news without corporate interests. **http://world.mediamonitors.net**

Center for Politics The Center for Politics is dedicated to the proposition that government works better when politics works better. **www.centerforpolitics.org**

Campaign Advertising

The mass media have become essential tools not only for national political leaders. Even candidates for state and many local offices have media advisers. Critics note that this techno-politics has serious downsides. In the age of television, photogenic candidates have an unfair built-in advantage. According to the critics, good looks rather than good ideas sway the electorate. Perhaps more serious, in some critics' view, is that slick presentation is more important than substance when it comes to 15-second TV spots.

Can candidates buy their way into office with advertising? While a candidate who vastly outspends another would seem to have an advantage, well-heeled campaigns can fail. In the most expensive U.S. Senate campaign in history, in New Jersey in 2000, Jon Corzine spent $60 million. He won. But in 1994 Michael Huffington spent $18 million on a California campaign for the U.S. Senate, and lost to Diane Feinstein, who spent only $9 million.

In presidential campaigns too, no correlation has been established between winning and media spending. **Herbert Alexander,** a University of Southern California political scientist who tracks campaign spending, noted that George Bush outspent Bill Clinton $43 million to $32 million in 1992 and lost. Ross Perot also outspent Clinton, buying almost $40 million in media time and space. In 1988, however, Bush outspent Michael Dukakis $32 million to $24 million and won. The data point to campaign advertising being only one of many variables in elections.

Herbert Alexander ■ His studies have concluded that media advertising is only one of many variables in political campaigns.

The fact remains, however, that a political campaign has a cost of admission. Candidates need media exposure, and a campaign without advertising would almost certainly be doomed.

It would be a mistake to conclude that political advertising has no effect. A major 1976 study by **Thomas Patterson and Robert McClure** concluded that 7 percent of the people in a 2,700-person sample were influenced by ads on whether to vote for Richard Nixon or George McGovern for president. While that was a small percentage, many campaigns are decided by even slimmer margins. The lesson from the Patterson-McClure study is that political advertising can make a critical difference.

Free Airtime

media ONLINE **The Living Room Candidate** A history of presidential campaign commercials from 1952–2000, from the American Museum of the Moving Image. **http://livingroomcandidate.movingimage.us**

The :30 Second Candidate PBS takes a look at the world of political advertising. **www.pbs.org/30secondcandidate/front.html**

Thomas Patterson and Robert McClure ■ Effect of political advertising on voters is critical only in close campaigns.

Television advertising accounts for most of candidates' campaign budgets, which has put growing pressure on candidates to raise funds to buy the time. This pressure has resulted in campaign finance irregularities that end up haunting candidates later. Many political observers, for example, questioned whether Al Gore's 2000 presidential hopes could survive the Buddhist Temple fund-raising scandal back during the 1996 Clinton-Dole campaign. Not surprisingly, Gore became an advocate of requiring television stations to give free airtime to candidates.

One proposal, from the Center for Governmental Studies in Los Angeles, would require stations to give two hours to candidates in the 60 days before an election. To allay station objections to losing revenue, the center proposed tax credits to offset station costs. Broadcasters still objected on numerous grounds. Shelby Scott, of the American Federation of Television and Radio Artists, said, "I don't want any more 30-second spots. I don't think they inform the electorate." Other television people noted that political ads, which are sold at cheap rates, would displace more lucrative commercial ads. Broadcasters also noted a coerciveness in being required to give free airtime to political candidates, noting that stations are beholden to the federal government for their licenses to remain in business.

CHAPTER 19 Wrap-Up

No one denies that the news media are influential in U.S. governance and politics, but the influence generally is indirect through media-savvy opinion leaders. Even so, the media are powerful players in public life because they shape the public's agenda by reporting some issues and ignoring or downplaying others. The media also frame issues and prime how people see the issues.

Questions for Review

1. What does the term *fourth estate* mean?
2. How do the news media influence people on political issues?
3. How do media agenda-setting and priming work?
4. How do government leaders manipulate media coverage?
5. What lessons do we know so far about campaign blogs?

Questions for Critical Thinking

1. Who are opinion leaders in your life? How do they influence your views?
2. What personal values would influence you as a news reporter who sets public agendas and frames issues and primes how people see them?

3. What perils face a reporter who accepts information off the record from one source and later receives the same information on deep *background from another source?*
4. Considering the dynamics in government-media relations, what are the prospects for plans to require television to give free airtime to political candidates?
5. If you were managing a television network's news coverage of a presidential campaign, what instructions would you give your reporters?
6. What would you advise a 2008 presidential candidate about heavy blogging?

Deepening Your media LITERACY

Is the Internet changing the government-media landscape?

STEP 1 Think about how a lack of electricity in Iraq might be reported by a U.S. television network, a U.S. newspaper and an Iraqi blogger.

Dig Deeper

STEP 2 If you were the press secretary for the president of the United States, how would you try to shape the media coverage of the issue of lack of electrical power in Iraq? Write a list of your ideas. Would your methods change for each kind of media? Would you try anything special for the blogger? What if the blogger were an American soldier stationed in Iraq?

What Do You Think?

STEP 3 Answer these questions:

1. How can the Internet serve as a media watchdog?
2. How can you evaluate the credibility of Internet blogs or political sites?
3. Can a blogger be an opinion leader? Or is an opinion leader someone who reads the blogs?
4. Who is setting the agenda: the blogger, the reader or the subject of the blog?

Keeping Up to Date

Professional journals that carry articles on media coverage of political issues and governance include *Columbia Journalism Review, Quill* and *American Journalism Review.*

Ongoing discussion on media responsibility also appears in the *Journal of Mass Media Ethics.*

For Further Learning

Helen Thomas. *Watchdogs of Democracy? The Waning Washington Press Corps and How It Has Failed the Public.* Scribner/Lisa Dew, 2006.

Thomas, a veteran White House reporter, blames an adversarial news media on an unholy alliance of big government and big business to control the news, sometimes subtly, sometimes not.

David D. Perlmutter. "Political Blogs: The New Iowa?" *Chronicle of Higher Education* (May 26, 2006). Pages B6–B8.

Perlmutter, a political scientist, examines the potential of blogs in presidential campaigns. He has as many questions as answers about this new medium in candidates' quivers.

Craig Crawford. *Attack the Messenger: How Politicians Turn You Against the Messenger*. Littlefield, 2005.

Crawford, a *Congressional Quarterly* columnist, examines White House policies in the Bush administrations to undermine the mainstream news media.

Eric Alterman. *When Presidents Lie: A History of Official Deception and Its Consequences.* Viking, 2004.

Alterman, a columnist for *Nation* magazine, says governance moved into a post-truth era with the administration of George W. Bush. His case studies are earlier: Franklin Roosevelt and the Yalta accords, John Kennedy and the Cuban missile crisis, Lyndon Johnson and the Tonkin Gulf incident, and Ronald Reagan and Iran-Contra illegalities.

Claes H. de Vreese. "The Effects of Frames in Political Television News on Issue Interpretations and Frame Salience," *Journalism and Mass Communication Quarterly* (Spring 2004), pages 36–52.

De Vreese, a Dutch scholar, looks at framing in television news coverage of proposals to enlarge the European Union. Vreese includes good discussion on framing as a media phenomenon.

David Brock. *The Republican Noise Machine: Right-Wing Media and How It Corrupts Democracy.* Crown, 2004.

Brock, once a conservative commentator but no longer, offers a partisan critique in which he posits right-wing talking points and bluster to weekly strategy meetings of arch-conservative Grover Norquist. His targets include Fox News. Also, he blames mainstream media for succumbing to right-wing pressure to avoid tough questions and instead offering uncritical "balance" of views—a he-said, she-said approach that falls short of identifying truth.

Ken Auletta. "Vox Fox," *New Yorker* (May 26, 2003), pages 58–73.

Auletta, who specializes in media subjects, is less than flattering in this extensive profile on Fox News creator and one-time Republican political adviser Roger Ailes.

Stephen D. Reese, Oscar H. Grady Jr. and August E. Grant, editors. *Framing Public Life: Perspectives on Media and Our Understanding of the Social World.* Erlbaum, 2001.

A collection on important observations on framing in mass communication.

Elizabeth M. Perse. *Media Effects and Society.* Erlbaum, 2001.

Perse, a communication scholar, offers an advanced overview of studies on media effects, including their effect on public opinion and voting.

Stephen J. Wayne. *The Road to the White House, 2000.* Palgrave, 2001.

Wayne, a scholar, includes campaign finance and the growing importance of money for television buying and media exposure.

Waiting for the Judge Jon Lech Johansen waits for his case to begin in a Norway court. The U.S. movie industry had gone after DVD Jon, as he came to be called, for publishing code that enabled others to copy disks. He was acquitted.

chapter 20 Mass Media Law

In this chapter you will learn:

- The heart of U.S. mass media law is the First Amendment's guarantee of free expression.
- Only rarely may the government prohibit expression.
- Anyone who is falsely slandered by the mass media may sue for libel.
- The mass media generally may not intrude on someone's solitude.
- The news media may cover the courts and government however they see fit.
- Obscenity is not protected by the First Amendment, but pornography is.
- Copyright law protects intellectual property from being stolen from its owners.

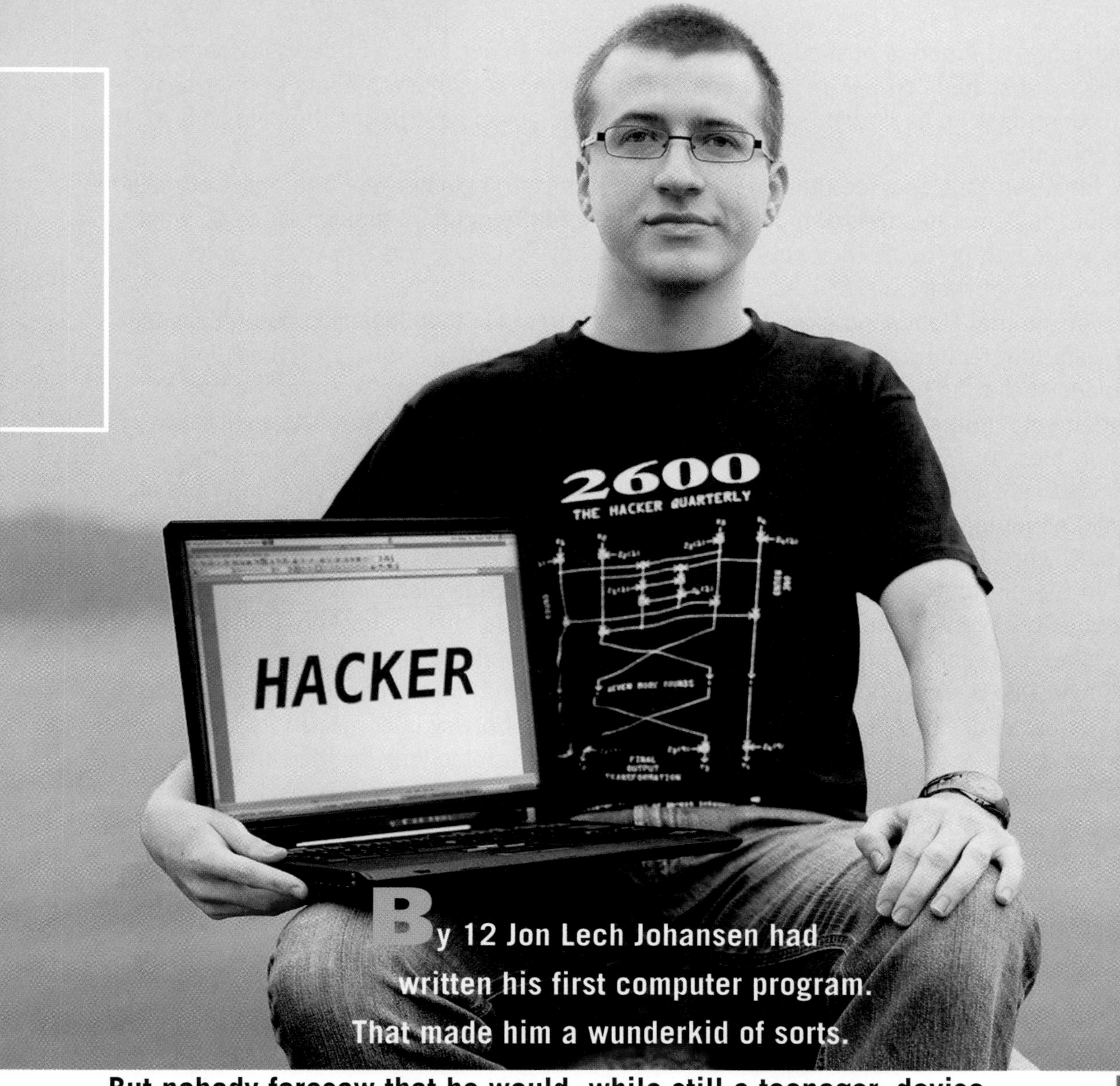

By 12 Jon Lech Johansen had written his first computer program. That made him a wunderkid of sorts.

But nobody foresaw that he would, while still a teenager, devise programs that would shake the billion-dollar Hollywood movie industry to its core. His genius, also, would make him a folk hero to millions of movie-lovers worldwide.

Jon-Lech, as he came to be lionized in his native Norway, began his trek to notoriety unwittingly. He loved movies. By 15 he owned 360 DVDs. Some he bought at jacked-up Norwegian prices because Hollywood's geographical coding prevented European computers from playing U.S.-issued versions. Other DVDs he bought from U.S. sources, and with coding he invented, he played them on his computer in Oslo. It all was perfectly legal in Norway. He recalls reveling at his accomplishment when he first ripped copies of *The Matrix* and *The Fifth Element.*

"Why shouldn't others share my enjoyment?" he asked himself. A week later he posted his coding on the Internet.

Hollywood went ballistic, recognizing that Jon-Lech's coding could be used to bypass the encrypting that prevented their DVD movies from being easily swapped through file-sharing. The revenue loss could be devastating. The Motion Picture

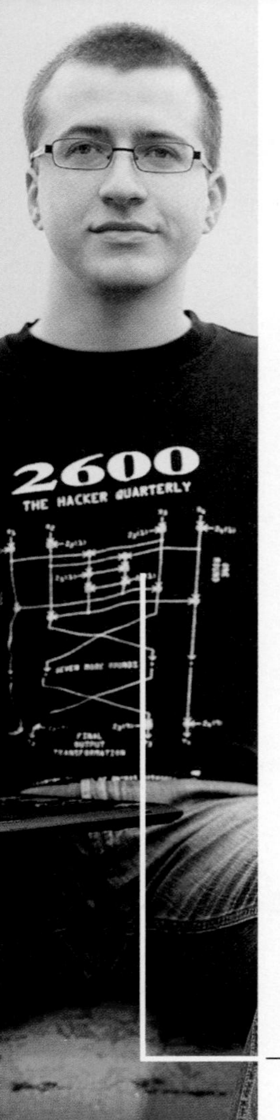

Association of America pushed Norwegian authorities to act. Police raided the Johansen home, confiscated Jon-Lech's computer, and put him through seven hours of interrogation. Confident he had done nothing wrong, Jon-Lech even gave police the password to his computer.

Johansen thus became the vortex of a continuing struggle between the rights of mega-media conglomerates that own creative material and the rights of individuals to do what they want with products they buy—in this case copying DVDs, and also music, to play on any number of their own devices.

For the trial Hollywood executives flew to Oslo to argue that Johansen had unleashed software that facilitated movie piracy and could put the movie industry in ruins. Johansen responded that he had committed no wrong-doing, let alone piracy, and that he had a fundamental human right of free expression to share his coding however he wanted. In effect, he said: "Go after the pirates, not me." Jon-Lech fancied himself a consumer advocate, allowing people to use their DVD purchases as they wanted—on computers at home, on laptops on the road, on handheld devices anywhere else. The court agreed. In fact, when the prosecution appealed, the court again agreed.

In the run-up to the trial, Jon-Lech supporters worldwide distributed t-shirts and neckties printed with his software. In the May Day parade in Oslo, backers carried a banner "Free DVD-Jon." The issue inspired a haiku. Meanwhile, more than 1 million copies of his anti-DVD encryption software had been downloaded from Johansen's site.

For better or worse, depending on your perspective, Norway later revised its laws to forbid software that could be used to undermine copyright protections, as the United States had done earlier at the behest of giant media companies. But the issue lives on, as you will discover in this chapter on mass media law. The chapter includes the most pressing media law dilemma in the early 21st century—the protection of intellectual property.

The U.S. Constitution

studypreview **The First Amendment to the U.S. Constitution bars the government from limiting freedom of expression, including expression in the mass media, or so it seems. However, for the first 134 years of the amendment's existence, it appeared that the states could ignore the federal Constitution and put their own restrictions on free expression because it did not apply to them.**

media ONLINE **Electronic Frontier Foundation** Defending freedom in a digital world. **www.eff.org**

First Amendment Handbook This online version of the Reporter's Committee for Freedom of the Press handbook has introductory sections on libel, privacy, news-gathering, access and copyright. **www.rcfp.org/handbook**

First Amendment Center Everything you want and more regarding the First Amendment, including current news headlines and the First Amendment Library. **www.firstamendmentcenter.org**

First Amendment

The legal foundation for freedom of expression in the United States is the **First Amendment** to the Constitution. The amendment, penned by **James Madison,** boiled down the eloquence of Benjamin Franklin, Thomas Jefferson and earlier libertarian thinkers during the American colonial experience to a mere 45 words: "Congress shall make no law respecting an establishment of religion, or prohibiting the free exercise thereof; or abridging the freedom of speech, or of the press; or of the right of the people peaceably to assemble, and to petition the Government for a redress of grievances."

The amendment, which became part of the Constitution in 1791, seemed a definitive statement that set the United States apart from all other nations at the time in guaranteeing that the government wouldn't interfere with free expression. It turned out, however, that the First Amendment did not settle all the questions that could be raised about free expression. This chapter looks at many of these unsettled issues and attempts to clarify them.

First Amendment ■ Bars government from limiting free expression.

James Madison ■ Author of the First Amendment.

media TIMELINE

LANDMARKS IN MEDIA LAW

1791 States ratified the First Amendment, the freedom of expression section of U.S. Constitution.

1901 Iowa Supreme Court ruled performers must accept criticism of performances.

1919 Justice Oliver Wendell Holmes coined the "Fire!" in a crowded theater example for prior restraint.

1930 Court overruled the import ban on *Ulysses.*

1931 U.S. Supreme Court banned prior restraint in *Near* v. *Minnesota.*

1964 U.S. Supreme Court ruled that public figures can sue for libel only if the media were reckless.

1968 U.S. Supreme Court ruled local community standards determine obscenity.

1971 U.S. Supreme Court banned prior restraint in the Pentagon Papers national security case.

2003 Recording industry cracks down on piracy downloads from the Internet.

Scope of the First Amendment

The First Amendment explicitly prohibited only Congress from limiting freedom of expression, but there was never a serious legal question that it applied also to the executive branch of the national government. There was a question, however, about whether the First Amendment prohibited the states from squelching freedom of expression.

From the early days of the Republic, many states had laws that limited freedom of expression, and nobody seemed to mind much. In fact, all the way through the 1800s the First Amendment seemed largely ignored. Not until 1925, when the U.S. Supreme Court considered the case of **Benjamin Gitlow,** was the First Amendment applied to the states. In that case Gitlow, a small-time New York agitator, rankled authorities by publishing his "Left Wing Manifesto" and distributing a Socialist paper. He was arrested and convicted of violating a state law that forbade advocating "criminal anarchy." Gitlow appealed that the First Amendment to the U.S. Constitution should override any state law that contravenes it, and the U.S. Supreme Court agreed. Gitlow, by the way, lost his appeal on other grounds. Even so, his case was a significant clarification of the scope of the First Amendment.

Prior Restraint

studypreview **When the government heads off an utterance before it is made, the government is engaging in prior restraint. Since the 1930s the U.S. Supreme Court has consistently found that prior restraint violates the First Amendment. At the same time the Court says there may be circumstances, though rare, in which the public good would justify such censorship.**

Public Nuisances

The U.S. Supreme Court was still finding its voice on First Amendment issues when a Minnesota case came to its attention. The Minnesota Legislature had created a "public nuisance" law that allowed authorities to shut down "obnoxious" newspapers. The Legislature's rationale was that government has the right to remove things that work against the common good: Just as a community can remove obnoxious weeds, so can

American Civil Liberties Union Working hard to defend civil liberties. **www.aclu.org**

Benjamin Gitlow ■ His appeal resulted in a ban on state laws that restrict freedom of expression.

mediaPEOPLE

Jay Near

Jay Near and Howard Guilford, who started a scandal sheet in Minneapolis in 1927, did not have far to look for stories on corruption. Prohibition was in effect, and Minneapolis, because of geography, was a key U.S. distribution point for bootleg Canadian whisky going south to Chicago, St. Louis and other cities. Police and many officials were knee-deep in the illicit whisky trade and bribery.

Hearing about the kind of newspaper that Near and Guilford had in mind, the crooked police chief, aware of his own vulnerability, told his men to yank every copy off the newsstands as soon as they appeared. The *Saturday Press* thus became the first U.S. newspaper banned even before a single issue had been published. Even so, Near and Guilford put out weekly issues, each exposing scandals.

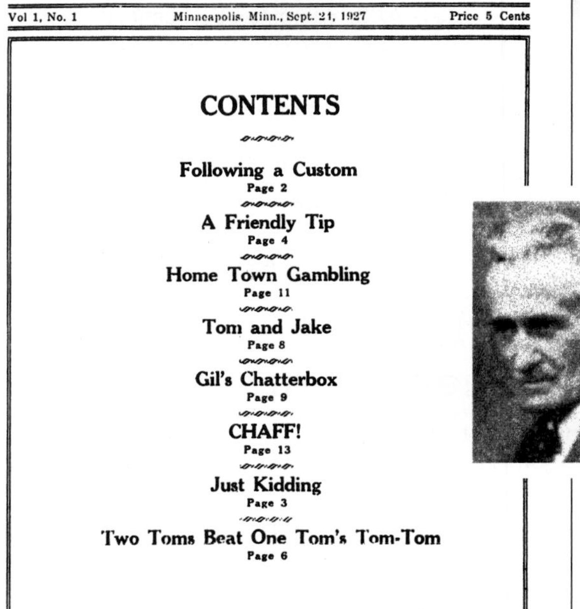

The Saturday Press

Vol 1, No. 1 | Minneapolis, Minn., Sept. 21, 1927 | Price 5 Cents

CONTENTS

Following a Custom
Page 2

A Friendly Tip
Page 4

Home Town Gambling
Page 11

Tom and Jake
Page 8

Gil's Chatterbox
Page 9

CHAFF!
Page 13

Just Kidding
Page 3

Two Toms Beat One Tom's Tom-Tom
Page 6

1927 Scandal Sheet Page One of Jay Near and Howard Guilford's inaugural issue looked bland enough, but inside were stories that infuriated officials. The officials eventually declared the *Saturday Press* a public nuisance and shut it down to head off further incriminating coverage of local corruption. In the landmark court case that resulted, *Near* v. *Minnesota,* the U.S. Supreme Court ruled that such prior restraint was unconstitutional.

Two months after the first issue of the *Saturday Press,* Floyd Olson, the prosecutor, was fed up. He went to court and obtained an order to ban Near and Guilford from producing any more issues. Olson based his case on a 1925 Minnesota gag law that declared that "a malicious, scandalous and defamatory newspaper" could be banned as a public nuisance.

Despite their crusading for good causes, Near and Guilford's brand of journalism was hard to like. Both were bigots who peppered their writing with references to "niggers," "yids," "bohunks" and "spades." Could they get away with saying such things in print?

The U.S. Supreme Court said "yes" in a landmark decision known as *Near* v. *Minnesota.* The court said that no government at any level has the right to suppress a publication because of what it might say in its next issue. Except in highly exceptional circumstances, such as life-and-death issues in wartime, legal action against a publication can come only after something has been published—not before.

Jay Near ■ His appeal resulted in a strong ruling against government prior restraint on expression.

Howard Guilford ■ Colleague of Jay Near in producing the *Saturday Press.*

Robert McCormick ■ Chicago *Tribune* publisher who supported *Near* v. *Minnesota* appeal.

American Civil Liberties Union ■ Backed *Near* v. *Minnesota.*

prior restraint ■ Prohibiting expression in advance.

it remove obnoxious "rags." In 1927 in Minneapolis, authorities used the law to padlock the *Saturday Press,* a feisty scandal sheet owned by **Jay Near** and **Howard Guilford.**

Most people would agree that the *Saturday Press* was obnoxious, especially its racist hate-mongering. Other people, however, including publisher **Robert McCormick** of the Chicago *Tribune* and the fledgling **American Civil Liberties Union,** saw another issue. In their thinking, the First Amendment protected all expression from government interference, no matter how obnoxious. They also were bothered that government, in this case the county prosecutor, was the determiner of what was obnoxious.

Three and one-half years after the *Saturday Press* was silenced, the U.S. Supreme Court, in a 5-to-4 decision, threw out the Minnesota law. The Court ruled that **prior restraint,** prohibiting expression before it is made, was disallowed under the U.S.

Constitution. Said Chief Justice **Charles Evans Hughes:** "The fact that the liberty of the press may be abused by miscreant purveyors of scandal does not make any less the immunity of the press from previous restraint in dealing with official misconduct."

The decision was a landmark limitation on governmental censorship, although the Court noted, as it always does in such cases, that protection for the press "is not absolutely unlimited." The Court has always noted that it can conceive of circumstances, such as a national emergency, when prior restraint might be justified.

media ONLINE

Media Center at New York Law School This law school site contains background about cases, statutes and scholarly papers related to media law and regulation. **www.nyls.edu/pages/107.asp**

Silha Center for the Study of Media Ethics and Law This site of the University of Minnesota contains articles, news and links related to issues of media law and regulation. **www.silha.umn.edu**

The Reporters Committee for Freedom of the Press A nonprofit organization that provides resources and free legal assistance to journalists. **www.rcfp.org**

Allowable Abridgments

In its wisdom the U.S. Supreme Court has avoided creating a rigid list of permissible abridgments to freedom of expression. No matter how thoughtfully drafted, a rigid list could never anticipate every situation. Nonetheless, the Supreme Court has discussed circumstances in which censorship is sometimes warranted.

National Security The federal government jailed dozens of antiwar activists during World War I. Many appealed, prompting the U.S. Supreme Court to consider whether the First Amendment's prohibition against government limitations should be waived in wartime. A federal prosecutor had gone after **Charles Schenck** of Philadelphia, general secretary of the Socialist Party, and his wife, **Elizabeth Baer,** for handing out leaflets aimed at recently drafted men. The pamphlets made several points:

- The draft violated the 13th Amendment, which prohibits slavery.
- The draft was unfair because clergy and conscientious objectors, like Quakers, were exempted.
- The war was being fought for the profit of cold-blooded capitalists who, the leaflets claimed, controlled the country.
- Draftees should join the Socialists and work to repeal the draft law.

Charles Evans Hughes ■ Chief justice who wrote the decision in *Near* v. *Minnesota.*

Charles Schenck ■ His arrest resulted in the U.S. Supreme Court's first First Amendment opinion in 1919.

Elizabeth Baer ■ Socialist pamphleteer; codefendant with her husband, Charles Schenck.

NEW YORK, SUNDAY, JUNE 13, 1971 — 75¢ beyond 50-mile zone from New York City, except Long Island. Higher in air delivery cities. — BQLI 50 *CENTS*

Vietnam Archive: Pentagon Study Traces 3 Decades of Growing U. S. Involvement

By NEIL SHEEHAN

A massive study of how the United States went to war in Indochina, conducted by the Pentagon three years ago, demonstrates that four administrations progressively developed a sense of commitment to a non-Communist Vietnam, a readiness to fight the North to protect the South, and an ultimate frustration with this effort—to a much greater extent than their public statements acknowledged at the time.

The 3,000-page analysis, to which 4,000 pages of official documents are appended, was commissioned by Secretary of Defense Robert S. McNamara and covers the American involvement in Southeast Asia from World War II to mid-1968—the start of the peace talks in Paris after President Lyndon B. Johnson had set a limit on further military commitments and revealed his intention to retire. Most of the study and many of the appended documents have been obtained by The New York Times and will be described and presented in a series of articles beginning today.

Three pages of documentary material from the Pentagon study begin on Page 35.

Though far from a complete history, even at 2.5 million words, the study forms a great archive of government decision-making on Indochina over three decades. The study led its 30 to 40 authors and researchers to many broad conclusions and specific findings, including the following:

¶That the Truman Administration's decision to give military aid to France in her colonial war against the Communist-led Vietminh "directly involved" the United States in Vietnam and "set" the course of American policy.

¶That the Eisenhower Administration's decision to rescue a fledgling South Vietnam from a Communist takeover and attempt to undermine the new Communist regime of North Vietnam gave the Administration a "direct role in the ultimate breakdown of the Geneva settlement" for Indochina in 1954.

¶That the Kennedy Administration, though ultimately spared from major escalation decisions by the death of its leader, transformed a policy of "limited-risk gamble," which it inherited, into a "broad commitment" that left President Johnson with a choice between more war and withdrawal.

¶That the Johnson Administration, though the President was reluctant and hesitant to take the final decisions, intensified the covert warfare against North Vietnam and began planning in the spring of 1964 to wage overt war, a full year before it publicly revealed the depth of its involvement and its fear of defeat.

¶That this campaign of growing clandestine military pressure through 1964 and the expanding program of bombing North Vietnam in 1965 were begun despite the judgment of the Government's intelligence community that the measures would not cause Hanoi to cease its support of the Vietcong insurgency in the South, and that the bombing was

Continued on Page 38, Col. 1

NIXON CRITICIZED

Vast Review of War Took a Year

U.S. URGES INDIANS AND PAKISTANIS TO USE RESTRAINT

Calls for 'Peaceful Political Accommodation' to End Crisis in East Pakistan

FIRST PUBLIC APPEAL

Statement Is Said to Reflect Fear of Warfare if Flow of Refugees Continues

By TAD SZULC
Special to The New York Times

WASHINGTON, June 12—The United States appealed today to India and Pakistan to exercise restraint and urged the Pakistanis to restore normal conditions in East Pakistan through "peaceful political accommodation."

It was the first public statement by the United States on the situation in the subcontinent

Neil Sheehan

Daniel Ellsberg

Pentagon Papers Story In 1971, when the New York *Times* began running a detailed series on the blundering U.S. policy on Vietnam over a quarter of a century, the federal government ordered the newspaper to stop. Because the series was based on secret documents, taken illegally from the Pentagon by researcher Daniel Ellsberg, the government claimed that national security would be jeopardized by the appearance of additional installments. The *Times* appealed, and the U.S. Supreme Court concluded that freedom of the press outweighed the government's concern.

As the government prosecutor saw it, the leaflets encouraged insubordination and disloyalty in the military, even mutiny. The Supreme Court agreed that the government can take exceptional prerogatives when the nation is at war. Schenck and Baer lost.

Since *Schenck* in 1919 the Court has repeated its point that national security is a special circumstance in which government restrictions can be justified. Even so, the Court's thinking has evolved in specifics, and many scholars believe that Schenck and Baer today would have prevailed. Support for this assessment of the Court's revised thinking came in an important 1972 case, during the Vietnam war, when the Court overruled the government for threatening the New York *Times* for a series of articles drawn from classified defense documents. In the so-called **Pentagon Papers** case, the Court said the people's right to know about government defense policy was more important than the government's claim that the *Times* was jeopardizing national security.

Public Endangerment In the Schenck case the eloquent Justice **Oliver Wendell Holmes** wrote these words: "The most stringent protection of free speech would not protect a man in falsely shouting 'Fire' in a crowded theater and causing panic." His point was that the First Amendment's ban on government abridgment of freedom of expression cannot be applied literally. Holmes was saying that reasonable people agree that there must be exceptions. Since then lesser courts have carved out allowable abridgments. Some have been endorsed by the Supreme Court. On other cases the Court has been silent, letting lower-level court decisions stand.

Pentagon Papers ■ Case in which the government attempted prior restraint against the New York *Times*.

Oliver Wendell Holmes ■ Justice who wrote that shouting "Fire!" in a crowded theater would be justification for abridgment of freedom of speech rights.

Walter Chaplinsky ■ Namesake for the case in which the Fighting Words Doctrine was defined.

Fighting Words Doctrine ■ The idea that censorship can be justified against insulting provocation to violence.

In a 1942 New Hampshire case the police were upheld in jailing **Walter Chaplinsky,** who had taken to the streets to deride religions other than his own as "rackets." Somebody called the police. Chaplinsky then turned his venom on the marshal who showed up, calling him, in a lapse of piety, "a God-damned racketeer" and "a damned fascist." From these circumstances emerged the **Fighting Words Doctrine.** The court said someone might be justified taking a poke at you for using "fighting words," with perhaps a riot resulting. Preventing a riot was a justification for halting someone's freedom of expression. Again, whether courts today would uphold Chaplinsky being silenced is debated among legal scholars. Nonetheless, the Fighting Words Doctrine

Martyred Political Prisoner

Eugene Debs, a Socialist Party leader, had run four times for the presidency, in 1900, 1904, 1908 and 1912. He ran a fifth time, in 1920—this time from prison. Here, party officials pose with Debs at the prison after notifying him that he had been nominated. He had been sent to jail for making an antiwar speech, a conviction that was upheld by the U.S. Supreme Court because of special national security considerations in time of war. Debs's 1920 campaign photograph showed him in prison garb with bars in the background—the martyred political prisoner. He won almost 1 million votes. A year later, President Warren Harding pardoned Debs, who by then was aged and ailing.

Clarence Brandenburg

Clarence Brandenburg worked by day as a television repair man in a suburb of Cincinnati. By night he was an Ohio Ku Klux Klan leader. One day, in the mid-1960s, he called a reporter for a Cincinnati television station and invited a television crew to a rally.

About a dozen hooded figures, some with firearms, burned a large wooden cross. There were no spectators—just the Klansmen and the news crew. The only record of what Brandenburg said is the news film. Although the sound on the film is not always clear, it seemed that Brandenburg's speech rambled and was loaded with non sequiturs and imprecise, sometimes nonsensical expressions and words. Derogatory things were said about blacks and Jews. Brandenburg urged sending "niggers" back to Africa and Jews to Israel. Here are some passages transcribed from the news film:

"This is an organizers' meeting. We have had quite a few members here today which are—we have hundreds, hundreds of members throughout the State of Ohio. I can quote from a newspaper clipping from the Columbus, Ohio, *Dispatch,* five weeks ago Sunday morning. The Klan has more members in the State of Ohio than does any other organization.

"We're not a revengent organization, but if our President, our Congress, our Supreme Court, continues to suppress the white, Caucasian race, it's possible that there might have to be some revengeance taken.

"We are marching on Congress July the Fourth, 400,000 strong. From there we are dividing into groups, one to march on St. Augustine, Florida, the other group to march into Mississippi. Thank you."

Authorities who saw the television news coverage decided to act. Soon Brandenburg was indicted for violating a 1919 Ohio law that barred violence directed at the government. This law made it a crime to advocate "violent means to effect political and economic change that endangers the security of the state." Brandenburg was convicted. In 1969, however, the U.S. Supreme Court found 9-0 in his favor. The court said the First Amendment protects advocating ideas, including the overthrow of the government. This protection, however, stops short of unlawful acts. The court was making an important distinction between advocacy of ideas and advocacy of unlawful action. In other words, you may teach and advocate overthrow but you can't do it. Nor can you prod someone else into doing it.

In short, the state needs to prove a real danger exists. In Brandenburg's case, such was impossible. Although his muddled expressions may have seemed to advocate violence against leaders of the national government, his prosecutors could not seriously argue that Brandenburg was a real threat to the republic. Whatever violence Brandenburg advocated was hardly imminent. The woods in southwest Ohio were a long way from the Potomac, and there was no way the prosecutors could demonstrate that violence was likely.

from *Chaplinsky* remains as testimony to the Court's willingness to consider public safety as a value that sometimes should outweigh freedom of expression as a value.

The courts also accept time, place and manner limits by the government on expression, using the **TPM Standard.** Cities can, for example, ban newsracks from busy sidewalks where they impede pedestrian traffic and impair safety, as long as the restriction is content-neutral—an important caveat. A newspaper that editorializes against the mayor cannot be restricted while one that supports the mayor is not.

Incitement Standard

Since the first Supreme Court First Amendment decision in 1919, the Court has moved to make it more difficult for the government to interfere with freedom of expression. In an important case, from the perspective of free-expression advocates, the Court overturned the conviction of a white racist, **Clarence Brandenburg,** who had been jailed after a Ku Klux Klan rally in the woods outside Cincinnati. Brandenburg had said hateful and threatening things, but the Court, in a landmark decision in 1969, significantly expanded First Amendment protection for free expression. Even the advocacy of lawless actions was protected, according to the Brandenburg decision, as long as it's unlikely that lawlessness is imminent and probable. This is called the **Incitement Standard.** The distinction was that advocacy is protected up to the brink that

TPM Standard ■ Government may control the time, place and manner of expression as long as limits are content-neutral.

Clarence Brandenburg ■ Ku Klux Klan leader whose conviction was overturned because his speech was far-fetched.

Incitement Standard ■ A four-part test to determine whether an advocacy speech is constitutionally protected.

lawlessness is incited. According to the Incitement Standard, authorities can justify silencing someone only if:

- The statement advocates a lawless action.
- The statement aims at producing lawless action.
- Such lawless action must be imminent.
- Such lawless action must be likely to occur.

Unless an utterance meets all four tests, it cannot be suppressed by the government.

Hate Speech

Emotions run high on First Amendment issues when national security is at stake or when expression is obnoxious or even vile. The Supreme Court, however, takes the position that a society that is free and democratic cannot have a government that silences somebody just because that person's views don't comport with mainstream values. In effect, the court says that people need to tolerate a level of discomfort in a society whose core principles value freedom of expression.

This point, made in the Brandenburg case, has come up in Court decisions against **hate-speech** laws that grew out of the political-correctness movement of the 1990s. Especially notable was *R.A.V.* v. *St. Paul.* Several punks had burned a cross, KKK style, on the lawn of a black family in St. Paul, Minnesota. They were caught and convicted under a municipal ordinance against "hate speech." One of them, identified only as R.A.V. in court documents, appealed to the U.S. Supreme Court on First Amendment grounds. The Court found that the ordinance was aimed at the content of the expression, going far beyond allowable time, place or manner restrictions. The decision was a slap at the political-correctness movement's attempts to discourage language that can be taken offensively.

Flag Burning

In another controversial application of toleration for offensive expression the Supreme Court has recognized burning of a U.S. flag as expression that is protected from government interference. Although revisited many times in the courts, the main Supreme Court decision goes back almost a quarter of a century. At the 1984 Republican national convention in Dallas, **Joey Johnson** marched with a hundred or so other protesters to City Hall. There he doused a U.S. flag with kerosene and lit it. Johnson's supporters chanted: "America, the red, white and blue, we spit on you." The flag burning was a powerful gesture, a political gesture, against President Ronald Reagan, whom the Republicans were renominating. Johnson was arrested and convicted under a Texas law, similar to laws in many states, that forbade defacing the flag.

The U.S. Supreme Court found that the arrest was wrong. Said Justice William Brennan: "If there is a bedrock principle underlying the First Amendment, it is that the government may not prohibit the expression of an idea simply because society finds the idea itself offensive or disagreeable."

Defamation

study preview **When the mass media carry disparaging descriptions and comments, they risk being sued for libel. The media have a strong defense if the libel was accurate. If not, there can be big trouble. Libel is a serious matter. Not only are reputations at stake when defamation occurs, but also losing a suit can be so costly that it can put a publication or broadcast organization out of business.**

hate speech ■ Offensive expressions, especially those aimed at racial, ethnic and sexual-orientation minorities.

Joey Johnson ■ Flag-burning protester whose conviction was overturned on First Amendment grounds.

Joey Johnson
Flag-burning protester whose conviction was overturned on First Amendment grounds.

The Libel Concept

If someone punched you in the face for no good reason, knocking out several teeth, breaking your nose and causing permanent disfigurement, most courts would rule that your attacker should pay your medical bills. If your disfigurement or psychological upset causes you to lose your job, to be ridiculed or shunned by friends and family or perhaps to retreat from social interaction, the court would probably order your attacker to pay additional amounts. Like fists, words can cause damage. If someone writes false, damaging things about you, you can sue for **libel.** Freedom of speech and the press is not a license to say absolutely anything about anybody.

If a libeling statement is false, the utterer may be liable for millions of dollars in damages. The largest jury award to date, in 1997 against the *Wall Street Journal,* was almost twice the earnings that year of the *Journal*'s parent company, Dow Jones Inc. The award was reduced substantially on appeal, but the fact remains that awards have grown dramatically in recent years and can hurt a media company seriously.

Reckless Disregard

Elected officials have a hard time winning libel suits today. Noting that democracy is best served by robust, unbridled discussion of public issues and that public officials are inseparable from public policy, the U.S. Supreme Court has ruled that public figures can win libel suits only in extreme circumstances. The Court has also said that people who thrust themselves into the limelight forfeit some of the protection available to other citizens.

The key court decision in developing current U.S. libel standards originated in an advertisement carried by the New York *Times* in 1960. A civil rights coalition, the Committee to Defend Martin Luther King and the Struggle for Freedom in the South, escalated its antisegregationist cause by placing a full-page advertisement in the *Times.* The advertisement accused public officials in the South of violence and illegal tactics against the civil rights struggle. Although the advertisement was by and large truthful, it was marred by minor factual errors. Police Commissioner L. B. Sullivan of Montgomery, Alabama, filed a libel action saying that the errors damaged him, and he won $500,000 in an Alabama trial. On appeal to the U.S. Supreme Court, the case, ***New York Times* v. *Sullivan,***

libel ■ A written defamation.

New York Times* v. *Sullivan ■ Libel case that largely barred public figures from the right to sue for libel.

mediaPEOPLE

Joseph Gutnick

Australian Miner Joseph Gutnick, who made a fortune in gold and diamonds and became prominent in his native Australia, objected when a U.S. magazine linked him falsely to shady money-laundering through a bogus Israeli charity. He sued.

Had Joseph Gutnick been a U.S. citizen and seen himself accused of money-laundering in the business magazine *Barron's,* he might have sputtered in anger but not much else. In 1964 the U.S. Supreme Court made it near impossible for public figures, like Gutnick, to sue for libel. The decision, *New York Times* v. *Sullivan,* was a major departure from libel laws in other democracies. In Australia, for example, the law is much more protective of reputations, even of prominent people.

Gutnick read the *Barron's* story at his home in Victoria, Australia, on a *Barron's* web site. He sued the U.S. publisher of *Barron's,* Dow Jones, and did so in an Australian court. Under Australian law his prominence in the mining industry, politics and philanthropy was immaterial to whether he had been wrongfully defamed. He won an apology from Dow Jones and $450,000.

The Gutnick case raised a question about whether one country can impose its libel laws on messages originating in another country. It's a significant question with the global growth in communication facilitated by the Internet. The short answer: Yes.

Even though Dow Jones had a mere 1,700 Internet subscribers in Australia, the company was indeed doing business there. That made it subject to Australian law, just as is any other company choosing to do business in another country.

Critics of the decision said the open and global nature of the Internet should make an exception to the maxim "When in Rome do as the Romans do." Australian law, according to these critics, should not govern American journalism. Their argument was that one country's restrictive laws, like those of Australia, could end up limiting what people have access to in other societies, like the United States, where the law encourages more robust public dialogue. Worse, as these critics saw the Gutnick case, the patchwork of laws in 190-some countries on the planet could force Internet publishers to gear their products to the country with the most restrictive laws. Think China. Think Saudi Arabia.

Whatever the objections, however, the reality is that multinational media companies now are more careful to filter material that could be problematic in other countries. It's not a matter of Australian law, for example, restricting free expression in the United States. It's possible for Internet publishers to filter their content geographically to comply with local law without diluting what they publish elsewhere—and they do. Legal scholars Jack Goldsmith and Tim Wu, in their book *Who Controls the Internet,* say that Internet publishers are accepting the reality that their legal staffs need to be as responsible for local compliance of Internet messages as for other aspects of doing business abroad: "These are simply the costs of doing international business."

How hobbling is the Gutnick lesson on most Internet users—students? Chatroom participants? Porn purveyors? Web-page operators? Bloggers? Goldsmith and Wu: "Far from being subject to multiple laws, these persons are immune from every law but their own." Most of us have no connection to Australia or any other country other than where we live.

---

became a landmark in libel law. The Supreme Court said that the importance of "free debate" in a democratic society generally was more important than factual errors that might upset and damage public officials. To win a libel suit, the Court said, public officials needed to prove that damaging statements were uttered or printed with the knowledge that they were false. The question in the *Sullivan* case became whether the *Times* was guilty of "**reckless disregard** of the truth." The Supreme Court said it was not, and the newspaper won.

Questions lingered after the *Sullivan* decision about exactly who was and who was not a public official. The courts struggled for definition, and the Supreme Court eventually changed the term to *public figure.* In later years, as the Court refined its view on issues raised in the *Sullivan* case through several decisions, it remained consistent in giving the mass media a lot of room for error, even damaging error, in discussing government officials, political candidates and publicity hounds.

reckless disregard ■ Supreme Court language for a situation in which public figures may sue for libel.

- **Government officials.** All elected government officials and appointed officials with high-level policy responsibilities are public figures as far as their performance in office is concerned. A member of a state governor's cabinet fits this category. A cafeteria worker in the state capitol does not.
- **Political candidates.** Anyone seeking public office is subject to intense public review, during which the courts are willing to excuse false statements as part of robust, wide-open discussion.
- **Publicity hounds.** Court decisions have gone both ways, but generally people who seek publicity or intentionally draw attention to themselves must prove "reckless disregard of the truth" if they sue for libel.

How far can the media go in making disparaging comments? It was all right, said a Vermont court, when the Barre *Times Argus* ran an editorial that said a political candidate was "a horse's ass, a jerk, an idiot and a paranoid." The court said open discussion on public issues excused even such insulting, abusive and unpleasant verbiage. Courts have generally been more tolerant of excessive language in opinion pieces, such as the Barre editorial, than in fact-based articles.

media ONLINE **What Would You Do?** Test your knowledge of media libel by walking through several scenarios and making the decisions media professionals make every day. **www.hfac.uh.edu/comm/media_libel/wwyd**

Media Law Resource Center, Inc. A New York nonprofit clearinghouse for information about libel law in the United States. **www.medialaw.org**

Comment and Criticism

People flocked to see the **Cherry Sisters'** act. Effie, Addie, Jessie, Lizzie and Ella toured the country with a song and dance act that drew big crowds. They were just awful. They could neither sing nor dance, but people turned out because the sisters were so funny. Sad to say, the Cherry Sisters took themselves seriously. In 1901, desperate for respect, the sisters decided to sue the next newspaper reviewer who gave them a bad notice. That reviewer, it turned out, was Billy Hamilton, who included a lot of equine metaphors in his piece for the Des Moines *Leader:* "Effie is an old jade of 50 summers, Jessie a frisky filly of 40, and Addie, the flower of the family, a capering monstrosity of 35. Their long skinny arms, equipped with talons at the extremities, swung mechanically, and anon waved frantically at the suffering audience. The mouths of their rancid features opened like caverns, and sounds like the wailings of damned souls issued therefrom. They pranced around the stage with a motion that suggested a cross between the *danse du ventre* and the fox trot—strange creatures with painted faces and hideous mien. Effie is spavined, Addie is stringhalt, and Jessie, the only one who showed her stockings, has legs with calves as classic in their outlines as the curves of a broom handle."

Cherry Sisters ■ Complainants in a case that barred performers from suing critics.

Fair Comment and Criticism
Upset with what an Iowa reviewer had written about their show, the Cherry Sisters sued. The important 1901 court decision that resulted said that journalists, critics and anybody else can say whatever they want about a public performance. The rationale was that someone who puts on a performance for public acceptance has to take a risk also of public rejection.

The outcome of the suit was another setback for the Cherrys. They lost in a case that established that actors or others who perform for the public must be willing to accept both positive and negative comments about their performance. This right of **fair comment and criticism,** however, does not make it open season on performers in aspects of their lives that do not relate to public performance. The *National Enquirer* could not defend itself when entertainer Carol Burnett sued for a story that described her as obnoxiously drunk at a restaurant. Not only was the description false (Carol Burnett abstains from alcohol), but Burnett was in no public or performing role at the restaurant. This distinction between an individual's public and private life also has been recognized in cases involving public officials and candidates.

Trespass, Fraud and Libel

An emerging legal tactic against the news media for disparaging coverage is not libel but trespass and other laws. In 1998 the Utah Restaurant Association sued television station KTVX for a report on roaches in restaurant kitchens and unsanitary food handling and storage. Wesley Sine, attorney for the restaurants, did not sue for libel. Sine argued instead that it was illegal for news reporters to go into a private area, like a kitchen, without permission.

Such end-runs around libel law worry media people. The defenses that usually work in libel cases are hard to apply if the media are sued over disparaging reports on grounds other than libel. This was a factor in a case involving the Food Lion supermarket chain that resulted in a $5.5 million jury verdict against ABC television. Food Lion was riled over a 1992 report on rats and spoilage in store backrooms as well as unfair labor practices. In its suit Food Lion never challenged ABC's accuracy. Rather, Food Lion said, among other things, that ABC had committed fraud by sending undercover reporters to get on the Food Lion payroll to investigate the backrooms. On appeal, the damages against ABC were reduced almost to zero—a moral victory for ABC, but it took seven years and lots of expensive lawyers.

Privacy Law

study preview **The idea that people have a right to limit intrusions on their privacy has been taking form in U.S. law through much of this century. In general, permission is not required in news coverage, although the courts have been consistent in saying that there are limits on how far news reporters can go with their cameras and in writing about personal information.**

Intruding on Solitude

Using **privacy law,** the courts have recognized a person's right to solitude and have punished overzealous news reporters who tap telephone lines, plant hidden microphones, use telephoto lenses and break into homes and offices for stories. In general, reporters are free to pursue stories in public places and, when invited, in private places. Sometimes the courts have had to draw the line between public and private places. Here are some examples:

- **A hospital room. Dorothy Barber** entered a Kansas City hospital with a metabolic disorder. No matter how much she ate, she lost weight. One day, two newspaper reporters, one with a camera, paid Barber a visit for a story and took a picture without permission. United Press International distributed the photograph, showing Dorothy Barber in her hospital bed, and *Time* magazine ran the picture. The caption read: "The starving glutton." Barber sued *Time* and won. The court said that reporters have a right to pursue people in public places, but the right of privacy protects a person in bed for treatment and recuperation.

fair comment and criticism ■ Doctrine that permits criticism of performers, performances.

privacy law ■ Recognizes a right to be left alone.

Dorothy Barber ■ Successfully sued when photos of her in the hospital were published.

- **Inside a private business.** A Seattle television photographer wanted to videotape a pharmacist charged with Medicaid fraud, but the man would not cooperate. The photographer then set himself on the sidewalk outside the pharmacy and filmed the pharmacist through a front window. The pharmacist sued, charging the television station with photographic eavesdropping, but the court dismissed the suit, ruling that the photographer recorded only what any passerby was free to see. The outcome would have been different had the photographer gone into the shop, a private place, and taped the same scene without permission.
- **Expectation of privacy.** Some intrusion cases have hinged on whether the person being reported on had "a reasonable expectation of privacy." Someone lounging nude at a fenced-in backyard pool would have a strong case against a photographer who climbed a steep, seldom-scaled cliff with a telephoto lens for a picture. A similar case can be made against hidden cameras and microphones.

Harassment

By being in a public place, a person surrenders most privacy protections, but this does not mean that journalists have a right to hound people mercilessly. **Ron Galella,** a freelance celebrity photographer, learned this lesson—or should have—in two lawsuits filed by **Jacqueline Kennedy Onassis.** Galella stalked the former First Lady, darting and jumping and grunting at her to catch off-guard facial expressions that would make interesting photographs that he could sell to magazines and photo archives. Mrs. Onassis became Galella's specialty, but he also was building a photo file on the Kennedy children. Galella broke Mrs. Onassis' patience in 1973 when he frightened a horse ridden by young John Kennedy and the horse bolted. John Kennedy escaped serious injury, but Mrs. Onassis asked her Secret Service protection detail to intervene to prevent Galella from endangering her children. Not long thereafter, the guards and Galella got into a tussle. Galella filed a $1.3 million suit, claiming that he had been roughed up and that the guards were interfering with his right to earn a livelihood. He also claimed that his First Amendment rights were being violated. Mrs. Onassis responded with a $1.5 million suit, asking for an injunction to halt Galella.

A federal judge acknowledged that Galella could photograph whomever he wanted in public places and write stories about them but that the First Amendment could not justify incessant pursuits that "went far beyond the reasonable bounds of news gathering." The judge said that harassment was impermissible, and he ordered Galella to stay 300 feet from the Onassis and Kennedy homes and the schools of the Kennedy children, 225 feet from the children in public places and 150 feet from Mrs. Onassis.

Nine years later, Mrs. Onassis returned to court to object to Galella's continuing overzealous journalistic techniques. He was found in contempt of court for violating the 1973 order on 12 separate occasions. The Onassis-Galella issue was a further recognition that a **right to be left alone** exists among other constitutional rights, including the right of a free press.

Journalism Law

study preview **The Constitution gives journalists great liberty in covering trials, seeking access to information held by the government.**

Court Coverage

News media have great liberty under the First Amendment to cover events as they see fit. Such was the case with **Sam Sheppard,** a Cleveland osteopath who was convicted of murder amid a media circus. Even when he was acquitted after 12 years in prison,

Ron Galella ■ Celebrity photographer.

Jacqueline Kennedy Onassis ■ Successfully barred a photographer from hounding her children, herself.

right to be left alone ■ Principle underlying most privacy cases and law.

Sam Sheppard ■ Plaintiff in a case in which judges were told that they, not the news media, are responsible for a fair trial.

it was too late for him. He was unable to reestablish his medical practice. He died, a ruined man, a few years later.

A free press does not come without cost, and some people, like Sheppard, end up paying dearly. It is from such cases, however, that we learn the implications of the First Amendment and how to sidestep some of the problems it creates. When the U.S. Supreme Court ordered a new trial for Sheppard in 1966, it declared that it is the responsibility of the courts to assure citizens a fair trial regardless of media irresponsibility. The justices were specific about what the judge presiding at Sheppard's trial could have done. Among options:

- Seat only jurors who have not formed prejudicial conclusions.
- Move the trial to another city not so contaminated by news coverage.
- Delay the trial until publicity has subsided.
- Put jurors under 24-hour supervision so they will not have access to newspapers and newscasts during the trial.
- Insist that reporters respect appropriate courtroom decorum.
- Order attorneys, litigants and witnesses not to talk with reporters.
- Issue gag orders against the media but only in "extraordinary circumstances."

In other cases the U.S. Supreme Court has allowed actions against the media to preclude unfavorable, prejudicial coverage of hearings, but those involve unusual circumstances. In the main the news media have First Amendment-guaranteed access to the courts and the freedom to cover court stories regardless of whether the courts are pleased with the coverage. The same applies to news coverage of government in general.

Sunshine Laws

Implicit in any democracy is that public policy is developed in open sessions where the people can follow their elected and appointed leaders as they discuss issues. Every state has an open meeting law that specifically declares that legislative units, including state boards and commissions, city councils, school boards and county governing bodies, be open to the public, including journalists. The idea is for public policy to be created and executed in the bright sunshine, not in the secrecy of back rooms. For this reason laws such as open meeting laws are often called **sunshine laws.**

Open meeting laws vary. Some insist that almost every session be open. Others are not nearly as strict with the state legislatures that created them as they are with city, county and school units and with state executive agencies. Some of these laws proclaim the virtues of openness but lack teeth to enforce openness. In contrast, some states specify heavy fines and jail terms for public officials who shut the doors. Here are provisions of strong open meeting laws:

- Legislative units are required to meet at regular times and places and to announce their agendas ahead of time.
- Citizens can insist on quick judicial review if a meeting is closed.
- Closed sessions are allowed for only a few reasons, which are specifically identified, such as discussion on sensitive personnel matters, collective bargaining strategy and security arrangements.
- Any vote in a closed session must be announced immediately afterward.
- Decisions made at a closed meeting are nullified if the meeting is later declared to have been closed illegally.
- Penalties are specified for any official who illegally authorizes a closed meeting.

Besides open meeting laws, the federal and state governments have open record laws to ensure public access to government documents. These laws are important to journalists in tracking policy decisions and actions that they could not cover personally. Journalists especially value documents because, unlike human sources, documents do not change their stories.

sunshine laws ■ Require government meetings, documents be open.

The federal **Freedom of Information Act** was passed in 1966, specifying how people could request documents. Since 1974 federal agencies have been required to list all their documents to help people identify what documents they are seeking and help the agencies locate them quickly. Despite penalties for noncompliance, some agencies sometimes drag their feet and stretch the FOI Act's provisions to keep sensitive documents off-limits. Even so, the law was a landmark of legislative commitment to governmental openness that allowed only a few exceptions. Among those exceptions are:

- Documents classified to protect national security.
- Trade secrets and internal corporate information obtained on a confidential basis by the government.
- Preliminary drafts of agency documents and working papers.
- Medical and personnel files for which confidentiality is necessary to protect individual privacy.
- Police files that, if disclosed, might jeopardize an investigation by tipping off guilty people or, worse, falsely incriminating innocent people.

Obscenity and Pornography

study preview **Despite the First Amendment's guarantee of freedom of expression, the U.S. government has tried numerous ways during this century to regulate obscenity and pornography.**

Import Restrictions

A 1930 tariff law was used as an import restriction to intercept James Joyce's *Ulysses* at the docks because of four-letter words and explicit sexual references. The importer, **Random House,** went to court, and the judge ruled that the government was out of line. The judge, **John Woolsey,** acknowledged "unusual frankness" in *Ulysses* but said he could not "detect anywhere the leer of the sensualist." The judge, who was not without humor, made a strong case for freedom in literary expression: "The words which are criticized as dirty are old Saxon words known to almost all men, and, I venture, to many women, and are such words as would be naturally and habitually used, I believe, by the types of folks whose life, physical and mental, Joyce is seeking to describe. In respect to the recurrent emergence of the theme of sex in the minds of the characters, it must always be remembered that his locale was Celtic and his season Spring."

Woolsey was upheld on appeal, and *Ulysses,* still critically acclaimed as a pioneer in stream-of-consciousness writing, remains in print today.

Postal Restrictions

Postal restrictions were used against a 1928 English novel, *Lady Chatterley's Lover,* by D. H. Lawrence. The book was sold in the United States in expurgated editions for years, but in 1959 **Grove Press** issued the complete version. Postal officials denied mailing privileges. Grove sued and won.

In some respects the Grove case was *Ulysses* all over again. Grove argued that Lawrence, a major author, had produced a work of literary merit. Grove said the explicit, rugged love scenes between Lady Chatterley and Mellors the gamekeeper were essential in establishing their violent yet loving relationship, the heart of the story. The distinction between the *Ulysses* and *Lady Chatterley* cases was that one ruling was against the customs service and the other against the postmaster general.

media ONLINE **Center for Democracy and Technology** The Center works for freedom of expression and at the same time right to privacy on the Internet and other new communications media.
www.cdt.org

Lady Chatterley's Lover Download it free and judge for yourself.
www.book999.com/ENGLISH%20300/Contents/English%20Literature/D.%20H.%20Lawrence%20%20(1855–1930)/Lady%20Chatterley's%20Lover

Freedom of Information Act ■ Requires many federal documents to be available to public.

Random House ■ Fought against censorship of James Joyce's *Ulysses.*

John Woolsey ■ Judge who barred import law censorship of *Ulysses.*

Grove Press ■ Fought against censorship of D. H. Lawrence's *Lady Chatterley's Lover.*

Communications Decency Act

The federal government's latest foray into systematically regulating media content were ill-conceived communications decency laws in 1996 and 1999. Without hearings or formal debate, Congress created the law to keep smut away from children who use the Internet. Although hardly anyone defends giving kids access to indecent material, the law had two flaws: the difficulty of defining indecency and the impossibility of denying questionable material to children without restricting freedom of speech for adults.

Definition Through history the courts have found it impossible to define indecency clearly. Before a Philadelphia federal appeals court that reviewed the 1996 Communications Decency Act, witnesses from the Justice Department testified that the law went ridiculously far. The law, they said, required them to prosecute for certain AIDS information, museum exhibits, prize-winning plays and even the *Vanity Fair* magazine cover of actress Demi Moore nude and pregnant.

Access When it reviewed the 1996 Communications Decency Act, the U.S. Supreme Court noted that the Internet is the most democratic of the media, enabling almost anyone to become a town crier or pamphleteer. Enforcing the law would necessarily inhibit freedom of expression of the sort that has roots in the Revolution that resulted in the creation of the Republic and the First Amendment, the court said. The 7-2 decision purged the law from the books.

How, then, are government bans of indecency on radio and television justified but not on the Internet? Justice John Stevens, who wrote the majority Supreme Court opinion, said the Internet is hardly as "invasive broadcasting." The odds of people encountering pornography on the Internet are slim unless they're seeking it, he said. Underpinning the Court's rejection of the Communications Decency Act was the fact that the Internet lends itself to free-for-all discussions and exchanges with everybody participating who wants to, whereas other media are dominated by carefully crafted messages aimed at people whose opportunity to participate in dialogue with the message producers is so indirect as to be virtually nil.

Pornography versus Obscenity

Since the *Ulysses* and *Lady Chatterley* cases, much more has happened to discourage federal censorship. The U.S. Supreme Court has ruled that pornography, material aimed at sexual arousal, cannot be stopped. Import and postal restrictions, however, still can be employed against obscene materials, which the Court has defined as going beyond pornography. Obscenity restrictions apply, said the Court, if the answer is yes to *all* of the following questions:

- Would a typical person applying local standards see the material as appealing mainly for its sexually arousing effect?
- Is the material devoid of serious literary, artistic, political or scientific value?
- Is sexual activity depicted offensively, in a way that violates state law that explicitly defines offensiveness?

Censorship Today

study preview **Local governments have tried numerous ways to restrict distribution of sexually explicit material. Local libraries and schools also sometimes act to ban materials, but these attempts at censorship are not restricted to obscenity and pornography. Anything to which a majority of a local board objects can be fair game.**

Local Censorship

Municipalities and counties have tried heavy-handed restrictions against sexually explicit publications and video material, generally without lasting success. Outright bans fail if they are challenged in the courts, unless the material is legally obscene. The U.S. Supreme Court spoke on this issue after Mount Ephraim, New Jersey, revised zoning laws to ban all live entertainment from commercial areas. The Court said the rezoning was a blatant attempt to ban lawful activities, and the decision was widely interpreted to apply to porn shops and other businesses that are often targets of local censorship campaigns. A federal court applied the same reasoning when it threw out a Keego Harbor, Michigan, zoning ordinance that forbade an adult theater within 500 feet of a school, church or bar. In Keego Harbor there was no site that was not within 500 feet of a school, church or bar.

Some local governments have been innovative in acting against sexually explicit materials. One successful approach has been through zoning laws to rid neighborhoods of porn shops by forcing them into so-called **war zones.** Owners of adult-oriented businesses generally have been pleased to go along. By complying, they face less heat from police and other official harassment. The courts have found that war zone ordinances are legitimate applications of the principle underlying zoning laws in general, which is to preserve and protect the character of neighborhoods. So just as local governments can create single-residence, apartment, retail and other zones, they also can create zones for adult bookstores and theaters.

An opposite zoning approach, to disperse these kinds of businesses instead of concentrating them, has also been upheld in court. In Detroit an ordinance insists that a 1,000-foot space separate "problem businesses," which include porn shops, adults-only theaters, pool halls and cabarets. This is all right, say the courts, as long as it does not exclude such businesses entirely.

Unlike the publishers in the landmark *Ulysses* and *Lady Chatterley* cases, in recent years book publishers have not taken the initiative against local restrictions aimed at pornography distributors and porn shops. Litigation is expensive, and major publishing houses do not produce porn-shop merchandise. Magazine publishers, notably *Playboy* and *Penthouse,* have fought some battles, but the issue has become fragmented since the Supreme Court's insistence that local standards be a measure of acceptability. Because what is obscene to people in one town might not be obscene to people in another, it is impossible for the producers of nationally distributed books and magazines to go after all the restrictive local actions.

Library and School Boards

Local libraries sometimes decide to keep certain books off the shelves, usually because of content that offends the sensitivities of a majority of the library board. This kind of censorship survives challenges only when legal obscenity is the issue, which is seldom. Also, the wide availability of banned books renders library bans largely symbolic.

Some school boards still attempt censorship, although there is little support in the courts unless the issue is legal obscenity, which is rare. Whatever latitude school boards once had was strictly limited in 1982 when the U.S. Supreme Court decided against the Island Trees, New York, school board after several members had gone into the high school library and removed 60 books. Among them were *The Fixer* by Bernard Malamud and *Laughing Boy* by Oliver Lafarge, both of which had won Pulitzer Prizes. School board members argued that the 60 books were anti-American, anti-Semitic, anti-Christian and "just plain filthy." The Court did not accept that. School boards, said the Court, "may not remove books from library shelves simply because they dislike the ideas in those books and seek their removal to prescribe what shall be orthodox in politics, nationalism, religion or other matters of opinion."

media ONLINE

Banned Books Online Hosted at the University of Pennsylvania, this web site examines books that have been targets of censorship in the United States.
http://digital.library.upenn.edu/books/banned-books.html

Index on Censorship Bimonthly magazine delivering articles on freedom of expression from respected writers around the world.
www.indexonline.org

Student Press Law Center A resource on media law issues involving student media.
www.splc.org

war zones ■ Neighborhoods where pornography is permitted.

Copyright Myths This web site addresses ten common copyright myths.
www.templetons.com/brad/copymyths.html

Copyright Website Real-world, practical and relevant copyright information for anyone interested.
www.benedict.com

The IP Mall Franklin Pierce Law School presents this collection of resources on intellectual property issues.
www.ipmall.fplc.edu

U.S. Copyright Office Home of the Digital Millennium Act. Also provides information on how copyright works and how to obtain it.
www.copyright.gov

Copyright

studypreview **Mass media people are vulnerable to thievery. Because it is so easy for someone to copy someone else's creative work, copyright laws prohibit the unauthorized re-creation of intellectual property, including books, music, movies and other creative production.**

How Copyright Works

Congress has had a **copyright law** on the books since 1790. The law protects authors and other creators of intellectual property from having someone profit by reproducing their works without permission. Permission is usually granted for a fee.

Almost all books have copyright protection the moment they are created in a tangible form. So do most movies, television programs, newspaper and magazine articles, songs and records and advertisements. It used to be that a creative work needed to be registered with the Library of Congress for a $10 fee. Formal registration is no longer required, but many people still do it for the fullest legal protection against someone pirating their work.

The current copyright law protects a creative work for the lifetime of the author plus 70 years. After the 70 years a work enters what is called the **public domain,** and anyone may reproduce it without permission. Under a 2003 version of the law, the term is longer for corporations with interests in characters, like Disney's Mickey Mouse.

The creator of an original work may sell the copyright, and many do. Authors, for example, typically give their copyright to a publisher in exchange for a percentage of income from the book's profits.

Infringement Issues

copyright ■ Protects intellectual property from theft.

public domain ■ Intellectual property that may be used without permission of the creator or owner.

What constitutes a copyright infringement has generated a litany of fascinating albeit quirky cases. One involved the 40-million copy bestseller *The Da Vinci Code*. Author Dan Brown drew on a hypothesis advanced in an earlier historical work that Jesus Christ and Mary Magadelene married and their son then married into French nobility. Historians

Mona Lawsuit

The author of *The Da Vinci Code,* Dan Brown, enters a London hearing on whether he leaned too heavily on an earlier book for the architecture of his story. The judge found for Brown. The claimants had claimed that Brown stole ideas and even characters for *Da Vinci* from them. The judge sent them packing.

Richard Leigh and Michael Baigent went to court alleging that Brown stole "the whole architecture" of their book, *The Holy Blood and the Holy Grail,* as well as a smattering of specifics. Brown responded that he had acknowledged the Leigh-Baigent work and that fiction, such as his work, would be hobbled as a literacy form if it were barred from drawing on history. His advocates asked rhetorically whether Shakespeare should be faulted for his historical dramas, like *Julius Caesar.*

Substantial Similarity One issue in infringement cases is whether there is substantial similarity. Although the Da Vinci case was heard in British courts, where copyright law is slightly variant from U.S. laws, a two-part test generally is used to sort through the question of substantial similarity.

- Are the general ideas similar?
- If so, is the expression of ideas similar?

The answer to both must be yes to establish substantial similarity.

This two-part test was used in a case brought by Sid and Marty Krofft, creators of H.R. Pufnstuf, against the McDonald's hamburger chain. The Kroffts claimed that McDonald's had copied the Living Island of the Pufnstuf television series for McDonaldland advertisements. It didn't help McDonald's that a former Krofft employee had designed McDonaldland.

Was the general idea the same? This was a no-brainer. Living Island and McDonaldland were mystical places populated with strange, amusing beings.

Was the expression of the general idea substantially similar? Topographically they were similar with trees, caves, a pond, a toad and a castle. Both were governed by mayors with huge, round heads and long, wide mouths. Both mayors were arrested by Keystone Cop characters. Both lands were plagued by crazy scientists and multi-armed evil creatures. Both had trees with human faces that talked. McDonald's lost.

Ideas as Free A bedrock fundamental in copyright law is that an idea cannot be copyrighted, only the physical expression of the idea. A dance step, for example, cannot be copyrighted, but a video of the dance can be. In the *Da Vinci* case, Dan Brown argued that the idea of Christ marrying and siring a child had been floated for centuries and hardly could be protected by copyright law. The judge agreed.

Piracy

The underlying rationale for legal protection for intellectual property through copyright laws has been called into question by massive downloading of music and video from the Internet, which became possible in the late 1990s with greater bandwidth capacities and other new technology. Cary Sherman, president of the Recording Industry Association of America, put the issue bluntly in 2003 when the association began suing people who downloaded music without permission: "We simply cannot allow online piracy to continue destroying the livelihoods of artists, musicians, songwriters, retailers and everyone in the music industry." His point was that the entire music industry had been built on an economic foundation of people paying to acquire music. Suddenly, that foundation was crumbling.

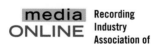

Recording Industry Association of America Trade group working to protect copyrighted music and enforce intellectual property regulations. **www.riaa.com/default.asp**

The issue was economic. Sales of recorded music were plummeting as people by the millions built their music libraries with free, albeit illegal, downloads. Related to economics was a broader issue of creativity. The founders of the Republic built copyright protection into the U.S. Constitution so that creative people, including authors, poets and composers, would have a financial incentive to make their creative contributions that enrich society. Without the financial incentive, musicians and others might opt to do other things with their talent, time and energies, and society would end up culturally the poorer for it.

The record industry's legal actions in 2003 began with suits against 261 people that RIAA claimed were sharing large amounts of music over the Internet. The association promised there would be thousands more suits and began subpoenaing colleges to turn over computer records to identify students who were engaged in the practice. The suits were risky. The industry was aware that companies that go on major legal offenses against customers can expect a backlash. To offset the risk from its aggressive legal tactics, the association offered amnesty to music-swappers who signed affidavits that they wouldn't do it any more.

With album packages approaching $20 retail, record-makers recognized that the incentive for pirates was partly of their own making. "What do you expect with exorbitant pricing?" fans asked. Addressing criticism, some record-makers cut prices and squeezed retailers to take less profits. Also, some record-makers licensed Internet suppliers like Apple to sell downloads at relatively low charges. Ninety-nine cents a song was common. These initiatives were designed not only to reduce piracy, but also to maintain the copyright-based financial infrastructure on which the whole music industry was based.

Meanwhile, the movie industry also was losing sales to downloads, although, because movie downloading requires so much time, the drain was far less than the record industry's. For Hollywood the main problem remained video copying, mostly in Asia and the Middle East for bootlegging back to the United States and other markets nationwide. Book publishers had a similar piracy problem with illicit printers, mostly in Asia. Both the movie and book industry focused their antipiracy programs at encouraging local law-enforcement officials to use their own, often-ignored copyright laws to crack down on illicit copying in their countries.

CHAPTER 20 Wrap-Up

The U.S. mass media enjoy great freedom under the First Amendment, which forbids the government from impinging on freedom of expression. Even so, the freedom has limits. When the First Amendment guarantee of a free press runs against the constitutional guarantee of a free trial, there is a conflict of values that must be resolved. This is also true when the mass media violate someone's right to be left alone, which, although not an explicit constitutional guarantee, has come to be recognized as a basic human right. An understanding of mass media law and regulation involves studying how the U.S. judicial system, headed by the U.S. Supreme Court, has reconciled conflicting interests. In short, the First Amendment is not inviolate.

Questions for Review

1. Why is the First Amendment important to mass media in the United States?
2. In what situations may the government exercise prior restraint to silence someone?
3. Who can sue the mass media for libel?
4. Do the mass media face limits on intruding on an individual's privacy?
5. How is obscenity different from pornography?
6. How did a U.S. Supreme Court decision pretty much end federal concern about pornography?
7. How does copyright law protect intellectual property from being stolen from its owners?

Questions for Critical Thinking

1. How can any restriction on freedom of expression by the mass media or by individuals be consistent with the absolutist language of the First Amendment?
2. Define censorship. In a strict sense, who is a censor?
3. What lessons about prior restraint are contained in *Near* v. *Minnesota* (1931) and *New York Times Co.* v. *United States* (1971)?
4. How do authors and creators of other intellectual property copyright their works, and why do they do it?
5. What is the trend with local censorship by library boards and school boards?

Deepening Your media LITERACY

Is local censorship a good thing?

STEP 1 Sometimes the decisions of the U.S. Supreme Court seem to be in conflict. Think about a local school, its library and its school board.

Dig Deeper

STEP 2 The U.S. Supreme Court has said that communities cannot outright ban sexually explicit material, at the same time allowing local zoning laws that restrict where the material is distributed. This gives some people, like school boards, the impression that control over offensive material is a local matter, and they reason that it's therefore OK to censor books and other material in the school library.

What Do You Think?

STEP 3 Compare the reasons you can think of in favor of local censorship to the reasons you can think of against it. Explain why the U.S. Supreme Court has always decided that books that local school boards claim might be "filthy" cannot be censored or pulled off the shelves. Do you think the Supreme Court is being faithful to the U.S. Constitution in its decisions on local censorship? Why or why not?

Keeping Up to Date

Censorship News is published by the National Coalition Against Censorship.

Media Law Bulletin tracks developments in media law.

News Media and the Law is published by the Reporters' Committee for Freedom of the Press.

Media Law Reporter is an annual collection of major court cases.

Student Press Law Reports, from the Student Press Law Center, follows events in the high school and college press and broadcast media.

The *Wall Street Journal* has a daily law section that includes media cases.

For Further Learning

Jack Goldsmith and Tim Wu. *Who Controls the Internet.* Oxford, 2006.

Goldsmith and Wu, legal scholars, debunk the idea that the Internet will usher in a new human order that empowers individuals while neutering the authority of traditional nation-states. The major nation-states, they argue, have properly taken over management of the Internet and a avoided an anarchy.

Lawrence Lessig. "Google's Tough call," *Wired* (November 2005), page 130.

Lessig, a contributing editor, compactly makes a case for Google to pursue its Print Library Project full bore. Lessig portrays book publishers as greedy Luddites that want to wring profits from technology they spurned by remaining wedded to their archaic business models.

Alan Murray. "Google Library Is Great for the World," *Wall Street Journal* (October 26, 2005), page A2.

Murray, a columnist, sees U.S. publishers objections to the Googlization of all the books in the English languages is a niggling roadblock. One way or the other, he says, the Google Print Library will be built.

Ellen Alderman and Caroline Kennedy. *The Right to Privacy.* Knopf, 1995.

Alderman and Kennedy, both lawyers, track the evolving concept of privacy through all the major cases.

Robert J. Wagman. *The First Amendment Book.* Pharos, 1991.

This lively history of the First Amendment is a solid primer on the subject.

Clark R. Mollenhoff. "25 Years of *Times* v. *Sullivan*," *Quill* (March 1989), pages 27–31.

A veteran investigative reporter argues that journalists have abused the landmark *Sullivan* decision and have been irresponsibly hard on public figures.

Phillip Nobile and Eric Nadler. *United States of America vs. Sex: How the Meese Commission Lied about Pornography.* Minotaur, 1986.

Nobile and Nadler, editors of the *Penthouse* magazine spin-off *Forum*, discredit the 1986 attorney general's report on pornography, which called for stricter laws against adult material. They argue that the commission ignored and distorted scientific evidence on the effects of pornography.

Michael Gartner. "Fair Comment," *American Heritage* (October–November 1982), pages 28–31.

Gartner, a television and newspaper executive, delights in digging up the details of the colorful Cherry Sisters case that decided that almost anything could be said about public performances.

Fred W. Friendly. *Minnesota Rag: The Dramatic Story of the Landmark Supreme Court Case That Gave New Meaning to the First Amendment.* Random House, 1981.

A colorful account of the *Near* v. *Minnesota* prior-restraint case.

Sanford Ungar. *The Papers & the Papers: An Account of the Legal and Political Battle Over the Pentagon Papers.* Dutton, 1975.

Ungar, a news reporter, provides a comprehensive chronology of a major prior-restraint case.

Jim DeFede

Reflexively, Miami *Herald* columnist Jim DeFede did what seemed right when a suicidal friend called. He taped the call. But in Florida taping a call without permission is against the law. But does being illegal make an act necessarily wrong? Such are the issues that make ethics essential to understand.

chapter 21 Ethics and the Mass Media

In this chapter you will learn:

- **Mass media ethics codes cannot anticipate all moral questions.**
- **Mass media people draw on numerous moral principles, some inconsistent with each other.**
- **Some mass media people prefer process-based ethics systems, while some prefer outcome-based systems.**
- **Potter's Box is a useful tool to sort through ethics issues.**
- **Some mass media people confuse ethics, law, prudence and accepted practices.**
- **Dubious mass media practices confound efforts to establish universal standards.**

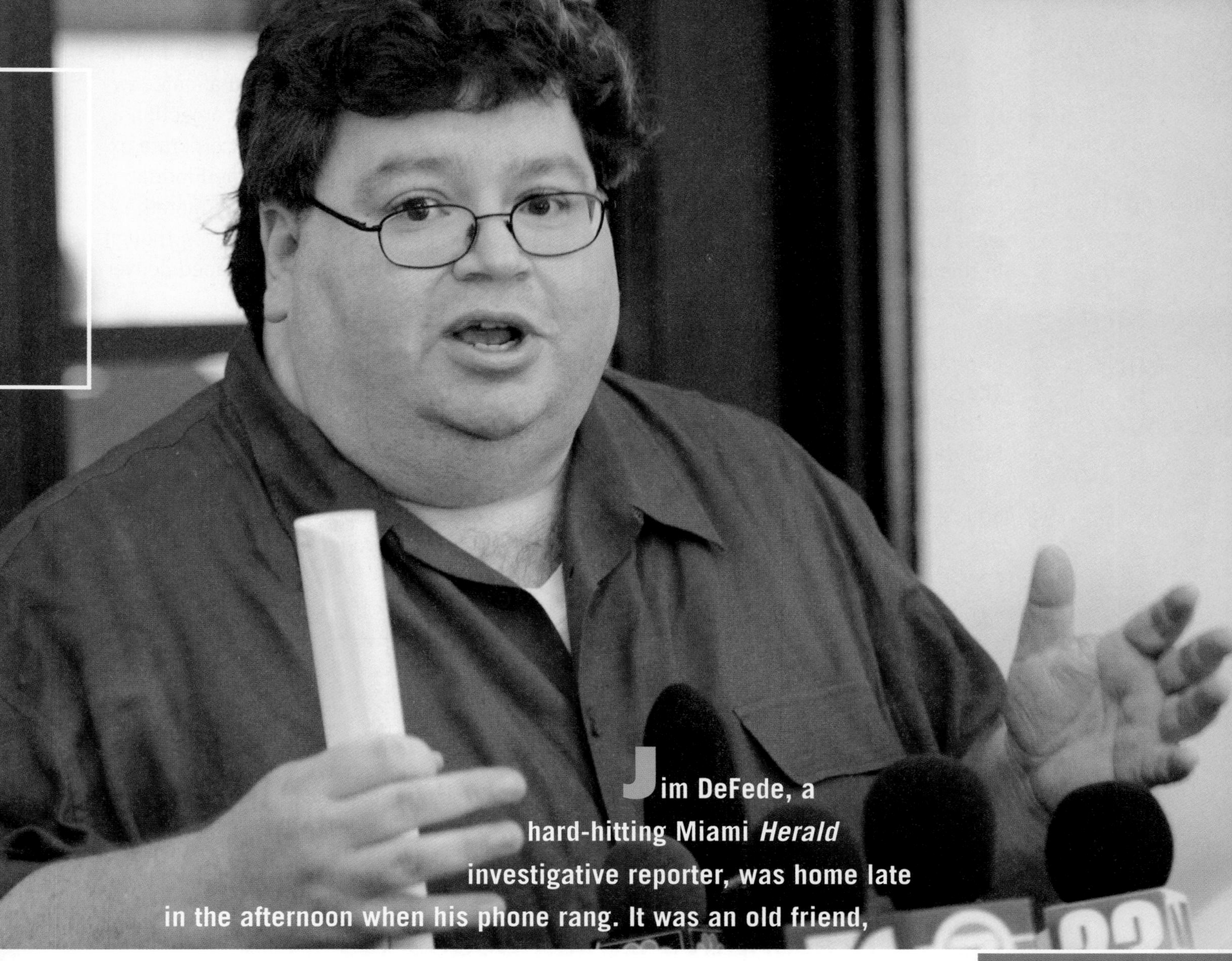

Jim DeFede, a hard-hitting Miami *Herald* investigative reporter, was home late in the afternoon when his phone rang. It was an old friend, former city and county Commissioner Arthur Teele Jr. Teele was distraught that another newspaper had outed him for trysts with a transvestite prostitute. "What did I do to piss off this town?" Teele asked. The transvestite allegation had followed 26 charges of fraud and money-laundering. Teele said he was being smeared by prosecutors. He was afraid the transvestite story would hurt him with "the ministers and the church."

Worried about his friend's anguish, DeFede turned on his telephone recorder to record his pain. He also asked if Teele wanted go public that the prosecutors were using the media to smear him. Teele said no, but the discussion meandered back and forth to a potentially explosive story for which Teele said he had documents. A couple hours later Teele called and said he was leaving the documents for DeFede. Then he hung up, put a pistol to his head, and shot himself dead.

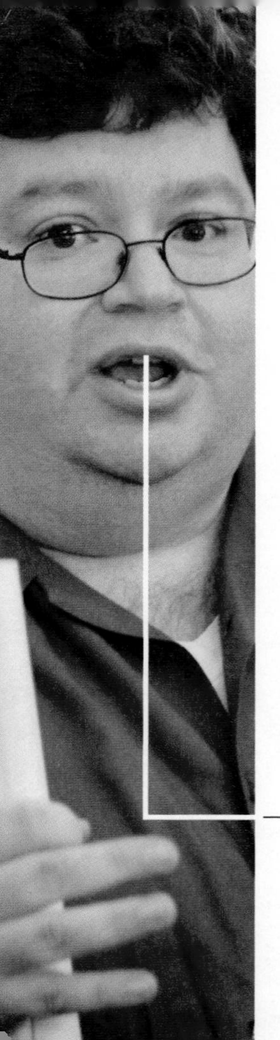

DeFede briefed his editor, Judy Miller, who told him to write a Page One story. In the meantime, higher executives at the *Herald* realized that DeFede had violated a state law that forbid taping a telephone conversation without permission. Over Miller's objections, publisher Jesus Diaz Jr. and corporate attorney Robert Beatty and two other corporate executives decided to fire DeFede—even though the *Herald* had once fought the Florida law, even though anyone who calls a reporter implicitly is consenting to being quoted, even though tape-recording is just a more detailed form of note-taking—and even though, in this case, *Herald* executives decided to draw on DeFede's notes from the taped conversation to be used in a Page One story on the suicide.

If indeed DeFede had acted unethically, then how about the *Herald* that drew on his information from the phone call? And how's this for a twist to make the issue murkier? The state's attorney cleared DeFede of violating the anti-recording stature. Also, only 12 states, including Florida, have such a law. If what DeFede did was unethical in Florida, is it less so in the 38 states that don't have such restrictions?

Clearly, the law and ethics don't coincide lockstep, which is a major issue in media ethics. In this chapter you will learn tools that have been developed through the centuries to sort through complexities posed by dilemmas of right and wrong, when choosing a course has downsides as well as upsides.

The Difficulty of Ethics

studypreview **Mass media organizations have put together codes of ethics that prescribe how practitioners should go about their work. Although useful in many ways, these codes neither sort through the bedeviling problems that result from conflicting prescriptions nor help much when the only open options are negative.**

Prescriptive Ethics Codes

The mass media abound with **codes of ethics.** The earliest was adopted in 1923, the **Canons of Journalism of the American Society of Newspaper Editors.** Advertising, broadcast and public relations practitioners also have codes. Many newcomers to the mass media make an erroneous assumption that the answers to all the moral choices in their work exist in the prescriptions of these codes, a stance known as **prescriptive ethics.** While the codes can be helpful, ethics is not so easy.

The difficulty of ethics becomes clear when a mass communicator is confronted with a conflict between moral responsibilities to different concepts. Consider:

code of ethics ■ Statement that defines acceptable, unacceptable behavior.

Canons of Journalism of the American Society of Newspaper Editors ■ First media code, 1923.

prescriptive ethics ■ Follow the rules and your decision will be the correct one.

privacy ■ Respect for privacy common in ethics codes.

timeliness ■ A virtue in most news ethics codes.

Respect for Privacy The code of the Society of Professional Journalists prescribes that reporters will show respect for the dignity, **privacy,** rights and well-being of people "at all times." The SPJ prescription sounds excellent, but moral priorities such as dignity and privacy sometimes seem less important than other priorities. The public interest, for example, overrode privacy in 1988 when the Miami *Herald* staked out presidential candidate Gary Hart overnight when he had a woman friend in his Washington townhouse.

Commitment to Timeliness The code of the Radio-Television News Directors Association prescribes that reporters be "**timely** and accurate." In practice, however, the virtue of accuracy is jeopardized when reporters rush to the air with stories. It takes time to confirm details and be accurate—and that delays stories and works against timeliness.

Being Fair The code of the Public Relations Society of America prescribes dealing **fairly** with both clients and the general public. However, a persuasive message prepared on behalf of a client is not always the same message that would be prepared on behalf of the general public. Persuasive communication is not necessarily dishonest, but how information is marshaled to create the message depends on whom the PR person is serving.

Conflict in Duties

Media ethics codes are well-intended, usually helpful guides, but they are simplistic when it comes to knotty moral questions. When media ethicians Clifford Christians, Mark Fackler and Kim Rotzoll compiled a list of five duties of mass media practitioners, some of these inherent problems became obvious.

Duty to Self Self-preservation is a basic human instinct, but is a photojournalist shirking a duty to subscribers by avoiding a dangerous combat zone?

Self-aggrandizement can be an issue too. Many college newspaper editors are invited, all expenses paid, to Hollywood movie premieres. The duty-to-self principle favors going: The trip would be fun. In addition, it is a good story opportunity, and as a free favor, it would not cost the newspaper anything. However, what of an editor's responsibility to readers? Readers have a right to expect writers to provide honest accounts that are not colored by favoritism. Can a reporter write fairly after being wined and dined and flown across the continent by movie producers who want a gung-ho story? Even if reporters rise above being affected and are true to conscience, there are the duty-to-employer and the duty-to-profession principles to consider. The newspaper and the profession itself can be tarnished by audience suspicions, no matter whether they are unfounded, that a reporter has been bought off.

Duty to Audience Television programs that reenact violence are popular with audiences, but do they do a disservice because they frighten many viewers into inferring that the streets are more dangerous than they really are?

Tom Wicker of the New York *Times* tells a story about his early days as a reporter in Aberdeen, North Carolina. He was covering a divorce case involving one spouse chasing the other with an ax. Nobody was hurt physically, and everyone who heard the story in the courtroom, except the divorcing couple, had a good laugh. "It was human comedy at its most ribald, and the courtroom rocked with laughter," Wicker recalled years later. In writing his story, Wicker captured the darkly comedic details so skillfully that his editor put the story on Page 1. Wicker was proud of the piece until the next day when the woman in the case called on him. Worn-out, haggard, hurt and angry, she asked, "Mr. Wicker, why did you think you had a right to make fun of me in your paper?"

The lesson stayed with Wicker for the rest of his career. He had unthinkingly hurt a fellow human being for no better reason than to evoke a chuckle, or perhaps a belly laugh, from his readers. To Wicker the duty-to-audience principle would never again transcend his moral duty to the dignity of the subjects of his stories. Similar ethics questions involve whether to cite AIDS as a contributor to death in an obituary, to identify victims in rape stories and to name juveniles charged with crimes.

Duty to Employer Does loyalty to an employer transcend the ideal of pursuing and telling the truth when a news reporter discovers dubious business deals involving the

fairness ■ A virtue in most media ethics codes.

mediaPEOPLE

Charlie Gay

Unusual among U.S. newspapers, the Shelton, Washington, *Journal* prints the names of rape victims and even gets into X-rated details in covering trials. The publisher, Charlie Gay, knows the policy runs against the grain of contemporary news practices. It's also, he says, "good basic journalism."

Rape Names Editor Charlie Gay sees a journalistic duty to include victim names in rape stories.

Most newsrooms shield the names of rape victims, recognizing a notion, flawed though it is, that victims invite the crime. This stigma sets rape apart from other crimes, or at least so goes one line of thinking. Thus, naming should be at the victim's discretion, not a journalist's. To that, Charlie Gay says balderdash. Silence and secrecy only perpetuate stigmas, he says. As he sees it, only with the bright light of exposure can wrongheaded stigmas be cleansed away.

Gay says the journalist's duty is to tell news fully and fairly. "If we did follow a policy of no victims' names, we'd be horribly unfair to the other party, the person who's picked up for the crime and who is innocent until proved guilty," he says. It's unfair reporting to be "stacking everything against the accused." In a speech to the Shelton Rotary Club, Gay said: "The *Journal* is reporting a crime and a trial. We're not trying to protect one party or make judgments about one party." The ideal to Gay is full, fair, detailed stories that inform without prejudicing.

The *Journal*'s victim-naming policy has rankled many Shelton people for years. Readers' letters flood the opinion page with every new rape case. The newspaper has been picketed. Critics have called for advertisers to boycott the paper and for readers to cancel subscriptions.

The state Legislature responded in 1992. After lengthy debate about whether naming names should be outlawed, the Legislature decided to bar reporters from naming child victims. The law was later ruled unconstitutional. It violated the First Amendment because government was abridging freedom of the press. The flap, however, demonstrated the intensity of feelings on the subject.

Police, prosecutors and social workers generally want names withheld, saying that some victims won't come forward for fear of publicity. Gay is blunt about that argument: The job of the press is to report the news, not to make the job of government easier. He says it is the job of government agents, including police and social workers, to persuade victims to press charges. Although decidedly with a minority view, Gay has some support for including names and gripping detail in reporting sex crimes. Psychologist Robert Seidenberg, for example, believes that rape victims may be encouraged to report the crime by reading the accounts of victims with whom they can relate because details make compelling reading that helps them sort through their own situation more clearly.

For a thorough discussion of the issue, including the interview with Charlie Gay from which this Media People box was drawn, see Richard J. Riski and Elinor Kelley Grusin's research article "Newspaper's Naming Policy Continues Amid Controversy," in the Fall 2003 issue of the *Newspaper Research Journal*.

parent corporation? This is a growing issue as the mass media become consolidated into fewer gigantic companies owned by conglomerates. In 1989, for example, investigative reporter Peter Karl of Chicago television station WMAQ broke a story that General Electric had manufactured jet engines with untested and sometimes defective bolts. Although WMAQ is owned by NBC, which in turn is owned by General Electric, Karl's exclusive, documented and accurate story aired. However, when the story was passed on to the network itself, Marty Ryan, executive producer of the *Today* show, ordered that the references to General Electric be edited out.

Duty to the Profession At what point does an ethically motivated advertising-agency person blow the whistle on misleading claims by other advertising people?

Duty to Society Does duty to society ever transcend duty to self? To the audience? To the employer? To colleagues? Does ideology affect a media worker's sense of duty to society? Consider how Joseph Stalin, Adolf Hitler and Franklin Roosevelt would be covered by highly motivated communist, fascist and libertarian journalists.

Are there occasions when the duty-to-society and duty-to-audience principles are incompatible? Nobody enjoys seeing the horrors of war, for example, but journalists may feel that their duty to society demands that they go after the most grisly photographs of combat to show how horrible war is and, thereby, in a small way, contribute to public pressure toward a cessation of hostilities and eventual peace.

Promoting Self-Interest

It didn't surprise anybody much that the reviews from online book retailer Amazon.com were enthusiastic. Most were drawn from book jacket blurbs. Amazon.com, after all, was in the business of promoting books and sales.

When the Washington *Post* started an online bookstore in 1998, its credibility was jeopardized. The *Post* created an ethics problem for itself: Would its reviews be driven by the influential critical comment, sometimes negative, that had traditionally marked its arts section, or would the *Post,* like Amazon.com, gravitate toward upbeat, favorable reviews that were likelier to sell books?

To its credit, Amazon.com permits readers to post reviews, critical and otherwise. To find these reviews, however, you need to scroll down past the sales pitch for the title.

Media Ethics

studypreview **Media ethics is complicated by the different performance standards that mass media operations establish for themselves. This is further complicated by the range of expectations in the mass audience. One size does not fit all.**

Media Commitment

A single ethics standard is impossible to apply to the mass media. Nobody holds a supermarket tabloid like *News of the World,* which specializes in celebrities being visited by aliens, to the same standard as the New York *Times.* Why the difference? Media ethics, in part, is a function of what a media operation promises to deliver to its audience and what the audience expects. The *News of the World* commitment is fun and games in a tongue-in-cheek news context. The New York *Times* considers itself a "Newspaper of Record." There is a big difference.

CNN touts accuracy in its promotional tagline: "News You Can Trust." Explicitly, the network promises to deliver truthful accounts of the day's events. CNN establishes its own standards. A lapse, like a misleading story, especially if intentional or the result of sloppiness, represents a broken promise and an ethics problem.

A media organization's commitments may be implicit. Disney, for example, has cultivated an image of wholesome products with which the whole family can be comfortable. It's a commitment: Nothing bordering on smut here.

Radio-Television News Directors Association The association's current code of ethics, adopted in 1987.
www.rtnda.org/ethics/coe.shtml

Society of Professional Journalists Includes the society's code of ethics, links to *Quill* magazine and other journalistic resources.
www.spj.org

Code of Ethics Guidelines and codes from U.S. news organizations regarding various ethical issues in the newsroom.
www.asne.org/ideas/codes/codes.htm

Center for the Study of Ethics in the Professions Links to codes of ethics for all kinds of organizations around the world.
http://ethics.iit.edu/codes

EthicNet Databank of European codes of ethics for journalism.
www.uta.fi/ethicnet

Audience Expectation

The audience brings a range of ethics expectations to media relations, which further thwarts any attempt at one-size-fits-all media ethics. From a book publisher's fantasy science fiction imprint, readers have far different expectations than they do from NBC

News, which, except for plainly labeled opinion, is expected to deliver unmitigated nonfiction.

A range in the type of messages purveyed by the mass media also bespeaks a variety of ethics expectations. Rarely is falsity excusable, but even the courts allow puffery in advertising. The news releases that public relations people produce are expected, by their nature, to be from a client's perspective, which doesn't always coincide with the perspective expected of a news reporter.

Media messages in the fiction story tradition don't unsettle anyone if they sensationalize to emphasize a point. Sensationalistic exaggeration in a serious biography, however, is unforgivable.

Ethics as an Intellectual Process

A set of rules, easily memorized and mindlessly employed, would be too easy. It doesn't work that way. Ethics, rather, needs to an intellectual process of sorting through media commitments, audience expectations and broad principles. But even on broad principles there is more.

Moral Principles

study preview **Concern about doing the right thing is part of human nature, and leading thinkers have developed a great number of enduring moral principles over the centuries. The mass media, like other institutions and also like individuals, draw on these principles, but this does not always make moral decisions easy. The principles are not entirely consistent, especially in sorting through dilemmas.**

The Golden Mean

Aristotle ■ Advocate of the golden mean.

golden mean ■ Moderation is the best course.

The Greek philosopher **Aristotle,** writing almost 2,400 years ago, devised the **golden mean** as a basis for moral decision-making. The golden mean sounds simple and straightforward: Avoid extremes and seek moderation. Modern journalistic balance and fairness are founded on this principle.

The golden mean's dictate, however, is not as simple as it sounds. As with all moral principles, application of the golden mean can present difficulties. Consider the federal law that requires over-the-air broadcasters to give equal opportunity to candidates for public office. If one candidate buys 30 seconds at 7 p.m. for $120, a station is obligated to allow other candidates for the same office to buy 30 seconds at the same time for the same rate. On the surface this application of the golden mean, embodied in federal law, might seem to be reasonable, fair and morally right, but the issue is far more complex. The equality requirement, for example, gives an advantage to candidates who hold simplistic positions that can be expressed compactly. Good and able candidates whose positions require more time to explain are disadvantaged, and the society is damaged when inferior candidates win public office.

Golden Mean The Greek thinker Aristotle told his students almost 2,400 years ago that right courses of action avoid extremes. His recommendation: moderation.

Although minute-for-minute equality in broadcasting can be a flawed application of the golden mean, Aristotle's principle is valuable to media people when making moral decisions, as long as they do not abdicate their power of reason to embrace formulaic tit-for-tat measurable equality. It takes the human mind, not a formula, to determine fairness. And therein lies the complexity of the golden mean. No two human beings think exactly alike, which means that applying the golden mean involves individuals making judgment calls that are not necessarily the same. This element of judgment in moral decisions can make ethics intellectually exciting. It takes a sharp mind to sort through issues of balance and fairness.

Universal Law Immanuel Kant, an 18th-century German philosopher, urged people to find principles that they would be comfortable having applied in all situations. He called these principles *categorical imperatives.*

"Do unto Others"

The Judeo-Christian principle of "**Do unto others** as you would have them do unto you" appeals to most Americans. Not even the do-unto-others prescription is without problems, however. Consider the photojournalist who sees virtue in serving a mass audience with a truthful account of the human condition. This might manifest itself in portrayals of great emotions, like grief. But would the photojournalist appreciate being photographed herself in a grieving moment after learning that her own infant son had died in an accident? If not, her pursuit of truth through photography for a mass audience would be contrary to the "do-unto-others" dictum.

Categorical Imperatives

About 200 years ago, German philosopher **Immanuel Kant** wrote that moral decisions should flow from thoroughly considered principles. As he put it, "Act on the maxim that you would want to become universal law." He called his maxim the categorical imperative. A **categorical imperative,** well thought out, is a principle that the individual who devised it would be willing to apply in all moral questions of a similar sort.

Kant's categorical imperative does not dictate specifically what actions are morally right or wrong. Moral choices, says Kant, go deeper than the context of the immediate issue. He encourages a philosophical approach to moral questions, with people using their intellect to identify principles that they, as individuals, would find acceptable if applied universally.

Kant does not encourage the kind of standardized approach to ethics represented by professional codes. His emphasis, rather, is on hard thinking. Says philosopher Patricia Smith, of the University of Kentucky, writing in the *Journal of Mass Media Ethics,* "A philosophical approach to ethics embodies a commitment to consistency, clarity, the principled evaluation of arguments and unrelenting persistence to get to the bottom of things."

Journal of Mass Media Ethics This journal addresses ethical situations in mass communication.
www.jmme.org

Media Watchdogs A collection of online media monitoring sources, from the University of Texas.
www.utexas.edu/coc/journalism/SOURCE/j363/watchdogs.html

"Do unto others" ■ Judeo-Christian principle for ethical behavior.

Immanuel Kant ■ Advocated the categorical imperative.

categorical imperative ■ Follow principles as if they had universal application.

John Stuart Mill ■ Advocated utilitarianism.

principle of utility ■ Best course bestows the most good for the most people.

Utilitarian Ethics

In the mid-1800s British thinker **John Stuart Mill** declared that morally right decisions are those that result in "happiness for the greatest number." Mill called his idea the **principle of utility.** It sounds good to many of us because it parallels the democratic principle of majority rule, with its emphasis on the greatest good for the greatest number of people.

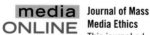

By and large, journalists embrace Mill's utilitarianism today, as evinced in notions like the *people's right to know,* a concept originally meant to support journalistic pursuit of information about government, putting the public's interests ahead of government's

Utilitarianism American journalists tend to like 19th-century British thinker John Stuart Mill's utilitarianism, which favors actions that result in the greatest good for the greatest number of people. This approach to ethics dovetails well with majority rule and modern democracy.

interests, but which has come to be almost reflexively invoked to defend pursuing very personal information about individuals, no matter what the human toll.

Pragmatic Ethics

John Dewey, an American thinker who wrote in the late 1800s and early 1900s, argued that the virtue of moral decisions had to be judged by their results. Dewey's **pragmatic ethics,** like other ethics systems, has problems. One is that people do not have perfect crystal balls to tell them for sure whether their moral actions will have good consequences.

Egalitarian Ethics

In the 20th century, philosopher **John Rawls** introduced the **veil of ignorance** as an element in ethics decisions. Choosing a right course of action, said Rawls, requires blindness to social position or other discriminating factors. This is known as **egalitarianism.** An ethical decision requires that all people be given an equal hearing and the same fair consideration.

To Rawls a brutal slaying in an upscale suburb deserves the same journalistic attention as a similarly brutal slaying in a poor urban neighborhood. All other things being equal, a $20,000 bank burglary is no more newsworthy than a $20,000 embezzlement.

John Dewey ■ Advocate of pragmatism.

pragmatic ethics ■ Judge acts by their results.

John Rawls ■ Advocated egalitarianism.

veil of ignorance ■ Making decisions with a blind eye to extraneous factors that could affect the decision.

egalitarianism ■ Treat everyone the same.

Hutchins Commission ■ Advocated social responsibility as goal and result of media activities.

social responsibility ■ Making decisions that serve society responsibly.

Social Responsibility Ethics

The **Hutchins Commission,** a learned group that studied the U.S. mass media in the 1940s, recommended that journalists and other media people make decisions that serve the society responsibly. For all its virtues the **social responsibility** system, like all ethics systems, has difficulties. For one thing decision-makers can only imperfectly foresee the effects of their decisions. It is not possible to predict with 100 percent confidence whether every decision will turn out to be socially responsible. Also, well-meaning people may differ honestly about how society is most responsibly served.

media TIMELINE

MEDIA ETHICS

400 B.C. Aristotle laid out the golden mean.

20s Jesus Christ articulated "Do unto others as you would have them do unto you."

1785 Immanuel Kant advanced the categorical imperative.

1865 John Stuart Mill proposed utilitarianism.

1903 John Dewey advanced pragmatism.

1919 Upton Sinclair exposed newsroom abuses in his novel *The Brass Check.*

1923 American Society of Newspaper Editors adopted a media ethics code.

1947 Hutchins Commission urged the media to be socially responsible.

1971 John Rawls advanced the veil of ignorance.

John Dewey He saw decisions as ethical if the ascertainable outcomes were good.

John Rawls He favored putting a blind eye to all issues except rightness and wrongness.

Process versus Outcome

study preview **The various approaches to ethics fall into two broad categories: deontological ethics and teleological ethics. Deontologists say people need to follow good rules. Teleologists judge morality not by the rules but by the consequences of decisions.**

Deontological Ethics

The Greek word *deon,* which means "duty," is at the heart of **deontological ethics,** which holds that people act morally when they follow good rules. Deontologists feel that people are duty bound to identify these rules.

Deontologists include people who believe that Scripture holds all the answers for right living. Their equivalent among media practitioners are those who rely entirely on codes of ethics drafted by organizations they trust. Following rules is a prescriptive form of ethics. At first consideration, ethics might seem as easy as following the rules, but not all questions are clear-cut. In complicated situations the rules sometimes contradict each other. Some cases are dilemmas with no right option—only a choice among less-than-desirable options.

Deontological ethics becomes complicated, and also more intellectually interesting, when individuals, unsatisfied with other people's rules, try to work out their own universally applicable moral principles.

Robert Hutchins His commission elevated social responsibility as a factor in ethics decisions.

deontological ethics ■ Good actions flow from good processes.

media ONLINE **Accuracy in Media** A media watchdog organization, AIM critiques the work of journalists from a conservative political perspective.
www.aim.org

Fairness & Accuracy in Reporting FAIR is a liberal media watch group that criticizes media for their allegedly biased coverage of minorities, women, and labor. FAIR's site provides reports and a variety of links.
www.fair.org/index.php

Center for Media and Public Affairs The Center for Media and Public Affairs describes itself as "a nonpartisan, nonprofit research organization in Washington, D.C., which conducts scientific studies of the news and entertainment media."
www.cmpa.com

The Media Institute TMI is a research foundation and think tank that supports three purposes: freedom of speech, a competitive media industry and excellence in journalism.
www.mediainstitute.org

Poynter Online The Poynter Institute for Media Studies is a nonpartisan, nonprofit organization that studies media ethics, management, and graphics. It conducts seminars on a variety of these topics.
www.poynter.org

Here are some major deontological approaches:

- **Theory of divine command.** This theory holds that proper moral decisions come from obeying the commands of God, with blind trust that the consequences will be good.
- **Theory of divine right of kings.** This theory sees virtue in allegiance to a divinely anointed monarch.
- **Theory of secular command.** This theory is a nonreligious variation that stresses allegiance to a dictator or other political leader from whom the people take cues when making moral decisions.
- **Libertarian theory.** This theory stresses a laissez-faire approach to ethics: Give free rein to the human ability to think through problems, and people almost always will make morally right decisions.
- **Categorical imperative theory.** This theory holds that virtue results when people identify and apply universal principles.

Teleological Ethics

Unlike deontological ethics, which is concerned with the right actions, teleological ethics is concerned with the consequences of actions. The word **teleology** comes from the Greek word *teleos,* which means "result" or "consequence."

Teleologists see flaws in the formal, legalistic duty to rules of deontologists, noting that great harm sometimes flows from blind allegiance to rules.

Here are some major teleological approaches:

- **Pragmatic theory.** This theory encourages people to look at human experience to determine the probable consequences of an action and then decide its desirability.
- **Utilitarian theory.** This theory favors ethics actions that benefit more people than they damage—the greatest good for the greatest number.
- **Social-responsibility theory.** This theory judges actions by the good effect they have on society.

Situational Ethics

Firm deontologists see two primary flaws in teleological ethics:

- Imperfect foresight.
- Lack of guiding principles.

Despite these flaws, many media practitioners apply teleological approaches, sometimes labeled **situational ethics,** to arrive at moral decisions. They gather as much information as they can about a situation and then decide, not on the basis of principle but on the facts of the situation. Critics of situational ethics worry about decisions governed by situations. Much better, they argue, would be decisions flowing from principles of enduring value. With situational ethics the same person might do one thing one day and on another day go another direction in a similar situation.

Consider a case at the *Rocky Mountain News* in Denver. Editors learned that the president of a major suburban newspaper chain had killed his parents and sister in another state when he was 18. After seven years in a mental hospital the man completed college, moved to Colorado, lived a model life and became a successful newspaper executive. The *Rocky Mountain News* decided not to make a story of it. Said a *News* official, "The only reason for dredging up [his] past would be to titillate morbid curiosity or to shoot down, maliciously, a successful citizen."

However, when another newspaper revealed the man's past, the *Rocky Mountain News* reversed itself and published a lengthy piece of its own. Why? The newspaper that broke the story had suggested that *News* editors knew about the man's past and had decided to protect him as a fellow member of the journalistic fraternity. *News* editors denied that their motivation was to protect the man. To prove it, they reversed their

theory of divine command ■ Proper decisions follow God's will.

theory of divine right of kings ■ Proper decisions follow monarch's will.

theory of secular command ■ Good decisions follow ruler's will.

libertarian theory ■ Given good information and time, people ultimately make right decisions.

teleology ■ Good decisions are those with good consequences.

situational ethics ■ Make ethics decisions on basis of situation at hand.

decision and published a story on him. The *News* explained its change of mind by saying that the situation had changed. *News* editors, concerned that their newspaper's credibility had been challenged, thought that printing a story would set that straight. Of less concern, suddenly, was that the story would titillate morbid curiosity or contribute to the destruction of a successful citizen. It was a classic case of situational ethics.

Flip-flops on moral issues, such as what happened at the *Rocky Mountain News,* bother critics of situational ethics. The critics say that decisions should be based on deeply rooted moral principles—not immediate, transient facts or changing peripheral contexts.

Potter's Box

studypreview **Moral problems in the mass media can be so complex that it may seem there is no solution. While ideal answers without any negative results may be impossible, a process exists for identifying a course of action that integrates an individual's personal values with moral principles and then tests conclusions against loyalties.**

Four Quadrants

A Harvard Divinity School professor, **Ralph Potter,** devised a four-quadrant model for sorting through ethics problems. The quadrants of the square-like model, called **Potter's Box,** each pose a category of questions. Working through these categories helps to clarify the issues and leads to a morally justifiable position. These are the quadrants of Potter's Box:

Ralph Potter ■ Ethicist who devised the Potter's Box.

Potter's Box ■ Tool for sorting through the pros and cons of ethics questions.

Situation In Quadrant 1 the facts of the issue are decided. Consider a newsroom in which a series of articles on rape is being developed and the question arises whether to identify rape victims by name. Here is how the situation could be defined: The

Ralph Potter

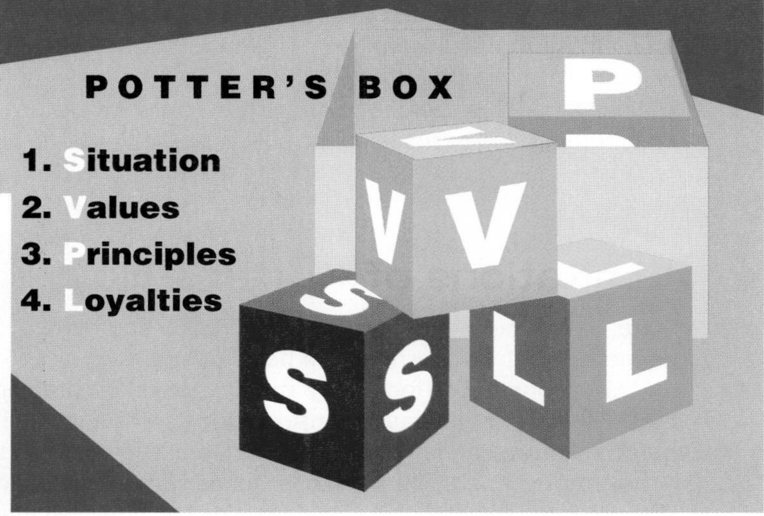

Clarifying Process Potter's Box offers four categories of questions to help develop morally justifiable positions. Ralph Potter, the divinity professor who devised the categories, said to start by establishing the facts of the situation. Then identify the values that underpin the options, recognizing that some values may be incompatible with others. Then consider the moral principles that support each of the values. Finally, sort through loyalties to all the affected interests. Potter's Box is not a panacea, but it provides a framework for working through ethics issues in a thorough way.

newspaper has access to a young mother who has been abducted and raped and who is willing to describe the assault in graphic detail and to discuss her experience as a witness at the assailant's trial. Also, the woman is willing to be identified in the story.

Values Moving to Quadrant 2 of Potter's Box, editors and reporters identify the values that underlie all the available choices. This process involves listing the positive and negative values that flow from conscience. One editor might argue that full, frank discussion on social issues is necessary to deal with them. Another might say that identifying the rape victim by name might discourage others from even reporting the crime. Other positions: Publishing the name is in poor taste. The newspaper has an obligation to protect the victim from her own possibly bad decision to allow her name to be used. The purpose of the rape series can be accomplished without using the name. Readers have a right to all the relevant information that the newspaper can gather. An editor who is torn between such contrary thoughts is making progress toward a decision by at least identifying all the values that can be posited.

Principles In Potter's Quadrant 3, decision-makers search for moral principles that uphold the values they identified in Quadrant 2. John Stuart Mill's principle of utility, which favors the majority over individuals, would support using the victim's name because it could add poignancy to the story, enhancing the chances of improved public sensitivity and perhaps even lead to improved public policy, all of which, Mill would say, outweigh the harm that might come to an individual. On the other hand, people who have used Immanuel Kant's ideas to develop inviolable operating principles—categorical imperatives—look to their rule book: We never publish information that might offend readers. One value of Potter's Quadrant 3 is that it gives people confidence in the values that emerged in their debates over Quadrant 2.

Loyalties In Quadrant 4 the decision-maker folds in an additional layer of complexity that must be sorted through: loyalties. The challenge is to establish a hierarchy of loyalties. Is the first loyalty to a code of ethics, and if so, to which code? To readers, and if so, to which ones? To society? To the employer? To self? Out of duty to self some reporters and editors might want to make the rape series as potent as possible, with as much detail as possible, to win awards and bring honor to themselves and perhaps a raise or promotion or bigger job with another newspaper. Others might be motivated by their duty to their employer: The more detail in the story, the more newspapers it will sell. For others their duty to society may be paramount: The newspaper has a social obligation to present issues in as powerful a way as possible to spur reforms in general attitudes and perhaps public policy.

Limitations of Potter's Box

Potter's Box does not provide answers. Rather, it offers a process through which the key elements in ethics questions can be sorted out.

Also, Potter's Box focuses on moral aspects of a problem, leaving it to the decision-maker to examine practical considerations separately, such as whether prudence supports making the morally best decision. Moral decisions should not be made in a vacuum. For example, would it be wise to go ahead with the rape victim's name if 90 percent of the newspaper's subscribers would become so offended that they would quit buying the paper and, as a result, the paper would go out of business?

Other practical questions can involve the law. If the morally best decision is to publish the name but the law forbids it, should the newspaper proceed anyway? Does journalistic virtue transcend the law? Is it worth it to publish the name to create a First Amendment issue? Are there legal implications, like going to jail or piling up legal defense costs?

Is it worth it to go against accepted practices and publish the victim's name? Deciding on a course of action that runs contrary to tradition, perhaps even contrary to some ethics codes, could mean being ostracized by other media people, whose decisions might have gone another way. Doing right can be lonely.

Ethics and Other Issues

studypreview **Right and wrong are issues in both ethics and law, but ethics and law are different. Obedience to law, or even to professional codes of ethics, will not always lead to moral action. There are also times when practical issues can enter moral decisions.**

Differentiating Ethics and Law

Ethics is an individual matter that relates closely to conscience. Because conscience is unique to each individual, no two people have exactly the same moral framework. There are, however, issues about which there is consensus. No right-minded person condones murder, for example. When there is a universal feeling, ethics becomes codified in law, but laws do not address all moral questions. It is the issues of right and wrong that do not have a consensus that make ethics difficult. Was it morally right for *USA Today* to initiate coverage of tennis superstar Arthur Ashe's AIDS?

Ethics and law are related but separate. The law will allow a mass media practitioner to do many things that the practitioner would refuse to do. Since the 1964 *New York Times* v. *Sullivan* case the U.S. Supreme Court has allowed the news media to cause tremendous damage to public officials, even with false information. However, rare is the journalist who would intentionally push the *Sullivan* latitudes to their limits to pillory a public official.

The ethics decisions of an individual mass media practitioner usually are more limiting than the law. There are times, though, when a journalist may choose to break the law on the grounds of ethics. Applying John Stuart Mill's principle of "the greatest good," a radio reporter might choose to break the speed limit to reach a chemical plant where an accident is threatening to send a deadly cloud toward where her listeners live. Breaking a speed limit might seem petty as an example, but it demonstrates that obeying the law and obeying one's conscience do not always coincide.

media ONLINE **Journalism Ethics Cases Online** These cases address a variety of ethical problems faced by journalists, including privacy, conflict of interest, reporter–source relationships, and the role of journalists in their communities. **www.journalism.indiana.edu/gallery/Ethics**

Silha Center for the Study of Media Ethics and Law This site of the University of Minnesota contains articles, news and links related to issues of both ethics and the law. **www.silha.umn.edu**

Accepted Practices

Just as there is not a reliable correlation between law and ethics, neither is there one between accepted media practices and ethics. What is acceptable at one advertising agency to make a product look good in photographs might be unacceptable at another. Even universally **accepted practices** should not go unexamined, for unless accepted practices are examined and reconsidered on a continuing basis, media practitioners can come to rely more on habit than on principles in their work.

Prudence and Ethics

Prudence is the application of wisdom in a practical situation. It can be a leveling factor in moral questions. Consider the case of Irvin Leiberman, who had built his *Main Line Chronicle* and several other weeklies in the Philadelphia suburbs into aggressive, journalistically excellent newspapers. After being hit with nine libel suits, all costly to defend, Leiberman abandoned the editorial thrust of his newspapers. "I decided not to

accepted practices ■ What media do as a matter of routine, sometimes without considering ethics implications.

prudence ■ Applying wisdom, not principles, to an ethics situation.

mediaPEOPLE

Ted Cohen

During the political ascendancy of George W. Bush, rumors abounded about his partying when he was younger. But aside from anecdotal stories, many from detractors, the facts were never nailed down. As a presidential candidate in 2000, Bush said that, at his wife's urging, he had long since sworn off the bottle. He wouldn't say more. There were stories that the powerful Bush family had bought off officials and called in favors to protect a wayward son. For many voters it was all distant and therefore irrelevant. Others were bothered by murkiness in the past of a presidential candidate and wanted clarifications.

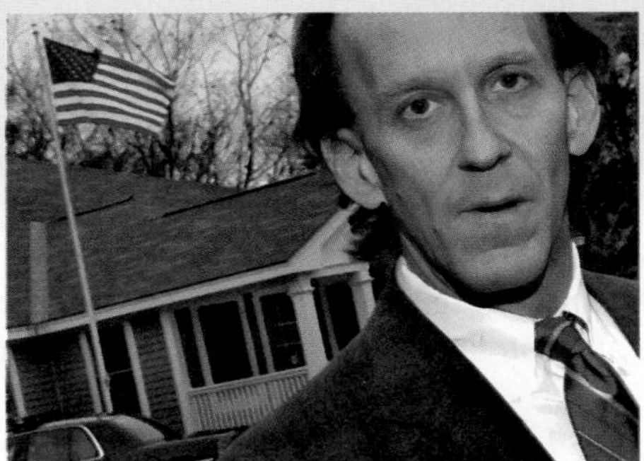

Ted Cohen His ethics dilemma was between an obligation as a news reporter to telling the whole story, in this case about George W. Bush's history of drunkenness, and to conforming with his employer's instructions not to.

In Portland, Maine, reporter Ted Cohen, searching through old court documents, realized that he had unearthed some of Bush's past when he found a drunk-driving conviction during a George W. visit at the family retreat at nearby Kennebunkport. The conviction was years back, when Bush was in his 30s, an age at which such an incident could hardly be dismissed as a youthful indiscretion. More telling, Bush had been silent about it despite continuing questions about his personal history.

At the Portland *Press Herald* Ted Cohen's editors killed his story, saying it was old news. At age 50, a seasoned reporter with 25 years at the *Press Herald*, Cohen didn't like being lectured on what was and wasn't news.

Cohen faced an ethical dilemma: Was he bound by a moral obligation to his employer? Or was he bound more by a moral obligation to the public, which had a legitimate right to a full and honest history about a candidate for the most powerful office on the planet? Was he bound by an obligation to his family and also himself to be gainfully employed so he could be a provider? Such are the thorny conflicts that make ethics excruciating: Damned if you do, damned if you don't.

Cohen struggled with the issues, then decided to give his story to a competitor, television station WPXT across town. Five days before the election the story broke nationally. That every network, newsmagazine and newspaper went with it was a vindication of Cohen's news sense despite the fact that his bosses at the *Press Herald* were chagrined and embarrassed.

Did Cohen do right? Right-minded, well-intentioned people can come down on both sides, which is what makes ethics both intellectually challenging and bedeviling. Often there are no easy rules, just conflicting values.

In Ted Cohen's case he says that his bosses at the *Press Herald* began harassing him after his story broke elsewhere. At one point he was suspended, then reassigned. He pointed also to an intrusion on a vacation and rejected overtime claims. Three and a half years later, after union grievances and a complaint to a state employment agency, Cohen said he was worn down. He left the paper. In a news story in the Portland *Phoenix* two of Cohen's bosses said that he was "a disgruntled employee" who was making "false and misleading statements." Cohen responded with a libel suit.

Whether the courts exonerate Cohen or his old bosses, or neither, is a legal question that won't settle the ethics issue in the Bush drunk-driving conviction revelation.

---

do any investigative work," he said. "It was a matter of either feeding my family or spending my whole life in court." Out of prudence Leiberman decided to abandon his commitment to hard-hitting, effective journalism.

Courageous pursuit of morally lofty ends can, as a practical matter, be foolish. Whether Irvin Leiberman was exhibiting a moral weakness by bending to the chilling factor of libel suits, which are costly to fight, or being prudent is an issue that could be debated forever. The point, however, is that prudence cannot be ignored as a factor in moral decisions.

Unsettled, Unsettling Issues

study preview **When mass media people discuss ethics, they talk about right and wrong behavior, but creating policies on ethics issues is not easy. Many standard media practices press the line between right and wrong, which muddies clear-cut standards that are universally applicable and recognized. There is further muddiness because many ethics codes confuse unethical behavior and behavior that may appear unethical but is not necessarily so.**

Plagiarism

Perhaps the most fiercely loyal media fans are those who read romance novels and swear by a favorite author. In an Internet chatroom in 1997, romance writer Janet Dailey found herself boxed into an admission that she had plagiarized from rival writer Nora Roberts. There is no scorn like that of creative people for those who steal their work, and Roberts was "very, very upset." HarperCollins recalled *Notorious,* Dailey's book that contained the plagiarism, and Roberts' fans, many of them long-time Dailey detractors, began a hunt for other purloined passages.

What is **plagiarism?** Generally, it's considered passing off someone else's creative work as your own, without permission. It's still plagiarism if it's changed a bit, as was Dailey's loose paraphrasing.

media ONLINE **Plagiarism** This group is dedicated to fighting online plagiarism, especially in education. **www.plagiarism.org**

The fact that Dailey's 93 books over 20 years had sold an average of more than 2 million each made the scandal all the juicier. In the end Roberts proposed a financial settlement, and the proceeds went to promote literacy.

Everyone agrees that plagiarism, a form of thievery, is unethical, but the issue is not simple. The fact is that in many media, people draw heavily on other people's ideas and work. Think about sitcom story lines that mimic each other or the bandwagon of movies that follow an unexpected hit with an oddball theme that suddenly becomes mainstream. Journalists, most of whom consider themselves especially pristine compared to their media brethren, have standard practices that encourage a lot of "borrowing."

Among factors that make journalists uncomfortable when pressed hard on plagiary questions are:

- Institutionalized exchanging of stories.
- The role of public relations in generating news stories.
- Monitoring the competition.
- Subliminal memory and innocent recall.

Swapping Stories Some creative work, like scholarship, requires that information and ideas be attributed to their sources. Journalists are not so strict, as shown by story swapping through the Associated Press. The AP picks up stories from its members and distributes them to other members, generally without any reference to the source. Some publications and broadcasters do not even acknowledge AP as the intermediary.

Conditioned by 150 years of the AP's being a journalistic model and under pressure to gather information quickly, many journalists have a high tolerance for "borrowing." When the Chicago *Tribune* was apologizing for a story cribbed from the Jerusalem *Post,* for example, one of the writer's colleagues defended the story: "Everybody rewrites the Jerusalem *Post*. That's how foreign correspondents work."

Incredible as it seems, journalistic tolerance for plagiarism once even allowed radio stations to pilfer the local newspaper for newscasts. Sometimes you could hear the announcer turning the pages. A sad joke that acknowledged this practice was that some stations bought their news at 50 cents a copy, which was cheaper than hiring reporters to cover the community. So pervasive was the journalistic tolerance for "borrowing" that few newspapers protested even mildly when their stories were pirated.

plagiarism ■ Using someone else's work without permission or credit.

News Releases In many newsrooms the plagiarism question is clouded further by the practice of using news releases from public relations people word for word without citing the source. Even in newsrooms that rewrite releases to avoid the embarrassment of running a story that is exactly the same as the competition's, it is standard practice not to cite the source. Public relations people, who are paid for writing favorable stories on their clients, have no objections to being plagiarized, and news organizations find it an easy, inexpensive way to fill space. Despite the mutual convenience, the arrangement raises serious questions of ethics to which many in the media have not responded. The practice leaves the false impression that stories originating with news releases actually originated with the news organization. More serious is that the uncredited stories are a disservice to democracy. Marie Dunn White, in the *Journal of Mass Media Ethics,* wrote: "In order for the reader to evaluate the information he or she is receiving correctly and completely, he or she must know which information came from a press release and, therefore, may be biased."

Monitoring the Competition Competitive pressure also contributes to fuzziness on the plagiarism issue. To avoid being skunked on stories, reporters monitor each other closely to pick up tips and ideas. Generally, reporters are not particular about where they pick up information as long as they are confident that it is accurate. For background, reporters tap newsroom libraries, databases, journals, books and other sources, and in the interest of not cluttering their stories, they do not use footnotes.

Subliminal Memory Covering breaking events has its own pressure that puts journalists at special risk. Almost every journalist who writes under the pressure of a deadline has had the experience of writing a story and later discovering that phrases that came easily at the keyboard were actually somebody else's. In their voracious pursuit of information reporters store phrases and perhaps whole passages subliminally in their memories. This happened to a drama critic at the St. Paul, Minnesota, *Pioneer Press,* who was horrified when a reader pointed out the similarity between his review of a play and an earlier review of the same play in the New York *Times.* Once aware of what he had done unwittingly, the critic offered his resignation. His editors instead moved him to the copy desk.

The muddiness on the issue of journalistic plagiarism is encapsulated in the fact that the Society of Professional Journalists' ethics code makes a flat statement that plagiarism is "dishonest and unacceptable" but then sidesteps the knotty part of the issue by declining to define *plagiarism.*

Misrepresentation

Janet Cooke's meteoric rise at the Washington *Post* unraveled quickly the day after she received a Pulitzer Prize. Her editors had been so impressed with her story "Jimmy's World," about a child who was addicted to heroin, that they nominated it for a Pulitzer Prize. The gripping tale began: "Jimmy is 8 years old and a third-generation heroin addict, a precocious little boy with sandy hair, velvety brown eyes and needle marks freckling the baby-smooth skin of his thin brown arms." Janet Cooke claimed that she had won the confidence of Jimmy's mother and her live-in male friend, a drug dealer, to do the story. Cooke said she had promised not to reveal their identities as a condition for her access to Jimmy.

Museum of Hoaxes Offers a section on misrepresentative journalism, including stories on Janet Cooke and Jayson Blair.
www.museumofhoaxes.com

The story, which played on the front page, so shocked Washington that people demanded that Jimmy be taken away from his mother and placed in a foster home. The *Post* declined to help authorities, citing Cooke's promise of confidentiality to her sources. The mayor ordered the police to find Jimmy with or without the newspaper's help, and millions of dollars in police resources went into a door-to-door search. After 17 days the police gave up knocking on doors for tips on Jimmy. Some doubts emerged at the *Post* about the story, but the newspaper stood behind its reporter.

Janet Cooke ■ Classic case of representing fiction as truth.

Janet Cooke, 25 when she was hired by the *Post,* had extraordinary credentials. Her résumé showed a baccalaureate degree, magna cum laude, from Vassar; study at the Sorbonne in Paris; a master's degree from the University of Toledo; abilities in several languages; and two years of journalistic experience with the Toledo *Blade.* Said Ben

James Frey

Frying Frey Talk-show host Oprah Winfrey gave an influential endorsement to Jim Frey's book, *A Million Little Pieces,* and for a while defended him from criticism that he had concocted pivotal parts in the supposedly nonfiction story line. Winfrey abruptly changed her position and, in an ambush on her television show, withdrew her endorsement and humiliated the unsuspecting Frey.

If you write a memoir, and you make a lot of it up, is it still a memoir? Traditionally, memoirs are true stories from a person's life, but author James Frey challenged that notion with his runaway bestseller, *A Million Little Pieces.*

Frey wrote about his supposed time spent in jail, his drug addiction and rehabilitation. The book, which overflows with vulgar and graphic language, was picked by Oprah Winfrey's book club, and it shot to the top of the best-seller lists. Next to the latest Harry Potter book, Frey's book sold more copies in the United States in 2005 than any other title—3.5 million copies by January of 2006. By then Frey owned a $2.5 million Manhattan apartment and an Amagansett summer house. Reported the web site The Smoking Gun: "Frey has become something of a literary rock star, attracting crowds at book signings that jam stores to capacity."

It was The Smoking Gun that first reported that Frey had fabricated much of his life story. At first Winfrey stood by Frey, but she changed her mind and devoted an entire show to rebuking him publicly, declaring, "I believe the truth matters."

"Memoir writing is not like mathematics," said Nan A. Talese, Frey's editor at Doubleday. "I am not at all dismayed. The truth is that the book has helped people enormously."

In his appearance on *Larry King Live,* Frey conceded that he had stretched the truth, but he dismissed it as no big deal, saying the "essential truth" of his book was more important than the facts.

Eventually, both Talese and Frey issued apologies, but the damage to the reputation of the book industry had been done. "The book industry has been deeply embarrassed, and I think that her [Winfrey's] show pointed up the disconnect between publishing and the real world," said Sara Nelson, editor-in-chief of *Publishers Weekly.*

Writer Diane Cole of *US News and World Report* points out that "literary fabrications have a centuries-old history, and yarn-spinning memoirists can point to no less a predecessor than Ernest Hemingway." But, and she says it's an important *but,* Hemingway prefaced *A Moveable Feast* with this: "If the reader prefers, this book may be regarded as fiction. But there is always the chance that such a book of fiction may throw some light on what has been written as fact."

Months before the Frey scandal erupted, Frey told *Publishers Weekly* that his next work would be a novel about life in contemporary Los Angeles. "I'm looking forward to showing people that I can write fiction." But as Cole concludes, "Honesty carries its own long tail. Riverhead Books, the publisher with whom James Frey had signed for two new books, has dropped the deal."

Bradlee, editor of the *Post:* "She had it all. She was bright. She was well spoken. She was pretty. She wrote well." She was black, which made her especially attractive to the *Post,* which was working to bring the percentage of black staff reporters nearer to the percentage of blacks in its circulation area.

"Jimmy's World" was published in September 1980. Six months later, the Pulitzer committee announced its decision and issued a biographical sheet on Janet Cooke. The Associated Press, trying to flesh out the biographical information, spotted discrepancies right away. Janet Cooke, it turned out, had attended Vassar for one year but had not been graduated with the honors she claimed. The University of Toledo had no record of awarding her a master's. Suddenly, doubts that had surfaced in the days immediately after

media ONLINE **New York *Times*** You can get the abstract of the May 11, 2003 article "Correcting the Record" about Jayson Blair for free, but there's a fee for the full 7000+ word article.
www.nytimes.com

"Jimmy's World" was published took on a new intensity. The editors sat Cooke down and grilled her on the claims on which she was hired. No, she admitted, she was not multilingual. The Sorbonne claim was fuzzy. More important, they pressed her on whether there was really a Jimmy. The interrogation continued into the night, and finally Janet Cooke confessed all: There were no confidential sources, and there was no Jimmy. She had fabricated the story. She resigned, and the *Post,* terribly embarrassed, returned the Pulitzer.

In cases of outright fabrication, as in "Jimmy's World," it is easy to identify the lapses in ethics. When Janet Cooke emerged briefly from seclusion to explain herself, she said that she was responding to pressures in the *Post* newsroom to produce flashy, sensational copy. Most people found the explanation unsatisfying, considering the pattern of deception that went back to her falsified résumé.

There are **misrepresentations,** however, that are not as clearly unacceptable. Much debated are the following.

Staging News To attract favorable attention to their clients, public relations people organize media events, a practice known as **staging news.** These are designed to be irresistible to journalists. Rallies and demonstrations on topical issues, for example, find their way onto front pages, magazine covers and evening newscasts because their photogenic qualities give them an edge over less visual although sometimes more significant events. The ethics question is less important for publicists, who generally are up front about what they are doing. The ethics question is more serious for journalists, who claim that their job is to present an accurate, balanced account of a day's events but who regularly overplay staged events that are designed by publicists to be photogenic and easy to cover.

media ONLINE **Project Censored** A collection of allegedly under-reported news stories and a call to action to critique corporate media.

www.projectcensored.org

Re-creations A wave of **reality programs** on television that began in the late 1980s featured **reenactments** that were not always labeled as such. Philip Weiss, writing in *Columbia Journalism Review,* offered this litany: shadows on the wall of a woman taking a hammer to her husband, a faceless actor grabbing a tin of kerosene to blow up his son, a corpse in a wheelbarrow with a hand dangling, a detective opening the trunk of a car and reeling from the smell of a decomposing body. Although mixing re-creations with strictly news footage rankles many critics, others argue that it helps people understand the situation. The same question arises with docudramas, which mix actual events and dramatic re-creations.

Selective Editing The editing process, by its nature, requires journalists to make decisions on what is most worth emphasizing and what is least worth even including. In this sense, all editing is selective, but the term **selective editing** refers to making decisions with the goal of distorting. Selective editing can occur in drama too, when writers, editors and other media people take literary license too far and intentionally misrepresent.

Fictional Methods In the late 1960s many experiments in media portrayals of people and issues came to be called the **new journalism.** The term was hard to define because it included so many approaches. Among the most controversial were applications of fiction-writing methods on topical issues, an approach widely accepted in book publishing but suddenly controversial when it appeared in the news media. Character development became more important than before, including presumed insights into the thinking of people being covered. The view of the writer became an essential element in much of this reporting. The defense for these approaches was that traditional, facts-only reporting could not approach complex truths that merited journalistic explorations. The profound ethics questions that these approaches posed were usually mitigated by clear statements about what the writer was attempting. Nonetheless, it was a controversial approach to the issues of the day. There was no defense when the fictional approach was complete fabrication passing itself off as reality, as in "Jimmy's World."

misrepresentations ■ Deception in gathering or telling information.

staging news ■ Creating an event to attract news media attention and coverage.

reality programs ■ Broadcast shows with a nonfiction basis.

reenactments ■ Re-creating real events.

selective editing ■ Misrepresentation through omission and juxtaposition.

new journalism ■ Mixing fiction techniques with nonfiction.

case STUDY

Prepackaged News: Who Funds Advocacy?

On five different television stations during one week in January 2006, "reporter" Kate Brookes brought viewers in Texas, Nevada, Louisiana, Illinois and Missouri a story on the "ethanol boom." The all-positive feature provided testimony from two industry experts, an ethanol plant builder and a local corn farmer.

Viewers were not told that Kate Brookes was really a publicist for Medialink, one of the country's largest providers of video news releases.

Brookes' VNR was blended into the newscasts of the five stations, who replaced the visuals with their own local-branded graphics and introduced Brookes as if she were on their news teams. All five stations overlaid their own text onto the video. Four of them edited the story slightly for length. None of them, however, added any original reporting or mentioned the scientific, economic or environmental debates about ethanol. None of them told their viewers that the story was produced by publicists and funded by Siemens, a German-based industrial giant with a direct financial stake in the ethanol business.

As the number of reporters decreases and the workload per reporter increases, the VNR business is booming. So is the business of producing ANRs, audio news reports, and SMTs, satellite media transmissions. In an SMT, a local anchor can conduct an interview via satellite through a service provided by a publicity firm, complete with scripted questions. Some firms also provide whole shows, like TVA Productions' syndicated newsmagazine programs *Business World News, Political World News* and *Health World News.*

According to an April 2006 report by the Center for Media Democracy, *Fake TV News: Widespread and Undisclosed,* most VNRs are produced for corporations. The study found that the broadcast PR firms clearly and accurately disclosed the client and funding information, but of the 87 instances of VNR use studied, only once was there even partial disclosure. "Worse, every TV station actively disguised VNRs as their own journalistic products. That's direct violation of professional guidelines and a betrayal of the public trust."

Following the release of the CMD study, the Radio-Television News Directors Association strongly urged station managements to review and strengthen their policies to require complete disclosure of any outside material used in news programming.

In February 2005 the Government Accountability Office found that VNRs funded by government agencies violate legal provisions that ban "covert propaganda." The Justice Department under the Bush administration claimed the "so-called covert propaganda prohibition does not apply where there is no advocacy of a particular viewpoint." What counts as advocacy? The Government Accountability Office concluded that production and distribution of prepackaged news stories that conceal the agency's role in producing the story is covert propaganda. It said the law is violated by using federal money to produce propaganda.

The RTNDA cautions against government intrusion in determining news content because it would undermine First Amendment values. "Determining the content of a newscast, including when and how to identify sources, is at the very heart of the responsibility of electronic journalists, and these decisions must remain far removed from government involvement or supervision."

Know Thy Source The upbeat side of ethanol production is half of the story that industry publicists fed local television stations in video news releases disguised as news and with no on-air indication as to the real source. Despite the ethics issue in stealth-sourced VNRs, studies have identified many stations that use them as expensive ways for stations to fill newscasts.

WHAT DO YOU THINK?

1. How does a television station using a VNR differ from a newspaper using a press release?
2. Is there any difference in using a VNR about a new neighborhood playground and one about a new prescription drug?
3. Is it okay to use part of a VNR in a station's own story without identifying its source?
4. Should there be a law requiring disclosure of client and funding information for VNRs? Would it undermine our First Amendment values?

Gifts, Junkets and Meals

In his 1919 book ***The Brass Check,*** a pioneer examination of newsroom ethics, **Upton Sinclair** told how news people took bribes to put stories in the paper. Today all media ethics codes condemn gifts and certainly bribes. Even so, there are still people who curry favor with the mass media through gifts, such as a college sports publicist who gives a fifth of whisky at Christmas to a sports writer as a gesture of good will. Favors can take many forms: media-appreciation lunches; free trips abroad, known as **junkets,** especially for travel writers; season passes to cover the opera; discounts at certain stores.

Cultural differences can complicate saying no. In Saudi Arabia, where gifts are a common custom, officials for years gave expensive watches, often Rolexes costing as much as $20,000, to Western reporters. Jihad al-Kahzen, of the Arabic-language daily *Al-Hayat* in Beirit, told the U.S newspaper trade journal *Editor & Publisher:* "If they like you, sometimes they give you his-and-her watches." To refuse a gift can be taken as an insult. Gradually, as more reporters, true to Western journalistic standards, declined Saudi watches, Saudis learned that gift-giving was problematic for journalists, who were concerned about their credibility being compromised. The practice has faded, although reports about gift Rolexes still surface from time to time.

Despite the consistent exhortation of the ethics codes against gifts, favors, free travel and special treatment and privileges, there is nothing inherently wrong in taking them if they do not influence coverage and if the journalist's benefactor understands that. The problem with favors is more a practical one than one of ethics. Taking a favor may or may not be bad, but it *looks* bad. Many ethics codes do not make this important distinction. One that does is the code of the Associated Press Managing Editors, which states: "Journalists must avoid impropriety and *the appearance of impropriety* as well as any conflict of interest or *the appearance of conflict.* They should neither accept anything nor pursue any activity that might compromise or *seem to compromise* their integrity" [italics added]. The APME admonitions at least recognize the distinction between the inherent wrongness of impropriety, which is an ethics question, and the perception that something may be wrong, which is a perception that is unwise to encourage but is not necessarily unethical.

While ethics codes are uniform in prohibiting **freebies,** as gifts and favors are called, many news organizations accept free movie, drama, concert and other tickets, as well as recordings, books and other materials for review. The justification is usually that their budgets allow them to review only materials that arrive free and that their audiences would be denied reviews if the materials had to be purchased. A counterargument is that a news organization that cannot afford to do business right should not be in business. Many news organizations insist on buying tickets for their reporters to beauty pageants, sports events and other things to which there is an admission fee. A frequent exception occurs when a press box or special media facility is available. With recordings, books and free samples, some media organizations return them or pass them on to charity to avoid any appearance that they have been bought off.

When junkets are proposed, some organizations send reporters only if they can pay the fare and other expenses. The Louisville *Courier-Journal* is firm: "Even on chartered trips, such as accompanying a sports team, or hitchhiking on a State Police plane, we insist on being billed for our pro-rata share of the expense." An exception is made by some news organizations for trips that they could not possibly arrange on their own, such as covering a two-week naval exercise aboard a ship.

Some media organizations address the issue of impropriety by acknowledging favors. Many quiz shows say that "promotional consideration" has been provided to companies that give them travel, lodging and prizes. Just as forthright are publications that state that reviews are made possible through season passes or free samples. Acknowledging favors does not remove the questions, but at least it is up front.

The Brass Check ■ 1919 book that exposed newsroom corruption.

Upton Sinclair ■ Author of *The Brass Check.*

junket ■ Trip with expenses paid by someone who may expect favors in return.

freebies ■ Gift for which the giver may expect favor in return.

CHAPTER 21 Wrap-Up

Moral decision-making is rooted in conscience, which makes it highly individual. Attempts to bring order to moral issues in journalism and the mass media have included codes of ethics. These codes identify behaviors that are recognized as ethically troublesome, but because they are generalized statements, the codes cannot anticipate all situations. There is no substitute for human reason and common sense.

Questions for Review

1. Why cannot ethics codes anticipate all moral questions? And does this limit the value of codes for mass media people?
2. List and explain moral principles that mass media people can use to sort through ethics questions.
3. How can mass media people come to different conclusions depending on whether they use process-based or outcome-based ethics?
4. How is Potter's Box a useful tool to sort through ethics issues?
5. Is ethics the same as law? As prudence? As accepted practice?
6. Discuss dubious mass media practices that are inconsistent with many moral principles.

Questions for Critical Thinking

1. How is the social responsibility approach teleological?
2. As someone who reads newspapers and watches newscasts, would you favor deontological or teleological ethics? Which is easier? Which system do you think most journalists prefer?
3. Can you identify the ethics principle or system most associated with Aristotle? Immanuel Kant? John Stuart Mill? John Dewey? John Rawls? Robert Hutchins?
4. How can codes of ethics help mass media people to make the right decisions? Do codes always work? Why or why not?
5. A candidate for mayor tells a news reporter that the incumbent mayor is in cahoots with organized crime. What should the reporter do before going on the air with this bombshell accusation? Why?
6. Can media people ever defend breaking the law as ethical?
7. Is there a difference between ethics and accepted practices?

Deepening Your media LITERACY

Is objectivity a duty?

STEP 1 Write down your definition of an objective journalist. Be sure to include whose duty the objective journalist should serve: self, audience, employer, profession and/or society.

Dig Deeper

STEP 2

1. Describing Oprah Winfrey's influence, Gloria Steinem, femininist and founder of *Ms.* magazine, said: "Of course, her refusal to be uniformly negative—a frequent definition of objectivity—is exactly what keeps her influence from being taken seriously." How is the journalist who reports uniformly negative news serving his or her duty to the audience? To his or her employer? To society?
2. Media critic Benjamin Radford says that many journalists apply a form of agnostic objectivity, which is ultimately uninformative. "Amid all the finger pointing, contradicting experts, and dueling statistics, the journalist's role turns from claim analyzer to claim deliverer . . . a reporter's job is to help separate the wheat from the chaff; instead, they usually just present two different piles of chaff for the viewer to look at and choose from." Is it OK for a journalist to leave it to the audience to judge the truth of what he or she writes? Why? How is the journalist who reports two sides of an issue without telling the viewer that one of them is not based on fact serving the journalist's duty to himself or herself? To the journalist's employer? To the audience? To society?

What Do You Think?

STEP 3 Answer these questions:

1. Should a prescriptive code defining objectivity include the journalist's duty? Which one(s)? Do you think a prescriptive code defining objectivity would work in all cases, for all journalists? Why or why not?

2. How should a journalist reconcile conflicting duties when trying to be objective?
3. Do you think Gloria Steinem has a valid point about objectivity?
4. What do you think of Benjamin Radford's criticism about how he perceives many of today's journalists exercise objectivity?

Keeping Up to Date

Ethicists sort through moral dilemmas involving mass communication in the scholarly *Journal of Mass Media Ethics.*

Many trade and professional journals also deal with media ethics, including *Quill, Columbia Journalism Review* and *American Journalism Review.*

For Further Learning

Bernard Goldberg. *Bias.* Regnery, 2002.
Goldberg, a former CBS television reporter, fuels the claim that major U.S. news media have a liberal slant. The book quickly became a best-seller.

Clifford G. Christians, Kim B. Rotzoll and Mark Fackler. *Media Ethics,* Sixth edition. Longman, 2002.
These scholars are especially good at describing Kant's categorical imperative and other philosophical systems on which media ethics can be based.

Lori Robertson. "Ethically Challenged," *American Journalism Review* (March 2001), pages 20–29.
Robertson, the *Review*'s assistant managing editor, explores a rash of newspaper plagiarism incidents. In an accompanying article (pages 31–35), by Valerie Basheda, *AJR* managing editor, deals with crediting news organizations that did the original work on a story that's being revisited or updated.

Colin Sparks and John Tulloch, editors. *Tabloid Tales: Global Debates over Media Standards.* Rowman & Littlefield, 2000.
Sparks and Tulloch, British scholars, have collected articles and essays on news coverage that dwells on highly personal details of people's lives.

Joe Strupp. "Policing Plagiarism," *Editor & Publisher* (August 7, 2000), pages 19–22.
Strupp, an *E&P* associate editor, surveys newspaper plagiarism cases. Mark Fitzgerald, in an accompanying article, "Why They Do It?" (pages 23–24), consults experts on what motivates plagiarism.

Robert E. Denton Jr., editor. *Political Communication Ethics: An Oxymoron?* Praeger, 2000.
Denton, a political scientist, pulls together essays from leading thinkers campaigns, media discourse and advertising. The role of the Internet is examined.

Ron F. Smith. *Groping for Ethics in Journalism,* Fourth Edition. Iowa State University Press, 1999.
Smith, a journalism professor, draws on case studies for principles to address journalistic ethics issues in all mass media.

Carl Hausman. *The Decision Making Process in Journalism.* Nelson-Hall, 1990.
Hausman, a journalism professor, provides a checklist to help sort the way through ethics problems.

Janet Malcolm. *The Journalist and the Murderer.* Knopf, 1990.
Malcolm argues that journalists exploit their sources of information, using the relationship of author Joe McGinniss and a convicted murderer for the book *Fatal Vision.*

Ralph B. Potter. "The Structure of American Christian Responses to the Nuclear Dilemma, 1958–1963."
Potter describes what came to be known as Potter's Box in his Harvard University doctoral dissertation in 1965.

Index

Page numbers in italics refer to the online chapters available on MyMassCommLab, **www.mymasscommlab.com,** and on the secure Companion Web Site, **www.ablongman.com/vivian8e,** which requires a passcode.

A&E cable network (*see* Arts & Entertainment)
A&R (*see* artist and repertoire)
AARP The Magazine, 85, 88, 90, 96
ABC (*see* American Broadcasting Company)
ABC (*see* Audit Bureau of Circulations)
abolitionism, 33, 74
Abramoff, Jack, 265, 266
Abu Ghraib, 235, 236
Abyss, The, 129
Academy Awards, 134, 135, 136, 275
access
  Internet, 207, 210, 211, 216
  photographers, *22-17*
accuracy, 214
Acme Newspictures, *22-12*
acoustic recording, 105
ACT (*see* Action for Children's Television)
Action for Children's Television (ACT), 379
Adams, Ansel, *22-10*
Adams, John, 228
adaptations, cross-media, 320
Ad Council, 282, 297–298, 399
advance against royalties, 43
advergames, 288
adversarial public relations, 258, 272–273
advertisers
  largest, 281
  role in advertising, 284
advertising, 278–303
  account executive, 283
  agencies (see advertising agencies)
  attack, 450
  books and, 14
  brands, 288, 289–290, 293
  cigarettes, 87, 296, 299
  classified, 3
  clutter, 286, 291, 299
  codes, 282, 297
  costs, 14
  creative director, 283
  creativity, 283, 299
  defined, 4
  democracy and, 281
  development of, 281–283
  dot-coms, 213
  effectiveness, 286, 291, 300
  financial basis of media, 14–15
  gatekeeping, 295–296
  globalization, 296
  Google, 288–289
  government, 16–17, 296, 297, 298–299
  illustrating, *22-11*
  Industrial Revolution and, 282
  infomercials, 292
  Internet, 212–213, 288, 289
  institutional, 268
  issues, 299–300
  magazine, 286
  make-goods, 190
  market segments, 290–291
  media plans, 285
  motivational research, 293–294
  negative, 450
  news and, 244
  newspapers, 56, 70, 73, 281, 285–286
  online, 283, 286–287, 288
  origins of, 281–283
  placement of ads, 285–287
  political, 452, 454–456
  positioning, 290–291
  product placement, 196–197, 292, 293
  prosperity and, 280–281
  psychology and, 293–295
  public relations and, 267–268
  radio, 196, 282
  redundancy, 291
  regulation, 295–299
  research, 293–295
  self-regulation, 296–298
  spending by medium, 286
  stealth, 291–292
  technology and, 281–282
  television, 172–173, 189–191, 191–192, 195–197, 286
  under-the-radar, 291–292
  upfront, 190
  viral, 292
Advertising Age, 81, 91
advertising agencies, 283–284
  brand manager, 284
  commission contract, 284
  compensation, 284
  equity contract, 284
  performance contract, 284
advertorials, 272–273
affiliates
  radio, 152, 153
  television, 182
Aftermath/Shady record label, 104
Agence France-Presse, 420
agencies
  coverage of government, 450
  news, 419–421
agenda-setting, 383–384, 397, 442
Ager, Milton, 310
agnostic, platform, 1–2
aggressive stimulation theory, 376
Aguilera, Christina, 321
AIDS, 5
airtime, free political, 456
airways as public, 152
Akeelah and the Bee, 127
Al Rojo Vivo con María Celeste, 183
albums, music, 112
Albuquerque *Tribune,* 228
alcohol, 4
Alda, Alan, 173
Alexander, Herbert, 455
Al-Ghwell, Hafed, 40
Alice Cooper, 110
Alien and Sedition acts, 228
aliteracy, 46
Alka-Seltzer, 291
All Things Considered, 165–166, 249
All for You, 103
All You magazine, 90
alternative media, 11, 19
AM (*see* amplitude modulation)
Amazing Race, 305
Amazon.com, 31
ambivalent media relations, 271–272
AMC movie-house chain, 137, 139
American Association of Advertising Agencies, 297
American Bicycling Journal, 314
American Broadcasting Company (ABC), 13, 14, 21, 115, 171, 175, 181, 182, 185, 188, 190, 193, 273, 314
American Civil Liberties Union, 462
Amistad, 135
An American Exodus: A Record of Human Erosion, 22-11
American Heritage, 35
American Journalism Review, 77
American Legion magazine, 90
American Magazine, 8, 83
American Marconi, 350
American Media, 80–82, 90
American Profile, 87
American Society of Magazine Editors, 97
American Society of Newspaper Editors, 410
American Textile Reporter, 91
American Turf Register, 314
America Online (AOL), 24, 25, 175, 180, 188, 189, 209
Amistad, 135
amplification, 359
amplitude modulation (AM), 150
analog television, 179
Andreessen, Marc, 10, 202, 203, 208, 209
Antonioni, Michelangelo, 141
anxiety, information, 384–385
AOL (*see* America Online)
AOLWarner, 191
AP (*see* Associated Press)
Apple, 105, 107, 113, 114, 115
Apple recording label, 104
Apprentice, The, 23
APR accreditation, 276
Arbitron, 149, 326
Arbuckle, Fatty, 140
Areopagitica, 23-9
Aristotle, 376, 486
Arledge, Roone, 185, 314
Armageddon, 305
Armstrong, Edwin, 150
Armstrong, Lance, 17
Army, U.S., 17
ARPAnet, 205
Arrangement, The, 46
Arrarás, María Celeste, 181
Arriba la Vida Foundation, 5
art, media content as, 319–320, 390–394
artist and repertoire (A&R), 111–112
artistic freedom, 110–111
Arts & Entertainment network (A&E), 95
ASCAP (*see* American Society of Composers, Authors and Performers)
Asics brand, 373
Associated Press (AP), 231, 234, 262, 419, 420, *22-1* to *22-2, 22-12*
Atlanta, Georgia, *Daily World,* 74
Atlantic magazine, 97
Atlantic recording label, 103
attack ads, 452
audience
  analysis, 340–343
  audits, 332–333
  donations, 16
  focus groups, 339
  galvanic skin checks, 339
  passivity, 368
  prototype research, 340
  ratings, 333–338
  ratings technology, 334
  reaction, 339–340
  size, 332–338
audion tube, 150
Audit Bureau of Circulations (ABC), 55, 76, 285, 327
Auletta, Ken, 21
auteur, 319
authentic performance, 308
authoritarianism, *23-2, 23-3* to *23-7*
authors, 41–43, 45
autistic perception, 371
Ayer, Wayland, 282–283

Baby Boomers, 341
Baby and Child Care, 37
background, news on, 248
Bad Boy recording label, 103
Bad Boys II, 128, 137
Baer, Elizabeth, 463
Bagdikian, Ben, 21–22, 27
Balter, Dave, 300
Baltimore *Sun,* 58, 67, 77
Bamboo Lingerie, 291
bands, garage, 112

Bandura, Albert, 376, 377
bandwidth, 208–210
Bangkok, 117
BankOne Park, 314
Bantam, 34
Barber, Dorothy, 470
Bardeen, Jack, 204
Barnak, Oscar, *22–7*
Barnes & Noble, 35, 36, 42, 318
Barnouw, Erik, 350
Barnum, P. T., 260, 274
barrages, advertising, 291
The Basketball Diaries, 373
Bassett, Angela, 127
Batman, 38, 39, 373, 393
Bazin, Andre, 319
BBC (*see* British Broadcasting Corporation)
BBDO advertising agency, 284
B. Dalton, 35, 36
Beastie Boys, 103
Beatles, 104, 108, 115
Bechtel, 273
Becker, Carl, *23–11*
Benetton brand, 292
Bennett, H. H., *22–6*
Bennett, James Gordon, 228, 230, 231, 313
Bennett, William, 4, 110
Berliner, Emile, 105, 107
Bernard, T. N., *22–10*
Bernays, Edward, 274
Berners-Lee, Tim, 207
Bernstein, Carl, 251
Berry, D. F., *22–10*
Bertelsmann, 34, 422
Besinger, Jeanine, 305
Best Buy, 113, 114
best-sellers, books, 48–49
BET (*see* Black Entertainment Network)
Better Homes and Gardens, 37, 88, 97
Bettmann Archives, *22–16*
bias, journalistic, 240–242
Bible, Gutenberg, 6–7
bicycle racing, 314
Big Four recording companies, 103
Big Three television companies, 182, 185–186, 195
Billboard, 91
billboards, 336
binding influence, of mass media, 4–6
Bismarck, Otto von, *23–5*
black
  audience, 98
  music, 311
  newspapers, 74–75
Black, Bill, 312
Black, Danilo, 76
Blackboard Jungle, 312
Black Entertainment Network (BET), 25, 184
Black Hawk Down, 305
Black Like Me, 32
Black Pirate, The, 126, 128
blackout, news, 448
Black Panthers, 246
black weeks, 338
Blair, Jayson, 67, 496, 497
Blair Witch Project, 134
blaxploitation, 307
block booking, 132, 133
blockbusters, books, 44
blogs, 217–218, 250
Blowup, 141
Bly, Nellie, 232, 233
BMG (*see* Sony BMG)
BoBo Doll studies, 377
Body Fashions, 91
body watch, 448
Bogart, Leo, 299
Bohn, Thomas, 352, 418
Bok, Edward, 282, 296
Bollywood, 428–429
Bolt of Fate: Benjamin Franklin and His Electric Kite Hoax, 32
book clubs, 35
Book-of-the-Month Club, 35
books, 28–51
  advertising and, 15
  agents, 43
  authors, 41–43
  best-seller lists, 48–49
  blockbusters, 44
  chains, 36
  clubs, 35
  consolidation of industry, 34
  current issues and, 32–33
  defined, 7
  direct-mail retailing, 35–36
  electronic, 40
  elitist measures of, 49–50
  evaluating, 48–49
  formats, 39–40
  history and, 30–31
  industry, 33–36
  influence of, 30–33
  issues, 44–47
  major publishers, 34
  mall stores, 36
  national development and, 31
  paperback, 39
  populist measures of, 48
  print-on-demand, 31, 40, 41
  products, 36–39
  professional, 37
  publishers, 33–35, 43
  quality measures, 48–49
  reference, 37
  retailing, 35–36
  science and, 30
  selection criteria, 44–46
  small publishers, 34–35
  social reform and, 30
  superstores, 36
  textbooks, 37–38
  time spent reading, 3
  trade, 37
  vanity press, 35
  web retailing of, 36
Books-A-Million 36
bookstores
  independent, 35
  mall, 36
  superstores, 36
Boom Box, 313
Borders, 36
Bordwell, David, 305
Boston *Gazette*, *22–2*
Boston *Globe*, 2, 58, 59, 60, 67, 77, 82
Boston *News-Letter*, 282
Bourke-White, Margaret, 86, 93, *22–11*, *22–13*
Bowie, David, 110
Bowling for Columbine, 134
boxing, 314
box office, 125, 137
boycott, information, 273–274
Boyz N Da Hood, 103, 373
Boyz II Men, 349
Bradford, Andrew, 8, 83
Brady, Mathew, *22–8* to *22–9*
Brandenburg, Clarence, 465
Brando, Marlin, 123
brands, 289–290, 292
Brass Check, The, 500, *23–10*
Brattain, Walter, 204
Brazile, Donna, 439
Brenston, Jackie, 312
brevity in news, 446
bribery, *23–5*
Brill, Steven, 13, 21
Brinkley, John, 153
Britain, 427–428
British Broadcasting Corporation (BBC), 20
British Invasion, 108
broadcasting (*see* radio; television)
Broadcast Ratings Council, 338
broadsheet, 56, 57
Brokeback Mountain, 124, 125, 137
Bronfman, Edgar Jr., 103
Bronx, 108
Brown, Christy, 136
Brown, Dan, 320, 476–477
Brown, Les, 314
browser, 208
Bruckheimer, Jerry, 193, 304–306
BSkyB, 20, 410, 422
Buchwald, Art, 46
Budweiser, 172, 191
bunching, advertising, 291
bundled transmission, 167, 168
Bundy, Ted, 377
Burden, Don, 440
Burke, Edmund, 438
Burke, James, 269, 270
Burnett advertising agency, 284
Burrow-Giles v. *Sarony*, *22–15*
Burson-Marsteller, 264, 268, 269
Bush, George W., 4, 9, 124, 135, 173, 194, 235, 236, 400, 439, 443, 494, 499
BusinessWeek magazine, 88
Butch Cassidy and the Sundance Kid, 310

Cable News Network (CNN), 13, 228, 248–249, 420, 421, 422
Cable-Satellite Public Affairs Network (C-SPAN), 248
cable television, 15, 175–180, 184, 187–189, 190–191
Cakewalk Sonar, 113
Caldwell, Earl, 246
Caldwell, Erskine, 86
Calvin and Hobbes, 94
Cambridge Press, 31
cameras, *22–6* to *22–8*
Cameron, James, 123, 143
campaign coverage, 451–452
Campbell, Joseph, 282
Canham, Erwin, 65
Cantril, Hadley, 366, 368, 371–372
CapCities Communications, 185
Capitol recording label, 103, 111
Capra, Frank, 130, 131
captures, digital, *22–5*
carbon nanotubes, 210
Carlin, George, 47, 318
Carl's Jr., 18
Carmaggedon, 381
Carmike movie-house chain, 139
Carnegie Commission on Educational Television, 191
Carson, Rachel, 32
cartridge, eight-track, 105
Caruso, Enrico, 274
Cash, Johnny, 107, 312
cassette, recorded, 105
catalytic theory, 377
categorical imperatives, 487
Catmull, Edwin, 129
CATV (*see* community-antenna television)
caveat emptor, 295
caveat venditor, 295
Caxton, William, 282
CBC (*see* Canadian Broadcasting Corporation)
CBS (*see* Columbia Broadcasting System), 14, 21, 131, 181, 182, 185, 239, 371–372, 363–364
CD (*see* compact disk)
cell phone, 180, 189, 197
censorship, 473–476, *23–5*
  gaming and, 319
  movies and, 139–142
Center for Media and Public Affairs, 391, 490
Central Intelligence Agency (CIA), 236
Cerf, Vint, 206
chains
  bookstore, 36
  movie house, 126, 138, 139
  newspaper, 58–60
  radio, 157–160
  television, 181, 182
change, mass media and, 402–403
channel
  noise, 357
  scarcity, 155
Chaplinsky, Walter, 464
Charlie's Angels, 128, 137
Charles, Ray, 117
Charren, Peggy, 379
chatrooms, 396
chemical technology, 8
Cheney, Dick, 236, 270
Cherry Sisters, 469–470
Chicago, 136
Chicago *Daily Defender*, 74
Chicago *Sun-Times*, 60, 62
Chicago *Tribune*, 55, 56, 57, 58, 67, 68, 77, *22–3*
Children's Internet Protection Act (2000), 220
Child Online Protection Act (1996), 220
children, sexual content and, 318–319
Children's Internet Protection Act (2000), 220
Chile, 236
Chili Pepper magazine, 83
China, 20, 285, 424–427
Chingy, 103
Chirac, Jacques, 48
Christian Science Monitor, 16, 57, 61
Chronicle of Higher Education, 49
Chronicles of Narnia, 128
CIA (*see* Central Intelligence Agency)
Cimono, Michael, 134

Cincinnati Consulting Consortium, 299, 301
Cinemark movie-house chain, 139
Cinemax, 317
circulation
audits, 332
newspaper, 55, 70–71, 7 6–77
pass-along, 286
penetration, 76–77
as revenue, 15–16
Circus Maximus, 306
Citizen Kane, 23-12
civil rights, 397
Civil War, 33, 39, 74, 83, 431, *22-8* to *22-9*
Clark, Alfred, 129
Clark, Jim, 209
Classification and Rating Administration, 142
Clear Channel, 21, 113
Cleveland *Plain Dealer,* 58, 60
clickthrough, 213, 288
Clinton, Bill, 4, 43, 439, 442, 445, 455
Clinton, Hillary, 194, 319, 453
Clio awards, 299
clustering, 71–72
clutter, ad, 286, 299
CNN (*see* Cable News Network)
CNN Effect, 442–443
coaxial cable, 181, 183
Coca-Cola, 197
codes
advertising, 297
ethics, 482–483
cognitive dissonance, 396–397
Cohen, Ted, 494
Cohn & Wolf, 268
cohort analysis, 340–341
Coldplay, 117
Colgate brand, 290
college textbooks, 37
Collier's magazine, 84, 92
Colombia, 135, 430–431
Columbine High School massacre, 373
The Color Purple, 135
Colton, Michael, *22-3*
Columbia Broadcasting System (CBS), 14, 21, 131, 181, 182, 185, 239, 371, 363
Columbia-DuPont Awards, 167
Columbia Journalism Review, 23, 235, 250, 358
Columbia movie studio, 132, 133, 138
Columbia recording company, 103, 105, 108
Comcast, 21
Come Away With Me, 117
comic books, 38–39
comics, *22-3* to *22-4*
communication
components, 349–351
linear, 202
mass, 202, 346–361
types, 348–349
web, 202
Communication Daily, 92
communication process, 348–360
Communications Decency Act, 474
communicators, mass, 350–351
communist political system, *23-2, 23-7* to *23-8*
community-antenna television (CATV), 175, 176, 177, 188, 190
compact disk (CD), 10, 105, 106, 108
compression, 205, 209
computer-generated imagery (CGI), 128, 129
Con Air, 305
concentric circle model, 352–354
concept album, 112
concerts, recording industry and, 112
conferences, news, 264, 267, 444, 449
confidence level, 329–330
confidential news sources, 228, 245–248
conflict in news, 445
conglomeration, 19–25, 234, 409–411, *22-3*
Congress, news coverage of, 450
consensible nature of news, 243
conservative media, 20
consistency theory, 370
consolidation, book industry, 34
Constitution, U.S., 460–461
consumer economics, 280
consumer magazines, 85–89
Consumer Reports magazine, 86
consumption, media, 3
contemporary transmission, 401–402
content analysis, 344
content-distribution model, 12–13
contingency planning, 267
convergence, technology, 215–217
Cooke, Janet, 77, 496–498
cool-hot model, 11
Cooper, Alice (*see* Alice Cooper)
Coors Field, 314
Cop Killer, 110
Cops, 13
copycat entertainment, 320
copyright, 476–478, *22-15* to *22-16*
Corbis photo agency, *22-16*
Cornell University, 9
Corning Glass, 208
corporate policy and news, 244–245
corporate
ideology, 411
radio, 158–160
Corporation for Public Broadcasting (CPB), 165–166, 191, 194–195
Corset and Underwear Review, 91
Cosmopolitan magazine, 5, 80–82, 88
cost per thousand (CPM), 93, 285
Costello, Elvis, 196
Cotton Bowl, 113
counterculture newspapers, 73–74
Counting Crows, 196
courts, news coverage of, 471–472
Cousins, Norman, 94
Cox, Ana Marie, 218
Cox media chain, 21
CPB (*see* Corporation for Public Broadcasting)
CPM (*see* cost per thousand)
Crain Communications, 91
creative director, 283
Creel, George, 261
Crest brand, 301
Creswell, Munsell, Fultz & Zirbel, 268
Crisis, 74
crisis management, 267
crooner, 106
Crosby, Bing, 308, 312
Crossley, Archibald, 327
cross-media adaptations, 320
Crossroads Guitar Concert, 113
Crouching Tiger, Hidden Cruelty, 183
Cruise, Tom, 12
Crystallizing Public Opinion, 274
CSI, 193, 304, 305, 307
C-SPAN (*see* Cable-Satellite Public Affairs Network)
Cuba, 5, 232, *22-1* to *22-2*
Cuban, Mark, 126, 127
cultural
enrichment, global, 415
imperialism, 411–415
intrusion, 411–416
subversiveness, 411
transmission, 400–402
culture
books as repository of, 31
media and, 4–6, 390–394
wars, 124
cumulative effects theory, 366–367
Customer Is Always Right, The, 39
CW network (Columbia Warner), 186–187, 190
cyberpornography, 219–220
cylinders, recording, 105

Daguerre, Louis, *22-4*
daguerreotype, *22-4*
Dailey, Janet, 455
DaimlerChrysler, 281
Dallas, 311
Dallas Mavericks, 127
Dallas, Texas, *Morning News,* 67, 77
dance music, 106
dark fiber, 206
Darwin, Charles, 258
databases, marketing, 72
Da Vinci Code, The, 321, 476–477
Davis, Elmer, 258, 261
Davis, Gray, 437
Davis, Lanny J., 247
Davis, Kenneth, 39
Davis, Stacy, 378–379
Davison, W. P., 367
Day, Ben, 228, 229
Day to Day, 249
DBS (*see* direct-broadcast satellite)
DC comics, 38
d-cinema, 126
Death of Literature, The, 44
Debs, Eugene, 464
decency, 318
decoding, 355
deep background, 248
defamation, 466–470
Defense Department, U.S., 8, 205, 433
Def Jam, 103, 109
DeFleur, Melvin, 367–368
De Forest, Lee, 150, 151, 161, 350
de Graff, Robert, 39
Dell, 34, 410, 422
delivery systems, television, 175–180
CATV, 175
satellite delivery, 175–179
video on demand, 180
demassification, 18–19
magazine, 92–96
music, 112
democracy,
advertising and, 281
public relations and, 257
demographic, 333, 340
Dempsey, Patrick, 395
Deng Xiaoping, 20
Denisoff, Serge, 111
Dentsu advertising agency, 284
deontological ethics, 489–490
Depression (*see* Great Depression)
deregulation, 155, 217, 421
desensitizing theory, 380–381
Des Moines *Register,* 58, 59
Desperate Housewives, 172, 193, 301, 336, 337
Detroit *Free Press,* 263, 439
Detroit *News,* 58, 59, 262, 263, 449
Devils & Dust, 108
Dewey, John, 488, 489
Dewey, Thomas, 329
Diana, Princess, 4
Diario-La Prensa, El, 75, 76
Diario las Americas, 76
Dias, Al, *22-1* to *22-2, 22-14*
DiCaprio, Leonardo, 373
Dichter, Ernest, 294
Dickson, William, 8, 125, 128
Die Another Day, 292
diffusion of innovation, 220
digital captures, *22-5*
digital divide, 211
digital DJs, 313
digital technology
integration, 10
Internet, 204–210
movies and, 126, 127, 138, 139
newspapers and, 56
recording, 105, 107
telecommunication and, 205, 208
television, 127, 175, 179
digital video disc (DVD), 105
Diller, Barry, 24, 72, 186, 221
direct-broadcast satellite (DBS), 179, 188
direct mail, books and, 35–36
DirecTV, 20, 21, 175, 178, 179, 180, 188, 317, 410, 422
Discovery Channel, 15
Dish network, 188, 317
Dish satellite television, 179, 180
Disney animated films, 126, 128
Disney ABC, 171, 185, 190, 422
Disney-Apple alliance, 180
Disney Channel, 190
Disney and Miramax, 136
Disney-Pixar merger, 121–122, 171
Disney, Walt, 128, 131, 132
distribution-content model, 12
diversion function, 369–370
diversity in news, 399
Divided in Death, 45
divine command theory, 490

divine right of kings, 490, *23-7*
Dixie Chicks, 104, 111, 112, 310
documentaries, 130–131
documentary photography, *22-8* to *22-11*
Dolorita in the Passion Dance, 139, 140
donations, audience, 16
Doors, 103
dot-com, 10, 203, 212
Doubleday, 34, 410, 422, 497
Double Helix, 35
Douglas, Kirk, 141
Douglass, Fredrick, 74
"do unto others," 487
Dow, Charles, 61, 62
Dow Jones, 58, 467, 468
Doyle, Leonard, 235
Dr. Dre, 104
Dreamworks, 134, 135
DualDisc, 108
DUB magazine, 95
DuBois, W. E. B., 74
Dumenco, Simon, 97
Dumont, Allen, 182, 186
DVD (*see* digital video disc)
DVD Audio, 108
dynamic routing, 211

earn out on royalties, 43
Eastman, George, 125, 126, *22-7*
Eastwood, Clint, 134
eavesdropping, 374–375
e-books, 30, 40, 41, 410, 411
EchoStar, 21, 179, 188
Eclectic Readers, 32
economics
mass media, 14–19, 418
newspaper, 234
television, 189–191
Edelman, 263, 264
Eddy, Mary Baker, 61, 64–65
Edison, Thomas, 8, 9, 10, 105, 106, 107, 137, *22-7*
editing, selective, 498
Editor & Publisher, 58, 70, 71, 240, 500
educational television (ETV), 191
Eisenstadt, Alfred, *22-15*
El Secreto De Selena, 183
electrical recording (music), 105–106
electromagnetic spectrum, 149
electronic books, 40
electronic delivery, 69
Electronic Frontier Foundation, 460
Electronic Media, 91
electronic scanning, 173
Elektra recording label, 103
el-hi textbooks, 37
elitist-populist model, 13–14
Elks magazine, 90
Elle magazine, 88, 410, 422
Ellegirl magazine, 88
Ellsberg, Daniel, 463
embedded reporters, 433
Emerson, Ralph Waldo, 89
Eminem, 104
encoding, 354
Enhanced Versatile Disc (EVD), 425
enlightened self-interest, 257, 258
Enlightenment, 23-9
entertainment, 306–323
gaming as, 315–317
genres, 307
history, 306–307
media function, 3–4
music, 307
performance as, 308–309
production line, 320
radio, 160
sports, 307
storytelling, 307
technology and, 306–307
trends and fads, 309–311
entertainment-information model, 11–12
Entertainment Tonight, 251
Entertainment Weekly, 96, 365
environmental noise, 357–358
Epic recording label, 103
Epstein, Daniel Mark, 123
Epstein, Jason, 40
equal time rule, 440
Escondido *North County Times,* 53
Esperanto, 415–416
ESPN, 95, 175, 190, 191, 314, 334, 415
Esquire magazine, 88, 97
Espresso Machine, 40
E.T., 128, 136, 137
ethics, mass media, 482–502
accepted practices, 493
audience expectation of, 485–486
categorical imperative, 487, 490
codes, 482–483
conflicts in, 483–484
deontological, 489–490
difficulty of, 482–485
divine command theory, 490
duties, 483–484
freebies, 500
gifts, 498–500
golden mean, 486
intellectual process, 486
junkets, 498–500
law and, 493
libertarianism, 490
media commitment to, 485
misrepresentation, 496–498
moral principles, 486–488
plagiarism, 495–496
Potter's box, 491–493
pragmatism, 488, 490
prescriptive, 482
privacy, 482–483
prudence and, 493–494
reenactments, 498
secular command theory, 490
selective editing, 498
situational, 490–491
social responsibility, 488–490
staging news, 498
teleological, 490
utilitarianism, 488, 490
ETV (*see* educational television)
EVD (*see* Enhanced Versatile Disc)
Everybody Has a Story, 239, 240
Execution of Mary Queen of Scots, The, 129
Exposition Press, 35
exposure, selective, 370–371, 384
Exodus, 141
The Exorcist, 381
Explorations, 389
extrapolation, statistical, 329

Fahrenheit 9/11, 134, 136
Fairbanks, Douglas, 126, 128, 134
fair comment and criticism, 469–470
fairness, 483
fairness doctrine, 155, 440
Fallaci, Oriana, 250
Fallows, James, 20, 446
Family Christian, 36
Family Circle magazine, 86, 88, 421
Famous Players Company, 133
Fanning, Shawn, 100–102
Farm Security Administration, U.S., *22-11*
Farnsworth, Philo, 8, 173, 174, 175, 181
Faulkner, William, 48, 320
FCC (*see* Federal Communications Commission)
Federal Communications Commission (FCC), 109, 151, 152, 155, 159, 175, 179, 194, 357, 440
Federal Emergency Management Administration, 4
federal government coverage, 448–450
Federalist Papers, 227–228
Federal Radio Commission, 152
Federal Trade Commission, 282, 298, 376
FedEx Field, 292
feedback, 359–360
Feshbach, Seymour, 376
Fessenden, Reginald, 150
FHM magazine, 89
fiber, dark, 206
Fiberoptic Link Around the Globe (FLAG), 221
fiber optic cable, 208–209
fiction, pulp, 321
Field & Stream, 89, 370, 371
560 Cent, 95, 104
Fighting Words Doctrine, 464
file-sharing, 114
film (*see also* movies)
photographic, *22-6* to *22-8*
filters, 358
Filthy Words, 318, 319
Finding Nemo, 122, 171
First Amendment, 140, 141, 151, 152, 193–194, 228, 246, 439–440, 460–461, *23-10*
Fitzgerald, F. Scott, 34, 320
Fitzgerald, Penelope, 13
500-channel universe, 5–6, 195
FLAG (*see* Fiberoptic Link Around the Globe)
flag burning, 466, 467
Flaherty, Robert, 130, 131
flights, advertising, 291
flu (*see* influenza)
flush factor, 338
FM (*see* frequency modulation)
focus groups, 338, 339
Folio magazine, 96, 97
folk music, 311–312
Food and Drug Administration, U.S., 298
Food & Wine magazine, 93
Forbes magazine, 16, 86
Ford, John, 133
foreign language newspapers, 75–76
For Me magazine, 90
Fort Peck dam, 86, 93, *22-13*
45-rpm records, 105
Foster, Lawrence, 269
Foster, Stephen, 310
fourth branch, 438–439
four theories of the press, *23-2* to *22-3, 23-16*
fourth estate, 438–439
Fox movie studio, 126, 132
Fox News Channel, 186, 191–192
Fox television, 13, 14, 20–21, 181, 185–186, 187, 190
framing, 443
France, 406–408, 414
Franco, Francisco, 274, *23-5*
Franken, Al, 164, 167, 308
Franklin, Benjamin, 8, 32, 74, 83, 460, *22-2*
fraud, 470
free airtime (political), 456
freebie, 500
Freed, Alan, 312
freedom, artistic, 110–111
Freedom House, 416–417
Freedom of Information Act, 473
Free Speech, 238
frequency modulation (FM), 150
Freud, Sigmund, 293
Frey, James, 497
Friday Night Fights, 314
Friedman, Jane, 41
Friedman, Thomas, 212, 409
Fronteras de la Noticia, 76
Fuller, Bonnie, 80–82, 88
Futureworld, 129
FX cable network, 22

Gable, Clark, 123
Galella, Ron, 471, *22-17*
Gallup, George, 326, 327, 328, 329
Gallup polls, 326, 327
galvanic skin checks, 338, 339
gaming, 315–317
advertising and, 287–288
censorship and, 319
movies and, 315
music and, 316
gangsta
lit, 309
rap, 104, 110
Gannett media chain, 13, 58–59, 75, 181, 440, 450
Gans, Herbert, 239, 390, 391
Garageband recording software, 113
garage bands, 112
Gardner, Alexander *22-10*
Garcia, Mario, 76
Garrett, Paul, 257, 258, 262
gatekeeping, 248, 295–296, 359
gatekeeper-regulator hybrids, 357
Gay, Charlie, 484
Geffen, David, 103, 134, 135
Geffen Records, 103
Gelbman, Leslie, 45
General Electric, 12, 13, 21, 24–25, 132, 185
General Magazine, 8

General Motors, 134, 173, 179, 257, 258, 262, 263, 273, 281
Generation X, 340
Generation Y, 98
genres, 307
geodemographics, 341–342
Gerbner, George, 366, 378, 382
Gerry, Elbridge, *22–3*
Getler, Michael, 235–236
Getty Images, *22–16*
Gibson, Mel, 45, 125
Gilder, George, 69
Ginsberg, Sam, 318
Ginza district, 296
Gitlow, Benjamin, 461
Gladiator, 134
Glamour magazine, 81
globalization
  advertising and, 296
  conglomeration, 409–411
  effects of, 411
  Friedman model, 409
  Internet and, 410–411
  mass media, 406–435
global village, 389–390, 403
Goddard, Morrill, *22–3*
Godey's Lady's Book, 88, 89
Godfather, 123, 311
Godzilla vs. The Thing, 141
Goebbels, Joseph, 293, *23–5*
Goldberg, Gary, 22
Golden Mean, 486–487
Goldmark, Peter, 107, 112
gold record, 117
Gone With the Wind, 37, 43, 44, 128, 143
Gonzáles, Elián, *22–1* to *22–2, 22–14*
Good Housekeeping magazine, 88
Good Morning America, 21, 449
Good Will Hunting, 136
Google, 31, 288–289, 407–408
Google Library Project, 47–48, 215
Gordy, Berry, 104
Gore, Al, 226, 446
Gorton, George, 437
Gotta Let You Go, 312
governance and mass media, 436–456
government
  advertising, 16–17, 296, 297, 298–299
  federal news, 448–450
  issues with media, 454–456
  local news, 453
  manipulation of news, 446–448
  relations with media, 439–440
  state news, 450–451
  subsidies, 16
Government Printing Office, 31
Graff, Robert de, 39
Grammy awards, 117
Grann, Phyllis, 45
Grapes of Wrath, 49, 392
graphic novels, 38–39
Great Depression, 92, 107, 257, 262, 447, *22–10* to *22–11*
Greece, *23–10*
Greeley, Horace, 228, 230
Green Day, 112
Green Hornet, 292
Grey advertising agency, 284
Grey's Anatomy, 495
Griffin, John Howard, 32, 396,
Griffith, D. W., 134, 319
Grokster, 102, 107, 114
Gross, Terry, 165
Grosvenor, Gilbert, 83, 84–85
group communication, 348–349
Grove Press, 473
Guantánamo, 454
Guess brand, 292
Guess Journal, 292
Guideposts magazine, 86
Guilford, Howard, 462
Gunsmoke, 311, 380
Guns N' Roses, 103, 109
Guns of August, 43
Gupta, Sanjay, 13
Gutenberg, Johannes, 6–7, 82, 30, 31, 207, 215, 281, *22–2, 23–3*
Gutnick, Joseph, 468

Hachette Filipacchi, 90, 422
Hale, Sara Josepha, 83, 88, 89
Haley, Bill, 312
halftone, 9, *22–4* to *22–5*
Hamilton, Andrew, 227
Hamilton, Billy, 469
Hanks, Tom, 134
Hannity, Sean, 147, 164
harassment, 471
Harcourt, 34
Hardee's, 18
Harding, Warren, 161, 464
Harlequin books, 33, 45, 320, 321
Harper & Row, 20
HarperCollins, 18, 20, 34, 41, 455, 495
Harper's magazine, 97
Harper's Weekly, 83, 84
Harris, Ben, 8, 227
Harris polls, 59, 326, 327
Harry Potter and the Chamber of Secrets, 137
Harry Potter and the Goblet of Fire, 137
Harry Potter and the Half-Blood Prince, 42
Harry Potter and the Sorcerer's Stone, 42, 128, 137
Hart, Gary, 482
Hart, Michael, 31
Hartman, Steve, 239
Hartnett, Josh, 39
Harvard, John, 31
Harvard University, 31
Harvard University Press, 34
Harvest of Shame, 131
Harwood, Richard, 54
Hastings, 36
hate speech, 466
Hathaway brand, 290
Havas advertising agency, 284, 420
Hawthorne, Nathaniel, 82, 89
Hays, Will, 140
HBO (*see* Home Box Office)
Hearst, William Randolph, 58, 232–233, 384
Heaven's Gate, 134
Hefner, Hugh, 83, 84, 88
Hello Nasty, 103
Henderson, Fletcher, 311
Henry VIII, *23–3* to *23–4*
Hersh, Seymour, 236, 237
Hiebert, Ray, 352, 418
high art, 390
highbrow, 391
highbrow slicks, 97
High Country, The, 380
high-definition radio, 168
Hill & Knowlton, 263, 264, 268
hillbilly music, 311–312
historical transmission, 400–401
hit, 213, 287
Hitter, The, 108
Hobbit, The, 37
Hogan's Alley, *22–3*
Holder, Dennis, 94
Hollywood (*see also* movies), 10, 140
Holmes, Oliver Wendell, 89, 461, 464
Holocaust, 86, 135
Holtzbrinck, 34
Home Box Office (HBO), 14, 175, 177, 178, 187, 188, 415
HBO Olé, 422
hometown dailies, 68
Home Shopping Network, 72
home video, 3, 15, 125
homophyly, 356
Honolulu *Advertiser,* 60
Honolulu *Star-Bulletin,* 60
Horgan, Steve, *22–5*
hot-cool model, 11
Houghton Mifflin, 25
House Un-American Activities Committee, U.S., 140
Houston *Chronicle,* 55, 67
Houston Rockets, 285
Howard Johnson restaurants, 294, 295
Howard, Ron, 134
HTML (*see* Hypertext markup language)
HTTP (*see* hypertext transfer protocol)
Hubbard, Stanley, 179
Hughes, Charles Evans, 161, 463
Hulk, The, 128, 137
Hunger in America, 131
Hurricane Katrina, 4, 272, 443
Hutchins Commission, 488, *23–12* to *23–13*
Hutchins, Robert, 489, *23–12* to *23–13*
hypertext, 208
hypertext markup language (HTML), 208
hypertext transfer protocol (HTTP), 208
hyping, 338

IBOC (*see* in-band, on-channel)
IBM, 205, 210
Ice T, 110–111
ideology, corporate, 411
Illinois Power, 273
I Love Lucy, 185
image dissector, 174
image consulting, 266
imperialism, cultural, 412–414
import restrictions, 473
In2TV, 180, 188, 189
in-band, on-channel, 168
incitement standard, 465–466
In Death series, 45
independent bookstores, 35
independent producers, 12, 134
India, 412–413, 428–429
Indiana Jones, 135
individual selectivity, 370–372
influenza, 106
information boycott, 273, 274
infomercials, 292
informational filter, 358
information anxiety, 384–385
information pollution, 384
infotainment, 12, *22–3*
initiating role of media, 372
innovation, diffusion, 220
Institute of American Public Opinion, 326
institutional advertising, 268
InStyle magazine, 80
integrated marketing, 267–268
integration, vertical, 13, 22
Interfax, 419, 420
internalization, 355–356
International Herald Tribune, 2, *22–4*
Internet, 200–222
  access, 207, 210, 211, 216
  accuracy, 214
  advertising, 212–213, 288, 289
  audience measures, 334–335
  bandwidth, 208–210
  blogs, 217–218, 250
  books and, 29
  carbon nanotubes, 210
  chatrooms, 396
  Children's Internet Protection Act, 220
  clickthrough, 465
  compression and, 205, 209
  convergence, technology, 215
  copyright and, 477–478
  evaluating, 213–214
  fiber optic cable, 208–209
  globalization and, 410–411
  hit, 213
  inequities, global, 220–221
  influence of, 202–203
  magazines, 95–96
  melding media, 215–217
  mesh networks, 211
  miniaturization and, 205
  newspapers and, 70–71
  pornography, 219–220, 474
  privacy and, 219
  public policy, 217–221
  reshaping of, 210–211
  scope of, 203
  site, 203
  streaming, 209–210
  technology, 8, 204–210
  terminology, 203
  ultrawideband, 211
  universal access, 220
  visit, 213
  Webby, 213
  wi-fi, 211
  World Wide Web and, 206–208
Internet Service Providers (ISP), 206–207
interpersonal communication, 348
Interpretative Reporting, 37
Interscope recording label, 103, 110
Interstate Commerce Commission, 258
interviews, in research, 333–334
intrapersonal communication, 348

intrusion, cultural, 411–416
inverted pyramid, 230
investigative reporting, 84, 251
Investor's Daily, 64
iPod, 11, 105, 107, 112, 114–115, 125, 156–157, 171, 172, 175, 180, 189
Iraq war 400
  antiwar music, 310
  desensitizing and, 381
  embedded reporters, 433
  reporting and, 228, 235, 236, 239, 433, 443
Island recording company, 103
It Happened One Night, 123
iTunes, 107, 110, 112, 113, 114–115
Ives, Frederick, 9, *22–4*

Jack Daniels brand, 290
Jackson, Alan, 95
Jackson, Curtis, 104
Jackson, Janet, 103, 194
Jackson, Michael, 242
Jackson, William Henry, *22–10*
James I, *23–7*
Japan, 414, 429
Jaws, 135
Jay-Z, 103
jazz, 110
Jazz, 194
jazz journalism, 233
Jazz Singer, The, 125, 126, 128
Jefferson, Thomas, 227, 228, 460
Jobs, Steve, 114, 115, 121, 128, 170, 171–172
"Join or Die," *22–2*
Johnson & Johnson, 269–270, 271, 281
Johnson, Joey, 466–467
Johnson, Robert, 184
Jones, Edward, 61, 62
Jones, George, 66
Jones, Norah, 117
Jones, Paula, 442
journalism (*see also* news)
  law, 471–473
  telephone book, 72
  jazz, 233
Joyce, James, 317
Juice, 373
jukebox, 106, 107
junction transistor, 204
Jungle, The, 84
Jurgensen, Karen, 61
Jurassic Park, 135
Justice Department, U.S., 133

Kael, Pauline, 380
Kaiser Aluminum, 273
Kaminski, Janusz, 135
Kant, Immanuel, 487, 488
Katrina, Hurricane, 4, 272, 443
Katzenberg, Jeff, 134
Kazaa, 114
KDKA radio, Pittsburgh, 151, 161, 314
Keillor, Garrison, 166
Kellogg, Ansell, 421
Kernan, Alvin, 44
Kennedy, John, 447
Ketchum public relations agency, 265, 276
Key, Wilson Bryan, 294, 295
Kilgore, Barney, 63
Kill Bill, 136, 373
The Killers, 103
King of Rock, 108
King, Stephen, 31, 37, 356, 391
KING television, Seattle, *22–17*
Kinsley, Michael, 96
Kiplinger Washington Newsletter, 92
Kissinger, Henry, 236
Knight-Ridder, 2, 75
Kodak, *22–7*
Kodak Image Bank, *22–16*
Kohut, Andy, 331
Kovacs, Myles, 95
Kroc, Joan, 164, 165–166
Kroger groceries, 293, 298
Ku Klux Klan, 465
Kucinich, Dennis, 183
Kuralt, Charles, 239

labeling of music, 109–110
Ladies' Home Journal, 88, 282, 296
Ladies' Magazine, 83, 88, 89
Land, Edwin, *22–7*
Landis, James, 42
Landmark movie chain, 126, 127, 138
landscape photography, *22–10*
Lange, Dorothea, *22–11*
Lardner, Ring Jr., 141
Lasseter, John, 120–122
Lasswell, Harold, 352, 364
Lava recording label, 103
law
  ethics and, 493
  mass media, 458–479
Law & Order, 192, 374
Lawrence, D. H., 473
Lazarsfeld, Paul, 365, 366, 441, 442
Lazarsfeld Studies, 368
leaks, 447
Ledbetter, James, 268
Lee, Ang, 124
Lee, Debra L., 184
Lee Enterprises, 18, 52–54, 58
Lee, Ivy, 258, 259–260, 270, 274
Lee, Peggy, 111, 112, 312
Lee, Spike, 134, 319
Lee, Tommy, 401
Legacy recording label, 103
legals, 16
Legion of Decency, 140, 141
Leica camera, *22–8*
Leitz, Ernst, *22–7*
Leno, Jay, 437
Leo Burnett advertising agency, 284, 290
Leonard, Matt, 129
Let That Be the Reason, 309
Letterman, David, 173
Levin, Gerald, 110–111, 175–178
Lewis, Jerry Lee, 312
Lexis, 203, 206
libel, 466–470
  concept of, 467
  New York Times v *Sullivan,* 66–67, 467
  public figures and, 461
libertarianism, 416, 417, *23–2, 23–9* to *23–10*
licensing, 13, 92, 109, *23–5*
Lichter, Linda, 395
Lichter, Robert, 361, 445
Lieberman, Joseph, 110, 319
Life magazine, 83, 85, 86, 87, 92–93, *22–7, 22–12, 22–15*
Life of a Fireman, 127
lightning news, 230
Lil' Kim, 103
Lima, Jineth Bedoya, 430
Limbaugh, Rush, 4, 147, 164, 166, 167
Lincoln, Abraham, 33, 41, 135, 385
Lincoln *Journal Star,* 58, 374
Lion King, 122
Lippmann, Walter, 364, 366, 371
literacy, 30–31
  AND BOOKS, 30–31
  media, 1–27
  rates (U.S.), 46
  visual, 9
literature, genres of, 309
Live Wire, 109
LL Cool J, 109, 112
lobbying, 261–263, 265–266, 451
Loeb, William, *23–15*
Loews movie house chain, 139
London *Financial Times,* 415
London, Jack, 421
London *Independent,* 57, 235, 236
London *Times,* 57, 236
Longfellow, Henry Wadsworth, 89
Long Island *Newsday,* 55, 58, 71, 72
long-play record (LP), 112
Looking Good Now magazine, 90
Look magazine, 92, *22–12*
Lopez, Jennifer, 103, 365
Lord, Daniel, 140
Los Angeles *La Opinion,* 76
Los Angeles *Times,* 55, 58, 62, 67, 69, 77, 331
Loudcloud, 209
Louis, Joe Hill, 312
Louisville *Courier Journal,* 58, 59, 71
Lovejoy, Elijah, *23–11*
low art, 390–391, 392, 394
lowbrow, 392
lowest common denominator, 192, 290
low-power radio, 159
LP (*see* long-play record)
Lucas, George, 121, 126, 128, 129, 135
Luce, Henry, 83, 86, 92, 314, *22–7*
Luckovich, Mike, *22–3*
Ludlow Massacre, 260
Lumière, Auguste and Louis, 126, 138 *22–13*
Luna, Diego, 135
Lydia E. Pinkham brand, 296
Lyon, Matthew, 228

MacDonald, Dwight, 390, 391
MacDougall, Curtis, 37
MacDougall, Kent, 91
Macmillan, 43
Madison, James, 227, 460
Madison, Wisconsin, *State Journal,* 71
magazines, 80–99 (*see individual magazine titles*)
  advertising and, 83, 285–286
  audience, 82
  consumer, 85–89
  circulation, 85–86
  competition, new, 95
  consumer, 85–89
  demassification and, 92–96
  defined, 7
  elitist measures, 97–98
  evaluating, 96–98
  influence of, 82–83
  Internet, 95–96
  investigative reporting and, 84
  as media innovators, 84–85
  men's, 88–89
  nationhood and, 82–83
  newsletters, 92
  newsmagazines, 86–87
  non-newsrack, 89–92
  personality profiles and, 84
  photojournalism and, 84–85, *22–12* to *22–13*
  populist measures, 96–97
  quality measures, 97–98
  Reader Usage Measure (RUM), 98
  reporting and, 84
  sponsored, 90–91
  time spent reading, 3
  trade journals, 91–92
  university, 16
  women's magazines, 88
  'zines, 96
Mailer, Norman, 73
Maine, 232
Maines, Natalie, 310
mainstream media (MSM), 10–11
make-goods, 190
Malcolm X, 134
Manilow, Barry, 112
manipulation of news, 446
Manning, Selvage & Lee, 265, 276
March of the Penguins, 131
Marconi, Guglielmo, 149, 151
Mares, Marie-Louise, 378–379
Marie Claire, 81
margin of error, 328–329
marketing
  books and, 44–46
  databases, 72
marketplace of ideas, 23–9
market segments, 290–291
Marvel comics, 38
Marx, Karl, *23–7, 23–8*
mascots, in sports, 374
*M*A*S*H,* 141
Massachusetts Institute of Technology, 396
mass communication, 346–361
  models, 352–353
  photography in, *22–1* to *22–18*
Mass Communications, 347
Mass Communications and American Empire, 412
mass communicators, 350–351
mass media
  advertising, 14–19
  alternative, 19
  binding influence of, 4–6
  change, and, 402–403
  chemical, 8
  colonial, 8
  companies, largest U.S., 21
  conglomeration, 19–25
  conservative, 20
  consumption, 3
  culture and values, 4–6, 390–394

demassification, 18–19
economic foundation, 14–19
effects, 362–387
electronic, 8
entertainment source, 3–4
ethics, 482–502
functions, 368–370
governance and, 436–457
global, 406–435
importance of, 2–4
influence, 441
information source, 3, 441
law, 458–479
liberal, 20
mainstream (MSM), 10–11
marketing of, 46
models, 11–14
monopolies, 21–22
morality and, 397–400
nation states and, 408–409
new media, 10–11
obsessions, 445–446
ownership, 19–25
persuasive forum 4
pervasiveness of, 2–3
photo essay and, 83
political systems and, *23-1* to *23-17*
postal rates and, 83
print, 6–8
promotion, 46
research, 324–345
society and, 390–405
technology, 6–10
timeline, 83
underground, 11
mass messages, 351
MathBlaster, 25
Matrix Reloaded, 128, 137
Maus: A Survivor's Tale, 39
Maxim magazine, 89, 97, 365
Maxwell, Joseph, 105, 107
Mays, Lowry, 149
Maytag brand, 290
Mazzarella, avid, 61
MCA, 103, 104
McCall's magazine, 88
McCann-Erickson advertising agency, 284
McCarthyism, 140
McCartney, Paul, 112
McClure, S. S., 421
McClure's magazine, 83, 84
McCombs, Maxwell, 365, 366
McCormick, Robert, 56, 61, 462, *23-12*
McDonald's, 268
McGinn, Colin, 123
McGraw-Hill, 91, 281
McGuffey, William Holmes, 31, 32, 49
McKinley, William, *22-13*
McKnight, Brian, 103
McLendon, Gordon, 160, 161, 162
McLuhan, Marshall, 388, 403
McLure, Robert, 456
McMahan, Harry, 299
McMahon, Vince, 314
Mead Data Central, 206
mean world syndrome, 382
media
brand names, 423
cognitive dissonance and, 396–397
mass, 351
melding, 215–217
kit, 269
plans, 285
relations with government, 439–440
relations (in public relations), 269–274
research, 324–345
status quo and, 395–396
media effects
on audience, 368
on children, 372
on governance, 442–446
mass media, 362–387
societal, 372–375, 382
studies, 364–368
and violence, 375
media-induced ritual, 394–395
mediated performance, 308
medium, defining, *22-6*
Méliès, Georges, 127
melding, media, 215–217
Melville, Herman, 31
Men's Fitness, 82
men's magazines, 88–89
Mercury Theater on the Air, 363–364
Meredith, 35
Merrill, John, 417
mesh networks, 211
messages, mass, 351
Messier, Jean-Marie, 25
metal type, movable, 6
meters in research, 333, 334, 335–336
Metro Boston, 2
metropolitan dailies, 67–68
Meyrowitz, Joshua, 375, 376
MGM, 133, 134, 138
Miami *Diario las Americas,* 76
Miami *Herald,* 58, 67
Miami *Nuevo Herald,* 75, 76
Miami University, 32
Microsoft, 21, 96, 209, 216, 219, 287, 315, 423, 424
microwave relays, 181, 183
middlebrow, 392
Mill, Charles, 92
Mill, John Stuart, 487–488, 492
Miller, Frank, 38–39
Miller Standard, 318
Ming, Yao, 285, 413
minimalist effects theory, 365–366
Minneapolis *Star Tribune,* 58, 60, 67
Miracle, The, 140, 141
Miramax, 136
misrepresentation, 496–498, *22-16, 22-17*
Mitzelfeld, Jim, 262–263
mixing, sound, 113
Miyamato, Shigeru, 312
M model, *22-6*
mobile television, 195–196
Mobil Oil, 258, 272–273
mobisode, 195
Moby-Dick, 31
models
bipolar, 416
change, 418–419
compass, 417
content-distribution, 12–13
continuum, 416–417
elitist-populist, 13–14
entertainment-information, 11–12
global, 416–419
hot-cool, 11
mass media, 11–14
subsystem, 419
Modern Bride, 87
Mondale, Walter, 439
Monday Night Football, 14, 185, 395
Montana Sky, 45
Mood Logic, 313
Moore, Demi, 365, 474
Moore, Gordon, 210
Moore, Michael, 134, 136
Moore, Scotty, 312
Moore's Law, 210
morality, 399
Morning Edition, 165, 166, 249
Morpheus, 114
Morse, Samuel, 228, 230, 231
Mortal Kombat, 315, 381
Mosaic, 208, 209
Mötley Crüe, 109
motion pictures (*see* movies)
motivational research, 294
Motor Trend magazine, 86, 95
Motown, 103, 104, 422
Mount Pleasant, Iowa, *News,* 46
movable metal type, 6–7, 8, 31
movies, 120–145
advertising and, 14
big budget, 128
block booking, 132
box office sales, 125, 137
censorship, 139–142
chains, movie house, 126, 137, 138, 139
criticism, 143
cultural influence of, 123–124, 137
d-cinema, 126
distribution, 136–137
documentaries, 130–131
exhibition, 137–139
experience of, 122–123
global data, 414
home video and, 15
importance of, 122–123
independent producers, 134
industry structure, 181–189
major studios, 132, 134
newsreels, 126, 128
palaces, 138
photography and, 125–126
political, 450
product placement, 196–197
quality measures, 143
rating code, 142
revenue, 125, 128, 137
studio system, 132, 133, 320
technology, 125–126
television and, 132, 174
time spent watching, 3
violence, 380
MP3, 105, 107, 156
MSNBC, 190, 219
MTV (*see* Music Television)
MTV Overdrive, 180
muckraking, 84
multinational companies, 409
multiplexing, 168, 209
multistep flow, 365, 441
multisystem operator (MSO), 188
Munich, 135
muniwireless, 211
Murdoch, Rupert, 20–21, 34, 186, 188, 216, 325–326, 409–411, 422, 455
Muren, Dennis, 129
Murrow, Edward R., 161, 163, 185
music (*see also* recorded music)
artistic freedom, 110–111
black, 311–312
demassification of, 112
entertainment, as, 311–313
folk, 311–312
hillbilly, 312
influence of recorded, 102–103
labeling, 109–110
licensing, 477–478
multimedia, 312–313
objectionable, 109–111
rock 'n' roll, 106, 107, 108, 312
swapping, 102, 103, 105, 107, 114
MusicLand, 114
Music Television (MTV), 25, 69, 180, 190, 191, 242, 243, 316, 318, 370, 415, 422, 423
My Lai massacre, 235, 236
My Left Foot, 136
My Life, 43
My Name Is Red, 432
MY Network, 187
Myrick, Daniel, 134
Myspace.com, 114

NAB (*see* National Association of Broadcasters)
NACS (*see* National Association of College Stores)
Nadeau, Jerry, 17
Nader, Ralph, 32
Nanook of the North, 131
nanotubes, carbon, 210
Napster, 100, 101–103, 113, 114, 115
narcoticizing dysfunction, 366
narrative model, 352
NASCAR, 17, 255–256
Nash, Gary, 32
Nast, Thomas, *22-3*
The Nation, 450
National Advertising Review Council, 297
National Association of Broadcasters (NAB), 109, 155, 194, 299, 357
National Association of College Stores (NACS), 38
National Book Award, 48, 391
National Broadcasting Company (NBC), 13, 14, 21, 181, 182, 183–185, 190, 282, 350, 422
National Collegiate Athletic Association, 374
national development
books and, 31
magazines and, 82–83
National Enquirer, 30, 82, 87, 242, 251
National Era, 33
National Geographic, 83, 84, 85, 86, 90–91
National Geographic Society, 131, *22-12, 22-16*
National Magazine Awards, 97
National Public Radio (NPR), 16, 165–166, 194, 241, 249

National Review, 97
National Science Foundation, 205
National Treasure, 305
nation states, 408–409
Natural Health, 82
natural law, *23-9*
NBC (*see* National Broadcasting Company, Radio Corporation of America)
NBC Universal (*see* National Broadcasting Company)
Near, Jay, 462, 463
Near v. *Minnesota,* 461–463
negative ads, 452
negative option, 35
Nelly, 321
Nelson, Willie, 310
Netscape, 10, 203, 204, 209, 219
networks (*see individual networks*)
  radio, 153–154
  television, 175, 178, 182–187
Neuharth, Allen, 60, 61
Neumann, Elisabeth-Noelle, 366–367
Newark *Star Ledger,* 58, 450
Newhouse media chain, 58, 71
New Jack City, 373
new journalism, 498
New Federalism, 451
new media, 10–11
New Media Monopoly, The, 22
New Republic magazine, 23, 96, 97
news, 224–253
  accuracy in, 251–252
  agencies, 419–420
  advertiser influence on, 244
  balance in, 251–252
  bias in, 240–242
  blackout, 448
  breaking, 161–162
  brevity in, 446
  briefing, 449, 450
  Colonial Period, 227
  combat, 431–433
  competition, 243
  concepts, 234–237
  on condition, 245–246
  conferences, 444, 449
  confidentiality, 246–247
  conflict in, 445
  consensible nature of, 243
  corporate policy and, 244
  defined, 3
  diversity and, 399
  economics, 234
  election, 446–447
  embedded, 433
  ethnocentrism in, 239
  European model, 234–235
  exploratory, 251
  fairness in, 251–252
  flow, 242, 249
  gatekeeping, 248
  headline service, 162
  hole, 68, 77, 241–242
  influences on, 243–245
  interpretation in, 252
  investigative, 251
  live, 249–250
  nonstop coverage, 249
  obsessions, 445–446
  objectivity, 234, 235, 237
  packages, 162
  Partisan Period, 232
  Penny Period, 229–232
  pools, 432–433
  quality, 251–252
  radio, 161–163
  rice-roots, 431
  scandals in, 445
  secretary, 449
  services, 420–421
  social order and, 240
  soft, 251
  source pressure, 245
  staffing, 242
  staging, 498, 245
  television, 173, 186
  trends, 249–251
  truth and, 234–237
  U.S. model, 234
  values, 242
  variables, 242–243
  war, 431–433
  Yellow Period, 232–233
News Corporation, 12, 13, 20, 21, 132, 422, 428
Newsday, 55, 58, 71 72
news hole, 68, 77, 241–242
newsletters, 92, 448, 450
newsmagazines, 64, 86–87
Newspaper Advertising Bureau, 299
Newspaper Guild, 60
Newspaper Research Journal, 484
newspapers (*see individual titles*)
  absentee ownership, 59
  advertising, 54, 56, 65, 70–71, 285, 286
  alternative, 72–76
  black, 74–75
  broadsheet, 56, 57
  chains, 58–60
  clustering, 71–72
  circulation, 53–54, 68–69, 76–77
  colonial, 8
  content, 55
  counterculture, 73–74
  daily, 60–65, 67–72
  defined, 7
  digital technology, 56
  electronic delivery, 69
  evaluating, 76–78
  foreign language, 75–76
  future, 68, 69
  hometown, 67–68
  importance of, 54–55
  industry dimensions, 54–55
  Internet and, 70–71
  inverted pyramid, 230, 231
  local autonomy and, 59
  metropolitan dailies, 67–68
  minority, 73–76
  national dailies, 60–65
  penetration, 76–77
  photography, *22-12*
  production, 56
  products, 56–58
  quality indicators, 77–78
  rural, 73
  salaries, 60
  shoppers, 73
  Sunday editions, 55
  supplements, 86, 87–88
  tabloids, 56–58, 62, 80–82
  television and, 54
  time spent reading, 3
  weekend supplements, 86, 87–88
  weekly, 54, 71, 72–73
newsreels, 126, 128
news releases, 268, 271
Newsweek magazine, 86, 88, 97, 296
New York *Daily Challenge,* 74
New York *Daily Graphic,* 9
New York *Daily News,* 13, 55, 56, 60, 61, 62, 67, 68, 233, 296, 444, *22-3, 22-12*
New York *El Diario-La Prensa,* 75, 76
New Yorker magazine, 83, 84, 87, 97, 124, 143, 236
New York *Graphic, 22-4, 22-11*
New York *Herald,* 230, 313
New York magazine, 93
New York *Post,* 55
New York *Sun,* 56, 228, 229, 231, 234 282
New York *Times,* 1–2, 13, 14, 42, 49, 55, 58, 61, 65–67, 77, 97, 143, 236, 246, 288, 326, 393, 409
New York Times v. *Sullivan,* 66, 423, 467–469
New York *Tribune,* 230, *22-11*
New York University, 274
New York *Village Voice,* 61, 73–74
Nexis, 203, 206
NFL Monday Night Football, 14, 185, 395
Nichi Bei Times, 75
Nickelodeon cable network, 25, 190, 191, 423
Nielsen, A. C., 327
Nielsen ratings, 325–327
Niépce, Joseph, 9, 126, *22-4*
nigger music, 109
9/11 attacks, 4, 219, 369
Nine Inch Nails, 3
Nitty Gritty Dirt Band, 310
Nixon, Richard, 67, 194, 251, 442, 447, 448, 451, 456
Nobel Prize, 48
noise, 357
nonstop news, 249
Northeastern University, 101
North Star, 74
Northwestern University, 98
Northwood, 89
Notorious, 495
Novak, Michael, 173
novels, graphic, 38–39
NPR (*see* National Public Radio)
NTV (Russia), 429–430
Nuendo, 113
Nuevo Herald, El, 75–76
N.W.A., 108

objectivity, 234, 235, 237
O'Brien, Conan, 173
O'Brien, Soledad, 443
obscenity, 317, 318, 458, 461, 474–475
obsessions, news, 445–446
Ochs, Adolph, 233
Ocean Spray brand, 298
Odyssey recording label, 103
off-record, 248
Ogilvy, David, 280, 290, 295
Ogilvy & Mather advertising agency, 284, 290
Ogilvy PR Group, 265, 268, 276
Olson, Floyd, 462
ombuds, *23-14*
Omnicom, 263, 284
Onassis, Jacqueline Kennedy, 471
on-demand radio, 156
Onitsuka Tiger, 373
online advertising, 286–287
On the Origin of Species, 32, 258
On the Road, 239
open media relations, 269–270, 271
OperaBabes, 103
Opinion, La, 76
opinion leaders, 365, 441
opinion surveys, 326–332, 344
Oppenheim, Ellen, 98
Oprah (*see* Winfrey, Oprah)
Orbison, Roy, 107, 312
Oscars (*see* Academic Awards)
Ottaway newspapers, 58
Outcault, Richards, *22-3*
Outside magazine, 97
over-air television, 181, 182, 190
overnights, 334
overwhelming, as PR technique, 448
ownership, of mass media, 19–25
Oxford University Press, 34, 35
Ozzie and Harriet, 311
Ozzie awards, 97

Pacifica radio, 318
Page, Arthur, 258, 263
Paine, Thomas, 402, *23-10*
Paley, William, 154, 182, 185
Pamuk, Orhan, 432
paperback books, 39, 40
Parade newspaper supplement, 8, 85, 87–88, 96
Paramount decision, 132–134, 138
Paramount movie studio, 133
parasocial interaction, 369
Parents Music Resource Center, 109
Park, Robert, 383, 442
Parke, Fred, 129
Partisan Period, 227–229
pass-along circulation, 286
The Passion of the Christ, 46, 125
passivity
  audience, 368
  media-induced, 385
Pathfinder, 83, 95–96
Patterson, Joseph, 56, 61, *22-12*
Patterson, Thomas, 456
pay per view (PPV), 177, 188
Payne Fund Studies, 368
PBS (*see* Public Broadcasting Service)
Pearl Harbor, 128, 137, 305
Pearl Jam, 310
Pearson, 34, 422, 423
Peckinpah, Sam, 380
peer review, 214, 241
peer-to-peer sharing (P2P), 102
Pencil of Nature, The, 22-4
PEN/Faulkner Award, 48
Penguin, 34, 423
Pennsylvania Railroad, 259
Penny Period, 229–232
Pentagon Papers, 67, 461, 463–464
People magazine, 80–82, 88, 96, 251
people meters, 327, 333–334, 338

perception, selective, 370, 371–372
Perestroika, 429–430
performance
authentic, 308
mediated, 308
Perkins, Carl, 107, 312
Perkins, Maxwell, 34, 46
persistence of vision, 125, 174, *22–7*
personality profiles, 84
persuasive photography, *22–11* to *22–12*
pervasiveness of mass media, 2–3
Peterson, Theodore, *23–2*
Petkus, Neil, 129
Pew polls, 331
Pfizer, 281
Phantom Menace, The, 126, 138
Philadelphia *Daily News,* 60, 70
Philadelphia *Inquirer,* 60, 67, 70
Philadelphia *Zeitung,* 75
Philips recording company, 105
Phillips, Sam, 312
Phonograph, 8, 105, 106, 107
photo agencies, *22–16*
photo essay, *22–7*
photography (*see also* visual messages)
access, *22–17*
instant, *22–7*
invention of, *22–4* to *22–5*
issues, *22–15* to *22–18*
landscape, *22–10*
movies and, 125–126
persuasive, *22–11* to *22–12*
privacy, *22–17* to *22–18*
reality photography, *22–12* to *22–14*
photojournalism, 84–85, 86, 93, *22–7*
photo op, 245, 254, 438, 451
physical filter, 358
Pickford, Mary, 133, 134
Pinnacle Nuendo, 113
PIPSA, *23–5*
piracy, 102, 114, 115–117, 460, 461, 477–478
Pirates of the Caribbean, 305
Pirsig, Robert, 41–43
Pittsburgh, *Post-Gazette,* 60
Pixar, 121–122, 128, 171–172
pixel, *22–5*
plagiarism, 495–496
platform agnostic, 1–2
platform for privacy preference (P3P), 219
platinum, record, 117
Playboy magazine, 13, 83, 84, 88, 213
playlists, 112, 156, 157, 160
PlayStation, 15, 316
Pocket Books, 39
podcasting, 116, 156, 158, 201–202
Poe, Edgar Allan, 82, 89
P.O.G. Records, 109
Polaroid, *22–8*
policy analysis, 344
political
campaign coverage, 451–452
communication, 266
favors, 455
political systems, mass media and, *23–1* to *23–17*
polling industry, 326–327
Polygram recording label, 422
pop art, 391, 392–394
Popoff, Peter, 182
Popular Mechanics, 89
Popular Science, 89
population in surveys, 327
populism, political, 436–438
pornography, 188, 219–220, 318–319, 473–474, 475
Porter, Edwin, 127
Portier, Sidney, 124
Portillo, Lourdes, 130
Portland *Phoenix,* 494
Portrait in Death, 45
positioning, 290–291
Postal Act of 1879, 82
postal restrictions, 473
Postal Service, U.S., 16, 17, 298
Post-War Generation, 340–341
Potter's Box, 491–493
Potter, Ralph, 491–493
Pound, Ezra, 35
powerful effects theory, 364–365
PPV (*see* pay per view)
pragmatism, 488
Preminger, Otto, 141
prescriptive ethics, 482–483
presidential coverage, 445
Presley, Elvis, 107–108, 312, 370
pressure groups, 357
PRI (*see* Public Radio International)
Price, Bella, 90
priming, 443–445
Prince, 104
Princess Diana, 4, *22–17*
print media
technology, 6–8
visual integration with, 9
print-on-demand, 31, 40, 41
prior restraint, 461–466
Prinze, Freddie, Jr., 188
privacy, *22–17* to *22–18*
ethics and, 482
Internet and, 219
law, 470–471
PRIZM, 327, 341
proactive media relations, 270–271
probability sampling, 327–330
Process and Effect of Mass Communication, The, 347–348
Procter & Gamble, 173, 272, 280, 281, 301
production line entertainment, 320
product placement, 191, 196–197, 292, 293
professional books, 37
profits, media, *23–14* to *23–25*
programming
black community, for, 184
cable 188
digital, 179
educational, 182
exclusive, 175, 177, 178
government role in, 194–195
live, 185
local, 186, 194
lowest common denominator, 192
national, 181
network, 182, 195
prime-time, 186
public television, 191
syndicate, 186
Project Gutenberg, 31
PR (*see* public relations)
prosocial socialization, 372, 375
prosperity and advertising, 280–281
prototype research, 340
PRSA (*see* Public Relations Society of America)
prudence, 493
pseudo-event, 451
psychographics, 327, 342–343
psychological filter, 358
psychology in advertising, 293–295
P3P (*see* platform for privacy preference)
P2P (*see* peer-to-peer sharing)
Public Broadcasting Service (PBS), 16, 191, 194–195
public domain, 476
Public Enemy, 108
publicity, 265
public interest, convenience and necessity, 152
public nuisance, 461–462
public policy, Internet, 217–221
public radio, 165–166
Public Radio International (PRI), 160, 166
public relations (PR), 254–277
adversarial, 258, 273–274
advertising and, 267–268
advertorials, 272
agencies, 264
alternative names, 276
ambivalent media relations, 272
certification, 276
contingency planning, 267
crisis management, 267, 270
defined, 4, 256–257
democracy and, 257
external, 263–264
image consulting, 266
information boycott, 273–274
institutional advertising, 268
internal, 264
lobbying, 262–263, 265
media kit, 269
media relations, 269–274
open media relations, 269
origins of, 258–263
overwhelming, as technique, 270, 448
policy role, 263
political, 266
proactive media relations, 270–271
professionalization, 273–276
promotion, 265
puffery, 260
social Darwinism and, 258–259
services, 264–268
standards, 276
structure of, 263–264
whitewashing, 275
World War I and II, 261
Public Relations Society of America (PRSA), 257, 258, 274, 276
public television, 191, 194
publishers, books, 33–35, 43
Publishers Weekly, 49, 300, 497
puffery, 260, 298
Pulitzer, Joseph, 56, 77, 228, 232–233, 314
Pulitzer chain, 53–54
Pulitzer Prize, 2, 48, 65, *22–14*
pulp fiction, 321
Pulp Fiction, 136
Puritans, 31
Putnam, 45

quality
books and, 48–49
newspapers and, 76–78
movies and, 143
radio, 167
question-answer interview, 83
Quigley, Martin. 140
Quill magazine, 91, 215, 430, 485
Quinley, Hal, 300
Quintanilla, Selena, 130
quiz shows, 320
quota sampling, 330

radio, 146–169
advertising, 196, 282
affiliates, 175
amplitude modulation (AM), 150
bundled transmission, 168
chains, 157
channel scarcity, 155
characteristics, U.S., 154–155
children and, 318
corporate radio, 157–160
decency, 318
deregulation, 155
entertainment, 160
frequency modulation (FM), 150
high-definition, 168
industry, 150–157
influence, 148–149
iPod and, 156
low-power, 159
marketplace concept, 155
networks, 153–154
news, 161–163
on-demand, 156
Pacifica case, 318
playlists, 157
podcasting, 156
public, 165–166
quality, 167
regulation, 152, 155
satellite, 10, 151, 156
scope, 149
subscription, 15
talk programming, 163–164
technology, 149–159
television and, 174, 181
time spent listening, 3
trusteeship rationale, 151
voice tracking, 157
Radio Corporation of America (RCA), 105, 107, 108, 154, 174, 175, 181, 350
Ramos, Jose, 5
Random House, 28–30, 34, 473
rap, 108–109
ratings
billboard, 336
broadcast, 333
Internet, 220, 334
movie, 142
technology, 334
R.A.V. v. *St. Paul,* 466

Rawls, John, 488, 489
Raymond, Henry, 61
RCA (*see* Radio Corporation of America)
Reader's Digest, 35, 83, 85, 88, 93, 96
Reader Usage Measure (RUM), 98
Reagan, Ronald, 155, 217, 299, 385, 400, 466
reality photography, *22–12* to *22–14*
reality shows, 498
"Rebirth" advertisement, 15
recall, selective, 371
reckless disregard, 468–469
recorded music, 100–119
  acoustic recording, 105
  albums, 112
  British Invasion and, 108
  companies (see each by name), 103
  demassification, 112
  digital, 106
  DualDisc and, 108
  electrical recording, 105–106
  evaluating companies, 117–118
  file-sharing and, 114
  formats, 105
  genres, 305
  indie labels, 103–104
  industry, scope of, 102–103
  influence of, 102–103
  innovations, 104–108
  jukebox and, 107
  major labels, 103
  National Association of Broadcasters and, 109
  objectionable music, 109–111
  Parents Music Resource Center and, 109
  performer influence, 106–108
  piracy, 115–117
  rap and, 108–109
  regulatory pressure and, 109–110
  rockabilly and, 107–108
  rock 'n' roll and, 108
  sound mixing, 113
  streaming and, 107, 114–117
  technology, 104–106
  television and, 180, 196, 197
  time spent listening, 3
  touring and, 112–113
Recording Industry of America (RIAA), 102, 114, 115, 117
Redbook magazine, 88
Red Hot Romance, 140
Red Record, A, 238
redundancy, 291
Reed Elsevier, 34, 422, 423
reenactments, 498
Reeve, Christopher, 359
Reeve, Dana, 359
Reeves, Rosser, 290
reference books, 37
Regal movie-house chain, 139
regional reporters, 450
regulation
  advertising, 295–299
  broadcasting, 439–440
  Internet, 440
  music, 109–111
  print media, 440
  radio, 152
  television, 192–194
Reid, Robert, 37
Reid, William, 140
religion, *23–10*
Remember the Titans, 305
Remington, Frederic, 233
reporting, investigative, 84
research
  applied versus theoretical, 343–344
  audience size, 332–338
  cohort analysis, 340–341
  content analysis, 344
  demographic, 340
  effects studies, 344, 364–368
  evaluating surveys, 330–331
  geodemographics, 341–342
  media, 324–345
  media-sponsored, 343–344
  motivational, 293–294
  opinion surveys, 344
  policy analysis, 344
  polling industry, 326–327
  probability sampling, 327–330
  prototype, 340
  psychographics, 342–343
  quota sampling, 330
  ratings technology, 334
  scholarship, 344
  straw polls, 331–332
  theoretical, 344
  uses and gratifications, 368–370
retention, selective, 370371
Reuters, 420
Reynolds, Glenn, 219
Rhimes, Shonda, 395
rhythm and blues, 311
RIAA (*see* Recording Industry of America)
rice-roots reporting, 431
Rifleman, The, 380
right to be left alone, 471
Rinehart, Richard, 56
Ripley, Alexandra, 43, 44
Riski, Richard J., 484
ritual, media-induced, 394–395
RKO movie studio, 133, 138
Roaring Twenties, 109
Robb, J. D., 44, 45
Robbin, Jonathan, 327, 341
Robe, The, 126
Roberts, Nora, 45
Robertson, Eleanor Jean, 45
RoboCop 2, 39
Rock, The, 305
rockabilly, 107–108
Rock Around the Clock, 312
Rockefeller, John D. Jr., 260
rock 'n' roll, 107, 108, 312
Rocky, 311
Rodriguez, Robert, 39
Roger and Me, 134
Rolaids brand , 290
role models, 372–373
Rolling Stone magazine, 14, 18, 84, 86, 88, 117
Rolling Stones, 112, 341
Romper Room, 379
Ronstadt, Linda, 112
Roosevelt, Franklin, 447, 485
Roosevelt, Theodore, 84, 259
Rosentiel, Tom, 23
Rosie magazine, 88
Ross, Harold, 83, 84
routing, 211
roving photographer, 332
Rowling, J. K., 37, 42
Roxio Boom Box, 313
royalties, 43
RUM (*see* Reader Usage Measure)
Rum: A Social and Sociable History of the Real Spirit of 1776, 32
Rumsfeld, Donald, 236
Run-D.M.C., 108
Russell, A. J., *22–10*
Russia, 429–430
Rutledge, Kathleen, 374

Saatchi & Saatchi advertising agency, 284, 291
Saba photo agency, *22–16*
SACD (*see* Super Audio CD)
sample selection, 328
sample size, 327
San Francisco *Chronicle,* 60
San Francisco *Examiner,* 57, 62, 232
San Francisco *Nichi Bei Times,* 75
San Jose, California, *Mercury News,* 77, 286
Sánchez, Eduardo, 134
Santa, 103
Saralegui, Cristina, 5
Sarnoff, David, 150, 151, 181, 182, 185, 350
satellite
  radio, 10, 155–156
  television, 15, 175–179
Saturday Evening Post, 82, 83, 92, *22–12*
Saturday Press, 462
Saturday Review, 94
Saudi Arabia, 115, 500
Saving Private Ryan, 134, 135
SBC Communications, 281
Scarlett, 43, 44
Scary Movie 3, 136
Scheiner, Elliot, 113
Schenck, Charles, 463
Schild, Steve, 367
Schiller, Herbert, 412, 415
Schindler's List, 135
Schlesinger, Arthur, 227
Schlitz brand, 290
Schmertz, Herb, 258, 272–273, 274
Scholastic, 42
Schramm, Wilbur, 346–348, 376, 378, *23–2*
Schwarzenegger, Arnold, 436–438
Sci-Fi Channel, 25
scribist monks, 6
Scribner, Charles, 34, 46
Seagram, 103
Search Inside, 215
secular command theory, 490
selective editing, 498
selective exposure, 370–371
selective perception, 371–372
selective recall, 371–372
selective retention, 371–372
selectivity, individual, 370–372
self-regulation, advertising, 296–298
self-righting process, *23–9*
semantic noise, 357
semiconductor, 204
Seven Sister magazines, 88
78-rpm records, 105
sex, 316–318
  children, 318–319
  decency requirements, 318
Sex, Lies and Videotape, 136
Shakespeare in Love, 136
Shannon, Claude, 352, 353
Shannon-Weaver communications model, 352
Sharpton, Al, 325
Shaw, Don, 365, 366, 442
Sheehan, Cindy, 400
Sheehan, Neil, 463
shelf life, 286
Shelton, Marley, 39
Sheppard, Sam, 471
Sheridan, Nicollette, 301
shield laws, 246
Shigeru Miyamoto, 316
shock jock, 156, 158
Shockley, William, 204
shoppers, 73
Shuster, Joe, 38
Siebert, Frederick, *23–2*
Siegel, Jerry, 38
Silent Spring, 32
Silhouette books, 45
Silicon Graphics, 209
Simon, Paul, 310
Simon & Schuster, 23, 33, 34
Simple Plan, 108
Simpsons, The, 20, 186, 310, 311
Sinatra, Frank, 107, 312
Sin City, 38, 39
Sinclair, Upton, 84, 488, 500, *23–12*
Sinclair television chain, 17
Singer, Bryan, 129
Sinners in Silk, 140
Sister, 109
site, Internet, 203
situational ethics, 490
60 Minutes, 131, 244, 337
Ski magazine, 93
Skinner, Otis, 274
Sky Global, 13
Slate web site, 96
Smith, James Todd (LL Cool J), 109
Smithsonian magazine, 89, 90, 91
Smokey Bear, 298
Smyth, Frank, 430
Snoop Dogg, 103, 156
Snow, Tony, 449
Snow White, 46, 126, 128
Snyder, Ruth, 62
social Darwinism, 258–259
socialization function, 369, 372–375
social order, 240
social reform, books and, 30
social responsibility, 417, 488, 489, 490, *23–2, 23–12* to *23–16*
society and mass media, 390–405
Society of Business Press Editors, 92
Society of Professional Journalists, 92, *22–14*
Soderbergh, Steven, 136
Solid Gold, 111
Sonar recording software, 113
Sontag, Susan, 391, 392, 393
Sony, 132, 142
Sony BMG, 103, 108
Sony Nashville recording label, 103
Sopranos, The, 104, 315
sound bite, 446

sound recordings (*see* recorded music)
Sousa, John Phillip, 106, 308
Southeastern Oklahoma State University, 374
space shifts, 195
Spartacus, 141
Sperlock, Morgan, 130–131
Spider-Man, 38, 128, 137, 315, 320
Spielberg, Steven, 134, 135, 310
Spiegelman, Art, 39
Spock, Benjamin, 37
sponsored link, 288
sponsored magazines, 90–91
sports, 313–316
  advertisers, 314
  audience, 314
  Internet, 314
Sports Illustrated, 88, 95, 96, 314
Springsteen, Bruce, 103, 108
staging news, 498
standard advertising unit (SAU), 56
Standard Oil, 83, 84, 260
standard television technology, 173–175
Stanton, Edwin, 431
Staples sports arena, 68
Star Academy, 413
Starlight Express, 308
Star TV, 20, 188, 413, 410, 422
Star Wars, 126, 128, 129, 138, 315
Star Wars: The Phantom Menace, 126, 138
Stationers Company, *23-5*
statistical extrapolation, 326, 329
status conferral, 359, 365–366, 397
Steel, Danielle, 37, 356
Stefani, Gwen, 103
Steffens, Lincoln, 84
Stein, Joel, 306
Steinbeck, John, 49
stereo recording, 107
Stereo Review, 93
stereotyping, 373–374
Stern, Howard, 147, 152, 156, 158, 167
Stewart, Jon, 10, 47, 124, 173, 196
stimulation, 354
  aggressive, 376, 377
St. Louis *Post-Dispatch,* 53, 58, 232
St. Martin's Press, 34, 119, 309
Stockbridge, Nellie, *22-10*
Stock Market photo agency, *22-16*
stonewalling, 448
storytelling, 307, 309
St. Paul, Minnesota, *Pioneer Press,* 60, 496
St. Petersburg, Florida, *Times,* 77
Story of Human Communication, The, 348
Stowe, Harriet Beecher, 31, 33, 44, 82, 89
Strait, George, 103
Strauss, Robert, 331, 345
straw polls, 331–332
streaming, 107, 114–117, 209–210
Stringer, Howard, 20
Stringer, Vickie, 309
Stryker, Roy, *22-11*
studio system, 132, 133, 320
studios, movie, 132–134
Stuff magazine, 89
subception, 294
subliminal advertising, 294–295
subscription radio, 156
subscription television, 15
subsidies, government, 16
Subtext, 92
subversiveness, 411
Sullivan, L. B., 66, 467
Sulzberger, Arthur J., 1–2
Sun recording label, 104, 107, 312
sunshine laws, 472–473
Super Audio CD (SACD), 108
Super Bowl, 14, 282, 314, 318
Superman Returns, 129
Super Size Me, 130
superstation, 187
supplements, newspaper weekend, 86, 87–88
Supreme Court
  Iowa, 461
  Tennessee, 238
  U.S., 67, 102, 107, 114, 132, 133, 138, 140, 141 242, 246, 318, 400, 440, 461, 462, 463, 464, 465–466, 467–468, 474, 475
SurfWatch, 220
surveillance function, 368–369
surveys
  evaluating, 330–331
  opinion, 326–332, 344
sweeps, 338
swooner, 106
Sword in the Stone, The, 121
Syma photo agency, *22-16*
syndicates, 188, 422, *22-3*

tabloid newspapers, 56–58, 62, 80–82
Talbot, William Fox, *22-4*
talkers, 164
talk radio, 163–166
Tarantino, Quentin, 136, 373
Tarbell, Ida, 83, 84
Target Center, 314
Taylor, Paul, *22-11*
TBS (*see* Turner Broadcasting System)
TBWA ad agency, 15
technology
  compression, 205, 209
  digital, 127, 175, 179
  entertainment and, 306–307
  mass media, 3–4
  miniaturization, 205
  movies, 123–126
  direct-broadcast satellite (DBS), 179, 188
  photographic, *22-3* to *22-5*
  radio, 149–150
  recording, 104–106
  television, 173–175
  voice transmission, 150, 151
TechnoMetrica, 441
Teen Vogue, 88
Telecommunications Act (1996), 155, 157, 203, 216, 217
telenovela, 187
teleological ethics, 490
telephone book journalism, 72
Televisa, 414, 422
television, 170–199
  advertising, 172–173, 189–191, 191–192, 195–197, 286
  affiliate-network relations, 182–187
  analog, 179
  cell phone and, 180, 189, 196
  chains, 181
  cable, 15, 175–180, 184, 187–189, 190
  CATV, 175
  cultural impact, 172–173
  delivery systems, 175–180
  digital, 127, 175, 179
  future, 310
  global village and, 403
  independent stations, 421
  influence of, 172–173
  magazines and, 93
  microwave relays, 181, 183
  mobile, 195–196
  mobisode, 195
  movies and, 132, 174
  news, 173, 186, 421–422
  newspapers and, 54
  over-air stations, 181, 182, 190
  product placement, 196–197
  programming *(see also as main heading),* 175, 177–179
  public, 191
  radio and, 174, 181
  technology, 8, 173–175
  reality, 23
  satellite, 15, 175–179
  signals, 176
  space shifts, 195
  structure of industry, 181–189
  superstation, 187
  technology, 173–180
  TiVo, 180, 195–197, 292, 293
  video on demand, 180
  violence, 193–194
  webisode, 195–196
Tellis, Gerald, 300
Terminator 2, 129
Terminator 3, 128, 137
terrorism (*see also* 9/11 attacks), 4, 219, 369
Texas Monthly, 93
textbooks, 37–38
Thelma and Louise, 310
theory
  aggressive stimulation, 376
  authoritarian, *23-2, 23-3* to *23-7*
  catalytic, 377–378
  communist, *23-2, 23-7* to *23-8*
  consistency, 370
  cumulative effects, 366–367
  desensitizing, 380–381
  four theories of the press, *23-2* to *23-3, 23-16*
  future of, 367–368
  libertarian, 490, *23-2, 23-9* to *23-10*
  minimalist effects, 365–366
  powerful effects, 364–365
  social responsibility, 488, 490, *23-2, 23-12* to *23-16*
  uses and gratifications, 344, 368–370
35-millimeter film, *22-7*
33 1/3-rpm record, 105
This Week, 59
Thomas, Helen, 444
Thomas, Parnell, 140
Thompson, Hunter S., 88, 99
Thomson (book publisher), 34
384 in surveying, 327–328
Thurman, Uma, 373
Tilley, Eustace, 97
timeline, media technology, 8
timeliness, 483
Time magazine, 14, 35, 83, 86, 96, 97, 470, *22-16* to *22-17*
Time, Place and Manner Standard (TPM), 465
Times Mirror, 331
Time Warner, 12, 13, 21, 24, 25, 83, 87, 95–96, 110, 132, 179, 186, 187, 188, 190, 281, 317, 325, 342, 422
Times v. *Sullivan,* 66, 423, 467–469,
Tinny, James, 74
Titanic, RMS 150, 350
Titanic, 123, 128, 137, 143
TiVo, 180, 195–197, 292, 293
Tolkien, J. R. R., 37
Tonight Show, 185, 437
Tony Stone photo agency, *22-16*
Tornillo opinion, 440
Totenberg, Nina, 249, 400
touring, record industry and, 112–113
Toy Story, 121, 122, 128, 171
TPM (*see* Time, Place and Manner Standard)
trade journals, 91–92, 452
trailing, advertising, 291
transistor, junction, 204
transmission, 355
trespass, 470
trial balloons, 447
Tribune Company (*see* Chicago *Tribune)*
Trio cable channel, 190
Triple Crown books, 309
Tritt, Travis, 103
Trout, Jack, 290, 302
Truman & Smith, 32
Trumbo, Dalton, 141
Trump, Donald, 23
trusteeship rationale, 151–152
truth, *23-6* to *23-7, 23-8, 23-9, 23-11*
Tuchman, Barbara, 43
Tucker, Tom, 35
Turkle, Sherry, 395
Turner, Ted, 21, 175, 178, 187, 316
Turner, Tina, 103
Turner Broadcasting System, 175
TVB, 414, 422
TV Guide magazine, 20, 88, 198
Twain, Mark, 31, 34, 121
Tweed, William Marcy, 66
Tweedle-Le-Dee, Tilden-Dum, *22-3*
20th Century Fox, 13, 20, 126, 132, 185, 186, 187
Twisted Sister, 103
Two-Bit Culture: The Paperbacking of America, 39
two-step flow, 365, 441
Twyn, John, *23-1*
Tylenol, 269–270
type, movable metal, 6

Uhlan, Ed, 35
ultrawideband, 211
Ulysses, 317, 461, 473, 474, 475

Uncle Tom's Cabin, 31, 33, 44, *22-11*
underground media, 11
Unger, Leslie, 275
Ungurait, Donald, 352, 418
Unification Church, 16, 67
unique selling proposition (USP), 290
United Artists, 134
United Negro College Fund, 298
United Paramount Network (UPN), 185, 186
United Paramount Theaters, 185
United Press International, 470
Universal, 13, 24–25, 132, 135, 138, 185 (*see also* National Broadcast Company; General Electric)
Universal Music, 103, 104
Universal Resource Locator (URL), 207–208
University of California at Los Angeles, 206, 381
University of California at San Diego, 377
University of North Carolina, 54, 411
University of Virginia, 33
Unknown American Revolution, The, 32
Unsafe at Any Speed, 32
UPN (*see* United Paramount Network)
URL (*see* Universal Resource Locator)
USA Networks, 190
USA Today, 2, 55, 58, 60–62
USA Weekend, 87
U.S.-based media companies, 422
uses and gratifications, 344, 368–370
U.S. government (*see agencies by name*)
U.S. News & World Report, 86, 87, 206, 240
USP (*see* unique selling proposition)
Us Weekly magazine, 2, 19–21, 80–82, 251
Utica *Observer-Dispatch*, 60
utilitarianism, 487–488
U2, 112
UWB (*see* ultrawideband)
Uzbekistan, 242

Vallee, Rudy, 308
VALS (*see* Values and Life-Styles)
Values and Life-Styles (VALS), 327, 342–343
values, news, 237–242
Vanderbilt, William Henry, 258
Vanidades magazine, 5
vanity press, 35
variables, news, 242–243
Vassar, Matthew, 89
veil of ignorance, 488
Ventura, Jesse, 436
Verizon, 175, 180, 191, 281
Veronica Guerin, 305
vertical integration, 13, 22
VFW magazine, 90
Viacom 21, 132, 180, 181, 184, 185, 186, 187, 190, 422
Vicary, Jim, 294
video news services, 420–421
video on demand (VOD)
  cable VOD, 180
  satellite VOD, 180
  wireless downloading, 180
  computer downloads, 180
  Internet video, 180
Vietnam war, 67, 236, 384, 431–432, 464
Village Voice, 61, 73, 74
violence, 193–194, 375–382
  in music, 108, 109
  and gaming, 319
  and ratings, 142
  studies, 381–382
  television, 193–194, 366
Violence Assessment Monitoring Project, 382
viral advertising, 292
Virgin recording label, 103
visual communication, *22-1* to *22-18*
  cameras, *22-7*
  celluloid, *22-6* to *22-7*
  comics, *22-3* to *22-4*
  creative, *22-15*
  documentary photography, *22-8* to *22-11*
  early media illustrations, *22-2* to *22-3*
  evaluating, *22-14*
  frontier photography, 22-9 to *22-10*
  illustrating advertisements, *22-11*
  image ownership, *22-15* to *22-16*
  imitative, *22-15*
  instant photography, *22-7*
  integration with print media, 9–10
  issues, *22-15* to *22-18*
  landscape photography, *22-10*
  magazine, *22-12* to *22-13*
  misrepresentation, *22-16* to *22-17*
  moving visuals, *22-12* to *22-14*
  newspaper, *22-12*
  persuasive photography, *22-11* to *22-12*
  reality photography, *22-12* to *22-14*
  stopping motion, *22-6*
visual messages, *22-1* to *22-18*
Vitascope, 137, *22-7*
Vivendi, 24–25, 103, 422
voice transmission, 150, 151

Wallace, Dewitt and Lila, 83, 87
Wall Street Journal, 2, 14, 49, 55, 61, 62–64, 242, 293
Wal-Mart, 46–47, 89, 90, 114, 125, 271–272, 293
Walton, Sam, 271–272
WAM music downloads, 113, 114
Warner Books, 24, 34, 43,44
Warner Brothers, 128, 132, 319
Warner Brothers television network (WB), 185, 186, 187
Warner Lambert, 290
Warner Music, 103, 110, 119
War Office, U.S., 131
War of the Worlds, 362–364, 371–372
"War of the Worlds" Study, 368
war zones, 475
Washingtonian, 93
Washington *Post*, 55, 67–68, 77, 224–226, 235, 442, 485
Washington *Times*, 16, 67
watchdog role, 439, 448–452
Watergate scandal, 67, 224–226, 228, 247, 251, 442, 448
Watson, James, 35
waves, advertising, 291
WB, (*see* Warner Brothers television network)
WBAI radio, New York, 318
Weaver, Pat, 185
Weaver, Warren, 352, 353
web
  advertising, 212–213, 288, 289
  books and, 36
  time spent with, 3
  technology, 8, 204–210
  television and, 178, 196
Webber, Andrew Lloyd, 308
Webby awards, 213
WebTV, 178
Wednesday Night Fights, 314
weekly newspapers, 54, 71, 72–73
Weinstein, Bob and Harvey, 136
Weiss, E. B., 299
Welles, Orson, 362–364, 371–372
Wells, H. G., 362–364
Wells-Barnett, Ida, 238
Western influence, 415
White Castle, The, 432
White House news, 241–242, 458–450
whitewashing, 274
Whiting, Susan, 324–326
Who Wants to Be a Millionaire, 320
Why We Fight, 130, 131
Wide World of Sports, 185, 314
Wi-Fi, 11, 211, 429
Wild Bunch, The, 380
Wilder, Billy, 133
Wild Wild West, 307
William Morrow, 42
Williams, Ian, 32
Williams, Pete, 270, 448
Williams, Robbie, 103
Winfrey, Oprah, 5, 46, 173, 310, 4446, 497
Winona Online Democracy, 367
wireless, muni, 211
Without a Trace, 305, 337
Wolf, Don, 73
Woman's Day magazine, 88, 422
women's magazines, 88
Wonder, Stevie, 196
Wonkette, 218
Woodward, Bob, 248, 251
Woolsey, John, 473
World Bank InfoShop, 40
World Is Flat, The, 32
World Trade Center, 249
World War I, 75, 106, 137, 261, *22-15*
World War II, 86, 161, 261, 340, 431, *22-13*, *22-15*
World Wide Web, 206–210
World Wrestling Entertainment, 314
World Wrestling Federation, 314
WPXT television, 494
wrestling, 314
WWP Group, 268

X&Y, 117
Xbox, 316, 423
XFL football, 307
X-Men, The, 320

yacht racing, 313
Yanjing beer, 285
Yankelovich Partners, 300
yellow journalism, 232–233, *22-3*
Yellow Kid, 233, *22-3*
Yellow Period, 232–233
YM magazine, 81, 88
You Have Seen Their Faces, *22-11*
Young & Rubicam (Y&R), 268

zapping, 338
Zeitung, 75
Zenger, John Peter, 227, 228
Zen and the Art of Motorcycle Maintenance, 41–43
'zine, 292
zipping, 338
Zukor, Adolph, 132, 133
Zworykin, Vladimir, 174, 181

Photo Credits

Page xxviii: AP/Wide World Photos; 1: AP/Wide World Photos; 2: AP/Wide World Photos; 5: PEOPLE EN ESPANOL © 1996 Time Inc. All rights reserved.; 7R: North Wind Picture Archives; 7L: North Wind Picture Archives; 9L: Brooks Kraft/ Corbis; 9R: SSPL/The Image Works; 12: AP/Wide World Photos; 15L: Courtesy Discovery Networks Europe; 15R: Photo by Dimitri Daniloff; 16: Photograph provided courtesy of Syracuse University. All rights reserved.; 17R: AP/Wide World Photos; 17L: Ezra Shaw/Getty Images; 18: CKE Restaurants, Inc.; 20: James Knowler/Reuters/Corbis; 22R: Ted Streshinsky; 22L: David M. Grossman; 23: Trump Prod./Mark Burnett Prod./The Kobal Collection; 25: Reuters NewMedia, Inc./Corbis; 28: Ara Koopelian; 29: Ara Koopelian; 30: Ara Koopelian; 32L: Culver Pictures, Inc.; 32R: The Granger Collection; 33R: Mary Evans Picture Library/The Image Works; 33L: Time Life Pictures/ Mansell/Getty Images; 39: Rico Torres, The Kobal Collection; 40T: Polymer Vision; 40B: On Demand Books LLC.; 41: Jonathan Saunders; 42: Jeff/Mitchell/: Reuters; 45L: John Earle Photography; 45R: Backyard Publications, LLC for Inside Annapolis Magazine; 47BR: Jacket Design © GTC Art & Design, Jacket Illustration by Anton Markous. The Last Supper (After) Leonardo da Vinci © A.K.G. Berlin/Superstock; WHEN WILL JESUS BRING THE PORK CHOPS? © George Carlin. Published by Hyperion; 47TR: Cover of THE DAILY SHOW WITH JON STEWART PRESENTS AMERICA (THE BOOK) by Jon Stewart. Copyright © 2004 by Busboy Productions, Inc. By permission of Warner Books, Inc.; 47T: John Alphonse/Aurora; 48R: AP/ Wide World Photos; 49R: Copyright 2005, The Chronicle of Higher Education. Reprinted with permission.; 49L: Copyright © 2006 "The New York Times Company." "Reprinted by Permission."; 52: Jeff Cook of the Quad Times; 53: Jeff Cook of the Quad Times; 54: Jeff Cook of the Quad Times; 57R: © 2003 Bob Adelman; 57L: Reprinted with permission of the Chicago Tribune, copyright Chicago Tribune, all rights reserved; 61L: USA TODAY. October 26, 2005. Reprinted with Permission.; 61R: Scott Maclay/The Freedom Forum; 62L: The New York Daily News; 62R: The New York Daily News; 63L: Reproduced by permission of The Wall Street Journal, © 2006 Dow Jones & Company, Inc. All Rights Reserved Worldwide.; 63R: The Wall Street Journal; 64R: Reproduced with permission from the September 25, 2006 issue of The Christian Science Monitor (http: //www.csmonitor.com/). © 2006 The Christian Science Monitor. All rights reserved.; 64L: The Granger Collection; 66R: Copyright © 2006 by The New York Times Co. Reprinted with permission.; 66TL: Copyright © 2006 "The New York Times Company." "Reprinted by Permission."; 66BL: Copyright © 2006 "The New York Times Company." "Reprinted by Permission."; 69: Brian W. Smith/Time Pix/Getty Images; 70: THE BOONDOCKS © 2006 Aaron McGruder. Dist. By UNIVERSAL PRESS SYNDICATE. Reprinted with permission. All rights reserved.; 73R: Courtesy of the Library of Congress; 73L: Courtesy of the Library of Congress; 74R: Courtesy Nichi Bei Times; 74L: Copyright © 2001 San Jose Mercury news. All rights reserved. Reproduced with permission.; 76: FRONTERAS is a joint venture of Universal Press Syndicate in the United States and Danilo Black in Mexico. Used by permission. All rights reserved.; 81: Star Photo Department; 82: Star Photo Department; 85: Cover/hologram photo-illustration by Tom Schaefges. Cover images used with permission of National Geographic Society. © National Geographic Society; 86: Courtesy of Margaret Bourke-White Estate/Life Magazine. © Time Inc./Getty Images; 87R: Arnold Newman/Getty Images; 87L: Reprinted with permission from Reader's Digest. Copyright © 2005 The Reader's Digest Assn., Inc.; 89: The Granger Collection; 90R: Courtesy Isobel McKenzie-Price; 90L: Courtesy Isobel McKenzie-Price; 93R: George Strock/: Getty Images; 93L: TimePix/: Getty Images; 94: Copyright © 1998 Watterson. Reprinted with the permission of Universal Press Syndicate. All rights reserved.; 96: Slate.com and Washingtonpost. Newsweek Interactive. All Rights Reserved.; 97: Rea Irvin/The New Yorker. Copyright © 1925 The New Yorker/Conde Nast Publications. reprinted by permission. All Rights Reserved.; 100: AFP/: Getty Images; 101: AFP/Getty Images; 102: AFP/Getty Images; 104: Kevin Winter/Getty Images; 106L: UPI/Corbis; 106R: Corbis; 107: AP/Wide World Photos; 108: Courtesy of Columbia Records; 109: AP/Wide World Photos; 110L: AP/Wide World Photos; 110R: John Stanton/Getty Images; 111R: AP/Wide World Photos; 111L: Hulton Archive/Getty Images; 113: Jordan Forteau; 115TL: Royalty Free/Corbis; 115TR: Kim KulishCorbis; 115B: Napster logo and marks reprinted with the permission of Napster, LLC.; 116: Kim Kulish/Corbis; 117: Reuters/Corbis; 120: Xavier Torres Bacchette/Corbis Outline; ; 122: Fred Prouser/ReutersLandov; 123: Buena Vista/Courtesy Everett Collection; 124: Focus Films/Everett Collection; 127: Vince Bucci/Getty Images; 129T: Warner Bros/DC Comics/The Picture Desk; 129B: Gregg Segal Photography; 130: Courtesy Lourdes Portillo. Photo by Rene Cardona; 131L: AP/Wide World Photos; 131R: Hulton Archive/ Getty Images; 133: Photofest; 133: Everett Collection; 135: © Dreamworks/Courtesy Everett Collection; 136: Photo by Robert Millard/ZUMA Press © Copyright 2001 by Robert Millard; 140: AP/Wide World Photos; 141L: Everett Collection; 141BR: AP/Wide World Photos; 141TR: CinemaPhoto/Corbis; 146: Rose Prouses/Reuters/Landov; 147: Rose Prouses/ Reuters/Landov; 148: Rose Prouses/Reuters/Landov; 150L: Bettmann/Corbis; 150R: Corbis; 153: UPI/Corbis; 156: XM Satellite Radio; 158: AP/Wide World Photos; 159: Photo by Sara Chapman. Photo originally appeared in the NDSU newspaper The Spectrum.; 161: AP/Wide World Photos; 163: AP/ Wide World Photos; 164R: Kevin Winter/Getty Images; 164L: Larry Downing/Reuters/Corbis; 165: Courtesy of "Fresh Air with Terry Gross," produced in Philadelphia by WHYY. Photograph by Miles Kennedy.; 166: AP/Wide World Photos; 170: Liz Hafalia/San Francisco Chronicle/Corbis; 171: Liz Hafalia/ San Francisco Chronicle/: Corbis; 172: Corbis; 172: Liz Hafalia/San Francisco Chronicle/: Corbis; 174: UPI/Corbis;

177: The Cable Center; 178R: NASA; 178L: AP/Wide World Photos; 180: © ABC/Courtesy Everett Collection; 183: AP/Wide World Photos; 184: Robert Galbraith/ReutersCorbis; 187: Paul Hawthorne/Getty Images; 188: Frazer Harrison/Getty Images; 192: Universal TV/Wolf Film/The Kobal Collection; 193: CBS/Landov; 196TR: Dick Locher and Mike Killian. Copyright Tribune Media Services. Reprinted with permission.; 196TL: LG Electronics MobileComm USA, Inc.; 197: NBCU Photo Bank; 200: © 2005 Shawn G. Henry; 201: © 2005 Shawn G. Henry; 202: © 2005 Shawn G. Henry; 204: AP/Wide World Photos; 205: Kevin R. Morris; 206: AP/Wide World Photos; 207: AP/Wide World Photos; 209: Justin Sullivan/Getty Images; 210L: © 2004-2005 Geoffrey R. Hutchison, licensed under a Creative Commons license.; 210R: AP/Wide World Photos; 216: AP/Wide World Photos; 218R: Courtesy Gawker Media; 218L: Courtesy Gawker Media ; 219: Photo by Christian Lange; 220: Hannah Belitz, photographer; 221: M. Kaia Sand; 221: M. Kaia Sand; 227: North Wind Picture Archives; 229R: Corbis; 229L: North Wind Photo Archive; 231: Matthew Brady/Henry Guttmann/Getty Images; 232TR: Culver Pictures, Inc.; 232BR: Culver Pictures, Inc.; 232L: Corbis; 233T: Culver Pictures, Inc.; 233B: Corbis; 235: Courtesy of Michael Getler. The Washington Post.; 236: Matt Dellinger/The New Yorker; 238: The Granger Collection; 246: AP/Wide World Photos; 247: AP/Wide World Photos; 250: Rocket Racing League; 250: AP/Wide World Photos; 254: Rocket Racing League; 255T: Rocket Racing League; 260L: Colorado Historical Society; 260R: AP/Wide World Photos; 261L: The Granger Collection; 261R: AP/Wide World Photos; 262: General Motors Corp. Used with permission, GM Media Archives; 265: Stephen Crowley/The New York Times; 266: AP/Wide World Photos; 268: McDonald's Corporation; 270R: Kevin Horan/Chicago; 270L: Abe Frajndlich; 272R: Eli Reichman/Time Life Pictures/Getty Images; 272L: Nicholas Kamm/AFP/Getty Images; 274: UPI/Corbis; 275: AP/Wide World Photos; 278: Fred R. Conrad/The New York Times; 279: Fred R. Conrad/: The New York Times; 280: Fred R. Conrad/The New York Times; 285: AP/Wide World Photos; 287: DaimlerChrysler/Screenshot from Tony Hawk's Pro Skater 2 courtesy of Activision Publishing, Inc. © 2000 Activision Publishing, Inc. All Rights Reserved.; 289L: Google, Inc.; 289R: Copyright 2005 by The New York Times Co. Reprinted with permission.; 291: Bamboo, Inc.; 292: Ogilvy & Mather, London; 293: CBS/Landov; 295L: Dr. Wilson Bryan Key; 295R: From The Clam-Plate Orgy by Wilson Bryan Key; 296: Tom Wagner/Corbis/SABA Press Photo, Inc.; 297: Office of National Drug Control Policy/Ad Council; 301: Laura Cavanaugh/Landov; 304: Paul Hawthorne/Getty Images; 305: Paul Hawthorne/Getty Images; 306: Paul Hawthorne/Getty Images; 307: Robert Voets/CBS/Courtesy Everett Collection; 309R: Artria Books/Simon & Schuster; 309L: Derrick Blakely; 310: Bryan Bedder/Getty Images; 313: Courtesy Roxio; 316: Robert Galbraith/Reuters/Landov; 318: Ted Streshinsky/Corbis; 321: Frank Micelotta/Getty Images; 324: AP/Wide World Photos; 325: AP/Wide World Photo; 326: AP/Wide World Photos; 328L: The Gallup Organization; 328R: AP/Wide World Photos; 331: Andrew Kohut, Director of the Pew Research Center for the People and the Press; 332: The Pew Research Center for the People and the Press; 334: AP/Wide World Photos; 335: The Arbitron Company, NY; 336L: Nielsen Media Research; 336R: Nielsen Media Research; 337: Republished with permission from Broadcasting & Cable, March, 2003, a Reed Business Publication; 339: Douglas Burrows/Getty Images; 346: The East-West Center; 347: The East-West Center; 348: The East-West Center; 349R: AP/Wide World Photos; 349L: Sam Jones Photography; 350: UPI/: Corbis; 355: Jacques Chenet/Woodfin Camp & Associates; 358: Reprinted from Columbia Journalism Review, September/October 2005. © 2005 by Columbia Journalism Review.; 359: Peter Kramer/Getty Images; 362: Culver Pictures; 363: Culver Pictures; 364: Culver Pictures; 367L: Patrick Seeger/dpa/Landov; 367R: Courtesy Steve Schild; 373: A Band Apart/MIiramax/The Kobal Collection; 374L: Lincoln Journal Star Library; 374R: AP/Wide World Photos; 377: Bettmann/Corbis; 379: AP/Wide World Photos; 380: Evening Standard/Hulton-Archive/Getty Images; 381L: Everett Collection, Inc.; 381R: © 1998 SCi ISales Curve Interactive Limited; 382: Kyle Cassidy/Annenberg School of Communication; 388: Corbis; 389: Corbis; 390: Corbis; 391: AP/Wide World Photos; 393L: NYP Holdings, Inc.; 393R: Copyright 2006 by The New York Times Co. Reprinted with permission.; 395: Kevin Winter: Getty Images for AFI; 395R: Center for Media and Public Affairs; 396: Photo by Louis Fabian Bachrach; 397: AP/Wide World Photos; 398: Emilio Flores/Getty Images; 399: National Fair Housing Alliance/Ad Council; 400: AP/Wide World Photos; 401: Frank Micelotta/Getty Images; 406: John Schults/Reuters; 407: John Schults/Reuters; 408: John Schults/Reuters; 409: Win McNamee/Getty Images for Meet the Press; 410: Roger L. Wollenberg/UPI/Landov; 412: SIO/UCSD Photo; 413: FETHI BELAID/AFP/Getty Images; 424: AFP/AFP/Getty Images; 425: AP/Wide World Photos; 427: China Photos/Getty Images; 428: Courtesy of Video Sound, Inc., NJ; 430: Reuters/Luis Ramirez/Colombia Press/Corbis/Sygma; 432: AP/Wide World Photos; 433: Jim Bourg/Reuters-Landov; 436: AP/Wide World Photos; 437: Fred Prouser/Reuters/Landov; 438: Fred Prouser/Reuters/Landov; 439: Paul J. Richards/AFP/Getty Images; 443: Courtesy CNN; 444: Eduardo Sverdlin/UPI/Landov; 447L: UPI/Corbis; 447R: Getty Images; 449: Stefan Zakin/UPI/Landov; 453R: Courtesy of Daily Kos; 453L: Courtesy of Daily Kos; 458: Len Irish; 459: Len Irish; 460: Len Irish; 462R: Star Tribune/Minneapolis-St. Paul, 2004; 462L: From the Collection of the Minnesota Historical Society; 463L: © The New York Times Co. Reprinted by permission.; 463BR: AP/Wide World Photos; 463BL: AP/Wide World Photos; 464: Underwood & Underwood/Corbis; 467: Time Life Pictures/Getty Images; 468: Norm Betts/Bloomberg News/Landov; 469: State Historical Society of Iowa-Iowa City; 476R: AP/Wide World Photos; 476L: HO/AFP/Getty Images; 478: AP/Wide World Photos; 480: AP/Wide World Photos; 481: AP/Wide World Photos; 482: AP/Wide World Photos; 483: Big Pictures; 484: Courtesy Charlie Gay; 486: Corbis; 487: North Wind Picture Archives; 488: North Wind Picture Archives; 489TR: Courtesy Harvard News Office; 489BR: Fritz Goro/Time Life Pictures/Getty Images; 489TL: Bettmann/Corbis; 491: Office of Communications at Harvard Divinity School; 494: AP/Wide World Photos; 494: David A. Rodgers; 497L: Ulf Anderson/Getty Images; 497R: Tim Boyle/Getty Images; 499: Neal Ulevich/Bloomberg News/Landov